Chapter Opening Cases

▶ Each chapter begins with a case scenario about an actual company, product, or situation that illustrates key concepts discussed in the chapter.

▶ *Marketing Implication Sections*

For every major concept discussed, marketing implication sections show how consumer behavior applies to the practice of marketing, including such basic marketing functions as market segmentation, target market selection, positioning, market research, promotion, price, product, and place decisions.

▶ *Current and Cutting-Edge Coverage*

In addition to providing a balanced perspective, including both psychological (micro) and sociological (macro) topics on the field of consumer behavior, the text provides the most up-to-date research possible. This includes several novel chapters that often do not appear in other textbooks: "Symbolic Consumer Behavior," "Knowing and Understanding," and "The Dark Side of Consumer Behavior and Marketing."

▶ *Emphasis on Globalization and E-Commerce*

Interwoven throughout the text are many cross-cultural examples as well as information on how the Internet has impacted consumer behavior. The wealth of these examples throughout the text emphasizes the text's practical and contemporary orientation.

D0146747

Consumer Behavior

Fifth Edition

Consumer Behavior

Wayne D. Hoyer
University of Texas at Austin

Deborah J. MacInnis
University of Southern California

SOUTH-WESTERN
CENGAGE Learning

Australia • Brazil • Japan • Korea • Mexico • Singapore • Spain • United Kingdom • United States

SOUTH-WESTERN
CENGAGE Learning™

Consumer Behavior, Fifth Edition
Wayne D. Hoyer, Deborah J. MacInnis

Vice President of Editorial, Business:
Jack W. Calhoun

Vice President/Editor-in-Chief:
Melissa Acuña

Executive Editor: Mike Roche

Senior Developmental Editor:
Joanne Dauksewicz

Marketing Manager: Mike Aliscad

Senior Content Project Manager:
Colleen A. Farmer

Marketing Communications Manager:
Sarah Greber

Media Editor: John Rich

Senior First Print Buyer: Diane Gibbons

Production Service: Pre-Press, PMG

Senior Art Director: Stacy Shirley

Internal Designer: Jean Hammond

Cover Designer: Jennifer Roycroft,
Roycroft Design

Photo Manager: Jennifer Meyer Dare

Photo Researcher: Julie Low

Cover Images: Image Copyright Mike
Flippo, 2008; Image Copyright marianad,
2008; Image Copyright Anton Gvozdikov,
2008; Image Copyright Elena Uspenskaya,
2008. All images used under license from
Shutterstock.com.

For product information and technology assistance, contact us at
Cengage Learning Customer & Sales Support, 1-800-354-9706
For permission to use material from this text or product,
submit all requests online at **www.cengage.com/permissions**
Further permissions questions can be emailed to
permissionrequest@cengage.com

Exam*View*® is a registered trademark of eInstruction Corp. Windows is a registered trademark of the Microsoft Corporation used herein under license. Macintosh and Power Macintosh are registered trademarks of Apple Computer, Inc. used herein under license.

© 2008 Cengage Learning. All Rights Reserved.

Cengage Learning WebTutor™ is a trademark of Cengage Learning.

Library of Congress Control Number: 2008935578

ISBN-13: 978-0-547-07992-9

ISBN-10: 0-547-07992-3

Instructor's Edition ISBN 13: 978-0-324-83428-4

Instructor's Edition ISBN 10: 0-324-83428-4

South-Western
5191 Natorp Boulevard
Mason, OH 45040
USA

Cengage Learning products are represented in Canada by Nelson Education, Ltd.

For your course and learning solutions, visit **academic.cengage.com**

Purchase any of our products at your local college store or at our preferred online store **www.ichapters.com**

Printed in the United States of America
1 2 3 4 5 6 7 13 12 11 10 09

To my wonderful family, Shirley, David, Stephanie, and Lindsey, to my parents Louis and Doris, and to our puppies Casey and Daphne for their tremendous support and love. To all of you, I dedicate this book.

Wayne D. Hoyer
Austin, Texas
September 2008

To my loving family and devoted friends. You are my life-spring of energy and my center of gravity.

Deborah J. MacInnis
Los Angeles, California
September 2008

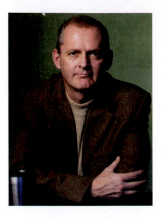

Wayne D. Hoyer

Wayne D. Hoyer is the James L. Bayless/William S. Farish Fund Chair for Free Enterprise in the McCombs School of Business at the University of Texas at Austin. He received his Ph.D. in Consumer Psychology from Purdue University in 1980. Wayne has published over 60 articles in various publications including the *Journal of Consumer Research, Journal of Marketing, Journal of Marketing Research, Journal of Advertising Research*, and *Journal of Retailing*. A 1998 article in the *Journal of Marketing Research* (with Susan Broniarczyk and Leigh McAlister) won the O'Dell Award in 2003 for the article that had the most impact in the marketing field over that five-year period. In addition to Consumer Behavior, he has co-authored two books on the topic of advertising miscomprehension. Dr. Hoyer's research interests include consumer information processing and decision making (especially low-involvement decision making), customer relationship management, and advertising effects (particularly miscomprehension and the impact of humor). He is a former associate editor for the *Journal of Consumer Research* and serves on nine editorial review boards including the *Journal of Marketing, Journal of Marketing Research, Journal of Consumer Research*, and *Journal of Consumer Psychology*. Dr. Hoyer is a member of the American Psychological Association, the Association for Consumer Research, and the American Marketing Association. His major areas of teaching include consumer behavior, customer strategy, and marketing communications. He has also taught internationally at the University of Mannheim, the University of Muenster, and the Otto Beisheim School of Management (all in Germany), the University of Bern in Switzerland, and Thammasat University in Thailand. He has also been a research fellow at the University of Cambridge (UK).

Deborah J. MacInnis

Debbie MacInnis (Ph.D., University of Pittsburgh 1986) is the Charles L. and Ramona I. Hilliard Professor of Business Administration and Professor of Marketing at the University of Southern California in Los Angeles, CA. She has previously held positions as Chairperson of the Marketing Department and Vice Dean for Research. Debbie has published papers in the *Journal of Consumer Research, Journal of Marketing Research, Journal of Marketing, Journal of Personality and Social Psychology, Psychology and Marketing*, and others in the areas of marketing communications, information processing, imagery, emotions, and branding. She is an Associate Editor for the *Journal of Consumer Research* and the *Journal of Consumer Psychology*. She has also served as a member of the editorial review boards of the *Journal of Consumer Research, Journal of Marketing Research, Journal of Marketing*, and *Journal of the Academy of Marketing Sciences* and has won outstanding reviewer awards from these journals. She has also served on the editorial review boards of other journals in marketing and business. Debbie has served as Conference Co-Chair, Treasurer, and President of the Association for Consumer Research. She has also served as Vice President of Conferences and Research for the Academic Council of the American Marketing Association. She has received major awards for her research, including the Alpha Kappa Psi and Maynard awards, given to the best practice- and theory-based articles respectively published in the *Journal of Marketing*.

Debbie's research has also been named as a finalist for the Practice Prize Competition for contributions to marketing, and the Converse Award for significant long-term contributions to marketing. She has been named recipient of the Marshall Teaching Innovation Award, the Dean's Award for Community, and the Dean's Award for Research from the Marshall School of Business. Her classes have won national awards through the SAA National Advertising Competition. Debbie's major areas of teaching include consumer behavior and integrated marketing communications. Debbie lives in Los Angeles with her husband and two children.

Brief Contents

Contents

Chapter 3   Exposure, Attention, and Perception   69

Chapter 4   Knowledge and Understanding   91

Part 3   The Process of Making Decisions   193

Chapter 8   Problem Recognition and Information Search   194

Chapter 9   Judgment and Decision Making Based on High Effort   219

Chapter 13   Social Class and Household Influences   325

Chapter 14   Psychographics: Values, Personality, and Lifestyles   355

Chapter 18   Ethics, Social Responsibility, and the Dark Side of Consumer Behavior and Marketing   469

Preface

At just about every moment of our lives, we engage in some form of consumer behavior. When we watch an ad on TV, talk to friends about a movie we just saw, brush our teeth, go to a ball game, buy a new CD, or even throw away an old pair of shoes, we are behaving as a consumer. In fact, being a consumer reaches into every part of our lives.

Given its omnipresence, the study of consumer behavior has critical implications for areas such as marketing, public policy, and ethics. It also helps us learn about ourselves—why we buy certain things, why we use them in a certain way, and how we get rid of them.

In this book we explore the fascinating world of consumer behavior, looking at a number of interesting and exciting topics. Some of these are quickly identified with our typical image of consumer behavior. Others may be surprising. We hope you will see why we became stimulated and drawn to this topic from the very moment we had our first consumer behavior course as students. We hope you will also appreciate why we choose to make this field our life's work, and why we developed and continue to remain committed to the writing of this textbook.

Why the New Edition of This Book?

There are a number of consumer behavior books on the market. An important question concerns what this book has to offer and what distinguishes it from other texts. As active researchers in the field of consumer behavior, our overriding goal was to continue providing a treatment of the field that is up to date and cutting edge. There has been an explosion of research on a variety of consumer behavior topics over the last twenty years. Our primary aim was to provide a useful summary of this material for students of marketing. However, in drawing on cutting-edge research, we wanted to be careful not to become too "academic." Instead, our objective is to present cutting-edge topics in a manner that is accessible and easy for students to understand.

Specific changes and improvements to the fifth edition of this book include:

- ▶ Shorter length and more streamlined prose, making the content easier for students to process

- ▶ Coverage of the latest research from the academic field of consumer behavior

- ▶ New end-of-chapter cases, giving students the opportunity to discuss real-world consumer issues and to apply and use the concepts discussed in each chapter

- ▶ New coverage of research and behavioral concepts related to such topics as emotions, post-decision regret, decision framing, privacy, and obesity

- ▶ Numerous new advertisements offering concrete illustrations of consumer behavior concepts in action

- ▶ Numerous new examples highlighting how all kinds of organizations use consumer behavior in their marketing efforts

▶ New database analysis exercises offering students an opportunity to make marketing decisions based on consumer demographics and behavior styles

Textbook Features

As award-winning teachers, we have tried to translate our instructional abilities and experience into the writing of this text. The following features have been a natural outgrowth of these experiences.

Conceptual Model First, we believe that students can learn best when they see the big picture—when they understand what concepts mean, how they are used in business practice, and how they relate to one another. In our opinion, consumer behavior is too often presented as a set of discrete topics with little or no relationship to one another. We have therefore developed an overall conceptual model that helps students grasp the big picture and see how the chapters and topics are themselves interrelated. Each chapter is linked to other chapters by a specific model that fits within the larger model. Further, the overall model guides the organization of the book. This organizing scheme makes the chapters far more *integrative* than most other books.

Practical Orientation, with an Emphasis on Globalization and E-commerce Another common complaint of some treatments of consumer behavior is that they reflect general psychological or sociological principles and theories, but provide very little indication of how these principles and theories relate to business practice. Given our notion that students enjoy seeing how the concepts in consumer behavior can apply to business practice, a second objective of the book was to provide a very practical orientation. We include a wealth of contemporary real-world examples to illustrate key topics. We also try to broaden students' horizons by providing a number of international examples. Given the importance of online consumer behavior, we also provide a number of examples of consumer behavior in an e-commerce context.

Current and Cutting-Edge Coverage Third, we provide coverage of the field of consumer behavior that is as current and up to date as possible (including many of the recent research advances). This includes several *novel chapters* that often do not appear in other textbooks: "Symbolic Consumer Behavior," "Knowing and Understanding," "Low Effort Attitude Change," "Low Effort Decision Making," and "Ethics, Social Responsibility, and the Dark Side of Consumer Behavior and Marketing." These topics are at the cutting edge of consumer behavior research and are likely to be of considerable interest to students.

Balanced Treatment of Micro and Macro Topics Fourth, our book tries to provide a balanced perspective on the field of consumer behavior. Specifically we give treatment to both psychological (micro) consumer behavior topics (e.g., attitudes, decision making) and sociological (macro) consumer behavior topics (e.g., subculture, gender, social class influences). Also, although we typically teach consumer behavior by starting with the more micro topics and then moving up to more macro topics, we realize that some instructors prefer the reverse sequence. The *Instructor's Manual* therefore provides a revised table of contents and model that shows how the book can be taught for those who prefer a macro first, micro second approach.

Broad Conceptualization of the Subject Fifth, we present a broad conceptualization of the topic of consumer behavior. While many books focus on what products or services consumers *buy*, consumer behavior scholars have recognized that the topic of consumer behavior is actually much broader. Specifically, rather than studying buying per se, we recognize that consumer behavior includes a *set* of decisions (what, whether, when, where, why, how, how often, how much, how long) about *acquisition* (including, but not limited to buying), *usage*, and *disposition* decisions. Focusing on more than what products or services consumers buy provides a rich set of theoretical and practical implications for our both understanding of consumer behavior and the practice of marketing.

Finally, we consider the relevance of consumer behavior to *many constituents*, not just marketers. Chapter 1 indicates that CB is important to marketers, public policy makers, ethicists and consumer advocacy groups, and consumers themselves (including students' own lives). Some chapters focus exclusively on the implications of consumer behavior for public policy makers, ethicists, and consumer advocacy groups. Other chapters consider these issues as well, though in less detail.

Content and Organization of the Book

One can currently identify two main approaches to the study of consumer behavior: a "micro" orientation, which focuses on the individual psychological processes that consumers use to make acquisition, consumption, and disposition decisions, and a "macro" orientation, which focuses on group behaviors and the symbolic nature of consumer behavior. This latter orientation draws heavily from such fields as sociology and anthropology. The current book and overall model have been structured around a "micro to macro" organization based on the way we teach this course and the feedback that we have received from reviewers. (As mentioned previously, for those who prefer a "macro to micro" structure, we provide in the *Instructor's Manual* an alternative Table of Contents that reflects how the book could be easily adapted to this perspective.)

Chapter 1 presents an introduction to consumer behavior and provides students with an understanding of the breadth of the field, and its importance to marketers, advocacy groups, public policy makers, and consumers themselves. It also presents the overall model that guides the organization of the text. An enrichment chapter, which follows Chapter 1, describes the groups who conduct research on consumers. It also describes methods by which consumer research is conducted.

Part I, "The Psychological Core," focuses on the inner psychological processes that affect consumer behavior. We see that consumers' acquisition, usage, and disposition behaviors and decisions are greatly affected by the amount of effort they put into engaging in behaviors and making decisions. Chapter 2 describes three critical factors that affect effort: the (1) *motivation* or desire, (2) *ability* (knowledge and information), and (3) *opportunity* to engage in behaviors and make decisions. In Chapter 3, we then examine how information in consumers' environments (ads, prices, product features, word-of-mouth communications, and so on) is internally processed by consumers—how they come in contact with these stimuli (*exposure*), notice them (*attention*), and *perceive* them. Chapter 4 continues by discussing how we compare new stimuli to our knowledge of existing stimuli, a process called *categorization*, and how we attempt to understand or *comprehend* them on a deeper level. In Chapters 5 and 6, we see how attitudes are formed and changed depending on whether the amount of effort consumers devote to forming an attitude is high or low and whether attitudes are cognitively or affectvely based. Finally, because consumers often must recall the information they have previously stored in order to make decisions, Chapter 7 looks at the important topic of consumer *memory*.

Whereas Part I examines some of the internal factors that influence consumers' decisions, a critical domain of consumer behavior involves understanding how consumers make acquisition, consumption, and disposition decisions. Thus, in Part II we examine the sequential steps of the consumer decision-making process. In Chapter 8, we examine the initial steps of this process—*problem recognition* and *information search*. Similar to the attitude change processes described earlier, we next examine the consumer decision-making process, both when *effort is high* (Chapter 9) and when it is *low* (Chapter 10). Further, in both chapters we examine these important processes from both a cognitive and an affective perspective. Finally, the process does not end after a decision has been made. In Chapter 11 we see how consumers determine whether they are *satisfied* or *dissatisfied* with their decisions and how they *learn* from choosing and consuming products and services.

Part III reflects a "macro" view of consumer behavior that examines how various aspects of *culture* affect consumer behavior. First, we see how consumer diversity (in terms of age, gender, sexual orientation, region, ethnicity, and religion) can affect consumer behavior (Chapter 12). Chapter 13 then examines how *social class* and *households* are classified and how these factors affect acquisition, usage, and disposition behaviors. Chapter 14 then examines how external influences affect our personality, lifestyle, and values, as well as consumer behavior. Chapter 15 considers how, when, and why the specific *reference groups* (friends, work group, clubs) to which we belong can influence acquisition, usage, and disposition decisions and behaviors.

Part IV, "Consumer Behavior Outcomes," examines the effects of the numerous influences and decision processes discussed in the previous three sections. Chapter 16 builds on the topics of internal decision making and group behavior by examining how consumers adopt new offerings, and how their *adoption* decisions affect the spread or *diffusion* of an offering through a market. Because products and services often reflect deep-felt and significant meanings (e.g., our favorite song or restaurant), Chapter 17 focuses on the interesting topic of *symbolic consumer behavior*.

Part V, "Consumer Welfare" covers two topics that have been of great interest to consumer researchers in recent years. Chapter 18 examines *ethics, responsibility, and the "dark side" of consumer behavior* and focuses on some negative outcomes of consumer-related behaviors (compulsive buying and gambling, prostitution, etc.) as well as marketing practices that have been the focus of social commentary in recent years. Finally, an additional chapter can be found on the website for this book. That chapter discusses *consumerism and public policy* issues that are relevant to consumer behavior.

Pedagogical Advantages

Based on our extensive teaching experience, we have incorporated a number of features that should help students learn about consumer behavior.

Chapter Opening Cases Each chapter begins with a case scenario about an actual company or situation that illustrates key concepts discussed in the chapter and their importance to marketers. This will help students grasp the "big picture" and understand the relevance of the topics from the start of the chapter.

Chapter Opening Model Each chapter also begins with a conceptual model that shows the organization of the chapter, the topics discussed, and how they relate both to one another and to other chapters. Each model reflects an expanded picture of one or more of the elements presented in the overall conceptual model for the book (described in Chapter 1).

Marketing Implication Sections Numerous *Marketing Implications sections* are interspersed throughout each chapter. These sections illustrate how various consumer behavior concepts can be applied to the practice of marketing, including such basic marketing functions as market segmentation, target market selection, positioning, market research, promotion, price, product, and place decisions. An abundance of marketing examples (from both the US and abroad) provide concrete applications and implementations of the concepts to marketing practice.

Marginal Glossary Every chapter contains a set of key terms that are both highlighted in the text and defined in margin notes. These terms and their definitions should help students identify and remember the central concepts described in the chapter.

Abundant Use of Full-Color Exhibits Each chapter contains a number of illustrated examples, including photos, advertisements, charts, and graphs. These illustrations help to make important topics personally relevant and engaging, help students remember the material, and make the book more accessible and aesthetically pleasing, thereby increasing students' motivation to learn. All diagrams and charts employ full color, which serves to both highlight key points and add to the aesthetic appeal of the text. Each model, graph, ad, and photo also has an accompanying caption that provides a simple description and explanation of how the exhibit relates to the topic it is designed to illustrate.

End-of-Chapter Summaries The end of each chapter provides students with a simple and concise summary of topics. These summaries are a good review tool to use with the conceptual model to help students to get the big picture.

End-of-Chapter Questions Each chapter includes a set of review and discussion questions designed to help students recall and more deeply understand the concepts in the chapter.

End-of-Chapter Cases Each chapter ends with a short case that describes an issue pertinent to the topics discussed in the text. By applying chapter content to real-world cases, students have a chance to make the concepts we discuss more concrete. Many of the cases involve brands that consumers are familiar with, heightening engagement with the material.

Complete Teaching Package

A variety of ancillary materials have been designed to help the instructor in the classroom. All of these supplements have been carefully coordinated to support the text and provide an integrated set of materials for the instructor. The Instructor's Manual, Test Bank, and PowerPoint programs can be found on the Instructor's

Resource CD-ROM. Instructor Manual, Test Bank files, and Lecture Outline Power-Points can also be found on the Instructor's Companion Site.

Instructor's Manual The *Instructor's Manual*, prepared by Professor Carol Bruneau, has been completely revised and updated to provide a thorough review of material in the text as well as supplementary materials that can be used to expand upon the text and enhance classroom presentations. An alternate table of contents and consumer behavior model for presenting the text in a "macro to micro" approach has been provided as well as different sample syllabi. Included for each chapter are a chapter summary; learning objectives; a comprehensive chapter outline; answers to review and discussion questions; answers to end-of-chapter cases; suggestions and guidelines for end-of-chapter exercises, including Internet exercises; additional discussion questions; and several suggested classroom activities. Classroom activities include questions for each chapter that stimulate group discussion, suggestions for bringing additional examples (videos, readings, etc.) into the classroom, and special experiential activities created by Professor Sheri Bridges, with detailed guidelines for facilitation.

Online Test Bank An extensive test bank prepared by Professor Carol Bruneau is available to assist the instructor in assessing student performance. The test bank has been expanded and revised to reflect the new edition content and includes a mix of both conceptual and applied questions for each chapter. Each test bank question provides a text page reference and has been tagged for AACSB requirements.

Online Test Bank, Diploma Format This electronic version of the printed Test Bank allows instructors to generate and change tests easily on the computer. The program will print an answer key appropriate to each version for the test you have devised, and it allows you to customize the printed appearance of the test.

PowerPoint Presentation Package A package of professionally developed Power-Point slides is available for use by adopters of this textbook. Two versions of the PowerPoints are available to provide instructors with maximum flexibility. The Lecture PowerPoints outline the text content, including key figures and tables; while specially tagged premium slides include additional print ads and other supplementary content that does not appear within the textbook. Instructors who have access to PowerPoint can edit slides to customize them for their classrooms.

Videos A completely new video package has been provided to supplement and enliven class lectures and discussion. Videos include many real-world scenarios that illustrate certain concepts in a given chapter. The clips are intended to be interesting, to ground the concepts in real life for students, and to provide an impetus for stimulating student input and involvement. A Video Guide is also available to help instructors integrate the videos with various text chapters.

WebCT For instructors teaching an online or hybrid course, WebCT course cartridges are available. This special offering provides unique exercises that give students first-hand experience using PRIZM® $_{NE}$ data resources. Students will be able to use this ground-breaking methodology to practice making solid, cost-effective marketing decisions about market size, site selection, direct mail, and other targeted communications.

Student and Instructor Companion Sites

Companion web sites enhance the book content and provide additional information, guidance, and activities. The student companion site provides a number of resources to help students study and test their learning. Interactive Flashcards allow students to study key terms and concepts, while the Interactive Quiz section of the site gives students an opportunity to prepare for in-class exams through chapter self-assessments. For instructors, the companion site provides a set of Lecture PowerPoints, as well as an online Instructor Manual and Test Bank files.

Acknowledgments

Special recognition is extended to Marian Wood, whose assistance was instrumental to the completion of this project. Her tireless work on this project is greatly appreciated. We have also been extremely fortunate to work with a wonderful team of dedicated professionals from Cengage Learning. We are very grateful to Joanne Dauksewicz, Fred Burns, Colleen Farmer, and Julie Low whose enormous energy and enthusiasm spurred our progress on this Fifth Edition. We also appreciate the efforts of Carol Bruneau of The University of Montana for her work on the Instructor's Manual and Test Bank; John Eaton of Arizona State University for his contributions to the online Interactive Quizzes and creation of the PRIZM Database Analysis Exercises; and Sheri Bridges at Wake Forest University for her work on the Experiential Exercises, The quality of this book and its ancillary package has been helped immensely by the insightful and rich comments of a set of researchers and instructors who served as reviewers. Their thoughtful and helpful comments had real impact in shaping the final product. In particular, we wish to thank:

Larry Anderson
Long Island University

Mike Ballif
University of Utah

Sharon Beatty
University of Alabama

Sandy Becker
Rutgers Business School

Russell Belk
University of Utah

Joseph Bonnice
Manhattan College

Timothy Brotherton
Ferris State University

Carol Bruneau
University of Montana

Margaret L. Burk
Muskingum College

Carol Calder
Loyola Marymount University

Paul Chao
University of Northern Iowa

Dennis Clayson
University of Northern Iowa

Joel Cohen
University of Florida

Sally Dibb
University of Warwick

Richard W. Easley
Baylor University

Richard Elliott
Lancaster University

Abdi Eshghi
Bentley College

Frank W. Fisher
Stonehill College

Ronald Fullerton
Providence College

Philip Garton
Leicester Business School

Peter L. Gillett
University of Central Florida

Debbora Heflin
Cal Poly - Pomona

Elizabeth Hirschman
Rutgers University

Raj G. Javalgi
Cleveland State University

Harold Kassarjian
UCLA

Patricia Kennedy
University of Nebraska - Lincoln

Robert E. Kleine
Arizona State University

Stephen K. Koernig
DePaul University

Scott Koslow
University of Waikato

Robert Lawson
William Patterson University

Phillip Lewis
Rowan College of New Jersey

Kenneth R. Lord
SUNY - Buffalo

Peggy Sue Loroz
Gonzaga University

Bart Macchiette
Plymouth State College

Michael Mallin
Kent State University

Lawrence Marks
Kent State University

David Marshall
University of Edinburgh

Ingrid M. Martin
California State University, Long Beach

Anil Mathur
Hofstra University

A. Peter McGraw
University of Colorado, Boulder

Matt Meuter
California State University, Chico

Martin Meyers
University of Wisconsin - Stevens Point

Vince Mitchell
UMIST

Lois Mohr
Georgia State University

Risto Moisio
California State University, Long Beach

Rebecca Walker Naylor
University of South Carolina

James R. Ogden
Kutztown University

Thomas O'Guinn
University of Illinois

Marco Protano
New York University

Judith Powell
Virginia Union University

Michael Reilly
Montana State University

Anja K. Reimer
University of Miami

Gregory M. Rose
The University of Mississippi

Mary Mercurio Scheip
Eckerd College

Marilyn Scrizzi
New Hampshire Technical College

John Shaw
Providence College

C. David Shepherd
University of Tennessee, Chattanooga

Robert E. Smith
Indiana University

Eric Richard Spangenberg
Washington State University

Bruce Stern
Portland State University

Barbara Stewart
University of Houston

Jane Boyd Thomas
Winthrop University

Phil Titus
Bowling Green State University

Carolyn Tripp
Western Illinois University

Rajiv Vaidyanathan
University of Minnesota, Duluth

Stuart Van Auken
California State University, Chico

Kathleen D. Vohs
University of Minnesota

Janet Wagner
University of Maryland

John Weiss
Colorado State University

Tommy E. Whittler
University of Kentucky

Carolyn Yoon
University of Michigan

An Introduction to Consumer Behavior

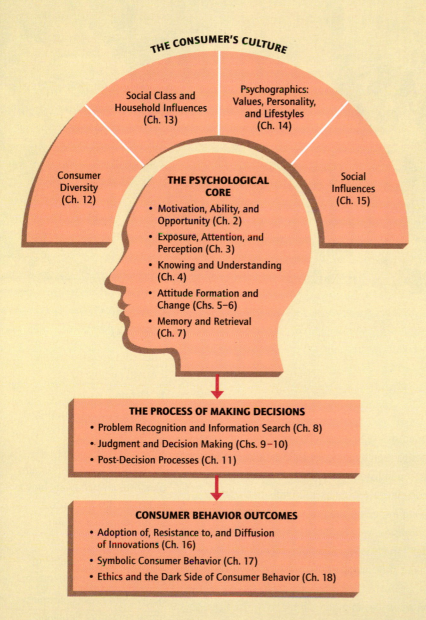

THE CONSUMER'S CULTURE

Social Class and Household Influences (Ch. 13)

Psychographics: Values, Personality, and Lifestyles (Ch. 14)

Consumer Diversity (Ch. 12)

THE PSYCHOLOGICAL CORE
- Motivation, Ability, and Opportunity (Ch. 2)
- Exposure, Attention, and Perception (Ch. 3)
- Knowing and Understanding (Ch. 4)
- Attitude Formation and Change (Chs. 5–6)
- Memory and Retrieval (Ch. 7)

Social Influences (Ch. 15)

THE PROCESS OF MAKING DECISIONS
- Problem Recognition and Information Search (Ch. 8)
- Judgment and Decision Making (Chs. 9–10)
- Post-Decision Processes (Ch. 11)

CONSUMER BEHAVIOR OUTCOMES
- Adoption of, Resistance to, and Diffusion of Innovations (Ch. 16)
- Symbolic Consumer Behavior (Ch. 17)
- Ethics and the Dark Side of Consumer Behavior (Ch. 18)

In Part One, you will learn that consumer behavior involves much more than purchasing products. In addition, you will find out that marketers continuously study consumer behavior for clues to who buys, uses, and disposes of what products as well as clues to when, where, and why they do.

Chapter 1 defines consumer behavior and examines its importance to marketers, advocacy groups, public policy makers, and consumers themselves. It also presents the overall model that guides the organization of this text. As this model indicates, consumer behavior covers four basic domains: (1) the psychological core, (2) the process of making decisions, (3) the consumer's culture, and (4) consumer behavior outcomes and issues. In addition, you will read about the implications of consumer behavior for marketing decisions and activities.

The Enrichment Chapter focuses on consumer behavior research and its special implications for marketers. You will learn about various research methods, types of data, and ethical issues related to consumer research. With this background, you will be able to understand how consumer research helps marketers develop more effective strategies and tactics for reaching and satisfying customers.

Chapter 1

Understanding Consumer Behavior

INTRODUCTION

Land of the Rising Trends

When Google wants to learn how cell phone users search the Internet, it looks at Japan, where 100 million consumers use phones to search online for train timetables, videos of pop stars, and more. Google's marketers watch and listen while cell phone users conduct searches, narrow down results, and react to website layouts. After users complained that maps loaded slowly and were difficult to navigate, Google sped up the process and added arrows to facilitate faster navigation. "People's expectations are very high here compared [with those of people in] other regions," explains a manager. "That's why we get good feedback." With good feedback, Google can make changes to meet consumers' expectations and maintain its position in the global search-engine market.

Japan is the land of rising trends in fashion as well as in high-tech services. The Swedish retail chain H&M has opened its doors in Tokyo to keep an eye on what local high school girls wear, as have Abercrombie & Fitch and other clothing retailers. LeSportsac's designers seek inspiration for new handbags by observing the preferences of trend-setting Tokyo teens. "I can see something happen in Tokyo and watch the ripple effect across the Pacific to New York and then watch as it goes back to L.A.," says a LeSportsac executive who visits Japan regularly in search of new product ideas.[1]

Google, LeSportsac, H&M, and other companies know that their success depends on understanding consumer behavior and trends so that they can create goods and services that consumers will want, like, use, and recommend to others. This chapter provides a general overview of (1) what consumer behavior is, (2) what factors affect it, (3) who benefits from studying it, and (4) how marketers apply consumer behavior concepts. Because you are a consumer, you probably have some thoughts about these issues. However, you may be surprised at how broad the domain of consumer behavior is, how many factors help explain it, and how important the field is to marketers, ethicists and consumer advocates, public policy makers and regulators, and consumers like yourself. You will also get a glimpse of the marketing implications of consumer behavior, previewing how we will connect consumer behavior concepts with practical applications throughout this book.

Defining Consumer Behavior

Consumer behavior
The totality of consumers' decisions with respect to the acquisition, consumption, and disposition of goods, services, time, and ideas by human decision-making units (over time).

If you were asked to define **consumer behavior,** you might say it refers to the study of how a person buys products. However, this is only part of the definition. Consumer behavior really involves quite a bit more, as this more complete definition indicates:

> *Consumer behavior reflects the totality of consumers' decisions with respect to the acquisition, consumption, and disposition of goods, services, activities, experiences, people, and ideas by (human) decision-making units [over time].*[2]

This definition has some very important elements, summarized in Exhibit 1.1. Here is a closer look at each element.

Consumer Behavior Involves Goods, Services, Activities, Experiences, People, and Ideas

Consumer behavior means more than just the way that a person buys tangible products such as bath soap and automobiles. It also includes consumers' use of services, activities, experiences, and ideas such as going to the doctor, visiting a festival, signing up for yoga classes, taking a trip, donating to UNICEF, and checking for traffic before crossing the street (an idea championed by New York City's "Cars hurt, stay alert" campaign).[3] In addition, consumers make decisions about people, such as voting for politicians, reading books written by certain authors, seeing movies starring certain actors, and attending concerts featuring favorite bands.

Offering A product, service, activity, or idea offered by a marketing organization to consumers.

Another example of consumer behavior involves choices about the consumption of time, such as whether to watch a certain television program (and for how long), and the use of time in ways that show who we are and how we are different from others.[4] Many consumers like the excitement of watching a sports event live on TV rather than waiting to watch a tape-delayed version later, for instance.[5] Because consumer behavior includes the consumption of many things, we use the simple term **offering** to encompass these entities.

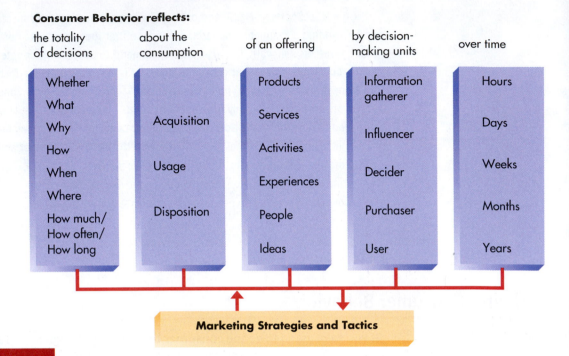

Consumer Behavior reflects:

the totality of decisions	about the consumption	of an offering	by decision-making units	over time
Whether		Products	Information gatherer	Hours
What		Services		
Why	Acquisition		Influencer	Days
How		Activities		
When	Usage	Experiences	Decider	Weeks
Where				
How much/ How often/ How long	Disposition	People	Purchaser	Months
		Ideas	User	Years

Marketing Strategies and Tactics

What Is Consumer Behavior?

Consumer behavior reflects more than the way that a product is acquired by a single person at any one point in time. Think of some marketing strategies and tactics that try to influence one or more of the dimensions of consumer behavior shown in this exhibit.

Acquisition The process by which a consumer comes to own an offering.

Usage The process by which a consumer uses an offering.

Disposition The process by which a consumer discards an offering.

Consumer Behavior Involves More Than Buying

The manner in which consumers buy is extremely important to marketers. However, marketers are also intensely interested in consumer behavior related to using and disposing of an offering:

- *Acquiring.* Buying represents one type of **acquisition** behavior. As shown later in this chapter, acquisition includes other ways of obtaining goods and services, such as leasing, trading, and sharing. It also involves decisions about time as well as money.[6]

- *Using.* After consumers acquire an offering, they use it, which is why **usage** is at the very core of consumer behavior.[7] Whether and why we use certain products can symbolize something about who we are, what we value, and what we believe. The products we use at Thanksgiving (for example, pumpkin pie, whether made from scratch or store bought) may symbolize the event's significance and how we feel about our guests. The music we enjoy (Shakira or Andrea Bocelli) and the jewelry we wear (Swatch watches or belly button rings) can also symbolize who we are and how we feel. Moreover, marketers must be sensitive to when consumers are likely to use a product,[8] whether they find it effective,[9] and how they react after using it—do they spread positive or negative word-of-mouth reviews about a new film, for instance?[10]

- *Disposing.* **Disposition,** how consumers get rid of an offering they have previously acquired, can have important implications for marketers.[11] Eco-minded consumers often seek out biodegradable products made from recycled materials or choose goods that do not pollute when disposed of. Municipalities are also interested in how to motivate earth-friendly disposition.[12] Marketers see profit opportunities in addressing disposition concerns. For instance, consumers who renovate their kitchens can install new counters made from recycled materials such as ShetkaStone, which is made from recycled paper.[13]

Consumer Behavior Is a Dynamic Process

The sequence of acquisition, consumption, and disposition can occur over time in a dynamic order—hours, days, weeks, months, or years, as shown in Exhibit 1.1. To illustrate, assume that a family has acquired and is using a new car. Usage provides the family with information—whether the car drives well, is reliable, and does little harm to the environment—that affects when, whether, how, and why members will dispose of the car by selling, trading, or junking it. Because the family always needs transportation, disposition is likely to affect when, whether, how, and why its members acquire another car in the future.

Entire markets are designed around linking one consumer's disposition decision to other consumers' acquisition decisions. When consumers buy used cars, they are buying cars that others have disposed of. From eBay's online auctions to Goodwill Industries' secondhand clothing stores, from consignment stores to used book stores, many businesses exist to link one consumer's disposition behavior with another's acquisition behavior.

Consumer Behavior Can Involve Many People

Consumer behavior does not necessarily reflect the action of a single individual. A group of friends, a few coworkers, or an entire family may plan a birthday party or decide where to have lunch. Moreover, the individuals engaging in consumer behavior can take on one or more roles. In the case of a car purchase, for example, one or more family members might take on the role of information gatherer by researching different models. Others might assume the role of influencer and try to affect the outcome of a decision. One or more members may take on the role of purchaser by actually paying for the car, and some or all may be users. Finally, several family members may be involved in the disposal of the car.

Consumer Behavior Involves Many Decisions

Consumer behavior involves understanding whether, why, when, where, how, how much, how often, and for how long consumers will buy, use, or dispose of an offering (look back at Exhibit 1.1).

Whether to Acquire/Use/Dispose of an Offering

Consumers must decide whether to acquire, use, or dispose of an offering. They may need to decide whether to spend or save their money when they earn extra cash.[14] How much they decide to spend may be influenced by their perceptions of how much they recall spending in the past.[15] They may need to decide whether to order a pizza, clean out a closet, or go to a movie. Some decisions about whether to acquire, use, or dispose of an offering are related to personal goals, safety concerns, or a desire to reduce economic, social, or psychological risk.

What Offering to Acquire/Use/Dispose of

Consumers make decisions every day about what to buy; in fact, each U.S. household spends an average of $127 per day on goods and services.[16] In some cases we make choices among product or service *categories*, such as buying food versus downloading new music. In other cases we choose between *brands*, such as whether to buy an iPhone or a Samsung cell phone. Our choices multiply daily

Exhibit 1.2

Consumer Spending, By Age

Consumers born in different years have different needs and spend different amounts on necessities and non-necessities.

Consumers Born In	Annual Average Spending per Household	Annual Average Spending on Housing, Food, and Transportation	Annual Average Spending on Entertainment, Reading, and Alcohol
1982 and later	$28,181	$18,941	$1,867
1972–1981	$47,582	$32,290	$2,976
1962–1971	$57,476	$37,611	$3,574
1952–1961	$57,563	$35,816	$3,515
1942–1951	$50,789	$31,337	$3,290
1941 and earlier	$35,058	$21,764	$1,983

Source: Adapted from "Age of Reference Person: Average Annual Expenditures and Characteristics," *Consumer Expenditure Survey Anthology 2006*, U.S. Department of Labor, U.S. Bureau of Labor Statistics, Table 3, *www.bls.gov.*

as marketers introduce new products, sizes, and packages. Exhibit 1.2 shows some of the spending patterns of consumers in particular age groups.

Why Acquire/Use/Dispose of an Offering

Consumption can occur for a number of reasons. Among the most important reasons, as you will see later, are the ways in which an offering meets someone's needs, values, or goals. Some consumers have body parts pierced as a form of self-expression, while others do it to fit into a group. Still others believe that body piercing is a form of beauty or that it enhances sexual pleasure.[17]

Sometimes our reasons for using an offering are filled with conflict, which leads to some difficult consumption decisions. Teenagers may smoke, even though they know it is harmful, because they think smoking will help them gain acceptance. Some consumers may be unable to stop acquiring, using, or disposing of products. They may be physically addicted to products such as cigarettes or alcoholic beverages, or they may have a compulsion to eat, gamble, or buy.

Why Not to Acquire/Use/Dispose of an Offering

Marketers also try to understand why consumers do *not* acquire, use, or dispose of an offering. For example, consumers may delay buying a personal video recorder because they doubt that they can handle the technology or they doubt that the product offers anything special. They may believe that technology is changing so fast that the product will soon be outdated. They may even believe that some firms will go out of business, leaving them without after-sale support or service. At times, consumers who want to acquire or consume an offering are unable to do so because what they want is unavailable.Ethics can also play a role. Some consumers may want to avoid products made in factories with questionable labor practices or avoid movies downloaded, copied, and shared without permission.[18]

How to Acquire/Use/Dispose of an Offering

Marketers gain a lot of insight by understanding how consumers acquire, consume, and dispose of an offering.

Ways of Acquiring an Offering How do consumers decide whether to acquire an offering in a store or mall, online, or at an auction?[19] How do they decide whether to

Acquisition Method	Description
Buying	Buying is a common acquisition method used for many offerings.
Trading	Consumers might receive a product or service as part of a trade. Example: Trading in old DVDs as partial payment for new DVDs.
Renting or leasing	Instead of buying, consumers rent or lease cars, tuxedos, furniture, vacation homes, and more.
Bartering	Thousands of consumers (and businesses) exchange goods or services without having money change hands.
Gifting	Gifting is common throughout the world. Each society has many gift-giving occasions as well as informal or formal rules dictating how gifts are to be given, what is an appropriate gift, and what is an appropriate response to a gift.
Finding	Consumers sometimes find goods that others have lost (hats left on the bus, umbrellas left in class) or thrown away.
Stealing	Because various offerings can be acquired through theft, marketers have developed goods and services to deter this acquisition method, such as alarms to deter car theft.
Sharing	Another method of acquisition is by sharing or borrowing. Some types of "sharing" are illegal and border on theft, as when consumers copy and share movies.

Exhibit 1.3

Eight Ways to Acquire an Offering

There are many ways that consumers can acquire an offering.

pay with cash, a check, a debit card, a credit card, or an electronic system such as PayPal, which online shoppers use to buy goods and services worth $47 billion annually?[20] These examples relate to consumers' buying decisions, but Exhibit 1.3 shows that consumers can acquire an offering in other ways.

Ways of Using an Offering   In addition to understanding how consumers acquire an offering, marketers want to know how consumers use an offering.[21] For obvious reasons, marketers want to ensure that their offering is used correctly. For example, makers of camera phones need to educate consumers about how to print images, not just e-mail them.[22] Improper usage of offerings like cough medicine or alcohol can create health and safety problems.[23] Because consumers may ignore label warnings and directions on potentially dangerous products, marketers who want to make warnings more effective have to understand how consumers process label information. Some consumers collect items, a situation that has created a huge market for buying, selling, transporting, storing, and insuring collectible items.[24]

Ways of Disposing of an Offering   Finally, consumers who want to dispose of offerings have several options:[25]

▶ *Find a new use for it.* Using an old toothbrush to clean rust from tools or making shorts out of an old pair of jeans shows how consumers can continue using an item instead of disposing of it.

▶ *Get rid of it temporarily.* Renting or lending an item is one way of getting rid of it temporarily.

▶ *Get rid of it permanently.* Throwing away an item gets rid of it permanently, although consumers may instead choose to trade it, give it away, or sell it.

However, some consumers refuse to throw away things that they regard as special, even if the items no longer serve a functional purpose.

When to Acquire/Use/Dispose of an Offering

The timing of consumer behavior can depend on many factors, including our perceptions of and attitudes toward time itself. Consumers may think in terms of

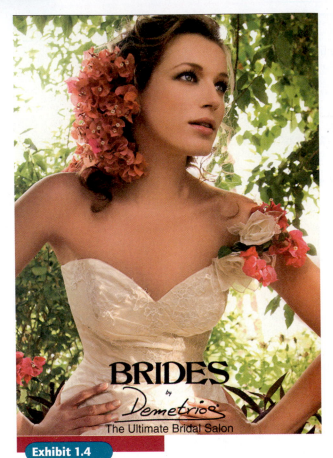

Exhibit 1.4

Transitions

Getting married is a major life transition that (like other transitions) stimulates consumption of entirely new offerings.

whether it is "time for me" or "time for others" and whether acquiring or using an offering is planned or spontaneous.[26] In cold weather, our tendency to rent DVDs, call for a tow truck, or shop for clothes is greatly enhanced while we are less likely to eat ice cream, shop for a car, or look for a new home. Time of day influences many consumption decisions, which is the reason why many McDonald's outlets stay open late to cater to hungry night-owls and workers getting off late shifts or going to early shifts.[27]

Our need for variety can affect when we acquire, use, or dispose of an offering. We may decide not to eat yogurt for lunch today if we have already had it every other day this week. Transitions such as graduation, birth, retirement, and death also affect when we acquire, use, and dispose of offerings. For instance, we buy wedding rings, wedding dresses, and wedding cakes only when we get married. When we consume can be affected by traditions imposed by our families, our culture, and the area in which we live.

Decisions about when to acquire or use an offering are also affected by knowing when others might or might not be buying or using it. Thus, we might choose to go to the movies or the gym when we know that others will *not* be doing so. In addition, we may wait to buy until we know something will be on sale; even if we have to line up to buy something popular, we are likely to continue waiting if we see many people joining the line behind us.[28] At times, we will acquire an item for later consumption. In fact, waiting to consume a pleasurable product such as candy increases our enjoyment of its consumption, even though we may be frustrated by having to wait to consume it.[29]

Another decision is when to acquire a new, improved version of a product we already own. This can be a difficult decision when the current model still works well or has sentimental value. However, marketers may be able to affect whether and when consumers buy upgrades by providing economic incentives for trading up from older products.[30]

Where to Acquire/Use/Dispose of an Offering

As Exhibit 1.4 suggests, transitions such as graduation, birth, retirement, and death also affect when we acquire, use, and dispose of offerings. Consumers have more choices of where to acquire, use, and dispose of an offering than they have ever had before, including making purchases in stores, by mail, by phone, and over the Internet. Shopping habits are changing as more consumers buy groceries, clothing, and other products at multiline superstores such as Wal-Mart.[31] The Internet has changed where we acquire, use, and dispose of goods. Shoppers spend $175 billion online every year—a figure that's growing by 20 percent or more annually.[32] Many consumers buy online because they like the convenience or the price.[33] Circuit City and other retailers even let customers go to local stores to pick up or return merchandise purchased online.[34] And as eBay's success shows, the Internet provides a

Exhibit 1.5

Bonus Packs

Promotions like bonus packs prompt consumers to buy and perhaps use more of an offering than they otherwise would.

convenient and often profitable way of disposing of goods that are then acquired by others.

In addition to acquisition decisions, consumers also make decisions about where to consume various products. For example, the need for privacy motivates consumers to stay home when using products that determine whether they are ovulating or pregnant. On the other hand, wireless connections allow consumers in public places to make phone calls, check e-mail, read news headlines, play computer games, and download photos or music from anywhere in the world. Consumers can even make charitable donations via cell phone.[35]

Finally, consumers make decisions regarding where to dispose of goods. Should they toss an old magazine in the trash or the recycling bin? Should they store an old photo album in the attic or give it to a relative? Older consumers, in particular, may worry about what will happen to their special possessions after their death and about how to divide heirlooms without creating family conflict. These consumers hope that mementos will serve as a legacy for their heirs.[36] A growing number of consumers are recycling unwanted goods through recycling agencies or nonprofit groups or giving them directly to other consumers through websites like Freecycle.org.[37]

How Much, How Often, and How Long to Acquire/Use/Dispose of an Offering

Consumers must make decisions about how much of a good or service they need; how often they need it; and how much time they will spend in acquisition, usage, and disposition.[38] Usage decisions can vary widely from person to person and from culture to culture. For example, consumers in India drink an average of only 5 nine-ounce bottles of soft drinks per year, whereas consumers in China drink 17, and consumers in America drink 280.[39]

Sales of a product can be increased when the consumer (1) uses larger amounts of the product, (2) uses the product more frequently, or (3) uses it for longer periods of time. Bonus packages such as the one shown in Exhibit 1.5 may motivate consumers to buy more of a product, but does this stockpiling lead to higher consumption? In the case of food products, consumers are more likely to increase consumption when the stockpiled item requires no preparation.[40] Usage may also increase when consumers sign up for flat-fee pricing covering unlimited consumption of telephone services or other offerings. However, because many consumers who choose flat-fee programs overestimate their likely consumption, they often pay more than they would have paid with per-usage pricing.[41]

Some consumers experience problems because they engage in more acquisition, usage, or disposition than they should. For example, they may have a compulsion to overbuy, overeat, smoke, or gamble too much. Many of us make New Year's resolutions to stop consuming things we think we should not consume or to start consuming things we think we should consume. Hence, researchers have recently given attention to understanding what affects consumers' abilities to control consumption temptations and what happens when self-control falters.[42]

Consumer Behavior Involves Feeling and Coping

Consumer researchers have studied the powerful role that emotions play in consumer behavior.[43] Positive and negative emotions as well as specific emotions like hope,[44] fear,[45] regret,[46] guilt,[47] embarrassment,[48] and general moods[49] can affect how consumers think, the choices they make, how they feel after making a decision, what they remember, and how much they enjoy an experience. Emotions like love sometimes describe how we feel about certain brands or possessions.[50] Consumers often use products to regulate their feelings—as when a scoop of ice cream seems like a good antidote to a bad quiz score.[51] Researchers have also studied how service employees' emotions can subconsciously affect consumers' emotions.[52] And low-level emotions can be very important in low-effort situations (e.g., the low-level feelings we get from viewing a humorous ad).

Because issues related to consumer behavior can involve stress, consumers often need to cope in some way.[53] Researchers have studied how consumers cope with difficult choices and an overwhelming array of goods from which to choose;[54] how consumers use goods and services to cope with stressful events[55] like having cancer; and how they cope with losing possessions due to divorce, natural disasters, moving to a residential-care facility, and other incidents.[56] They have even studied the coping behavior of certain market segments, such as low-literacy consumers who often find it challenging to understand the marketplace without being able to read.[57]

What Affects Consumer Behavior?

The many factors that affect acquisition, usage, and disposition decisions can be classified into four broad domains, as shown in the model in Exhibit 1.6: (1) the psychological core, (2) the process of making decisions, (3) the consumer's culture, and (4) consumer behavior outcomes. Although the four domains are presented in separate sections of this book, each domain is related to all the others. For example, to make decisions that affect outcomes like buying new products, consumers must first engage in processes described in the psychological core. They need to be motivated, able, and have the opportunity to be exposed to, perceive, and attend to information. They need to think about this information, develop attitudes about it, and form memories.

The cultural environment also affects what motivates consumers, how they process information, and the kinds of decisions they make. Age, gender, social class, ethnicity, families, friends, and other factors affect consumer values and lifestyles and, in turn, influence the decisions that consumers make and how and why they make them. In the following overview, we illustrate the interrelationships among the domains with an example of a vacation decision.

The Psychological Core: Internal Consumer Processes

Before consumers can make decisions, they must have some source of knowledge or information upon which to base their decisions. This source—the psychological

A Model of Consumer Behavior

Consumer behavior encompasses four domains: (1) the consumer's culture, (2) the psychological core, (3) the process of making decisions, and (4) consumer behavior outcomes and issues. As the exhibit shows, Chapters 2–18 of this book relate to the four parts of this overall model.

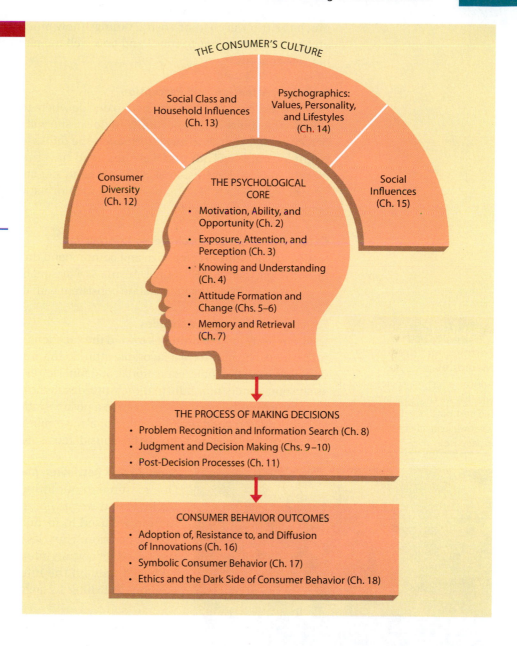

THE CONSUMER'S CULTURE

Social Class and Household Influences (Ch. 13)

Psychographics: Values, Personality, and Lifestyles (Ch. 14)

Consumer Diversity (Ch. 12)

Social Influences (Ch. 15)

THE PSYCHOLOGICAL CORE
- Motivation, Ability, and Opportunity (Ch. 2)
- Exposure, Attention, and Perception (Ch. 3)
- Knowing and Understanding (Ch. 4)
- Attitude Formation and Change (Chs. 5–6)
- Memory and Retrieval (Ch. 7)

THE PROCESS OF MAKING DECISIONS
- Problem Recognition and Information Search (Ch. 8)
- Judgment and Decision Making (Chs. 9–10)
- Post-Decision Processes (Ch. 11)

CONSUMER BEHAVIOR OUTCOMES
- Adoption of, Resistance to, and Diffusion of Innovations (Ch. 16)
- Symbolic Consumer Behavior (Ch. 17)
- Ethics and the Dark Side of Consumer Behavior (Ch. 18)

core—covers motivation, ability, and opportunity; exposure, attention, and perception; categorization and comprehension of information; and attitudes about an offering.

Having Motivation, Ability, and Opportunity

Consider the case of a consumer named Jessica who is deciding on a ski vacation. In Jessica's mind, the vacation decision is risky because it will consume a lot of money and time, and she does not want to make a bad choice. Therefore, Jessica is motivated to learn as much as she can about various vacation options, think about them, and imagine what they will be like. She has put other activities aside to give herself the opportunity to learn and think about this vacation. Because Jessica already knows how to ski, she has the ability to determine what types of ski vacations she would find enjoyable. Whether she focuses on concrete things (how much the trip will cost) or abstract things (how much fun she will have) depends on how soon she plans to travel and how well the place she plans to visit fits with her self-concept.[58]

Exposure, Attention, and Perception

Because Jessica is greatly motivated to decide where to go on vacation and because she has the ability and opportunity to do so, she will make sure she is exposed to, perceives, and attends to any information she thinks is relevant to her decision. She might look at travel ads and websites, read travel-related articles, and talk with friends and travel agents. Jessica will probably not attend to *all* vacation information; however, she is likely to be exposed to information she will never consciously perceive or pay attention to.

Categorizing and Comprehending Information

Jessica will attempt to categorize and comprehend the information she does attend to. She might infer that Kitzbühel, Austria, is a reasonably priced vacation destination because a website shows information consistent with this interpretation.

Forming and Changing Attitudes

Jessica is likely to form attitudes toward the vacations she has categorized and comprehended. She may have a favorable attitude toward Kitzbühel because a website describes it as affordable, educational, and fun. However, her attitudes might change as she encounters new information. Attitudes do not always predict our behavior. For example, although many of us have a positive attitude toward working out, our attitude and our good intentions do not always culminate in a trip to the gym. For this reason, attitudes and choices are considered as separate topics.

Exhibit 1.7

Forming and Retrieving Memories

Ads can affect our choices, but whether we choose something the next time may depend on what we remember about our experiences.

Forming and Retrieving Memories

One reason that our attitudes may not predict our behavior is that we may or may not remember the information we used to form our attitudes when we later make a decision. Thus, Jessica may have *formed* memories based on certain information, but her choices will be based only on the information she *retrieves* from memory, as Exhibit 1.7 suggests.

The Process of Making Decisions

The processes that are part of the psychological core are intimately tied to the second domain shown in Exhibit 1.6; the process of making decisions. The process of making consumption decisions involves four stages: problem recognition, information search, decision making, and post-purchase evaluation.

Problem Recognition and the Search for Information

Problem recognition occurs when we realize that we have an unfulfilled need. Jessica realized that she needed a vacation, for example. Her subsequent search for information gave her insight into where she might go, how much

To over 960 destinations across the world…

With its young fleet, superior service and the unique Turkish hospitality, Turkish Airlines is now a member of Star Alliance. Now while flying to over 960 destinations across the world, you can earn more miles with your Miles&Smiles card and benefit from even more exclusive advantages.

TURKISH AIRLINES

www.thy.com | 1-800-874-8875   A STAR ALLIANCE MEMBER

the vacation might cost, and when she might travel. She also examined her financial situation. Elements of the psychological core are invoked in problem recognition and search because once Jessica realizes that she needs a vacation and begins her information search, she is exposed to information, attends to and perceives it, categorizes and comprehends it, and forms attitudes and memories.

Making Judgments and Decisions

Jessica's decision is characterized as a *high-effort decision,* meaning that she is willing to invest a lot of time and to exert mental and emotional energy in making it. She identifies several criteria that will be important in making her choices: the trip should be fun and exciting, safe, educational, and affordable. Not all decisions involve a lot of effort. Jessica also faces low-effort decisions such as what brand of toothpaste to take on the trip.

Again, the psychological core is invoked in making decisions. With a high-effort decision, Jessica will be motivated to expose herself to lots of information, think about it deeply, analyze it critically, and form attitudes about it. She may have lasting memories about this information because she has thought about it so much. Consumers are not always aware of what they are thinking and how they are making their choices, so Jessica might not be able to explain what affected her choices (background music in a travel agency might even be an influence).[59] Yet the emotions she thinks she will experience from different options (excitement, relaxation) may well influence her ultimate choice.[60] With a low-effort decision, such as what brand of toothpaste to buy, she would probably engage in less information search and process information less deeply, resulting in less enduring attitudes and memories.

Making Post-Decision Evaluations

This step allows the consumer to judge, after the fact, whether the decision made was the correct one and whether to purchase that offering again. When she returns from her vacation, Jessica will probably evaluate the outcome of her decisions. If her expectations were met and if the vacation was everything she thought it would be, she will feel satisfied. If the vacation exceeded her expectations, she will be delighted. If it fell short of them, she will be dissatisfied. Once again, aspects of the psychological core are invoked in making post-decision evaluations. Jessica may expose herself to information that validates her experiences, she may update her attitudes, and she may selectively remember aspects of her trip that were extremely positive or negative.

The Consumer's Culture: External Processes

Why did Jessica decide to go on a skiing trip in the first place? In large part, our consumption decisions and how we process information are affected by our culture. **Culture** refers to the typical or expected behaviors, norms, and ideas that characterize a group of people. It can be a powerful influence on all aspects of human behavior. Jessica had certain feelings, perceptions, and attitudes because of the unique combination of groups to which she belongs and the influence they have on her values, personality, and lifestyle.

Culture The typical or expected behaviors, norms, and ideas that characterize a group of people.

Diversity Influences

Jessica is a member of many regional, ethnic, and religious groups that directly or indirectly affect the decisions she makes. For example, although her decision to ski at

Exhibit 1.8

Vacation

The word "vacation" means different things to different people. Your idea of a "relaxing getaway" may be quite different from someone else's. Can you see how factors like social class, ethnic status, economic conditions, group affiliations, and gender affect the kinds of vacations we are likely to find attractive? These examples show that some marketers are successful precisely because they understand what their customers value.

On vacation, would you like to . . .

Tour the World by Motorcycle?   See Europe or Asia from behind the handlebars of a motorcycle riding up and down highways, mountain passes, and country roads. You'll need $3,000, at least seven days, and considerable stamina to handle long days of riding and parking a 600-pound bike—but the views are breathtaking.

Work Up a Sweat and Then Get Pampered?   At a high-activity spa, you can learn to surf, practice yoga positions, hike sandstone canyons, or kickbox during the day. Nights are for pampering: After a healthy gourmet meal, rest your feet, take a class, or just retire to your featherbed. Price tag, including three meals: $200–$540 per day.

Be a Rancher?   Visit one of the more than 100 ranches in Wyoming and Montana, choosing from a rustic cabin at $150 per day or a luxurious room priced at $275 per day, including hearty chow. Help herd cattle, fix fences, take trail rides, or simply enjoy the Western scenery.

Play with Penguins?   Be one of only 15,000 tourists who visit Antarctica in a year. Start with a long plane ride to South America, followed by a cruise through the icy waters of the Drake Passage. Learn about the flora and fauna; then go ashore to see penguins and seals at play. Expect to pay $5,000 and up for a 12-day cruise.

Sources: Rosalind S. Helderman, "Lessons from the Bottom of the World," *Washington Post*, December 23, 2004, p. T3; Perri Cappell, "Going Mobile: Can't Shake the 'Easy Rider' Fantasy?" *Wall Street Journal*, December 20, 2004, p. R7; Marcy Barack, "Destination: Wyoming; Ranch Life Can Spoil a Manicure," *Los Angeles Times*, July 11, 2004, p. L13.

a place far from home is fairly typical for a working woman from North America, a consumer from a developing nation or a single woman from a different culture may not have made the same choice. Also, her age, gender, and educational background may all affect her impressions of what constitutes a good vacation, accounting for her interest in a European ski trip. Consider the vacation choices shown in Exhibit 1.8, and try to imagine the background factors that predispose consumers to choose these as vacation options.

Social Class and Household Influences

Because Jessica is a member of the upper middle class and has moved in with her parents, these social and household influences may have had an effect on her decision to go to a luxurious European ski resort with friends rather than go skiing with her family at a rustic ski area near home.

Values, Personality, and Lifestyles

The choices Jessica makes are based, in part, on her beliefs, her personality, and her activities, interests, and opinions. Thus, she may be attracted to a European ski trip because she wants a vacation that she thinks will be exciting and out of the ordinary. She also anticipates that this vacation will test her ability to manage on her own and give her a sense of accomplishment.

Reference Groups and Other Social Influences

Reference group A group of people we compare ourselves with for information regarding behavior, attitudes, or values.

When Jessica sees groups of others she perceives as similar to herself, she regards them as **reference groups,** people whose values she shares and whose opinions she values (see Exhibit 1.9). She might also want to emulate the behavior of people whom she admires and to listen to the advice they offer through *word of mouth.* Thus, athletes, musicians, or movie stars sometimes serve as reference

got milk?

Busy Body.
Actress, model,
mother, health nut,
spokesperson,
role model. How
does a busy mom
get it all done?
I exercise, eat right
and drink milk.
Studies suggest the
nutrients in 3 glasses
of lowfat or fat
free milk a day
can help maintain
a healthy weight.
Plus the protein
helps build muscle
for a lean body.
Done.

milk your diet

Exhibit 1.9

Influence of Reference Groups

Reference groups are people whose values we share and whose opinions we value.

Symbols External signs that we use to express our identity.

groups, influencing how we evaluate information and the choices we make. Reference groups can also make us feel as if we should behave in a certain way. Jessica may feel some pressure to go to Kitzbühel because her friends think that doing so is cool. In addition, Jessica's personality may affect her decisions. Because she is an extrovert and a moderate risk taker, she wants a vacation that is exciting and allows her to meet new people.

Consumer Behavior Outcomes and Issues

As Exhibit 1.6 shows, the psychological core, decision-making processes, and the consumer's culture affect consumer behavior outcomes such as the symbolic use of products and the diffusion of ideas, products, or services through a market. They also influence and are influenced by issues of ethics and social responsibility as well as the dark side of marketing and consumer behavior.

Consumer Behaviors Can Symbolize Who We Are

The groups we belong to and our sense of self can affect the **symbols** or external signs we use, consciously or unconsciously, to express our identity. For example, while skiing, Jessica may wear a North Face parka and Bollé goggles to communicate her status as an experienced skier. She might also take home objects that symbolize her vacation, such as postcards and T-shirts.

Consumer Behaviors Can Diffuse Through a Market

After Jessica makes her vacation decision, she may tell others about her prospective trip, which, in turn, could influence their vacation decisions. In this way, the idea of going to Kitzbühel on vacation may diffuse, or spread, to others. Had Jessica resisted going to Kitzbühel (perhaps because she thought it was too expensive or too far away), she might have communicated information that would make others less likely to vacation there. Thus, the diffusion of information can have both negative and positive effects for marketers.

The Dark Side of Marketing and Consumer Behavior, Ethics, and Social Responsibility

Certain consumer behaviors and certain marketing practices may be problematic to the consumer and/or to society. For instance, compulsive buying can have severe financial consequences for the consumer and his or her family. Lack of self-control over such behaviors can make consumers feel bad about themselves as well.[61] Other behaviors of concern include stealing, buying or selling through black markets, and underage drinking or smoking. Marketing can have a dark side, as

well. Key ethical issues are whether companies should advertise to children, whether marketing efforts promote obesity, whether advertising affects self-image, and whether marketing invades consumers' privacy. In addition, the environmental consequences of products and marketing are of increasing concern to consumers, regulators, and companies worldwide. For example, consumer research on disposition behavior has the potential to affect programs that conserve natural resources. Exhibit 1.10 shows an ad that aims to educate consumers about the benefits of recycling.

Who Benefits from the Study of Consumer Behavior?

Why do people study consumer behavior? The reasons are as varied as the four different groups who use consumer research: marketing managers, ethicists and advocates, public policy makers and regulators, and consumers.

Marketing Managers

The study of consumer behavior provides critical information to marketing managers for developing marketing strategies and tactics. The American Marketing Association's definition of **marketing** shows why marketing managers need to learn about consumer behavior:

Marketing A social and managerial process through which individuals and groups obtain what they need and want by creating and exchanging products and value with others.

> *Marketing is the activity, set of institutions, and processes for creating, communicating, delivering, and exchanging offerings that have value for customers, clients, partners, and society at large.*

As this definition makes clear, marketers need consumer behavior insights to understand what consumers and clients value; only then can they develop, communicate, and deliver appropriate goods and services. See the Enrichment Chapter for more about marketing research.

Ethicists and Advocacy Groups

Marketers' actions sometimes raise important ethical questions. Concerned consumers sometimes form advocacy groups to create public awareness of inappropriate practices. They also influence other consumers as well as the targeted companies through strategies such as media statements and boycotts. For example, Mothers Against Violence in America is one of several groups protesting video games that feature physical violence. The video game industry's Entertainment Software Rating Board labels games with designations such as *M* (mature, for persons 17 and older). Despite such labeling, advocacy groups are concerned that younger teens can easily acquire and play games intended for older consumers.[62] We explore various ethical issues throughout this book and go into more detail in Chapter 18.

Public Policy Makers and Regulators

Consumer behavior can be quite useful to legislators, regulators, and government agencies in developing policies and rules to protect consumers from unfair, unsafe, or inappropriate marketing practices. In turn, marketers' decisions are affected by these public policy actions. Consider the regulatory limits on tobacco marketing that are designed to discourage underage consumers from smoking and to inform consumers of smoking's health hazards. The United States, European Union, and other areas ban cigarette advertising on television and radio and in certain other media; they also require warning labels on each pack.[63]

Understanding how consumers comprehend and categorize information is important for recognizing and guarding against misleading advertising. For instance, researchers want to know what impressions an ad creates and whether these impressions are true. They also want to know how marketing influences consumers' decisions to comply with product usage instructions, such as using medical treatments as prescribed.[64] And consumer behavior research helps government officials understand and try to improve consumer welfare.[65]

Academics

Consumer behavior is important in the academic world for two reasons. First, academics disseminate knowledge about consumer behavior when they teach courses on the subject. Second, academics generate knowledge about consumer behavior when they conduct research focusing on how consumers act, think, and feel when acquiring, using, and disposing of offerings. In turn, such academic research is useful to marketing managers, advocacy groups, regulators, and others who need to understand consumer behavior.

Consumers and Society

An understanding of consumer behavior can help make a better environment for consumers. For example, research indicates that we better understand the differences among brands when we can view a chart, matrix, or grid comparing brands and their attributes.[66] Thus, matrices such as those presented in *Consumer Reports* are likely to help many consumers make better decisions.

Product, service, and communications developments to protect certain consumer segments have also grown out of understanding how consumers behave. Many people want to protect children against inappropriate advertising or guard themselves against invasion of privacy. Some companies have changed their marketing voluntarily, whereas others have waited until legislators, regulators, or advocacy groups forced them to make changes in their marketing. Finally, research on disposition behavior has the potential to aid recycling programs and other activities related to environmental protection, as discussed in Chapter 18.

Marketing Implications of Consumer Behavior

As you learn about consumer behavior, you may wonder how marketers use different consumer behavior concepts and findings. Starting with Chapter 2, you will find numerous sections titled "Marketing Implications" that illustrate how marketers apply consumer behavior concepts in the real world. In general, consumer research helps marketers to develop product-specific plans as well as broader strategies for market segmentation, targeting, and positioning and to make decisions about the components of the marketing mix.

Developing and Implementing Customer-Oriented Strategy

Marketing is designed to *provide value to customers.* Thus, marketers must conduct research to understand the various groups of consumers within the marketplace so that they can develop a strategy and specific offerings that will provide such value. Once they develop and implement a suitable strategy, marketers need research to determine how well it is working and whether it is delivering the expected results (such as increasing market share or improving profits).

How Is the Market Segmented?

What one consumer values in a product may not be the same as what another consumer values. Consider the market for plug-in battery chargers. Energizer conducted consumer research and "found that how people use chargers is very different," says a marketing manager. Women said they wanted an easy-to-use charger that is "instantly understandable," whereas men disliked chargers that were too simplistic. Energizer therefore developed the Dock & Go for men, with lights that show when the charging is underway and when it is complete, and the Easy Charger for women, with readouts that show each stage of the charging cycle.[67] Consumer research helps marketers understand the different groups that make up a market and whether they can make an offering to appeal to one or more of these groups.

How Profitable Is Each Segment?

Consumer research can help marketers identify consumers who have needs that are not being met and can reveal the size and profitability of each segment. When Best Buy researched its customer base, the retailer identified a number of segments and created *personas*, names and descriptions to personify each segment's characteristics. It named one profitable segment "Buzz" (young men who enjoy new technology and like to buy new electronics gadgets) and one unprofitable segment "Devil" (consumers who buy items on sale and resell them online). The company then remodeled its stores and retrained its salespeople to focus on consumers who fit the "Buzz" persona.[68]

What Are the Characteristics of Consumers in Each Segment?

After determining how the market is segmented and whether it is potentially profitable, marketers need to learn about the characteristics of consumers in each segment, such as their age, education, and lifestyle. This information helps marketers project whether the segment is likely to grow or to shrink over time, a factor that affects future marketing decisions. For example, sales of fitness goods and services are expected to rise as aging baby boomers strive to stay fit.

Are Customers Satisfied with Existing Offerings?

Marketers often do considerable research to learn whether consumers are currently satisfied with the company's offerings. Harley-Davidson executives regularly ride with members of the Harley Owners Group to find out firsthand what satisfies motorcycle buyers and what else they are looking for. Combining this information with data from other research helps the company come up with new product ideas and promote new bikes to current and potential customers.[69]

Selecting the Target Market

Understanding consumer behavior helps marketers determine which consumer groups are appropriate targets for marketing tactics and how heavy users of a product differ from light users.[70] Marketers also need to identify who is likely to be involved in acquisition, usage, and disposition decisions. Although Virgin Mobile mainly targets teenagers and young adults who use cell phones, its research shows that parents are often the decision makers. Its research also shows that family plans can be more costly than parents realize. "The message we're trying to get out is: When they use family plans, parents are handing [teens] a credit card with an antenna on it," says a company official.[71]

Positioning

Another strategic choice is deciding how an offering should be positioned in consumers' minds. The desired image should reflect what the product is and how it differs from the competition. For example, Newman's Own's slogan, "Shameless exploitation in pursuit of the common good," reflects the company's positioning of itself as the upstart food brand that donates all its profits to charity.

How Are Competitive Offerings Positioned?

Marketers sometimes conduct research to see how consumers view other brands in comparison with their own and then plot the results on a graph called a *perceptual map*. Brands in the same quadrant of the map are perceived as offering similar benefits to consumers. The closer companies are to one another on the map, the more similar they are perceived to be, and hence, the more likely they are to be competitors.

How Should Our Offerings Be Positioned?

Companies use consumer research to understand what image a new offering should have in the eyes of consumers and what messages will effectively support this image.[72] The positioning should suggest that the product is superior in one or more attributes valued by the target market.[73] For example, Toyota's target market for the Scion is car buyers in their twenties and thirties. Through research, Toyota learned that these consumers expect good value for their money, like distinctive styling, and want to customize their cars. The Scion's positioning touches on all of these elements, especially the self-expression aspect that has become a key differentiator.[74]

Should Our Offerings Be Repositioned?

Consumer research can help marketers reposition existing products (i.e., change their image). Consider how the World Gold Council, a trade group, decided to reposition gold jewelry. Through research, the council determined that women enjoy wearing fine gold jewelry, but they didn't perceive available products as either exciting or stylish. The Council therefore recommended that jewelers create pieces with updated, edgier styling, and it repositioned gold jewelry through ads tapping into the positive feelings women have about wearing gold.[75]

Developing Products and Services

Developing products and services that satisfy consumers' wants and needs is a critical marketing activity. Marketers apply consumer research when making a number of decisions about products.

What Ideas Do Consumers Have for New Products?

First, marketers need to design an offering that matches what consumers want. In some cases, customers collaborate on the development of new offerings. Consider what happened when Häagen-Dazs invited consumers to suggest new ice cream flavors. From the hundreds of ideas submitted, the company chose Sticky Toffee Pudding—a flavor that proved so popular it has become part of the regular line instead of a limited-time-only offering.[76]

What Attributes Can Be Added to or Changed in an Existing Offering?

Marketers often use research to determine when and how to modify or tailor a product to meet the needs of new or existing groups of consumers. For example, Virgin Mobile asked 2,000 of its teenage customers about their color preferences for cell phones. Originally, the company was planning to make an all-white cell phone—building on the popularity of the original white Apple iPod digital music player—but the teens rejected that idea as "a knockoff" and asked for a blue phone with a silver interior, which Virgin Mobile put into production.[77]

What Should Our Offering Be Called?

Consumer research plays a vital role in product and brand naming decisions. For instance, Burger King introduced the BK Stacker (a sandwich with layers of burgers and cheese) after research showed that hamburger lovers wanted a "really indulgent meat-and-cheese burger," says a Burger King executive.[78] This offering's name is consistent with research suggesting that brands should be easy to understand and remember and reflect key benefits (like stacks of burgers and cheese).

What Should Our Package and Logo Look Like?

Many marketers use consumer research to test alternative packaging and logos. Research shows, for instance, that consumers are likely to think that food (including cookies) is good for them if it comes in green packaging.[79] This information is valuable in the design of packages for products with a "healthy" positioning. Research is also vital in decisions about changing packaging and logos. For instance, WD-40 repackaged its X-14 household cleaning products to better communicate the brand's positioning as the "bathroom cleaning expert."[80]

Making Promotion and Marketing Communications Decisions

Research can help companies make decisions about promotional/marketing communications tools, including advertising, sales promotions (premiums, contests, sweepstakes, free samples, coupons, and rebates), personal selling, and public relations.

What Are Our Advertising Objectives?

Consumer research can be very useful in determining advertising objectives. It may reveal, for example, that few people have heard of a new brand, suggesting that the advertising objective should be to enhance brand-name awareness. If research indicates that consumers have heard of the brand but don't know anything about it, the advertising objective should be to enhance brand knowledge. If consumers know the brand name but don't know the characteristics of the brand that make it desirable, the advertising should aim to enhance brand knowledge and encourage positive attitudes about it. And if consumers know neither the brand name nor the product's benefits, the advertising should educate the target market about both.

What Should Our Advertising Look Like?

Research can help marketers determine what words and visuals would be most effective and most memorable in advertising. A brand name is better remembered when placed in an ad that has interesting, unusual, and relevant visuals. If the visuals are interesting but unrelated to the product, consumers may remember the visuals but forget the product's name. Moreover, marketers can research how different groups respond to different wording. For example, saying a product is a good "value for the money" does not work in Spain. Instead, marketers use the phrase "price for product."[81] And research shows that marketers who use e-mail to boost website traffic should customize messages based on their knowledge of different consumers in the target market.[82]

Where Should Advertising Be Placed?

When marketers select specific media vehicles in which to advertise, they find demographic, lifestyle, and media usage data very useful. As noted earlier, research shows that more people split their time among many different media and that many people use recording technology to avoid commercials. Knowing this, marketers are choosing media with better targeting or more consumer exposure in mind. A growing number of firms are using sponsorship of cause-related events (such as the Avon Walk for Breast Cancer) to reach target audiences.[83]

When Should We Advertise?

Research may reveal seasonal variations in purchases due to weather-related needs, variations in the amount of discretionary money consumers have (which changes, for instance, before and after Christmas), holiday buying patterns, and the like. ConAgra Foods advertises its Banquet Crock-Pot Classics ready-to-cook frozen foods during fall and winter because consumers use slow-cookers more often during those seasons.[84]

Has Our Advertising Been Effective?

Finally, advertisers can research an ad's effectiveness at various points in the advertising development process. Sometimes marketers or ad agencies conduct advertising *copy testing* or *pretesting,* testing an ad's effectiveness before it appears in public. If the objective is creating brand awareness and the tested ad does not enhance awareness, the company may replace it with a new ad. Effectiveness research can also take place after the ads have been placed in the media, such as conducting tracking studies to see whether ads have achieved particular objectives over time.

What About Sales Promotion Objectives and Tactics?

When developing sales promotions, marketers can use research to identify sales promotion objectives and tactics. For example, after OfficeMax discovered that consumers didn't see much difference among the big office-supply retailers, it tried to make OfficeMax stand out during the year-end holiday buying period. It launched a branded, interactive Elf Yourself website for consumers' enjoyment that created a buzz and drew more than 200 million visitors during two holiday seasons. Follow-up research revealed that more than one-third of these visitors were influenced to shop at OfficeMax.[85] Research can also prevent such pitfalls as offering coupons to certain consumers who won't redeem them for fear of looking stingy.[86]

When Should Sales Promotions Take Place?

Companies can also use consumer research to time their sales promotions. Del Monte Beverages, maker of World Fruits juices, conducted research to learn more about its U.K. target market. The company discovered that those in the segment of frequent purchasers, men and women ages 25 to 44, usually take two vacations per year, preferably to foreign destinations. To boost brand awareness and sales, World Fruits launched a "Win an Exotic Adventure with a Twist" promotion during the winter months, when members of this segment are thinking about vacations.[87]

Have Our Sales Promotions Been Effective?

Consumer research can answer this question. OfficeMax counted the number of visitors to its Elf Yourself site and researched visitors' shopping intentions. Del Monte can compare brand awareness after the World Fruits promotion with pre-promotion levels, for instance, and measure pre- and post-promotion market share. Research can also indicate whether a free sample has been more effective than a price promotion, whether a free gift enhances value perceptions and purchase intentions, and how consumers react after a sales promotion has been discontinued.[88]

How Many Salespeople Are Needed to Serve Customers?

By tracking store patronage at different times of the day or on different days of the week, retailers can determine the appropriate number of store personnel needed to best serve customers.

How Can Salespeople Best Serve Customers?

Finally, research can help managers make decisions about selecting salespeople and evaluating how well they serve customers. For example, similarity between the consumer and a salesperson or service provider can influence whether customers comply with these marketing representatives.[89] Other studies indicate that how a salesperson presents a product will affect consumers' attitudes toward the salesperson and what consumers learn about the product.[90]

Making Pricing Decisions

The price of a product or service can have a critical influence on consumers' acquisition, usage, and disposition decisions. It is therefore very important for marketers to understand how consumers react to price and to use this information in pricing decisions.

What Price Should Be Charged?

Why do prices often end in 99? Consumer research has shown that people perceive $9.99 or $99.99 to be cheaper than $10.00 or $100.00. Perhaps this is one reason why so many prices end in the number 9.[91] Although economic theory suggests that a decrease in price will increase the likelihood of purchase, too low a price can make consumers suspect the product's quality.[92] In general, consumers respond better to a discount presented as a percentage off the regular price (e.g., 25 percent subtracted from the original cost) than to a discount presented as a specific amount of money subtracted from the regular price (originally $25, now only $15).[93] Research shows that consumers have complicated reactions to pricing. For example, if catalog customers can save $8 on shipping charges, they will spend an average of $15 more on catalog purchases—a finding that has caused some catalog marketers to absorb shipping fees.[94]

Also, when making a purchase, consumers consider how much they must pay in relation to the price of other relevant brands or to the price they previously paid for that product, so marketers must be aware of these reference prices.[95] When buying multiple units of a service for one bundled price (such as a multiday ski pass), consumers may not feel a great loss if they use only some of the units because they have difficulty assigning value to each unit. In addition, when consumers buy multiple products for one bundled price (such as a case of wine), they are likely to increase their consumption because unit costs seem low.[96] According to research, how much consumers will pay for a given item can even be affected by the price of unrelated products they happen to see first. Thus, the price you would be willing to pay for a T-shirt may vary, depending on whether the prices you noticed for shoes in the store next door were high or low.[97] Finally, studies indicate that consumers have differing perceptions of what a product is worth, depending on whether they are buying or selling it. Sellers should therefore avoid this *endowment effect;* that is, they should not set a higher price than buyers are willing to pay.[98]

How Sensitive Are Consumers to Price and Price Changes?

Research also suggests that consumers have different views of the importance of price. Some consumers are very price sensitive, meaning that a small change in price will have a large effect on consumers' willingness to purchase the product. Cruise lines, for example, have found that lower prices help fill their ships.[99] Other consumers are price insensitive and thus likely to buy an offering regardless of its price. Demand for brewed coffee generally remains steady despite price increases, a situation that means Starbucks is unlikely to lose many customers when it raises its coffee prices.[100] Marketers can use research to determine which consumers are likely to be price sensitive and when. For fashion or prestige goods, a high price symbolizes status. Thus, status-seeking consumers may be less sensitive to a product's price and pay more than $50 for a T-shirt with a prestigious label.

When Should Certain Price Tactics Be Used?

Research also reveals when consumers are likely to be most responsive to various pricing tactics. For example, consumers have traditionally been very responsive to price cuts on bed linens during January. These "white sales" are effective because consumers have come to anticipate them and are unlikely to buy linens after Christmas without a financial incentive to do so.

Making Distribution Decisions

Another important marketing decision involves how products are distributed and sold to consumers in retail stores. Here, too, marketers can use consumer research.

Where Are Target Consumers Likely to Shop?

Marketers who understand the value consumers place on time and convenience have developed distribution channels that allow consumers to acquire or use goods and services whenever and wherever it is most convenient for them. For example,

24-hour grocery stores, health clubs, and catalog ordering and online ordering systems give consumers flexibility in the timing of their acquisition, usage, and disposition decisions. As another example, consumers can now shop for cars through the Internet, auto brokers, and warehouse clubs and at giant auto malls and used-car superstores as well as at traditional auto dealerships.

How Should Stores Be Designed?

Supermarkets are generally designed with similar or complementary items stocked near one another because research shows that consumers think about items in terms of categories based on products' similar characteristics or use. Thus, stores stock peanut butter near jelly because the products are often used together. Consumer research can also help marketers develop other aspects of their retail environments. Studies show that bright colors and up-tempo music make consumers move quickly through a store; subdued colors and quiet music have the opposite effect.[101] Store design also depends on whether consumers are shopping for fun or seeking to quickly accomplish a particular task like buying a certain item.[102] Knowing that some consumers simply like to shop, retailers are increasingly creating more exciting and aesthetically pleasing store environments.[103]

Stores and websites can be designed to convey a very specific image. Apple's stores are open and modern, with plenty of gadgets for shoppers to test. The "genius bar," staffed by tech experts, is in the back, drawing customers through the store (and past attractive displays) when they need advice. "We wanted an atmosphere that was inviting—not intimidating—forward-looking, warm, interactive," explains the head of Apple retail operations.[104]

Summary

Consumer behavior involves understanding the set of decisions (what, whether, why, when, how, where, how much, and how often) that an individual or group of consumers makes over time about the acquisition, use, or disposition of products, services, ideas, or activities. The psychological core exerts considerable influence on consumer behavior. A consumer's motivation, ability, and opportunity affect his or her decisions and influence what a consumer is exposed to, what he or she pays attention to, and what he or she perceives. These factors also affect how a consumer categorizes or interprets information, how he or she forms and changes attitudes, and how he or she forms and retrieves memories. Each aspect of the psychological core has a bearing on the consumer decision-making process, which involves (1) problem recognition, (2) information search, (3) judgment and decision making, and (4) evaluation of level of satisfaction with the decision.

Consumer behavior is also affected by the consumer's culture and by the typical or expected behaviors, norms, and ideas of a particular group. Consumers belong to a number of groups, share their cultural values and beliefs, and use their symbols to communicate group membership. Consumer behavior can be symbolic and express an individual's identity. In addition, consumer behavior is indicative of how forcefully or quickly an offering can spread throughout a market.

Marketers study consumer behavior to gain insights that will lead to more effective marketing strategies and tactics. Ethicists and advocacy groups are also keenly interested in consumer behavior, as are public policy makers and regulators who want to protect consumers from unsafe or inappropriate offerings. Consumers and society can both benefit as marketers learn to make products more user-friendly and to show concern for the environment. Finally, studying consumer behavior helps marketers understand how to segment markets and how to decide which to target, how to position an offering, and which marketing-mix tactics will be most effective.

Questions for Review and Discussion

1. How is consumer behavior defined?

2. What three broad categories of consumer activity do marketers and researchers study in consumer behavior?

3. What are some of the factors in the psychological core that affect consumer decisions and behavior?

4. What are some of the external processes that influence consumer decisions and behavior?

5. How is *marketing* defined?

6. How do public policy decision makers, advocacy groups, and marketing managers use consumer research?

7. What kinds of questions can marketers use consumer behavior research to answer?

CL Visit http://cengage.com/marketing/hoyer/ ConsumerBehavior5e to find resources that are available to help you study for the course.

CONSUMER BEHAVIOR CASE

Swatch Makes Time for Luxury

From plastic to platinum—the wristwatch company known for fun fashion accessories is now focusing on the watch as a status symbol. When Switzerland-based Swatch Group was founded in 1983, popularly priced quartz watches made by Japanese firms had taken considerable market share from traditional Swiss watch brands. Swatch's bold idea for recapturing share was to combine colorful cases, bands, and faces into eye-catching watches that were functional, affordable, and fashionable. The company began introducing an ever-changing array of new models, which helped consumers begin to think about wristwatches as both trendy and collectible. It also decided to restrict some models to certain geographic areas. This encouraged consumers to be on the lookout for new Swatches when traveling and to snap up models not sold in stores at home.

The idea of building a wardrobe of watches caught on. Consumers—particularly women—quickly became accustomed to buying Swatch watches as they would any fashion accessory, on impulse or to match particular outfits. Showing off new and unusual Swatch models—especially those not locally available—became another way to express individuality and status. Soon Swatch's success attracted the attention of rivals that entered the market with a wide range of inexpensive watches for everyday wear.

To avoid the profit-sapping problems of this intense competition, Swatch made another bold decision. Without abandoning its basic $35 Swatch models, the company started acquiring established quality brands such as Omega and Hamilton. It also bought super-luxury brands

such as Breguet, which offers hand-made, limited-edition watches priced as high as $500,000. The posh image of these brands brought a new dimension to Swatch's corporate reputation and new possibilities for marketing more watches to more segments.

Now the company can cater to buyers seeking an extraordinary piece of jewelry for themselves or to give as a special gift—buyers for whom price is a secondary consideration. Swatch's high-end brands can also satisfy the needs of wealthy consumers who get in a buying mood while on vacation and choose fancy watches in exclusive boutiques or airport duty-free shops. Knowing that more luxury watches are sold to men than to women, Swatch has also partnered with the Tiffany jewelry retail chain to design and market high-quality women's watches as fashion accessories.

To connect with customers beyond the purchase of a single wristwatch and strengthen brand loyalty, Swatch has been using a variety of marketing communications. Its luxury brand ads appear in magazines geared to high-income consumers. It publishes *Voice*, a twice-yearly lifestyle magazine, to inform customers about fashion trends, special Swatch events, new product news, and more. Its online newsletter keeps customers updated on the latest styles and trends. On the Swatch website, enthusiasts can click to join the Swatch club and gain access to members-only products, contests, collectible watches, blogs, photos, and videos. In addition, Swatch mounts special events for customers all over the world, such as a beach-theme party in Austria and a weekend pirate-theme cruise in Turkey.

Thanks to its portfolio of more than a dozen brands and a global chain of 600 stores, Swatch has become the world's leading watch marketer. Its annual sales have risen to $5 billion, despite mixed global economic conditions. In fact, luxury watches now account for more than half of Swatch's profits, and the company is readying more fine-jewelry accessories under its status-symbol brands. Still, competition from high-end brands such as Patek Philippe, Piaget, Cartier, and Bulgari has become more intense over the years. Will Swatch continue to thrive in such a highly pressured environment? Only time will tell.[105]

Case Questions

1. What role does the consumer's culture seem to be playing in Swatch's marketing strategy?
2. Explain, in terms of internal consumer processes, why Swatch puts so much emphasis on marketing communications.
3. Under what circumstances would the decision to buy a Swatch watch be a high-effort decision? A low-effort decision?

Developing Information About Consumer Behavior

INTRODUCTION

Understanding China's "Technology Tribes"

Of the more than 40 million PCs sold in China every year, 10 million bear the Lenovo brand. But this fast-growing market is drawing global competitors like Hewlett Packard and Dell. Lenovo, which bought IBM's PC division in 2005, is defending itself by marketing new products created through a deeper understanding of the needs, expectations, and aspirations of Chinese PC users.

Lenovo hired the research and design firm Ziba to study how Chinese consumers buy, use, think about, and feel about PCs. Ziba researchers observed how consumers in China spent their time, how they made major purchases, and how they used technology products. They asked consumers to photograph their activities during one weekday and one leisure day, with special attention to use of technology products. The researchers studied fashion trends and other influences on product styling and interviewed consumers about the benefits they sought from technology products.

After analyzing all the data, Ziba researchers identified five segments or "technology tribes" with differing needs, attitudes, and behaviors: Social Butterflies, Relationship Builders, Upward Maximizers, Deep Immersers, and Conspicuous Collectors. Lenovo chose to target all but the Conspicuous Collectors with new products such as modular, multimedia desktop

PCs (for Deep Immersers) and smaller notebook PCs (for Relationship Builders). Building on its success in China's consumer market, Lenovo has expanded to targeting consumers in other parts of Asia plus those in Europe and the United States, where its ThinkPad laptops already have a loyal following.[1]

Consumer behavior research helps marketers such as Lenovo determine what customers need, how they behave, and how they feel. Just as important, research can guide marketers in determining how to profitably satisfy consumer needs through decisions about segmentation, targeting, positioning, and the marketing mix. This chapter opens with a description of the tools that marketers use to collect information about consumers. Next, you will learn about the types of entities that use consumer research. Finally, you will be introduced to some ethical issues related to consumer research, a topic covered in more detail in Chapter 18, "Ethics, Social Responsibility, and the Dark Side of Consumer Behavior and Marketing."

Consumer Behavior Research Methods

Primary data Data originating from a researcher and collected to provide information relevant to a specific research project.

Secondary data Data collected for some other purpose that is subsequently used in a research project.

Researchers collect and analyze two types of data for marketing purposes: primary and secondary. Data collected for its own purpose is called **primary data.** When marketers gather data using surveys, focus groups, experiments, and the like to support their own marketing decisions, they are collecting primary data. Data collected by an entity for one purpose and subsequently used by another entity for a different purpose is called **secondary data.** For example, after the government collects census data for tax purposes, marketers can use the results as secondary data to estimate the size of markets in their own industry.

A number of tools are available in the consumer researcher's "tool kit" for gathering primary data, some based on what consumers say and some on what they do. Researchers may collect data from relatively few people or compile data from huge samples of consumers. Each of these tools can provide unique insights that, when combined, reveal very different perspectives on the complex world of consumer behavior. This is research with a purpose: to guide companies in making more informed decisions and achieving marketing results.[2]

Surveys

Survey A written instrument that asks consumers to respond to a predetermined set of research questions.

One of the most familiar research tools is the **survey,** a written instrument that asks consumers to respond to a predetermined set of research questions. Some responses may be open-ended, with the consumer filling in the blanks; others may ask consumers to use a rating scale or check marks. Surveys can be conducted in person, through the mail, over the phone, or by using the Web. Procter & Gamble, for example, conducts about 1,500 online consumer surveys every year and obtains results 75 percent faster than it does with traditional survey methods—at half the cost.[3]

Although companies often undertake specialized surveys to better understand a specific customer segment, some organizations carry out broad-based surveys that are made available to marketers. The U.S. Bureau of the Census is a widely used source of demographic information. Its Census of Population and Housing, conducted every ten years, asks U.S. consumers questions regarding their age, marital status, gender, household size, education, income, and home ownership. This database, available online (*www.census.gov*), in libraries, or on CD-ROM, helps marketers learn about population shifts that might affect their offerings or their industry.

Survey data can also tell marketers something about media usage and product purchase. Mediamark Research Incorporated conducts yearly surveys (in English and Spanish) with more than 26,000 consumers, asking about their media habits, demographics, and product purchases.[4] Researchers are even studying how to encourage survey response. In one study, more consumers completed the survey when the package was topped by a Post-It note asking them to participate.[5]

Focus Groups

Focus group A form of interview involving 8 to 12 people; a moderator leads the group and asks participants to discuss a product, concept, or other marketing stimulus.

Unlike a survey, which may collect input from hundreds of people responding individually to the same questionnaire, a **focus group** brings together groups of 6 to 12 consumers to discuss an issue or an offering (see Exhibit EN.1). Led by a trained moderator, participants express their opinions about a given product or topic, which can be particularly useful in identifying and testing new product ideas. Focus groups provide qualitative insights into consumer attitudes as opposed to the quantitative (numerical) data resulting from surveys. Anheuser-Busch fine-tunes its Bud Light commercials for the Super Bowl by showing them to dozens of focus groups in the months leading up to the game.[6]

A related technique is the computer-based focus group, in which consumers go to a computer lab where their individual comments are displayed anonymously on a large screen for viewing by the group. This method can help researchers gather information on sensitive topics, as can focus groups conducted by telephone or online rather than in person. However, the anonymity prevents researchers from collecting other relevant data, such as nonverbal reactions conveyed by facial expressions and body language that would be available in a traditional focus group.

Some companies convene customer advisory boards, small groups of customers that meet with marketing and service executives once or twice a year (face to face, online, or by phone) to discuss offerings, competitive products, future needs, acquisition and usage problems, and related issues. Board meetings serve not just as research but also as a tool for strengthening customer relations.[7] To illustrate, Premier Bank of Tallahassee, Florida, asks its two customer boards for feedback on branch services, new product ideas, and community involvement.[8]

Interviews

Like focus groups, interviews involve direct contact with consumers. Interviews are often more appropriate than focus groups when the topic is sensitive, embarrassing, confidential, or emotionally charged. They provide more in-depth data than surveys when the researcher wants to "pick consumers' brains." For instance, when Volvo sought closer connections with car buyers, its ad agency interviewed valet parking attendants around the world to get a well-rounded picture of Volvo owners. The agency learned that Volvo customers are "doers"—more concerned with what they do than with what they have—and value togetherness and sharing. This research helped the agency create a new Volvo campaign with the theme "Life is better lived together."[9]

In some interviews, researchers ask customers about the process they use to make a purchase decision. One research company assigns professional interviewers to tape-record consumers' thoughts while they shop for groceries. This research

helps marketers understand how factors in the shopping environment affect purchasing. For example, a company might learn that a consumer didn't buy a certain cereal because it was placed too close to the laundry detergent.[10]

Traditional interviews require a trained interviewer who attempts to establish rapport with consumers. Interviewers also note nonverbal behaviors like fidgeting, voice pitch changes, and folded arms and legs as clues to whether the respondent is open to the discussion or whether certain questions are particularly sensitive. Researchers often record interviews for later transcription so they can examine the results using qualitative or quantitative analysis. Sometimes researchers videotape nonverbal responses that cannot be captured in the transcription process and analyze the interviews later to identify patterns or themes.

Storytelling

Storytelling A research method by which consumers are asked to tell stories about product acquisition, usage, or disposition experiences. These stories help marketers gain insights into consumer needs and identify the product attributes that meet these needs.

Another tool for conducting consumer research is **storytelling,** in which consumers tell researchers stories about their experiences with a product. At Patagonia, researchers collect consumer stories about backpacking and other outdoor experiences for use in developing the company's catalogs. Storytelling not only provides information relevant to the marketing of the product but also shows that Patagonia is in touch with its customers and values what they say.[11]

Although storytelling involves the real stories of real consumers, sometimes marketers ask consumers to tell or write stories about hypothetical situations that the marketer has depicted in a picture or scenario.[12] The idea is that a consumer's needs, feelings, and perceptions are revealed by the way he or she interprets what is depicted in the picture or scenario. For example, researchers may show a picture of a woman at the entrance to a Hot Topic store with a thought bubble above her head and ask consumers to write what they imagine the woman is thinking. Such stories can reveal what consumers think of a particular store, purchase situation, and so on.

Photography and Pictures

Some researchers use a technique in which they show pictures of experiences that consumers have had in order to help consumers remember and report experiences more completely.[13] Researchers may also ask consumers to draw or collect pictures that represent their thoughts and feelings about the topic at hand (the way Lenovo had consumers photograph their daily interactions with technology products). Still another practice is to ask consumers to assemble a collage of pictures that reflects their lifestyles. Researchers then ask about the pictures and the meaning behind them or have the consumer write an essay, which can help integrate the images and thoughts suggested by the pictures.[14]

For example, Wrigley's marketers asked teenagers to select pictures and write a story about Juicy Fruit Gum. The company learned that teens chewed the gum when they craved sweets. With this insight, Wrigley's ad agency launched the "Gotta Have Sweet" campaign—and Juicy Fruit sales climbed.[15]

Diaries

Asking consumers to keep diaries can provide important insights into their behavior, including product purchasing and media usage. Diaries often reveal how friends and family affect consumers' decisions about clothes, music, fast foods, videos, concerts, and so on. When Unilever was planning a new deodorant, it asked a group of women to keep an "armpit diary" noting how often they shaved, what their underarms looked like, and how frequently they used deodorant. Finding that the women were concerned about the condition of their underarm skin, Unilever created a moisturizing deodorant product and promoted its skin-care benefits.[16]

The research firm NPD Group asks more than 3 million consumers worldwide to maintain online diaries tracking their purchases in dozens of product categories. Companies buy NPD's diary data to learn whether consumers are brand loyal or brand switching and whether they are heavy or light product users. By linking the data with demographic data, marketers can also learn more about these consumers. Burger King, for example, can use the NPD system to look at burger consumption by age group, geographic location, and even time of day, information that helps the chain better target or change promotions, plan new products, and make other decisions.[17]

Experiments

Consumer researchers can conduct experiments to determine whether certain marketing phenomena affect consumer behavior. For example, they might design an experiment to learn whether consumers' attitudes toward a brand are affected by the brand name as opposed to factors such as product features, package, color, logo, room temperature, or the consumer's mood. By measuring emotional arousal, salivation levels, and eye movements of participants, marketers may determine which ads are most arousing and attention getting or which products are preferred. Ford used brain scanning technology as a way to gauge European consumers' reactions to a new vehicle in development.[18]

With experiments, researchers randomly assign consumers to receive different "treatments" and then observe the effects of these treatments. For example, consumers might be assigned to groups that are shown different brand names. The researchers collect data about participants' attitudes toward the name and compare attitudes across groups. In a taste-test experiment, they might randomly assign consumers to groups and then ask each group to taste a different product. Comparing evaluations of the product across the groups will show which product is preferred.

An important aspect of such experiments is that the groups are designed to be identical in all respects except the treatment, called the **independent variable.** Thus, in a taste-test experiment, only the taste of the food or beverage is varied. Everything else is the same across groups—consumers eat or drink the same amount of the product, at the same temperature, from the same kind of container, in the same room, in the presence of the same experimenter, and so on. After consumers taste and rate the product, researchers can compare the groups' responses to see which taste is preferred. Because the groups are identical in all other respects, researchers know that any differences between the two groups are caused by the treatment (the food's taste).

Field Experiments

Although experiments are often conducted in controlled laboratory situations, sometimes marketers conduct experiments in the real world, known as "field experiments." One type of field experiment, a **market test,** reveals whether an offering is likely to sell in a given market and which marketing-mix elements most effectively enhance sales. Suppose marketers want to determine how much advertising support to give to a new product. They could select two test markets of a similar size and demographic composition and spend a different amount of money on advertising in each market. By observing product sales in the two markets over a set period, the marketers would be able to tell which level of advertising expenditure resulted in higher sales.

All marketing-mix elements can be market tested. P. F. Chang's China Bistro, a restaurant chain, recently tested a new dinner menu in its Dallas restaurant. The results were so successful that the company added the menu to 45 of its other restaurants. [19]

Conjoint Analysis

Many marketers use the sophisticated research technique of **conjoint analysis** to determine the relative importance and appeal of different levels of an offering's attributes. To start, researchers identify the attributes of the offering, such as package size, specific product features, and price points. Next, they determine the levels to be tested for each attribute (such as large or small size). Then they ask consumers to react to a series of product concepts that combine these attributes in different ways.

For example, researchers might ask how likely consumers are to buy a large package of Tide laundry detergent that has added stain removal power and costs $4.75; they might also ask how likely consumers are to buy a small package of Tide that does not have added stain removal power and costs $2.50. By analyzing the responses to different combinations, the researchers can see how important each attribute (e.g., size, price) is and the level of a given attribute that customers prefer. Academic researchers have used this methodology to understand, among other things, how much weight consumers give to environmental factors versus price and other attributes when they buy wooden furniture.[20]

Observations

At times, researchers observe consumers to gain insight into potentially effective product, promotion, price, and distribution decisions (see Exhibit EN.2). The maker of Huggies disposable diapers, Kimberly-Clark, uses observational research to see how consumers react to new packaging and new shelf positions as they "shop" in virtual store environments customized to look like specific chain stores. The results not only help Kimberly-Clark's marketers make product and promotion decisions;

Independent variable The "treatment" or the entity that researchers vary in a research project.

Market test A study in which the effectiveness of one or more elements of the marketing mix is examined by evaluating sales of the product in an actual market, e.g., a specific city.

Conjoint analysis A research technique to determine the relative importance and appeal of different levels of an offering's attributes.

Exhibit EN.2

Observational Research

At the Fisher-Price Playlab, researchers observe children's reactions to determine whether the children like Fisher-Price toys.

Ethnographic research
In-depth qualitative research using observations and interviews (often over repeated occasions) of consumers in real world surroundings. Often used to study the meaning that consumers ascribe to a product or consumption phenomenon.

they also help Wal-Mart, Target, and other retailers make decisions about buying and displaying Kimberly-Clark products.[21]

Some marketers use tracking software to observe which websites consumers visit, which pages they look at, how long they visit each site, and related data. By analyzing consumer browsing patterns, researchers can determine how to make websites more user friendly and how to better target online advertising as well as how to make other decisions about online marketing activities.[22] However, privacy advocates are concerned that tracking software—especially when used without the consumer's knowledge or consent—is intrusive. In response, companies are posting privacy policies and, in some cases, allowing consumers to view and edit collected data or even "opt out" of tracking systems.[23]

Some companies conduct **ethnographic research,** in which researchers interview, observe (and perhaps videotape) how consumers behave in real-world surroundings. When Coleman wanted to expand from camping stoves to gas barbecue grills, its researchers visited homes to observe men (who typically act as outdoor cooks) talking with friends and family as they used a grill. The research revealed that the act of grilling evoked nostalgia for camping experiences. As a result, Coleman downplayed technical specifications such as BTUs and promoted its grill as the centerpiece of "a relaxing ritual" in the "backyard oasis."[24]

Purchase Panels

Sometimes marketers try to understand consumer behavior by tracking what consumers buy on different purchase occasions. This kind of research, conducted by IRI and other firms, simply records whether a behavior occurred; for instance, Campbell Soup uses IRI to track soup purchases in U.S. stores.[25] Such behavioral data may be collected from special panel members, from a representative sample of the general population, or from the marketer's target market. Every time panel members go shopping, the cash register records their purchases. By merging purchase data with demographic data, marketers can tell who is purchasing a product, whether those consumers are also buying competitors' products, and whether a coupon or other sales promotion was involved. Marketers can also use these data to determine whether, for example, the shelf space allocated to a product, or added advertising in the test area, affected panel members' purchases.

A growing number of firms, including Del Monte Foods, Procter & Gamble, and Coca-Cola, also conduct research through a proprietary online purchase panel. For instance, Del Monte's research firm set up the password-protected "I Love My Dog" website and invited 400 dog owners to participate in answering questions about dog food products. Feedback from participants helped Del Monte select flavors for its Snausages Breakfast Bites dog treats.[26]

Database Marketing

Marketers can dig deeper into consumer behavior if they combine different forms of consumer research into a common database. This database might contain

Data mining Searching for patterns in a company database that offer clues to customer needs, preferences, and behaviors.

information about targeted consumers' demographics and lifestyles combined with data about their purchases in various product categories over time, their media habits, and their usage of coupons and other promotional devices. Using **data mining,** the company then searches for patterns in the database that offer clues to customer needs, preferences, and behaviors.[27]

Wal-Mart is at the cutting edge of the data-mining movement. It follows every piece of merchandise from warehouse to store shelf by using radio frequency identification tags. Every item sold at the checkout is recorded, along with the item's price, the time of sale, and the store location. These data are reported to Wal-Mart hourly and daily by product, by category, by store, by supplier, and so on. Wal-Mart also analyzes what else goes into the shopping cart, store by store and region by region, for clues to pricing products in different categories. Finally, data mining helps the company identify promising new store locations and profile each store's shoppers so it can stock the right assortment of goods in appropriate quantities.[28]

More marketers are collecting consumer data online for promotional purposes, such as to plan e-mail messages or build website traffic. Although e-mail is fast and cheaper than other communication methods, consumers are inundated with electronic messages. Therefore, to trigger a response, an e-mail campaign must be based on consumer needs—for instance, it might provide information the consumer requested—and should tailor the content and timing to each individual.[29] For instance, after consumers agree to receive e-mail from Frederick's of Hollywood, which markets women's lingerie, the company customizes messages based on the pages and products viewed by each consumer. This customization helps the company retain customers and build sales.[30]

It is even possible to use clickstream data from websites to analyze consumer behavior. One study looked at consumers' use of websites to buy automobiles and found that the best predictor of purchase was not the use of sophisticated decision-making aids or the number of repeat visits consumers made to the site but rather how long they browsed and navigated through the site.[31] Database marketing and data mining have raised concerns about invasion of consumer privacy, however; see Chapter 18 for more detail.

Neuroscience

Neuroscientists are seeking to understand consumer behavior by looking at brain activity using functional magnetic resonance imaging (fMRI). To do this, they examine which parts of the brain become activated when consumers are engaging in activities such as making a decision, viewing an ad, or selecting an investment.[32] For instance, Christian Dior used fMRI research to test consumers' reactions to music, colors, and ad placement when planning its highly successful introductory campaign for J'Adore perfume. Although neuroscience research raises concerns about manipulation, one advertising executive notes: "Observing brain activity and setting up models for behavior is not the same as forcing a brain into making a consumption decision."[33]

Types of Consumer Researchers

Many entities use market research to study consumer behavior for different reasons, as shown in Exhibit EN.3. Organizations such as consumer goods and service companies, ad agencies, and marketing research firms conduct research to make decisions about marketing a specific product or service. Government organizations

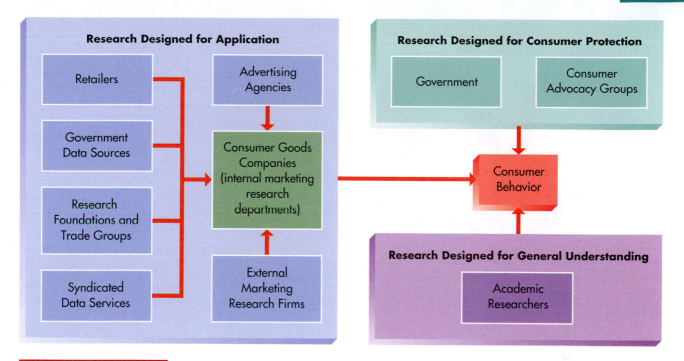

Research Designed for Application

Retailers

Government Data Sources

Research Foundations and Trade Groups

Syndicated Data Services

Advertising Agencies

Consumer Goods Companies (internal marketing research departments)

External Marketing Research Firms

Research Designed for Consumer Protection

Government

Consumer Advocacy Groups

Consumer Behavior

Research Designed for General Understanding

Academic Researchers

Exhibit EN.3

Who Conducts Consumer Research?

A number of different organizations conduct research on consumers, although they differ in their objectives. Some do research for application, some for consumer protection, and some for obtaining general knowledge about consumers.

collect consumer information so as to set laws designed to protect consumers. Academics conduct research to protect consumers or simply to understand why and how consumers behave as they do.

In-house Marketing Research Departments

The benefits of conducting "in-house" research (conducted by the company for the company) are that the information collected can be kept within the company and that opportunities for information to leak to competitors are minimized. However, internal departments are sometimes viewed as less objective than outside research firms since they may have a vested interest in the research results. For example, employees may be motivated to show that the company is making good decisions, a situation that may unwittingly bias the nature of their research or the outcomes they report. Consequently, some companies use outside research companies to gather their consumer research.

External Marketing Research Firms

External research firms often help design a specific research project before it begins. They develop measuring instruments to measure consumer responses, collect data from consumers, analyze the data, and develop reports for their clients. As you saw in the chapter-opening example, Lenovo hired Ziba to study PC users in China as a first step toward designing new products for that fast-growing market.

Some marketing research firms are "full service" organizations that perform a variety of marketing research services; others specialize in a particular type of research. GfK Custom Research North America, for instance, conducts media research, brand awareness research, and other consumer behavior research. In its Starch Ad Readership studies, dozens of readers of a specific magazine go through a recent issue with a trained interviewer. The interviewer asks whether consumers have seen each ad in the issue and whether they saw the picture in each ad,

Exhibit EN.4

A "Starched" Ad

Companies like Starch collect data on what, if anything, consumers remember from an ad. The numbers noted on the stickers placed at the top of the ad indicate the percentage of respondents sampled who remembered having seen or read various parts of the ad.

read the headline, read the body copy, and saw the ad slogan. The company compiles reports about the percentage of respondents who saw each part of each ad and sells the results to advertisers who want to determine whether their ads were seen and read more than other ads in the issue or in the product category. Exhibit EN.4 shows an ad for which STARCH scores have been tabulated.

Advertising Agencies

Some advertising agencies have departments to test advertising concepts as part of the service they provide to clients. On behalf of retailer Best Buy, the La Comunidad ad agency has used ethnographic research to study how Hispanic parents and their tech-savvy teenagers decide on consumer electronics purchases. The results helped the agency create Spanish-language TV commercials. They acknowledge that new technology can be intimidating and showcase Best Buy's expertise in helping customers select the right electronics product for the entire family.[34]

Agencies may also conduct advertising pretesting, using drawings of ads or finished ads, to make sure that an ad is fulfilling its objectives *before* it is placed in the media. In addition, agencies often conduct tracking studies to monitor advertising effectiveness over time. Tracking studies can determine whether the percentage of target market consumers who are aware of a brand has changed as a function of the amount, duration, and timing of its advertising.

Syndicated Data Services

Syndicated data services are companies that collect and then sell the information they collect, usually to firms that market products and services to consumers. For example, the Yankelovich Monitor study collects data on consumer lifestyles and social trends using 90-minute interviews at the homes of approximately 2,500 adults. Its annual reports describing current and projected lifestyle trends help advertising agencies and company marketers develop content for promotional messages, choose media, identify new product ideas, plan positioning strategy, and make other marketing decisions.

Nielsen is a syndicated data service that tracks the TV viewing habits of thousands of participating U.S. households using three techniques: (1) diaries, (2) TV set-top people meters that record which household member is viewing and when, and (3) set-tuning devices that record whether a TV set is on or off and the channel it is tuned to.[35] Based on these data, Nielsen assigns a rating that indicates the number and percentage of all households watching a particular TV program, and a specific commercial, along with demographic analyses of the audience. This is how advertisers know how many viewers tuned in to watch the Super Bowl, for instance.[36]

By combining demographic and TV viewing behavior, Nielsen can also examine who is watching which shows. Networks, cable stations, and independent channels use this information to determine whether TV shows should be renewed and how much they can charge for advertising time on a particular show. In general, advertisers will pay more to advertise on very popular shows (those with higher Nielsen ratings). Advertisers who buy Nielsen data can assess which TV shows they should advertise in, basing their decisions on how well the audience's demographic characteristics match the sponsor's target market. Nielsen also conducts research into consumers' use of the Internet, video games, mobile devices, and other media that carry ad messages.[37]

Retailers

Large retail chains often conduct consumer research. By using electronic scanners to track sales of a brand or product category, they can determine which are their best- and worst-selling items and see how consumers respond to coupons, discounts, and other promotions. Because salespeople often interact directly with customers, retailers sometimes use research to measure customer satisfaction and determine how they can improve service quality. Observing emerging trends can help retailers plan ahead for new products. For example, Target has employees who travel internationally to spot new consumer trends in clothing, home decorating, and so on.[38]

Research Foundations and Trade Groups

Research foundation A nonprofit organization that sponsors research on topics relevant to the foundation's goals.

Many research foundations and trade groups collect consumer research. A **research foundation** is a nonprofit organization that sponsors research on topics relevant to the foundation's goals. As an example, the nonprofit Advertising Research Foundation seeks to improve the practice of advertising, marketing, and media research. It sponsors conferences and publishes reports related to research in these areas.[39] The Marketing Science Institute is another nonprofit organization that sponsors academic research studies to uncover information useful to companies.

Trade group A professional organization made up of marketers in the same industry.

Specialized trade groups may also collect consumer research to better understand the needs of consumers in their own industries. A **trade group** is an organization formed by people who work in the same industry, such as the Recording Industry Association of America, a group whose members are involved in the recorded music industry through recording, distribution, or retailing activities. This organization has sponsored a host of research projects, including studies to understand how American music tastes have changed over the years.

Government

Although government agencies do not use research to help market an offering, businesses frequently use government research for marketing purposes, as when they examine census data to estimate the size of various demographic markets. Government studies by agencies such as the Consumer Products Safety Commission, the Department of Transportation, and the Food and Drug Administration are specifically designed for consumer protection. As an example, the Federal Trade Commission (FTC) conducts research on potentially deceptive, misleading, or fraudulent advertising. The FTC once conducted research to determine whether consumers might have been misled by ads claiming that one slice of Kraft cheese was made from five ounces of milk. The FTC worried that consumers might infer that the cheese had as much calcium as five ounces of milk (which it did not) or that Kraft cheese was superior to its competitors in terms of calcium content (which it was not).[40] Research can also help resolve court cases involving marketing issues such as whether consumers are confusing a new product's trademark with an established product's trademark, a situation that could hurt the established brand.[41]

Consumer Organizations

Independent consumer organizations also conduct research, generally for the purpose of protecting or informing consumers. Consumers Union is an independent, nonprofit testing and information organization designed to serve consumers. The organization publishes the well-known *Consumer Reports* magazine. Many of the products described in *Consumer Reports* are tested in Consumers Union's independent product-testing lab, and the results are posted on the organization's website (*www.consumersunion.org*).

Academics and Academic Research Centers

Although academic research involving consumers can be used for marketing and may have implications for public policy, studies often are designed simply to enhance our general understanding of consumer behavior. Much of the research reported in this book describes state-of-the-art academic studies. Some academic research centers focus on a specific aspect of consumer behavior. For example, to learn more about media consumption, researchers from Ball State University's Center for Media Design observed 101 consumers from the time they woke up until the time they went to sleep. They found that consumers actually spend more time with TV, radio, newspapers, and online media than is reflected in conventional media research.[42] Another example is the Restaurant of the Future, on the campus of Wageningen University in the Netherlands, where researchers experiment with lighting, plates, food arrangement, and other details to see their effects on what and how much students and faculty eat.[43]

Ethical Issues in Consumer Research

Although marketers rely heavily on consumer research in the development of successful goods and services, the conduct of this research raises important ethical issues. As the following sections show, consumer research has both positive and negative aspects.

The Positive Aspects of Consumer Research

Both consumers and marketers can benefit from consumer research. Consumers generally have better consumption experiences, and marketers can learn to build stronger customer relationships by paying attention to consumer research.

Better Consumption Experiences

Because consumer research helps marketers become more customer focused, consumers can have better designed products, better customer service, clearer usage instructions, more information that helps them make good decisions, and more satisfying postpurchase experiences. Consumer research (by government and consumer organizations) also plays a role in protecting consumers from unscrupulous marketers.

Potential for Building Customer Relationships

Research can help marketers identify ways of establishing and enhancing relationships with customers through a better understanding of their needs, attitudes, and behavior. Interestingly, U.S. consumers have a more favorable view of marketing today than they did in the 1980s and 1990s, particularly in regard to retailing and distribution.[44] Being aware of these kinds of broad trends in consumer sentiment is a good foundation from which to approach relationship building.

The Negative Aspects of Consumer Research

Consumer research is a very complex process with a number of potentially negative aspects. These include the difficulty of conducting research in foreign countries, the high costs of conducting research, concerns about invasion of privacy, and the use of deceptive practices.

Tracking Consumer Behavior in Different Countries

Marketers who want to research consumer behavior in other countries face special challenges. For instance, focus groups are not appropriate in all countries or situations. U.S. marketers often put husbands and wives together in a focus group to explore attitudes toward products like furniture. However, this approach won't work in countries like Saudi Arabia, where women are unlikely to speak freely and are highly unlikely to disagree with their husbands in such settings. Focus groups must also be conducted differently in Japan, where cultural pressures dictate against a person's disagreeing with the views of a group.

Although telephone interviewing is common in the United States, it is far less prevalent in Third World countries. Marketers must also consider a country's literacy rate when planning survey research. At a minimum, researchers should word questions carefully and check to ensure that the meaning is being accurately conveyed by first translating questions into the other language and then translating them back into English.

Companies may not be able to directly compare secondary data gathered in another country with data gathered in the United States, in part because of different collection procedures or timing. Countries may also use different categorization schemes for describing demographics like social class and education level. Moreover, different or fewer syndicated data sources may be available in other countries, a situation that limits the research available to marketers.

Potentially Higher Marketing Costs

Some consumers worry that the process of researching consumer behavior leads to higher marketing costs, which in turn translate into higher product prices. Some marketers, however, argue that they can market to their customers more efficiently if they know more about them. For example, product development, advertising, sales promotion costs, and distribution costs will be lower if marketers know exactly what consumers want and how to reach them.

Invasion of Consumer Privacy

A potentially more serious and widespread concern is that in the process of conducting and use of research—especially database marketing—marketers may invade consumers' privacy. Consumers worry that marketers know too much about them and that personal data, financial data, and behavioral data may be sold to other companies or used inappropriately without their knowledge or consent. See Chapter 18 and the bonus online chapter about public policy for more discussion of this important issue.

Deceptive Research Practices

Finally, unscrupulous researchers may engage in deceptive practices. One such practice is lying about the sponsor of the research (e.g., saying it is being conducted by a nonprofit organization when it is really being conducted by a for-profit company). Another deceptive practice is promising that respondents' answers will remain anonymous when in fact the company adds identifying information to the data in order to be able to market to these consumers later on. Unscrupulous researchers may also promise to compensate respondents but fail to deliver on this promise.[45]

Summary

Consumer research is a valuable tool that helps marketers design better marketing programs, aids in the development of laws and public policy decisions regarding product safety, and promotes our general understanding of how consumers behave and why. Researchers use a variety of techniques, including collecting data on what consumers say and what they do. These tools may involve data collection from relatively few individuals or from many individuals and may study consumers at a single point in time or track their behavior across time.

Some companies have internal marketing research departments to collect data; others use external research firms to conduct studies. Advertising agencies and syndicated data services are two types of outside agencies that conduct consumer research. Large retail chains often use electronic scanners to track sales of a brand or product category. Research foundations, trade groups, the government, consumer organizations, academics, and academic research centers also collect consumer information. Research supports a consumer-oriented view of marketing and can help companies improve consumption experiences and strengthen customer relationships. However, critics say research may invade consumers' privacy and lead to higher marketing costs; in addition, unscrupulous marketers can misuse consumer information.

Questions for Review and Discussion

1. How do researchers use surveys, focus groups, interviews, storytelling, and neuroscience to learn about consumer behavior?
2. How do experiments differ from field experiments?
3. Why do researchers use observation and purchase panels to study consumer behavior?
4. How is primary data different from secondary data?
5. What are some of the positive and negative aspects of consumer research?

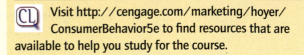 Visit http://cengage.com/marketing/hoyer/ConsumerBehavior5e to find resources that are available to help you study for the course.

CONSUMER BEHAVIOR CASE

OfficeMax Asks How Shoppers Shop—and More

How can a retailer bring in more shoppers, encourage them to browse and buy more, and gain their long-term loyalty despite competition from two major rivals? Competing against Staples and Office Depot, OfficeMax is in just such a situation. Although the office-supply retailer draws many business buyers, it is also popular among consumers who need paper and envelopes, pens and pencils, file storage supplies, photocopying and printing, and home-office essentials such as printers, scanners, computers, software, desks, and chairs.

Every time a shopper buys any item in any OfficeMax store, the company's information system captures all of the details—the amount of the sale, the product(s) and quantities purchased, the store location, the time of day, and so on—and stores them in its huge database. Analyzing sales data helps the retailer's marketers determine, for instance, which products tend to be purchased together and when and where certain products are particularly popular.

What no database can show, however, is how Office-Max shoppers navigate through the store and what influences their movements from front to back and from aisle to aisle. OfficeMax's marketers needed to know more about how its customers shop, with their goal being to redo the stores to increase customer satisfaction and boost sales. According to the chief merchandising officer, "The experience [Office Max creates] by scientifically understanding how [its] customers interact with [its] stores can make a big difference."

The market research firm hired by OfficeMax to study shopper behavior began observing what people did from the moment they entered one of its stores to the moment they left. Did shoppers pick up a shopping bag? Did they turn left or right after entering? Which departments did they visit and in what order? Which displays did they examine, and how long did they browse?

After observing how shoppers behaved in several OfficeMax stores, the researchers told the company that many shoppers were confused about the store layout, in part because they could not see beyond the high shelving used to store and display some products. Moreover, the aisles were arranged in a grid, which made it difficult for some shoppers to quickly identify where to look for specific product categories. Based on their findings, the researchers recommended that OfficeMax replace its straight aisles with a "racetrack" loop to guide shoppers around the store. They also suggested featuring high-priced gadgets such as computers and digital cameras in the center of the loop.

OfficeMax acted on these research findings and changed its store layout. It did away with the aisle grid and formed a central highlighted area for computers and other electronics. In addition, the retailer set up a few other zones along the racetrack loop, each organized around a particular product category. To see how the changes were working, the researchers observed shoppers in newly revamped stores. Now, because more products and displays were more visible from the racetrack loop, more than half of the shoppers browsed to the back wall, whereas in the original research only one-third of the shoppers were observed doing so.

OfficeMax has also used research to develop new store-brand products and to fine-tune promotions. The first time that OfficeMax put up its holiday "Elf Yourself" website, where visitors could personalize an animated elf by using their own photos, observers noted how many visitors came to the site, how long they stayed, and how many created elves. The second year, after OfficeMax added new features such as personalized voice messages, research showed that the site drew twice as many visitors as it had the previous year—drawing 60 million people in all. Reinforced by in-store communications and online advertising, the campaign achieved its goal of building brand excitement and store traffic.[46]

Case Questions

1. Identify the types of consumer research used by OfficeMax and the research firm it hired. Why were these appropriate for the company and its situation?
2. What kind of research would help OfficeMax gauge the attitudes and feelings of current customers and noncustomers toward its brand?
3. Suppose OfficeMax was considering the use of either purchase panels or diaries to gain a better understanding of its customers' buying behavior. Which method, if either, would you recommend, and why?

The Psychological Core

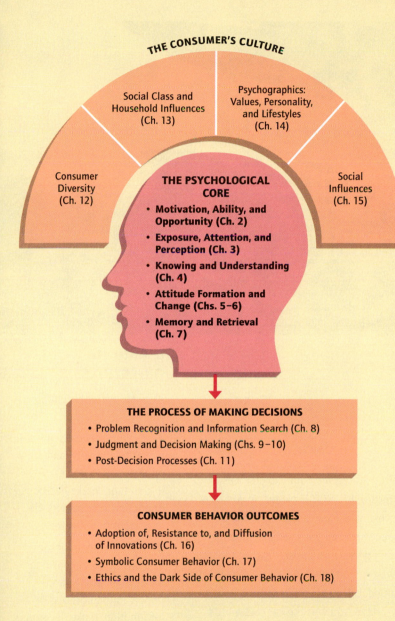

THE CONSUMER'S CULTURE

Social Class and Household Influences (Ch. 13)

Psychographics: Values, Personality, and Lifestyles (Ch. 14)

Consumer Diversity (Ch. 12)

Social Influences (Ch. 15)

THE PSYCHOLOGICAL CORE
- **Motivation, Ability, and Opportunity (Ch. 2)**
- **Exposure, Attention, and Perception (Ch. 3)**
- **Knowing and Understanding (Ch. 4)**
- **Attitude Formation and Change (Chs. 5–6)**
- **Memory and Retrieval (Ch. 7)**

THE PROCESS OF MAKING DECISIONS
- Problem Recognition and Information Search (Ch. 8)
- Judgment and Decision Making (Chs. 9–10)
- Post-Decision Processes (Ch. 11)

CONSUMER BEHAVIOR OUTCOMES
- Adoption of, Resistance to, and Diffusion of Innovations (Ch. 16)
- Symbolic Consumer Behavior (Ch. 17)
- Ethics and the Dark Side of Consumer Behavior (Ch. 18)

Consumer behavior is greatly affected by the amount of effort that consumers put into their consumption behaviors and decisions. Chapter 2 describes three critical factors that affect effort: the (1) motivation, (2) ability, and (3) opportunity consumers have to engage in behaviors and make decisions. Chapter 3 discusses how consumers come into contact with marketing stimuli (exposure), notice them (attention), and perceive them.

Chapter 4 continues the topic by discussing how consumers compare new stimuli with their existing knowledge and attempt to understand or comprehend the information they take in on a deeper level. Chapter 5 describes what happens when consumers exert a great deal of effort in forming and changing attitudes. Chapter 6 discusses how attitudes can be influenced when consumer effort is low. Finally, because consumers are not always exposed to marketing information when they actually need it, Chapter 7 focuses on memory and how consumers retrieve information.

Chapter 2

Motivation, Ability, and Opportunity

INTRODUCTION

The Toyota Prius Zooms into the Fast Lane

When Toyota first launched the Prius in the United States, the Ford Explorer was in its heyday. The year was 2000, and Ford sold a record 445,000 Explorers. In a market dominated by rugged SUVs and pickup trucks, few consumers knew anything about the innovative hybrid electric-gasoline engine that powered the small Prius sedan. However, some had heard about earlier electric cars that couldn't go very far or very fast without being plugged in for recharging, and many routinely evaluated cars in terms of horsepower. Therefore, Toyota's introductory campaign focused on educating buyers about the Prius's environmentally friendly under-the-hood technology, one reason why the car cost a little more than comparable sedans.

Over the next few years, Toyota's advertising continued to explain the hybrid engine to consumers but also emphasized low emissions, high mileage, and the fact that they would "never have to plug it in." As the price of gasoline climbed higher and public concern about global warming heated up, the Prius's sales soared, and demand outstripped supply for a time. Prius became the best-selling car in places like Portland, Oregon, where consumers enthusiastically embraced eco-friendly products. Once Toyota caught up with the demand, its new ads announced, "Your Prius is ready," calling the car "America's most fuel-efficient car." By 2007,

LEARNING OBJECTIVES

After studying this chapter, you will be able to

1. Explain why consumers' motivation, ability, and opportunity to process information, make decisions, or engage in behaviors are important to marketers.

2. Identify the influences and outcomes of consumer motivation, ability, and opportunity to process information, make decisions, and engage in behaviors.

the Prius was outselling the Ford Explorer in the U.S. market and had become "a symbol for something more than just a car," according to the Prius product marketing manager.[1]

Toyota understands that consumer motivation, ability, and opportunity exert a powerful influence on a consumer's acquisition, usage, and disposition decisions. This chapter examines motivation, ability, and opportunity in detail. Exhibit 2.1, an overview of the chapter, shows that motivated individuals may invest a lot of thought and activity in reaching their goals.

Motivation to process information, make a decision, or engage in a behavior is enhanced when consumers regard something as (1) personally relevant; (2) consistent with their values, needs, goals, and emotions; (3) risky; and/or (4) moderately inconsistent with their prior attitudes. Toyota encourages Prius buyers to see the car as consistent with their save-the-planet values, their goals of saving money, and their self-concept as people who can make a difference. On the other hand, consumers also have to weigh the car's higher price against the money they'll save on gas in the long run.

Whether motivated consumers actually achieve a goal depends on whether they have the *ability* to achieve it, which is based on (1) their knowledge and experience; (2) cognitive style; (3) complexity of information; (4) intelligence, education, and age; and, in the case of purchase goals, (5) money. Toyota, for instance, went to great lengths to provide information that clarified how the Prius was different from electric cars and regular sedans. Achieving goals like processing information also depends on whether consumers have the *opportunity* to achieve the goal. If the goal is to process information, opportunity is determined by (1) time, (2) distractions, and (3) the amount, repetition, and control of information to which consumers are exposed. So Toyota, realizing that the Prius was different, used many marketing communications and repeated its messages to give consumers the opportunity to learn about the novelty of the car.

Consumer Motivation and Its Effects

Motivation An inner state of arousal that provides energy needed to achieve a goal.

Motivation is defined as "an inner state of arousal," with the aroused energy directed to achieving a goal.[2] The motivated consumer is energized, ready, and willing to engage in a goal-relevant activity. For example, if you learn that a much-anticipated video game will go on sale next Tuesday, you may be motivated to be at the store early that morning. Consumers can be motivated to engage in behaviors, make decisions, or process information, and this motivation can be seen in the context of acquiring, using, or disposing of an offering. Let's look first at the effects of motivation, as shown in Exhibit 2.1.

High-Effort Behavior

One outcome of motivation is behavior that takes considerable effort. For example, if you are motivated to buy a good car, you will research vehicles online, visit dealerships, take test drives, and so on. Likewise, if you are motivated to lose weight, you will buy low-fat foods, eat smaller portions, and exercise. Motivation not only drives behaviors consistent with a goal but also creates a willingness to expend time and energy engaging in these behaviors. Thus, someone motivated to buy a new video game may earn extra money for it, drive through a snowstorm to reach the store, and then wait in line for an hour to buy it.

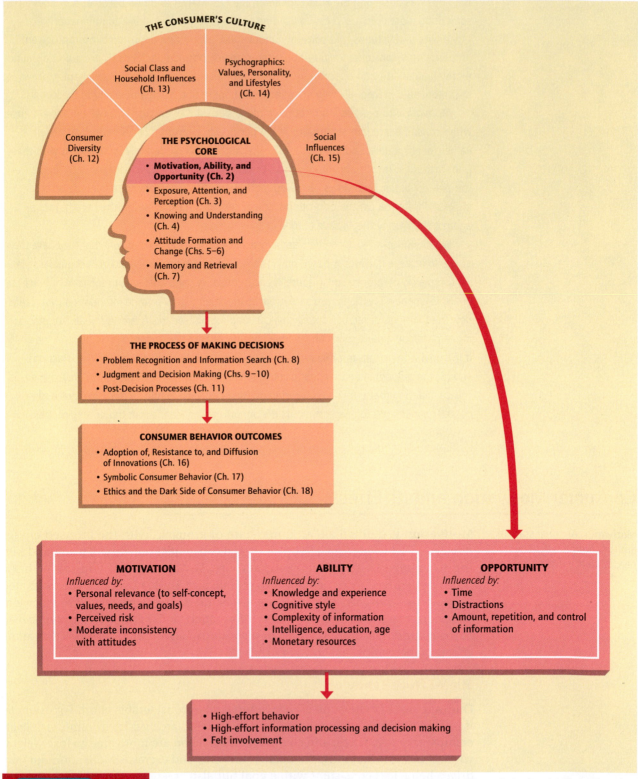

THE CONSUMER'S CULTURE

Social Class and Household Influences (Ch. 13)

Psychographics: Values, Personality, and Lifestyles (Ch. 14)

Consumer Diversity (Ch. 12)

THE PSYCHOLOGICAL CORE
- **Motivation, Ability, and Opportunity (Ch. 2)**
- Exposure, Attention, and Perception (Ch. 3)
- Knowing and Understanding (Ch. 4)
- Attitude Formation and Change (Chs. 5–6)
- Memory and Retrieval (Ch. 7)

Social Influences (Ch. 15)

THE PROCESS OF MAKING DECISIONS
- Problem Recognition and Information Search (Ch. 8)
- Judgment and Decision Making (Chs. 9–10)
- Post-Decision Processes (Ch. 11)

CONSUMER BEHAVIOR OUTCOMES
- Adoption of, Resistance to, and Diffusion of Innovations (Ch. 16)
- Symbolic Consumer Behavior (Ch. 17)
- Ethics and the Dark Side of Consumer Behavior (Ch. 18)

MOTIVATION
Influenced by:
- Personal relevance (to self-concept, values, needs, and goals)
- Perceived risk
- Moderate inconsistency with attitudes

ABILITY
Influenced by:
- Knowledge and experience
- Cognitive style
- Complexity of information
- Intelligence, education, age
- Monetary resources

OPPORTUNITY
Influenced by:
- Time
- Distractions
- Amount, repetition, and control of information

- High-effort behavior
- High-effort information processing and decision making
- Felt involvement

EXHIBIT 2.1

Chapter Overview: Motivation, Ability, and Opportunity

Motivation, ability, and opportunity (MAO) to engage in various consumer behaviors is affected by many factors. Outcomes of high MAO include (1) goal-relevant behavior, (2) high-effort information processing and decision making, and (3) felt involvement.

High-Effort Information Processing and Decision Making

Motivation also affects how we process information and make decisions.[3] When consumers are highly motivated to achieve a goal, they are more likely to pay careful attention to it, think about it, attempt to understand or comprehend goal-relevant information, evaluate that information critically, and try to remember it for later use. Doing all this takes a lot of effort. For example, if you are motivated to buy a new video game, you might scour newspaper ads looking for a sale. If someone mentions a store that lets people reserve a game in advance, you might actively try to get the store's name and phone number.

However, when consumers have low motivation, they devote little effort to processing information and making decisions. For example, your motivation to purchase the best pad of paper on the market is likely to be low. You wouldn't devote much attention to learning about the characteristics of paper pads, nor would you think about what it would be like to use various types of pads. Once in the store, you are unlikely to spend much time comparing brands. You may use decision-making shortcuts, such as deciding to buy the cheapest brand or the same brand you bought the last time.[4] The purchase of most common grocery products falls into the same category.

Most research on consumer behavior has focused on consumers' motivation to process information *accurately*, as just described. However, recent research has focused on a different type of motivation involved in information processing that is called **motivated reasoning.** When consumers engage in motivated reasoning, they process information in a biased way so that they can obtain the particular conclusion they want to reach.[5]

Motivated reasoning Processing information in a way that allows consumers to reach the conclusion that they want to reach.

For example, if your goal is to lose weight, and you see an ad for a diet product, you might process the ad in a biased way to convince yourself that the product will indeed work for you. If we want to believe that we are not vulnerable to the ill effects of smoking, we may be more likely to smoke if we are aware that there are smoking cessation products on the market that are touted as "remedies." Because there are remedies to help us stop smoking, we can use motivated reasoning to convince ourselves that smoking must not be so bad after all.[6]

As another example, because we want to think about good things that can happen to us rather than bad things, we may underestimate the likelihood of facing problems such as becoming ill—and fail to take preventive steps to avoid doing so.[7] We may be particularly prone to motivated reasoning when our egos are at stake or when we desperately hope to achieve a particular goal (like weight loss) or avoid a negative outcome (like becoming ill).[8] The concept of motivated reasoning is rather new, so most of the discussion that follows focuses on the motivation to process information accurately.

Felt Involvement

A final outcome of motivation is that it evokes a psychological state in consumers called *involvement.*

Researchers use the term **felt involvement** to refer to the psychological experience of the motivated consumer.[9]

Felt involvement Self-reported arousal or interest in an offering, activity, or decision.

Types of Involvement

Felt involvement can be (1) enduring, (2) situational, (3) cognitive, or (4) affective.[10]

Enduring involvement exists when we show interest in an offering or activity over a long period of time.[11] Car enthusiasts are intrinsically interested in cars and

Enduring involvement Long-term interest in an offering, activity, or decision.

exhibit enduring involvement in them. Enthusiasts engage in activities that reveal this interest (e.g., going to car shows, reading car magazines, visiting dealerships). In most instances, consumers experience **situational (temporary) involvement** with an offering or activity. For example, consumers who exhibit no enduring involvement with cars may be involved in the car-buying process when they are in the market for a new car. After they buy the car, their involvement with new cars declines dramatically.

Researchers also distinguish between cognitive and affective involvement.[12]

Cognitive involvement means that the consumer is interested in thinking about and processing information related to his or her goal. The goal therefore includes learning about the offering. A sports enthusiast who is interested in learning all she can about pitching ace Pedro Martinez would be exhibiting cognitive involvement.

Affective involvement means that the consumer is willing to expend emotional energy in or has heightened feelings about an offering or activity. The consumer who listens to music to experience intense emotions is exhibiting affective involvement.

Objects of Involvement

As many of this chapter's examples indicate, consumers may exhibit cognitive and/or affective involvement in objects. These objects can include *a product or retail category* such as cars or cosmetic stores or can involve *experiences* such as white-water rafting.[13] You might be involved with clothing because you enjoy shopping for such products and see them as important for your self-expression (see Exhibit 2.2).[14]

Consumers can also exhibit cognitive and/or affective *involvement with a brand* by being emotionally attached to it, as one might be with a particular musical band or one's iPod. When one is emotionally attached to and involved with a brand, one views the brand as an extension of oneself and feels a great deal of passion toward the brand.[15] Consumers can also be *involved with ads* that are interesting or relevant to them.[16] In Japan, ads that emphasize interpersonal relationships, social circumstances, and nonverbal expressions generate more involvement than ads with clearly articulated and spoken messages.[17] Consumers may also be *involved with a medium* (like TV, newspapers, or the Internet) or with a particular article or show in which an ad is placed. *American Idol*, which has logged 600 million viewer votes per season, generates a lot of involvement, as does the Super Bowl.[18] A person may get so involved in interacting with a particular company's website that he or she may view it as "play."[19]

Consumers involved in certain decisions and behaviors are experiencing **response involvement.**[20] For example, consumers may be highly involved in the process of deciding between brands. Because consumers can be involved with many different entities, it is important to specify the *object of involvement* when using the term *involvement*. For instance, consumers who are involved with brands because they are attached to them are unlikely to be involved in deciding which brand to buy since they already think their brand is the best. Similarly, consumers can be very involved in an ad because it is funny or interesting, yet they may not be involved in the advertised brand because they are loyal to another brand.

We are motivated to behave, process information, or engage in effortful *decision making* about things that we feel are personally relevant. And we will experience considerable involvement when buying, using, or disposing of them. Think about all the behaviors that you engaged in when deciding where to go to college—obtaining applications and information packets, searching the Web, visiting campuses, weighing the information about each school, and deciding where to go.

Situational involvement
Temporary interest in an offering, activity, or decision, often caused by situational circumstances.

Cognitive involvement
Interest in thinking about and learning information pertinent to an offering, activitiy, or decisions.

Affective involvement
Interest in expending emotional energy and evoking deep feelings about an offering, activity, or decision.

Response involvement
Interest in certain decisions and behaviors.

1. It gives me pleasure to shop for clothes.
2. I can think of instances in which a personal experience was affected by the way I was dressed.
3. Because of my personal values, I feel that clothing ought to be important to me.
4. I enjoy buying clothes for myself.
5. I rate my dress sense as being of high importance to me.
6. Clothes help me express who I am.
7. I attach great importance to the way people are dressed.
8. It is true that clothing interests me a lot.
9. *The kind of clothes I buy do not reflect the kind of person I am.*
10. I buy clothes for the pleasure they give me, not others.
11. *Clothing is a topic about which I am indifferent.*
12. *Clothing is not part of my self-image.*
13. Relative to other products, clothing is the most important to me.
14. Buying clothes feels like giving myself a gift.
15. *I am not at all interested in clothes.*

Source: From Nina Michaelidou and Sally Dibb, "Product Involvement: An Application in Clothing," *Journal of Consumer Behavior,* no. 5, 2006, pp. 442–453.

You probably found the task of making this decision personally involving and were interested, enthusiastic, and perhaps anxious and overwhelmed during the process. Finally, we are also motivated to think deeply about issues pertinent to a given decision when we believe we will have to justify or explain our decisions.[21]

What Affects Motivation?

Because motivation can affect outcomes of interest to marketers (like goal-relevant behaviors such as purchasing, effortful information processing, and felt involvement; see Exhibit 2.1) it is important for marketers to understand what affects motivation. If they know what creates motivation, they may be able to develop marketing tactics to influence consumers' motivation to think about, be involved with, and/or process information about their brand or ad. Exhibit 2.1 shows that a key driver of motivation is personal relevance. In turn, personal relevance is affected by how relevant something like a brand or an ad is to consumers' (a) self-concepts, (b) values, (c) needs, and (d) goals.

Personal Relevance

Personal relevance
Something that has a direct bearing on the self and has potentially significant consequences or implications for our lives.

A key factor affecting motivation is the extent to which something is **personally relevant**—that is, the extent to which it has a direct bearing on and significant implications for your life.[22] For example, if you learn that your laptop computer's battery is being recalled because it can overheat and cause a fire, you will probably find this issue to be personally relevant. Careers, college activities, romantic relationships, a car, an apartment or house, clothes, and hobbies are likely to be personally relevant because their consequences are significant for you. Research indicates that the prospect of receiving a customized (and therefore more personally relevant) product will motivate consumers to disclose private information, although they are less likely to reveal details that could be embarrassing.[23] People perceive something as personally relevant when it is consistent with their values, needs, goals, and emotions. This relevance fuels their motivation to process information, make decisions, and take actions.

Consistency with Self-Concept

Self-concept Our mental view of who we are.

Something may be personally relevant to the extent that it bears on your **self-concept,** or your view of yourself and the way you think others view you. Self-concept helps us define who we are, and it frequently guides our behavior. [24] Note that different parts of a self-concept can be salient at different times. [25] When we buy clothing, we are often making a statement about some aspect of who we are—such as a professional, a student, or a sports fan. To illustrate, some consumers find brands like Harley-Davidson to be relevant to their self-concept. *Red*, a U.K. women's magazine, makes itself relevant by appealing to the reader's self-concept as busy and productive but entitled to small indulgences. [26] In a similar way, reality TV shows can be relevant when viewers identify with the lives of the people on the show. [27]

Values

Values Beliefs about what is right, important, or good.

Consumers are more motivated to attend to and process information when they find it relevant to their **values**—beliefs that guide what people regard as important or good. Thus, if you see education as very important, you are likely to be motivated to engage in behaviors that are consistent with this value, such as pursuing a degree. (You'll read more about values in Chapter 14.)

Needs

Needs An internal state of tension caused by disequilibrium from an ideal/desired physical or psychological state.

Consumers also find things personally relevant when they have a bearing on activated needs. A **need** is an internal state of tension caused by disequilibrium from an ideal or desired state.

For example, at certain times of the day, your stomach begins to feel uncomfortable. You realize it is time to get something to eat, and you are motivated to direct your behavior toward certain outcomes (such as opening the refrigerator). Eating satisfies your need and removes the tension—in this case, hunger. Once you are motivated to satisfy a particular need, objects unrelated to that need seem less attractive. Thus, if you are motivated to fix your hair because you're having a bad hair day, a product such as styling gel will seem more attractive and important than will popcorn or another snack. [28] Needs can also lead us away from a product or service: You might stay away from the dentist because you want to avoid pain.

What needs do consumers experience? Psychologist Abraham Maslow's theory groups needs into the five categories shown in Exhibit 2.3: (1) physiological (the need for food, water, and sleep); (2) safety (the need for shelter, protection, and security); (3) social (the need for affection, friendship, and acceptance); (4) egoistic (the need for prestige, success, accomplishment, and self-esteem); and (5) self-actualization (the need for self-fulfillment and enriching experiences). [29] Within this hierarchy, lower-level needs generally must be satisfied before higher-level needs become activated. Thus before we can worry about prestige, we must meet lower-level needs for food, water, and so on.

Although Maslow's hierarchy brings useful organization to the complex issue of needs, some critics say it is too simplistic. First, needs are not always ordered exactly as in this hierarchy. Some consumers might place a higher priority on buying lottery tickets than on acquiring necessities such as food and clothing. Second, the hierarchy ignores the intensity of needs and the resulting effect on motivation. Finally, the ordering of needs may not be consistent across cultures. In some societies, for instance, social needs and belonging may be higher in the hierarchy than egoistic needs.

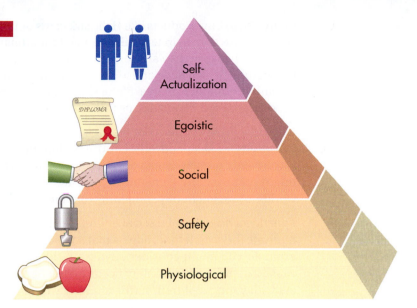

Exhibit 2.3

Maslow's Hierarchy of Needs

Maslow suggested that needs can be categorized into a basic hierarchy. People fulfill lower-order needs (e.g., physiological needs for food, water, sleep) before they fulfill higher order needs.

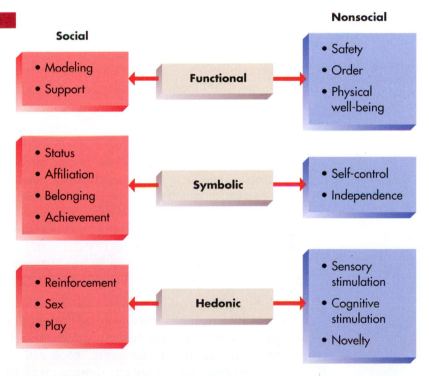

Exhibit 2.4

Categorizing Needs

Needs can be categorized according to whether they are (1) social or nonsocial and (2) functional, symbolic, or hedonic in nature. This categorization method helps marketers think about consumers' needs.

Types of Needs

Another way to categorize needs is as (1) social and nonsocial needs or as (2) functional, symbolic, and hedonic needs[30] (see Exhibit 2.4).

▶ *Social needs* are externally directed and relate to other individuals. Fulfilling these needs thus requires the presence or actions of other people. For example, the need for status drives our desire to have others hold us in high regard; the need for support drives us to have others relieve us of our burdens; the need for modeling reflects a wish to have others show us how to behave. We may be motivated to buy products like Hallmark cards or use services such as MySpace.com because they help us achieve a need for affiliation.[31] Other products may be valued because they are consistent with our need for status or our need to be unique. We also have antisocial needs—needs for space and psychological distance from other people. Plane seats that are too close together violate our need for space and motivate us to escape the confining environment.

▶ *Nonsocial needs* are those for which achievement is not based on other people. Our needs for sleep, novelty, control, uniqueness, and understanding, which involve only ourselves, can affect the usage of certain goods and services. We might purchase the same brand repeatedly to maintain consistency in our world—or we might buy something different to fulfill a need for variety.

Functional needs Needs that motivate the search for offerings that solve consumption-related problems.

▶ *Functional needs* may be social or nonsocial (see Exhibit 2.4). **Functional needs** motivate the search for products that solve consumption-related problems. For example, you might consider buying a product like a car with side airbags because it appeals to your safety needs (a functional, nonsocial need). For mothers with young children, hiring a nanny would solve the need for support (a functional, social need).

Symbolic needs Needs that relate to how we perceive ourselves, how we are perceived by others, how we relate to others, and the esteem in which we are held by others.

▶ *Symbolic needs* affect how we perceive ourselves and how we are perceived by others. Achievement, independence, and self-control are **symbolic needs** because they are connected with our sense of self. Similarly, our need for uniqueness is symbolic because it drives consumption decisions about how we express our identity.[32] The need to avoid rejection and the need for achievement, status, affiliation, and belonging are symbolic because they reflect our social position or role. For example, some consumers wear Jimmy Choo shoes to express their social standing.

Hedonic needs Needs that relate to sensory pleasure.

▶ *Hedonic needs* include needs for sensory stimulation, cognitive stimulation, and novelty (nonsocial hedonic needs) and needs for reinforcement, sex, and play (social hedonic needs). These **hedonic needs** reflect our inherent desires for sensory pleasure. If the desire is intense enough, it can inspire fantasizing about specific goods, simultaneously pleasurable and discomforting.[33] Consumers may buy perfume for the sensory pleasure it can bring or go to luxury shopping areas like the Shoppes at Palazzo in Las Vegas for the eye-catching ambiance.[34] For the same reason, products containing fake fat failed because they did not meet consumers' hedonic needs—they tasted bad.

▶ *Needs for cognition and stimulation* also affect motivation and behavior. Consumers with a high need for cognition[35] (a need for mental stimulation) enjoy being involved in mentally taxing activities like reading and deeply processing information when making decisions. People with a low need for cognition may prefer activities that require less thought, such as watching TV, and are less likely to actively process information during decision making. In addition, consumers often need other kinds of stimulation. Those with a high optimum stimulation level enjoy a lot of sensory stimulation and tend to be involved in shopping and seeking brand information.[36] They also show heightened involvement in ads. Consumers with thrill-seeking tendencies enjoy activities like skydiving and white-water rafting. In contrast, consumers who feel overstimulated want to get away from people, noise, and demands—a desire revealed in the popularity of vacations at monasteries and other sanctuaries.

Characteristics of Needs

Each of the preceding needs has several characteristics:

- *Needs are dynamic.* Needs are never fully satisfied; satisfaction is only temporary. Clearly, eating once will not satisfy our hunger forever. Also, as soon as one need is satisfied, new needs emerge. After we have eaten a meal, we might next have the need to be with others (the need for affiliation). Thus, needs are dynamic because daily life is a constant process of need fulfillment.

- *Needs exist in a hierarchy.* Although several needs may be activated at any one time, some assume more importance than others. You may experience a need to eat during an exam, but your need for achievement may assume a higher priority—so you stay to finish the test. Despite this hierarchy, many needs may be activated simultaneously and influence your acquisition, usage, and disposition behaviors. Thus, your decision to go out for dinner with friends may be driven by a combination of needs for stimulation, food, and companionship.

- *Needs can be internally or externally aroused.* Although many needs are internally activated, some needs can be externally cued. Smelling pizza cooking in the apartment next door may, for example, affect your perceived need for food.

- *Needs can conflict.* A given behavior or outcome can be seen as both desirable and undesirable if it satisfies some needs but fails to satisfy others. The result is called an **approach-avoidance conflict** because you both want to engage in the behavior and want to avoid it. Teenagers may experience an approach-avoidance conflict in deciding whether to smoke cigarettes. Although they may believe that others will think they are cool for smoking (consistent with the need for belonging), they also know that smoking is bad for them (incompatible with the need for safety).

- An **approach-approach conflict** occurs when someone must choose between two or more equally desirable options that fulfill different needs. A consumer who is invited to a career-night function (consistent with achievement needs) might experience an approach-approach conflict if he is invited to see a basketball game with friends (consistent with affiliation needs) on the same evening. This person will experience conflict if he views both options as equally desirable.

- An **avoidance-avoidance conflict** occurs when the consumer must choose between two equally undesirable options, such as going home alone right after a late meeting (not satisfying a need for safety) or waiting another hour until a friend can drive her home (not satisfying a need for convenience). Neither option is desirable, which creates conflict.

Approach-avoidance conflict A feeling of conflictedness about acquiring or consuming an offering that fulfills one need but fails to fulfill another.

Approach-approach conflict A feeling of conflictedness about which offering to acquire when each can satisfy an important but different need.

Avoidance-avoidance conflict A feeling of conflictedness about which offering to acquire when neither can satisfy an important but different need.

Identifying Needs

Because needs influence motivation and its effects, marketers are keenly interested in identifying and measuring them. However, consumers are often unaware of their needs and have trouble explaining them to researchers. Inferring consumers' needs based only on their behaviors is also difficult because a given need might not be linked to a specific behavior. In other words, the same need (for example, affiliation) can be exhibited in various and diverse behaviors (visiting friends, going to the gym), and the same behavior (going to the gym) can reflect various needs (affiliation, achievement). Consider the activity of shopping. One study found that when women shop in drugstores, they are seeking information about items that provide peace of mind (satisfying needs for safety and well-being). When they shop in club stores like Costco or Price Chopper, they are seeking adventure and entertainment (satisfying the need for stimulation).[37]

Inferring needs in a cross-cultural context is particularly difficult. For example, some research indicates that U.S. consumers use toothpaste primarily for its cavity-reducing capabilities (a functional need). In contrast, consumers in England and some French-speaking areas of Canada use toothpaste primarily to freshen breath (a hedonic need). French women drink mineral water so they will look better (a symbolic need), whereas German consumers drink it for its health powers (a functional need).[38]

Given these difficulties, marketers sometimes use indirect techniques to uncover consumers' needs.[39] One technique is to ask consumers to interpret a set of relatively ambiguous stimuli such as cartoons, word associations, incomplete sentences, and incomplete stories. Using Exhibit 2.5, one consumer might reveal needs for esteem by interpreting the man in the cartoon as thinking, "My friends will think I'm really cool for riding in this car!" Another might reveal needs for affiliation by filling in the cartoon with "I could take all my friends for rides with me."

When one study asked cigarette smokers why they smoked, most said they enjoyed it and believed that smoking in moderation was fine. However, when they were given incomplete sentences like "People who never smoke are _____," respondents filled in the blanks with words like *happier* and *wiser.* And when given sentences like "Teenagers who smoke are _____," respondents answered with words like *crazy* and *foolish.* These smokers were clearly more concerned about smoking than their explicit answers indicated.[40]

SURVEY

A. Cartoon drawing:
What do you think the people in this cartoon are thinking?

B. Sentence completion:
Fill in the blanks with the first word that comes to your mind:

1. The perfect gift _____.

2. The gifts I still treasure _____.

3. If I give a gift to myself _____.

C. Tell a story:
Tell a story about the gift being unwrapped in this picture.

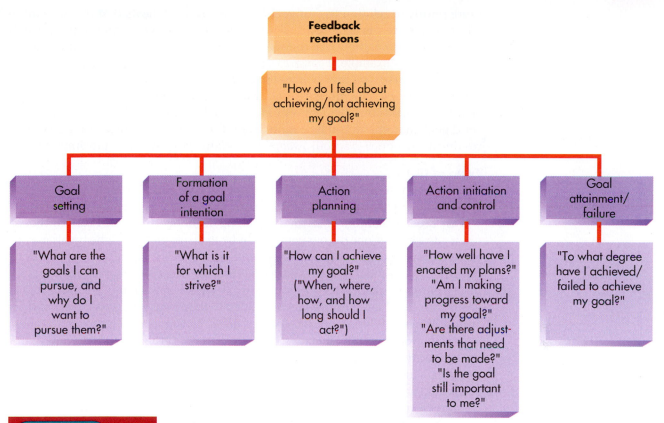

Feedback reactions

"How do I feel about achieving/not achieving my goal?"

Goal setting	Formation of a goal intention	Action planning	Action initiation and control	Goal attainment/ failure
"What are the goals I can pursue, and why do I want to pursue them?"	"What is it for which I strive?"	"How can I achieve my goal?" ("When, where, how, and how long should I act?")	"How well have I enacted my plans?" "Am I making progress toward my goal?" "Are there adjustments that need to be made?" "Is the goal still important to me?"	"To what degree have I achieved/ failed to achieve my goal?"

Exhibit 2.6

Goal Setting and Pursuit in Consumer Behavior

The process of setting and pursuing goals is circular: How a person feels about achieving or not achieving a goal affects what new goals that person sets and why. This process affects the individual's motivation to initiate or continue behaviors relevant to the goal that has been set.

Goals

Goals Outcomes that we would like to achieve.

Goals are also an important influence on personal relevance and motivation (see Exhibit 2.1).[41] A **goal** is a particular end state or outcome that a person would like to achieve. You might have goals for saving money, enrolling in a class you want to take, or taking someone special to dinner.

Goal Setting and Pursuit

Goal setting helps consumers figure out what they need to do to attain a goal.[42] As shown in Exhibit 2.6, goal-attainment activities follow a certain sequence. After we set a goal (such as to lose four pounds this month), we are motivated to form a goal intention, plan to take action (identify low-fat foods and join a gym), implement and control the action (through diet and exercise), and evaluate success or failure in attaining the goal (checking weight at the end of the month). We use what we learn by achieving or not achieving the goal as feedback for future goal setting. Thus, setting and pursuing goals help to drive behavior.

Goals and Effort

Consumers vary in how much effort they will exert to achieve a goal. You might want to lose weight but might not put much effort into doing so. Furthermore, if you perceive that you have failed in achieving a goal (such as saving a certain amount of money), you will be less motivated and, subsequently, perform even more poorly in relation to that goal.[43] Some research shows that the amount of effort people exert to achieve a goal depends not only on how important the goal is to them but also on how well they are doing in achieving other, potentially unrelated, goals. For example, if you are making progress toward a goal of getting a good grade in a course, you may be more likely to also pursue a different goal, such as starting a new exercise routine.[44] The amount of effort people put into achieving a goal also depends on whether they have feedback demonstrating their progress toward goal attainment. You'll be more likely, for example, to stick with an exercise routine if you notice that your strength and endurance are constantly improving.[45]

Types of Goals

Goals can vary in whether they are *concrete or abstract*. Some goals are concrete. They are specific to a given behavior or action and determined by the situation at hand. If you are tired, one of your goals for the evening might be to go to bed early. If you are often late for class, one of your goals might be to arrive on time. Other goals may be more abstract and endure over a long period, such as being a good student or looking beautiful.[46] Consumers can also have goals that are described as *promotion-focused* or *prevention-focused*. With promotion-focused goals, consumers are motivated to act in ways to achieve positive outcomes; that is, they focus on hopes, wants, and accomplishments. With prevention-focused goals, consumers are motivated to act in ways that avoid negative outcomes; they focus on responsibilities, safety, and guarding against risks. To illustrate, if you were going to buy a new car, would you focus on how much fun you would have driving it (promotion-focused goal) or on how much you would have to pay for insurance (prevention-focused goal)? Alternatively, if you were trying to diet, would you be more likely to focus on how good you would feel if you avoided that slice of cake or how bad you would feel if you ate it?[47]

In addition, consumers frequently have *goals to regulate how they feel*. If you feel depressed, you might have a goal of trying to make yourself feel better, perhaps by eating an ice cream cone or going to the movies. These goals describe why consumers who are feeling sad may think that "retail therapy" will cheer them up.[48] Moreover, consumers also regulate their feelings by thinking about how to sequence their consumption activities so as to gain maximal pleasure. For example, when you are on vacation, you are likely to set a plan of what you want to do first, second, and third so that you can maximize the overall pleasure of the day.[49]

And consumers can have *goals to regulate what they do* (not just how they feel). For example, if you have been doing just a little too much partying, you might try to regulate your behavior by partying less and hitting the books harder. In trying to control your behavior, you hope that you can achieve goals that will be important to you (like getting a good grade).[50]

Goals and Emotions

Goals are important because the extent to which our goals are met or thwarted affects how we feel: Whether we feel good or bad about something depends on whether it is consistent or inconsistent with our goals. According to **appraisal theory,** our emotions are determined by how we think about or "appraise" a situation or outcome. As Exhibit 2.7 shows, appraisal theory proposes that we feel positive emotions like pleasure and pride when an outcome is consistent with our goals.

Appraisal theory also posits that other appraisal dimensions affect how we feel—dimensions like normative/moral compatibility (is the outcome relevant to what is expected of us or what we should do?), certainty (is the outcome certain to occur or not?), and agency (was I the cause of the outcome, did someone else or the

Appraisal theory A theory of emotion that proposes that emotions are based on an individual's assessment of a situation or an outcome and its relevance to his or her goals.

Caused by...	Good for Me (consistent with my goals)		Bad for Me (inconsistent with my goals)		
	Certain	Uncertain	Certain	Uncertain	
Self	Pride	Hope Excitement	Guilt Shame	Fear Anxiety	Relevant to what I should do or should have done
	Happiness	Hope Excitement	Distress	Fear Anxiety	Irrelevant to what I should do or should have done
Other	Admiration Love	Hope Excitement	Contempt Disgust Envy	Fear Anxiety	Relevant to what I should do or should have done
	Gratitude Love	Hope Excitement	Anger Enraged Resentful	Fear Anxiety	Irrelevant to what I should do or should have done
Environment	Satisfied Relieved Delighted	Hope Excitement Interest Challenge	Disappointed Threatened Frustrated Regret	Fear Anxiety	Relevant to what I should do or should have done
	Pleased Delighted Relieved	Hope Excitement	Miserable Bored	Fear Anxiety	Irrelevant to what I should do or should have done
Not Sure	Glad Delighted	Hope Excitement	Pity	Fear Anxiety	Relevant to what I should do or should have done
	Happiness Joy	Hope Excitement	Sadness Miserable	Fear Anxiety	Irrelevant to what I should do or should have done

Exhibit 2.7
Appraisal Theory

Source: Adapted from Allison Johnson and David Stewart, "A Re-Appraisal of the Role of Emotion in Consumer Behavior: Traditional and Contemporary Approaches," *Review of Marketing Research* 1 (New York: M.E. Sharpe, 2005), pp. 3–34.

environment cause it, or did it happen by chance?). To illustrate Exhibit 2.7, we might feel proud when a good outcome happens, we are the cause of that outcome, and the outcome is consistent with what we should have done. In contrast, we might feel sad when an outcome is inconsistent with our goals and we see it as being caused by the situation or by bad luck.[51] Still applying appraisal theory, marketers should recognize that sometimes actions and outcomes create specific emotions rather than general feelings of goodness or badness. If a product doesn't work, consumers might feel guilty, angry, sad, or frustrated, depending on who is seen as being responsible for the product's not working. Because emotions play a powerful role in attitudes, choices, and satisfaction, the discussion of appraisal theory will continue in later chapters.[52]

MARKETING IMPLICATIONS

Marketers can enhance consumers' motivation to process promotional material by making the information as personally relevant as possible and appealing to consumers' self-concepts, values, needs, or goals. Salespeople can explore consumers' underlying reasons for making a purchase and tailor sales pitches to those reasons. Research indicates that the prospect of receiving a customized (and therefore more personally relevant) product will motivate consumers to disclose private information.[53] Consumers who value advancement or achievement will find an ad more personally relevant if it appeals to those values. The American Red Cross and other groups are targeting adults aged 17 to 24 to stimulate affective involvement with the act of donating blood—not an easy task because this activity "is not on their radar screens, and there is no reason for them to care about the issue," says a blood center spokesperson. To encourage affective involvement, the organization's ad campaign carries the tag line "Saving the world isn't easy. Saving a life is. Just one pint of blood can save up to three lives."[54] Appealing to the value of saving a life should be particularly motivating to consumers.

In advertising, messages can use a narrative structure to stimulate narrative processing, helping consumers connect the advertised brand with their self-concept.[55] Consumers tend to think more about messages that match their self-concept.[56] Thus, if you see yourself as being extroverted, you are likely to be stimulated to process an ad if it portrays a brand appropriate for extroverted people.

Consumers' needs and goals have particular relevance to marketers:

▶ *Segment based on needs and goals.* Marketers can use needs or goals to segment markets, such as the need for healthier foods. Kellogg and other food manufacturers have introduced whole-grain breakfast cereals in response to federal dietary recommendations encouraging consumers to eat more whole-grain foods.[57]

▶ *Create new needs or goals.* Marketers can attempt to create new needs or goals. To illustrate, the Italian automaker Ferrari launched its F-1 Clienti program to create a need for a new car-racing experience. Customers willing to pay $1 million (or more) to buy a retired Ferrari racecar can drive it on Grand Prix courses and be tutored by a racing champion and supported by a professional pit crew. According to Ferrari, the F-1 Clienti program allows customers to have "an experience they can't get elsewhere."[58]

▶ *Develop need- and goal-satisfying offerings.* Marketers can also identify currently unfulfilled needs or goals or can develop better alternatives to satisfy needs and goals. For example, the Quacker Factory company identified a need among middle-aged suburban women for enjoyable, comfortable, reasonably priced clothing that is attractive but neither revealing nor clingy. In satisfying this need for self-expression—many customers own two dozen Quacker Factory items—the company satisfied another need: the need for affiliation. Women wearing the company's distinctive clothing call "Quack, quack, quack" greetings to each other when they meet.[59] Chapter 16 explains more about research and the development of new products.

▶ *Manage conflicting needs or goals.* Companies can develop new products or use communications to resolve need conflicts. For instance, the marketers of Propecia, a prescription tablet for treating male baldness, must promote the drug's benefits while also countering the perception that it will reduce sexual desire.[60]

Exhibit 2.8

Consumer Goals

Consumers are more likely to be involved in ads when brands are touted as relevant to consumers' goals (e.g., losing weight).

burn more calories with every step™

earth

Working out starts the moment you walk in Earth® footwear. Our Kalsø® Negative Heel Technology® positions your toes 3.7° higher than your heels—helping tone, firm, and strengthen your body*—to get "summer legs" all year round. Learn more by viewing our educational video on-line at www.earthfootwear.com.

▶ *Appeal to multiple goals and needs.* Marketers may want to create bundled offerings that allow consumers to achieve more than one goal or satisfy more than one need during a single consumption episode.[61] The Subway sandwich chain launched a Fresh Resolutions program that would help consumers achieve their weight-loss goals while also promoting its sandwiches to satisfy consumers' hedonic needs and cravings for variety.[62]

▶ *Enhance communication effectiveness.* By suggesting that the offering fulfills or is relevant to a need or goal, marketers can increase the likelihood that consumers will process the message and engage in desired behaviors. The makers of Head and Shoulders shampoo, for example, recognize that consumers have a strong need to be accepted by others. The manufacturer effectively appeals to this need by suggesting that having dandruff will lead to social rejection. Thus, addressing needs is an effective way of positioning a product or service.[63]

▶ *Appeal to goals.* Marketers launching a new product might want to target consumers with promotion-focused goals. Why? Buying a new product may bring many new benefits, but there are also potential costs in making the change—money, switching costs, learning costs, uncertainty about making the right choice. Prevention-focused consumers are more likely to preserve the status quo by staying with the option they know, so they are less receptive to new products.[64] Further, knowing that consumers have goals to make themselves feel better, marketers might show how their products can improve the target market's mood—an appeal quite common in ads for spas and other indulgence-related products. Finally, marketers can help consumers achieve their self-control goals, as seen in the way Weight Watchers and other weight-loss organizations offer tips and tools for maintaining self-control when eating as well as feedback on progress toward reaching the goal (see Exhibit 2.8).

▶ *Manage consumers' emotions.* Finally, motivation and goals help marketers understand how they can manage consumers' emotions. The inability to fly out of an airport at the scheduled time is definitely goal incongruent from a consumer's standpoint. However, an airline can influence whether passengers feel angry or disappointed about the situation by communicating that the plane is not taking off because of safety concerns or inclement weather (agency is due to the situation), not because of airline incompetence (agency is due to the airline). Marketers can also manage consumers' emotions by promoting their products as mood-regulating devices, as might be true of a chocolate company that promotes its product as a source of gratification or a cruise line that promotes its cruises as a way for customers to make themselves feel happy. ◖▬▬◗

Perceived Risk

Exhibit 2.1 shows that another factor of consumers' motivation to process information about a product or brand is **perceived risk,** the extent to which the consumer is uncertain about the personal consequences of buying, using, or disposing of an offering.[65]

If negative outcomes are likely or positive outcomes are unlikely, perceived risk is high. Consumers are more likely to pay attention to and carefully process marketing communications when perceived risk is high. As perceived risk increases, consumers tend to collect more information and evaluate it carefully.

Perceived risk can be associated with any product or service, but it tends to be higher (1) when little information is available about the offering, (2) when the offering is new, (3) when the offering has a high price, (4) when the offering is technologically complex, (5) when brands differ fairly substantially in quality and might cause the consumer to make an inferior choice, (6) when the consumer has little confidence or experience in evaluating the offering, or (7) when the opinions of others are important, and the consumer is likely to be judged on the basis of the acquisition, usage, or disposition decision.[66]

Perceptions of risk vary across cultural groups. In particular, high levels of risk tend to be associated with many more products in less-developed countries, perhaps because the products in these countries are generally of poorer quality.[67] Also, perceived risk is typically higher when travelers purchase goods in a foreign country.[68] In addition, risk perceptions vary within a culture.[69] For example, Western men take more risks in stock market investments than women take, and younger consumers take more risks than older ones take. Clearly the women and older consumers in these examples perceive greater risks with various decisions.

Types of Perceived Risk

Researchers have identified six types of risk[70]

Performance risk Uncertainty about whether the offering will perform as expected.

> ▶ **Performance risk** reflects uncertainty about whether the product or service will perform as expected. General Motors reassures used car buyers who are concerned about this risk by advertising that its certification program screens out severely damaged or heavily repaired cars.[71]

Financial risk The extent to which buying, using, or disposing of an offering is perceived to have the potential to create financial harm.

> ▶ **Financial risk** is higher if an offering is expensive, such as the cost of buying a home. When consumers perceive high product-category risk due to high price levels, research suggests that their buying decisions can be improved if they research offerings using websites such as Epinions.com.[72]

Physical or safety risk The extent to which buying, using, or disposing of an offering is perceived to have the potential to create physical harm or harm one's safety.

> ▶ **Physical (or safety) risk** refers to the potential harm a product or service might pose to one's safety. Many consumer decisions are driven by a motivation to avoid physical risk (see Exhibit 2.9). For example, consumers often shy away from buying perishable groceries that have passed the stated expiration date because they are afraid of getting sick from eating spoiled food.[73]

Social risk The extent to which buying, using, or disposing of an offering is perceived to have the potential to do harm to one's social standing.

> ▶ **Social risk** is the potential harm to one's social standing that may arise from buying, using, or disposing of an offering. According to research, antismoking ad messages that conveyed the severe social disapproval risk of smoking cigarettes were more effective in influencing teens' intentions not to smoke than ad messages stressing the health consequences of smoking, such as disease.[74]

Psychological risk The extent to which buying, using, or disposing of an offering is perceived to have the potential to create negative emotions or harm one's sense of self.

> ▶ **Psychological risk** reflects consumers' concern about the extent to which a product or service fits with the way they perceive themselves. For example, if you see yourself as an environmentalist, buying disposable diapers may be psychologically risky.

Time risk Uncertainties over the length of time consumers must invest in buying, using, or disposing of the offering.

> ▶ **Time risk** reflects uncertainties about the length of time that must be invested in buying, using, or disposing of the product or service. Time risk may be high if the offering involves considerable time commitment, if learning to use it is a lengthy process, or if it entails a long commitment period (such as joining a health club that requires a three-year contract).

Risk and Involvement

As noted earlier, products can be described as either high- or low-involvement products. Some researchers have classified high- versus low-involvement products in terms of the amount of risk they pose to consumers. Consumers are likely to be more involved in purchasing products such as homes and computers than in

"I never thought I would need **my Road ID**...I was wrong!"
-- Andrea U., Gilroy, CA

Carrying ID during your daily workout could save your life - just ask Andrea. It's not something we like to think about, but accidents DO happen while exercising. In an emergency, wearing ID may be the only thing you have to guarantee immediate contact of family members and proper medical treatment. If you can't speak for yourself, your Road ID™ will. Make sure you take Road ID™ with you whenever and wherever you exercise. Visit our website to read more about Andrea and others who have benefited from wearing Road ID™. While you're there, find out more about our entire line durable Road ID™ products and how to purchase Road ID™ for the active people in your life.

www.RoadID.com   800-345-6336

RoadID™
Be seen wearing it.

Exhibit 2.9

Perceived Risk

Consumer products and services are often touted as ways to avoid risky outcomes.

purchasing picture frames or coffee because the former generate higher levels of performance, financial, safety, social, psychological, or time risk and can therefore have more extreme personal consequences.

High risk is generally uncomfortable for consumers. As a result, they are usually motivated to engage in any number of behaviors and information-processing activities to reduce or resolve risk. To reduce the uncertainty component of risk, consumers can collect additional information by conducting online research, reading news articles, engaging in comparative shopping, talking to friends or sales specialists, or consulting an expert. Consumers also reduce uncertainty by being brand loyal (buying the same brand that they did the last time), ensuring that the product should be at least as satisfactory as their last purchase.

In addition, consumers attempt to reduce the consequence component of perceived risk through various strategies. Some consumers may employ a simple decision rule that results in a safer choice. For example, someone might buy the most expensive offering or choose a heavily advertised brand in the belief that this brand is of higher quality than other brands. When decision risk is high, consumers may be willing to consider less conventional alternatives, particularly when they do not trust traditional products or practices. For example, consumers who believe that conventional medical treatments are too technological or dehumanizing may be open to other healing alternatives.[75]

MARKETING IMPLICATIONS

When perceived risk is high, marketers can either reduce uncertainty or reduce the perceived consequences of failure. AstraZeneca reassures consumers about the use of its cholesterol-lowering medication, Crestor, by explaining the benefit in the ad headline "Good news for your arteries. Bad news for plaque." The rest of the company's information-heavy print ads educate consumers about how Crestor slows the buildup of plaque, helping to reduce uncertainty about the product and its performance.

When risk is low, consumers are less motivated to think about the brand or product and its potential consequences. Marketers sometimes need to enhance risk perceptions to make their messages more compelling. For instance, the Scottish government runs nationwide ad campaigns every winter to remind consumers that flu can be deadly and to urge them to reduce their risk by getting vaccinated.[76] Interestingly, consumers do not always see a particular action as risky, even when it is. For example, many people fail to realize the risks of unprotected sex, a situation that explains why condom sales are not higher. Marketers can also enhance consumers' understanding of how behavior can create risky negative outcomes. When consumers think about the role their own behavior plays in acquiring AIDS, they are more likely to follow the advice in ads about reducing that risk.[77]

Inconsistency with Attitudes

A final factor affecting motivation, shown in Exhibit 2.1, is the extent to which new information is consistent with previously acquired knowledge or attitudes. We tend to be motivated to process messages that are moderately inconsistent with our knowledge or attitudes because such messages are perceived as moderately threatening or uncomfortable. Therefore, we try to eliminate or at least understand this inconsistency.[78] For example, if a consumer sees a car ad that mentions slightly negative information about the brand she currently owns—such as the brand's getting lower gas mileage than a competitor—she will want to process the information so that she can understand and perhaps resolve the uncomfortable feeling.

On the other hand, consumers are less motivated to process information that is highly inconsistent with their prior attitudes. Thus, someone who is loyal to the Heinz brand would not be motivated to process information from a comparative ad suggesting that Heinz is bad or that other brands are better. The consumer would simply reject the other brands as nonviable options.

Consumer Ability: Resources to Act

Ability The extent to which consumers have the resources needed to make an outcome happen.

Motivation may not result in action unless a consumer has the ability to process information, make decisions, or engage in behaviors. **Ability** is defined as the extent to which consumers have the necessary resources to make the outcome happen.[79] If our ability to process information is high, we may engage in active decision making. As shown in Exhibit 2.1, knowledge, experience, cognitive style, complexity of information, intelligence, education, age, and money are factors that affect consumers' abilities to process information about brands and make decisions about and engage in buying, usage, and disposition.

Product Knowledge and Experience

Consumers vary greatly in their knowledge about an offering.[80] They can gain knowledge from product or service experiences such as ad exposures, interactions with salespeople, information from friends or the media, previous decision making or product usage, or memory. A number of studies have compared the information-processing activities of consumers who have a lot of product knowledge or expertise with those of consumers who do not.[81] One key finding is that knowledgeable consumers, or "experts," are better able to think deeply about information than are equally motivated but less knowledgeable consumers, or "novices." These differences in prior knowledge clearly affect how consumers make decisions. For example, consumers trying to lease a car rarely understand the concept of capitalized costs (the figure used to determine lease payments), how these costs are determined, or the need to negotiate lower costs to lower their payments. The inability to understand these costs may result in a less than optimal decision.[82]

According to research, novices and experts process information in different ways.[83] Experts can process information stated in terms of attributes (what the product has—such as a 200-gigabyte hard drive), whereas novices process information better when it's stated in terms of benefits (what the product can do—such as store a lot of data). Novices may be able to process information when marketers provide a helpful analogy (e.g., can hold a library's worth of data).[84] In particular, an analogy is persuasive when consumers can transfer their knowledge of one product's attributes to an unfamiliar product and can allocate the resources needed to process this mapping.[85]

Also, consumers may have difficulty evaluating a service provider when they lack product knowledge or experience (or simply because the service outcome is not easy to evaluate, such as whether the doctor provided the best possible advice). In such situations, consumers may judge service providers using *heuristics*, simple cues or rules of thumb such as whether the medical staff was friendly or whether the examination room was clean and in good order.[86]

Cognitive Style

Consumers can differ in *cognitive style*, or their preferences for ways information should be presented. Some consumers are adept at processing information visually, whereas others prefer to process information verbally. For example, some consumers prefer to check a map, and others prefer to read directions when planning to reach a destination.

Complexity of Information

The complexity of the information to which consumers are exposed can also affect their ability to process it. Individuals may be stymied when information gets too technical or complicated; as information becomes more complex, people's ability to process it decreases. What makes information complex? Studies indicate that consumers find technical or quantitative information more difficult to handle than nontechnical and qualitative data,[87] a situation that inhibits processing. Many technological and pharmaceutical products entail complex information. In addition, research shows that messages containing pictures without words tend to be ambiguous and therefore hard to process.[88] Marketers can, however, use visualization tools to communicate complex information so consumers can more easily process it. For instance, SmartMoney.com's MarketMap helps consumers understand stock market trends at a glance by grouping stocks by industry and assigning colors to convey performance (brighter greens mean sharper stock price increases; brighter reds mean steeper stock price declines) (Also see Exhibit 2.10).[89]

Information may also be complex if the individual must sift through a huge volume of it. More consumers look online for complex information about health or medicines because Web search functions help them search efficiently. Knowing this, the patient advocacy group Citizens for the Right to Know maintains an English-language site (*rtk.org*) and a Spanish-language site (*espanol.rkt.org*) to help consumers find complex information about health-plan coverage.[90]

Intelligence, Education, and Age

Intelligence, education, and age have also been related to the ability to process information and make decisions. Specifically, consumers who are more intelligent and more educated can better process more complex

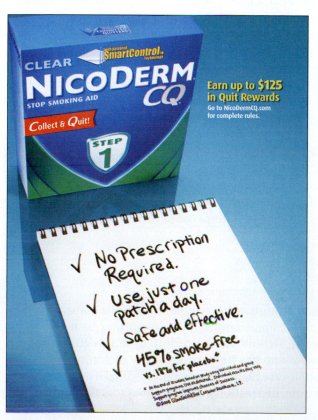

information and make decisions. Age also accounts for differences in processing ability. Older children seem to be more sensitive to the fact that the benefits of searching for information sometimes outweigh the costs, whereas younger children don't seem to have this same ability.[91] Old age has been associated with a decline in certain cognitive skills and thus reduced ability to process information. In one study, older consumers took more time to process nutrition information and made decisions that were less accurate than those of younger consumers.[92]

Money

Obviously, the lack of money also constrains consumers who might otherwise have the motivation to engage in a behavior that involves acquisition. Although motivated consumers who lack money can still process information and make buying decisions, they are definitely constrained in their immediate ability to buy from marketers.

MARKETING IMPLICATIONS

Factors affecting ability suggest several implications for marketers. First, marketers should be sure that target consumers have sufficient prior knowledge to process marketing communications. If not, the company may need to develop educational messages as a first step. Marketers also need to be sensitive to the potentially different processing styles, education levels, and ages of target consumers. For example, highly motivated but visually oriented parents may not be able to assemble toys for their children if the written instructions are too complex and thus incompatible with their processing style. IKEA's furniture assembly instructions are appropriate for a broad audience because they include no words, having only illustrations and numbers.

Providing information enhances consumers' abilities to process it, make decisions, and act on those decisions. TheKnot.com has become popular because it offers comprehensive information about all kinds of goods, services, and advice to help engaged couples plan their weddings, from buying invitations and choosing a gown to ordering the wedding cake and arranging the honeymoon.[93]

Knowing that a lack of money constrains purchase behaviors, marketers can facilitate first-time and repeat buying by providing monetary aid. Car manufacturers have enhanced consumers' purchasing ability—and boosted sales—by offering low- or no-down-payment programs, low financing rates, and rebates. Marketers can also provide education and information (through advertising, websites, point-of-purchase displays, and other communications) that help consumers better process information, make more informed decisions, and engage in consumption behaviors.

Consumer Opportunity

The final factor affecting whether motivation results in action is consumers' opportunity to engage in a behavior. For example, a consumer may be highly motivated to work out and have sufficient money to join a health club (ability); however, he may be so busy that he has little opportunity to actually go. Thus, even when motivation and ability are high, someone may not take action or make decisions because of lack of time, distractions, and other factors that impede the ability to act.

Time

Time can affect the consumer's opportunity to process information, make decisions, and perform certain behaviors. Some studies show that time-pressured consumers are more likely to buy things for themselves during the Christmas season because this is one of the few opportunities they have to shop.[94] Time affects leisure-time consumption behavior as well. Knowing that would-be gardeners have little time (or patience) to plant, weed, and water, companies are successfully marketing seed-embedded mats, low-maintenance plants, and fast-maturing trees.[95]

Consumers under time pressure to make a decision will engage in limited information processing. For example, a consumer who has to buy 30 items during a 15-minute grocery shopping trip will not have time to process a lot of information about each item. Time-pressured consumers not only process less information but also put more weight on negative information and are quicker to reject brands because of negative features.[96] When motivation to process information is low, consumers feeling moderate time pressure will tend to process information systematically. However, if time pressure is quite high or quite low, consumers are unlikely to process details systematically.[97] The more time consumers have to think about consumption problems, the more creative they tend to be at coming up with novel solutions.[98] In an advertising context, consumers have limited opportunity to process information when a message is presented in a short period; when they cannot control the pace of message presentation, as is the case with TV and radio ads; or when they fast-forward through commercials.[99]

Distraction

Distraction refers to any aspect of a situation that diverts consumers' attention. For example, an important exam can divert a consumer's attention from a yoga class she really wants to take. If someone talks while a consumer is viewing an ad or making a decision, that distraction can inhibit the consumer's ability to process the information. Certain background factors in an ad, such as music or attractive models, can also distract consumers from an advertised message.[100] Consumers may be distracted from TV commercials if the program during which the commercials appear is very involving.[101] Distraction seems to influence the effect of consumers' thoughts on their choices, not the effect of their emotions on choices.[102]

Amount, Repetition, and Control of Information

The amount of information present can also affect consumers' opportunity to process a message. Moreover, whereas consumers' ability to process information is limited by time, distraction, and the quality and complexity of the information, one factor—repetition—actually enhances it.[103] If consumers are repeatedly exposed to information, they can more easily process it because they have more chances to think about, scrutinize, and remember the information. Advertisers who use television and radio, in particular, must therefore plan to get their messages to the target audience more than once in order to enhance the opportunity for processing. However, research suggests that when a brand is unfamiliar, consumers may react negatively to repeated advertising, thereby reducing communication effectiveness. In contrast, consumers show more patience for repetition of ads attributed to known, familiar brands.[104]

Consumers remember and learn more when they can control the flow of information by determining what information is presented, for how long, and in what order. With print ads, for example, consumers have a lot of control over which messages they pay attention to, how long they spend processing each message, and the order in which they process the messages. They have more opportunity to select what is appropriate for their own needs and goals, process the information, and apply it to consumption decisions. In contrast, consumers exposed to radio or TV commercials have no such control, so they have less opportunity to process and apply the information.[105] As consumers become proficient in controlling the information flow, they can put more effort into processing the content rather than focusing on the control task.[106]

MARKETING IMPLICATIONS

Often marketers can do little to enhance consumers' opportunities to process information, make careful decisions, or engage in purchase, usage, or disposition behaviors. For example, advertisers cannot make living rooms less distracting during TV commercials or give consumers more time for shopping. However, companies can play some role in enhancing opportunity.

▶ *Repeating marketing communications* (up to a point) increases the likelihood that consumers will notice and eventually process them. Marketers can also increase the likelihood of processing by presenting messages at a time of day when consumers are least likely to be distracted and pressed for time. Messages should be stated slowly and in simple terms so consumers can understand them. One caution: Although repetition increases the opportunity to process information, it can also reduce consumers' motivation to process it!

▶ *Reducing time pressure* can lessen distractions for consumers. For example, stores may extend their hours so consumers can shop when they are least distracted and least time pressured. Many catalog companies and all online shopping sites accept orders 24 hours a day. Marketers can also offer ancillary services, such as extended shopping or service hours, that remove time constraints.

▶ *Reducing the time needed to buy, use, and learn about a product or service* allows consumers more opportunities to process information and act on their decisions. Charles Schwab, for example, reduces learning time on its website by allowing consumers to enter questions in plain English.[107] In stores, clear signs and directories help consumers locate goods more quickly and increase the likelihood that they will actually buy the goods.

Summary

Motivation reflects an inner state of arousal that directs the consumer to engage in goal-relevant behaviors, effortful information processing, and detailed decision making. We are motivated to notice, approach, and think about things that are important and personally relevant. Motivated consumers often experience affective or cognitive involvement. In some cases, this involvement may be enduring; in other cases, it may be situational, lasting only until the goal has been achieved. Consumers can also be involved with product categories, brands, ads, the media, and consumption behaviors. Consumers experience greater motivation when they regard a goal or object as personally relevant—meaning that it relates to their self-concepts, values, needs, and goals; when it entails considerable risk; or when it is moderately inconsistent with their prior attitude.

Even when motivation is high, consumers may not achieve their goals if their ability or opportunity to do so is low. If consumers lack the knowledge or experience, intelligence, education, or money to engage in a behavior, process information—especially complex information—or make a decision, they cannot achieve a goal. In addition, they may not achieve the goal if they are attending to information that is incompatible with their processing styles. Highly motivated consumers may also fail to achieve goals if lack of time, distractions, insufficient information, or lack of control over information flow limits the opportunity to do so.

Questions for Review and Discussion

1. How is motivation defined, and how does it affect felt involvement?
2. What are some objects of involvement for consumers?
3. What determines the ranking of needs in Maslow's hierarchy?
4. What types of goals do consumers have?
5. According to appraisal theory, what do emotions have to do with goals?
6. How does perceived risk affect personal relevance, and what are six types of perceived risk?
7. In what ways can ability affect consumer behavior?
8. Identify some of the elements that contribute to consumer opportunity for processing information and making decisions.

CL Visit http://cengage.com/marketing/hoyer/ConsumerBehavior5e to find resources that are available to help you study for the course.

CONSUMER BEHAVIOR CASE

What's in Store at Umpqua Bank

Umpqua Bank wants to be more than a dependable, knowledgeable financial institution where consumers pop in to use the ATM, make a deposit, or apply for a loan. Founded in 1953, the bank had just five branches and $140 million in deposits in 1994 when Ray Davis became CEO with the vision of making Umpqua "the world's greatest bank." Since then, by expanding geographically and acquiring other banks, Umpqua has grown to more than $7 billion in deposits and now does business through 147 "stores" in Oregon, Washington, and California.

Each store is a "community hub" where people can spend a few minutes sipping Umpqua-brand coffee, listening to local music selected by Umpqua, or surfing the Web using Umpqua's free Wi-Fi Internet access. With lots of light, comfortable seating, a coffee bar, a television screen, and a teller area styled like the reception desk of an upscale hotel, an Umpqua store is nothing like the formal, stuffy stereotype of an old-fashioned bank branch.

Old-fashioned banks would never launch a summer program to teach youngsters how to run a lemonade stand, offer them $10 in start-up money, give them hints about advertising and pricing, and lend out kid-friendly folding lemonade stands to young entrepreneurs.

Looking ahead, today's lemonade tycoon may very well become tomorrow's satisfied customer. As one Umpqua executive notes: "Kids have come back to the store to try to repay their loan, but we encourage them to open a savings account."

Top-notch service is another Umpqua hallmark and competitive point of differentiation. In addition to teaching employees the ins and outs of financial products, the bank sends them to customer-service courses provided by the Ritz-Carlton—the hotel chain world-famous for its superlative service. Emphasizing its service helps the bank build long-term relationships by connecting with customers on a more personal level.

The Innovation Lab in Portland, Oregon, is Umpqua's latest innovation. Working with technology leaders such as Intel, Microsoft, and Cisco, Umpqua has created this cutting-edge store as a testing ground for new ideas. "When people think of technology, they often think of it as something that makes things go faster," observes CEO Ray Davis. Instead of simply thinking "fast," Davis says the bank asks, "How can we use technology as a tool to enhance the customer experience? In banking, the challenge is how to keep the delivery system relevant."

The Innovation Lab is both people friendly and efficient. It features a huge touch-screen multimedia plasma wall where customers can obtain detailed product information and listen to podcasts about various services. Another interactive wall offers ever-changing information on community activities and volunteer programs. In another section of the store, the Computer Café, stocked with the latest laptops, is available for customer use. The bank has even set up a website where local business owners can network with each other. Umpqua is studying the ways that customers react to these and other innovations with an eye toward launching the most successful new ideas in its other stores.

Umpqua's unusual approach to banking has attracted tens of thousands of new customers, hundreds of millions of dollars in new deposits, and the attention of financial institutions across the United States and beyond. As it works toward achieving the CEO's vision of becoming the world's greatest bank, Umpqua aims to give its customers a great banking experience and more. "We provide a very clear alternative to the traditional banking experience," Davis states. "It's fun, interesting, entertaining, exciting. It's like going to Disney World."[108]

Case Questions

1. How does Umpqua enhance consumer motivation by making itself personally relevant to customers?
2. Explain, in consumer behavior terms, how the Innovation Lab enhances customers' ability to process information about banking products and services.
3. What is Umpqua doing to enhance consumers' opportunity to process information about financial services?

Exposure, Attention, and Perception

JENS, WÄHLEN SIE, VON WEM SIE STEHLEN MÖCHTEN.

INTRODUCTION

Going After Gamers: Advertising in Video Games

Advertising in video games is becoming big business for big brands: Players of *Tiger Woods* video games tee off with Nike golf clubs; players of *Tony Hawk* video games text each other using Nokia cell phones. The clothing retailer H&M had its products featured in *The Sims 2 H&M Fashion Stuff* video game. As the company's U.S. advertising manager explains, "It gives [their] existing customers an opportunity to take the fashion they love in the real world and interact with it in a whole new way." Similarly, Burger King launched its *Sneak King* video game because "Interacting with [its] characters in the games is actually more engaging than just sitting back in your chair and watching a Super Bowl commercial," notes the company's head of global marketing.

By 2011, expenditures for advertising in video games could reach $1 billion as more marketers learn how to reach out to consumers in nontraditional ways. For instance, one advertising agency studying ads in the *Rainbow Six* game found that an ad's on-screen position was more important than its size: A small Carl's Jr. ad placed close to the focal point of the action attracted more notice than a larger Mazda ad placed near the top of the screen. The agency also found that ads with motion attracted more attention than static ads.[1] But questions remain. First, are in-game ads overly intrusive? Second, are players less resistant to in-game ads? Third, do people change their attitudes or behavior as a result of viewing such ads? Research shows that product placement in video games can increase brand recall. However, if players find a game frustrating or boring, this response can influence their feelings about a brand advertised in that game.[2]

In consumer behavior terms, in-game advertising is all about exposure, attention, and perception. If consumers are to register any message after being exposed to an ad in some medium, they must perceive and pay attention to it. Whether they do so depends on a host of factors described in this chapter. As Exhibit 3.1 indicates, these issues are important because they affect what consumers comprehend, what attitudes they have, and what they remember after exposure to and attention paid to ads. They also affect what decisions they make and what actions they take after doing so.

Exposure

Exposure The process by which the consumer comes in physical contact with a stimulus.

Marketing stimuli Information about offerings communicated either by the marketer via ads, salespeople, brand symbols, packages, signs, prices, and so on or by nonmarketing sources, e.g., the media or word of mouth.

Before any type of marketing stimulus can affect consumers, they must be exposed to it. **Exposure** refers to the process by which the consumer comes into physical contact with a stimulus (see Exhibit 3.1). **Marketing stimuli** are messages and information about products or brands and other offerings communicated by either the marketer (via ads, salespeople, brand symbols, packages, signs, prices, and so on) or by nonmarketing sources (e.g., the media, word of mouth). Consumers can be exposed to marketing stimuli at the buying, using, or disposing stages of consumption. Because exposure is critical to influencing consumers' thoughts and feelings, marketers must ensure that consumers are exposed to stimuli that portray their offering in a favorable light.

(MARKETING IMPLICATIONS)

Marketers start the process of gaining exposure by selecting media, such as radio, product placements, and the Internet, and by developing communications for reaching targeted consumers. Visa USA, for instance, reaches out to travelers, sports fans, affluent shoppers, and other groups through messages in broadcast, print, and online media as well as through Olympic sponsorship and product placements. The company uses Spanish-language messages on its website, in print media, and in broadcast media to reach Hispanic consumers. Visa avoids television when targeting wealthy consumers because this group tends to record programs for later viewing and may zip through commercials. Instead, its Visa Signature card ads appear in upscale magazines such as *Condé Nast Traveler* and business magazines such as *The Economist.* Visa has also arranged to co-brand print and online ads with selected retailers such as Banana Republic. The Visa card has even replaced paper money in an updated version of the Game of Life.[3]

Factors Influencing Exposure

The *position of an ad within a medium* can affect exposure. Consumers' exposure to magazine ads is greatest when they appear on the back cover because the ads are in view whenever the magazine is placed face down. Also, consumers are most likely to be exposed to ads placed next to articles or within TV programs that interest them.[4] Exposure to commercials is greatest when they are placed at the beginning or end of a commercial break within a program because consumers either are still involved in the program or are waiting for the program to come back on.

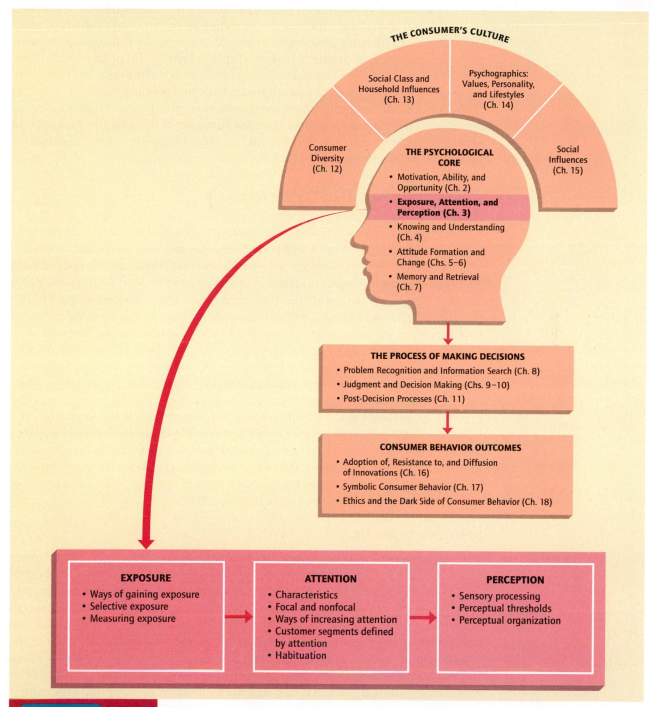

THE CONSUMER'S CULTURE

Social Class and
Household Influences
(Ch. 13)

Psychographics:
Values, Personality,
and Lifestyles
(Ch. 14)

Consumer
Diversity
(Ch. 12)

**THE PSYCHOLOGICAL
CORE**
• Motivation, Ability, and
Opportunity (Ch. 2)
• **Exposure, Attention, and
Perception (Ch. 3)**
• Knowing and Understanding
(Ch. 4)
• Attitude Formation and
Change (Chs. 5–6)
• Memory and Retrieval
(Ch. 7)

Social
Influences
(Ch. 15)

THE PROCESS OF MAKING DECISIONS
• Problem Recognition and Information Search (Ch. 8)
• Judgment and Decision Making (Chs. 9–10)
• Post-Decision Processes (Ch. 11)

CONSUMER BEHAVIOR OUTCOMES
• Adoption of, Resistance to, and Diffusion
of Innovations (Ch. 16)
• Symbolic Consumer Behavior (Ch. 17)
• Ethics and the Dark Side of Consumer Behavior (Ch. 18)

EXPOSURE
• Ways of gaining exposure
• Selective exposure
• Measuring exposure

ATTENTION
• Characteristics
• Focal and nonfocal
• Ways of increasing attention
• Customer segments defined
by attention
• Habituation

PERCEPTION
• Sensory processing
• Perceptual thresholds
• Perceptual organization

Exhibit 3.1

**Chapter Overview:
Exposure, Attention,
and Perception**

Consumers do some processing of a stimulus (e.g., an ad, brand) once they have been exposed to it,
pay attention to it, and perceive its characteristics. Once it has been perceived, consumers may examine it more closely.

Some advertisers sponsor commercial-free TV programs in which the company
gets product placement within the show or airs a single ad before or after the show.
Moreover, *product distribution* and *shelf placement* affect consumers' exposure
to brands and packages. The more widespread the brand's distribution is (the more

stores in which the product is available), the greater the likelihood that consumers will encounter it. Likewise, the product's location or the amount of shelf space allocated to it can increase consumers' exposure to a product. Consumers are most likely to be exposed to products that are displayed at the end of an aisle or those that take up a lot of shelf space. Products placed from waist to eye level get more exposure than those placed higher or lower. Exposure also increases for products placed at locations in the store where all consumers must go and spend time. For example, sales of some products increase because of their higher exposure in point-of-purchase displays at checkout counters in supermarkets, automotive stores, and restaurants.[5]

MARKETING IMPLICATIONS

In addition to the traditional ways of reaching consumers, such as using strategic placement of TV commercials or effective product displays and shelf placement, marketers are testing other ways of gaining exposure for marketing stimuli. Kellogg noticed sales increases after promoting its cereals and snacks on the Wal-Mart TV Network, which has 125,000 screens that reach 130 million shoppers in 3,100 Wal-Mart stores.[6] Advertising in media such as airlines' in-flight entertainment programs, shopping carts, hot air balloons, and turnstiles at sports arenas is another way of increasing exposure.

Some cash-strapped city governments are allowing companies to place ads on public buses, garbage trucks, and taxis and even in subway tunnels. In China, Beijing bus shelters and subway stations are plastered with ads for Internet sites and other offerings.[7] In England, Panasonic helps defray its transportation costs by selling advertising space on its delivery trucks.[8] Using "human directionals"—people in crazy outfits who stand on street corners waving their hands and shouting information—is one way that retailers and home developers affect consumers' exposure to a store or housing development. E-mail marketing is another way of increasing exposure. Although Internet users resent uninvited messages from companies, many will agree to receive e-mail or instant messages if they can control their timing.[9]

Selective Exposure

While marketers can work very hard to affect consumers' exposure to certain products and brands, ultimately consumers, not marketers, control whether their exposure to marketing stimuli occurs or not. In other words, consumers can actively seek certain stimuli and avoid others. Readers of *Vogue* magazine are more likely to selectively expose themselves to fashion-oriented ads, whereas readers of *Car and Driver* choose to look at different kinds of ads. Some consumers try to ignore the ads altogether. Online, a growing number of Internet users have software to block "pop-up" ads that would otherwise open while a Web page is loading.[10] One reason consumers want to avoid ads is that they are exposed to so many that they cannot possibly process them all. Consumers avoid ads for product categories that they do not use (this action indicates that the ads are irrelevant to them); they also tend to avoid ads they have seen before because they know what these ads will say.

Consumers' avoidance of marketing stimuli is a big problem for marketers.[11] One survey reveals that 54 percent of U.S. consumers and 68 percent of German consumers avoid ads.[12] During a TV ad, consumers can leave the room, do something else—many surf the Web while watching TV, for instance[13]—or avoid it entirely by zipping and zapping. With **zipping,** consumers record TV shows and fast-forward through the commercials when viewing the shows later

Zipping Fast-forwarding through the commercials recorded on a VCR or DVR.

Exhibit 3.2	
A Look at Zipping	
U.S. households with digital video recorders (DVRs)	20%
Recorded programming viewed in households with DVRs	80%
Amount of advertising viewers fast-forward through while viewing recorded programs	70%
Amount of all advertising viewers fast-forward through in households with DVRs	55%
Amount of all advertising viewers fast-forward through in all U.S. households	11%
Wasted advertising expenditure	$5.5 billion

Exhibit 3.2

A Look at Zipping
These numbers show why advertisers are concerned about products like DVRs that make zipping (fast-forwarding through TV commercials) easy.

Source: Susan Thea Posnock, "It Can Control Madison Avenue," *American Demographics,* February 2004, p. 31.

(see Exhibit 3.2). Consumers zip through up to 75 percent of the ads in recorded shows—yet they can still identify the brand or product category of many ads in shows they zip through.[14] Although digital video recorders now allow consumers to skip ads easily, users choose to watch specific ads that seem relevant and interesting, especially eye-catching ads for forthcoming movies.[15]

Zapping Use of a remote control to switch channels during commercial breaks.

With **zapping,** consumers avoid ads by switching to other channels during commercial breaks. Approximately 20 percent of consumers zap at any one time; more than two-thirds of households with cable TV zap regularly. Men zap significantly more than women do. People are more likely to zap commercials at the half-hour or hour mark than during the program itself.[16] Knowing this, television networks are trying to hold viewers by using such techniques as airing 30-second or 60-second minimovies in the middle of a commercial block.[17]

Many parents want to limit their children's exposure to ads because youngsters have difficulty distinguishing between ad messages and other types of media content. Marketers who advertise sugary or fatty foods have come under fire in many countries as concerns mount over childhood obesity, for example.[18] One marketer taking steps to respond to this criticism is Kraft Foods, which has stopped advertising Oreos and similar snacks during TV shows targeted at children under 12 years old.[19] However, limiting children's exposure to ads for inappropriate products—such as R-rated movies—is not easy because of massive multimedia campaigns that simultaneously appear on TV, billboards, and other media.

Now the rising tide of unsolicited ad exposure has created a backlash among consumers, leading to government action. Millions of consumers have added their phone numbers to the Federal Do Not Call Registry to avoid unwanted telemarketing pitches. Consumers can now opt out of receiving unsolicited catalogs by registering on websites like *www.catalogchoice.org.*[20] Many states have antispam statutes, and federal law forbids marketers from sending unsolicited commercial messages via e-mail, wireless phones, and pagers. Nevertheless, experts say that spam continues to clog consumers' e-mail in-boxes.[21] This situation has opened new opportunities for companies to market offerings that isolate spam messages and block ads during Internet use.

MARKETING IMPLICATIONS

Marketers want to get their messages or products noticed without alienating consumers, a real challenge when consumers feel bombarded by marketing stimuli. Therefore, small and large marketers alike are testing media not yet saturated with advertising. For instance, Dell and Subway have tried promotions via cell phone, sometimes called the "third screen" (TV and the computer monitor are the other two).[22]

Moosejaw Mountaineering, a Michigan sporting goods retailer, invites customers to sign up for cell-phone text messages about sales and contests.[23] ◖▬▮◗

Measuring Exposure

Why would advertisers pay nearly $3 million for a single 30-second spot during the Super Bowl? In part, they do it because projections of exposure measurements indicate that hundreds of millions of consumers around the world will watch the game. Marketers are very interested in determining which media will generate exposure to their marketing stimuli and whether the desired exposure rates have actually been reached.

As discussed in the online Enrichment Chapter that follows Chapter 1, many marketers use data from specialized research firms to track consumers' exposure to TV, radio, billboards, websites, and other media. Still, marketers are clamoring for more complete and accurate measures. For example, traffic counters can track how many cars drive by a billboard every day, but they cannot count how many people are in each car. Nor can they track pedestrians or determine whether anyone actually looked at the billboard. Now researchers are testing devices for counting how many people pass billboards or transit ads and learning about the people's characteristics and behaviors.[24] For TV advertisers, TiVo is conducting research to learn how often viewers zip and zap as well as which ads are being viewed.[25]

How to measure exposure to websites and online advertising is a big concern. At present, advertisers have no way of knowing exactly how many consumers see an Internet ad, although they can track the number of people who click through to reach an ad. Earlier measures of online audiences, such as page views—the number of pages that people see—do not account for newer technologies that let users view a marketer's content on multiple sites (such as YouTube). Marketers are therefore pushing for standardization in the way that Internet exposure levels are measured so they can fine-tune their targeting and better measure the results of marketing campaigns.[26]

Attention

Attention The process by which an individual allocates part of his or her mental activity to a stimulus.

While exposure reflects whether consumers encounter a stimulus, **attention** reflects how much mental activity they devote to a stimulus (see Exhibit 3.1). A certain amount of attention is necessary for information to be perceived—for it to activate people's senses. Furthermore, after consumers perceive information, they may pay more attention to it and continue with the higher-order processing activities discussed in the next few chapters. This relationship between attention and perception explains why marketers need to understand the characteristics of attention and find ways of enhancing consumers' attention to marketing stimuli.

Characteristics of Attention

Attention has three key characteristics: (1) it is selective, (2) it is capable of being divided, and (3) it is limited.

Attention Is Selective

Selectivity means that we decide what we want to focus on at any one time. At any given time, we are exposed to a potentially overwhelming number of stimuli. When we go to a store, for example, we are exposed to numerous products, brands, ads, displays, signs, and prices all at the same time. Because we cannot examine all these marketing stimuli simultaneously, we must determine which to focus on.

Research shows that people pay less attention to things they have seen many times before.[27] Attention can also be affected by goals: If we look at a product's package with the goal of learning how to use it, we may be more likely to read the directions than to read about its ingredients.[28] Because attention is selective, consumers searching for information online can decide what to focus on—which is why American Airlines and other firms buy sponsored links alongside search engine results.[29]

Attention Can Be Divided

A second important aspect of attention is that it is capable of being divided. Thus, we can parcel our attentional resources into units and allocate some to one task and some to another. For example, we can drive a car and talk at the same time. We can allocate attention flexibly to meet the demands of things in our environment, but we also have the potential to become distracted when one stimulus pulls our attention from another. If we are distracted from a product or ad, the amount of attention we devote to it will be greatly reduced.[30] Knowing that viewers can divide their attention, TV networks reinforce their brands and flash on-screen reminders of upcoming shows during other programs. "Viewers are more confused than ever about what is on TV and when it is on," says a CBS executive. "It is incumbent on us to help them navigate our programming."[31]

Attention Is Limited

A third, and critical, aspect of attention is that it is limited. Although we may be able to divide our attention, we can attend to multiple things only if processing them is relatively automatic, well practiced, and effortless.[32] Imagine that you are watching TV and, at the same time, listening to your friends talk. If the conversation turns serious, you will need to turn down the TV so you can devote your attention to your friends. The fact that attention is limited explains why consumers browsing in an unfamiliar store are less likely to notice new products than when those same consumers browse in a familiar store. Consumers will inevitably miss some products when they try to pay attention to many unfamiliar products.

Focal and Nonfocal Attention

These three characteristics of attention raise questions about whether we can attend to something in our peripheral vision even if we are already focusing on something else. For example, when we read a magazine article, can we process the information in an adjacent ad—even if our eyes are concentrating on the article and we are not aware of the ad? When we drive down the highway, can we process any information from a roadside billboard if we are focusing only on the road?

Preattentive Processing

Preattentive processing
The nonconscious processing of stimuli in peripheral vision.

To the extent that we can process information from our peripheral vision even if we are not aware that we are doing so, we are engaged in **preattentive processing.** With preattentive processing, most of our attentional resources are devoted to one thing, leaving very limited resources for attending to something else. We devote just enough attention to an object in our peripheral vision to process *something* about the object. But because attention is limited, we are not aware that we are absorbing and processing information about that object.

Hemispheric Lateralization

Our ability to process information preattentively depends on (1) whether the stimulus in peripheral vision is a picture or a word and (2) whether it is placed in the right or left visual field (to the right side or the left side of the object on which we are

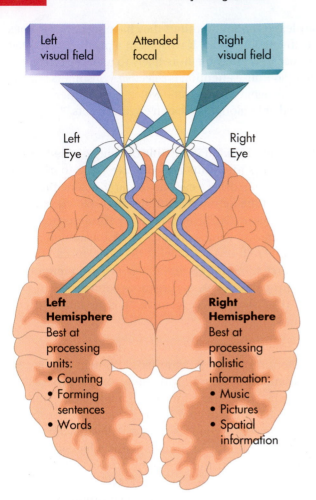

Left visual field

Attended focal

Right visual field

Left Eye

Right Eye

Left Hemisphere
Best at processing units:
• Counting
• Forming sentences
• Words

Right Hemisphere
Best at processing holistic information:
• Music
• Pictures
• Spatial information

Exhibit 3.3

Hemispheric Lateralization

The two hemispheres of our brain specialize in processing different types of information. When a stimulus is in focal vision, it is processed by both hemispheres. When it is in peripheral vision (i.e., it is not being focused on), it is processed by the opposite hemisphere. Information presented in the left visual field is therefore processed by the right hemisphere.

focused). These factors are influential because of how the two halves of the brain—the two hemispheres—process information (see Exhibit 3.3). The right hemisphere is best at processsing music, grasping visual and spatial information, forming inferences, and drawing conclusions. The left hemisphere is best at processing units that can be combined, performing tasks such as counting, processing unfamiliar words, and forming sentences.[33]

Interestingly, stimuli placed in the right visual field (ads on the right side of the focal article or billboards on the right side of the road) tend to be processed by the left hemisphere; those in the left visual field tend to be processed by the right hemisphere. Stimuli on which we focus directly are processed by both hemispheres. These findings suggest that people will most likely preattentively process stimuli such as pictures in ads if the pictures are placed to the left of a magazine article because the processing takes place in the right hemisphere—the hemisphere that is best at processing visual stimuli. Likewise, stimuli such as brand names or ad claims are most likely to be preattentively processed if they are placed in the right visual field because they will be processed by the left hemisphere. Studies confirm that consumers' ability to preattentively process pictures, brand names, or claims in ads depends on whether the ad is in the right or left visual field.[34]

Preattentive Processing, Brand Name Liking, and Choice

Although we may notice and devote some minimal level of processing to stimuli placed in peripheral vision, an important question is whether such preattentively processed stimuli affect our liking for an ad or brand or our decisions to buy or use a particular brand. In fact, some research suggests that consumers will like the same brand name more if they have processed it preattentively than if they have not been exposed to it at all.[35] Preattentive processing makes a brand name familiar, and we tend to like things that are familiar.[36]

Other evidence suggests that stimuli processed preattentively can affect consumer choices. In one study, consumers were more likely to consider choosing a product if they had previously been preattentively exposed to an ad containing that product than if they had not been exposed to the ad. In this case, preattentive processing of the ad affected consumers' consideration of the product, even though they had no memory of having seen the ad.[37]

(MARKETING IMPLICATIONS)

Although consumers can process information preattentively, the information will have more impact when consumers devote full attention to it. Unfortunately, a marketing stimulus competes with many other types of stimuli (including other marketing stimuli) for consumers' attention. Moreover, consumers may have limited motivation and opportunity to attend to marketing stimuli in the first place. Consequently, marketers often need to take steps to attract consumers' attention by making the stimulus (1) personally relevant, (2) pleasant, (3) surprising, and/or (4) easy to process.

1. *Make stimuli personally relevant.* One of the most powerful ways for a stimulus to be perceived as personally relevant is for it to appeal to your needs, values, emotions, or goals.[38] If you are hungry, you are more likely to pay attention to food ads and packages. Ski enthusiasts who join the SkiSpace.com social networking site are apt to find its travel and gear ads more relevant because they appeal to skiers' needs and goals.[39] A second way to make stimuli personally relevant is by showing sources similar to the target audience. You are more likely to notice individuals whom you perceive as similar to yourself.[40] Many ads feature "typical consumers," hoping that consumers will relate to these individuals and thereby attend to the ad.

   A third way to make stimuli personally relevant is using dramas—ministories that depict the experiences of actors or relate someone's experiences through a narrative in one or more ads—to enhance consumers' attention. A fourth way to draw a consumer into the ad is to ask rhetorical questions—those asked merely for effect.[41] No one expects an answer to a rhetorical question like "How would you like to win a million dollars?" because the answer is obvious. These questions appeal to the consumer by including the word *you* and by asking the consumer (if only for effect) to consider answering the question.

2. *Make stimuli pleasant.* Because people tend to approach things that are inherently pleasant, marketers can increase consumers' attention to marketing stimuli by

   ▶ *Using attractive models.* Ads containing attractive models have a higher probability of being noticed because the models arouse positive feelings or a basic sexual attraction.[42] To get noticed, Singapore Airlines' ads and website feature attractive flight attendants wearing sarong uniforms.[43] Clearly, individual differences influence people's opinions about what is attractive. For example, although some people enjoy seeing naked bodies in advertisements, other viewers find these images offensive. Cross-cultural differences also account for what is considered attractive. Ultrathin models represent a Western standard of beauty; elsewhere in the world, such models would be perceived as poor, undernourished, and unattractive.

   ▶ *Using music.* Familiar songs and popular entertainers have considerable ability to attract us in pleasant ways.[44] As one example, General Motors has used music by Led Zeppelin, Hum, and other groups to reach out to prospective Cadillac buyers. Music, says the head of one of GM's ad agencies, is "often the best way to generate immediate recognition or elicit strong emotions and feelings."[45]

   ▶ *Using humor.* Humor can be an effective attention-getting device.[46] For example, Puccino's Café catches the eye of consumers walking past its U.K. coffee bars with mock warning signs stating: "Smile on server's face may be fake."[47] Note that although roughly one in five TV ads contains humor, some are more successful at getting viewers to laugh (and pay attention throughout the message) than others.[48]

3. *Make stimuli surprising.* Consumers are likely to process a stimulus when it is surprising due to its novelty, unexpectedness, or puzzling nature.

   ▶ *Using novelty.* We are more likely to notice any marketing stimulus (a product, package, or brand name) that is new or unique—because it stands out relative to other stimuli around us. Direct mail and e-mail advertising are relatively new to Chinese consumers, for example, so they not only pay attention; they also open such messages far more often than U.S. and European consumers do.[49] Companies can attract attention

HIDDEN VALLEY® is a registered trademark of The HV Food Products Company. Used with permission.

MAKES VEGETABLES DELECTABLE™

visit HiddenValley.com

Exhibit 3.4

Capturing Attention
Consumers are more likely to pay attention to ads with unexpected elements.

Prominence The intensity of stimuli that causes them to stand out relative to the environment.

using novel advertising formats such as magazine ads with graphics that appear to move or digital messages that freeze when surrounding messages continue to move.[50] Although novel stimuli attract attention, we do not always like them better. For example, we may dislike food with a taste that differs from those of foods we usually eat. Thus, the factors that make a stimulus novel may not be the same factors that make it likable.

▶ *Using unexpectedness.* Unexpected stimuli may not necessarily be new to us, but their placement or content differs from what we are used to, arousing curiosity and causing us to analyze them further to make sense of them (see Exhibit 3.4).[51] In fact, unexpectedness can affect the extent to which consumers perceive an ad as humorous.[52] For example, slapstick comedy has nothing to do with banking, so consumers are apt to notice the funny Provident Bank TV ads in which a monkey drops a banana peel that later trips up a bank manager.[53] Also, research shows that women, in particular, may be responsive to messages that use mild erotica to call attention to social causes such as combating AIDS.[54]

▶ *Using a puzzle.* Visual rhymes, antitheses, metaphors, and puns are puzzles that attract attention because they require resolution. Consumers tend to think more about ads that contain these elements. However, consumers from other cultural backgrounds may have difficulty understanding some puns and metaphors in U.S. ads that American consumers can easily comprehend.[55] Although ads that use a puzzle may capture attention, they are not necessarily effective in achieving other objectives (like persuasion) if consumers cannot solve the puzzle.

4. *Make stimuli easy to process.* Although personal relevance, pleasantness, and surprise attract consumers' attention by enhancing their motivation to attend to stimuli, marketers can also enhance attention by boosting consumers' ability to process the stimuli. Four characteristics make a stimulus easy to process: (1) its prominence, (2) its concreteness, (3) the extent to which it contrasts with the things that surround it, and (4) the extent to which it competes with other information.

▶ *Prominent stimuli.* Prominent stimuli stand out relative to the environment because of their intensity. The size or length of the stimulus can affect its **prominence.** For example, consumers are more likely to notice larger or longer ads than to notice smaller or shorter ones.[56] This is why larger ads in yellow pages directories generate more phone calls than smaller ads.[57] Pictures in an ad capture attention regardless of their size; increasing the amount of ad space devoted to text increases the viewers' attention to the entire message.[58] Making words prominent by using boldface text also enhances consumers' attention. In addition, loud sounds can enhance prominence. TV and radio stations sometimes turn up the volume for commercials so that they will stand out relative to the program; loud music played during ads can serve the same purpose.

Prominence is also evident in marketers' use of large or multiple in-store displays. After Dole installed additional coolers to display its fruits in supermarkets, its

Concreteness and Abstractness

We may pay more attention to things that are concrete and capable of generating images than we do to things that are abstract and difficult to represent visually.

Concrete Words	Abstract Words
Apple	Aptitude
Bowl	Betrayal
Cat	Chance
Cottage	Criterion
Diamond	Democracy
Engine	Essence
Flower	Fantasy
Garden	Glory
Hammer	Hatred
Infant	Ignorance
Lemon	Loyalty
Meadow	Mercy
Mountain	Necessity
Ocean	Obedience

Source: Allan Paivio et al., *Journal of Experimental Psychology*, Monograph Supplement, January 1968, pp. 1–25. Copyright © 1968 by the American Psychological Association. Adapted with permission.

Concreteness The extent to which a stimulus is capable of being imagined.

sales results in those stores improved by more than 25 percent. And the California Tree Fruit Commission has found that expanding display size by just 1 percent can boost sales of the featured foods by about 19 percent.[59] Also, movement makes an ad more prominent, which is the reason why attention to commercials tends to be enhanced when the ad uses dynamic, fast-paced action.[60]

▶ *Concrete stimuli.* Stimuli are easier to process if they are concrete rather than abstract.[61] **Concreteness** is defined as the extent to which we can imagine a stimulus. Notice how easily you can develop images of the concrete words in Exhibit 3.5 compared with your response to the abstract words. Concreteness applies to brand names as well. Among brands of well-known dishwashing liquids, the name Sunlight is much more concrete than the names Dawn, Joy, or Palmolive. That concreteness may give Sunlight an advantage over the others in attention-getting ability.

▶ *Contrasting stimuli.* A third factor that makes stimuli easier to process is contrast (see Exhibit 3.6). Color newspaper ads are more likely to capture attention because they are surrounded by black and white, just as a black-and-white TV ad is likely to stand out when aired during shows broadcast in color. For contrast, some winemakers put images of unusual animals on their labels to help their bottles stand out on the shelf.[62] Although research shows that consumers are more likely to consider yellow pages ads in which color is used only for the sake of attracting attention, they are more likely to actually call the firms when the color enhances the product's appeal in an appropriate manner.[63]

▶ *The amount of competing information.* Finally, stimuli are easier to process when few things surround them to compete for your attention.[64] You are more likely to notice a billboard when driving down a deserted rural highway than when in a congested, sign-filled city, just as you are more likely to notice a brand name in a visually simple ad than in one that is visually cluttered.

Customer Segments Defined by Attention

One set of researchers asked the following question: If we do pay attention to things that are relevant, pleasant, surprising, and easy to process, can we identify groups or segments of consumers who are more affected by relevance, pleasantness, surprise, and ease of processing? The answer to this question appears to be yes. Researchers identified a group of consumers who paid minimal attention to an ad because the elements in the ad were not relevant to them. A second group focused on things in the ad that were visually pleasant, such as the picture. The last group spent the longest time looking at the ad and devoted equal amounts of time to the picture, package, headline, and body text. One reason for their attention may be that they viewed the product as personally relevant and its purchase as potentially risky. Hence the consumers needed sustained attention to properly evaluate the ad's information.[65]

Contrast and Attention

The Palmolive bottle stands out and attracts attention only when its color contrasts with (is different from) that of the bottles surrounding it. What implications does contrast have for merchandising products?

Habituation

Habituation The process by which a stimulus loses its attention-getting abilities by virtue of its familiarity.

When a stimulus becomes familiar, it can lose its attention-getting ability, a result called **habituation.** Think about the last time you purchased something new for your apartment or room (such as a plant or picture). For the first few days, you probably noticed the object every time you entered the room. As time passed, however, you probably noticed the item less and less, and now you probably do not notice it at all. You have become habituated to it.

MARKETING IMPLICATIONS

Habituation poses a problem for marketers because consumers readily become habituated to ads, packages, and other marketing stimuli. A good solution is to alter the stimulus every so often, which is the reason that many advertisers develop multiple ads that communicate the same basic message but in different ways. Thus, Toyota, Honda, and other car companies are combining conventional mass-media messages with ads in video games, on car-shopping and video-sharing websites, and delivered via mobile devices.[66] Habituation also explains why marketers sometimes change product packaging to attract consumers' attention anew.

Perception

Perception The process by which incoming stimuli activate our sensory receptors: eyes, ears, taste buds, skin, and so on.

After we have been exposed to a stimulus and have devoted at least some attention to it, we are in a position to perceive it. **Perception** occurs when stimuli are registered by one of our five senses: vision, hearing, taste, smell, and touch.

Perceiving Through Vision

What arouses our visual perception?

- *Size and shape.* Size attracts attention. When choosing among competing products, consumers tend to buy products in packages that appear to be taller than others; even the ratio of the dimensions of rectangular products or packages can subtly affect consumer preferences.[67] Moreover, consumers perceive that packages in eye-catching shapes contain more of a product.[68]

- *Lettering.* The size and style of the lettering on a product or in an ad can attract attention and support brand recognition and image.[69] The distinctive Wendy's script, for instance, is eye-catching and instantly identified with the name of the hamburger chain.

- *Color.* Color is an extremely important factor in visual perception. Research suggests, in fact, that color determines whether we see stimuli.[70] A given color can be described according to hue, saturation, and lightness. *Hue* refers to the pigment contained in the color. Colors can be classified into two broad categories or color hues: warm colors such as red, orange, and yellow; and cool colors such as green, blue, and violet. *Saturation* (also called *chroma*) refers to the richness of the color, leading to distinctions such as pale pink or deep, rich pink. *Lightness* refers to the depth of tone in the color. A saturated pink could have a lot of lightness (a fluorescent pink) or a lot of darkness (a mauve).

- *Effects of color on physiological responses and moods.* Color can also influence our physiological responses and moods. Color psychologists have discovered that warm colors generally encourage activity and excitement, whereas cool colors are more soothing and relaxing. Thus, cool colors are more appropriate in places such as spas or doctors' offices, where it is desirable for consumers to feel calm or to spend time making decisions.[71] Warm colors are more appropriate in environments such as health clubs and fast-food restaurants, where high levels of activity are desirable.[72] One study found that deeper and richer colors (greater saturation) and darker colors evoked more excitement than did less deep and lighter colors.[73]

▶ *Color and liking.* Colors can have a great effect on consumers' liking of a product. Dirt Devil vacuum cleaners now come in fashion colors like Harbour Sky (blue) and Plum; Hamilton Beach blenders are available in Moroccan Red, Seabreeze (blue), and Apple (green).[74]

MARKETING IMPLICATIONS

Because colors can strongly influence attention to and liking of a product, marketers often rely on the advice of "color forecasters" when deciding which colors to use in products and on packages.[75] For example, the Color Association of the United States and the Color Marketing Group tell manufacturers and designers which colors consumers are likely to prefer two or three years into the future. These forecasts are very important: The right color can make consumers believe they are buying products that are very current. Researchers have also found differences among social classes in color preferences. Hot, bright colors have historically appealed to lower-end markets, whereas deep, rich colors have historically appealed to higher-end markets.[76]

Perceiving Through Hearing

Sound represents another form of sensory input. A major principle determining whether a sound will be perceived is its auditory intensity.[77] Consumers are more likely to notice loud music or voices and stark noises. When the announcer in a radio or TV ad speaks more quickly, the faster pace disrupts consumers' processing of the information, yet a low-pitched voice speaking syllables at a faster-than-normal rate actually induces more positive ad and brand attitudes.[78] When a company uses one person to speak the voice-over lines during many of its ads or plays the same jingle in many commercials, consumers come to associate those sounds with the product or brand. McDonald's and other firms consciously seek to define a certain *sonic identity*—using sounds such as music or particular voices to support a brand's image.[79] Further, consumers infer product attributes and form evaluations using information gleaned from hearing a brand's sounds, syllables, and words, a process known as *sound symbolism*.[80]

MARKETING IMPLICATIONS

Fast music, like that played at aerobics classes, tends to energize; in contrast, slow music can be soothing. The type of music being played in a retail outlet can have an interesting effect on shopping behavior.[81] Specifically, a fast tempo creates a more rapid traffic flow, whereas a slow tempo can increase sales as much as 38 percent because it encourages leisurely shopping (although consumers tend to be unaware of this influence on their behavior).[82] However, a fast tempo is more desirable in restaurants because consumers will eat faster, thereby facilitating greater turnover and higher sales.[83] Music can also affect moods.[84] Likable and familiar music can induce good moods, whereas discordant sounds and music in a disliked style can induce bad moods. This effect is important to note because, as you will see in later chapters, bad moods may affect how people feel about products and consumption experiences.[85]

Perceiving Through Taste

Food and beverage marketers must stress taste perceptions in their marketing stimuli. For example, the major challenge for marketers of low-calorie and low-fat products is to provide healthier foods that still taste good. However, what tastes good to one person may not taste good to another, and consumers from different cultural backgrounds may have different taste preferences. Interestingly, tasting or sampling a product is the in-store marketing tactic that most influences consumer purchasing, even though stand-alone in-store displays for particular brands—perceived through vision—are the marketing tactic that shoppers notice the most.[86] Exhibit 3.7 shows the influence of various in-store tactics perceived through vision, hearing, touch, and taste.

Exhibit 3.7

In-Store Marketing Tactics

Although stand-alone displays and product sampling were noted most often by customers, sampling most often influenced purchase.

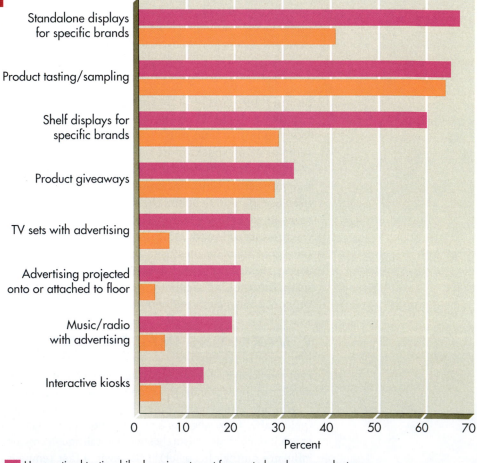

Have noticed tactic while shopping at most frequented package-goods store.

Tactic has influenced purchase among respondents who noticed two or more tactics.

MARKETING IMPLICATIONS

Marketers often try to monitor consumers' tastes through taste tests. Many food and beverage products are thoroughly taste tested before they are introduced. Ads or food packages sometimes ask consumers to compare the product's taste with that of competing products. To encourage product trial in the U.K. market, Kellogg's Nutri-Grain snack bars recently featured a taste challenge with a money-back guarantee.[87] However, consumers are not always good at discerning taste, so marketers should consider adding descriptive words or pictures to marketing communications about foods, restaurants, and the like.[88] To engage consumers, sometimes marketers mention taste in an unexpected way. For instance, the slogan of Buckley's Cough Mixture is "It Tastes Awful. And It Works."[89]

Perceiving Through Smell

If you were blindfolded and asked to smell an item, you would probably have a hard time identifying it; most consumers do.[90] However, consumers also differ in their ability to label odors. Compared with younger consumers, the elderly have a harder time identifying smells,[91] and men in general are worse at the task than are women.[92] Marketers are concerned with the effects of smell on consumer responses, product trial, liking, and buying.

Effects of Smells on Physiological Responses and Moods

Like the other senses, smell produces physiological and emotional responses. For example, the smell of peppermint is arousing, and the smell of lily of the valley is relaxing.[93] Some studies show that people can feel tense or relaxed depending on whether or not a scent is present and what it is.[94] This theory has been key to the development of aromatherapy. Some of our most basic emotions are also linked to smell. For example, children hate having their security blankets washed, in part because washing removes the smells that comfort the child. In addition, the smell of the ocean or of freshly baked cookies can revive very emotional and basic childhood memories.[95]

Smells and Product Trial

Companies can expose consumers to marketing stimuli through their sense of smell (see Exhibit 3.8). Smell (often in combination with other sensory perceptions) can entice consumers to try or buy a food product. Krispy Kreme designs its outlets so that customers can smell—and see—the doughnuts coming fresh out of the oven.[96] Scratch-and-sniff advertisements expose consumers to fragrances and other types of products that involve the use of smell. Research suggests that scents in the air can be effective stimuli when related to the product being sold. Thus, a flowery aroma would be more appropriate for a lingerie store than for a coffee bar.[97] Also, some perfume and cologne ads are doused with the product to increase sensory processing. However, this technique can backfire if consumers are offended by scented ads or have allergic reactions to the smells.

Smell and Liking

Retailers also realize that smells can attract consumers. For example, Bronner's Christmas Wonderland in Frankenmuth, Michigan, puts consumers in the holiday shopping mood by using a machine that sends pine fragrance into the air throughout the tree department during December.[98] Similarly, grocery retailers often locate in-store bakeries so that the aroma of fresh bread can be smelled at the main store entrance.

Smell and Buying

Research has found that providing a pleasant-smelling environment can have a positive effect on shopping behavior by encouraging more attention to relevant stimuli that consumers encounter and encouraging consumers to linger longer.[99] In one study, shoppers in a room smelling of flowers evaluated Nike shoes more positively than did consumers in an odor-free room.[100] Tesco, a U.K. grocery chain, seeks to stimulate coffee purchases by fitting its store-brand coffee packages with special aroma-releasing valves that let the scent waft out.[101]

MARKETING IMPLICATIONS

Obviously, we like some products—for example, perfumes and scented candles—for the smells they produce. However, we may like other products, such as mouthwashes and deodorants, because they mask aromas. Procter & Gamble's Febreze started as an odor eliminator and now offers fragrance-enhancing products for the home and laundry.[102] However, smell does not always work to the marketers' advantage: Some consumers may dislike the scent in the ambient retail environment or find it irritating. In addition, some consumers value particular products because they have no smell, such as unscented deodorants, carpet cleaners, and laundry detergents. Finally, consumers' preferences for smells differ across cultures. Spices that are commonly used in one culture can literally make consumers in another ill. Only one smell (cola) is universally regarded as pleasant, a finding that is good news for companies like Coke and Pepsi that are expanding globally.[103]

Exhibit 3.8

Perception Through Smell

Some products are valued because of the smells they evoke (or mask).

Glade

Smells like the real thing.
Made with essential oils extracted fresh from nature.

Perceiving Through Touch

Touch (both what we touch with our fingers and the way that things feel to us as they come in contact with our skin) is a very important aspect of many products and services, although individual preferences for touch vary.[104] Depending on how we are touched, we can feel stimulated or relaxed. And research has shown that consumers who are touched by a salesperson are more likely to have positive feelings and are more likely to evaluate both the store and the salesperson positively. In addition, customers who are touched by the salesperson are more likely to comply with the salesperson's requests.[105] However, the effectiveness of being touched in sales situations differs from culture to culture. Compared with U.S. consumers, those in Latin America are more comfortable with touching and embracing. In Asia, however, touching between relative strangers is seen as inappropriate.[106]

Consumers like some products because of their feel (see Exhibit 3.9). Some consumers buy skin creams and baby products for their soothing effect on the skin, or they go to massage therapists to experience tactile sensations and feel relaxed. In fact, research shows that consumers who have a high need for touch tend to like products that provide this opportunity.[107] When considering products with material properties, such as clothing or carpeting,

Dreft.com

*Gentle as a
mother's touch*

Exhibit 3.9

Perception Through Touch

The way a product feels can influence whether consumers choose it.

Absolute threshold The minimal level of stimulus intensity needed to detect a stimulus.

Differential threshold/just noticeable difference (j.n.d.) The intensity difference needed between two stimuli before they are perceived to be different.

Weber's law The stronger the initial stimulus, the greater the additional intensity needed for the second stimulus to be perceived as different.

consumers prefer goods they can touch and examine in stores more than products they can only see and read about online or in catalogs.[108] Clearly, the way clothing feels when worn is a critical factor in consumers' purchasing decisions for those products. Knowing that consumers prefer to try products before they buy them, the REI chain of sporting goods stores invites shoppers to test any product on display, from boots to bicycles.[109]

When Do We Perceive Stimuli?

Our senses are exposed to numerous inputs at any given time. To perceive each one would be overwhelming and extremely difficult. Fortunately, our sensory processing is simplified by the fact that many stimuli do not enter our conscious awareness. For us to perceive something, it must be sufficiently intense. Stimulus intensity is measured in units. The intensity of a smell can be measured by the concentration of the stimulus in a substance or in the air. Stimulus intensity of sounds can be measured in decibels and frequencies, and stimulus intensity of colors can be measured by properties like lightness, saturation, and hue. In the area of touch, stimulus intensity can be measured in terms of pounds or ounces of pressure.

Absolute Thresholds

The **absolute threshold** is the minimum level of stimulus intensity needed for a stimulus to be perceived. In other words, the absolute threshold is the amount of intensity needed for a person to detect a difference between something and nothing. Suppose you are driving on the highway and a billboard is in the distance. The absolute threshold is that point at which you can first see the billboard. Before that point, the billboard is below the absolute threshold and not sufficiently intense to be seen.

Differential Thresholds

Whereas the absolute threshold deals with whether or not a stimulus can be perceived, the **differential threshold** refers to the intensity difference needed between two stimuli before people can perceive that the stimuli are *different*. Thus, the differential threshold is a relative concept; it is often called the **just noticeable difference (j.n.d.)**. For example, when you get your eyes checked, the eye doctor often shows you a row of letters through different sets of lenses. If you can detect a difference between the two lenses, the new lens is different enough to have crossed the differential threshold.

The psychophysiologist Ernst Weber first outlined the basic properties of the differential threshold in the nineteenth century. **Weber's law** states that the stronger the initial stimulus, the greater the additional intensity needed for the second stimulus to be perceived as different. This relationship is outlined in the following formula:

$$\frac{\Delta s}{S} = K$$

where S is the initial stimulus value, Δs is the smallest change (Δ) in a stimulus capable of being detected, and K is a constant of proportionality.

To illustrate, imagine that consumer testing found that 1 ounce would need to be added to a 10-ounce package before consumers could notice that the two packages weighed different amounts. Suppose we now have a 50-ounce box and want to know how much we must add before consumers could detect a difference. According to Weber's law, $K = 1/10$ or 0.10. To determine how much would need to be added, we would solve for Δs as follows:

$$\frac{\Delta s}{50} = 0.10$$

The answer is 0.10 of the package weight, or 5 ounces.

MARKETING IMPLICATIONS

Absolute Threshold

The obvious implication is that consumers will only consciously perceive a marketing stimulus when it is sufficiently high in intensity to be above the absolute threshold. Thus, if images or words in a commercial are too small or the sound level is too low, consumers' sensory receptors will not be activated, and the stimulus will not be consciously perceived.

Differential Threshold

The differential threshold has two important marketing implications.

1. Sometimes marketers *do not* want consumers to notice a difference between two stimuli. Marketers of nonalcoholic beers, for example, have hoped that consumers would not be able to tell the difference between the tastes of real and nonalcoholic beers.[110] Some marketers might not want consumers to notice that they have decreased a product's size or increased its price, a situation that raises ethical concerns. For example, some consumers were unhappy when they noticed that Nips had reduced the amount of candy in its value pack from 5.5 ounces to 4 ounces.[111]

2. In other instances marketers *do* want consumers to perceive a difference between two stimuli. For example, McDonald's once increased the size of its regular hamburger patty by 25 percent but left the price the same, hoping that consumers would notice the change.[112] Many marketers hope that consumers can tell the difference between an old and an improved product. However, sometimes consumers cannot make the distinction because differential thresholds vary from sense to sense. For example, since our sense of smell is not well developed, we often fail to differentiate the smell of two versions of the same object.

Subliminal Perception

The concept of the perceptual threshold is important for another phenomenon—subliminal perception. Suppose you are sitting at a movie and are being exposed to messages like "Eat popcorn" and "Drink Coke." However, each message is being shown on the screen for only a fraction of a second, so short a time that you are not consciously aware of it. Stimuli of this type, presented below the threshold level of

Subliminal perception The activation of sensory receptors by stimuli presented below the perceptual threshold.

awareness, are called *subliminal messages,* and our perception of them is called **subliminal perception.**

Subliminal perception is different from preattentive processing. With preattentive processing, our attention is directed at something other than the stimulus—for instance, at a magazine article instead of an ad in our peripheral vision. With subliminal perception, our attention is directed squarely at the stimulus that is being presented subliminally. Also, with preattentive processing, the stimulus is fully present—if you shift your attention and look directly at the ad or billboard, you can easily see it. In contrast, subliminal stimuli are presented so quickly or are so degraded that the very act of perceiving them is difficult.

MARKETING IMPLICATIONS

The question of whether stimuli presented subliminally affect consumers' responses has generated considerable controversy in the marketing field. A widely known but fraudulent study in the advertising industry claimed that consumers at a movie theater had been subliminally exposed to messages on the movie screen that read "Eat popcorn" and "Drink Coke." Reportedly, exposure to these subliminal messages influenced viewers' purchase of Coke and popcorn.[113] Although advertising agencies deny using such stimuli, and the original popcorn-Coke study has been discredited, some people claim that marketers are brainwashing consumers and attempting to manipulate them. These people also believe that ads containing such stimuli are effective.[114]

Exhibit 3.10

Perceptual Organization

Our eyes naturally focus on information in the foreground as opposed to the background of an ad.

JIL SANDER

T +1 800 704 7317

Does Subliminal Perception Affect Consumer Behavior?

Research suggests that subliminal perception has limited effects on consumers.[115] Such stimuli have not been found to arouse motives like hunger. Nor do subliminally presented sexual stimuli affect consumers' attitudes or preferences. Research has also failed to show that subliminal stimuli affect consumers' explicit memory of ads or brands. As a result, the advertising community tends to dismiss subliminal perception research.

Interestingly, however, there is some evidence that stimuli presented below the threshold of conscious perception can reach our sensory registers. Researchers have found that if consumers are subliminally exposed to a word (e.g., *razor*), they will recognize that word faster than they recognize words to which they have not been exposed subliminally.[116] Moreover, some preliminary evidence suggests that stimuli perceived subliminally can affect consumers' feelings. Consumers in one study were found to have stronger responses to ads with sexual subliminal implants than to those without them.[117] Thus, stimuli perceived subliminally are somehow analyzed for their meaning, and they can elicit primitive feeling responses. However, these effects do not appear to be strong enough to alter consumers' preferences or to make an ad or brand more memorable. Exposing consumers to the message at or above the threshold level of awareness should have just as much if not more impact than subliminal stimuli, making the use of subliminal stimuli unnecessary.[118] Now researchers are using neuroscience to continue investigating whether subliminal advertising works.[119]

How Do Consumers Perceive a Stimulus?

Some research has focused on how individuals organize or combine the visual information they perceive. Consumers tend not to perceive a single stimulus in isolation; rather, they organize and integrate it in the context of the other things around it. Also, many stimuli are really a complex combination of numerous simple stimuli that consumers must organize into a unified whole using **perceptual organization** (see Exhibit 3.10). This process represents a somewhat higher, more meaningful level of processing than simply having stimuli register on our sensory receptors. Four basic principles related to perceptual organization are figure and ground, closure, grouping, and bias for the whole.

The principle of **figure and ground** suggests that people interpret incoming stimuli in contrast to a background. The figure is well defined and in the forefront—the focal point of attention—whereas the ground is indefinite, hazy, and in the background. People tend to organize their perceptions into figure-and-ground relationships, and the manner in which this process occurs will determine how the stimulus is interpreted. Advertisers should therefore plan for important brand information to be the figure, not the background, and not let the background detract from the figure. Advertisers often violate this principle when using sexy or attractive models in ad messages, with the result being that the model becomes the figure and focal point, leaving the product or brand unnoticed.

Closure refers to the fact that individuals have a need to organize perceptions so that they form a meaningful whole. Even if a stimulus is incomplete, our need for closure will lead us to see it as complete. We therefore try to complete the stimulus. The key to using the need for closure, then, is to provide consumers with an incomplete stimulus. For example, putting a well-known television ad on the radio is an effective way to get consumers to think about a message. The radio version of the ad is an incomplete stimulus, and consumers' need for closure leads them to picture the visual parts of the ad. Likewise, severely cropping objects in ads so that they appear ambiguous may be one way of getting consumers to think about what the object is and to gain closure.[120]

Grouping refers to the fact that we often group stimuli to form a unified picture or impression, making it easier to process them. We view similar or nearby objects as belonging together. Marketers can often influence the image or perception of a product or service by grouping it with other stimuli. In Exhibit 3.6, the two groups of yellow bottles are seen as being different from the green bottle. In advertising, companies sometimes include more than one brand or product in a message to generate exposure through grouping. In merchandising, marketers often create a unified impression by displaying related items as a group. Consumers may perceive a table setting as elegant when the napkins, napkin holders, wine goblets, silverware, dishes, and serving bowls are cleverly grouped.

Perceptual organization The process by which stimuli are organized into meaningful units.

Figure and ground According to this principle, people interpret stimuli in the context of a background.

Closure According to this principle, individuals have a need to organize perceptions so that they form a meaningful whole.

Grouping The tendency to group stimuli to form a unified picture or impression.

Bias for the whole The tendency to perceive more value in a whole than in the combined parts that make up a whole.

Bias for the whole is the principle that consumers perceive more value in the whole of something than in two or more parts that are equivalent to the whole. Thus, you are more likely to make a $20 purchase if you have two $5 bills and a $10—and less likely to make the purchase if you have a single $20 bill. In other words, your bias for the whole (the single $20 bill) makes you less willing to spend it.[121] Flight attendants on Cathay Pacific Airlines ask passengers whether they will contribute their leftover foreign coins to UNICEF. Simply asking for spare change, the airline has collected more than $1 million for UNICEF since 1991.[122]

Summary

For a marketing stimulus to have an impact, consumers must be exposed to it, allocate some attention to it, and perceive it. Consumers need a basic level of attention to perceive a stimulus before they can use additional mental resources to process the stimulus at higher levels (something we explore in the next chapter). Exposure occurs when the consumer is presented with a marketing stimulus. Knowing that consumers' exposure to marketing stimuli is selective, marketers use a variety of tactics to increase stimulus exposure.

Attention occurs when the consumer allocates processing capacity to the stimulus. Attention is selective, divided, and limited. Using tactics such as product placement does not guarantee that consumers will directly attend to marketing stimuli, although consumers may attend to such stimuli preattentively. Making a marketing stimulus personally relevant, pleasant, surprising, or easy to process enhances its attention-getting properties. Consumers perceive a stimulus by using one of their five senses: vision (through size and color stimuli), hearing (through sound intensity, pitch, pace, and other characteristics), taste (especially for food and beverages), smell (affecting responses, moods, trial, liking, and buying), and touch (affecting responses, moods, and liking).

Perceptual thresholds determine the point at which stimuli are perceived. The absolute threshold is the lowest point at which an individual can experience a sensation. The differential threshold is the minimal difference in stimulus intensity needed to detect that two stimuli are different. The differential threshold is important both when marketers do not want consumers to notice a difference between two stimuli (as in a

size decrease) and when they do (as in the case of product improvements). Consumers can sometimes perceive things outside of their conscious level of awareness, a phenomenon called *subliminal perception,* but this seems to have a limited impact on consumers' motives or behaviors. Finally, perceptual organization occurs when consumers organize a set of stimuli into a coherent whole, affected by the principles of figure and ground, closure, grouping, and bias for the whole.

Questions for Review and Discussion

1. How do zipping and zapping affect consumers' exposure to stimuli such as products and ads?

2. What is attention, and what are its three key characteristics?

3. In what ways do prominence and habituation affect consumer attention?

4. What is perception, and what methods do we use to perceive stimuli?

5. Differentiate between the absolute threshold and the differential threshold, and explain how these concepts relate to Weber's law.

6. Name four principles of perceptual organization and explain why marketers need to know about them.

CL Visit http://cengage.com/marketing/hoyer/ConsumerBehavior5e to find resources that are available to help you study for the course.

Heinz Is Looking for Attention

From upside-down bottles and wacky-colored ketchups to unusual store displays and customer-created television commercials, H. J. Heinz is definitely looking for attention. Although Heinz sells 650 million bottles of ketchup each year, the company is anything but complacent about keeping its brands and products in the public eye. One way it does this is by using special in-store displays. To catch the eye of tailgaters browsing in Sam's Club and other warehouse stores, the company has created cardboard displays shaped like the back of a pickup truck and filled them with grab-and-go picnic packs of Heinz ketchup, mustard, and relish.

When Heinz introduces new products and packaging, it gains more shelf space, attracts attention, and highlights each item's appeal to the senses. Its E-Z-Squirt Ketchup, in vivid, child-friendly colors like green, purple, and blue, was a standout on store shelves. Its organic ketchup comes in an upside-down squeeze bottle with a green lid that sets the product apart while linking it to the category of natural and organic foods. Heinz is also developing a sweeter variety of tomato for future ketchup products.

However, what appeals to consumers' taste buds in one country may not appeal in those in another country. "Consumer tastes are still very local," observes a Heinz executive, "[which is the reason why] we still like our recipes to be very locally tweaked, even in ketchup." Chefs, scientists, designers, engineers, and marketers work together to create and taste-test new ketchups and other food products at the Heinz Global Innovation and Quality Center outside Pittsburgh, Pennsylvania. The result is untraditional new flavors keyed to specific markets, such as the chili ketchup and sweet onion ketchup recently launched in U.K. stores. The center also hosts a "supermarket" where marketers can observe how consumers behave as they walk down aisles filled with products by Heinz and competing firms.

With so many food products vying for attention in advertising media and on supermarket shelves, getting consumers to notice a ketchup ad—let alone act on it—is another key challenge. Heinz communicates through numerous messages running in print and broadcast media as well as online; it also uses in-store and in-restaurant communications to reinforce brand image and loyalty. Heinz has also sponsored Top This TV contests in which consumers submit homemade 30-second commercials featuring Heinz ketchup, which are then posted on YouTube for viewing and voting. The top prize is $57,000 (a play on "Heinz 57 varieties") and a spot on national TV for the winning commercial.

To encourage participation and wave the brand banner, Heinz promotes these contests on its ketchup labels, on TV, in print, and online. Hundreds of consumers uploaded entries to the first two contests; many of these commercials, including those created by the finalists, are still available on YouTube and on Heinz's *topthistv.com* website. Media coverage and word-of-mouth buzz spread the contest message quickly and kept people talking about the homemade commercials even after the voting was over and the winners had been announced.

Heinz also mounted a contest to gain community attention and involve U.S. students and teachers with the brand and its communications. The Ketchup Creativity contest invited students in grades 1 through 12 to submit artwork for Heinz single-serve packets. From more than 15,000 entries, the judges chose 12 winners to have their artwork displayed on millions of Heinz ketchup packets. Each winner received a $750 scholarship; each winner's school received $750 worth of Heinz ketchup and $750 worth of art supplies. Student-created artwork made the winning ketchup packets stand out and added to the visual appeal of a product that rarely gets the spotlight to itself.[123]

Case Questions

1. Using the concepts discussed in this chapter, explain how Heinz has been successful in generating exposure and capturing attention. What other ideas would you suggest Heinz try to foster exposure, attention, and perception?

2. In terms of exposure, attention, and perception, what are some of the potential disadvantages of Heinz's Top This TV contests?

3. Do you think that Heinz will gain long-term benefits from holding a contest for students that focused on the visual appeal of designing single-serve ketchup packets? Explain your answer.

Chapter 4

Knowledge and Understanding

LEARNING OBJECTIVES

After studying this chapter, you will be able to

1. Describe the connection between consumer knowledge and consumer understanding, explain what affects these processes, and show why marketers must take both into account.

2. Discuss how and why concepts like schemas, associations, images, categories, and prototypes are relevant to marketers.

3. Distinguish between categorization and comprehension and describe how product features, price, and other marketing elements can induce consumers to make inferences about products.

INTRODUCTION

Ringing Up the Engagement Ring Market

The diamond ring has long been an engagement tradition in the United States and a mainstay of Tiffany, the jewelry store famous for its blue gift boxes. In Europe, however, couples have preferred colored gemstone rings—until now. Today, couples in Europe and the United Kingdom are increasingly choosing diamond solitaires, as are their counterparts in Japan and China. "The engagement-ring phenomenon has gone worldwide," observes the CEO of De Beers, the global market-leader in diamonds.

Many companies want engaged couples everywhere to think about diamond rings when they think about getting married. Bulgari created a line of distinctive engagement rings for Japanese customers; Cartier's fourteen stores in China feature special "bridal bars" where couples can sip champagne while they compare dazzling diamonds. LVMH, the French luxury-goods company, has teamed with De Beers to open De Beers Diamond Jewellers stores in major cities worldwide. De Beers originated the well-known slogan "A diamond is forever" and also promotes its own Forevermark brand of diamonds through magazine ads and its *forevermark.com* website.[1]

In the preceding chapter, you learned how consumers pay attention to and perceive things. This chapter goes a step further, asking how consumers understand the world around them. To answer this question, we need to know how consumers relate what they observe to what they already know—their prior knowledge. Consumers who see a diamond ring may associate it with things like love and expensive jewelry. Moreover, cues like blue boxes and the Forevermark brand add to each jewelry store or brand's personality and help consumers distinguish one from another. And based on prior knowledge, consumers can categorize brands and products. Thus, some may see the Tiffany engagement ring as the prototypical piece of diamond jewelry, itself a subset of the jewelry category. Finally, consumers' knowledge helps them interpret and understand jewelry ads and websites—all topics discussed in this chapter.

Overview of Knowledge and Understanding

Knowledge content Information we already have in memory.

As Exhibit 4.1 shows, there are two broad domains of prior knowledge: knowledge content (stored information) and knowledge structure. In turn, prior knowledge is used for understanding (categorizing and comprehending) new information.

Knowledge content reflects the information consumers have already learned about brands, companies, product categories, stores, ads, people, how to shop, how to use products, and so on. Companies sometimes use marketing to develop, add to, or change consumers' knowledge content; increasingly, companies try to link their brands to other knowledge that consumers may have, as illustrated in Exhibit 4.1.[2] **Knowledge structure** describes how consumers organize knowledge.

Knowledge structure The way in which knowledge is organized.

Consumers often organize knowledge into categories, storing similar things in the same category. For example, the names of certain brands of toothpaste, such as Rembrandt, may be stored in a category called *whitening toothpastes*. In addition, this brand, along with others such as Crest and Colgate, may be stored in a more general category called *toothpaste*. All these toothpaste brands along with dental floss and related products might then be stored in an even broader category called *dental hygiene products*.

Categorization The process of labeling or identifying an object. Involves relating what we perceive in our external environment to what we already know.

Comprehension The process of deepening understanding. Involves using prior knowledge to understand more about what we have categorized.

Prior knowledge is essential for two aspects of consumer understanding: categorization and comprehension (see Exhibit 4.1). **Categorization** is the process of labeling or identifying an object that we perceive in our external environment based on the object's similarity to what we already know. Thus, we might label Trident gum as a dental hygiene product instead of a candy product and relate it to our knowledge of other dental hygiene products. **Comprehension** is the process of using prior knowledge to understand more about what has been categorized. For example, we might relate the picture, headline, and ad copy in a Trident ad or website and understand that "Trident gum is good for teeth and can achieve some of the same benefits as brushing."

We say that we "know" something when we have encountered it before and have somehow come to understand what it means and what it is like.

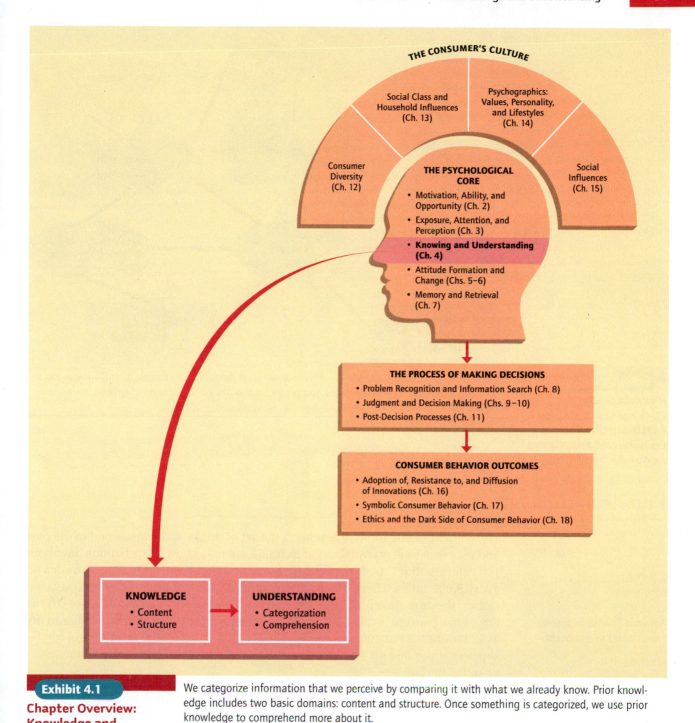

THE CONSUMER'S CULTURE

Social Class and Household Influences (Ch. 13)

Psychographics: Values, Personality, and Lifestyles (Ch. 14)

Consumer Diversity (Ch. 12)

THE PSYCHOLOGICAL CORE
- Motivation, Ability, and Opportunity (Ch. 2)
- Exposure, Attention, and Perception (Ch. 3)
- **Knowing and Understanding (Ch. 4)**
- Attitude Formation and Change (Chs. 5–6)
- Memory and Retrieval (Ch. 7)

Social Influences (Ch. 15)

THE PROCESS OF MAKING DECISIONS
- Problem Recognition and Information Search (Ch. 8)
- Judgment and Decision Making (Chs. 9–10)
- Post-Decision Processes (Ch. 11)

CONSUMER BEHAVIOR OUTCOMES
- Adoption of, Resistance to, and Diffusion of Innovations (Ch. 16)
- Symbolic Consumer Behavior (Ch. 17)
- Ethics and the Dark Side of Consumer Behavior (Ch. 18)

KNOWLEDGE
- Content
- Structure

UNDERSTANDING
- Categorization
- Comprehension

Exhibit 4.1

Chapter Overview: Knowledge and Understanding

We categorize information that we perceive by comparing it with what we already know. Prior knowledge includes two basic domains: content and structure. Once something is categorized, we use prior knowledge to comprehend more about it.

Knowing therefore has to do with our prior knowledge—both what we have encountered (knowledge content) and the way in which that knowledge is organized (knowledge structure). Further, we tend to direct our consumption and search behaviors in ways that take full advantage of such prior knowledge.[3]

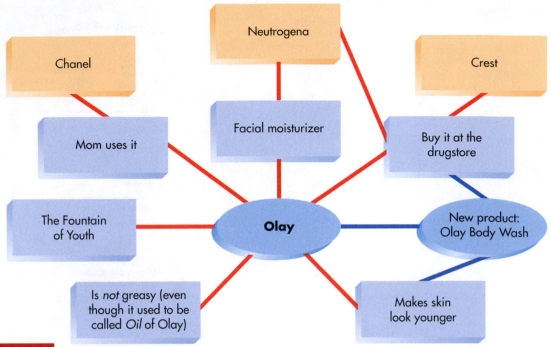

Exhibit 4.2

Marketers Use Ads, Packages, and Product Attributes to Enhance Consumers' Knowledge About an Offering

Marketers often want consumers to know more about their products (for example, that Olay now has a new body wash product). Ads, packages, and product attributes are useful ways of getting this knowledge across.

Knowledge Content

Schema The set of associations linked to a concept.

The content of our knowledge reflects the set of things we have learned in the past and may consist of many facts. For example, we may know that a banana has about 100 calories, that Utah is the Beehive State, and that we need to change a car's oil every 5,000 miles. These pieces of information are not stored as random facts; rather, they are linked to or associated with a concept. The set of associations linked to a concept is called a ***schema***.[4] A schema for the concept *banana* has many associations—it has 100 calories, is yellow, and bruises easily, and the peel can be slippery if stepped on. A schema is elaborated when we have many associations linked to the concept.

Schemas, Associations, and Brand Equity

The associations in schemas can be described along several dimensions.[5]

- ▶ *Types of associations.* Consumers have many *types of associations.* One schema for banana might include associations that reflect (1) the attributes of a banana (yellow, long, soft, contains a lot of potassium), (2) its benefits (nutritious, low in fat), (3) people who eat it (athletes who lose a lot of potassium through sweating), (4) times when it is eaten (as a snack), (5) places it is eaten (at home, at school), (6) ways it is eaten (peeled, sliced), (7) places where it is purchased (at a grocery store), (8) places where it is grown (in South America), and so on.

▶ *Favorability.* Associations can also be described in terms of their *favorability.* The notion that a banana has 100 calories might be evaluated as favorable. The fact that eating too many can make one constipated might not be evaluated as favorable.

▶ *Uniqueness.* Associations vary in their *uniqueness*—that is, the extent to which they are also related to other concepts. "Greasiness" is not unique to McDonald's, but the Golden Arches and Ronald McDonald are.

▶ *Salience.* Associations vary in their *salience,* or how easily they come to mind. For example, a consumer might always retrieve the association of Golden Arches upon hearing the McDonald's name. Less salient associations may be retrieved only in certain contexts. Thus, the association that McDonald's offers wrap sandwiches may be less salient than other associations, and a consumer may think about it only if someone starts talking about sandwiches.[6]

▶ *Abstractness.* Associations in schemas can also vary in terms of how abstract or concrete they are.

Types of Schemas

We have schemas for many entities. The banana example is an illustration of a *product category* schema; however, we also have schemas for *brands* (see Exhibit 4.2). For example, consumers' schema for the Payless ShoeSource retail chain may include low price and a rather limited selection, although the company is using ads to add "fashion" to consumers' schema of Payless.[7] Consumers often use associations with brands and other product features to predict what the benefits of the product will be.[8] We have schemas for *people* (mothers, Alex Rodriguez, working-class people) plus schemas for *stores,* although the associations linked to Payless may be quite different from the associations linked to Nordstrom. We have schemas for *salespeople* (cosmetics salesperson, car salesperson), *ads* (Coke ads, Geico ads), *companies* (Starbucks, IBM), *places* (DisneyWorld, Vail), *countries* (South Africa, Germany), and *animals* (cougar, moose). We even have a schema for ourselves, called a *self-schema,* and sometimes consider whether a brand's schema fits with the schema we have of ourselves.[9]

Images

Brand image A subset of salient and feeling-related associations stored in a brand schema.

An image is a subset of associations that reflect what something stands for and how favorably it is viewed.[10] For instance, our **brand image** of McDonald's may be favorable, and it may include such associations as a family-friendly place and fast food. An image does not represent *all* the associations linked to a schema—only those that are most salient and that make the brand different from others in the category. Thus, although we may know that McDonald's serves some low-fat foods, this knowledge need not be used to form our brand image. We also have images for other marketing entities like stores, companies, places, and countries.[11] Exhibit 4.3 shows brands around the world that have very well-known brand images.

Brand personality The set of associations that reflect the personification of the brand.

Schemas can include associations that reflect the **brand's personality**—that is, the way that the consumer would describe the brand if it were a person.[12] Consumers from one study described the Whirlpool brand as gentle, sensitive, quiet, good-natured, flexible, modern, cheerful, and creative. Researchers found that these

Rank	Brand	Known for
1	Coca-Cola	Soft drinks
2	Microsoft	Software
3	IBM	Computer services
4	General Electric	Diversified electronic products
5	Nokia	Consumer electronics
6	Toyota	Automotives
7	Intel	Computer technology
8	McDonald's	Fast-food restaurants
9	Disney	Media
10	Mercedes	Automotives

Source: The *BusinessWeek/*Interbrand Annual Ranking of the Best Global Brands 2007.

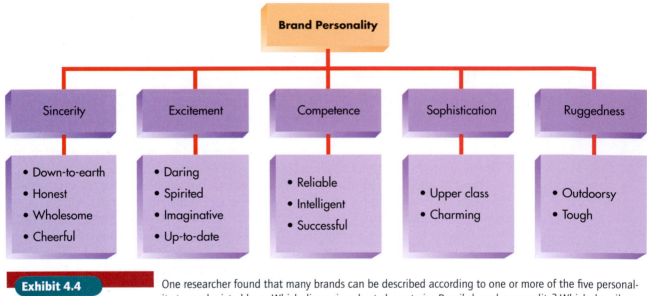

Exhibit 4.4

A Brand Personality Framework

One researcher found that many brands can be described according to one or more of the five personality types depicted here. Which dimensions best characterize Pepsi's brand personality? Which describe the personalities of Dell? Volkswagen? Google? Smucker's?

associations suggested a modern and family-oriented suburban woman who is neighborly, successful, attractive, and action oriented. Whirlpool's personality was quite different from KitchenAid's, whose name personified a smart, aggressive, glamorous, wealthy, elegant, and fashionable career woman.[13] When Whirlpool expanded in Europe, it used advertising to create a brand personality linked to powerful goddesses. Whirlpool later adapted this successful campaign for U.S. markets, where it targets working mothers.[14]

As you might expect, a celebrity endorser's personality can reinforce associations with the endorsed brand's personality.[15] Brand personalities can also be embodied in brand characters like Charlie the Tuna and the Geico gecko. One study found that many brands could be described according to their position on the dimensions shown in Exhibit 4.4. Because brand personalities have cultural meaning and reflect cultural values, a global brand may be perceived slightly differently in different cultures.[16] Finally, brand personalities can be updated based on consumers' exposure to new information.[17]

MARKETING IMPLICATIONS

Schemas, images, and personalities are clearly important to consumer knowledge. These associations are important to marketers too because brands that have strong and desirable images are more valuable to companies. That is, they contribute to *brand equity* or the value of the brand to the company.[18] Because the images of liked brands can translate into strong brand loyalty, marketers need to identify and understand the various associations that consumers link to a particular brand.[19] Note that consumers as young as middle-school age start associating brand images with their images of themselves.[20] Understanding the associations that consumers see as part of themselves or want to see as part of themselves helps marketers develop brand images, change them, and protect them.

Creating new schemas, images, and personalities

When an offering is new, the marketer has to create a schema, image, and/or personality to help consumers understand what it is, what it can do for them, and how it differs from competing offerings. Creating schemas is especially important for new products because consumers may not yet understand what these new products are or what they offer.

Creating schemas and images for a company is also important so that consumers understand the general types of products produced by the firm. Georgia-based AFLAC, for instance, offers supplemental health and accident insurance. Consumers did not know much about AFLAC until it gained a concrete personality by featuring a duck mascot in its advertising. Within a year, AFLAC had increased its brand recognition among Americans to 90 percent—and its U.S. sales soared.[21]

Schemas, images, and personalities can sometimes be created by means of brand extensions, licensing agreements, and brand alliances.

▶ A brand extension occurs when a firm uses the brand name of a product with a well-developed image, like Oreo cookies, on a product in a different category, such as Oreo Candy Bites, which belong to the candy category.

▶ Licensing occurs when a firm sells the rights to the brand name to another company that will use the name on its product. For example, Chrysler has licensed the Jeep brand to be used on baby strollers, clothing, wheelbarrows, luggage, and other items.[22]

▶ A brand alliance occurs when two companies' brand names appear together on a single product, as in Häagen-Dazs Baileys Irish Cream ice cream (see Exhibit 4.5).

One consequence of brand extensions, license agreements, and alliances is that consumers develop an image for the new brand by transferring to it their associations and favorable feelings from the original brand's schema.[23] If consumers think Jeep vehicles are rugged and reliable, they may infer that Jeep wheelbarrows will be rugged and reliable, too. If consumers like a brand initially, these feelings will influence their evaluations of later brand extensions.[24] However, firms need to be careful about which associations they want to transfer to the brand extension. Promoting a brand extension's attributes can focus consumers' attention on the attributes, not the brand, and make the extension seem less attractive.[25]

Exhibit 4.5

Brand Alliances
Häagen-Dazs and Baileys Irish Cream come together in this brand alliance (also called a co-branding strategy).

Consumers tend to like brand extensions more when the product fits in some way with the parent brand or with the set of brands in the brand family and when they really like the parent brand.[26] The fit between brand extension and parent brand or family may be based on similar attributes or benefits, usage goals, or targets.[27] Although consumers in different cultures may have differing perceptions of how a brand extension fits with the parent brand or family, they tend to like the extension more when they perceive a better fit.[28] Sometimes consumers must expend effort to understand how a brand extension relates to its parent brand or brand family. Thus, evaluations can be affected by consumers' MAO, that is, their *motivation*, *ability*, and *opportunity* (concepts described in Chapter 2), to understand the fit between the brand extension and the parent brand.[29] Consumers' evaluations of brand extensions can also be affected by whether or not they are in a good mood and how involved they are in processing information about the brand.[30]

One concern about brand extensions is that they may make the brand schema less coherent and may dilute the brand's image.[31] If the Jeep name appears on too many different products—wheelbarrows, clothing, luggage—consumers may be confused about what Jeep stands for. On the other hand, sometimes consumers accept a brand extension better when the brand name is already linked to products that are quite different from one another. This happens because consumers may find some attributes or benefits of at least one of the product categories that make it seem like the brand extension is a good product.[32]

Although existing brands can affect consumers' perceptions of a brand extension, marketing messages about a brand extension can sometimes influence consumers' perceptions of the existing brand(s) as well.[33] For example, if a consumer has a bad experience with Jeep luggage, those negative feelings may affect his or her image of Jeep vehicles. Given these potential problems, marketers need to be concerned about the long-term effects of using these strategies.[34]

At a more fundamental level, creating associations linked to an offering helps to position the offering so that consumers understand what it is and what it is competing against. Snacks made by Newman's Own Organics, for instance, are associated with organic ingredients and health-food stores, associations that differentiate them from competing snack brands such as Frito-Lay snacks, which are sold in supermarket chains.

Developing existing schemas, images, and personalities

Although marketers must sometimes create new schemas, in other cases they must develop or elaborate a schema—that is, add information to an existing schema so that consumers understand more about it.[35] Then, over time, consistent advertising can help develop and reinforce long-term brand schemas.[36] There are three ways to develop schemas:

1. Use multiple brand extensions. Although Arm & Hammer was once associated only with baking soda, the extension of the brand to such categories as kitty litter, carpet deodorizer, and refrigerator deodorizer has reinforced its deodorizing image.

2. Link the product to sponsorship of an appropriate sporting event. Doing this strengthens and develops the existing schema and brand personality.[37]

3. Highlight additional features and benefits. Nalgene develops schemas by promoting its reusable water bottles as lightweight, leakproof, trendy, and earth-friendly.[38]

Changing schemas, images, and personalities

Sometimes consumers' schemas, images, and brand personalities contain associations that require change. When a brand or product image becomes stale, outdated, or linked to negative associations, marketers need to find ways to add new and positive associations.

Shimano America, which makes bicycle components, helped change the bicycle's image from a high-tech and highly engineered machine to one that is fun and easy to ride. Shimano's new Coasting bicycles are engineered to shift automatically so that riders do not have to worry about switching gears, yet the bikes look like the kind of two-wheelers that anyone can ride. Consequently, the new bikes have reinvigorated sales and have attracted new buyers.[39]

Protecting brand images

Brand images may be threatened during crises that involve potential harm, such as reports of contaminated products or health problems that are linked to specific products. St. Joseph Aspirin, which originally made low-dose children's aspirin, faced this challenge after doctors discovered that children who took the aspirin for viral infections might develop deadly Reye's syndrome. The company kept the St. Joseph brand but instead targeted adults who want to take low-dose aspirin to reduce their risk of strokes and heart problems. To build on positive associations that had been formed when today's adults had been given St. Joseph's aspirin as children, the company returned to an older package design.[40]

The way that a company responds to a crisis affects its brand image, but research indicates that consumers' prior expectations also play a critical role. Companies whose customers held a strong, positive image of the brand prior to the crisis suffered less image damage than did companies whose customers had lower expectations. Therefore, firms with weaker brand images should act aggressively to support their brands after a crisis.[41] Interestingly, firms with a "sincere" brand personality may have difficulty reestablishing strong customer relations after a crisis because fundamental perceptions of the brand have deteriorated. In contrast, firms with an "exciting" brand personality may have an easier time reinvigorating customer relationships after a crisis because consumers are less surprised by nonroutine experiences with such brands.[42] Finally, distribution activities can also affect brand image: Consumers displeased by a store's price increase on one brand may feel negatively toward other brands sold in that store.[43]

Scripts

Script A special type of schema that represents knowledge of a sequence of actions involved in performing an activity.

Schemas represent our knowledge about objects or things.[44] A **script** is a special type of schema that represents our knowledge of a sequence of actions involved in performing an activity. For example, you may have a script for how to arrange roses bought from the store: You open the cellophane wrapping, get scissors, fill a vase with water, run the roses under water, cut them, and arrange them in the vase. This knowledge helps you accomplish tasks quickly and easily. But when you do something for the first time, such as assembling a piece of Ikea furniture, not having a script may prolong the task.

(MARKETING IMPLICATIONS)

Scripts help marketers understand how consumers buy and use an offering. In turn, marketers use this knowledge to make marketing decisions that improve products or services. Marketers may also perform tasks that are part of consumers' scripts. In other cases, marketers may want consumers to consider using a particular brand or product as part of a scripted activity—incorporating hands-free devices as part of their cell phone usage script, for example. Interactive advertising and shopping, as well as offers and services delivered by cell phone, are changing the way that consumers perform scripted activities such as processing ads and buying goods and services. Hallmark.com, for instance, offers an e-mail reminder service to alert consumers about upcoming birthdays, anniversaries, or other important occasions that involve sending greeting cards.

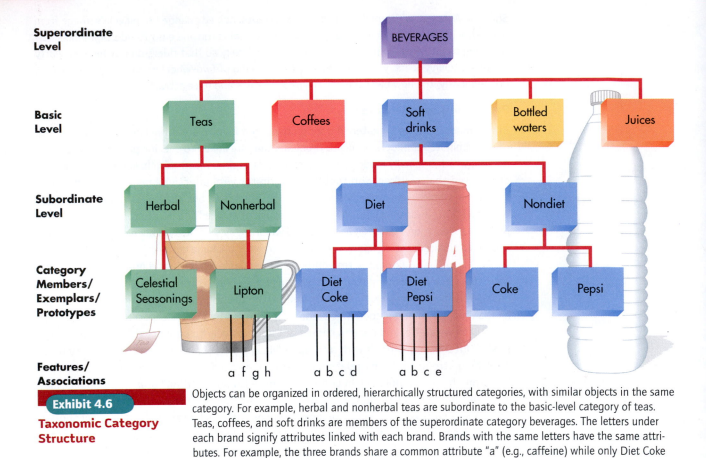

Superordinate Level

Basic Level

Subordinate Level

Category Members/ Exemplars/ Prototypes

Features/ Associations

BEVERAGES

Teas — Coffees — Soft drinks — Bottled waters — Juices

Herbal — Nonherbal — Diet — Nondiet

Celestial Seasonings — Lipton — Diet Coke — Diet Pepsi — Coke — Pepsi

a f g h   a b c d   a b c e

Exhibit 4.6

Taxonomic Category Structure

Objects can be organized in ordered, hierarchically structured categories, with similar objects in the same category. For example, herbal and nonherbal teas are subordinate to the basic-level category of teas. Teas, coffees, and soft drinks are members of the superordinate category beverages. The letters under each brand signify attributes linked with each brand. Brands with the same letters have the same attributes. For example, the three brands share a common attribute "a" (e.g., caffeine) while only Diet Coke and Lipton share attribute "b" (e.g., artificial sweetener).

Knowledge Structure

Although schemas and scripts reflect the content of what we know, our lives would be utter chaos if we did not have some way of organizing or structuring our knowledge. Fortunately, as shown in the next sections, we are adept at organizing our knowledge and categorizing information.

Categories and Their Structure

Taxonomic category A group of objects that are classified in an orderly and often hierarchically based scheme based on their similarity to one another.

Objects can be organized into **taxonomic categories**.[45] A taxonomic category is a specifically defined division within an orderly classification of objects with similar objects in the same category. For example, although we have schemas for Coke, Pepsi, Diet Coke, and so on, these schemas can be clustered in a category called *soft drinks*. Moreover, we may use subcategories to cluster specific brands and separate them from others. Thus, we might have one subcategory for diet soft drinks and a different subcategory for nondiet soft drinks. In turn, soft drinks may be part of a larger beverage category that also includes coffees, teas, juices, and bottled waters, as shown in Exhibit 4.6.

Graded Structure and Prototypicality

Things within the same taxonomic category share similar features, and the features they share are different from the features of objects in other categories. So a category member such as Diet Coke shares many associations with members of its own category of diet colas but shares few associations with members of other categories. In Exhibit 4.6, Diet Coke has associations a–d, and Diet Pepsi has many but not all of the same associations (a–c and e). Lipton tea has associations a and f–h; hence it has few associations in common with Diet Coke.

Even though category members share similar features, not every member is perceived to be an equally good category member. For example, you might perceive a robin to be a better example of the category *bird* than a flamingo is. Likewise, you might view Coke as a better example of a soft drink than Sierra Mist is. The fact that category members vary in how well they are perceived to represent a category illustrates the principle of **graded structure.**[46]

Graded structure The fact that category members vary in how well they represent a category.

Prototype The best example of a cognitive (mental) category.

Within a category, you as a consumer can rank specific category members according to how well you believe they represent the category. The category **prototype** is that category member perceived to be the best example of the category. Thus, a robin is a prototypical bird, and iPod is a prototypical digital music player. Exhibit 4.7 identifies brands generally regarded as prototypes in their product categories.

What Affects Prototypicality?

Several factors affect whether a consumer regards something as a prototypical category member.[47] The first is shared associations: A prototype shares the most associations with other members of its own category and shares the fewest with members from different categories. Potato chips are a prototypical snack food because they have associations common to many snack foods (good taste, crunchy, salty, finger food, high in carbohydrates and fats) and few associations in common with other categories such as *dinner foods.*

Exhibit 4.7		

Prototypical Brands

Brands viewed as the best examples of a product category are called *prototypical brands.* Prototypical brands tend to have many features in common with other brands in the category, are encountered frequently, and may have been the first entrant in the product category.

Product Category	Prototypical Brands
Children's entertainment	Disney
Laundry detergent	Tide
Digital music player	iPod
Cell phone	Nokia
Toothpaste	Crest
Electronics	Sony
Peanut butter	Skippy
Tuna fish	Starkist
Soup	Campbell's
Bologna	Oscar Mayer
Ketchup	Heinz
Bleach	Clorox
Greeting cards	Hallmark
Motorcycle	Harley-Davidson
Grape jelly	Welch's
Gelatin	Jell-O
Hamburgers	McDonald's
Baby shampoo	Johnson & Johnson
Tools	Black & Decker
Cold cereal	Kellogg's
Tissue	Kleenex
Acetaminophen	Tylenol
Hook-and-loop fastener	Velcro
Online retailer	Amazon.com

A second feature that affects prototypicality is the frequency with which an object is encountered as a category member. Amazon.com is a prototypical Internet retailer because consumers frequently encounter its name when online or when searching for online sources of books. The first or "pioneer" brand in a category—such as Amazon—may also be a prototype because it sets a standard against which later brands are compared.[48]

MARKETING IMPLICATIONS

Prototypes are the main point of comparison used by consumers to categorize a new brand. Therefore, a brand can develop its identity by being positioned as being either similar to or different from the prototype.

▶ *Positioning a brand as similar to the category prototype* is appropriate when the goal is to appeal to a broad segment of consumers. Because the prototype best defines the category and is well liked, a new brand positioned as being similar to it may appeal to that same (large) segment of consumers. Thus, consumers may well have a positive response to copycat products that look similar to the prototype.[49] Comparative advertising may be a useful tool for making a brand seem similar to a prototype. If a challenger brand such as Barnesandnoble.com comes into the market and directly compares itself with Amazon.com, the challenger may be seen as similar to the prototype.[50]

▶ *Positioning away from the prototype* is a good way to differentiate a brand. For instance, targeting U.S. consumers in their twenties, Toyota positions its Scion xB as having more distinctive styling than the popular Honda Civic.[51] This tactic works when the brand differs from others (particularly from the prototype) and when the point of difference offers a credible reason for buying. It is also appropriate when appealing to consumers with specific needs. Positioning a brand away from the prototype can also work with pricing because consumers judge whether a product's price is high or low by comparing it with the prices of several category members, not just with the price of the prototype.[52]

Correlated Associations

Although graded structure reflects one way that knowledge is structured, another way depends on whether the associations linked to category members are *correlated*, or go together. For example, consumers might expect a cake with rich flavor to have high calories or expect nationally advertised brands to be of higher quality than local ones. With automobiles, consumers may expect a big car to be less fuel efficient than a smaller car. Although these attributes may be correlated in consumers' minds, they may or may not actually be true of a specific brand. Thus, knowledge about **correlated associations** can significantly affect consumers' inferences about a new brand and the kinds of communications marketers need to make to overcome potentially false inferences.

Correlated associations The extent to which two or more associations linked to a schema go together.

When consumers are developing a schema or when they are confronted with ambiguous information, they can mistakenly believe that if a product in a particular category has a type of attribute, other products in that category have similar attributes.[53] To understand these illusory correlations, consider this example: Just as some smokers mistakenly thought that "clean" smokeless cigarettes were safer than regular cigarettes, they may also mistakenly believe that low-toxin and natural cigarettes are safer.[54] Advertising that capitalizes on these illusory correlations raises ethical issues, as Chapter 18 discusses. On the other hand, companies need to address inaccuracies that affect their marketing activities, as you will see in this chapter's case about Hyundai.

Exhibit 4.8

Example of Hierarchical Structure

When products are organized in stores in a way that corresponds to our mental categories (e.g., the "dairy" aisle, with "milk," "cheese," and "cream" products clustered together), we can find things more easily.

Consumers also use prior knowledge to estimate the likelihood that two events will occur together. For example, you may believe that once a car stops at a red light, you can cross the street. Although these two events often go together, this situation is not always true, as we know from traffic accidents. According to research, prior expectations influence the accuracy of these judgments.[55] If you fly regularly, you may know that taxis are often waiting outside of airports. Hence, you may be surprised and unhappy to find no taxis waiting to take you to your hotel when you arrive at a local airport in Costa Rica.

Hierarchical Structure

Superordinate level The broadest level of category organization containing different objects that share few associations but are still members of the category.

Basic level A level of categorization below the superordinate category that contains objects in more refined categories.

Subordinate level A level of categorization below the basic level that contains objects in very finely differentiated categories.

A final way in which taxonomic categories are structured is hierarchically. As Exhibit 4.6 indicates, taxonomic categories can be hierarchically organized into basic, subordinate, and superordinate levels. The broadest level of categorization is the **superordinate level,** where objects share a few associations but also have many different ones. Diet Coke and Fiji bottled water, both in the beverages category, have some common associations but many that are different.

Finer discriminations among these objects are made at the **basic level.** Beverages might be more finely represented by categories such as teas, coffees, and soft drinks. The objects in the teas category have more in common with each other than they do with objects in the coffee category. The finest level of differentiation exists at the **subordinate level.** For example, soft drinks might be subdivided into categories of diet and nondiet soft drinks. Here, members of the diet soft-drink category have more associations in common with each other than they do with members of the nondiet category. Consumers can organize information in categories quite flexibly; for beverages, they may consider whether soft drinks are diet or nondiet, colas or not colas, caffeinated or decaffeinated.

Consumers use more associations to describe objects in a progression from the superordinate to the basic to the subordinate levels. They may apply associations such as "drinkable" and "used throughout the day" to all members of the beverages category. However, other associations—"carbonated, served cold, sold in six-packs"— describe members of the soft-drink category and still more associations of "no calories" and "artificial sweeteners" describe members at the subordinate diet-drink level.

MARKETING IMPLICATIONS

Understanding consumers' hierarchical category structure helps marketers identify their competitors. It also gives marketers a tool for analyzing and influencing consumers' perceptions of category attributes and prototypical products.[56] Although consumers often make choices among brands at the basic or subordinate level, sometimes they choose from brands that belong to a common superordinate category. If you are deciding whether to order a pizza or snack on microwave popcorn, you are making a decision about products that belong to two different basic categories within the snack superordinate-level category. The brands in both categories might be compared based on higher-order attributes that link the brands to the same superordinate-level category (convenience, price, taste). And although pizza restaurants might not normally consider popcorn brands as competitors, they are in this situation.

▶ *Establishing a competitive position.* By understanding consumers' superordinate-category structure, marketers can glean a broad view of their competition and use this understanding to establish an appropriate competitive position; they can also determine which attributes to emphasize so that consumers will properly categorize their offering. For example, if a nonalcoholic beer is positioned as a subordinate category of beer, its advertising should not only stress features central to beer (great beer taste) but also promote associations that put it in this subordinate category (has no alcohol).

▶ *Designing retail stores and sites.* Basic, subordinate, and superordinate category levels have implications for consumer information search and the design of retail stores and sites (see Exhibit 4.8). Generally, grocery stores are designed so that objects in taxonomically similar categories are shelved together, as are items in the same basic- and subordinate-level categories. Thus, most grocery stores have a dairy (superordinate level) section with shelves for milk, yogurt, cheese, and so on (basic level). Within each of these sections are subordinate categories of items such as low-fat, nonfat, and whole milk. Retail websites also group products according to category (such as cameras or books). Placing items in ways that are consistent with the structure of consumers' knowledge helps consumers find products efficiently. This is the reason why White Wave markets its Silk soymilk by packaging it in milk cartons and placing it in the refrigerated milk section of stores.[57]

Goal-Derived Categories

Goal-derived category
Things that are viewed as belonging in the same category because they serve the same goals.

In addition to creating taxonomic categories, consumers may also organize their prior knowledge in **goal-derived categories.** A goal-derived category contains things that consumers view as similar because they serve the same goal,—even though they belong to different taxonomic categories.[58] For example, when traveling on an airplane, you might regard in-flight movies, blankets, and peanuts as being in the same category because all are part of the goal-derived category "things that make air travel more pleasant." Because consumers have many goals, they can have many goal-derived categories. For example, if you are on a diet, you might form a category for "foods to eat on a diet."

Consumers frequently encounter certain goals and therefore have firmly established categories for those goals. For example, if you give a lot of parties, the goal-derived category of "things to buy for a party" probably consists of a fairly stable and constant set of products. In contrast, you may create relevant categories on a situation-by-situation basis for less frequently encountered goals. However, category structure is flexible: the same object can be part of a goal-derived category and part of a taxonomic category. Thus, Diet Coke might be part of the taxonomic categories diet colas, soft drinks, and beverages and also be a member of the following goal-derived categories: things to have for lunch, things to take on a picnic, and things to drink at a ball game.

Like taxonomic categories, goal-derived categories exhibit graded structure. Consumers regard some members as better examples of a particular category than others when those members best achieve the goals of the category. For example, lettuce is lower in fat and calories, so it is a better example of foods to eat when on a diet than baked crackers. Because goal-derived categories exhibit graded structure, consumers can also identify prototypes of goal-derived categories. As with taxonomic categories, the frequency with which an item is encountered as a category member affects its prototypicality. We tend to classify lettuce as a prototype for foods to eat when on a diet and would probably rate it as more prototypical than a food that is equally appropriate but encountered less frequently—like kohlrabi.

Construal Level Theory

How we think about or understand things can also vary in terms of the level at which we think about (or construe) something. According to construal level theory, we can think about a product or an action in terms of high-level or low-level construals.[59] Adopting the former means that we think about something in terms of its abstract features. For example, an activity like "studying" could be thought of abstractly (a high-level construal) as "furthering my education" or concretely (a low-level construal) as "making sure I get an A on the marketing quiz." The idea of purchasing a table for our living room could be construed of abstractly as "making the room look more beautiful" or concretely as "having a place to put my coffee when I watch TV."

Notice that the abstract construals fit into a superordinate goal-derived category while the concrete ones fit into a more subordinate goal-derived category. With abstract, high-level constructs, we do not tend to think about the context. In the studying case, we are just thinking about furthering our education, not about getting an A on a particular marketing quiz, a thought that does consider the context. The abstract, high-level construals are tied to our general goals while the concrete, low-level construals are not.

The choices we make can be based on either high- or low-level construals. However, which we tend to use depends on whether we are making a decision about what to do right now or are deciding about something we might do in the future.[60] When we make a choice about something that we will do *right now,* our choices tend to be based on *low-level construals.* For example, if we are trying to decide whether to go to Cabo san Lucas or Mazatlan over spring break next week, we are more likely to consider specific and concrete aspects of the decision (e.g., how expensive are the flights?) and how feasible it is for us to do this right now (do I have the money to pay for it?). In contrast, when we make a decision about things that will happen in the distant future (e.g., should I go to Cabo san Lucas or Mazatlan over spring break next year?), we use high-level construals (how much do I need to relax?) and focus more on desirability (how much fun will I have?) than on feasibility.

Our focus on different aspects of the decision, depending on the timing, can explain why we thought as we did as we get ready to execute a decision we made a long time ago (e.g., why did I decide to go home for spring break when I have so much work to do at school?).[61] In addition, just having a set of brands present at the time that we are making a choice about the future makes us focus on more concrete, low-level construals. What this means is that the brands consumers think they will prefer in the future are actually the ones they do prefer by the time they obtain the brand.[62]

MARKETING IMPLICATIONS

Positioning an offering as relevant to a goal can be an important marketing objective. To illustrate, in Japan, Nestle's Kit Kat brand translates into something like "If I try, I will win." Thus, Kit Kat candy bars are positioned as "lucky things to eat before school exams."[63] Wal-Mart discounts all kinds of goods and services—including gasoline—to maintain its prototypical position in the goal-derived category of "saving money."

Supermarkets also apply goal-derived category structures when planning store design. Many stores display baby bottles, diapers, baby food, and juice in the same aisle despite these products' taxonomic differences (diapers are usually seen as similar to tissue, baby juice as similar to juice for older kids, and baby food as similar to other foods). But these products are part of a goal-derived category—"things you need to take care of a baby." Parents can therefore easily find the items they need and decide which brands to buy. Similarly, websites can be designed with consumers' goal-derived categories in mind; a travel site might allow consumers with different travel goals to search efficiently for options such as safaris, barge vacations, and so on. They might also include not just flight options but also hotel and rental car options since all are consistent with the "pleasant travel" goal-derived category.

Why Consumers Differ in Their Knowledge

Background factors affecting consumers' knowledge structure and content include the culture in which the consumer lives and the consumer's level of expertise.

Culture

The culture of which consumers are a part affects their knowledge in many ways:

- *Different associations linked to a concept.* The associations that consumers link to a concept may vary considerably across cultures.[64] In Europe, the Philips brand is associated with consumer electronics while in U.S. markets Philips is closely associated with light bulbs, which it also makes.[65]

- *Different category members.* Although consumers may have similar goal-derived categories such as "things to have for breakfast," cultural groups vary considerably in what they regard as relevant category members. In the United States, category members might include cereal, bagels, fruit, and eggs; in Japan, category members include fish, rice, and pickled vegetables (see Exhibit 4.9).

- *Different category prototypes.* Category prototypes and members may vary across cultures, requiring companies to position brands differently in different cultures. In the Netherlands, Heineken beer is regarded as Budweiser is in the United States—frequently encountered and prototypical. In the United States, however, Heineken's associations are linked with the concept of an imported, expensive,

Exhibit 4.9

Cultural Differences in Goal-Derived Categories

What we would include in the goal-derived category of "things to eat for breakfast" varies from one culture to the next.

high-status beer, so these associations put Heineken in a subordinate category. Because the beer brands have different competitors in the two markets, the same positioning strategy is unlikely to work equally well in both countries.

- *Different correlated associations.* Culture may also affect whether associations are correlated and the direction of their correlation. For example, U.S. megastores like Costco and Wal-Mart tend to price products lower than small stores do because the large stores are often discounters. In India and Sri Lanka, however, large stores tend to price products higher to cover higher overhead costs.

- *Different goal-derived categories.* Consumers in different cultures not only may have different members in goal-derived categories but, in fact, also may have different goal-derived categories. For example, the goal to have clothing that looks sexy is not likely to apply in cultures with strict religious values.

Expertise

Consumers vary in their ability to process information based on how much prior knowledge they have. Experts are people whose prior knowledge is well developed, in part because they have had a lot of experience and familiarity with an object or a task. Experts' knowledge differs from that of novices in several ways.[66] First, experts' overall category structures are more developed than the category structures of nonexperts. They also have more categories and more associations with concepts within a category, and they understand whether associations in a category are correlated. In addition, they learn which brands might be appropriate for different usage situations, organize such information by product subcategories, and are less motivated to learn about a new product than are nonexperts.[67] Experts have more subordinate-level categories and can therefore make finer distinctions among brands. For example, car experts would have many subordinate categories for cars, such as vintage cars and roadsters. Note that consumers are sometimes overconfident in their knowledge and think that they know more than they actually do.[68]

Another important point is that when experts are exposed to a marketing message, they form expectations against which they evaluate their actual experiences with that product. If a product fails to measure up to their expectations, experts are more likely to perceive a wider discrepancy between the experience and their message-generated expectations than nonexperts will.[69] Still, people who consider themselves to be experts tend to both search for information and make decisions differently than do those who do not consider themselves to be experts, situations that in turn affect how companies market to these groups.

Using Knowledge to Understand

Consumers' decisions are not influenced by their simply attending to and perceiving stimuli. Individuals must also interpret or give meaning to the objects they perceive in light of their prior knowledge.

Categorization

A first step in this process occurs when consumers categorize an object. Categorization occurs when consumers use their prior knowledge to label, identify, and classify something new. Consumers might categorize MacBook as a type of computer, eBay as a site for bidding on merchandise, and *Entertainment Tonight* as a source for getting the scoop on celebrities. Once we have categorized an object, we know what it is, what it is like, and what it is similar to. How we categorize an offering has many implications for marketers since categorization affects how favorably we evaluate an offering, what we compare it with, the expectations we have for it, whether we will choose it, and how satisfied we may be with it. Research shows, for instance, that consumers exposed to brand extensions can more quickly categorize the parent brand correctly. Given the speed at which consumers are exposed to marketing stimuli when shopping, this faster categorization can be an advantage for marketers.[70]

Consumers do not always categorize offerings correctly. For example, Japanese women initially and incorrectly categorized *Good Housekeeping* magazine as a magazine for housemaids.[71] Timberland helps consumers put its boots in the goal-derived category of "brands that make the world better" through its advertising slogan "Make it better." One of Timberland's ads was dotted with seeds labeled with the words *Plant me* to demonstrate the company's concern for conservation.[72] If consumers encounter a product or service provider that does not seem to fit the category stereotype (such as a male arts and crafts counselor), they may elaborate more on the information about that provider. And if they categorize that provider as a member of the category, they may infer that the provider has features or attributes typical of the category.[73]

Once consumers have categorized an offering, they may not be able to categorize it differently. The California Dried Plum Board changed the name of prunes to *dried plums*. "Unfortunately, the stereotype among the women that we're targeting is of a medicinal food for their parents rather than a healthful, nutritious food for women who are leading an active lifestyle," explains the executive director. The industry's research shows that women aged 35 to 50 much prefer the dried plum name; the challenge now is to encourage consumers to recategorize this offering.[74]

MARKETING IMPLICATIONS

Categorization is a basic psychological process that has far-reaching implications for marketers, including the following:

▶ *Inferences.* If we see a product as a member of a category, we may infer that the product has features or attributes typical of that category. For example, we may infer that a cell phone does not take very good pictures—an inference that may not always be correct. Thus, marketers of new products should help consumers categorize the product in a way that positively influences their perceptions of it, such as selling the phone in the photography department instead of in the electronics department of a store.[75]

▶ *Elaboration.* Categorization influences how much we think about something. We tend to be more motivated to think about or process information that we have trouble categorizing. We are more motivated to watch ads that are different from the typical ad, and we are more motivated to think about products that look different from others in the category.[76] Seeing a Honda Accord with a spoiler and racing stripes might prompt elaboration because these features suggest a mixture of the sports car and compact car categories.

▶ *Evaluation.* Categorization influences how we feel about an object, also known as our *affect* toward it. Once we categorize something as a member of a category, we may simply retrieve our evaluation of the category and use it to assess the object.[77] For example, if we hate lawyers and see an ad for a lawyer, we may use our category-based affect and decide that we hate this one, too. Likewise, if our category for chocolate bars contains positive affect, we may retrieve and use this affect to evaluate a new brand in the category.

▶ *Consideration and choice.* Whether and how we label an offering affects whether we will consider buying it. If a new phone/fax/printer is categorized as a phone, we will consider it if we are in the market for a phone. If it is categorized as a printer, we won't consider it if we are in the market for a phone.

▶ *Satisfaction.* Categorization has important implications for consumer expectations and satisfaction.[78] If we categorize something as a skin moisturizer, we will expect it to be as good as most moisturizers. If it is not, we are likely to be dissatisfied. ◀▬

Comprehension

While categorization reflects the process of identifying an entity, comprehension is the process of extracting higher-order meaning from it. Marketers are concerned with the two aspects of comprehension. The first is **objective comprehension**— whether the meaning that consumers take from a message is consistent with what the message actually stated. The second is **subjective comprehension,** the different or additional meaning consumers attach to the message, whether or not these meanings were intended.[79]

Objective and Subjective Comprehension

Objective comprehension reflects whether we accurately understand the message a sender intended to communicate. Interestingly, many people miscomprehend marketing messages due to the way the information is presented (its language) or differences between the sender's and the receiver's prior knowledge—or both. Subjective comprehension reflects what we understand whether or not it is accurate. Marketing mix elements such as price and advertising can play a powerful role in influencing what we think a message is saying. You may infer that a certain brand of dental gum is as powerful at whitening teeth as whitening toothpastes are

Objective comprehension
The extent to which the receiver accurately understands the message a sender intended to communicate.

Subjective comprehension
Reflects what we understand, regardless of whether this understanding is accurate.

because the package art has white sparkles, the model in the ad has very white teeth, and the package displays terms like *whitening agent.* Yet the product may not be a powerful whitening agent, and the words on the package may not actually say that it is. The inferences that consumers make and the reasons certain communications prompt these inferences raise some important public policy implications.

Miscomprehension

Miscomprehension Inaccurate understanding of a message.

Although marketing communications such as ads and packaging are often fairly simple to comprehend, consumer research reveals that getting consumers to achieve objective comprehension can sometimes be quite a challenge for marketers. **Miscomprehension** occurs when consumers inaccurately receive the meaning contained in a message. Several studies have found a surprisingly high level of miscomprehension of TV and magazine ads, across all demographic segments. The estimated rate of objective comprehension was only about 70 percent for TV ads and 65 percent for print ads. Moreover, the rates of miscomprehension for directly asserted information and implied information were fairly equal, as were miscomprehension rates for programming, editorial material, and advertising.[80]

In addition to miscomprehending advertising messages, consumers sometimes miscomprehend product descriptions and usage instructions. AFLAC recently changed its advertising after research showed that consumers didn't understand its insurance offerings. Although the duck is still in AFLAC ads, the ads now focus on the benefits of the company's insurance with messages like "When I'm hurt and miss work, AFLAC gives me cash to help pay the bills that my health insurance doesn't pay."[81]

Effect of MAO

Consumers may not comprehend a marketing message when they have low motivation and limited opportunity to process it, when the message is complex or shown for only a few seconds, or when the message is viewed only once or twice.[82] Experts are better able to comprehend information about a highly innovative product when prompted by marketing messages that help them make the connections and tap existing knowledge in more than one category.[83] Regarding ability, one study found that although consumers want to see nutritional information on packaging (implying high motivation to process it), most do not comprehend it once they have read it.[84] Still, comprehension may improve with expertise and ability, which is the reason that adults often better comprehend the finer points of a message than young children do.[85]

Effect of the Culture

The culture in which consumers live can also affect comprehension and miscomprehension (see Exhibit 4.10). Low-context cultures such as those in North America and northern Europe generally separate the words and meanings of a communication from the context in which it appears. Consumers in these cultures place greater emphasis on what is said than on the surrounding visuals or the environmental context of the message. But in high-context cultures (such as many in Asia), much of a message's meaning is implied indirectly and communicated visually rather than stated explicitly through words. The message sender's characteristics, such as social class, values, and age, also play an important role in the interpretation of a message.[86]

Because cultures differ in the ways that they attend to the content and context of the message, we might expect differences in consumers' comprehension of the same message across cultures. For example, when the Michigan-based Big Boy

Exhibit 4.10

Importance of Visuals in High-Context Cultures

In high-context cultures much of a message's meaning is implied indirectly and communicated visually rather than stated explicitly through words.

就没有杀害。 **WildAid**

fast-food chain opened its first restaurant on a busy street in Thailand, some local customers mistook its giant Big Boy statue for a religious icon.[87] Language differences further raise the possibility of miscomprehension; in fact, marketers risk miscomprehension if they do not use language as consumers in a culture do. In India, for example, so many people mix Hindi and English that advertisers are doing the same in their messages. Thus, Pepsi ads in India say, "Yeh Dil Maange More" (translation: "The heart wants more"), and Coke's slogan there is "Life ho to aisi" (translation: "Life should be like this").[88]

Culture also affects the meaning consumers attach to words.[89] For example, in the United Kingdom, a *billion* is "a million million," whereas in the United States a billion means "a thousand million." Likewise, in the United Kingdom, a movie that is a *bomb* is a "success"; elsewhere the term means a "failure." One U.S. airline promoted its "rendezvous lounges" in Brazil; however, among the Brazilians the phrase implied "a room for lovemaking."

Improving Objective Comprehension

Fortunately, consumer researchers have provided some guidelines for improving objective comprehension.[90] One is to keep the message simple. Another is to repeat the message—stating it multiple times within the same communication and repeating it on multiple occasions. Presenting information in different forms, such as both visually and verbally in a TV commercial, can help consumers form an accurate mental picture.[91] Research shows that consumers who have had more exposure to marketing communications will be better able to process information about the brand and have more positive attitudes toward it.[92] Ease in perceiving and processing information is known as **perceptual fluency.**

Perceptual fluency The ease with which information is processed.

Subjective Comprehension

Subjective comprehension describes the meanings consumers generate from a communication, whether or not these meanings were actually intended.[93] Public policy makers are often concerned because what consumers take away from an ad may be different from what the ad objectively states. Not long ago, the Federal Trade Commission raised concerns about a KFC ad that was thought to be misleading.

The ad said that two KFC fried chicken breasts contain less fat than a Burger King Whopper sandwich. Although the ad was accurate in saying that KFC chicken breasts have less total fat and saturated fat than a Whopper, the FTC noted that two KFC breasts have triple the transfat and cholesterol of a Whopper. "For consumers to obtain healthier choices, we must make sure that the companies promote their products honestly," said the head of the FTC.[94]

Some researchers describe subjective comprehension in terms of several comprehension levels. In this scheme each level indicates more thinking or elaboration.[95] For example, suppose a consumer sees an ad for a front-loading washing machine. She may infer that a high-efficiency laundry detergent is needed to make the machine work properly. Adding to her elaboration of the machine, she may think that ordinary detergent will not be completely rinsed away, meaning that she would have to wash the clothes again, an activity that defeats the purpose of buying a high-efficiency washer. She may further elaborate that because the machine offers high efficiency and uses less water, her water bills will be much lower (if she uses the right detergent), a situation that will in turn allow her to save money for a vacation.

(MARKETING IMPLICATIONS)

Like categorization, subjective comprehension involves some interaction between what is in a message and what consumers already know. As a result, a marketer can strongly influence what consumers subjectively perceive from a message by designing or structuring it in a way that is consistent with their prior knowledge. Sometimes when consumers know little about a new product, marketers may be able to convey information effectively by drawing an analogy between the product and something with similar benefits. For example, a marketer may try to communicate the idea that a particular brand of boots is waterproof, soft, and lightweight by using the analogy of a duck.[96]

Marketers are often successful in designing an ad so that consumers form the "correct" inferences about the offering. At times, however, marketers may (knowingly or unknowingly) create inferences that do not accurately characterize a product or service and result in miscomprehension.[97] Situations in which marketers deliberately create false inferences raise important ethical and legal implications, as discussed in Chapter 18. ▬▬

Consumer Inferences

Specific elements of the marketing mix can work with consumers' prior knowledge to affect the correct or incorrect inferences they make about an offering. The following sections describe how brand names and symbols, product features and packaging, price, distribution, and promotion can affect the inferences consumers make about products.

Brand Names and Brand Symbols

Subjective comprehension of a marketing communication can be based on the inferences consumers make from a brand symbol. The Pillsbury Dough Boy has slimmed down over the years because the company's marketers were afraid that consumers would infer that he was fat from eating Pillsbury products. Even the typeface used in a brand name can create inferences.[98]

Brand names can create subjective comprehension and inferences. For example, alphanumeric brand names like BMW's X6 tend to be associated with technological sophistication and complexity. In addition, consumers tend to make inferences when they evaluate a brand extension by carrying over certain features linked to the parent brand.[99] Moreover, foreign brand names may create inferences based on cultural categories and stereotypes. Häagen-Dazs, a German-sounding name, may evoke favorable associations when applied to ice cream even though the product is manufactured in the Bronx. Marketers should therefore not only consider linguistic factors when translating brand names for another culture but also examine how consumers in that culture process different types of brand names.[100]

Descriptive names can also create inferences. Brand names such as Obsession for perfume and Speedo for bathing suits may create inferences about the particular brand's benefits.[101] Companies marketing products whose quality cannot be observed can communicate quality by offering a warranty, selling through a credible retailer, or forging an alliance with another reputable brand. Under these circumstances, consumers are likely to infer that the allied product would lose its reputation or its future profits if the quality claims were untrue.[102]

Inferences Based on Misleading Names and Labels Although some brand names may accurately characterize a product's attributes and benefits, others have been called misleading because they create false inferences about the product's benefits. For example, consumers may infer that "lite" olive oil has fewer calories when it is really only "lite" in color.[103] This confusion has prompted the development of labeling laws to ensure that product names and ingredients accurately describe the offering. The U.S. Department of Agriculture has enacted regulations standardizing the use of the term *organic*. The term is restricted to crops that have been untouched by herbicides, pesticides, or fertilizers for at least three years or to livestock raised without antibiotics or hormones.[104]

Inferences Based on Inappropriate or Similar Names Some brand names lead to inappropriate inferences about the product. One gas company came up with the new name Enteron, but it later learned that *enteron* is a real word that means "the alimentary canal" (i.e., intestines), giving a different meaning to the term *gas*.[105] The challenge for Web-based marketers is to find a name that suggests what they do and one that helps them stand out in the crowd. "A fanciful name that is well branded—and examples of this are plentiful: Intel, Yahoo!—will resonate in the consumer's mind and conjure the supplier of specific products and services," says one Web marketing expert. "A generic domain name lacks that distinctive association."[106]

Sometimes brand or company names are too similar, so consumers may inadvertently infer that the brands are similar or made by the same company. Typically these situations create legal battles, with companies fighting over who can use the original brand name. For instance, after the Culinary Institute of America sued the American Culinary Institute for trademark infringement and unfair competition, the latter organization adopted a new corporate name and trademark.[107]

Product Features and Packaging

Consumers can also subjectively comprehend aspects of an offering based on inferences they make from the product and the way that it is packaged.

Inferences Based on Product Attributes Knowledge that two attributes tend to be correlated in a product category may lead consumers to infer that the presence of one attribute in a brand implies the presence of the other. Thus, consumers may infer that a product with a low repair record also has a long warranty.[108] Consumers also may make inferences about products based on package size. A consumer who encounters a large, multipack item may use prior knowledge about the correlation between price and package size to infer that the large-sized brand is also a good buy.[109]

Consumers make taste inferences based on nutritional information presented about food products, inferences that affect their buying and consumption decisions.

MEDITERRANEAN STYLE
DINNERS SO FRESH TASTING,
ITALIAN CHEFS
WANT TO HIDE THEM.

Exhibit 4.11

Inferences Based on Country of Origin

We make inferences about the characteristics or the quality of products based on their name and the country in which they are made.

Some research shows that consumers who are given nutritional information about a product are more likely to see it as healthier than when they are not given nutritional information. However, they will also infer that the healthier product will not taste as good as an unhealthier product.[110] Moreover, consumers infer that products with unusual flavors or color names are better than products that use common flavors or color names.[111]

When two companies form a brand alliance for marketing purposes, consumers tend to infer that the attributes of the two brands are similar even when only one of the brands is completely described in an ad.[112] When consumers are searching for information about whether a product will deliver a particular benefit, exposure to irrelevant attributes leads to inferences that the product will not necessarily perform as desired.[113] In highly competitive categories, where differences among products seem minimal, consumers may infer that although the dominant brand is good on observable attributes it has a disadvantage on some unobservable attribute.[114]

Inferences Based on Country of Origin Knowledge about a product's country of origin can affect the way consumers think about it (see Exhibit 4.11).[115] Just as we stereotype people based on where they were born, we stereotype products based on where they were made. Research shows that consumers in developing countries infer higher quality for brands perceived as foreign.[116] Consumers may have a more positive response to products made in countries with reputations for high-quality manufacturing.

However, if consumers dislike a country because of its political or social policies, they may have a more negative response to its products.[117] In one study, Japanese consumers inferred that the quality of Japanese-made products was higher than the quality of American-made products—even when the Japanese products were not superior. This preference for own-country origin explains why marketing by Kao stresses the company's Japanese roots as it defends its dominance of the Japanese diaper market against competition from U.S. brands.[118] Exhibit 4.12 shows the three most important positive attributes of products for which Japanese consumers' buying decisions are influenced by Japan's being the country of origin. Consumers are more likely to make inferences about a brand based on its country of origin when they are unmotivated to process information about that brand or when their processing goal guides attention toward origin information.[119]

Inferences Based on Package Design Package characteristics can also create inferences. Although consumers may make inferences about one brand if its packaging looks much like that of the category prototype, they do not necessarily react negatively to the copycat brand.[120] At the same time, packaging can suggest a brand's uniqueness. To differentiate its Iron City Beer from bottled imported lagers, Pittsburgh Brewing packages it in long-necked 12-ounce aluminum bottles with the brand name

Exhibit 4.12

Made in Japan

The superior points or positive aspects of products made in Japan, for the top products for which "made in Japan" is a factor when making a purchase choice.

Top Six Products that Are Chosen with Emphasis on Whether or Not They Were Made in Japan	Top Aspect	Second Aspect	Third Aspect
No.1 Domestic home appliances	Efficiency	Durability, hard to break	Service and maintenance
No.2 Food items for cooking	Safety	Efficiency (good taste, flavor)	Ease of use
No.3 Processed food items, such as sweets, etc.	Safety	Efficiency (good taste, flavor)	Relative cheapness, familiarity
No.4 Cars	Service and maintenance	Efficiency	Durability, hard to break
No.5 Medical care items	Safety	Efficiency	Service and maintenance
No.6 Personal computers	Service and maintenance	Efficiency	Durability, hard to break

Source: From Hitami Taira, "More Japanese People 'Want Made in Japan,'" *Japan Close-Up,* December 2004, p. 31. Reprinted with permission of PHP Institute, Inc.

boldly lettered on the front. In addition, the aluminum bottles have pop-off tops (not pop tabs) and are designed to chill more quickly than glass or plastic bottles.[121]

Sometimes packages are designed to look like the packages of well-known brands. Walkers, a U.K. cracker manufacturer, once complained that the packaging of Tesco's Temptations snacks, marketed by the Tesco supermarket chain, was perhaps too much like that of Walkers' Sensations snacks. Although the furor soon subsided, *Grocer,* an industry magazine, observed that the package colors were almost identical—with Tesco's colors indicating different flavors than Walkers' colors did—and that the two packages had similar imagery, such as potatoes in the foreground of a rustic country scene.[122]

Inferences Based on Color We have color categories stored in prior knowledge: The category of green things includes mint, grass, trees, and leaves as members and has associations like refreshing, new, organic, peaceful, and springlike. Because of this category-based knowledge, consumers may infer that a brand of toothpaste that is green or that comes in a green package is refreshing, minty, and healthy. Knowing that colors can create inferences, some firms legally protect the color of their brand to prevent other firms from using that color on their products. This strategy also reduces the possibility that consumers will categorize the product incorrectly or draw false inferences about a knockoff product. To illustrate, Owens-Corning has trademarked its pink home-insulation products.[123]

Because category content varies with culture, the meanings associated with colors and consumers' inferences based on color will also vary.[124] For example, Western consumers associate white with purity and cleanliness, whereas in Asian countries white signifies death. Green is popular in Muslim countries but is negatively perceived in Southwest Asia. Black has negative overtones in Japan, India, and Europe but is perceived positively in the Middle East. Marketers must therefore consider these cultural differences when marketing in other cultures.

Price

At times, consumers make inferences about a product or service based on its price. For example, category-based knowledge suggests that price and quality are correlated, so a consumer may infer that a high-priced product is also high in quality.[125] Consumers often make this inference when they believe that brands differ in quality, when they perceive that choosing a low-quality product can be risky, and when they have no information about the brand's quality before they buy it.[126] When consumers use price as a shortcut to infer quality, they may overestimate. the relationship between price and quality.[127] However, consumers do not always make price-quality inferences.[128] Additionally, when consumers receive a product as a free gift with the purchase of another item, they infer that the gift has a lower value and will therefore expect to pay less for the product when it is offered separately.[129]

Retail Atmospherics and Display

Category-based knowledge about retail design, displays, layout, merchandising, and service can also affect consumers' inferences. For example, the inferences you make when walking into a warehouse-type store like Costco are likely to be different from the inferences you make entering a more upscale, service-oriented store like Nordstrom's. Research indicates that an aesthetically pleasing retail atmosphere causes consumers to infer positive quality perceptions of socially communicative products such as gifts, but not of utilitarian products such as household appliances.[130] Consumers also infer differences among brands based on the ways that products are displayed in stores. Further, the display context can lead consumers to rely less on their prior knowledge and more on external cues—meaning that a brand's positioning could be undermined by a store's inappropriate retail display decisions.[131] Exhibit 4.13 shows that lighting and signs are the two atmospheric elements that consumers say exert the most influence on their in-store behavior.

Atmospherics are a major tool used by retailers to develop, elaborate, and change their store images. When fashion firm Comme des Garcons opened stores in Berlin, Barcelona, and other European cities, it deliberately chose locations outside traditional shopping districts. Untouched by architects, each store was clearly

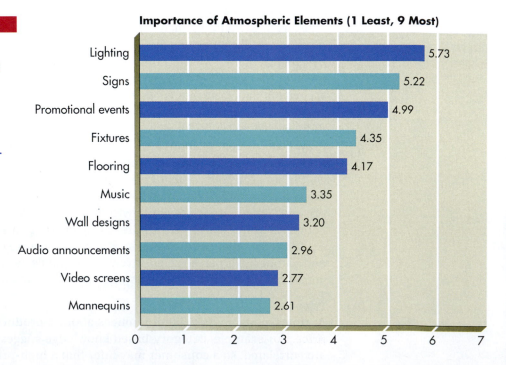

Exhibit 4.13

Which Atmospheric Elements Exert the Most Influence?

Certain atmospheric elements are perceived by consumers to impact their shopping and buying behavior.

Importance of Atmospheric Elements (1 Least, 9 Most)

Lighting	5.73
Signs	5.22
Promotional events	4.99
Fixtures	4.35
Flooring	4.17
Music	3.35
Wall designs	3.20
Audio announcements	2.96
Video screens	2.77
Mannequins	2.61

recognizable from the nearly raw décor, just the kind of edgy urban context the firm wanted for displaying its avant-garde clothing.[132]

Advertising and Selling

Advertising and selling efforts clearly affect the inferences consumers make about an offering. In personal selling and advertising, inferences can be based on body language. An advertisement that shows a woman touching a man's hand for longer than a second could lead us to believe that they are romantically involved. Consumers might infer that a salesperson with a weak handshake is not interested in their business. The nonverbal aspects of communication are particularly important in Asian cultures.[133] In Japan, for example, a verbal "yes" might mean "no"; the speaker's body language communicates the true intent.[134] In addition, consumers who feel that a salesperson is deliberately trying to persuade, and not just inform, them—especially by the use of hard-sell or pressure-selling tactics—may be less likely to buy the product.[135]

Physical space, or the distance between people, may also be interpreted differently in different cultures. Compared with Westerners, Asians tend to leave more distance between people and prefer limited physical contact. A U.S. salesperson who is accustomed to less space and more contact may give Asian consumers the impression of being pushy and unacceptably physical. However, compared with U.S. consumers, Latin American consumers are comfortable with less distance between people and may infer that a U.S. salesperson who maintains more distance is standoffish.[136]

Pictures

Advertisers frequently use pictures to stimulate inferences. Research suggests that pictures may be more effective at generating inferences when consumers have sufficient opportunity to process their meaning.[137] At the same time, the lack of pictures or words in ads can spark inferences of modernity, honesty, and sophistication.[138]

Language

Just as specific words like brand names or adjectives can affect consumers' inferences, the way in which words are structured into sentences can also affect subjective comprehension.[139] The word structure of the hypothetical ad in Exhibit 4.14 can lead to the following (potentially incorrect) inferences:

▶ *Juxtaposed imperatives.* The headline contains two sentences placed next to one another (juxtaposed). Consumers might interpret the headline as saying,

---

Exhibit 4.14

A Hypothetical Car Ad

The way that a message is worded can affect our inferences. What do you think this ad is saying? Is it really saying what you think it says? How does the wording affect what you comprehend?

Headline:	**Experience luxury and sportiness at its finest. It's the AD7 from Starfire.**
Body copy:	Automotive World's toughest tests found that no other brand gives you more than Starfire's AD7. It performs better than the Porsche in interior comfort, has better braking ability than the RX7, has a smoother ride than the Corvette, and it's less expensive.
Tag:	**Starfire's AD7. Nobody gives you more.**

"The Starfire AD7 gives you luxury and sportiness at its finest," even though the ad does not actually make this statement.

▷ *Implied superiority.* Another inference commonly made from advertising is implied superiority. The statement "nobody gives you more," as in the exhibit, could be technically true if all brands offered equal performance benefits.

▷ *Incomplete comparisons.* Ads sometimes provide a comparison but leave the object or basis of comparison either incomplete or ambiguous, which can lead to incorrect inferences.[140] The statement "it's less expensive" in Exhibit 4.14, for example, does not indicate what the Starfire AD7 is less expensive than. Is it less expensive than the other brands listed in the ad, last year's model, or the most expensive car on the market?

▷ *Multiple comparisons.* Some ads make comparisons with multiple brands. For example, the ad states that the Starfire AD7 performs better than a Porsche in interior comfort, better than an RX7 in braking ability, and better than a Corvette in smoothness of ride. However, consumers may infer that the AD7 is better than all these brands in terms of all these attributes. Readers may also infer that the Porsche offers the best interior comfort because it is the standard for comparison. Note that the ad could still technically be true if the Porsche were less comfortable than an RX7 and a Corvette but only marginally less comfortable than the AD7.

Ethical Issues

These inferences raise a number of ethical questions. On the one hand, marketers are apparently able to use marketing mix elements (such as brand name, visuals, price, store atmosphere, and ad copy) not only to make their brand look better but also to mislead consumers. On the other hand, some may argue that consumers allow themselves to be misled by marketers and that marketers cannot be held accountable for consumers' inaccurate inferences and miscomprehension. What do you think? See Chapter 18 for more discussion of the potential negative effects of marketing.

Summary

We understand something in the environment by relating it to our prior knowledge. Knowledge content is represented by a set of associations about an object or an activity linked in schemas and scripts. Understanding the content of consumers' knowledge is important because marketers are often in the position of creating new knowledge—that is, developing brand images or personalities, creating brand extensions, or positioning a brand—as well as developing consumers' existing knowledge or changing their knowledge through repositioning.

Our knowledge is also organized or structured into categories. Objects in one category are similar to objects in the same category and different from objects in other categories. Objects within a category exhibit graded structure, meaning that some are better examples of the category than are others. The prototype is the best example. Knowledge may be hierarchically organized, with similar objects organized in basic, subordinate, or superordinate levels of categorization, and objects within a category may have associations that are correlated. Categorization plays a role in construal level theory, which holds that behavior is affected by how abstractly consumers think about something and how immediately they face a choice. Categories may also be organized around things that serve similar goals. Both cultural systems and level of expertise affect consumer knowledge.

Prior knowledge combined with information from the external environment affects how we categorize something and what we comprehend. Categorization has far-reaching implications for what we think about a product, how we feel about it, what we expect from it, and whether we choose and will be satisfied with it. One way of thinking about comprehension is to ask whether consumers accurately understand what was stated in a message, a concept called *objective comprehension*. Limited motivation, ability, and/or opportunity to attend to and process a message often affect comprehension. *Subjective comprehension* refers to what consumers think they know or have understood from a message, which may not always match what a message states. Consumers may fail to accurately understand a message because they form inferences based on marketing elements. Unscrupulous marketers take advantage of consumers' tendencies to make inferences and deliberately mislead consumers, a practice that raises ethical and legal issues.

Questions for Review and Discussion

1. What is a schema, and how can the associations in a schema be described?

2. How do brand extensions, licensing, and brand alliances relate to schemas, brand images, and brand personalities?

3. What is a category prototype, and what affects prototypicality?

4. What does it mean to say that consumers organize knowledge according to goal-derived categories?

5. How do culture and expertise affect a consumer's knowledge base?

6. In what way is objective comprehension different from subjective comprehension and miscomprehension?

7. What are some examples of ways in which a company can use the marketing mix, in combination with consumers' prior knowledge, to affect the inferences consumers make about a product?

CL Visit http://cengage.com/marketing/hoyer/ ConsumerBehavior5e to find resources that are available to help you study for the course.

CONSUMER BEHAVIOR CASE

Hyundai Accelerates New Image Marketing

Hyundai is speeding toward a new brand image with a $150 million advertising campaign and a new upscale sedan intended to compete with the top German and Japanese luxury brands. In the late 1980s, when the South Korean car company first entered the U.S. market, it used its vehicles and communications to create a brand image of affordability. That budget image helped Hyundai increase its sales in the United States throughout the 1990s and beyond. By 2008, the firm was selling nearly 500,000 cars in U.S. markets each year and enjoying especially strong demand for its low-priced Elantra and Accent models.

Now Hyundai's long-term goal is to broaden its appeal beyond the budget segment and to target U.S. buyers who want a better car and are willing to pay for it. The company invested $540 million in designing, developing, and manufacturing its new rear-wheel-drive Genesis sedan. Its engineers and designers studied luxury sedans from Cadillac, Lexus, Mercedes, and BMW

and then set out to "build a car to wow consumers," says a Hyundai executive. The firm contracted with suppliers such as Bosch and Harman Becker, which sell parts to many European luxury car brands, to produce critical elements such as the engine controls and the sound system. As a result, the Genesis boasts a stylish design, a powerful V8 engine, a well-appointed dashboard, a music-lover's audio system, and a price tag well below comparable competing models.

However, moving upscale will be challenging because U.S. consumers still think of Hyundai as a budget brand. "Hyundai doesn't have product issues; Hyundai has brand issues," observes a Hyundai Motor America's vice president for marketing. "Unless we give people a compelling reason to shuffle the brand deck, they'll stand with the brands they know rather than make that switch."

To reshape its brand image, Hyundai hired Goodby, Silverstein & Partners to come up with a multimedia campaign focusing on product attributes that suggest quality and reliability. The campaign asks questions like "Shouldn't a car have more air bags than cupholders?" (which Hyundai's cars do) and makes statements like "A five-year warranty says a lot about the car. A 10-year warranty says a lot about the car company" (because Hyundai's cars are covered by a 10-year warranty). All the ads end with an invitation for consumers to "Think about it" and get more information at Hyundai's *thinkaboutit.com* website.

As part of the campaign, Hyundai bought two Super Bowl commercial spots to introduce its Genesis sedan to the widest possible audience. In one ad, actor Jeff Bridges tells viewers, "We're pretty sure that Mercedes, BMW, and Lexus aren't going to like it very much" as the Genesis drives over mountain roads and zooms along on a test track.

Jeff Goodby, who heads the ad agency that created the campaign, explains that the messages "emphasize the quality and integrity of the cars" rather than high-lighting their price advantages. "Largely because the cars have been improved so much in the last three, four years, if you dismissed them then, you haven't seen the best of them," he says. "So all we want to do is get people to look at the facts, think about it, and ask them to make up their own minds."

Can Hyundai change its brand's image by replacing negative associations with positive associations? Will encouraging consumers to elaborate on the brand and categorize it with more upscale competitors change consumers' inferences, and make consumers consider the Genesis? Solid U.S. sales for the Genesis and sales increases for all other Hyundai models will be the final measure of whether the campaign has been effective.[141]

Case Questions

1. Why would Hyundai have a voice-over stating, "We're pretty sure that Mercedes, BMW, and Lexus aren't going to like it very much" in a Genesis ad?
2. How is Hyundai using the country of origin to influence consumers' inferences about the Genesis?
3. In terms of knowledge and understanding, how is the introduction of the upscale Genesis sedan likely to affect how consumers think about lower-priced Hyundai models?

Attitudes Based on High Effort

Chapter 5

LEARNING OBJECTIVES

After studying this chapter, you will be able to

1. Discuss how marketers can apply various cognitive models to understand and influence consumers' attitudes based on high-effort thought processes.

2. Describe some of the methods for using the communication source and the message to favorably influence consumers' attitudes.

3. Explain how and why a company might try to change consumers' attitudes by influencing their feelings.

INTRODUCTION

Endorsed by . . . Tomorrow's Sports Superstars

Startups like Half Pint Skateboards and established firms like Element Skateboards are seeking an edge in the $5 billion skateboard industry through sponsorships that link their brands with promising young athletes. Drake Riddiough was only eight when he joined the Half Pint Skateboards team. He is also sponsored by DC Shoes, which makes footwear for skateboarding, snowboarding, and other sports—more markets in which athlete endorsements can influence buying decisions. Even up-and-coming equestrians are being sponsored: 18-year-old Georgie Spence, who aspires to represent the United Kingdom in a future Olympics, has support from Mapei, which makes floor coverings.

More companies see the drama and emotion of sports competition as a way to connect with consumers, create new beliefs, and influence attitudes to foster positive feelings. For example, Chipotle Mexican Grill became a major sponsor of what is now the Slipstream/Chipotle Professional Cycling Team after the team instituted an extremely strict anti-drug program. According to Chipotle's marketing director, this dedication to integrity has much in common with the chain's "Food with Integrity" program of serving eco-friendly produce from family farms. The idea is to remind consumers of this integrity every time that team cyclists speed toward the finish line wearing the Chipotle brand.[1]

These sports sponsorships illustrate several important points that stem directly from the concepts covered in the preceding chapter. Consumers probably have certain beliefs about businesses such as Chipotle Mexican Grill and Half Pint Skateboards that are based on the mental associations they have linked to them (how the burritos taste, how the skateboards look). These beliefs can affect consumers' attitudes (whether they like a certain restaurant or a certain kind of skateboard) and their behavior (whether they will drive further to get to that restaurant or to a store that carries that skateboard). Finally, attitudes can be based on the offering's functional features (such as fresh, natural ingredients or durable materials) or the emotional aspects (feeling good about supporting family farms or helping young athletes). How marketers like Chipotle and Half Pint help consumers form positive attitudes toward their brands based on new beliefs and associations—to affect buying decisions—are central issues addressed in this chapter.

What Are Attitudes?

Attitude A relatively global and enduring evaluation of an object, issue, person, or action.

An **attitude** is an overall evaluation that expresses how much we like or dislike an object, issue, person, or action.[2] Attitudes are learned, and they tend to persist over time. Our attitudes also reflect our overall evaluation of something based on the set of associations linked to it. This is the reason why we have attitudes toward brands, product categories, ads, people, stores, activities, and so forth.

The Importance of Attitudes

Cognitive function How attitudes influence our thoughts.

Affective function How attitudes influence our feelings.

Connative function How attitudes influence our behavior.

Attitudes are important because they (1) guide our thoughts (the **cognitive function**), (2) influence our feelings (the **affective function**), and (3) affect our behavior (the **connative function**). We decide which ads to read, whom to talk to, where to shop, and where to eat, based on our attitudes. Likewise, attitudes influence our behavior in acquiring, consuming, and disposing of an offering. Thus, marketers need to change attitudes in order to influence consumer decision making and change consumer behavior.

The Characteristics of Attitudes

Favorability The degree to which we like or dislike something.

Attitude accessibility How easily an attitude can be remembered.

Attitude confidence How strongly we hold an attitude.

Attitude persistence How long our attitude lasts.

Attitude resistance How difficult it is to change an attitude.

Attitudes can be described in terms of five main characteristics: favorability, attitude accessibility, attitude confidence, persistence, and resistance. **Favorability** refers to how much we like or dislike an attitude object. **Attitude accessibility** refers to how easily and readily an attitude can be retrieved from memory.[3] If you went to a movie last night, you can probably remember fairly easily what your attitude toward it was, just as you can easily remember your attitude toward an important object, event, or activity (such as your first car).

Attitudes can also be described in terms of their strength, or **attitude confidence.** In some cases we hold our attitudes very strongly and with a great deal of confidence, whereas in other cases we feel much less certain about them. Attitudes may also vary in their **persistence,** or endurance. The attitudes we hold with confidence may last for an extremely long time, whereas others may be very brief. In addition, attitudes can be described in terms of their **resistance** to subsequent change.[4] Consumers may change attitudes easily when they are not loyal to a particular brand or know little about a product. However, attitude change is more difficult when consumers are brand loyal or consider themselves experts in the product category.

Ambivalence When our evaluations regarding a brand are mixed (both positive and negative).

Finally, attitudes may be described in terms of **ambivalence,** as when we have strong positive evaluations of one aspect of a brand and strong negative evaluations of other aspects of the brand. Interestingly, someone else's opinion will tend to influence us more when our attitudes are ambivalent, even when we do not see that person as being particularly knowledgeable about the product or category. So if you are shopping, and you can find both good and bad reasons to buy the product, you may be more influenced to buy it if a friend encourages you to do so.[5]

Forming and Changing Attitudes

Marketers can better create or influence consumers' attitudes toward new offerings and novel behaviors when they understand how attitudes are formed. This understanding also helps marketers plan strategies for changing consumer attitudes about existing offerings and established behaviors. Exhibit 5.1 summarizes general approaches to attitude formation and change processes that are discussed in this and the next chapter.

The Foundation of Attitudes

As Exhibit 5.1 shows, one approach to attitude formation suggests that attitudes are based on *cognitions (thoughts)* or beliefs.[6] This means that attitudes can be based on thoughts we have about information received from an external source (such as advertising, salespeople, the Internet, or a trusted friend) or on information we recall from memory. One study shows that ad messages with information about product function—what a product's features can do, for example—can provoke thinking about the product and stimulate positive product attitudes.[7]

A second approach suggests that attitudes are based on *emotions*. Sometimes we have a favorable attitude toward an offering simply because it feels good or seems right. Likewise, we can acquire attitudes by observing and vicariously experiencing the emotions of others who use an offering. For example, if you see that people riding skateboards are having fun, you may believe that if you rode one, you would, too. In fact, research suggests that both the hedonic aspect (related to the experience of product use) and the utilitarian aspect (related to the product's function) affect attitudes toward product categories and individual brands.[8]

The Role of Effort in Attitude Formation and Change

How much extensive thinking or *elaboration* consumers put forth affects their attitude formation and change processes as well. As discussed in Chapter 2, consumers may sometimes have high motivation, ability, and opportunity (MAO) to process information and make decisions. When MAO is high, consumers are more likely to devote a lot of effort toward and become quite involved in forming

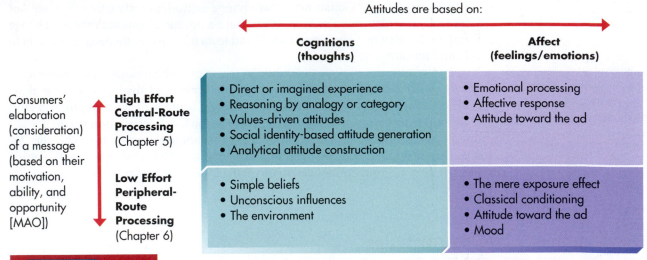

Attitudes are based on:

	Cognitions (thoughts)	Affect (feelings/emotions)
High Effort Central-Route Processing (Chapter 5)	• Direct or imagined experience • Reasoning by analogy or category • Values-driven attitudes • Social identity-based attitude generation • Analytical attitude construction	• Emotional processing • Affective response • Attitude toward the ad
Low Effort Peripheral-Route Processing (Chapter 6)	• Simple beliefs • Unconscious influences • The environment	• The mere exposure effect • Classical conditioning • Attitude toward the ad • Mood

Consumers' elaboration (consideration) of a message (based on their motivation, ability, and opportunity [MAO])

Exhibit 5.1

General Approaches to Attitude Formation and Change

Consumers can form attitudes in four basic ways, depending on whether elaboration is high or low and whether the processing is cognitive or affective. This chapter examines the ways in which attitudes can be formed and changed when consumer effort is high.

Central-route processing
The attitude formation and change process when effort is high.

Peripheral-route processing
The attitude formation and change process when effort is low.

or changing attitudes and making decisions. Some researchers have used the term **central-route processing** to describe the process of attitude formation and change when thinking about a message requires some effort.[9] Processing is central because consumers' attitudes are based on a careful and effortful analysis of the true merits or central issues contained within the message. As a result of this extensive and laborious processing, consumers form strong, accessible, and confidently held attitudes that are persistent and resistant to change.

When MAO is low, however, consumers' attitudes are based on a more tangential or superficial analysis of the message, not on an effortful analysis of its true merits. Because these attitudes tend to be based on peripheral or superficial cues contained within the message, the term **peripheral-route processing** has been used to describe attitude formation and change that involves limited effort (or low elaboration) on the part of the consumer.

This chapter focuses on several ways in which consumers form and change attitudes when effort (i.e., MAO) is high. The next chapter focuses on how consumers form and change attitudes when effort is low. Because attitudes tend to be more accessible, persistent, resistant to change, and held with confidence when consumers' MAO to process information is high, much of the chapter focuses on what affects the favorability of consumers' attitudes.

As shown in Exhibit 5.2, when consumers are likely to devote a lot of effort to processing information, marketers can influence consumer attitudes either (1) *cognitively*—influencing the thoughts or beliefs they have about the offering or (2) *affectively*—influencing the emotional experiences consumers associate with the offering. Furthermore, marketers can try to influence consumers' attitudes through characteristics of the source used in a persuasive communication, the type of message used, or some combination of both. After attitudes are formed, they may play a powerful role in influencing consumers' intentions and actual behavior.

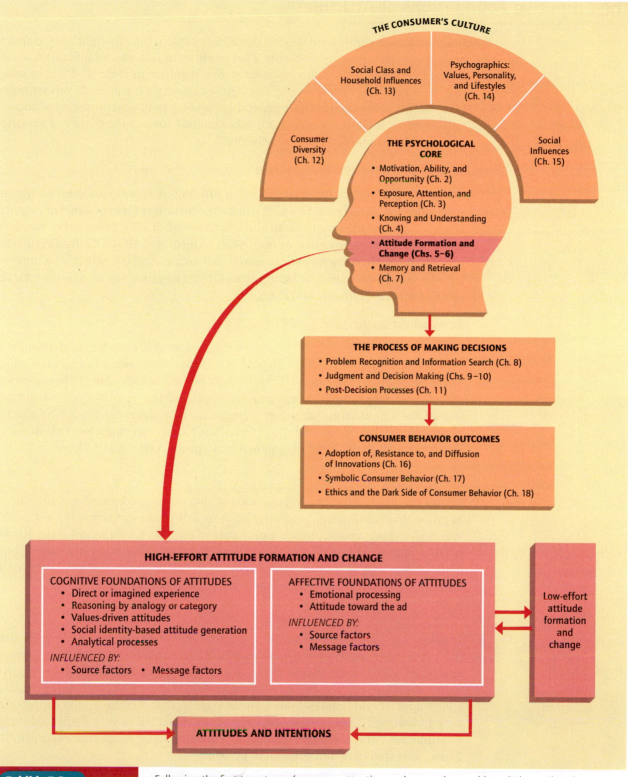

Exhibit 5.2

Chapter Overview: Attitude Formation and Change, High Consumer Effort

Following the first two stages (exposure, attention, and perception; and knowledge and understanding), consumers can either form or change their attitudes. This chapter explains how consumers form high-effort attitudes based on both cognition and affect. It also shows how marketers can influence attitudes through source factors and message factors.

The Cognitive Foundations of Attitudes

Researchers have proposed various theories to explain how thoughts are related to attitudes when consumers devote a lot of effort to processing information and making decisions. This section focuses on five cognitive models: (1) direct or imagined experience, (2) reasoning by analogy or category, (3) values-driven attitudes, (4) social identity-based attitude generation, and (5) analytical processes of attitude construction, including expectancy-value models such as the theory of reasoned action and the theory of planned behavior.

Direct or Imagined Experience

Elaborating on actual experience with a product or service (or even imagining what that experience could be like) can help consumers form positive or negative attitudes. You are likely to form an attitude after test-driving a new car or watching a movie preview, for instance, or even likely to form an attitude by imagining what it would be like to drive that car or watch that movie. And you will have a more favorable attitude toward that laptop brand if you use imagery to elaborate on the positive aspects of buying and using it.[10]

Reasoning by Analogy or Category

Consumers also form attitudes by considering how similar a product is to other products or to a particular product category. If you have never sipped a chilled bottle of Starbucks Frappuccino, but you think it might be similar to the hot Starbucks coffees that you like, for example, your reasoning would lead you to form a positive attitude toward the Frappuccino. As another example, if a new digital camera is advertised as having the versatile functionality of a Swiss Army knife, you might form a positive attitude toward it because the analogy involves a product you like (the knife).[11]

Values-Driven Attitudes

Another way that attitudes are generated or shaped is based on individual values.[12] Suppose that environmental protection is one of your most strongly held values. When you think about buying a new pair of sneakers, you might have a more positive attitude about a brand that uses recycled materials than you would about a brand that uses materials that cannot be recycled. Here, your values drive the formation of your attitude toward a particular brand or product.

Social Identity-Based Attitude Generation

The way that consumers view their own social identities can play a role in forming their attitudes toward products or brands. If you consider yourself a very serious sports fan, for instance, that may be a defining aspect of your identity. In turn, you will tend to form positive attitudes toward a brand or product (such as the brand of sports apparel endorsed by your favorite athlete) that enables you to express this social identity.[13] Thus, consumers who see themselves as very dedicated skateboarding fans may form positive feelings toward Drake Riddiough's sponsor, DC Shoes, after watching him perform in person.

Analytical Processes of Attitude Formation

Consumers sometimes use a more analytical process of attitude formation in which, after being exposed to marketing stimuli or other information, they form

Cognitive responses Thoughts we have in response to a communication.

attitudes based on their cognitive responses. **Cognitive responses** are the thoughts a person has when he or she is exposed to a communication, which may take the form of recognitions, evaluations, associations, images, or ideas.[14] Suppose a man sees an ad for the impotency drug Cialis. In response, he might think, "I really need a product like this," "This product will never work," or "The guy in the ad was paid to praise this product." These spontaneously generated thoughts will, according to cognitive response models, influence his attitude toward Cialis.[15] Positive thoughts can have a favorable impact on attitudes, whereas negative thoughts can have a negative effect.

Cognitive Responses to Communications

According to the cognitive response model, consumers exert a lot of effort in responding to the message—enough effort to generate counterarguments, support arguments, and source derogations.

Counterarguments (CAs) Thoughts that disagree with the message.

Support arguments (SAs) Thoughts that agree with the message.

Source derogations (SDs) Thoughts that discount or attack the source of the message.

- **Counterarguments (CAs)** are thoughts that express disagreement with the message. In the earlier example of a man seeing an ad for Cialis, such thoughts might be "This product will never work" or "This product will not cure my problem."

- **Support arguments (SAs)** are thoughts that express agreement with the message. The man may think "This sounds great" or "I really need a product like this."

- **Source derogations (SDs)** are thoughts that discount or attack the message source. Seeing the Cialis ad, the man might think "The guy is lying" or "The guy in the ad was paid to say this."

Counterarguments and source derogations, in particular, result in a less favorable initial attitude or resistance to attitude change. Thoughts like "It will never work" or "The guy was paid to say this" are likely to lead to a negative attitude toward Cialis. However, consumers do not blindly accept and follow suggestions made in persuasive messages; rather, they may use their knowledge about marketers' goals or tactics to effectively cope with or resist these messages.[16] In fact, consumers do think about how marketers try to influence consumer behavior—and, in turn, these thoughts allow consumers to formulate counterarguments or support arguments in response to marketing activities.[17] Moreover, the presence of support arguments ("This sounds great") results in positive attitudes toward the offering.

Research shows that when consumers resist persuasion and become aware of their own resistance, this awareness reinforces their initial attitudes. In high-elaboration situations, consumers confronted with a persuasive message that conflicts with their own attitudes will generate counterarguments that strengthen their initial attitudes—but only when the message is from an expert source.[18]

MARKETING IMPLICATIONS

Although marketers want consumers to be exposed to and to comprehend their marketing messages, they also want consumers' responses to be positive rather than negative. Consumers who generate counterarguments and source derogations will have weak or even negative attitudes toward an offering. To combat this reaction, marketers should test consumers' cognitive responses to their communications before placing ads in the media. By asking consumers to think aloud while they view the ad or to record their thoughts right after seeing it, marketers can classify the responses, identify problems, and strengthen the message.

Consumers tend to generate more counterarguments and fewer support arguments when the message content differs from what they already believe. Thus, a message supporting handgun control will generate a lot of counterarguments among National Rifle Association members. This **belief discrepancy** creates more counterarguments because consumers want to maintain their existing belief structures and do so by arguing against the message.[19] Consumers also generate more counterarguments and fewer support arguments when the message is weak. For example, saying that Gillette disposable razors come in many colors is not a strong and compelling reason to buy one. In such a situation, consumers may derogate the source (Gillette) or generate counterarguments ("Who cares about color?").[20]

Consumers come up with more support arguments and fewer counterarguments when they are involved with the TV program in which a commercial appears. The program distracts consumers from counterarguing, enhancing the persuasive impact of the message.[21] Another way to decrease counterarguments is through the *disrupt-then-reframe technique*. Disrupting consumers' cognitive processing of the communication in an odd but subtle way ("$4 a day—only 400 pennies per day") clears the way for more effective persuasion when the message is reframed (with a statement such as "this is an incredible bargain").[22] Finally, consumers react more favorably to communications when they are in a good mood: They often want to preserve this mood, so they resist counterarguing.[23]

Expectancy-Value Models

Expectancy-value models are analytical processes that explain how consumers form and change attitudes based on (1) the beliefs or knowledge they have about an object or action and (2) their evaluation of these particular beliefs.[24] According to this model, you might like a Volkswagen because you believe it is reliable, modestly priced, and stylish—and you think it is good for a car to have these traits.

The expectancy-value model known as the **theory of reasoned action (TORA)** provides an expanded picture of how, when, and why attitudes predict consumer behavior, particularly in the United States.[25] As shown in Exhibit 5.3, the model proposes that **behavior (B)** is a function of a person's **behavioral intention (BI)**, which in turn is determined by (1) the person's **attitude toward the act (A_{act})** and (2) the **subjective norms (SN)** that operate in the situation. Consistent with most expectancy-value models, A_{act} is determined by the consumer's *beliefs* (b_i) about the consequences of engaging in the behavior and the consumer's *evaluation* (e_i) of these consequences. Subjective norms are determined by the consumer's *normative beliefs* (NB_i)—or what the consumer thinks someone else wants him or her to do—and the consumer's *motivation to comply* (MC_i) with this person.

Note that the TORA model takes into account how other people in the social environment influence consumer behavior. In some situations, **normative influences** from others can play a powerful role in how people behave. Also, trying to predict behavioral intentions from attitudes, as in the TORA model, is much easier than trying to predict actual behaviors because many situational factors could cause a consumer not to engage in an intended behavior.[26] For example, you may *intend* to buy a Volkswagen, but you may not because you are short of money.

The TORA model assumes that attitudes are accessible since they can only guide behavior if consumers can retrieve them. Attitude confidence and less ambivalence will also increase the relationship between attitudes and behavior.[27] In addition, an extension of TORA, the **theory of planned behavior,** seeks to

---

Belief discrepancy When a message is different from what consumers believe.

Expectancy-value model A widely used model that explains how attitudes form and change.

Theory of reasoned action (TORA) A model that provides an explanation of how, when, and why attitudes predict behavior.

Behavior (B) What we do.

Behavioral intention (BI) What we intend to do.

Attitude toward the act (A_{act}) How we feel about doing something.

Subjective norms (SN) How others feel about our doing something.

Normative influences How other people influence our behavior through social pressure.

Theory of planned behavior An extension of the TORA model that predicts behaviors over which consumers perceive they have control.

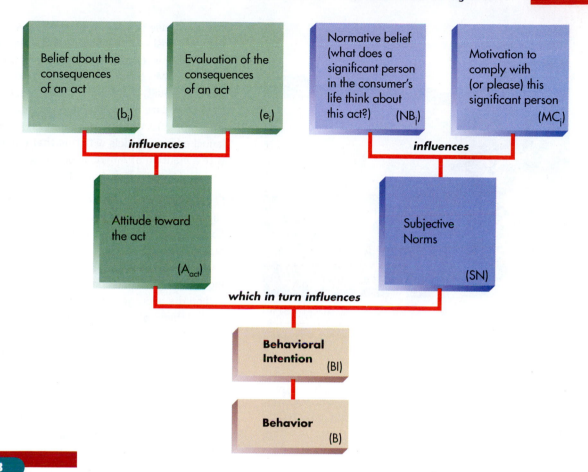

Exhibit 5.3

The Theory of Reasoned Action

TORA is an expectancy-value model that proposes how beliefs influence attitudes and norms, which in turn affect behavior.

predict behaviors over which consumers have incomplete control by examining their perceived behavioral control.[28] For instance, older consumers who see an ad promoting the health benefits of taking blood pressure medication will be more likely to obtain and take the product if they form a positive attitude toward making this change, form intentions to change, and perceive that they have some control over this consumption behavior.

MARKETING IMPLICATIONS

Marketers need to understand not only what attitudes consumers have but also why consumers have these attitudes and how these attitudes can be changed. The TORA model, for instance, is useful for analyzing the reasons why consumers may like or dislike an offering, whether they intend to engage in or resist a behavior, and who else might be influential and therefore should also be targeted.

Such models also provide useful guidance on how marketers can change attitudes, intentions, and (marketers hope) behavior through these major strategies:

1. *Change beliefs.* One possible strategy would be to change the strength of the beliefs that consumers associate with the consequences of acquiring an offering. Marketers could try to (1) strengthen beliefs that the offering has positive, important consequences or (2) lessen the belief that it has negative consequences. Although marketers

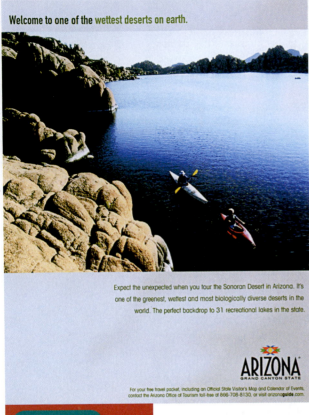

Welcome to one of the wettest deserts on earth.

Expect the unexpected when you tour the Sonoran Desert in Arizona. It's one of the greenest, wettest and most biologically diverse deserts in the world. The perfect backdrop to 31 recreational lakes in the state.

ARIZONA
GRAND CANYON STATE

For your free travel packet, including an Official State Visitor's Map and Calendar of Events, contact the Arizona Office of Tourism toll-free at 866-708-8130, or visit arizonaguide.com.

Exhibit 5.4

Arizona's Wet Desert

Most people believe that Arizona is a dry desert. This ad offers a new belief that Arizona has a wet region as well.

commonly use this strategy when consumers are more likely to consider the message, inducing such change is not easy when consumers have strong prior beliefs. For instance, GM's Saturn brand originally stood for small, American-built, reasonably priced cars. But Saturn was slow to update its styling, and the brand lost much of its luster. To change consumers' beliefs, GM has launched new models with ads that emphasize styling with a mention of American-made appeal: "Don't buy it because it's American. Buy it because it's amazing."[29]

2. *Change evaluations.* Another way to change attitudes is to change consumers' evaluations of the consequences. Consumers' attitudes become more positive when their beliefs are more positive or less negative. The American Chemistry Council, an industry group, is using advertising to change consumers' attitudes toward chemicals. "When the average person thinks about chemicals, [he or she] thinks about risks and hazards instead of benefits," observes the head of Nova Chemicals. "We've got to bridge that gap." The "essential2" campaign explains that chemicals are essential ingredients in many products that enhance consumers' quality of life.[30] Interestingly, research shows that a campaign promoting a product category winds up changing the relative importance of the attributes that consumers use to evaluate brands in that category.[31]

3. *Add a new belief.* A third strategy is to add a new belief altogether that would make the consumer's attitude more positive. This strategy is particularly effective when a brand has existing features that are considered inferior, quality perceived to be lower, or a higher price than that of its competitors.[32] Note that adding novel attributes to a low-complexity product is likely to encourage positive beliefs and a more positive attitude toward that product.[33] For instance, consumers may form a positive attitude toward Amazon.com's Kindle, a wireless electronic book reader priced higher than the competing Sony Reader, when they find out that Kindle can also access e-mail and retrieve blogs. Another example is illustrated in the ad in Exhibit 5.4.

4. *Encourage attitude formation based on imagined experience.* Marketers can communicate information through ads featuring vivid language, detailed pictures, or instructions to encourage consumers to imagine the experience. Doing this may produce positive brand attitudes as long as consumers are good at imagining things and as long as they focus on positive aspects rather than potentially negative aspects.[34] For example, Blendtec's "Will it blend?" videos, posted on YouTube, show the company's blenders ripping apart iPods and cell phones. These videos help consumers imagine how well the appliance will "blend a margarita and get rid of that big chunk of ice," says Blendtec's director of marketing.[35]

5. *Target normative beliefs.* Another strategy is to develop communications that specifically target strong normative beliefs as a way of influencing behavior. Northern Illinois University has successfully used a normative campaign to reduce heavy

drinking by letting students know that most students have fewer than five drinks when partying.[36] On the other hand, condom ads have been unsuccessful in increasing sales because they have *not* stressed normative beliefs (what others will think of you if you do not use them).[37] The importance of normative beliefs does, however, vary across cultures. In countries that stress group values over those of the individual (such as Japan, among other Asian nations), appeals to normative beliefs take on greater significance.[38]

How Cognitively Based Attitudes Are Influenced

As Exhibit 5.2 indicates, both the communication source and the message influence how favorable a consumer's attitude will be. Here we explore how marketing communications can affect consumers' cognitively based attitudes when the processing effort is extensive.

Communication Source

Among consumers who process information extensively, those with attitudes based on cognitions are likely to be influenced by believable information. This means that marketing messages must be credible to generate support arguments, restrict counterarguments and source derogations, and increase belief strength. Several factors, including source credibility and company reputation, enhance the credibility of a message.

Source Credibility

Credibility Extent to which the source is trustworthy, expert, or has status.

In many marketing messages, information is presented by a spokesperson, usually a celebrity, an actor, a company representative, or a real consumer. In a sales situation, the salesperson is a spokesperson for the company and the offering. Both the **credibility** of these sources and the credibility of the company influence consumers' attitudes.[39] According to research, consumers tend to evaluate product information more thoughtfully when source credibility is low than when source credibility is high.[40]

Sources are credible when they have one or more of three characteristics: trustworthiness, expertise, and status. First, someone perceived as trustworthy is more likely to be believed than someone who is not. Because consumers tend to see other consumers' opinions as less biased than persuasive words from official sources, they will check product reviews posted on BizRate.com and other websites where consumers comment on offerings.[41]

Second, we are more likely to accept a message from someone perceived as knowledgeable or as *an expert* about the topic than from someone who has no experience with it. A salesperson who demonstrates extensive product knowledge will be more credible than an uninformed one. Third, someone with a high position or social status can also be perceived as credible; this is the reason why many firms feature their CEOs or founders in their ads. In Latin America, having products endorsed by famous and respected people is an effective technique, particularly in Venezuela and Mexico. Pepsi, for example, features the Latin pop star Shakira in some Spanish-language ads.[42]

Research shows that credible sources have considerable impact on the acceptance of the message when consumers' prior attitudes are negative, when the message deviates greatly from their prior beliefs, when the message is complex or difficult to understand, and when there is a good "match" between product and endorser, as there is between preteen skateboarder Drake Riddiough and his footwear sponsor, DC Shoes.[43] Moreover, source credibility can influence consumer attitudes by influencing consumers' confidence in their thoughts about the ad message.[44]

Yet credible sources will have less impact when consumers hold their existing attitude with confidence (so that even a credible source will not convince them otherwise) and when they have a high degree of ability to generate their own conclusions from the message (they have a lot of product-relevant knowledge, particularly if it is based on direct experience).[45] Also, consumers are less likely to believe that a source is credible when the source (e.g., a celebrity) endorses multiple products.[46] Finally, trust is an important element of credibility for spokescharacters such as the GEICO gekko or Pillsbury Doughboy. Specifically, trust in a spokescharacter results in favorable brand attitudes if the consumer has had little experience with that brand.[47]

MARKETING IMPLICATIONS

Robert DeNiro and George Foreman have been successful endorsers because consumers perceive these celebrities as honest and straightforward.[48] Likewise, consumers might perceive a salesperson who has an "honest face" as a credible source of information. Ordinary people can also be perceived as credible endorsers. Companies such as Home Depot and Wal-Mart have featured employees in their advertising campaigns because the employees add realism and, in many cases, are similar to the target market.[49] In addition, Latin American consumers tend to give positive evaluations to ads featuring real people.[50]

Because of their skill, sports figures like Peyton Manning, Andy Roddick, and Serena Williams have been successful expert sources for athletic apparel and equipment as well as for other products.[51] Expert sources can also be popular, another factor that can contribute to an effective ad. Interestingly, one survey indicated that women endorsers are often seen as more popular and credible than male endorsers.[52] However, the company or product risks losing some credibility if a celebrity endorser gets into trouble or quits. Nike, for instance, cancelled its endorsement contract with football star Michael Vick after he pleaded guilty to charges of illegal dog-fighting.[53]

However, a low-credibility source *can* be effective in some circumstances. In particular, if a low-credibility source argues against his or her own self-interest, positive attitude change can result.[54] Political ads, for example, often feature a member of the opposing party who endorses a rival candidate. In addition, the impact of a low-credibility source can actually increase over time (assuming the message is powerful). This **sleeper effect** occurs because the consumer's memory of the source can decay more rapidly than his or her memory of the message.[55] Thus, consumers may remember the message but not the source.

Sleeper effect Consumers forget the source of a message more quickly than they forget the message.

Company Reputation

When marketing communications do not feature an actual person, consumers judge credibility by the reputation of the company delivering the message.[56] People are more likely to believe—and change their attitudes based on— messages from companies with a reputation for producing quality products, dealing fairly with consumers, or being trustworthy. Online, a company can enhance its reputation and engender positive reactions by sponsoring content on relevant websites; banner ads highly targeted to a site's audience can also elicit positive attitudes toward the company.[57] More specifically, a brand's perceived trustworthiness exerts more influence on consumers' consideration and behavior than its expertise.[58]

MARKETING IMPLICATIONS

Knowing that reputation influences consumer perceptions and credibility, many companies devote considerable time and money to developing a positive image through corporate advertising. As shown in Exhibit 5.5, a company's environmental record can affect buyers' attitudes and behavior. Many firms use advertising and public relations to communicate their involvement in environmental initiatives. For instance, the energy company BP has spent millions of dollars on an image-building "Beyond Petroleum" ad campaign showcasing its environmental conservation activities.[59]

The Message

Just as consumers evaluate whether or not the source is credible when their processing effort is high, they also evaluate whether or not the message is credible. Three factors affect the credibility of a message: the quality of its argument, whether it is a one-sided or two-sided message, and whether it is a comparative message.

Argument Quality

Strong argument A presentation that features the best or central merits of an offering in a convincing manner.

One of the most critical factors affecting whether a message is credible concerns whether it uses strong arguments.[60] **Strong arguments** present the best features or central merits of an offering in a convincing manner. Messages can also present supporting research or endorsements, such as the *Good Housekeeping* Seal or *Consumer's Digest* Best Buy designation (see Exhibit 5.6). Strong arguments are

---

Exhibit 5.5

Is the Company Eco-Friendly?

Depending on their gender and region of the country, consumers vary in their views of the importance of a company's eco-friendliness when making their decisions.

GOOD COMPANY

Whereas Westerners have a reputation for being earth conscious, Northeasterners are actually more impressed by companies known for being eco-friendly.

Percentage of Americans who say that the following factors would influence their decision to buy a given product:

	GENDER		REGION			
	Men	Women	Northeast	Midwest	South	West
Safe for the environment	76%	84%	83%	81%	78%	80%
Company is known for using environmentally friendly practices	65%	75%	78%	71%	68%	67%
Company is known for treating workers well	62%	69%	67%	63%	69%	60%
Portion of sale goes to charity	46%	62%	53%	58%	56%	50%

Source: Reprinted with permission from the October 2003 issue of *American Demographics.* Copyright Crain Communications, Inc. 2003.

Carpet you'll love from a name you already know and TRUST.

Good Housekeeping™

Carpet One has worked closely with the Good Housekeeping Institute to develop carpet that will fit your family's lifestyle. Tested for durability, safety and quality. Good Housekeeping Carpet is backed by the prestigious Good Housekeeping Seal. Now the name you already know and trust brings you a collection of beautiful and comfortable carpet, available exclusively at Carpet One stores.
For a Carpet One store near you, call 1-800-CARPET-1 or visit carpetone.com.
Good Housekeeping is a trademark of Hearst Communications, Inc.

CARPET ONE
More Floors. More Choices.

Exhibit 5.6

Argument Quality: Good Housekeeping Seal

When a company announces that its products or services have won awards or endorsements from independent organizations such as *Good Housekeeping* the company's advertising can become more credible and convincing to consumers.

likely to be more persuasive if consumers are exposed to such messages after thinking about what they could have done differently to avoid a purchasing experience that led to an undesirable outcome.[61] In addition, strong arguments have a greater effect on behavioral intentions when consumers focus on the process of using the product rather than on the outcome of using it, especially for low- to moderate-involvement products.[62] Combining a strong argument with an implicit conclusion in an ad message engenders more favorable brand attitudes and buying intensions among consumers with a high need for cognition.[63] Moreover, consumers are more persuaded by a message containing a strong argument when they devote sufficient cognitive resources to processing the information.[64]

Infomercials—commercial messages that can last 30 to 60 minutes—allow companies enough time to fully explain complicated, technologically advanced, or innovative goods and services. Numerous firms, including Nikon and Humana Healthcare, have successfully used infomercials to present strong arguments and sell offerings. Internet advertising enables companies to supplement complicated messages with convincing information and to have a positive impact on consumers.[65]

(MARKETING IMPLICATIONS)

If messages are weak, consumers are unlikely to think that they offer credible reasons for buying. Saying that a person should buy a particular brand of mattress because it comes in decorator fabrics is not very convincing. Nevertheless, messages do not always have to focus on substantive features of a product or service. Less important features can actually play a key role in influencing consumers' attitudes when brands are similar and many competitors emphasize the same important attributes.[66] Also, a message should match the amount of effort consumers want to use to process it. A message that is too simple or too complicated is unlikely to be persuasive.[67]

One- versus Two-Sided Messages

One-sided message A marketing message that presents only positive information.

Two-sided message A marketing message that presents both positive and negative information.

Most marketing messages present only positive information. These are called **one-sided messages.** In some instances, however, a **two-sided message,** containing both positive and negative information about an offering, can be effective. For example, Buckley's Cough Mixture is marketed throughout North America using blunt two-sided ad messages such as "It tastes awful. And it works" and "Disgustingly effective."[68] Like strong arguments, two-sided messages may affect consumers' attitudes by making the message more credible (that is, they increase belief strength) and reducing counterarguments. When consumers see negative information in an ad, they are likely to infer that the company is honest, a belief that adds to source credibility.[69] By providing reasons for consumers to be interested in the offering despite these problems, the ad encourages consumers to add a new belief. Note that the persuasive effect of two-sided messages depends, in part, on how much negative information is presented and on the interplay of negative and positive attributes.[70]

MARKETING IMPLICATIONS

Two-sided messages seem to be particularly effective (1) when consumers are initially opposed to the offering (they already have negative beliefs) or (2) when they will be exposed to strong countermessages from competitors.[71] Two-sided messages are also well received by more intelligent consumers, who prefer neutral, unbiased messages. The Hardee's restaurant chain once used a campaign both to acknowledge consumers' complaints and to introduce its new Thickburgers. The campaign's slogan, "It's how the last place you'd go for a burger will become the first," was a direct appeal to transform negative attitudes into positive attitudes.[72] However, the use of two-sided advertising is not always in the marketer's best interest. In general, the positive effects of two-sided messages on brand attitudes occur only if the negative message is about an attribute that is not extremely important. ◼▬

Comparative Messages

Comparative messages Messages that make direct comparisons with competitors.

Comparative messages show how much better the offering is than a competitor's. Two types of comparative messages have been identified.[73] The most common type is the *indirect comparative message*, in which the offering is compared with those of unnamed competitors (such as "other leading brands" or "Brand X"). This strategy can improve consumers' perceptions of a moderate-share brand relative to other moderate-share brands (but not to the market leader).[74] Marketers must remember, however, that the effectiveness of comparative advertising differs from culture to culture.[75] In Korea, a culture that values harmony, comparative advertising seems overly confrontational and is rarely used, whereas this technique is frequently used in the United States.

With *direct comparative advertising*, advertisers explicitly name and attack a competitor or set of competitors on the basis of an attribute or benefit. This approach is usually used when the offering has a feature that is purportedly better than that of a competitor's. For instance, Apple has used ads to compare its easy-to-use computer operating systems with those made by Microsoft for PCs.[76] Salespeople frequently use this technique to convince consumers of the advantages of their offering over the competition. Comparative advertising is also used in political campaigns, where it generates more counterarguments and fewer source derogations than negative political advertising does. This result may be due to the different styles of information processing that the two types of messages encourage.[77] However, consumers exposed to negative political messages find them less useful for decision making and have more negative attitudes toward political campaigns than do consumers exposed to positive political advertising.[78]

In general, direct comparative messages are effective in generating attention and brand awareness and in positively increasing message processing, attitudes, intentions, and behavior.[79] (See Exhibit 5.7.) They do not, however, have high credibility, as noted earlier. These messages are particularly effective for new brands or low-market-share brands attempting to take sales away from more popular brands.[80] Advertising for the new or low-share brand can enhance consumers'

In the race against teething pain,
30 minutes is too long to wait...

Baby Orajel Wins!

Baby Orajel works on contact to relieve teething pain instantly, not up to 30 minutes like Children's Tylenol, Children's Advil or Hyland's, which all have to work their way through a baby's system to start to provide relief.

Baby Orajel is fast, safe & effective. No wonder it's the #1 pediatrician recommended brand. In fact, it's trusted by more moms & pediatricians than all other teething brands combined.

Nothing beats Baby Orajel

Use as directed. Another fine product from © Del Pharmaceuticals 2008. For information: 1-800-952-5080 or www.babyorajel.com. Tylenol® is a registered trademark of McNeil. Advil® is a registered trademark of Wyeth Consumer Healthcare. Hyland's™ is a trademark of Hyland's Inc. and are not associated with Del Pharmaceuticals, Inc. or its products.

Exhibit 5.7

Comparative Advertising

One type of strong argument is to make a direct comparison with the competition. In this comparative ad, Baby Orajel provides a strong reason why its brand is better than the three named brands.

attitudes by highlighting how the brand is different from or better than other brands, giving consumers a credible reason for purchasing it. In fact, comparative advertising that stresses differentiation can spur consumers to note the dissimilarities of competing brands.[81] Messages comparing two brands perceived as dissimilar will elicit more elaboration, especially among consumers with a low need for cognition, precisely because the brands are different.[82]

Comparative messages are especially effective when they contain other elements that make them believable—such as a credible source or objective and verifiable claims (a strong argument)[83]—and when the featured attribute or benefit is important within the product category.[84] Still, a message that indirectly indicates a brand's superiority on featured attributes when compared with all competitors is more effective at positioning that brand within the overall market than a noncomparative or direct comparison ad is.[85] Also, consumers who originally receive information in a noncomparative ad and are then exposed to a comparative ad will revise their evaluations more than they will when subsequently exposed to another noncomparative ad.[86] Comparative ads that refer to competitors in a negative way are perceived as less believable and more biased; they cause consumers to develop more counterarguments and fewer support arguments than do comparative ads without negative competitive references.[87]

Marketers should also consider consumers' goals when preparing comparative ads. Promotion-focused consumers, whose goal is to maximize their gains and positive outcomes, will be more responsive to claims that Brand X is superior to Brand Y; prevention-focused consumers, who want to minimize their loss and risk, will be more skeptical of superiority claims and more responsive to claims that Brand X is similar or equivalent to Brand Y.[88] Note that positively framed comparative messages (Brand X performs better than Brand Y) are more effective for promotion-focused consumers, whereas negatively framed messages (Brand Y has more problems than Brand X) are more effective for prevention-focused consumers.[89] Positively framed comparative messages encourage more cognitive processing and prompt consumers to consider other brand information—sparking their buying intentions if the additional information supports the positive argument.[90]

MARKETING IMPLICATIONS

Direct comparative messages are best used when consumers' MAO to process the message is high. When MAO is high, consumers exert more effort in processing the message and are less likely to confuse the advertised brand with its competition.[91] Further, when consumers use analytical processing, a comparative ad will be more persuasive than a noncomparative ad; when consumers use imagery processing, a noncomparative ad will be more persuasive.[92] The Subway sandwich chain has used comparative messages urging consumers to "buy our sandwich instead of their hamburger," says one of its marketing executives, a directive that helps consumers make a decision between fast-food categories based on attributes such as nutrition.[93] Bear in mind that comparative messages are not useful in changing a consumer's negative first impression of a brand or company, however.[94]

All information contained in a comparative message must be factual and verifiable; otherwise, competitors may consider taking legal action. Although comparative ads are widely used in the United States and Latin America, they are illegal in some countries and closely regulated in the European Union.[95] Some consumers dislike comparative advertising. Japanese consumers, for example, respond better to a softer sell than they do to comparative ads.[96] Finally, messages that compare a company's new, improved product to the same company's original product will be effective only when the improved functions are seen as atypical for that product. Otherwise, consumers are likely to discount the novelty of the new functionality.[97]

The Affective (Emotional) Foundations of Attitudes

Affective involvement
Expending emotional energy and heightened feelings regarding an offering or activity.

Most of the early consumer research on attitudes when MAO and processing effort are high has focused on the cognitive models of attitude formation. Now, however, researchers are recognizing that consumers might exert a lot of mental energy in processing a message on an emotional basis. Emotional reactions, independent of cognitive structure, may serve as a powerful way of creating attitudes that are favorable, enduring, and resistant to change.[98] This section examines when and how attitudes can be changed through consumers' feelings when MAO and processing effort are high.

When **affective involvement** with an object or decision is high, consumers can experience fairly strong emotional reactions to or engagement with a stimulus. *Engagement* refers to the extent to which consumers are emotionally connected to a product or ad.[99] A high level of engagement means strong feelings that can, in turn, influence attitudes. In this case the consumer's *feelings* act as a source of information, and consumers will rely on these feelings to evaluate the stimulus.[100]

Feelings are more likely to influence attitude change when they fit with or are viewed as relevant to the offering.[101] For example, someone who is in love might have a *more positive attitude* toward an expensive perfume than someone who is not experiencing this emotion would. Feelings can also be a factor when consumers see others experiencing strong emotion while using an offering or when situational factors hamper the consumer's effort to develop a cognitive attitude.[102] Thus, consumers under severe time pressure could simply recall a previous emotional experience rather than develop a cognitive attitude.

In marketing situations, certain factors can activate experiences or episodes from memory that may be associated with strong emotions.[103] For example, you might experience positive emotions such as joy and excitement if you suddenly see an ad for the car you just bought. If you are a dog lover, you might experience affective involvement toward a message featuring a cute dog. It is small wonder that dogs have, in fact, been included in print advertising for decades.[104]

i promise
to go where you go

canine cuisine in 15 gourmet flavors
love them back with **cesar**

Exhibit 5.8

Man's Best Friend in Advertising

Pet owners feel strong emotions toward their dogs. Thus, a picture of a cute dog can be used to stimulate these strong emotions.

Affective responses When consumers generate feelings and images in response to a message.

Emotional appeals Messages designed to elicit an emotional response.

Attitudes can also be formed through an emotional route to persuasion called *regulatory fit*. Recall that Chapter 2 identified two types of goals consumers might have—promotion- and prevention-focused. Consumers with promotion-focused goals are motivated to act in ways to achieve positive outcomes, focusing on hopes, wants, and accomplishments. In contrast, consumers with prevention-focused goals are motivated to act in ways that avoid negative outcomes, focusing on responsibilities, safety, and guarding against risks.

Research suggests that a consumer's attitude toward a product depends on the fit between the consumer's goal and the strategies available to achieve that goal. For example, a promotion-focused consumer who sees an ad showing how great it feels to drive a certain car (i.e., the ad fits her promotion goal) will be more persuaded than if the ad emphasized safety features. The ad emphasizing safety would, in fact, be more persuasive for consumers with prevention-focused goals. Why? People just feel right when there is a fit between their regulatory goals and the strategies available to help them achieve their goals. This feeling makes them more certain about their attitude evaluation and more likely to regard their attitude or choice as valuable.[105]

When consumers are emotionally involved in a message, they tend to process it on a general level rather than analytically.[106] This process involves the generation of images or feelings, called **affective responses** (or ARs),[107] rather than cognitive responses. In fact, affective responses are generally more influential than cognitive responses in shaping consumers' attitudes toward trying a product.[108] Affective responses are particularly important when the ad builds toward a "peak emotional experience."[109] Consumers can either recall an emotional experience from memory or vicariously place themselves in the situation and experience the emotions associated with it.[110] These feelings will then influence their attitudes. Consumers focused on goals involving their hopes and aspirations tend to rely on their affective responses to an ad, whereas consumers focused on their responsibilities and obligations tend to rely more on message content.[111]

Cross-cultural differences can also influence the effectiveness of **emotional appeals.** One study found that messages evoking ego-focused responses (such as pride or happiness) led to more favorable attitudes in group-oriented cultures, whereas empathetic messages led to more positive attitudes in individualistic cultures.[112] The reason for this apparent reversal is that the appeal's novelty or uniqueness increases the motivation to process and consider the message.

Negative emotions sometimes have a positive effect on attitude change. In one study, the exposure to a public service announcement about child abuse initially created negative emotions (sadness, anger, fear) but then led to a feeling of empathy, and this response led to a decision to help.[113] In addition, consumers can actively try to avoid making decisions associated with strong negative emotions by making choices to minimize these emotions.[114]

Note that cognition can still influence whether experienced feelings will affect consumer attitudes. For feelings to have a direct impact on their attitudes, consumers must cognitively link them to the offering.[115] To illustrate, if you saw a bank ad showing a tender scene of a father holding his baby, you might experience an immediate emotional response (warmth and joy). However, this feeling will affect your attitude toward the bank only if you consciously make a connection between the feeling and the bank ("This bank makes me feel good" or "I like this bank because it cares about people"). Also, an advertising message that relies on emotional appeal will be more effective in helping heavy users of the product access the brand name than in helping light users access the brand name.[116]

MARKETING IMPLICATIONS

Marketers can try to influence emotions as a way of affecting consumer attitudes. In particular, marketers can try to ensure that the emotions experienced in a particular situation will be positive. Car salespeople, for example, may try to do everything possible to make customers happy so that they will develop positive attitudes toward the dealer and the car. The importance of creating positive emotions also explains why airlines, financial institutions, and other service providers place a high value on being friendly. Southwest Airlines has earned a customer-friendly reputation because, says its president, "we just kill them [passengers] with kindness and caring and attention."[117]

Marketing communications can potentially trigger strong emotions in consumers, although the ability to trigger these emotions is typically quite limited—ads are better at creating low-level moods than they are at creating intense emotions. Think about how commercials that show people enjoying themselves in a McDonald's restaurant seek to put viewers in a good mood. Nevertheless, in situations in which affective involvement in the product or service is often high, marketers may be able to generate the images and feelings necessary to change attitudes. This outcome most often occurs in categories in which a strong pleasure-seeking or symbolic motivation is present—when feelings or symbolic meanings are critical. To illustrate, Mercedes has traded its informational advertising approach for a more emotional appeal. ◼️

How Affectively Based Attitudes Are Influenced

When MAO and effort are high and attitudes are affectively (emotionally) based, several strategies shown in Exhibit 5.1 can be employed to change attitudes. As with cognitively based attitudes, marketers can use characteristics of the source and the message to change consumers' attitudes by affecting their emotions.

The Source

Attractiveness A source characteristic that evokes favorable attitudes if a source is physically attractive, likable, familiar, or similar to ourselves.

Perceived **attractiveness** is an important source characteristic affecting high-effort emotionally based attitudes. Research on source attractiveness suggests that when consumers' MAO and effort are high, attractive sources tend to evoke favorable attitudes if the sources are appropriate for the offering category (e.g., a luxury automobile, fashion, cosmetics, and beauty treatments).[118] This effect has been

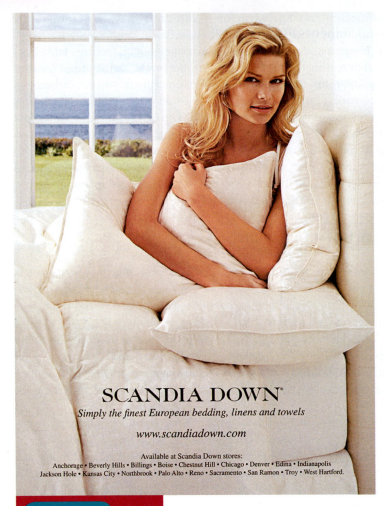

Exhibit 5.9

The Importance of Attractiveness

Ads often use attractive models to stimulate positive feelings toward the ad and the product. This ad for Scandia Down is a good example.

Match-up hypothesis The idea that the source must be appropriate for the product/service.

called the **match-up hypothesis** (the source should match the offering). The relevant attractive source probably enhances attitudes, either by making the ad informative and likable or by affecting consumers' beliefs that the product must be good. A source that is attractive but not relevant can distract the consumer from the message's ideas.[119]

American Express uses a variety of attractive and expert sources to communicate the benefits of its credit cards to consumers. In one recent campaign—"Are you a cardmember?"—Olympic champion snowboarder Shaun White is shown booking flights to snow-bound destinations using reward points he earned with his American Express card. "I need to be able to travel where I want, when I want," he tells the audience.[120] Research suggests that the match-up hypothesis may be even more powerful for expert sources than for attractive sources, the reason why White's endorsement of snowboard clothing made by Burton may be particularly effective.[121]

The relationship between attractiveness and attitude change applies to selling encounters as well. Consumers perceive physically attractive salespeople as having more favorable selling skills and are more likely to yield to their requests.[122] Customers also tend to be attracted to and to buy from salespeople whom they perceive as similar to themselves.[123]

MARKETING IMPLICATIONS

Although attractiveness is most often thought of in terms of physical features, sources can also be attractive if they are perceived as similar, likable, or familiar (in terms of physical appearance or opinions).[124] Basketball star Yao Ming has proven so likable (and become so familiar) that he now endorses a wide variety of offerings, including Reebok sneakers, Visa credit cards, and Coca-Cola soft drinks. Ming's celebrity has made him a valuable endorser in his home country, where he promotes the China Unicom cell-phone firm.[125]

The Message

Just as marketers can use characteristics of the source to understand and influence affective processing, they can also use characteristics of the message to influence consumers. In particular, emotional appeals and fear appeals are two important message characteristics.

Emotional Appeals

Marketers sometimes attempt to influence consumers' attitudes by using appeals that elicit emotions such as love, desire, joy, hope, excitement, daring, fear, anger, shame, or rejection. Disgust can be a powerful emotion that, even when stimulated unintentionally through humor or another aspect of an ad message, can engender negative attitudes and purchase intentions toward a brand or company.[126] The positive emotions are intended to attract consumers to the offering, whereas the negatives are intended to create anxiety about what might happen if consumers do not use the offering.

Messages can also present situations that express positive emotions with the hope that consumers will vicariously experience these emotions. In these situations marketers can induce consumers to imagine how good the product will make them feel or look. As an example, one ad for the impotency drug Viagra shows a happy dancing couple.[127] Similarly, McDonald's Happy Meals ads concentrate on the emotions surrounding this offering. "For parents, Happy Meal means happy memories; for kids, it means fun, favorite toys, and [entertainment] properties, and favorite food," explains a McDonald's executive. "The area between those is 'special moments,' which gave us the line 'Happy Meals for happy times.'"[128] When consumers are drawn into a message through warm, positive feelings, they become more interested and their attitudes become more positive toward the ad, especially if the message is affectively intense.[129] Yet emotional appeals based on conflicting emotions (such as happiness and sadness) can result in less favorable attitudes among consumers who are less accepting of such contradictions.[130]

However, emotional appeals may limit the amount of product-related information consumers can process.[131] This result can occur because consumers may be thinking more about feeling good than about the product's features, a situation that inhibits cognition about the product and its benefits. Thus, emotional appeals are more likely to be effective when the emotional arousal relates to product consumption or usage, an occurrence that is common when hedonic or symbolic motivations are important. Volvo switched the focus of some of its campaigns away from safety and toward "driving pleasure and excitement"—also adding the "Enjoy life" slogan—because the brand had developed such a strong image of a safe and stodgy vehicle.[132] Research suggests that emotional appeals more effectively influence consumer behavior when the type of product being advertised has been on the market for some time. In contrast, ads featuring expert sources and strong arguments are more effective for products in younger markets.[133]

MARKETING IMPLICATIONS

Typically, marketers attempt to arouse emotions by using techniques such as music, emotional scenes, visuals, sex, and attractive sources. In India, a commercial for Airtel wireless phone services seeks to connect emotionally with consumers by showing a special moment between father and son.[134] In the United Kingdom, commercials for Vicks Cough Syrup avoid medical terminology and instead focus on scenes and dialogue that emphasize emotional aspects of comfort, care, and wellness.[135] Note, however, that arousing emotions is a challenge unless the message has personal relevance for the consumer.[136]

Fear Appeals

Fear appeals Messages that stress negative consequences.

Fear appeals attempt to elicit fear or anxiety by stressing the negative consequences of either engaging or not engaging in a particular behavior. By arousing this fear, marketers hope consumers will be motivated to think about the message and behave in the desired manner.[137] But is fear an effective appeal? Early studies found that fear appeals were ineffective because consumers' perceptual defense helped them block

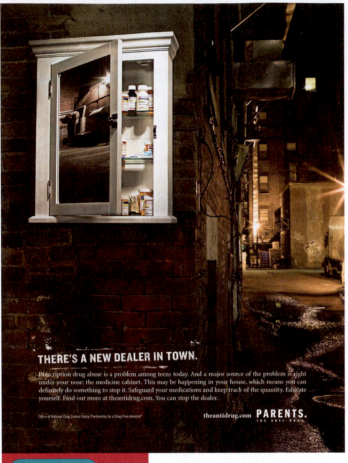

THERE'S A NEW DEALER IN TOWN.

Prescription drug abuse is a problem among teens today. And a major source of the problem is right under your nose: the medicine cabinet. This may be happening in your house, which means you can definitely do something to stop it. Safeguard your medications and keep track of the quantity. Educate yourself. Find out more at theantidrug.com. You can stop the dealer.

Office of National Drug Control Policy/Partnership for a Drug-Free America®

theantidrug.com **PARENTS.**
THE ANTI-DRUG.

Exhibit 5.10

Fear Appeal

Ads can use fear appeals to motivate consumers to action. This ad tries to generate fear among parents regarding teenage prescription drug abuse.

Terror management theory (TMT) A theory which deals with how we cope with the threat of death by defending our world view of values and beliefs.

out and ignore the message (due to its threatening nature).[138] This research provides one explanation of why the surgeon general's warning on cigarette packages and ads has been largely ineffective. However, more recent research indicates that fear appeals can work under certain conditions.[139] For example, fear appeals that evoke guilt, regret, or challenge can motivate behavior because they play to feelings of self-accountability that are experienced when the consumer does or does not do something, such as applying sunscreen to avoid cancer.[140]

Terror management theory (TMT) provides additional insight into the use of fear appeals. According to this theory, we develop a worldview of values and beliefs to cope with the terror of knowing that we will die someday, despite our innate impulse toward self-preservation. To avoid being paralyzed by anxiety, we may respond to messages that highlight the threat of death by more strongly defending our worldview. A high-fear appeal using a threat of fatal consequences may be ineffective, therefore, because consumers elaborate so much on the threat that they cannot process the message's suggested change in behavior. So the nature of the fear appeal—specifically, whether it makes mortality more salient—can influence consumers' emotions, their elaboration, and their attitudes.[141]

MARKETING IMPLICATIONS

When can fear appeals be effective? First, the appeal must suggest an immediate action that will reduce the consumer's fear. Second, the level of fear must be generally moderate.[142] If the fear induced is too intense (as it was in early studies), the consumer's perceptual defense will take over and the message will not have an impact. Third, at higher levels of involvement, lower levels of fear can be generated because the consumer has a higher motivation to process the information.[143] Factors such as personality, product usage, and socioeconomic status also have an impact on the effectiveness of fear appeals.[144] Finally, the source providing the information must be credible; otherwise, the consumer can easily discount the message by generating counterarguments and source derogations.

Attitude Toward the Ad

Attitude toward the ad (A_{ad}) Whether the consumer likes or dislikes an ad.

Although most attitude research has focused on consumers' attitude toward the brand, some evidence suggests that the overall **attitude toward the ad (A_{ad})** in which the brand is advertised will influence consumers' brand attitudes and behavior.[145] In other words, if we see an advertisement and like it, our liking for the ad may rub off on the brand and thereby make our brand attitude more positive.

Most A_{ad} research has been done in the context of low-effort processing. However, researchers are finding that A_{ad} can also have an impact when consumers devote considerable effort to processing the message. Three major factors have been found to lead to a positive A_{ad} in this context.[146]

First, more *informative* ads tend to be better liked and to generate positive responses.[147] These reactions to the ad will, in turn, have a positive influence on brand attitudes, a factor called the **utilitarian** (or **functional**) **dimension.** For example, consumers often like promotions on the Internet because these are seen as more informative than promotions in other media. On the other hand, consumers may have negative attitudes toward ads that are not informative. A good example is the rising negativity toward political ads that are viewed as "mudslinging" and that provide little useful information about the candidates.[148]

Second, consumers can like an ad if it creates positive feelings or emotions (the **hedonic dimension**).[149] We tend to like ads that either make us feel good or elicit positive experiences from our memory. This positive attitude can transfer to the brand and make our beliefs about the brand (b_i) more positive as well.[150] Marketers are also using a variety of techniques to make online advertising seem hip and fun. Ford, for example, recently launched a series of eight-minute advertising Webisodes, "Meet the Lucky Ones," featuring ten quirky characters who have Mercury cars in their lives (usually in the background). Aimed at younger buyers—women particularly—this Internet campaign was supplemented by online diaries kept by the fictional characters, inviting more involvement and cognition—and giving consumers a more positive view of the Mercury brand. The result: Mercury's various websites logged more visitors and more requests for information during the campaign.[151]

Third, consumers can like an ad because it is interesting—that is, it arouses curiosity and attracts attention. When consumers exert a lot of effort and thoughtfully elaborate on a message, it can be viewed as interesting and generate a positive A_{ad}. This factor helps explain the success that teen-oriented retailer Pacific Sunwear has had in building online sales through ever-changing promotions, including free music downloads, celebrity interviews, and "win your wish list" contests. "We view our website as a venue for us to communicate with our customers," says the company's director of e-commerce. "It's more than just for shopping." Bringing consumers back to the website again and again reinforces brand awareness, generates a positive attitude toward Pacific Sunwear, and builds sales.[152]

Utilitarian (functional) dimension When an ad provides information.

Hedonic dimension When an ad creates positive or negative feelings.

When Do Attitudes Predict Behavior?

Marketers are interested not only in how attitudes are formed and can be changed but also in knowing whether, when, and why attitudes will predict behavior. The TORA model comes closest to providing this information by predicting which factors affect consumers' behavioral intentions. However, as previously noted, what we intend to do does not always predict what we actually will do. Therefore, marketers also need to consider which factors affect the attitude-behavior relationship. These are some of the factors that affect whether a consumer's attitudes will influence his or her behavior:

- *Level of involvement/elaboration.* Attitudes are more likely to predict behavior when cognitive involvement is high and consumers elaborate or think extensively about the information that gives rise to their attitudes.[153] Attitudes also tend to be strong and enduring and therefore more predictive of a consumer's behavior when affective involvement is high. Thus, attitudes toward emotionally charged issues such as owning a handgun or getting an abortion tend to be strongly held and related to behavior. What if consumers are faced with inconsistencies about a brand and learn, for example, that it rates higher against competitors on one attribute but lower on another attribute? Here, the attitude-behavior relationship is weakened if consumers do not attempt to resolve the inconsistency through elaboration.[154]

▶ *Knowledge and experience.* Attitudes are more likely to be strongly held and predictive of behavior when the consumer is knowledgeable about or experienced with the object of the attitude.[155] When making a computer decision, for example, an expert is more likely to form an attitude that is based on more detailed and integrated information than is a novice. This attitude would then be more strongly held and more strongly related to behavior.

▶ *Analysis of reasons.* Research shows that asking consumers to analyze their reasons for brand preference increases the link between attitude and behavior in situations in which behavior is measured soon after attitudes are measured. Marketers should take this finding into account when planning consumer research to support a new product introduction.[156]

▶ *Accessibility of attitudes.* Attitudes are more strongly related to behavior when they are accessible or "top of mind."[157] Conversely, if an attitude cannot be easily remembered, it will have little effect on behavior. Direct experience (product usage) generally increases attitude accessibility for attributes that must be experienced (e.g., tasted, touched), whereas advertising can produce accessible attitudes for search attributes (e.g., price, ingredients), especially when the level of repetition is high.[158] Also, consumers asked about their purchase intentions toward a product in a particular category are more likely to choose brands toward which they have positive and accessible attitudes; research itself can make attitudes more accessible for brands in that category, thereby changing behavior.[159]

▶ *Attitude confidence.* As noted earlier, sometimes we are more certain about our evaluations than we are at other times. Therefore, another factor affecting the attitude-behavior relationship is attitude confidence. Confidence tends to be stronger when the attitude is based either on a greater amount of information or on more trustworthy information. And when we are confident, our attitudes are more likely to predict our behaviors.[160] Not surprisingly, strongly held attitudes have more influence on consumers' consideration and choice of brand alternatives than weakly held attitudes.[161]

▶ *Specificity of attitudes.* Attitudes tend to be good predictors of behavior when we are very specific about the behavior that they are trying to predict.[162] Thus, if we wanted to predict whether people will take skydiving lessons, measuring their attitudes toward skydiving in general would be less likely to predict behavior than would measuring their attitudes specifically toward skydiving lessons.

▶ *Attitude-behavior relationship over time.* When consumers are exposed to an advertising message but do not actually try the product, their attitude confidence declines over time. Marketers should therefore plan their advertising schedules to reactivate consumer attitudes and attitude confidence through message repetition. On the other hand, trial-based brand attitudes are likely to decline over time even though advertising-based attitudes do not. As a result, marketers should use communications to reinforce the effects of the trial experience and thereby reactivate the attitude.[163]

◐ *Emotional attachment.* The more emotionally attached consumers are to a brand—the more they feel bonded or connected to it—the more likely they will be to purchase it repeatedly over time. In fact, such consumers are more willing to pay a price premium for the brand to which they are committed and remain loyal even if it is involved in a product crisis such as a recall.[164] Also, consumers who are emotionally attached to a brand will be aroused by negative information about that brand, which in turn will motivate them to generate more counterarguments against the negative information.[165]

◐ *Situational factors.* Intervening situational factors can prevent a behavior from being performed and can thus weaken the attitude-behavior relationship.[166] You might have a very positive attitude toward a Porsche, but you might not buy one because you cannot afford to. In another situation, if you had gone to buy the car, your attitude might not have resulted in a purchase if it had not been in stock at the dealership. In other circumstances, the usage situation may alter the attitude. For example, your attitudes toward different wines might depend on whether you are buying wine for yourself or for a friend.

◐ *Normative factors.* According to the TORA model, normative factors are likely to affect the attitude-behavior relationship. For example, you may like going to the ballet, but you may not go because you think your friends will make fun of you for doing so. Although your attitude is positive and should lead to the behavior of attending the ballet, you are more motivated to comply with normative beliefs.

◐ *Personality variables.* Finally, certain personality types are more likely to exhibit stronger attitude-behavior relationships than are others. Individuals who like to devote a lot of thought to actions will evidence stronger attitude-behavior relationships because their attitudes will be based on high elaboration thinking.[167] Also, people who are guided more by their own internal dispositions (called *low self-monitors*) are more likely to exhibit similar behavior patterns across situations and therefore more consistent attitude-behavior relationships.[168] People who are guided by the views and behaviors of others (called *high self-monitors*), on the other hand, try to change their behavior to adapt to every unique situation. Thus, a high self-monitor's choice of beer might depend on the situation; a low self-monitor would choose the same beer regardless of the circumstances.

Summary

When consumers' MAO to engage in a behavior or to process a message is high, consumers tend to devote considerable effort to forming their attitudes and to message processing. An attitude is a relatively global and enduring evaluation about an offering, issue, activity, person, or event. Attitudes can be described in terms of their favorability, accessibility, confidence, persistence, and resistance. Consumers' thoughts and feelings in response to this situation can affect their attitudes, through either a cognitive or an affective route to persuasion.

Five types of cognitive models show how thoughts relate to attitudes in high-consumer-effort situations: (1) direct or imagined experience, (2) reasoning by analogy or category, (3) values-driven attitudes, (4) social identity-based attitude generation, and (5) analytical processes of attitude construction, including expectancy-value models such as the theory of reasoned action and the theory of planned behavior. Under the cognitive response model, consumers exert a lot of effort in responding to the message— enough effort to generate counterarguments, support arguments, and source derogations. Under elaborative processing, messages can be effective if they have a credible source or a strong argument, present positive and negative information (under certain circumstances), or involve direct comparisons (if the brand is not the market leader).

Consumers can experience emotions when they are affectively involved with a communication or when the message involves an emotional appeal. In either case the consumer processes the communication, and the positive or negative feelings that result can determine attitudes. When attitudes are affectively based, sources that are likable or attractive can have a positive impact on affective attitude change. Emotional appeals can affect communication processing if they are relevant to the offering. Fear appeals, a type of emotion-eliciting message, are explained, in part, by terror-management theory. A consumer's attitude toward the ad (A_{ad}) can play a role in the attitude change process if the ad is informative or associated with positive feelings. The A_{ad} can then rub off on brand beliefs and attitudes.

Finally, attitudes will better predict a consumer's behavior when (1) involvement is high, (2) knowledge is high, (3) reasons are analyzed, (4) attitudes are accessible, (5) attitudes are held with confidence, (6) attitudes are specific, (7) the attitude-behavior relationship does not decline over time, (8) emotional attachment is high, (9) no situational factors are present, (10) normative factors are not in operation, and (11) we are dealing with certain personality types.

Questions for Review and Discussion

1. What are attitudes, and what three functions do they serve?

2. How do expectancy-value models seek to explain attitude formation?

3. What role does credibility play in affecting consumer attitudes based on cognitions?

4. What are the advantages and disadvantages of offering a two-sided message about a product?

5. Contrast emotional and fear appeals. Why is each effective? Which do you consider most compelling for products in which you are interested?

6. What three factors may lead to a positive attitude toward the ad (A_{ad}) when consumers devote a lot of effort to processing a message? How can marketers apply these factors when designing advertising messages?

CL Visit http://cengage.com/marketing/hoyer/ ConsumerBehavior5e to find resources that are available to help you study for the course.

CONSUMER BEHAVIOR CASE

GEICO Makes Its Case for Savings and Service

GEICO is the number-four U.S. car insurance firm, behind State Farm, Allstate, and Progressive, yet its $500 million annual budget for marketing communications is by far the industry's largest. GEICO uses this budget to great advantage with a wide variety of messages in a variety of media to influence consumers' attitudes toward its insurance offerings, which include coverage for cars, motorcycles, homes, and recreational vehicles. In a product category in which consumers do not switch from one brand to another without considerable thought, GEICO's communications give drivers something to think about and steer them toward positive brand attitudes.

The company's messages use strong arguments focusing on savings and service to get consumers thinking about the cost of car insurance. Some of its comparative messages show exactly how much money a particular consumer saved by switching from a competing insurance company to GEICO, information that enhances the product's believability. In a variation on this theme, many of its comparative ads say that "fifteen minutes could save you fifteen percent." This message encourages consumers to calculate how much less they could be paying for car insurance if they were GEICO customers. It also reassures consumers by telling them that making the switch to GEICO will be quick and easy.

Every ad not only mentions the brand name but also gives GEICO's toll-free phone number or its website (or both)—a call to action for consumers to take the next step and get a free quote, read more about specific types of policies, or contact customer service with just a click or a call, day or night. Messages about GEICO's high levels of customer satisfaction and brand loyalty have more credibility because they are based on expert sources named on the website: The University of Michigan's American Customer Satisfaction Index and the Brand Keys Customer Loyalty Engagement Index.

To support its aggressive expansion into motorcycle insurance, GEICO recently set up MyGreatRides.com as a social networking website for motorcycle enthusiasts. The idea is to provide an online forum for motorcycle owners to post upcoming events, exchange views about favorite bike brands, and show off their tricked-out rides. Although the GEICO brand is nowhere to be found on the website, the company sees it as an investment in learning how consumers think and feel about everything related to their bikes, including insurance. "If we can learn more about the needs of motorcycle riders and what kind of service they expect, we think it will help us with our current customers and potential ones," says GEICO's director of motorcycle products.

GEICO's Corporate Community Citizens program fosters positive consumer attitudes through the company's involvement with local causes and organizations. Not only does GEICO donate money to nonprofit groups all around the United States; its employees also volunteer their time for causes such as Habitat for Humanity home-building projects, Bikers for Tykes motorcycle rally fundraisers, and Big Brothers/Big Sisters activities. One of GEICO's many auto

safety initiatives is the Safety Belt Poster Contest, in which school-age children submit artwork for posters that remind drivers about the importance of buckling up for safety. Local efforts such as these link the GEICO name with worthwhile causes that touch an emotional chord with consumers.

Despite increased competition from its larger rivals, GEICO's approach to marketing car and motorcycle insurance has been extremely effective. The company currently serves more than 7 million customers and, according to J.D. Power & Associates studies, enjoys high brand awareness as well as the highest new-customer acquisition rate among the major insurers. Watch for GEICO to keep driving toward higher market share by reaching out to car and motorcycle drivers all over the United States.[169]

Case Questions

1. Does GEICO appear to be using marketing communications to change consumers' beliefs, change their evaluations, add a new belief, encourage attitude formation based on imagined experience, or target normative beliefs? Explain your answer.

2. What role does source credibility play in GEICO's marketing communications?

3. Do you agree with GEICO's decision not to show its brand on the MyGreatRides.com website? How do you think this decision is likely to affect the website's visitors' attitudes toward GEICO?

Chapter 6

Attitudes Based on Low Effort

INTRODUCTION

Those Funny, Quirky, Sexy Beer Commercials

The computer screen and the television screen are major battlegrounds for beer commercials that seek to make consumers smile, give them something to think about, or simply attract their attention. When seconds count, many beer commercials rely on humor, quirkiness, sex, or—sometimes—benefits to connect with the audience.

Market leader Anheuser-Busch, for example, is so well known for its clever and humorous Budweiser and Bud Light commercials that some Super Bowl viewers talk about its latest ads almost as much as they talk about the game. Posted on the company's product websites, the Super Bowl commercials used to draw about 700,000 viewers per year. Now, added to blogs and video-sharing sites like YouTube, the ads draw tens of millions of viewers throughout the year.

Sex is also a staple of beer commercials. Knowing that beer consumption rises during warm weather, Coors has run summertime campaigns featuring curvy ladies, hoping that younger consumers would like seeing sexy women, feel good about Coors Light, and buy more of it. Imported brands such as Beck's also use sex in advertising. Traditionally, Beck's commercials focused on the brand's German brewing tradition. After the firm switched to black-and-white commercials featuring scantily clad women and throaty voice-overs, its sales surged. "You are

LEARNING OBJECTIVES

After studying this chapter, you will be able to

1. Outline some issues marketers face in trying to change consumers' attitudes when processing effort is low.

2. Explain the role of unconscious influences on attitudes and behavior in low-effort situations.

3. Discuss how consumers form beliefs based on low processing effort and explain how marketers can influence those beliefs.

4. Describe how consumers form attitudes through affective reactions when cognitive effort is low.

148

5. Highlight how marketers can use the communication source, message, and context to influence consumers' feelings and attitudes when processing effort is low.

going to see beautiful women in beer advertising until that no longer becomes relevant to the target," says a Beck's executive. "We've aspired to be more tasteful rather than crass."[1]

The different approaches used by Anheuser-Busch, Coors, and Beck's illustrate how marketers can influence attitudes even when consumers devote little effort to processing a message. Because consumers tend not to actively process message arguments or become emotionally involved in messages about beer, marketers must use other techniques to create positive evaluations of their brands, raise awareness of need situations, and stimulate purchasing and consumption. This chapter discusses how marketers apply techniques such as sex, humor, attractive sources, and emotion to influence attitudes when consumers make little effort to process the message.

High-Effort versus Low-Effort Routes to Persuasion

When consumers are either unwilling or unable to exert a lot of effort or devote many emotional resources to processing the central idea behind a marketing communication, we characterize it as a *low-effort situation*. Here, consumers are unlikely to think about what the product means to them, relate empathetically to the characters in the ad, or generate arguments against or in support of the brand message. When processing effort is low, consumers are passive recipients of the message and usually do not form strong beliefs or accessible, persistent, resistant, or confident attitudes. In fact, attitudes formed under low-effort processing may not even be stored in memory, allowing consumers to form attitudes anew each time they are exposed to a message.[2] Marketers must therefore use a strategy that takes into account these effects of lower-level processing.

Peripheral route to persuasion Aspects other than key message arguments that are used to influence attitudes.

Peripheral cues Easily processed aspects of a message, such as music, an attractive source or picture, or humor.

One approach is to create communications that use a different route. Instead of focusing on the key message arguments, the message will be more effective if it takes the **peripheral route to persuasion.**[3] Processing is called *peripheral* when consumers' attitudes are based not on a detailed consideration of the message or their ability to relate to the brand empathetically but on other easily processed aspects of the message, such as the source or visuals, called **peripheral cues.** In particular, consumer attitudes can persist over time if peripheral cues such as visuals are related to the offering.[4]

Just as there are both cognitive and affective routes to persuasion when processing effort is high, so too can consumers form low-effort attitudes in both a cognitive and an affective manner. Marketers can try to design their ads to enhance the likelihood that consumers' thoughts (the cognitive base), feelings (the affective base), or both will be favorable. Exhibit 6.1 provides a framework for thinking about the peripheral bases of consumer behavior, including unconscious influences on attitude formation and change.

Marketers need to understand how consumers form attitudes with low effort because, in most cases, consumers will have limited MAO to process marketing communications. Think about the countless marketing messages you receive every day. How many actually attract your attention and stimulate you to think about the ad and the way that you feel about the offering? When the television is on, do you channel-surf during commercials or tune them out because they feature products you do not care about? These behaviors pose challenges for marketers.

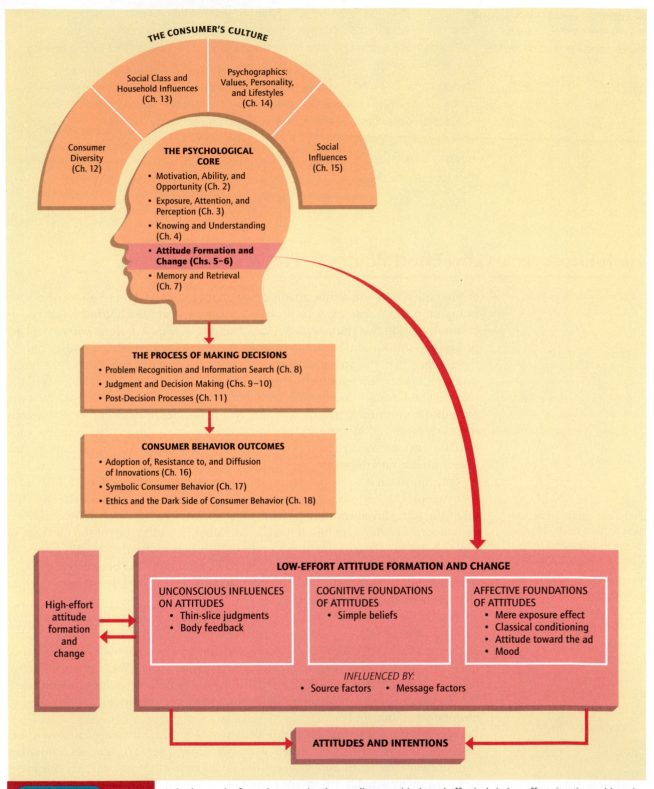

Chapter Overview: Attitude Formation and Change: Low Consumer Effort

Attitudes can be formed unconsciously as well as cognitively and affectively in low-effort situations, although not in the same way as they are in high-effort situations. Low-effort cognition involves simple beliefs, and affect involves mere exposure, classical conditioning, attitude toward the ad, and mood. Marketers can also influence consumer attitudes cognitively and affectively using source, message, and context factors.

Unconscious Influences on Attitudes When Consumer Effort Is Low

Recent research indicates that much processing in low-effort situations occurs below conscious awareness. This means that consumers form attitudes on both cognitive and affective bases without being aware of how or why they have done so. For example, a consumer browsing in a store may unconsciously be affected by various aspects of the shopping environment.[5] Two unconscious influences receiving particular attention from researchers are thin-slice judgments based on brief observations and cues from body feedback.

Thin-Slice Judgments

Thin-slice judgments Evaluations made after very brief observations.

Thin-slice judgments are assessments consumers make after brief observations despite receiving minimal information input. Studies show that consumers can form surprisingly accurate impressions through thin-slice judgments, even though they are not doing so on a conscious level.[6] For example, a consumer may unconsciously form an assessment about a salesperson after a minute or less of observation or interaction. (This same effect may occur when students judge a professor's class performance after brief observation.) Such an assessment can influence the consumer's decision to buy and satisfaction with the sale. At the same time, an overabundance of information, knowledge, or analysis can impair this kind of intuitive assessment.[7]

Body Feedback

Even though consumers may not consciously monitor their own physical reactions, body feedback can influence attitudes and behavior in some circumstances. According to research, consumers who were induced to nod had more positive evaluations of positively valenced brands; when induced to shake their heads, consumers had more negative evaluations. Similarly, pushing up on a table led to more positive evaluations; pushing down led to more negative evaluations. However, consumers must know the meaning of the body feedback they experience in order to explain their behavior. If they do not recognize that nodding signals agreement, this feedback cue will have no effect on their attitude or behavior.[8]

MARKETING IMPLICATIONS

Marketers can try to enhance thin-slice judgments and induce positive body feedback, even though consumers will not be consciously aware of these influences. Some entertainment websites like iTunes invite consumers to listen to snippets of songs or watch movie trailers, hoping that this brief exposure will help consumers form a positive impression of these samples and ultimately lead to a purchase. Applying body feedback theory, many marketers make product packaging intriguing or attractive enough to cause consumers to reach out and pick up a product. Also, marketers should aim to have consumers read ad copy from top to bottom (and then from bottom to top) to simulate nodding "yes." Such body movements could tip the scale in favor of a purchase if the consumer already has a positive perception of the product. Applying unconscious influences in marketing can be tricky, however, because of their complex interactions with conscious influences.[9]

Cognitive Bases of Attitudes When Consumer Effort Is Low

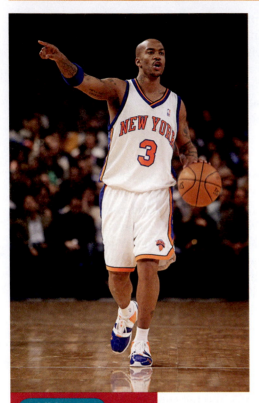

Exhibit 6.2

Stephon Marbury Wearing Starbury Sneakers

Stephon Marbury (pictured here) wears his Starbury sneakers in games to show consumers that he really does care about this brand.

Simple inferences Beliefs based on peripheral cues.

Heuristics Simple rules of thumb that are used to make judgments.

Frequency heuristic Belief based simply on the number of supporting arguments or amount of repetition.

Truth effect When consumers believe a statement simply because it has been repeated a number of times.

Chapter 5 explained how consumers' beliefs form an important cognitive basis for their attitudes. When processing effort is low, attitudes may be based on a few simple and not very strong beliefs because consumers have not processed the message deeply. Interestingly, because these beliefs are not very strong, marketers may actually be *more* successful in changing them than when processing effort is high.

The attitudes of low-effort consumers may be less resistant to attack than those of high-effort consumers because the low-effort people may "let their guard down" and not resist the message or develop counterarguments. So a company that wants to change consumers' false beliefs about a product will be more successful if it uses a direct refutation to rebut a direct product claim.[10] In addition, ads that focus consumers on the process of using the advertised product make consumers more likely to think about a plan to buy the product—and open the way to persuasion by strong message claims.[11]

When processing effort is low, consumers may acquire simple beliefs by forming **simple inferences** based on simple associations. For example, consumers may infer that a brand of champagne is elegant because it is shown with other elegant things, such as a richly decorated room or a woman in an evening dress. If an ad is perceived to be similar to the prototypical ad for a product or service category, consumers may believe that the offering is just like the prototypical brand and may develop similar attitudes toward both.[12] Inferred beliefs may also come from consumers' superficial analysis of the product's brand name, country of origin, price, or color.

In addition, consumers can form simple beliefs based on attributions or explanations for an endorsement.[13] If consumers attribute an endorsement to a desire to earn a lot of money, they will not find the message believable. The ad is apt to be credible if consumers perceive that the endorser truly cares about the offering. For example, basketball star Stephon Marbury does more than lend his name to the $14.98 Starbury line of sneakers marketed by the Steve & Barry's retail chain—he wears them in games (see Exhibit 6.2). "We want to prove that they are all good enough quality for an NBA star to wear," explains Steve & Barry's CEO.[14]

Finally, consumers can aid judgments by forming **heuristics,** or simple rules of thumb, that are easy to invoke and require little thought.[15] For example, consumers could use the heuristic "If it is a well-known brand, it must be good" to infer that brands with more frequent ads are also higher in quality.[16] A special type of heuristic is the **frequency heuristic,** with which consumers form a belief based on the number of supporting arguments.[17] They may think, "It must be good because there are ten reasons why I should like it." Research also indicates that consumers are likely to have stronger beliefs about a product when they hear the same message repeatedly, which is known as the **truth effect.**[18] Rather than thinking about and evaluating the information, consumers use familiarity with the message to judge its accuracy ("This 'rings a bell,' so it must be true").

How Cognitive Attitudes Are Influenced

Marketers need to consider multiple factors when trying to influence cognitive attitudes. There are the strength and importance of consumers' beliefs. Another factor is the likelihood that consumers will form favorable beliefs based on the inferences, attributions, and heuristics they use in processing the message. In designing communications that overcome these hurdles, marketers must consider three major characteristics of a communication: (1) the source, (2) the message, and (3) the context in which the message is delivered.

Communication Source

Characteristics of the source play an important role in influencing consumers' beliefs when processing effort is low. Credible sources can serve as peripheral cues for making a simplified judgment, such as "Statements from experts can be trusted" or "Products endorsed by an expert must be good."[19] Note that source expertise is used here as a simple cue in judging the credibility of the message, and unlike the case in high-effort situations, little cognitive effort is required to process the message. Marketers may also increase the chances that consumers will believe the endorsement of a product by using an endorser who does not advertise many other products.

The Message

The message itself can influence attitudes in a number of ways when consumers' processing effort is low.

Category- and Schema-Consistent Information

Many elements of a communication affect the inferences that consumers make about a message. For example, consumers may infer that a brand has certain characteristics based on its name ("Healthy Choice soups must be good for me"). They may make inferences about quality based on price, as discussed earlier, or about attributes based on color, such as when blue suggests coolness. Thus, in designing ads for low-effort consumers, marketers pay close attention to the immediate associations consumers have about easily processed visual and verbal information. These associations are likely to be consistent with category and schema information stored in the consumer's memory.

Many Message Arguments

The frequency heuristic can also affect consumers' beliefs about the message. As a simplifying rule, consumers do not actually process all the information but form a belief based on the number of supporting arguments. For example, Russell Stover encourages candy lovers to form a belief about its Net Carb candies based on ads featuring three message arguments: the candy is low in carbohydrates, it is full of chocolate flavor, and it is "good enough to be called Russell Stover." Note that low-effort attitudes can be affected by how easily consumers remember the message arguments. Simply being able to recall some of the arguments can enhance a consumer's preference for the advertised brand.[20]

Simple Messages

In low-processing situations, a simple message is more likely to be effective because consumers will not have to process a lot of information. Marketers often

Exhibit 6.3

Simple Message

When effort is low, consumers will not process a lot of information. In these cases, advertisers need to provide simple messages such as this one for Ft. Lauderdale's website.

Self-referencing Relating a message to one's own experience or self-image.

Mystery ad An ad in which the brand is not identified until the end of the message.

want to convey basic information about why a particular brand is superior, especially when a point of differentiation distinguishes it from the competition. Thus, rather than overloading low-processing consumers with details, marketers should use a simple message with one or two key points (see Exhibit 6.3). When Glad advertises its ForceFlex garbage bags, the words and pictures focus on one simple point: the bags stretch when stuffed, but they do not break. When marketing food products on the basis of convenience, marketers should focus attention on one important functional benefit through a literal, direct assertion, such as "ready in just 15 minutes."[21]

Involving Messages

Marketers will sometimes want to *increase* consumers' situational involvement with the message to ensure that the information is received. One common strategy is to increase the extent to which consumers engage in **self-referencing,** or relating the message to their own experience or self-image.[22] A self-referencing strategy can be effective in developing positive attitudes and intentions, especially if it is used at moderate levels and involvement is not too low.[23]

Remembering and using the consumer's name in a personal selling context will also increase purchase behavior.[24] Consumers will have more favorable attitudes toward a brand that is highly descriptive on a personality dimension that they consider important or self-descriptive.[25] New Balance, which makes high-performance sneakers, does not use celebrity endorsers but instead puts the focus on consumers' passion for doing their best at sports they love, a dimension with which many consumers identify.[26] A mainstream ad with dominant culture cues may stimulate self-referencing among members of a subculture as well as among members of the dominant culture and lead to favorable ad attitudes. If the ad has subcultural cues rather than dominant culture cues, however, it will induce self-referencing and positive ad attitudes only among subculture members.[27]

MARKETING IMPLICATIONS

Marketers can increase self-referencing by (1) directly instructing consumers to use self-reference ("Think of the last time you had a good meal . . . "), (2) using the word *you* in the ad, (3) asking rhetorical questions ("Wouldn't you like your clothes to look this clean?"),[28] or (4) showing visuals of situations to which consumers can easily relate. When a rhetorical question in an ad attracts special attention, however, consumers wonder why the question is there, shifting their processing effort to the message style instead of the message content.[29]

The **mystery ad** (also called the "wait and bait" ad), which does not identify the brand until the end, if at all, is another way to arouse consumers' curiosity and involvement. Some movies use mystery ads to build audience interest in advance of their

What do you see?
It might be your future.

Do you think there are many ways to look at a problem? As well as an opportunity? We want people who look at the future and are excited by the possibilities. See for yourself. www.ey.com

CONSULTING · TAX · ASSURANCE   ≡‖ ERNST & YOUNG
FROM THOUGHT TO FINISH.™

©1999 ERNST & YOUNG LLP

Exhibit 6.4

Increasing Active Processing

This ad tries to draw consumers into the message by challenging them to look at the image in different ways.

Incidental learning Learning that occurs from repetition rather than from conscious processing.

release dates. In particular, the mystery ad is effective in generating category-based processing and storing brand associations in memory.[30]

Marketers can also employ other techniques to increase situational involvement and processing effort. Online marketers can use avatars to induce more arousal and involve consumers in the website experience.[31] Scratch-and-sniff print ads often increase processing effort because many consumers cannot resist trying something new. Also, inviting consumers to experience simulated product usage online increases involvement and advertising effectiveness more than an online ad message alone would.[32] This reaction is the reason why the Lego site features interactive games that invite players to create virtual animals and cities using virtual Lego blocks—these activities demonstrate the product's functionality and the fun of playing with the blocks.[33] In Exhibit 6.4, Ernst & Young draws consumers into its message by challenging them to look at the illustration in different ways. ◖▬▬◗

Message Context and Repetition

Although source and message factors can influence consumers' attitudes, the context in which the message is delivered can affect the strength of consumers' beliefs and the prominence (or salience) of those beliefs for the consumers. In particular, a company can use message *repetition* to help consumers acquire basic knowledge of important product features or benefits, enhancing the strength and salience of their beliefs. Consumers do not try to process this information actively; rather, the constant repetition increases recall through effortless or **incidental learning.** For example, you may have a prominent belief about milk's health benefits because you have been repeatedly exposed to the long-running "Got Milk?" milk mustache ad campaign.[34]

Repetition may enhance brand awareness, make a brand name more familiar,[35] make it easier to recognize in the store, increase the likelihood that consumers will remember it and be better able to process it when making a purchasing decision,[36] and increase consumers' confidence in the brand.[37] Third, as you have seen, repetition can make claims more believable (the truth effect)—an effect that gets even stronger when ads are spaced out over time.[38] And fourth, TV commercials that air within the context of similar programming (i.e., humorous ads aired during comedy shows) are more likable and better understood by consumers expending low processing effort.[39] Similarly, ads that fit into the context of the magazines in which they appear elicit more positive feelings and are better remembered than ads not in tune with magazine context.[40]

Affective Bases of Attitudes When Consumer Effort Is Low

The establishment of low-level beliefs based on peripheral cues is not the only way that consumers can form attitudes about brands with little effort. Attitudes can also be based on consumers' affective or emotional reactions to these easily processed peripheral cues. These low-effort affective processes may be due to (1) the mere exposure effect, (2) classical conditioning, (3) attitude toward the ad, and (4) consumer mood.

The Mere Exposure Effect

Mere exposure effect When familiarity leads to a consumer's liking an object.

According to the **mere exposure effect,** we tend to prefer familiar objects to unfamiliar ones.[41] Therefore, our attitudes toward an offering such as a new style of clothing should change as we become more and more familiar with it, regardless of whether we perform any deep cognitive analysis of it. The mere exposure effect may explain why many of the top 30 brands in the 1930s are still in the top 30 today. It also explains why the music industry likes to have recordings featured on the radio or in TV music videos. Through repeated exposure, consumers become familiar with the music and come to like it.

Because most demonstrations of the mere exposure effect have occurred in tightly controlled laboratory studies, some experts question whether it generalizes to the real world.[42] It is also possible that repeated exposure reduces uncertainty about the stimulus or increases consumers' opportunity to process it[43] and that these factors (rather than mere familiarity) are what affect consumers' attitudes. However, research shows that mere exposure can help an unknown brand compete against other unknown brands if product performance characteristics are equivalent and consumers invest little processing effort at the time of brand choice.[44] Also, when consumers can easily process the information from a stimulus to which they have been exposed in the past, they mistakenly believe that the ease in processing is due to liking, truth, or acceptability.[45]

(MARKETING IMPLICATIONS)

If the mere exposure effect is valid, marketers may be able to enhance consumers' liking of a new product or service by repeatedly exposing consumers to the offering or messages about it. Research suggests that when consumers' MAO is low, marketers need creative tactics for increasing consumers' exposure to products and messages, perhaps by using the right medium, the right placement within the medium, optimal shelf placement, and sampling.

Consistent with the mere exposure effect, some smaller companies are embarking on ad campaigns to develop and maintain brand-name familiarity. For instance, now that Massachusetts regulations allow competition among auto insurers, local firms such as Arbella Insurance Group of Quincy are launching ad campaigns to support their brands

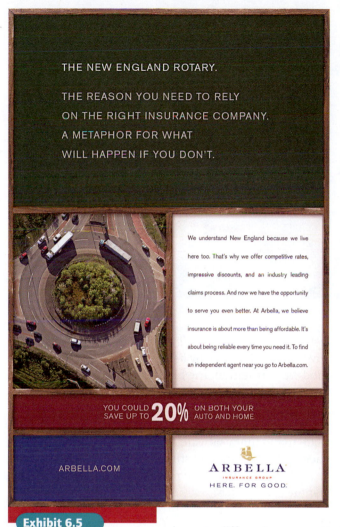

THE NEW ENGLAND ROTARY.

THE REASON YOU NEED TO RELY
ON THE RIGHT INSURANCE COMPANY.
A METAPHOR FOR WHAT
WILL HAPPEN IF YOU DON'T.

We understand New England because we live here too. That's why we offer competitive rates, impressive discounts, and an industry leading claims process. And now we have the opportunity to serve you even better. At Arbella, we believe insurance is about more than being affordable. It's about being reliable every time you need it. To find an independent agent near you go to Arbella.com.

YOU COULD SAVE UP TO **20**% ON BOTH YOUR AUTO AND HOME

ARBELLA.COM

ARBELLA
INSURANCE GROUP
HERE. FOR GOOD.

Exhibit 6.5

Arbella's Ad Campaign
Companies strive to develop well-known brand names. Arbella Insurance Group is attempting to do this with ads like the one pictured here.

Wearout Becoming bored with a stimulus.

Classical conditioning Producing a response to a stimulus by repeatedly pairing it with another stimulus that automatically produces this response.

and their independent insurance agents, as in Exhibit 6.5. "We've heard from our agents that it helps them to have a recognizable brand, a company name that people know and associate with positive attributes," says John Donohue, Chairman, President, and Chief Executive Officer, Arbella Insurance Group.[46]

Some companies pay to have their logos displayed at sporting events, knowing that there will be repeated exposures as race cars go around the track or players move around on the field. However, repeated exposures will build familiarity and liking only up to a point.[47] After this, consumers typically experience **wearout,** which means they become bored with the stimulus, and brand attitudes can actually become negative.[48] In fact, once a persuasive ad has effectively reached the targeted consumer segment, wearout causes a loss of persuasiveness.[49] When consumers are familiar with a brand, however, wearout may occur later.[50] Also, the use of rational arguments to promote a well-known brand in a mature product category tends to be less effective than the use of affectively based tactics because consumers have been exposed to the product information many times before.[51] Still, in low-effort processing situations, brand evaluations do not suffer when consumers are repeatedly exposed to messages about product features.[52]

Marketers can overcome wearout by creating different executions for the same message or variants on the same offering; this is the reason why many advertisers develop a series of ads rather than a single execution.[53] The goal is to get the same message across in many different ways, as Kraft Foods does by rotating five brief, funny commercials about grilled cheese sandwiches to promote its Kraft Singles cheese slices.[54] The mere exposure effect may not be the only reason that repetition affects brand attitudes. When repetition allows consumers greater opportunity to process information about specific aspects of the brand and the ways that it relates to other brands in the category, brand attitudes improve.[55]

Classical Conditioning

One way of influencing consumers' attitudes without invoking much processing effort is **classical conditioning.** Classical conditioning became well known from a study in the 1900s by the Russian scientist Ivan Pavlov. Normally, hungry dogs will salivate automatically just at the sight of food. Pavlov discovered that he could condition hungry dogs to salivate at the sound of a bell. How did he do that?

According to Pavlov, the food was an *unconditioned stimulus (UCS),* and the salivation response to the food was an *unconditioned response (UCR)* (see Exhibit 6.6). A stimulus is unconditioned when it automatically elicits an involuntary response. In this situation, the dogs automatically salivated when they

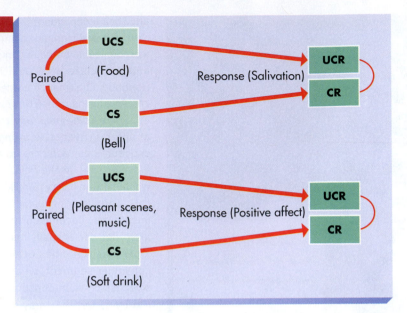

Exhibit 6.6

Classical Conditioning

These diagrams illustrate the basic process of classical conditioning. An unconditioned stimulus, or UCS (e.g., food or pleasant scenes), will automatically produce an unconditioned response, or UCR (e.g., salivation or positive affect). By repeatedly pairing the UCS with a conditioned stimulus, or CS (e.g., a bell or soft drink), the CS can be conditioned to produce the same response, a conditioned response, or CR (e.g., salivation or positive affect). Can you think of any other situations in which this process occurs?

saw meat powder. In contrast, a *conditioned stimulus (CS)* is something that does not automatically elicit an involuntary response by itself. Until Pavlov rang the bell at the same time that the food was presented, the bell alone could not make the dogs salivate. By repeatedly pairing the conditioned stimulus (the bell) with the unconditioned stimulus (the meat powder), the involuntary unconditioned response (salivation) was created. The dogs associated the food and the bell so closely that eventually just the ringing bell made them salivate. Because the response could now be evoked in the presence of the conditioned stimulus, the response was said to be a *conditioned response (CR)*. (This is the same phenomenon that makes cats come running when they hear the can opener.)

MARKETING IMPLICATIONS

Classical conditioning theory is sometimes used to explain the effectiveness of marketing communications. Here, however, the unconditioned response is not a physiological one like salivating but a psychological one like an emotion. Certain unconditioned stimuli (such as a happy scene or a catchy jingle) automatically elicit an unconditioned emotional response such as joy. By repeatedly pairing one of these unconditioned stimuli with a conditioned stimulus such as a brand name, marketers may be able to evoke the same emotional response (now the conditioned response) to the conditioned stimulus, the brand name itself. Similarly, consumers might be conditioned to have a negative emotional response to an offering such as cigarettes if ads by health advocacy groups repeatedly show the product with stimuli that automatically elicit a negative emotional response (such as pictures of stained teeth).

In one of the first consumer studies to demonstrate classical conditioning, subjects viewed a slide of a blue or beige pen that was matched with a one-minute segment of either pleasant or unpleasant music. Subjects who heard pleasant music selected the pen they viewed with that music 79 percent of the time, whereas only 30 percent of those who heard the unpleasant music selected the pen they had viewed.[56]

Although these findings could be interpreted in different ways (subjects may have done what they thought the experimenter wanted them to do, or the music may have put the consumers in a better mood),[57] more recent and more tightly controlled studies have found support for classical conditioning. For example, by using unconditioned stimuli such as *Star Wars* music and pleasing pictures, experimenters have affected consumers' attitudes toward such conditioned stimuli as geometric figures, colas, and toothpaste.[58] Research also shows that attitudes created by classical conditioning can be fairly enduring over time.[59]

These studies suggest that conditioning is most likely to occur under the following circumstances:

▶ The conditioned stimuli–unconditioned stimuli link is relatively novel or unknown. This is the reason why marketers often use unique visuals, such as pictures of beautiful scenery, exciting situations, or pleasing objects, as unconditioned stimuli to create positive feelings.

▶ The conditioned stimulus precedes the unconditioned stimulus *(forward conditioning)*. Conditioning is weaker when the unconditioned stimulus is presented first *(backward conditioning)* or at the same time as the conditioned stimulus *(concurrent conditioning)*.

▶ The conditioned stimulus is paired consistently with the unconditioned stimulus.

▶ The consumer is aware of the link between the conditioned and unconditioned stimuli.

▶ A logical fit exists between the conditioned and unconditioned stimuli, such as between golfer Tiger Woods and Nike, the sports brand he has endorsed for many years.[60]

Interestingly, the first condition can cause problems for marketers because unconditioned stimuli are often well-known celebrities, music, or visuals for which consumers possess many associations. This finding might suggest that using highly visible celebrities is not as effective a strategy for creating a classical conditioning effect. Other research indicates that the problem can be overcome by using highly familiar stimuli such as popular songs and personalities because they elicit very strong feelings in many situations. Some marketers do not shy away from endorsers associated with multiple brands. Tiger Woods endorses a number of brands, yet Gatorade recently signed him to endorse a line of sports drinks.[61]

Attitude Toward the Ad

Another concept that has been useful in understanding the affective bases of attitudes in low-effort situations is the consumer's attitude toward the ad (A_{ad}). Sometimes consumers like an ad so much that they transfer their positive feelings from the ad to the brand.[62] Thus, you may decide that you really like Pepsi because its soft-drink ads are humorous or that you like AT&T products because the company's wireless phone ads are interesting.

One study found that consumers' beliefs or knowledge about the brand did not fully account for brand attitudes and that A_{ad} provided a significant additional explanation—brands with liked ads were evaluated more favorably.[63] Furthermore, research in India, Greece, Denmark, New Zealand, and the United States revealed that the A_{ad} principle was globally applicable.[64] An Advertising Research Foundation project suggests that consumers' attitudes toward ads may be the best indicator of advertising effectiveness.[65]

The **dual-mediation hypothesis** is a somewhat more complex explanation of the relationship between consumers' liking of an ad and brand attitude

Dual-mediation hypothesis
Explains how attitudes toward the ad influence brand attitudes.

Exhibit 6.7

The Dual-Mediation Hypothesis

This hypothesis explains how attitudes toward the ad (A_{ad}) can influence attitudes toward the brand (A_b) and intentions (I_b). When you read an ad, you can have responses (C_{ad}) that are both cognitive (this ad has information about a brand) and affective (positive feelings from finding the ad). These responses may cause you to like the ad (A_{ad}), a reaction that can then either (1) make you more accepting of brand beliefs (C_b), leading to a more positive brand attitude (A_b); or (2) give you positive feelings that transfer over to the brand (I like the ad, so I like the brand). Both processes lead to an increase in intention to purchase.

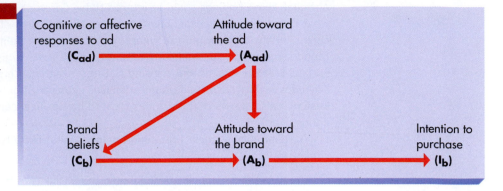

Cognitive or affective responses to ad (C_{ad}) → Attitude toward the ad (A_{ad})

Brand beliefs (C_b)

Attitude toward the brand (A_b)

Intention to purchase (I_b)

(see Exhibit 6.7).[66] According to this hypothesis, consumers can have a favorable attitude toward an ad either because they find it believable or because they feel good about it. Thus, the dual-mediation hypothesis proposes that A_{ad} can affect brand attitudes (A_b) either through believability or liking. These responses, in turn, may positively affect consumers' intentions to purchase (I_b).

MARKETING IMPLICATIONS

The clear implication of the attitude-toward-the-ad theory is that by providing ads that are pleasing, marketers may be able to make consumers' brand attitudes more positive as well. Thus, by using techniques such as humor, music, pleasant pictures, and sex (all of which will be discussed in more detail shortly), marketers can encourage positive attitudes toward the ad. Procter & Gamble, for example, is relying on ads with drama or emotion to strengthen relationships with consumers of household products like laundry detergent.[67]

In addition, the effect of ad attitudes on brand attitudes may depend on whether consumers already have a strong attitude toward the brand. When brands are well known and attitudes about them have been formed, consumers may not like the brand more just because they like the ad. However, when brands are new or not well known, consumers' liking of the ad can play a more significant role in their liking of the brand.[68] Studies also suggest that the effect of attitude toward the ad on attitude toward the brand dissipates over time.[69] As memory of the ad fades, liking of the ad and the brand becomes weaker.

Mood

Affective attitudes can also be influenced by the consumer's mood. Here, a stimulus creates a positive or a negative mood; in turn, this mood can affect consumers' reactions to any other stimulus they happen to evaluate. Thus, we are more likely to say that we like something if we are in a good mood or say that we dislike something if we are in a bad mood. Mood can therefore bias attitudes in a *mood-congruent direction*. Note that mood is different from classical conditioning because mood (1) does not require a repeated association between two stimuli and (2) can affect consumers' evaluations of any object, not just the stimulus.

According to one study, consumers in a good mood who have a tentative preference for a certain brand tend to ignore negative information about that brand as well as information about a competitor.[70] Another study found that although consumers tend to like a brand extension less when the product is not very similar to the parent product, consumers in a good mood are more likely to like a brand extension that is moderately similar to the parent product than consumers who are not in a good mood.[71] A good mood can act as a resource by increasing elaboration, helping consumers think creatively and see relationships among brands. Specific emotions, not just a general good or bad mood, can also influence attitudes when MAO is low, as long as the emotions are consistent with the consumer's goals.[72] Moreover, consumers in a good mood tend to give more weight to positive information when evaluating a product, whereas consumers in a bad mood give more weight to negative information.[73]

Researchers examining how lighting influences mood have found that brighter in-store lighting tends to increase the extent to which shoppers examine and handle merchandise.[74] Brighter lighting does not, however, increase the amount of time consumers spend shopping or the number of purchases they make. Color is also a factor. Warm colors such as red, orange, and yellow tend to be more stimulating and exciting, whereas cool colors such as blue, green, and violet tend to be more soothing.[75] A salesperson's mood can influence consumers as well. Consumers in a bad mood are likely to feel worse and downgrade their judgments of the product being sold when they interact with salespeople who seem to be happy (unless the decision is so important that they are motivated to shake off the effects of their bad mood).[76]

Consumers may like a brand better when they are put in a good mood by its ads or the programs in which the ads appear. Research has focused on the kinds of emotions or moods that ads invoke and the variety of ways these factors might affect consumers' ad and brand attitudes.[77] One study identified three major categories of affective responses: (1) *SEVA* (surgency, elation, vigor, and activation), which is present when the communication puts the consumer in an upbeat or happy mood; (2) *deactivation feelings*, which include soothing, relaxing, quiet, or pleasant responses; and (3) *social affection*, which are feelings of warmth, tenderness, and caring.[78] Another study found that ad-induced feelings of warmth and humor could have a direct and positive impact on brand attitudes.[79] Thus, when ads for Huggies disposable diapers picture tender moments between babies and parents, they may also generate positive feelings for the brand.

MARKETING IMPLICATIONS

On the assumption that mood affects consumer behavior, retailers can use physical surroundings and the behavior of store employees to put consumers in a good mood. Warm colors are more likely to draw customers to an outlet but can also create tension, whereas cool colors are more relaxing but do not attract customers.[80] Therefore, when the goal is to stimulate quick purchases or activity, warm colors are more appropriate, a situation that explains why the discount stores Target and Costco use a red-based color scheme. Warm colors are also appropriate for health clubs, sports stadiums, and fast-food restaurants, where a high level of activity and energy is desirable.

Cool colors are more appropriate when the goal is to have consumers feel calm or spend time deliberating. The color schemes of stores that sell expensive merchandise are a good example. Apple's modernistic stores are decorated in white, black, and shades of grey to provide a clean, uncluttered environment for showcasing high-tech products to millions of shoppers.[81]

How Affective Attitudes Are Influenced

When consumers apply little processing effort and form attitudes based on feelings, the same three factors that influence cognitive reasoning also influence affective attitudes: the communication source, the message, and the context. Again, these factors are based on low-effort processes such as mere exposure, classical conditioning, attitude toward the ad, and mood.

Communication Source

Under conditions of low effort, two factors play a major role in determining whether or not the communication source evokes favorable affective reactions: its physical attractiveness and its likability. These two factors help to explain why marketers like to feature celebrities in ads, as in Exhibit 6.8.

Attractive Sources

Many ads feature attractive models, spokespersons, or celebrities, reflecting the long-held belief that beauty sells—especially in the beauty business. Research studies generally support this notion. When consumers' motivation to process an advertised message is low, attractive sources enhance the favorability of consumers' brand attitudes regardless of whether the message arguments are strong or weak.[82] Consumers also rate ads with attractive models as more appealing, eye-catching, impressive, and interesting than ads with unattractive models. These ratings may affect consumers' attitudes toward the products these models sponsor.[83]

Moreover, attractiveness can have beneficial effects on advertiser believability and actual purchase.[84] These effects can occur for both male and female models (consumers are most strongly attracted to models of the opposite sex) and have been found to operate for direct-mail responses, point-of-purchase displays, and personal-selling interactions.[85] Race may be an important factor as well.[86] One study showed that African American consumers who identified strongly with African American culture responded more favorably to ads with African American models. Attractive sources make a difference in personal selling, too. In one study, consumers had more positive attitudes and stronger buying intentions when attractive salespeople stated their intention to persuade than they did when unattractive salespeople were involved.[87]

Note that in the context of high affective involvement, attractive sources directly influence brand-based attitudes because the sources are directly relevant to the product being considered (perfume, fashion, lingerie, etc.) and are thus a central part of the message. In the context of low-effort processing, attractive sources serve as a peripheral cue used to increase situational involvement and to generate a positive attitude toward the ad.

Exhibit 6.8

Influence of Communication Source

Companies use popular movie stars or celebrities to generate positive feelings toward the ad and the product. A good example is this Samsonite ad which features Danica Patrick.

Samsonite
Life's a Journey

Life's like a TRACK.
It's the TURNS
that make it worthwhile.

Danica Patrick, racing driver.
She travels with Silhouette 10 Spinner.
Four wheel steering, one smooth ride.

samsonite.com

Likable Sources

The likability of the source can influence affective attitudes.[88] For instance, the Japanese cosmetics company Shiseido has found Angelina Jolie to be a likable and attractive endorser for lipsticks.[89] Consumers also have more favorable attitudes toward brands that use likable celebrity voice-overs.[90] Likable sources may serve as unconditioned stimuli, create a positive mood that affects consumers' evaluations of the ad or brand, and make consumers feel more positive about the endorsed product. Sometimes the source can be physically unattractive but have features or a personality that consumers like. We tend to like people of average looks because they are more similar to ourselves and we can relate to them. In addition, disabled people are effective, likable endorsers for companies such as Sears because marketers want to represent human diversity and because consumers admire courageous individuals.[91]

Celebrity Sources

Physical attractiveness and likability explain why celebrities and well-known cartoon characters are among the most widely used sources. In this case, the presence of celebrities essentially increases the likelihood that consumers will like the ad (A_{ad}). In particular, celebrity sources can be effective when they are related to the offering (the match-up hypothesis).[92] Basketball star LeBron James, for instance, has a $90 million contract to endorse Nike athletic shoes.[93] Teenage consumers find athletes to be especially influential endorsers: the sports stars stimulate discussion about the brand and encourage brand loyalty.[94]

Spokescharacters of long tenure sometimes need updating to remain attractive to contemporary eyes. That is the reason why the Brawny man, who appears on Georgia-Pacific's paper towels, got a makeover, with new hair color, new hair style, and new clothing.[95] Spokescharacters may engender trust even if they are not directly relevant to the advertised product; trust, in turn, influences brand attitude.[96] Spokescharacters may be most effective in ads for hedonic services such as restaurants.[97]

Nonprofit organizations also use celebrities to attract attention and influence attitudes. Nicole Kidman and other celebrity endorsers for UNICEF "are of huge value," says the nonprofit's head of celebrity relations. "When a celebrity talks, people listen; there is no better messenger."[98] Using a celebrity endorser entails some risk because the spokesperson might become ill, break the law, or have another problem that could put the brand in a negative light. Yet research shows that a company can actually enhance its reputation by associating with an endorser who is perceived by consumers as having little blame for a problem (such as falling ill).[99]

The Message

Just as the source can influence consumers' feelings and moods, so too can characteristics associated with the message. These message characteristics include pleasant pictures, music, humor, sex, emotional content, and context.

Pleasant Pictures

Marketers frequently use pleasant pictures to influence consumers' message processing. Visual stimuli can serve as a conditioned stimulus, affect consumers' mood, or make an ad likable by making it interesting. Research has generally supported the view that pleasant pictures can affect ad and brand attitudes when they are processed peripherally, beyond the effect they have on consumers' beliefs about the product.[100] A picture of a sunset, for instance, can influence the choice of a soft drink.[101] Many advertisers use high-powered special effects rivaling those seen in movies for their television and online ads. A key goal of Internet advertising is to look cool, thereby creating positive feelings about the ad.[102]

Music

Music is frequently used as a communications tool by many companies, including General Motors and Victoria's Secret (which have used Bob Dylan's music to promote Cadillacs and women's apparel, respectively).[103] Further, the use of music is progressing beyond the traditional use of the "jingle." Sometimes the music ads become popular and drive album sales, as was the case with U2, whose album *How to Dismantle an Atomic Bomb* became a huge hit after the song "Vertigo" was featured in an iPod TV commercial.[104]

The popularity of music as a marketing device should not be surprising given that music has been shown to stimulate a variety of positive effects.[105] First, music can be an effective conditioned stimulus for a classical conditioning strategy. Intel, NBC, and other brands use musical "tags" to serve as retrieval cues and add to the brand identity. Second, music can put the consumer in a positive mood and lead to the development of positive attitudes. Third, music can be effective in generating positive feelings such as happiness, serenity, excitement, and sentimentality. Fourth, background music in ads can stimulate emotional memories of experiences or situations.[106] If a song in an ad reminds you of your high school days or of an old boyfriend or girlfriend, the emotions associated with these memories may transfer to an ad, brand, store, or other attitude object. Several studies have found that music can have a positive effect on purchase intentions.[107]

Whether or not music evokes a positive affective response depends on the music's structure. Exhibit 6.9 shows several musical characteristics and the emotional responses they may elicit. The style of music used and the product meanings it conveys can vary considerably across different cultures.[108] Marketers must therefore be careful to match their music to the desired affective responses.

Humor

An ad can use humor in many different ways, including puns, understatements, jokes, ludicrous situations, satire, and irony. Humor is common in TV advertising: 24 to 42 percent of all commercials contain some form of humor.[109] Although not as widespread in other media as in television, use of humor is nevertheless extensive, particularly in radio.[110] The popularity of humor as a message device is not surprising because it increases consumers' liking of the ad and the brand.[111]

Exhibit 6.9

Musical Characteristics For Producing Various Emotional Expressions

Research has pinpointed the specific effect that various aspects of music can have on feelings. As shown here, the mode, tempo, pitch, rhythm, harmony, and volume of music can influence whether individuals feel serious, sad, sentimental, serene, humorous, happy, excited, majestic, or frightened.

	Emotional Expression								
Musical Element	**Serious**	**Sad**	**Sentimental**	**Serene**	**Humorous**	**Happy**	**Exciting**	**Majestic**	**Frightening**
MODE	Major	Minor	Minor	Major	Major	Major	Major	Major	Minor
TEMPO	Slow	Slow	Slow	Slow	Fast	Fast	Fast	Medium	Slow
PITCH	Low	Low	Medium	Medium	High	High	Medium	Medium	Low
RHYTHM	Firm	Firm	Flowing	Flowing	Flowing	Flowing	Uneven	Firm	Uneven
HARMONY	Consonant	Dissonant	Consonant	Consonant	Consonant	Consonant	Dissonant	Dissonant	Dissonant
VOLUME	Medium	Soft	Soft	Soft	Medium	Medium	Loud	Loud	Varied

Source: Gordon C. Bruner, "Music, Mood, and Marketing," *Journal of Marketing*, October 1990, p.100. Reprinted by permission.

Humor appears to be more appropriate for low-involvement offerings in which generating positive feelings about the ad is critical.[112] Humor is also most effective when it is tied or related to the offering. Otherwise, consumers will only pay attention to the humor and ignore the brand.[113] In fact, consumers will have higher recall of an ad when the humor is strong and relates to the message.[114] Consumers who feel the need to seek out amusement and wittiness will develop more favorable attitudes toward humorous ads—and may have less favorable attitudes toward ads with lower levels of humorous content.[115] How consumers react during a TV ad affects their evaluations of the message as well. Consumers in one study rated TV ads as more humorous when the ad created surprise followed by a humorous response.[116]

MARKETING IMPLICATIONS

Humor tends to work best on TV and radio because these media allow for greater expressiveness than do other media.[117] Unilever has used tongue-in-cheek ads to great effect in building Axe into a major men's personal care brand, prompting rival Procter & Gamble to start running humorous ads for its Old Spice brand.[118] However, humor is more effective with certain audiences than with others. In particular, younger, more educated males tend to respond most positively—apparently because aggressive and sexual types of humor appear more frequently than other types of humor, and men enjoy this type of humor more than women do.[119] Also, humor appears to be more effective for consumers who have either a lower need for cognition or a positive attitude toward the advertised brand.[120]

Finally, humor can be used effectively throughout the world. One study examined humorous ads from Germany, Thailand, South Korea, and the United States and found that most humorous ads in all four countries contained the same basic structure—contrasts between expected/possible and unexpected/impossible events.[121] However, ads in Korea and Thailand tended to emphasize humor related to group behavior and unequal status relationships, whereas ads in the other two countries focused the humor on individuals with equal status. In all four countries, humor was more likely to be used for marketing pleasure-oriented products. In addition, not all countries appear to employ humor more often for low-involvement products than for high-involvement ones. German and Thai ads, for example, used humor equally for both types of products, and U.K. firms tend to use humorous ads more than U.S. firms do.[122]

Sex

Sex as a communication technique appears in two major forms: sexual suggestiveness and nudity. Sexual suggestiveness involves situations that either portray or imply sexual themes or romance. SSL International, the world's largest condom manufacturer, has switched from fear appeals to suggestiveness. Now radio ads for its Durex brand of condoms include flirtatious banter between male and female voices, and its Internet banner ads rely on innuendo.[123] Another use of sex is through nudity or partial nudity, a technique often used by brands in the fragrance industry.[124] Exhibit 6.10 shows an ad from Germany that employs this technique. Interestingly, research shows that consumers prefer mildly provocative ads and that such ads can even be effective in promoting social causes that have some connection to sex (match-up hypothesis).[125]

Exhibit 6.10
Nudity in Advertising

Sometimes ads contain naked or scantily clad models to generate attention or elicit consumers' emotions toward a product or service. Here we see an ad from Germany for a mineral water that states, "Water in its finest form." The naked model attracts attention and emphasizes the other copy point: that this water does a lot to enhance health.

Although the percentage of ads with sexual overtones has not changed over the years, the type of sex appeal depicted has. From 1964 to 1984, the use of sex in the United States became more overt and blatant.[126] As the country became more conservative in the late 1980s, ads became lighter, more playful, and subtler—suggestive rather than blunt.[127] In recent years, public response and regulatory scrutiny have prompted some advertisers to tone down their use of sexual references and imagery.[128]

MARKETING IMPLICATIONS

Research on sexual themes in messages suggests that they can be effective in several ways. Sexual messages attract the consumer's attention[129] and can evoke emotional responses such as arousal, excitement, or even lust, which in turn can affect consumers' moods and their attitudes toward the ad and brand.[130] Funny ads featuring sexy women drawn to men wearing Axe-brand body spray have been quite effective for Unilever.[131]

For some consumers, however, sexual messages can create negative feelings such as embarrassment, disgust, or uneasiness, any of which would have a negative effect. In particular, women are more likely to react negatively to ads with sexy female models.[132] Women also react more negatively to nudity in general, but more positively to suggestiveness.[133] Men are much more likely than women to buy a product featured in an ad with sexual content. Yet 61 percent of the respondents in one study said they would be less likely to buy products advertised with sexual imagery. In this research, 53 percent of the respondents preferred love imagery over sex imagery in advertising.[134]

One survey indicated that 84 percent of females and 72 percent of males believe that TV ads place too much emphasis on sex.[135] In another survey, 49 percent said they have been embarrassed in front of friends or family by sexy TV ads, and 47 percent indicated they would not buy a product if they found an ad offensive.[136] The lesson for marketers is that sexual themes should be used carefully and not be demeaning, sexist, or offensive.

Whether consumers will have a positive or negative reaction to a sexual ad often depends on whether the sexual content is appropriate for the product/service. One study found that using a seductive model to sell body oil was very appealing, but having a nude model endorse a ratchet set was not.[137] Thus, sexual themes would be relevant for products such as perfume, cologne, suntan lotion, and lingerie but inappropriate for tools, computers, and household cleaners.

Finally, consumer reaction to sexual messages varies from culture to culture. In some societies, such as in Europe, sexual attitudes are fairly open, and the use of sex in advertising is more widespread than it is in other countries. In other areas (such as Muslim and Asian countries), attitudes are more conservative, and the use of sex is much more restricted. Showing intimacy and kissing, as is done in many ads in the United States, would be totally inappropriate and even offensive in many Asian countries.[138] Consumers in different countries reacted differently to a public-service ad for breast cancer awareness in which men admired an attractive woman wearing a sundress while an announcer stated, "If only women paid as much attention to their breasts as men do." Japanese consumers appreciated the humor, but French consumers disliked the sexual overtones and light treatment of a serious problem.[139]

Emotional Content

Marketers can plan communications to accommodate or enhance consumers' existing MAO and processing effort in the presence of cognitive attitudes. The same holds true for affective attitudes, which is where emotionally involving messages come into play.

Transformational advertising Ads that try to increase emotional involvement with the product or service.

One special type of emotional message is called **transformational advertising**.[140] The goal of a transformational ad is to associate the experience of using the product with a unique set of psychological characteristics. These ads try to increase emotional involvement by making the use of the product or service a warmer, more exciting, more pleasing, and richer experience as opposed to the approach taken by informational ads, which seek only to present factual information. Coca-Cola, for example, uses transformational advertising to convey that "Coke is a part of the pleasure of everyday life, the pleasure of aliveness, relaxation, and being connected," says the company's chief marketing officer. The upbeat Coke Side of Life ads feature the trademark Coke bottle to reinforce the idea that "Coke is about happiness in and around the bottle."[141]

Dramas Ads with characters, a plot, and a story.

Dramas can also increase emotional involvement in a message. A drama message has characters, a plot, and a story about the use of the product or service.[142] This type of message aims to involve consumers emotionally and influence positive attitudes through both sympathy and empathy.[143] Unilever advertises its Sunsilk hair-care products during reruns of *Sex and the City* using "Lovebites," a series of two-minute dramas about a young woman juggling work, dating, and life, including handling her hair. Ratings indicate that the *Sex and the City* viewers also stay tuned to watch "Lovebites" during the commercial breaks.[144]

Message Context

The program or editorial context in which an ad appears can affect consumers' evaluation of the message. First, ads embedded in a happy TV program may be evaluated more positively than those in sad programs, especially if the ads are emotional.[145] Similarly, how well we like the program can affect our feelings about the ad and the brand.[146] One explanation of this reaction is that the programs influence us to process information in a manner consistent with our mood. Or, according to the excitation transfer hypothesis, we may mistakenly attribute to the ad our feelings about the TV program.[147]

One note of caution: A TV program can become too arousing and can therefore distract viewers from the ads. In an interesting study that compared consumers' reactions to ads broadcast during the Super Bowl, ad responses in the winning city were inhibited in contrast to those in the losing and neutral cities.[148] Another study shows that placing ads in violent programs can inhibit processing and ad recall.[149]

Summary

Marketers can use a variety of techniques to change consumers' attitudes when motivation, ability, and opportunity (MAO) are low and consumers use little effort to process information, make decisions, or engage in behavior. Often consumers form attitudes unconsciously, without being aware of how or why they have done so. Two unconscious influences in low-effort situations are thin-slice judgments and body feedback. When attitudes of low MAO consumers are based on cognitive processing, the message should affect their beliefs, which may be formed by simple inferences, attributions, or heuristics. Marketers can also affect the salience, strength, or favorability of consumers' beliefs on which attitudes are based. Source credibility, information consistent with the offering category, the number of message arguments, simple arguments, and repetition can all influence beliefs.

According to the mere exposure effect, when effort (MAO) is low, consumers' attitudes toward an offering become more favorable as they become more familiar with it. Classical conditioning predicts that consumers' attitudes toward an offering (the conditioned stimulus) are enhanced when it is repeatedly paired with a stimulus (the unconditioned stimulus) that evokes a positive emotional response (the unconditioned response). This reaction is most likely to occur when the unconditioned stimulus is novel, when the consumer is aware of the link when the conditioned and unconditioned stimuli fit together, and when the conditioned stimulus precedes the unconditioned one. If consumers like an ad, these positive feelings may be transferred to the brand. Consumers' moods and their tendency to evaluate an offering in accordance with their moods can also affect their attitudes.

Finally, marketers can use marketing communications to induce favorable attitudes based on affective processes when consumers' motivation, ability, opportunity, and effort are low. Characteristics of the source (attractiveness, likability), the message (attractive pictures, pleasant music, humor, sex, emotionally involving messages), and the context (repetition, program or editorial context) can all influence affective attitudes.

Questions for Review and Discussion

1. How can unconscious influences affect consumer attitudes and behavior in low-effort situations?

2. What role do source, message, context, and repetition play in influencing consumers' cognitive attitudes in low-effort situations?

3. What is the mere exposure effect, and why is it important to consumers' affective reactions?

4. How does classical conditioning apply to consumers' attitudes when processing effort is low?

5. Explain the dual-mediation hypothesis. What are the implications for affecting consumers' brand attitudes?

6. In low-effort situations, what characteristics of the message influence consumers' affective response?

7. What are the advantages and disadvantages of featuring celebrities in advertising messages?

CL Visit http://cengage.com/marketing/hoyer/ ConsumerBehavior5e to find resources that are available to help you study for the course.

CONSUMER BEHAVIOR CASE

Tugging on Shoppers' Heartstrings

J.C. Penney and Wal-Mart want shoppers to know how much they care. Good prices and good selection are still important, but with so many choices on the street and on the Web, retailers really have to fight for attention in today's crowded marketplace. This reason explains why Penney's and Wal-Mart are using marketing communications to build an emotional connection with consumers.

"Everybody out there is doing product-focused advertising," explains J.C. Penney's chief marketing officer. "What we learned is that no matter how well you do that, it does not break through the clutter." So the department store's advertising agency, Saatchi & Saatchi, tried something a little different. Its employees spent several days tagging along with more than 50 women to learn firsthand what these consumers were doing, thinking, and feeling as they went about their daily lives.

What emerged from this research was a communications focus on consumers, exemplified by the advertising slogan "Every day matters." In line with this slogan, the agency created a series of touching, dialogue-free commercials featuring brief but moving glimpses of moments from daily life. Each commercial was set to a song with intriguing lyrics and unfolded without sponsor identification until the final seconds.

The first commercial in the campaign showed a young couple and their two children getting ready for the day, with a hint of gift-giving in the sparkle of diamond jewelry passing from husband to wife. The commercial had no voice-over, a situation that freed viewers to focus their attention on the heartwarming visuals and enjoy the catchy song, "So Say I." In one of the Christmas ads, parents and children walked along snow-covered streets (and a diamond gift made a brief appearance) as the song "All That I Want" played in the background. Viewers could not be sure what they were watching because Penney's logo did not appear until the very end of the commercial—and then only briefly. The entire campaign was acclaimed for its creativity and use of music, many of the commercials wound up with thousands of viewers on YouTube, and many of the songs became instant iTunes hits. Penney's also posted a series of online episodes on its website, hoping that teenagers would find the content amusing and pass the word to their friends and classmates.

When this unusual campaign began, not everyone in the Penney's organization was sure that it would work. "Sometimes we run ads that we don't totally understand, and they have been home runs with the customer," notes the chief marketing officer. In his view, "if you are doing the same old warmed-over product-based stuff that everyone else is doing, you are wasting your money."

Wal-Mart, best known for its discount prices, is also seeking more emotional bonds with its customers. The yellow smiley-face that appeared in Wal-Mart's communications for so many years is now gone. Instead, the Martin Agency, which handles the retail giant's advertising, is using communications to drive home the benefit of what consumers can do with the money they save

by shopping at Wal-Mart, with this theme reflected in the retailer's new slogan, "Save Money. Live Better."

For instance, the company's Christmas commercials portrayed Wal-Mart shoppers enjoying the feeling of being able to give brand-name gifts to loved ones because of the store's low prices. "It's great to save money, but the feeling you get giving the bike the kid wants is the payoff," says Wal-Mart's chief marketing officer. In the end, he says moving away from a simple low-price message has been important because the company has been "trying to make sure there is an emotional connection and not just an empty promise of 'Save, save, save.'"[150]

Case Questions

1. How is J.C. Penney using mood to influence consumers' affective attitudes?
2. By withholding the sponsor's name until the end of its commercials, J.C. Penney adds a sense of mystery to its ads. Do you think this is a good approach for a retailer to take? Explain your answer by using consumer behavior concepts from this chapter.
3. How is Wal-Mart seeking to influence consumers' cognitive and affective attitudes with its new ads and new slogan "Save Money. Live Better"?

Memory and Retrieval

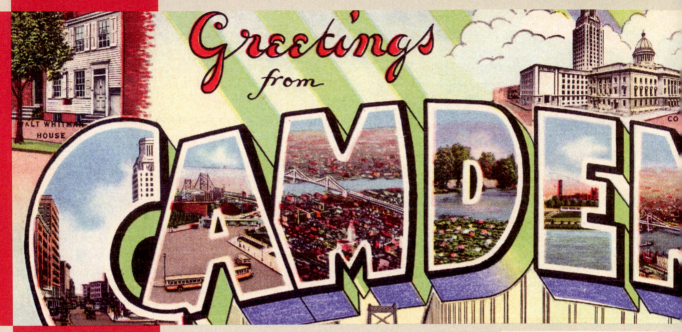

INTRODUCTION

Déjà Vu All Over Again: Nostalgia Marketing

Entrepreneur Molly Robbins is marketing children's clothing to parents who smile when they remember the Italian mouse puppet Topo Gigio that was popular in the 1960s. Evoking the past to promote brands and products with decades of history behind them, a strategy known as *nostalgia marketing,* is helping small businesses as well as multinational giants increase sales and profits today. Robbins' firm markets clothing featuring brand images once known throughout Latin America, including Topo Gigio and De La Rosa candy. "These are products from my youth in Mexico, and [they] bring back fond memories," she says, adding that marketing this apparel "is not just about the brands; it is about the memories they bring to you." Mervyns and other major stores carry the line, which primarily targets Latino consumers but also has a broader attraction because of the appealingly retro graphics.

Other marketers are using old brands, symbols, images, logos, slogans, or jingles to create positive attitudes for their products through nostalgia. Food marketers such as Chicken of the Sea and Campbell Soup are resurrecting vintage jingles to jog consumers' memories. Nostalgia marketing is common in other countries as well. Nostalgic for the years when East Germany was separate from West Germany, some German consumers are snapping up foods, clothing, and other products that remind them of the old days.

Similarly, Russians in their twenties and thirties who feel nostalgic for the old U.S.S.R. are buying fashions featuring hammer-and-sickle designs.[1]

What is driving the popularity of nostalgia marketing? Consumers in today's fast-paced, information-intensive age are feeling overwhelmed by the new and unfamiliar, a situation that leaves them more receptive to familiar products, songs, and images. Reminders of familiar offerings can also enhance brand awareness and brand knowledge because consumers already have personal memories associated with these offerings. Many of these memories reflect a happier and more peaceful time. Seeing an old ad, hearing an old brand name, or catching a few notes from an old jingle reminds consumers of their positive feelings about this earlier time and generates positive attitudes toward both the ad and the advertised brand.[2] All these concepts are covered in this chapter.

What Is Memory?

Consumer memory A personal storehouse of knowledge about products and services, shopping, and consumption experiences.

Retrieval The process of remembering or accessing what we have stored in memory.

Consumer memory is a vast personal storehouse of knowledge about products, services, shopping excursions, and consumption experiences. In essence, memory reflects our prior knowledge. **Retrieval** is the process of remembering or accessing what we have stored in memory.

We all store and remember information about things, experiences, and evaluations. Specifically, we might remember what brands, products, services, and companies we have used in the past (things); what we paid; the features of these products or services; how, where, when, and why we bought and used them (experiences)[3]; and whether or not we liked them (evaluations). We can store and remember information about old products we have disposed of, such as a favorite car we sold. We also have memories of special occasions—for example, a concert we attended with friends to celebrate a birthday. The information we store and retrieve is learned from many sources—marketing communications, the media, word of mouth, and personal experience.

We discussed certain aspects of memory and retrieval in the preceding three chapters. Chapter 4 noted that information stored in memory affects whether and how we interpret and categorize objects. Chapters 5 and 6 indicated that attitudes are part of our memory—they represent stored summary evaluations of objects. Moreover, we can and often do recall attitudes when we make decisions. As we shall see in subsequent chapters, memory also affects decision making. You may decide to buy season tickets to a sporting event because you can vividly remember what a good time you had when you went before with your friends. Alternatively, you may receive information about an offering at one time and use that information to make purchase, usage, or disposition decisions at another time.

What Are the Types of Memory?

Memory represents more than the prior knowledge that we discussed in Chapter 4, however. Exhibit 7.1 indicates three types of memory: sensory memory (echoic and iconic memory), short-term memory (imagery and discursive processing), and long-term memory (autobiographical and semantic memory). Let us look at what each type of memory means.

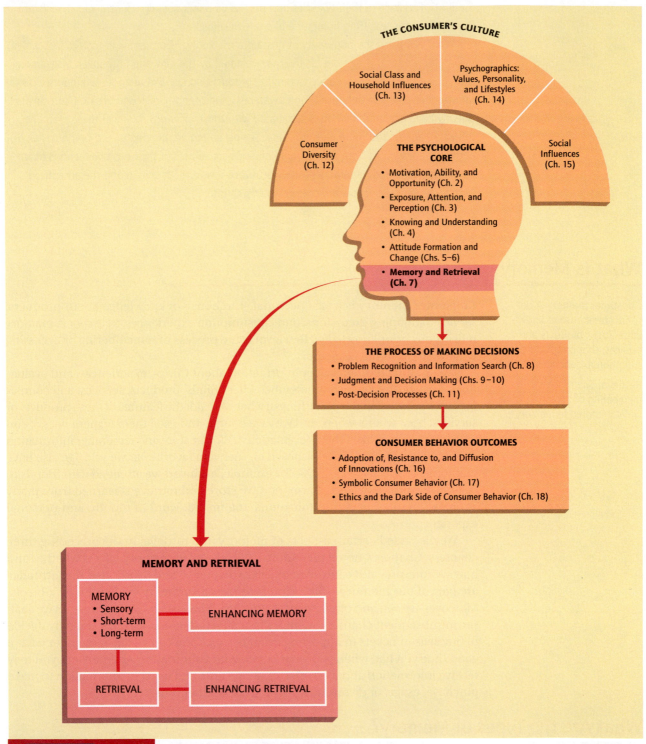

Exhibit 7.1

Chapter Overview: Memory and Retrieval

Research has identified three types of memory: sensory memory, short-term memory (STM), and long-term memory (LTM). Once information is in memory, it can then be retrieved (recognized or recalled). This chapter shows (1) what influences the transfer of information from STM to LTM and (2) what affects the likelihood that information will be retrieved from memory.

Sensory Memory

Assume for a minute that as you are talking to the person seated next to you at a dinner party, you happen to overhear other guests talking about a new movie you want to see. You do not want to appear rude, so you try to pay full attention to your dinner partner, but you really want to hear what the others are saying about the movie. Even though you cannot listen to both conversations simultaneously, you can store, for a relatively short period, bits and pieces of the other conversation. So you might be listening to your dinner partner but switch your attention to the other conversation once you hear the word *amazing*. As another example, assume that you are doing your homework in front of the TV. Your roommate comes in and says, "That's a great commercial!" Although you have not been listening, right after your roommate makes this statement, you realize that you heard the words *Coca-Cola*. You realize it is a Coke commercial, and you say, "Yeah, I really like that one, too."

Sensory memory Sensory experiences stored temporarily in memory.

The ability to store sensory experiences temporarily as they are produced is called **sensory memory.** Sensory memory uses a short-term storage area called the *sensory store*. Sensory memory operates automatically, and if we quickly switch our attention to our sensory store, we may be able to interpret what is in it.

Echoic memory Very brief memory for things we hear.

Iconic memory Very brief memory for things we see.

Our sensory store can house information from any of the senses, but **echoic memory**—memory of things we hear—and **iconic memory**—sensory memory of things we see—are the most commonly studied.[4] The Coke example illustrates echoic memory. Here is another example: You may have found that when someone asks you a question, and you are not really listening, you can say, "What did you say?" and actually "play back" what the person said. Iconic memory is at work when you drive by a sign and see it quickly, only to realize after you have driven past that it was a sign for Applebee's.

Information in sensory memory is stored in its actual sensory form. In other words, we store the word *amazing* as it sounds, and we store it exactly, not as a synonym. Information in sensory memory is also short-lived, generally lasting from a quarter of a second to several seconds.[5] If the information is relevant, we will be motivated to process it further, and it may enter what is called *short-term memory*. However, if we do not analyze that information, it is lost.

Short-Term Memory

Short-term memory (STM) The portion of memory where incoming information is encoded or interpreted in light of existing knowledge.

Short-term memory (STM) is the portion of memory where we "encode" or interpret incoming information.[6] The processes of knowing and understanding discussed in Chapter 4 occur in short-term memory. As you read this book, you are using your short-term memory to comprehend what you read. You also use short-term memory when you watch a TV commercial or make a decision in a store. Short-term memory is very important because it is where most of our information processing takes place. Short-term memory can be hurt when we are distracted by other information.[7]

Imagery and Discursive Processing

Discursive processing The processing of information as words.

Imagery processing The processing of information in sensory form.

The information in short-term memory can take one of several forms. When we think about an object—say, an apple—we might use **discursive processing** and represent it with the word *apple*. Alternatively, we could represent it visually as a picture of an apple or in terms of its smell, its feel, what it sounds like when we bite into it, or what it tastes like. Representing the visual, auditory, tactile, gustatory, and/or olfactory properties of an apple uses **imagery processing.**[8] Unlike the case of discursive processing, an object in imagery processing bears a close resemblance to the thing being represented.[9] Therefore, if you were asked to imagine an apple and a car, imagery processing would ensure that you preserve their relative sizes.

Information represented either as words or images can be elaborated, or thought about more deeply.[10] When MAO is low, short-term memory might consist of a simple reproduction of an object—for example, the word *skier* or a picture of a skier. When MAO is high, however, consumers can use elaborated imagery processing to engage in daydreams, fantasies, visual problem-solving, or elaborated discursive processing to think about upcoming events or work out solutions to current problems. For example, if you are thinking about a skiing vacation, you may develop an elaborate fantasy about lounging around the fireplace at a resort hotel, drinking hot cider, feeling the ache of your tired muscles, and enjoying the company of your friends. You might also use discursive processing to compare the prices and attributes of various resorts.

Characteristics of Short-Term Memory

Short-term memory has two interesting characteristics:

- ▶ *Short-term memory is limited.* We can hold only a certain number of things in short-term memory at any one time. For example, if you have to go to the store right now to buy two items, chips and hot dogs, you'll probably be able to remember what to buy. But suppose you have to buy nine items: chips, hot dogs, coffee, cookies, baking soda, plastic wrap, toothpaste, spaghetti sauce, and dog food. Chances are high that you will forget one or more of these items unless you make a shopping list.

- ▶ *Short-term memory is short-lived.* The information held in short-term memory is very short-lived unless that information is transferred to long-term memory. Unless we actively try to remember information, it will be lost. This phenomenon explains why we sometimes learn someone's name only to forget it two minutes later.

MARKETING IMPLICATIONS

Short-term memory, particularly imagery processing, has four key implications for marketers:

1. *Imagery processing can affect product liking and choice.* The vacation we choose, for example, may be greatly influenced by what we imagine it will be like. We value some of the products we buy (for example, novels or music) because of the imagery they provide.[11] In fact, consumers who immerse themselves in thoughts of using a product or having an experience similar to one simulated in an ad will tend to have positive attitudes toward the ad and the product.[12] Thus, a product's ability to stimulate multisensory imagery might affect how much we like (or dislike) that product.

2. *Imagery can stimulate memories of past experiences.* We value some things that help us re-experience a past consumption experience. Thus, you might keep a sports program or ticket stub because the imagery it evokes allows you to relive the event. As another example, Microsoft recently released an updated, high-definition Pac-Man video game, a product that may stimulate some consumers to create imagery of using the old Pac-Man game (see Exhibit 7.2).[13]

Exhibit 7.2

Stimulating Memories of Past Experiences

The new Pac-Man video game may stir up memories of past experiences with the old Pac-Man game.

3. *Imagery can affect how much information we can process.* Adding more information, like providing lists of attributes, can hurt discursive processing by creating information overload. However, adding information can help imagery processing because the additional information helps us flesh out the image. Bluenile.com, for example, encourages imagery by letting consumers zoom in on the diamond jewelry it sells to get a closer look,[14] a tactic that might help consumers better imagine what it might be like to own or give the jewelry as a gift.

4. *Imagery may affect how satisfied we are with a product or consumption experience.* We may create an elaborate image or fantasy of just what the product or consumption experience will be like (how great we will look in a new car or how relaxing a vacation will be) only to find that it does not materialize in the way that we had imagined. If reality does not confirm our imagery, we may feel dissatisfied. Realizing this possibility, some marketers help consumers establish realistic imagery. For example, on the Sherwin-Williams website, consumers can "paint" rooms in a virtual home so that they can envision the product's effect before they actually buy the paint.

Long-Term Memory

Long-term memory (LTM)
The part of memory where information is placed for later use; permanently stored knowledge.

Autobiographical or episodic memory Knowledge we have about ourselves and our personal experiences.

Long-term memory (LTM) is that part of memory where information is permanently stored for later use. Research in cognitive psychology has identified two major types of long-term memory: autobiographical and semantic memory.[15]

Autobiographical Memory

Autobiographical, or **episodic, memory** represents knowledge we have about ourselves and our past.[16] It includes past experiences as well as emotions and sensations tied to these experiences. These memories tend to be primarily sensory, mainly involving visual images, although they may also include sounds, smells, tastes, and tactile sensations. We may have autobiographical memories that relate to product acquisition, such as a shopping trip to find a specific product or the role that this product has played in our personal history.[17] And we may have autobiographical memories regarding consumption or disposition, such as attending a particular concert or throwing away a well-worn but loved product.

Because each individual has a unique set of experiences, autobiographical memory tends to be very personal and idiosyncratic. If you were asked to remember the road test you took when you got your driver's license, you might have stored in long-term memory the sequence of events that occurred on that day: what car you drove, what your route was, how nervous you were, what your instructor told you to do, and what happened after you passed (or failed!).

Semantic Memory

A lot of what we have stored in memory is not related to specific experiences. For example, we have memory for the concept called "cola." We know that colas are liquid, come in cans and bottles, are fizzy and brown in color, and are sweet. This knowledge is true of all colas. It is not tied to any particular brand of cola.

Semantic memory General knowledge about an entity, detached from specific episodes.

Knowledge about the world that is detached from specific episodes is called **semantic memory.** To illustrate, semantic memory regarding numbers can influence our perception of prices and, therefore, our intention to buy.[18]

MARKETING IMPLICATIONS

Much of the knowledge we have stored in cognitive categories reflects semantic memory. Thus, many of the marketing implications previously presented about knowledge stored in categories (see Chapter 4) also relate to semantic memory. Autobiographical memory, however, is also important to marketers.

Affecting decision making

Each consumer has a large storehouse of consumer-related memories that can influence how products and services are evaluated. For example, if you ate at a particular restaurant and found a hair in your food, the memory of this experience might prevent you from eating there again. Positive experiences would have the opposite effect. When selecting a restaurant, you might recall a previous visit in which the food was fabulous or the service incredible—memories that would clearly influence your decision about eating there again. We also have memories of how much we paid for something,[19] and this memory can affect our future choices; we will not buy something we think we paid too much for last time.

Promoting empathy and identification

Autobiographical memories can play a role in creating identification with characters or situations in ads. For example, if a Hefty ad can make consumers think about incidents in which their own garbage bags split open, consumers may be better able to relate to an ad showing inferior bags splitting apart while Hefty bags remain strong. Exhibit 7.3 also promotes identification.

Cueing and preserving autobiographical memories

As the chapter opening example suggested, consumers value some products because they promote autobiographical memories by creating feelings of nostalgia—a fondness for the past.[20] Consumers often find it important to preserve memories of graduations, the birth of a child, and so on. Entire industries for products such as digital cameras and photo printers focus on consumers' desires to document

Exhibit 7.3

Promoting Identification
Consumers who want a green lawn can identify with the situation illustrated in this ad.

WE'VE BEEN THERE. From gardening tools to hedge trimmers to lawn care supplies, we have the tools, products and advice you need to get your yard in its best shape ever.

True Value.
START RIGHT. START HERE.®

startrightstarthere.com

these autobiographical memories. The scrapbooking industry, based on products that help consumers preserve memories, has become a $2.6 billion business.[21] Consumers in many cultures want to preserve autobiographical memories.[22] Consumers who have moved from one country to another sometimes build shrines in their houses to remind them of the culture they left behind. Around the world, consumers highly value possessions that remind them of their friends, their family, and the important events in their lives.

Reinterpreting memories

Research shows that advertising can even affect autobiographical memories, such as how a consumer remembers past experiences with the advertised product.[23] One study had consumers sample good- and bad-tasting orange juices and then watch ads that described the products' good taste. Those exposed to the ads remembered the bad-tasting juice as being better tasting than it actually was.[24]

How Memory Is Enhanced

Because we must attend to something before we can remember it, many of the factors that affect attention (described in Chapter 3) also affect memory. Several additional processes, including *chunking, rehearsal, recirculation,* and *elaboration,* also affect memory.[25] These processes are useful for influencing short-term memory or for increasing the likelihood that information will be transferred to long-term memory—with important implications for marketers.

Chunking

Chunk A group of items that can be processed as a unit.

Traditionally, researchers have believed that the most individuals can process in short-term memory at any one time is three to seven "chunks" of information. Later studies suggest that the number may be closer to three or four.[26] A **chunk** is a group of items that is processed as a unit. For example, phone numbers are typically grouped into three chunks: the area code, the exchange, and four numbers.

Rehearsal

Rehearsal The process of actively reviewing material in an attempt to remember it.

Whereas chunking reduces the likelihood that information will be lost from short-term memory, rehearsal also affects the transfer of information to long-term memory. **Rehearsal** means that we actively and consciously interact with the material that we are trying to remember. We can either silently repeat the material or actively think about the information and its meaning, as we would do when studying for an exam. In marketing contexts, rehearsal is likely to occur only when consumers are motivated to process and remember information. If you are motivated to find food ingredients that are associated with good health you might study them so that you will not forget them.

Recirculation

Recirculation The process by which information is remembered via simple repetition without active rehearsal.

Information can also be transferred to long-term memory through the process of **recirculation.** Just as water is recirculated when it goes through the same pipe again and again, information is recirculated through your short-term memory when you encounter it repeatedly. Unlike rehearsal, with recirculation we make no

Creamy Jif has more fresh roasted peanut taste than any other leading creamy brand.

Choosy Moms Choose

Jif

Visit www.jif.com for recipes.
©2003 The J.M. Smucker Company

Exhibit 7.4

Recirculation
We might remember Jif peanut butter simply because we have seen it so many times before. Additional images of Jif further this recirculation process.

Elaboration Transferring information into long-term memory by processing it at deeper levels.

active attempt to remember the information. If we do remember, it is because the information has passed through our brain so many times. For example, because you have seen it so often, you probably remember the brand of mayonnaise that your mom buys. Note that brand recall is greater when information is repeated at different times rather than when it is presented over and over at one time.[27] Recirculation may be at work in Exhibit 7.4.

Elaboration

Finally, information can be transferred into long-term memory if it is processed at deeper levels, or **elaborated.**[28] We can try to remember information through rote memorization or rehearsal; however, this type of processing is not always effective. If you have ever memorized material for an exam, you probably noticed that you forgot most of what you had learned within two or three days. More enduring memory is established when we try to relate information to prior knowledge and past experiences. If you see an ad for a new product, for instance, you might elaborate on the ad information by thinking about how you would use the product in your day-to-day life. As a result, you may have a better memory for the brand and what the ad said about it.

MARKETING IMPLICATIONS

Marketers can apply chunking, rehearsal, recirculation, and elaboration to help consumers remember their brands, communications, or offerings.

Chunking

Marketers can increase the likelihood that consumers will hold information in short-term memory and transfer it to long-term memory by providing larger bits of information that chunk together smaller bits. For example, acronyms reduce several pieces of information to one chunk. Brand names like KFC and H&M are examples of chunking in a marketing context. Similarly, marketers can facilitate consumers' memory for telephone numbers by providing words rather than individual numbers or digits (800-GO-U-HAUL). Advertisements might draw conclusions that summarize or chunk disparate pieces of information into a single attribute or benefit. An ad that discusses a food product's calorie, fat, sodium, and sugar content might chunk this information into a conclusion about the product's healthfulness.

Rehearsal

When motivation is low, marketers may use tactics such as jingles, sounds, and slogans to perpetuate rehearsal. Under Armour, which makes sports apparel, created ads featuring men's cleats making distinctive click-clack sounds and the slogan "Click-Clack: I think you hear us coming."[29] Sometimes these techniques work too well, as you may know from going through the day singing a commercial's jingle. Rehearsal is not always good for marketers.

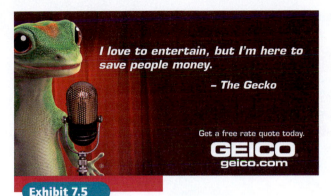

I love to entertain, but I'm here to save people money.

– The Gecko

Get a free rate quote today.

GEICO
geico.com

Exhibit 7.5

Tactics to Enhance Elaboration

GEICO's unusual choice of a gecko as spokescharacter for its insurance is intended to make consumers connect GEICO to gecko.

One study found that consumers who rehearsed the price paid for a product on the last occasion by writing it down (when paying by check or entering the amount into financial management software, for example) were less inclined to buy it.[30] The memory of the price probably highlighted what consumers had to give up to obtain the product.

Recirculation

Recirculation is an important principle for marketing because it explains why repetition of marketing communications affects memory, particularly in low-involvement situations.[31] Marketers can strengthen the effect of recirculation by creating different ads that repeat the same basic message. To illustrate, a slogan like "Chevy, an American revolution" is likely to be memorable after you have been exposed to it on many occasions, even though the ad content may change over time.

Recirculation can also explain why communications that repeat the brand name frequently, either within an ad or across communications, produce better brand name memory. Knowing that preteens like to play video games over and over again, the head of marketing for Burton Snowboard says his firm's snowboards and gear are featured in Sony video games for one reason: "Repetition, repetition, repetition."[32] According to research, planning spaced exposures by alternating messages in involving media such as TV commercials and less involving media such as billboards can be highly effective.[33] However, when one brand repeatedly advertises product claims that are similar to claims promoted repeatedly by a close competitor, the repetition may actually confuse consumers rather than enhance memory.[34]

Elaboration

Several strategies familiar from previous chapters enhance the likelihood that consumers will elaborate on information. For example, unexpected or novel stimuli can attract attention and induce elaboration.[35] GEICO's unusual choice of a gecko as spokescharacter for its insurance is intended to make consumers think about the connection (see Exhibit 7.5). Also, an advertising agency study indicates that consumers who pay attention to a particular TV program and think about it are more likely to remember its commercials.[36] Older people may have less ability to elaborate on information from marketing messages, perhaps because their short-term memory is more limited. Children may elaborate less because they have less knowledge, which makes it more difficult for them to think extensively about an ad message.[37] Elaboration may also explain why moderate levels of humor in an ad enhance both encoding and retrieval of the product's claims, whereas strong humor inhibits elaboration of the claims.[38]

What Is Retrieval?

In Chapter 4, you learned that knowledge is organized into categories and linked to associations. These categories and associations also relate to the concepts of memory and retrieval.

Semantic or associative network A set of associations in memory that are linked to a concept.

Organization of Long-Term Memory

Memory researchers think about long-term memory, or prior knowledge, as a series of **semantic (or associative) networks.** Exhibit 7.6 represents one consumer's memory

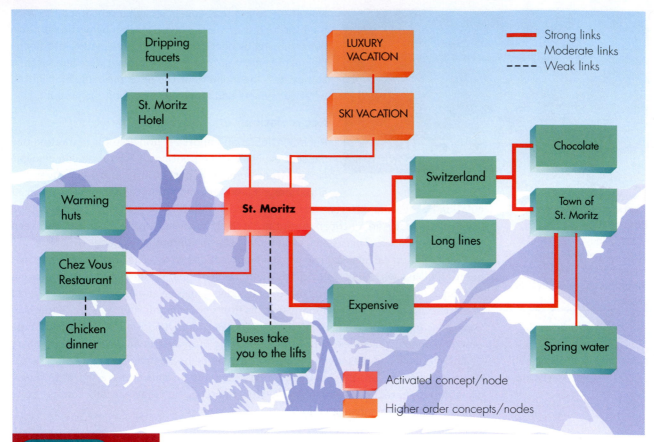

Exhibit 7.6

A Semantic (or Associative) Network

A semantic network is a set of concepts connected by links. When one concept is activated, others may become activated via the links. Concepts connected by strong links are more likely to activate each other than are those connected by weak links.

(or prior knowledge) about the category called "vacations," specifically the associations the consumer has to a St. Moritz ski vacation, a member of the "ski vacation" category. That category, in turn, is part of the higher order "luxury vacation" category. The St. Moritz ski vacation concept is connected to a set of links (called *associations* and *beliefs* in previous chapters). How did these links get there? They were learned and remembered based on personal experiences or information that the consumer had heard or read. Some links represent autobiographical memories; others represent semantic memory. The group of associations or links connected to the "St. Moritz ski vacation" concept is called a *semantic* (or *associative*) *network*.

Notice that in Exhibit 7.6, the links in the semantic network vary in strength. Strong links, depicted by the thick lines, are firmly established in memory. Others, depicted by the dashed lines, are weakly established in memory. Some links are strong because they have been rehearsed, recirculated, chunked, and elaborated extensively. Others are weak because they have been encountered infrequently, have not been accessed in a long time, or have been processed on a very limited basis. The entire semantic network represents what is available in this consumer's memory as a "St. Moritz ski vacation."

The Semantic Network

We have a lot of information in our memory, but we are only able to retrieve or access some of it at any given time.[39] We have all been in situations in which we try to remember something but cannot. Two factors about the semantic network affect what we remember: trace strength and spreading of activation.[40]

Trace Strength

Trace strength The extent to which an association or link is strongly or weakly linked to a concept in memory.

Accessible The extent to which an association or link is retrievable from memory.

The first factor affecting the semantic network is the strength of the links or associations, known as **trace strength.** The stronger the link that connects information to the category, the more **accessible** the information is and the easier it is to retrieve from memory. You are more likely to remember that BMW is "the ultimate driving machine" if you have a strong association connecting the car with its slogan. Marketers often try to strengthen our memory links. For example, after research revealed that most U.S. consumers believe that family-owned firms make products that consumers can trust, S. C. Johnson & Son added the tag line "A Family Company" to its advertising and packaging. Doing this helped the maker of Glade, Raid, and Windex strengthen the association of its products with family ownership in the minds of consumers.[41] The more marketers can engage in recirculation, or encourage consumers to rehearse or elaborate on information, the greater the likelihood that the link will be strengthened and that consumers will be able to retrieve that information.

Spreading of Activation

Spreading of activation The process by which retrieving one concept or association spreads to the retrieval of a related concept or association.

A second factor explaining what gets retrieved from memory is called **spreading of activation.** Think of a semantic network as a kind of electric network. Strong links have the potential for generating high-voltage current, and weak links have the potential for generating low-voltage current. Using the example in Exhibit 7.6, if a concept like "St. Moritz" is activated in the consumer's semantic network, the strong link between "St. Moritz" and "expensive" will activate or make the consumer think about "expensive." Because the current connecting "St. Moritz" and "expensive" is very strong, the electrical potential from this current will spread to adjacent items in the semantic network, particularly along strong links. Following Exhibit 7.6, this spreading of activation will likely lead the consumer to remember the town of St. Moritz. The activation of the concept "St. Moritz" may also activate "Switzerland" and "long lines." Activation from "Switzerland" may, in turn, spread to the concept "chocolate."

Of course, concepts like "Switzerland," "chocolate," and "expensive" are linked to many semantic networks, not just to one. Our consumer may think about chocolate when prompted to think about St. Moritz, but chocolate may be strongly linked to other semantic networks that can be cued through spreading of activation. This consumer may start thinking that she recently bought chocolate at a Godiva store, a recollection that may lead her to remember a friend she saw there, which may in turn remind her that she should write to her friend. Spreading of activation explains why we sometimes have seemingly random thoughts as the activation spreads from one semantic network to another.

MAO can influence spreading of activation. If motivation and opportunity to process information are high, the number of activated links can also be quite high. On the other hand, when motivation or opportunity is low, only the closest and strongest links might be activated. Individuals with more knowledge about a concept will have a greater ability to process a more detailed semantic network, bringing forth any number of associations.[42]

Because strong links enhance an item's accessibility from memory, they are very important to marketers. The weak links are not unimportant, however.

Activation spreads to every link in the semantic network, although the activation may not be sufficient to cause consumers to remember an item. A concept that has been activated but not enough to make it retrievable from memory is said to have been **primed.** It has been given a jump-start. Suppose our consumer is trying to remember how she got to the lifts at St. Moritz. The "buses" link is not strongly established in her memory. Activating "St. Moritz" might prime the "buses" concept, but the activation is too weak for the consumer to remember the buses. If she later drives by a school, the activation of the "school" concept might cue "buses," and this activation might be sufficient for her to remember that she got to the ski lift in St. Moritz by taking a bus.

Prime Activation of a node in memory, often without conscious awareness.

Retrieval Failures

Trace strength and spreading of activation help to explain forgetting—the failure to retrieve information from memory. Forgetting is a fact of life. You might forget to get your car serviced or forget that you are cooking hard-boiled eggs (until they explode). Retrieval failures clearly affect consumers' purchase, consumption, and disposition behaviors.

Decay

Decay The weakening of memory nodes or links over time.

In some cases, we forget things because trace strength fades; that is, memory links **decay** over time, often because they have not been used. Thus, we tend to forget events from childhood because they happened so long ago. Decay is reduced when we are repeatedly exposed to the information through recirculation or when we retrieve it often from memory. Sometimes the details or attributes of the information we have learned decay.[43] For example, we might have heard many details about a new movie, such as what the plot was about and who starred in it. However, later we may remember only something general about it ("I've heard it was good").

The fact that consumers can forget attributes explains some interesting marketing phenomena. For example, consumers may have equally strong memories for brands about which they have heard either very bad or very good things. They forget the information stated about the brands; all they remember is that the brands were in the news. Forgetting also explains the sleeper effect, discussed in Chapter 5, in which consumers show more positive attitudes toward a bad ad as time passes. Researchers believe that over time, consumers forget that an ad lacked credibility and simply remember what the source said about the brand. In essence, memory for the source decays more rapidly than memory for the message.[44]

Interference

Interference That which causes us to confuse which features go with which brand or concept due to semantic networks being too closely aligned.

Spreading of activation and trace strength explain a second cause of forgetting: interference.[45] **Interference** occurs when semantic networks are so closely aligned that we cannot remember which features go with which brand or concept. Suppose you are watching a car ad that focuses on the car's safety. If you have a lot of information about similar cars stored in memory, you might confuse which attribute is associated with which car. In addition, when consumers see ads that look similar, the similarity interferes with brand recall.[46] Competitive advertising also affects interference. When an established brand is promotes a new attribute, consumers' knowledge of the brand's old attributes can interfere with retrieval of information about the new one. Yet when competitive advertising is present, consumers are able to suppress older attribute information and effectively retrieve the new attribute information, an accomplishment that works to the brand's advantage.[47]

Interference also affects marketing across cultures. For instance, a study of how interference affects bilingual consumers concluded that second-language messages are not retrieved as well as first-language messages. To reduce interference, marketers should therefore use visual and textual cues that reinforce each other. This tactic helps consumers process second-language messages, thereby improving retrieval.[48]

Moreover, interference can result when one concept is activated so frequently that we cannot activate a different one. Suppose you are trying to recall the ten items that you have on your grocery list. Chances are good that you can recall several items very easily and a few more with some difficulty, but the last ones are probably impossible to remember. This situation results because in trying to remember the missing items, you keep remembering the items you have already recalled, and these recollections interfere with your ability to activate the missing ones.[49] Repeatedly activating the memory trace for the items you have remembered inhibits activation of the other items.

Primacy and Recency Effects

Primacy and Recency effect The tendency to show greater memory for information that comes first or last in a sequence.

Decay and interference can be used to explain **primacy and recency effects**—that is, the fact that the things we encountered first or last in a sequence are often those most easily remembered. As an example of primacy effects, you are likely to remember the first ad you saw during a commercial break because there was no other advertising information to interfere with it. That information may also be less likely to decay if you rehearse it. The primacy effect explains why, when you study for an exam, you tend to remember best the material you studied first.

As an example of recency effects, you are more likely to remember what you ate for breakfast this morning than what you ate a week ago because (1) this morning's information has not yet decayed, and (2) there is much less information interfering with the retrieval of this information. Considering primacy and recency effects, many advertisers believe that the best placement for an ad is either first or last in a commercial sequence or in a magazine. Some research supports the importance of being first; evidence in support of being last is not as strong.[50]

Retrieval Errors

What we do remember is not always accurate or complete; our memory may be subject to distortion or confusion. You might remember that your friend told you about a great new movie, but it was really your neighbor who told you about it. Memory may be selective, meaning that we retrieve only some information, often the information that is either very positive or very negative. In anticipating a vacation, you may remember the good things that happened on your last vacation but not the bad things. Finally, memory may be distorted. If you had a bad product experience, you may later remember experiences that were bad but that did not actually happen. Perhaps you remember that a waitress who treated you badly at a restaurant clunked your coffee down loudly on the table. While this "memory" is consistent with the "bad waitress" experience, it might not have actually happened.[51] And virtual interaction with a product leads to more false memories because it generates vivid images that consumers later come to believe were real occurrences.[52]

What Are the Types of Retrieval?

Consumers can retrieve information through two retrieval systems: explicit and implicit memory.

Explicit Memory

Explicit memory Memory for some prior episode achieved by active attempts to remember.

Explicit memory is memory of some prior episode achieved by active attempts to remember it. In this situation, you are consciously trying to remember something that happened in the past. For example, you would use explicit memory to remember what you ordered during a recent trip to In-N-Out. Consumers try to retrieve information from explicit memory by either recognizing it or recalling it.

Recognition The process of determining whether a stimulus has or has not been encountered before.

▶ **Recognition** occurs when we can identify something we have seen before, such as brand recognition (we remember having seen the brand before) and ad recognition (we remember having seen the ad before). Brand recognition is particularly critical for in-store decisions because it helps us identify or locate the brands we want to buy. Logos on brands or packages may be particularly effective at enhancing brand recognition. You may not recall which brand of shampoo you buy but you might recognize it once you see it on the store shelf.

Recall The ability to retrieve information from memory.

▶ **Recall** involves a more extensive activation of the links in memory, as when we see a Pepsi display and use recall to retrieve knowledge about Pepsi as input for decision making. *Free recall* exists when we can retrieve something from memory without any help, such as what we had for dinner last night. *Cued recall* exists if we are asked the same question (What did we have for dinner last night?) but need a cue (Was it a vegetarian dish?).

Implicit Memory

Implicit memory Memory for things without any conscious attempt at remembering them.

Sometimes we remember things without conscious awareness, a phenomenon called **implicit memory.** Suppose as you drive down the highway at high speed, you pass a billboard bearing the word *Caterpillar* (tractors). Later you are asked whether you remember seeing a billboard and, if so, what was on it. You do not remember seeing a billboard, let alone what it was for; you have no explicit memory of it. But if you are asked to say the first word you can think of that begins with *cat-*, you might answer "caterpillar." You might have encoded something about the billboard without being aware of even having seen it.

How can you have implicit memory of something you cannot explicitly remember? Your brief exposure to the Caterpillar name activated or primed the word *caterpillar* in your memory. The activation level was not strong enough for the name to be consciously retrieved; however, when you are asked for a word that begins with *cat-*, this activation brings *caterpillar* to mind.

(MARKETING IMPLICATIONS)

Retrieval is clearly an important concept for marketers.

Retrieval as a communication objective

Some marketing communications aim to increase recall of the brand name, product attribute, or brand benefit.[53] Other communications aim to increase consumers' recognition of the brand name, logo or brand symbol, package, advertisement, ad character, brand benefit, and so on. Newer competitors in an established industry work particularly hard to increase consumers' memory for their brand names. Under Armour, best known for men's sports apparel, now targets women with ads that incorporate unique sounds—in this case, "Boom Boom Tap"—to facilitate retrieval.[54]

Retrieval affects consumer choices

One study found that Japanese consumers' use of a bank declined as their recognition of the name of the bank declined.[55] Getting consumers to recognize or recall specific claims or slogans is also critical. Furthermore, knowing and remembering this information may serve as useful input to consumers' attitudes, and consumers may invoke this information when making choices among brands.

However, the most memorable ads are not necessarily the most effective. You may remember an ad because it was particularly bad, not because it increased your desire to buy the advertised brand. Nor are memorable ads necessarily effective at achieving objectives such as linking information to the specific brand. In one study, consumers who watched the Super Bowl and its commercials incorrectly attributed the advertising slogan of one telecommunications firm to as many as 13 other companies.[56] And not all marketers are interested in recall. For example, although consumers cannot always recall a product's actual price, they can recognize when a price is a good deal.[57]

Recognition and recall relate to advertising effectiveness

Marketers need to develop appropriate measures of recognition, recall, and implicit memory for testing advertisement and brand name effectiveness.[58] Exhibit 7.7 shows this kind of research. For example, if you are thinking about where you might go for lunch today, the list of restaurants you will consider will probably depend on those you can recall from memory. In such cases, marketers should use message strategies that encourage consumers to think about the brand and product, a process that enhances recall at the moment when choices are actually being made.[59]

Implicit memory is also important to marketers. Although ad agencies typically measure consumers' explicit memory by what they recall and recognize from an ad, the concept of implicit memory suggests that consumers may have some memory of

Exhibit 7.7	Rank	Brand	Ad Description
Recall Research The table to the right shows research on the most recalled new ads between February 25 and March 23, 2008.	1	Oreo	Young boy and father eat cookies with milk together over video chat; good night, Buddy; good morning, Dad
	2	Reese's	Peanut Butter Egg—Peanut butter jar and chocolate rabbit nuzzle; puff of smoke creates peanut butter eggs
	3	TGI Friday's	Ultimate Recipe Showdown Menu—Guy Fieri introduces dishes inspired by Food Network's Ultimate Recipe Showdown champion
	4	Burlington Coat Factory	Easter Savings Event—Families in Easter scenes; huge savings on boys' suits; the largest selections for girls
	5	AT&T	Man shoots basketball in bar; hi, I'm Chuck's phone; Chuck can't answer because he's an idiot; NCAA Final Four tickets

Source: © 2004–2008 IAG Research, http://www.iagr.net/data_total_market.jsp.

information in an advertising message even if they do not recognize or recall it. Thus, advertisers may try to use measures of implicit memory to gauge whether their ads have affected consumers' memory.

Consumer segments and memory

Although retrieval is an important objective for marketers, not all consumers can remember things equally well. In particular, older consumers have difficulty recognizing and remembering brand names and ad claims. ▬▬

How Retrieval Is Enhanced

Given the importance of retrieval, marketers need to understand how they can enhance the likelihood that consumers will remember something about specific brands. Consumers cannot recognize or recall something unless it is first stored in memory; chunking, rehearsal, and similar factors increase the likelihood that an item will be stored and available for retrieval. Four additional factors—some related to trace strength and spreading of activation—also affect retrieval: (1) the stimulus itself, (2) what it is linked to, (3) the way it is processed, and (4) the characteristics of consumers.

Characteristics of the Stimulus

Retrieval is affected by the salience (prominence) of the stimulus (the message or message medium). It is also affected by the extent to which the item is a prototypical member of a category, whether it uses redundant cues, and the medium that is used to convey information.

Salience

Something is salient if it stands out from the larger context in which it is placed because it is bright, big, complex, moving, or prominent in its environment (see Exhibit 7.8).[60] If you saw a really long commercial or a multipage ad, it might be salient relative to the short commercials or single-page ads that surround it. A visually complex figure in an ad will be salient relative to a simple background, and an animated Internet ad will be salient relative to motionless ones. Also, ads and demonstrations that offer consumers specific criteria for evaluating the promoted product as compared with competing products enhance the salience of those attributes. As a result, consumers can more easily encode and retrieve information based on those salient attributes.[61]

The salience of a stimulus affects retrieval in several ways. Salient objects tend to attract attention, drawing attention away from things that are not salient. Because they are prominent, salient stimuli also induce greater elaboration, thereby creating stronger memory traces.[62] This phenomenon might explain why some research has shown that consumers tend to remember longer commercials better than shorter ones and bigger print ads better than smaller ones.[63]

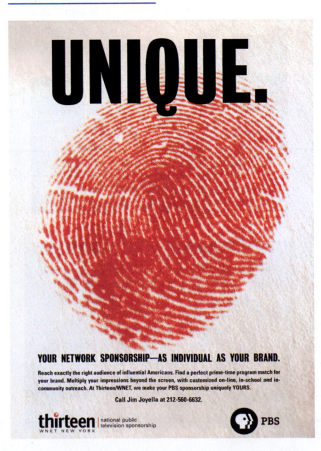

Prototypicality

We are better able to recognize and recall prototypical or pioneer brands in a product category (see Chapter 4 for a discussion of prototypicality). Because they have been frequently rehearsed and recirculated, the memory trace for prototypical brands is strong. These brands are also likely to be linked to many other concepts in memory, making their activation highly likely. The fact that we tend to remember these brands may explain why they have been so successful over time and why so many companies fight to establish themselves as category leaders.[64] Coca-Cola, for example, uses marketing to establish itself as the market leader in many countries. Thanks to in-store promotions and other techniques, its Femsa subsidiary has dramatically increased sales in Mexico. Consumers there now drink more Coca-Cola per capita than consumers in any other nation—3,200 ounces per year—making the brand the prototypical soft drink.[65]

Redundant Cues

Memory is enhanced when the information items to be learned seem to go together naturally. Thus, our memory of brand names, advertising claims, and pictures presented in ads is better when these elements convey the same information. Marketers can also enhance consumers' memory for brands by advertising two complementary products together (such as Special K with Tropicana orange juice) and explaining why they naturally go together.[66] Research indicates that event sponsorship enhances memory when the brand is prototypical—due to its prominence in the marketplace—and when the event relates to the brand's core meaning. Even if no clear link exists between the event and the sponsor, sponsor recall can be improved if the company explains (elaborates for the consumer) why the sponsorship makes sense.[67] Furthermore, because of redundancy between the spokesperson and the product category, recall is enhanced when a spokesperson is relevant to the product (as when model Petra Nemcova endorses Rampage, as shown in Exhibit 7.9).[68]

The Medium in Which the Stimulus Is Processed

Advertisers often wonder whether certain media are more effective than others at enhancing consumer memory, an area that researchers are still exploring. Currently, advertisers are trying to determine whether spending money on Internet ads is a good use of advertising dollars. Some research suggests that consumers tend not to look at or remember Internet ads, whereas other studies suggest that these ads can be as or even more effective in generating brand memory than ads shown in traditional media.[69]

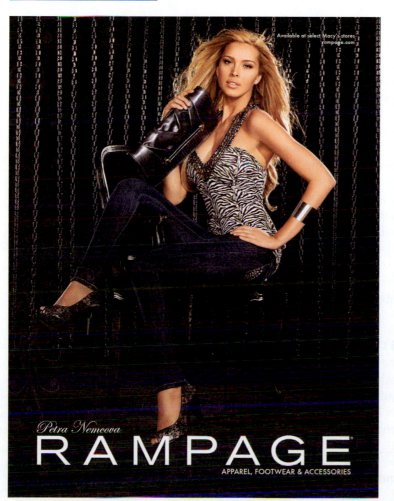

Exhibit 7.9

Redundant Cues

Memory is enhanced when the information items to be learned seem to go together naturally.

Available at select Macy's stores
rampage.com

Petra Nemcova

RAMPAGE

APPAREL, FOOTWEAR & ACCESSORIES

What the Stimulus Is Linked To

Retrieval cue A stimulus that facilitates a node's activation in memory.

Retrieval can also be affected by what the stimulus is linked to in memory. The associative network concept explains a related way of facilitating retrieval—providing retrieval cues. A **retrieval cue** is a stimulus that facilitates the activation of memory.[70] For example, if you want to remember to go to a sale at Macy's, you might leave a note on your desk that says, "Macy's." The note serves as a retrieval cue when you see it some time later and remember the sale.

Retrieval cues can be generated internally or externally. Internally, a thought can also cue another thought, as in "Today is December 8. Oh, my gosh, it's Mom's birthday!" An external stimulus such as a vending machine, a Web banner, or an in-store display could also serve as a retrieval cue—"Oh, there's the new candy bar I've been hearing about." These same retrieval cues can be used to activate images stored in autobiographical memory. If you see an ad for your favorite brand of ice cream, this cue might activate both your positive feelings about ice cream and your memory of past experiences with it. Pictures or videos of ourselves engaging in an activity can serve as powerful retrieval cues to stimulate memories.[71] However, effective retrieval cues may differ from culture to culture. One study found that sounds serve as more effective retrieval cues for English-language ads, whereas visuals serve as more effective retrieval cues for Chinese-language ads.[72]

Brand Name as a Retrieval Cue

One of the most important types of retrieval cues is the brand name.[73] If we see brand names such as Panasonic, Kellogg, and Reebok, we can retrieve information about these and related brands from memory. In particular, revealing the brand name early in an ad message is likely to strengthen the memory association between the brand and the consumer's evaluation of the message content, an effect that influences retrieval.[74] Yet the impact of a brand name as a retrieval cue is not the same for recognition as it is for recall.[75] Unfamiliar brands have a retrieval advantage when the name of the brand fits well with the product function, whereas familiar brands have a retrieval advantage when the name features unusual spelling.[76] Images closely related to the brand name also serve as retrieval cues.[77]

If marketers want consumers to *recognize* the brand on the store shelf, it is important to have high-frequency words or names to which consumers have been heavily exposed—for example, Coast or Crest. On the other hand, if the goal is to have consumers *recall* the brand and its associations, it is more important to have brand names that (1) evoke rich imagery (Passion or Old El Paso), (2) are novel or unexpected (Ruby Tuesday's or Toilet Duck), or (3) suggest the offering and its benefits (Minute Rice or PowerBook).

Other Retrieval Cues

Along with brand names, logos and packages can also act as retrieval cues. The picture of the girl with the umbrella is likely to cue consumers to remember the Morton seasoning products depicted in Exhibit 7.10. Category names are another type of retrieval cue. Thus, encountering the product categories "cars," "cookies," or "computers" might cue the names of specific brands from these categories from memories. Moreover, the visual properties of typefaces can serve as retrieval cues to the advertised product's benefits. This response is the reason why fast-food companies like Wendy's use distinctive and instantly recognizable lettering for their brand names.[78]

When it comes to salt, she's got it covered.

The Morton Salt girl.
Let her shake things up in your kitchen.
With salts and seasonings for every occasion,
she has that little something that makes a big difference.
For our entire line of salts and recipe ideas, see *mortonsalt.com*.
© 2002 Morton International, Inc.

Exhibit 7.10

The Package as Retrieval Cue

Packages sometimes contain information that helps consumers remember what they saw in an ad. The girl with the umbrella (who shows that Morton salt still pours even when it rains) is used as a retrieval cue on all Morton seasoning products.

MARKETING IMPLICATIONS

Retrieval cues have implications for consumers' purchasing decisions. Consumers often remember very little advertising content when they are actually making a decision in the store.[79] The reason this happens is that advertising is typically seen or heard in a context completely different from the purchase environment. One way to handle this problem is to place a cue from the ad on the brand's package or on an in-store display in order to activate advertising-related links in memory.[80] Thus, packages are sometimes labeled "as seen on TV." Another strategy is to place well-known cues from ads on the package, such as the bear on Snuggle fabric softener or "scrubbing bubbles" on S. C. Johnson's bathroom cleaner.

Retrieval cues also have important implications for marketers. First, these cues can affect what consumers remember from ads.[81] Some research has shown that the most effective retrieval cues match the cues actually used in an ad. Therefore, if an ad uses a picture of an apple, then a picture of an apple and not the word *apple* is the most effective retrieval cue. If the ad uses a particular word, then that word and not a picture of what it represents is the most effective retrieval cue. Other research has shown that music is an effective retrieval cue for ad content, affecting consumers' memories of pictures in an ad.

Some marketers have developed features to help consumers generate their own retrieval cues. For example, Hallmark.com offers a free reminder service to consumers who register and then list the people and special occasions they want to remember (by sending greeting cards or in other ways). The site will send an e-mail reminder of each birthday, anniversary, or other noteworthy occasion well in advance. This service not only acts as a retrieval cue but also facilitates searching and decision making—issues discussed in the next set of chapters. ◖▬▭

How a Stimulus Is Processed in Short-Term Memory

Another factor affecting retrieval is the way that information is processed in short-term memory. One consistent finding is that messages processed through imagery tend to be better remembered than those processed discursively. For instance, research shows that older consumers' memory for information from advertising can be improved if they form a mental image of things in the ad, such as the claims that it makes. Imagery apparently creates a greater number of associations in memory, which, in turn, enhance retrieval.[82] The reason for this phenomenon may be that things processed in imagery form are processed as pictures *and* as words. This **dual coding** provides extra associative links in memory, thereby enhancing the likelihood that the item will be retrieved. Information encoded verbally, however, is processed just one way—discursively—so it has only one retrieval path.

Dual coding The representation of a stimulus in two modalities, e.g., pictures and words in memory.

Nevertheless, imagery processing is not necessarily induced by pictures alone. When you read a novel, you can often generate very vivid images about the story and its characters. In this way, verbal information can also possess imagery-generating properties. Inducing imagery via pictures, high-imagery words, or imagery instructions may result in dual coding.[83] Dual coding is one reason that marketers often use the audio portion of well-known TV ads as radio commercials. When consumers hear the familiar verbal message, they may provide their own imagery of the visual part. The fact that they have engaged in coding of both the verbal message and its associated visuals facilitates retrieval of one if the other is present.

In the case of print ads, the ability of consumers to retrieve memories of earlier presentations of an ad strengthens memory traces of that message. However, varying ad format and content when messages appear at longer intervals will decrease the likelihood that consumers can retrieve memories of earlier presentations during the later presentations.[84]

Consumer Characteristics Affecting Retrieval

Finally, consumers' mood and expertise can affect retrieval.

Mood

Mood has some very interesting effects on retrieval.[85] First, being in a positive mood can enhance our recall of stimuli in general. Second, we are more likely to recall information that is consistent with our mood. In other words, if we are in a positive mood, we are more likely to recall positive information. Likewise, if we are in a negative mood, we will recall more negative information. From a marketing perspective, if an advertisement can influence a consumer's mood in a positive direction, the recall of relevant information may be enhanced when the consumer is feeling good.

Several explanations account for these mood effects. One is that feelings consumers associate with a concept are linked to the concept in memory. Thus, your memory of DisneyWorld may be associated with the feeling of having fun. If you are in a mood for fun, the "fun" concept may be activated, and this activation may spread to the concept of "Disney World."[86] Research also suggests that people process information in more detail when mood is intense than when it is not. More detailed processing leads to greater elaboration and higher levels of recall.[87]

Furthermore, mood influences both elaboration and rehearsal, two processes that enhance memory. Thus, consumers in a positive mood are more likely to readily learn brand names and engage in brand rehearsal.[88]

Expertise

Chapter 4 mentioned that compared with novices, experts have more complex category structures in memory with a greater number of higher- and lower-level categories and more detail within each category. Therefore, experts' associative networks are more interconnected than the networks of novices. The complex linkages and the spreading of the activation concept explain why experts can recall more brands, brand attributes, and benefits than novices.[89]

Summary

Memory consists of three memory stores. Sensory memory (iconic and echoic) involves a very brief analysis of incoming information. Short-term memory represents active working memory and involves imagery and discursive processing. Long-term memory represents the permanent memory store, covering both autobiographical and semantic memory. Consumers will lose information from the sensory store and from short-term memory if they do not further process the information.

Long-term memory can be represented as a set of semantic networks with concepts connected by associations or links. Although long-term memory reflects what we have stored, not everything in memory is equally accessible, indicating that memory and retrieval are different phenomena. To enhance the likelihood that information is stored in long-term memory and to reduce the likelihood that stored information will be lost, marketers can enhance memory using chunking, recirculation, rehearsal, and elaboration.

Retrieval is the process of remembering information stored in memory. Consumers can retrieve information when concepts are activated in memory, making the information accessible. Concepts may also be activated by the spreading of activation. Even if the activation is not sufficient to retrieve an item, it may be sufficiently strong to prime the concept in memory, making that concept more easily retrievable when other cues are present. People forget because of retrieval failures (due to decay, interference, primacy and recency effects) or because they may retrieve information that is not accurate.

There are two types of retrieval tasks: those that ask whether we can remember things we have previously encountered—an explicit memory task—and those that *reveal* the memory of things for which we have no conscious memory—an implicit memory task. Because of their importance to retrieval, both recall and recognition serve as objectives for marketing communications, influence consumer choice, and have important strategic implications. Factors that facilitate recognition and recall include the characteristics of the information (its salience, prototypicality, and redundancy), what it is linked to (retrieval cues), the way that it is processed (particularly in imagery mode), and the characteristics of consumers (mood, expertise).

Questions for Review and Discussion

1. How are sensory, short-term, and long-term memory linked?

2. What techniques can enhance the storage of information in long-term memory?

3. Why are some links in a semantic or associative network weak, whereas others are strong?

4. How can retrieval failures and errors affect consumer memory?

5. How does recognition differ from recall?

6. What is implicit memory, and how can it affect a consumer's ability to retrieve a brand name?

7. How do mood and expertise affect retrieval of memories?

CL Visit http://cengage.com/marketing/hoyer/ConsumerBehavior5e to find resources that are available to help you study for the course.

Remember the Apple

Thanks to a steady stream of innovative products combining user-friendly technology and elegant design, Apple's bite of the consumer electronics market has been getting a little larger year by year. Once it hit the iPod sales jackpot, however, Apple's brand took a major leap forward in public awareness and cachet—a leap that has also boosted sales of Apple's other products.

Apple has a history of zigging when the rest of the industry is zagging. The Apple brand is fun, unique, and memorable because it is such a departure from brands that sound serious and corporate. The company's original name, Apple Computer (changed to Apple a few years ago), helped reinforce the link between the seemingly whimsical "apple" and the concept of computers. Apple's Macintosh computer has always stood out because it looks different from other personal computers and relies on software that even novices can learn. Like every Apple product, the Mac and its packaging sport the company logo, an apple with one bite taken out of it.

Then came the iPod. Apple didn't invent digital music devices, but it did take them to a new level of style and convenience with the iPod, which debuted in 2001. Backed by music-driven advertising, the player with the white ear buds immediately became the product of choice for many consumers. Newer models such as the iPod Nano and the iPod Touch have continued the tradition of adding new features and updating the styling to make the product even more irresistible to current customers and to new buyers alike. Today Apple sells $8 billion worth of iPods every year and earns millions from its iTunes online store, where customers can buy songs, movies, TV shows, and other downloadable entertainment products.

And then came the iPhone, a new combination of mobile phone, iPod, and wireless Internet/e-mail appliance with a large, colorful touch screen for one-finger operation and accessories like the iPod's well-known white ear buds. Prompted by extensive publicity and introductory ads touting the sleek phone's smart features and trendy look, buyers lined up for days to get the first iPhones in 2007. Within months, Apple began a second round of advertising to encourage non-iPhone customers to switch from their current phones. Rather than focusing exclusively on the product, this campaign showcased customers talking about how they use their iPhones.

The iPhone was an instant success: Apple sold 4 million units in the product's first six months and, with a price cut, sales have continued to be strong. But something else happened during those six months that Apple had not anticipated. With so many shoppers browsing Apple stores in search of iPhones and iPods, the company began to sell many more Macintosh computers. Although Apple's share of the worldwide personal computer market remains below 5 percent, it has room to grow as the Mac momentum builds.

Since then, Apple has expanded Macintosh distribution and stepped up advertising in all media to make the most of the high awareness and popularity of its brand. One campaign, titled simply "Get a Mac," targeted consumers who use non-Mac computers by presenting humorous commercials about the features that make the Mac easier to use than competing products. This campaign also ran in the United Kingdom and Japan, with local actors and content customized for each culture. As with every Apple ad, these Mac ads closed with a shot of the apple logo.

Both sales revenue and profits are rising as Apple bites more deeply into the global market for personal computers, mobile phones, digital music players, and other electronics. The key to building demand across product categories is to help consumers remember the Apple.[90]

Case Questions

1. Use the concepts of trace strength and spreading of activation to explain why the Apple brand is memorable. What does Apple do to strengthen trace strength, and why is doing this important for the company's long-term success?
2. How has the iPod's prototypicality affected the Apple brand?
3. Why would Apple change to new advertising right after the introduction of the iPhone? Explain, using your knowledge of memory and retrieval.

The Process of Making Decisions

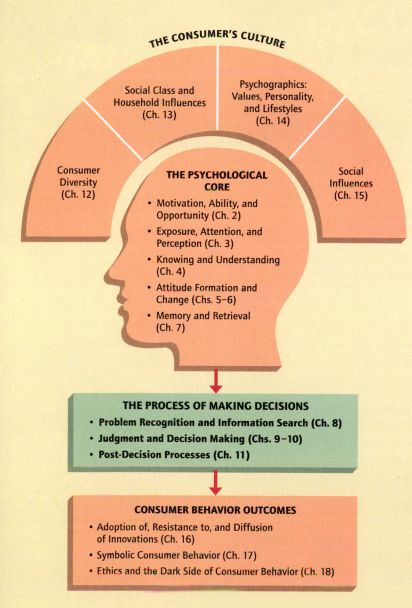

THE CONSUMER'S CULTURE

Social Class and Household Influences (Ch. 13)

Psychographics: Values, Personality, and Lifestyles (Ch. 14)

Consumer Diversity (Ch. 12)

Social Influences (Ch. 15)

THE PSYCHOLOGICAL CORE
- Motivation, Ability, and Opportunity (Ch. 2)
- Exposure, Attention, and Perception (Ch. 3)
- Knowing and Understanding (Ch. 4)
- Attitude Formation and Change (Chs. 5–6)
- Memory and Retrieval (Ch. 7)

THE PROCESS OF MAKING DECISIONS
- Problem Recognition and Information Search (Ch. 8)
- Judgment and Decision Making (Chs. 9–10)
- Post-Decision Processes (Ch. 11)

CONSUMER BEHAVIOR OUTCOMES
- Adoption of, Resistance to, and Diffusion of Innovations (Ch. 16)
- Symbolic Consumer Behavior (Ch. 17)
- Ethics and the Dark Side of Consumer Behavior (Ch. 18)

Part Three examines the sequential steps in the consumer decision-making process. Chapter 8 explores the initial steps of this process—problem recognition and information search. Consumers must first realize they have a problem before they can begin the process of making a decision about solving it. They must then collect information to help make this decision.

As with attitude change, decision making is affected by the amount of effort consumers expend. Chapter 9 examines the decision-making process when consumer effort is high and explores how marketers can influence this extensive decision process. Chapter 10 focuses on decision making when consumer effort is low and discusses how marketers can influence this kind of decision process. Chapter 11 looks at how consumers determine whether they are satisfied or dissatisfied with their decisions and how they learn from choosing and consuming products and services.

Chapter 8

Problem Recognition and Information Search

INTRODUCTION

Awesome or Awful? Read the Review

With more than 30,000 new products being launched every year, how can consumers locate suitable offerings, learn more about each, and narrow their choices without walking through every store on the planet? Millions of consumers let their fingers do the clicking around the Internet to check product reviews and ratings. Expert reviews and ratings from trusted sites such as those sponsored by AAA and *Consumer Reports* provide objective information. But consumer reviews are the big attractions on shopping agents such as Shopping.com, PriceGrabber.com, and Retrovo.com, where reviews appear alongside detailed product descriptions, buyers' guides, and price comparisons.

Online, consumer reviewers assign stars or a number to rate a product and add comments such as "Easy to use!" or "Not worth the money." To help would-be buyers determine which write-ups are most credible, consumers rate other consumers' reviews on most sites. Retrovo.com takes a slightly different approach to rating electronic gadgets. It analyzes all online expert and consumer feedback for a particular item, then posts a single rating (positive, neutral, negative, or undecided). Amazon.com, Bass Pro Shops, and Best Buy are only some of the retail websites that encourage consumers to post reviews—both raves and rants—for all to read.[1]

LEARNING OBJECTIVES

After studying this chapter, you will be able to

1. Describe how consumers recognize a consumption problem and show why marketers must understand this part of the decision-making process.

2. Discuss what happens when consumers conduct an internal search to solve a consumption problem and identify some of the ways in which marketers can affect internal searches.

3. Explain why and how consumers conduct an external search to solve a consumption problem.

4. Identify opportunities and the challenges that marketers face in trying to influence such searches.

Online reviews are increasingly important elements in the early stages of the consumer decision-making process. Suppose Lindsey, a typical consumer, cannot get her camera to work when she is on vacation. Disappointed, she realizes that she needs a replacement (problem recognition, as shown in Exhibit 8.1). Once she comes home, Lindsey tries to recall what she knows about camera brands and features (internal information search). However, knowing that her information is outdated, she checks magazine ads and articles and looks up camera reviews online (external information search). Sometimes, as in this example, problem recognition, internal information search, and external information search proceed sequentially; at other times, these processes occur simultaneously or in a different order. However they occur, these three stages are useful in explaining the basic processes that characterize consumer decision making.

Problem Recognition

Problem recognition The perceived difference between an actual and an ideal state.

Ideal state The way we want things to be.

Actual state The way things actually are.

The consumer decision process generally begins when the consumer identifies a consumption problem that needs to be solved ("I need a new camera" or "I would like some new clothes"). **Problem recognition** is the perceived difference between an ideal and an actual state. This is a critical stage in the decision process because it motivates the consumer to action.

The **ideal state** is the way that consumers would like a situation to be (having an excellent camera or wearing attractive clothing). The **actual state** is the real situation as consumers perceive it now. Problem recognition occurs if consumers become aware of a discrepancy between the actual state and the ideal state ("My camera is too old" or "My clothing is out of date"). Exhibit 8.2 shows how a marketer contrasts the ideal and the actual states. The greater the discrepancy between the actual and the ideal states, and the higher the level of motivation, ability, and opportunity (MAO), the more likely consumers are to act. If consumers do not perceive a problem, their motivation to act will be low.

Problem recognition relates to consumption and disposition as well as to acquisition. Consumers can recognize problems such as needing to decide what to make for dinner, which item of clothing to wear, or whether to replace an old appliance. Reckitt Benckiser tapped into problem recognition when it discovered that consumers were disposing of dark-colored clothing that faded after repeated washing. In response, the company introduced Woolite Dark Laundry as a detergent that cleans without affecting clothing color.[2] Because problem recognition stimulates many types of consumer decision making, it is important to understand what contributes to differences between the ideal and the actual states.

The Ideal State: Where We Want to Be

Where do we get our notion of the ideal state? Sometimes we rely on simple expectations, usually based on past experience, about everyday consumption and disposition situations and how products or services fulfill our needs. For example,

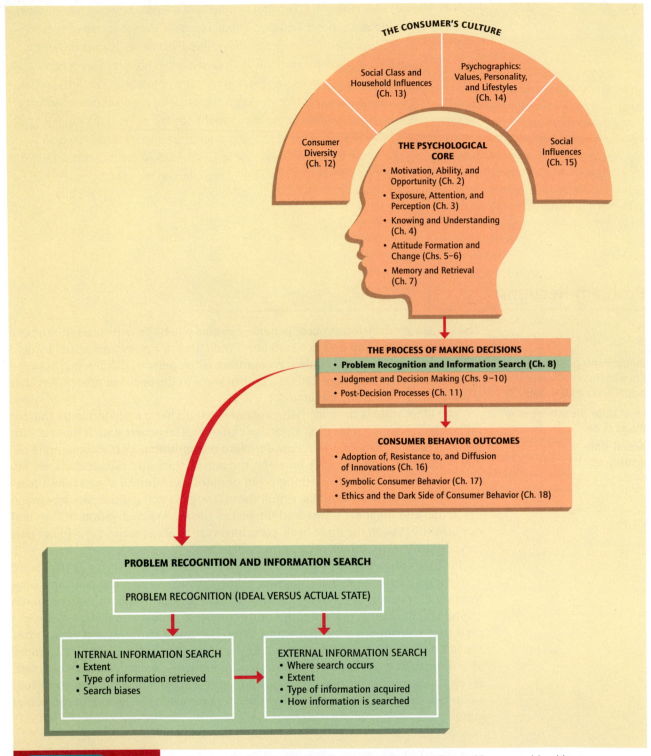

THE CONSUMER'S CULTURE

Social Class and Household Influences (Ch. 13)

Psychographics: Values, Personality, and Lifestyles (Ch. 14)

Consumer Diversity (Ch. 12)

Social Influences (Ch. 15)

THE PSYCHOLOGICAL CORE
- Motivation, Ability, and Opportunity (Ch. 2)
- Exposure, Attention, and Perception (Ch. 3)
- Knowing and Understanding (Ch. 4)
- Attitude Formation and Change (Chs. 5–6)
- Memory and Retrieval (Ch. 7)

THE PROCESS OF MAKING DECISIONS
- **Problem Recognition and Information Search (Ch. 8)**
- Judgment and Decision Making (Chs. 9–10)
- Post-Decision Processes (Ch. 11)

CONSUMER BEHAVIOR OUTCOMES
- Adoption of, Resistance to, and Diffusion of Innovations (Ch. 16)
- Symbolic Consumer Behavior (Ch. 17)
- Ethics and the Dark Side of Consumer Behavior (Ch. 18)

PROBLEM RECOGNITION AND INFORMATION SEARCH

PROBLEM RECOGNITION (IDEAL VERSUS ACTUAL STATE)

INTERNAL INFORMATION SEARCH
- Extent
- Type of information retrieved
- Search biases

EXTERNAL INFORMATION SEARCH
- Where search occurs
- Extent
- Type of information acquired
- How information is searched

Exhibit 8.1

Chapter Overview: Problem Recognition and Information Search

The first step in the consumer decision-making process involves problem recognition (the consumer recognizes a problem that needs to be solved). Next, the consumer searches for information to solve the problem either internally from memory or externally from outside sources (such as experts, magazines, or ads). How much consumers search, what they search for, and the process they go through while searching are all discussed in this chapter.

Your day.

Your new way.

Richer aroma.   Bigger flavor.

Try today's Taster's Choice, from Nescafé., the world's biggest name in coffee. With new, richer aroma and more flavor than ever, it's sure to please all your senses. So, enjoy!

TastersChoice.com

Advantage You.™

Taster's Choice

Exhibit 8.2

Ideal vs. Actual State

This ad is a good illustration of problem recognition and the difference between the actual and ideal state. The actual state is a hectic day (like a tornado). The ideal state is a calm day, which can be achieved by drinking a nice cup of Taster's Choice coffee.

we consider how we might look in certain clothes, how clean our house should be, how much fun it would be to vacation in a particular location, which old products we should keep, and so on. The ideal state also can be a function of our future goals or aspirations. For example, many consumers might want to drive a car that will provide them with social status (a Lexus, Mercedes, or Porsche) or to join a club that will bring them admiration or acceptance by others.

Both expectations and aspirations are often stimulated by our own personal motivations—what we want to be based on our self-image—and by aspects of our own culture. Some societies are more materialistic than others, and therefore the desire for many goods and services may be greater in those cultures. Likewise, social class can exert an influence: many consumers want to be accepted by members of their class or to raise their social standing, leading them to aspire to a higher ideal state. Reference groups also play a critical role because we strive to be accepted by others and because reference groups serve as a guide to our behavior.

Finally, major changes in personal circumstances, such as getting a promotion or becoming a parent, can instigate new ideal states. When you graduate and start a new job, you are likely to develop new ideal states related to where you live, what you wear, what you drive, and so forth. Newly affluent consumers in Vietnam, for example, are increasingly interested in buying world-famous status-symbol brands such as Gucci and Louis Vuitton.[3]

The Actual State: Where We Are Now

Like our perception of the ideal state, our perception of the actual state can be influenced by a variety of factors. Often these are simple physical factors, such as running out of a product, having a product malfunction (the cell phone breaks) or become obsolete (the digital music player has insufficient storage), or unexpectedly needing a service (a cavity requires dental work). Needs also play a critical role. If you are hungry or thirsty or if friends make fun of your clothes, your actual state would not be acceptable. Finally, external stimuli can suddenly change your perceptions of the actual state. If someone tells you that Mother's Day is next Sunday, for example, you might suddenly realize that you have not bought a card or present yet. Or opening your closet door may make you realize the closet is too full.

MARKETING IMPLICATIONS

Marketing can help put consumers in a state of problem recognition and motivate them to start the decision process, leading them to acquire, consume, or dispose of a product or service. In general, marketers use two major techniques to try to stimulate problem

Exhibit 8.3

An Ideal State

Consumers who shop at upscale stores want the ideal state of a fashionable yet reusable shopping bag. Stores like Lord & Taylor are providing them with these bags so they can achieve this ideal state.

recognition. First, they can attempt to create a new ideal state. Thirty years ago, few people gave much thought to the performance or style of their athletic shoes. Today we are bombarded with marketing messages featuring athletic shoes that will make us run faster, jump higher, and look more fashionable—a new ideal state.

Second, marketers can try to encourage our dissatisfaction with the actual state, as Saks Fifth Avenue did by fostering shoppers' dissatisfaction with ordinary shopping bags. When Saks created boldly stylish, eco-friendly, reusable bags to hold purchases, it encouraged consumers to view free bags as personal statements about fashion and environmental consciousness. Now Lord & Taylor (Exhibit 8.3) and other competitors are also giving away carefully designed shopping bags with every purchase.[4]

Whether they create a new ideal state or stimulate dissatisfaction with the actual state, marketers are more likely to have their offering chosen if they position it as the solution to the consumer's problem. For example, the British food chain Pret A Manger has become successful because, as the French name suggests, its fresh-daily takeout meals are "ready to eat"—solving the office worker's problem of finding a quick, healthy, affordable lunch.[5]

Internal Search: Searching for Information from Memory

Internal search The process of recalling stored information from memory.

After problem recognition has been stimulated, the consumer will usually begin the decision process to solve the problem. Typically, the next step is **internal search.** As you saw in Chapter 7, almost all decision making involves some form of memory processing. Consumers have stored in memory a variety of information, feelings, and past experiences that can be recalled when making a decision.

Because consumers have limited capacity or ability to process information—and because memory traces can decay over time—consumers are likely to recall only a small subset of stored information when they engage in internal search. Researchers are investigating (1) the extent of the search, (2) the nature of the search, and (3) the process by which consumers recall information, feelings, and experiences and enter them into the decision process.

How Much Do We Engage in Internal Search?

The degree of internal search can vary widely from the simple recall of only a brand name to more extensive searches through memory for relevant information, feelings, and experiences. On a general level, researchers know that the effort consumers devote to internal search depends on their MAO to process information. Thus, consumers will attempt to recall more information when felt involvement, perceived risk, or the need for cognition is high. In addition, consumers can engage in active internal search only if the information is stored in memory. Consumers with a greater degree of knowledge and experience therefore have a greater ability to search internally. Finally, consumers can recall information from memory only if they have the opportunity to do so. Time pressure or distractions will limit internal search.

The cure for Cabin Fever.

Start your spring thaw now. Miller Chill. The light beer brewed with a hint of lime and salt.

Exhibit 8.4

Creating Dissatisfaction with the Actual State

This ad for Miller Chill creates dissatisfaction with the actual state (being cooped up in the winter) and suggests the use of the product to achieve the ideal state (feeling good).

Consideration or evoked set The subset of top-of-mind brands evaluated when making a choice.

What Kind of Information Is Retrieved from Internal Search?

Much of the research on the role of internal search in consumer judgment and decision making has focused on what is recalled. Specifically, researchers have examined the recall of four major types of information: (1) brands, (2) attributes, (3) evaluations, and (4) experiences.[6]

Recall of Brands

The set of brands that consumers recall from memory whenever problem recognition has been stimulated is an important aspect of internal search that greatly affects decision making. Rather than remembering all available brands in any given situation, consumers tend to recall a subset of two to eight brands known as a **consideration** or **evoked set.**[7] For example, someone buying bottled water might consider Perrier and Poland Spring rather than all possible brands. With product proliferation, however, the number of offerings has increased dramatically. Nestlé alone offers more than 50 water brands (including Perrier and Poland Spring), a situation that increases competition for inclusion in the consideration set.[8]

In general, the consideration set consists of brands that are "top of mind," or easy to remember, when a consumer is making a decision. Some U.S. consumers fly rather than take the train—even when taking the train is faster and cheaper—simply because they do not consider the possibility of train travel. Conversely, in India, airlines are using marketing to encourage consumers to consider flying rather than taking the train or bus when they travel long distances.[9] A small consideration set is usually necessary because consumers' ability to recall brand information decreases as the size of the set increases. However, even if they do not recall the entire set from memory, stored information aids the recognition process. For example, stored information can help consumers recognize services in the yellow pages or identify brands on the shelf. This is the reason why Nestlé is using TV advertising to make its Aero chocolate bar more memorable to U.K. consumers. "With 50 or 60 brands [for consumers] to choose from, our key objective was to get Aero into consumers' consideration set," says an executive at Nestlé's ad agency.[10]

Studies indicate that consideration sets vary in terms of their size, stability, variety, and *preference dispersion* (the equality of preferences toward brands or products in the set). On more familiar occasions and in more familiar locations, such as when buying snacks at the local movie theater, consumers have consideration sets that are less stable, are larger in size, and have slightly more variety. In such situations, consumers tend to have stronger preferences for one or two items in the consideration set. This phenomenon suggests that a company should enhance its product's linkage with an occasion or situation familiar to consumers—such as eating on the run—to increase the chance that the product will be retrieved from memory as part of the consideration set.[11]

According to research, brands that are recalled are more likely to be chosen.[12] However, a brand's simply being recalled does not guarantee that it will be in a consumer's consideration set because consumers can recall a number of brands and then reject undesirable alternatives. Also, consumers' choices can be altered by the simple manipulation of which brands they recall, even though this manipulation may not change their product preferences. Thus, if consumers cannot recall brands from memory to form a consideration set, the set will tend to be determined by external factors such as the availability of products on the shelf or the suggestions of salespeople.[13]

Researchers have looked at the following factors that increase the possibility of consumers' recalling a particular brand during internal search and including that brand in their consideration set:

- *Prototypicality.* When consumers engage in internal search, they more easily recall brands that are closest to the prototype or that most resemble other category members, making these more likely to be included in the consideration set than brands that are not typical of the category.[14] For example, Armor All created the category of automotive protectant, and it has become the dominant brand not only in the United States but also in Mexico, Canada, Germany, Japan, and Australia.[15] This brand is more likely than other brands to be in the consideration set when problem recognition for the product exists.

- *Brand familiarity.* Well-known brands are more easily recalled during internal search than unfamiliar brands because the memory links associated with these brands tend to be stronger. As a result, companies need to repeat marketing communications continually to keep brand awareness high and associations strong. In Asian cultures, ads with high-meaning pictures and words (e.g., Superman fences with a picture of Superman) are very effective in increasing brand-name recall.[16] Even in low-MAO situations in which little processing occurs, incidental ad exposure can increase the likelihood of a brand's inclusion in the consideration set.[17] This explains why global brands such as Sony, McDonald's, and Coca-Cola have high familiarity worldwide and are likely to be in many consumers' consideration sets. Brand familiarity helps consumers recognize which of the many brands in the store should be attended to and reduces misidentification of brands.[18]

- *Goals and usage situations.* As discussed in Chapter 5, consumers have goal-derived and usage-specific categories in memory, such as drinks to bring to the beach, and the activation of these categories will determine which brands they recall during internal search.[19] Therefore, marketers can attempt to associate products with certain goals and usage situations. For example, Western Union—already known for secure, instant funds transfer—wants immigrants to associate its brand with the positive feeling of helping relatives by sending money home. Its advertising tag line, "sending so much more than money," reinforces both goal and usage.[20]

- *Brand preference.* Brands toward which the consumer has positive attitudes tend to be recalled more easily and tend to be included in the consideration set more often than brands that evoke negative attitudes.[21] This tendency highlights the importance of developing positive brand attitudes. Unilever's Dove brand, for instance, has been associated with moisturizing since the soap debuted in 1955. Dove has fostered positive attitudes about its brand through ads that celebrate the real beauty of real women.[22]

> *Retrieval cues.* By strongly associating the brand with a retrieval cue, marketers can increase the chance that the brand will be included in the consumer's consideration set. Think of the McDonald's Golden Arches or the Target red-and-white bull's-eye. Packaging can be an important retrieval cue for food products; this is the reason why Listerine comes in a distinctive squared-off bottle and Coca-Cola's hourglass bottle still appears in the company's promotions.[23]

Recall of Attributes

For a variety of reasons, we access only a small portion of the information stored in memory during internal search. Often we cannot remember specific facts about a product or service because our memory of details decreases over time. Thus, the attribute information we recall tends to be in summary or simplified form rather than in its original detail. We would be more likely to remember that a car gets good gas mileage or that filling the tank is not expensive than to remember the actual miles per gallon the car gets or the exact price of the gas.

Nevertheless, consumers can often recall *some* details when they engage in internal search, and the recalled attribute information can strongly influence their brand choices.[24] As a result, researchers have been very interested in determining which factors influence the recall of attribute information in the information search and decision-making processes. These are some of the major variables they have identified:

> *Accessibility or availability.* Information that is more accessible or available—having the strongest associative links—is the most likely to be recalled and entered into the decision process.[25] Information that is perceived as being easy to recall is also more likely to be accessible.[26] Simply reminding consumers of the ease of information retrieval can affect their judgments in some situations.[27] Marketers can make information more accessible by repeatedly drawing attention to it in communications or by making the information more relevant.[28]

Diagnostic information That which helps us discriminate among objects.

> *Diagnosticity.* **Diagnostic information** helps us distinguish objects from one another. If all brands of computers are the same price, then price is not diagnostic, or useful, when consumers are making a decision. On the other hand, if prices vary, consumers can distinguish among them, so the information is diagnostic.[29] If information is both accessible and diagnostic, it has a very strong influence in the decision-making process.[30] However, if accessible information is not diagnostic, it is less likely to be recalled.
>
> Research shows that negative information tends to be more diagnostic than positive or neutral information because the former is more distinctive.[31] Because most brands are associated with positive attributes, negative information makes it easier for consumers to categorize the brand as different from other brands. Unfortunately, consumers tend to give negative information greater weight in the decision-making process, increasing the chances that alternatives with negative qualities will be rejected. Therefore, marketers should avoid associating their offerings with negative information, plan a two-sided message campaign that counters the negative information, or divert attention away from the negative feature. In addition, marketers can identify which attributes tend to be most diagnostic for a particular product or service category and seek a competitive advantage on one or more of these attributes. This is what Toyota did with its highly fuel-efficient and earth-friendly Prius.[32]

Exhibit 8.5

Recall of Attributes

The iPod Nano has four very distinctive or vivid features: small size, circular control pad, bright colors, and white ear buds.

Salient attributes Attributes that are "top of mind" or more important.

Attribute determinance Attributes that are both salient and diagnostic.

▶ *Salience.* Research has clearly shown that consumers can recall very **salient** (prominent) **attributes** even when their opportunity to process is low.[33] The Apple iPod's distinctive circular control pad and white ear buds serve as salient attributes for consumers interested in digital music players, for example. In addition, price is a highly salient attribute for many consumers. Note that consumers do not always have a strong belief about the salience of an attribute.[34] Thus, a marketer of stereo systems can improve consumers' recall of its products' sound quality by providing information that makes this attribute more salient, an action that in turn facilitates brand choice.[35] By repeatedly calling attention to an attribute in marketing messages, marketers can increase a product's salience and its impact on the decision.[36] For example, in light of recent research, winemakers now promote the positive health benefits of drinking red wine, such as a lower incidence of heart disease among red wine drinkers.[37]

▶ However, an attribute can be highly salient but not necessarily diagnostic. If you are buying a watch, for example, the attribute "tells time" would be highly salient but not very diagnostic. For information to be recalled and entered into the decision, it must have **attribute determinance,** which means the information is both salient and diagnostic.[38] Glad Products' ForceFlex line of stretchy-yet-strong trash bags is made from plastic embossed with distinctive diamond shapes to reinforce the salience and diagnosticity of the strength attribute.[39]

▶ *Vividness.* Vivid information is presented as concrete words, pictures, or instructions to imagine (e.g., imagine yourself on a tropical beach) or through word-of-mouth communication. For example, a picture of a hand holding the credit-card-sized iPod Nano is vivid information (see Exhibit 8.5). Vivid information is easier to recall than less dramatic information, but it only tends to influence judgment and decision making when consumers have not formed a strong prior evaluation, especially one that is negative.[40] Also, vividness affects attitudes only when the effort required to process the information matches the amount of effort the consumer is willing to put forth.[41] Otherwise, vivid and nonvivid information affect consumer attitudes in about the same way.

▶ *Goals.* The consumer's goals will determine which attribute is recalled from memory. For example, if one of your goals in taking a vacation is to economize, you are likely to recall price when considering possible vacation destinations. Marketers can identify important goals that guide the choice process for consumers and can then position their offerings in the context of these goals, such as offering economy vacation packages.

Recall of Evaluations

Because our memory for specific details decays rapidly over time, we find overall evaluations or attitudes (that is, our likes and dislikes) easier to remember than specific attribute information. In addition, our evaluations tend to form strong associative links with the brand. This tendency is the reason that it is important for a marketer to encourage positive attitudes toward its brand or offering, whether it is a product, service, person, or place. For example, the "Uniquely Singapore" ad campaign features tourists talking about how much they enjoyed Singapore. The city-state also provides financial incentives for companies filming movies and TV shows in Singapore, with the goal of "creating more awareness of Singapore and generating buzz in a competitive tourism market," says an official.[42]

Online processing When consumer are actively evaluating a brand as they view an ad for it.

Evaluations are also more likely to be recalled by consumers who are actively evaluating the brand when they are exposed to relevant information. For example, if you are ready to buy a new computer and suddenly see an ad for a particular brand, you will probably determine whether you like the brand when you see the ad. This activity is called **online processing.**[43] Afterward, you will more likely recall this evaluation rather than the specific information that led to it. Many times, however, consumers do not have a brand-processing goal when they see or hear an ad. In such cases they do not form an evaluation and are therefore better able to recall specific attribute information, assuming that their involvement was high and the information was processed.[44] Moreover, consumers are more likely to use on-line processing in evaluating family brands when the brands within that family have low variability and share many attributes.[45]

Recall of Experiences

Internal search can involve the recall of experiences from autobiographical memory in the form of specific images and the effect associated with them (see Exhibit 8.6).[46] Like information in semantic memory, experiences that are more vivid, salient, or frequent are the most likely to be recalled. For example, if you have an experience with a product or service that is either unusually positive or unusually negative, you are likely to recall these vivid experiences later. Furthermore, if you repeatedly have a positive experience with a product or service, it will be easier to recall. For example, some bowling alleys now offer loud music and flashing lights to appeal to younger bowlers and make the experience more fun, exciting, and memorable.[47] Research suggests that although advertising may affect how accurately consumers can recall their product experiences, their recall of the product's evaluations is not necessarily affected.[48]

(MARKETING IMPLICATIONS)

Obviously marketers want consumers to recall positive experiences related to certain products or services. Marketers often deliberately associate their products or services with common positive experiences or images to increase their recall from consumers' memory. Prudential and Sony are just two of many firms that film ads at the Grand Canyon because it is the "quintessential breathtaking experience," and they hope that consumers will tie this positive memory to their brands.[49]

Is Internal Search Always Accurate?

In addition to being influenced by factors that affect what we recall, we all have processing biases that alter the nature of internal search. These search biases can sometimes lead to the recall of information that results in a less-than-optimal judgment or decision. Three biases have important implications for marketing: confirmation bias, inhibition, and mood.

Confirmation bias Tendency to recall information that reinforces or confirms our overall beliefs rather than contradicting them, thereby making our judgment or decision more positive than it should be.

Confirmation Bias

Confirmation bias refers to our tendency to recall information that reinforces or confirms our overall beliefs rather than contradicting them, thereby making our judgment or decision more positive than it should be. This phenomenon is related to the concept of *selective perception*—we see what we want to see—and occurs because we strive to maintain consistency in our views. When we engage in internal search, we are more likely to recall information about brands we like or have previously chosen than information about brands we dislike or have rejected. Furthermore, when the confirmation bias is operating, we are more likely to recall positive rather than negative information about favored brands. This response can be a problem because, as mentioned earlier, negative information tends to be more diagnostic.

Nevertheless, we sometimes recall contradictory evidence. In fact, we may recall moderately contradictory information because we had consciously thought about it when we first tried to understand it.[50] In most instances, however, consumers tend to recall information that reinforces their overall beliefs.

Inhibition

Another internal search bias is associated with limitations in consumers' processing capacity.[51] In this case, all the variables that influence the recall of certain attributes—such as accessibility, vividness, and salience—can actually lead to the **inhibition** of recall for other diagnostic attributes.[52] In buying a house, for example, a consumer might recall information such as the selling price, number of bathrooms, and square footage, but he or she may not recall other important attributes such as the size of the lot. Inhibition can also lead to a biased judgment or decision because consumers may remember but still ignore important and useful information.

Inhibition The recall of one attribute inhibiting the recall of another.

Mood

You saw in Chapter 7 that consumers engaged in internal search are most likely to recall information, feelings, and experiences that match their mood.[53] With this knowledge in mind, advertisers are aware that marketing communications that put consumers in a good mood through the use of humor or attractive visuals can enhance the recall of positive attribute information.

(MARKETING IMPLICATIONS)

From a marketing perspective, confirmation bias presents a real problem when consumers search internally for only positive information about the competition. One way marketers attack this problem is to draw attention to negative aspects of competitive brands through comparative advertising. Apple has done this with ads comparing its easy-to-use computer operating systems with those made by Microsoft for PCs.[54] By presenting comparative information in a convincing and credible way, marketers may be able to overcome confirmation bias.

Inhibition is an important aspect of internal search for two reasons. First, consumers may not always consider key aspects of a brand when making a decision because they recall other, more accessible attributes instead. If these nonrecalled attributes reflect features that differentiate the brand from others (i.e., if the attributes are diagnostic), the company may want to highlight them in marketing communications. Marketers can sometimes offset the effect of their brand's disadvantages and/or their competitors' advantages by drawing attention to more vivid or accessible attributes. For example, ads for Cervana deer meat stress that venison is tasty, tender, and low in fat, deflecting attention from the belief that it tastes too gamey.[55]

LIFE HAS
ITS MOMENTS...

Happy Birthday to me

A special moment with Julie

...MAKE THEM
UNFORGETTABLE

WWW.PANDORA-JEWELRY.COM

PANDORA™
UNFORGETTABLE MOMENTS

Exhibit 8.6

Recall of Experiences

Ads sometimes try to evoke positive memories or experiences. This ad for Pandora tries to get consumers to remember good moments with their mothers or with their daughters.

External search The process of collecting information from outside sources, e.g., magazines, dealers, ads.

Prepurchase search A search for information that aids a specific acquisition decision.

Ongoing search A search that occurs regularly, regardless of whether the consumer is making a choice.

External Search: Searching for Information from the Environment

Sometimes a consumer's decision can be based entirely on information recalled from memory. At other times, information may be missing or some uncertainty may surround the recalled information. Then consumers engage in an **external search** of outside sources, such as dealers, trusted friends or relatives, published sources (magazines, pamphlets, or books), advertisements, the Internet, or the product package. Consumers use external search to collect additional information about which brands are available as well as about the attributes and benefits associated with brands in the consideration set.

Two types of external search are prepurchase search and ongoing search. **Prepurchase search** occurs in response to the activation of problem recognition. As an example, consumers seeking to buy a new car or truck can get information by visiting dealers, searching Edmunds.com and other websites, checking quality rankings, talking to friends, and reading *Consumer Reports*.[56] **Ongoing search** occurs on a regular and continual basis, even when problem recognition has not been activated.[57] A consumer might consistently read automotive magazines, visit automotive websites, and go to car shows because he or she has a high degree of enduring involvement in cars. Exhibit 8.7 contrasts these two types of searches.

Researchers have examined five key aspects of the external search process: (1) the source of information, (2) the extent of external search, (3) the content of the external search, (4) search typologies, and (5) the process or order of the search.

Where Can We Search for Information?

For either prepurchase or ongoing search, consumers can acquire information from five major categories of external sources:[58]

▶ *Retailer search.* Visits or calls to stores or dealers, including the examination of package information or pamphlets about brands; in particular, consumers believe they save time by going to stores that are clustered together.[59]

▶ *Media search.* Information from advertising, online ads, manufacturer-sponsored websites, and other types of marketer-produced communications.

▶ *Interpersonal search.* Advice from friends, relatives, neighbors, coworkers, and/or other consumers, whether sought in person, by phone, online, or in another way.

▶ *Independent search.* Contact with independent sources of information, such as books, non-brand-sponsored websites like Shopping.com, government pamphlets, or magazines.

▶ *Experiential search.* Using product samples or product/service trials (such as a test-drive) or experiencing the product online.

Types of Information Searches

Consumers can engage in two major types of external search. Prepurchase search occurs in response to problem recognition; the goal is to make better purchase decisions. Ongoing search results from enduring involvement and occurs on a continual basis (independent of problem recognition). In the latter consumers search for information because they find searching enjoyable (they like to browse).

	Prepurchase Search	Ongoing Search
Determinants	• Involvement in the purchase • Market environment • Situational factors	• Involvement with the product • Market environment • Situational factors
Motives	To make better purchase decisions	• Build a bank of information for future use • Experience fun and pleasure
Outcomes	• Increased product and market knowledge • Better purchase decisions • Increased satisfaction with the purchase outcome	• Increased product and market knowledge leading to – future buying efficiencies – personal influence • Increased impulse buying • Increased satisfaction from search, and other outcomes

Traditionally, retailer and media searches, followed by experiential search, have been the most frequently used forms of search. These increase when a consumer's involvement is higher and knowledge is lower.[60] This finding is significant for marketers because such sources are under their most direct control. Other research indicates that consumers browse two or more sources of information (such as the Internet and catalogs) before making a buying decision.[61] Therefore, marketers and retailers should ensure that their brand information is consistent across the various sources.[62]

Consumers increase their use of interpersonal sources as their brand knowledge decreases. Apparently, when consumers' knowledge is limited, they are motivated to seek out the opinions of others. Furthermore, when consumers believe that their purchase and consumption of certain items (usually hedonic or symbolic products and services such as fashion, music, and furniture) will be judged by others, they tend to seek out interpersonal sources.[63]

Experiential search is also critical for hedonic products and services. Given the importance of sensory stimulation, consumers want to get a "feel" for the offering, so they often try on clothing or listen to a stereo before they buy. Chipotle Mexican Grill relies heavily on free samples when it opens a new store. At one New York City store opening, it spent $35,000 to give away burritos to 6,000 people. The cost was worthwhile because "the response to food is almost always positive," explains the marketing director.[64]

Cultural characteristics play a role in external search as well. According to research, consumers who are members of subcultural groups and not culturally assimilated—fully integrated into the surrounding culture—tend to conduct a wider search of external sources. And members of subcultural groups who identify with the surrounding culture are more likely to search for information among media advertisements. Thus, marketers should create informative advertising messages when targeting these consumer segments.[65] Although independent search tends to increase as available time increases, time spent on this type of search is generally quite minimal.

Internet Sources

Without leaving their keyboards, consumers can use the Internet to search through mounds of data online, locate any details needed to make purchase decisions, and buy. In fact, consumers can use the Internet to get information from all five of the sources just mentioned (see Exhibit 8.8). Sometimes consumers search for specific information; at other times they simply browse.[66] One study suggests that women and older consumers visit websites longer than others do.[67] Speed, user control, and two-way communication capability are key elements of website interactivity for conducting online searches.[68] Interestingly, consumers may perceive that a site downloads quickly when its color has a relaxing effect.[69]

In general, consumers who have a pleasant experience with a company's website will have more positive attitudes toward the site and its brands.[70] Consumers report higher satisfaction and stronger buying intentions when searching and shopping on sites that use an avatar—an animated "person"—to deliver information.[71] Internet ads can be especially effective for encouraging current customers to buy again. Research shows that the number of exposures to Internet ads, number of websites visited, and number of pages viewed all have a positive effect on repeat purchasing.[72]

In addition to conducting keyword searches on sites such as Google, consumers can use shopping agents such as Shopping.com to organize their search results according to price, retail source, and other attributes. However, consumers do not always accurately assess whether a shopping agent's recommendations are appropriate and effective in a particular buying situation. Thus, consumers may make poor buying decisions by using an inferior shopping agent and by choosing offers they should have avoided.[73] Also, when consumers using a shopping agent receive recommendations about unfamiliar products, they check additional recommendations for familiar products as a context in which to evaluate the unfamiliar products.[74] Over time, analyzing consumers' buying patterns can improve shopping agents' recommendations.[75] Still, consumers who make numerous visits to a website may not buy even when the site offers tools to help them make better decisions.[76]

Exhibit 8.8

Using the Internet for Information Searching

In today's market, many consumers (like these London shoppers) have access to almost unlimited amounts of information over the Internet.

Information Overload

Consumers today have access to so much information that they can actually become overloaded. Depending on the way in which the information is structured, an overload can lead to a decline in decision quality.[77] Some search sites therefore apply more efficient search techniques that prioritize results by identifying the most popular or frequently accessed sites.[78] An ordered list with the "best" result presented first may actually encourage consumers to keep exploring less-than-optimal options, resulting in less-than-optimal buying decisions. On the other hand, consumers whose searches uncover increasingly better options may have more positive brand evaluations and be motivated to search for superior choices.[79]

Search sites such as About.com have subject-matter experts selecting the most important information and narrowing the choice set according to specific criteria. Shopping agents bring order to results by presenting items according to price or another attribute selected by the user. Although some retailers try to thwart shopping agents, believing the price comparisons are too easy, a growing number are paying for links or ads on popular shopping sites so that they can make it into the consumer's choice set.[80]

Simulations

Advances in technology and graphics have dramatically improved the online experience. Website developers can now simulate the retail experience as well as product trials by creating sites that incorporate special and interactive effects including audio, video, zoom, panoramic views, streaming media, and three-dimensional product representations that can be manipulated.[81] Creating a virtual product experience has a positive effect on consumer product knowledge and brand attitude, thereby reducing perceived risk and increasing purchase intention.[82] Realtor.com, a real estate site, offers virtual tours of 3 million houses for sale, allowing consumers to simulate a personal visit.[83]

The Online Community

Often people with a common interest or condition related to a product or service go online to share ideas by using websites, text chat, and other tools.[84] Research indicates that the most common interactions focus on product recommendations and how-to-use-it advice.[85] Often this information can be very influential in the consumer's decision process because it is not controlled by marketers and is therefore seen as more credible. Knowing this dynamic, Jeff Bezos, founder of Amazon.com, does not try to prevent consumers from posting negative reviews of products. Even though the company may lose a few sales, Bezos sees his site as an online community of "neighbors helping neighbors make purchase decisions."[86]

An increasing number of retailers and manufacturers are tracking consumers' online information search and purchase patterns to provide additional assistance and recommendations. For example, consumers who rent or download movies from Netflix are encouraged to rate them so that the site can recommend other movies based on what each consumer liked and didn't like. Each movie description also includes an overall rating from the Netflix community. These ratings are Netflix's way of adding movies to the consideration set and providing more information for consumer decision making.

MARKETING IMPLICATIONS

Consumers are buying online more frequently, making bigger purchases, and choosing a wider variety of products than they did in the early days of the Internet. Still, online marketers tend to be less successful when shoppers cannot judge the quality of a product such as a sofa (as the defunct furniture retailer Living.com found out) or when consumers perceive that the delivery cost is high relative to the cost of individual items such as groceries (as the defunct online grocer Webvan.com found out).[87] Facilitating extended searches for even inexpensive items like books can boost sales significantly, as Amazon.com learned with its "Search Inside the Book" feature, which lets consumers read pages from individual books.[88] When shopping for homes and other major purchases, many consumers use the Internet to search for information and then complete the purchase in person, although a small number will buy with a click or call without any personal experience of the offering.[89]

Many consumers see product choice as riskier when they lack access to experiential information until after they have completed an online purchase.[90] Sometimes consumers search but then abandon their online shopping carts because of frustration over the time and effort needed to check out; some do not buy because they get no information about shipping fees and taxes until they reach the final screen.[91] RugSale.com, an online retailer of area rugs, slashed its cart-abandonment rate by reducing the number of pages consumers needed to view to finalize a purchase. Its homepage trumpets free shipping on purchases and returns, so consumers know the policy before they click to buy.[92]

To learn which online tactics are most effective for their site and products, marketers track consumers' search and purchase behaviors using appropriate measurements. As one example, an Internet retailer like RugSale.com tracks how many would-be buyers abandon their carts before they complete the purchase; an online advertiser tracks the percentage of consumers exposed to each ad who actually click to read more.[93] Exhibit 8.9 shows some common measures of consumer activity online. Note that marketers need specific strategies for specific local and regional markets because activities that are effective with U.S. consumers will not be effective everywhere. As an example, few Chinese consumers use credit cards to buy online; retail websites must therefore arrange for payment through bank-backed systems or other trusted methods.[94]

Exhibit 8.9

Selected Measures of Online Consumer Activity

Marketers are very interested in the ways that consumers search online. Here are some common measures used to measure and evaluate this activity.

Measurement	Purpose
Ad impressions	To determine the opportunity for communication by tracking how many consumers are exposed to a particular Web ad.
Unique visitors	To determine the extent of message exposure by measuring how many different consumers visit the site during a given period.
Click-through rate	To determine ad effectiveness by tracking the number of consumers exposed to a message who actually click on it for additional ad information.
Percentage of repeat visits	To determine consumer loyalty by tracking the number of visitors in a given period who have visited the site previously.
Frequency of visits	To determine consumer loyalty by tracking how often each visitor visits the site in a given period.
Top entry page	To determine message and offer effectiveness by tracking the first page on which most visitors enter the site.
Top exit page	To determine message and offer effectiveness plus interactivity response by tracking the page from which most visitors leave the site.
Visitor path	To determine message and offer effectiveness plus interactivity response by tracking, in page order, the ways that consumers navigate the site.
Conversion rate	To determine offer effectiveness by tracking the percentage of visitors who actually buy.
Cart abandonment rate	To determine offer and interactivity effectiveness by tracking the percentage of visitors who put items in their shopping carts but fail to complete the checkout process.
Mouse movement	To determine interest and interactivity by identifying the place on a web page or ad where a visitor moves the mouse and how long the mouse remains in one spot.

Sources: Michael Totty, "So Much Information . . . " *Wall Street Journal,* December 9, 2002, p. R4; Subodh Bhat, Michael Bevans, and Sanjit Sengupta, "Measuring Users' Web Activity to Evaluate and Enhance Advertising Effectiveness," *Journal of Advertising,* Fall 2002, pp. 97–106.

How Much Do We Engage in External Search?

Much of the research on external search has concentrated on examining how much information consumers acquire prior to making a judgment or decision. One of the key findings is that the degree of search activity is usually quite limited, even for purchases that are typically considered important.[95] With more consumers shopping online, search activity is increasing because online sources are very convenient. Nevertheless, information search can vary widely from a simple hunt for one or two pieces of information to a very extensive search relying on many sources. In an attempt to explain this variance, researchers have identified a number of causal factors that relate to our motivation, ability, and opportunity to process information.

Motivation to Process Information

As the motivation to process information increases, external search will generally be more extensive. Six factors increase our motivation to conduct an external search: (1) involvement and perceived risk, (2) the perceived costs of and benefits resulting from the search, (3) the nature of the consideration set, (4) relative brand uncertainty, (5) attitudes toward the search, and (6) the level of discrepancy of new information.

▶ *Involvement and perceived risk.* To understand how involvement relates to external search, recall the distinction from Chapter 2 between situational involvement—a response to a particular situation—and enduring involvement—an ongoing response. Higher situational involvement will generally lead to a greater prepurchase search,[96] whereas enduring involvement relates to an ongoing search regardless of whether problem recognition exists.[97] Thus, consumers with high enduring involvement with cars are more likely to read automotive magazines, visit car shows and car-related websites, and seek out other information about cars on a regular basis.

Because perceived risk is a major determinant of involvement, it should not be surprising that when consumers face riskier decisions, they engage in more external search activity. One of the key components of perceived risk is uncertainty regarding the consequences of behavior, and consumers use external search as a way to reduce this uncertainty.[98] Consumers are more likely to search when they are uncertain about which brand to choose than when they are uncertain about a brand's specific attribute. Consumers also search more when they are evaluating services rather than products because services are intangible and hence perceived as more uncertain.[99] Finally, consumers will have higher motivation to search if the consequences are more serious, such as those entailing high financial or social risk. This situation explains why consumers often search more extensively for information about higher-priced products or services.

▶ *Perceived costs and benefits.* External search activity is also greater when its perceived benefits are high relative to its costs.[100] In these situations, consumers who search will benefit by reducing their uncertainty and increasing the likelihood of their making a better decision, obtaining a better value, and enjoying the shopping process. The costs associated with external search are time, effort, inconvenience, and money (including traveling to stores and dealers). All these factors place psychological or physical strain on the consumer. In general, consumers tend to continue searching until they perceive that the costs outweigh the benefits. The desire to reduce searching costs explains why many supermarkets now offer a variety of nontraditional items like electronics and furniture, becoming places "where people do all their gift shopping."[101] As noted earlier, consumers who uncover increasingly better options will be motivated to keep searching for superior options.[102] Even so, consumers tend to minimize their initial search investment, delay further searches after making a choice, and underestimate the future costs (both search and usage) of switching to another offering.[103]

▶ *Consideration set.* If the consideration set contains a number of attractive alternatives, consumers will be motivated to engage in external search to decide which alternative to select. On the other hand, a consideration set that contains only one or two brands reduces the need to search for information.

▶ *Relative brand uncertainty.* When consumers are uncertain about which brand is the best, they are more motivated to engage in external search.[104]

▶ *Attitudes toward search.* Some consumers like to search for information and do so extensively.[105] These consumers generally have positive beliefs about the value and benefits of their search. In particular, extensive search activity appears to be strongly related to the belief that "when important purchases are made quickly, they are regretted."[106] Other consumers simply hate searching and do little of it.

Researchers have identified two groups of Internet searchers.[107] Experienced searchers are the most enthusiastic and heaviest users of the Internet, whereas moderate and light users see it as a source of information only, not a source of entertainment or fun. To appeal to the latter group, some companies have created interesting and engaging games to stimulate consumers to search.[108]

▶ *Discrepancy of information.* Whenever consumers encounter something new in their environment, they will try to categorize it by using their stored knowledge. If a stimulus does not fit into an existing category, consumers will try to resolve this incongruity by engaging in information search, especially when incongruity is at a moderate level and the consumer has limited knowledge about the product category.[109] Consumers are likely to reject highly incongruous information.[110] Marketers can capitalize on this tendency by introducing moderate discrepancies between their brand and other brands. For example, an ad for Miele vacuum cleaners displayed the phrase "Lung Damage Control." This feature is not normally associated with vacuum cleaners (a moderate discrepancy), so the message may motivate consumers to search and discover that the brand has filters to control pollution and allergens.[111]

The same general process applies to the search for information about new products. If a new product is moderately discrepant or incongruent with existing categories of products, the consumer will be motivated to resolve this discrepancy.[112] In particular, consumers explore the most salient attributes in greater depth rather than search for a lot of additional attributes. From a marketing perspective, this behavior suggests that positioning new products as moderately different from existing brands may induce consumers to search for more information that might, in turn, affect their decision-making process. A good example is a DVD player that can also record as compared with those that only play prerecorded DVDs. This moderate discrepancy between the types of players might stimulate consumers to search for additional product information that could ultimately affect their decision to buy.

Ability to Process Information

External search is also strongly influenced by the consumer's ability to process information. Researchers have studied the ways that three variables affect the extent of external information search: (1) consumer knowledge, (2) cognitive abilities, and (3) demographic factors.

▶ *Consumer knowledge.* Common sense suggests that expert consumers search less because they already have more complex knowledge stored in memory. However, research results on this subject have been mixed.[113] Part of the problem stems from the way that *knowledge* is defined. Some studies have measured *subjective knowledge,* the consumer's perception about what he or she knows relative to what others know. *Objective knowledge* refers to the actual information stored in memory that can be measured with a formal knowledge test. Researchers have linked objective knowledge to information search, although both types of knowledge are somewhat related. One study found that subjective knowledge influences the locations where consumers search for information as well as the quality of their choices.[114]

Specifically, several studies have found an inverted-U relationship between knowledge and search.[115] Consumers with moderate levels of knowledge search the most. They tend to have a higher level of motivation and at least some basic knowledge, which helps them to interpret new information. Experts, on the other hand, search less because they have more knowledge stored in memory, and they also know how to target their search to the most relevant or diagnostic information, ignoring that which is irrelevant—except when the search involves new products. Because experts have more developed memory structures, they have an advantage when learning novel information and can acquire more information about new products.

▶ *Cognitive abilities.* Consumers with higher basic cognitive abilities, such as a high IQ and the ability to integrate complex information, not only are more likely to acquire more information than consumers with little or no knowledge but also are able to process this information in more complex ways.[116]

▶ *Demographics.* As researchers continue to investigate whether certain types of consumers search more than others, they have discovered a few consistent patterns. For instance, consumers with higher educations tend to search more than less educated consumers do. This situation results because consumers with more education have at least moderate levels of knowledge and better access to information sources than the less educated do.[117]

Opportunity to Process Information

Consumers who have the motivation and ability to search for information must still have the opportunity to process that information before an extensive search can take place. Situational factors that might affect the search process include (1) the amount of information, (2) the information format, (3) the time available, and (4) the number of items being chosen.

▶ *Amount of information available.* In any decision situation, the amount of information available to consumers can vary greatly, depending on the number of brands on the market, the attribute information available about each brand, the number of retail outlets or dealers, and the number of other sources of information, such as magazines or knowledgeable friends. In general, consumers do more searching as the amount of available information increases, suggesting that the Internet can generate greater external search. If information is restricted or not available, however, consumers have a hard time engaging in extensive external search.

Nutrition Facts
Serving Size 3/4 Cup (27g)

Amount Per Serving	Cereal	With 1/2 Cup Skim Milk
Calories	90	130
Calories from Fat	10	10

	% Daily Value	
Total Fat 1g*	**2%**	**2%**
Saturated Fat 0g	**0%**	**0%**
Trans Fat 0g	**0%**	**0%**
Cholesterol 0mg	**0%**	**0%**
Sodium 190mg	**8%**	**11%**
Potassium 85mg	**2%**	**8%**
Total Carbohydrate 23g	**8%**	**10%**
Dietary Fiber 5g	**20%**	**20%**
Sugars 5g		
Protein 2g		

Vitamin A	0%	4%
Vitamin C	10%	15%
Calcium	0%	15%
Iron	2%	2%

Exhibit 8.10

Information Format

Public policy makers have tried to make nutrition labels easier for consumers to understand and use by improving the format of this information. How easy do you think it is to understand the nutrition information in this exhibit?

> *Information format.* The format in which information is presented can also strongly influence the search process. Sometimes information is available from diverse sources or locations, but consumers must expend considerable effort to collect it. When buying insurance, for example, consumers may have to contact different agents or companies to collect information about individual policies. In contrast, presenting information in a manner that reduces consumer effort can enhance information search and usage, particularly when the consumer is in the decision mode.[118] For example, in an effort to increase the use of nutritional information, researchers provided a matrix that makes this information easier for consumers to search (see Exhibit 8.10), thereby improving opportunity.[119] A related study found that consumers increase their use of nutritional information when the rewards of good nutrition are made more explicit.[120] In addition, consumers will engage in more leisurely exploratory searches if the information surrounding an object is visually simple and uncluttered.[121]

> *Time availability.* Consumers who face no time restrictions have more opportunity to search. If consumers are under time pressure, however, they will severely restrict their search activity.[122] Further, consumers will spend less time getting information from different sources as time pressure increases.[123] Time pressure is one of the main reasons that consumers search and shop on the Internet. One study found that when consumers revisit a website for search reasons, they spend less total time on the site because they look at fewer pages, not because they spend less time looking at each page.[124]

> *Number of items being chosen.* When consumers are making a decision about multiple items, research suggests that they will conduct a more extensive search with less variability in search patterns than if the decision involves the purchase or use of only one item.[125]

MARKETING IMPLICATIONS

The extent to which consumers search for external information has important implications for marketing strategy. If many consumers tend to search extensively for a particular product or service, marketers can facilitate this process by making information readily available and easily accessible at the lowest cost and with the least consumer effort. To do this, marketers should consider redesigning their product packaging, websites, ads, and other promotional materials to add information that will alter consumers' attitudes and change their buying behavior. Look at how Bankrate improved its website's visibility. The company, which tracks credit card and mortgage rates and posts personal finance articles, analyzed the keywords that consumers use to search for financial information.

By including keywords such as *mortgage rates* in page headlines and titles, Bankrate was able to improve its website's ranking in search results.[126] Exhibit 8.11 shows how a company uses a kiosk to make birth control information easily available.

Companies should also provide information about salient and diagnostic attributes, particularly if the brand has a differential advantage. Otherwise, if consumers cannot get the information they need, they may eliminate the brand from their consideration set. Novices, in particular, tend to be influenced by visual cues such as pictures and colors that focus their attention on selected attributes, a factor that affects their external search and, ultimately, their brand choices.[127]

Moreover, marketers can segment the market for a product or service according to search activity. For example, one study identified six clusters of searchers in the purchase of a car.[128] Another found that consumers who search online for cars are younger and better educated and conduct more searches than those who do not use the Internet—and that they would have searched more extensively if they could not have used the Internet.[129] In high-tech markets, older consumers tend to search information channels that provide fairly uncomplicated information, whereas better educated consumers tend to search all information channels.[130] Determining which search activities are commonly used for a particular product helps marketers plan to meet the information needs of their targeted consumers. Low-search consumers, for example, will focus on getting a good deal, whereas high searchers will need a lot of attention and information to offset their low levels of confidence and prior satisfaction. Marketers can be very selective in providing low searchers with information, emphasizing only those attributes that are most salient and diagnostic.

Marketers can attempt to stimulate external search by providing information in a highly accessible manner. Barnes & Noble, for instance, has in-store kiosks where shoppers can search for specific books, see how many copies are in stock, find their location in the store, and place orders for out-of-stock items.[131] As another example, consumers with web-enabled cell phones can locate and contact a local Office Depot store by logging on to the retailer's website, entering a zip code, and clicking on the store's phone number to get connected.[132] Such opportunities for additional search may lead low searchers to information that will change their attitudes and affect their buying decisions. Marketers can also provide consumers with incentives to search. For example, after Gap.com posted an online coupon good only in Gap stores, the chain's stores were flooded with consumers clutching coupons as they examined merchandise.[133]

What Kind of Information Is Acquired in External Search?

Researchers are interested in the types of information that consumers acquire during an external search because this information can potentially play a crucial role in influencing the consumers' judgments and decision making. When searching external sources, consumers usually acquire information about brand name, price, and other attributes.

▶ *Brand name* is the most frequently accessed type of information because it is a central node around which other information can be organized in memory.[134] Thus, when we know the brand name, we can immediately activate other relevant nodes. For example, we can draw on prior knowledge and associations if we know the brand name is Allstate.

▶ *Price* is often the focus of consumer search because it tends to be diagnostic and can be used to make inferences about other attributes such as quality and value.[135] One study found that when price and quality are not directly correlated for a product category, consumers who use quality-screening agents to search for purchase options online are actually more sensitive to price differences.[136] Yet the search for price is less important than we might expect (due to the low overall extent of search), and it does not become more important when price variations increase and costs are higher.[137] The importance of price can also depend on the culture. For example, compared to other countries, consumers in Japan have not traditionally been fond of discounters. However, this has changed as many now seek out bargains in low-price stores such as Uniqlo.[138]

Other Attributes

After searching for brand name and price, consumers will search for additional information, depending on which attributes are salient and diagnostic in the product or service category. Consumers are more likely to access information that is relevant to their goals. For example, if a major goal in choosing a vacation is to maximize excitement, a consumer would probably collect information about a location's available activities, nightlife, and visitors. When consumers switch goals from one purchase occasion to the next, as when looking for an economy car instead of one that is fast, the search they perform for the second task is more efficient because they can transfer the knowledge from the first task.[139]

Is External Search Always Accurate?

Consumers can be just as biased in their search for external information as they are during internal search. In particular, consumers tend to search for external information that confirms rather than contradicts their overall beliefs. In one study, consumers with a strong price-quality belief tended to search more for higher priced brands.[140] Unfortunately, confirmation bias can lead consumers to avoid important information, resulting in a less-than-optimal decision outcome. Thus, if a lower priced, high-quality brand were available, consumers might never acquire information about it and therefore never select it for purchase.

How Do We Engage in External Search?

External search follows a series of sequential steps that can provide further insight into the consumer's decision. These steps include orientation, or getting an overview of the product display; evaluation, or comparing options on key attributes; and verification, or confirming the choice.[141] Researchers have examined the order of information acquisition during evaluation, in particular, because they assume that information acquired earlier in the decision process plays a more significant role than information acquired later.[142] For example, once a brand emerges as the leader early in the search process, subsequent information acquisition and evaluation are distorted in favor of that brand.[143]

Search Stages

Consumers access different sources and use different decision criteria at different stages of the search process. In the early stages, mass media and marketer-related sources tend to be more influential, whereas interpersonal sources are more critical when the actual decision is made.[144] Early in a search, consumers are more likely to access information that is especially salient, diagnostic, and goal related. However, if they can recall salient, diagnostic information from memory, they will have little need to search for it externally. Therefore, consumers will search first for information on attributes that provoke greater uncertainty or are less favorable.[145]

Early in a search, consumers will use simpler criteria to screen out options and then apply more detailed decision rules later in the search process. How highly a brand ranks early in the search may have little influence on the likelihood that the consumer will select it later in the process.[146] Because consumers tend to search first for brands with a higher perceived attractiveness, it is important for marketers to encourage positive brand attitudes. Consumers who are new to a product or service category will start by searching for information about low-risk, well-known brands; search lesser known brands; and then consolidate the information leading to a preference for brands that provide the greatest utility.[147]

Searching by Brand or Attribute

Searching by brand Collecting information on one brand before moving to another.

Searching by attribute Comparing brands on attributes, one at a time.

Two major types of processes are (1)**searching by brand,** in which consumers acquire all the needed information on one brand before moving on to the next, and (2) **searching by attribute,** in which consumers compare brands in terms of one attribute at a time, such as by price.[148] Consumers generally prefer to process by attribute because doing so is easier.

Consumers are very sensitive to the manner in which information is stored in memory and the format in which it is presented in the store.[149] If information is organized by brand, as is the case in most stores where all the information is on packages, consumers will process information by brand. Experts, in particular, tend to process by brand because they have more brand-based knowledge. The fact that consumers are accustomed to processing by brand may bias processing, however, even when information is organized by attribute.[150] In addition, different search strategies affect consumers' decision processes differently.[151] Consumers who process by brand remain high in uncertainty until the very end of the search process, whereas those who search by attribute gradually reduce their uncertainty.

Nevertheless, consumers with less knowledge will take advantage of opportunities to process by attribute, such as by viewing information in a matrix in *Consumer Reports* or in another format that simplifies searching. One study found that presenting lists of nutritional information in the grocery store is popular with consumers. The *Consumer Reports* Rating Charts, which provide information about the top brands and best buys in various product categories in a simple format, are popular sources of information. As noted earlier, search engines and shopping agents also make it easier for consumers to process by attribute, especially by price.

(MARKETING IMPLICATIONS)

Marketers have to make the specific information that consumers seek easily and readily available by emphasizing it in advertising, on a package, in pamphlets, on websites, or through the sales force. It is important to remember that consumers are less likely to choose a brand that performs poorly on attributes that are accessed frequently. Therefore, marketers should be sure that their offerings perform well on attributes that are heavily accessed, including price. When marketers promise to match the lowest price that consumers can find, such policies spark more extensive searching when search costs are low (as consumers look for the lowest price) but less extensive searching when search costs are high (and consumers perceive that the policy signals low prices).[152] Finally, companies can pay search sites such as Google to make brand information available in a prominently positioned sponsored link when consumers perform certain keyword searches. ◖▬▬◗

Summary

This chapter examined the three initial stages of the consumer judgment and decision-making process. Problem recognition, the first stage, is the perceived difference between an ideal state and the actual state. When a discrepancy between these two states exists, the consumer may be motivated to resolve it by engaging in decision making.

Internal search is the recall of information, experiences, and feelings from memory. The extent of internal search generally increases as motivation, ability, and opportunity increase. Aspects of an offer that are more salient, diagnostic, vivid, and related to goals are generally the most likely to be recalled. Several biases exist in internal search: confirmation bias, in which information that reinforces our overall beliefs is remembered; inhibition, in which the recall of some information can inhibit the recall of other attributes; and mood, our tendency to recall mood-congruent information.

When consumers need more information or are uncertain about recalled information, they engage in external search, acquiring information from outside sources through prepurchase search (in response to problem recognition) or ongoing search (which continues regardless of problem recognition). During external search, consumers can acquire information from retailers, the media, other people, and independent sources and by experiencing the product. Retailer and media searches account for the highest level of search activity, but interpersonal sources increase in importance as consumer knowledge decreases and normative factors increase.

Consumers will conduct a more extensive search when they have a higher motivation and opportunity to process information. Situational factors affect the consumer's opportunity to process the information.

Brand name and price are the most accessed attributes in an external search. Consumers also tend to exhibit a confirmation bias in their external search. More salient and diagnostic information tends to be accessed earlier. Finally, consumers tend to process either by brand or by attribute. Attribute search is easier and preferred, but often the information is not organized to facilitate such processing.

Questions for Review and Discussion

1. How does a discrepancy between the ideal state and the actual state affect consumer behavior?

2. What factors affect the inclusion of brands in the consideration set, and why would a company want its brand in the consideration set?

3. How does confirmation bias operate in internal and external searches for information?

4. What six broad groups of sources can consumers consult during external search? Where does the Internet fit in these groups?

5. How do involvement, perceived risk, perceived costs and benefits, and the consideration set affect a consumer's motivation to conduct an external search?

6. When would a consumer be more likely to conduct an external search by brand rather than by attribute? Which search process would a marketer prefer consumers to use—and why?

> CL Visit http://cengage.com/marketing/hoyer/ ConsumerBehavior5e to find resources that are available to help you study for the course.

Using Cell Phones for Price and Product Comparisons

Calling all shoppers: For quick and easy comparisons of products and prices, just grab that cell phone and search for information from anywhere at any time. Cell phones are also being used to search out which local stores stock particular items, to learn about the latest sales, and to receive notices about future retail promotions and discounts. In short, searching for information by cell phone can help consumers better understand and evaluate their options, improve their product and market knowledge, formulate or narrow down their consideration set, and feel better about having made an informed decision.

Users of Frucall, for example, can compare prices via cell phone in three ways. First, they can call a toll-free number, enter the UPC code or brand and model number of a specific item, and then listen as Frucall's system reads back the best prices for that item available through online retailers. A second way to use Frucall is to send the numeric UPC code in a text message to Frucall, which then replies with a text message containing online price comparisons for that item. A third way is to use a web-enabled phone to search the Frucall site for price comparisons.

In addition, Frucall users can check product ratings and merchant ratings, save their search results to check later, ask to be alerted when a product goes on sale, or press a button to buy right away. Extras such as gift suggestions by category and price, listings of recent products searched by other users, wish lists, and product recommendations add to Frucall's value as a prepurchase source of information.

Whether they are already at the mall or just thinking about going on a shopping trip, consumers can find out whether a product is available in local stores by using a cell phone or the Web to check NearbyNow. Stores in 200 malls have opened their inventory to searches by NearbyNow so that consumers can determine whether a product in a certain size or color is in stock at a nearby mall, check the prices for items in different mall stores, and even reserve products for purchase and pickup within a few days.

Rather than going to the mall and wandering from store to store to find something, leaving empty-handed, or making a purchase only to find the same product selling for a lower price in a different mall store, NearbyNow users can use their cell phones to do a little more research and plan ahead. They will know exactly which store to visit, what is in stock, and what each store charges for an item before they shop; they can also sign up to receive special offers from mall merchants in their area. These services are especially helpful for consumers who enjoy shopping in person rather than online or who are in such a hurry that they cannot wait for an online retailer to ship the merchandise.

Consumers who call for a bargain will find many discounts and choices at Cellfire. Hundreds of U.S. stores and restaurants like Hollywood Video, Domino's Pizza, Hardee's, Supercuts, and T.G.I. Friday's offer discounts to Cellfire users, as do major marketers like Procter & Gamble, Kimberly-Clark, and General Mills. After registering, users simply browse the discount offers, go to a participating store or restaurant, click on the Cellfire coupon they want to redeem, and show the phone screen to the salesperson or cashier. This way, price-conscious consumers know they will get a good deal at the checkout counter just by having their cell phones handy—no scissors needed.[153]

Case Questions

1. Why might information overload be a concern for consumers who use Frucall to research a particular purchase? What would you recommend that Frucall do to avoid creating this problem?

2. Knowing that consumers may skip a shopping trip if the item they want is not available at the local mall, why would a mall retailer agree to open its inventory to NearbyNow users?

3. Who is more likely to use a service like Cellfire, and why? Your answer should consider the consumer's motivation, ability, and opportunity (MAO) to process information.

Judgment and Decision Making Based on High Effort

Chapter 9

LEARNING OBJECTIVES

After studying this chapter, you will be able to

1. Distinguish between judgment and decision making, and indicate why both processes are important to marketers.

2. Explain how cognitive decision-making models differ from affective decision-making models and why marketers are interested in both types of models.

3. Identify the types of decisions faced by consumers in high-effort situations and discuss how marketers can try to influence these decisions.

INTRODUCTION

Racing Toward Higher Vehicle Sales in Thailand

Thailand is a land of opportunity—and fierce competition—for nearly every major automotive manufacturer, even though car ownership is not nearly as widespread as it is in more developed countries. In Thailand, the ratio of vehicles to consumers is 1:12, far below the world average of 1:4 and the U.S. average of 1:2.5. However, Thais are passionate about their vehicles, listing them as the fifth necessity behind food, lodging, medicine, and clothing. In fact, Thailand is the world's second-largest market for pickup trucks, trailing only the United States.

Ford, General Motors, Mercedes, Toyota, Honda, Suzuki, Nissan, and other automakers are racing toward higher sales in Thailand by learning more about how consumers decide to buy. For example, many consumers have a positive impression of U.S.-made sport-utility vehicles, but only wealthy Thais can afford these imported models—and many of these people do not do their own driving. Also, the back seat of such vehicles is not designed for those who spend the day conducting business over the phone while their drivers navigate potholes. Thus, comfort, status, and brand image may explain why Mercedes-Benz holds a large share of the luxury-car market in Thailand. Also, Thai consumers, driven by concern for the environment, are increasingly interested in new vehicles that are more fuel-efficient and less polluting than older cars.[1]

4. Outline the ways that consumer characteristics, decision characteristics, and other people can influence high-effort decisions.

How Thai consumers buy cars and trucks points up the importance of knowing the types of judgments that consumers make (such as that imported vehicles are well made) and the criteria that most influence consumers' decisions (comfort, price, what others think or say about the purchase, and so on). They must know the brands that consumers are thinking about buying too, because those are the brands that are the marketer's competitors. In addition, marketers must understand the emotions and feelings that influence consumer decisions (e.g., that a car makes you feel good). This chapter examines high-effort judgments and decisions (see Exhibit 9.1), the kind of judgments and decisions that consumers make when their motivation, ability, and opportunity to process information relevant to the decision are high. By carefully analyzing the factors that enter into judgment and decision making, marketers can acquire valuable insights that help them develop and market offerings to consumers.

High-Effort Judgment Processes

Judgments Evaluations of an object or estimates of likelihood of an outcome or event.

Decision making Making a selection among options or courses of action.

Think about the last time you went to a restaurant. While reviewing the menu, you probably considered some items and thought about how good they would be before making your final choice. You were making **judgments** – evaluations or estimates regarding the likelihood of events. Judgment is a critical input into the decision process, but it is not the same as **decision making,** which involves making a selection among options or activities.

In a consumer context, *judgments* are evaluations or estimates regarding the likelihood that products and services possess certain features or will perform in a certain manner.[2] Judgments do not require a decision. Thus, if you see an ad for a new Italian restaurant, you can form a judgment as to whether you will like it, how different it will be from other Italian restaurants, or how expensive it will be. These judgments can serve as important inputs into your decision about whether to eat at the restaurant, but they do not require that you decide whether to go there or not.

Judgment and decision making can also involve different processes.[3] For example, one study found that consumers searched attributes in a different order when they were making judgments than when they were making decisions.[4] Another found that whether consumers' familiarity with a product helped or hurt the amount of information they could recall about it depended on whether they were making judgments or making decisions about the brands.[5] Given the importance of judgment in consumers' information processing, marketers need to understand judgments about (1) likelihood and (2) goodness or badness.

Judgments of Likelihood and Goodness/Badness

Estimations of likelihood Judging how likely it is that something will occur.

One kind of judgment is an **estimation of likelihood,** our determination of the probability that something will occur. Estimations of likelihood appear in many consumer contexts. For example, when we buy a good or service, we can attempt to estimate the likelihood that it will break down, the likelihood that others will like it, and the likelihood that it will satisfy our needs. When we view an ad, we can assess the likelihood that it is truthful.

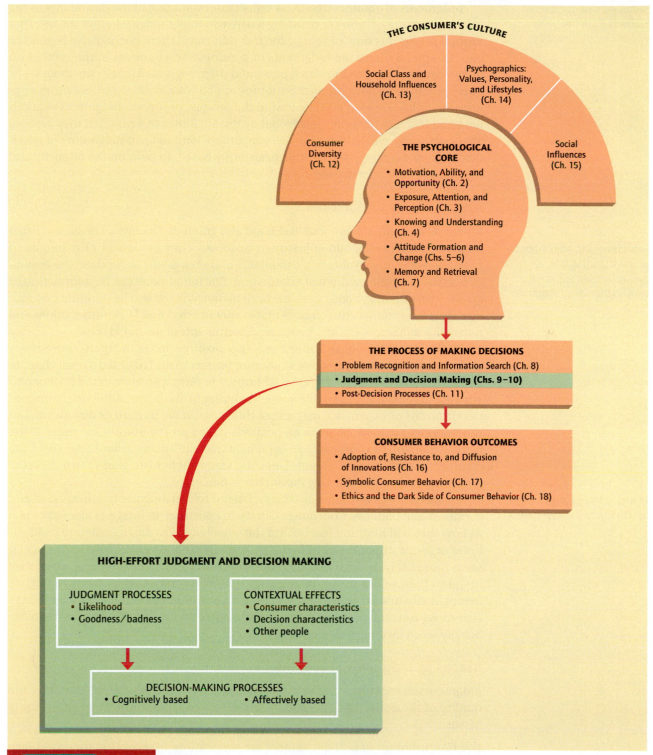

THE CONSUMER'S CULTURE

Social Class and
Household Influences
(Ch. 13)

Psychographics:
Values, Personality,
and Lifestyles
(Ch. 14)

Consumer
Diversity
(Ch. 12)

THE PSYCHOLOGICAL
CORE
• Motivation, Ability, and
Opportunity (Ch. 2)
• Exposure, Attention, and
Perception (Ch. 3)
• Knowing and Understanding
(Ch. 4)
• Attitude Formation and
Change (Chs. 5–6)
• Memory and Retrieval
(Ch. 7)

Social
Influences
(Ch. 15)

THE PROCESS OF MAKING DECISIONS
• Problem Recognition and Information Search (Ch. 8)
• **Judgment and Decision Making (Chs. 9–10)**
• Post-Decision Processes (Ch. 11)

CONSUMER BEHAVIOR OUTCOMES
• Adoption of, Resistance to, and Diffusion
of Innovations (Ch. 16)
• Symbolic Consumer Behavior (Ch. 17)
• Ethics and the Dark Side of Consumer Behavior (Ch. 18)

HIGH-EFFORT JUDGMENT AND DECISION MAKING

JUDGMENT PROCESSES
• Likelihood
• Goodness/badness

CONTEXTUAL EFFECTS
• Consumer characteristics
• Decision characteristics
• Other people

DECISION-MAKING PROCESSES
• Cognitively based   • Affectively based

Exhibit 9.1

**Chapter Overview:
Judgment and Decision
Making Based on High
Consumer Effort**

After problem recognition and search, consumers can engage in some form of judgment or decision making, which can vary in terms of processing effort (from high to low). This chapter looks at high-effort judgment and decision processes. Judgments are estimates of how likely something is to occur or how good or bad something is. These serve as inputs into decision making, which can be cognitively or affectively based. Contextual effects also influence this process.

Judgments of goodness/badness Evaluating the desirability of something.

Judgments of goodness/badness reflect our evaluation of the desirability of the offering's features. If you are planning a trip, you might judge whether the fact that Europe is cold this time of year or the fact that travel there is expensive is good or bad. Chapter 6 discussed judgments of goodness and badness in the section on high-effort attitudes. The research presented there suggested that a consumer combines judgments about product attributes or actions associated with a product to form an evaluation of or attitude toward the product or service. Judgments of goodness and badness not only are affected by the attributes of a product; they are also affected by how we feel. Specifically, consumers tend to form judgments of goodness or badness more quickly and consistently based, in part, on the intensity and direction of their affective responses.[6]

Anchoring and Adjustment

Anchoring and adjustment process Starting with an initial evaluation and adjusting it with additional information.

When making judgments about likelihood and goodness/badness, consumers often employ an **anchoring and adjustment process.**[7] They first anchor the judgment based on some initial value (see Exhibit 9.2) and then adjust or "update" the evaluation as they consider additional information. The initial value can be information or an affective response readily available from memory; it can also be attribute information from the external environment that is encountered first.[8] Consumer values and normative influences can also be strong determinants of the initial value.

To illustrate, Starbucks Coffee has a very positive image in Japan—one survey ranks it at the top of all Japanese restaurant brands.[9] This factor led a local chain to name its coffee brand "Seattle Coffee," hoping to form a positive initial anchor and encourage consumers to see the shops as similar to Starbucks. Additional information from ads or experience may adjust this initial value upward or downward, but the judgment is more likely to be positive, based on the Starbucks image. If the prior evaluation of Starbucks had been negative, the anchor would probably have resulted in a negative judgment. Thus, the same anchor can lead to two different judgments, depending on how the anchor is perceived.

Imagery Imagining an event in order to make a judgment.

Imagery, or visualization, also plays a major role in judgments of likelihood and goodness and badness. Consumers can try to construct an image of an event, such as how they will look and feel behind the wheel of a new car, to estimate its likelihood or judge its goodness or badness. Visualizing an event can actually make it seem more likely to occur because consumers may form a positive bias when they imagine themselves using the product.[10] Imagery may also lead consumers to overestimate how satisfied they will be with a product or service.[11] Imagery may also cause consumers to focus on vivid attributes and weigh those attributes more heavily when forming judgments.[12]

Biases in Judgment Processes

Judgments are not always objective. Biases and other factors may compromise the quality of the consumer's decision[13] and affect consumer judgment in a variety of ways:

● *Confirmation bias.* If consumers are susceptible to a confirmation bias (see Chapter 8), they will focus more on judgments that confirm what they already believe and will hold those judgments with more confidence. They may ignore information that runs counter to their judgments. Of course, overweighting confirming information and underweighting contrary information in forming judgments can reduce consumers' tendencies to search for more information

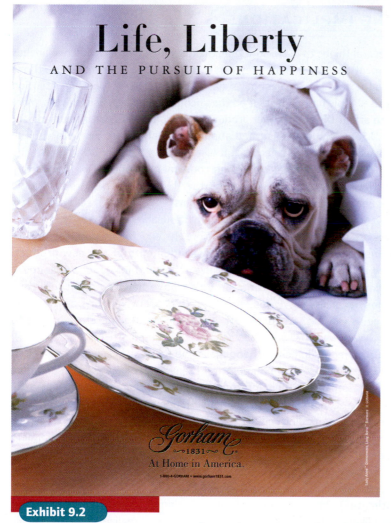

Life, Liberty
AND THE PURSUIT OF HAPPINESS

Gorham
—1831—
At Home in America.
1-800-4-GORHAM • www.gorham1831.com

Exhibit 9.2

Anchoring a Judgment
The light humor created by the unhappy dog who does not get to lick the plate attempts to prime consumers with positive feelings. Marketers hope consumers will then evaluate Gorham china positively as well.

because they believe they know almost everything about the product.[14] Therefore, the confirmation bias can set consumers up for making less-than-optimal choices.

▶ *Self-positivity bias.* Consumers can make judgments about the extent to which they or others are vulnerable to having bad things happen to them (e.g., contracting AIDS, getting into an automobile accident). Interestingly, research finds that consumers have a self-positivity bias when making these judgments about the likelihood that bad outcomes will happen. That is, they tend to believe that bad things are more likely to happen to other people than to themselves. As such, they might not process messages that suggest that they themselves might be vulnerable to risks.[15] This is bad news for some marketers (e.g., health-care marketers, insurance marketers) who want to remind consumers that bad things can indeed happen to them.

▶ *Negativity bias.* With a negativity bias, consumers give negative information more weight than positive information when they are forming judgments. Consumers seem to weigh negative information more heavily in their judgments when they are forming opinions about something that is very important to them and for which they wish to have as accurate a judgment as possible (e.g., which college to attend). But consumers do not engage in a negativity bias when they are already committed to a brand. For example, if you love the school you are now attending, you are unlikely to think much about (or may even discount) any negative information you hear about it.[16]

▶ *Mood and bias.* Mood can bias consumer judgments in several ways.[17] First, your mood can serve as the initial anchor for a judgment. If you are in a good mood when shopping for a CD, you will probably respond positively to any new music that you hear. Second, moods bias consumers' judgments by reducing their search for and attention to negative information. The reason for this phenomenon is that consumers want to preserve their good mood, and encountering negative information may not serve that goal. Third, mood can bias judgments by making consumers overconfident about the judgments they are reaching.[18]

▶ *Prior brand evaluations.* When consumers judge a brand to be good based on their past exposure to it, they may subsequently fail to learn (and view as important) information about the brand's attributes that affect its actual quality.[19] In effect, the favorable brand name "blocks" learning about quality-revealing product attributes that should affect consumers' judgments.

MARKETING IMPLICATIONS

Marketers can do several things to make sure that their brand serves as a positive anchor in anchoring adjustment decisions. First, they can focus consumers' attention on those attributes that place the brand as the best in its class. For example, by focusing attention on styling and easy use, Apple has made its iPod the anchor for digital music players. Marketers can also try to affect the set of other products that consumers use in their adjustment.[20] To affluent U.S. consumers concerned about personal safety, for instance, the spacious $300,000 Mercedes Maybach may seem overly showy when compared with the more discreet Bentley GT luxury coupe. By getting consumers to anchor on the Bentley and then focus on the Maybach (as opposed to other brands), marketers can guide choices to favor the Bentley. Perhaps this process explains why Mercedes sells only a few hundred Maybachs yearly, whereas Bentley sells several thousand coupes yearly.[21]

When consumers are exposed to a brand extension, the existing brand name and its positive associations often serve as the anchor for judgments of the new product. A product's country of origin can also serve as an anchor and influence subsequent judgments.[22] For example, domestic brands in China have had to mount vigorous marketing campaigns because many consumers prefer Western versions of the same product, which serve as the anchor. Local soft-drink makers are therefore having to compete against such well-known U.S. brands as Coca-Cola and Pepsi-Cola.[23]

Marketers can also affect judgments of goodness and badness in several ways. First, making consumers feel good (e.g., by manipulating their moods or *priming* consumers with positive feelings before giving them information) will lead them to evaluate the offering more positively.[24] Second, marketers can affect judgments of goodness and badness by asking consumers to imagine the attributes or benefits of a product or service. A particular kind of pizza will be judged as better than other kinds when consumers imagine how delicious it tastes. It will be judged as worse when consumers imagine the grease it might have floating on the top of it.

Finally, marketers can affect consumers' perceptions of how probable things are (i.e., likelihood estimates). Research shows that consumers primed to consider their family ties are more likely to take a financial risk because they realize that their family can help cushion a monetary loss. However, consumers are less likely to take a social risk when thinking about family ties because of the way that a negative outcome might affect their family.[25] Marketers can also try to reduce consumers' self-positivity judgments. A study on consumers' self-positive bias regarding the likelihood that they could contract AIDS was reduced when consumers were shown that people very similar to them have also gotten AIDS and when they were made to think about actions that they engage in that could result in getting AIDS.[26] Enumerating many (versus few) risk behaviors that can make a person vulnerable to a bad outcome (e.g., contracting AIDS) can also reduce his or her self-positivity bias.[27]

High-Effort Decisions and High-Effort Decision-Making Processes

Acquisition, usage, and disposition all involve some sort of consumer decision—even if the decision is not to select any of the alternatives, which may happen when a great deal of uncertainty exists.[28] In some cases, the consumer first makes a decision about whether or not to buy and then focuses on the selection decision.[29] The selection decision can, in turn, involve other decisions such as decisions about (a) what offerings to

Exhibit 9.3

Types of Decisions that Consumers Face in High-Effort Situations

In high effort situations, consumers are often confronted with a variety of different types of decisions to make. This exhibit outlines the major ones.

- Deciding which brands to consider
  - Consideration set
- Deciding what is important to the choice
  - Goals
  - Time
  - Framing
- Deciding what offerings to choose
  - Thought-based decisions
    - Brands
    - Product attributes
    - Gains and losses
  - Feeling-based decisions
    - Appraisals and feelings
    - Affective forecasts
- Deciding whether to make a decision now
  - Decision delay
- Deciding when alternatives cannot be compared

consider, (b) what factors are important to the choice, (c) what choice to actually make, (d) whether to make a decision now or to delay a decision, and (e) how to make choices when alternatives cannot be compared. We consider each of these kinds of decisions in this chapter (see Exhibit 9.3). When consumers' motivation, ability, and opportunity (MAO) to process information relevant to a decision are high, consumers put a lot of effort into making these decisions.

Deciding Which Brands to Consider

Consumers today face more options than ever before.[30] With so many available options, they often find themselves first deciding whether brands fall into an **inept set** (those that are unacceptable), an **inert set** (those they treat with indifference), and a **consideration set** (those they want to choose among; see Chapter 8).[31]

The consideration set is very important to marketers because it affects what brands consumers are choosing among and hence whom the marketer is competing against. Decisions tend to be easier when the consideration set contains brands that can be easily compared.[32] Still, just because a brand is in a consideration set does not mean that it will get much of the consumers' attention.[33] But if it does get a lot of attention, consumers are more likely to select it and to be willing to pay more for it than for the other alternatives.[34] If they focus on one brand at a time, they tend to judge that brand more positively than they would the average of the best brands within that category.[35]

A consumer's evaluation of a brand in the consideration set depends on the other brands to which it is compared. If one brand is clearly more attractive or dominant than the others, making a choice does not require much effort. Changing the alternatives in the consideration set can, however, have a major impact on the consumer's decision, even without a change in preferences.[36] For example, a good brand can look even better when an inferior brand is added to the consideration set. This **attraction effect** occurs because the inferior brands increase the attractiveness of the dominant brand, making the decision easier.[37]

Inept set Options that are unacceptable when making a decision.

Inert set Options toward which consumers are indifferent.

Consideration set The subset of top-of-mind brands evaluated when making a choice.

Attraction effect When adding of an inferior brand to a consideration set increases the attractiveness of the dominant brand.

MARKETING IMPLICATIONS

The most important implication is that it is critical for a company to get its brand into the consumer's consideration set; otherwise, there is little chance that the brand will be chosen. Repetition of the brand name and messages in marketing communications are needed to ensure that the brand name is "top of mind." Another way to try to gain an advantage is by promoting comparisons of the brand with inferior rather than with equal or superior competitors (see Exhibit 9.4). Doing this maximizes the attraction effect and results in a more positive evaluation of the brand. Also, marketers can increase sales of a high-margin item simply by offering a higher-priced option.[38] Thus, Panasonic could increase the sales of a $179 microwave oven by offering a slightly larger model at $199. The higher-priced model might not sell well, but it would make the lower-priced model look like a good deal. ▬◖

Deciding Which Criteria Are Important to the Choice

Before consumers can choose a specific offering from among a set of brands in a consideration set, they need to determine which criteria are relevant to the decision and how important each criterion is to their decision. The relevance and importance of various decision criteria, in turn, depend on consumers' goals, the timing of their decision, and how the decision is framed or represented.

Goals

Goals clearly affect the criteria that will drive a consumer's choice. For example, if you are trying to choose between having chips or carrot sticks for a snack, you will focus on different attributes if your goal is to "eat something that is on my diet" instead of "eat something that makes me feel good." You are likely to use different decision criteria when buying beer for yourself than when buying beer for a party. You might buy lower-priced beer for a party because you need a large quantity, but you might be more concerned about image as well.

When the goal is to make a decision, consumers may judge products with unique, positive attributes and shared negative attributes as more favorable than products with unique, negative attributes that share positive attributes.[39] If the goal is flexibility in choice, the consumer will seek out a large assortment of choices; if the goal is to simplify the choice, the consumer will seek out a small assortment.[40] Consumers whose goal is to influence others will use different criteria when choosing among brands than those used by consumers who do not have this goal.[41]

In addition, consumers' goals may change during the decision process. For example, before you go to a store, you may be less certain about what you want to buy—but once you are in the store, your goals may become more certain and concrete.[42] Whether the consumers' goals are prevention- or promotion-focused will also affect their decisions. Promotion-focused consumers, whose goal is to maximize gains and positive outcomes, will put more emphasis on whether they

Exhibit 9.4

Consideration Set

Sometimes a higher-priced option can make a lower-priced option look like a better deal, as is the case with these cameras.

think they have the skills and capacity to use the product to achieve the goal they seek and put less emphasis on the effectiveness of the product itself. Prevention-focused consumers, who are more risk-averse, emphasize the product's efficacy rather than their own skills and capacities to use it.[43]

Time

The timing of a decision also affects which criteria drive our choices. As you learned in Chapter 4, *construal level theory* relates to how we think about (or construe) an offering. Whether we use high-level (abstract) or low-level (concrete) construals depends on whether we are making a decision about what to buy/do right now or about something we might buy/do in the future.[44] If the decision is about something we will buy or do immediately (e.g., what restaurant to go to right now), our choices tend to be based on *low-level construals*—specific, concrete elements such as how close it is to home, how much dinner will cost there, and who is coming along. The opposite is true for decisions we anticipate making later: our criteria tend to be more general and abstract (e.g., which restaurant will create the best dining experience). When the decision outcome will be realized far in the future, consumers may consider the hedonic aspects of a decision (how good it will make me feel) to be more important than the more rational aspects of the decision (can I really afford it?).[45]

Framing

Decision framing The initial reference point or anchor in the decision process.

The way in which the task is defined or represented, **decision framing,** can affect how important a criterion is to our choice. For example, a frame for a car purchase might be (1) buy an economical car I can afford or (2) buy a car that will impress my friends. Clearly different criteria will be employed in these two situations. Because the frame serves as the initial anchor in the decision process, all subsequent information is considered in light of that frame.

Early research on framing studied people's willingness to take risks in a gamble. Results showed that people are more willing to take risks when a choice is framed as avoiding a loss rather than as acquiring a gain.[46] Other research has found that messages framed in terms of loss are more persuasive when consumers are in a good mood, whereas messages framed in terms of gain are more persuasive when consumers are in a bad mood.[47] Framing gains and losses also applies to buying and selling: When the outcomes are equally positive, buyers feel better about not losing money while sellers feel better about achieving gains. But when the outcomes are equally negative, buyers feel worse about losses while sellers feel worse about not gaining anything.[48]

Decisions can also be framed in terms of how the problem is structured in the external environment, such as whether beef is presented as 75 percent lean or as 25 percent fat.[49] Framing the time period can affect decisions as well. Consumers perceive health hazards as being more immediate and concrete if they are framed as occurring every day but regard them as less immediate and more abstract if they are framed as occurring every year.[50] In another study, industrial buyers who used low price as an initial reference point were less willing to take risks than buyers with a medium- or high-price point.[51] Likewise, consumers react more positively when marketers frame the cost of a product as a series of small payments (pennies a day) instead of as a large one-time expense.[52] Moreover, a product framed in the context of higher-priced

Exhibit 9.5

Goal-Related Marketing

Sometimes ads try to stimulate purchase by relating to consumers' personal goals, such as losing weight. This ad for The Skinny Cow illustrates this tactic.

options will be judged as being less expensive than one framed in the context of lower-priced options.[53]

Whether a decision is framed positively (How good is this product?) or negatively (How bad is this product?) influences the evaluation differently.[54] Consumers are more likely to choose a brand with negatively framed claims about a competitor when elaboration is low, but higher elaboration may lead them to conclude that the tactics being used are unfair.[55]

Priming certain attributes, such as reliability and creativity, can significantly alter consumers' judgments of both comparable alternatives like different brands of cameras and noncomparable alternatives like computers and cameras.[56] This priming causes consumers to focus their processing on specific attributes rather than on abstract criteria. Priming hedonic or symbolic attributes—such as associations—with political concerns (e.g., reduce toxic waste) rather than with functional ones (e.g., no more hassles) can produce a higher willingness to pay for items or social programs.[57] Consumers primed to respond to a question about liking a product (i.e., one framed positively) answered more quickly than when they were primed to respond to a question about disliking a product (one framed negatively).[58]

MARKETING IMPLICATIONS

Goals, decision timing, and framing have important implications for positioning and market segmentation. First, marketers can position an offering as being consistent with consumers' goal-related or usage categories. That way, marketers can influence the way that consumers frame the decision, and consumers will be more likely to consider the brand and important related information (see Exhibit 9.5). For example, the SMART car is marketed as the car for intercity driving and parking on the small streets of European cities. Second, marketers can identify and market to large segments of consumers who have similar goal-related or usage-context categories. Thus, the $150 SK-II Air Touch electric makeup applicator is marketed to women who want their faces to look flawless.[59]

Another marketing strategy is to frame or reframe the decision. For example, targeting recent immigrants, Western Union reframed the use of its money-transfer services to emphasize the emotional aspect of sending money to family members still at home rather than focus on the speed or cost of the transaction.[60] Sales promotions generally are more successful when framed as gains rather than as a reduced loss—consumers prefer getting something free rather than getting a discount. And consumer decisions can be framed by the location of products in the store, a strategy that influences comparisons. For example, placing wine next to gourmet foods may frame the consumer's decision more broadly as planning to have a nice, romantic meal rather than simply as buying a bottle of wine.

Deciding What Brand to Choose: Thought-Based Decisions

Researchers have proposed various decision-making models, each of which may accurately describe how consumers make these high-effort decisions. Being opportunistic and adaptive, consumers do not follow a uniform process every time they make a decision.[61] Instead, they choose a model or use bits and pieces of various models, depending on the situation, and they may employ one or more decision rules, sometimes just because they want a change.[62] Furthermore, the choices consumers make may be related to other choices. For example, making one decision (buying a computer) can lead to yet another decision (buying a printer).[63]

Cognitive decision-making models describe how consumers systematically use information about attributes to reach a decision. Researchers also recognize that consumers may make decisions on the basis of feelings or emotions, using **affective decision-making models.**[64] Therefore, marketers need to know how consumers make choices when the decision is either cognitive or more emotional in nature.

Decision-making styles can vary across cultures.[65] Some North Americans, for example, tend to be analytical, rely on factual information, and search for solutions to problems. In contrast, in Asian cultures, and particularly in Japan, logic is sometimes less important than the *kimochi*—the feeling. Similarly, many Saudi Arabians are more intuitive in their decision making and avoid persuasion based on empirical reasoning. Russians may place more emphasis on values than on facts, and Germans tend to be theoretical and deductive. In North American and European cultures, decisions are usually made by individuals who control their own fate. In Asian cultures, the group is of primary importance, and actions are regarded as arising at random or from other events rather than as being controlled by individuals.

Cognitive models describe the processes by which consumers combine information about attributes to reach a decision in a rational, systematic manner. Two types of cognitive models are (1) compensatory versus noncompensatory and (2) brand versus attribute (see Exhibit 9.6).

With a **compensatory model,** consumers evaluate how good each of the attributes of the brands in their consideration set is (i.e., they make judgments about goodness and badness) and weight them in terms of how important the attributes are to their decisions. The brand that has the best overall score (attribute goodness times importance summed across all of the brand's attributes) is the one consumers choose. This is a kind of mental cost-benefit analysis in which a negative evaluation of one attribute can be compensated for (hence the name *compensatory*) by the positive features on others. To illustrate, for some U.S. consumers, a negative feature of Chinese products is that they are not made in America. However, this evaluation can be overcome if the products rate highly on other criteria deemed important, such as price.

With a **noncompensatory model,** consumers use negative information to evaluate brands and immediately eliminate from the consideration set those that are inadequate on any one or more important attributes.[66] These models are called *noncompensatory* because a negative rating on a key attribute eliminates the brand, as is the case when some U.S. consumers reject a product because it is foreign-made. Noncompensatory models require less cognitive effort than compensatory models do because consumers set up **cutoff levels** for each attribute and reject any brand with attribute rankings below the cutoff. Thus, if brands in consumers'

Cognitive decision-making models The process by which consumers combine items of information about attributes to reach a decision.

Affective decision-making models The process by which consumers base their decision on feelings and emotions.

Compensatory model A mental cost-benefit analysis model in which negative features can be compensated for by positive ones.

Noncompensatory model Simple decision model in which negative information leads to rejection of the option.

Cutoff levels For each attribute, the point at which a brand is rejected with a noncompensatory model.

Exhibit 9.6

Types of Cognitive Choice Models

Cognitive decision-making models can be classified along two major dimensions: (a) whether processing occurs one brand at a time or one attribute at a time, and (b) whether they are compensatory (bad attributes can be compensated for by good ones) or noncompensatory (a bad attribute eliminates the brand).

	Compensatory	Noncompensatory
Processing by Brand	Multiattribute models	Conjunctive model Disjunctive model
Processing by Attribute	Additive difference model	Lexicographic model Elimination-by-aspects model

consideration set are similar in attractiveness, they must put more effort into making a decision and will probably use a compensatory model.[67]

MARKETING IMPLICATIONS

Given that different models can lead to different choices, marketers may sometimes want to change the process by which consumers make a decision. For example, if most consumers are using a compensatory strategy, switching them to a noncompensatory strategy may be advantageous, particularly if competitors' products have a major weakness. By convincing consumers not to accept a lower level of an important attribute—that is, not to compensate for the attribute—marketers might prompt some consumers to reject competitors' products from consideration. Consider Steve & Barry's $14.98 Starbury sneakers, named after basketball star Stephon Marbury. Seeing Marbury wear these sneakers during big games has prompted some consumers to reject higher-priced sneakers in favor of Starbury sneakers.[68]

When consumers reject a brand using a noncompensatory strategy, marketers can try to switch them to using a compensatory strategy by arguing that other attributes compensate for a negative. To illustrate, advertising for high-priced, premium brands often stresses the reasons why its offerings are worth the extra money so that consumers do not reject them on price alone.

Decisions Based on Brands

In making a decision, consumers may evaluate *one brand at a time*. Thus, a consumer making a laptop purchase might collect information about an Apple model and make a judgment about it before moving on to the next brand. This type of **brand processing** occurs frequently because the environment—advertising, dealerships, and so on—is often organized by brands.

Much research has focused on brand-based compensatory models, also called **multiattribute expectancy-value models.**[69] One multiattribute model, the theory of reasoned action (TORA), was discussed in Chapter 5. Note that when considering multiple attributes, consumers tend to give more weight to those that are compatible with their goals.[70] Multiattribute models can be emotionally taxing as well as cognitively taxing when consumers need to make tradeoffs among attributes.[71] For instance, consumers facing emotionally difficult tradeoffs between price and quality may cope by choosing the offering with the best quality.[72] Some consumers may simply avoid making trade offs between conflicting attributes.[73]

Using a **conjunctive model,** consumers set up *minimum* cutoffs for *each* attribute that represent the absolute lowest value they are willing to accept.[74] For example, a

Brand processing Evaluating one brand at a time.

Multiattribute expectancy-value model A type of brand-based compensatory model.

Conjunctive model A noncompensatory model that sets minimum cutoffs to reject "bad" options.

Exhibit 9.7

Which Apartment Would You Choose?

Imagine that you visited five apartments (A, B, C, D, and E) and were trying to decide which to rent. You have determined what attributes you get (cost is the most important attribute followed by size and then location). After visiting each apartment, you rate how good each apartment is on each attribute. Which apartment would you rent if you used the following decision rules? Note that different decision rules can lead to different choices.

Evaluations of brands as good or bad based on information retrieved from memory or generated through external search (5 = very good on this attribute; 1 = not at all good on this attribute).

Importance weight of this attribute based on needs, values, goals (higher score means more important: weights add up to 100).

Evaluative Criteria	A	B	C	D	E	Importance
Cost	5	3	4	4	2	35
Size	3	4	5	4	3	25
Location	5	5	5	2	5	20
View	1	3	1	4	1	15
Has a pool	3	3	4	3	5	5

Apartment Chosen Based on the:
1. Compensatory Model (sum of Eval x Imp) _____
2. Conjunctive Model (set minimum cutoff of 2) _____
3. Disjunctive Model (set acceptable cutoff of 3) _____
4. Lexicographic Model (compare on EC in order of Imp) _____
5. Elimination by Aspects Model (set acceptable cutoff of 3) _____

Answers: 1 = C; 2 = B or D; 3 = B; 4 = A; 5 = B

consumer might want to pay less than $20 per month to finance a brief vacation and therefore reject an alternative with a higher monthly cost. Thus, the Carnival cruise line has arranged financing to allow consumers to charge a $299 three-day cruise and pay $14 per month for two years. "Some people still perceive cruising as too expensive," says a Carnival executive. "This just helps us get over that hurdle."[75] Because the cutoffs represent the bare minimum belief strength levels, the psychology of a conjunctive model is to rule out unsuitable alternatives (i.e., get rid of the "bad ones") as soon as possible, something that consumers do by weighing negative information.

Disjunctive model A noncompensatory model that sets acceptable cutoffs to find options that are "good."

The **disjunctive model** is similar to the conjunctive model, with two important exceptions. First, the consumer sets up *acceptable* levels for the cutoffs—levels that are more desirable (i.e., find the "good ones"). So even though $20 per month may be the highest monthly payment a consumer will accept for a vacation, $14 per month may be more acceptable. Second, the consumer bases evaluations on several of the *most important* attributes rather than on all of them, putting the weight on positive information. Using the descriptions provided above, see if you can decide which brand you would choose from among the set of brands in Exhibit 9.7, using first the multiattribute decision-making model, then the conjunctive, and finally the disjunctive model. Note that consumers may use several of these decision-making models. When the consideration set is large, they might use the conjunctive or disjunctive model to eliminate undesirable brands and then make their final choice among the brands that remain, using the multiattribute model.[76]

MARKETING IMPLICATIONS

Brand-based compensatory models help marketers understand which alternatives consumers may choose or reject and the beliefs that consumers have about the outcomes or attributes associated with a product. If consumers do not strongly believe that

DISCOVER THE POWER OF **PROTEIN** IN THE LAND OF **LEAN BEEF**

BeefItsWhatsForDinner.com | Funded by The Beef Checkoff

Promoting Compensatory Attributes

Sometimes marketers try to overcome the negative features of a product by focusing on positive features (a compensatory process). Here the positive feature of beef (protein) is stressed to overcome its negative health image.

Attribute processing
Comparing brands, one attribute at a time.

Additive difference model
Compensatory model in which brands are compared by attribute, two brands at a time.

Lexicographic model A noncompensatory model that compares brands by attributes, one at a time in order of importance.

positive outcomes or attributes are associated with a decision, marketers should stress these outcomes or attributes through marketing in order to strengthen consumers' beliefs (see Exhibit 9.8). The tiny, no-frills Tata Nano car marketed in India is the world's lowest-priced car. Tata promotes the Nano's fuel efficiency and four-person passenger capacity to compensate for the car's small size and lack of air conditioning, power brakes, and other amenities.[77]

Marketers can address shortcomings by altering the product and communicating its improvements to consumers. However, when companies make changes to remove competitive disadvantages, they may draw consumers away from competitive offerings, but they may also be reducing differentiation. Therefore, marketers should consider the long-term effects of improvements.[78]

Decision models can also help marketers better plan marketing communications, especially comparative ads. Research shows that consumers with little commitment to a brand will put more weight on negative information because they perceive it as more diagnostic.[79] For instance, Home Depot competes with Lowe's and other rivals that advertise good service and product selection. To counter negative perceptions of its customer service, Home Depot hired plumbing and electrical experts to work in its stores and switched to night restocking so that its employees could focus on customers.[80]

Decisions Based on Product Attributes

The previous discussion described how consumers make choices when they first process information one brand at a time. Here, we discuss **attribute processing,** which occurs when consumers compare across brands *one attribute at a time,* such as comparing each brand on price. Although most consumers prefer attribute processing because it is easier than brand processing, they cannot always find information available in a manner that facilitates it. This situation accounts for the increasing popularity of shopping agents. One study found that the inclusion of an attribute in a shopping agent's recommendations list gives that attribute more prominence.[81]

According to the **additive difference model,** brands are compared by attribute, *two brands at a time.*[82] Consumers evaluate differences between the two brands on each attribute and then combine them into an overall preference. This process allows tradeoffs between attributes—that is, a positive difference on one attribute can offset a negative difference on another.

With the **lexicographic model,** consumers order attributes in terms of importance and compare the options one attribute at a time, starting with the most important. If one option dominates, the consumer selects it. In the case of a tie, the consumer proceeds to the second most important attribute and continues in this way until only one option remains. A tie can occur if the difference between two options on any attribute is below the just noticeable difference: one brand priced at $2.77 and one priced at $2.79 would likely be regarded as being tied on price.

Elimination-by-aspects model Similar to the lexicographic model but adds the notion of acceptable cutoffs.

The **elimination-by-aspects model** is similar to the lexicographic model but incorporates the notion of an *acceptable cutoff*.[83] This model is not as strict as the lexicographic model, and more attributes are likely to be considered. Consumers first order attributes in terms of importance and then compare options on the most important attribute. Those options below the cutoff are eliminated, and the consumer continues the process until only one option remains. Again using the information shown in Exhibit 9.7, think about which brand you would select if you were to use the various decision models described in this exhibit.

MARKETING IMPLICATIONS

The additive difference model helps marketers determine which attributes or outcomes exhibit the greatest differences among brands and use this knowledge to improve and properly position their brand. If a brand performs below a major competitor on a certain attribute, the company needs to enhance consumers' beliefs about that product's superiority. On the other hand, if a brand performs significantly better than competitors on a key attribute, marketers should enhance consumer beliefs by positioning the offering around this advantage. To illustrate, the South African fast-food restaurant Africa Hut has become popular because it differs from all other competitors on one key attribute: It serves traditional local dishes such as pap (corn porridge) and malam-agodu (tripe).[84]

If many consumers are employing a lexicographic model, and a brand is weak on the most important attribute, the company needs to improve this feature in order to have its brand selected. Also, marketers can try to change the order of importance of attributes so that a major brand advantage is the most critical attribute.

Identifying consumers' cutoff levels can be very useful for marketers. If an offering is beyond any of the cutoffs that many consumers set, it will be rejected frequently. This result means marketers must change consumers' beliefs about these attributes. For example, more consumers in China are considering SUVs because of the vehicles' cargo capacity and the large-vehicle safety factor, but they are also very price-conscious. ZXAuto and other local manufacturers therefore make SUVs similar to Japanese or American models but price them lower than the cost of foreign models.[85] Marketers can also influence brand choice by affecting how attributes are framed (i.e., whether they are framed negatively or positively). Consumers may not like or choose a brand that is framed as having 25 percent fat and may like a brand framed as being 75 percent lean better. While both brands have the same amount of fat, one is framed in terms of a positive (lean); the other in terms of a negative (fat).[86]

Decisions Based on Gains and Losses

The previous discussion describes the different types of models that consumers can use to make decisions. However, research shows that the decisions consumers make also depend on whether the consumer is motivated to seek gains or to avoid losses. According to *prospect theory*, losses loom larger than gains for consumers even when the two outcomes are of the same magnitude.[87] For example, when asked to set a price for an item to be exchanged, sellers typically ask for a much higher price (because they are experiencing a loss of the item) than buyers are willing to pay (gaining the item). This has been called the **endowment effect** because ownership increases the value (and loss) associated with an item.

Endowment effect When ownership increases the value of an item.

YOU CAN FINALLY GET ALL THOSE BARELY USED BOTTLES OuT of YoUR HaiR.

NO WORRIES GUARANTEE

NOW, NATURALLY RADIANT HAIR IS GUARANTEED.*
Dazzling radiance in one use, or your money back. That's our No Worries Guarantee. Call 1-8-NO-WORRIES or visit aussie.com

*1.8 NO WORRIES. Satisfaction guaranteed. Call within 30 days with receipt. Aussie ©2008 P&G

aussie®
Add Some Roo To Your Do.®

Exhibit 9.9

Reducing Risk

Sometimes marketers try to reduce consumer risk in buying the product by providing guarantees, as in this ad for Aussie.

Similarly, consumers have a much stronger reaction to price increases than to price decreases and may be more reluctant to upgrade to higher-priced durable items. Thus, consumers may avoid making decisions to a greater degree when a decision involves losses relative to gains. This effect has been demonstrated across a variety of products/services including wine, lottery tickets, basketball tickets, and pizza toppings.

In addition, the consumer's promotion- and prevention-focused goals will impact this process. For instance, prevention-focused consumers tend to preserve the status quo instead of making a decision that will result in a change because they want to avoid losses. In contrast, promotion-focused consumers are more willing to try new things if they think that changing from the status quo will help them achieve their goals of growth and development.[88]

MARKETING IMPLICATIONS

Prospect theory has a number of important marketing implications. First, consumers will be more risk averse and unwilling to buy the product when the decision involves losses. Thus, marketers must make a effort to reduce risks and potential losses. This situation is one of the key reasons that manufacturers and retailers make offers such as the "full money–back guarantee" or "no money down for 12 months with no interest" as well as provide warranty programs (see Exhibit 9.9). Second, consumers will react more negatively to price increases or higher-priced items than they will react positively to price decreases. Thus, marketers need to carefully consider the amount of the price increase (i.e., the greater the increase, the stronger the negative reaction). Further, this suggests that if possible, marketers should try to frame these increases as gains rather than losses (i.e., the increased benefit the consumer might get from the higher-priced item).

Deciding What Brand to Choose: High-Effort Feeling-Based Decisions

Affective decision making
Decisions based on feelings and emotions.

Just as consumers can make high-effort thought-based decisions, so too can they make high-effort feeling-based decisions. With **affective decision making,** consumers make a decision because the choice feels right rather than because they have made a detailed, systematic evaluation of offerings. Or they may decide that the chosen option feels like a perfect fit, regardless of their prior cognitive processing.[89] Consumers who make decisions based on feelings tend to be more satisfied afterward than those who make decisions based on product attributes.[90] Moreover, emotions can also help thought-based decision making since emotions can help consumers gather their thoughts and make judgments more quickly.[91]

As you saw in Chapter 6, brands can be associated with positive emotions such as love, joy, pride, and elation as well as with negative emotions such as guilt, hate, fear, anxiety, anger, sadness, shame, and greed. These emotions can be recalled to play a central role in the decision process, particularly when consumers perceive them as relevant to the offering.[92] This affective processing is frequently experience-based.[93] In other words, consumers select an option based on their recall of past experiences and the associated feelings. When consumers choose among brands in memory, they must work harder to process information, so their feelings carry considerable weight. In contrast, when they choose among brands based on information in ads or other external stimuli, they can focus more on the offering's attributes and less on their feelings.[94]

Consumer feelings are particularly critical for offerings with hedonic, symbolic, or aesthetic aspects.[95] Feelings also influence decisions about what we will consume and for how long.[96] We tend to buy offerings that make us feel good more often and for longer periods than we buy offerings that do not have these effects. Note that consumers sometimes buy a product, such as jewelry, simply to make themselves feel better. In other situations, they may make a choice because of a negative feeling, buying a product out of guilt or shame.

Appraisals and Feelings

As you saw in Chapter 2, *appraisal theory* examines how our emotions are determined by the way that we think about or "appraise" the situation, a field being explored by many researchers.[97] This theory also explains how and why certain emotions (including those carried over from previous decisions) can affect future judgments and choices. People who are fearful tend to see more risk in new situations than do people who are angry, for example. In situations involving disposition of objects, people who are disgusted tend to view this activity as an opportunity to get rid of their current possessions while people who are sad tend to view it as an opportunity to change their circumstances.[98] Even the emotional reaction to a desired product's being out of stock can affect a consumer's feelings about and appraisals of subsequent purchases in the same environment.[99]

Affective Forecasts and Choices

Affective forecasting A prediction of how you will feel in the future

Consumers' predictions of what they will feel in the future—**affective forecasting**—can influence the choices they make today. For instance, someone may buy a dishwasher after forecasting the relief she will feel at having an appliance to handle this time-consuming chore. You may decide to go to Mexico instead of Colorado over spring break because you think the Mexico trip will make you feel more relaxed. As shown in Exhibit 9.10, we can forecast (1) how we think we will

---

Exhibit 9.10

Affective Forecasting

Affective forecasting occurs when consumers try to predict how they will feel in a future consumption situation. Specifically, they try to predict what feelings they will have, how strongly these feelings will be, and how long the feelings will last.

What Will I Feel?	How Much Will I Feel It?	How Long Will I Feel This Way?
• Valence (good or bad) • Nature of feeling (specific emotion such as happiness, regret, guilt, shame)	• Intensity	• Duration

feel as a result of a decision, (2) how intensely we will have this feeling, and (3) how long this feeling will last. Any one of these forecasts can affect our decision about whether to go to Mexico. It is important to remember that affective forecasting is not always accurate, however, and that we can be wrong about any or all of the above-noted forecasts.[100] Consequently, after our vacation, instead of feeling relaxed, we may feel stressed; instead of feeling extremely relaxed, we may feel only mildly relaxed; or instead of feeling relaxed for a week, our postvacation feelings of relaxation may only last until we reach home (and see the pile of work we now have to do).

While anticipating post-decision levels of happiness (or relaxation, as illustrated in the example above) can impact the choices consumers make, so too can anticipated regret about making a wrong decision impact the choices consumers make. For instance, if they are participating in an auction and anticipate feeling deep regret should another bidder win, consumers will place a higher bid on an item than they would otherwise have placed.[101] Similarly, consumers who anticipate regret at later finding out that today's sale price was better than a future sale price are more likely to buy the item on sale now.[102]

Imagery

Imagery plays a key role in emotional decision making[103] Consumers can attempt to imagine themselves consuming the product or service and can use any emotions they experience as input for the decision (see Exhibit 9.11). In choosing a vacation, you can imagine the excitement you might experience by being in each destination. If these images are pleasant (or negative), they will exert a positive (or negative) influence on your decision process. Imagery can also ignite consumer desire for and fantasizing about certain products.[104] Inviting consumers to interact with a product through an online demonstration can evoke vivid mental images of product use and increase purchase intentions.[105]

Adding information actually makes imagery processing easier because more information makes it easier for consumers to form an accurate image (whereas it may lead to *information overload* under cognitive processing). For instance, consumers who see an ad asking them to imagine how good they would feel using the advertised product are likely to react positively and like the product more.[106] Moreover, imagery encourages brand-based processing because images are organized by brand rather than by attribute. Also, companies that design new products by encouraging customers to imagine or create a new image rather than recall one from memory can produce more original product designs.[107]

Exhibit 9.11

Stimulating Imagery Through Advertising

Ads sometimes try to induce consumers to imagine themselves in certain situations. When they do, consumers may experience the feelings and emotions that are associated with this situation. This ad for Yankee Candle may stimulate the positive feelings of being in a beautiful forest in autumn.

THERE ARE PLACES WHERE AUTUMN LASTS AS LONG AS YOU WANT IT TO.

Save up to 25% on select Autumn Housewarmers at all Yankee Candle stores and participating Yankee Candle retailers. Let our true-to-life scents take you there. For a location near you, call 800.243.1776, or shop online at yankeecandle.com

YANKEE CANDLE
where will our scents take you?

MARKETING IMPLICATIONS

Marketers can employ a variety of advertising, sales, and promotional techniques to add to the emotional experience and imagery surrounding an offering. Good service or pleasant ambiance in a hotel, restaurant, or store, for example, can produce consumers' positive feelings and experiences that may influence their future choices. This is why the Ritz-Carlton hotel chain spends so much time and money training its 35,000 employees to deliver exemplary service and make every guest feel pampered.[108]

Nike has long used imagery to help consumers feel the excitement and satisfaction of excelling in the sports activities they love. Its "Just Do It" campaign famously offered encouragement to athletes of all ages and abilities. Similarly, its "Become Legendary" campaign linked the youthful aspirations of now-established superstars like Derek Jeter with the introduction of a new Air Jordan top-performance sneaker.[109]

Additional High-Effort Decisions

In addition to deciding which brands to include in a consideration set, deciding what is important to the choice, and deciding what offerings to choose, consumers in high-effort situations face two more key decisions. First, should they delay the decision or make it right now? And second, how can they make a decision when the alternatives cannot be compared?

Decision Delay

If consumers perceive the decision to be too risky or if it entails an unpleasant task, they may delay making a decision.[110] Another reason for delaying a decision is if consumers feel uncertain about how to get product information.[111] Delaying a decision can affect a consumer's evaluation of brands that have features in common, regardless of whether those features are positive or negative. Specifically, the delay seems to make the shared features easier to recall and therefore has a greater impact on consumers' evaluations of the brands being considered.[112]

MARKETING IMPLICATIONS

Should marketers encourage consumers to decide on a purchase right away? Many sales promotion techniques, including coupons and discounts, are available only to consumers who act quickly. On the other hand, if consumers delay making their decisions, marketers may have more time to offer additional information to bolster the chances that their brand will be chosen. Apple used this strategy to good advantage when it hyped the introduction of its iPhone months in advance of product availability. By the time the product was actually available, many consumers were willing to wait for hours just for the chance to be among the first to buy the iPhone.[113]

Decision Making When Alternatives Cannot Be Compared

Consumers sometimes need to choose from a set of options that cannot be directly compared on the same attributes. For instance, you might be trying to select entertainment for next weekend and may have the choice of going to the movies, eating at a nice restaurant, renting a video, or attending a party. Each alternative has different attributes, making comparisons among them difficult.

Using Attribute-Based Strategies for Noncomparable Options

Sometimes consumers have trouble making noncomparable choices, such as choosing from different vacation destinations, so they use abstract attributes like "fun" or "beauty."

Noncomparable decisions The process of making decisions about products or services from different categories.

Alternative-based strategy Making a noncomparable choice based on an overall evaluation.

Attribute-based strategy Making noncomparable choices by making abstract representations of comparable attributes.

In making these **noncomparable decisions,** consumers adopt either an alternative-based strategy or an attribute-based strategy.[114] Using the **alternative-based strategy** (also called *top-down processing*), they develop an overall evaluation of each option—perhaps using a compensatory or affective strategy—and base their decision on it. For example, if you were deciding on weekend entertainment, you could evaluate each option's pros and cons independently and then choose the one you liked the best.

Using the **attribute-based strategy,** consumers make comparisons easier for themselves by forming abstract representations that will allow them to compare the options (Exhibit 9.12). In this type of bottom-up processing, the choice is constructed or built up. To make a more direct comparison of options for an entertainment decision, for example, you could construct abstract attributes for them such as "fun" or "likelihood of impressing a date." Because using abstractions simplifies the decision-making process, consumers tend to use them even when the options are easy to compare.[115]

Note that both strategies can be employed in different circumstances. When the alternatives are less comparable, consumers tend to use an alternative-based strategy because it is harder for them to create attribute abstractions.[116] Alternative-based strategies also suit consumers who have well-defined goals because they can easily recall the various options and their results. For example, if your goal is to find enjoyable things to do with a date, you could immediately recall a set of options like going to a movie or eating out, along with your overall evaluation of each option. You would then pick the option with the strongest evaluation. On the other hand, when consumers lack well-defined goals, they tend to use attribute-based processing.

Remember that price is often the one attribute on which alternatives can be compared directly. Consumers typically use price to screen alternatives for the consideration set rather than as the main basis of comparison among noncomparable alternatives. Thus, when selecting from among entertainment alternatives, you might use cost to generate a set of options that are reasonably affordable, then use an alternative- or attribute-based strategy to make the final decision.

MARKETING IMPLICATIONS

Because of the way that consumers approach noncomparable decisions, marketers should look at each product's or brand's competition in broad terms as well as understand how the product or brand stacks up to specific competitors. For example, when consumers are deciding where to go on vacation, their alternatives may reflect competition between different types of destinations (such as cities or beaches), activities (such as going to museums or going surfing), and so on. Therefore, marketers might identify the abstract attributes that consumers use to make these noncomparable evaluations.

For instance, stressing an attribute like "fun" could make it easier for consumers to compare products. Also, communications about destinations like Scotland could feature multiple attributes (golf courses, fishing areas, historic landmarks) and suggest how visiting the destination will fit the "fun" attribute.[117] Pricing is also an important marketing tactic for getting a brand into the consideration set when consumers cannot directly compare the attributes of various alternatives. Thus, tourism marketers often use pricing promotions to attract consumers' attention and encourage them to make further comparisons based on their goals or on individual attributes.

What Affects High-Effort Decisions?

As you have seen, consumers can use many different strategies when making decisions. However, the best strategy to use for making a specific decision depends on the consumer and the nature of the decision.[118] This final section looks at how characteristics of (a) consumers, (b) the situation they are in, and (c) the group that they are a part of can affect their decisions.

Consumer Characteristics

Characteristics associated with consumers—such as their expertise, mood, extremeness aversion, time pressure, and metacognitive experiences—can affect the decisions they make.

Expertise

Consumers are more likely to understand their preferences and decisions when they have detailed consumption vocabularies—meaning that they can articulate exactly why they like or dislike the brands that they do. For example, a consumer who is an expert in wine may know that he or she likes wines that are buttery, dry, and smooth, whereas a novice might not know how to articulate these preferences.[119] Consumers who have this "consumption vocabulary" can use more attributes and information when making a decision. Expert consumers have more brand-based prior experience and knowledge and, as a result, tend to use brand-based decision strategies.[120] These consumers know how to identify relevant information and ignore irrelevant attributes in their decision making. When consumers consider complex information, they may simplify the processing task by focusing more on brand effects and less on attributes, especially if they face more than one complex choice task.[121]

Mood

Consumers who are in a reasonably good mood are more willing to process information and take more time in making a decision than those who are not in a good mood.[122] When in a good mood, consumers pay closer attention to the set of brands being considered and think about a higher number of attributes connected with each brand, a process that can result in more extreme (positive or negative) evaluations.[123] Another study showed that consumers in a high-arousal mood—feeling excited or very sad, for instance—tend to process information less thoroughly. Recall is also affected: Consumers in a bad mood are more likely to accurately recall what a marketing message said, a factor that may affect what attributes they consider when making their choices.[124]

Mood can also influence how positively consumers judge products and their attributes.[125] One study found that when consumers' moods were subconsciously influenced by music, consumers in a good mood rated a set of audio speakers more positively than did consumers in a bad mood.[126] Interestingly, consumers may deliberately manipulate their moods to help themselves improve their decision performance.[127] Finally, consumers in a good mood are more willing to try new products because they perceive lower probabilities of incurring losses.[128]

Time Pressure

As time pressure increases, consumers initially try to process information relevant to their choices faster.[129] If doing this does not work, they base their decision on fewer attributes and place heavier weight on negative information, eliminating bad alternatives by using a noncompensatory decision strategy. Time pressure, one of the major reasons that consumers fail to make intended purchases, can reduce shopping time and the number of impulsive purchases.[130] Time pressure also affects consumers' decisions to delay their choices.[131] Moreover, whether a consumer is present- or future-oriented can lead to different motivations and choices for different products.[132] *Present-oriented consumers* want to improve their current well-being and prefer products that help them to do so, such as relaxing vacations and entertaining books. *Future-oriented consumers* want to develop themselves and select life-enriching vacations and books.

Extremeness Aversion

Extremeness aversion
Options that are extreme on some attributes are less attractive than those with a moderate level of those attributes.

Consumers tend to exhibit **extremeness aversion,** meaning that options for a particular attribute that are perceived as extreme will seem less attractive than those perceived as intermediate. This tendency is the reason that people often find moderately priced options more attractive than options that are either very expensive or very inexpensive. For example, retailer Williams-Sonoma offered one bread-making unit at $275 and then added a second unit priced 50 percent higher. Introducing the more expensive unit doubled the sales of the first unit.[133]

When consumers see the attributes of one alternative as being equally dispersed (rather than very close together or very far apart), they will view this alternative as the compromise option even when it is not at the overall midpoint among options.[134] According to the **compromise effect,** a brand will gain share when it is seen as the intermediate or compromise choice rather than as an extreme choice.[135] Also, consumers prefer a brand with attributes that score equally well on certain criteria more than a brand that has unequal scores across attributes, a phenomenon known as **attribute balancing.**[136]

Compromise effect When a brand gains share because it is an intermediate rather than an extreme option.

Attribute balancing Picking a brand because it scores equally well on certain attributes rather than faring unequally on these attributes.

Metacognitive Experiences

Metacognitive experiences
How the information is processed beyond the content of the decision.

One final set of consumer characteristics that affects the decision-making process is that of **metacognitive experiences.** These are factors based on our decision-processing experience, such as how easy it is to recall information in memory and to form thoughts as well as how easy it is to process new information.[137] Metacognitive experiences affect decisions beyond formal knowledge by influencing retrieval ease, inferences, and biases. Thus, it is not just the content of the information that influences the decision; rather, *how* this information is processed is also critical.

According to one study, the pleasant experience of being able to process a brand name easily can lead to a consumer's favorable attitudes toward that brand. Yet in some cases in which consumers can process information about the brand more easily—such as seeing the mention of product benefits in an ad message—they may develop less favorable attitudes toward the brand because they may attribute that ease of processing to the persuasiveness of the information rather than to the attractiveness of the brand itself. Other studies have found that individuals are more likely to regard a statement as true when it is printed in an easy-to-read color or if the words rhyme.[138] In short, metacognitive experiences affect choices in concert with stimuli and consumer characteristics such as mood.[139]

Characteristics of the Decision

In addition to consumer characteristics, decision characteristics can affect how consumers make their choices. Two decision characteristics of particular note are the availability of information on which to base a decision and the presence of trivial attributes.

Information Availability

The amount, quality, and format of the information can affect the decision-making strategy that consumers use. When a consumer has more information, the decision becomes more complex, and the consumer must use a more detailed decision-making strategy, such as the multiattribute choice strategy. Having more information will lead to making a better choice only up to a point, however; after that, the consumer will experience information overload.[140] For example, pharmaceutical firms are legally required to provide detailed prescription information and to disclose side effects of medications in their ads, yet the amount of such information can be overwhelming.

If the information provided is useful and relevant to our decision criteria, decision making is less taxing, and we can make better decisions.[141] Essentially, we can narrow the consideration set relatively quickly because we can focus on those attributes that are most important to our decision. Hence, it is better for marketers to focus on providing relevant information, not just more information. If the information provided is not useful or if some information is missing, we will need to infer how the product might rate on that attribute, perhaps by using other attributes of the brand in question to make that inference.[142]

If the available information is ambiguous, consumers are more likely to stay with their current brand than to risk purchasing a new competitive brand—even a superior one.[143] Consumers also can compare numerical attribute information faster and more easily than they can compare verbal information.[144] For example, to help parents select video games, a group of manufacturers developed a numerical rating system to indicate the amount of sex and violence in their games. Finally, decisions are sometimes affected by information about attributes to which consumers have been exposed in a previous choice.[145]

Information Format

The format of the information—the way that it is organized or presented in the external environment—can also influence the decision strategy that consumers use. If information is organized by brand, consumers will likely employ a brand-based decision-making strategy such as a compensatory, conjunctive, or disjunctive model. If information is organized by attribute or in a matrix, consumers can use an attribute-processing strategy. For example, one study found that organizing yogurt by flavor instead of by brand encouraged more comparison shopping on the basis of attribute processing.[146] Sometimes consumers will even restructure information into a more useful format, especially in a matrix. One study found that consumers were less likely to choose the cheapest brand of consumer electronics product when the offerings were organized by model (similar offerings by different companies grouped together) rather than by brand.[147] Thus, companies with high-priced brands would want the display to be organized by model, and companies offering low-priced brands would prefer a brand-based display.

The presence of a narrative format for presenting information about brands can also impact consumers' choices. When researchers presented consumers with a narrative message about vacations, the consumers used holistic processing to sequence and evaluate the information. The narrative structure is similar to the way in which consumers acquire information in daily life, so processing was easier. In processing the narrative, consumers did not consider individual features, a situation that meant negative information had less impact.[148]

Trivial Attributes

Consumers sometimes finalize decisions by looking at trivial attributes. For example, if three brands in the consideration set are perceived as equivalent with the exception that one contains a trivial attribute, the consumer is likely to choose the brand with the trivial attribute (arguing that its presence may be useful). If, however, two of the three brands in the consideration set have a particular trivial attribute, the consumer is likely to choose the one without that attribute (arguing that the attribute is unnecessary). In both cases, the trivial attribute was used to complete and justify the decision.[149]

Group Context

Finally, consumers' decisions can be affected by the presence of a group, such as when a group of people is dining out and each member is deciding what to order. As each group member makes a decision in turn, he or she attempts to balance two sets of goals: (1) goals that are attained by the individual's action alone *(individual alone)* and (2) goals that are achieved depending on the actions of both the individual and the group *(individual group)*.[150] Because consumers may have to choose a different alternative to achieve each set of goals, they cannot always achieve both sets of goals simultaneously in group settings.

In a group, consumers face three types of individual-group goals, as shown in Exhibit 9.13:

- ▶ *Self-presentation.* Consumers seek to convey a certain image through the decisions they make in a group context. When consumers want to use unique choices as positive self-presentation cues or to express their individuality, the result will be variety seeking at the group level. Yet consumers are often more concerned about social norms and therefore make similar choices to blend in, resulting in uniformity at the group level.

- ▶ *Minimizing regret.* Consumers who are risk averse and want to minimize regret will tend to make choices that are similar to those made by the rest of the group, leading to uniformity at the group level. Making this choice allows group members to avoid any disappointment they might feel if someone else's choice seemed better than their own.

- ▶ *Information gathering.* Consumers can learn more about the different choices each has made through interaction with other group members. Whether members actually share choices or simply share their reactions, the result is variety

Goal Classes that Affect Consumer Decision Making

Consumers are not always able to achieve both individual-alone and individual-group goals when making decisions in the context of a group. Trying to achieve individual-group goals can result in either group variety or group uniformity, while trying to achieve individual-alone goals allows the consumer to satisfy his or her own taste through the decision.

Note. — In cases where informational social influence is present during the decision process, an outcome of group uniformity or variety seeking can result.

in the totality of choices within the group when consumers see information gathering as a priority. However, when group members are more concerned with self-presentation or loss aversion than with information gathering, they will make similar choices, resulting in group uniformity.

When making a decision in a group context, we try to balance these three individual-group goals with our individual-alone goals. In most group situations, the result is group uniformity, even though individual members may ultimately feel less satisfied by the outcome.

MARKETING IMPLICATIONS

Marketers can develop some interesting strategies by understanding how consumer characteristics affect high-effort decisions. One technique is to sell a new, improved model alongside the old model at the same price, a tactic that makes the new one look better. In addition, marketers need to think about the information in their ads and on their packaging because irrelevant information can sometimes influence consumers' decisions—even in the presence of more relevant information.[151]

Providing the right amount of information at the right time is a challenge marketers face all over the world. One study found that consumers in Romania and Turkey have experienced great confusion in judging quality and making choices because "there are so many alternatives now."[152] Marketers should therefore present a few key points, not a flood of information. However, providing too little information can also hamper decision making, resulting in poorer quality decisions and a lower level of satisfaction. A lack of both products and information has been a major problem in some former communist countries.[153]

Finally, marketers can use communications to make individual-group goals a higher priority in group situations, leading to more uniformity of choice in favor of the advertised brand. Beer marketers, for instance, often show group members enjoying only the advertised brand, an image that reinforces strong social norms and encourages consumers to order that brand when they drink in a social setting.

Summary

Judgments involve forming evaluations or estimates—not always objective—of the likelihood of the occurrence of events, whereas decisions entail choosing from among options or courses of action. Two types of judgments are judgments of likelihood and judgments of goodness or badness, both of which can be made by recalling past judgments using imagery or an anchoring and adjustment process.

Once they recognize a problem, consumers may address it by using cognitive decision-making models (deciding in a rational, systematic manner) or affective decision-making models (deciding on the basis of their feelings or emotions). Consumers face a number of other decisions in high-effort situations: which brands to consider (developing the consideration set), what is important to the choice (how it is affected by goals, decision timing, and decision framing), what offerings to choose, whether to make a decision now, and what to do when alternatives cannot be compared.

In thought-based decisions about offerings, consumers may use compensatory or noncompensatory models, process by brand or by attribute, and consider gains versus losses. Feeling-based decisions about offerings may rely on appraisals and feelings, affective forecasts and choices, and imagery. Finally, three types of contextual factors that can influence the decision process are (1) consumer characteristics, (2) decision characteristics, and (3) the presence of a group.

Questions for Review and Discussion

1. How does consumer judgment differ from consumer decision making?

2. What is the anchoring and adjustment process, and how does it affect consumer judgment?

3. How do consumers use compensatory and noncompensatory decision-making models?

4. Explain how consumers use their goals, decision timing, and framing to decide which criteria are important for a particular choice.

5. Why do marketers need to know that attribute processing is easier for consumers than brand processing?

6. How do appraisals and feelings as well as affective forecasting influence consumer decision making?

7. What three contextual elements affect consumer decision making?

CL   Visit http://cengage.com/marketing/hoyer/ConsumerBehavior5e to find resources that are available to help you study for the course.

CONSUMER BEHAVIOR CASE

Winnebago Wants RV Owners to Get on the Road

Will high gasoline prices and uncertain economic conditions keep consumers from buying recreational vehicles and motor homes to enjoy the romance of the open road with all the comforts of home? The profits of Winnebago Industries of Forest City, Iowa, are riding on the answer to this question. Winnebago has been making and selling RVs and motor homes since 1958 under the Winnebago and Itasca brands. Its annual sales are approaching $900 million, and its brands account for a sizable share of the 350,000 RVs and motor homes bought by U.S. consumers every year.

Winnebago's marketing experts recognize that choosing a motor home with a price tag as high as $300,000 (or as low as $60,000) is not an easy decision. Many potential customers consider traveling in motor homes an affordable way to see the country by driving through scenic spots and parking at campgrounds along the way rather than paying to stay in motels and eat in restaurants. When gasoline prices were low, consumers were less concerned about fuel efficiency because of the money they were saving by camping. As gasoline prices have increased, however, so has demand for RVs that get better mileage and help customers achieve their dreams of traveling without breaking their budgets.

In response, Winnebago has developed more fuel-efficient models and offered a number of financial incentives to sweeten the deal, including a choice of either a rebate or cash toward filling the gas tank on certain models. It also maintains a list of dealers who will rent Winnebago models. Although some consumers will choose to rent to avoid the expense of ownership, this option also gives would-be customers a chance to try the vehicle and to experience Winnebago traveling before they make their final choice of which brand and model to buy.

Today's buyers often want a Winnebago or Itasca for more than camping. The CEO says the company's typical customer "is someone 55 to 70 years of age who has been in retirement mode or who is looking for an RV for leisure travel or wants one to help with pursuing another hobby—like following the NASCAR circuit or tailgating at a favorite football team's [games] on weekends." Knowing how buyers plan to use their RVs enables Winnebago to include appropriate features on various models. Some models are basic while others are fully outfitted with kitchen and laundry appliances, computer networks, sound systems, and other amenities suitable for what may become a second home on wheels. "We make sure that nobody's roughing it too much," notes Winnebago's CEO.

Consumers researching Winnebago's offerings can go to the company's website to learn how to choose an RV or motor home, click for 360-degree virtual tours of various Winnebago and Itasca vehicles, and compare detailed specifications of each model. They can also watch a slide show to see the craftsmanship involved in manufacturing a Winnebago product or request a video version of the factory tour. And they can buy all kinds of caps, shirts, jackets, accessories, and other items emblazoned with the Winnebago brand logo to make a statement about their lifestyle.

Finally, the company encourages a sense of community by inviting buyers to become members of the Winnebago-Itasca Travelers Club. More than 19,000 customers have joined to enjoy benefits such as receiving a monthly newsletter; gathering with other Winnebago customers at local club meetings; attending national and statewide events such as the annual Grand National Rally in Forest City; and taking advantage of member discounts on vehicle insurance, roadside assistance, campgrounds, and more. Through special-interest groups within the travelers' club, members can find like-minded individuals who share their interests in golfing, singing, bowling, or extended RV trips.[154]

Case Questions

1. In what ways does Winnebago help consumers imagine themselves inside one of its motor homes or RVs and enjoying the lifestyle that comes with such a product?

2. Why would Winnebago offer a slide show and video of its factory tour?

3. Explain, in terms of thought-based decisions, why Winnebago should promote the improved gas mileage of its fuel-efficient models.

4. Are there any emotional aspects related to the Winnebago decision process? If so, how does Winnebago influence these emotions?

Chapter 10

Judgment and Decision Making Based on Low Effort

INTRODUCTION

Jones Soda Bottles Brand Loyalty

Are loyal Jones Soda customers drawn to its quirky soft drinks or to its irreverent image? Both have helped build Jones into a $56 million company. Unique soda flavors like Crushed Melon and Christmas Tree and cheeky brands like Whoop Ass energy drink set Jones apart from the big cola companies. The labels on Jones Soda bottles, which feature photos taken by consumers, are another point of differentiation. Even photos not chosen for labels are posted on the brand's multimedia website, where visitors can click to vote for their favorites and play games, buy branded merchandise such as skateboards, and get the latest news about snowboarders, surfers, and other extreme athletes sponsored by Jones.

The brand's irreverent image has also been shaped by its distribution strategy. At first, Jones Sodas were available only in skateboard shops, tattoo parlors, music stores, and other retail locations where soft drinks are not usually found. Then the company was able to get its sodas into larger outlets such as Barnes & Noble bookstores and Panera Bread restaurants and ultimately was able to expand to more than 15,000 U.S. stores, including some mainstream supermarkets. And because Jones regularly introduces offbeat flavors like Turkey and Gravy, when Jones's loyal customers hanker for something new, they now have many choices of flavors, bottles with new labels, and places to buy.[1]

LEARNING OBJECTIVES

After studying this chapter, you will be able to

1. Identify the types of heuristics that consumers can use to make simple judgments.

2. Explain why marketers need to understand both unconscious and conscious decision-making processes in low-effort situations.

3. Show how the hierarchy of effects and operant conditioning explain consumers' low-effort decision making.

4. Discuss how consumers make thought-based low-effort decisions using performance-related tactics, habit, brand loyalty, price-related tactics, and normative influences.

5. Describe how consumers make affect-based low-effort decisions using feelings as a simplifying strategy, brand familiarity, variety seeking, and impulse purchasing.

The various ways that consumers act toward Jones Soda illustrate several factors discussed in this chapter. When consumers have low motivation, ability, and opportunity (MAO) to process information (as when purchasing everyday products like soft drinks), their judgment and decision processes are different and involve less effort than when MAO is high (as when buying luxury goods). Consumers may simplify their decisions by repeatedly buying a brand they like. Or they may be guided by their feelings toward a familiar brand or bottle (in this case, with labels featuring consumer-contributed photos). Some consumers may simply be in the mood for variety, such as a new flavor. Also, the brand can try to increase the excitement (or situational involvement) by offering games, merchandise, and news on its website or through other sources. This chapter examines the nature of low-effort judgment and decision making, as shown in Exhibit 10.1. The focus here is on the cognitive and affective shortcuts or heuristics that consumers use to make judgments and decisions, as well as on how consumers make unconscious and conscious decisions in low-effort situations.

Low-Effort Judgment Processes

Chapter 9 showed that when effort is high, consumers' judgments—such as estimations of likelihood and goodness/badness—can be cognitively complex. In contrast, when MAO is low, individuals are motivated to simplify the cognitive process by using heuristics, or rules of thumb, to reduce the effort involved in making judgments.[2] Two major types of heuristics are representativeness and availability.

The Representativeness Heuristic

Representativeness heuristic Making a judgment by simply comparing a stimulus with the category prototype or exemplar.

One way that consumers can make simple estimations or judgments is to make comparisons with the category prototype or exemplar. This categorization process is called the **representativeness heuristic.**[3] For example, if you want to estimate the likelihood that a new mouthwash is of high quality, you might compare it with your prototype for mouthwashes, such as Listerine. If you see that the new brand is similar to the prototype, you will assume that it is also of high quality. This is the reasoning behind packaging many store brands so that they look similar to leading brands in various product categories. The retailers hope that the outward similarity will suggest to the consumer that the store products possess the same good qualities.

Like any shortcut, the representativeness heuristic can also lead to biased judgments. For instance, consumers who see McDonald's as the prototype of a hamburger restaurant may assume that it offers no healthy foods or cannot make a good salad. To overcome these biased judgments, McDonald's has added quality salads, wraps, and desserts made with high-quality vegetable and fruit ingredients.[4]

The Availability Heuristic

Availability heuristic Basing judgments on events that are easier to recall.

Judgments can also be influenced by the ease with which instances of an event can be brought to mind, a shortcut called the **availability heuristic.**[5] Consumers are more likely to recall more accessible or more vivid events, a tendency that influences their judgments—even though they may be unaware of this effect.[6] To illustrate, suppose that years ago you purchased a DVD player that needed constant repair.

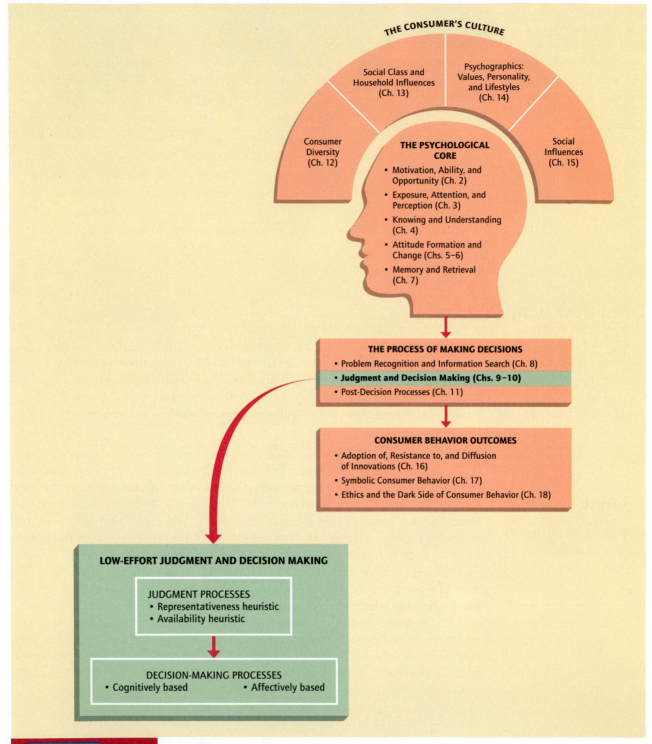

Exhibit 10.1

Chapter Overview: Judgment and Decision Making: Low Consumer Effort

In low-effort processing situations, consumers tend to use heuristics or ways of simplifying the judgment or decision. Both cognitively based heuristics (performance-based tactics, habit, price-related tactics, brand loyalty, and normative influences) and affectively based heuristics (affect-related tactics, variety seeking, and impulse) are used to make decisions.

Today you may still recall your anger and disappointment when you see this brand. Your experiences greatly color your estimations of the quality of this brand, even though the brand might actually have few breakdowns today. Word-of-mouth communication is another example of accessible information that leads to use of the availability heuristic. If a friend says she had problems with a certain brand of DVD player, this information is likely to affect your estimates of the brand's quality, even though her experience might have been an isolated event.

Base-rate information How often an event really occurs on average.

These judgments are biased because we tend to ignore **base-rate information**—how often the event really occurs—in favor of information that is more vivid or accessible. One study demonstrated this effect in the context of estimating the probability that refrigerators would break down.[7] One group was given a set of case histories told by consumers, and another was given actual statistics about the incidence of appliance breakdown. People who read the case histories provided breakdown estimates that were 30 percent higher than those of the statistics group. Another study found that consumers can use both base-rate and case information, but their judgment depends on how the information is structured.[8] As case history information becomes more specific, consumers rely less on base rates. Another reason that we do not use more base-rate information is that it is often not available.

Law of small numbers The expectation that information obtained from a small number of people represents the larger population.

A related bias is the **law of small numbers,** whereby people expect information obtained from a small sample to be typical of the larger population.[9] If friends say that a new CD by a particular group is really good or that the food at a particular restaurant is terrible, we believe that information, even if most people do not feel that way. In fact, reliance on small numbers is another reason that word-of-mouth communication can be so powerful. We tend to have confidence that the opinions of friends or relatives are more reflective of the majority than they may actually be.

MARKETING IMPLICATIONS

Both the representativeness and availability heuristics are important to marketers.

The representativeness heuristic

This heuristic suggests that companies position offerings close to a prototype that has positive associations in consumers' minds. However, when the shortcut leads to a judgment that is negatively biased, marketers must take steps to overcome it. In the 1960s, electronics made in Japan were considered the prototype for poor-quality merchandise. Japanese firms spent many years producing and heavily marketing high-quality products to overcome this bias. Korean companies have faced the same bias until quite recently.[10] This situation explains why Samsung Electronics markets its brand as one of high quality and high style.[11]

The availability heuristic

Marketers can attempt either to capitalize on or to overcome the availability bias. To capitalize, they can provide consumers with positive and vivid product-related experiences through the use of marketing communications, or they can ask consumers to imagine such situations. Both strategies will increase consumers' estimates that these events will occur. Or marketers can attempt to stimulate positive word-of-mouth communication. For instance, some TV networks are offering "widgets," picture-in-picture viewers that consumers can post on their blogs or social networking pages to showcase clips or characters from favorite TV shows, a practice that gets their friends talking about the shows.[12]

Marketers can attempt to overcome the availability bias by providing consumers with base-rate information about the general population. If this information is vivid and specific (such as "chosen 2 to 1 over its competitors"), it can help consumers make a less biased judgment. The Internet is an excellent vehicle for providing base-rate information. To illustrate, consumers interested in buying books or music at Amazon.com can see a summary rating and read reviews submitted by other consumers. The availability bias is also a common problem in the context of sweepstakes and lotteries. Although the likelihood of their winning is exceedingly small, consumers often overestimate the odds because they are exposed to highly vivid and available images of winners in the media. Regulators have attempted to overcome this bias by requiring marketers to clearly post the odds of winning.

Low-Effort Decision-Making Processes

Most low-effort judgment and decision situations are not very important in consumers' lives relative to other decisions in their lives (career, marriage, and so on). Clearly, career and family decisions are far more important than deciding which toothpaste or peanut butter to buy. Thus, the consumer usually does not want to devote a lot of time and effort to these relatively mundane decisions.[13] So how do consumers make decisions in these low-elaboration situations? Researchers suggest that such decisions are sometimes made unconsciously and sometimes consciously, but with little effort.

Unconscious Low-Effort Decision Making

In some low-effort situations, consumers may make a decision without being consciously aware of how or why they are doing so. Such unconscious choices may be strongly affected by environmental stimuli such as the fragrance of a perfume in a department store.[14] With "all of the other senses, you think before you respond, but with scent, your brain responds before you think," observes one expert.[15] Other environmental stimuli that might trigger choices and behavior without the consumer's being consciously aware of the effect are brand logos, certain places or social situations, and the presence of other people.[16]

Some researchers argue that certain choices represent goal-related behavior (e.g., buying fast food), even though consumers are pursuing the goal almost automatically, without conscious thought.[17] Others point out that although many consumer behaviors operate on a conscious level, unconscious choices and behaviors are also important, even if poorly understood and unpredictable.[18] More research is needed to explain how and why consumers use unconscious decision making.

Conscious Low-Effort Decision Making

Traditional hierarchy of effects Sequential steps used in decision making involving thinking, then feeling, then behavior.

Low-effort hierarchy of effects Sequence of thinking-behaving-feeling.

In the discussion of high-effort decision making in Chapter 9, you saw that consumers have certain beliefs about each alternative that are combined to form an attitude that leads to a conscious behavior or a choice. The consumer engages in *thinking*, which leads to *feelings*, which result in *behaving*, a progression known as the hierarchy of effects. However, studies show that this **traditional hierarchy of effects** does not apply to all decision-making situations.[19]

Instead, researchers have proposed a **hierarchy of effects for low-effort situations** that follows a *thinking-behaving-feeling* sequence.[20] The consumer enters the decision process with a set of low-level beliefs based on brand familiarity and knowledge obtained from repeated exposures to advertising, in-store exposure, or prior usage. In the absence of any attitude, these beliefs serve as the foundation for the decision or behavior.. After making the decision and while using the product, the consumer evaluates the brand and may or may not form an attitude, depending on how strongly the brand is liked or satisfies needs.

Some researchers have challenged the belief-behavior link in the low-involvement hierarchy, saying that consumers sometimes base a decision solely on how they feel rather than on what they think.[21] For example, you might select a flavor of gum or a new DVD based on positive feelings rather than on beliefs or knowledge. Here, the sequence would be feeling, behaving, and thinking. This type of decision making, which clearly does occur, suggests that consumers can process in both a cognitive and an affective manner—a factor in many low-elaboration situations.

Using Simplifying Strategies When Consumer Effort Is Low

Low-effort purchases represent the most frequent type of decisions that consumers make in everyday life (Exhibit 10.2). One in-store study of laundry detergent purchases found that the median amount of time taken to make a choice was only 8.5 seconds.[22] A study of coffee and tissues found very low levels of decision activity, particularly among consumers who purchased the product frequently and had a strong brand preference.[23] Some research has examined consumer decision processes across a number of product categories and has even questioned whether there is any decision process at all.[24] Other research suggests that if you have low motivation and ability, you may simply delegate a buying decision by asking a friend or someone else to make the decision. Of course, the outcome will depend on how well the other person knows you.[25]

Under low motivation and low processing opportunity, how a marketing message is framed will influence how consumers react. A negatively framed marketing message is more effective than a positively framed message under MAO, for instance.[26] Research also shows that consumers with a low need for cognition are more susceptible to the influence of a negatively framed message.[27]

Exhibit 10.2

Low-Effort Purchases

Grocery shopping is an activity that involves low effort or motivation to process and, as a result, most consumers do not like to spend a lot of time in the stores.

And when a decision is framed in terms of subtracting unwanted options from a fully loaded product, consumers will choose more options with a higher total option price than they will if the decision is framed in terms of adding wanted items to a base model.[28]

A decision process probably does occur in low-effort situations, but it is simpler, involves less effort, and is qualitatively different from processes that occur when MAO is high. Two other factors influence the low-MAO decision process. First, the goal is not necessarily to find the best possible brand, called *optimizing*, as is the case with high-elaboration decisions. To optimize here would require more effort than consumers are typically willing to expend. Instead, consumers are more willing to **satisfice,** to find a brand that is good enough to simply satisfy their needs. The effort required to find the best brand may simply not be worth it.[29]

Satisfice Finding a brand that satisfies a need even though the brand may not be the best brand.

Second, most low-elaboration decisions are made frequently and repeatedly. In these decisions, consumers may rely on previous information and judgments of satisfaction or dissatisfaction from past consumption. Think of all the times that you have purchased toothpaste, breakfast cereal, and shampoo. You have acquired information by using these products and by seeing ads, talking to friends, and so forth. Instead of searching for information every time you are in the store, you can simply remember previous decisions and use that information to make your next choice.

Choice tactics Simple rules of thumb used to make low-effort decisions.

In these common, repeat-purchase situations, consumers can develop decision heuristics called **choice tactics** for quick, effortless decision making.[30] Rather than comparing various brands in detail, consumers apply these rules to simplify the decision process. The study of laundry detergents mentioned earlier supports this view.[31] When consumers were asked how they made their choices, several major categories of tactics emerged, including *price tactics* (it's the cheapest or it's on sale), *affect tactics* (I like it), *performance tactics* (it cleans clothes better), and *normative tactics* (my mother bought it). Other studies have identified *habit tactics* (I buy the same brand I bought last time), *brand-loyalty tactics* (I buy the same brand for which I have a strong preference), and *variety-seeking tactics* (I need to try something different). Research has found similar patterns in Singapore, Germany, Thailand, and the United States.[32]

Consumers can develop a choice tactic for each repeat-purchase, low-elaboration decision in the product or service category. If the consumer's decision is observed only once, it will appear very limited. Because all prior purchases serve as input to the current decision, it is important to look at a whole series of choices and consumption situations to fully understand consumer decision making. Thus, low-effort decision making is very dynamic in nature.

MARKETING IMPLICATIONS

For effective marketing, companies need to understand unconscious and conscious decision making in low-effort situations.

Unconscious decision making

Because environmental stimuli strongly influence unconscious choices, many stores and restaurants scent the air with aromas that serve as unconscious reminders of certain products or situations. Sony Style stores make female shoppers feel at home by scenting the air with a combination of orange, vanilla, and cedar.[33] Marketers can also use music, displays, and other sensory cues.

Conscious decision making

By advertising frequently, a company can help consumers develop a basic awareness of its brand and brand claims. Based on this familiarity, consumers may pick up the brand with little effort the next time that they shop for a product in that category. In addition, marketers can cater to consumers who use price tactics by highlighting special sales or special values, as do many stores that offer "buy one, get one free" as an inducement to stock up. As you saw in the opening example, consumers who use variety seeking may respond well to new flavors offered by a trusted brand. ●▬

Learning Choice Tactics

Operant conditioning The view that behavior is a function of reinforcements and punishments received in the past.

To understand low-elaboration decision making, marketers need to know how consumers learn to apply choice tactics. Certain concepts from the behaviorist tradition in psychology are relevant to understanding the way that consumers learn. **Operant conditioning** views behavior as a function of previous actions and of the reinforcements or punishments obtained from these actions.[34] For example, while you were growing up, your parents may have given you a reward for making good grades or an allowance for mowing the lawn. You learned that these were good behaviors, and you were more likely to do these things again because you had been rewarded for them.

Reinforcement

Reinforcement usually comes from a feeling of satisfaction that occurs when we as consumers perceive that our needs have been adequately met. This reinforcement increases the probability that we will purchase the same brand again. For example, if you buy Liquid Tide and are impressed by its ability to clean clothes, your purchase will be reinforced, and you will be more likely to buy this brand again. In one study, past experience with a brand was by far the most critical factor in brand choice—more important than quality, price, and familiarity.[35] Other research has shown that the information that consumers receive from product trials tends to be more powerful and influential than that received from advertising.[36] The thoughts and emotions experienced during a trial can have a particularly powerful influence on evaluations.[37] Reinforcement in the form of frequent-buyer rewards can also be effective. One study found that consumers actually accelerated their purchasing as they got closer to earning an reward.[38]

Note that consumers often perceive few differences among brands of many products and services.[39] Thus, they are unlikely to develop a strong positive brand attitude when no brand is seen as clearly better than another. As long as the consumer is not dissatisfied, the choice tactic he or she used will be reinforced. Suppose you buy the cheapest brand of paper towels. If this brand at least minimally satisfies your needs, you are likely to buy the cheapest brand again—and it may be a different brand next time. Thus, reinforcement can occur for either the brand or the choice tactic.

Punishment

Alternatively, consumers can have a bad experience with a product or service, form a negative evaluation of it, and never purchase it again. In operant conditioning terms, this experience is called *punishment*. If you did something bad when you were growing up, your parents may have punished you to make sure that you would not behave that way again. In a consumer context, punishment occurs when a brand does not meet our needs and we are dissatisfied, so we learn not to buy that brand again. Punishment may also lead consumers to reevaluate the choice tactic and use a different tactic for the next purchase. If you buy the cheapest brand of trash bags, and the bags burst when you take out the trash, you could either employ a new tactic (buy the most expensive or the most familiar brand) or upgrade your tactic (buy the cheapest *national* brand).

Repeat Purchase

Consumers learn when the same act is repeatedly reinforced or punished over time, a process summarized in Exhibit 10.3. This process occurs whenever we buy a common, repeat-purchase product. Thus, we learn and gradually acquire a set of choice tactics that will result in making a satisfactory choice in each decision situation. Decision-making models have traditionally ignored the key role of consumption in the decision process, focusing more attention on the processing that occurs immediately prior to the decision. But clearly what takes place while the product is being consumed has important implications for future acquisition, usage, and disposition decisions. In other words, whether the consumer forms a positive or negative evaluation of the brand or tactic can be an important input into future decisions.

Choice Tactics Depend on the Product

The choice tactics we use often depend on the product category that we are considering.[40] For example, we might be brand loyal to Heinz ketchup but always buy the cheapest trash bags. The tactic we learn for a product category depends on which brands are available and our experiences with them. The amount of advertising, price variations, and the number and similarity of brands also influence the type of tactic that we employ.[41] Interestingly, the study from Singapore mentioned

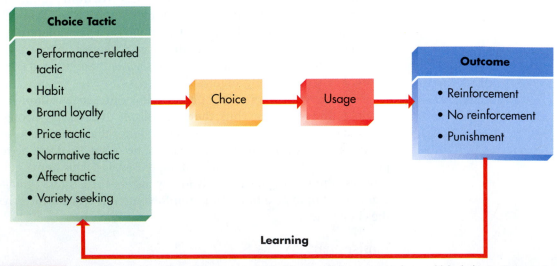

Choice Tactic
- Performance-related tactic
- Habit
- Brand loyalty
- Price tactic
- Normative tactic
- Affect tactic
- Variety seeking

Choice → Usage

Outcome
- Reinforcement
- No reinforcement
- Punishment

Learning

Exhibit 10.3
The Learning Process

This diagram shows how the outcome of a decision can help consumers learn which choice tactic to apply in a given situation. After consumers apply one of the seven basic types of tactics to make a choice, they take the brand home and use it. During consumption, they can evaluate the brand, an action that results in one of three basic outcomes: reinforcement (satisfaction leading to positive attitude and repurchase), no reinforcement (leading to tactic reinforcement, but no attitude toward the brand), or punishment (leading to a negative attitude, no repurchase, and tactic re-evaluation).

earlier found a greater similarity in the tactics that consumers use for the same product in different cultures (the United States and Singapore) than in tactics that they use for different products in the same culture.[42] In general, our experiences help us learn what works for each product, and we use these tactics to minimize our decision-making effort for future purchases.

Low-Effort Thought-Based Decision Making

Each tactic consumers learn for making low-elaboration decisions can have important implications for marketers. As in high-elaboration decisions, these strategies can be divided into two broad categories: thought-based and feeling-based decision making. This section examines cognitive-based decision making, which includes performance-related tactics, habit, brand loyalty, price-related tactics, and normative influences.

Performance as a Simplifying Strategy

Performance-related tactics
Tactics based on benefits, features, or evaluations of the brand.

When the outcome of the consumption process is positive reinforcement, consumers are likely to use **performance-related tactics** to make their choices. These tactics can represent an overall evaluation (works the best) or focus on a specific attribute or benefit (gets clothes cleaner, tastes better, or has quicker service). Satisfaction is the key: Satisfied consumers are likely to develop a positive evaluation of the brand or service and repurchase it based on its features.

MARKETING IMPLICATIONS

A principal objective of marketing strategy should be to increase the likelihood of satisfaction through offering quality (Exhibit 10.4). Only then can a brand consistently achieve repeat purchases and loyal users. For instance, Starbucks recently closed all 7,000 of its U.S. stores for three hours of training to be sure baristas make the chain's coffee drinks the same way every time. Employees also brushed up on their product presentation and customer-contact skills.[43]

Advertising can play a central role in influencing performance evaluations by increasing the consumer's expectation of positive reinforcement and satisfaction and lessening the negative effects of an unfavorable consumption experience.[44] Because we see what we want to see and form our expectations accordingly, marketers should select product features or benefits that are important to consumers, help to differentiate the brand from competitors, and convince consumers that they will be satisfied if they buy the product. To illustrate, Gillette's Venus Embrace razor has five blades and a wraparound moisture strip for a smooth, close shave. This combination of features sets the Gillette razor apart from the competing Schick Quattro for Women razors, which has four blades.[45]

Sales promotions such as free samples, price deals, coupons, or premiums (gifts or free merchandise) are often used as an incentive to get the consumer to try an offering. Marketers hope that if consumers find the product satisfactory, they will continue to buy it after the promotions end. However, these strategies only work if product performance satisfies and reinforces the consumer. They will not overcome dissatisfaction due to poor product quality or other factors. Snapple failed in Japan despite heavy promotion because Japanese consumers did not like the drink's cloudy appearance and the stuff floating in the bottle.[46] Another caution is that consumers may perceive a price

**BAND-AID® Brand
TOUGH-STRIPS® WATERPROOF**

Up to 2x stronger than
ordinary waterproof bandages,
TOUGH-STRIPS® WATERPROOF bandages
have Super-Stick adhesive and a unique
fiber reinforcement material for all-day staying
power. Waterproof protection that stays tough,
no matter what comes your way.

Johnson & Johnson

Exhibit 10.4

Emphasizing Product Quality

Sometimes marketers influence consumers' performance expectations for a brand by providing them a simple point of differentiation regarding what the product can do. Here Band-Aid sets the expectation that it is tough and waterproof.

Habit Doing the same thing time after time.

Shaping Leading consumers through a series of steps to create a desired response.

promotion as a signal of lower quality when they are not category experts, when the promotion is not typical of the industry, and when the brand's past behavior is inconsistent.[47]

Habit as a Simplifying Strategy

Humans are creatures of **habit.** Once we find a convenient way of doing things, we tend to repeat it without really thinking: following the same routine every morning, driving the same route to work or school, shopping at the same stores. We do these things because they make life simpler and more manageable.

Sometimes consumers' acquisition, usage, and disposition decisions are based on habit, too. Habit is one of the simplest, most effortless types of consumer decision making, characterized by (1) little or no information seeking and (2) little or no evaluation of alternatives. However, habit does not require a strong preference for an offering; rather, it simply involves repetitive behavior and regular purchase.[48] Decision making based on habit also reduces risk.[49] Consumers know the brand will satisfy their needs because they have bought it a number of times in the past. Research supports the effect of habit on low-priced, frequently purchased products. Yet the longer consumers wait to make their next purchase in a product category, the less likely they are to buy the brand that they habitually purchase.[50]

MARKETING IMPLICATIONS

Habit-based decision making has several important implications for marketers who want to develop repeat-purchase behavior and to sell their offerings to habitual purchasers of both that brand and competing products.

Developing repeat-purchase behavior

Getting consumers to acquire or use an offering repeatedly is important because repeat purchases lead to profitability. Marketers can use an operant conditioning technique called **shaping** that leads consumers through a series of steps to a desired response: purchase.[51] Companies often use sales promotions to shape repeat purchasing. First, they might offer a free sample to generate brand trial, along with a high-value coupon to induce trial (see Exhibit 10.5 for product samples from Thailand). The next step might be to provide a series of lower-value coupons to promote subsequent repurchase, hoping that when the incentives end, consumers will continue to buy the product by habit.

Marketing to habitual purchasers of other brands

Another major marketing goal is to break consumers' habits and induce them to switch to the company's brand. Because the habitual consumer does not have a strong brand preference, this goal is easier to achieve than it is for brand-loyal consumers. For example, the European company Eat Natural makes cereal bars intended for all-day

Exhibit 10.5

Free Samples

Here are three samples of skin products from Thailand, where sampling is a frequently used marketing tool. Many samples are given out in shopping centers. What type of product samples do you receive?

snacking. "We know people who have them as breakfast, an 11 A.M. snack, or at lunch with a sandwich," says a company executive. Therefore, Eat Natural has its products displayed near healthy snacks (rather than breakfast cereals) to attract consumers who might otherwise buy rice cakes or similar foods.[52]

Sales promotion techniques to induce brand switching include pricing deals, coupons, free samples, and premiums intended to capture consumers' attention and get them to try the new brand. Procter & Gamble has used coupons generated at the supermarket checkout to target users of a competing dishwashing product. Shoppers who bought Electrasol Tabs received a coupon for a free box of P&G's Cascade Power Tabs.[53] Once the old habit is broken, consumers may continue to purchase the new brand—in this case, Cascade—either because they like it or because they have developed a new habit.

Marketers can also break habits by introducing *a new and unique benefit* that satisfies consumers' needs better than existing brands. This differential advantage then needs to be heavily advertised to get the word out to consumers. For instance, finding that its customers crave more bacon on their burgers, Wendy's has introduced the Baconator, with six strips of bacon on top of two hamburger patties and two slices of cheese. The product name and its advertising both highlight the extra bacon in each sandwich.[54]

Finally, *distribution policies* are very important for habitual purchasing. In general, the greater the amount of shelf space a brand has in the store, the more likely the brand is to get consumers' attention. A product's location may be enough to capture the habitual consumer's attention and plant the idea in his or her mind to buy something else. An end-of-aisle display may increase a brand's sales by 100 to 400 percent.[55] In one study, eye-catching displays increased sales of frozen dinners by 245 percent, laundry detergent by 207 percent, and salty snacks by 172 percent.[56] In another study, sales of cough and cold syrups rose by 35 percent with in-store promotions linked to a point-of-purchase brand display.[57] Thus, marketers often try to develop interesting displays, such as the award-winning units shown in Exhibit 10.6.

Marketing to habitual purchasers of one's own brand

Marketers do not want repeat-purchase customers to break their buying habits. Because habitual consumers are susceptible to competitors' deals, marketers need to offer comparable deals to build resistance to switching. This situation explains why a fare cut by any one airline is usually matched immediately by all of its major competitors.

Exhibit 10.6

Award-Winning Displays

By designing eye-popping displays, marketers hope to capture consumers' attention at retail and change their buying habits. This reaction can occur because habitual consumers typically do not have a strong preference for their usual brand. Can you think of any displays that have caught your attention recently?

Distribution and inventory control are also important tactics used to prevent habitual consumers from switching to another brand. Without a strong preference, consumers are more likely to break the habit and buy another brand if their usual brand is out of stock rather than to go to another store. In one study, 63 percent of consumers said they would be willing to buy another brand of groceries and canned foods if their preferred brand were not available.[58] Widespread distribution can ensure that the consumer is not forced to buy something else, one reason why Jones Soda sought supermarket distribution. Finally, advertising can induce resistance to switching. By occasionally reminding the consumer of a reason for buying the brand and keeping the brand name "top of mind," marketers may be able to keep consumers from switching.

Brand Loyalty as a Simplifying Strategy

Brand loyalty Buying the same brand repeatedly because of a strong preference for it.

Brand loyalty occurs when consumers make a conscious evaluation that a brand or service satisfies their needs to a greater extent than others do and decide to buy the same brand repeatedly for that reason.[59] Essentially, brand loyalty results from *very* positive reinforcement of a performance-related choice tactic. Brand loyalty can also develop when a consumer becomes skillful in using a particular offering, such as a specific brand of money-management software. Faced with the learning curve needed to switch to a different brand of software, the consumer tends to remain brand loyal because of *cognitive lock-in*.[60]

Note that the level of commitment to the brand distinguishes brand loyalty from habit. The stronger this evaluation becomes over time, the higher the degree of brand loyalty. If you buy Heinz ketchup and decide that it is thicker and tastes better than other brands, you will purchase it again. If this evaluation is reinforced repeatedly, you will develop strong brand loyalty. Consumers can also be **multibrand loyal,** committed to two or more brands that they purchase repeatedly.[61] For example, if you prefer and purchase only Coke and Sprite, you exhibit multibrand loyalty for soft drinks.

Multibrand loyalty Buying two or more brands repeatedly because of a strong preference for them.

Brand loyalty results in low-effort decision making because the consumer does not need to process information when making a decision and simply buys the same brand each time. However, because of their strong commitment to the brand or service, brand-loyal consumers have a relatively high level of involvement with the *brand* whether their involvement with the product or service category is high or low. Thus, even though ketchup might typically be thought of as a low-involvement product, the brand-loyal consumer can exhibit a high level of involvement toward the brand Heinz.

MARKETING IMPLICATIONS

Brand-loyal consumers form a solid base on which companies can build brand profitability. By identifying the characteristics of these consumers, marketers might discover ways to strengthen brand loyalty. Unfortunately, doing this is difficult because marketers cannot obtain a general profile of the brand-loyal consumer that applies to all product categories.[62] In fact, brand loyalty depends on the product category; the consumer who is loyal for ketchup may not be loyal for peanut butter. This situation means that marketers must assess brand loyalty for each specific category.

Identifying brand-loyal customers

One way that marketers can identify brand-loyal consumers is to focus on consumer purchase patterns. Consumers who exhibit a particular sequence of purchases (three to four consecutive purchases of the same brand) or proportion of purchases (seven or eight out of ten purchases for the same brand) are considered brand loyal.[63] The problem is that because brand loyalty involves both repeat purchases *and* a commitment to the brand, purchase-only measures do not accurately distinguish between habitual and brand-loyal consumers. To truly identify the brand-loyal consumer, marketers must assess both repeat-purchase behavior and brand preference. In one study, a measure that looked only at repeat-purchase behavior identified more than 70 percent of the consumer sample as brand loyal. Adding brand preference as a qualifier reduced the percentage to less than 50 percent.[64]

With the availability of scanner data and online buying information, marketers now have a wealth of information about consumer purchase patterns that they can analyze to understand how coupons or pricing changes affect buying. Nevertheless, firms that want to study brand loyalty should be measuring both purchase patterns and preference.

Developing brand loyalty

Companies seek to develop brand loyalty because they know these customers have a strong brand commitment and are more resistant to competitive efforts and switching than other consumers are. However, the widespread use of pricing deals in the United States has gradually eroded consumer loyalty toward many brands, leading more consumers to buy on the basis of price. Therefore, marketers are now striving to develop consumer loyalty through nonprice promotions. (Note that in Europe, firms use fewer price promotions, and brand loyalty has remained relatively stable.[65])

Developing brand loyalty through product quality

One obvious and critical way to develop brand loyalty is to satisfy the consumer with a high-quality product (see Exhibit 10.7). Consumers may also become brand loyal to high-quality brands that are perceived to be priced fairly, a result that explains why some companies have lowered prices on major brands.[66]

When it comes to powering your digital camera
⊖ the negatives and positives ⊕
may surprise you

Energizer
LITHIUM

Up to 600 pictures
over the life of two batteries

Existing Lithium Chemistry

Use them up
and throw them away

Buy two more

Use them up
and throw them away

Buy two more

Use them up
and throw them away

Buy two more

Use them up
and throw them away

Buy two more

Use them up
and throw them away

Buy two more

Use them up

DURACELL
• RECHARGEABLE

Up to 5,000 pictures
over the life of two batteries

Advanced Rechargeable Technology

Recharge in 15 minutes

Keep and recharge
100's of times

**RECHARGEABLES
REINVENTED**

DURACELL
⊕ TRUS±ED EVERYWHERE ⊖

© 2008 P&G

Exhibit 10.7

**Using Quality to
Encourage Brand Loyalty**

Having high-quality products is
a key way to develop brand loyalty. This is what Duracell is
stressing in this ad for their
batteries.

Price-related tactics Simplifying decision heuristics that are
based on price.

Developing brand loyalty through sales promotions

Many companies cultivate brand loyalty through sales promotions such as discount coupons and giveaways. Frequent-buyer programs build loyalty by encouraging consumers to buy a product or service repeatedly so that they can earn points toward free trips or other rewards. Marketers must take care in planning loyalty rewards and program requirements. The reward should have some brand connection if it is to increase acces- sibility of favorable brand associations. However, if the reward is too valuable, it will draw more attention than the brand itself.[67] Also, consumers perceive more value in a loyalty program when they think that they have an advantage in earning points.[68] Moreover, consum- ers who must do more to earn loyalty points will tend to choose luxury rewards (especially when they feel guilty about luxury consumption).[69]

Marketing to brand-loyal consumers of other brands

Marketers want to induce brand-loyal users of com- petitive brands to switch to their brands. However, be- cause these consumers are strongly committed to other brands, getting them to switch is extremely dif- ficult. As a result, it is usually better to avoid these consumers and to try to market toward nonloyal or ha- bitual consumers, except when a brand has a strong point of superiority or differentiation when compared with the competition. In this case the superior attribute might be enough to persuade brand-loyal consumers to switch. For instance, Subway promotes its sandwich variety and healthy ingredients: "We have 14 million combinations when you do the math with all of the different veggie and sauce combinations," says an executive.[70]

Price as a Simplifying Strategy

Consumers are most likely to use **price-related tactics** such as buying the cheapest brand, buying the brand on sale, or using a coupon when they perceive few differences among brands and when they have low involvement with the brands in the consider- ation set. One study found that nine out of ten shoppers entered the store with some strategy for saving money (see Exhibit 10.8).[71] Although price is a critical factor in many decisions, consumers generally do not remember price information, even for a brand they have just selected.[72] This reaction occurs because price information is always available in the store, so consumers have little motivation to remember it. Note that consumers who worry about losing money are more concerned about price, whereas those who are sensitive to gains look at brand features as well as price.[73]

MARKETING IMPLICATIONS

Sometimes marketers mistakenly assume that consumers always look for the lowest possible price. Although this assumption is true in some instances, a more accurate

Exhibit 10.8

Money-Saving Strategies

Consumers can use different types of money-saving strategies in their shopping. Which type of shopper are you?

HOW CONSUMERS SHOP

Practical Loyalists	29%
Look for ways to save on the few brands and products she or he will buy anyway	
Bottom-Line Price Shoppers	26%
Buy the lowest-priced item, with little or no regard for brand	
Opportunistic Switchers	24%
Use coupons or sales to decide among brands and products that fall within a considered set	
Deal Hunters	13%
Look for the best bargain and are not brand loyal	
Nonstrategists	8%
Do not spend the time or effort to strategize	

Zone of acceptance The acceptable range of prices for any purchase decision.

statement is that consumers have a **zone of acceptance** regarding what constitutes an appropriate range of prices for a particular category.[74] As long as the brand falls within this price range, consumers will consider it but reject brands falling either above or below the range. For instance, consumers initially shunned wipe products because they cost more than paper towels and cleaning fluids. After marketers began promoting the benefits of germ-killing and convenience, consumers began to buy the products— although some still use price as a primary criterion for choice.[75]

Consumers may reject low-priced products because they infer that something is wrong with the products. Buyers would be suspicious of a pair of expensive designer jeans on sale for $9.99. As noted earlier, consumers sometimes use price as a heuristic to judge quality (higher price means higher quality). Framing is another factor: Under low motivation and low processing opportunity, consumers will respond more to a negatively framed message than to a positively framed one.[76] Retailers must also consider that consumers view store design (layout and ambiance) as a pricing cue and expect higher prices at stores that look upscale.[77] Finally, when stores that have high selling costs advertise low prices, the revenue generated may not justify the increased cost of servicing the customers who respond.[78]

Price Perceptions

Consumer perceptions play an important role in the use of price-related tactics. Remember that for consumers to perceive two prices as different, the variation must be at or above the just noticeable difference. Thus, consumers might not care if one brand of toothpaste is priced at $1.95 and another at $1.99. Consumers also compare a product's price with an internal reference price for such products that is based on past prices paid, competing product prices, and other factors, including incidental products in some cases.[79] Typically, consumers use a range of prices rather than a single price point when they think of products.[80]

In addition, perceptual processes play a role in the consumer's reaction to different price points. Research has consistently indicated that consumers perceive odd prices (those ending with an odd number) as significantly lower than even prices (those ending with an even number); a DVD priced at $15.99 will be perceived as less expensive than one priced at $16.00.[81] Consumers who see a much higher-priced item in a catalog that also has moderately priced products will form a higher reference point for the moderately priced items.[82]

Consumers tend to be more responsive to price decreases than they are to price increases.[83] Lowering the price of an offering will increase sales to a greater degree than increasing price by the same amount will decrease sales. Moreover, when a company heavily discounts a product on an infrequent basis, consumers will perceive the average price as lower than if the product goes on sale often but with less of a price reduction.[84] One study found that when companies establish a purchase or time limit, consumers perceive the deal as more valuable, but only when motivation to process is low.[85]

How companies describe the deal can also make a difference. One study found that comparing the sale price to the "regular price" worked better in the store, whereas comparison to competitors' prices was more effective at home.[86] Also, paying for products in a foreign currency (as when traveling) affects price perceptions and spending behavior: When the foreign currency is valued as a multiple of the home-country currency (such as 40 Indian rupees = $1), consumers tend to spend more than when the foreign currency is valued as a fraction (such as .4 Bahraini dinar = $1).[87] Finally, consumers tend to perceive a price increase as less fair if they learn about it from a personal source (such as a sales rep) rather than from nonpersonal sources such as a store sign.[88]

The Deal-Prone Consumer

Deal-prone consumers
Consumers who are more likely to be influenced by price.

Marketers are interested in identifying **deal-prone consumers** because this segment is suitable for more directly targeted price-related strategies, but research findings on this issue have been mixed. One study found that deal-prone consumers are more likely to be lower-income, older, and less educated than non-deal-prone consumers; other studies have found that higher-income consumers have better access to price information and are therefore more able to act on it.[89] Part of the problem is that consumers react differently to different types of deals: Some will be more responsive to coupons, whereas others will be more responsive to price cuts and to rebates.[90]

MARKETING IMPLICATIONS

Marketers can use a variety of pricing techniques, including coupons, price-offs, rebates, and two-for-ones, as long as the savings are at or above the just noticeable difference and within the zone of acceptance.

Deals

The importance of deals is evidenced by the deep price cuts supermarkets have made, spurred by stiff competition from Wal-Mart, Costco, and other discounters. Many brands have lowered their prices in response to competition from store brands, which are promoted as being equal in quality to national brands but priced lower. Although many shoppers like shopping online because they can search for price deals, some companies prefer not to attract consumers who use price-comparison sites. The head of marketing for John Lewis Direct, a U.K. catalog company, says, "Customers recruited from these sites have generally been the least profitable, as they don't come back. They are often seeking the cheapest deals . . . and show little loyalty."[91]

The importance of value

Many consumers are looking for good value—that is, a high-quality brand at a good price (see Exhibit 10.9). Fast-food chains such as Burger King, McDonald's, and Taco Bell therefore seek to satisfy consumers by offering special "value meals." Value does not always mean lower price: Consumers will pay more if they believe the offering provides an important benefit.[92] European consumers, for instance, will pay more for the convenience of premeasured laundry detergent tablets marketed under such well-known brands as Wisk and Tide.[93] One way for marketers to deliver value without lowering prices is to provide a differential benefit and convince consumers that the brand is worth the extra cost. For example, Colgate bet—correctly—that consumers would pay more for Total toothpaste, which has a special germ-fighting ingredient.[94]

Special pricing

If marketers use pricing deals too often, consumers will perceive the special price as the regular price and will not buy unless the brand is on sale—resulting in lost profits. This result has happened in the past to food chains such as Arby's. Too many deals can also damage brand loyalty as consumers become too deal oriented and switch brands more often. Thus, deals tend to work best when used intermittently and selectively. Lower brand loyalty has become a major concern in numerous product categories in the United States and is the reason that many firms want to move toward brand-building strategies such as advertising and sampling.[95]

The use of pricing deals also varies with the country. Coupons are common in the United States: Nearly 50 percent of all retailers use them, and consumers save $3 billion annually by redeeming coupons.[96] Online coupon sites such as RedPlum.com draw 20 million visitors every year.[97] The trend in the United Kingdom and Italy has been toward fewer coupons of higher value.[98] Coupons are not used in every country; retailers will not accept them in Holland and Switzerland, and the retail infrastructure in Russia and Greece cannot accommodate them.

Price consciousness is not static

Consumers tend to be more price conscious in difficult economic times than in times of prosperity. In the sluggish Japanese economy, discount stores and coupons are growing more popular in a country that once scorned both.[99] In China, consumers have become even more price conscious now that Wal-Mart and other discount retailers are expanding there.[100]

Normative Influences as a Simplifying Strategy

Sometimes other individuals can influence consumers' low-elaboration decision making. A college freshman may buy the brand of laundry detergent that his mother

Exhibit 10.9

Price as a Simplifying Strategy

Sometimes companies stress low price and good value in their ads, like this one from Burger King which highlights their $1 offer for a BK Spicy CHICK'N CRISP sandwich.

Normative choice tactics
Low-elaboration decision
making that is based on
others' opinions.

uses at home; a sophomore might buy clothing that her friends like. Our use of such **normative choice tactics** can result from (1) *direct influence*, in which others try to manipulate us; (2) *vicarious observation*, in which we observe others to guide our behavior; and (3) *indirect influence*, in which we are concerned about the opinions of others. Normative tactics are particularly common among inexperienced consumers who have little knowledge. Online communication can increase the importance of normative influence in decision making because consumers can contact each other so easily.

MARKETING IMPLICATIONS

If normative tactics are particularly evident in a product or service category, companies can emphasize these motivations in advertising. A good example of this strategy is an ad for Ritz crackers that shows how pleased party guests will be when you "serve it on a Ritz." Consumers often buy expensive imported products to impress others. Marketers can also attempt to stimulate word-of-mouth communication, as described in Chapter 15.

Low-Effort Feeling-Based Decision Making

The final category of low-effort strategies covers decisions that are based more on feelings than on cognitive processing. These types of strategies include affective tactics, variety seeking, and impulse purchasing.

Feelings as a Simplifying Strategy

Affect Low-level feelings.

At times, consumers will select a brand or service because they like it, even though they may not know why. This behavior relies on very basic, low-level feelings, or **affect.** Affect differs from cognitive strategies such as performance-related attitudes in that it does not necessarily result from a conscious recognition of need satisfaction and is usually weaker than an attitude. Simply being in the presence of someone you like who is smiling happily can make you smile and feel happy—and, in turn, can have a positive influence on your evaluation of a product.[101]

Affect is most likely to be part of the decision process when the offering is hedonic (rather than functional) and when other factors, such as performance evaluations, price, habit, and normative influences, are not in operation. If you buy Heinz ketchup because it best satisfies your needs or if you usually buy only the cheapest brand of paper towels, affect is less likely to influence your decision. However, when these factors do not operate in low-effort situations, affect can play a central role.

Affect-related tactics Tactics
based on feelings.

Affect referral A simple type
of affective tactic whereby we
simply remember our feelings
for the product or service.

Affect-related tactics use a form of category-based processing.[102] In other words, we associate brands with global affective evaluations we recall from memory when making a choice, a process called **affect referral** or the "How do I feel about it?" heuristic.[103] For instance, when we hear the name *Starbucks*, we might associate it with general feelings of happiness, and we might decide to get coffee there based on these feelings rather than on a detailed evaluation of Starbucks. In one study, consumers choosing between a healthy dessert and a less healthy chocolate cake chose the dessert associated with the most positive affect (the cake) when they had little opportunity to think about the choice. When they had more time to think, they chose the healthier dessert, a reaction that suggests that affect referral is more of a factor under low processing effort.[104] Another study found that positive feelings toward promotions can also transfer not only to the promoted product but to unrelated products as well.[105]

Exhibit 10.10

Co-Branding

Sometimes companies engage in co-branding by advertising two different brands together. Here we see a joint ad from Sony and Harlequin books.

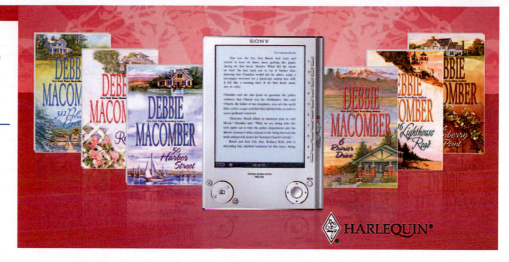

Whenever a consumer encounters a new brand, he or she can also compare it with other brands in the same category. To the extent that the new brand is similar to previously encountered brands, the affect associated with that category can be transferred to the new instance and influence choice.[106] On the other hand, if the new brand is perceived as being dissimilar, the consumer is more likely to switch to piecemeal processing, evaluating attributes in the manner described in Chapter 9.[107] For example, Listerine Whitening Quick Dissolving Strips, which help whiten teeth but disappear within a few minutes, lack the tingling Listerine flavor that some people dislike. Because the product's name, benefit, and flavor are unlike those of traditional Listerine mouthwash, consumers may be able to evaluate the attributes of the new product on their own merits.[108]

Brand Familiarity

Brand familiarity Easy recognition of a well-known brand.

Affect can also be generated from **brand familiarity** (through the mere exposure effect). In one study, beer drinkers with well-established brand preferences could not distinguish their preferred brand from others in a blind taste test.[109] However, when the beers were identified, consumers rated the taste of their preferred brand significantly higher than that of the others. Another study found that "buying the most familiar brand" was a dominant choice tactic for inexperienced purchasers of peanut butter. Even when the quality of the most familiar brand was manipulated to be lower than that of unfamiliar brands, consumers still greatly preferred the familiar brand.[110] Another study found that brand name was a more important heuristic cue in low-elaboration situations than in high-elaboration ones.[111]

These findings were replicated in a study in Singapore, suggesting that the impact of brand familiarity may be a cross-cultural phenomenon.[112] Coca-Cola is a household name due, in part, to its consistent, highly visible marketing.[113] Yet aggressively promoted local brands such as Crazy Cola that work hard to gain brand familiarity are outselling Coke and other global brands in Siberia and other areas.

Co-branding An arrangement by which the two brands form a partnership to benefit from the power of both.

Many companies now engage in **co-branding,** an arrangement by which two brands form a partnership to benefit from the combined power and familiarity of the two (see Exhibit 10.10).[114] Kellogg sometimes puts two of its own brands on a single product, such as Eggo Froot Loops, which are waffles with cereal bits.[115] Liquor companies are using co-branding to get around advertising restrictions by placing their name on food (one example: Jack Daniel's Grill with TGI Friday's).[116]

MARKETING IMPLICATIONS

Given that feelings can play an important role in the decision process, marketers can attempt to create and maintain brand familiarity, build category-based associations, and generate affect through advertising that creates positive attitudes toward the ad. By creating positive affect toward their brand, marketers can increase the probability that, all other things being equal, their brand will be selected.

Affect plays a key role in determining aesthetic responses to marketing stimuli, especially when visual properties are the only basis for judgment. In Yellow Pages advertising, for example, consumers are more likely to consider firms with color ads and more likely to call those with product-enhancing color.[117] One study showed that two key aspects of a product's design generate more positive affective responses to the product.[118] These are **unity,** which means that the visual parts of the design connect in a meaningful way, and **prototypicality,** which means that the object is representative of its category.

Brands that have positive cross-cultural affect can be marketed internationally. The U.S. image has benefited many firms that market in China; for instance, KFC dominates the fast-food category.[119] Similarly, positive affect for Italian cooking has helped Barilla capture 25 percent of the pasta market in the United States.[120] In particular, hedonic offerings—those that involve style or taste—rely heavily on affective associations.

Unity When all the visual parts of a design fit together.

Prototypicality When an object is representative of its category.

Variety seeking Trying something different.

PUMP, PAINT & GO!

NIC'S STICKS
PAINT & GO NAIL LACQUER

LONG-WEARING • FAST-DRYING • FITS IN POCKET OR PURSE

Nicōle
by O·P·I

Available at select Target stores.

Decision Making Based on Variety-Seeking Needs

Another common consumer-choice tactic in low-effort situations is to try something different, a phenomenon called **variety seeking** (see Exhibit 10.11). A consumer might regularly buy Johnson's baby shampoo but one day have an urge to try Pantene shampoo—then return to the baby shampoo for later purchases. Consumers seek variety for two major reasons: *satiation* and *boredom*.[121] If you had the same food for dinner every night or listened to only one CD over and over, satiation would occur, driving you to do something different. Consumer decisions that occur repeatedly can become monotonous; this result explains why some consumers switch for the sake of change, even though they would have derived more immediate enjoyment from repeating their usual choice.[122] Another reason consumers seek variety in public situations is because they anticipate that others will evaluate their decision more positively.[123] Consumers may engage in variety seeking because they perceive the costs of switching to a new product to be lower than do consumers who are not variety seekers.[124]

However, variety seeking is not expressed in every product category. It is most likely to occur when involvement is low, there are few differences among brands, and the product is more hedonic than functional.[125] It also tends to occur when consumers become satiated with a particular sensory attribute of a product, such as its smell, taste, touch, and visual appearance.[126] Marketers can therefore reduce consumers' boredom simply by providing more variety in a product category.[127]

Consumers are motivated to relieve their boredom because their level of arousal falls below the **optimal stimulation level** *(OSL)*—an internal ideal level of stimulation.[128] Repetitive purchasing causes the internal level of stimulation to fall below the OSL, and buying something different is a way of restoring it. In addition, certain consumers need more stimulation and are less tolerant of boredom than others are. These **sensation seekers** are more likely to engage in variety seeking and to be among the first to try new and trendy products; therefore, these consumers are a good market for new offerings.[129]

Note that purchasing something different is only one way to seek stimulation. Consumers can also express their variety drive by engaging in vicarious exploration.[130] **Vicarious exploration** occurs when consumers collect information about a product, either by reading or talking with others or by putting themselves in stimulating shopping environments. For example, many people like to go to stores simply to look around or browse—not to buy, just to increase their stimulation.

> **Optimal stimulation level (OSL)** The level of arousal that is most comfortable for an individual.
>
> **Sensation seekers** Those who actively look for variety.
>
> **Vicarious exploration** Seeking information simply for stimulation.

MARKETING IMPLICATIONS

Marketers should recognize consumers' need for variety and accommodate these needs appropriately, as Jones Soda does by introducing new flavors and new bottle labels on a regular basis. Marketers can attempt to induce brand switching among variety seekers by encouraging consumers to "put a little spice into life" and try something different. Stevens Point Brewery now offers a variety 12-pack with two bottles each of its six types of beer.[131] However, consumers may not like *too* much variety. Note that simply altering the way that the product assortment is presented (how items are arranged on the store shelves, for example) can increase consumers' perceptions of variety and trigger higher consumption, a finding that is particularly relevant for food retailers.[132]

Buying on Impulse

> **Impulse purchase** An unexpected purchase based on a strong feeling.

Another common decision process that has a strong affective component is the **impulse purchase,** which occurs when consumers suddenly decide to purchase something they had not planned on buying. Impulse purchases are characterized by (1) an intense or overwhelming feeling of having to buy the product immediately, (2) a disregard for potentially negative purchase consequences, (3) feelings of euphoria and excitement, and (4) a conflict between control and indulgence.[133] Consumers in Asian countries, where interdependence and emotional control are emphasized, tend to engage in less impulse purchasing than do consumers in Western countries, where personal independence and hedonistic pleasures are emphasized.[134] Impulse purchasing and consumption, especially when related to unfulfilled pleasure-seeking needs, are often triggered by the consumer's exposure to an external stimulus, such as an in-store display, a Web ad, or a TV ad with a phone number.[135]

Some research suggests that impulse purchases are prompted by a failure of consumers' self-control.[136] Applying self-control is taxing, a factor that explains why consumers who exert self-control in one area—such as not eating sweets while dieting—may be less able to maintain self-control in another area and will therefore buy something on impulse.[137] Making a series of decisions can deplete consumers' self-control even further.[138] Yet consumers may be unable to control impulse purchasing even when they engage in a great deal of conscious processing.[139]

Researchers estimate that anywhere from 27 to 62 percent of consumer purchases can be considered impulse buys.[140] However, it is important to distinguish between impulse buying and partially planned purchases, or those for which the consumer has an intention to buy the product category but uses the store display to decide which brand to select. When this distinction is made, the proportion of impulse purchases is usually lower.[141] The tendency to engage in impulse purchasing varies; some consumers can be considered highly impulsive buyers, whereas others are not.[142] The tendency to buy on impulse is probably related to other traits such as general acquisitiveness and materialism, sensation seeking, and a liking for recreational shopping.[143] If the costs of impulsiveness are made salient or if normative pressure such as the presence of others with negative opinions is high, consumers will engage in less impulse purchasing.[144] Finally, the presence of peers increases the urge to make impulse purchases, while the presence of family members has the opposite effect.[145]

(MARKETING IMPLICATIONS)

Many stores organize their merchandise to maximize impulse purchases. Card shops position commonly sought items such as greeting cards near the back so that consumers will have to pass a number of displays containing higher-margin impulse items to get to them. As discussed earlier, eye-level and eye-catching displays, including end-of-aisle displays and blinking lights, can increase sales dramatically—mostly of impulse items.[146] Package design can also increase impulse purchases—the reason that packages of NXT shaving gel and after-shave glow on the shelf with the power of battery-operated lights.[147]

Impulse purchasing tends to decline in difficult economic times. In Japan, for example, where a lengthy economic recession has led many consumers to buy only what they need, marketers have repositioned certain products as necessities rather than as impulse items.[148] On the other hand, some U.S. consumers still splurge on selected luxuries when money is tight, trading up to premium brands such as Starbucks coffee.[149]

Summary

This chapter examined the nature of consumer judgment and decision making when motivation, ability, and opportunity—and consequently elaboration—are low. In these situations, consumers often make judgments using simplified heuristics or decision rules. When using the representativeness heuristic, consumers base their judgments on comparisons to a category prototype. When using the availability heuristic, they base their judgments on accessibility of information.

Sometimes low-effort decisions are made unconsciously, sometimes consciously. Unconscious decisions may be strongly affected by environmental cues.

Conscious low-effort decision making can follow a hierarchy of effects in which thinking leads to behaving and results in feeling; in contrast, the hierarchy of effects for high-effort decision making is typically thinking-feeling-behaving. For simplicity, consumers making low-effort decisions may satisfice rather than optimize. They may also devise choice tactics over repeat purchase occasions through a process similar to operant conditioning. Cognitively based choice tactics include performance, habit, brand loyalty, price, and normative influences; affective-based choice tactics include affect referral, brand familiarity, variety seeking, and impulse buying.

Questions for Review and Discussion

1. How do base-rate information and the law of small numbers bias judgments made on the basis of the availability heuristic?

2. How is the high-effort hierarchy of effects similar to and different from the low-effort hierarchy?

3. What operant conditioning concepts apply to consumer learning?

4. Why is quality an important ingredient in cognitive-based decision making?

5. What is brand loyalty, and what role does it play in low-effort decision making?

6. How do price and value perceptions affect low-effort decision making?

7. When is affect likely to be more of a factor in low-effort decision making?

8. If habit is a simplifying strategy, why do consumers sometimes seek variety?

CL Visit http://cengage.com/marketing/hoyer/ConsumerBehavior5e to find resources that are available to help you study for the course.

CONSUMER BEHAVIOR CASE

Try It, You'll Like It: Sampling

Sampling has emerged as a critical marketing technique for a long list of companies, from Starbucks and Stew Leonard's to Viva and Vitamin Water. In a bid to broaden its appeal beyond lovers of espresso and similar beverages, Starbucks recently introduced its everyday Pike Place Roast coffee with free 8-ounce sample cups in all of its 7,100 U.S. stores. During the same week, some McDonald's units in Starbucks' hometown of Seattle began offering free samples of the new McDonald's espresso and latté drinks—an attempt to attract consumers who want something more than an everyday cup of coffee. This is only one example of McDonald's using sampling to encourage trial of a new menu item. For instance, when it offered samples of its new premium-roast coffee, the company experienced a 15 percent increase in chainwide coffee sales.

Many fast-food restaurants have found sampling to be effective in inducing trial and purchase. For instance, Wendy's once held a nationwide hamburger sampling tour to attract noncustomers by giving away thousands of free hamburgers at special events along with gift cards good for free hamburgers in local Wendy's restaurants. "It's one thing to talk about a hamburger," says a Wendy's executive. "It's another thing to actually try it." Pizza Hut held "Free Slice of Pizza Day" not long ago so that customers could try its improved hand-tossed pizzas. On the first day of spring, Dunkin' Donuts gave away 3 million cups of iced coffee throughout the country to signal the start of the iced-coffee-drinking season.

Stew Leonard's, a grocery chain based in Norwalk, Connecticut, always has some sampling going on in its four stores: free cups of chicken chili or clam chowder handed out at the front entrance, fresh-squeezed orange juice offered in the produce section, and free cookies piled high in the bakery section. "It's an expensive form of advertising because of the extra labor and staff involved," says the CEO. "But it's also good business. We usually double or triple sales of featured products." And, he adds, customers who try something and enjoy it may very well buy it the next time they shop at Stew Leonard's.

Kimberly-Clark has used sampling to get consumers to feel the softness and strength of its Viva paper towels. In thinking about how to give away a single paper towel as a sample, the company's advertising agency suggesting stitching it into magazines like *Every Day with Rachel Ray* and *Reader's Digest* so that readers could rip the towel out and try it for themselves. At the same time, Kimberly-Clark arranged to distribute Viva coupons at supermarket checkouts. These kinds of marketing tactics have helped Viva boost market share and become the number-two brand in the paper-towel market behind Bounty, the market leader.

Stores and magazines are not the only places where consumers can experience sampling. College students on Florida beaches for spring break are a prime target audience for samples distributed by companies seeking to start or reinforce a brand relationship. Some samples are handed out at hotel registration desks along with room keys. Others are the focus of contests and experiential activities. Students who participate in the "Sand Castle Demolition" contest stomp through sand structures and dig deep for hidden bottles of Vitamin Water, for instance. In Neutrogena's Acne Stress Control tent, students can try out Acne Stress Control Power-Foam Wash, register to win a big gift basket of samples, and stay for a free massage. Marketers also use these contacts as an opportunity to research students' likes and dislikes, shopping habits, and brand preferences, looking for insights that will make their sampling programs even more effective during next year's spring break.[150]

Case Questions

1. Why is sampling a good marketing tool to influence low-effort decisions?
2. In terms of choice tactics, explain the risk that Starbucks takes if consumers who sample Pike Place coffee do not like it.
3. Why would Kimberly-Clark arrange to distribute coupons in supermarkets at the same time that it had Viva towel samples stitched into magazines?
4. What role might normative influences play in the product decisions made by students who receive samples during spring break?

Chapter 11

Post-Decision Processes

LEARNING OBJECTIVES

After studying this chapter, you will be able to

1. Distinguish between the dissonance and the regret that consumers may experience after acquisition, consumption, or disposition.

2. Explain how consumers can learn from experience and why marketers need to understand this post-decision process.

3. Discuss how consumers judge satisfaction or dissatisfaction with their decisions about acquisition, consumption, or disposition.

4. Describe how consumers may dispose of something, why this process is more complex for meaningful objects, and what influences consumer recycling behavior.

INTRODUCTION

The Treasure Hunt Is On at Costco

Who would pay for the privilege of shopping in a no-frills warehouse store? Costco's 52 million customers gladly pay an annual membership fee—and they are so satisfied and loyal that nearly 90 percent of them renew year after year. In fact, membership is on the rise as more consumers search out bargain-priced brand-name foods, books, electronics, gasoline, and other goods and services at Costco's 540 stores or on its website. While low prices are a major attraction, customers also enjoy the fun of hunting down one-time deals on anything from diamond rings to designer jeans.

Another reason for Costco's success is its generous return policy. Anything can be returned for a refund at any time; even the membership fee will be refunded if a customer is dissatisfied. The only exceptions are electronic items like TVs, cameras, computers, and iPods, which cannot be returned after 90 days. Costco's research shows that most electronic products are returned because customers cannot figure out how to operate them, so the retailer now offers free technical assistance and a two-year warranty to demonstrate its commitment to providing complete satisfaction.[1]

The Costco example illustrates several key topics in this chapter. First, it highlights the importance of customer satisfaction as the foundation of a successful business. Second, it shows how customer satisfaction depends on good performance, creating positive feelings, and perceptions of equity (a fair exchange). Third, it illustrates how consumers learn about offerings by experiencing them directly, as customers do when shopping in Costco or using its website. Finally, it demonstrates how a business can counter customer dissatisfaction by offering warranties, technical support, and a generous return policy. All of these phenomena occur after the consumer has made a decision. This chapter examines the four post-decision processes shown in Exhibit 11.1: dissonance and regret, consumer learning, satisfaction/dissatisfaction, and disposition—all of which have important implications for marketers.

Post-Decision Dissonance and Regret

Consumers are not always confident about their acquisition, consumption, or disposition decisions. They may feel uncertain about whether they made the correct choice or may even regret the decision that they made, as the following sections show.

Dissonance

Post-decision dissonance
A feeling of anxiety over whether the correct decision was made.

After you make an acquisition, consumption, or disposition decision, you may sometimes feel uncertain about whether you made the correct choice. You might wonder whether you should have bought a shirt or dress other than the one you did, or whether you should have worn something else to a party, or whether you should have kept an old teddy bear instead of throwing it away. **Post-decision dissonance** is most likely to occur when more than one alternative is attractive and the decision is important.[2]

Post-decision dissonance can influence consumer behavior because it creates anxiety that the consumer would like to reduce, especially when motivation, ability, and opportunity (MAO) are high. One way of reducing dissonance is to search for additional information from sources such as experts and magazines. This search is very selective and is designed to make the chosen alternative more attractive and the rejected ones less attractive, thereby reducing dissonance.

Regret

Post-decision regret A feeling that one should have purchased another option.

Post-decision regret occurs when consumers perceive an unfavorable comparison between the performance of the chosen option and the performance of the options not chosen . If you consider three cars before making your purchase decision and then find out that the resale value of the car that you bought is much lower than that of either of the two options, you may regret your

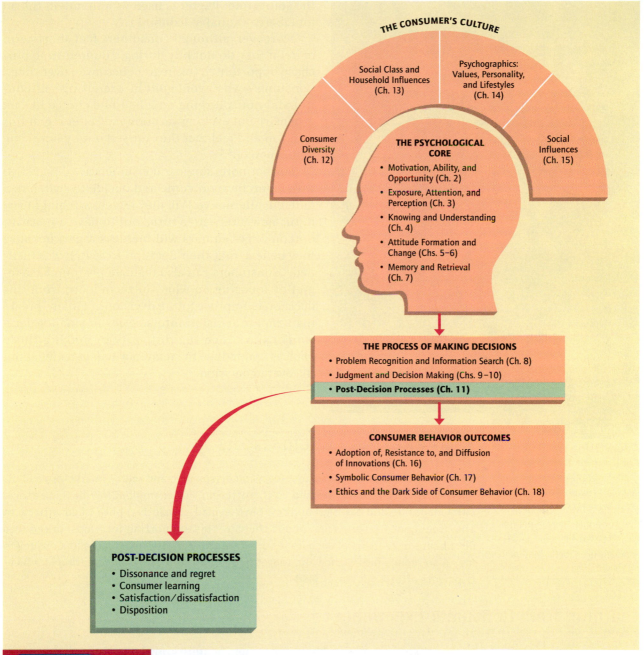

THE CONSUMER'S CULTURE

Social Class and Household Influences (Ch. 13)

Psychographics: Values, Personality, and Lifestyles (Ch. 14)

Consumer Diversity (Ch. 12)

THE PSYCHOLOGICAL CORE
- Motivation, Ability, and Opportunity (Ch. 2)
- Exposure, Attention, and Perception (Ch. 3)
- Knowing and Understanding (Ch. 4)
- Attitude Formation and Change (Chs. 5–6)
- Memory and Retrieval (Ch. 7)

Social Influences (Ch. 15)

THE PROCESS OF MAKING DECISIONS
- Problem Recognition and Information Search (Ch. 8)
- Judgment and Decision Making (Chs. 9–10)
- Post-Decision Processes (Ch. 11)

CONSUMER BEHAVIOR OUTCOMES
- Adoption of, Resistance to, and Diffusion of Innovations (Ch. 16)
- Symbolic Consumer Behavior (Ch. 17)
- Ethics and the Dark Side of Consumer Behavior (Ch. 18)

POST-DECISION PROCESSES
- Dissonance and regret
- Consumer learning
- Satisfaction/dissatisfaction
- Disposition

Exhibit 11.1

Chapter Overview: Post-Decision Processes

The decision does not end after consumers have made a choice or purchase. Consumers can experience dissonance (anxiety over whether they made the correct decision) or regret after a purchase, learn about the offering by using it, experience satisfaction or dissatisfaction with it, and eventually dispose of it.

purchase and wish that you had chosen one of the other cars. In fact, research indicates that you may feel regret even if you have no information about the unchosen alternatives—especially if you cannot reverse your decision, have a negative outcome from your chosen alternative, or have made a change from

THE WIND'S WHIPPING
AND THE LIGHTS ARE OUT.

THIS IS NO TIME TO BE
READING THE FINE PRINT ON
YOUR INSURANCE POLICY.

Storms are trouble. But even more troubling is being hassled on your insurance claim. Liberty Mutual is quick to act and follow through with 24/7 claims assistance, plus emergency board-up and 48-hour property replacement services. Taking responsibility to be there when you need us most. That's our policy. For home, auto, or life insurance, call 1.800.4LIBERTY or visit libertymutual.com

Auto Home Life   Responsibility. What's your policy?

Liberty Mutual.

Exhibit 11.2

Advertising Based on Feelings of Regret

Sometimes ads try to stimulate feelings of regret. A good example is this ad which suggests that consumers may regret not having an excellent insurance company like Liberty Mutual in troubled times.

the status quo. Regret is used as a theme in the ad for Liberty Mutual in Exhibit 11.2.

Moreover, although consumers feel short-term regret if they do not buy during a limited-time purchase opportunity, this regret goes away over time.[4] Consumers who avoid guilt by exercising self-control and not splurging on a hedonic choice like an expensive but exciting vacation may later regret this decision and feel that they missed out by not living in the moment.[5]

Furthermore, suppose consumers are dissatisfied with a purchase outcome and decide to switch to a different alternative. Will they regret switching? Even if this new alternative turns out to have a negative outcome, consumers will feel less regret because they believe that their decision to switch was justified.[6] Consumers can also regulate postpurchase regret by focusing on what they can learn from this decision to improve future decisions.[7] Finally, breaking a major decision into a series of smaller decisions can reduce the difficulty of making those choices and reduce the tendency to feel regret about the overall decision.[8]

MARKETING IMPLICATIONS

By helping consumers reduce post-decision dissonance and regret, marketers can diminish negative feelings related to the offering. For example, BMW buyers receive *BMW Magazine* and can sign up for a BMW e-mail newsletter, both filled with facts and "feel good" information about the car. This supporting information reduces dissonance or regret and encourages positive attitudes toward the brand. Consumers may also reduce dissonance and regret by reading supporting information in advertisements after a purchase.

Learning from Consumer Experience*

Earlier chapters explained how consumers acquire knowledge through processes such as information search, exposure to marketing communications, and observation of others. From a practical perspective, we most often think about this type of consumer learning because much of it is under the direct control of the company, which provides information through marketing communications. However, these efforts are often limited because of their low credibility.[9] Consumers assume that these messages are intended to persuade them to buy the offering and are therefore generally skeptical about the marketing claims.

Experiences that occur during acquisition, consumption, or disposition, however, can be equally—if not more—important sources of consumer knowledge for

---

* Some of this section draws heavily from an article by Stephen J. Hoch and John Deighton, "Managing What Consumers Learn from Experience," *Journal of Marketing*, April 1989, pp. 1–20.

several reasons. First, the consumer tends to be more motivated to learn under these circumstances. Actually experiencing an event is more involving and interesting than being told about it, and the consumer has more control over what happens. Simply investigating the various alternatives is a learning experience. However, if consumers become too attached to the alternatives during the decision process, they may feel uneasy after making a choice because they had to forgo the other alternatives.[10]

Second, information acquired from experience is more vivid and therefore easier to remember than other types of information.[11] However, the information gained from experiential learning is not always accurate and may, in fact, be biased and erroneous.[12] Information about attributes that must be experienced through taste, touch, or smell exerts a stronger influence on consumers' future behavior when it comes from experience or product trial than when it is acquired from ads or word of mouth.[13] An ad can state that a product will taste good, but actually eating it is more likely to generate a strong attitude. On the other hand, repeated exposure to ads can approximate the effect of direct experience when it comes to search or informational attributes such as price or ingredients, resulting in consumers holding strong beliefs about those characteristics.[14]

A Model of Learning from Consumer Experience

Hypothesis testing Testing out expectations through experience.

Consumers can learn from experience by engaging in a process of **hypothesis testing.** On the basis of past experience or another source such as word of mouth or advertising, consumers can form a hypothesis or expectation about a product or service, a consumption experience, or a disposition option and then set out to test it. Such hypotheses are important because without them consumers are less likely to gather the evidence that they need to learn. Researchers have proposed that consumers go through four basic stages in testing hypotheses for learning: (1) **hypothesis generation,** (2) exposure to evidence, (3) encoding of evidence, and (4) integration of evidence and prior beliefs (see Exhibit 11.3). The following example illustrates these four stages.

Hypothesis generation Forming expectations about the product or service.

Suppose a consumer sees an ad for a new Steve Carrell movie. She also remembers some of his previous movies, such as *Get Smart*. Based on all this information, she generates a hypothesis about the quality of the new movie ("It must be great"). Next, she seeks out **exposure to evidence** to either confirm or disprove this hypothesis by going to see the new movie. While watching it, she can assess whether or not it is in fact great, a step called **encoding the evidence.** After watching the movie, the consumer can **integrate the evidence** with her existing knowledge or beliefs. If she really likes it, confirming her hypothesis, she may have learned that "you can always count on a Steve Carrell movie to be great." However, if she does not like it, she may form the new belief that "not all Carrell films are great, and I must be careful in the future."

Exposure to evidence Actually experiencing the product or service.

Encoding of evidence Processing the information one experiences.

Integration of evidence Combining new information with stored knowledge.

Consumers can form hypotheses in relation to any aspect of consumer behavior: acquisition ("buying from eBay will be fun"), consumption ("listening to the concert will be fun"), or disposition ("getting rid of used textbooks will be easy"). Learning from experience is also important when consumers use a shopping agent or react to recommendations from retail sites such as Amazon.com. Using feedback from repeated hypothesis tests, the agent or site learns what the consumer likes and can present more appropriate options.[15]

The consumer's hypothesis and experience of brand personality also influence learning. If a firm with a "sincere" brand personality suffers a crisis, it may have difficulty reconnecting with customers because its fundamental perceptions of the

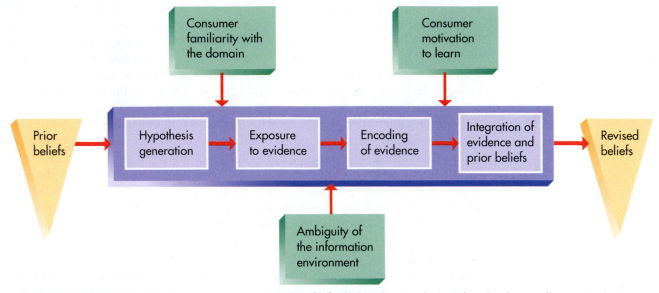

Exhibit 11.3

A Model of Learning from Experience

Consumers can acquire a lot of information about products and services by actually experiencing them. This learning process starts with prior beliefs (such as "Steve Carrell movies are great"). Upon seeing an ad for a new Steve Carrell movie, the consumer can generate hypotheses ("I'll bet this new movie is good"), get exposure to the evidence (see the movie), encode the evidence (evaluate whether or not it is good), and integrate the evidence with prior beliefs (relate the current evaluation to past perceptions). If the movie is not good, the consumer will revise his or her beliefs (not all Steve Carrell movies are good). This entire process is influenced by consumer familiarity, motivation to process, and the ambiguity of the information.

brand have deteriorated. However, firms with an "exciting" brand personality may reinvigorate customer relationships more easily after a crisis because consumers are less surprised by nonroutine experiences with such brands.[16]

What Affects Learning from Experience?

Four factors affect learning from experience: (1) motivation, (2) prior familiarity or ability, (3) ambiguity of the information environment or lack of opportunity, and (4) processing biases.

Motivation

When consumers are motivated to process information, they will generate a number of hypotheses and seek out information to confirm or disprove them, actively engaging in the process of learning from experience. Consider what happened when shoppers told QVC.com that they could not judge a certain handbag's size from the product photo. The company quickly posted photos showing women of different heights holding the purse. This information helped consumers learn more about the purse; in fact, those who viewed the photos were more likely to buy the purse than those who did not view the photos.[17] Note that when motivation is low, consumers will generate few or no hypotheses and will be less likely to learn unless the learning process involves the simpler processes of classical or operant conditioning (see Chapters 6 and 10). Still, marketers can facilitate learning when motivation is low, as shown later in this chapter.

Prior Knowledge or Ability

Consumers' prior knowledge or ability affects the extent to which they learn from experience. When knowledge is high, consumers are likely to have well-defined beliefs and expectations and are therefore unlikely to generate new hypotheses. Also, experts are less likely than those with moderate knowledge to search for information.[18] Both of these factors inhibit learning. In contrast, low-knowledge consumers lack skills to develop hypotheses to guide the learning process.[19] Without guiding hypotheses, consumers have difficulty collecting evidence and learning. Thus, moderately knowledgeable consumers are the most likely to generate hypotheses and learn from experience. Interestingly, experts do have an advantage in learning information about new products and services due to their more extensive knowledge base.[20]

Ambiguity of the Information Environment or Lack of Opportunity

Ambiguity of information
When there is not enough information to confirm or disprove hypotheses.

Some situations do not provide the opportunity for consumers to learn from experience, which means that consumers may lack sufficient information to confirm or disprove hypotheses.[21] Such **ambiguity of information** occurs because many offerings are similar in quality and consumers can glean little information from the experience. Moreover, making the initial choice in a context of ambiguity affects consumers' certainty about the decision and, if the actual experience is uninformative, can lead to persistent preferences for the chosen option's attributes.[22]

Ambiguous information can strongly affect consumers' ability to learn from experience. When consumers have difficulty determining product quality (for such products as beer and motor oil), they tend to support their hypotheses with information from advertising or word of mouth. Because consumers cannot disprove the information by experiencing the product, they see the product as being consistent with their prior expectations.[23] Thus, for many years consumers believed that Listerine prevented colds because the claim could not be disproved by usage. Obviously, the marketer in such a situation has an unfair advantage, a situation that explains why deception in advertising is an important topic.

On the other hand, when evidence is unambiguous and the product is clearly good or bad, consumers base their perceptions on actual experience and learn a great deal. Unambiguous information tends to be better remembered and to have more impact on future decisions.[24] When evidence is ambiguous, evaluations by both experts and novices are strongly influenced by country-of-origin expectations (e.g., knowing that a product was made in Japan), but when evidence is unambiguous, experts ignore this information and make evaluations based on actual quality.[25]

Processing Biases

The confirmation bias and overconfidence can pose major hurdles to the learning process, particularly when evidence is ambiguous.[26] Specifically, these biases inhibit learning by making consumers avoid both negative and highly diagnostic information. For example, a consumer who believes that all Japanese products are of high quality may ignore contrary evidence and learn nothing new about these products. Also, negative information is important to the learning process because it provides a more balanced picture of the situation and allows consumers to more accurately test hypotheses. Research has also shown that the acquisition of disproving evidence has a strong and rapid impact on consumer learning.[27]

Exhibit 11.4

Encouraging Learning to Facilitate Switching

Sometimes marketers can encourage learning about their brand in order to get consumers to switch. Here Huggies offers a diaper test, which helps consumers to learn about the quality of the brand.

Top dog A market leader or brand that has a large market share.

Underdogs Lower-share brands.

MARKETING IMPLICATIONS

Ambiguous information and processing biases often inhibit consumer learning about products and services. These biases have important strategic implications, depending on the offering's market position.[28]

Top-dog strategies

A product, service, or business that is the market leader or has a large market share is called a **top dog.** Limitations on learning are advantageous to top dogs because consumers will simply confirm existing beliefs and expectations and be overconfident, particularly when the motivation to learn is low. When motivation to learn is high, the consumer will try to acquire information that could be disproving and lead to a switch. To avoid this, the top dog can state specific claims that justify consumers' evaluation of the brand. Or the top dog can encourage consumers not to acquire new information, which is called *blocking exposure to evidence.* If top-dog evidence is unambiguous, the consumer simply needs reinforcement of messages telling why the brand is satisfying—called *explaining the experience*—and encouragement to try it. The McDonald's advertising slogan "I'm Lovin' It" is a good example.

Underdog strategies

Underdogs (lower-share brands) want to encourage consumer learning because new information may lead consumers to switch brands. When consumers are not motivated, underdogs can instigate learning through comparisons of their brand with the market leader, side-by-side displays, or information provided online. The underdog needs a strong and distinct advantage if it is to overcome overconfidence and confirmation biases (see Exhibit 11.4).

Second, marketers can create expectations and use promotions to provide the actual experience for consumers. If the evidence is ambiguous, consumers' expectations are not likely to be disconfirmed. For example, Walnut Crest advertised to create expectations for its Chilean Merlot wine by encouraging U.S. consumers to take the "$1,000,000 Taste Challenge" and arranged for restaurants to offer taste comparisons of its product with higher-priced wines.[29] Finally, facilitating product trial is critical when consumers' motivation to learn is low and the evidence is unambiguous because the evidence will lead to a positive learning experience (see Exhibit 11.5).

How Do Consumers Make Satisfaction or Dissatisfaction Judgments?

After consumers have made acquisition, consumption, or disposition decisions, they can evaluate the outcomes of their decisions. If their evaluations are positive—if they believe their needs or goals have been met—they feel

Exhibit 11.5

Facilitating Trial

Sometimes ads try to stimulate a trial of the product or service (e.g. through coupons or deals) because this will lead to a positive learning experience, such as booking travel through CheapTickets.

Satisfaction The feeling that results when consumers make a positive evaluation or feel happy with their decision.

Dissatisfaction The feeling that results when consumers make a negative evaluation or are unhappy with a decision.

satisfaction. Thus, you could feel satisfied with the purchase of a new DVD player, a haircut, a buying experience, a salesperson, or a retail outlet.[30] When consumers have a negative evaluation of an outcome, they feel **dissatisfaction.** Dissatisfaction occurs if you did not enjoy a movie, were unhappy with a salesperson, or wished you had not thrown something away. Dissatisfaction can be related to feelings of tolerance, distress, sadness, regret, agitation, and outrage.[31]

Most of the research on satisfaction and dissatisfaction has focused on offerings that consumers can evaluate on *utilitarian dimensions*, or how well the product or service functions (good or bad), as well as on *hedonic dimensions*, or how the product makes someone feel (happy, excited, delighted, sad, regretful, or angry).[32] In judging satisfaction, consumers make a conscious comparison between what they thought would happen and the actual performance.[33] Satisfaction also varies with consumer involvement, consumer characteristics, and time.[34] High-involvement consumers tend to express higher satisfaction immediately after a purchase, probably due to their more extensive evaluation, but their satisfaction declines over time. Lower-involvement consumers exhibit lower satisfaction at first, but their satisfaction increases with greater usage over time.

MARKETING IMPLICATIONS

Customer satisfaction is critical to business success because satisfied customers are willing to pay higher prices, particularly if they buy the product repeatedly.[35] They are also more likely to remain customers, be brand loyal, and be committed to the product.[36] Also, they will tell others about their experiences, increasing the likelihood that those consumers will then buy the product.[37] Attracting new customers is more expensive than marketing to existing customers, a situation that means retaining satisfied customers is cost-efficient.[38] When the product category is important to the consumer, satisfaction can also lead to more frequent purchasing, especially when it is convenient for the consumer to buy.[39] And consumers tend to spend more on the brand with which they are satisfied when they make purchases in that product category.[40] For instance, Disney has calculated that the long-term value of a loyal customer of its theme parks is $50,000.[41] Thus, some studies have been able to link customer satisfaction with company profitability.

Not surprisingly, many companies actively monitor customer satisfaction. For example, Holiday Chevrolet in St. Cloud, Florida, uses telephone surveys to gauge customer satisfaction one day after a car has been serviced or purchased.[42] The American Customer Satisfaction Index (ACSI) monitors satisfaction with a variety of industries and firms

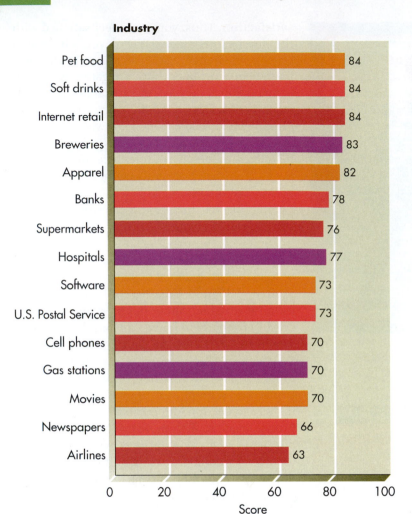

Industry

Industry	Score
Pet food	84
Soft drinks	84
Internet retail	84
Breweries	83
Apparel	82
Banks	78
Supermarkets	76
Hospitals	77
Software	73
U.S. Postal Service	73
Cell phones	70
Gas stations	70
Movies	70
Newspapers	66
Airlines	63

Score (0 — 20 — 40 — 60 — 80 — 100)

Note: Higher scores indicate higher satisfaction.

Source: Data from ACSI, 2007.

Exhibit 11.6

The American Consumer Satisfaction Index

The ACSI measures customer satisfaction performance across a variety of different industries. Here are a few examples.

Disconfirmation The existence of a discrepancy between expectations and performance.

Expectations Beliefs about how a product/service will perform.

Performance The measurement of whether the product/service actually fulfills consumers' needs.

(see Exhibit 11.6). Marketers should also aim for satisfaction when responding to customers' questions and concerns because (1) these tend to be highly loyal customers and (2) these consumers will influence others through word of mouth after the contact.[43]

Finally, marketers must understand the roots of dissatisfaction because of the potential for negative outcomes such as negative word-of-mouth communication, complaints, and lower sales and profits. If a department store loses 167 customers a month, it will lose $2.4 million in sales (and $280,000 in profit) in just one year.[44] One study found that it takes 12 positive experiences to overcome a single negative one and that the cost of attracting a new customer is five times the cost of keeping an existing one.[45]

Satisfaction/Dissatisfaction Based on Thoughts

Just as consumers make decisions based on thoughts and feelings, they also judge satisfaction or dissatisfaction based on thoughts and feelings. Thought-based judgments of satisfaction/dissatisfaction can relate to (1) whether consumers' thoughts and expectations about the offering are confirmed or disconfirmed by its actual performance, (2) thoughts about causality and blame, and (3) thoughts about fairness and equity.

Expectations and Performance: The Disconfirmation Paradigm

As diagrammed in Exhibit 11.7, **disconfirmation** occurs when there is a discrepancy, positive or negative, between our prior expectations and the product's actual performance (see the red arrows in the exhibit).[46] In this case, **expectations** are desired product/service outcomes and include "pre-consumption beliefs about overall performance, or . . . the levels or attributes possessed by a product (service)."[47] For example, you might expect a Japanese car to be reliable and fuel efficient, expectations based on advertising, inspection of the product, prior experience with similar offerings, and the experiences of other referent consumers.[48]

Performance measures whether these expected outcomes have been achieved. Performance can either be *objective*—based on the actual performance, which is fairly constant across consumers—or *subjective*—based on individual feelings, which can vary across consumers. The objective performance of a car describes how well it runs and how economical its gas mileage is, whereas subjective performance might include an assessment of how stylish it is or "how good it makes me feel." Better-than-expected performance leads to a *positive disconfirmation* and to

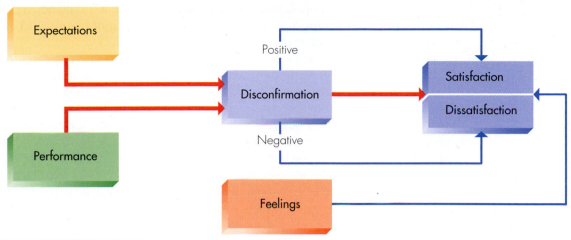

Exhibit 11.7

The Disconfirmation Paradigm

Here the disconfirmation paradigm shows how satisfaction or dissatisfaction can occur. Using an example of a new Steve Carrell movie, the consumer enters the situation with expectations ("Steve Carrell movies are entertaining"). Once she sees the movie, she can evaluate it (performance). If she finds it more entertaining than she expected, positive disconfirmation has occurred, and she will be satisfied. If the movie is less entertaining than she expected, a negative disconfirmation and dissatisfaction will result. Expectations (the likelihood of seeing the movie as entertaining), performance (whether the movie actually is good), and feelings (positive or negative emotions experienced during viewing) will also affect satisfaction/dissatisfaction (independent of disconfirmation).

satisfaction. If performance is as good as expected, a *simple confirmation* has occurred, and this condition will also lead to satisfaction. In contrast, if performance is lower than expected, the result is *negative disconfirmation* and dissatisfaction.

Customers' evaluation of services is also susceptible to disconfirmation.[49] Here, customers have expectations related to price and service performance and to intangible characteristics of the facilities and the personnel.[50] One way online retailers such as Amazon can avoid dissatisfaction is by providing plenty of information, such as stating the cutoff date for ordering merchandise to be delivered by Christmas.[51] Research also finds that if consumers participate in a service expecting to achieve a goal such as weight loss, they are more satisfied when they successfully follow the instructions and achieve the goal.[52]

Although the disconfirmation paradigm is similar to the learning process, satisfaction and dissatisfaction are based on a formal evaluation, whereas the learning process may not be. Also, satisfaction need not be transaction-specific and is subject to change—in fact, it can be affected by social influences such as family members and may be closely related to consumers' satisfaction with their own lives.[53] Consumers who have many choices will feel more satisfied when they decide on an option that turns out well, and they can give themselves credit for making a good decision (but they will be dissatisfied if they choose an option that turns out to be bad because they will blame themselves for making a bad decision).[54]

Interestingly, consumers who have many choices may be optimistic about their chosen product's performance at first, but this optimism will fade over time.[55] When consumers expect to evaluate an offering, they will pay closer attention to negative aspects during consumption and therefore will provide less favorable quality and satisfaction evaluations—unless they have low expectations at the outset.[56] Also, customers who buy at a discount may perceive that they benefit less from the product's consumption than if they had paid full price.[57] Even when price has no bearing on a product's quality, consumers' beliefs about the price-quality relationship will affect their experience of the product's performance.[58]

Exhibit 11.7 shows that performance, expectations, and feelings can affect satisfaction, *independent* of disconfirmation (as reflected by the blue arrows).[59] To fully understand why satisfaction or dissatisfaction occurs, we must account for all these dimensions together and separately. The simple fact that a product performs well will have a positive influence on satisfaction, independent of expectations.[60] Likewise, the poor performance of a product or service alone can lead to dissatisfaction.[61] If you buy a new digital music player, and it does not work well, you could be dissatisfied—even without having had any prior expectations about it. How feelings affect satisfaction and dissatisfaction will be explored later in this chapter.

MARKETING IMPLICATIONS

Based on the disconfirmation paradigm, better performance leads to fulfilled expectations and satisfaction. Expectations created by marketers about product performance can also influence satisfaction or dissatisfaction. Raising consumers' expectations of how well the product or service will perform can increase ratings of product performance.[62] When Pizza Hut first opened in China, pizza was unfamiliar to most Chinese consumers. The firm therefore created tabletop cards to inform diners that pizza is a healthy food with natural ingredients, creating positive expectations.[63] On the other hand, marketers are setting themselves up for a potential negative disconfirmation and dissatisfaction if customer expectations are too high, and companies make promises they cannot keep.

Providing consumers with a good warranty or guarantee can create positive expectations that will lead to satisfaction.[64] For instance, Pinemoor West Golf Course in Englewood, Florida, differentiates itself by guaranteeing that golfers can complete a round in less than four and a half hours. Staff members deliver golf carts and load golf bags to save customers time and effort. [65]

Causality and Blame: Attribution Theory

Attribution theory A theory of how individuals find explanations for events.

Attribution theory explains how individuals think about explanations for or causes of effects or behavior.[66] In a marketing context, when a product or service does not fulfill consumers' needs, they will attempt to find an explanation based on three factors:

- ▸ *Stability.* Is the cause of the event temporary or permanent?

- ▸ *Focus.* Is the problem consumer or marketer related?

- ▸ *Controllability.* Is the event under the customer's or marketer's control?

Customers are more likely to be dissatisfied if the cause is perceived to be permanent, marketer related, and not under the customer's control. Suppose you find a crack in the windshield of your new car. If you perceive that this is only a chance or temporary occurrence, beyond the control of the marketer (maybe a rock hit the window while you were driving) or perhaps your own fault, you will probably not be dissatisfied. On the other hand, if you discover that many other consumers have had a similar problem—that is, the cause is more permanent, company related, and under the company's control—you will probably be dissatisfied.

Attribution theory also applies to services. For instance, consumers were dissatisfied with a travel agent if the problem they had experienced was permanent and under the firm's control.[67] In a study of passengers delayed at an airport, attributions were found to explain the desire either to complain or to fly the same airline again. If consumers saw the delay as permanent and under the airline's control, they were more likely to complain and less likely to fly the airline again.[68] Consumers who can choose whether to participate in a service are likely to attribute at least part of any negative outcome to their own involvement, whereas they will attribute a good part of any positive outcome to their own participation.[69] Satisfaction with services also depends on whether the consumer holds the company responsible for the outcome and believes the outcome stems from a stable or unstable cause.[70] Finally, consumers are more satisfied when companies exert extra effort to serve them, even when the offerings are not that great.[71]

MARKETING IMPLICATIONS

Attribution theory can provide marketers with guidance in how to deal with potential or existing perceptions of consumer dissatisfaction. If the cause of the dissatisfaction actually is permanent, marketer related, and under the marketer's control, something must be done to correct the problem or provide the consumer with restitution. In the banking industry, many banks are marketing value-added services such as financial advice, stock quotes, and bill payment in an attempt to satisfy customers.[72]

Fairness and Equity: Equity Theory

Equity theory A theory that focuses on the fairness of exchanges between individuals, which helps in understanding consumer satisfaction and dissatisfaction.

Equity theory focuses on the nature of exchanges between individuals and their perceptions of these exchanges. In marketing, it has been applied to examining the exchange between a buyer and a seller or a more general institution.[73] According to equity theory, consumers form perceptions of their own inputs and outputs into a particular exchange and compare these perceptions with their perceptions of the inputs and outputs of the salesperson, dealer, or company. For example, when buying a car, a consumer's inputs might include information search, decision-making effort, psychological anxiety, and money. The output would be a satisfactory car. Seller inputs might include a quality product, selling effort, and a financing plan; seller output might be a fair profit.

Fairness in the exchange The perception that people's inputs are equal to their outputs in an exchange.

For equity to occur, the buyer must perceive **fairness in the exchange.** Thus, the car buyer might perceive a fair exchange if he or she purchased a desirable car at a fair price. Satisfaction is even higher if consumers perceive that they have gotten a bargain.[74] Consumers will be dissatisfied if they perceive inequity in an exchange—for example, if the salesperson did not pay enough attention to the buyer. For equity to occur, the consumer must perceive that the seller is also being dealt with fairly. Nevertheless, fairness perceptions tend to be self-centered, biased more toward buyer outcomes and seller inputs, than to buyer inputs and seller outcomes.[75]

Moreover, research shows that consumers judge the equity of the payment exchanged for service usage by asking themselves, "Am I using this service enough, given what I pay for it?" They will perceive the exchange as more equitable when they have high expectations of service usage levels at first or when the service performance exceeds their normative expectations. When they perceive the price/usage exchange to be more equitable, they will be more satisfied.[76] Also, perceptions of equity can shift over time. For instance, as the end of a car's warranty period approaches, owners become increasingly dissatisfied with attributes they believe can be remedied; in turn, these attributes become more highly related to product quality satisfaction.[77]

Equity theory complements the disconfirmation paradigm in that equity theory specifies another way dissatisfaction can occur. In other words, both types of processes can operate at the same time. However, whereas the disconfirmation paradigm focuses on expectations and performance, equity theory is concerned with more general interpersonal norms governing what is wrong or right and with a consideration of the outcomes for both the seller and the buyer.

MARKETING IMPLICATIONS

As long as consumers perceive that their inputs and outputs are equitable in relation to those of the seller, they will be satisfied. This reaction is true in terms of the offering itself as well as in terms of interactions with employees when resolving a complaint. In other words, consumers who perceive that they have been treated fairly in the complaint process will be more satisfied, more likely to buy again, and more likely to spread positive word of mouth.[78] However, if an inequity exists, consumers will be dissatisfied.

Marketers must work toward providing fair exchanges, even though consumers' perceptions of fairness tend to be biased toward themselves. One area in which marketers can directly affect equity perceptions is the salesperson-customer interaction. Salespeople must make every effort to ensure that their inputs match customer inputs by listening to consumer needs, answering questions, and trying to provide a good deal.

Promotions can also increase perceptions of fairness in an exchange. Offering a lower price or a free gift with purchase can make consumers feel that they are getting more out of the exchange. In addition, companies must ensure that outputs are satisfactory by providing a quality product at a fair price, as Target's loyal customers are satisfied by the store's value-priced designer housewares.

Satisfaction/Dissatisfaction Based on Feelings

Consumers can also judge satisfaction and dissatisfaction on the basis of feelings, specifically (1) experienced emotions (and coping with these emotions) and (2) mispredictions about emotions.

Experienced Emotions and Coping

Post-decision feelings
Positive or negative emotions experienced while using the products or services.

The positive and negative **post-decision feelings** we experience help to explain satisfaction or dissatisfaction judgments (independent of disconfirmation, as you saw in Exhibit 11.7).[79] If we feel good (or bad) while using a product or service, we are more likely to be satisfied (or dissatisfied), independent of our expectations and evaluations of its performance. Consumers who are happy or content are most likely to be satisfied, followed by those who experience pleasant surprise. In fact, most consumers around the world find enjoyment and satisfaction in their buying experiences. One study found that more than 90 percent of durable-goods purchases were associated with positive feelings.[80] Dissatisfaction is most likely to strike consumers who feel angry or upset, followed by those who experience unpleasant surprise.[81] Feelings expressed by service employees also affect customer

Active Coping	**Expressive Support Seeking**	**Avoidance**
ACTION COPING • I concentrate on ways the problem could be solved • I try to make a plan of action RATIONAL THINKING • I analyze the problem before reacting • I try to control my emotions POSITIVE THINKING • I try to look on the bright side of things	EMOTIONAL VENTING • I take time to express my emotions • I delve into my feelings to understand them INSTRUMENTAL SUPPORT • I ask friends with similar experience what they did • I try to get advice from someone about what to do EMOTIONAL SUPPORT • I seek out others for comfort • I rely on others to make me feel better	AVOIDANCE • I avoid thinking about it • I try to take my mind off of it by doing other things DENIAL • I deny that the event has happened • I refuse to believe that the problem has occurred

Exhibit 11.8

Coping with Dissatisfaction Due to Consumption Problems

Consumers may cope with dissatisfaction through active coping, expressive support seeking, or avoidance.

Source: Adapted from Adam Duhachek, "Coping: A Multidimensional, Hierarchical Framework of Responses to Stressful Consumption Episodes," *Journal of Consumer Research* 32, June 2005, pp. 41–53.

satisfaction. When employees appear to be expressing genuinely positive emotions, consumers are more satisfied with the service encounter.[82]

Consumers who are dissatisfied with a purchase, consumption, or disposition decision may need to cope with the feelings of stress that dissatisfaction involves.[83] How they cope depends on whether they feel threatened or challenged by the stress and whether they think that they have the motivation, ability, and opportunity to deal with it. For example, a consumer might cope with a technological product failure by reading the instruction manual (active coping), by calling a friend who knows that technology (instrumental support seeking), or by denying that the failure has occurred (see Exhibit 11.8).

Consumers' satisfaction evaluations also tend to be tied to specific consumption situations—we may be satisfied (or not) with the offering as we are using it at the current time. Even if we are satisfied now, however, we may not be satisfied the next time we use it. Thus, satisfaction differs from an attitude, which is relatively enduring and less dependent on the specific situation.[84] In addition, research shows that feelings tend to have more influence on satisfaction judgments early on, but this influence decreases over time. Conversely, thoughts have more influence on satisfaction judgments as time goes on.[85] Note that a post-decision evaluation can differ from a pre-decision evaluation in that after using the product, a consumer may judge different attributes and cutoff levels than he or she did before.[86] For example, after trying frozen microwave pizza, you might decide that you like the taste less than you thought you would.

Mispredictions About Emotions

While post-decision feelings can affect satisfaction judgments, so too can the difference between how we thought the product would make us feel and how it actually makes us feel, a phenomenon known as **affective forecasting.** In other words, we tend to be more dissatisfied not only when a product fails to perform as we thought it would but also when a product makes us feel worse than we forecast that

Affective forecasting When we try to predict how a product will make us feel.

Exhibit 11.9

Enhancing the Coping Process

The minor-league baseball team St. Paul Saints tries to make its fans, or customers, feel good by engaging in a variety of activities, such as reading to young-sters and signing autographs.

it would. This phenomenon may be a fairly common occurrence because people tend to be poor predictors of how decisions, experiences, and outcomes will make them feel.[87]

MARKETING IMPLICATIONS

Marketers should make sure that customers' feelings about trying, buying, and using their offerings are as positive as possible. Some marketers use promotions to increase consumers' positive feelings. As seen in Exhibit 11.9, the St. Paul Saints, a minor-league baseball team, gives fans a good feeling about the team through promotions such as having players read to young fans in center field and signing autographs.[88] Businesses and nonprofits can build relationships with consumers and contributors by encouraging their involvement and identification with the organization through communications and other activities.[89] Knowing that dissatisfied consumers may feel stress, companies can aid in the coping process by providing a feedback mechanism and expert advice. For example, the Genius Bar experts in Apple stores stand ready to listen to customer com-plaints or inquiries and to offer knowledgeable ideas and solutions.

Responses to Dissatisfaction

Marketers must understand the nature of consumers' responses to dissatisfaction because a variety of mostly negative consequences can result. Specifically, dissatis-fied consumers can decide to (1) take no action, (2) discontinue purchasing the product or service, (3) complain to the company or to a third party and perhaps return the item, or (4) engage in negative word-of-mouth communication.[90] The last two behaviors are of special interest to consumer researchers.

Complaints

Surprisingly, the majority of dissatisfied consumers do not complain.[91] Nevertheless, even a few consumer complaints can indicate marketing-related problems that need attention. When consumers complain, they can voice their dissatisfaction to a manufacturer, the retailer, regulatory agencies, or the media. Sometimes consumers seek formal redress through legal means or from governmental agencies. Thus, marketers need to focus on when complaints are likely to occur and which consumers tend to complain.

Complaining is more likely when motivation, ability, and opportunity are high. It is also more likely as the level of dissatisfaction or the severity of the problem increases.[92] In equity theory terms, the unfairness of the exchange is higher, and the consumer is more motivated to act.[93] However, the severity of the dissatisfaction alone does not explain complaining behavior. In particular, consumers are less likely to act if they perceive that complaining will take a lot of time and effort, that their chances of benefiting from doing so are low, or that the offering is insignificant.[94]

The more the blame or attribution for dissatisfaction is placed on someone else, particularly on the company or on society in general, the greater the motivation and likelihood of complaining.[95] Thus, consumers are more likely to complain when they feel removed from the problem—that is, when the perceived cause is permanent, marketer related, and volitional.[96] If dissatisfaction is so strong that complainers want "revenge" against the company, they will even resort to a suboptimal alternative, such as switching to a more costly competing product.[97]

You might expect that consumers who are aggressive and self-confident would be more likely to complain than those who are not[98] or that consumers with more experience or knowledgeability about how to complain might be more likely to do so than their less savvy counterparts. Neither idea has been strongly supported by evidence, although findings suggest experience may influence the likelihood of consumer complaints. Consumers are more likely to complain when they have the time and formal channels of communication to do so.

Research suggests that there are four types of complainers.[99] *Passives* are the least likely to complain. *Voicers* are likely to complain directly to the retailer or service provider. *Irates* are angry consumers who are most likely to engage in negative word of mouth, stop patronage, and complain to the provider but not to a third party such as the media or government. *Activists* engage heavily in all types of complaining, including to a third party. Activists can now reach thousands of people by posting negative comments on blogs or on websites.[100]

(MARKETING IMPLICATIONS)

Although a large percentage of consumers do not complain, it is still in the marketer's best interests to be responsive when any consumers do. Speedy response is important: 57 percent of the consumers in one survey said that how quickly a website responds to e-mail influences their decision to buy from that site in the future.[101] However, 45 percent of the big companies included in a recent study did not tell consumers how quickly they could expect a response to an e-mailed complaint or inquiry.[102] Clearly, consumers will be more satisfied and more likely to buy again if they get a speedy response, especially if it involves getting money back or a fair exchange/refund policy.

Dissatisfied consumers who have been treated fairly can become even more loyal in the future. For example, a consumer who set up a complaint website to publicize his problems with a Sony electronics product converted the site to an enthusiastic fan site after the company resolved the problem.[103] However, if consumers experience more than one problem with a company, their satisfaction and repurchase intent will drop, even if the problems are quickly resolved. In fact, they will rate the second problem as even more severe than the first and are more likely to see a pattern in which the company is to blame.[104] Thus, not only do companies need an efficient and responsive mechanism for handling problems; they also must make changes to avoid similar lapses in the future.

Positive disconfirmation of warranty and service expectations—a better-than-expected response—can result in satisfaction with the complaint resolution.[105] Also note that sometimes a company may want to encourage complaints because dissatisfied consumers who do not complain are more likely to stop buying.[106] But when companies are too responsive to complaints—that is, too eager to please—customers may be more likely to complain, even when a complaint is not justified, because they perceive a greater likelihood of compensation.[107] Still, by encouraging complaints when they are justified and by actively managing customer problems, the company can retain valued consumers. ▬▬

Responding to Service Recovery

If customers are dissatisfied, marketers need to find ways of making up for this dissatisfaction to win back the customers' business. How consumers will respond to service recovery efforts will depend on their expectations.[108] When consumers expect to maintain a good relationship despite a mishap, the business should sincerely apologize and promise to prevent such mishaps in the future. When consumers expect to respond aggressively and to control the situation, the business should take their complaints seriously, give them choices, and help them feel in control. When consumers expect a rational response based on costs and benefits, the business should offer a discount or some other benefit to restore some level of satisfaction.

(MARKETING IMPLICATIONS)

Research indicates that consumers prefer service recovery efforts that correspond to the type of failure experienced.[109] In the case of inattentive service, for instance, restoring good service and quickly apologizing can reduce dissatisfaction and help restore satisfaction. When dissatisfied consumers perceive that the cause of the service problem is permanent, marketer related, and under the firm's control when in fact it is not, marketers need to correct these misperceptions. Providing consumers with logical explanations for service failure, especially if it was not the company's fault, or providing some form of compensation such as a gift or refund can often reduce consumers' feelings of dissatisfaction.[110] ▬▬

Responding by Negative Word of Mouth

Negative word-of-mouth communication The act of consumers saying negative things about a product or service to other consumers.

When consumers are unhappy with a product or service, they are often motivated to tell others in order to relieve their frustration and to convince others not to purchase the product or to do business with the company. **Negative word-of-mouth communication** is more likely to occur when the problem is severe, when consumers are unhappy with the company's responsiveness, and when consumers perceive that the company is at fault.[111] Negative word of mouth can be troublesome because it tends to be highly persuasive and very vivid (and therefore easily remembered) and because consumers place great emphasis on it when making decisions.[112] It also may influence other consumers to stop (or never begin) doing business with the company. Negative word of mouth can go global as consumers air gripes on blogs and on websites such as PlanetFeedback.com.[113] These sites are a potential threat to businesses because they are available to consumers worldwide, and the information may be unfair, nasty, or inappropriate.[114]

MARKETING IMPLICATIONS

Marketers need to be responsive to negative word of mouth, make an effort to identify the reason for or source of the difficulty, and take steps to rectify or eliminate the problem with restitution or communications. Consider how Hertz handled a chorus of consumer complaints about a proposed $2.50 reservation fee on vehicles rented in the United States. The company had been seeking to offset higher costs, but it announced that it would not institute the fee after hundreds of consumers protested to Hertz and on Internet message boards.[115]

Is Customer Satisfaction Enough?

Although customer satisfaction should be an extremely important goal for any firm, some have questioned whether satisfaction alone is enough to keep customers loyal. As evidence, they point out that 65 to 85 percent of customers who defect to competitors' brands say that they had been either satisfied or very satisfied with the product or service they left.[116] When consumers are not strongly satisfied, they are more prone to defect.[117] Other studies have found a low correlation between satisfaction and repurchase.[118] Thus, customers may need to be "extremely satisfied" or need a stronger reason in order to stay with a brand or company.[119] Moreover, loyalty depends on whether the product is competitively superior, consumers find its superiority desirable, and the product can be part of a social network that the company is able to maintain.[120]

Customer retention The practice of keeping customers by building long-term relationships.

A key goal for any marketer should therefore be **customer retention,** the practice of working to satisfy customers with the intention of developing long-term relationships with them. A customer-retention strategy attempts to build customer commitment and loyalty by continually paying close attention to all aspects of customer interaction, especially after-sales service. See Exhibit 11.10 for a good example of this strategy. Customer loyalty programs can, over the long term, strengthen relationships with customers and increase purchasing.[121] Specifically, profits can be increased through repeat sales, reduced costs, and referrals.[122] Customer relationship management systems can

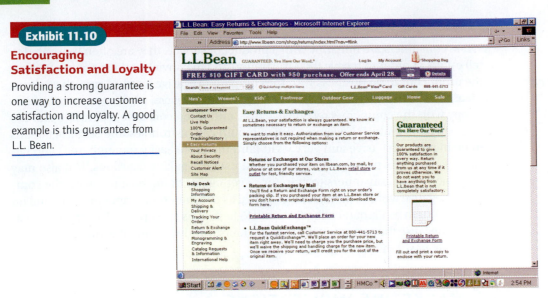

Exhibit 11.10

Encouraging Satisfaction and Loyalty

Providing a strong guarantee is one way to increase customer satisfaction and loyalty. A good example is this guarantee from L.L. Bean.

help companies learn more about their customers, information that, in turn, helps marketers better serve, satisfy, and retain customers.[123]

MARKETING IMPLICATIONS

Given the cost of acquiring new customers and the potential profit in repeat purchasing, companies should take steps such as the following to retain their customers:[124]

▶ *Care about customers.* Two-thirds of consumers defect because they believe that the company does not care about them. Thus, a little caring can go a long way. One Starbucks customer raves about the personal attention: "They actually smile and remember you. They treat you like a friend. I think a lot of companies could learn from them."[125]

▶ *Remember customers between sales.* Companies can contact consumers to make sure that they are not having any problems with the offering or to acknowledge special occasions such as birthdays. The owner of the Number 5 Restaurant in Auckland, New Zealand, e-mails a weekly newsletter and calls customers to ask how they liked their dining experience. "These things don't cost us a lot, but [they] make the customer feel considered and special," she says.[126]

▶ *Build trusting relationships.* Provide consumers with expertise and high-quality offerings. This is how Craigslist draws 30 million consumers monthly who post or read classified ads for jobs, apartments, and other commodities on its 450 city-specific websites. "I just want to provide the kind of customer service that I'd appreciate in other companies," founder Craig Newmark explains. "If you give people an environment where they can trust each other and be fair, for the most part, then people almost always return that trust."[127]

▶ *Monitor the service-delivery process.* Companies should make every effort to respond and show concern when an offering requires service or repairs. After the owner of Mr. Magic Car Wash in Mt. Lebanon, Pennsylvania, saw that customers were frustrated by waiting in long lines, he set up two lanes. The automated lane is for customers who want a regular wash and are using a refillable payment card. The full-service lane is for customers whose cars need extra attention. This change increased customer satisfaction and loyalty.[128]

▶ *Provide extra effort.* Companies that put special effort into satisfying customers are more likely to build lasting relationships than companies that do the minimum. Dell, for instance, set up a service center in China to offer technical support so that local customers could have their systems "back up and running as quickly as possible," says a Dell vice president.[129] ●━

Disposition

At the most basic level, *disposition* is the throwing away of meaningless or used-up items without giving the action much thought, yet research shows that disposition is actually a much richer and more detailed process.[130] We tend to think of possessions as physical things, but they can be defined much more broadly as anything that reflects an extension of the self, including one's body and body parts, other persons, pets, places, services, time periods, and events. For example, you could end a relationship, give a friend an idea, donate an organ, abandon an unhealthy lifestyle, use up all your leisure time, or discontinue your Costco membership. Thus, the study of disposition relates to all of these types of possessions.

Many options are available when a consumer decides that a possession is no longer of immediate use, as outlined in Exhibit 11.11.[131] Note that disposition can be *temporary* (loaning or renting the item) or *involuntary* (losing or destroying the item).[132] Here we will focus on permanent, voluntary disposition.

Consumers often have logical and reasonable motives behind their disposition actions.[133] For example, people sell things to earn an economic return and come out ahead. In contrast, they may choose to donate something without getting a tax deduction, or they may pass an item along out of a desire to help someone as well as a desire not to let the product go to waste. Situational and product-related factors can also affect disposition options.[134] For example, when consumers have limited time or storage space, they may be more likely to dispose of a possession by throwing it away, giving it away, or abandoning it (see Exhibit 11.12). Consumers disposing of a possession of high value are likely to sell it or to give it to someone special rather than to throw it away. In general, the frequency of different disposition behaviors varies by product category.

Research has examined how consumers dispose of unwanted gifts.[135] They can be laterally recycled (swapped, sold, or passed on to someone else), destroyed, or returned. Destruction is a way of getting revenge against the giver but is usually more of a fantasy than a real action. Retailers need to be aware that returning a gift to a store can be a negative emotional experience for consumers. Disposition can involve more than one individual, as when consumers give old clothes to someone, sell a car, or participate in a neighborhood cleanup, or it can consist of activities of a collective or societal nature, such as recycling waste water.[136]

Disposing of Meaningful Objects

Although disposition often means simply getting rid of unwanted, meaningless, or used-up possessions, the process is more involved for certain significant items. Possessions can sometimes be important reflections of the self that are infused with significant symbolic meaning.[137] They define who we are, and they catalog our personal history.[138] In these situations, disposition involves two processes: physical detachment and emotional detachment.

A TAXONOMY OF VOLUNTARY DISPOSITION

Methods	Personal Focus	Interpersonal Focus	Societal Focus
Give away: usually to someone who can use it.	Necessarily requires another person as receiver.	Donate body organs; give clothes to the needy; give a baby up for adoption; give an idea to a friend.	Give land to new settlers; give surplus food to the poor; give military advice to an ally.
Trade or exchange it for something else.	Skin grafts; trade sleep time for work time; trade work time for shopping for bargains.	Trade a car; trade stock; barter; exchange ideas with a colleague; switch boyfriends/girlfriends. Swap meets.	Trade tanks for oil; exchange effluent water for a golf course.
Recycle: convert it to something else.	Convert barn beams to paneling; make a quilt of scraps; eat turkey sandwiches after Thanksgiving.	Recycle newspapers; recycle aluminum cans; manufacturers' recycling of defective parts.	Recycle waste water; convert a slum to a model neighborhood; recycle war ruins as national monuments.
Sell: convert it to money.	Necessarily requires another person as buyer; prostitution; sell one's artwork; sell ideas.	Businesses; sell blood; sell ideals to attain political goals.	Sell wheat; sell weapons; sell land.
Use up: consumption is equivalent to disposal.	Eat food; drive car using up the fuel; shoot ammo; spend one's time; burn wood.	Use employee's time and energy; use someone else's money; use the neighbor's gas.	Use natural fuels or electricity; use a nation's productive capacity; use people as soldiers in wars.
Throw away: discard in a socially acceptable manner.	Put things in the trash; flush the toilet; use a garbage disposal; discard an idea.	Neighborhood cleanup; divorce; end a relationship; resign or retire from a job.	Dump garbage in the oceans; bury nuclear waste.
Abandon: discard in a socially unacceptable manner.	Abandon car on the roadside; abandon morals; abandon an unhealthy, unhappy lifestyle.	Abandon one's child or family; abandon a pet on someone's doorstep; abandon another's trust.	Abandon Vietnam; abandon the Shah of Iran; abandon old satellites in space; abandon the poor.
Destroy: physically damage with intent.	Tear up personal mail; commit suicide; burn house down; shred old pictures.	Raze a building; murder; euthanasia; cremation; abort a child; commit arson.	Conduct war; genocide; execute prisoners; carry out a revolution; burn a flag.

Exhibit 11.11

Disposition Options

Disposition often means throwing things away; however, there are many additional ways of disposing of an offering (e.g., give away, trade, recycle). In addition, disposition can involve one person (personal focus), two or more people (interpersonal focus), or society in general (societal focus).

Physical detachment Physically disposing of an item.

Emotional detachment Emotionally disposing of a possession.

Source: Melissa Martin Young and Melanie Wallendorf, "Ashes to Ashes, Dust to Dust: Conceptualizing Consumer Disposition of Possessions," in Proceedings, Marketing Educators' Conference (Chicago, American Marketing Association, 1989), pp. 33–39. Reprinted by permission.

We most often think of disposition in terms of **physical detachment,** the process by which the item is physically transferred to another person or location. However, **emotional detachment** is a more detailed, lengthy, and sometimes painful process. Often, consumers remain emotionally attached to possessions long after they have become physically detached. For example, it may take a person years to come to grips with selling a valued house or car. Giving up a baby or pet for adoption is an example of difficult emotional detachment that sometimes results in grief and mourning. In fact, some pack rats have a difficult time disposing of even minimally valued possessions—as evidenced by overflowing basements, closets, and garages. Even when an item can be traded in for a discount on a new replacement, emotional attachment enhances the value consumers perceive in the old item, complicating the disposition and purchase decision.[139]

The disposition process can be particularly important during periods of role transition, such as puberty, graduation, and marriage.[140] In these instances consumers dispose of possessions that are symbols of old roles. Upon getting married, for example, many people dispose of items that signify old relationships, such as pictures, jewelry, and gifts. The disposition of shared possessions is a critical process during divorce. Two types of such disposition have been identified: *disposition to break free*, in which the goal is to free oneself from the former relationship, and *disposition to hold on*, in which the intent is to cling to possessions with the hope that the relationship can be repaired.[141] Consumers also specify how their possessions will be distributed upon their death. This can include giving away valued items to important family members, other individuals, and organizations such as charities and schools as well as distributing monetary wealth through a will.

MARKETING IMPLICATIONS

Marketers need to understand disposition for several reasons. First, disposition decisions often influence later acquisition decisions. Thus, someone who must buy a new refrigerator because the old one stopped working may decide that the old one did not last long enough and may eliminate this brand from future consideration. By understanding why consumers dispose of older brands, particularly when a problem has occurred, marketers may be able to improve their offerings for the future.

Second, marketers have become interested in the way that consumers trade, sell, or give away items for secondhand purchases through used-merchandise retail outlets and websites, flea markets, garage sales, and classified ads in newspapers and online. Flea markets are popular, not only because they are a different way of disposing of and acquiring products but also because of the hedonistic experience they provide.[142] Consumers enjoy searching and bargaining for items, the festive atmosphere—almost like a medieval fair—and the social opportunities. This enjoyment is also true of consumers who use sites such as eBay and Craigslist to search for and buy goods.

Third, product disposition behaviors can sometimes have a major impact on society in general. For example, if product life can be extended by getting consumers to trade or resell items, waste and resource depletion could be reduced. Fourth, by examining broad disposition patterns, marketers can gain important insights. For example, one study examined household garbage to identify group differences in food consumption.[143] Researchers found that the region of the country accounted most strongly for differences in consumption patterns, followed by cultural status. For instance, people consume more beans in the southwestern United States because Mexican food is more popular in that region.

Recycling

Because of concerns about conserving natural resources, studying disposition behaviors can provide valuable insights for the development of recycling programs (see Exhibit 11.13). In light of this fact, a number of researchers have been interested in examining factors that relate to recycling.[144] For instance, studies show that attitudes toward recycling influence waste recycling and recycling shopping behaviors.[145] The most useful variables in understanding consumer recycling are motivation, ability, and opportunity to recycle.

Motivation to Recycle

Consumers are more likely to recycle when they perceive that the benefits outweigh the costs, including money, time, and effort.[146] Immediate benefits or goals include avoiding filling up landfills, reducing waste, reusing materials, and saving the environment. Higher-order goals are to promote health and avoid sickness, achieve life-sustaining ends, and provide for future generations.[147] These benefits are likely to vary across segments. For example, focusing on environmental effects may have little meaning in neighborhoods where violence is a major problem.[148] Also, consumers who perceive that their efforts will have an impact are more motivated to recycle than consumers who do not.[149] Having a clean, convenient place to bring recyclable materials improves consumer motivation as well.

Ability to Recycle

Consumers who know how to recycle are more likely to do so than those who do not.[150] One study of German consumers found that a lack of knowledge led to incorrect disposal and therefore less recycling.[151] Consumers must also possess general knowledge about the positive environmental effects of recycling and must remember to recycle as part of their daily routine.

Exhibit 11.13

What Do U.S. Consumers Recycle?

Car batteries are by far the most recycled products in the United States.

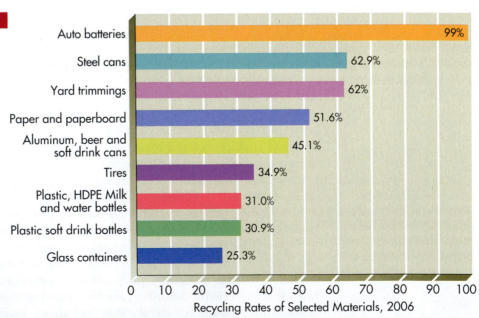

Material	Recycling Rate
Auto batteries	99%
Steel cans	62.9%
Yard trimmings	62%
Paper and paperboard	51.6%
Aluminum, beer and soft drink cans	45.1%
Tires	34.9%
Plastic, HDPE Milk and water bottles	31.0%
Plastic soft drink bottles	30.9%
Glass containers	25.3%

Recycling Rates of Selected Materials, 2006

Source: U.S. Environmental Protection Agency, *www.epa.gov/epaoswer/non-hw/muncpl/facts.htm*

Opportunity to Recycle

If separating, storing, and removing recyclable materials is difficult or inconvenient, consumers will usually avoid doing so. A program in Germany that offered color-coded, large plastic containers on wheels for recyclable materials was quite successful. In addition, consumers must break old waste disposal habits and develop new recycling behaviors. Providing easy-to-use containers also helps consumers in this regard. Also, consumers who buy products such as soft drinks for consumption on the go have fewer opportunities to recycle the empty bottles and cans.[152]

MARKETING IMPLICATIONS

Marketers can facilitate recycling by increasing consumers' MAO to recycle. Special incentives such as contests can increase motivation. Communications that focus on the negative consequences of not recycling and that are conveyed in person are especially effective in increasing motivation.[153] The only drawback is that these techniques must be reintroduced periodically because their effects are usually temporary.

Marketers can increase consumers' ability to recycle by teaching them how to recycle through personally relevant and easy-to-remember communications from community or block leaders, flyers, or public service announcements. Also, offering tags to place on the refrigerator door can remind consumers to recycle.[154] Providing separate containers so that recyclable items can easily be put out and collected along with the trash can increase the opportunity to recycle. Offering easily recycled products is another way to increase the opportunity to recycle. Finally, making products and packaging as environmentally friendly as possible—and promoting the benefits of doing so—can help marketers attract consumers who like the convenience of *not* having to recycle.

Summary

Consumers sometimes develop post-decision dissonance—a feeling of anxiety or uncertainty regarding a purchasing decision after it has been made. On occasion, they may feel regret when they perceive an unfavorable comparison between the performance of the chosen option and the performance of the unchosen options. These feelings of regret can directly influence the consumer's intention to buy the same product in the future. Consumers can learn from experience through hypothesis testing, in which they try to confirm or disprove expectations by actually engaging in acquisition, consumption, or disposition of a product. This process is influenced by motivation, prior knowledge (familiarity), ambiguity of information, and two types of biases: the confirmation bias and overconfidence.

Satisfaction is both a subjective feeling and an objective evaluation that a decision has fulfilled a need or goal. Dissatisfaction occurs when consumers have negative feelings and believe that their goals or needs have not been fulfilled. Thought-based judgments of satisfaction/dissatisfaction can relate to (1) whether consumers' thoughts and expectations about the offering are confirmed or disconfirmed by its performance (the disconfirmation paradigm), (2) thoughts about causality and blame (attribution theory), and (3) thoughts about fairness and equity (equity theory). Consumers also judge satisfaction and dissatisfaction on the basis of feelings, specifically (1) experienced emotions (and coping with these emotions) and (2) mispredictions about emotions.

Consumers can respond to dissatisfaction by complaining, reacting to service recovery, and engaging in negative word of mouth. Finally, consumers can dispose of products in various ways, actions that have important implications for marketing strategy and for an understanding of consumer behavior. Recycling, one form of disposition, depends on consumers' motivation, ability, and opportunity to act.

Questions for Review and Discussion

1. How does post-decision dissonance differ from post-decision regret, and what effect do these have on consumers?

2. Describe how consumers acquire information about goods and services by learning from their experiences with the commodities.

3. How do expectations and performance contribute to disconfirmation?

4. Define *attribution theory* and *equity theory,* and explain how they relate to dissatisfaction.

5. Why is complaining important to marketers, and how should complaints be handled?

6. What influence can experienced emotions and mispredictions about emotions have on consumer satisfaction or dissatisfaction?

7. In what eight ways can consumers dispose of something?

8. Why is it important for marketers to consider both physical and emotional detachment aspects of consumer disposition?

CL Visit http://cengage.com/marketing/hoyer/ ConsumerBehavior5e to find resources that are available to help you study for the course.

Service Recovery Helps JetBlue Fly Higher

JetBlue Airways knows that every flight represents another opportunity to satisfy passengers and to win or reinforce their loyalty. Based at New York's JFK Airport, JetBlue sent its first jet taxiing down the runway in 2000 and now flies to dozens of U.S. cities plus vacation spots in the Caribbean. The airline prides itself on its low fares and friendly service with extras that many low-cost carriers do not offer. Its jets feature roomy leather seats, satellite TV and satellite radio for everyone, and free Dunkin' Donuts coffee on all flights.

It's small wonder that loyal customers have voted JetBlue to the top of many industry surveys and choose to fly the airline whenever they can. Nor has JetBlue been shy about trumpeting its awards and raising customers' expectations for a superior travel experience from start to finish. Delivering on its service promises has helped JetBlue increase its annual revenues to nearly $3 billion.

But what happens when JetBlue customers arrive at the airport expecting an easy flight and instead find themselves sleeping in the terminal or trapped on a parked jet? This service nightmare started when an ice storm struck New York on Valentine's Day in 2007. Believing that the storm would soon pass and that some flights would then be able to take off, JetBlue allowed

passengers to board nine planes, sealed the doors, and sent the jets out toward the runway. As the storm continued to pound the airport, JetBlue kept the jets parked near the runway. The storm raged on, food and water ran out, the bathrooms got dirty, but the jets stayed put for as long as nine hours, until JetBlue brought them back to the terminal and let the angry passengers off.

That day, JetBlue canceled more than 250 flights and stranded thousands of passengers in its JFK terminal. The next day was not much better because JetBlue could not get enough planes and crew members to New York quickly enough to fly the stranded passengers to their destinations. Nor could planes stuck in New York get out to the other cities served by JetBlue, a predicament that disrupted the airline's entire schedule. Two days after the storm, the airline had to halt service to 11 cities and cancel 23 percent of its flights while it moved planes and people into position. In all, more than 1,000 flights were canceled in a five-day period, leaving JetBlue customers outraged and frustrated.

However, even as this service nightmare was making headlines across the country, the airline's top executives were taking steps to unravel the mess, prevent a recurrence, and address the firestorm of customer dissatisfaction. "This is going to be a different company because of this," vowed the CEO. "It's going to be expensive. But what's more important is to win back people's confidence." Within days, JetBlue announced its Customer Bill of Rights, which provides refunds or vouchers for customers whose flights have been canceled or delayed and pledges to get passengers off planes if they've been waiting to take off for more than five hours.

In all, JetBlue paid out $40 million in vouchers and refunds to customers affected by the storm. However, the bigger challenge was to repair its tarnished reputation. Just weeks after the storm, *BusinessWeek* magazine removed JetBlue from its 2007 listing of Customer Service Champs; before the crisis, the airline would have been number 4. JetBlue kept promoting its Customer Bill of Rights, added more customer-service representatives, trained its workforce to deal more effectively with delays, and redoubled its efforts to satisfy every customer on every flight. These service recovery steps are paying off: JetBlue's revenues have been growing, and it captured the number 7 spot on *BusinessWeek's* listing of Customer Service Champs in 2008.[155]

Case Questions

1. Use the disconfirmation paradigm to explain why you think that JetBlue should or should not be raising customer expectations by promoting its service as competitively superior.
2. How was the speedy implementation of a Customer Bill of Rights likely to affect the post-decision feelings of customers holding JetBlue tickets for future flights?
3. Were JetBlue customers affected by the storm likely to feel dissonance or regret? Why?
4. Could JetBlue have done anything differently to make customers happier?

The Consumer's Culture

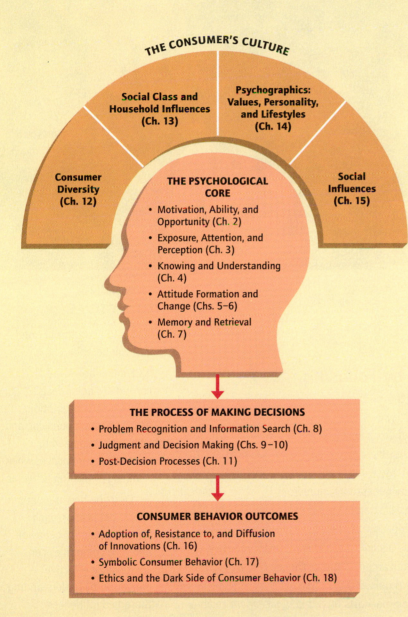

THE CONSUMER'S CULTURE

Social Class and Household Influences (Ch. 13)

Psychographics: Values, Personality, and Lifestyles (Ch. 14)

Consumer Diversity (Ch. 12)

Social Influences (Ch. 15)

THE PSYCHOLOGICAL CORE
- Motivation, Ability, and Opportunity (Ch. 2)
- Exposure, Attention, and Perception (Ch. 3)
- Knowing and Understanding (Ch. 4)
- Attitude Formation and Change (Chs. 5–6)
- Memory and Retrieval (Ch. 7)

THE PROCESS OF MAKING DECISIONS
- Problem Recognition and Information Search (Ch. 8)
- Judgment and Decision Making (Chs. 9–10)
- Post-Decision Processes (Ch. 11)

CONSUMER BEHAVIOR OUTCOMES
- Adoption of, Resistance to, and Diffusion of Innovations (Ch. 16)
- Symbolic Consumer Behavior (Ch. 17)
- Ethics and the Dark Side of Consumer Behavior (Ch. 18)

Part Four reflects a "macro" view of consumer behavior, examining how various aspects of the consumer's culture affect behavior. Chapter 12 focuses on diversity, specifically on the roles that age, gender, sexual orientation, and regional, ethnic, and religious influences play in consumer behavior. Chapter 13 explores how social class is determined in various cultures and how, in turn, it affects consumer decisions and behaviors. The chapter also looks at various types of households and families and how household members influence acquisition and consumption decisions.

The combination of diversity, social class, and household influences can affect our values, personality, and lifestyle, the topics covered in Chapter 14. Moreover, as Chapter 15 explains, our behavior and decisions can be influenced by certain individuals, specific groups (such as friends, coworkers, club members) and various media. All of these factors influence consumer behavior and therefore have many implications for marketers.

Chapter 12

Consumer Diversity

LEARNING OBJECTIVES

After studying this chapter you will be able to

1. Explain how the consumer's age affects acquisition, consumption, and disposition behavior, and why marketers need to consider age influences when planning marketing activities.

2. Describe how gender and sexual orientation each affects consumer behavior and how companies can create more effective marketing by understanding these two influences.

3. Discuss how regional, ethnic, and religious influences can affect consumer behavior and why marketers must consider such influences when targeting specific groups.

INTRODUCTION

Connecting with Customers by Focusing on Quinceañera Celebrations

Marketers like the Disneyland Resort, Royal Caribbean Cruises, and Hallmark are connecting with Hispanic American consumers by focusing on the *quinceañera,* the traditional Hispanic celebration of a girl's coming of age when she turns 15. Even though their families have been in the United States for many generations, numerous Hispanic Americans continue the custom of presenting (introducing as an adult) a young lady of 15 in her Catholic church and then at a party for family and friends.

Marketing *quinceañera*-related offerings has become a $400 million U.S. industry, especially strong in regions with large Hispanic American populations. *Quince Girl,* a magazine founded in 2005, carries articles and ads to help girls and their parents plan this special celebration. California's Disneyland Resort, for example, hosts three big *quinceañera* celebrations every month, priced at $7,500 and up. Royal Caribbean Cruises partners with travel agencies to customize *quinceañera* cruises for as many as 1,200 people per party. Mattel sells a special *Quinceañera* Barbie, and Hallmark sells *quinceañera* greeting cards. However, even as some Hispanic American teens are looking forward to their *quinceañera,* others are adopting U.S. customs by choosing a "Sweet 16" party or getting a car rather than celebrating with a party for their fifteenth birthday.[1]

This example illustrates several diversity influences that affect consumer behavior, all of which are discussed in this chapter (see Exhibit 12.1). First, age and gender can be factors in acquisition and consumption: A *quinceañera* triggers many purchases and results in the consumption of a variety of offerings. Second, the region in which consumers reside—within the United States or elsewhere in the world—can influence their behavior. Finally, consumer behavior can vary among subgroups of individuals with unique patterns of ethnicity and religion because of their different traditions, customs, and preferences. For instance, *quinceañera* cakes favored by families with roots in Mexico may differ from those of families with roots in Chile or Nicaragua. Clearly, to develop and implement effective marketing strategies and tactics, companies must understand how these diversity influences affect consumers.

How Age Affects Consumer Behavior

Marketers often segment consumers by age. The basic logic is that people of the same age are going through similar life experiences and therefore share many common needs, experiences, symbols, and memories, which, in turn, may lead to similar consumption patterns.[2] Regardless of country, age groups are constantly shifting as babies are born, children grow up, adults mature, and people die. This section opens with an overview of U.S. age trends and continues with an examination of four major age groups being targeted by marketers: (1) teens and Generation Y, also called the "millenniums"; (2) Generation X; (3) boomers; and (4) seniors.

Age Trends in the United States

The median age of U.S. consumers, which was 30 years in 1980, is currently 36.4 years, reflecting a huge bulge in the 40- to 60-year-old population. Adults aged 18 and over now make up 75 percent of the overall U.S. population (see Exhibit 12.2). Thanks in part to better medical care and healthier lifestyles, people are living longer, making the senior market an attractive target for marketers. The number of adults aged 20 to 34 (spanning Generations X and Y) had been declining, but that trend is turning around, opening new opportunities for marketers to build and sustain brand loyalty during these critical household formation years.[3]

Teens and Generation Y

Your own experience may confirm that this segment has considerable influence in household purchases and enjoys a good deal of financial independence. Given the high number of two-career families and single parents, teens often shop for themselves and are responsible for more decisions than previous generations were.[4] They tend to do more shopping on weekends, and females shop more than males do.[5] Friends are a major source of information about products, and socializing is one of the major reasons that teens like to shop. Many teens and Gen Yers discuss

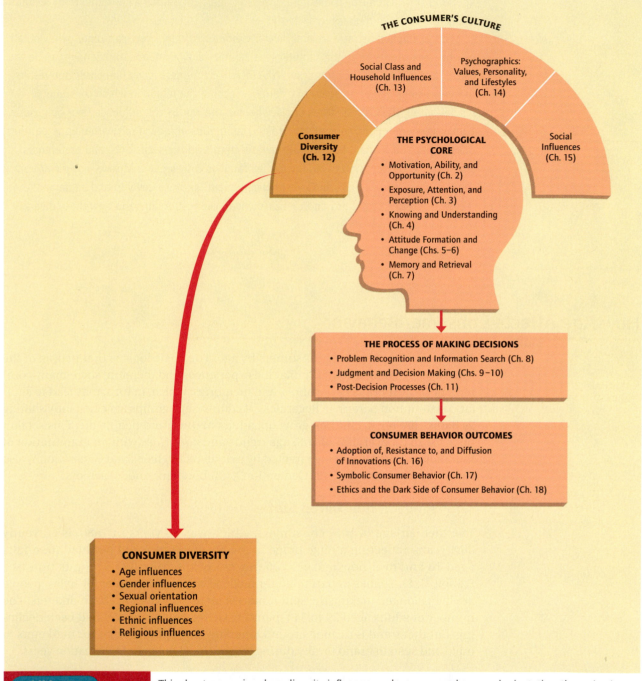

THE CONSUMER'S CULTURE

Social Class and
Household Influences
(Ch. 13)

Psychographics:
Values, Personality,
and Lifestyles
(Ch. 14)

**Consumer
Diversity
(Ch. 12)**

**THE PSYCHOLOGICAL
CORE**
- Motivation, Ability, and
  Opportunity (Ch. 2)
- Exposure, Attention, and
  Perception (Ch. 3)
- Knowing and Understanding
  (Ch. 4)
- Attitude Formation and
  Change (Chs. 5–6)
- Memory and Retrieval
  (Ch. 7)

Social
Influences
(Ch. 15)

THE PROCESS OF MAKING DECISIONS
- Problem Recognition and Information Search (Ch. 8)
- Judgment and Decision Making (Chs. 9–10)
- Post-Decision Processes (Ch. 11)

CONSUMER BEHAVIOR OUTCOMES
- Adoption of, Resistance to, and Diffusion
  of Innovations (Ch. 16)
- Symbolic Consumer Behavior (Ch. 17)
- Ethics and the Dark Side of Consumer Behavior (Ch. 18)

CONSUMER DIVERSITY
- Age influences
- Gender influences
- Sexual orientation
- Regional influences
- Ethnic influences
- Religious influences

Exhibit 12.1

**Chapter Overview:
Consumer Diversity**

This chapter examines how diversity influences such as age, gender, sexual orientation, the region in
which one lives, ethnic groups, and religion can affect consumer behavior.

brands in text messages, instant messages, blogs, social networking, and online
reviews.[6] Having grown up with recycling, many in this segment consider a product's environmental impact before buying.

A common teen "culture" is spreading around the world, although marketers
must take care not to overlook localized culture and its effects on teen consumer
behavior.[7] A study of teens in 44 countries reveals common characteristics and
attitudes that cross national boundaries in six distinct segments.[8] The "Thrills and

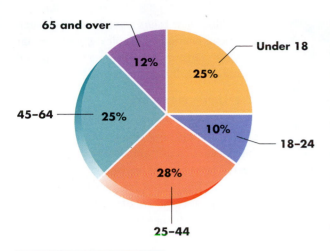

Exhibit 12.2

The U.S. Population by Age

Consumers up to the age of 18 comprise 25 percent of the U.S. population; by comparison, consumers aged 65 and older comprise just 12 percent of the population.

Generation Y Mini population explosion from the children of baby boomers.

Chills" segment, including teens in the United States, Germany, and other countries, consists of fun-seeking, free-spending consumers from middle-class or upper-class backgrounds. Teens in the "Resigned" segment, covering Denmark, Korea, and other countries, are alienated from society and have low expectations of the future and of material success. High-aspiration teen "World Savers" in Hungary, Venezuela, and several other countries are characterized by their altruism and good grades. Ambitious teen "Quiet Achievers" in Thailand, China, and other nations conform to societal norms. "Bootstrappers" in Nigeria, Mexico, the United States, and other countries are family-oriented achievement seekers with hopes and dreams for the future. Finally, dutiful and conforming "Upholders" in Vietnam, Indonesia, and other nations seek a rewarding family life and uphold traditional values.

Teens as well as consumers born during the years 1979 through 1994 are part of **Generation Y.** Generation Y is media and tech savvy, using PCs, the Internet, cell phones, DVD players, and many other high-tech products to communicate, play games, do homework, and shop.[9] Among consumers under 24 years old, for example, the market for cell phones tops $16 billion annually; many in their twenties have no phone other than a cell phone.[10] Approximately 4 million U.S. consumers reach the age of 21 every year, making them eligible for adult offerings such as liquor that are off-limits to younger consumers.[11]

MARKETING IMPLICATIONS

The number of U.S. teens is expected to reach 30 million by 2015.[12] (See Exhibit 12.3.) Their personal purchasing power is a substantial $108 billion, not counting $47 billion more in family purchases.[13] Around the world, the similarity of teens' tastes, attitudes, and preferences for music, movies, clothing, and video games is partly due to popular entertainment and partly due to the Internet. Nonetheless, teens in different regions exhibit some differences, a phenomenon that marketers must research before addressing local tastes and behaviors.[14]

Brand loyalty

The fact that initial purchases of many offerings are made during the teenage years is also important since brand loyalties established at this time may carry into adulthood. For example, 50 percent of female teens have developed cosmetic brand loyalties by the age of 15.[15] McDonald's reinforced brand loyalty among teens and twenty-something consumers worldwide before the summer Olympic games in Beijing through an online multiplayer game called *The Lost Ring*. "Our goal is really about strengthening our bond with the global youth culture," explained the company's global chief marketing officer.[16]

Positioning

Some marketers position their products as helpful for dealing with the adolescent pressures of establishing an identity, rebelling, and being accepted by peers. In the United Kingdom and in Asia, credit and debit card companies are targeting teens under age 16 because they are more likely than their parents to use their cards and buy online.[17] As you know, teens can also be trendsetters, particularly in areas such as fashion and music; this is the reason why companies such as Coca-Cola and Pepsi are constantly researching what teens want.[18] However, teen tastes can change very quickly, and popular products or stores may become overexposed and can quickly lose their cachet.[19]

Advertising messages

Effective advertising often incorporates symbols, issues, and language to which teens can relate. Because music and sports tend to be the universal languages of teenagers, popular music and sports figures are frequently featured in ads. However, teens are often wary of blatant attempts to influence them.[20] Thus, messages need to talk *to* teens, not at them. Furthermore, because they have grown up with videos and computers, today's teens seem to process information faster than older consumers do.[21] As a result, they prefer short, snappy phrases to long-winded explanations. For example, an antismoking ad campaign used the tagline "Tobacco: tumor-causing, teeth-staining, smelly puking habit."[22] Using slang can sometimes be dangerous, however, because if a phrase is out-of-date by the time that the ad appears, the offering will look "uncool." Also, many teenagers are less concerned about advertising than they are about price.

Media

Marketers can target Generation Y through certain TV networks, TV programs, magazines, radio stations, and the Internet.[23] Marketers of sports-related products can reach teens through special-interest magazines, TV shows, and websites devoted to snowboarding and other sports.[24] However, teens tend not to be loyal to individual sites unless there is a specific appeal. This tendency explains why Nike and Alloy post new videos and interactive features to draw teens back to their websites again and again.[25]

Other marketing activities

Some marketers reach teens through recreation or special events. Heeling Sports, which makes sneakers with retractable wheels, sends teen product ambassadors to perform at amusement parks, malls, skate parks, and college campuses. It also has its teams post videos on YouTube to generate buzz.[26] In addition, marketers are rethinking their distribution strategies to get their products into stores where teens and Generation Y consumers shop. For example, Viacom's Simon Spotlight Entertainment division decided to sell teen-oriented books through the clothing chain Urban Outfitters.[27]

Exhibit 12.3

Targeting Teens (or Generation Y)

This ad for Honda Civic targets Generation Y by highlighting the music group Panic at the Disco (popular with this segment).

Generation X

Generation X Individuals born between 1965 and 1976.

Individuals born from 1965 to 1976 are often called **Generation X.** Within this diverse group of 49 million, some underachievers at 30 or beyond still hang on to their Generation X "angst," while older members of this group are building careers, having families, and buying homes.[28] Nonetheless, Xers who believe that they may not be able to match or surpass their parents' level of success may feel a bit disillusioned and less materialistic than other age groups. In fact, compared with consumers who were 30 to 40 years old a decade ago, fewer Xers own their own homes today.[29] Nevertheless, they tend to find success and achievement in being at the cutting edge of technology and try to balance their work and personal lives.

Some Xers are boomerang kids, returning home to live after college or not moving out until they are well into their thirties to save money.[30] Because parents pay for many essentials, boomerang kids have more discretionary income to spend on entertainment and are more likely to buy items like a new car or electronics than are Xers who must pay utility bills and other housing costs. Boomerangers feel less pressure to settle down than earlier generations did and often delay marriage. This trend has led to closer relationships with parents, who are often seen as friends or roommates. Boomerangers also influence family decisions to remodel or expand the house, creating opportunities for construction firms, furniture manufacturers, and other marketers.[31]

MARKETING IMPLICATIONS

The Generation X market represents more than $120 billion in spending power. This group takes the time to research a purchase and likes to customize offerings to their personal needs and tastes.[32] It is a key segment for music, movies, budget travel, beer and alcohol, fast food, clothing, athletic shoes, and cosmetics.[33] Xers are also important targets for marketers of electronic gadgets, online services, and other tech-related offerings.

Advertising messages

Born and bred on TV, Xers tend to be cynical about obvious marketing techniques.[34] They sometimes find objectionable ads that contain exaggerated claims, stereotypes, unpopular products like cigarettes and alcohol, and sexually explicit, political, religious, or social messages. However, Xers do react positively to messages they see as clever or in tune with their values, attitudes, and interests. For example, Toyota uses hip-hop and heavy metal songs in car commercials targeting Xers.[35] (See also Exhibit 12.4.)

Media

Marketers can reach Xers through media vehicles such as popular or alternative music radio stations and network or cable TV, although this group watches less TV than other groups do.[36] Ads in music-related publications and messages displayed at concerts, sporting events, and popular vacation spots can also be effective. Thus, Mountain Dew, among other companies, sponsors extreme sporting events and teams to reach Xers through special interests.[37] Increasingly, marketers are using the Internet to reach these Web-savvy consumers.[38]

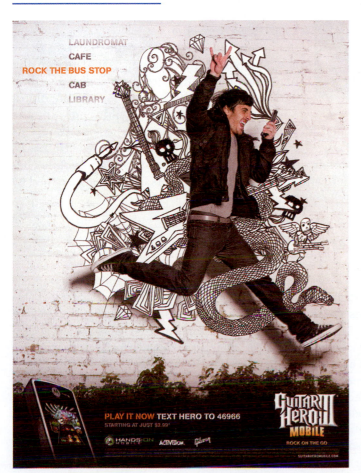

Be a leader. Give back, create change, and build a better future. Each of us can make a difference. www.paulmitchell.com Only in salons and Paul Mitchell schools. Printed on post-consumer recycled paper.

Exhibit 12.5

Targeting Boomers

Marketers often try to target and appeal to the values of baby boomers since they comprise a large segment that has great economic power. This ad for Paul Mitchell is a good example.

Baby boomers Individuals born between 1946 and 1964.

To promote its car insurance, State Farm has run fast-paced ads on Rollingstone.com and other sites that target Xers.[39]

Boomers

The 78 million **baby boomers** born between 1946 and 1964 make up the largest demographic group in the United States. Because of their numbers and the fact that many are in their peak earning years, boomers have a lot of buying power and are an influential consumer segment. Although boomers are a diverse group, they share many common experiences of the 1960s and 1970s, when they grew up. Boomers strongly value individualism and want the freedom to do what they want, when and where they want.[40] Most boomers grew up with TV and as they get older, tend to watch it more. They also spend more time browsing the Internet than other groups do.[41]

Some researchers have identified five subgroups of boomers based on five-year divisions (1946–1951, 1951–1956, and so on). Others suggest three subsegments: leading boomers (born 1946–1950), core boomers (1951–1959), and trailing boomers (1960–1964). Consumers in these subgroups have life experiences in common and may share more attributes with each other than with other segments.[42] If this is true, the oldest and youngest subgroups would tend to be the most different—especially since the oldest are now seniors. Research suggests that boomers around the world, like teens around the world, share certain attitudes and values (see Exhibit 12.5). For example, a majority of U.K. boomers believe that life today is more stressful than it was 50 years ago—a view echoed by most boomers in Mexico, France, and Hong Kong.[43]

MARKETING IMPLICATIONS

Because baby boomers have so much buying power, they are the target for many products and services, including cars, housing, travel, entertainment, recreational equipment, and motor homes.[44] Harley-Davidson has profited by producing heavyweight motorcycles—priced at $17,000 or more—for this segment.[45] Boomers are heavy consumers of financial services as they look toward retirement and simultaneously pay for their children's college educations.[46] Time-pressured boomers still like fast food, but many are buying gourmet sandwiches from Panera and other restaurant chains as a healthier and more varied alternative to burgers and fries.[47]

Some firms are developing offerings specifically for the needs of baby boomers. For example, apparel marketers have created jeans in larger sizes and different styles to accommodate the middle-aged physique.[48] The Chico's chain has grown to more than 450 stores by specializing in loose-fitting casual clothing for baby-boom women.[49]

Personal care products, fitness goods and services, cosmetic surgery, and similar offerings are especially attractive to boomers who are sensitive to the idea of aging.[50] For example, Procter & Gamble has been successful with anti-aging Olay facial creams and cleansers for boomer women.[51]

Seniors

Gray market Individuals over 65.

In the **gray market** of consumers over 65, women outnumber men because women tend to live longer.[52] Because information-processing skills tend to deteriorate with age, seniors are less likely to search for information and more likely to have difficulty remembering information and making more complex decisions.[53] Thus, they tend to engage in simpler, more schematic processing.[54] Furthermore, poor recognition memory makes some seniors susceptible to the "truth effect" (believing that often-repeated statements are true—see Chapter 6).[55] As a result, they may need help or education when making decisions.[56]

Exhibit 12.6

Targeting Seniors
Today's seniors think younger than those of previous generations. This ad targets seniors by stressing this value.

MARKETING IMPLICATIONS

Seniors represent a critical and growing market for health-related products and services and for retirement communities (particularly in warmer states).[57] In general, seniors tend to be brand-loyal, tend to know more about brands from long-standing experience, may not search extensively when planning high-ticket purchases, and have less motivation and cognitive capacity to deal with new, unfamiliar brands.[58]

Marketing communications

Marketers can target boomers through the use of media geared to this group's interests, including oldies rock 'n' roll radio and TV programs, activity-specific publications and TV shows, and lifestyle-related events such as home shows and sporting events.[59] Seniors perceive ads with positive older role models as more credible than those with younger models.[60] However, because of America's youth culture, seniors are less likely to appear in ads—or to be depicted positively—although this situation has been changing over time.[61] Therefore, ads should show seniors as active, contributing members of society (see Exhibit 12.6), and messages should focus on only a few key attributes. Also, older consumers like and can better recall messages that focus on avoiding negative emotions, possibly because they want to avoid the negative outcomes that are associated with age.[62]

Specialized sales techniques and promotions

Retailers can design their outlets to provide a more age-friendly shopping environment for boomers and seniors, with features such as wider aisles and well-lit aisles and parking lots.[63] Seniors value service, a factor that explains why the Chico's retail chain

You're never too young to start thinking about not acting your age.

Have a retirement vision—even if it's to act like a kid again. As a Fortune 500® company with over $70 billion in assets under management,* we can help you plan for what's ahead. How will you thrive in retirement? Tell us at thrivent.com/retirement.

Let's thrive. Thrivent Financial *for Lutherans*

offers personalized assistance.[64] Marketers in many product and service categories offer senior citizen discounts to attract and retain customers in this segment.[65] However, because older consumers who seek social interaction from telemarketing calls may not recognize fraudulent offers, education and protection are needed to help this segment avoid being victimized by scams (as discussed in the online chapter).[66]

How Gender and Sexual Orientation Affect Consumer Behavior

Clearly males and females can differ in traits, attitudes, and activities that can affect consumer behavior. The following sections discuss a few key issues that have been the focus of consumer research because complete coverage of the contrasts between men and women is beyond the scope of this text. Remember that these sections describe only general tendencies, which are subject to considerable individual variation.

Sex Roles

In most cultures, men and women are expected to behave according to sex-role norms learned very early in childhood. Until recently, males in Western society were expected to be strong, assertive, and emotionless. They were the primary breadwinners and were guided by **agentic goals** that stress mastery, self-assertiveness, and self-efficacy.[67] Women, on the other hand, have been guided more by **communal goals** of forming affiliations and fostering harmonious relations with others and have been expected to be relatively submissive, emotional, and home oriented.

On a very general level, men tend to be more competitive, independent, externally motivated, and willing to take risks.[68] Expressing "man-of-action" masculinity may take the form of hypercompetitive breadwinner behavior or a rebel approach (including entrepreneurial breadwinner behavior).[69] In contrast, women tend to be cooperative, interdependent, intrinsically motivated, and risk averse. Over time, however, female and male roles have been evolving. In particular, more U.S. women are delaying marriage and childbearing in favor of building a career. This trend has led to higher standards of living for women and to changes in women's attitudes, particularly an emphasis on independence.[70] More women are vacationing alone and rejecting traditional roles related to submissiveness, homemaking, and sexual inhibition.

Traditional sex roles are changing in many countries, even those that are very conservative and male dominated. For example, in India, where arranged marriages are still the norm, women's attitudes toward careers, marriage, and the family are undergoing radical changes as more women build careers—especially in high-tech firms—and seek independence.[71] However, sex roles and appropriate behavior may vary from one culture to another. In the United States, for example, some men feel uncomfortable hugging each other, whereas this behavior is widely accepted in European and Latin societies, often as a greeting. Sex roles in ads can provoke differing responses as well: For example, women in the Czech Republic react less favorably to ads in which female models are depicted in roles that seem superior to those of male models.[72]

Gender and Sexual Orientation

Gender refers to a biological state (male or female), whereas **sexual orientation** reflects a person's preference toward certain behaviors. *Masculine* individuals

---

Agentic goals Goals that stress mastery, self-assertiveness, self-efficacy, strength, and no emotion.

Communal goals Goals that stress affiliation and fostering harmonious relations with others, submissiveness, emotionality, and home orientation.

Gender Biological state of being male or female.

Sexual orientation A person's preference toward certain behaviors.

The perfect trip starts at southwest.com/gaytravel

Southwest Airlines® is proud to offer a section of our web site dedicated to the gay and lesbian community. At southwest.com/gaytravel, you'll find helpful information on gay-friendly destinations, special deals, and events around the country along with travel tips to fabulous places. Whether it's business or pleasure, Southwest is taking freedom to new heights.

SOUTHWEST
southwest.com/gaytravel

Exhibit 12.7

Targeting Gay and Lesbian Consumers

Companies are increasingly targeting gay and lesbian consumers. A good example is this ad for Southwest Airlines.

(whether male or female) tend to display male-oriented traits, and *feminine* individuals tend toward female characteristics. In addition, some individuals can be *androgynous,* having both male and female traits. Sexual orientations are important because they can influence consumer preferences and behavior. For example, women who are more masculine tend to prefer ads that depict nontraditional women.[73]

An increasing number of marketers are using sexual orientation to target gay and lesbian consumers for a wide range of offerings (Exhibit 12.7). In part, this strategy is due to a dramatic rise in the number of same-sex U.S. households. According to Census Bureau statistics, the United States has more than 601,000 same-sex households (304,000 gay male couples and 297,000 lesbian couples), primarily in large metropolitan areas such as San Francisco and New York City.[74] Although gay and lesbian consumers tend to dislike and distrust ad messages more than heterosexual consumers do, they are likely to respond to sexual orientation symbols in advertising, such as red AIDS ribbons, and to ads that "reflect their lives and culture."[75] They respond to marketing that they perceive as gay friendly (and condemn apparently antigay marketing activities).[76] For example, ads promoting Philadelphia tourism with the theme "Come to Philadelphia. Get your history straight and your nightlife gay" were well received by gay consumers.[77]

Differences in Acquisition and Consumption Behaviors

Despite sex-role changes, men and women still exhibit a number of differences in their consumption behaviors. Women are more likely to engage in a detailed, thorough examination of a message and to make extended decisions based on product attributes (similar to high MAO decision making), whereas men are selective information processors, driven more by overall themes and simplifying heuristics (similar to low-MAO decision making).[78] Men tend to be more sensitive to personally relevant information (consistent with agentic goals), and women pay attention to both personally relevant information and information relevant to others (consistent with communal goals).[79]

Whereas men are more likely to use specific hemispheres of their brain for certain tasks (the right side of the brain for visual and the left side for verbal), women use both hemispheres of their brain for most tasks. Men also appear to be more sensitive to trends in positive emotions experienced during consumption, such as feeling enthusiastic and strong, whereas women display a tendency for negative emotions, such as feeling scared and nervous.[80] In addition, men and women differ in the symbolic meaning that they attach to products and services.[81] Women are more likely to have shared brand stereotypes for fashion goods, whereas men are more consistent in their images of automobiles.

In general, American women see shopping as a pleasurable, stimulating activity and a way of obtaining social interaction, whereas men see shopping merely as a way of acquiring goods and as a chore, especially if they hold traditional sex-role stereotypes. These patterns also hold true in other countries such as Turkey and the Netherlands. Finally, men and women tend to exhibit different eating patterns. In particular, women are more likely to engage in **compensatory eating**—responding to depression or making up for deficiencies such as a lack of social contact by eating.[82]

Compensatory eating
Making up for depression or lack of social contact by eating.

MARKETING IMPLICATIONS

Obviously, many products (such as clothing for men and feminine hygiene products for women) are geared toward gender-specific needs. In addition, certain offerings may be perceived as being more appropriate for one gender than for the other. A tie or gun may be seen as more masculine, whereas a food processor or hand lotion may be seen as more feminine. However, some products are becoming less sex-typed as sex roles evolve. For example, more than 12 percent of Harley-Davidson's motorcycle sales are to women, and the company is attracting even more women customers with new, low-slung bikes and special riding clinics.[83] Meanwhile, Nivea is successfully marketing skin-care products specially formulated for men.[84]

Targeting a specific gender

Marketers often target a particular gender. In Russia, Damskaya vodka targets 24- to 45-year-old women with a graceful lavender bottle and the ad slogan "Between us girls."[85] Lowe's has renovated its U.S. stores with brighter lighting and more informative displays to attract women do-it-yourselfers. "Women are information gatherers—they want the stores to be inspirational," explains a manager.[86]

Studies show that men and women respond differently to emotional advertising.[87] In line with changing sex roles, men in ads are increasingly shown in emotional and caring roles, whereas women are appearing more frequently in important situations and professional positions. A study of magazine ads found a similar trend in Japan as well.[88] Yet traditional roles have not disappeared: In China, where women are increasingly assertive and independent, men are now drawn to marketing that "suggest[s] or reinforce[s] a feeling of control," says an advertising agency manager.[89] Research shows that ads targeting men for a gender-specific product such as perfume (purchased as a gift) are more effective when a male spokesperson is used. In contrast, ads targeting women who buy perfume for themselves are more effective with a female spokesperson.[90]

Media patterns

Some sex differences still exist in media patterns. Marketers can reach men through certain TV programs, especially sports, and magazines such as *Sports Illustrated, Esquire,* and car and motorcycle publications. To reach female fitness enthusiasts in Malaysia, Nike has sponsored special events with demonstrations of kickboxing, wall climbing, and other sports.[91] Women are more likely than men to watch soap operas and home shopping networks, a tendency that explains why women's personal care products are often advertised in these media.[92] Some companies are launching websites for gender-specific products or a gender-specific audience, such as NikeWomen.com. ●━━

How Regional Influences Affect Consumer Behavior

Because people tend to work and live in the same area, residents in one part of the country can develop patterns of behavior that differ from those in another area. For example, a consumer from New England might enjoy lobster and skiing, whereas someone from Texas may prefer barbecues and rodeos. This section explores how the region in which people live can affect their consumer behavior, both within the United States and in various regions across the world.

Regions Within the United States

Although we can speak of an overall American culture, the United States is a vast country in which various regions have developed distinctive identities based on differing ethnic and cultural histories. For example, California and the Southwest were originally part of Mexico and therefore reflect a Mexican character; the Southwest also has Native American and frontier roots. The eastern seaboard from New England to Georgia reflects the region's roots as the original 13 British colonies. The great expanses of the West and Northwest are reflected in the free-spirited personalities of these regions, and the Deep South from Louisiana to Florida owes some of its character to agriculture as well as to the Confederacy's rebellion during the Civil War. Finally, the Midwest is noted for its farms and agriculture.

These statements represent very broad generalizations. Although each region also has many unique influences and variations that are too numerous to mention, regional differences can affect consumption patterns. Immigration patterns, such as a large number of Mexican-born consumers moving into California and Texas, can add ethnic influences to certain regions as well.[93] For instance, due to a strong Mexican influence, consumers in the Southwest prefer spicy food and dishes such as tortillas and salsa (see Exhibit 12.8). Interestingly, some Tex-Mex

Exhibit 12.8

Regional Influences

Sometimes strong regional influences can spread to other areas. For example, chips and salsa are a popular appetizer in Mexican restaurants in the Southwest. In turn, these restaurants are popular throughout the United States and in other parts of the world.

foods, including nachos and chili dogs, were first developed in the United States and then became popular in Mexico.[94]

Because considerable variation exists in values and lifestyles among consumers within a region, researchers have looked for ways to describe consumers on the basis of more specific characteristics, a technique called *clustering*.

Clustering is based on the principle that "birds of a feather flock together."[95] This notion suggests that consumers in the same neighborhood tend to buy the same types of cars, homes, appliances, and other products or services.[96] Systems such as Mosaic (from Experian) and PRIZM NE (from Claritas) group areas and neighborhoods into more precise clusters based on consumers' similarities on demographic and consumption characteristics. These systems can define a cluster according to similarity of income, education, age, household type, degree of urbanity, attitudes, and product/service preferences, including the type of car owned and preferred radio format.

Clustering The grouping of consumers according to common characteristics using statistical techniques.

For example, PRIZM NE has identified 66 U.S. consumer segments. Here is a sampling:[97]

- *Upper Crust.* This segment consists of wealthy couples who are 45 years old or older, live in suburban areas, and have at least a college education.

- *Urban Achievers.* These are lower-middle-income, city-dwelling single consumers who are under 35 years old and have a high school or college education.

- *Kid Country, USA.* This segment consists of lower-middle-income families living in towns, headed by adults under the age of 45 who have a high school education.

- *Mobility Blues.* These downscale consumers live in smaller cities, are under the age of 35, and have a high school education.

MARKETING IMPLICATIONS

Marketers can develop an offering or communication to appeal to different regions of the United States. McDonald's sells bratwurst in Minnesota, burritos in California, and lobster sandwiches in Maine.[98] Many marketers in Texas infuse their ads with a western flavor, whereas ads directed toward the East Coast may take on a more urban theme. Also, some products are identified with certain regions: Florida orange juice, Hawaiian macadamia nuts, Maine lobsters, and Texas beef are a few examples. Smaller firms catering to local tastes can develop a loyal following in certain regions. Even though Frito-Lay sells more potato chips across America than all of its smaller competitors combined, Utz potato chips are popular in Pennsylvania and Jays potato chips are popular in Chicago.[99]

Marketers can use clustering systems to help find new customers, learn what their customers like, develop new products, buy advertising, locate store sites, and target consumers through media.[100] The Gannett newspaper chain has successfully boosted response levels by using PRIZM to target direct-mail subscription promotions.[101] Retailers can use clustering to identify neighborhoods of consumers most likely to purchase certain merchandise. Petco, which sells pet products, uses clustering to pinpoint neighborhoods where home ownership is high because "usually renters don't own animals," a manager says.[102] Clustering systems are also available for other countries. Experian's Global Mosaic system clusters consumers into a few common lifestyle categories so that global marketers can target consumers with similar characteristics in different parts of the world.[103]

Regions Across the World

Clearly, the area of the world in which a consumer resides can influence consumption patterns; as we have learned, cross-cultural variations exist in just about every aspect of consumer behavior. For instance, the most Coca-Cola is consumed in North America, followed by Latin America and the European community. The lowest consumption occurs in Asia, the Middle East, and Africa. Some nations are strongly associated with certain products (such as beer in Germany and sushi in Japan) while the consumption of specific types of products is forbidden in other regions. Drinking alcohol and smoking are not allowed in Muslim countries, and religious restrictions forbid the consumption of pork in Israel and beef in India.

Cultural influences also affect behaviors such as patience. Consumers in Western cultures tend to be less patient and value immediate consumption more than consumers in Eastern cultures do, for instance.[104] In a broader sense, the ways in which cultures differ can affect how consumers think and behave. These differences can be viewed along three main dimensions:

▶ *Individualism versus collectivism.* Consumers from cultures high in individualism (many Western cultures) put more emphasis on themselves as individuals than as part of the group; consumers from cultures high in collectivism (many Eastern cultures) emphasize connections to others rather than their own individuality.[105] Marketers might apply this distinction to the way in which they depict consumers in ads for each culture—as ruggedly individual or as part of a group, for instance.

▶ *Horizontal versus vertical orientation.* Consumers from cultures with a horizontal orientation value equality, whereas consumers from cultures with a vertical orientation put more emphasis on hierarchy.[106] This distinction is especially important to marketers of status-symbol products that will appeal to consumers influenced by vertical orientation.

▶ *Masculine versus feminine.* Consumers from masculine cultures (such as the United States) tend to be more aggressive and focused on individual advancement; in contrast, consumers from feminine cultures (such as Denmark) tend to be more concerned with social relationships.[107] Therefore, advertising with aggressive themes is more likely to strike a chord in masculine cultures than in feminine cultures.

All the consumers in a particular culture may not be affected by cultural influences in the same way, however. The extent of the influence depends on how each consumer processes information and the personal knowledge that he or she relies on when making a judgment.[108]

MARKETING IMPLICATIONS

Marketers need to understand global differences in consumer behavior so that they can alter marketing strategy, where necessary, to appeal to specific regions and countries. For example, money-back guarantees give U.S. consumers confidence, but Latin Americans do not believe them because they never expect to get their money back. Also, the strategies of using famous endorsers or being the official product of a sporting event are much more effective in Venezuela and Mexico than in the United States.

Many companies adjust their marketing activities to accommodate global consumer differences.[109] To draw consumers in Japan, where stores are generally small, Office Depot had to downsize its cavernous warehouse stores and reduce the number of

Exhibit 12.9

Regional Marketing

McDonald's adapts its promotions to different regions of the world. This Hello Kitty plush doll giveaway was popular in Asian regions such as Hong Kong.

office-supply products on the shelves.[110] And Procter & Gamble developed different versions of a TV ad for Pampers disposable diapers to account for variations in slang and accent in different regions of the German-speaking world. Not heeding important cross-cultural differences can embarrass a company and cause its products to fail. In Germany, Vicks had to change its brand name to *Wicks* because the former term is slang for sexual intercourse. Finally, marketers should remember that, as in the United States, consumers in different parts of one country may exhibit different types of consumer behavior (see, for example, Exhibit 12.9). Consumers in Beijing and Shanghai prefer different foods, for instance—differences common in many of China's 2,000 cities.[111]

How Ethnic Influences Affect Consumer Behavior

Ethnic influences are another major factor that affects consumer behavior. It is important to emphasize that the generalizations about ethnic groups discussed in this chapter are only broad group tendencies and may or may not apply to individual consumers. Marketing to any consumer group requires careful research to get beyond stereotypes and to identify specific characteristics and behavioral patterns that can be addressed using appropriate strategies and tactics.

Individuals from many different cultures have come to America over the years. This long history of immigration has created not only a unique national culture but also a number of subcultures or **ethnic groups** within the larger society. Members of these ethnic groups share a common heritage, set of beliefs, religion, and experiences that set them apart from others in society. Larger groups include the Hispanic, African American, Asian, Italian, Irish, Jewish, Scandinavian, and Polish subcultures.

These groups are bound together by cultural ties that can, in turn, strongly influence consumer behavior. Moreover, through the process of **acculturation,** members of a subculture must learn to adapt to the host culture. During acculturation, consumers acquire knowledge, skills, and behavior through social interaction, by modeling the behavior of others, and through reinforcement or receipt of rewards

Ethnic groups Subcultures with a similar heritage and values.

Acculturation Learning how to adapt to a new culture.

for certain behaviors.[112] Acculturation is strongly influenced by family, friends, and institutions such as the media, place of worship, and school and combines with traditional customs to form a unique consumer culture. Meanwhile, members of a larger culture who like to learn about new cultures and think that cultural diversity is important will, at times, adopt a subculture's ethnic-oriented products.[113] Racism can have the opposite effect, prompting racist consumers to avoid products associated with particular ethnic groups.[114]

Ethnic Groups Within the United States

The majority of U.S. consumers (commonly referred to as *Anglos*) can trace their ancestry back to one or more European nations. However, immigration and population trends are leading to greater diversity within the United States. By 2010, the three largest ethnic groups within the U.S. population will be Hispanic Americans (15.5 percent of the population), African Americans (13.1 percent), and Asian Americans (4.6 percent).[115] By 2030, nearly half of the youth population of the United States will be non-Anglo—primarily Hispanic (see Exhibit 12.10).[116]

Clearly, U.S. population trends have huge implications for marketers. Collectively, the three main U.S. subcultures will soon control nearly $4 trillion in buying power as these groups continue to grow much faster than the general U.S. population.[117] Small wonder that many firms are targeting certain ethnic groups with appropriate marketing approaches. However, marketers need not focus on only one group. They can target several cultures at the same time.

Multicultural marketing
Strategies used to appeal to a variety of cultures at the same time.

Multicultural marketing, the use of strategies that simultaneously appeal to a variety of cultures, is quite popular. SoftSheen-Carson, which originally specialized in hair-care products for African American consumers, has broadened its focus through multicultural marketing. "Because we are a culture that comes in many hues," says the firm's president, "the advertising should be reflective of the multi-hues that we come in."[118] This approach requires both long-term commitment and consideration of ethnic groups from the outset, not as an afterthought.[119]

Ethnic Composition of Under-18 U.S. Consumers

In the coming years, the non-Anglo youth population will continue to grow much faster than the Anglo youth population in the United States. By 2030, non-Anglo youngsters under 18 will comprise nearly half of the total U.S. youth population.

We are the World
Ethnic kids and teens are fueling growth in the youth market.

(UNDER AGE 18)	2001	2010	2020	2030	% CHANGE (2001–2030)
Total Youth	71.0 mil	72.5 mil	77.6 mil	83.4 mil	+18%
Hispanic	11.3 (16%)	13.7 (16%)	17.2 (22%)	21.0 (25%)	+85%
Non-Hispanic White	45.2 (64%)	42.7 (59%)	42.4 (55%)	42.3 (51%)	−6%
Non-Hispanic Black	10.7 (15%)	11.3 (16%)	12.2 (16%)	13.2 (16%)	+24%
Asian/ Pacific Islander	3.2 (5%)	4.0 (6%)	5.0 (7%)	6.1 (7%)	+94%
Other Non-Hispanic	0.7 (1%)	0.7 (1%)	0.8 (1%)	0.9 (1%)	+27%

(in millions, % of total youth)   *Percentages may not equal 100 due to rounding*

Source: U.S. Census Bureau; calculations by American Demographics

Hispanic American Consumers

Hispanic Americans represent one of the largest, most diverse, and fastest-growing ethnic groups in the United States today, more than 42 million strong with a median age of 27, well below the overall U.S. median age of 36.4.[120] This subculture can be divided into four major groups: Mexican Americans (58.5 percent), living primarily in the Southwest and California; Puerto Ricans (9.6 percent), centered in New York; Central and Southern Americans (8.6 percent); and Cuban Americans (3.5 percent), located primarily in southern Florida.[121]

Hispanics can also be divided into several groups based on their level of acculturation to the host culture: (1) the *acculturated,* who speak mostly English and have a high level of assimilation; (2) the *bicultural,* who can function in either English or Spanish; and (3) the *traditional,* who speak mostly Spanish.[122] The rate of acculturation can be slow, usually taking four generations because 80 percent of all Hispanics marry other Hispanics. Yet some Hispanic Americans resist assimilation and desire to maintain their ethnic identity.[123]

Intensity of ethnic identification How strongly people identify with their ethnic group.

The consumer's level of acculturation affects consumption patterns, as does the **intensity of ethnic identification.**[124] Consumers who strongly identify with their ethnic group and are less acculturated into the mainstream culture are more likely to exhibit the consumption patterns of the ethnic group. Strong Hispanic identification leads to a higher level of husband-dominant decisions (discussed in greater detail in Chapter 13).[125] Furthermore, strong identifiers are more likely to be influenced by radio ads, billboards, family members, and coworkers and are less likely than weak identifiers to use coupons.[126]

MARKETING IMPLICATIONS

Hispanic Americans have a combined buying power of more than $800 billion.[127] Marketers are using a variety of activities to serve this segment, as the following examples show.

Product development

Marketers are building customer loyalty by developing offerings specifically for Hispanic Americans. Frito-Lay created zestier Doritos snacks for the Hispanic American segment. Within a year, the products were ringing up more than $100 million in annual sales.[128] California-based Newhall Laboratories specializes in fruit-scented hair-care products developed especially for Hispanic American consumers.[129]

Media targeting

Because Hispanic Americans tend to be concentrated in certain areas and share a common language, many can be targeted in Spanish-language media, including TV, radio, print, billboards, and websites. Thus, when Miller Brewing wanted to boost sales of its beer to Hispanic Americans, it arranged with the Spanish-language TV network Univision to sponsor World Cup soccer matches and boxing programs.[130] ESPN Deportes airs sports programming to appeal to specific subsegments of the Hispanic American market, such as Mexican soccer matches and Dominican baseball games.[131]

Advertising messages

More marketers are developing ads targeting Hispanic Americans, including Procter & Gamble, AT&T, and Toyota.[132] Advertising is particularly important in this segment because many Hispanics prefer prestigious or nationally advertised brands (see Exhibit 12.11). When Hanes started an ad campaign targeting Hispanic consumers in Chicago and San Antonio, its pantyhose sales increased by 8 percent.[133]

Una buena tradición debe continuar.

Porque tus hijos también se merecen un jugo natural como el que te daba tu mamá. Juicy Juice de Nestlé. Sigue la tradición natural.

Exhibit 12.11

Hispanic American Consumers

Some marketers target specific subcultures. This ad for Nestlé Juicy Juice targets Hispanic consumers.

Accommodation theory The more effort one puts forth in trying to communicate with an ethnic group, the more positive the reaction.

Hispanic Americans tend to react positively to ads using ethnic spokespeople, who are perceived as more trustworthy, leading to consumers' having more positive attitudes toward the brand being advertised.[134] This strategy is most effective in environments in which ethnicity is more salient (i.e., the group is in the minority).[135] Ads that draw attention to ethnicity can trigger "ethnic self-awareness" and generate more favorable responses from the targeted group.[136] Marketers who develop ads specifically for Hispanic Americans or other groups should realize that although members of the overall culture also may be exposed to the ads, they are unlikely to react in the same way as the targeted group does because they are less familiar with the cues in the ads.[137] Also, some advertisers try to make ethnic representation in ads proportional to the group's size relative to the general population.[138]

Accommodation theory can also apply when marketers develop advertising for Hispanics. This theory predicts that the more effort a source puts into communicating with a group— for example, by using role models and the native language— the greater the response by members of this group and the more positive their feelings. Therefore, advertising in Spanish increases perceptions of the company's sensitivity toward and solidarity with the Hispanic community, creating consumers' positive feelings toward the brand and the firm.[139]

However, using Spanish messages exclusively can lead to negative ad perceptions. Many ads directed toward Hispanic Americans are delivered in English because these consumers are often bilingual or highly acculturated. An even more effective strategy may involve using both English and Spanish, the method employed by Anheuser-Busch when it plans its TV commercials for Hispanic Americans.[140] When an ad targeting Hispanic Americans mixes English and Spanish, it is likely to be more persuasive if the text is mainly in Spanish with one word switched to English instead of mainly in English with one Spanish word. Note that consumers may like a code-switching message less if it mixes words incorrectly.[141]

Distribution

More marketers are tailoring distribution to Hispanic American consumers. La Curacao department stores in Los Angeles and Carnival grocery stores in Texas are two of the many retailers that target Hispanic American shoppers.[142] Building on this subculture's focus on the family, the Target retail chain positions children's clothing near the front of its stores in areas with a high Hispanic American population.[143]

African American Consumers

More than 39 million African Americans live in the United States, with a median age of 30 years old (compared with the overall U.S. population median age of 36.4 years old).[144] African Americans represent a large and diverse group consisting of many subsegments across different levels of income and education, occupations, and regions. Among African American households, nearly 30 percent have an income of $50,000 or higher, 46 percent are homeowners, and more are single-parent families headed by women than are found in the general population. The South is home to more than half of all African American consumers, with a high proportion living in major urban areas. Nearly 15 percent of African Americans have college degrees, compared with 24 percent of the overall U.S. population.[145]

As with any subculture, African American consumers have some similarities to the general population and also differ in certain ways. For example, African Americans are more likely to believe that people should feel free to live, dress, and look the way that they want to.[146] They also do not necessarily aspire to assimilate with the majority culture.[147] However, as incomes rise, a strong desire to preserve a cultural identity also develops. A defining element in the consumption patterns of African Americans is the importance of style, self-image, and elegance. Consumption patterns are also related to a strong desire to be recognized and show status. According to research, African Americans often buy premium brands of boys' clothing to make a statement about themselves.[148]

MARKETING IMPLICATIONS

African American consumers have a total buying power exceeding $800 billion.[149] They respond positively to offerings and communications targeted toward them and are less likely to trust or buy brands that are not advertised.[150]

Product development

Many marketers focus primarily on products for the unique needs of the African American market. For example, SoftSheen-Carson and African Pride have created hair-care brands for this market.[151] Marketers that make products for the broader U.S. population are now branching out to also design products specifically for black consumers, as evidenced by clothing manufacturers that are designing styles deemed more flattering for the physique of African American women.

Media targeting

African Americans watch more TV and have more positive attitudes toward ads than do Anglo consumers.[152] Research shows that strong ethnic identifiers among African American consumers act more positively than weak identifiers to ads placed in racially targeted media.[153] In fact, 82.3 percent of African American consumers seek out information from magazines specifically aimed at them.[154] Thus, the Lincoln Navigator SUV is marketed to African American consumers through ads in *Black Enterprise, Ebony,* and other magazines with high readership in this segment.[155] TV networks such as Black Entertainment Television and targeted websites such as BET.com also reach this segment.[156]

Advertising messages

Some of the largest U.S. advertisers, including General Motors, Procter & Gamble, and Johnson & Johnson, are investing in ad campaigns specifically for this segment.[157] As noted earlier, subcultures such as African Americans will identify more strongly and have more positive evaluations when the advertising source is of the same ethnic group as the target.[158] Therefore, marketers must take the unique values and expectations of African Americans into account when planning communications, especially since consumers in this segment pay attention to the ways that they are represented in ads.[159]

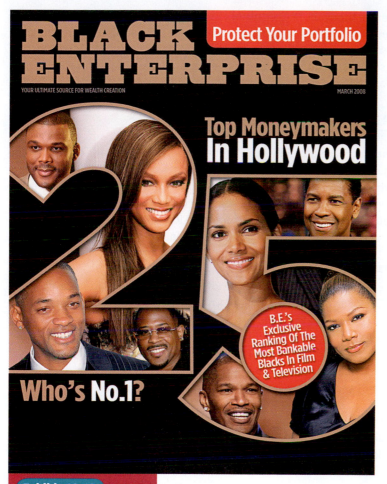

Exhibit 12.12

Marketing to African American Consumers

Some communications target African-American consumers like this one for *Black Enterprise* magazine.

Marketers must also be aware of the effect that African American models and actors in ads may have on consumers outside the targeted segment. According to Coors's director of ethnic marketing, the company's targeted advertising has boosted the beer's overall sales, not just its sales to African American consumers, "because African American consumers in urban markets have a lot of influence on what's cool with the general market."[160] On the other hand, one study found that some Anglo consumers had less favorable attitudes and were less likely to purchase the product when ads featured African American rather than Anglo actors.[161] This problem is more pronounced when Anglo consumers are prejudiced toward non-Anglos. Yet research suggests that younger Anglo consumers are more accepting of non-Anglo actors, a factor that may reduce the problem over time.[162]

Distribution

Marketers can also adjust distribution strategies to appeal to African American consumers. In areas where African Americans represent more than 20 percent of the population, J.C. Penney has developed "Authentic African Boutiques" that offer clothing, handbags, hats, and other accessories imported from Africa.

Asian American Consumers

America's 12 million Asian Americans are the third largest and the fastest growing major subculture in the country, with a median age of 33.2 years old.[163] The largest concentrations are in California cities, New York City and its suburbs, and Hawaii, where more than 65 percent of the population is of Asian descent. Growth has also been high in other urban areas, including Chicago and Washington, D.C.[164] The Asian American community consists of people from more than 29 countries, from the Indian subcontinent to the Pacific Ocean, each with its own values and customs. The six largest groups include immigrants from China, the Philippines, India, Korea, Vietnam, and Japan.[165] In light of this tremendous diversity, marketers should research the specific subsegment they wish to target.

One common denominator of most Asian cultures is the strong emphasis on the family, tradition, and cooperation.[166] These consumers shop frequently and enjoy shopping with friends. They want brand names and are willing to pay for top quality, even though they react positively to bargains. Also, Asian Americans frequently recommend offerings to friends and relatives.[167] For example, Consolidated Restaurants in Seattle ran a two-week campaign in Japanese on mainstream radio stations. "We know there is a significant Japanese population that's bilingual and they're going to talk to each other," says the marketer behind the campaign.[168] Asian Americans are more than twice as likely as the average consumer to check prices and products on the Internet before they buy.[169] Consumers in this group also tend to save money, be highly educated, have higher computer literacy, and hold a higher percentage of professional and managerial jobs than the general population does.[170] More than half live in integrated suburbs as opposed to ethnic areas such as a Chinatown, and most tend to be highly assimilated by the second and third generations.

MARKETING IMPLICATIONS

Because Asian Americans are a rapidly growing group with buying power approaching $450 billion in annual purchases, this subculture is attractive to many marketers.[171] Another reason for the attraction is that the median income of Asian Americans is nearly $55,000, well above the overall U.S. median income of $43,000. Moreover, 22 percent of Asian American households have an annual income of $100,000 or more, compared with 14 percent of overall U.S. households earning at this income level.[172]

Product and service development

Marketers are increasingly developing more offerings for Asian Americans.[173] To accommodate 48 busloads of Asian Americans who go to Mohegan Sun in Connecticut every day from Boston and New York, the casino has created a special section featuring 46 tables of Asian games like Sic Bo plus food kiosks styled like Hong Kong street vendors.[174] Yet caution is needed to avoid missteps: One company mistakenly offered golf balls in a four-pack instead of the usual three-pack, not knowing that the word *four* is unlucky because it sounds similar to the word for death in both Japanese and Chinese.

Media targeting

To reach this diverse group, marketers often use native-language newspapers, magazines, broadcast and cable TV, radio, and the Internet. Ford has employed this strategy, placing newspaper ads in Mandarin, Korean, and Cantonese and running TV commercials in Cantonese, Mandarin, and Vietnamese.[175] Charles Schwab has a Chinese-language version of its brokerage website, and HSBC, a global bank, has sponsored the Chinese-language World Cup soccer site.[176] (See also Exhibit 12.13.)

Advertising messages

Messages delivered to Asian Americans in their native language are often more effective than those delivered in English. Despite the diversity of languages within this subculture, marketers may find the effort worthwhile when many consumers from a single subgroup are concentrated in an area. For instance, Toyota dealers in Seattle air commercials on the International Channel in Mandarin, Cantonese, Tagalog, Vietnamese, and Korean.[177] Taking advantage of the popularity of Yao Ming and other basketball stars recruited from China, the National Basketball Association has promoted the sport with ads in Chinese-language newspapers in

Exhibit 12.13

Asian American Consumers

Some media target Asian American consumers. Here is Ford's Chinese-language version of its website.

six U.S. cities.[178] Asian Americans tend to respond to subtle messages that focus on tradition, the family, and cooperation as well as to ads featuring Asian models.[179]

Promotions and distribution

Linking promotions and signage to the language, interests, or lifestyles of a particular Asian American group can be quite successful. The Pacific Place shopping center in Seattle draws Japanese American shoppers by printing coupons and special offers in English on one side and Japanese on the other. After the Boston Red Sox signed Japanese baseball star Daisuke Matsuzaka, some restaurants and businesses put up signs in Japanese to attract Japanese American fans on their way to Fenway Park.[180] ▬

Ethnic Groups Around the World

Ethnic subcultures exist in many nations. Although it is beyond the scope of this book to discuss each of the numerous ethnic groups around the world, a few examples illustrate their importance and the challenges and opportunities of reaching specific groups within a particular country.

In Canada, the French-speaking subculture has unique motivations and buying habits.[181] Compared with the rest of the Canadian population, French Canadians use more staples for original or "scratch" cooking; drink more soft drinks, beer, wine, and instant beverages; and consume fewer frozen vegetables, diet drinks, and hard liquor. Patriotism and ethnic pride are extremely strong, and these themes have been successfully incorporated into marketing to this subculture by McDonald's, KFC, and others.[182]

The former Soviet Union was a diverse country, with more than 100 different ethnic groups speaking more than 50 different languages. The breakup of this large nation yielded a number of countries with strong ethnic cores, including Russia, the Baltic countries (Lithuania, Estonia, and Latvia), Belorussia, and Ukraine.

In Thailand more than 80 percent of the population is of Thai origin, but several sizable ethnic subcultures still flourish. The largest, 10 percent of the population,

Exhibit 12.14

Ethnic Subcultures Around the World

Ethnic subcultures exist in many countries, including Thailand, where 10 percent of the population has Chinese roots.

has Chinese roots (Exhibit 12.14), and this segment has influenced the Thai culture to a significant degree.[183] Chinese consumers in Thailand exert a powerful economic force because they own many businesses; their influence is also felt in art, religion, and food. Other, smaller, ethnic groups in Thailand include people of Laotian, Indian, and Burmese origin.

India has a diverse ethnic population, with more than 80 languages and 120 dialects spoken in the country. Some villagers need travel only 30 miles from home to reach a destination where they are not able to speak the language. KFC and Pizza Hut, both owned by Yum Brands, have done well in India by customizing their American-style menus to the tastes of consumers in specific cities, using local ingredients and flavors that appeal to each subsegment.[184]

The Influence of Religion

A final type of subculture is based on religious beliefs. Religion provides people with a structured set of beliefs and values that serve as a code of conduct or guide to behavior. It also provides ties that bind people together and make one group different from another. According to research, the majority of Americans are either Protestant or Catholic. In comparison, only a small fraction of Americans identify themselves as being Jewish, Mormon, Muslim, or a follower of another religion.[185]

Although individual differences certainly come into play, some religious influences or traditions can affect consumer behavior. Born-again Christians, for instance, are less likely to buy on credit, purchase national brands, or attend rock concerts and movies.[186] Religion can also prevent consumption of certain products or services. Mormons are prohibited from using liquor, tobacco, and caffeine, including cola. Orthodox Jews do not eat pork or shellfish, and all meat and poultry to be consumed must be certified as kosher. Muslims cannot eat pork or drink liquor. Catholic consumers may choose to abstain from eating meat on Fridays during the season of Lent.

Religious subcultures are clearly present in many parts of the world. In India, for example, most of the population is Hindu, but large groups of Muslims, Christians, and Sikhs exhibit different patterns of consumption. Because Hindus are predominantly vegetarian, Indian manufacturers of food and cosmetics must use vegetable-based rather than animal-based oils and shortening in their products. The Sikh religion forbids the consumption of beef and tobacco, and the sales of such products are low in areas where many Sikhs live. Finally, the color green has significance for Muslims, a factor that has led to its frequent use on product packages for this group.

MARKETING IMPLICATIONS

Marketers can segment the market by focusing on religious affiliation, delivering targeted messages and promotions or using certain media to deliver them. They can target Christian consumers through religious radio stations, cable TV networks, and TV programs, which reach millions of U.S. consumers. A number of marketers reach Christian consumers through Salem Communications' Christian music radio stations, publications, and websites.[187] In addition, marketers can advertise in one of the many publications geared to specific religious affiliations.

Marketing tactics should demonstrate understanding and respect for the targeted group's beliefs and customs, a strategy that will also generate positive word of mouth. Wal-Mart met with local Islamic leaders for two years before opening a Supercenter near

Detroit with foods and other products appropriate for the many Muslim consumers in the area. Most of the new store's employees speak at least two languages, so they can assist shoppers from many backgrounds. Wal-Mart has even asked Hallmark to develop greeting cards specifically for Muslim consumers.[188]

Marketers can also distribute religious products through specialized stores such as King's House in Scottsdale, Arizona. More religious institutions are opening gift shops, snack bars, and even fitness centers, providing distribution opportunities for suitable goods and services.[189] Some marketers use religious themes in their marketing efforts, such as selling special products or packages during religious holidays. However, some marketers avoid products or messages with overt religious meaning. The teen retail chain Hot Topic will not sell clothing bearing religious symbols. "If someone who isn't familiar with our store walks by our window display and is offended by what [he or she sees], we won't carry it," explains the general merchandise manager.[190]

Summary

Six major aspects of consumer diversity have important effects on consumer behavior: age, gender, sexual orientation, regional differences, ethnic differences, and religious differences. Age is a key factor because people of the same age have similar life experiences, needs, symbols, and memories that may lead to similar consumption patterns. Teens and Generation Y consumers in their twenties have significant spending power and influence family purchasing. Generation X consumers were born between 1965 and 1976. Baby boomers, born from 1946 to 1964, are the largest age category in the United States. Seniors are the 50-and-older segment.

Gender differences also affect consumer behavior, including the influence of changing sex roles. Men and women differ in terms of their consumer traits, information-processing styles, decision-making styles, and consumption patterns. In addition, more marketers are using sexual orientation to target gay and lesbian consumers for various goods and services.

Consumption patterns may differ in various regions of the United States and the world, leading some marketers to tailor their strategies specifically to these regions. Clustering helps marketers describe consumers in different regions based on similar demographic and consumption characteristics rather than on geographic location only. The three largest U.S. ethnic groups are African Americans, Hispanic Americans, and Asian Americans. Many marketers are taking a multicultural approach, trying to appeal to several subcultures instead of just one. Finally, religious values and customs can influence consumer behavior and form the basis of some marketing strategies.

Questions for Review and Discussion

1. What type of U.S. consumers are in the Generation X, Generation Y, and baby boomer segments?

2. What is the difference between gender and sexual orientation, and why is this distinction important for marketers?

3. What is clustering, and why do marketers use it?

4. What are the three main subcultures within the U.S. population?

5. How do acculturation and intensity of ethnic identification affect consumer behavior?

6. Define the *accommodation theory*, and explain its importance for marketers who target Hispanic Americans.

7. Why would a company adopt multicultural marketing rather than target a single subculture?

8. Why do marketers have to consider regional influences when targeting consumers within the United States or in another country?

9. Identify some of the ways in which religion can influence consumer behavior.

CL Visit http://cengage.com/marketing/hoyer/ConsumerBehavior5e to find resources that are available to help you study for the course.

CONSUMER BEHAVIOR CASE

Can Canned Soup Translate?

The first time that New Jersey–based Campbell Soup tried to market its soups in China, consumers simply did not buy them. It was the early 1990s, and Campbell's marketers saw a huge sales opportunity in a populous nation that sips a lot of soups—more than 241 servings per person per year, or 320 billion servings in all. In contrast, U.S. consumers swallow some 14 billion soup servings per year.

Traditionally, the vast majority of Campbell's sales have come from U.S. markets, where soup is about as mature as a product category can be. With sales growth slowing at home, the company saw great potential for marketing soups to the large and increasingly affluent population in China. However, instead of researching local buying and consumption patterns to see whether changes would be necessary, Campbell decided to export its current line of condensed soups to China. The cans sat and sat on store shelves, and eventually the company withdrew from the market.

The second time that Campbell planned to market soups to Chinese consumers, in 2007, its marketers did a lot of homework in the months leading up to its product introductions. Its researchers traveled to different regions of China to see how consumers make soup at home and to ask about food consumption habits and preferences. They learned that Chinese consumers almost always make soup from scratch. Although consumers add monosodium glutamate (MSG) to enhance the flavor of homemade soup, the additive can cause headaches and other health problems. Chinese consumers "know [MSG] is not good for them, and they're looking for an alternative," says the head of Campbell's international division. Using these findings, the company did not add MSG to its broths.

As part of its research, Campbell provided women in Shanghai with different broths and sample recipes to get their reactions. Not everyone used the recipes—in fact, one woman said the broth would be a good substitute for oil and water when stir-frying. The researchers concluded that Chinese consumers were likely to use Campbell's soups mainly as a base for meat, vegetable, and noodle dishes rather than as a soup course. They also determined that, like their counterparts in many nations, Chinese consumers would be interested in the time-saving convenience of premade broths.

Campbell's product experts cooked up two types of all-natural, low-fat broths to market in China under the Swanson brand. One was a strongly flavored clear chicken broth that research showed Chinese consumers would prefer. The second was an even more full-bodied broth made from chicken, pork, and ham. To introduce these new products, Campbell marketers arranged to give away 10 million samples plus recipe flyers in major cities. Knowing that cell phones are extremely popular in China, they also created text-message promotions to build the Swanson brand and to encourage product trial and repurchase.

Following up on their research, Campbell's marketers decided to distribute the new products in two stages. First, they planned to sell the broths in large supermarkets, supporting the campaign with in-store demonstrations to show how well the products work as a base for soup and vegetable dishes. As the Swanson brand and image became better established, the second stage would be to distribute the broths through smaller grocery stores.

Campbell's second foray into the China market has gone smoothly, and the company is also expanding into Russia, where it launched several new soups tailored specifically to that country's consumption habits and supported by sampling and coupons to stimulate trial and repurchase. Today, Campbell rings up $7 billion annually through sales in 120 countries. What will it need to do to market to the soup customers of tomorrow?[191]

Case Questions

1. What is the difference between consumer behavior with regard to soup in China and in your own country?

2. Do you agree with Campbell's two-stage distribution plan for marketing its new soups in China? Explain your answer.

3. For Campbell, what are the likely marketing implications of gender, age, and regional influences on the way that consumers buy and use soup in China?

4. Now that Campbell is using text messages to advertise the Swanson brand in China, should it use the same promotional technique in Russia?

Social Class and Household Influences

Chapter 13

LEARNING OBJECTIVES

After studying this chapter, you will be able to

1. Define the social class hierarchy and identify the major determinants of social class standing.

2. Explain how social class influences consumer behavior and why marketers must consider these influences when planning strategy and tactics.

3. Discuss three key forces that are, over time, changing social class structure in many countries.

4. Describe the various types of households and families, and explain how the family life cycle and other forces affect household structure.

INTRODUCTION

Marketing to India's Growing Middle Class

The 100 million-plus consumers of India's middle class represent a large, lucrative, and rapidly expanding market for cars, cell phones, air travel, and many other goods and services. During the 1990s, India accounted for less than 1 percent of the world's car sales. Now, thanks to middle-class buying power, India accounts for 2.4 percent of world car sales as local firms like Tata Motors compete with global firms like Hyundai and Honda for market share. Tata's Nano, the world's lowest-priced car, is a no-frills transportation option for families that might otherwise perch children on a motorcycle's handlebars or ride on public buses.

Cell phones are another high-sales area: More than 211 million people are already subscribers, and sales are multiplying rapidly as income rises and families seek to stay in touch by phone. With more Indian consumers seeking employment in the cities and traveling outside the country for work and pleasure, demand for air travel has increased significantly. This development is pitting local full-service carriers like Jet Airways against local discounters like Kingfisher Airlines and well-regarded international rivals like Singapore Airlines. As Jet Airways' founder observes, "Many Indians have the money, and they want quality service when they fly internationally—standards not lower than Singapore [Airlines] and Cathay [Pacific Airways]."[1]

5. Outline the roles that household members play in acquisition and consumption decisions, and show how companies can use their knowledge of these roles to market more effectively.

This example illustrates how social class and household influences can affect consumer behavior (see Exhibit 13.1). The concept of social class implies that some people have more power, wealth, and opportunity than others do, a situation that makes a difference in what and how consumers buy. Among India's middle-class consumers are college graduates, business and government managers, storekeepers, and farmers whose occupational opportunities and rising incomes allow them to buy and use more and better products and services than they ever have before. Another consideration is the influence that family members have on decisions about purchasing expensive items like cars (i.e., buying a Nano instead of buying a motorcycle or taking a bus) and making travel plans. As you read this chapter, remember that the generalizations about social class and household are broad group tendencies and may or may not apply to individual consumers.

Social Class

Social class hierarchy The grouping of members of society according to status high to low.

Most societies have a **social class hierarchy** that confers higher status to some classes of people than to others. These social classes consist of identifiable groups of individuals whose behaviors and lifestyles differ from those of members of the other classes. Members of a particular social class tend to share similar values and behavior patterns. Note that social classes are loose collections of individuals with similar life experiences, not formal groups with a strong identity.[2]

Many societies view these distinctions as important because they recognize that everyone has a necessary role to play in order for society to function smoothly. However, some roles, such as medical doctor or executive, are more prestigious and more valued than others, such as toll taker or janitor. Nevertheless, the concept of social class is not inherently negative. Even with the inequalities, social class distinctions can help individuals determine what their role in society is or what they would like it to be (their aspirations). Furthermore, all levels of the social class hierarchy make an important contribution to society.

Types of Social Class Systems

Most societies have three major classes: high, middle, and lower. Often, however, finer distinctions are made. The United States, for example, is typically divided into the seven levels presented in Exhibit 13.2, with up to 70 percent of the population concentrated in the middle classes.[3] Although most societies have some kind of hierarchical structure, the size and composition of the classes depend on the relative prosperity of a particular country.[4]

Compared with the United States, Japan, and Scandinavia have an even larger and more predominant middle class with much smaller groups above and below. This distribution means that there is greater equality among people in those two countries than in other societies. The Japanese structure represents a concerted government effort to abolish the social class system and mix together people from all levels of society.[5] Yet the very competitive and selective Japanese educational system still restricts entry to higher status corporate and government positions.

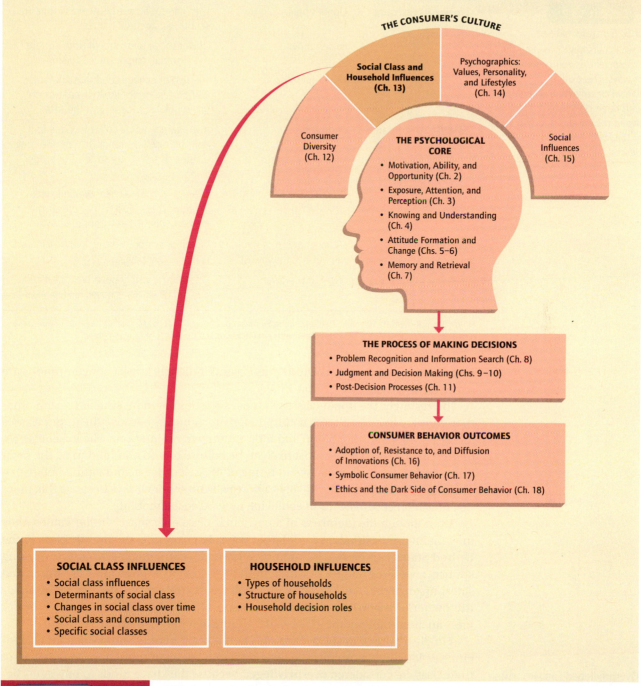

THE CONSUMER'S CULTURE

Social Class and Household Influences (Ch. 13)

Psychographics: Values, Personality, and Lifestyles (Ch. 14)

Consumer Diversity (Ch. 12)

THE PSYCHOLOGICAL CORE
- Motivation, Ability, and Opportunity (Ch. 2)
- Exposure, Attention, and Perception (Ch. 3)
- Knowing and Understanding (Ch. 4)
- Attitude Formation and Change (Chs. 5–6)
- Memory and Retrieval (Ch. 7)

Social Influences (Ch. 15)

THE PROCESS OF MAKING DECISIONS
- Problem Recognition and Information Search (Ch. 8)
- Judgment and Decision Making (Chs. 9–10)
- Post-Decision Processes (Ch. 11)

CONSUMER BEHAVIOR OUTCOMES
- Adoption of, Resistance to, and Diffusion of Innovations (Ch. 16)
- Symbolic Consumer Behavior (Ch. 17)
- Ethics and the Dark Side of Consumer Behavior (Ch. 18)

SOCIAL CLASS INFLUENCES
- Social class influences
- Determinants of social class
- Changes in social class over time
- Social class and consumption
- Specific social classes

HOUSEHOLD INFLUENCES
- Types of households
- Structure of households
- Household decision roles

Exhibit 13.1

Chapter Overview: Social Class and Household Influences

This chapter examines social class and household influences on consumer behavior. The first section discusses the determinants of social class (e.g., occupation, education, income), changes in social class over time, and how social class affects consumption. Next is a discussion about household influences on consumer behavior, including the various types of households, trends in household structure, and the decision roles that household members play in acquiring and using an offering.

Upper Americans	Upper-upper	The "capital *S* society" world of inherited wealth, aristocratic names
	Lower-upper	Newer social elite, drawn from current professional, corporate leadership
	Upper-middle	The rest of college graduate managers and professionals; lifestyle centers on private clubs, causes, and the arts
Middle Americans	Middle class	Average-pay white-collar workers and their blue-collar friends: live on the "better side of town," try to "do the proper things"
	Working class	Average-pay blue-collar workers; lead "working class lifestyle" whatever the income, school, background, or job
Lower Americans	"A lower group of people but not the lowest"	Working, not on welfare; living standard is just above poverty
	"Real lower-lower"	On welfare, visibly poverty stricken, usually out of work (or have "dirtiest jobs")

Source: From Richard P. Coleman, "The Continuing Significance of Social Class to Marketing," *Journal of Consumer Research,* December 1983, p. 277. Reprinted with permission of The University of Chicago Press.

In developing areas such as Latin America and India, the largest concentrations are in the lower classes (see Exhibit 13.3).

Interestingly, the upper classes in most societies are more similar to each other than they are to other classes within their own countries because the upper classes tend to be more cosmopolitan and international in orientation.[6] The lower classes, on the other hand, are the most likely to be culture bound and tend to be the most different from the other classes in terms of lifestyles, dress, and eating behaviors. The middle classes are most likely to borrow from other classes because this practice may represent a means of achieving upward social mobility.

Even though the members of a particular class may share similar values, they may maintain these values in different ways. For example, the middle class in the United States can be represented by a lower-level manager with a nonworking spouse, a working couple in which both partners have office jobs, an unmarried salesperson, a divorced parent with a college degree supporting two children, or the owner of a bowling alley. All of these individuals might strive for a better life—an important middle-class value—but take different paths to get there.

Finally, a particular social class may contain different economic substrata. Specifically, families whose income level is 20 to 30 percent more than the median of their class are considered **overprivileged** because they have funds to buy items beyond the basic necessities.[7] **Class average** families have an income level that is average for their social class and can therefore afford the type of symbols expected for their status, such as a house, a car, and appropriate clothing. The **underprivileged,** whose incomes are below the median, have trouble meeting class expectations.

Overprivileged Families with an income higher than the average in their social class.

Class average Families with an average income in a particular class.

Underprivileged Families below the average income in their class.

Social Class Influences

Social class structures are important because they strongly affect norms and values and, therefore, behavior. Given that members of a social class interact regularly with each other (both formally and informally), people are more likely to be influenced

Exhibit 13.3

Class Structure by Culture

The relative sizes and structures of social classes vary by culture. Japan and Scandinavia, for example, are characterized by a large middle class with few people above or below it. India and Latin America, on the other hand, have a greater proportion of individuals in the lower classes. The United States has a large middle class but also has significant proportions in the upper and lower classes.

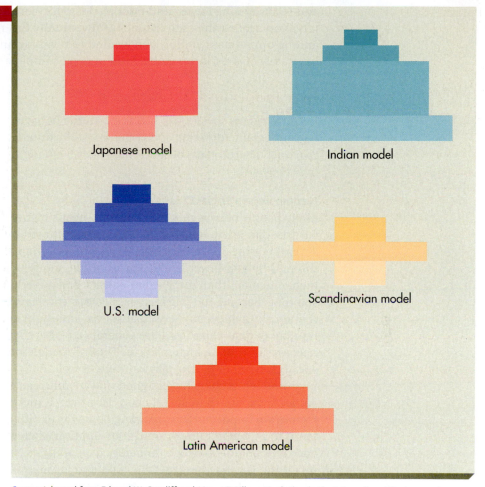

Japanese model

Indian model

U.S. model

Scandinavian model

Latin American model

Source: Adapted from Edward W. Cundiff and Marye T. Hilger, *Marketing in the International Environment* (Englewood Cliffs, N.J.: Prentice-Hall, 1988) and Marieke K. de Mooij and Warren Keegan, *Advertising Worldwide* (Englewood Cliffs, N.J.: Prentice-Hall, 1991), p. 96.

by individuals in their own social class than by those in other classes. Note that social class influence is not a cultural straitjacket; it merely reflects the fact that people with similar life experiences are likely to exhibit similar lifestyles and behaviors.[8]

The norms and behaviors of consumers in one class can also influence consumers in other social classes. A commonly cited theory of class influence is the **trickle-down effect,** whereby lower classes copy trends that begin in the upper classes. As one example, clothing styles adopted by the upper class often become popular with other groups. The trickle-down effect occurs because those in lower classes may aspire to raise their social standing by emulating the higher classes. They also accept upper-class influence if they lack the cultural knowledge to make their own judgments of what is and is not acceptable.[9] For example, the middle class often looks to the upper class for guidance on cultural matters of music, art, and literature.

More recently, however, the universal validity of the trickle-down theory has been questioned. In some instances, a **status float** can occur, whereby trends start in the lower and middle classes and then spread upward. This phenomenon has occurred with tattoos, which began in the lower classes and moved into the upper classes. It also happened with blue jeans, which first gained popularity in the 1950s

Trickle-down effect Trends that start in the upper classes and then are copied by lower classes.

Status float Trends that start in the lower and middle classes and move upward.

and 1960s among lower- and middle-class U.S. youths because they symbolized rebellion against the establishment.[10] Eventually this message gained popularity among upper-class youths who wanted to revolt against their parents, and jeans ultimately evolved into a global fashion item, complete with designer labels.

How Social Class Is Determined

Examining how social class affects consumer behavior requires a way of classifying consumers into different social classes. Unfortunately, this is a complex task, and the exact determinants of social class have been the subject of considerable debate over the years.

Income versus Social Class

Many people believe that more money means higher social standing. You may be surprised to learn, however, that income is not strongly related to social class for several reasons.[11] First, income levels often overlap social classes, particularly at the middle and lower levels. For example, many U.S. blue-collar workers have higher incomes than some white-collar workers, yet they do not have higher social standing. Second, income increases greatly with age, but older workers do not automatically achieve higher social status. Finally, in many countries an increasing number of dual-career families generate a higher than average income but do not necessarily attain a higher status. Thus, although income is one factor related to social class, other factors play key roles as well.

Some researchers have argued that income can be a better predictor of consumer behavior than social class. However, a more common view is that both factors are important in explaining behavior in different situations.[12] Social class tends to be a better predictor of consumption when it reflects lifestyles and values and does not involve high monetary expenditures, such as purchasing clothes or furniture. For example, middle-class and lower-class consumers favor different styles of furniture, but middle-class consumers tend to spend more money on home furnishings even when the income levels of both classes of consumers are roughly similar. Income, on the other hand, is more useful in explaining the consumption of offerings unrelated to class symbols—such as boats—but that do involve substantial expenditures. Both social class and income are needed to explain behaviors that involve status symbols and significant expenditures such as buying a house or car.

Although income cannot explain social class, social class can often explain how income is used. As one illustration, upper-class consumers are more likely to invest money, whereas the lower classes are more likely to rely on savings accounts in banks. The key point is that social class aids in the understanding of consumer behavior and that social standing is determined by a variety of factors in addition to income.

Occupation and Education

The greatest determinant of class standing is occupation, particularly in Western cultures. Specifically, some occupations, especially those that require higher levels of education, skill, or training, are viewed as higher in status than others (see Exhibit 13.4). Moreover, individuals with the same occupation tend to share similar income, lifestyles, knowledge, and values. Researchers can easily measure occupation by asking consumers what they do for a living. They can then code the responses and compare them with published scales of occupational prestige, such as the widely used socioeconomic index (SEI) or the Nam and Powers scale.[13]

Occupation	Score	Occupation	Score
Legislator	96	Librarian	53
Physician	94	Livestock farmer	49
Dentist	89	Hotel manager	38
Information technology manager	75	Hairdresser	31
Civil engineer	74	Motor mechanic	30
Human resource manager	70	Firefighter	29
Sales and marketing manager	66	Chef	27
School teacher	65	Toolmaker	25
Social worker	60	Plumber	24
Accountant	58	Domestic housekeeper	17
Journalist	57	Truck driver	12
Police officer	54	Waiter	10

Source: Adapted from Julie McMillan and F. L. Jones, "The ANU3_2 Scale: A Revised Occupational Status Scale for Australia," *Journal of Sociology*, March 2000, Appendix on pp. 69–80.

Exhibit 13.4

Status Levels of Selected Occupations in Australia

A variety of indexes have been developed to classify different occupations in terms of their status level. This exhibit presents the status scores of a sample of occupations, using an index developed for Australia. What major factors do you think cause some occupations to be high in status and others to be low?

Inherited status Status that derives from parents at birth.

Earned status Status acquired later in life through achievements.

Note that the perceived status of an occupation may vary from culture to culture. Compared with their situation in the United States, for example, professors have higher status in Germany, Japan, China, Thailand, and Nigeria because those countries place more emphasis on education. Engineers typically have higher status in developing countries than they do in developed countries because of the important role engineering plays in integrating industry and technology into society.

Education also plays a critical role because it is one of the key determinants of occupation and therefore social class. In fact, educational attainment is considered the most reliable determinant of consumers' income potential and spending patterns.[14] The median income of an average U.S. household headed by someone with a college degree (or more advanced education) is $71,400, double the median income of a high school graduate's household. Highly educated consumers not only earn more, but they also read and travel more, are healthier, and are often more receptive to new offerings than the rest of the population.[15]

A college degree is particularly important for gaining entry into higher-status occupations. More than 66 percent of people with bachelor's or advanced degrees are in managerial or professional occupations, compared with 22 percent who have only some college education.

Other Indicators of Social Class

Factors such as area of residence, possessions, family background, and social interactions can also indicate class level. The neighborhood in which we live and the number and types of possessions we have are visible signs that often communicate class standing. In terms of family background, researchers distinguish between **inherited status,** which is adopted from parents at birth, and **earned status,** which is acquired later in life from personal achievements.[16] Inherited status is the initial anchor point from which values are learned and from which upward or downward mobility can occur. As mentioned previously, members of a social class often interact with each other, so the company we keep also helps us to identify our social standing.

The relative importance of these determinants of social class varies from country to country. In formerly communist countries such as Romania, for example, money and possessions are now the strongest determinants of social standing, as opposed to the former criterion of position in the Communist party.[17] In the Arab world, status is determined primarily by social contacts and family position, both of which are considered far more important than money.[18]

Social Class Indexes

All of the preceding factors must be taken into account to determine social class standing, and sociologists have developed a number of indexes to accomplish this task. Older tools such as the *Index of Status Characteristics* and the *Index of Social*

Computerized Status Index (CSI) A modern index used to determine social class through education, occupation, residence, and income.

Status crystallization When consumers are consistent across indicators of social class income, education, occupation, etc.

Position have been criticized as being out-of-date and inappropriate for gauging the status of dual-career households.[19] Therefore, researchers now use more current indexes such as the **Computerized Status Index (CSI).** This index assesses consumers' education, occupation, area of residence, and income.

When consumers are consistent across the various dimensions, social class is easy to determine and **status crystallization** occurs. Sometimes, however, individuals are low on some factors but high on others. Thus, a new doctor from an inner-city neighborhood might be inconsistent on factors such as occupation, income, neighborhood, and family background. Consumers in such situations can experience stress and anxiety because they do not know exactly where they stand.[20] It is also difficult for marketers to neatly categorize such consumers into one social class or another.

How Social Class Changes over Time

Social class structures are not necessarily static, unchanging systems. Three of the key forces producing an evolution in social class structures in many countries are (1) upward mobility, (2) downward mobility, and (3) social class fragmentation.

Upward Mobility

Upward mobility Raising one's status level.

In many cultures, consumers can raise their status level through **upward mobility,** usually by educational or occupational achievement (Exhibit 13.5). In other words, lower- or middle-class individuals can take advantage of educational opportunities, particularly a college education, to gain entry into higher-status occupations. "Education is the biggest ticket to the middle class," says one economist about upward mobility opportunities for lower-class consumers.[21] In the United States, more than one-third of the children of blue-collar workers are college graduates and have about a 30 percent chance of raising their occupational status.[22] However, the percentage of U.S. college graduates from poverty-level households has remained below 5 percent for decades, reflecting the challenge of paying for college and the difficulty of bridging the gap between the lower and middle classes while in college.[23]

Clearly, upward mobility is not guaranteed. The lower classes, particularly some minorities, still face limited economic and cultural resources as well as limited educational opportunities and are statistically less likely than are the upper classes to have access to higher-status occupations.[24] Individuals from higher-status families are twice as likely to maintain their status as members of lower classes are to achieve a higher status. Even after achieving upward mobility, an individual's behavior can still be heavily influenced by his or her former class level because the behaviors associated with the social class in which people grow up are strongly learned.[25]

Note that the degree of upward mobility may vary across cultures. Typically, Western nations offer the most opportunities for upward advancement, although opportunities for upward mobility have actually decreased in Canada and the United States during some periods.[26] In formerly communist countries, old party and state bureaucrats have formed the new upper classes because they have the skills and economic knowledge to thrive in the modern environment.[27] In Arab countries, the upper and middle classes are growing rapidly as a result of oil money

Your towels –
Personally monogrammed.

Your bathrobe –
Pure silk.

Your spa products –
French lavender.

Your faucet –
ShowHouse®
by Moen®

SHOW HOUSE
by MOEN

Live wonderfully.™

To see more ShowHouse designs, visit ShowHouse.Moen.com

Exhibit 13.5

Social Class Mobility

Sometimes ads show symbols of upward mobility. This ad for ShowHouse is a good example.

Downward mobility Losing one's social standing.

Status panic The inability of children to reach their parents' level of social status.

Social class fragmentation The disappearance of class distinctions.

and an increase in Western college education.[28] The size of the middle class has been exploding in many developing countries because international trade is making affordable goods more available, dual-career families are earning greater income, and more professionals such as managers and accountants are needed to support growing economies.[29]

Downward Mobility

Downward mobility, or moving to a lower class, is an increasing trend in some industrialized societies. In the past 20 years, millions of U.S. families have slid downward as jobs were sent overseas or were eliminated by technology and companies lowered wages or laid off workers.[30] Although many parents dreamed of providing their children with a better life and higher status, some children may have difficulty reaching their parents' status level, a phenomenon labeled **status panic.**[31] Meanwhile, because of increasing material desires, more upper-middle- and middle-class families are having difficulty maintaining a lifestyle characteristic of their status level. Even households with sizable retirement portfolios can feel the pinch when stock market gyrations erode the value of their holdings, which in turn can affect current consumption behavior and consumption patterns after retirement.[32]

Downward mobility creates disappointment and disillusionment. People in this situation face a constant struggle to provide for their family, fight off depression, and maintain their dignity. Sometimes acquisition and consumption can help protect personal self-worth. For example, a consumer might buy a new truck or other item to feel good about himself or herself.[33] Because middle-class consumers in Japan are accustomed to conveying status through the purchase of luxury goods, many still spend lavishly despite the country's prolonged economic problems.[34] Alternatively, downward mobility can lead to a loss of possessions, such as a prized car or home, or to a decrease in consumption if people choose to spend less on items that are less important.

Social Class Fragmentation

Interestingly, the old social class distinctions are beginning to disintegrate—a phenomenon called **social class fragmentation**—due to several factors.[35] First, both upward and downward mobility have blurred class divisions. Second, the increased availability of mass media, especially TV and the Internet, is exposing consumers worldwide to the values and norms of diverse classes and cultures, leading some people to incorporate the idiosyncrasies of these groups into their own behavior. A third reason for social class fragmentation is that advances in communication

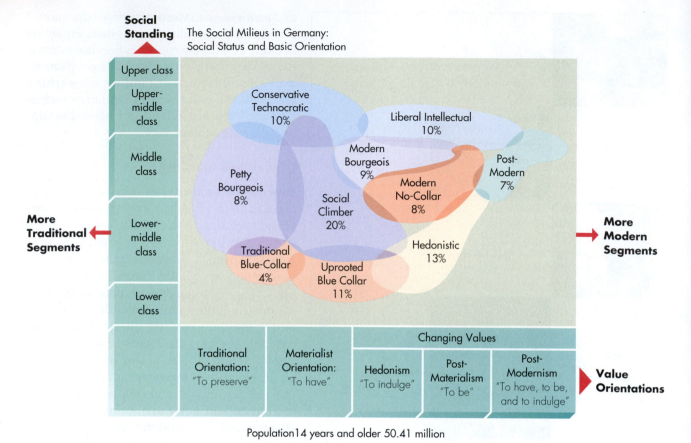

The Social Milieus in Germany:
Social Status and Basic Orientation

Population 14 years and older 50.41 million

1. Conservative-Technocratic Milieu
2. Petty Bourgeois Milieu
3. Traditional Blue-Collar Milieu
4. Uprooted Blue-Collar Milieu
5. Social Climber Milieu
6. Modern Bourgeois Milieu
7. Liberal-Intellectual Milieu
8. Modern No-Collar Milieu
9. Hedonistic Milieu
10. Post-Modern Milieu

Exhibit 13.6

German Social Classes

This exhibit is a detailed depiction of social class structure in German society. The 10 groups are characterized along two dimensions: social standing (low to upper-middle class) and value orientations (traditional to very modern values).

technology have increased interaction across social class lines, as when Internet users chat online without regard to social class. These factors have led to the emergence of many social class subsegments with distinct patterns of values and behavior. The United States now has dozens of classes ranging from the suburban elite (super-rich families) to the hardscrabble (poor, single-parent families).[36] Similar trends are occurring in other countries as well. Exhibit 13.6 shows some traditional and emerging classes in Germany.

How Does Social Class Affect Consumption?

Social class is often viewed as a cause of or motivation for consumer acquisition, consumption, and disposition behaviors. This section examines three major topics: (1) conspicuous consumption and status symbols, (2) compensatory consumption, and (3) the meaning of money.

Conspicuous Consumption and Status Symbols

Conspicuous consumption, also related to social class, is an attempt to offset deficiencies or a lack of esteem by devoting attention to consumption.[37] Conspicuously consumed items are important to their owner because of what they tell others.[38] Only if these items are visible will the message be communicated. According to research, both uniqueness and conformity play a role in conspicuous consumption.[39] Another explanation, from *terror management theory,* suggests that such materialism helps relieve consumers' anxiety over the inevitability of death.[40]

Conspicuous consumption can be observed in most social classes.[41] Individuals at all levels can "keep up with the Joneses"—acquiring and displaying the trappings that are characteristic of a respected member of their class. In the Arab world the newly rich upper classes engage in the conspicuous consumption of items such as airplanes. Conspicuous consumption competition also occurs in formerly communist countries, where someone who cannot keep up with others might be "the shame of the village."[42]

In addition, consumers can engage in **conspicuous waste.** For example, wealthy individuals may buy houses they never use, pianos that no one plays, and cars that no one drives.[43] However, some consumers are moving away from conspicuous consumption toward "experience facilitators" or items and pastimes that set them apart from the crowd.[44] For example, many consumers who have satisfied their desire for material possessions are paying for out-of-the-ordinary experiences, such as adventure travel tours.[45]

Status Symbols and Judging Others

Highly related to conspicuous consumption is the notion that people often judge others on the basis of what they own. In other words, goods or services become **status symbols** to indicate their owners' place in the social hierarchy.[46] Someone who owns an expensive watch or car will likely be viewed as upper class. Among the super-rich, a custom-built yacht equipped with helicopter or mini-sub is becoming a must-have status symbol.[47] Taking an expensive cruise indicates status in Thailand; the same is true of having a rock garden or a golf club membership in Japan. In Brazil, eating in a fast-food restaurant such as Burger King is a status symbol for lower-middle-class consumers.[48]

Consumers' quest to acquire items that reflect not only their current social class but also their class aspirations can explain some acquisitions and consumption behavior. Middle-class consumers, for example, typically want to own a nice house in a respectable neighborhood so that others will judge them in a positive manner. By acquiring items that members of their own social class cannot typically afford,

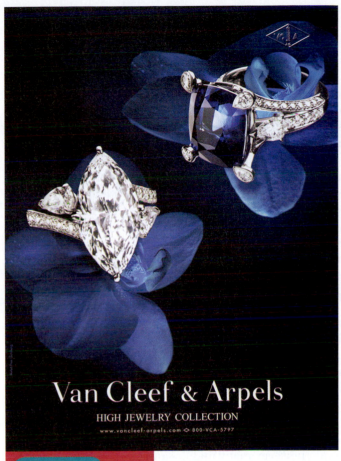

Exhibit 13.7

Conspicuous Consumption

Sometimes consumers buy items because they signal a message of status or eliteness to others. This might be a reason to buy expensive jewelry like that offered by Van Cleef & Arpels.

Conspicuous consumption The acquisition and display of goods and services to show off one's status.

Conspicuous waste Visibly buying products and services that one never uses.

Status symbols Products or services that tell others about someone's social class standing.

consumers can increase their perception of self-worth. Depictions of the material success of peers can spur the desire for luxurious status symbols as well.[49] Even relatively affordable luxuries—like a $6 Panera sandwich or the lowest-priced Mercedes car—"enable less affluent consumers to trade up to higher levels of quality, taste, and aspiration," says a Boston Consulting Group expert. "These are the luxuries that continue to sell even when the economy is shaky, because they often meet very powerful emotional needs."[50]

Parody display Status symbols that start in the lower social classes and move upward.

Fraudulent symbols Symbols that become so widely adopted that they lose their status.

Interestingly, status symbols can sometimes move in a reverse direction, which is called a **parody display**.[51] For example, middle- and upper-class Brazilians feel hip if they practice capoeira, a blend of dance and martial arts that was traditionally popular among members of the lower class.[52] In addition, if certain status symbols become widely possessed, they can lose their status connotations and become **fraudulent symbols**. For example, recognizing that luxury brands are often copied to produce low-price knockoffs for the mass market, Coach and others have redesigned their products with subtler logos. The new products are unmistakably upscale but don't "scream 'Coach, Coach, Coach,'" observes a Coach designer.[53]

Compensatory Consumption

Compensatory consumption The consumer behavior of buying products or services to offset frustrations or difficulties in life.

Compensatory consumption behavior, also related to social class, is an attempt to offset deficiencies or a lack of esteem by devoting attention to consumption.[54] A consumer who is experiencing frustration or difficulties, particularly in terms of career advancement or status level, may compensate for this lack of success by purchasing desired status symbols, such as a car, house, or nice clothes. These acquisitions help restore lost self-esteem.

Traditionally, compensatory consumption typified the acquisition patterns of the working classes, who would mortgage their future to buy a house, car, and other status symbols. More recently, however, many middle- and upper-middle-class U.S. consumers have exhibited compensatory consumption behavior. Some of these consumers have not enjoyed the level of career advancement and prosperity that their parents did, due in part to increased job competition, corporate downsizing, and economic uncertainty. To offset their disappointment, a number of consumers will seek gratification through compensatory consumption.[55] Knowing this tendency, some companies have created offerings that are somewhat more affordable than their existing luxury brands. Tiffany, for example, is opening mall stores to cater to middle-class buyers while continuing to sell more upscale jewelry through its original Tiffany stores.[56]

The Meaning of Money

An important concept related to social class is money. At the most basic level, economists define *money* as a medium of exchange or standard of payment. Under this view, money fulfills a very functional or utilitarian purpose, enabling people to acquire items needed for everyday living. Often, however, money comes to symbolize security, power, love, and freedom.

Consumers learn the meaning of money early in childhood. Parents easily discover that they can control their children by meting out rewards and punishments based on money and by buying or not buying things.[57] Children learn that if they behave, get good grades, or do their chores, their parents will buy things for them. This early learning later translates into adult life when money is viewed

Exhibit 13.8

Marketing a State Lottery

State lotteries are popular among certain classes because of the belief that "it could happen to anyone, including me." This belief illustrates the importance of money.

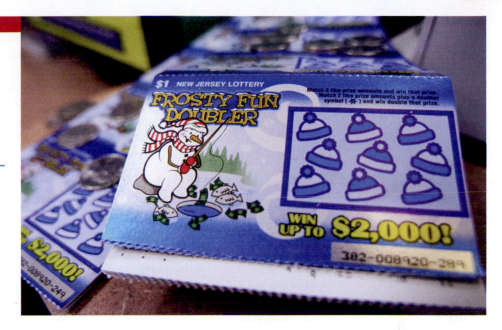

as a means of acquiring things that will bring not only happiness and fulfillment but also a sense of status and prestige. In some societies this belief can lead to an almost insatiable desire and quest for making money, which is enhanced by media coverage of those who have "made it" and by the belief that "it could happen to anyone, including me." This belief is one reason that state lotteries are popular among certain classes (Exhibit 13.8).

Marketers must understand money and what it stands for in order to understand consumption patterns. Money allows consumers to acquire status objects as indicators of social class standing. It is also viewed as a way to rise to a higher level by acquiring more. However, the ongoing increase in credit and debit card usage shows that money need not involve physical cash. Even in nations like Kenya, where cash has long been the accepted payment method, more consumers are qualifying for credit cards so that they can buy now and pay the bill later.[58] Shoppers in a growing number of nations can set up electronic wallets that enable them to easily make purchases online. Consumers in the Netherlands can sign up for the MiniTix electronic wallet and then just click to have the amount of any purchase electronically transferred to an online retailer.[59]

Of course, different consumers treat money in different ways. Some will spend money to acquire what they want now, whereas others will engage in self-denial to save. One study found that spenders tend to be healthier and happier than self-deniers, who tend to be unhappy about finances, personal growth, friends, and jobs.[60] Over time, consumers who consistently spend more than they have will be deeply in debt and may even have to declare bankruptcy.

Money As Both Good and Evil

Money can be perceived as the just reward for hard work and can lead to the acquisition of needed items, a higher quality of life, and the ability to help others and society in general. On the downside, the quest for money can lead to obsession, greed, dishonesty, and potentially harmful practices such as gambling, prostitution, and drug dealing (see Chapter 18). The quest for money can also lead to negative emotions such as anxiety, depression, anger, and helplessness.[61] Although people generally respect wealthy individuals, they often disdain the obsessive desire for money, a reaction that means wealthy people may feel alienated from others.[62] Moreover, individuals who do not share their wealth with others may be seen as selfish and greedy. Interestingly, consumers with yearly household incomes under $25,000 donate about 4 percent of their income to charities, whereas consumers with household incomes of $100,000 or more contribute less than 3 percent of their income to charities.[63]

Money and Happiness

The popular belief (especially in Western countries) that money can buy happiness is rarely true. After some people acquire tremendous wealth, money can become meaningless and no longer highly desired. Furthermore, wealthy people can often afford to hire others to handle many of the activities that they formerly enjoyed, such as gardening and do-it-yourself projects. And, of course, money simply cannot buy love, health, true friendship, and children, among other things. Thus, the relentless pursuit of money may not end in the fulfilled dreams that many think it will.

MARKETING IMPLICATIONS

Tapping into the desire for visible signs of upward mobility can be effective in marketing certain offerings. Not everyone can afford the $72,500 gem-encrusted Vertu cell phone, but even the $6,500 low-end model can symbolize status for newly wealthy consumers in Russia and China.[64] Targeting upper-class consumers who want to wear signs of wealth, Luxottica offers a $10,000 pair of designer sunglasses.[65] And among upper-middle-class consumers, the home elevator—priced at $25,000 and up—is becoming a popular status symbol.[66]

The use of credit and debit cards is rising in many nations, presenting both opportunities and challenges. In Russia, for instance, the use of such cards has risen dramatically and now accounts for an average of $4,000 in annual spending.[67] Credit-card debt is increasing not only in the United States but also in Australia, Canada, the United Kingdom, and elsewhere. However, excess use of credit is also contributing to higher consumer bankruptcy rates in those countries, a situation that raises ethical and public policy issues.

The Consumption Patterns of Specific Social Classes

Earlier sections examined how social class influences acquisition and consumption in general. This section extends the discussion by examining, in broad generalities, the consumption patterns of specific social classes. Although class distinctions are becoming blurred, for the sake of simplicity, this discussion will focus on (1) the upper class, (2) the middle class, (3) the working class, and (4) the homeless. Remember that these are broad tendencies; marketers must delve deeper to identify subsegments of consumers with specific and unique consumption patterns.

The Upper Class

Upper class The aristocracy, new social elite, and upper middle class.

The **upper class** of most societies is a varied group of individuals who include the aristocracy, the new social elite (or nouveaux riches), and the upper middle class (professionals). In the United States, the upper class usually means "old money" consumers—the 1 percent of U.S. society whose ancestors acquired wealth and power long ago and who now live on inherited money. These consumers tend to save and invest money more than members of other classes.[68] Still, many are price-conscious.[69] When shopping for holiday gifts, only 49 percent visit upscale stores; the remainder shop at midrange stores such as Macy's and at discount and outlet stores.[70] Upper-class consumers are also more likely than other classes to carefully research their purchases and to use product characteristics, not price, as an indicator of quality.

Although small, the upper class is diverse, and its members share a number of common values and lifestyles that relate to consumption behavior. These consumers tend to view themselves as intellectual, political, and socially conscious, leading to an increase in behaviors such as attending the theater, investing in art and antiques, traveling, and giving time and money to charities and civic issues.[71] Self-expression is also important, resulting in the purchase of high-quality, prestige brands in good taste. Rolls-Royce, which markets high-end cars like the $320,000 Phantom, says that its average customer has a net worth of more than $30 million.[72]

The nouveaux riches are upper-class consumers who have acquired a great deal of status and wealth in their own lifetimes. This group likes to collect items that are symbols of acquired wealth and power, such as furniture, art objects, cars, fine jewelry, or jets customized with luxurious interiors.[73] Most millionaires do not fit the traditional image of tycoons with stately mansions. One-third of all

Exhibit 13.9

Targeting Upper-Class Consumers

Some ads target upper-class consumers with luxury items like this one from Marlow Yachts.

U.S. households with assets topping $1 million are headed by consumers aged 39 and younger.[74] The average U.S. millionaire is 54 years old, is married with three children, and has an average household net worth of $9.2 million.[75] More than 1.1 million U.S. households have a net worth exceeding $5 million.[76]

The Middle Class

Middle class Primarily white-collar workers.

The U.S. **middle class** consists primarily of white-collar workers, many of whom have attended college (although some have not earned a degree). The values and consumption patterns of middle-class consumers vary, yet many look to the upper class for guidance on certain behaviors such as proper dining etiquette, clothing (especially important for those with aspirations of upward mobility), and popular leisure activities such as golf and tennis. This tendency extends to theater attendance, vacations, and adult education classes for self-improvement. Consumers in the middle class believe that they control their prospects and see opportunity in the future.[77] Middle-class values can also determine the types of products and brands that middle-class consumers acquire and consume. As just one example, compared with lower-class consumers, a higher percentage of middle-class consumers subscribe to premium cable channels.[78]

Similar middle-class behavior patterns have been found in other countries. For example, the middle class in Mexico has many similarities to the U.S. middle class, spending much of its disposable income on cars, clothing, vacations, and household goods. However, lower-middle-class households in Mexico have a lower average income (around $14,400) than that of their American counterparts.[79] In Russia, 5 million consumers make up the middle class, with an average monthly income of $500. Roughly 85 percent of this group own cars, and many prefer Western-brand fast-food restaurants.[80] In fact, the middle class is growing in many developing countries, particularly in India, China, Indonesia, and South Korea.[81]

The Working Class

Working class Primarily blue-collar workers.

The **working class** is mainly represented by blue-collar workers. The stereotype of a hard-hatted, middle-aged man is changing as the working class becomes younger, more ethnically diverse, more female, somewhat more educated, and more alienated from employers.[82] Working-class consumers depend heavily on family members for economic and social support in many areas, including job opportunities and advice—particularly for key purchases and help during difficult times.[83] As a result, they tend to have more of a local orientation socially, psychologically, and geographically than other classes. For example, working-class men exhibit strong preferences for local athletic teams, news segments, and vacations. The working class has also demonstrated strong resistance to changing sex roles, buying non-U.S.-made cars, and abandoning the macho symbol of a large, powerful car or truck.

Consumers in the working class are more likely to spend than to save; however, when they do save, many choose savings accounts over investments and seek financial stability.[84] In addition, working-class consumers are more likely to judge product quality on the basis of price (higher price means higher quality), to shop in mass merchandise or discount stores, and to have less product information when purchasing.[85] And they may exhibit distinctly different product preferences than those of consumers in other social classes. For instance, only 15 percent of U.S. adults with an income below $25,000 say they drink wine, compared with 52 percent of adults in the top income bracket and 28 percent in middle-income brackets.[86]

The Homeless

Homeless People at the low end of the status hierarchy.

At the low end of the status hierarchy are **homeless** consumers who lack shelter and live on the streets or in makeshift structures, cars, or vacant houses.[87] The homeless represent a sizable segment of society in some countries. Official U.S. estimates indicate that about 750,000 people are homeless on any given night, although other estimates of this population range as high as 7 million.[88] This growing group is made up primarily of drug and alcohol abusers, former mental patients, members of female-headed households, and people who have experienced financial setbacks. Homeless consumers are not necessarily unemployed: According to a survey in Austin, Texas, where an estimated 6,000 homeless people live, 51 percent of the respondents were employed but not earning enough to afford a permanent residence.[89]

An overriding characteristic of the homeless is the struggle for survival. With little or no income, homeless consumers have difficulty acquiring daily necessities such as food and medical care.[90] They are not helpless but rather are a "resourceful, determined, and capable group that proactively deals with its lack of resources in the consumer environment."[91] They tend to maintain their self-esteem by distancing themselves from more dependent individuals on welfare or in shelters and from institutions like the Salvation Army, accepting their street role identity, or telling fictitious stories about past or future accomplishments.[92]

A particularly important survival activity for homeless consumers is *scavenging*, finding used or partially used goods that others have discarded. Many vary their scavenging patterns to avoid detection as they move between areas to find the needed items, making this a mobile or nomadic society. Despite their poverty, most homeless consumers have some valued possessions, and they get the maximum use out of items, discarding something only if they have absolutely no further use for it.

MARKETING IMPLICATIONS

Social class can serve as an effective way of segmenting the market, thereby influencing product or service development, messages, media selection, and channel selection.

Product or service development

Social class motives and values can determine which offerings consumers desire. For example, to satisfy their need for prestige and luxury, many upper-class consumers prefer high-end automobiles, imported wines, fancy restaurants, exotic or deluxe vacations, and couture clothing. The working class, on the other hand, wants good quality at a fair price, and many offerings are designed to fulfill this desire. Examples include family-rate motels, buffet restaurants, and economy or used cars. In Mexico, the 823 stores in the Elektra chain cater to working-class customers by making credit available for purchases of televisions, appliances, and even cars.[93]

Sometimes marketers develop different product lines for different classes. Targeting middle- and upper-class consumers, Procter & Gamble has developed a premium line of Pampers disposable diapers, Baby Stages of Development, marketed on the basis of innovative features rather than price.[94] Also, marketers can create products that appeal

Cestello
18kt pink gold.

A private affair.

ROLEX
Cellini

Rolex Cestello in 18kt pink gold. Rolex, v. Cellini and Cestello are trademarks.
FOR THE NAME AND LOCATION OF AN OFFICIAL ROLEX CELLINI JEWELER NEAR YOU, PLEASE CALL 1-800-367-6539.

www.rolex.com   New York

Exhibit 13.10

Advertising a Status Symbol

The Rolex watch is a strong status symbol for upper-class consumers.

to consumers' aspirations for upward mobility. For example, the designer Michael Kors offers moderately priced clothing based on his high-end apparel line, fashions he calls "carpool couture" that "look aspirational."[95]

Messages

Advertisers targeting a particular social class within the larger population can be effective by tapping into the group's distinctiveness; when targeting the upper classes, for instance, the advertiser might suggest the group's status as a small, elite group (see Exhibit 13.10).[96] Other messages for the upper classes might focus on themes of "a just reward for hard work," "you've made it," or "pamper yourself because you deserve it." Certain offerings can be advertised as coveted status symbols; thus, Jaguar advertises its XJ8 as a car that wealthy consumers lust after because it combines "beauty and brains." Messages for the working class might take on a more localized orientation, focusing on home and friends as well as favored activities such as hunting and watching sports events. In addition, messages can use typical members of a social class as role models. The ad in Exhibit 13.11, for example, represents an appeal to the working class.

Media exposure

The classes differ in their exposure to certain media. Advertisers try to reach the upper classes, especially the nouveaux riches, through targeted magazines and newspapers such as *The Robb Report, Modern Luxury,* and *ForbesLife Executive Woman.*[97] Many upper-class consumers watch public TV stations and cultural shows and are more likely to fit the profile of the Internet shopper, with higher income and education.[98] Lower-class consumers tend to be heavy watchers of TV and less likely than other classes to read magazines and newspapers. Middle-class consumers, particularly those with only some college, are unique because they tend to be heavy TV watchers as well as magazine readers.

Channel selection

Marketers targeting upper-class consumers can make goods available through channels that sell exclusive merchandise with personalized service.[99] For example, the high-end Bijan boutique on Rodeo Drive in Los Angeles sells by appointment only, offering luxury clothing such as $1,000 men's silk ties.[100] Conspicuous consumption can play a role when consumers want to acquire items in the "correct" store, especially if they can be seen doing so.[101] Even mass merchandisers are selling products with a bit more snob appeal. Target sells "cheap chic" apparel and housewares very similar to those offered by pricier retailers.[102] Dollar stores such as Dollar Tree attract working-class consumers with value pricing of quality goods.

Exhibit 13.11

Working-Class Appeal

This ad appeals to working-class values and product preferences (i.e., having a large vehicle to tow things such as a trailer as well as having a "big fat juicy" cheeseburger).

Note of caution

Marketers have had difficulty in using social class as a segmentation variable for several reasons. As noted earlier, social class is difficult to assess because a variety of factors such as occupation and income can have opposite effects on class. Also, variations within a class make social class a better predictor of broad behavior patterns, such as conspicuous product–level choice, than of specific behaviors such as brand choice. Finally, because of social class fragmentation, traditional class distinctions may be becoming too broad to be truly useful. Therefore, marketers are using technology to segment markets and to target consumers more precisely through database marketing, the Internet, direct mail, and other tools.

How the Household Influences Consumer Behavior

Some researchers argue that the household itself is the most important unit of analysis for consumer behavior because households make many more acquisition, consumption, and disposition decisions than individuals do. This section defines families and households, examines the different types of households, describes the family life cycle, and looks at how families influence decisions and consumption.

Types of Households

A *family* is usually defined as a group of individuals living together who are related by marriage, blood, or adoption. The most typical unit is the **nuclear family,** consisting of a father, mother, and children. The **extended family** consists of the nuclear family plus relatives such as grandparents, aunts, uncles, and cousins. Nearly 4 million U.S. families have three or more generations of parents living with children and grandchildren.[103] In the United States we often think of *family* in terms of the nuclear family, whereas the extended family is the defining unit in many nations. Although the family is important almost everywhere in the world, some countries and cultures exhibit a stronger family orientation than others. In Japan and China, for example, the family is a focal point, and most people feel a very strong sense of obligation to it.[104]

Nuclear family Father, mother, and children.

Extended family The nuclear family plus relatives such as grandparents, aunts, uncles, and cousins.

Household is a broader term that includes a single person living alone or a group of individuals who live together in a common dwelling, regardless of whether they are related. This term includes cohabiting couples (an unmarried male and female living together), gay couples, and singles who are roommates. Because the number of households is on the rise—increasing by 1.35 million each year—marketers and researchers are increasingly thinking in terms of households rather than families.[105]

Household A single person living alone or a group of individuals who live together in a common dwelling, regardless of whether they are related.

The traditional stereotype of the American family consisted of a husband as the primary wage earner, a non-wage-earning wife at home, and two children under the age of 18. Today, because of later marriages, cohabitation, divorce, dual careers, boomerang children, people living longer, and a lower birth rate, the number of nontraditional families has greatly increased.[106] In fact, one-person households now outnumber households with children.[107] Meanwhile, the number of single-parent households headed by women has increased three times faster than the number of two-parent households.[108] Note that 29 percent of all U.S. households consist of married couples without children (either because of a conscious choice to have none or because the children have left home).[109] Exhibit 13.12 shows how U.S. households are changing.

Households and Family Life Cycle

Family life cycle Different stages of family life, depending on the age of the parents and how many children are living at home.

Households can further differ in terms of stage in the **family life cycle.** As shown in Exhibit 13.13, families can be characterized in terms of the age of the parents, the number of parents present, the age and number of children living at home, and so on.[110] Households may also consist of one or more unmarried singles, couples without children, and couples whose children are grown and gone. Changes such as death or divorce can alter household structure by, for instance, creating single-parent households, as the arrows in Exhibit 13.13 indicate.

Marketers must consider the great variation in needs over the family life cycle and the effect on consumer behavior within households. In general, spending increases as households shift from young singles to young married and then remains high until falling sharply at the older married or older single stages.[111] However, this pattern depends on what is purchased. New parents tend to spend more on health care, clothing, housing, and food (and less on alcohol, transportation, and education). The U.S. market for baby products alone is worth nearly $9 billion dollars.[112] As their families grow, parents spend more on housing and furnishings, child care, and related household services. Young empty nesters spend

	2000		2010		2000-2010
	number	percent	number	percent	percent change
All households	110,140	100.0 %	117,696	100.0 %	6.9 %
Families	77,705	70.6	80,193	68.1	3.2
Married couples	60,969	55.4	61,266	52.1	0.5
with children younger than 18*	24,286	22.1	23,433	19.9	−3.5
with children 18+ only	5,318	4.8	6,884	5.8	29.4
with no children	31,365	28.5	30,950	26.3	−1.3
Single fathers	1,523	1.4	1,660	1.4	9.0
Single mothers	7,473	6.8	7,779	6.6	4.1
Other families	7,741	7.0	9,488	8.1	22.6
Nonfamilies	32,434	29.4	37,503	31.9	18.0
Men living alone	10,898	9.9	12,577	10.7	15.4
Women living alone	16,278	14.8	18,578	15.8	14.1
Other nonfamilies	5,258	4.8	6,347	5.4	20.7

* Includes those with children both younger than age 18 and 18 and older.
Note: Numbers in thousands and percent of all households by type, 2000-2010; and percent change 2000-2010.
Numbers may not add to total due to rounding.

Exhibit 13.12

Changes in Household Types

The composition of U.S. households is changing. In particular, the segment of nontraditional families (singles living alone, couples without children, divorced families) is on the rise.

more on vehicles and clothing; older single households and couples spend more on home-based products, health care, and travel. Finally, households in the midst of a life cycle change are more likely to switch brand preferences and be more receptive to marketing efforts.[113]

However, these stages do not capture all types of households. Notably missing are same-sex couples and never-married single mothers, two important market segments. Gays and lesbians, for example, represent anywhere from 11 to 23 million consumers in the United States and are relatively affluent and highly educated (see Chapter 12).[114] In addition, more than 4 million women are never-married mothers between 15 and 44 years old.[115] Finally, as discussed in Chapter 17, more than 60 percent of U.S. households include a pet (cat, dog, or another animal) that is sometimes regarded as a very special family member and can therefore be an important influence on household spending.[116]

Changing Trends in Household Structure

Five main factors are altering the basic structure and characteristics of households. These include (1) delayed marriage, (2) cohabitation, (3) dual careers, (4) divorce, and (5) smaller families.

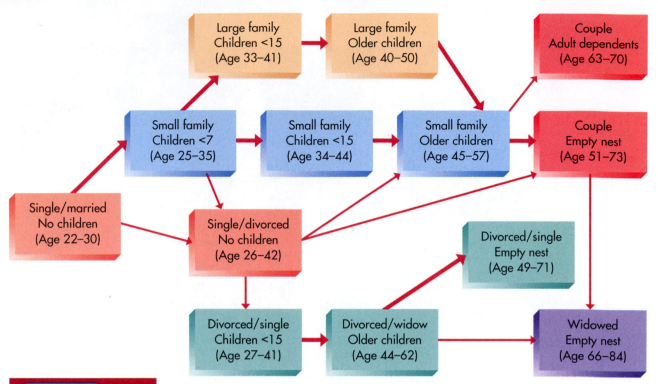

Source: Rex Y. Du and Wagner A. Kamakura, "Household Life Cycles and Lifestyles in the United States," *Journal of Marketing Research,* February 2006, Figure 1, p. 126.

Exhibit 13.13

Household Life Cycles in the United States

This chart depicts how households change as the family life cycle changes. Each box represents a stage in the family life cycle; each line and arrow represents a type of change (marriage, divorce, death, children entering or leaving, aging). Note that this diagram accounts for numerous possibilities (divorce, becoming a single parent, being a childless couple, never marrying). What stage is your family in right now?

Delayed Marriage

In many Western societies, an increasing number of individuals are either delaying or avoiding getting married. Today the median age at which U.S. men first marry is 27; for U.S. women, the median age is 25.[117] As a result, 27 percent of all U.S. households (27 million people, more women than men) consist of one person living alone.[118] Delayed marriage may occur because career is seen as a higher priority, because it is now more acceptable for a man and a woman to live together before marriage, or because consumers with college loans want to reduce their debt first.

The trend toward delayed marriage is important for marketers because single-person households exhibit unique consumption patterns. For example, single men spend more on alcohol, new cars, clothes, and education than married men do. Compared with married women, single women tend to spend more on new cars, shoes, entertainment, candy, and housing (to live in a safe area).[119] Singles tend to have more discretionary income and therefore can spend more than couples of the same social class and income level.[120] Not only do singles spend more on restaurant meals, but they also eat out more often.[121]

By delaying marriage, couples typically find themselves in a better financial position and can pay more for a home and furnishings, baby clothes, and housekeeping services than they would have if they had married earlier. Parents over age 35 with children under age 6 spend more than younger parents do on housing, furnishings, child care, transportation, and food. Also, when couples delay marriage, they also delay having children, a development that has led to an increase in the use of fertility drugs and the incidence of twins and triplets.[122]

Cohabitation

As a result of changing social norms, more consumers are deciding to live with members of the opposite sex outside marriage. Among the 5 million opposite-sex U.S. households, more than half have never been married. Most of the cohabitors (38 percent) are aged 25 to 34, and 20 percent are aged 35 to 44.[123] In addition, more than 600,000 U.S. households consist of same-sex couples.[124] Compared with married couples, cohabitating individuals tend to be more self-oriented. Many view possessions as personal rather than joint items in case the relationship does not endure.[125] Nevertheless, many unmarried partners share expenses, and because both individuals are likely to work, they often have higher discretionary income than do married couples of a similar age (with a nonworking spouse). Thus, unmarried couples are more frequent consumers of entertainment, transportation, and vacations than are married couples.

Dual-Career Families

The two major types of dual-career families are (1) those in which the woman seeks career advancement and personal fulfillment and (2) those in which the woman works out of financial necessity and considers her employment "just a job."[126] The woman in the latter group tends to be more like the traditional housewife in terms of outlook and behavior, whereas the woman in the former group is more contemporary and progressive.

Dual-career families have several important implications for consumer behavior. First, having two incomes increases discretionary spending.[127] Dual-career families tend to spend more than other families do on child care, eating out, and services in general (see Exhibit 13.14). Wives are contributing to the family finances, which allows them influence over household acquisition and consumption decisions for vacations, cars, housing, and other offerings.[128] Second, the increased burden of having both career and family, or *role overload*, leaves less time for cooking, housekeeping, shopping, and other activities. This is why dual-career families particularly value offerings that save time, such as microwaveable meals, prepared foods, housekeeping, child care, fast food, and food delivery services. Because women in such households have limited shopping time, they are more likely to be brand loyal, buy impulsively, and buy from catalogs or online.

Third, more husbands are taking on household responsibilities, including shopping, cooking, and—for a small but growing percentage of families—staying home to care for children.[129] As a result, more ads are geared toward men who are, for example, sharing some responsibility for household cooking. In Asia, however, such ads may prompt a negative response from both men and women because sex roles are viewed more traditionally, even though more men are handling more housework.

For women who want it all, we deliver.

- Medical/dental/vision coverage from day one
- Paid vacation, personal days and holidays
- 401(k) and profit sharing plans
- Backup Care
- Dependent care reimbursement
- Pregnancy, Health and Wellness course
- Prenatal exercise and Healthy Babies programs
- Adoption assistance

Own Your Career.

WORKING MOTHER 100 BEST COMPANIES 2008
(sixth consecutive year)

verizon wireless
We never stop working for you.

To learn about nationwide opportunities in a variety of fields, visit

verizonwireless.com/careers

We are an equal opportunity employer, m/f/d/v.

Divorce

More than four of every ten U.S. marriages are likely to end in divorce.[130] Although the trend has recently leveled off, many divorces still occur each year, and these separations have important implications for consumer behavior.[131] Going through a divorce represents a major transition in which consumers perform a number of critical tasks, such as disposing of old possessions, forming a new household, and creating new patterns of consumption.[132] Divorce can lead to a major change in lifestyle, and acquiring goods and services can be an integral part of forming a new identity and relieving stress during this transition. For example, a recently divorced consumer might buy a new house, car, furniture, or clothing; get a new hairstyle; or go to singles events to assume a new image or to feel better.

Divorce also influences household structure. If the couple was childless, the newly divorced often adopt many of the singles' acquisition and consumption patterns discussed earlier. However, these new singles are typically older and have greater discretionary income for housing, transportation, and clothing if they are working. Also, divorce creates single-parent families when children are involved. Estimates are that one in three families in the United States now has only one parent, and most of these families have a female head-of-household, although the proportion of single fathers is growing.[133] Because the single parent must earn an income and raise children, convenience offerings—such as packaged or fast foods—are a necessity.[134] Compared with their married counterparts, single parents are likely to have lower than average incomes, to spend relatively less on most things, and to be renters rather than homeowners.

Finally, divorced individuals with children are remarrying with greater frequency, creating more stepfamilies.[135] Demographers estimate that more than one-third of U.S. families are of this type. In nearly two-thirds of stepfamilies, children live with their biological mother; many such families are lower in income and education and are more youthful than intact families. Due to potential stress and conflicting emotions, about half these families will also end up in divorce. Like other households, stepfamilies can have unique consumption needs. For example, children who travel between families require duplicate supplies of clothes, toothbrushes, and toys.[136]

Smaller Families

In many countries, the average household size is getting smaller. In the United States, Boomer and Xer couples are having fewer children because of dual careers; financial burdens, and concern for overpopulation—some couples believe that having more than two children is socially irresponsible. The average family size in the United States is now 3.14 people.[137] Smaller family size means more discretionary income to spend on recreational items, vacations, education, toys, and entertainment. Smaller families also can spend more on each child. Childless married couples, one of the fastest-growing types of households, have more discretionary income than other households. Compared with couples who have children, childless couples spend more on food, restaurant meals, entertainment, liquor, clothing, and pets.[138]

(MARKETING IMPLICATIONS)

Products and services that offer convenience can be marketed specifically to dual-career and divorced households. Because more husbands from dual-career families and single or divorced men shop for groceries and other items, retailers are increasingly targeting men.[139] Wives in dual-career households have more clout in expensive decisions, so marketers of costly products and services must appeal to both husband and wife. Nontraditional families are also being targeted: Hallmark has developed greeting cards that deal with stepfamily and cohabitation relationships.[140]

Single men and women are an attractive target for many marketers. Some stores in the Trader Joe's grocery chain designate a special "Singles Night" and create romance-themed displays of chocolate and wine for customers who come to mix and mingle as they shop.[141]

Marketers are targeting same-sex couples through events like gay pride parades, ads in targeted magazines such as *Out* and *The Advocate,* specialized websites, billboards in select neighborhoods, and—increasingly—TV ads depicting same-sex couples.[142] Following the lead of Subaru, Ford, and other automakers, Cadillac has begun advertising its vehicles to gay consumers.[143] In openly targeting gay and lesbian consumers, however, some of these marketers have become targets of conservative groups and religious leaders opposed to homosexuality.[144] Marketers who target same-sex couples also must understand how these consumers make decisions; for instance, purchasing decisions by lesbian couples tend to be made in a more egalitarian manner than decisions in husband- or wife-dominated traditional households are.[145]

Roles that Household Members Play

Household decision roles Roles that different members play in a household decision.

A key aspect of households is that more than one individual can become involved in acquisition and consumption. This section discusses various elements of household consumer behavior, with particular emphasis on **household decision roles** and how household members influence decision processes.

In a multiperson household, members may perform a variety of tasks or roles in acquiring and consuming a product or service:

- *Gatekeeper* Household members who collect and control information important to the decision.

- *Influencer* Household members who try to express their opinions and influence the decision.

- *Decider* The person or persons who actually determine which product or service will be chosen.

- *Buyer* The household member who physically acquires the product or service.

- *User* The household members who consume the product.

Each role can be performed by different household members or by a single individual, subset of individuals, or the entire household. For example, in deciding which movie to rent or download, parents might make the final decision, but the children may play a role, either directly (by stating their preferences) or indirectly (when parents keep their children's preferences in mind). One parent may actually obtain the movie, but the entire family may watch (or consume) it. Parents are often the deciders and purchasers of items consumed by their children, such as clothing, toys, food, and movies. Similarly, more than 70 percent of men's underwear and fragrance is purchased by wives and girlfriends. Exhibit 13.15 divides household purchases into nine categories, depending on the decision maker and the user.

Instrumental roles Roles that relate to tasks affecting the buying decision.

Household decision roles can be **instrumental,** meaning that they relate to tasks affecting the buying decision, such as when and how much to purchase.

Exhibit 13.15

Buyers and Users

Household purchase decisions can be made by one, some, or all members of the family. Acquired products and services may be consumed by one, some, or all members. Here is an example of three cells that result from crossing these two factors. Can you think of examples that would fit into the other six cells?

A Purchase Decision Maker

		One member	Some members	All members
A Consumer	One member	1	2 Tennis racket	3
	Some members	4 Sugar Pops	5	6
	All members	7	8	9 Refrigerator

For Example:
1. Mom and Dad go to buy a new tennis racket for Mom. Dad advises Mom on her purchase. Some members are decision makers and one member is a consumer: cell 2.
2. Mom goes to the grocery store to buy Sugar Pops cereal for her children. She'll never eat the stuff. One member is a decision maker and some members are consumers: cell 4.
3. Mom, Dad, and the kids go to the department store to buy a refrigerator. All members are decision makers and all are consumers: cell 9.

Expressive roles Roles that involve an indication of family norms.

Roles can also be **expressive,** which means they indicate family norms, such as choice of color or style.[146] Traditionally, the husband fulfilled the instrumental role and the wife the expressive role, but sex-role changes are altering this pattern.

Conflict can often occur in fulfilling different household roles based on (1) the reasons for buying, (2) who should make the decision, (3) which option to choose, and (4) who gets to use the product or service.[147] For example, because all family members have increased their computer usage, conflict often arises over who gets to use the computer and for how long.[148] Conflict may also occur in decisions about "green" consumption, such as using organic food and conserving water or energy.[149] In general, households resolve conflicts through problem solving, persuasion, bargaining, and politics, with persuasion and problem solving the most frequently used methods.[150] Note, however, that resolution is often not systematic and rational, but rather a "muddling-through" process in which the household makes a series of small decisions to arrive at a solution.[151] Moreover, many households avoid rather than confront conflict.

Marketers should recognize that household decisions are more frequent in some circumstances than in others. Specifically, joint decisions are more likely when the perceived risk associated with the decision is high, the decision is very important, there is ample time to make a decision, and the household is young. In addition, household members can influence each other in terms of brand preferences and loyalties, information search patterns, media reliance, and price sensitivities.[152]

The Roles of Spouses

Husbands and wives play different roles in making decisions, and the nature of their influence depends on the offering and the couple's relationship. In examining husband-wife influence, a landmark study conducted in Belgium (and replicated in the United States) identified four major decision categories:[153]

Husband-dominant decision
Decision made primarily by the male head-of-household.

Wife-dominant decision
Decision made primarily by the female head-of-household.

Autonomic decision
Decision equally likely to be made by the husband or wife, but not by both.

Syncratic decision Decision made jointly by the husband and wife.

▶ A **husband-dominant decision** is made primarily by the male head-of-household (e.g., the purchase of lawn mowers and hardware).

▶ A **wife-dominant decision** is made primarily by the female head-of-household (e.g., children's clothing, women's clothing, groceries, and toiletries).

▶ An **autonomic decision** is equally likely to be made by the husband or the wife but not by both (e.g., men's clothing, luggage, toys and games, sporting equipment, and cameras).

▶ A **syncratic decision** is made jointly by the husband and wife (e.g., vacations, refrigerators, TVs, living room furniture, financial planning services, and the family car).

As spouses come closer to a final decision, the process tends to move toward syncratic decision making and away from the other three types, particularly for more important decisions. These role structures are only generalities, however; the actual influence exerted depends on many factors. First, a spouse will have greater influence when he or she brings higher financial resources to the family and when he or she has a high level of involvement in the decision.[154] Second, demographic factors, such as total family income, occupation, and education, are also related to the degree of husband-wife influence.[155] Combined, these factors provide a spouse with a perception of power in the decision-making situation. The higher the degree of perceived power, the more likely the spouse will exert influence.

When the family has a strong traditional sex-role orientation, certain tasks are stereotypically considered either masculine or feminine, and more decisions tend to be husband dominated than they are in less traditional families.[156] For example, Mexican American families tend toward a traditional orientation and husband-dominant decisions. However, sex-role changes, as noted earlier, are influencing husband-wife decisions. In Thailand, nearly half of the husbands surveyed said that they decided what foods their households would eat and that they did the family food shopping, a task traditionally considered part of the wife's role.[157] In the United States, joint decision making is most common among Anglo families, husband dominance is more likely in Japanese American families, and wife dominance is more prevalent in African American families.

Researchers have found support for the four major patterns of spousal decision roles in a number of countries, although the United States, France, and the Netherlands exhibited a higher level of joint decision making than did Venezuela and Gabon, where autonomous decisions were more prevalent.[158] Other aspects of spousal decision making have also been studied. For example, through the processes of **bargaining** (which involves a fair exchange) or **concession** (in which a spouse gives in on some points to get what he or she wants in other areas), couples tend to make equitable decisions that result from compromises.[159] Couples do not typically follow a formal, systematic process for making decisions; instead, they use an informal process in which they have limited awareness of each other's knowledge and decision strategy.[160] Husbands and wives are generally not good at estimating their spouse's influence and preferences, although each learns from the outcome of previous decisions and makes adjustments over time.[161]

Bargaining A fair exchange of preferences.

Concession Giving in on some points to get what one wants in other areas.

The Roles of Children

Children play an important role in household decisions by attempting to influence their parents' acquisition, usage, and disposition behavior. The most common stereotype is that children nag until their parents finally give in. Research finds that the success of such attempts depends on the type of offering, characteristics of the parents, age of the child, and stage of the decision process.[162] Children are more likely to use their influence for child-related products such as cereals, cookies, snacks, cars, vacations, and new computer technologies. For clothing and toys, children often use the argument that "everyone else has one," and because parents want to avoid being identified as "scrimpers," they will often give in.[163]

Interestingly, children consistently overestimate how much influence they have in most decisions.[164] Children tend to have less influence when parents are more involved in the decision process or are more traditional and conservative. Working and single parents, on the other hand, are more likely to give in because they face more time pressures.[165] When parents place more restrictions on TV watching, they tend to yield less, but children's attempts to influence parents increase as parents watch more TV with them.

Another important finding is that the older the child, the more influence he or she will exert.[166] One reason for this situation is that younger children tend to have lower involvement in the decision process, and parents are more likely to refuse younger children's requests. As evidence, teens believe that they have greater influence when the decision is important to them and the family. Older children also often generate their own income, giving them more power.[167] However, even when the family includes two or more children, parents still exert the most influence over decisions about buying and consuming new offerings.[168]

One study examined the strategies adolescents use in trying to influence parental and family decision making, which include bargaining (making deals), persuasion (trying to influence the decision in their favor), emotional appeals (using emotion to get what they want), and requests (directly asking).[169] Parents, in turn, can use not only the same strategies on their children but also expert (knowledge), legitimate (power), and directive (parental authority) strategies.

The type of household determines the nature of children's influence:

- Authoritarian households stress obedience.
- Neglectful households exert little control.
- Democratic households encourage self-expression.
- Permissive households remove constraints.

Children are more likely to have direct decision control in permissive and neglectful families and are more likely to influence decisions in democratic and permissive ones.[170] Also, children's influence varies at different stages of the decision process. It is greatest early in the decision-making process (problem recognition and information search) and declines significantly in the evaluation and choice phases.[171]

MARKETING IMPLICATIONS

Marketers need to recognize that household decision roles exist and may be performed by different household members. Thus, appealing only to deciders or purchasers may be a narrow and relatively ineffective strategy. Marketers who exclusively target children for toys or breakfast cereals, for example, ignore the fact that parents are usually influencers, deciders, and purchasers of these products. Therefore, marketers should determine which family members are involved in each acquisition decision and appeal to all important parties. To illustrate, the Kidzania theme park in Tokyo—designed for children from 2 to 15 years old—targets Japanese parents who want to give their children a taste of different careers. The entrance fee allows children to "play" at a variety of occupations, from dentistry to electrical engineering.[172]

More U.S. children are using the Internet for e-mail, visiting websites, and playing games in virtual worlds created especially for youngsters.[173] This development has created opportunities for established brands and newcomers alike. Disney's Club Penguin, loaded with children's games and activities, has 700,000 young members whose parents pay a monthly fee of $6.[174] Marketing to young children, in particular, raises ethical and legal issues; for that reason, websites for children under 13 must comply with the Children's Online Privacy Protection Act and obtain parental permission before collecting information from children. ⬤▬

Summary

Individuals in a society can be grouped into status levels (upper, middle, and lower), making up a social class hierarchy. Class distinctions are significant because members of a particular class share common life experiences and therefore also share values and consumer behavior patterns, although many variations occur within groups. Individuals are most likely to be influenced by members of their own class because they regularly interact with them. Still, influence can cross class lines through the *trickle-down effect* (when lower classes copy upper-class values and behavior) or the *status float effect* (when trends start in the lower classes and spread upward).

A variety of factors determine social class, the most critical of which are occupation and education. Researchers use a battery of items, such as the Computerized Status Index, to measure social class. Three major trends producing an evolution in social class structure are upward mobility, downward mobility, and social class fragmentation. Social class influences consumer behavior in three major ways: (1) through conspicuous consumption, the acquisition and display of status symbol offerings to demonstrate social standing; (2) through compensatory consumption, trying to offset some deficiency by engaging in greater than usual consumption; and (3) through the meaning of money.

Households include both families and unrelated people living together as well as singles. The proportion of nontraditional households has increased because of factors such as (1) later marriages, (2) cohabitation, (3) dual-career families, (4) divorce, and (5) smaller families. Households exert considerable influence on acquisition and consumption patterns. Members can play different roles in the decision process (gatekeeper, influencer, decider, buyer, and user). Also, husbands and wives vary in their influence in the decision process, depending on whether the situation is husband dominant, wife dominant, autonomic, or syncratic. Children can influence the decision process by making requests of parents. The nature of this influence partly depends on whether the household is authoritarian, neglectful, democratic, or permissive. In general, the older the child, the greater the influence.

Questions for Review and Discussion

1. What is the social class hierarchy?
2. What are the determinants of social class?
3. Why is social class fragmentation taking place?
4. Why would a consumer engage in conspicuous consumption and conspicuous waste?
5. How does parody display differ from status symbols?
6. Under what circumstances does compensatory consumption occur?
7. Why might a company develop different offerings for consumers in different social classes?
8. Define the terms *nuclear family*, *extended family*, and *household*.
9. What five key factors have altered the basic structure and characteristics of households?
10. What are the five roles that a household member may perform in acquiring and consuming something?

CL Visit http://cengage.com/marketing/hoyer/ConsumerBehavior5e to find resources that are available to help you study for the course.

Getting to Know Mom

What do families need, want, use, and buy? More marketers are getting to know Mom as they gather information about the acquisition and consumption preferences and patterns of households with children. Some companies monitor what moms are saying about products or problems on parenting websites and blogs. A growing number of marketers are sponsoring special areas on social networking sites geared toward mothers, their goal being to research specific questions or to generate feedback and word of mouth about certain brands.

For instance, Hasbro sponsors the Playskool Preschool Playgroup area on CafeMom.com, a networking site where moms exchange ideas about everything from baby talk and baby clothes to recipes and reading. More than 10,000 mothers have joined the Playskool area, where they post ideas about raising preschoolers and are also able to receive free Playskool samples. When Hasbro introduced its Kid Motion toy kit, the company sent samples to 5,000 members of the Playskool Preschool Playgroup. Hasbro learned from the reactions that recipients posted on CafeMom—and its product also benefited when moms talked up the product to other moms.

McDonald's created a Global Moms Advisory Panel to offer advice on its menu and its restaurants because "moms are so important to our business," says the chain's head of global marketing. "We intend to listen and learn from our Global Moms Panel, with the goal of providing the best possible experience for families in our restaurants around the world." KFC's Moms Matter! Advisory Board performs a similar function, serving as a sounding board for products and promotions under consideration. Looking for insights into future household trends, KFC's marketers also ask these moms about issues beyond eating out, such as how they manage daily stress and family responsibilities.

Johnson & Johnson reaches out to research mothers' needs and the role of household dynamics in several ways. It sponsors the BabyCenter.com networking site, where mothers post comments about all aspects of expecting and raising children. The site also features professional videos about pregnancy, child development, and other topics. J&J does not advertise on BabyCenter, although it does accept advertising from other marketers. To stimulate extended dialogue in person, J&J recently invited dozens of mothers who are active bloggers to a three-day Camp Baby conference in New Jersey. Discussions during and after the conference helped J&J's marketers better understand what moms think about, worry about, and look forward to. The dialogue continued long after the moms returned home because the participants blogged about the experience (providing J&J with valuable reactions), and company personnel also blogged about what they learned.

Procter & Gamble is another company that is actively seeking the input and insights of mothers. In particular, it wants to find out more about the needs and interests of moms who are 28 to 45 years old and have children who are 19 years old or younger. Vocalpoint, P&G's networking site, has recruited more than 600,000 moms who fit this demographic profile. Once they join, the moms receive P&G product samples, tell the company what they think about the products, and express their opinions in periodic focus groups and research surveys. Vocalpoint sends moms a weekly e-mail newsletter with updates about what is on the site and specific questions such as how and when they prefer to communicate their opinions. In addition, the site invites moms to get involved in word-of-mouth campaigns for P&G products such as Febreze air freshener and Dawn dishwashing foam. Not only is P&G getting to know moms; it is also getting moms to know its products and to spread the word about the products they like and use.[175]

Case Questions

1. From a marketing standpoint, what are the advantages and disadvantages of sponsoring a branded area on a networking site, such as the Playskool Preschool Playgroup, to engage a target audience?
2. J&J's Camp Baby was for moms only—no babies allowed. Would the company learn more about household influences by allowing children to accompany mom bloggers next time? Explain your answer.
3. Do you think Vocalpoint moms should be asked to respond to surveys about some P&G products and also be invited to promote certain P&G products through word of mouth? Why, or why not?
4. What are moms' roles in the family decision-making process? How might other family members play a role?

Psychographics: Values, Personality, and Lifestyles

Chapter 14

LEARNING OBJECTIVES

After studying this chapter, you will be able to

1. Define values and the value system, and show how they can be described.

2. Identify some values that characterize Western cultures, outline the main factors that influence values, and describe how values can be measured.

3. Discuss the personality characteristics most closely related to consumer behavior patterns and show why these are important from a marketing perspective.

4. Explain how lifestyles are represented by activities, interests, and opinions, and describe how psychographic applications in marketing combine values, personality, and lifestyle variables.

INTRODUCTION

The Lure of Luxury versus Back to Basics

Lured by luxury and back to basics—these contrasting trends are playing out around the world as consumers buy and use goods and services to express what is important to them, who they are, and how they live. Affluent consumers who buy high-end items like a $14,000 handbag to show off their financial success are the mainstay of luxury brands like Louis Vuitton and Gucci, which have their strongest sales outside North America. Meanwhile, a growing number of consumers are treating themselves to "affordable luxury" items such as a $300 Coach purse or a $6,900 BeefEater barbecue grill, perhaps to keep up with the Joneses or to indulge a hobby or interest.

Despite the lure of luxury, some consumers are turning away from brand cachet and going back to basics. Some are rebelling against what they see as too much emphasis on material things, some worry about wasting natural resources, some want to break out of the brand mold, and others simply want to save money. As a result, sales of private-label goods marketed by retailers such as Rite Aid have been rising (and raising stores' profit margins). Going back to basics can also mean buying a branded product for less in a discount store such as Wal-Mart or Costco. Even consumers who change their buying habits for environmental reasons can make a statement about themselves through their decisions. The eco-friendly Prius, for example, is so distinctive that no one could mistake it for an ordinary car.[1]

These dual trends illustrate the influence of values, personality, and lifestyles on consumer behavior, all topics discussed in this chapter. Values determine what products people feel are "right" to buy or own (whether they care more about acquiring possessions or saving the environment, for instance). If a consumer's personality leans toward frugality, he or she will put more emphasis on getting the most value for the price paid (hence the popularity of private-label brands). People who love cooking outdoors may view a fancy barbecue grill as a lifestyle necessity.

Psychographics A description of consumers based on their psychological and behavioral characteristics.

Together, values, personality, and lifestyles constitute the basic components of **psychographics,** the description of consumers based on their psychological and behavioral characteristics (see Exhibit 14.1). Traditionally, psychographics measured consumer lifestyles, but more modern applications also include the consumers' psychological makeup, values, personality, and behavior with respect to specific products (usage patterns, attitudes, and emotions). Marketers use psychographics to gain a more detailed understanding of consumer behavior than they can get from demographic variables like ethnicity, social class, age, gender, and religion.

Values

Values Enduring beliefs regarding what is right or wrong.

Values are enduring beliefs that a given behavior or outcome is good or bad.[2] For example, you may believe that it is good to be healthy, keep your family safe, have self-respect, and be free. As enduring beliefs, your values serve as standards that guide your behavior across situations and over time. Thus, how much you value the environment generally determines the extent to which you litter, recycle, or buy products made from recycled materials. Values are so ingrained that people are usually not conscious of them and have difficulty describing them.

Value system Our total set of values and their relative importance.

Our total set of values and their relative importance to us constitute our **value system.** The way that we behave in a given situation is often influenced by how important one value is to us relative to others.[3] For instance, deciding whether to spend Saturday afternoon relaxing with your family or exercising will be determined by the relative importance that you place on family versus health. You feel *value conflict* when you do something that is consistent with one value but inconsistent with another equally important value. This dynamic can be illustrated with the example of parents who place equal value on convenience and concern for the environment. They may experience value conflict if they buy disposable diapers for their babies. Consumers facing such decisions consider not only the product's immediate consumption outcomes but also the product's general effect on society, including how the manufacturer behaves (toward the environment, for instance).[4]

Because values are among the first things that children learn, value systems are often in place by age 10. As you will see in Chapter 15, people learn values through the process of socialization, which results from exposure to reference groups and other sources of influence.[5] You may therefore value education because your parents went to college and because they and your teachers encouraged this value. Because individuals learn values through exposure to others in institutions and cultures, people within the same group often hold similar values.

Acculturation is the process by which individuals learn the values and behaviors of a new culture (see Chapter 12). For example, immigrants arriving in the

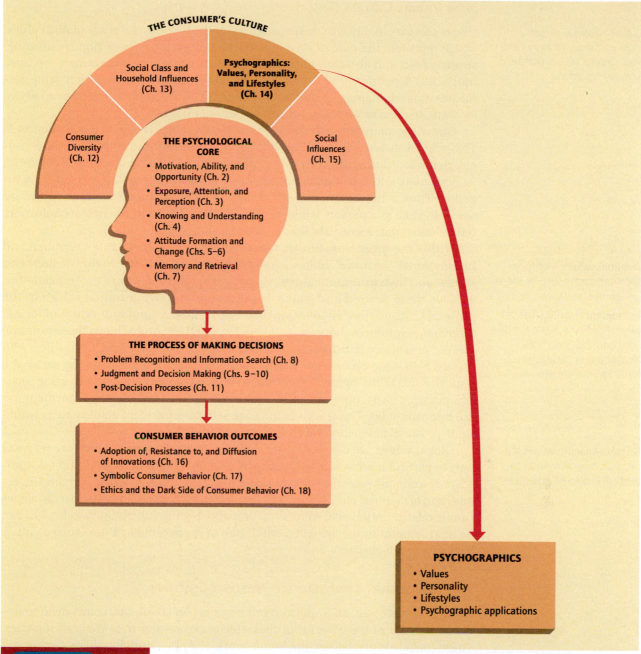

THE CONSUMER'S CULTURE

Social Class and Household Influences (Ch. 13)

Psychographics: Values, Personality, and Lifestyles (Ch. 14)

Consumer Diversity (Ch. 12)

THE PSYCHOLOGICAL CORE
- Motivation, Ability, and Opportunity (Ch. 2)
- Exposure, Attention, and Perception (Ch. 3)
- Knowing and Understanding (Ch. 4)
- Attitude Formation and Change (Chs. 5–6)
- Memory and Retrieval (Ch. 7)

Social Influences (Ch. 15)

THE PROCESS OF MAKING DECISIONS
- Problem Recognition and Information Search (Ch. 8)
- Judgment and Decision Making (Chs. 9–10)
- Post-Decision Processes (Ch. 11)

CONSUMER BEHAVIOR OUTCOMES
- Adoption of, Resistance to, and Diffusion of Innovations (Ch. 16)
- Symbolic Consumer Behavior (Ch. 17)
- Ethics and the Dark Side of Consumer Behavior (Ch. 18)

PSYCHOGRAPHICS
- Values
- Personality
- Lifestyles
- Psychographic applications

Exhibit 14.1

Chapter Overview: Psychographics: Values, Personality, and Lifestyles

Previous chapters demonstrated how membership in certain cultural groups (regional, ethnic, social class, and so on) can affect group behaviors. This chapter examines the effect of these cultural influences on an individual level—namely, on values (deeply held beliefs), personality (consumer traits), and lifestyles (behavioral patterns that are manifestations of values and personality). Each of these factors is useful in understanding consumer behavior; in addition, marketers often combine them to obtain an overall psychographic profile of consumers.

United States must learn new values to acculturate to American life. Consumers are more likely to adopt the values of a new culture if they view that culture as attractive and as having values similar to their own. Acculturation also happens faster when people in the new culture are cohesive, give a lot of verbal and nonverbal signals about what their values are, and express pride in the values that they hold.[6]

How Values Can Be Described

Global values A person's most enduring, strongly held, and abstract values that hold in many situations.

Values can vary in terms of their specificity. At the broadest level are **global values,** which represent the core of an individual's value system. These highly enduring, strongly held, and abstract values apply in many situations. For example, because much of U.S. political philosophy is based on the idea of freedom, that value permeates many domains of our lives. We believe in the freedom to speak, to go where we want, to dress as we please, and to live where we want.

One of the many ways of characterizing global values is depicted in Exhibit 14.2. This scheme divides global values into seven categories: maturity, security, prosocial behavior (doing nice things for others), restrictive conformity, enjoyment, achievement, and self-direction. Note that similar categories are placed close together. Thus, achievement and self-direction reflect a similar orientation toward the individual as a person, whereas prosocial behavior and restrictive conformity reflect values that relate to how an individual should deal with others.

Terminal values Highly desired end states such as social recognition and pleasure.

Instrumental values The values needed to achieve the desired end states such as ambition and cheerfulness.

Within the seven domains there are two types of global values: terminal and instrumental. **Terminal values** (shown with an asterisk) are highly desired end states, and **instrumental values** (shown with a plus sign) are those needed to achieve these desired end states. For example, the two terminal values in the prosocial category are equality and salvation. The instrumental values of loving, forgiving, helpfulness, honesty, and belief in God help one achieve these terminal values.[7] Also notice in Exhibit 14.2 that values tend to be polarized: Consumers who place a high value on one set of terminal values place less value on the set on the opposite side of the figure. This situation means that individuals who value security, maturity, and a prosocial orientation might place less value on enjoyment (on the opposite side). Those who emphasize self-direction and achievement would value prosocial behaviors and restrictive conformity less.

Domain-specific values Values that may only apply to a particular area of activities.

Global values are different from **domain-specific values,** which are relevant only to particular areas of activity, such as religion, family, or consumption. Materialism is a domain-specific value because it relates to the way that we view the acquisition of material goods. Although they differ, global and domain-specific values can be related in that achievement of domain-specific values (such as health) can be instrumental to the achievement of one or more global values (such as inner harmony or self-respect).

The Values that Characterize Western Cultures

Given that values are an important influence on behavior, marketers need to understand some of the values that characterize consumption in Western societies. These include materialism, the home, work and play, individualism, family and children, health, hedonism, youth, authenticity, the environment, and technology.

Materialism

Materialism Placing importance on money and material goods.

One value that has become increasingly prevalent in Western cultures is **materialism.**[8] In a materialistic society, people gauge satisfaction in terms of what they have or have not acquired in life and in terms of desired possessions. Materialistic individuals tend to value items like cars, jewelry, and boats. In contrast, symbolic items such as a mother's wedding gown, family mementos, and photos are more important to those low in materialism.[9] Materialistic consumers might believe that they would be happy if they had a bigger house, a nicer car, or more expensive clothes—beliefs that can lead to stress if family or life changes disrupt their financial situation.[10]

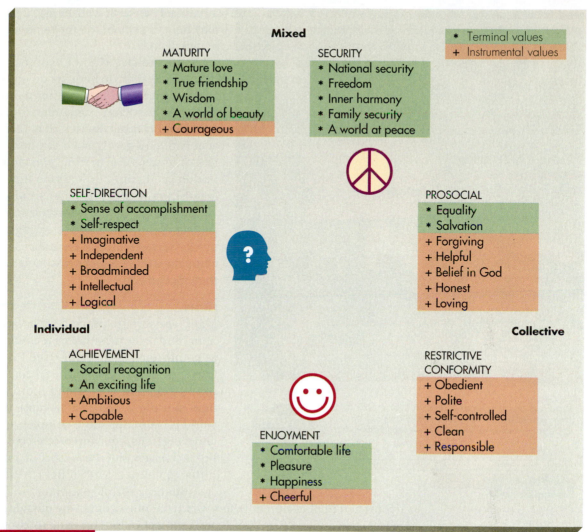

Exhibit 14.2

Global Values and Value Categories

One scheme for classifying global values identifies seven major categories. Some values are individual oriented (e.g., self-direction, achievement); others are more collective or group oriented (e.g., prosocial, restrictive conformity). Note that categories close to each other are similar; those farther apart are less so. Terminal values (or highly desired end states) are marked with an asterisk (*); instrumental values have a plus sign (+).

Materialism may relate to several of the terminal values noted in Exhibit 14.2. For example, possessions may be instrumental in achieving the higher-order value of social recognition. Or materialism may reflect a high value on accomplishment if people judge self-worth by what they have acquired or by their achievement of a comfortable life. According to **terror management theory,** materialism is rooted, in part, in consumers' drive to relieve anxiety over the inevitability of death by deriving self-esteem and status from acquiring and possessing things.[11] On the other hand, members of communes and certain religious orders have chosen a lifestyle that rejects material possessions.[12] Growing numbers of people have changed their priorities, rejected materialism, and simplified their lives by making and spending less. Research shows that the value conflict between the individual orientation of materialism and the group orientation of family-oriented values is associated with

Terror management theory
Theory that explains how individuals try to deal with anxiety over the inevitability of death.

Going out, made affordable.

With our selection of outdoor furniture to grills to fire pits, you can update your outdoor space and spend more time relaxing without exhausting your budget. Shop and compare with our free buying guides at Lowes.com/OutdoorLiving.

LOWE'S
Let's Build Something Together

Shown: Love Seat - Regency Brown #272809, Cushioned Chair - Regency Brown #272867, Side Table - Regency Brown #272868 (Regency color varies by market), Firepit - #256803, Grill - Perfect Flame #271573, Pavers - #182084.   For the store nearest you, call 1-800-993-4416.   © 2008 by Lowe's. All rights reserved. Lowe's and the gable design are registered trademarks of LF, LLC.

Exhibit 14.3

Placing a High Value on the Home

Consumers are placing a greater value on the home and are spending more time there. Thus, companies are increasingly appealing to this value. A good example is this ad for Lowe's Home Improvement.

a reduced sense of well-being, a finding that may help to explain the movement away from materialism.[13]

Nevertheless, U.S. consumers generally have a materialistic bent, as do consumers in Japan, China, and many other nations.[14] In a materialistic society, consumers will be receptive to marketing tactics that facilitate the acquisition of goods, such as phone-in or on-line orders, special pricing, convenient distribution, and communications that associate acquisition with achievement and status, like ads for a Rolex watch. Consumers also want to protect their possessions, creating opportunities for services such as insurance and security companies that protect consumers against loss, theft, or damage.

Home

Many consumers place a high value on the home and believe in making it as attractive and as comfortable as possible (see Exhibit 14.3). Currently, 69 percent of U.S. citizens own their own home, and they spend more time there than they did in the past. Because the outside world is becoming more complex, exhausting, and dangerous, consumers often consider their home a haven, but they also look for opportunities to connect with others.[15] The home is "command central"—a place to coordinate activities and pool resources before family members enter the outside world. For example, more than 70 million Americans use online banking to control family finances from their home computers.[16] Ikea has run an emotional global ad campaign reflecting how strongly people feel about their homes. "It marks commitment to putting the heart back into the home and serves as our manifesto for the future," says an Ikea marketing manager.[17]

Work and Play

Not everyone in every culture shares the same values of work and play. In the United States, consumers are working harder and longer than ever before, partly due to corporate downsizing and an emphasis on productivity. In fact, when career-minded consumers go on vacation, nearly half regularly communicate with work colleagues through cell phone, e-mail, and fax.[18] However, consumers increasingly value work for its instrumental function in achieving other values such as a comfortable lifestyle, family security, and accomplishing their life goals. Thus, the idea of valuing work itself and delaying gratification to the exclusion of leisure and pleasure is less characteristic of U.S. consumers than it was a century ago.

When people work longer hours, they value leisure time as much as they value money, and they will pay for services so that they can spend more nonwork time on leisure activities. For instance, the online grocery retailer FreshDirect has built a $200 million business serving New York City consumers who have better things to do than go to the supermarket.[19] Many consumers make leisure-time choices with the express purpose of getting completely away from work, a goal that has made remote vacation spots and spas more popular in recent years.[20]

Individualism

U.S. culture, in particular, has long placed a high value on individualism. The traditional "rugged individualist" consumer values independence and self-reliance, tending to see the individual's needs and rights as a higher priority than the group's needs and rights.[21] Marketers who target men for products such as hunting gear often use advertising imagery and words to make explicit the connection between owning and using these products and expressing rugged individualism. Despite the frontier roots of individualism in America, some consumers worry about violence and other possible negative consequences of unbridled individualism.

Even in a generally individualistic society, there are *allocentric* consumers who prefer interdependence and social relationships. In contrast, *idiocentric* consumers tend to put more emphasis on individual freedom and assertiveness. The behavior of these two types of consumers reflects such differences. Idiocentric consumers in the United States exhibit more interest in sports and adventure, financial satisfaction, gambling, and brand consciousness. Allocentric consumers exhibit more interest in health consciousness, group socializing, reading, and food preparation.[22]

Family and Children

Cultures also differ in the values that they place on their families and children. Parents in Europe and Asia, for example, tend to value education more than U.S. parents do. Among Asian middle-class families, educating children is second in priority only to providing food. Nevertheless, American consumers still place a high value on children (see Exhibit 14.4). Rather than move their families when they change jobs or get promoted, some parents commute to work in another city or state and use e-mail and other technologies to stay in touch with the other parent and their children during the week.[23]

U.S. parents are generally quite receptive to child-related products. Walt Disney has built a $4 billion business marketing princess clothing, accessories, movies, and theme-park experiences for little girls.[24] Personalized items are in high demand as indulgent parents or grandparents snap up Gund teddy bears monogrammed with a special baby's name and birth date or toddler sweatshirts emblazoned with the names of every family member—including Fido or Kitty.[25] Marketers are targeting children with an endless range of cereals, juices, desserts, soft drinks, and other snack products, not to mention toys, games, and other playthings.

Health

Many U.S. consumers place a high value on health due to reasons of self-esteem (the way the body looks) and concerns about longevity and survival. The value of health is reflected in the popularity of foods low in fat, calories, carbohydrates, salt, sugar, or cholesterol—as well as foods with special nutritional benefits. Gatorade drinks are marketed to consumers who work out or play sports since the products provide the benefit of replacing fluids and electrolytes.[26] Growing concern about pesticides, additives, food-related illnesses, and contaminants has enhanced demand for organic and vegetarian foods. Heinz is only one of many companies launching organic versions of foods such as ketchup (see Exhibit 14.5).[27] Yearly revenues at Whole Foods Market, which stocks only natural and organic grocery items, now top $6 billion.[28] In Europe, health concerns have led many consumers to resist genetically modified foods.[29]

Exhibit 14.4

Valuing Education

This ad is trying to appeal to consumers who value reading and education for children.

some students dream
of staying after school

Because those students are part of "Agilent Afterschool," a global program where real Agilent scientists and engineers volunteer their time to demonstrate how much fun science really can be. It's a balloon-powered car. An actual operating periscope you can build at home. It's how a light bulb turns on. It's igniting a spark in tomorrow's scientists and engineers. And it's just a small part of Agilent's ongoing efforts to enrich communities the world over.

www.agilent.com

Agilent Technologies

dreams made real

The emphasis on health has also paved the way for low-calorie and low-fat foods, health clubs, and diet aids. Just as Nabisco and other companies have successfully marketed 100-calorie snack-food packages for people who want to control portion size, firms like Wichita's Blue Dog Bakery are offering 100-calorie snack-food packs for dogs.[30] Magazines like *Health* and *Runners' World* also exemplify health values. CVS, Wal-Mart, and other retailers are opening in-store walk-in clinics offering basic medical services such as treating ear infections and providing flu shots.[31] Antismoking campaigns, bans on smoking in public places, and tobacco and alcohol warning labels in many Western nations are consistent with health values.

Values and behavior can differ, however. Although many Americans talk about a healthy diet, 33 percent of U.S. adults are obese as compared with 17 percent of European adults.[32] As controversy rages over the obesity epidemic, some marketers have been criticized for offering excessively large food portions or packages,

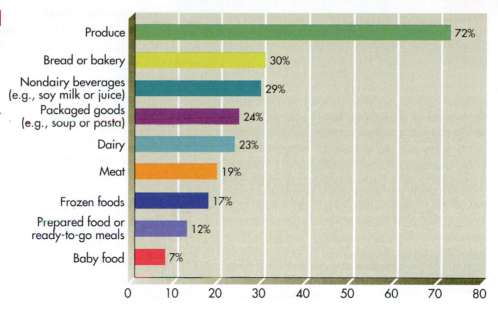

Exhibit 14.5

Most Popular Categories of Organic Foods

Consumers are increasingly buying organic foods. These are the most popular items.

Most Popular Categories of Organic Foods chart:

- Produce: 72%
- Bread or bakery: 30%
- Nondairy beverages (e.g., soy milk or juice): 29%
- Packaged goods (e.g., soup or pasta): 24%
- Dairy: 23%
- Meat: 19%
- Frozen foods: 17%
- Prepared food or ready-to-go meals: 12%
- Baby food: 7%

whereas others have come under fire for the ingredients they put into (or do not take out of) food products (see Chapter 18 for more on this issue). Criticism has prompted fast-food restaurants to post nutritional information on their websites and in their outlets and to add healthier menu items. For instance, McDonald's has added Happy Meals options such as Apple Dippers in the United States, yogurt in France, raisins in Australia, and grapes in Great Britain.[33] Meanwhile, offerings such as plus-size clothing have flourished.[34]

Hedonism

Hedonism The principle of pleasure seeking.

Consumers are increasingly operating on the principle of **hedonism,** or pleasure seeking, searching for goods, services, and experiences that simply make them feel good, such as luxury cars, home entertainment centers, and exciting vacations. For example, the hedonistic appeal of Tao Las Vegas, an upscale restaurant with an elegant atmosphere, roaming musicians, and delicacies such as Kobe beef, draws 600,000 customers yearly and brings in $55 million in annual revenue.[35] Hedonism has led to some interesting eating patterns that contradict health values, witnessed by the successes of Häagen-Dazs (the first super-premium ice cream) on the one hand and Healthy Choice low-fat foods (a $700 million brand) on the other.[36] Furthermore, despite their concerns about health, consumers will not switch to low-fat, low-calorie varieties unless they taste good. In fact, one study found that consumers possess an implicit intuition that healthy foods taste bad.[37] Thus, Splenda No Calorie Sweetener captured a 51 percent share of the U.S. market for sugar substitutes in just six years because consumers perceived its taste as being closer to that of sugar than were the tastes of competing products.[38]

Youth

Compared with other cultures, the United States has long placed a high value on youth, as evidenced by the wide range of offerings for combating or reducing signs of aging (think of wrinkle creams, hair coloring, and hair transplants). Cosmetic surgery is one of the fastest-growing medical specialties for both men and women. A strong youth orientation is also evident in Latin America, where consumers spend more than $1.6 billion a year on cosmetics, and in China, where consumers spend more than $20 billion on cosmetics (mainly on foreign brands).[39] Marketing communications also indicate the value placed on youth. Coca-Cola, for instance, has created special ads and a cell-phone-accessed website to promote its Sprite soft drink to teens around the world. "As early adopters of technology, teens also represent the single largest and most important consumer group of the Sprite brand," says Sprite's global brand director.[40]

Authenticity

People generally value authentic things, either the original article (such as the actual furniture that George Washington owned, which is displayed in his Mount Vernon home) or a faithful reproduction (furniture made to look like that of George Washington and shown in a museum or available for purchase).[41] Cheap knockoffs or counterfeits tend to be valued much less. Consumers may feel a close attachment to brands they perceive to be "authentic"—and may drop or even disparage brands that cease to seem authentic.[42] A service or experience may also be valued for its authenticity. For example, some consumers may perceive the experience of sipping espresso in a small, locally owned coffee shop as a more authentic experience than going to Starbucks, which has a global presence and a consistent in-store brand identity.

The Environment

Environmental protection has become an important value among U.S. and European consumers (see Exhibit 14.6), who are interested in conserving natural resources, preventing pollution, and supporting environmentally friendly goods, services, and activities. In one study, 87 percent of U.S. consumers said they would choose energy-saving features in a new home over better kitchen cabinets or other creature comforts.[43] The Toyota Prius is just one of a growing number of cars attracting buyers because they run more cleanly and deliver more fuel efficiency.[44] Among environmentally conscious consumers, 90 percent buy products with recycled parts or packaged in recycled materials. Many also buy from firms that offer earth-friendly products or contribute to environmental causes.[45] Businesses can profit from many aspects of environmental values. ReCellular, for instance, recycles 10 tons of cell phones every day, keeping them out of landfills.[46]

Technology

Consumers in many cultures are fascinated by technological advances. More than ever before, consumers in the United States, Japan, and other nations believe that computers, cell phones, digital cameras, and the Internet improve the quality of their lives. On the horizon are nanotech-enhanced products such as paint that does not peel and light yet powerful tennis rackets.[47] Nevertheless, technological changes can be so rapid that we have trouble keeping up, resulting in a renewed emphasis on

Exhibit 14.6

Valuing the Environment

Environmental concerns are an increasingly important value trend. Organizations like the SFI, Sustainable Forestry Initiative, are dedicated to this cause.

MEET THE NEW ENVIRONMENTALIST.

Millions of people have found a way to shop for the wood and paper products they need while still being good to our forests. They simply look for products with the SFI® label at all their favorite stores. From cereal boxes to paper towels to wood flooring:

- SFI labeled products come from forests managed to rigorous environmental standards.
- SFI standards conserve biodiversity and protect soil and water quality, as well as wildlife habitats.
- SFI forests are audited by independent experts to ensure proper adherence to the SFI Standard.
- SFI participants also plant more than 650 million trees each year to keep these forests thriving.

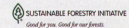 **SUSTAINABLE FORESTRY INITIATIVE**
Good for you. Good for our forests.

To learn more about the SFI Standard, visit www.sfiprogram.org

simplicity or at least on managing complexity. This trend is reflected in the rise of magazines like *Real Simple,* which shows readers how to remove some of the complexity from daily life. Still, products with features that work automatically are popular because they make it easier for consumers to use the products properly.[48] For example, many cell phones are programmed for voice activation so that consumers can make calls without pushing any buttons. Thus, consumers appear to value technology for what it can do to make their lives easier rather than for its own sake, making technology an instrumental rather than a terminal value.

Why Values Change

Because societies and their institutions are constantly evolving, value systems are also changing. In addition to the key trends already discussed, U.S. values are moving toward casualness in living, greater sophistication in behavior, a change in sex roles, and the desire to be modern.[49] Although the United States was different from Western Europe 100 years ago, both cultures (and to a certain extent Japan as well) are now becoming more similar in values, even though differences still exist. This increase in value consistency is driven in part by the increase in global communication. For example, Western Europeans regard some U.S. consumption patterns as attractive. Affluent Japanese consumers are starting to place greater value on personal preferences, a balanced life, and experiences and less value on traditional expectations, work, and possessions.[50]

Influences on Values

How do values differ across groups of consumers? This section explores the ways that culture, ethnicity, social class, and age can influence our values.

Culture and Values

People in different countries are exposed to different cultural experiences, a situation that leads to cross-cultural differences in values. One study found that the three most important values among Brazilians are true friendship, mature love, and happiness, whereas U.S. consumers named family security, world peace, and freedom.[51] Consumers in China place the most importance on values such as preserving the best that one has attained, being sympathetic to others, having self-control, and integrating enjoyment, action, and contemplation. A study of women in Germany, France, and the United Kingdom found that the value of "having a familiar routine" is most important for German women, but only tenth in importance for the British and twenty-third for the French.[52]

In a classic study, Geert Hofstede found that cultures can vary along four main value dimensions:[53]

- ▶ *Individualism versus collectivism.* The degree to which a culture focuses on the individuals rather than the group.

- ▶ *Uncertainty avoidance.* The extent to which a culture prefers structured to unstructured situations.

- ▶ *Masculinity versus femininity.* The extent to which a culture stresses masculine values (as defined by Hofstede) such as assertiveness, success, and competition over feminine values such as quality of life, warm personal relationships, and caring.

- ▶ *Power distance.* The degree to which a society's members are equal in terms of status.

All cultures can be classified according to these four dimensions. Understanding where a given culture falls may provide insight into cross-cultural differences. For example, research showed that tipping in restaurants is less likely to occur in countries where power distance and uncertainty avoidance are low, feminine values are strong, and individualism is high.[54] Another study found that humorous ad themes are more likely to focus on groups in collectivist societies like Thailand and South Korea and more likely to focus on unequal status relationships in countries with high power distance like the United States and Germany.[55] Finally, studies suggest that U.S. men use everyday consumption to support their view of themselves as men of action, a value in a culture high on masculinity.[56]

Ethnic Identification and Values

Ethnic groups within a larger culture can have some values that differ from those of other ethnic subcultures. As noted in Chapter 12, Hispanic Americans strongly value the family and home; similarly, African American and Asian American consumers place a high value on the extended family.[57] Consumers in different countries may have different ethnic values. For example, consumers in China tend to hold the traditional Confucian value of respect for older family members. Knowing this, Nestlé advertises milk-based meal supplements to adults by appealing to their respect and responsibility for aging parents.[58]

Social Class and Values

Different social classes hold specific values, as discussed in Chapter 13, which in turn affect their acquisition and consumption patterns. As countries in Eastern Europe and other nations embrace market economies, the size of the global middle class is increasing dramatically, along with middle-class values of materialism and a desire for less government control over their lives and greater access to information. Upper-upper-class consumers value giving back to society, a characteristic that explains why they become active in social, cultural, and civic causes. These consumers also prize self-expression as reflected in their homes, clothing, cars, and other forms of consumption.[59]

Age and Values

Members of a generation often share similar values that differ from those of other generations. For example, your grandparents may value security over hedonism, not because they are older but because they grew up during the Great Depression and suffered economic hardship as children. Many of that generation therefore view hedonic activities as frivolous and unacceptable. Baby boomers who grew up in the 1960s—a time of political upheaval, self-indulgence, and rebellion—value hedonism, morality, self-direction, and achievement.[60] Note that it is sometimes very difficult to distinguish values we acquire with age from those we learn from our era. Nevertheless, differences by virtue of age or cohort do exist, and they influence the way that we behave as consumers.

MARKETING IMPLICATIONS

Marketers need to understand how consumer values affect consumption patterns, market segmentation, new product development, ad development strategy, and ethics.

Reflection of Values

The Dove "Campaign for Real Beauty" and the film Evolution (image still pictured) ads have won awards and many customers for Dove because the messages reflect values and resonate with consumers.

Value segmentation The grouping of consumers by common values.

Consumption patterns

Consumers usually buy, use, and dispose of products in a manner consistent with their values.[61] Thus, marketers can know more about what consumers like if they understand their values. For example, those who value warm relationships with others are more likely to buy gifts and send cards than those who place less value on relationships.[62] When the U.K. supermarket chain Tesco studied its customers' values, it found such strong environmental concerns that it launched a program to label the carbon footprint of every product it sells.[63] However, marketers sometimes adopt an ethnocentric perspective, assuming that consumers in other cultures hold values similar to their own. Campbell's soup failed in South America because in that region, a mother's behavior is judged by her devotion to domestic duties. Serving canned soup is like saying you do not care enough about your family to make the soup yourself.

Market segmentation

Marketers can identify groups of consumers who have a common set of values that differ from those of other groups, a process called **value segmentation.** Even the market for something as basic as pencils can be segmented in this way. Faber-Castell, which sells 2 billion pencils every year, offers products for different value segments, including consumers who value quality, creativity, the environment, status, and style.[64] Marketers also can use values to understand the attributes that consumers in a particular segment may find important in a product and that may motivate them to choose one brand over another. (See Exhibit 14.7.) When buying clothes, individuals who value status might look for attributes like price and luxury, those who value fitting in with the crowd might look for clothing that is trendy, and those who value uniqueness might look for new or nonmainstream styles.

New product ideas

Values can also influence consumers' reactions to new and different products. The more a new product is consistent with important consumer values, the greater the likelihood of its success. For example, good-tasting, microwaveable, low-fat, and low-calorie frozen entrees have succeeded in part because these items are consistent with multiple values like hedonism, time, convenience, health, and technology. Time-saving devices like the Mr. Clean MagicReach cleaning tool tap into the value of using leisure time for fun; the product is advertised as a means to "take back your Saturday morning."[65]

Ad development strategy

Examining the target segment's value profile can help marketers design more appealing ads.[66] The more compatible the ad copy is with consumers' values, the more likely consumers are to become involved in the message and find it relevant. To illustrate, the

"Campaign for Real Beauty" promoting Unilever's Dove brand has won awards—and won over customers—because the messages reflect the target audience's values of beauty and authenticity.[67] Clearly, marketers must connect product attributes and benefits to consumer values because these represent the end state consumers desire to achieve—the driving force behind their consumption of the product. Marketers must also avoid communications that conflict with cultural values. For example, consumer groups in Thailand protested an ad that showed Hitler eating an inferior brand of potato chips and being transformed into a good guy by eating the advertised brand.[68]

Ethical considerations

Consumers use values to gauge the appropriateness of others' behaviors—including the behavior of marketers. For example, those who value morality might disapprove of products such as cigarettes and X-rated videos, consumption practices like prostitution and gambling, and sexually explicit ads. Consumers also evaluate marketers' behavior for fairness, ethics, and appropriateness.[69] As Chapter 18 explains, marketers should be aware that consumers may boycott, protest, or complain about practices that seem inconsistent with their values of fairness.

How Values Can Be Measured

To segment the market by values, marketers need some means of identifying consumers' values, gauging their importance, and analyzing changes or trends in values. Unfortunately, values are often hard to measure. One reason is that people do not often think about their values and may therefore have a hard time articulating what is really important to them. Another reason is that people may sometimes feel social pressure to respond to a values questionnaire in a certain way to make themselves look better in the eyes of the researcher. Therefore, marketers usually use less obtrusive or more indirect ways of assessing values.

Inferring Values from the Cultural Milieu

The least obtrusive way to measure values is to make inferences based on a culture's milieu. Advertising has often been used as an indicator of values.[70] Research examining the values portrayed in U.S. print ads between 1900 and 1980 revealed that practicality, the family, modernity, frugality, wisdom, and uniqueness were among the values that appeared most frequently. Researchers can also use ads to uncover cross-cultural differences and track trends in values. One study found that because the People's Republic of China, Taiwan, and Hong Kong are at different levels of economic development and have different political ideologies, different values were reflected in each country's ads.[71] At the time, ads from China focused on utilitarian themes and promised a better life, Hong Kong ads stressed hedonism and an easier life, and Taiwan ads fell between the other two. Now, with the economic changes occurring in China, the trend in local advertising is away from utilitarian themes and toward variety in products and product assurances.

Marketers can infer values just by looking at product names. Product names reflecting values of materialism (Grand Hyatt hotels), hedonism (Obsession perfume), time (Minute Rice), technology (Microsoft), and convenience (Reddi-wip topping) are common in the United States.

Values are also reflected in magazine titles (such as *Money*), book and movie titles, TV programs, the types of people regarded as heroes or heroines, and popular songs. Many people are concerned that violent song lyrics are an indication of a decline in values, for instance.

One criticism of cultural milieu as an indicator of values is that researchers never know whether culture reflects values or creates them. In light of this problem, researchers have introduced other methods to measure values.

Means-End Chain Analysis

Means-end chain analysis
A technique that helps us understand how values link to attributes in products and services.

Marketers can use the **means-end chain analysis** to gain insight into consumers' values by better understanding which attributes they find important in products. Armed with this information, researchers can work backward to uncover the values that drive consumer decisions.[72] One way to do this is through *value laddering*, determining the root values related to product attributes that are important to consumers.[73] Suppose a consumer likes light beer because it has fewer calories than regular beer. If a researcher asks why it is important to have a beer with fewer calories, the respondent might say, "Because I don't want to gain weight." If the researcher asks why not, the consumer might respond by saying, "I want to be healthy." If asked why again, the consumer might say, "Because I want to feel good about myself." This example is illustrated in the top line of Exhibit 14.8.

Note that this means-end chain has several potential levels. First, the consumer mentioned an important attribute followed by a concrete benefit that the attribute provides. Then the consumer indicated that this benefit was important because it served some instrumental value. This entire process is called a *means-end chain* because the attribute provides the means to a desired end state or terminal value (in this case, self-esteem).

Looking at Exhibit 14.8, you can also see that a particular attribute can be associated with very different values. For example, rather than valuing light beer for its health benefits, some consumers may like light beer because they drink it in a social context that leads to a greater sense of belonging. Second, the same value may be associated with very different products and attributes. Thus, attributes associated with both light beer and rice may appeal equally to the value of belonging. Third, a given attribute may be linked with multiple benefits and/or values, meaning that a consumer might like light beer because it makes her feel healthier and because it facilitates belonging.

Exhibit 14.8

An Example of Means-End Chains

According to the means-end chain analysis, product and service attributes (e.g., fewer calories) lead to benefits (e.g., I won't gain weight) that reflect instrumental values (e.g., helps make me healthy) and terminal values (e.g., I feel good about myself). This analysis helps marketers identify important values and the attributes associated with them. Can you develop a means-end chain for toothpaste or deodorant?

Product	Attribute	Benefit	Instrumental Value (driving force)	Terminal Valuel
Light beer (I)	Fewer calories	I won't gain weight.	Helps make me healthy	I feel good about myself (self-esteem).
Light beer (II)	Fewer calories Great taste Light taste	Less filling Enjoyable/relaxing Refreshing	Good times/fun Friendship Sharing	Belonging
Rice	Comes in boiling bag	Convenient No messy pan to clean up	Saves time	I can enjoy more time with my family (belonging).

Source: Adapted from Jonathan Gutman, "A Means-End Chain Model Based on Consumer Categorization Processes," *Journal of Marketing*, Spring 1982, pp. 60–72; Thomas J. Reynolds and John P. Rochan, "Means-End Based Advertising Research: Copy Testing Is Not Strategy Assessment," *Journal of Business Research*, March 1991, pp. 131–142.

Includes American Eagle® We know why you fly and AA.com are marks of American Airlines, Inc.

Your son's first visit from the tooth fairy.

We know why you fly

250,000 people. On 3,900 flights. Every day. Including one to the most important meeting of your day.

AmericanAirlines®
AA.com

Exhibit 14.9

American Airlines "We Know Why You Fly" Campaign

Sometimes marketers try to stress the strong values underlying consumer behavior. This ad for American Airlines "We Know Why You Fly" identifies one of the key values influencing the choice of an airline.

Rokeach Value Survey (RVS) A survey that measures instrumental and terminal values.

List of Values (LOV) A survey that measures nine principal values in consumer behavior.

Marketers can use means-end chain analysis to identify product attributes that will be consistent with certain values.[74] Not long ago, consumers generally considered sports cars to be expensive and uncomfortable, and ownership of them took on an aspect of "arrogance and irresponsibility." As a result, manufacturers began offering comfortable cars positioned for "people who have friends" in order to be more in line with current values.[75] The means-end chain model is also useful for developing advertising strategy. By knowing which attributes consumers find important and which values they associate with those attributes, advertisers can design ads that appeal to these values and emphasize related attributes. Note that the ad need not explicitly link a given attribute with a motive, but it can allow consumers to implicitly make the linkage (see Exhibit 14.9).

Finally, marketers can use the means-end chain to segment global markets and appeal to consumers on the basis of specific benefits and related values.[76] To market yogurt, for instance, a company could identify one segment that values health and reach this segment by focusing on product attributes such as low fat and could identify a second segment that values enjoyment and reach this segment through attributes such as fruit ingredients.

Value Questionnaires

Marketers can directly assess values by using questionnaires. Some types of questionnaires, such as the material values scale, focus only on specific aspects of consumer behavior.[77] Others cover a range of values. One of the best known of these is the **Rokeach Value Survey (RVS).** This questionnaire asks consumers about the importance that they attach to the 19 instrumental values and 18 terminal values identified in Exhibit 14.2. This questionnaire is standardized, and everyone responds to the same set of items, a procedure that helps researchers identify the specific values that are most important to a given group of consumers, determine whether values are changing over time, and learn whether values differ for various groups of consumers. One drawback is that some values measured by the RVS are less relevant to consumer behavior (such as salvation, forgiving, and being obedient). Some researchers have therefore recommended using a shortened form of the RVS containing only the values most relevant to a consumer context.[78]

Others have advocated the use of the **List of Values (LOV).** Consumers are presented with nine primary values and asked either to identify the two most important or to rank all nine values by importance. The nine values are (1) self-respect, (2) warm relationships with others, (3) sense of accomplishment, (4) self-fulfillment, (5) fun and enjoyment in life, (6) excitement, (7) sense of belonging, (8) being well respected, and (9) security.[79] The first six are internal values because they derive from the individual; the others are external values. The values can also be described in terms of whether they are fulfilled through interpersonal relationships (warm relationships with others, sense of belonging), personal factors (self-respect, being well respected, self-fulfillment), or nonpersonal things (sense of accomplishment, fun, security, and excitement).

In one study, the LOV predicted consumers' responses to statements that describe their self-reported consumption characteristics (e.g., "I am a spender, not a saver"), their actual consumption behaviors (the frequency with which they watch movies or the news, read certain magazines, and engage in activities like playing tennis), and their marketplace beliefs ("I believe the consumer movement has caused prices to increase"). Compared with the RVS, the LOV is a better predictor of consumer behavior, is shorter, and is easier to administer. Finally, the LOV is useful for identifying segments of consumers with similar value systems.[80]

Personality

Although individuals with comparable backgrounds tend to hold similar values, it is important to remember that people do not always act the same way even when they hold the same values. In listening to a sales pitch, one consumer may state demurely that she finds the product interesting but is not ready to make up her mind right now. Another might act more assertively, interrupting the salesperson midway through his pitch to indicate that she has no interest whatsoever in the product. Therefore, consumers vary in terms of their personality or the way in which they respond to a particular situation.

Personality An internal characteristic that determines how individuals behave in various situations.

Personality consists of the distinctive patterns of behaviors, tendencies, qualities, or personal dispositions that make one individual different from another and lead to a consistent response to environmental stimuli. These patterns are internal characteristics that we are born with or that result from the way we have been raised. The concept of personality helps us understand why people behave differently in different situations.

Research Approaches to Personality

The social sciences provide various approaches to studying personality. This section reviews five that consumer researchers apply: psychoanalytic approaches, trait theories, phenomenological approaches, social-psychological theories, and behavioral approaches.

Psychoanalytic Approaches

According to psychoanalytic theories, personality arises from a set of dynamic, unconscious internal struggles within the mind.[81] The famous psychoanalyst Sigmund Freud proposed that we pass through several developmental stages in forming our personalities. In the first stage, the oral stage, the infant is entirely dependent on others for need satisfaction and receives oral gratification from sucking, eating, and biting. At the anal stage, the child is confronted with the problem of toilet training. Then in the phallic stage, the youth becomes aware of his or her genitals and must deal with desires for the opposite-sex parent.

Freud believed that the failure to resolve the conflicts from each stage could influence one's personality. For example, the individual who received insufficient oral stimulation as an infant may reveal this crisis in adulthood through oral-stimulation activities like gum chewing, smoking, and overeating or by distrusting others' motives (including those of marketers). At the anal stage an individual whose toilet training was too restrictive may become obsessed with control and be overly orderly, stubborn, or stingy, resulting in neatly organized closets and records, list making, and excessive saving or collecting. These individuals may also engage in extensive information search and deliberation when making decisions. On the other hand, those whose training was overly lenient may become messy, disorganized adults.

Although some of Freud's theories were later questioned by many researchers, the key point is that the subconscious can influence behavior. Consequently, some advertising agencies conduct research to delve deep into consumers' psyches and uncover subconscious reasons why they buy a particular product.[82] This type of research led to the discovery of a deep-seated desire for milk that the dairy industry used in its "Got Milk?" campaign.

Trait Theories

Trait theorists propose that personality is composed of characteristics that describe and differentiate individuals.[83] For example, people might be described as aggressive, easygoing, quiet, moody, shy, or rigid. Psychologist Carl Jung developed one of the most basic trait theory schemes, suggesting that individuals could be categorized according to their levels of introversion and extroversion.[84] Introverts are shy, prefer to be alone, and are anxious in the presence of others. They tend to avoid social channels and may not find out about new products from others. They are also less motivated by social pressure and more likely to do things that please themselves. In contrast, extroverts are outgoing, sociable, and typically conventional.

Research in social psychology has found that five major personality traits tend to account for the most variance in personality (the "Big 5"): agreeableness, conscientiousness, emotional stability, openness, and extraversion.[85] Recent work has also found that the trait of stability, or consistency in behavior, when combined with the introversion/extroversion dimension, can be used as a basis to represent various personality types (see Exhibit 14.10). For example, a person who is reliable tends to be high on both introversion and stability. In contrast, a passive person is introverted but neither highly stable nor highly unstable. One interesting feature about this scheme is that the personality types identified by these two dimensions match the four temperaments identified by the Greek physician Hippocrates centuries ago—for example, a phlegmatic person is introverted and stable; a melancholic person is introverted and unstable.

Phenomenological Approaches

Phenomenological approaches propose that personality is largely shaped by an individual's interpretations of life events.[86] For example, according to this approach, depression is caused by the way that someone interprets key events and the nature of that interpretation rather than by internal conflicts or traits.

Exhibit 14.10

A Trait Conception of Personality Types

Consumers can be classified according to whether they have introverted or extroverted personality traits. These traits can lead to the identification of various personality types (e.g., moody, peaceful, lively, and aggressive). Interestingly, these traits can be collected into four major groups that correspond to the basic temperaments identified by the ancient Greek physician Hippocrates many centuries ago. How would you classify your personality according to this scheme?

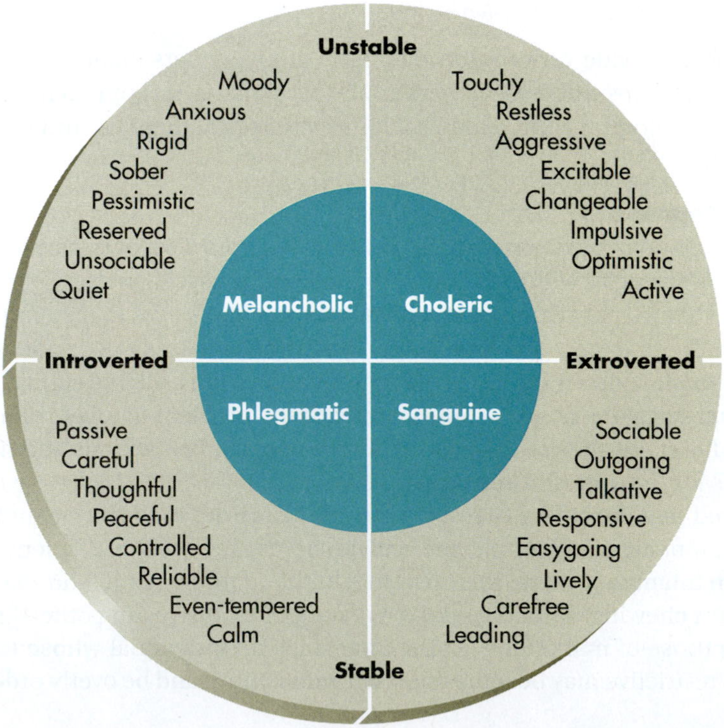

Locus of control How people interpret why things happen (internal versus external).

A key concept of the phenomenological approaches is **locus of control,** or people's interpretations of why specific things happen.[87] Individuals with an internal locus of control attribute more responsibility to themselves for good or bad outcomes, so they might blame themselves or see themselves as having been careless when a product fails. Externally controlled individuals place responsibility on other people, events, or places rather than on themselves. Thus, they might attribute product failure to faulty manufacturing or poor packaging.

Locus of control can heavily influence consumers' perceptions of satisfaction in a consumption experience and determine how the consumer feels. To illustrate, consumers who blame themselves for product failure might feel shame, whereas those who blame product failure on an external source might feel anger and irritation. In addition, someone's life theme or goals (concerns that we address in our everyday lives) can greatly influence the meanings that he or she derives from ads.[88] As a result, a person who is more concerned with family might interpret an ad differently than someone who is more concerned with his or her private self.

Social-Psychological Theories

Another group of theories focuses on social rather than biological explanations of personality, proposing that individuals act in social situations to meet their needs. The researcher Karen Horney, for instance, believed that behavior can be characterized by three major orientations.[89] *Compliant* individuals are dependent on others and are humble, trusting, and tied to a group. *Aggressive* individuals need power, move away from others, and are outgoing, assertive, self-confident, and tough-minded. *Detached* individuals are independent and self-sufficient but suspicious and introverted. These three orientations are measured by the CAD scale.[90] One study found that assertiveness and aggressiveness were significantly related to styles of interaction with marketing institutions.[91] In particular, highly assertive and aggressive people were likely to perceive complaining as acceptable and to enjoy doing it.

In social-psychological theory, researchers distinguish between state-oriented consumers, who are more likely to rely on subjective norms to guide their behavior, and action-oriented consumers, whose behavior is based more on their own attitudes.[92] Consumers also vary in terms of their attention to information that helps them compare themselves with others (social comparison information). Individuals high on this factor are more sensitive to normative pressure than are those low on this factor.

Behavioral Approaches

In contrast to other explanations of personality, behavioral approaches propose that differences in personality are a function of how individuals have been rewarded or punished in the past. According to behavioral approaches, individuals are more likely to have traits or engage in behaviors for which they have received positive reinforcement. They are less likely to maintain characteristics and behaviors for which they have been punished.[93] Thus, an individual might be extroverted because parents, caretakers, and other individuals rewarded outgoing behaviors and punished introverted behaviors. Likewise, a consumer might prefer colorful clothing if he or she previously received positive reinforcement for wearing it. Note that these behavioral approaches to personality involve the principles of operant conditioning discussed in Chapter 10.

Determining Whether Personality Characteristics Affect Consumer Behavior

Much of the consumer-related personality research has followed the trait approach and focused on identifying specific personality traits that explain differences in consumers' purchase, use, and disposition behavior. Although studies have attempted to find a relationship between personality and consumer behavior, personality is not always a good predictor of consumer behavior.[94] One major problem is that researchers developed many of the trait measurement instruments for identifying personality disorders in clinical settings, so these instruments may not be applicable for identifying traits related to consumption behaviors.

Although some studies have been problematic, other researchers believe that more reliable measures of traits, developed in a consumer context, would reveal a relationship.[95] For instance, researchers created a consumer self-confidence scale to examine how this trait affects the choice of higher-price alternatives.[96] Also, the association between personality and consumer behavior may be stronger for some types of consumer behavior than for others. For example, although personality may not be very useful in understanding brand choice, it may help marketers understand why some people are more susceptible to persuasion, particularly like a certain ad, or engage in more information processing. The ad in Exhibit 14.11 has personality appeal.

Marketers may also find personality more useful for targeting some product and service categories than others. In particular, our choice of offerings that involve subjective or hedonic features such as looks, style, and aesthetics may be somewhat related to personality. A good example is the selection of a greeting card, which represents a personal message and therefore is an extension of the sender's personality. Finally, certain types of personality traits may be more related to consumer behavior than others. As described below, these include optimal stimulation level, dogmatism, need for uniqueness, creativity, need for cognition, susceptibility to influence, frugality, self-monitoring behavior, national character, and competitiveness.

Optimal Stimulation Level

Some activities have the potential to provide some sort of physiological arousal. For example, you might feel more aroused when you speed on the highway, ride a roller coaster, see a scary movie, or go to new and unfamiliar surroundings. Things that are physically stimulating, emotionally energizing, or novel have arousal-inducing potential. However, highly stimulating activities are not always desirable. According to the theory of **optimal stimulation level (OSL),** people prefer things that are moderately arousing to things that are either too arousing or not arousing at all.[97] For example, you might prefer eating at a restaurant that offers moderately imaginative food to eating at one that offers boring food or one that offers unusual food.

Even though people generally prefer moderate levels of stimulation, individuals differ in the level of arousal they regard as moderate and optimal. Individuals with a low optimal stimulation level tend to prefer less arousing activities because they want to avoid going over the edge. In contrast, individuals with a high optimal stimulation level are more likely to seek activities that are very exciting, novel, complex, and different. Consumers with a high need for stimulation might enjoy activities like skydiving, gambling, and river rafting.[98] They are also more likely to be innovative and creative.

Individuals with high and low needs for stimulation also differ in the way in which they approach the marketplace. Those with high stimulation needs tend to

Optimum stimulation level (OSL) People's preferred level of stimulation, which is usually moderate.

Personality and Ad Appeal

Ad messages are often designed to appeal to certain personalities. This ad is directed to those who have a more adventurous personality.

it takes more than a click to go here*

*amen

OUTWARD BOUND®

IT'S IN YOU.

1 888 88 BOUND | WWW.OUTWARDBOUND.COM

© Outward Bound 2000

Outward Bound is a kick-it-into-high-gear,¹ do-it-yourself or it won't get done,² environmentally responsible³ adventure away from your parents.⁴

Key for parents: ¹Character building.²Confidence building.³Call for free, recycled paper catalog.⁴Vacation away from your teenager.

be the first to buy new products, to seek information about them, and to engage in variety seeking (buying something different).[99] They are more curious about the ads they see but may also be easily bored by them. These consumers are more likely to buy products associated with greater risk, enjoy shopping in malls with many stores and products, and prefer offerings that deviate from established consumption practices.

Dogmatism

Dogmatism A tendency to be resistant to change or new ideas.

Consumers can vary in terms of being open- or closed-minded. **Dogmatism** refers to an individual's tendency to be resistant to change and new ideas. Dogmatic, or closed-minded, consumers are relatively resistant to new products, new promotions, and new ads. In support, one study found that Nigerian consumers' acceptance of new products depended on how dogmatic the consumers were. The study also found that Muslims were more dogmatic than Christians.[100]

Need for Uniqueness

Need for uniqueness (NFU)
The desire for novelty through the purchase, use, and disposition of products and services.

Consumers who pursue novelty through the purchase, use, and disposition of goods and services are displaying a **need for uniqueness (NFU).**[101] A need for uniqueness covers three behavioral dimensions: creative choice counterconformity (the consumer's choice reflects social distinctiveness yet is one that others will approve of), unpopular choice counterconformity (choosing products and brands that do not conform to establish distinctiveness despite possible social disapproval), and avoidance of similarity (losing interest in possessions that become commonplace to avoid the norm and hence reestablish distinctiveness). In one study, consumers with a high need for uniqueness who were asked to explain their decisions made unconventional choices, showing that they were aware that their choices and reasoning were outside the norm.[102] Thus, consumers with a high need for uniqueness may avoid well-known global brands in favor of small, local brands.[103] They may also dispose of clothing that has become too popular in favor of emerging fashion trends, seek out handcrafted or personalized items, and customize products to their own specifications.

Creativity

In terms of consumer behavior, *creativity* means "a departure from conventional consumption practice in a novel and functional way."[104] For instance, if confronted with an everyday problem such as lacking the right ingredients to make dinner, a consumer high in creativity would locate substitutes. This solution would enable the consumer to complete the activity in a novel yet practical way. Such creativity enhances the consumer's mood as well.[105] The Kraft Foods website encourages creativity by offering videos demonstrating different cooking techniques, allowing consumers to search for recipes that use ingredients on hand, and inviting consumers to exchange ideas about dinner menus, dishes for entertaining, and more.

Need for Cognition

Need for cognition (NFC)
A trait that describes how much people like to think.

Consumers who enjoy thinking extensively about things like products, attributes, and benefits are high in the **need for cognition (NFC).**[106] Those with a low need for cognition do not like to think and prefer to take shortcuts or to rely on their feelings. Consumers with different needs for cognition differ in terms of their product interests, information search, and reaction to different ad campaigns. Specifically, those with a high need for cognition enjoy products and experiences that carry a serious learning and mastery component such as chess, educational games, and TV shows like *Jeopardy*. They derive satisfaction from searching for and discovering new product features and react positively to long, technically sophisticated ads with details about products or services. They might also scrutinize messages more carefully than other consumers do, considering the credibility or merits of the message.[107] Consumers with a low need for cognition, on the other hand, react more positively to short messages using attractive models, humor, or other cues. These individuals tend to make decisions that involve little thinking.

Susceptibility to Influence

Consumers also vary in their susceptibility to persuasion attempts, especially those that are interpersonal or face to face. Some consumers have a greater desire to enhance their image as observed by others and are therefore willing to be influenced or guided by them.[108] Consumers with lower social and information processing confidence tend to be more influenced by ads than are those with higher self-confidence.

The 2008 Honda Clearance

2008 Honda Accord LX

"Value is my middle name."

— *Mr. Opportunity*

Yes, it's Honda Clearance time again. And there's no better time to get a great deal on a shiny new Accord. See your Honda dealer today. And don't forget to tell them Mr. Opportunity sent you.

ShopHonda.com

© 2008 American Honda Motor Co., Inc.

Exhibit 14.12

Ad Appealing to Frugality

Some consumers possess the value of frugality, especially in tough economic times. Some ads stress this value, like this one from Honda.

National character The personality of a country.

Frugality

Frugality is the degree to which consumers take a disciplined approach to short-term acquisitions and are resourceful in using products and services to achieve longer-term goals. (Exhibit 14.12). Consumers who are high on frugality will, for example, pack leftovers for lunch at work (rather than buy take-out food or eat in a restaurant). Such consumers are less materialistic, less susceptible to the influence of others, and more conscious of price and value.[109] Sometimes governments or firms will actively encourage frugality to conserve scarce resources such as electric power.[110] The Japanese magazine *Hot Pepper* appeals to frugality with discount coupons and articles about saving money. "Four years ago when the magazine was first published, there were people who said, 'What are coupons?' or 'Discounts are petty,'" says a *Hot Pepper* executive. Now the featured stores and restaurants are seeing more traffic—and *Hot Pepper* has lots of competition for the attention of frugal-minded consumers.[111]

Self-Monitoring Behavior

Individuals differ in the degree to which they look to others for cues on how to behave. High self-monitors are typically sensitive to the desires and influences of others as guides to behavior, and low self-monitors are guided more by their own preferences and desires and are less influenced by normative expectations.[112] High and low self-monitors also differ in their responsiveness to advertising appeals. High self-monitors are more responsive to image-oriented ads and more willing to try and pay more for products advertised with an image consistent with high self-monitoring. In contrast, low self-monitors are generally more responsive to ads that make a quality claim and are more willing to try these products and pay extra for them.

National Character

Personality traits can sometimes be used to stereotype people of a particular country as having a **national character.** These characterizations represent only very broad generalizations about a particular country; obviously, individuals vary a great deal. To illustrate, French people and Italian people are often characterized as emotional and romantic, the British as more reserved; German, French, and U.S. citizens have been characterized as more assertive than their British, Russian, or Italian counterparts. German, British, and Russian consumers can be viewed as "tighter" compared with the "looser" French, Italian, and U.S. consumers.[113]

U.S. consumers are considered more impulsive, risk oriented, and self-confident than Canadians, who are stereotyped as more cautious, restrained, and reserved. Researchers have characterized how countries differ in their needs for achievement, levels of introversion and extroversion, perceptions of human nature, and flexibility.[114] Marketers must consider how differences in national character may influence reactions to advertising and other communications. For instance,

Nike had to pull a TV commercial in China featuring basketball star LeBron James fighting cartoon characters in martial arts attire after the Chinese government said the ad was insulting to national dignity.[115]

Competitiveness

The personality trait of competitiveness has been associated with the desire to outdo others through conspicuous consumption of material items such as electronic gadgets. It also plays a role in consumers' wanting to do better than others in a direct way (through a sport or by gambling, for instance) or an indirect way (such as when watching a sporting event).[116] Marketers who want to appeal to competitive consumers often use messages emphasizing the opportunity to be among the first to try or buy a new product or service.

MARKETING IMPLICATIONS

Because some personality traits may be related to consumption behavior, marketers can develop offerings and communications that appeal to various personality types. For example, ads targeting compliant or extremely self-monitoring consumers should focus on the approval of others, whereas ads and promotions appealing to high optimal stimulation-level consumers or those with a strong need for uniqueness might focus on trying something new and different. The magazine *Sole Collector* and the website niketalk.com (sponsored not by Nike but by sneaker enthusiasts) often feature hand-decorated athletic shoes and other one-of-a-kind sneakers, targeting consumers with a high need for uniqueness.[117] Targeting web-savvy consumers who have high stimulation needs and are competitive, MTV Networks has created a series of ever-changing online games and virtual worlds with contests, experiences, and product placements for brands such as Pepsi.[118]

Lifestyles

Lifestyles People's patterns of behavior.

Activities, interests, and opinions (AIOs) The three components of lifestyles.

Lifestyles relate closely to consumers' values and personality. Whereas values and personality represent internal states or characteristics, **lifestyles** are manifestations or actual patterns of behavior. In particular, they are represented by a consumer's **activities, interests, and opinions (AIOs),** as illustrated in Exhibit 14.13. What people do in their spare time is often a good indicator of their lifestyle. One consumer might like outdoor activities such as skiing, whereas another might prefer to surf the Web. Political opinions, ideology, and involvement also can affect acquisition, consumption, and disposition decisions.[119]

Consumers who engage in different activities and have differing opinions and interests may in fact represent distinct lifestyle segments for marketers. For instance, one lifestyle segment consists of people with an affinity for *nostalgia,* or the desire for old things.[120] This segment clearly represents a key market for old movies, books, and antiques. As another example, consumers who participate in extreme sports such as snowmobiling are a key market for companies that sell related equipment.[121]

Lifestyle research can help marketers understand how a product fits into consumers' general behavior patterns. For example, lifestyles related to cooking include Speed Scratch Cooking (using time-saving techniques and equipment to prepare meals) and Investment Cooking (cooking many dishes or a large quantity of food at once but storing some for later consumption).[122]

Exhibit 14.13

Activities, Interests, and Opinions

Lifestyles are represented by consumers' activities, interests, and opinions. Here are some major examples of each category. Note that these lifestyles provide a more detailed profile of consumers than their demographics do (the last column).

Activities	Interests	Opinions	Demographics
Work	Family	Themselves	Age
Hobbies	Home	Social issues	Education
Social events	Job	Politics	Income
Vacations	Community	Business	Occupation
Entertainment	Recreation	Education	Family size
Club membership	Fashion	Economics	Dwelling
Community	Food	Products	Geography
Shopping	Media	Culture	City size
Sports	Achievements	Future	Life cycle stage

Source: Joseph T. Plumer, "The Concept and Application of Life Style Segmentation," *Journal of Marketing*, January 1974, pp. 33–37. Reprinted with permission.

Finally, consumers in different countries may have characteristic lifestyles. For instance, compared with U.S. women, Japanese women are more home focused, less price sensitive, and less likely to drive.[123] Given these preferences, Japanese women would probably spend more time than U.S. women would preparing meals at home and would therefore pay more for products that enhance meal quality. Popular lifestyle activities among Russian consumers include going to the movies and theater and participating in sports like soccer, ice hockey, and figure skating.[124]

MARKETING IMPLICATIONS

Consumer lifestyles can have important implications for market segmentation, communication, and new product ideas.

Market segmentation

Marketers can use lifestyles to identify consumer segments for specific offerings. For example, targeting wine lovers with busy lifestyles, Francis Ford Coppola has introduced a single-serve can of sparkling wine, complete with convenient sipping straw.[125] Services such as day-care centers and housecleaning services save time and provide convenience, two benefits that particularly appeal to dual-career couples, working women, and other consumers with busy lifestyles.[126] At the other end of the spectrum, consumers who enjoy the slower pace of gardening are a lucrative target market for local garden centers as well as Home Depot and other retail giants.[127]

Lifestyle segmentation also has important cross-cultural implications. One study of 12 European countries used demographics, activities, media behavior, political inclinations, and mood to identify six Eurotype lifestyle segments: Traditionalists (18 percent of the population), Homebodies (14 percent), Rationalists (23 percent), Pleasurists (17 percent), Strivers (15 percent), and Trendsetters (13 percent).[128] Finally, marketers often monitor lifestyle changes to identify new opportunities. In Missouri, all branches of Fifth Third Bank are open extended hours—even on Saturdays and Sundays—so that time-stressed customers can handle transactions in person. "It should be just as easy for [customers] to get a home equity loan as it is to buy a pair of shoes," says the bank's president.[129]

Communications

Marketers can design ad messages and promotions to appeal to certain lifestyles, featuring products in the context of desired lifestyles.[130] Using the Internet can be a very targeted way to communicate with a variety of lifestyle segments, particularly those who surf the web most often. This is why JonesSoda.com, MyCoke.com, and other sites regularly post new features such as music and games to keep younger visitors returning again and again.

Finally, media usage patterns may be related to lifestyles.[131] For example, consumers who read magazines and newspapers tend to be educated and hold prestige jobs as well as being involved in the community and politics. Interestingly, consumers who love to surf the Internet also tend to be heavy TV watchers.[132] One national survey found connections between seemingly unrelated lifestyles and media usage, such as fishing enthusiasts tending to enjoy listening to Christian rock music and reading *Southern Living*.[133]

New product ideas

Often marketers can develop new product and service ideas by uncovering unfulfilled needs of certain lifestyle segments. For example, Bertolli recognized that the busy lifestyles of working couples left little time for shopping and cooking, yet many yearned for restaurant-quality dinners at home. In response, the company launched Dinner for Two, a line of frozen entrees with trendy touches such as portobello mushrooms. The package reinforces the positioning by showing a glass of wine next to the plate.[134]

Psychographics: Combining Values, Personality, and Lifestyles

This chapter opened by observing that psychographic research today combines values, personality, and lifestyle variables. To illustrate this key point, this last section provides a brief description of several psychographic applications in marketing.

VALS

Values and Life Style Survey (VALS) A psychographic tool that measures demographic, value, attitude, and lifestyle variables.

One of the most widely known psychographic tools is **VALS,** formerly known as **Values and Lifestyle Survey,** conducted by SRI Consulting Business Intelligence. VALS analyzes the behavior of U.S. consumers to create segments based on two factors. The first is resources, including income, education, self-confidence, health, eagerness to buy, intelligence, and energy level. The second is primary motivation. Consumers motivated by ideals are guided by intellectual aspects rather than by feelings or other people's opinions. Those who are motivated by achievement base their views on the actions and opinions of others and strive to win their approval. And those who are motivated by self-expression desire social or physical action, variety, activity, and personal challenge.[135]

Combining the resource and motivation variables, VALS has identified eight consumer segments (see Exhibit 14.14). At the low end of the resource hierarchy are Survivors, who have the lowest incomes. Their focus is on survival, so they are not described by a primary motivation. Believers are conservative and motivated by ideals; they have somewhat modest resources and, because they do not change easily, tend to prefer familiar, established products and brands. The other group motivated by ideals is the Thinkers, who are mature and well educated and who actively conduct information searches when planning purchases. Thinkers have more resources and are value oriented in their consumption practices.

Exhibit 14.14

VALS American Segments

VALS classifies consumers into eight major segments based on two dimensions: resources (education, income, intelligence, and so on) and primary motivation (ideals, achievement, self-expression), as described in this exhibit. Into which group would you fall?

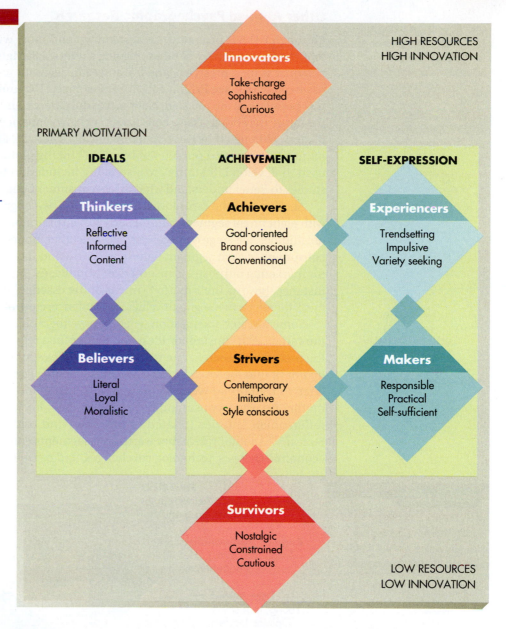

Innovators
Take-charge
Sophisticated
Curious

HIGH RESOURCES
HIGH INNOVATION

PRIMARY MOTIVATION

IDEALS

ACHIEVEMENT

SELF-EXPRESSION

Thinkers
Reflective
Informed
Content

Achievers
Goal-oriented
Brand conscious
Conventional

Experiencers
Trendsetting
Impulsive
Variety seeking

Believers
Literal
Loyal
Moralistic

Strivers
Contemporary
Imitative
Style conscious

Makers
Responsible
Practical
Self-sufficient

Survivors
Nostalgic
Constrained
Cautious

LOW RESOURCES
LOW INNOVATION

The two achievement-oriented segments are Strivers (who have limited discretionary income yet strive to emulate more successful people) and Achievers (who have higher resources, are focused on their work and families, and prefer status-symbol products). In the self-expression segment, Makers value self-sufficiency, buy basic products, and are focused on family, work, and constructive activities. Experiencers have more resources than Makers, stay active, seek stimulation and novelty, and spend money on socializing and entertainment. Innovators have the greatest resource base, with plenty of self-confidence, high incomes, and education, so they can indulge in all three primary motivations to some extent. These consumers will accept new products and technologies, and they choose upscale offerings reflective of their personal style.

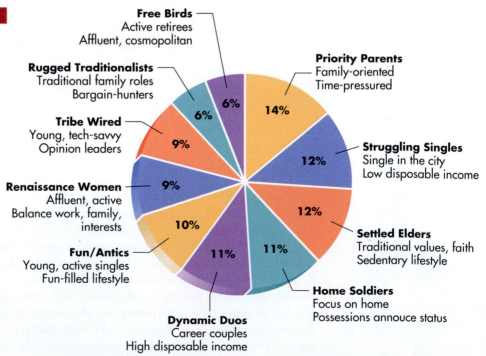

MARKETING IMPLICATIONS

Tools such as VALS, LifeMatrix, MindBase, and other psychographic applications can be useful for market segmentation, new product ideas, and ad development. Hyundai has used LifeMatrix data to segment the U.S. market for cars, identify the consumers most likely to buy its brand, choose the most effective media to reach these consumers, and create advertising messages that appeal to these consumers' values and interests.[141] Chris Bole, customer development manager for PowerBar, sees an opportunity to sell to Tribe Wired men by displaying its products in the personal grooming section of drugstores. He comments, "This would be a good example of 'How does this fit into a lifestyle?'"[142] Coors is using psychographics to target different beer-drinking segments in Boston with cable-TV ads that have different endings and with offers for different promotional events.[143]

Summary

Consumers learn values—enduring beliefs about things that are important—through the processes of socialization and acculturation. Our values exist in an organized value system, in which some are viewed as more important than others. Terminal values are desired end states that guide behavior in many situations, whereas instrumental values help people achieve those desired end states. Domain-specific values are relevant within a given sphere of activity.

Western cultures tend to highly value materialism, the home, work and play, individualism, family and children, health, hedonism, youth, authenticity, the environment, and technology. Marketers use value-based segmentation to identify groups within the larger market that share a common set of values that differ from those of other groups. Three methods for identifying value-based segments are inferring values based on the cultural milieu of the group, using the means-end chain analysis, and using questionnaires like the Rokeach Value Survey and the List of Values.

Personality consists of the patterns of behaviors, tendencies, and personal dispositions that make people different from one another. Approaches to the study of personality include (1) the psychoanalytic approach, which sees personality as the result of unconscious struggles to complete key stages of development; (2) trait theories, which attempt to identify a set of personality characteristics that describe and differentiate individuals; (3) phenomenological approaches, which propose that personality is shaped by an individual's interpretation of life events; (4) social-psychological theories, which focus on the ways that individuals act in social situations; and (5) behavioral approaches, which view personality in terms of behavioral responses to past rewards and punishments. Marketers are also interested in examining lifestyles, which are patterns of behavior or activities, interests, and opinions, for additional insight into consumer behavior. Finally, some marketing researchers use psychographic techniques involving values, personality, and lifestyles to predict consumer behavior.

Questions for Review and Discussion

1. Explain the differences among global values, terminal values, instrumental values, and domain-specific values.

2. What are the four main value dimensions along which national cultures can vary?

3. How do marketers use means-end chain analysis, the Rokeach Value Survey, and the List of Values?

4. How does the locus of control affect personality?

5. What are the three components of a consumer's lifestyle?

6. Define *psychographics*, and discuss its use and potential limitations.

CL Visit http://cengage.com/marketing/hoyer/ConsumerBehavior5e to find resources that are available to help you study for the course.

McDonald's Goes Upscale from Paris to Peoria

A Big Mac, fries, and . . . a cappuccino? These days, when consumers from Paris to Peoria go into a neighborhood McDonald's, they can order meals made from fresh, locally grown produce and sip more sophisticated beverages. Of course, the fast-food chain's well-known hamburgers are still the main attraction, but it is not just the food that is changing. The restaurants also look more luxe, some with sleek coffee bars and stylish armchairs that give customers a comfy place to linger over their lattés.

McDonald's plan to move upscale started in Europe, an area that accounts for nearly $4 out of every $10 that the company earns. Only a decade ago, however, McDonald's European sales were lagging as local consumers fretted over the few healthy choices and turned up their noses at the frumpy décor. The movement actually began in France, where people are famously particular about what they eat. "To make McDonald's and a Big Mac work in the country of slow food, we felt we had to pay more attention to space and showcasing," remembers Denis Hennequin, who was then in charge of McDonald's in France and now heads McDonald's in Europe.

Hennequin and his team started by modifying the menu for local tastes, introducing salads, desserts, and smoothies featuring fresh fruits and vegetables from French suppliers. They also cooked up new twists on McDonald's sandwiches, including cheeseburgers with French cheese and a hot ham-and-cheese sandwich called the Croque McDo, the chain's answer to France's popular Croque Monsieur sandwiches. To reinforce the idea that McDonald's was doing things differently, the company invited consumers to tour its restaurant kitchens and even meet with its produce suppliers.

The next step was to give McDonald's restaurants in France an updated, upscale look to showcase the more upscale menu and to invite consumers to savor the fast food. Hennequin set up a design studio in Paris to develop nine different restaurant décors, ranging from interiors with sleek, simple lines and neutral tones to colorful interiors with large pictures of freshly picked produce. In the new interiors, the designers replaced McDonald's usual bold red with a rich burgundy

and toned down the glaring neon lights for a more subtle look.

French consumers noticed the difference: sales at the McDonald's restaurants with new menus and interiors increased by nearly 5 percent. McDonald's then began giving its other European restaurants a menu and design makeover, a move that has boosted its sales growth in Europe by 15 percent. Now McDonald's customers in Lisbon can order soup for lunch or dinner while customers in London can settle back into leather seats and use wireless Internet access. Reflecting changing lifestyles, McDonald's is also stepping into the coffee culture in a big way. In Germany, where Starbucks is not yet a major force, the McCafé coffee bars located inside McDonald's restaurants dominate the market.

McDonald's has also brought its upscale movement to America, where the cappuccinos, iced coffees, and flavored teas served in its 1,000 McCafés are attracting many consumers who otherwise would have gone to nearby Starbucks outlets. An ever-growing menu of old favorites and newer alternatives like salads and wraps gives McDonald's customers more choices than ever before. Some of its U.S. restaurants now feature amenities such as big-screen TVs and fireplaces as well as wireless Internet access, letting customers relax and enjoy themselves if they have the time. "We really wanted to make sure that we were the customers' destination of choice," notes the chief operating officer, adding that this goal means providing "convenience, comfortable seating, [and] great locations, along with value and the right offerings."[144]

Case Questions

1. How do the changes that McDonald's has made to move upscale address changing consumer lifestyles?
2. What values seem to be reflected in the changes that McDonald's has made?
3. What aspects of personality do you think McDonald's marketers should pay particular attention to as they plan future menu and restaurant changes?

Social Influences on Consumer Behavior

Chapter 15

LEARNING OBJECTIVES

After studying this chapter, you will be able to

1. Explain how sources of influence differ in four key ways depending on whether they are delivered via mass media or personally, and whether they are delivered by marketers or others.

2. Discuss why marketers must pay particular attention to the influence of opinion leaders.

3. Outline the types and characteristics of reference groups and show how each can affect consumer behavior.

4. Distinguish between normative and informational influence, and discuss how marketers can use their knowledge of these types of influence for more effective marketing.

INTRODUCTION

Building Sales by Building Buzz

Building sales by building person-to-person buzz has become big business. BZZAgent, Tremor, and other specialized agencies now enlist consumer volunteers to help spread the word—without pay—about a brand or product. BZZAgent's 400,000 "agents" like the feeling of being the first to learn about something new; they, like the 230,000 teenage volunteers who belong to Tremor's network, can choose whom to tell, what to say (good or bad), and how to say it (via e-mail, blog, personal conversations, and so on).

When Philips wanted to increase sales of its Sonicare electric toothbrush following a nationwide TV campaign, the company hired BZZAgent for buzz marketing. Sonicare samples went out to 500 Atlanta-area BZZAgent participants so that they could try the product, form their own opinions, and then buzz about it to friends, relatives, and others. Because agents distributed discount coupons when they discussed the product, BZZAgent could track how many sales resulted from the buzzing. The test was so successful that Philips expanded the program to 30,000 agents and later to 45,000 agents.[1]

Sometimes the information that people provide, as **social influences,** can have a big impact on consumers. Information presented by some people can be very credible, and

Social influences Information by and implicit or explicit pressures from individuals, groups, and the mass media that affect how a person behaves.

some people can communicate a marketing message widely. Social influence is also powerful when individuals within groups are in frequent contact and have many opportunities to communicate information and perspectives in the way that BZZAgent's volunteers build buzz. Certain people have influence because their power or expertise makes others want to follow what they believe, do, or say. Groups can influence not only what people know but also what they do, affecting whether their behaviors are socially appropriate, socially inappropriate, and even personally destructive (such as the use of illicit drugs). Therefore, marketers need to understand what kinds of social entities create influence, what kinds of influence they create, and what effects their influence attempts can have on other consumers. Exhibit 15.1 summarizes the social influences that can affect consumers.

Sources of Influence

Many people learn about products through advertising, the Internet, publicity, samples and coupons, personal experience, people, and other sources. The phenomenon described in the chapter opener, *buzz marketing,* is the amplification of initial marketing efforts by the influence of third parties[2] (such as Tremor and BZZAgent agents). But which sources have the most impact, and why? Exhibit 15.2 offers some answers to these questions.

Marketing and Nonmarketing Sources

Influence can come from marketing and nonmarketing sources and can be delivered via the mass media or personally.

Marketing Sources Delivered via Mass Media

Marketing source Influence delivered from a marketing agent, e.g., advertising, personal selling.

Marketing sources that deliver influence through the mass media (cell 1 in Exhibit 15.2) include advertising, sales promotions, publicity, and special events. Macy's and Target try to influence your purchase behavior by promoting special sales in newspapers and on television. Companies often generate excitement for new offerings through special events and media coverage. Widespread publicity about Microsoft's Halo 3 video game prompted 1 million consumers to preorder the game months before its launch. In the days leading up to its actual introduction, thousands of consumers formed long lines outside stores to get their copies when the game went on sale at midnight.[3]

Marketing Sources Delivered Personally

Marketing sources can also deliver information personally (cell 2 in Exhibit 15.2). Salespeople, service representatives, and customer service agents are marketing sources of influence who deliver information personally in retail outlets, at consumers' homes or offices, over the phone, or via e-mail or online chat. In some situations, consumers will respond to a marketing agent, such as a salesperson, by making use of the agent's knowledge and assistance to further their personal goals. When consumers worry about undue persuasion, however, they will adopt

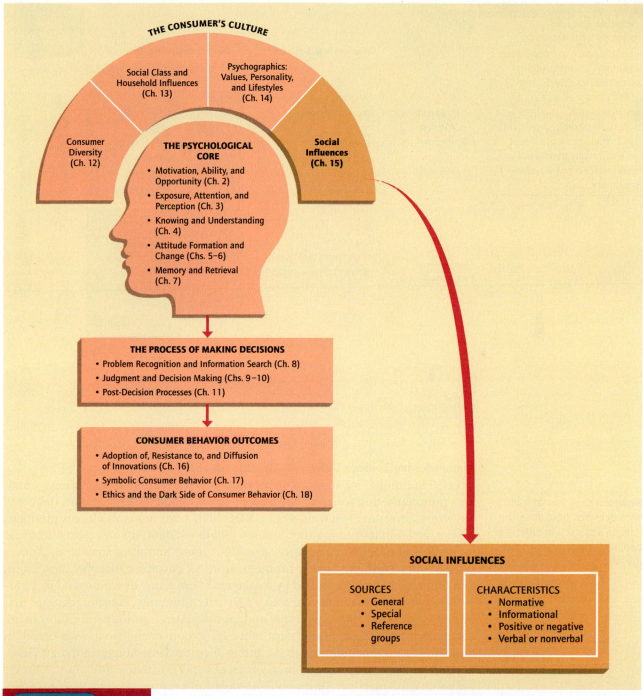

THE CONSUMER'S CULTURE

Social Class and
Household Influences
(Ch. 13)

Psychographics:
Values, Personality,
and Lifestyles
(Ch. 14)

Consumer
Diversity
(Ch. 12)

Social
Influences
(Ch. 15)

**THE PSYCHOLOGICAL
CORE**
- Motivation, Ability, and
  Opportunity (Ch. 2)
- Exposure, Attention, and
  Perception (Ch. 3)
- Knowing and Understanding
  (Ch. 4)
- Attitude Formation and
  Change (Chs. 5–6)
- Memory and Retrieval
  (Ch. 7)

THE PROCESS OF MAKING DECISIONS
- Problem Recognition and Information Search (Ch. 8)
- Judgment and Decision Making (Chs. 9–10)
- Post-Decision Processes (Ch. 11)

CONSUMER BEHAVIOR OUTCOMES
- Adoption of, Resistance to, and Diffusion
  of Innovations (Ch. 16)
- Symbolic Consumer Behavior (Ch. 17)
- Ethics and the Dark Side of Consumer Behavior (Ch. 18)

SOCIAL INFLUENCES

SOURCES
- General
- Special
- Reference
  groups

CHARACTERISTICS
- Normative
- Informational
- Positive or negative
- Verbal or nonverbal

Exhibit 15.1

**Chapter Overview:
Social Influences**

This chapter describes various sources of influence (general sources, special sources, and groups) and
how they exert influence (by providing normative or informational influence, by providing positive
and/or negative information, and by providing information verbally or nonverbally).

techniques to fend off unwanted attention.[4] Note that some buzz-building tactics
such as those in the opening example blur the line between marketing and nonmarketing sources. In the opening example, the buzz agents are not salespeople or
paid marketing representatives, yet they are working as volunteers on behalf of
marketers to deliver marketing messages.

Exhibit 15.2

Sources of Influence

Social influence can come from marketing or nonmarketing sources and can be delivered via the mass media or in person. Nonmarketing sources tend to be more credible. Information delivered via the mass media can reach many people but may not allow for a two-way flow of communication.

	Marketing Source	**Nonmarketing Source**	
Mass Media-Delivered	**1** Advertising Sales promotions Publicity Special events E-mail and websites Direct mail Cell phone	**2** News Critiques/reviews/blogs Program content External endorsements Cultural heroes/heroines Clubs/organizations Virtual communities	High / Low — Reach
Delivered Personally	**3** Salespeople Service representatives Customer service agents	**4** Family Friends Neighbors Casual acquaintances Classmates Coworkers	Low / High — Two-Way Communication

Special sources: Opinion leaders

Low ——————— **Credibility** ——————— High

Nonmarketing Sources Delivered via Mass Media

As cell 3 in Exhibit 15.2 shows, sources that are not working for marketing companies (**nonmarketing sources**) can also wield influence via mass media-delivered messages. Consumer behavior may be affected by news items about new products, movies, and restaurants; product contamination; accidents involving products; and incidences of product abuse or misuse. Consumers shopping for a new car may learn about recalls and quality problems from TV coverage, Internet sites, blogs, and other media not controlled by marketers.[5] Some may be influenced by information and opinions obtained through a virtual community, consumer groups that interact online to achieve personal and group goals.[6] Certain media sources are particularly influential. Many consumers, for instance, choose movies based on film critics' recommendations, make dining decisions based on restaurant reviews, make buying decisions based on *Consumer Reports* articles, and choose hotels based on the American Automobile Association's ratings. Celebrities and other well-known figures may also influence consumers' acquisition, usage, and disposition decisions.

Nonmarketing Sources Delivered Personally

Finally, consumer behavior is influenced by nonmarketing sources who deliver information personally (cell 4 in Exhibit 15.2).[7] Our consumer behavior can be affected by observing how others behave or by **word of mouth,** information about offerings communicated verbally by friends, family, neighbors, casual acquaintances, and even strangers. For instance, according to a Consumer

Nonmarketing source Influence delivered from an entity outside a marketing organization, e.g., friends, family, the media.

Word of mouth Influence delivered verbally from one person to another person or group of people.

Electronics Association survey, 64 percent of adults find out about new electronics products by talking with friends, family, or work associates; 65 percent of adults ask these people for recommendations when starting to research an electronics purchase.[8]

How Do These General Sources Differ?

The influence sources shown in Exhibit 15.2 differ in terms of their reach, capacity for two-way communication, and credibility. In turn, these characteristics affect how much influence each source can have with consumers.

Reach

Mass-media sources are important to marketers because they reach large consumer audiences. A 30-second TV commercial during the Super Bowl can reach more than 90 million people. Now satellite TV and radio, the Internet, cell phones, and other technologies are spreading marketing messages, product news, information about the behavior of public figures, and TV programs to an increasingly large audience, thus expanding marketers' reach dramatically.

Capacity for Two-Way Communication

Personally delivered sources of influence are valuable because they allow for a two-way flow of information. For example, a car salesperson may have more influence than a car ad because the salesperson can tailor sales information to fit the buyer's information needs, rebut counterarguments, reiterate important and/or complex information, ask questions, and answer the buyer's questions. Personal conversations are often more casual and less purposeful than mass-media-delivered information. During a conversation, people are less likely to anticipate what will be said and hence are less likely to take steps to avoid information inconsistent with their own frames of reference. Information from a personal source may also seem more vivid than information from the mass media because the person speaking somehow makes it more real, a factor that may make it more persuasive.[9]

Credibility

Whereas personal and mass-media sources differ in their reach and capacity for two-way communication, marketing and nonmarketing sources differ in their credibility. Consumers tend to perceive information delivered through marketing sources as being less credible, more biased, and manipulative. In contrast, nonmarketing sources appear more credible because we do not believe that they have a personal stake in our purchase, consumption, or disposition decisions. We are more likely to believe a *Consumer Reports* article on cars than information from a car salesperson (see Exhibit 15.3). Because nonmarketing sources are credible, they tend to have more influence on consumer decisions than marketing sources do.[10] David Pogue, a *New York Times* technology columnist, tells consumers to check reviews on independent sites like dcresource.com (maintained by a digital photography enthusiast) before buying a digital camera.[11]

Specific personal and mass-media sources vary in their credibility. We tend to believe information that we hear from people with whom we have close relationships, in part because their similarity to us (and our values and preferences) makes their opinions credible.[12] Certain people are also regarded as more credible than others because they are experts or are generally recognized as having unbiased opinions; Tiger Woods is a credible source for golf-related equipment, for instance.

Similarly, certain media have higher credibility because they base their opinions on carefully acquired and trustworthy information: Consumers are more likely to believe articles in *Time* magazine than articles in the *National Enquirer*.

MARKETING IMPLICATIONS

Marketers can build on these differences in credibility, reach, and two-way communication capability to influence consumer behavior in various ways.

Use nonmarketing sources to enhance credibility

When possible, marketers should try to have nonmarketing sources feature their offerings (see Exhibit 15.4). Testimonials and word-of-mouth referrals may have considerable impact, particularly if delivered through personal communications.[13] Likewise, the media have tremendous power to influence consumption trends and behavior and to alter perceptions. For example, *Teen Magazine* has worked with the American Cancer Society to carry stories that deride smoking. One publisher notes: "We have the power to lead those teens and tell them what brands are hot. . . . We need to leverage that power and make it cool not to smoke."[14]

Consumers cannot always determine whether information in the media is from a marketing or nonmarketing source because some magazine ads look like editorial content and some magazine articles mention the names of advertisers. On the other hand, consumers who visit the Allrecipes.com site—where brands such as Kraft sponsor some content—can tell that it is a nonmarketing source for home cooks to swap recipes and cooking tips.[15] Connecting with a virtual community that is structured around consumers' common interests (such as cooking) can be a credible, effective way for marketers to reach a targeted group.[16]

Use personal sources to enhance two-way communication

Marketing efforts may be more effective when personal information sources are used. Hosts of home shopping parties are credible as sales representatives because "people want to buy from people they like and know," says the head of Tastefully Simple, which sells gourmet foods through such parties.[17] Some companies encourage managers and employees to write blogs, informal online journals with personal opinions and ideas about various topics. Some of Wal-Mart's buyers now blog about products—what they like and what they don't like —because, says an official, "It puts real personality out there in a real conversation."[18]

Use a mix of sources to enhance impact

Because marketing and nonmarketing sources differ in their impact, the effect on consumers may be greatest when marketers use complementary sources of influence. A vitamin marketer, for example, found that although word of mouth had historically sustained the company, competition forced it to achieve greater reach through advertising. Similarly, given the competition from nonbank service providers, word-of-mouth referrals are less effective at enticing consumers to try or to stay with a particular bank.[19] Some companies are

---

Exhibit 15.3

Nonmarketing Sources Enhance Credibility

Nonmarketing sources of influence like *Consumer Reports* can have a powerful impact on consumers' purchase decisions because they are regarded as highly credible.

"Sign an organ donor card ... I did, and it's the best contract I've ever had!"

SUSAN SARANDON

"The National Kidney Foundation's donor card is a contract that's very special. It can have a great impact on your life...and eventually someone else's too.

Right now, nearly 90,000 Americans are on a waiting list for organ transplants. Due to a constant shortage of donors, the list grows longer and thousands more will die.

That's why I signed an organ donor card, and I'm asking you to do the same. You can make a difference. Contact the National Kidney Foundation for your free donor card and to learn more. Believe me, you'll feel like a star."

National Kidney Foundation
1-800-622-9010   www.kidney.org

Exhibit 15.4

Celebrities as Opinion Leaders

Nonmarketing sources can yield powerful influences because they are often seen as more objective and less biased.

Opinion leader An individual who acts as an information broker between the mass media and the opinions and behaviors of an individual or group.

Gatekeepers Sources that control the flow of information.

stimulating referrals by rewarding customers with discounts or prizes when they refer other people.[20]

Opinion Leaders

A special source of social influence is the **opinion leader,** someone who acts as an information broker between the mass media and the opinions and behaviors of an individual or group. Opinion leaders have some position, expertise, or firsthand knowledge that makes them particularly important sources of relevant and credible information, usually in a specific domain or product category. Thus, Serena Williams is an opinion leader for sports apparel, not for computers. In rural India, the village headman serves as an opinion leader for TVs, cell phones, and many things. "If I tell [the villagers] I like a particular brand, they'll go out and get it," says the headman of Kaler, a tiny town in Punjab.[21]

Opinion leaders are regarded as nonmarketing sources of influence, a perception that adds to their credibility. They are not necessarily well-known people; they may be friends and acquaintances or professionals like doctors, dentists, or lawyers who advise patients and clients. While film critics, restaurant reviewers, and *Consumer Reports* may be opinion leaders for some offerings, celebrities and models may be opinion leaders for other offerings. Opinion leaders are part of a general category of **gatekeepers,** people who have special influence or power in deciding whether a product or information will be disseminated to a market. For example, the Chinese government acts as a gatekeeper, prohibiting viewing of sexually explicit TV shows and music videos from other countries as well as politically sensitive blogs.[22]

Researchers studying opinion leaders have observed several characteristics.[23] Opinion leaders tend to learn a lot about products, are heavy users of mass media, and tend to buy new products when they are first introduced. Opinion leaders are also self-confident, gregarious, and willing to share product information. They may become opinion leaders because of an intrinsic interest in and enjoyment of certain products—in other words, they have enduring involvement with a product category.[24] Opinion leaders might also like the power of having information and sharing it with others, or they may communicate information because they believe that their actions will help others.[25]

Opinion leaders have influence because they generally have no personal stake in whether their opinions are heeded, so their opinions are perceived as unbiased and credible. They are also regarded as knowledgeable about acquisition, usage, and disposition options because of their product knowledge and experience. These characteristics explain why digital camera buyers value the comments of opinion leaders like David Pogue, a *New York Times* technology columnist, and why camera marketers want Pogue to review their products. However, simply because they serve as information brokers does not mean that information only flows from opinion leaders to consumers. Indeed, opinion leaders often get information by seeking it from consumers, manufacturers, and retailers.[26]

Whereas opinion leaders are important sources of influence about a particular product or service category, researchers have also identified another special source of influence—a **market maven,** someone who seems to have a lot of information about the marketplace in general.[27] A market maven seems to know all about the best products, the good sales, and the best stores.

Market maven A consumer on whom others rely for information about the marketplace in general.

MARKETING IMPLICATIONS

Marketers use several tactics to influence opinion leaders.

Target opinion leaders

Given their potential impact and the fact that they are both seekers and providers of marketplace information, an obvious strategy is to identify and target opinion leaders directly.[28] For instance, because Esther Bushell leads 10 book clubs in Connecticut, publishers send her early copies of new books and arrange for some authors to meet with Bushell and her clubs.[29]

Use opinion leaders in marketing communications

Although opinion leaders' influence may be less effective when delivered through a marketing source, their expertise and association can still support an offering. As an alternative, marketers may use a simulated opinion leader. For example, major TV networks do not allow medical professionals or actors playing them to endorse a product. Instead, Mentadent toothpaste has used dentists' wives, husbands, and children because their affiliation with real experts presumably gives them some credibility.[30] (See Exhibit 15.4.)

Refer consumers to opinion leaders

Marketers can and do ask consumers to contact a knowledgeable opinion leader. Many prescription drug ads do this by suggesting that consumers consult their doctors (opinion leaders) about how the advertised product can help them. One U.K. ad campaign for NiQuitin CQ Lozenges, a nicotine replacement therapy product, focused on pharmacists who can suggest products for consumers who want to quit smoking. After a month, recommendations by pharmacy personnel sales were 5 to 20 percent higher than before the campaign—and consumer sales increased by as much as 34 percent in some areas.[31]

Reference Groups as Sources of Influence

Social influence is exerted by individuals such as opinion leaders as well as by specific groups of people. A reference group is a set of people with whom individuals compare themselves for guidance in developing their own attitudes, knowledge, and/or behaviors.

Types of Reference Groups

Aspirational reference group A group that we admire and desire to be like.

Consumers may relate to three types of reference groups: aspirational, associative, and dissociative. **Aspirational reference groups** are groups we admire and wish to be like but are not currently a member of. For example, a younger brother may want to be like his older brother and other older children. According to one U.S. study, consumers aged 18 to 34 most often admire celebrities for their possessions, traits, or lifestyles.[32] Given the high respect accorded to education in Korea, teachers often serve as an aspirational reference group for students there.

Associative reference group A group to which we currently belong.

Associative reference groups are groups to which we actually belong, such as a clique of friends, an extended family, a particular work group, a club, or a school group. The gender, ethnic, geographic, and age groups to which you belong are also associative reference groups with whom you may identify (see Exhibit 15.5). Even consumers who think of themselves as individual-minded react well to products linked to appropriate associative reference groups.[33]

Associative reference groups can form around a brand, as is the case with clubs like the HOG (Harley Owners Group), which is made up of Harley-Davidson fans (see Exhibit 15.6). A **brand community** is a specialized group of consumers with a structured set of relationships involving a particular brand, fellow customers of that brand, and the product in use.[34] Members of a brand community not only buy the product repeatedly, but they are extremely committed to it, share their information and enthusiasm with other consumers, and influence other members to remain loyal.[35] Interestingly, such communities may survive even after the brand is discontinued.[36]

Brand community A specialized group of consumers with a structured set of relationships involving a particular brand, fellow customers of that brand, and the product in use.

Dissociative reference group A group we do not want to emulate.

Dissociative reference groups are groups whose attitudes, values, and behaviors we disapprove of and do not wish to emulate. "Gangsta rap" groups promoting violence are dissociative reference groups for some people. U.S. citizens serve as dissociative reference groups to religious groups in some Arab countries, and neo-Nazis serve as dissociative reference groups for many people in Germany and the United States. Research shows that country music fans are a dissociative reference group for some in the United States—even though these consumers may secretly like the music itself.[37] Note that the influence of dissociative reference groups can depend, in part, on whether a product is consumed in public or in private.[38]

Exhibit 15.5

High School Reference Groups

Researchers have found that no matter where you went to high school, the classmates you hung around with were likely to belong to one of five categories: elites, athletes, deviants, academics, and others. What category were you in, and what did students at your school call your group? What "other" groups existed in your school?

- **Elites** are high in peer status and social involvement and are somewhat involved in academics.
- **Athletes** are high in peer status and social involvement but only slightly involved in academics.
- **Deviants** are in the middle on peer status and social involvement and low on academic involvement. They tend to rebel against school.
- **Academics** are high in academic involvement, in the middle on peer status, and relatively low on social involvement.
- **Others** tend to be relatively low in peer status, social involvement, and academic involvement.

Source: Steve Sussman, Pallav Pokhrel, Richard D. Ashmore, and B. Bradford Brown, "Adolescent Peer Group Identification and Characteristics: A Review of the Literature," *Addictive Behaviors*, August 2007, pp. 1620–1627.

Exhibit 15.6

Customer-Centric Model of Brand Community

A consumer who is a member of a brand community thinks about brand names (e.g., Harley Davidson), the product category (e.g., motorcycles), other customers who use the brand (e.g., HOG members), and the marketer who makes and promotes the brand. James H. McAlexander, John W. Schouten and Harold Koenig (2002). "Building Brand Community", Journal of Marketing, 66(1), 38–54.

Customer-Centric Model of Brand Community

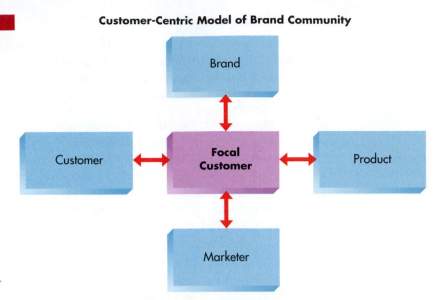

MARKETING IMPLICATIONS

The influence of various reference groups has some important implications for marketers.

Associate products with aspirational reference groups

Knowing their target consumers' aspirational reference group enables marketers to associate their product with that group and to use spokespeople who represent it. Because celebrities are an aspirational reference group for some, many companies use celebrities to endorse their products, as Nokia has done by hiring rappers to promote its cell phones to people who admire these rappers.[39]

Accurately represent associative reference groups

Marketers can also identify and appropriately represent target consumers in ads by accurately reflecting the clothing, hairstyles, accessories, and general demeanor of their associative reference groups.[40] To sell products like skateboards and mountain-climbing equipment, for example, many sports marketers develop promotions featuring actual skateboarders and mountain climbers.[41]

Help to develop brand communities

Harley-Davidson has built brand communities, partly through a special website for the Harley Owners Group and its 1 million worldwide members.[42] Another example is the Boston Red Sox baseball team, whose website is home to the Kid Nation and Red Sox Nation brand communities, with 35,000 members worldwide.[43]

Avoid using dissociative reference groups

When appropriate, companies should not use dissociative reference groups in their marketing. McDonald's decided to avoid using Ronald McDonald in its promotions in the Middle East because it knew that religious Muslims would not consider a zany, brightly colored clown to be an idol.[44] Similarly, some marketers drop celebrity spokespeople who commit crimes or exhibit other behavior that is offensive to the target market.

Characteristics of Reference Groups

Reference groups can be described according to the degree of contact, formality, and similarity among members; group attractiveness, as well as their density, degree of identification, and strength of the ties connecting members.

Degree of Contact

Reference groups vary in their degree of contact. We may have direct and extensive contact with some reference groups like our immediate circle of friends or family but may have less contact with others like gangsta rappers. Reference groups with which we have considerable contact tend to exert the greatest influence.[45] A group with which we have face-to-face interaction, such as family, peers, and professors, is a **primary reference group.** In contrast, a **secondary reference group** is one that may influence us even though we have no personal contact with most of its members. We may be members of groups like an Internet chat group or a musical fan club. Although we may interact with some members of the group only through such impersonal communication channels as newsletters, its behavior and values can still influence our behavior.

Primary reference group Group with whom we have physical face-to-face interaction.

Secondary reference group Group with whom we do not have direct contact.

Formality

Reference groups also vary in formality. Groups like fraternities, athletic teams, clubs, and classes are formally structured, with rules outlining the criteria for group membership and the expected behavior of members. For example, you must satisfy certain requirements—gaining admission, fulfilling class prerequisites—before you can enroll in particular college courses. Once enrolled, you must follow specified rules for conduct by coming to class on time and taking notes. Other groups are more ad hoc, less organized, and less structured. For example, your immediate group of friends is not formally structured and probably has no strict set of rules. Likewise, an informal group of local residents may form a neighborhood watch group. People who attend the same party or vacation on the same cruise also may constitute an informal group.

Homophily: The Similarity Among Group Members

Groups vary in their **homophily,** the similarity among the members. When groups are homophilous, reference-group influence is likely to be strong because similar people tend to see things in the same way, interact frequently, and develop strong social ties.[46] Group members may have more opportunity to exchange information and are more likely to accept information from one another. Because senders and receivers are similar, the information that they share is also likely to be perceived as credible.

Homophily The overall similarity among members in the social system.

Group Attractiveness

The attractiveness of a particular peer group can affect how much consumers conform to the group.[47] When members perceive a group as being very attractive, they have stronger intentions to conform to what the group does—even its illicit consumption behavior. This situation implies that making substance abusers seem less attractive may help U.S. children and teens resist illicit activities.

Density

Dense groups are those in which group members all know one another. For example, an extended family that gets together every Sunday operates as a dense social network. In contrast, the network of faculty at a large university is less dense

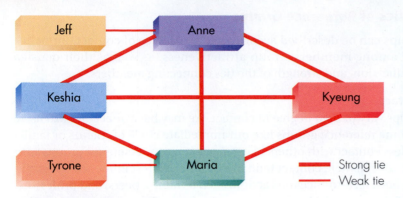

Strong tie
Weak tie

Exhibit 15.7

Tie-Strength and Social Influence

The thick red line shows that Anne has strong ties to three school friends: Maria, Kyeung, and Keshia. The thin red line indicates that Anne is less closely tied to Jeff, someone she knows from her health club. Another thin red line indicates that Maria does not have a close relationship with her distant cousin Tyrone. If you were a marketer, whom would you target in this network? Why?

Tie-strength The extent to which a close, intimate relationship connects people.

because its members have fewer opportunities to interact, share information, or influence one another. In Korea, network density varies by geographic area. A rural village may have high density because its families have known each other for generations whereas many of the 10 million residents of Seoul may not know one another, so network density there is low.

Degree of Identification

Some characteristics of an individual within a group contribute to the ways in which groups vary. One is the degree of identification that a consumer has with a group. Just because people are members of a group does not mean that they use it as a reference group. Even though people may be Hispanic or senior citizens, they need not necessarily regard similar individuals as part of their reference group.[48] The influence that a group has on an individual's behavior is affected by the extent to which he or she identifies with it. One study found that consumers who attend sporting events were more likely to buy a sponsor's products when they strongly identified with the team and viewed such purchases as a group norm.[49] Moreover, a marketing stimulus that focuses attention on consumers' identification with a certain group (such as ethnic or religious identity) and is relevant to that identification will more likely elicit a positive response.[50]

Tie-Strength

Another characteristic describing individuals within a group is **tie-strength.**[51] A strong tie means that two people are connected by a close, intimate relationship often characterized by frequent interpersonal contact. A weak tie means that the people have a more distant, nonintimate relationship with limited interpersonal contact. Exhibit 15.7 illustrates these concepts.

MARKETING IMPLICATIONS

The characteristics of reference groups have some important implications for marketers.

Understanding information transmission

Homophily, degree of contact, tie-strength, and network density can significantly influence whether, how much, and how quickly information is transmitted within a group. Within dense networks, in which consumers are in frequent contact and are connected by strong ties, information about acquiring, using, and disposing of an offering—or related offerings—is likely to be transmitted quickly. The best way for marketers to disseminate information rapidly within a market is to target individuals in dense networks characterized by strong ties and frequent contact.

Formal reference groups as potential targets

Formal reference groups can provide marketers with clear targets for marketing efforts. For example, Mothers Against Drunk Driving can target formal groups like local PTAs, school boards, and so on. To build anticipation for trips to Hong Kong Disneyland, Disney targeted the 70 million members of China's Communist Youth League, arranging storytelling programs and character visits.[52]

Homophilous consumers as targets

Marketers may use the concept of homophily to market their products. If you log on to Amazon.com and find a book you like, the recommendation system points you to more books you might like based on the purchases of consumers who bought the first book. The principle is that you might share the reading tastes of people that the site considers to be similar to you.

Targeting the network

Sometimes it makes sense for marketers to target the network itself. Verizon Wireless, for example, offers one large pool of monthly cell phone minutes to be shared among family members. Health clubs target networks when they offer consumers a discount if a friend joins. Marketers may also encourage referrals by asking consumers to "tell a friend about us."

Understanding the strength of weak ties

Although weak ties may seem to have little potential for marketers, the opposite is true. Because weak ties often serve as "bridges" connecting groups, they can play a powerful role in propagating information *across* networks. [53] In Exhibit 15.7, for instance, Maria is a bridge between her close friends and her distant cousin. Once she gives information to Tyrone, he can communicate it to others with whom he has ties. In fact, researchers have found that word of mouth spreads more effectively among people with weak ties; this phenomenon contributed to higher sales during a buzz marketing program for the Rock Bottom Restaurant and Brewery.[54]

Marketers can use weak ties to identify new networks for marketing efforts. For example, direct-selling organizations like Tupperware and Cutco and charitable groups like the American Cancer Society target individual consumers as selling (or fundraising) agents and rely on their interpersonal networks to reach others.[55] Individuals can tap not only consumers with whom they have strong ties but also those with whom they have weak ties. Girl Scouts sell cookies to friends and relatives as well as to neighbors, parents' coworkers, and people shopping at grocery stores. These are called **embedded markets** because the social relationships among buyers and sellers change the way that the market operates.[56] Thus, your social relationship with a seller may influence the way that you react to his or her selling efforts. You are more likely to buy Girl Scout cookies from a neighbor's daughter than from a girl you have never met because you want to remain on good terms with your neighbor. ▬◗

Embedded markets Markets in which the social relationships among buyers and sellers change the way the market operates.

Reference Groups Affect Consumer Socialization

One way that reference groups influence consumer behavior is through socialization, the process by which individuals acquire the skills, knowledge, values, and attitudes that are relevant for functioning in a given domain. **Consumer socialization** is the process by which we learn to become consumers and come to know the value of money; the appropriateness of saving versus spending; and how, when, and where products should be bought and used.[57] Through socialization, consumers learn consumption values as well as gain the knowledge and skills for consumption.[58] Consumer socialization can occur in many ways, as the following sections show.

Consumer socialization The process by which we learn to become consumers.

People as Socializing Agents

Reference groups like family and friends play an important role as socializing agents. Parents may, for example, instill values of thriftiness by directly teaching their children the importance of saving money, letting the children observe them being thrifty, or rewarding children for being thrifty. One study found that direct teaching was most effective for instilling consumer skills in younger children and observational learning was most effective for older children.

Intergenerational influence—information, beliefs, and resources being transmitted from one generation (parents) to the next (children)—affects consumers' acquisition and use of certain product categories and preferred brands (see Exhibit 15.8).[59] Research shows that children are using brand names as cues for consumer decisions by the time they are 12 years old.[60] Note that parenting styles and socialization patterns vary from culture to culture.[61] In individualistic cultures like Australia and the United States (see Chapter 14), in which many parents are relatively permissive, children develop consumer skills at an earlier age. In contrast, children in a collectivist culture such as India, in which parents tend to be stricter, understand advertising practices at a later age.

Moreover, parents affect socialization by influencing what types of products, TV programs, and ads their children are exposed to and how much control they have over buying products that they want. Some observers worry that exposure to these socializing agents encourages children to see the acquisition of material goods as a path to happiness, success, and achievement.[62] Some parents are very concerned about their children's exposure to violent and sexually explicit programming and products and actively regulate what their children watch and what games they play.[63] Even grandparents can play a powerful socializing role. This factor explains why the Office of National Drug Control Policy advertises to encourage grandparents to talk to their grandchildren about drugs. Grandparents' less emotionally charged relationship with their grandchildren sometimes makes them better information sources than parents.[64]

Exhibit 15.8

Intergenerational Influence

Kids, parents, and grandparents can influence one another's consumption decisions.

The effect of reference groups as socializing agents can change over time. Parents have substantial influence on young children, but their influence wanes as children grow older and interact more with their peers.[65] Similarly, your high school friends probably had a more powerful effect on your values, attitudes, and behaviors when you were a teen than they do now. Because we associate with many groups throughout our lives, socialization is a lifelong process.

The Media and the Marketplace as Socializing Agents

TV programs, movies and videos, music, video games, the Internet, and ads can also serve as socializing agents. Boys are sometimes depicted in ads as more knowledgeable, aggressive, active, and instrumental to actions than girls are; these sex role stereotypes can affect children's conceptions of what it is like to be a boy rather than a girl.[66] Consumer products may be used as socializing agents, a situation in which our childhood toys might have influenced who we are and what was expected of us.[67] Parents are likely to give boys sporting equipment, military toys, and vehicles. In contrast, they are more likely to give girls dolls, dollhouses, and domestic toys.[68] Studies show that children of 20 months can already distinguish "boy" toys from "girl" toys. These effects seem to occur at least in part because parents encourage the use of what they consider sex-appropriate toys and discourage cross-sex interests, especially for boys.[69] However, as children mature, they can become more suspicious of media and marketplace socializing agents; teens tend to be particularly skeptical of advertising claims.[70]

Normative Influence

Thus far you have learned about various sources of influence—general, special, and groups. These sources can exert two types of influence, normative and informational (see Exhibit 15.9). Assume that you are at a dinner interview with a prospective employer who tells you that she is a vegetarian. You may be reluctant to order beef, which you love, because you want to make a good impression.

Normative influence, which is what you experienced in the hypothetical example, is social pressure designed to encourage conformity to the expectations of others.[71] Chapter 5 discussed normative influences in the context of how they affect intentions and consumption decisions. The term *normative influence* derives from **norms,** society's collective decisions about what behavior should be. For example, we have norms for which brands and stores are "in" as well as norms that discourage stealing and impulse buying.[72] Morals also exert normative influence about what is right and wrong, and they can strongly influence attitudes—as they do in people's views of cigarette smoking, for example.[73]

Norms Collective decisions about what constitutes appropriate behavior.

Normative influence implies that consumers will be sanctioned, punished, or ridiculed if they do not follow the norms,[74] just as it also implies that they will be rewarded for performing the expected behaviors. To illustrate, a prospective boss may reward you with a job offer or deny you a job, depending on your behavior in the interview. Middle-school girls impose sanctions by treating classmates differently when they do not conform to the dress norm.[75]

How Normative Influence Can Affect Consumer Behavior

Normative influence can have several important effects on consumption behaviors.

Sources of Influence

SOURCES OF INFLUENCE
- Marketing or nonmarketing source
- Delivered personally or by mass media
- Differ in reach, capacity for two-way communication, credibility

SPECIAL INFLUENCE SOURCES
- Opinion leaders
- Market mavens

GROUPS AS INFLUENCE SOURCES
- Aspirational
- Associative
- Dissociative
- Groups vary in contact, formality, homophily, density, identification, tie-strength

Exert Influence

NORMATIVE INFLUENCE
- Can affect brand choice congruence, conformity, compliance, or reactance, ac1

INFORMATIONAL INFLUENCE
- Affected by characteristics of the product, the consumer, and the influencer

---

Exhibit 15.9

Sources of Influence and Types of Influence

Marketing and nonmarketing sources, special influence sources, and certain groups can affect consumer behavior by exerting normative and/or informational influences.

Brand-choice congruence Purchase of the same brand as members of a group

Conformity The tendency to behave in an expected way.

Brand-Choice Congruence and Conformity

Normative influence affects **brand-choice congruence**—the likelihood that consumers will buy what others in their group buy. If you compare the types of clothes, music, hairstyles, and cars that you buy with the selections of your friends, you will probably find that you and your friends make similar choices.[76] The presence of others can influence the enjoyment of shared stimuli (such as going to a movie together) and affect congruence as well.[77] Friends, relatives, and others in your social network may also influence the types of goods and services that you buy as gifts.[78] Simply rehearsing what to say in anticipation of discussing a particular brand purchase with others can change the way that consumers think and feel about the product and its features.[79]

Normative influence can also affect **conformity,** the tendency for an individual to behave as the group behaves. Conformity and brand-choice congruence may be related. For instance, you might conform by buying the same brands as others in your group do,[80] although brand-choice congruence is not the only way for you to conform. You may also conform by performing activities that the group wants you to perform, such as participating in initiation rites or acting in the way that the group acts. For example, your actions at a party might depend on whether you are there with your parents or your friends. In each case, you are conforming to a certain set of expectations regarding appropriate behavior. One study found that the norms established by social and brand relationships can influence consumer behavior as well.[81]

Pressures to conform can be substantial.[82] Research examining group pressure toward underage drinking and drug consumption found that students worried about how others would perceive them if they refused to conform to the group's expected behavior. Other studies have shown that conformity increases as more people in the group conform. However, identity-based thinking ("I am an environmentalist") is very strong and resistant to conformity pressures.[83] Note that conformity varies by culture. Compared with U.S. consumers, for example, Japanese consumers tend to be more group oriented and conform more to group desires.

Compliance versus Reactance

Compliance Doing what the group or social influencer asks.

Compliance, a somewhat different effect of normative influence, means doing what someone explicitly asks you to do. You are complying if, when asked, you fill out a marketing research questionnaire or purchase the products sold at a home party. Parents comply with children by purchasing foods or toys or allowing activities (such as parties) that kids request. In a virtual community, members may *not* comply as readily with the group's desires because the members are anonymous and can withdraw at will.[84]

Reactance Doing the opposite of what the individual or group wants us to do.

When we believe our freedom is being threatened, a boomerang effect occurs and we engage in **reactance**—doing the opposite of what a person or group wants us to do. For example, if a salesperson pressures you too much, you may engage in reactance by refusing to buy whatever he or she is trying to sell.[85] Reactance can occur in brand communities too. When a member feels too much pressure to perform certain rituals or assume certain roles, desire to participate in the community or buy the brand in the future may be lowered.[86]

Social-Relational Theory

According to social-relational theory consumers conduct their social interactions according to (1) the rights and responsibilities of their relationship with group members, (2) a balance of reciprocal actions with group members, (3) their relative status and authority, and (4) the value placed on different objects and activities. In turn, these relationships and their unspoken rules wield normative influence on consumer behavior.[87] For instance, consumers may regard as taboo transactions in which they are asked to pay for something held to have morally significant value, such as love, friends, family, or even votes in an election. Taboos based on cultural or historical elements may also apply to buying and selling transactions.[88]

What Affects Normative Influence Strength

The strength of normative influence depends on the characteristics of the product, the consumer, and the group to which the consumer belongs.

Product Characteristics

Reference groups can influence two types of decisions: (1) whether we buy a product within a given category and (2) what brand we buy. However, whether reference groups affect product and brand decisions also depends on whether the product is typically consumed in private or in public and whether it is a necessity or a luxury.[89] As Exhibit 15.10 shows, mattresses and hot-water heaters are considered privately consumed necessities, whereas digital cameras and DVD players are considered publicly consumed luxuries. This exhibit reflects predictions about when reference groups will affect these decisions.

One prediction is that because we must buy necessity items, reference groups are likely to have little influence on whether we buy such products. However, reference groups might exert some influence on whether we buy a luxury item. For example, your friends will probably not influence whether you buy tissues, a necessity you would buy in any case. But friends might influence whether you get an iPod, in part because luxury products communicate status—something that may be valued by group members. Also, luxury items may communicate your special interests and values and thus convey who you are and with whom you associate.

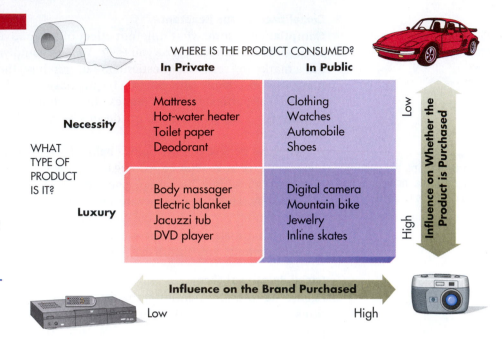

Exhibit 15.10

Reference Group Influences on Publicly and Privately Consumed Products

Reference groups tend to influence consumption of a *product category* only when the product is a luxury (not a necessity). Reference groups tend to influence consumption of a particular *brand* only when the product is consumed in public (not when it is consumed in private). Give some examples of your own to illustrate the matrix.

WHERE IS THE PRODUCT CONSUMED?

In Private   **In Public**

WHAT TYPE OF PRODUCT IS IT?

Necessity

| In Private | In Public |
| Mattress
Hot-water heater
Toilet paper
Deodorant | Clothing
Watches
Automobile
Shoes |

Luxury

| Body massager
Electric blanket
Jacuzzi tub
DVD player | Digital camera
Mountain bike
Jewelry
Inline skates |

Influence on Whether the Product is Purchased — Low / High

Influence on the Brand Purchased

Low   High

A second prediction is that products consumed in public—such as the cars we drive—give others the opportunity to observe which brand we have purchased (whether it is a Hummer or a Prius). In contrast, few people see which brand of mattress we buy because we consume this product in private. Different brand images communicate different things to people, so reference groups are likely to have considerable influence on the brand we buy when the product is publicly consumed but not when it is privately consumed. Moreover, a publicly consumed product provides opportunities for sanctions, whereas it would be difficult for groups to develop norms and sanctions for violations when the product is consumed privately. Therefore, reference groups influence product category choice for luxuries but not for necessities and they influence brand choice for products consumed in public but not for those consumed in private.[90]

The significance of the product to the group also affects normative influence.[91] Some products designate membership in a certain group. A varsity sports jacket may signify team membership and play a significant role in designating in-group and out-group status. The more central a product is to the group, the greater the normative influence the group exerts over its purchase. Finally, whether a product is perceived as embarrassing may also influence acquisition and consumption behavior that occurs in a more public setting.[92]

Consumer Characteristics

The personalities of some consumers make them readily susceptible to influence by others.[93] The trait of competitiveness, for instance, can influence conspicuous consumption behavior.[94] Thus, ads for high-end Dixie Chopper riding lawn mowers ask: "Do you want bragging rights? This mower will make you the envy of your competition."[95] Several researchers have developed the scale of "susceptibility to interpersonal influence," which includes the first six items shown in Exhibit 15.10. Consumers who are susceptible to interpersonal influence try to enhance their

Items Indicating Susceptibility to Interpersonal Influence

1. I rarely purchase the latest fashion styles until I am sure my friends approve of them.
2. If other people can see me using a product, I often purchase the brand they expect me to buy.
3. I often identify with other people by purchasing the same products and brands that they purchase.
4. To make sure that I buy the right product or brand, I often observe what others are buying and using.
5. If I have little experience with a product, I often ask my friends about the product.
6. I frequently gather information from friends or family about a product before I buy it.

Items Indicating Attention to Social Comparison Information

1. It is my feeling that if everyone else in a group is behaving in a certain manner, this must be the proper way to behave.
2. I actively avoid wearing clothes that are not in style.
3. At parties, I usually try to behave in a manner that allows me to fit in.
4. When I am uncertain about how to act in a social situation, I look to the behavior of others for cues.
5. I tend to pay attention to what others are wearing.
6. The slightest look of disapproval in the eyes of a person with whom I am interacting is enough to make me change my approach.

Exhibit 15.11

Measuring Susceptibility to Interpersonal Influence and Attention to Social Comparison Information

Individuals differ in whether they are susceptible to influence from others and whether they pay attention to what others do. What conclusions can you draw about yourself based on your answers to these questions? What implications do these questions have for marketers?

self-image by acquiring products that they think others will approve of. These consumers are also willing to conform to others' expectations about which products and brands to buy.

In addition, a personality characteristic called "attention to social comparison information" (ATSCI) is related to normative influence. Exhibit 15.11 shows several items from an ATSCI scale. People who are high on this personality trait pay close attention to what others do and use this information to guide their own behavior. For example, research shows that people feel lower self-esteem when they are exposed to idealized ad images of financial success or physical attractiveness.[96] When consumers are susceptible to normative influence, they tend to react more positively to communications highlighting product benefits that help them avoid social disapproval.[97]

Tie-strength also affects the degree of normative influence. When ties are strong, individuals presumably want to maintain their relationships with others, so they are therefore motivated to conform to the group's norms and wishes.[98] Normative influence is also affected by a consumer's identification with the group.[99] When a member of a group such as a family or subculture does not identify with that group's attitudes, behaviors, and values, normative reference-group influence will be weak.

Group Characteristics

Finally, the characteristics of the group can impact the degree of normative influence. One characteristic is the extent to which the group can deliver rewards and sanctions, known as the degree of reward power or **coercive power.**[100] To illustrate, your friends probably have more influence over your clothing choices than your neighbors do because friends have greater coercive power. That is, they are better able to deliver sanctions if they consider your clothing inappropriate or out of style.

Coercive power The extent to which the group has the capacity to deliver rewards and sanctions.

Group cohesiveness and group similarity also affect the degree of normative influence.[101] Cohesive groups and groups with similar members may communicate and interact on a regular basis. Thus, they have greater opportunity to convey normative influences and deliver rewards and sanctions. Also, research shows that if a company calls consumers' attention to their cultural identity, their increased awareness of their membership in a particular group can influence their decisions based on group norms.[102] Normative influence tends to be greater when groups are large and when group members are experts.[103] For example, you might be more inclined to buy a bottle of wine recommended by a group of wine experts than one recommended by a casual acquaintance.

MARKETING IMPLICATIONS

Marketers can take a variety of actions based on normative influences and the factors that affect their strength.

Demonstrate rewards and sanctions for product use/nonuse

Marketers may be able to create normative influence by using advertising to demonstrate rewards or sanctions that can follow from product use or nonuse. For example, beer or liquor ads sometimes show friends approving of the purchase or consumption of the advertised brand.

Create norms for group behavior

Marketing organizations may create groups with norms to guide consumers' behavior. Members of Weight Watchers who adhere to the norms (by losing weight) are rewarded with group praise. Because influence is greater when consumption is public, another strategy is to make a private behavior public. Having group discussions about eating behaviors is one way that Weight Watchers makes private information public.

Create conformity pressures

Marketers may also attempt to create conformity. For example, they may actively associate a product with a certain group so that their product becomes a badge of group membership. They may simulate conformity by showing actors in an ad behaving similarly with respect to a product, as some antismoking campaigns do by portraying teens who do not smoke.[104] Conformity may also be enhanced by publicizing others' conformity, a situation that happens at Tupperware parties and at charity fundraisers like telethons.

Use compliance techniques

Foot-in-the-door technique A technique designed to induce compliance by getting an individual to agree first to a small favor, then to a larger one, and then to an even larger one.

With the **foot-in-the-door technique,** marketers try to enhance compliance by getting a consumer to agree first to a small favor, then to a larger one, and then to an even larger one. For example, a salesperson may first ask a consumer his or her name and then ask what the person thinks of a given product. After complying with these requests, the consumer may be more inclined to comply with the salesperson's ultimate request to purchase the product.[105]

Door-in-the-face technique A technique designed to induce compliance by first asking an individual to comply with a very large and possibly outrageous request, followed by a smaller and more reasonable request.

With the **door-in-the-face technique,** the marketer first asks the consumer to comply with a very large and possibly outrageous request, then presents a smaller and more reasonable request. For example, a salesperson might ask a consumer whether she wants to buy a $500 piece of jewelry. When the consumer says no, the salesperson might then ask if she wants to buy a set of earrings on sale for only $25.[106] Because the consumer perceives that the requester has given something up by moving from a large to a small request, he or she may feel obligated to reciprocate by responding to the smaller request.

Even-a-penny-will-help technique A technique designed to induce compliance by asking individuals to do a very small favor—one that is so small that it almost does not qualify as a favor.

A third approach is the **even-a-penny-will-help technique.**[107] Here, marketers ask the consumer for a very small favor—so small that it almost does not qualify as a favor. Marketers collecting money for a charity may indicate that even a penny will help those in need. Salespeople making cold calls may tell prospective clients that even one minute of their time will be valuable. Because people would look foolish denying these tiny requests, they usually comply and, in fact, often give an amount appropriate for the situation.

Ask consumers to predict their behavior

Simply asking consumers to predict their own behavior in taking a certain action often increases the likelihood that they will actually behave in that way.[108] For example, a marketer of products containing recycled parts might ask consumers to predict their behavior in supporting the environment by buying or using products made with reclaimed materials.[109] This request may remind consumers that they have not been doing enough to live up to their own standards in supporting the environment—in turn, leading to purchases that will fulfill the consumers' self-prophecy.

Provide freedom of choice

Because reactance usually occurs when people feel that their freedom is being threatened, marketers need to ensure that consumers believe that they have freedom of choice. For example, a salesperson might show a consumer a variety of DVD players, discussing the advantages of each. In this situation the consumer will feel a greater sense of control over whether to buy at all, and if so, which item to buy.

Use expert service providers who are similar to target customers

Some research shows that consumers are more likely to comply with what a service provider asks (and be more satisfied with the outcome) when the provider and customer have similar attitudes and when the expert clarifies the customer's role.[110]

Informational Influence

Informational influence The extent to which sources influence consumers simply by providing information.

In addition to normative influence, reference groups and other influence sources can exert **informational influence** by offering information to help a person make decisions.[111] For example, chat groups on Internet travel sites exert informational influence by providing travel tips to prospective travelers. Friends exert informational influence by telling you which movie is playing at the local theater, and the media exert informational influence by reporting that certain foods may be health hazards.

How Informational Influence Can Affect Consumer Behavior

Informational influence can affect how much time and effort consumers devote to information search and decision making. If you can get information easily from a friend, you may be reluctant to conduct an extensive, time-consuming information search when making a decision. Therefore, if you want a new cell phone, and a trusted friend says that the one he just bought is the best he has ever had, you might simply buy the same one.

Factors Affecting Informational Influence Strength

The extent to which informational influence is strong or weak depends on the characteristics of the product, of the consumer and the influencer, and of the group.

Product Characteristics

Consumers tend to be susceptible to informational influence when considering complex products such as electronic appliances that consumers cannot easily understand how to use.[112] They are also more susceptible to informational influence when they perceive product purchase or usage to be risky.[113] Thus, consumers may be affected by information that they receive about cosmetic surgery, given its formidable financial and safety risks. Consumers may also be more open to informational influence when they themselves cannot tell the difference between brands.[114]

Consumer and Influencer Characteristics

Characteristics of both the consumer and the influencer affect the extent of informational influence. Such influence is likely to be greater when the source or group communicating the information is an expert,[115] especially if the consumer either lacks expertise or has had ambiguous experiences with the product. For example, given their lack of knowledge and confidence about the home-buying process, first-time home buyers may carefully consider the information conveyed by experts such as real estate agents. Personality traits, such as consumers' susceptibility to reference group influence and attention to social comparison information, also influence the extent to which consumers look to others for cues on product characteristics.[116]

Like normative influence, informational influence is affected by tie-strength. Individuals with strong ties tend to interact frequently, a situation that provides greater opportunities for consumers to learn about products and others' reactions to them. Note that informational influence may actually affect the ties between individuals. When people establish social relationships that involve sharing information, for example, they may become friends in the process.[117]

Finally, culture may affect informational influence. One study found that U.S. consumers were more likely than Korean consumers to be persuaded by information-packed ads. Because the Korean culture often focuses on the group and group compliance, Korean consumers may be more susceptible to normative influence than U.S. consumers are.[118]

Group Characteristics

Group cohesiveness also affects informational influence. Specifically, members of cohesive groups have both greater opportunity and perhaps greater motivation to share information.

MARKETING IMPLICATIONS

Marketers can apply informational influence in several ways.

Create informational influence by using experts

Because source expertise and credibility affect informational influence, marketers can use sources regarded as expert or credible for the product category, as Saucony does when it uses sports stars in its ads. (See Exhibit 15.12).

RYAN SHAY
1979-2007

RYAN,
THANK YOU FOR BEING AN INSPIRATION TO RUNNERS EVERYWHERE. ALTHOUGH
WE MOURN YOUR DEATH, WE CELEBRATE YOUR LIFE. WE'LL MISS YOU...
· YOUR SAUCONY FAMILY

Exhibit 15.12

Informational Influence from Experts

Athletes are often great endorsers for sports products because they exert influence by virtue of their expertise in the product category.

Valence Whether information about something is good (positive valence) or bad (negative valence).

Create a context for informational influence

Marketers should try to create a context for informational influence to occur. One way to do this is by hosting or sponsoring special product-related events where people can talk to one another about the company's products. Another way is to allow online chats or blogs in a special area of a product's or company's website. Marriott International's website invites public reaction to the CEO's regular blog posts and podcasts.[119]

Create informational and normative influence

Marketing efforts may be most successful when *both* normative and informational influences are involved. One study found that only 2 percent of consumers donated blood in the absence of any type of influence, but between 4 and 8 percent did so when either informational or normative influence was present. However, when both forms of influence were used, 22 percent of the consumers donated blood.[120] Also, because source similarity enhances both normative and informational influence, advertisers might enhance influence by using sources that are similar to their target audience. Using web-based recommendation systems is another approach to using both normative and informational influence.[121]

Descriptive Dimensions of Information

In the context of consumer behavior, information can be described by the dimensions of valence and modality.

Valence: Is Information Positive or Negative?

Valence describes whether the information is positive or negative. This distinction is very important because researchers have found that negative and positive information affect consumer behavior in different ways.[122] More than half of dissatisfied consumers engage in negative word of mouth. Moreover, dissatisfied consumers talk to three times more people about their bad experiences than satisfied consumers do about their good experiences.[123] People who like to post online comments about products react more to negative information than do people who read without posting—perhaps because the posters want to make it look like they have high standards.[124]

Researchers hypothesize that people pay more attention to and give more weight to negative information than they do to positive information.[125] Negative information may be diagnostic—that is, it has more significance because it seems to tell us how offerings differ from one another. Most of the information we hear about offerings is positive, so negative information may receive more attention because it is surprising, unusual, and different.[126] Negative information may also prompt consumers to attribute problems to the offering itself, not to the consumer who uses it.[127] Thus, if you learn that a friend got sick after eating at a new restaurant, you may attribute the outcome to bad food rather than to your friend's eating too much.

Modality: Does Information Come from Verbal or Nonverbal Channels?

Another dimension describing influence is the modality through which it is delivered—is it communicated verbally or nonverbally? Although norms about group behavior might be explicitly communicated by verbal description, consumers can also infer norms through observation. For instance, a consumer may learn that a particular brand of can openers is bad either by observing someone struggling with it or by hearing people discuss their experiences with the product.

The Pervasive and Persuasive Influence of Word of Mouth

Marketers are especially interested in word of mouth, which can affect many consumer behaviors. Your neighbor may recommend a hair stylist, or you may overhear a stranger say that Nordstrom's semiannual sale is next week.[128] Or you may go to a new movie because your friend said it was great. In fact, word of mouth before a movie is released and during its first week in theaters has been shown to strongly influence other consumers' movie-going intentions.[129] More than 40 percent of U.S. consumers ask family and friends for advice when selecting a doctor, a lawyer, or an auto mechanic, although men and women differ in how often they seek advice and from whom.[130] Moreover, research shows that positive word of mouth is more common than negative word of mouth.[131]

Not only is word of mouth *pervasive;* it is also more *persuasive* than written information is.[132] One study found that word of mouth was the top source affecting food and household product purchases. It was seven times more effective than print media, twice as effective as broadcast media, and four times more effective than salespeople in affecting brand switching.[133] Online forums, blogs, websites, and e-mail can potentially magnify the effect of word of mouth because consumers can tell others about good or bad experiences with just the click of a mouse. More than 15 million people are active bloggers, and many more read blogs.[134] Thus, many companies monitor mentions of their product on blogs and websites. Volkswagen, for instance, views blogs as "first, a listening post for [the company] and, second, as a medium or device by which we can state our position," according to the public relations manager.[135]

Viral marketing Rapid spread of brand/product information among a population of people.

Viral marketing, a rapid spread of brand/product information among a population of people, is powerful and credible because the source is not the marketer and because the message is delivered personally. The nonprofit Girl Scouts of America has used viral marketing to sell its cookies, for instance. It posts cookie commercials on YouTube and other sites where visitors can stumble across them and share them with other people. It also set up a MySpace page for the annual cookie sale, complete with profiles for Thin Mints and its other cookies.[136]

MARKETING IMPLICATIONS

Word of mouth can have a dramatic effect on consumers' product perceptions and an offering's marketplace performance. Many small businesses such as hairstylists, piano instructors, and preschools cannot afford to advertise and rely almost exclusively on word-of-mouth referrals. Doctors, dentists, and lawyers often rely heavily on word of mouth because they fear that extensive advertising will cheapen their professional image. Moreover, success in some industries (such as entertainment) is ultimately tied to favorable word of mouth.

Preventing and responding to negative word of mouth

Marketers must act to prevent negative word of mouth and to rectify it once it occurs.[137] Rather than ignoring complaints, firms that empathize with consumers' complaints and respond with free goods or in another meaningful way will be more successful at reducing negative word of mouth. For example, zoos have been under fire from activists who fear that animals are being mistreated. So when an alligator escaped over a wall before the Los Angeles Zoo opened one morning, zoo officials did not try to hide the escape. Instead, they called in the media to show that "he's a very smart, healthy gator."[138] In the event of a major crisis, companies must take definite steps to restore consumer confidence (see Exhibit 15.13).[139]

Engineering favorable word of mouth

In addition to creating quality offerings,[140] marketers can try to engineer favorable word of mouth by targeting opinion leaders and using networking opportunities at trade shows, conferences, and public events. For instance, Panasonic, Sony, and all of

Exhibit 15.13 **Restoring Public Trust** Professional crisis managers recommend these steps when a company is under siege.	DO:	DON'T:
	• *Recognize that speed is crucial.* "If you don't have an answer or a solution to the problem, you better be able to tell your audiences that you're working on one," says Rich Blewitt, president of Rowan & Blewitt.	• *Hide what you know.* Being one step behind when evidence of wrongdoing surfaces not only damages your credibility, but also hinders your ability to control the spin, says Victor Kamber, CEO of The Kamber Group.
	• *Place customers' interests above your own.* A company must "seem to want to come to the aid of the people in the crisis first, and [put] their own corporate interests last," says Larry Kramer, managing director at GCI Group.	• *Get tied down in the day-to-day details of running the company.* Make this crisis the No. 1 priority. "You've got to have a bunch of people who drop everything and just deal with this," says Mark Braverman, principal, CMG Associates Inc.
	• *Take a long-term view.* As the massive Tylenol recall showed, sacrificing a product's image in the short term can demonstrate responsibility over the long haul.	• *Forget that public perception is more important than reality.* Even if you've done nothing wrong but consumers think you have, their view is what matters, says Steven Fink, president of Lexicon Communications Corp.

their competitors mount elaborate displays to draw media and buyer attention to new products during the gigantic Consumer Electronics Show, which draws 140,000 attendees to Las Vegas every January.[141]

Handling rumors and scandals

Rumors are a special case of negative word of mouth.[142] Scandals can also touch off negative word of mouth—even affecting a company's competitors.[143] Companies should be aware of what consumers are saying about their brands and products,[144] offline and online, and be ready to deal with rumors and scandals.[145]

▷ *Do nothing.* Often companies prefer to do nothing because more consumers may actually learn about a rumor from marketers' attempts to correct it. However, this strategy can also backfire. When Nike was accused of condoning low wages and abusive conditions in its Asian factories, its image suffered when it did not respond vigorously to the attacks. The company has since responded in various ways, including putting links to labor standards on its website and severing ties with suppliers that violate those standards.[146]

▷ *Do something locally.* Some companies react locally, putting the rumor to rest on a case-by-case basis. Procter & Gamble sent a packet of information about its man-in-the-moon symbol, long rumored to connote devil worship, only to those consumers who called its hotline. In such cases, companies should brief staff members about the rumor and how they should respond to consumers.

▷ *Do something discreetly.* Companies may want to respond discreetly to a rumor. For example, when rumors circulated that oil companies were contriving oil shortages out of greed, the firms ran a public relations campaign highlighting their socially desirable activities. They did not mention the rumor, but the gist of the campaign clearly ran contrary to the rumor's content.

▷ *Do something big.* At times, companies may respond with all the media resources at their disposal. They may use advertising to directly confront and refute the rumor, create news refuting the rumor, conduct media interviews to communicate the truth, and hire credible outside opinion leaders to help dispel the rumor. When rumors circulated in Alaska that Interbake Foods was discontinuing Sailor Boy Pilot Bread, Interbake sent its regional business manager to Anchorage to set the record straight. He told the *Anchorage Daily News* that the crackers were being produced in a different factory with new ovens, and he distributed samples at a local Costco, requesting customer feedback.[147]

Tracking word of mouth

Whether word of mouth is positive (like referrals) or negative (like rumors), companies may want to try to identify the source of it. Marketers can find out where consumers heard the information and then ask all of those sources where, in turn, they heard the story.[148] Marketers can also ask consumers about specific details that they heard from the source to track the distortion of information and find the key sources perpetuating the distortions. Then the company can follow up by, for example, thanking or rewarding individuals who communicate positive word of mouth and provide referrals.

Summary

Consumers are influenced by many sources—marketing and nonmarketing, and those that are delivered through the mass media and those that are delivered personally. Consumers regard nonmarketing sources as more credible than marketing sources. Information delivered personally has less reach but more capacity for two-way communication than does information from mass-media sources. Marketers may want to target opinion leaders who are sources of influence because they are experts in a product category.

Reference groups, people with whom individuals compare themselves, may be associative, aspirational, or dissociative, and they can be described according to their degree of contact, formality, homophily, group attractiveness, density, identification, and tie-strength. Reference groups may play a powerful socializing role, influencing consumers' key actions, values, and behaviors.

These influence sources exert normative and informational influence. Normative influence tends to be greater for products that are publicly consumed, considered luxuries, or regarded as a significant aspect of group membership. Normative influence is also strong for individuals who tend to pay attention to social information. Social-relational theory suggests that the unspoken rules of relationships with group members wield normative influence on consumer behavior. Strong ties and identification with the group increase the likelihood that consumers will succumb to normative influences. Finally, normative influence is greater when groups are cohesive, members are similar, and the group has the power to deliver rewards and sanctions.

Informational influence operates when individuals affect others by providing information. Consumers are most likely to seek and follow informational influence when products are complex, purchase or use is risky, and brands are distinctive. The more expert the influencer and the more consumers are predisposed to listen to others, the greater the informational influence. Informational influence is also greater when groups are more rather than less cohesive. Social influence varies in valence and modality. Negative information is communicated to more people and given greater weight in decision making than positive information is. Marketers are particularly interested in word of mouth, both positive and negative.

Questions for Review and Discussion

1. How do sources of influence differ in terms of marketer domination and delivery?

2. Why do companies sometimes target opinion leaders for marketing attention?

3. What are the three types of reference groups, and how can these groups be described?

4. How might consumers respond to normative influence?

5. What three techniques can marketers use to encourage consumer compliance?

6. Differentiate between information valence and modality.

7. Why is word of mouth so important for marketers?

CL Visit http://cengage.com/marketing/hoyer/ ConsumerBehavior5e to find resources that are available to help you study for the course.

CONSUMER BEHAVIOR CASE

Who Makes the Call to Switch Carriers?

Whether they go with Sprint, T-Mobile, AT&T, Verizon Wireless, or another cell phone service carrier, consumers often choose and use a calling plan based on what their friends use. Although brand loyalty may play a role, many people are particularly concerned about whether they can call or text other in-network customers for free and when they can make or receive other calls without charge. It is a matter of dollars and sense: On some service plans, the cost of calling or texting friends who use other carriers—especially during periods of peak pricing—can add up quickly.

A growing number of consumers are making purchase and consumption decisions based on who is switched into or out of a carrier's network. These decisions are complicated by the fact that carriers usually require customers to sign a one- or two-year contract and pay a hefty fee if they want to switch carriers before the end of the contract. Once their contracts are up, however, some consumers will follow their friends from carrier to carrier, switching phones in the process, so that they can talk and text whenever they like. Friends who do not switch may wind up getting fewer calls and text messages, keeping their calls and messages short, or waiting to talk or text until off-peak hours.

For example, after a friend switched from Sprint to T-Mobile because so many in her group were using the carrier, one college student observed, "We used to talk every day all day. Now I only hear from her after 9 p.m. so that she doesn't use her minutes." To stay connected without spending a fortune, this student plans to sign with T-Mobile as soon as her contract with Sprint expires.

Carrier choices can bring in-network friends closer while impeding communications with out-of-network friends. "I try not to talk to those who don't have Sprint. I don't have minutes to waste," explains a 23-year-old Sprint customer. On the other hand, this customer became better friends with a casual acquaintance after both realized that with the Sprint network in common, they could call each other as often as they liked.

For their part, the carriers recognize that these dynamics can greatly influence decisions and usage. Sprint, for instance, moved the start of its "night" period up to 7 P.M. instead of using the 9 P.M. start time that many competitors have set, giving customers two additional hours of lower-priced, off-peak calling time. T-Mobile began offering a plan that allows customers to specify five out-of-network phone numbers that they can then call free at any time. More carriers are also introducing flat-rate plans with unlimited calling.

Not everyone wants to talk, however. Verizon Wireless examined its records and found that a growing number of its 66 million customers were using cell phones more for texting rather than for calling. In any given month, customers were sending more than 10 billion text messages (New Year's Day is Verizon Wireless's busiest text day of the year while Halloween is its busiest day for video and photo messages). On the basis of this research, the company introduced plans that allow for unlimited text, video, photo, and instant messages. Users on these plans pay for voice phone calls by the minute.

Because most cell phones are preset to work only on a specific network, switching carriers generally means switching phones. This change is not a big obstacle for consumers who want the latest technology, but it represents an extra expense—and a bit of a learning curve—for those who like their current cell phone. Because of this cost, Verizon Wireless recently opened its network to allow customers to "bring their own phones" (as long as the phones have been tested for compatibility).[149]

Case Questions

1. What characteristics of the reference group are likely to be involved when consumers switch to the cell phone service carrier used by most of their close friends?

2. How does normative influence affect carrier choice? What are the marketing implications for Sprint and other carriers?

3. What role is informational influence likely to play in a consumer's decision to switch carriers after his or her friends have switched?

Consumer Behavior Outcomes and Issues

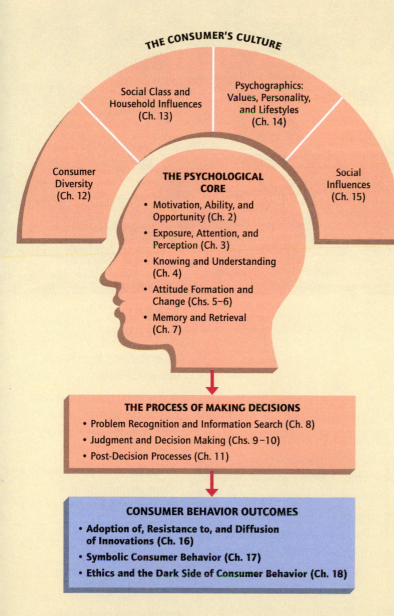

THE CONSUMER'S CULTURE

Social Class and Household Influences (Ch. 13)

Psychographics: Values, Personality, and Lifestyles (Ch. 14)

Consumer Diversity (Ch. 12)

Social Influences (Ch. 15)

THE PSYCHOLOGICAL CORE
- Motivation, Ability, and Opportunity (Ch. 2)
- Exposure, Attention, and Perception (Ch. 3)
- Knowing and Understanding (Ch. 4)
- Attitude Formation and Change (Chs. 5–6)
- Memory and Retrieval (Ch. 7)

THE PROCESS OF MAKING DECISIONS
- Problem Recognition and Information Search (Ch. 8)
- Judgment and Decision Making (Chs. 9–10)
- Post-Decision Processes (Ch. 11)

CONSUMER BEHAVIOR OUTCOMES
- Adoption of, Resistance to, and Diffusion of Innovations (Ch. 16)
- Symbolic Consumer Behavior (Ch. 17)
- Ethics and the Dark Side of Consumer Behavior (Ch. 18)

Part Five examines the outcomes of and issues related to many influences and processes discussed in Parts Two, Three, and Four. Chapter 16 builds on the topics of decision making and group processes by exploring how consumers adopt innovative offerings and how their adoption decisions affect the spread (diffusion) of a new offering through a market. This chapter also looks at factors that make a difference in consumers' resistance to an innovation, an adoption of an innovation, and the diffusion of an offering through a marketplace.

Chapter 17 discusses the fascinating topic of symbolic consumer behavior. Both goods and services can have deeply felt and significant meanings for consumers, symbolic meanings affected by rituals related to acquisition, consumption, and disposal. Moreover, the meaning of an offering can be transferred through gift giving.

Chapter 18 examines the dark side of consumer behavior and marketing, including some negative outcomes of acquisition behaviors (such as compulsive buying) and key ethical issues related to consumer behavior (such as whether marketing efforts promote obesity). This final chapter also explores important social responsibility issues in marketing.

Chapter 16

Adoption of, Resistance to, and Diffusion of Innovations

INTRODUCTION

A Taste for Innovation

How will hungry consumers react to new menu items? Panera Bread and McDonald's face this challenge all the time. Panera adds a new dish to its menu every eight weeks to boost sales and satisfy loyal customers who seek variety. When Panera's head of product development created a new salad not long ago, he noted growing consumer interest in whole grains and tasted some of the unusual ingredients used by chefs in chic restaurants. Putting these trends together, he created a grilled salmon salad with wheat berries and Meyer lemon juice that received a favorable response when tested in 30 Panera units. The salad is now on the menu in all 1,000 Panera units. The chain is also testing menu innovations to build its breakfast and dinner business.

McDonald's was targeting drive-through customers when its director of culinary innovation first cooked up a grab-and-go taco/quesadilla combination featuring chicken and melted cheese. The "tacadilla" did not do well in consumer tests, so the head chef revamped it, wrapping chicken strips, ranch sauce, shredded cheese, and lettuce in a flour tortilla. This Snack Wrap tested so well that it was launched in all U.S. markets within six months—a rapid entry when compared with the 18 to 24 months usually

LEARNING OBJECTIVES

After studying this chapter, you will be able to

1. Describe how innovations can be classified in terms of their type, the benefits they offer, and their breadth.

2. Explain how consumers adopt an innovation, why they might resist adoption, and why marketers must understand the timing of adoption decisions.

3. Define *diffusion* and discuss how diffusion curves relate to the product life cycle.

4. Outline the main factors that affect adoption, resistance, and diffusion, and show how marketers can use their knowledge of these factors to market more effectively.

needed to introduce a new menu item. It has become McDonald's most successful new product introduction ever.[1]

The way that restaurant chains develop and market new menu items illustrates some of the factors that influence consumers' decisions about innovative offerings, the subject of this chapter (see Exhibit 16.1). First the chapter describes types of innovations, which can vary in both novelty and benefits. The Snack Wrap, for instance, was new to McDonald's, distinctly different from the chain's usual hamburger fare, and offered the benefit of convenience. Next we examine what affects whether consumers will resist a new product (like McDonald's "tacadilla") or adopt it (like Panera's grilled salmon salad). The final section examines the factors affecting how quickly a new product spreads, or diffuses, through a market.

Innovations

The ability to develop successful new products is critical to a company's sales and future growth. Selling 10 million iPhones in the product's first year not only boosted Apple's profits; it also established the company as a formidable competitor in a lucrative product category in which it had had no previous experience.[2] Innovation is so important to Nestlé's future that the top management team receives monthly reports on the ten most promising products in development.[3] Given the role that new products play in a company's sales and profitability, it is very important for marketers to understand new products and what drives their success.

Defining an Innovation

Innovation An offering that is perceived as new by consumers within a market segment and that has an effect on existing consumption patterns.

A new product, or an **innovation,** is an offering that is new to the marketplace. More formally, an innovation is a product, service, attribute, or idea that consumers within a market segment perceive as new and that has an effect on existing consumption patterns.[4] McDonald's Snack Wrap was new to its drive-through customers, for instance. Services such as movie downloads and identity fraud insurance can be innovations, as can ideas. For example, social marketers have been active in persuading consumers to adopt such ideas as practicing safe sex and preventing bullying.

Products, services, attributes, packages, and ideas are innovations if they are *perceived* as being new by consumers, whether or not they actually are new. When Propecia was introduced as a drug to reduce male baldness, few consumers realized that it is really the same drug that is sold as Proscar and used to treat prostate problems.[5] On the other hand, although products can be marketed as new offerings, they can fail if consumers do not view them as providing any unique benefits.[6]

Marketers also define an *innovation* with respect to a market segment. Because of the nation's small home kitchens and ingrained traditions, the

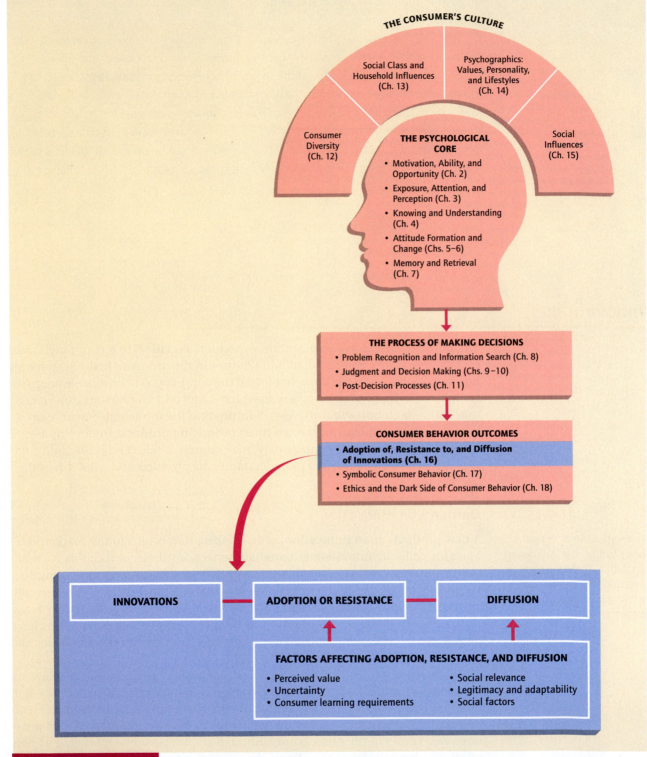

THE CONSUMER'S CULTURE

Social Class and
Household Influences
(Ch. 13)

Psychographics:
Values, Personality,
and Lifestyles
(Ch. 14)

Consumer
Diversity
(Ch. 12)

**THE PSYCHOLOGICAL
CORE**

• Motivation, Ability, and
  Opportunity (Ch. 2)

• Exposure, Attention, and
  Perception (Ch. 3)

• Knowing and Understanding
  (Ch. 4)

• Attitude Formation and
  Change (Chs. 5–6)

• Memory and Retrieval
  (Ch. 7)

Social
Influences
(Ch. 15)

THE PROCESS OF MAKING DECISIONS

• Problem Recognition and Information Search (Ch. 8)
• Judgment and Decision Making (Chs. 9–10)
• Post-Decision Processes (Ch. 11)

CONSUMER BEHAVIOR OUTCOMES

• **Adoption of, Resistance to, and Diffusion
  of Innovations (Ch. 16)**
• Symbolic Consumer Behavior (Ch. 17)
• Ethics and the Dark Side of Consumer Behavior (Ch. 18)

INNOVATIONS	ADOPTION OR RESISTANCE	DIFFUSION

FACTORS AFFECTING ADOPTION, RESISTANCE, AND DIFFUSION

• Perceived value
• Uncertainty
• Consumer learning requirements

• Social relevance
• Legitimacy and adaptability
• Social factors

Exhibit 16.1

**Chapter Overview:
Adoption of, Resistance
to, and Diffusion of
Innovation**

Consumers may decide to adopt (e.g., purchase) or resist adopting a new offering (an innovation). Diffusion reflects how fast an innovation spreads through a market. Adoption, resistance, and diffusion can be influenced by the type of innovation, its breadth, its characteristics, and the social system into which it is introduced.

automatic dishwasher is seen as an innovation in Japan, where only 7 percent of households own one.[7] Consumers in Third World countries may regard certain appliances and electronic gadgets as entirely new, even though Americans and consumers in other Western countries regard these items as near necessities.

Innovations can bring about changes in acquisition, consumption, and disposition patterns. Thanks to high-speed Internet access, a growing number of consumers are shopping online rather than visiting stores.[8] Microwave ovens have changed the way we cook, e-mail has changed the way we communicate, and digital cameras and camera phones have changed the way we take photographs and share them with others. Increased attention to recycling has brought about innovations such as recyclable and reusable packaging. Finally, online auction sites such as eBay provide an innovative way for consumers to dispose of unwanted items.

Marketers classify innovations in three main ways: in terms of (1) the innovation's type (2) the type of benefits it offers, and (3) its breadth.

Innovations Characterized by Degree of Novelty

One way to characterize innovations is to describe the degree of change that they create in our consumption patterns.[9]

Continuous innovation An innovation that has a limited effect on existing consumption patterns.

> A **continuous innovation** has a limited effect on existing consumption patterns; it is used in much the same way as the products that came before it. McDonald's Snack Wrap is an example of a continuous innovation. It has different ingredients and tastes different than other wraps do, but we eat it in much the same way that we eat other wraps. Not surprisingly, most new products are continuous innovations.

Dynamically continuous innovation An innovation that has a pronounced effect on consumption practices and often involves a new technology.

> A **dynamically continuous innovation** has a pronounced effect on consumption practices. Often these innovations incorporate a new technology. Digital cameras were dynamically continuous innovations when they were introduced because they changed the way that consumers viewed, stored, and printed pictures. The cameras have dramatically affected the sale of film and film processing services. Now fewer than 200 million rolls of film are sold each year, a steep decline from the more than 800 million rolls sold in 1999; because of lower demand, Stop & Shop and some other retailers have stopped offering photo processing services altogether.[10]

Discontinuous innovation An offering that is so new that we have never known anything like it before.

> A **discontinuous innovation** is a product so new that we have never known anything like it before.[11] Airplanes and Internet service were once discontinuous innovations that radically changed consumer behavior. Like dynamically continuous innovations, discontinuous innovations often spawn a host of peripheral products and associated innovations. For example, after microwave ovens were introduced, marketers began offering new pans, temperature probes, food products, and cookbooks tailored specifically for microwave cooking.

Based on these three broad innovation types—continuous, dynamically continuous, and discontinuous—innovations can be characterized more specifically according to their degree of novelty on a continuum of newness (see Exhibit 16.2). Discontinuous innovations are the most novel and require the most behavioral change, whereas continuous innovations are the least novel and require the least behavioral change.

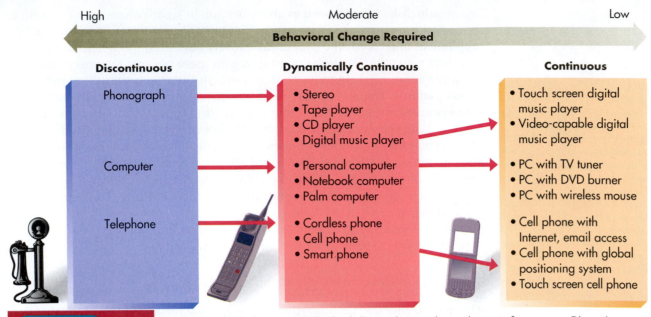

Behavioral Change Required

Discontinuous   **Dynamically Continuous**   **Continuous**

Phonograph

- Stereo
- Tape player
- CD player
- Digital music player

- Touch screen digital music player
- Video-capable digital music player

Computer

- Personal computer
- Notebook computer
- Palm computer

- PC with TV tuner
- PC with DVD burner
- PC with wireless mouse

Telephone

- Cordless phone
- Cell phone
- Smart phone

- Cell phone with Internet, email access
- Cell phone with global positioning system
- Touch screen cell phone

Exhibit 16.2

The Innovation Continuum

Innovations vary in how much behavioral change they require on the part of consumers. Discontinuous innovations (products that are radically new when they are first introduced) require considerable change in consumption patterns, whereas continuous innovations (often extensions of existing products) require very little change.

Innovations Characterized by Benefits Offered

In addition to their degree of novelty, innovations can be characterized by the type of benefits that they offer. Some new products, services, attributes, or ideas are **functional innovations** because they offer functional performance benefits that are better than those provided by existing alternatives. For example, hybrid vehicles are more fuel-efficient than traditional gasoline-powered vehicles, a functional performance benefit that saves consumers money on fuel costs and reduces pollution at the same time. Functional innovations often rely on new technology that makes the product better than existing alternatives.

Functional innovation A new product, service, attribute, or idea that has utilitarian benefits that are different from or better than those of alternatives.

Aesthetic or **hedonic innovations** are new products, services, or ideas that appeal to our aesthetic, pleasure-seeking, and/or sensory needs.[12] New forms of dance or exercise, new types of music, new clothing styles, and new types of food all qualify as aesthetic or hedonic innovations.

Aesthetic or **hedonic innovation** An innovation that appeals to our aesthetic, pleasure-seeking, and/or sensory needs.

Symbolic innovations are products, services, attributes, or ideas that have new social meaning. In some cases a symbolic innovation is a new offering that is used exclusively by a particular group of consumers. Using the innovation, therefore, conveys meaning about a consumer's group membership. New styles of clothing that convey membership in a particular ethnic, age, or gender group may be regarded as symbolic innovations.

Symbolic innovation A product, service, attribute, or idea that has new social meaning.

In some cases the meaning of the product, not the product itself, is new. For example, although condoms have been around for a long time, their meaning is now couched in terms of preventing the spread of AIDS as opposed to controlling conception. Earrings, once worn by women, are now fashionable for men as well. Finally, tattoos, once a symbol of machismo, have gained wide appeal and have different meanings among various consumer groups. Many new products also represent blends of innovation types. Nutrition bars are designed to offer the functional benefits of protein and vitamins, with the hedonic benefit of good taste. Exhibit 16.3 shows another example.

Innovations Characterized by Breadth

Finally, innovations can be characterized in terms of their *breadth*, or the range of new and different uses for a particular product. Baking soda, for example, has enjoyed a long life in part because it has innovation breadth; it has been used as a baking ingredient, a tooth polisher, a carpet deodorizer, and a refrigerator deodorizer. Teflon, originally developed to keep food from sticking to cookware, is now used in oven mitts and other kitchen accessories. It is also used in men's suits to help repel stains caused by spills.[13]

Adoption A purchase of an innovation by an individual consumer or household.

Resistance A desire not to buy the innovation, even in the face of pressure to do so.

Resistance versus Adoption

Because the success of their new offerings is so important to companies, marketers need to understand how a consumer or household chooses to buy or adopt an innovation. Initially, marketers are interested in learning whether consumers would even consider the **adoption** of an innovation or whether they would choose to resist buying it. Marketers also want to know how consumers adopt products and how they decide whether to buy an innovation. Finally, marketers are interested in learning when a consumer would buy an innovation in relation to when other consumers would purchase it.

Guardian angel.

POM WONDERFUL 100% POMEGRANATE JUICE

Want to have your own personal miracle worker? Drink POM Wonderful 100% Pomegranate Juice. It helps guard your body against free radicals, unstable molecules that emerging science suggests aggressively destroy healthy cells in your body and contribute to disease. POM Wonderful 100% Pomegranate Juice is supported by $23 million of initial scientific research from leading universities, which has uncovered encouraging results in prostate and cardiovascular health. Eight ounces a day is all you need to keep your body absolutely heavenly.

POM Wonderful 100% Pomegranate Juice. The Antioxidant Superpower.

Whether Consumers Adopt an Innovation

Adoption will take place only if consumers do not resist the innovation. Consumers who resist an innovation choose not to buy it, even in the face of pressure to do so.[14] Consumers sometimes resist adopting an innovation because it is simpler or seems preferable for them to continue using a more familiar product or service. **Resistance** may also be high if consumers think that using the new product would involve some risk. Battles between incompatible technology standards, for instance, have affected adoption of products such as DVD players over the past two decades.[15] Exhibit 16.4 shows that consumers often resist new technologies until they perceive that the negative effects from having to deal with something new are outweighed by the positive effects the new product might bring.[16] Research also indicates that consumers with low needs for change and cognition are most likely to resist innovations, whereas consumers with high needs for change and cognition are least likely to resist them.[17]

Note that resistance and adoption are separate concepts. An individual can resist purchasing an innovation without ever progressing to

Exhibit 16.4

Exhibit 16.4	Paradox	Description
Eight Central Paradoxes of Technological Products Consumers sometimes have mixed reactions to technologies because they create some of the paradoxes noted here. When the negative sides of these paradoxes are salient, consumers will likely resist an innovation.	Control/chaos	Technology can facilitate regulation or order, and technology can lead to upheaval or disorder.
	Freedom/enslavement	Technology can facilitate independence or fewer restrictions, and technology can lead to dependence or more restrictions.
	New/obsolete	New technologies provide the user with the most recently developed benefits of scientific knowledge, and new technologies are already or soon to be outmoded as they reach the marketplace.
	Competence/incompetence	Technology can facilitate feelings of intelligence or efficacy, and technology can lead to feelings of ignorance or ineptitude.
	Efficiency/inefficiency	Technology can facilitate less effort or time spent in certain activities, and technology can lead to more effort or time spent in certain activities.
	Fulfills/creates needs	Technology can facilitate the fulfillment of needs or desires, and technology can lead to the development or awareness of needs or desires previously unrealized.
	Assimilation/isolation	Technology can facilitate human togetherness, and technology can lead to human separation.
	Engaging/disengaging	Technology can facilitate involvement, flow, or activity, and technology can lead to disconnection, disruption, or passivity.

Source: From David Glen Mick and Susan Fornier, "Paradoxes of Technology: Consumer Cognizance, Emotions, and Coping Strategies," *Journal of Consumer Research* 25, September 1998, p. 126. Reprinted with permission of The University of Chicago Press.

the point of adoption. If an individual does adopt a product, he or she has presumably overcome any resistance to purchasing that might have existed initially. Marketers have to understand whether, why, and when consumers resist innovations—because the product will fail if resistance is too high. Typically, marketers can use a number of tactics to reduce consumers' resistance to an innovation. As discussed later in this chapter, the characteristics of the innovation, the social system in which the consumers operate, and marketing tactics all influence consumers' resistance to innovations.

How Consumers Adopt an Innovation

Whether consumers choose to adopt or resist an innovation depends, in part, on whether they are prevention-focused or promotion-focused. Prevention-focused consumers, whose priority is safety and protection, are more likely to resist new offerings because of the perceived risk and uncertainty new offerings entail.[18] Promotion consumers, whose priority is advancement and growth, are more likely to adopt new offerings, at least when the risks are not salient.[19]

High-effort hierarchy of effects A purchase of an innovation based on considerable decision-making effort.

The way in which consumers adopt innovations can vary, depending on whether the adoption decision is a high-effort or a low-effort one. The **high-effort hierarchy of effects,** illustrated in the top half of Exhibit 16.5, corresponds to the high-effort information search, attitude formation, judgment, and choice processes described in earlier chapters. Here, the consumer becomes aware of an innovation, thinks about it, gathers information about it, and forms an attitude based on this information. If his or her attitude is favorable, the consumer may try

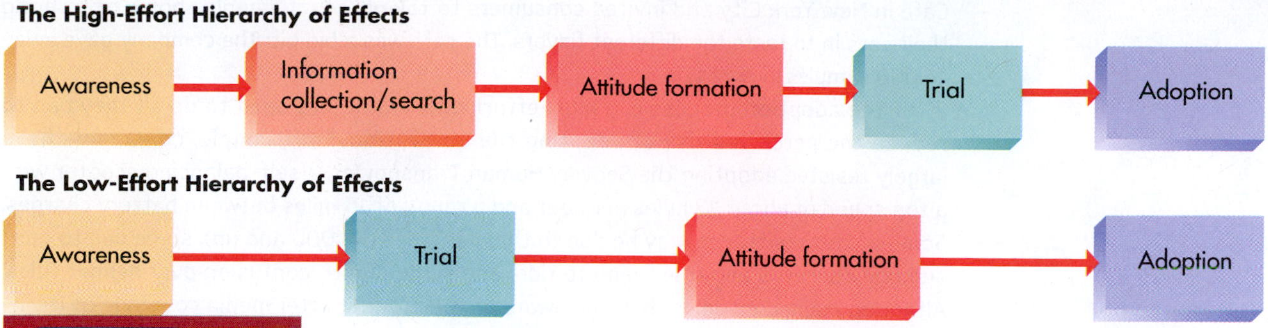

The High-Effort Hierarchy of Effects

Awareness → Information collection/search → Attitude formation → Trial → Adoption

The Low-Effort Hierarchy of Effects

Awareness → Trial → Attitude formation → Adoption

Exhibit 16.5

Adoption Decision Process

The amount of effort we engage in before we decide to adopt an innovation varies. In some cases we engage in considerable effort (e.g., extensive information search and evaluation of an offering). In other cases the adoption process involves limited effort. In such cases we first adopt the innovation and then decide whether we like it.

the product. If the trial experience is favorable, the consumer may decide to adopt the new product.

Consumers' motivation, ability, and opportunity (MAO) determine whether a high-effort adoption process occurs. A high-effort adoption process often takes place when consumers think the innovation incurs psychological, social, economic, financial, or safety risk. For example, the consumer may think that wearing a new style of clothing is socially risky and will wait for others to buy it first. In earlier times, consumers carefully considered the benefits of buying a DVD player because of the high cost of replacing an entire collection of videotapes or albums with DVDs.

Consumers are more likely to follow a high-effort decision-making process when the innovation is discontinuous (as opposed to continuous) because they know less about the innovation and must learn about it. Novice consumers need more information before they can understand and appreciate the benefits of a discontinuous innovation.[20] Also, a high-effort adoption process may be used when many people are involved in the decision, as in a family or an organization.[21]

When the new product involves less risk (as might be the case with a continuous innovation) and when fewer people are involved in the buying process, decision making may follow the **low-effort hierarchy of effects** illustrated in the bottom half of Exhibit 16.5. Here, consumers devote less decision-making effort to considering and researching the product before they try it, and then they form attitudes based on the trial. If their attitudes are positive, they may adopt the innovation. With a low-effort hierarchy of effects, the time between awareness of the innovation and its trial or adoption may be brief.

Low-effort hierarchy of effects A purchase of an innovation based on limited decision-making effort.

MARKETING IMPLICATIONS

Understanding whether consumers' adoption decisions are based on a high- or low-effort adoption process has important implications for marketers. For example, if the adoption involves low effort, marketers need to do all they can to encourage trial. Because the time between trial and purchase is low, trial may be very effective at encouraging consumers to buy the product. When Meow Mix launched Wet Pouches cat food, it set up the Meow Mix

Café in New York City and invited consumers to take product samples home or to bring their cats in to taste the different flavors. The café was a big hit: The company gave away 14,000 samples in only 12 days.[22]

If the adoption process is a high-effort one, marketers need to do all they can to reduce the perceived risk of adopting the innovation. For example, consumers have largely resisted adopting the Segway Human Transporter, a self-balancing scooter with a top speed of about 13 miles per hour and a range of 15 miles between battery charges. Some of this resistance may be due to the high price ($3,000 and up), some due to consumers' concerns about learning to ride, and some due to confusion over helmet rules. Although many consumers became aware of the product after media coverage of its introduction, relatively few have actually seen or tried riding a Segway. Still, media coverage of Segways used for tourism and other purposes has given consumers more information. The company is also giving every buyer free training as well as a video on scooter safety and a detailed instruction manual.[23]

When Consumers Adopt Innovations

Consumers differ in when they adopt an innovation. One framework identifies five adopter groups based on the timing of their adoption decisions, as shown in Exhibit 16.6.[24] The first 2.5 percent of the market to adopt the innovation are described as *innovators*. The next 13.5 percent are called *early adopters*. The next 34 percent are called the *early majority*. The *late majority* represent the next 34 percent of adopters. The last 16 percent of the market to purchase the product are called *laggards*.

Characteristics of Adopter Groups

The adopter groups tend to exhibit different characteristics, as shown in the exhibit. Research indicates, for example, that innovators who are enthusiastic about technology want to be the first to get a new high-tech product, even if there are a few bugs or inefficiencies.[25] Manufacturers of digital media centers—gadgets that

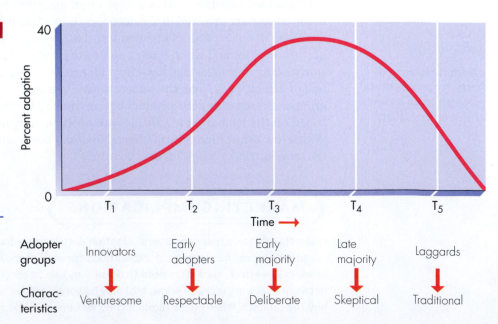

Exhibit 16.6

Profile of Adopter Groups

Researchers have identified five groups of consumers that differ in when they adopt an innovation relative to when others do. Innovators are the first in a market to adopt an innovation, and laggards are the last. Certain characteristics are associated with each adopter group.

connect or incorporate a PC, TV, stereo, and other components of a high-tech home entertainment center—initially targeted innovators.[26]

Early adopters are visionaries in the product category. They admire a technologically new product not so much for its features as for its abilities to create a revolutionary breakthrough in how things are done. One research company has suggested that approximately 16 percent of U.S. households are technologically advanced families—early adopters. These families want faster, newer, and more advanced products that help make home and work life more efficient and fun. Although they know that additional products that will follow the new product's introduction will likely be cheaper, faster, and easier to use than the innovation on the market right now, they do not want to wait for the future products. Technologically advanced families tend to be younger and better educated and to have more children than the average U.S. family.[27]

The early majority are pragmatists, seeking innovations that offer incremental, predictable improvements on an existing technology. Because they do not like risk, they care deeply about who is making the innovation and the reputation of the company. They are interested in how well the innovation will fit with their current lifestyle and the products they own now, and they are concerned about the innovation's reliability. They are price sensitive, and they are happy when competitors enter the market because they can then compare features and be more assured about the product's ultimate feasibility.

Late-majority consumers are more conservative, wary of progress, and rely on tradition. They often fear high-tech products, and their goal in buying them is to not get stung. They like to buy preassembled products that include everything in a single, easy-to-use package. Laggards, the slowest group to adopt, are skeptics. Although laggards may resist innovations, marketers can gain insights from understanding why this group is skeptical of an innovation. Why, for example, do some people shun PCs in favor of other methods of storing, analyzing, and communicating information? Do they fear losing or misplacing data not filed in printed form? Do they worry about information security or fear they will never learn to use the product properly? Knowing the answers to these questions can help firms market more effectively to this group. The answers can also help companies develop add-ons to the innovation that would resolve consumers' fears.

Application of Adopter Group Categories

An important implication of adopter groups is that if an innovation is to spread through the market, it must appeal to every group. Unfortunately, many potentially useful innovations have never gained mass-market appeal because the marketing efforts for them did not acknowledge the characteristics of the adopter groups. This result was the case with short-lived products such as the Apple Newtown pen computer and the Flooz system of online buying credits.[28]

Some researchers have criticized the five-category scheme of adopter groups because it assumes that these categories exist for all types of innovations. The critics say that there may be more or fewer categories, depending on the innovation.[29] Also, the assumption that the number of consumers in the adopter categories forms a bell-shaped curve may not be true. For example, instead of attracting the percentages of adopters that form the bell-shaped curve in Exhibit 16.6, certain products may attract the first 1 percent of adopters as innovators, the next 60 percent as early adopters, the next 30 percent as the early majority, the following 5 percent as the late majority, and the last 4 percent as laggards.

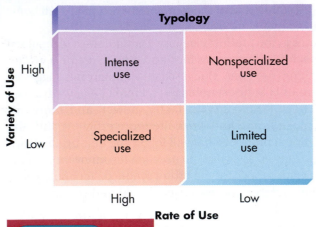

Exhibit 16.7

Use-Diffusion Patterns for Home Technology Innovations

In fact, some researchers have rejected the definition of *innovators* as a certain percentage of people who have adopted a product just after it comes on the market. These researchers believe that innovators are instead those who make a decision to buy a new product despite the fact that they have not heard about it from others.[30] Often such consumers do buy the product soon after it comes to market, but they do so based on their own feelings, not on the opinions of others.

Other research suggests that examining the rate of use and variety of use can help marketers understand how an innovation diffuses through the market.[31] As an example, the use-diffusion model in Exhibit 16.7 identifies specific types of users of home technology such as PCs: intense users (who have many uses for an innovation and show a high rate of use), specialized users (high rate of use but low variety of uses), nonspecialized users (high variety of uses but low rate of use), and limited users (low variety of uses and low rate of use).

MARKETING IMPLICATIONS

Whether or not marketers accept the five-category adopter scheme, they recognize that consumers who are the first to buy a new product are important for several reasons. First, because innovators adopt new products independently of the opinions of other people, they are more likely to be receptive to information about new products, including information provided by marketers. Second, by virtue of their experience with the innovation, they may also communicate information to others and thus exact normative and informational influence through the adoption decisions of others (see Chapter 15). Given these issues, many researchers want to better understand who innovators are and how they can be reached through marketing communications and appropriate media.

Demographics

Several of the demographic variables described in Chapters 12 and 13 have been linked with innovators.[32] For example, innovators tend to be younger, more affluent, and better educated than other consumers; laggards are older, have less income and education, and have lower occupational status. Religion is sometimes linked with innovation adoption. Amish consumers, for example, avoid many innovations, including cars, electricity, and telephones.

The link between these demographic variables and innovativeness makes sense. First, highly educated people tend to be heavier users of media and therefore tend to learn about new products earlier than less educated people do. Second, high-income consumers can afford to buy innovations, and they may perceive less financial risk in adopting something new. Demographic variables such as culture of origin have also been linked with innovativeness. Consumers in South Korea and Japan, for example, are regarded as innovators for new technology, a factor that explains why these markets have become launching sites for new high-tech offerings such as services delivered via broadband Internet access.[33]

Social influence

Innovators have been linked with the social influence factors discussed in Chapter 15.[34] They tend to have a great deal of social influence beyond their immediate groups, and they tend to be opinion leaders. Although this finding has not been observed in all research, it makes sense that innovators have influence because their opinions are shared with and respected by nonadopters.

Personality

Several personality characteristics have also been linked with the adoption of innovations.[35] For example, innovators are high in their need for stimulation, are inner directed, and are less dogmatic than other consumers. However, the relationships between personality traits and innovativeness are not very strong.[36] Innovators also do less planning and deliberate less than other consumers do when making buying decisions.[37]

Some researchers have proposed that rather than measuring "innate innovativeness" (as a personality trait), a better approach is to examine consumers' willingness to be innovative in a specific consumption domain. For example, an innovator of alternative music might respond positively to statements like "In general, I am among the first in my circle of friends to download a new alternative-rock CD album" or "I know the names of new alternative-rock acts before other people do." Innovators in the area of fashion, however, might not respond similarly to these statements.[38]

Cultural values

Adoption of innovations has been linked with culture of origin and the values tied to the culture. One study of 11 European countries found that innovativeness was associated with cultures that value individualism over collectivism, those that value assertiveness over nurturing, and those that value openness to change over conservatism.[39]

Media involvement

Other research has suggested that innovators are frequent users of the media and rely extensively on external information.[40] They tend to think of themselves as active seekers and disseminators of information.[41] This finding makes sense because to affect others' adoption decisions, innovators must not only get their information somewhere but must also be willing to transmit it.

Usage

Finally, innovators may be heavy users within the product category.[42] Consumers who frequently drink soft drinks may be innovators of new beverages because they are in the market often and hence are likely to notice these new products. In addition, innovators are usually experts in the product category, perhaps because of their usage and media involvement.

Diffusion

Diffusion The percentage of the population that has adopted an innovation at a specific point in time.

As increasing numbers of consumers in a market adopt an innovation, the innovation spreads or diffuses through the market. Whereas adoption reflects the behavior of an individual, **diffusion** reflects the behavior of the marketplace of consumers as a group. More specifically, diffusion reflects the percentage of the population that has adopted an innovation at a specific point in time. To illustrate, cell

phones are used by more than three-quarters of the population in the United States, Argentina, Chile, South Africa, and many European countries.[43] (See Exhibit 16.8.)

Because marketers are interested in successfully spreading their offering through a market, they want to understand two important diffusion issues: how an offering diffuses through the market and how quickly it does so.

How Offerings Diffuse Through a Market

One way to examine how offerings spread through a market is to look at the pattern of adoption over time. From the marketers' perspective, life would be easy if everyone adopted the new offering just as soon as it was introduced into the market. However, this occurrence is rarely the case; in fact, several diffusion patterns have been identified.

The S-Shaped Diffusion Curve

Some innovations exhibit an **S-shaped diffusion curve,** as shown in Exhibit 16.9(a).[44] Following this pattern, adoption of the products begins relatively slowly; as the exhibit shows, a relatively small percentage of the total market has adopted the prod-

Exhibit 16.8

Diffusion of Cell Phones

Cell phones are diffusing more quickly in Africa than in other parts of the world, encouraging more manufacturers and service providers to enter markets such as Botswana.

S-shaped diffusion curve A diffusion curve characterized by slow initial growth followed by a rapid increase in diffusion.

Exponential diffusion curve A diffusion curve characterized by rapid initial growth.

uct between time **1** and time **2** in the exhibit. After a certain period, however, the rate of adoption increases dramatically, with many consumers adopting the product within a relatively short period of time. Between times **2** and **3,** a dramatic increase occurs in the number of consumers adopting the product. Then adoptions grow at a decreasing rate, and the curve flattens out.

To illustrate, the diffusion of microwave ovens was initially very slow. Then it increased dramatically as consumers became more aware of and knowledgeable about microwave technology and marketers introduced more products compatible with microwave cooking (recipes, snacks, cookware, and so forth). Now there is general acceptance of the microwave, and many consumers have one in their house or office.

The Exponential Diffusion Curve

Another type of adoption curve is the **exponential diffusion curve,** illustrated in Exhibit 16.9(b).[45] In contrast to the S-shaped curve, the exponential diffusion curve starts out much more quickly, with a large percentage of the market adopting the product as soon as it is available. However, with each additional time period, the adoption rate increases at a slower pace.

Factors Affecting the Shape of the Diffusion Curve

Many factors influence the ultimate shape of the diffusion curve. In general, marketers might expect an S-shaped diffusion curve when the innovation is associated with some social, psychological, economic, performance, or physical risk. In such situations, consumers might wait to see how other people use and react to the

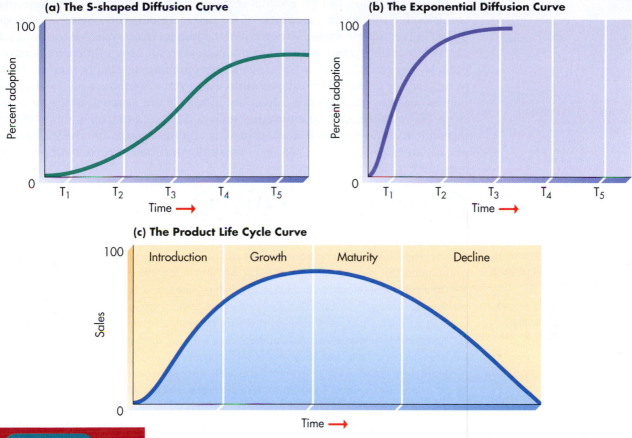

(a) The S-shaped Diffusion Curve

(b) The Exponential Diffusion Curve

(c) The Product Life Cycle Curve

Introduction | Growth | Maturity | Decline

Exhibit 16.9

Diffusion and Product Life Cycle Curves

Several diffusion patterns have been identified. (a) With an S-shaped diffusion curve, diffusion starts out slowly, increases rapidly, and then flattens out again. (b) With an exponential diffusion curve, many people adopt the innovation quickly. (c) The product life cycle curve depicts sales (not cumulative diffusion) of an offering over time.

innovation before adopting it. Diffusion may also be slow initially if consumers are not sure whether the product will be on the market for long or whether its use carries high switching costs. The diffusion of computers and CD players followed this S-shaped curve. An S-shaped diffusion pattern might also occur when consumers are physically far apart, do not discuss the innovation with others, or do not share the same beliefs.

In contrast, when the innovation involves little risk, when switching costs are low, when consumers are similar in their beliefs and values, and/or when people talk often about the product and quickly disseminate knowledge throughout the social system, the product may have a rapid takeoff period that follows the exponential curve for diffusion. Note that these curves reflect only the rate at which consumers in the market adopt a product, not the time period under analysis. In other words, an S-shaped or an exponential curve could reflect diffusion that has occurred over a 1-year or a 30-year period. Furthermore, the curves could reflect the diffusion of either a functional, symbolic, or hedonic innovation.

How Diffusion Relates to the Product Life Cycle

Product life cycle A concept that suggests that products go through an initial introductory period followed by periods of sales growth, maturity, and decline.

The **product life cycle** concept, illustrated in Exhibit 16.9(c), proposes that products initially go through a period of introduction, followed by relatively rapid growth as more competitors enter the market and more consumers adopt the product. With greater competition, weaker competitors drop out, and product sales plateau. At some point, however, consumer acceptance wanes, and product sales decline.

Product diffusion and the product life cycle are related but different concepts. Diffusion focuses on the *percentage of the market* that has adopted the product; diffusion is complete when 100 percent of the market has purchased the product. The product life cycle, on the other hand, deals with *sales of the product* over time. Moreover, diffusion curves are generally cumulative—that is, they continue to increase or at least level off over time. However, the product life cycle curve may decline as consumers decide not to purchase the product on future occasions. For instance, after an innovation such as the rotary-dial telephone diffused through an entire market, it was replaced by another innovation, the touch-tone phone, and sales of the old product eventually declined as the new innovation took hold.

MARKETING IMPLICATIONS

Fad A successful innovation that has a very short product life cycle.

Fashion A successful innovation that has a moderately long and potentially cyclical product life cycle.

Classic A successful innovation that has a lengthy product life cycle.

Marketers who understand a product's life cycle can try to prevent that product's decline—perhaps by finding new uses for it. For example, nylon has enjoyed a long life cycle given the myriad uses to which it has been put since its introduction in the 1940s—as an ingredient in clothing, rope, fishing lines, and so on. Rand McNally is extending the life cycle of its detailed maps by packaging them in printed atlases, offering them in software form, and offering them for download to Web-enabled cell phones.[46] To the extent that marketers develop new uses for a product or encourage use innovativeness, they can lengthen their product's life cycle.

Marketers can also try to diagnose the likely life cycle pattern of their offering. Just as diffusion curves differ, so too are there different product life cycle curves. A **fad** is a successful innovation that has a very short product life cycle. Pokemon cards, scooters, and certain diets are examples of fads. When energy drinks such as Red Bull became a fad, Pepsi, Coca-Cola, and others launched energy drinks to capitalize on consumer interest.[47] Some fads experience a revival years after their first appearance. Hula-Hoops came back, more than 40 years after the original fad, as a product to use to stay fit.[48]

A **fashion** or trend is a successful innovation with a lengthier and potentially cyclical life. For example, certain aesthetic styles like art deco run in fashion cycles, as do certain styles of clothing like cargo pants and platform shoes. Some types of foods, like Thai or Mexican, run in fashion cycles, as do certain consumption practices (e.g., breast versus bottle-feeding infants). Polynesian-style restaurants were popular in the 1950s but fell out of fashion within a few decades. Today, they are back in New York City, Dallas, and other cities where new "tiki" restaurants are opening (see Exhibit 16.10).[49] In contrast, a **classic** is a successful innovation that has a lengthy product life cycle. Jeans are an American classic, as are rock 'n' roll music, Coca-Cola, and hamburgers.

Although the terms *fad, fashion,* and *classic* have most often been applied to aesthetic or hedonic innovations, they can also describe functional and symbolic innovations because the life cycle of these innovations similarly can be variable.

Exhibit 16.10

Trend Toward Tiki

Polynesian-style restaurants like this one shown here are back in fashion.

Influences on Adoption, Resistance, and Diffusion

Knowing that innovations may diffuse quickly or slowly through a market and that the success of a new product depends on how many people within the market adopt it, marketing managers need to understand the factors affecting resistance, adoption, and diffusion. A number of factors, including characteristics of the innovation and of the social system into which it is introduced, are described below.

Characteristics of the Innovation

Characteristics of the innovation that can affect resistance, adoption, and diffusion include perceived value, benefits, and costs.

Perceived Value

Consumers perceive that an innovation has value if it offers greater perceived benefits or lower perceived costs than existing alternatives do. Products with high perceived value may be more readily adopted than those with low perceived value.

Perceived Benefits

Relative advantage Benefits in an innovation superior to those found in existing products.

An innovation's value to consumers is affected by its perceived **relative advantage,** the extent to which it offers benefits superior to those of existing products. Something new offers a relative advantage if it can help consumers avoid risks, fulfill their needs, solve problems, or achieve their goals—criteria that affect consumers' adoption decisions. In fact, research indicates that product advantage is one of the most important predictors of new-product success (see Exhibit 16.11).[50] Note that a relative advantage is something the product does for the consumer—not something that exists in the product. Thus, the relative advantage of hybrid cars such as the Toyota Prius lies not in their features but rather in the owners' ability to save money on gasoline and help save the environment.

However, if consumers do not perceive a new product's advantage over the benefits of existing alternatives or think the advantage is unimportant, the innovation will face resistance. Campbell Soup faced this situation, says a senior brand manager for Soup at Hand. "We launched a soup in a plastic package, which was on the market for three years," she says, "but the consumer could never understand what was different about the plastic package [as compared with] the can."[51]

Use innovativeness Finding use for a product that differs from the product's original intended usage.

Consumers are likely to perceive a product's benefits as being more valuable when they can adapt it for use in different contexts. **Use innovativeness** means using products in a new or creative way, as in the way that a consumer might use baking soda to solve problems like deodorizing a kitty litter box.[52] In fact, use innovativeness on the part of its customers led Arm & Hammer to introduce a new kitty litter deodorizer product.

Perceived Costs

Another aspect of the value of a product is its perceived costs. The higher the purchase cost, the greater the resistance, and hence the slower the diffusion. Consider hybrid gas-electric cars like the Prius, which tend to have a higher initial cost than comparable conventional cars do. Although the higher perceived cost slowed its adoption at first, the car's relative advantage became apparent after the pump price of gasoline skyrocketed, resulting in higher demand for fuel-efficient cars. In contrast, DVD players have experienced much more rapid diffusion as manufacturing efficiencies have brought costs and prices down.[53] Switching costs—the costs of changing from the current product to a new one—can also be an issue. Therefore, consumers who own many PlayStation games must weigh the perceived switching costs when they consider whether to buy a Nintendo Wii.

GEOX
THE SHOE THAT BREATHES

INTERNATIONAL PATENT
By combining a microperforated rubber sole and the breathable
waterproof membrane, the Geox system lets foot perspiration go
out through the sole thus keeping your feet dry and healthy.

575 MADISON AVENUE · NYC, NORTH BEVERLY DRIVE · CA
ALSO AVAILABLE AT GEOX SHOPS NATIONWIDE 1-866-610-GEOX   ·   GEOX.COM

Exhibit 16.11

Relative Advantage
Innovations that have a clear relative advantage tend to be adopted more quickly.

MARKETING IMPLICATIONS

If consumers do not perceive that an innovation has a relative advantage, marketers may need to add one by physically redesigning or reengineering the innovation.

Communicate and demonstrate the relative advantage

The company must educate consumers who do not understand a product or its relative advantages. When Amazon.com introduced its Kindle wireless reading device, the company posted video demonstrations on its website showing how the product works. For months after the reader's launch, the Amazon homepage included a link to those videos and to additional product information.[54] Another way to communicate an innovation's advantage is through highly credible and visible opinion leaders. Amazon did this by sending Kindle samples to influential reviewers at the *New York Times* and other leading media outlets.

Use price promotions to reduce perceived costs

If consumers perceive that a product is too costly, the company can use special price-oriented sales promotions such as price-offs, rebates, or refunds to reduce the perceived cost. FluMist, a nasal flu vaccine, offered a $25 mail-in rebate to increase adoption by reducing the product's perceived cost as compared with that of flu shots.[55] Marketers can also provide guarantees or warranties that make the product seem less expensive. Alternatively, the marketer may find a cheaper way to manufacture the product and pass on the savings in the form of lower prices for consumers, a strategy that marketers of digital watches used.

Provide incentives for switching

If innovations are not adopted because consumers think switching costs are high, marketers might provide incentives for switching. This situation explains why razor companies often give away free razor handles to get consumers to switch to new-generation blades. Companies might also use advertising to inform consumers about the costs associated with *not* switching. Finally, marketers might be able to force their innovation to become the industry standard, for instance, by having such high quality, ease of use, or low price that they become the dominant alternative.

Uncertainty

In addition to the characteristics of the innovation, uncertainty surrounding the innovation can affect its adoption, resistance, and diffusion. Several aspects of uncertainty are particularly important. One is doubt about what will become the standard in the industry. When Sony first introduced its PlayStation 3 game console, which included a Blu-ray DVD drive, a battle raged over whether Blu-ray or

HD DVD would be the new DVD industry standard. Sales lagged behind projections until Blu-ray won and became the industry standard.[56]

Another aspect is uncertainty about the relative advantage of a product that requires the consumer to make significant behavioral changes.[57] Consumers are often more uncertain about the usefulness of a discontinuous (vs. a continuous).[58] Surprisingly, giving consumers more information about a high-tech product that combines a new interface with new functionality actually makes consumers more uncertain about the product's advantages. This phenomenon may happen because consumers pay more attention to the new interface and, in processing the information, reason through the possible negative outcomes of product adoption.[59]

A third aspect of uncertainty is the length of the product life cycle. Consumers are more likely to resist buying a fad than a fashion or a classic. For example, you may forgo spending $80 on spike-heeled shoes if you think they will go out of style soon. Concern over life cycle length is quite legitimate in clothing and high-tech markets, where products are frequently changed or improved.

MARKETING IMPLICATIONS

When consumers resist innovations because they are worried about an offering's short life cycle, marketers might show how adaptable the product is and hence how likely it is to have a long life cycle. For example, marketers of digital video recorders can address consumers' fears of the product's rapid obsolescence by demonstrating how their products may be upgraded, connected to advanced systems, or used in other ways that extend the life cycle by continuing to deliver perceived value. ●━●

Consumer Learning Requirements

A third characteristic affecting resistance, adoption, and diffusion is consumer learning requirements—or what consumers need to do to use the innovation effectively. These learning requirements involve compatibility, trialability, and complexity.

Compatibility

Compatibility The extent to which an innovation is consistent with one's needs, values, norms, or behaviors.

Consumers often resist innovations because they see them as incompatible with their needs, values, norms, or behaviors.[60] The more **compatible** the innovation is with consumers' values, norms, and behaviors, the less their resistance and the greater the product diffusion. Clorox Disinfecting Wipes, a new-product hit, is compatible with the way that people have traditionally cleaned their kitchens and bathrooms, yet it also offers the relative advantage of convenience.[61] On the other hand, Ziploc Tabletops "semi-disposable" plates were not completely compatible with the consumer behavior of throwing away disposable plates after one use. They were more durable than typical disposable plates but priced in line with low-end permanent plates. As a result, S.C. Johnson eliminated the product less than two years after introducing it.[62] Exhibit 16.12 shows another example of compatibility.

Some potentially serious consequences can arise when an innovation is incompatible with consumers' values, goals, and behaviors. One case in particular is marketers' attempts to encourage bottle-feeding by mothers in the developing nations of Latin America, Africa, and Asia. Manufacturers' ads showed pictures of

Exhibit 16.12

Compatibility
Products diffuse through a market faster when they are compatible with consumers' norms, values, and behaviors.

Trialability The extent to which an innovation can be tried on a limited basis before it is adopted.

Complexity The extent to which an innovation is complicated and difficult to understand or use.

mothers with beautiful, fat, healthy babies. The ad copy read, "Give your baby love and Lactogen." (Lactogen is an infant formula.) The modern look of the ad was attractive to upper-income, well-educated consumers as well as to peasant families who aspired to be like the well educated. Unfortunately, most peasant families could not afford the expensive formula, so they diluted it with water, leaving their babies malnourished. Furthermore, they were unfamiliar with practices like sterilizing nipples and bottles; as a result, bacteria in these items made the babies sick. The lack of compatibility between the innovation and the consumers' behavior therefore caused unanticipated problems.[63]

Trialability

A second aspect of consumer learning requirements is the **trialability** of the innovation, the extent to which the product can be tried on a limited basis before it is adopted. Products like microwaveable meals can be tested and tasted in just a few minutes. However, trialability is virtually impossible with innovations like laser eye surgery. Because a trial allows a consumer to assess the product's relative advantages and potential risks, products that are easy to try tend to diffuse through the market more quickly than those that do not.

Trialability is often quite important to innovators and early adopters because they have little else on which to base the value of the innovation. Trialability can be less important for later adopters, who are likely to know many people who have already adopted the innovation and who can therefore speak to its efficacy.[64]

Complexity

Complexity is a final learning requirement related to adoption and diffusion. Diffusion is likely to be slow when consumers perceive they will have difficulty understanding or using a new product. Products that are loaded with many features may appear useful, yet the fact that they have so many features leads them to be perceived as being overly complex.[65] In fact, consumers may form a lower evaluation of a complex product with novel attributes because they worry about the time needed to understand the new features.[66] This perception is a problem for marketers because consumers tend to underestimate how well they can manage complexity.[67] Digital photography initially diffused at a relatively slow rate because consumers perceived complexity in learning to transfer digital images from the camera to the computer, figuring out the software for enhancing images, and printing high-quality photos.[68] Other products, such as DVR players, have diffused more rapidly, in part because they are easy to use.

MARKETING IMPLICATIONS

Marketers can use several tactics to reduce consumers' resistance to innovations.

Enhance compatibility or reduce complexity

Marketers may be able to reposition an innovation so that it is viewed as more consistent with consumers' needs and values. Campbell's soup enjoyed renewed popularity when it was repositioned away from taste and toward nutrition and low calories.[69] Sometimes, however, companies must redesign an offering to overcome incompatibility and reduce complexity. For example, the photo-sharing website Flickr houses more than 2 billion images contributed by users worldwide. To make it easier for consumers to find specific types of images, Flickr has added a feature that allows browsing by location as well as by keyword search. It also provides a virtual "how to" tour of the site and highlights key benefits of usage on its homepage.[70]

Educate about compatibility

Companies can use promotions to show how their innovations actually are compatible with consumers' needs, values, norms, or behaviors. For example, consumers in some developing nations are not used to modern medicine and the techniques employed to avoid diseases. One way that entities like the World Health Organization have dealt with this situation is to launch educational programs to demonstrate the value of vaccinations and the procedures that can stop disorders like diarrhea.[71] Advertising can also show how a new offering is easier to use or has more benefits than current alternatives do, even if it requires adopting new behaviors.

Use change agents

Another way to enhance perceived compatibility is to use change agents such as opinion leaders. Marketers in such diverse fields as farming equipment, medicine, and computers have aimed new products at influential and highly respected people who can be convinced of a new product's merits and who will then spread positive word of mouth to others.[72]

Fit with a system of products

Some marketers address incompatibility by designing the innovation to fit with a system of existing products. Procter & Gamble's Mr. Clean AutoDry car cleaning sprayer was designed to be hooked up to any garden hose, making the product simple and easy for consumers to use. The rate of diffusion was "beyond our wildest dreams," a P&G spokesperson comments.[73]

Force the innovation to be the industry standard

Marketers can sometimes work with regulators to require adoption of the innovation. For example, smoke detectors, seat belts, and lead-free gasoline are all innovations that have been forced into usage by government mandate. Manufacturers are introducing more hybrid cars because states' clean-air requirements are mandating zero-emission vehicles.[74]

Use promotions to enhance trialability

Companies can stimulate trial through various promotions. Free samples, for example, encourage trial by people who might otherwise resist using the product. When Nutra-Sweet was first introduced, its makers overcame potential trialability problems by sending millions of consumers free samples of gumballs sweetened with NutraSweet. The company chose this approach because NutraSweet is best experienced as an ingredient in food products, not as a stand-alone product.

Demonstrate compatibility and simplicity

Live demonstrations (at trade shows or conducted by salespeople) and demonstrations in ads and online videos can show a product's ease of use and its compatibility with consumers' needs, values, and behaviors. Sales of Blendtec's blenders increased by 500 percent after the firm posted videos on YouTube to demonstrate how rugged the blenders are and how quickly and easily they work.[75]

Simulate trial

At times, a company may need to simulate trial rather than have consumers actually try the product. On Benjamin Moore's website, consumers can use a "personal color viewer" to preview how different paint colors would look on the walls of different rooms.

Social Relevance

Social relevance The extent to which an innovation can be observed or the extent to which having others observe it has social cachet.

A fourth major factor that affects resistance, adoption, and diffusion is the innovation's **social relevance,** particularly its observability and social value. *Observability* is the extent to which consumers can see others using the innovation. In general, the more consumers can observe others using the innovation, the more likely they are to adopt it.[76] For example, a new shoulder strap designed to distribute the weight of a golf bag gained acceptance among caddies after they saw others using the product.[77] On the other hand, a new scale that announces your body weight is unlikely to be very observable because few people want to weigh themselves in public (or want others to hear their weight!).[78] Thus, diffusion is also affected by the public or private nature of the product, as described in Chapter 15.

Social value reflects the extent to which the product has social cachet, which means that it is seen as socially desirable and/or appropriate and therefore generates imitation, speeding diffusion. One study found that farmers adopted certain farming innovations because the innovations were expensive and thus had social prestige value. These studies also found that the earlier someone adopted the innovation, the more prestige was associated with it.[79] Consumers sometimes adopt aesthetic innovations like new fashions, hairstyles, and cars based on the social prestige they confer on the user.

Although social value may enhance diffusion, the diffusion of a product based on a prestige image may actually shorten its life cycle because once a product is adopted by the masses, it is no longer prestigious. For example, designer jeans, once associated with prestige and exclusivity, lost prestige when everyone in the market started to wear them.[80]

MARKETING IMPLICATIONS

Observability can be enhanced by the use of distinctive packaging, styling, and color or unique promotions,[81] using the attention and perception enhancement techniques described in Chapter 3. Also, associating the product with a well-known person (the way Gatorade Tiger is associated with golfer Tiger Woods) or creating ads to suggest that the consumer will be socially rewarded for using the product may enhance observability. An innovation's social relevance can be heightened through advertising—particularly advertising that ties product use with potential social approval. Finally, marketers can enhance social value by associating the product with some social entity, cause, or value. Having a new beverage serve as the official drink of the Olympic team might, for example, enhance its social value.

Legitimacy and Adaptability

Legitimacy The extent to which the innovation follows established guidelines for what seems appropriate in the category.

Legitimacy and adaptability also influence resistance, adoption, and diffusion, particularly for symbolic and aesthetic innovations.[82] **Legitimacy** refers to the extent to which the innovation follows established guidelines for what seems appropriate in the category. An innovation that is too radical or that does not derive from a legitimate precursor lacks legitimacy. For example, rock 'n' roll and later rap music were initially seen as deviant forms of music and thus diffused slowly. In contrast, part of the success of artists like k. d. lang stemmed from their ability to fuse two legitimate musical styles (country and rock) into a style that sounded new.

Adaptability The extent to which the innovation can foster new styles.

Adaptability, the innovation's potential to fit with existing products or styles, is another factor affecting adoption and diffusion (see Exhibit 16.13).[83] For example, certain fashion or furniture is highly adaptable because it can fit with a variety of other fashion or furniture trends. Some functional products, such as cell phones, have high adaptability because they can perform a variety of functions.

MARKETING IMPLICATIONS

Marketers may enhance legitimacy by demonstrating how the innovation came into being or marketing it in a way that is consistent with consumers' perceptions of what is appropriate for the category. Frito-Lay did this when it tried marketing Latin-flavored Doritos and Lay's chips to Hispanic Americans. Adoption was slow because the targeted consumers "were looking for authentic flavors but didn't expect to see them on those brands," says Frito-Lay's chief marketing officer. Instead, the firm started importing its Sabritones chile and lime wheat snacks from Mexico, initially stocking them only in stores serving Mexican American communities. Adoption was so enthusiastic that the product was soon made available in other outlets.[84]

Conversely, if consumers believe the product lacks adaptability, marketers can show that it has uses beyond its original function. For example, the makers of cranberry sauce ask consumers to consider other uses for their product besides serving it as a condiment at Thanksgiving dinner.[85]

Characteristics of the Social System

Innovations diffuse rapidly or slowly in part because of product characteristics and in part because of the characteristics of the social system into which they are introduced. Both the kinds of people in the target market and the nature of the relationships among the people in the social system will affect the innovation's acceptance.

Modernity The extent to which consumers in the social system have positive attitudes toward change.

▶ *Modernity.* Resistance, adoption, and diffusion are affected by the social system's **modernity,** the extent to which the system's consumers have a positive attitude toward change. Consumers in modern systems value science, technology, and education and are technologically oriented in terms of the goods produced and the skill of the labor force.[86] The more modern the social system, the more receptive its consumers are to new products.

▶ *Homophily.* The homophily, or overall similarity among members of the system, affects acceptance. Diffusion is generally faster when consumers in the market are highly similar in education, values, needs, income, and other dimensions.[87] Why? First, the more similar people's backgrounds are, the more likely they are to have similar needs, values, and preferences. Second, similar people are more likely to interact with one another and transmit information. Third, similar people tend to model each other. Also, normative influence is likely to be higher as homophily grows, increasing the pressure for adopting the innovation and speeding adoption and diffusion.

▶ *Physical distance.* Diffusion tends to be slower when members of the social system are spread apart. Some marketers in Japan have found that high school girls excel at setting trends. No doubt this ability is due to the physical and emotional proximity of girls and their tendency to talk about new products they have seen and used.[88] Likewise, an innovation may experience slower diffusion when consumers are physically separated.[89]

▶ *Opinion leadership.* As noted in Chapter 15, people with credibility, such as experts or opinion leaders, can have considerable influence on product adoption and diffusion because they may spread positive or negative product information to others.[90] One study analyzing the diffusion of information about family-planning practices among women in a Korean village found that opinion leaders were very important sources of information. Not only was the information communicated by these women important, but the opinion leaders also served as bridges connecting spatially related but separate cliques in the village.[91]

MARKETING IMPLICATIONS

Marketing efforts can influence resistance, adoption, and diffusion by affecting the social system. For example, if members of the target market are very different from one another, companies may need to use targeted communications that show the product's relevance to consumers' unique needs, values, or norms and may need to place the messages in specialized (target-market-specific) media to reach these consumers.

Companies might also identify consumers who have not adopted the innovation. According to research, nonadopters can be divided into three groups: (1) passive consumers who have tried the product but are unlikely to provide much information to others about it; (2) active rejectors who have tried the product but are likely to provide unfavorable word of mouth to others; and (3) potential adopters who have not yet tried the product but who may be influenced by active rejectors, active acceptors, or marketers. Different marketing strategies may be appropriate for different adopter and nonadopter groups.[92] If potential adopters are unaware of the innovation, for instance, advertising can help build awareness and encourage adoption. Product improvements may, however, be necessary to attract active rejectors.

Because marketing activities can influence diffusion by affecting both the innovation and the social system, it is not surprising that the more intensive the marketing effort, the faster the innovation spreads through a market.[93] As noted in Chapter 15, media coverage of an innovation (such as the iPhone) generally has more credibility than the company's communications do. Targeting opinion leaders and targeting the network, rather than the consumer, can also stimulate positive word of mouth, as can new product demonstrations at trade shows and in online videos. And marketers can take a number of steps to track word of mouth, generate positive word of mouth, and counteract negative word of mouth.

The Consequences of Innovations

Although innovations often offer relative advantages that may not have previously existed, they are not always good for society. One study examined the diffusion of the steel ax among a tribe of aborigines who lived in the Australian bush.[94] Before the innovation was introduced, the stone ax had served as the tribe's principal tool. It was used only by men and was awarded to them as a gift and as payment for work performed. It was generally regarded as a symbol of masculinity and respect. However, missionaries came into the social system with the steel ax and distributed it to men, women, and children. This distribution scheme disrupted the sex and age roles among tribal members and thus affected the social system.

Innovations may also have negative socioeconomic consequences. For example, a study examining the diffusion of the CAT scanner through the medical community identified two important sociological consequences. First, the innovation tended to diffuse to markets that were generally wealthy, leaving the technology unavailable to families who lived in poorer rural areas. Second, the innovation was expensive and was viewed as driving up health-care costs.[95] Given these types of unanticipated social and economic consequences, we as consumers should be careful to avoid adopting a universally pro-innovation bias.

Summary

Innovations are products, services, ideas, or attributes that consumers in a market segment perceive to be new. Innovations can be characterized as functional, symbolic, or hedonic and may vary in the degree of behavioral change their adoption requires. Product innovativeness ranges along a continuum from continuous to discontinuous. Innovations may represent fads, fashions, or classics and hence may exhibit a short, moderate, or long life cycle. Marketers can extend a product's life cycle by enhancing the breadth of the innovation and encouraging consumers to find innovative uses for familiar products.

Strategies for marketers of innovations include reducing consumers' resistance to innovations, facilitating consumers' adoption of the innovation, and affecting the diffusion of the innovation through the marketplace. A high-effort as opposed to low-effort hierarchy-of-effects adoption process occurs when the innovation is seen as risky. Some individuals, called *innovators*, are among the first to adopt new products independently of the decisions of other people. Companies may target innovators because their adoption of products influences other consumers' adoption decisions through word of mouth or social modeling.

Resistance, adoption, and diffusion are affected by the characteristics of the innovation and the social system into which it is introduced. Overcoming resistance is easiest when the innovation is perceived to provide value to consumers such as a relative advantage, low price, or low switching costs. Resistance will be lower when the innovation requires minimal learning and is highly compatible with consumers' existing needs, values, and behaviors; easy to try; easy to use; and low risk. Innovations viewed as high in social relevance, legitimacy, and adaptability encounter less resistance than those regarded as low in such factors. The characteristics of the social system in which the innovation operates also affect resistance, adoption, and diffusion. The denser the social network and the more homophilous consumers within the social system are, the more likely it is that adopters will transmit information to nonadopters, in turn affecting the likelihood of their adopting the product. However, it is possible that the diffusion of an innovation may entail some negative social and economic consequences.

Questions for Review and Discussion

1. How can innovations be described in terms of degree of novelty and types of benefits? How does the degree of novelty affect consumers' behavioral change?

2. What is the difference between adoption and diffusion? How does the concept of *resistance* relate to adoption?

3. Under what circumstances might a consumer follow the high-effort hierarchy of effects in adopting an innovation?

4. How can consumers be categorized in terms of their timing of adoption relative to that of other consumers?

5. What is the product life cycle, and how does it differ from product diffusion?

6. How do consumer learning requirements and social relevance affect resistance, adoption, and diffusion?

7. What characteristics of the social system affect an innovation's acceptance within a market?

CL Visit http://cengage.com/marketing/hoyer/ ConsumerBehavior5e to find resources that are available to help you study for the course.

CONSUMER BEHAVIOR CASE

The CFL: Coming Soon to a Light Socket Near You

In a nation with 4 billion light sockets, one light bulb per household can make a real difference. If every U.S. household replaced one ordinary incandescent light bulb with a compact fluorescent lamp (CFL), the energy saved would be enough to light 3 million homes. This single change would be the environmental equivalent of taking 800,000 cars off the road and preventing 450 pounds of greenhouse gases from reaching the atmosphere. Change a light bulb, help the planet, slash energy costs—sounds like a win–win situation.

Yet since the CFL's invention more than 30 years ago, it has been slow to catch on. Meanwhile, the incandescent light bulb, which was commercialized more than a century ago, still accounts for more than 90 percent of all light bulbs sold in the U.S. Why have CFLs not been more popular?

- *Higher price.* One big reason that CFLs have not been big sellers is because each costs five to seven times more than an incandescent light bulb does. A CFL can last up to twelve times as long as an incandescent

bulb does, and installing even a few will make a noticeable difference in a household's monthly electric bill. However, the initial outlay has discouraged many people from making the switch.

- *Not the same old light bulb.* A second reason is that CFLs do not work as well as incandescent bulbs do in certain circumstances, such as in fixtures outfitted with dimmers or in spotlights. Because the two types of bulbs are not completely interchangeable, consumers have to do at least a little research and possibly some experimentation to determine when they can and cannot install a CFL in place of an incandescent bulb. Instead, most consumers stay with what they know and keep buying the same type of bulbs they have always used.

- *Still too new.* Until very recently, few CFLs could be found on store shelves; those that were available had to compete with rows and rows of incandescent light bulbs. And CFLs were rarely featured in advertising. Despite some publicity, not everyone was getting the message about the CFL's energy efficiency and the long-term cost benefits of switching from incandescents.

- *Disposal concerns.* Because CFLs contain a minute amount of mercury, they must be handled like hazardous waste instead of being thrown away like ordinary light bulbs. Sylvania provides customers with special packaging to return burnt-out CFLs for recycling by dropping them off at FedEx Kinko's or at local post offices. However, even when consumers know about the benefits of CFLs, they may not know how to dispose of them safely.

Now the CFL is coming into its own amid a growing chorus of campaigns by retailers, manufacturers, utilities, and government agencies. Wal-Mart is putting a major marketing push behind CFLs, featuring them in ads and on the Web to encourage its 100 million customers to buy at least one new bulb. The retailer has even added CFLs to its back-to-school shopping list for eco-friendly products that it has posted on Facebook to reach "green teens." Utilities such as Pacific Gas & Electric in California have given away free CFLs or have offered CFLs at reduced prices to encourage customers to at least try the bulbs.

Major bulb manufacturers like General Electric, Philips, and Sylvania are helping to educate consumers about CFLs through on-package information and in marketing communications such as ads and media interviews. With new government standards calling for the phase-out of regular incandescent light bulbs over the next 10 years, manufacturers are also testing energy-efficient lighting alternatives such as low-heat incandescent bulbs, new halogen bulbs, and light-emitting diode (LED) bulbs. Soon light sockets all over America will be lit with CFLs and other new bulbs.[96]

Case Questions

1. Would you characterize the CFL as discontinuous, dynamically continuous, or continuous? How does this level of innovation help to explain why CFLs have diffused relatively slowly through the market?
2. Does the decision to adopt CFLs follow the high-effort or low-effort hierarchy of effects? What are the implications for marketers who make or retail CFLs?
3. How have the characteristics of the innovation and consumer learning requirements affected consumers' resistance to and adoption of CFLs?

Chapter 17

Symbolic Consumer Behavior

INTRODUCTION

Pampering Pets = Big Business

How much do Americans love their pets? Enough to spend $41 billion annually for pet-related goods, services, experiences, and activities—more than the total amount U.S. consumers spend to see movies, play video games, *and* buy music in a year. More than 60 percent of U.S. households have a pet, whether it is a cat, dog, fish, bird, rabbit, gerbil, lizard, pony, or another type of animal. Pampered pets are often treated as family members or an extension of their owners, who may name them, dress them in special clothing, buy them Christmas gifts, squirt perfume on them, photograph or videotape them, send cards to or from them, take them on vacation, get them massage therapy, and even buy them health insurance.

Pampering pets has created profitable opportunities for all kinds of businesses. Consumers who once felt sad or guilty about leaving a pet alone when they were at work or boarding a pet when they were traveling now seek out pet day-care services, pet-friendly hotels, and upscale boarding facilities like the TV-equipped private suites offered by PetSmart, the world's largest pet product retailer. Special pets need special food, a situation that explains why firms like Procter & Gamble and Nestlé spend $300 million a year advertising a huge variety of pet foods and invest millions more in researching new meals, treats, and packaging.

LEARNING OBJECTIVES

After studying this chapter, you will be able to

1. Discuss how products, special possessions, and consumption activities gain symbolic meaning and how this meaning is conveyed from one consumer to another.

2. Highlight how marketers can influence symbolic meaning.

3. Distinguish between sacred and profane entities, and show why this distinction is important for marketing strategy.

4. Understand the process of gift giving and describe how marketers can use knowledge of this process to market more effectively.

And if beloved pets get sick, many owners will open their wallets wide to pay for special treatments, hospital care, and drugs.[1]

Pets can have symbolic meaning, the focus of this chapter. The first section examines how symbolic meaning develops in products or consumption experiences, the functions symbolic consumption serve, and how symbolic consumption can affect our self-concept. The next section explains why some products are more meaningful than others. Some are special—even sacred—and require consumption practices to keep them so. The final section discusses how meaning is transferred from person to person through gift giving (see Exhibit 17.1). Knowing how symbolic meaning affects consumer behavior can help marketers develop and identify target markets, create needs-satisfying offerings, and plan appropriate communications.

Sources and Functions of Symbolic Meaning

To understand why some consumers pamper their pets, consider where the meaning associated with pets and related offerings comes from and what functions these offerings and practices fulfill. As shown in Exhibit 17.2, this meaning can stem from either our culture or ourselves as individuals.

Meaning Derived from Culture

Cultural categories The natural grouping of objects that reflect our culture.

Part of the meaning associated with products comes from our culture (see Exhibit 17.3).[2] Anthropologists suggest that we have **cultural categories** for such things as time (as in work time and leisure time), space (such as home, office, and safe or unsafe places), and occasions (such as festive versus somber events). We also have cultural categories that reflect characteristics of people, such as categories of gender, age, social class, and ethnicity.

Cultural principles Ideas or values that specify how aspects of our culture are organized and/or how they should be perceived or evaluated.

Implicit in cultural categories are **cultural principles**—ideas or values that specify how aspects of our culture are thought about and evaluated. For example, the cultural principles associated with "work time" dictate time that is structured, organized, and precise. The principles associated with "leisure time" are quite different. Cultural principles give meaning to products. This explains why the clothing we associate with work time is also more structured and organized than the clothing we associate with leisure time. In addition, we have categories for occasions, including festive (vibrant, active, and energetic) and somber (dark, quiet, and inactive) occasions. The clothing that we consider appropriate for those occasions mirrors these qualities.

We also have cultural principles linked with social status, gender, age, and ethnicity. For example, the category "women" has historically been associated with concepts like delicate, whimsical, expressive, and changeable. In contrast, the category "men" has historically been associated with concepts like disciplined, stable, and serious. Marketers make products and consumers use them in ways that are consistent with these principles. Thus, women's clothing has traditionally been more delicate, whimsical, expressive, and changeable than men's clothing. Exhibit 17.3 indicates that by matching product characteristics with cultural principles and categories, we transfer

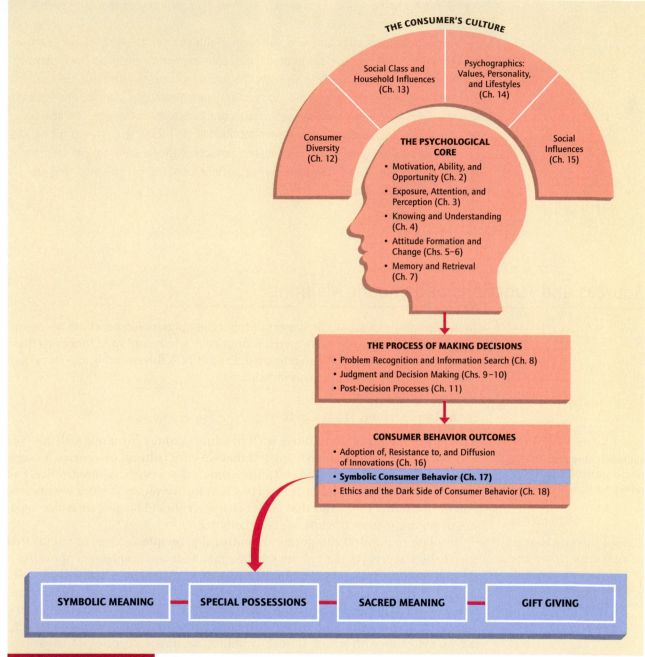

THE CONSUMER'S CULTURE

Social Class and Household Influences (Ch. 13)

Psychographics: Values, Personality, and Lifestyles (Ch. 14)

Consumer Diversity (Ch. 12)

Social Influences (Ch. 15)

THE PSYCHOLOGICAL CORE
• Motivation, Ability, and Opportunity (Ch. 2)
• Exposure, Attention, and Perception (Ch. 3)
• Knowing and Understanding (Ch. 4)
• Attitude Formation and Change (Chs. 5–6)
• Memory and Retrieval (Ch. 7)

THE PROCESS OF MAKING DECISIONS
• Problem Recognition and Information Search (Ch. 8)
• Judgment and Decision Making (Chs. 9–10)
• Post-Decision Processes (Ch. 11)

CONSUMER BEHAVIOR OUTCOMES
• Adoption of, Resistance to, and Diffusion of Innovations (Ch. 16)
• **Symbolic Consumer Behavior (Ch. 17)**
• Ethics and the Dark Side of Consumer Behavior (Ch. 18)

| SYMBOLIC MEANING | SPECIAL POSSESSIONS | SACRED MEANING | GIFT GIVING |

Exhibit 17.1

Chapter Overview: Symbolic Consumer Behavior

Products and consumption activities can symbolize something about ourselves and our relationships with others. In this chapter, we consider how products and consumption activities take on and communicate meaning. We also show how some possessions and consumption activities take on special or even sacred meaning. Finally, we discuss how gift giving can symbolize how we feel toward a gift recipient.

the meaning associated with the cultural principle to the product. For example, we might classify certain clothing as "feminine" or as "suitable for work" because we associate it with the corresponding cultural principles and categories.

Exhibit 17.3 also shows that many agents can play a role in this association and matching process. First, product designers and manufacturers introduce new products

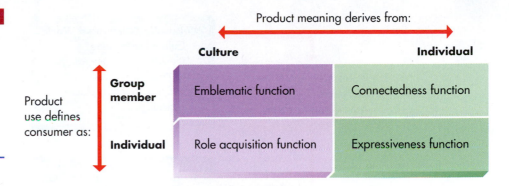

Exhibit 17.2

The Sources and Functions of Consumption Symbols

Consumers use products with various meanings to achieve a set of functions. Combined, these functions help define the consumer's self-concept.

with characteristics that reflect cultural principles. For example, the Harley-Davidson motorcycle has characteristics that make it "macho." This fit between cultural principles and offerings explains why U.S. consumers perceive a rodeo as more authentic if it reflects freedom, independence, and competition, qualities closely associated with the American West.[3] Marketers may also confer meaning by associating their offerings with certain cultural categories or myths. Therefore, Harley-Davidson develops clothing, accessories, and information that communicate what it means to be a "biker."[4]

Meaning also comes from nonmarketing sources. Specific people may serve as opinion leaders who shape, refine, or reshape cultural principles and the products and attributes they are linked to (see Chapter 15). For example, *Sex and the City* star Sarah Jessica Parker, who makes store appearances to promote her "Lovely" fragrance, may shape the type of products that women associate with sexual attractiveness.[5] Sometimes groups on the margins of society can be agents of change, as when brash, distinctive street-smart clothing worn by inner-city teens influences what mainstream designers produce.[6] Meaning derived from nonmarketing sources can sometimes go mainstream, as when Nike hired a former New York City graffiti artist to design a distinctive limited-edition athletic shoe.[7]

Journalists also shape cultural principles and the products associated with them. For example, restaurant reviewers may determine whether a restaurant is associated with principles like status, and style editors may determine whether clothes are associated with young and hip categories or with others. Magazines like *Runner's World* communicate meanings associated with the runner category, such as what runners are like, what they wear and eat, and what they like to do. Celebrities like Miley Cyrus can also create meaning in products by how they use them. Through all of these sources, the meaning inherent in the product is transferred to the consumer.

Meaning Derived from the Consumer

In addition to the way that products derive symbolic meaning from the culture, consumers can develop their own individual meanings associated with products. Whether meaning stems from (1) the culture or the consumer, however, consumption symbols can be used to say something (2) about the consumer as a member of a group or as a unique individual. Combining these two dimensions produces the emblematic, role acquisition, connectedness, and expressiveness functions of symbols described next.

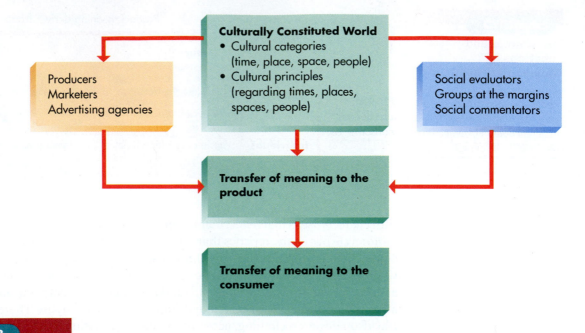

Culturally Constituted World
- Cultural categories (time, place, space, people)
- Cultural principles (regarding times, places, spaces, people)

Producers
Marketers
Advertising agencies

Social evaluators
Groups at the margins
Social commentators

Transfer of meaning to the product

Transfer of meaning to the consumer

Exhibit 17.3

Transfer of Meaning from the Culture to the Product and to the Consumer

Meaning that exists at the level of the culture (e.g., youthfulness) can become associated with a product (e.g., Burton snowboards). Both marketers and nonmarketers (e.g., opinion leaders, the media) can play a powerful role in this association process. The meaning associated with the product can in turn be transferred to the consumer who uses it.

Emblematic function The use of products to symbolize membership in social groups.

The Emblematic Function

Meaning derived from culture allows us to use products to symbolize our membership in various social groups—what we call an **emblematic function.** Dresses are associated with women, and clerical collars are associated with priests. The music we listen to may symbolize our age, and the car we drive may symbolize our social status. Consciously or unconsciously, we use brands and products to symbolize the groups to which we belong (or want to belong[8]). At the same time, people who observe us using these products may consciously or unconsciously categorize and make inferences about us and the groups to which we belong (see Chapter 4). Just by looking at someone and his or her possessions, we might be able to tell whether that person is a member of the "surfer," "fraternity type," or "rich kid" social categories.[9] In particular, offerings can serve as geographic, ethnic, or social class emblems.

Geographic Emblems

Products can symbolize geographic identification. For example, brightly colored, loose-fitting clothing symbolizes identification with sunnier regions of the United States, such as California, Arizona, and Hawaii. The outdoorsy clothing made by Roots symbolizes places like Canada.[10] Products may also symbolize geographic identification with a region even if they are used by people who live elsewhere.

Ethnic Emblems

Products and consumption activities can symbolize identification with a specific culture or subculture. African Americans sometimes wear African garb to symbolize identification with that culture. In India, Sikh men wear five Ks as symbols of their ethnic and religious affiliation: *kesh* (hair), *kada* (bangle), *kangha* (comb), *kacha* (underpants), and *kirpan* (dagger). Some consumers use ethnic emblems of other cultures or subcultures to differentiate themselves.

Consumers also use food to express ethnic identity. For example, grilled chicken, chicken mole, and steamed yellowfish reflect U.S., Mexican, and Chinese identities, respectively. Cornmeal serves as an ethnic emblem for Haitians immigrating to the United States.[11] In addition, we can express ethnic identification by how and when we eat. Cultures differ in whether all elements of the meal are served at once or one item at a time.[12] U.S. families typically eat dinner before 7:00 P.M., but dinnertime is much later in Spain and Italy.

Social Class Emblems

Products can also symbolize social class. In China, emblems of status include color TVs, cognac (for older consumers), and fine imported wine (for younger consumers).[13] Among wealthy American consumers, symbols of social class include helicopters, backyard golf courses, private airplanes, and palatial homes.[14] The cultural principles of upper-upper-class membership include characteristics of refinement, understated restraint, and discipline. So too do the products and consumption activities of this class.

Different social classes use different symbols in consumption rituals. For example, higher and lower social classes in the United States differ greatly in the types of clothing they wear at holiday time, the importance they place on etiquette, the types of serving dishes they use at formal family dinners, and even the way that they serve certain foods. Countering this type of social-class emblematic function, a growing number of U.S. schools (both public and private) require students to wear uniforms. The purpose of this policy is to help curb gang activity, remove social class emblems, reduce students' anxiety about keeping up with peers, and encourage identification with the school community.[15]

Gender Emblems

Food, clothing, jewelry, and alcoholic beverages are only some of the product categories associated with membership in the male and female gender categories. One study of consumers in France revealed that meat and certain other foods are viewed as "man" foods, whereas celery and other foods are viewed as "woman" foods. The way that a food is eaten also reflects its gender appropriateness: Steak and meats that may be cut roughly and chewed intensively are viewed in some cultures as more consistent with male characteristics.[16] Other researchers have found gender differences in food preferences, with boys preferring chunky peanut butter, for instance, and girls preferring the smooth variety. These preferences may be related to culturally derived associations with boys (rough) and girls (not rough).[17]

Large, rugged, powerful vehicles such as pickup trucks are often associated with male characteristics and, not surprisingly, marketed primarily to men. For instance, after Toyota redesigned its Tundra pickup truck, it launched the new product by sponsoring bass-fishing contests, livestock shows, and other events that attract men. It also offered free test drives at places that draw male shoppers, such as the sporting-goods chain Bass Pro Shops.[18]

Reference Group Emblems

Harley-Davidson merchandise is a good example of how products can serve as emblems of membership in a reference group (see Exhibit 17.4). One reason why Harley consumers adopt "outlaw" symbols is that they like being members of a reference group with a counterculture ideology and independence. In general, consumers like a reference group emblem (like a T-shirt with the Harley logo) more when an identity-consistent aspect of their self-concept (such as their image of themselves as fiercely independent) has been activated.[19] Varsity jackets, special hats, particular colors, or gang-designated jewelry may also symbolize reference group membership. Conversely, consumers may shun certain products to avoid being seen as members of a reference group—which, in turn, symbolizes membership in another reference group. In the auto business, a backlash against

Exhibit 17.4

Reference Group Emblems

Jeans, black boots, and black leather jackets are just some of the reference group emblems associated with being a "biker."

gas-guzzling SUVs is driving some consumers to buy fuel-efficient hybrid cars. Thus, these motorists become members of the group of consumers who act on their concerns about the environment by buying earth-friendly products.[20]

In addition to products, rituals are sometimes important indicators and affirmations of group membership. For example, rituals like attending graduation may reinforce our membership in the "college graduate" group. Other rituals serve as public confirmation that we have become members of a group. Among the upper-upper class, the debutante ball is a ritual that formally introduces 16-year-old girls into the group of women eligible for dating.[21]

MARKETING IMPLICATIONS

Marketers can play three roles in establishing the emblematic function of products.

Symbol development

Marketing can link a product and its attributes to a specific cultural category and its principles. When Toyota wanted to develop the symbolic associations of its redesigned Tundra pickup truck, it targeted opinion leaders it calls "true truckers," men who work in rugged situations like construction or ranching, because "they're the taste makers, the influentials," a Toyota executive explained.[22] Sometimes marketers need to ensure that product attributes are appropriately linked with cultural principles. Miller, for example, positioned the *lite* in Miller Lite as meaning "less filling and has fewer carbohydrates"—an appropriate attribute for men—rather than *diet*, which would have made the beer seem more feminine.[23]

Symbol communication

A company can use advertising to imbue a product with meaning through the setting for the ad (whether fantasy or naturalistic, interior or exterior, or rural or urban) and through other details such as the time of day and the types of people in the ad—their gender, age, ethnicity, occupation, clothing, body postures, and so on.[24] Each ad element reinforces the meaning associated with the product. This situation illustrates why ads for Toyota's redesigned Tundra showcased the pickup's brute strength and performance under harsh conditions, such as hauling extremely heavy loads.[25]

Symbol reinforcement

Firms can design other elements of the marketing mix to reinforce the symbolic image.[26] For instance, a company can use various pricing, distribution, and product strategies to maintain a product's status image. It may give the product a premium price, distribute it through outlets with an upscale image, and incorporate certain features that are appropriate only for the targeted segment. However, marketers may hurt a product's symbolic image if the elements of the marketing mix clash with each other.

Symbol removal

Some marketers have made a business of helping consumers erase symbols associated with groups with which they no longer identify. For example, the tattoo removal market is growing. Consumers often want tattoos removed because they are emblematic of an earlier time of life or an abandoned reference group and therefore impede the development of new personal identities.[27]

The Role Acquisition Function

In addition to serving as emblems of group membership, offerings can help us feel more comfortable in new roles. This function is called the **role acquisition function** (look back at Exhibit 17.2).

Role acquisition function The use of products as symbols to help us feel more comfortable in a new role.

Role Acquisition Phases

Consumers fill many roles in their lives, and these roles constantly change. You may currently occupy the role of student, son or daughter, brother or sister, and worker. At some point in your life (perhaps even now), you may occupy the role of husband or wife, uncle or aunt, parent, divorcee, grandparent, retiree, widow or widower, and so on.

People typically move from one role to another in three phases.[28] The first phase is *separation* from the old role. This often means disposing of products associated with the role we are leaving, the way that children give up security blankets in their transition from baby to child. Consumers who are breaking up a relationship may symbolize the relationship's end by giving away, throwing away, or destroying products that remind them of their former partners.[29] The second phase is the *transition* from one role to another, which may be accompanied by experimentation with new identities. During this transition, consumers may be willing to accept new possessions or styles that they otherwise would have rejected. Consumers may also construct a new identity through plastic surgery, dieting, new hairstyles, branding, body piercing, and tattooing. The final phase is *incorporation*, in which the consumer takes on the new role and the identity associated with it.

Use of Symbols and Rituals in Role Transitions

Exhibit 17.5 illustrates how and why we use symbols and rituals when we acquire a new role. We often feel uncomfortable with a new role because we are inexperienced in occupying it and have little knowledge about how to fulfill it. A common reaction is to use products stereotypically associated with that role. For example, MBAs who are insecure about their job prospects are more likely than other MBAs to use symbols generally associated with the role of a businessperson.[30] We often use a

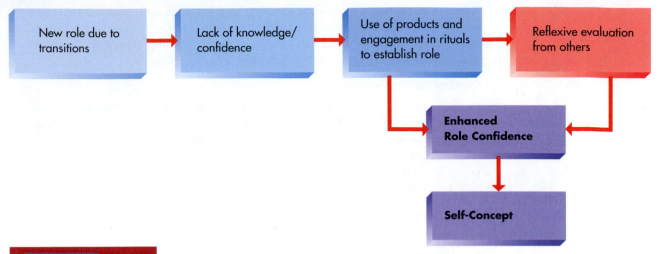

| New role due to transitions | → | Lack of knowledge/ confidence | → | Use of products and engagement in rituals to establish role | → | Reflexive evaluation from others |

Enhanced Role Confidence

Self-Concept

Exhibit 17.5

Model of Role Acquisition

When we first enter a new role (e.g., parenthood), we may lack some role confidence. As a result, we engage in activities (e.g., have baby showers) and buy groups of products (e.g., strollers) typically associated with that role. These activities and products, along with the way that others react to our behaviors, enhance our role confidence.

group of products to symbolize adoption of a new role. Having the right combination of products is important because without it we may not elicit the appropriate response from others. Imagine the reaction you would get at work if you wore white socks or sneakers with a business suit.

Rituals are an important part of role transitions. For example, a number of rituals mark the transition from single to married status in the United States—engagement party, wedding shower, bachelor party, rehearsal dinner, wedding, reception, and honeymoon—each with relevant enabling products.[31] The wedding itself includes clothing for the attendants, flowers, wedding gown, musicians, a photographer, and so on. Funeral rituals in different cultures involve symbolic consumption activities such as presenting or consuming special foods, buying flowers and cards, and displaying pictures or valuables that reflect on the deceased and the bereaved.[32]

Rituals often involve others whose participation helps validate the role transition. As Exhibit 17.5 shows, we use symbols and engage in rituals to get feedback from participants about whether we are fulfilling the role correctly. This feedback, called **reflexive evaluation,** helps us feel more confident in our role and thus validates our new status. Newly minted MBAs, for example, feel more confident in their role when experienced businesspeople acknowledge them as fellow businesspeople. The next section focuses on marital role transitions and products as symbols of this transition process.

Reflexive evaluation Feedback from others that tells us whether we are fulfilling the role correctly.

Marital Transitions

Products are often an important component in the transition from single to married status. As part of separating from the old phase, the couple must decide which of their possessions to dispose of and which to move to their new household. Often presents from old boyfriends or girlfriends are discarded, as are products symbolizing one's former single status. As part of the incorporation phase, the couple acquires new products that are culturally appropriate for the married role and that help them create a mutual history. Clearly, different cultures have different marital rituals. For example, the mother-in-law often gives the keys to the house to a Hindu bride following the wedding, symbolically handing over the charge of running the house.

A similar process operates in the transition from married to divorced status. Here, each person takes back what was his or hers, and they divide their joint possessions. People may deliberately dispose of possessions that remind them of the other person. As one set of researchers notes, "Jettisoning symbols of the ex-spouse . . . may be psychologically necessary in the process of ending the relationship."[33] Some people destroy possessions, an action that perhaps serves several functions—symbolically representing the destruction of the marriage, punishing the ex-spouse, and eliminating possessions that symbolize the marriage.

People may have difficulty fulfilling other symbolic functions as a result of ending a marriage. For example, one spouse may no longer have the conspicuous consumption items that once communicated social status. Thus, someone who loses a house and a car (two important symbols of social prestige) may feel a loss of identity. On the other hand, people may acquire products symbolic of their new single status during this role transition, as some people do by purchasing a sports car at this time.

Cultural Transitions

Consumers also may change roles when they move to a new culture, often abandoning or disposing of old customs and symbols and adopting new ones in the process. Research suggests that Mexican immigrants faced different and sometimes difficult experiences in moving to the United States.[34] Among these were living in densely grouped housing, shopping in stores with a sometimes overwhelming number of choices, and dealing with unfamiliar currency. Another study shows that Indians moving to the United States needed to acquire status symbols that they did not need in India, where caste and family designate class membership.[35]

Expatriates often face frustrating and formidable barriers to inclusion in a new culture. To reduce these barriers, they may participate in local events and rituals, adapt consumption to local customs, and become brand conscious, even though they may hold on to certain aspects of their home culture, like food, language, videos, photos, and jewelry.[36] Whether someone abandons or retains possessions that symbolize the old role may depend on how long the role is expected to last. The study of expatriates from India showed that consumers held onto possessions reminiscent of their culture of origin because they still considered the possibility of someday returning to India.

Social Status Transitions

Newly wealthy individuals, the "nouveaux riches," use possessions—usually ostentatious ones—to demonstrate their acquired status and validate their role. This behavior is consistent with the model of symbols and role transitions in Exhibit 17.5, which shows the importance of reflexive evaluation from others to indicate successful role performance. As one author notes, "Consumer satisfaction is derived from audience reactions to the wealth displayed by the purchaser in securing the product or service rather than to the positive attributes of the item in question."[37]

(MARKETING IMPLICATIONS)

Marketers can apply their knowledge of consumers' role transitions in several ways.

Role transitions and target consumers

Consumers in transition represent an important target market for many firms (see Exhibit 17.6). As Procter & Gamble's global marketing officer says, "Newlyweds are in

Exhibit 17.6

Role Transitions
Consumers who take on new roles often rely on products to help them feel more comfortable in their role status.

some ways the ultimate consumer."[38] Many companies target engaged couples who will soon buy offerings related to the wedding, honeymoon, and new housing. A campaign from De Beers's Diamond Trading Company targets women with messages reinforcing how wearing jewelry on different hands can symbolize marriage or self-expression. The tag line is "Your left hand says 'we.' Your right hand says 'me.'"[39]

Role transitions as a means for developing inventory

Because product disposition can be an important aspect of role separation, marketers of secondhand products can acquire inventory by marketing to people engaged in role transitions. For example, secondhand stores might target college students before graduation, knowing that in their role transitions many may wish to dispose of student-related paraphernalia such as furniture and clothing. Similarly, online auction sites such as eBay profit when consumers decide to dispose of items made obsolete or irrelevant by role transitions.

Role transitions and product promotions

Marketers may find it useful to promote their products as instrumental in incorporating a new role. For example, marketers tout everything from shower fixtures to stock shares as acceptable wedding gifts. Bloomingdale's is one of many retailers targeting partners planning same-sex marriages, and wedding registries are showing up in places as diverse as Ace Hardware and the Metropolitan Museum of Art stores.[40] Baby gift registries have become a $240 million business, helping new parents acquire products that are important to their new role.[41]

Selling product constellations

Marketers can stress the importance of groups of products to consumers in the process of role acquisition.[42] Businesses featuring product constellations include websites such as TheKnot.com and WeddingChannel.com, which offer access to one-stop shopping for wedding apparel, photographers, florists, limousines, catering companies, and related offerings. Company advertising can suggest that consumers will earn positive reflexive evaluation from others if they use an appropriate constellation of products associated with a given role.

Managing rituals

Marketers can also be instrumental in developing services that help in planning and implementing rituals surrounding transitions, as funeral homes do by performing services in the death ritual.

The Connectedness Function

Although the meaning of offerings that serve emblematic or role acquisition functions comes from the culture, product meaning can also come from the groups consumers belong to (review Exhibit 17.2).[43] Products and consumption activities

Connectedness function The use of products as symbols of our personal connections to significant people, events, or experiences.

that serve the **connectedness function** express our membership in a group and symbolize our personal connections to significant people, events, or experiences in our lives (see Exhibit 17.7). For example, you may particularly like a painting or a hat because it was a gift from a close friend. Heirlooms and genealogy studies connect people with their ancestors; family photos connect them to their descendants. People may also value concert programs, ticket stubs, and other souvenirs as reminders of special people, events, and places.[44]

Other products and acts can also symbolize connectedness. For instance, Chinese consumers use large round tables in restaurants to symbolize wholeness and the group's connectedness; Chinese New Year celebrations emphasize family ties. During Muslim feasts, everyone shares food from a community plate; those who ask for a separate plate are considered rude. Rituals such as the U.S. celebration of Thanksgiving may also symbolize connectedness. Often family members show their commitment by attending the Thanksgiving gathering—even if they have to travel long distances. Moreover, cultures like those of the United States and England emphasize family connectedness during the Christmas ritual. In other cultures, such as those of some Eskimo villages in Alaska, the Christmas ritual has more of a community focus.[45]

Each family maintains its own traditions that foster connectedness. Members often strongly resist deviating from these traditions (such as trying a new stuffing recipe). Many families foster connectedness by looking at old family photographs or videos and telling family stories. Other families pass certain cherished objects from one generation to the next as symbols of the family's connectedness, with each owner acting as guardian of the special possessions.[46] This sense of connectedness may not only reaffirm social ties but may also make us nostalgic about past times.

The Expressiveness Function

Expressiveness function The use of products as symbols to demonstrate our uniqueness—how we stand out as different from others.

As a symbol, a product has the potential to say something about our uniqueness.[47] This **expressiveness function** reflects how unique we are, not how we relate to other people. According to research, Eastern European youths like Western products because these offerings are used to create a distinct appearance that sets them

apart from others.[48] We express our unique personalities through offerings like clothing, home decoration, art, leisure activities, and food consumption. We might find certain product categories, such as hairstyles or music, particularly appropriate for indicating who we are as individuals.[49] Some consumers use body piercing, branding, and tattooing to symbolize their individuality and expressiveness.[50]

MARKETING IMPLICATIONS

The connectedness and expressive functions lead to several marketing implications. For example, marketers may wish to invoke feelings of nostalgia by connecting their product with people, places, or events (see Chapter 7). Marketers of toys and games, movies, and music have successfully encouraged consumers to connect these products with special times in their lives.[51] Pacific Cycle revived the Schwinn Sting-Ray bicycle brand to tap into family connectiveness by offering retro styles that Mom and Dad enjoyed as children. "This is an opportunity [for parents] to allow their kids to have similar experiences with a similar bike," says Kristen Rumble, who heads branding and creative services. In addition, marketers can suggest that their products enhance uniqueness. Pacific Cycle does this by joining with Orange County Choppers to offer accessories that can be used to customize Sting-Ray bikes. "It offers a hobby for a dad and his son, or even his daughter, too, to trick out a bike the way dad tricks out his car," Rumble notes.[52]

Multiple Functions

A given product may serve several of the functions we just described. A set of crystal wine goblets received as a wedding present from the bride's grandparents could serve an emblematic function because their high price tag communicates social status. They may also serve a role acquisition function, helping the newlyweds to internalize their new marital roles. Because they were a present from grandparents, the goblets may also serve a connectedness function—symbolizing the newlyweds' special relationship with their grandparents. Finally, if the goblets are personally appealing to the couple, they may symbolize the newlyweds' individual aesthetic tastes, thus also serving an expressiveness function. We are not always aware of a product's symbolic function. We may expect certain types of gifts when we go through role transitions like graduation and marriage, but we are probably not conscious of the fact that these products are helping us adjust to our new roles. Finally, we may really like an item that we received as a gift without realizing that we are reacting in this way because it serves as a reminder of the gift giver.

Symbols and Self-Concept

Actual identity schemas The set of multiple, salient identities that reflect our self-concept.

Ideal identity schema A set of ideas about how the identity would be indicated in its ideal form.

The symbolic functions of products and consumption rituals are important because together they help to define and maintain our self-concept, our mental conception of who we are.[53] Social identity theory proposes that we evaluate brands in terms of their consistency with our individual identities.[54] According to the theory, our self-concept can be decomposed into many separate identities called **actual identity schemas,** including student, worker, daughter, and so on. These identities may be driven, at least in part, by the roles that we fulfill. Some identities may be especially salient or central to our self-concept. Our actual identity may be shaped by an **ideal identity schema**—a set of ideas about how the identity that we seek would be realized in its ideal form.

Our actual and ideal identity schemas influence which products we use and which consumption practices we engage in, even among consumers who object to the overcommercialization of contemporary culture[55] (see Chapter 18 for more about the dark side of marketing). Our actual identity might affect which symbols of ourselves (such as family photos or personal mugs) we bring to our workplace to reflect who we are.[56]

The fact that possessions help to shape our identity may explain why people who lose their possessions in natural disasters or war and people who are in institutions like the military, nursing homes, or prisons sometimes feel a loss of identity.[57] Indeed, loss of possessions can induce a state of grief that resembles the death of a loved one. Some institutions, such as the military and prisons, deliberately strip individuals of their possessions to erase old identities.[58] On the other hand, millions of consumers have personal websites, blogs, and other online places where they use words, images, audio, links, and other elements to construct and project identities digitally, shaping and sharing their self-concept with cyberspace friends.[59]

MARKETING IMPLICATIONS

Marketers need to consider several implications stemming from the preceding concepts.

Marketing and the development of consumer self-concepts

Marketers can play a role in both producing and maintaining an individual's self-concept. Although products may help define who we are, we also maintain our self-concept by selecting products with images that are consistent with it. For example, a Karastan ad invites women to "Make a statement. Your own" by using the brand's carpeting to display their fashion sense in the home. "When they're in this mode, they're decorating divas," comments an executive at Karastan's ad agency.[60]

Product fit with self-concepts

Marketers should understand how their product fits with the identities of their target consumers and try to create a fit between the image of the brand and the actual or ideal identity of the consumer. The more similar a product's image is to a consumer's self-image, the more the consumer likes the product.[61] In Japan, Nissan markets a *kawaii* (cute) version of its Pino minicar, with touches like hubcaps in the shape of snowflakes, targeting young women who see themselves as cute and approachable.[62]

Product fit with multiple self-concepts

Because self-images are multifaceted, marketers must also determine whether products consistent with one aspect of the target customers' identity may be inconsistent with another aspect. For example, a new father may react negatively to disposable diapers because even though the product is consistent with his new parent identity, it is inconsistent with his environmentally conscious identity.

Advertising fit with self-concepts

Finally, ads should appeal to the identity concept appropriate for the targeted segment's gender and culture.[63] Thus, some ads that target women might emphasize mutual reliance, whereas some ads that target men might emphasize autonomy. Similarly, ads geared toward consumers in China might stress culturally appropriate themes of group goals and achievement, whereas ads for U.S. consumers might stress culturally appropriate themes of personal goals and achievement.

Special Possessions and Brands

We may feel emotionally attached to certain possessions (such as an afghan made by a family member) and certain brands (such as an Apple iPod) because we see them as part of ourselves.[64] However, some products come to hold a special, valued position in our minds, whether or not they are relevant to our self-concepts (see Exhibit 17.8).[65] For example, one consumer may regard his lawn mower as a special possession because it is very functional, whereas another may view her skis as special because they provide such enjoyment, yet neither consumer may view these items as relevant to their self-concept.[66] This section looks at what makes a brand or product special to a consumer.

Special Brands

A brand becomes special to consumers when they feel emotionally attached to it in some way. As this emotional connection strengthens, consumers become more likely to buy the special brand over and over again. Ultimately, a special brand may be able to command a price premium and will retain loyal customers even after a crisis such as a product recall.[67]

Exhibit 17.8

Special Possessions
Products like collectible coins can become special possessions to some consumers.

Types of Special Possessions

Although almost any possession can be special, researchers have found that special possessions typically fall into one of several categories: pets, memory-laden objects, achievement symbols, and collections.[68]

Pets

As illustrated in the opening example, U.S. consumers tend to regard their pets as very special. Now that 71 million U.S. households keep a pet, retailers such as PetSmart and Petco see higher demand for gourmet pet food and other premium products.[69] Petco's CEO states, "People keep projecting onto their animals how they feel about themselves and what they want in their own life. The premium pet-food craze very much reflects human interest in better diets."[70] Not every culture treats pets as special possessions. For example, cats and dogs are not treasured as pets in the Middle East, and dog owners in Korea typically feed their pets leftovers rather than dog food.

Memory-Laden Objects

Some products acquire special meaning because they evoke memories or emotions of special people, places, or experiences.[71] Examples include heirlooms, antiques, souvenirs, and gifts from special people. You may value a ticket stub—otherwise just a piece of paper—because it evokes memories of going to see your favorite band in concert.

Such possessions can be therapeutic for elderly people because they evoke links to other people and happy times. Several researchers report the case of an individual who had to sell a favorite automobile because of a divorce but saved the license plates as a memento of this special possession. Many consumers consider photographs special because they are reminders of special people, and they create "shrines" by displaying photos on bureaus, mantles, and pianos.[72] Possessions that symbolize connectedness clearly have the potential to become special.

Achievement Symbols

People also regard possessions that symbolize achievement as special. One researcher who studied the Mormon migration to Utah in the 1800s found that people often moved possessions that demonstrated competence. For example, men brought tools, and women brought sewing machines and other objects that had a practical function but also symbolized domestic achievement.[73] Modern-day symbols of achievement might include college diplomas, sports trophies, recognition plaques, or even conspicuously consumed items like Rolex watches or Porsches.

Collections

Collections are special possessions for many people. Common collectible items include model cars, sports memorabilia, seashells, minerals, coins, and childhood objects like baseball cards and dolls.[74] Uncommon collectibles include spark plugs and drain tiles. Firms like the Bradford Exchange, the Franklin Mint, GovMint.com, and the Danbury Mint produce collectible items for consumers, but rarity makes some items particularly special: A collector paid more than $1 million for a locomotive-shaped weather vane that came from the top of a train station in Rhode Island.[75]

Collectors often view their collections as extensions of themselves—sometimes symbolizing an aspect of their occupation, family heritage, or appearance. Researchers have studied a grocery store owner who collected antique product packages, an engineer who collected pocket watches, a woman named Bunny who collected rabbit replicas, and wealthy women who collected monogrammed silver spoons.[76] For some, collections represent a fantasy image of the self. For example, men who collect baseball cards may be keeping alive the fantasy of themselves as ball players. As is often the case with people who have special possessions, collectors tend to believe that they take better care of their collections than anyone else would.[77]

The Characteristics that Describe Special Possessions

Special possessions have several distinct characteristics.[78] First, consumers will not sell them at market value, if at all, and often buy special possessions with little regard for their price. We could never, for example, sell at any price our family pet or a quilt made by our grandmother. Collectors may pay exorbitant prices to acquire particularly sought-after objects like rare coins.

Second, special possessions (like our family dog) have few or no substitutes. Insurance may pay to replace furniture that was damaged in a fire, but new furniture cannot compensate for heirloom pieces that were passed down through generations. In fact, consumers see special possessions as irreplaceable because of their associations with certain events and people in the consumers' lives.[79] A third characteristic is that people will not discard special possessions, even when they lose their functional value. Children are often reluctant to part with security blankets and stuffed animals and will keep these favorite objects until they are mere threads of fabric. Do your parents still keep your old report cards and pictures that you drew for them?

Special possessions are not always used for their original purpose. Some people who buy Altoids "Curiously Strong" mints retain the tin container to keep small special possessions safe.[80] Some consumers believe that a prized possession will lose valued properties if it is used to fulfill its original function. One study described a woman who collected nutcrackers but would not consider using them to crack nuts.[81]

Finally, consumers frequently personify special possessions. Some name individual items in a collection, name their houses, or use a feminine or masculine pronoun when referring to their cars or boats. Perhaps even more significant, we may treat these possessions as though they were our partners, feeling such commitment and attachment that we are devastated by their loss.[82]

Why Some Products Are Special

Possessions take on special meaning for several reasons, including their symbolic value, mood-altering properties, and instrumental importance. Exhibit 17.9 shows more specific reasons that underlie these three general categories.

Exhibit 17.9

Reasons Why Possessions Are Special

Take a possession that you regard as special. Most likely it is special to you because it has symbolic value, mood-altering properties, and/or utilitarian value.

Take a possession that you regard as special, and answer the following questions using a 7-point scale (1 = not true of me; 7 = very true of me).

This possession is important to me because it . . .

Symbolic Value	Symbolizes personal history	Represents interpersonal ties Reminds me of particular events or places Is a record of my personal history
	Represents achievement	Required a lot of effort to acquire or maintain Reminds me of my skills, achievements, or goals Reminds me of my relationship with a particular person Reminds me of my family or a group of people that I belong to Represents my family heritage or history
	Facilitates interpersonal ties	Allows me to spend time or share activities with other people
	Demonstrates status	Has social prestige value Gives me social status Makes others think well of me
	Is self-expressive	Allows me to express myself Expresses what is unique about me, different from others
Mood-Altering Properties	Provides enjoyment	Provides enjoyment, entertainment, or relaxation Improves my mood Provides comfort or emotional security
	Is spiritual	Provides a spiritual link to divine or higher forces
	Is appearance related	Is beautiful or attractive in appearance Improves my appearance or the way I look
Utilitarian Value	Is utilitarian	Allows me to be efficient in my daily life or work Has a lot of practical usefulness Provides me freedom or independence
	Has financial aspects	Is valuable in terms of money

Source: Adapted from Marsha Richens, "Valuing Things: The Public and Private Meanings of Possessions," *Journal of Consumer Research* 21, December 1994, pp. 504–521.

- *Symbolic value.* Possessions may be special, in part, because they fulfill the emblematic, role adoption, connectedness, and expressiveness functions noted earlier in the chapter. For example, we may value art, heirlooms, and jewelry because they express our style or because they were gifts and tie us to special people.[83] Thus, consumers are very reluctant to part with a possession that has symbolic meaning because it was acquired from a much-loved family member or close friend.[84]

- *Mood-altering properties.* Possessions may be special because they have mood-altering properties. For example, trophies, plaques, collections, and diplomas can evoke feelings of pride, happiness, and joy.[85] Pets can evoke feelings of comfort. A consumer in one study described her refrigerator as a special possession because making snacks always cheered her up. Others cited music players and music as favorite possessions because these put consumers in a good mood.[86]

- *Instrumental importance.* Possessions may also be special because they are extremely useful. A consumer who describes her cell phone or computer as special because she uses it constantly to get things done throughout the day is referring to this possession's instrumental value.

Consumer Characteristics Affect What Is Special

Social class, gender, and age are among the background characteristics that affect the types of things that become special to each of us.

- *Social class.* One study examined the meanings that people of different social classes in England gave to their possessions. People in the business class were concerned about possessions that symbolized their personal history and self-development. Unemployed people were concerned about possessions that had utilitarian value.[87] In addition, consumers who aspire to a higher social class may use particular possessions to associate themselves with that social class, even misrepresenting those products to support the self-image of belonging to the higher class.[88]

- *Gender.* For men, products are special when they symbolize activity and physical achievement and when they have instrumental and functional features. On the other hand, women often value symbols of identity and products that symbolize their attachment to other people.[89] A study of consumers in Niger and the United States found that women's special possessions were those that symbolized their children's accomplishments or connected consumers to others. For U.S. women, these possessions included heirlooms and pictures; for the Nigerian women, they included tapestries, jewelry, and other items passed on through generations. Men chose objects that showed material comfort and possessions that indicated mastery over the environment.[90] Men are more likely to collect cars, books, and sports-related objects, and women are more likely to collect jewelry, dishes, and silverware.[91] Exhibit 17.10 identifies special possessions by gender and ages.

- *Age.* Although individuals have special possessions at all ages, what they regard as special changes with age. As Exhibit 17.10 shows, stuffed animals are very important for children, music and motor vehicles are highly prized among adolescents, and photographs take on increasing importance as consumers enter adulthood and old age.

Age	Males	Females
Middle childhood	Sports equipment* Stuffed animals Childhood toys Small appliances Pillows, blankets	Stuffed animals* Dolls Music Jewelry Books
Adolescence	Music Sports equipment Motor vehicles Small appliances Clothing	Jewelry Stuffed animals Music Clothing Motor vehicles Small appliances
Early adulthood	Motor vehicles Music Photographs Jewelry Memorabilia Artwork	Jewelry Photographs Motor vehicles Pillows, blankets Stuffed animals
Middle adulthood	Photographs Jewelry Books Sports equipment Motor vehicles Small appliances	Dishes, silverware Jewelry Artwork Photographs Memorabilia Furniture
Late adulthood	Small appliances Photographs Motor vehicles Artwork Sports equipment	Jewelry Dishes, silverware Photographs Religious Items Furniture

*Items are listed in order from most to least frequently cited.

Source: Adapted with permission from N. Laura Kamptner, "Personal Possessions and Their Meanings: A Life-Span Perspective," in ed. Floyd W. Rudmin, *To Have Possessions: A Handbook on Ownership and Property,* Special Issue, *Journal of Social Behavior and Personality* 6, no. 6, 1991, p. 215.

Rituals Used with Special Possessions

We often engage in rituals designed to create, energize, or enhance the meaning of special possessions. These rituals can occur at the acquisition, usage, or disposition stage of consumption.

Possession rituals Rituals we engage in when we first acquire a product that help to make it "ours."

At the acquisition stage, **possession rituals** enable the consumer to claim personal possession of new goods.[92] When you buy new jeans, for example, you may change the length, cut them at the knees, or add embellishments. You may adorn a new car with personal markers like personalized license plates, favorite CDs, a special scent, seat covers, and so on. When you move to a new house or apartment, you hang pictures, buy curtains, and position the furniture.

Possession rituals for previously owned goods include wiping away traces of the former owner.[93] For example, when you buy a new home, you thoroughly clean it, tear down old wallpaper, and take down personal markers like the name on the mailbox. However, it is not always possible to wipe away meaning. In China, for example, consumers often build new houses because of a sense that older structures are "contaminated" by the former occupants.

Grooming rituals Rituals we engage in to bring out or maintain the best in special products.

At the consumption stage, consumers may engage in **grooming rituals** to bring out or maintain the best in special products.[94] Some consumers spend hours washing and waxing their cars or cleaning house before visitors arrive. Sometimes the grooming ritual extends to you personally, as when you spend a lot of time making yourself look good for a special event.

Divestment rituals Rituals enacted at the disposition stage that are designed to wipe away all traces of our personal meaning in a product.

Finally, when the offering loses its symbolic meaning, consumers engage in **divestment rituals**—wiping away all traces of personal meaning.[95] For example, many people remove the address labels before giving away magazines that they subscribe to or delete personal files before selling or donating a computer. We might even get rid of a possession in stages, moving it from the living room to the basement before finally selling it or throwing it away.

Disposing of Special Possessions

People dispose of special possessions for different reasons and in different ways. Studies show that older consumers make disposition decisions when experiencing periods of crisis, when moving to an institution, when approaching death, and when marking rites of passage and progression—although some transfer special possessions only after death through a will. Sometimes the consumer hopes that giving the object to a relative will invoke memories, express love, or lead to a symbolic immortality; at other times the consumer seeks to control disposition decisions and timing. An older consumer generally considers which recipient will best appreciate the special object's meaning, continue to use or care for it, or uphold family traditions, or he or she may simply give it to the person who asks for it first.[96]

Sacred Meaning

Sacred entities People, things, and places that are set apart, revered, worshiped, and treated with great respect.

Profane things Things that are ordinary and hence have no special power.

Although many possessions are considered special, some are so special that they are viewed as sacred. **Sacred entities** are people, things, and places that are set apart, revered, worshiped, and treated with great respect. We may find such entities deeply moving, and we may feel anger and revulsion when they are not respected. In contrast, **profane things** are those that are ordinary and hence have no special power. Profane objects are often distinguished from sacred ones by the fact that they are used for more mundane purposes.[97]

Movie stars, popular singers, historic figures like John F. Kennedy and Martin Luther King Jr., and religious leaders such as the pope, Buddha, and Gandhi are regarded by many people as sacred. The sacred status of famous people is exemplified by the crowds visiting the graves of celebrities like Princess Diana and driving by or visiting homes of living or dead celebrities, such as Elvis's Graceland. Japanese and American baseball fans regard Seattle Mariners slugger Ichiro Suzuki as sacred. Suzuki paraphernalia is popular, Japanese reporters cover all his games, and fans travel from afar to watch him play.[98]

One reason why heirlooms and photographs of ancestors take on sacred status is that we may view our ancestors as heroes. A similar phenomenon explains why we treat items associated with famous statesmen such as George Washington and Winston Churchill as sacred. Although not part of our actual past, these heroes were instrumental in formulating national identities. Consumers demonstrate their reverence by visiting the places that mark these historic figures.[99]

Many consumers also regard as sacred such objects as national flags, patriotic songs, art, collections, family recipes, and the Bible and such places as museums, the

Alamo, the Taj Mahal, and the Great Wall of China (see Exhibit 17.11). These sacred objects and places evoke powerful emotions, sometimes causing people to weep or feel choked up when viewing them. In addition to sacred people, objects, and places, we may identify certain times and events, religious holidays, weddings, births, deaths, and grace before meals as sacred. Sacred entities involve some mystery or myth that raises them above the ordinary.[100] The pope, for example, is viewed as being almost godlike. And legendary figures such as Jim Morrison, Elvis Presley, Marilyn Monroe, and John F. Kennedy are associated with mystery. Second, sacred entities have qualities that transcend time, place, or space. When you enter the Alamo, you may feel as if you are back in the period when the historic fighting took place.

Sacred objects also possess strong approach/avoidance characteristics and create an overwhelming feeling of power and fascination. For example, you may simultaneously desire to be close to but also watch from a distance people you view as heroes and heroines. Encountering sacred entities may evoke certain feelings, such as ecstasy or the sense of being smaller and humbler than the sacred entity. For instance, some people may feel that they have accomplished little in life in comparison with the achievements of heroes like Martin Luther King Jr. Some people feel humbled by the mass of humanity represented by the Vietnam Memorial. Moreover, sacred objects can create strong feelings of attachment, such as the need to take care of and nurture the sacred entity. Often sacred objects involve rituals that dictate how we should behave in the object's presence, such as the right and wrong way to treat the American flag.

Sacredness may be maintained by scarcity and exclusivity.[101] For example, the sacred status of special works of art derives from their uniqueness and the fact that their high price maintains their exclusivity. Entities that were once sacred can be made profane if they are not treated with due respect or if their sacred status is eliminated through commercialization. We can feel anger and disgust at the profaning of a sacred person or sacred object. In one study, some *Star Trek* fans said they were "barely" able to "stand watching the show" because of the way that the series was being commercially exploited.[102]

(**MARKETING IMPLICATIONS**)

Marketers need to be aware of the sacred meanings of people, objects, places, and events.

Creating and maintaining sacredness

Sometimes marketers create sacredness in objects or people. For example, the promoters of a famous movie star might heighten his sacred status by creating or enhancing his mystery and myth, making him exclusive, and promoting the powerful emotional effect he has on people. Marketers may also help maintain sacredness—for example, by keeping the price of sacred objects like collections, fine art, and rare jewelry very high.

Avoiding the profaning of sacred objects

Unsophisticated marketers sometimes profane sacred objects through commercialization. Some consumers believe that Elvis Presley has been profaned by commercial Elvis paraphernalia. Selling religious trinkets outside the sacred properties of certain religious sites may profane these places as well.

Product involvement in sacred activities and rituals

In some cases, marketers sell products regarded as instrumental to the continuation or conduct of sacred occasions and rituals. Marketers like Hallmark Cards profitably capitalize on sacred rituals such as Christmas celebrations by selling products (tree ornaments, ribbons, wrapping paper, cards) regarded as important parts of these events.

The Transfer of Symbolic Meaning Through Gift Giving

This chapter has shown how consumers invest products, times, activities, places, and people with symbolic meaning. Some meanings enhance the special and/or sacred status of the product, and some are instrumental in developing or maintaining the consumer's self-concept. Another important aspect of symbolic consumption involves transferring meaning from one individual to another through gifts of physical goods (such as clothing) or experiences (such as a gift card for a restaurant).[103]

The Timing of Gifts

Some gift-giving occasions are culturally determined and timed. In the United States, these include Valentine's Day, Mother's Day, and Father's Day.[104] Koreans celebrate the 100th day of a baby's life, and families in China celebrate when a baby is one month old. Koreans also give gifts to elders and family members on New Year's Day. Consumers in cultures around the world also celebrate various gift-giving holidays such as Christmas, Hanukkah, and Kwanzaa.[105]

Some gift-giving occasions are culturally prescribed but occur at a time that is specific to each individual.[106] These are often the transitions discussed earlier: anniversaries, graduations, birthdays, weddings, bridal and baby showers, retirement parties, and religious transitions such as baptism, first communion, or bar mitzvah. Still other gift-giving occasions are ad hoc, as when we give gifts as part of a reconciliation attempt, to celebrate the birth of a child, to cheer up someone who is ill, or to thank someone for helping us.

Three Stages of Gift Giving

Gestation stage The first stage of gift giving, when we consider what to give someone.

Presentation stage The second stage of gift giving, when we actually give the gift.

Reformulation stage The final stage of gift giving, when we reevaluate the relationship based on the gift-giving experience.

Gift giving consists of three stages, as shown in Exhibit 17.12. In the **gestation stage,** we consider what to give the recipient. The **presentation stage** occurs with the actual giving of the gift. Finally, in the **reformulation stage,** we reevaluate the relationship based on the gift-giving experience.

The Gestation Stage

The gestation stage before a gift is given involves the motives for and emotions surrounding giving, the nature and meaning of the gift, the value of the gift, and the amount of time spent searching for the gift.

Motives for and Emotions Surrounding Giving   During the gestation stage we develop motives for gift giving.[107] On the one hand, people may give for altruistic reasons—to help or show love for the recipient. For example, a relative may give a large cash gift to help a young couple start their married life. We may also give for agnostic reasons because we derive positive emotional pleasure from the act of giving. Or we may give a gift for instrumental reasons, expecting the recipient to give something in return, as when a student gives a teacher a small gift in hopes of a higher grade. Consumers may also give for purely obligatory reasons because they feel the situation or the relationship demands it. Indeed, sometimes we do not react positively to gifts given by others because we now feel the obligation to reciprocate.

Sometimes we give gifts because we want to reduce guilt or alleviate hard feelings. In divorce, for example, the spouse who feels responsible for the breakup tends to give the partner more than a fair share in what is called *compensatory giving*.[108] Sometimes people have antagonistic motives for gift giving. For example, if you are invited to the wedding of someone you do not like, you might give the couple something you think is not very beautiful. Sometimes givers feel anxiety about giving a gift.[109] They may feel that the gift has to be absolutely perfect or worry if they lack the time or money to find a suitable gift.

The Appropriateness and Meaning of the Gift   The appropriateness of the gift depends on the situation and the relationship between the gift giver and the recipient. For example, a worker would not give a boss a gift of lingerie because such items are too personal. Likewise, you would not give good friends a token wedding gift because the relationship dictates something more substantial. Although token gifts may not be appropriate on a clearly defined gift-giving occasion, they can be highly significant when no gift is expected. Spontaneously giving a gift, even something small, can signify love and caring.[110]

Exhibit 17.12

A Model of the Gift-Giving Process

The process of gift giving can be described in terms of three stages: (1) the *gestation stage,* at which we think about and buy the gift; (2) the *presentation stage,* at which we actually give the gift; and (3) the *reformulation stage,* at which we reevaluate our relationship based on the nature of the gift-giving experience. At each stage we can identify several issues that affect the gift-giving process.

Gestation Stage
- Motives
- Nature of the gift
- Value of the gift
- Search time

Presentation Stage
- Ceremony
- Timing and surprise elements
- Attention to the recipient
- Recipient's reaction

Reformulation Stage
- Relationship bonding
- Reciprocation

Thus, you may feel quite touched when your significant other buys you "a little something." Token gifts are quite important for recipients with whom we do not have strong ties. It is appropriate and desirable to send holiday and birthday cards to people we see infrequently.[111]

The gift may also symbolize a particular meaning to the receiver.[112] For example, gifts can represent values we regard as appropriate for the recipient, such as domesticity for new brides and grooms or a new set of expectations. An engagement ring symbolizes expectations regarding commitment and future fidelity, just as giving golf clubs at retirement symbolizes expectations regarding future leisure. Gifts can also be symbolic of the self, as when giving a piece of art or something that the giver has created.

The Value of the Gift The value of the gift is an important element of the gift-selection process. You might splurge on a Mother's Day gift because you want your mother to know how much you love her. The consumer's culture can influence decisions about the value of a gift. In Japan, for example, people lose face if the gift they receive exceeds the value of the gift they have given.[113] Interestingly, consumers perceive that gifts they buy for others are more valuable, in economic terms, than gifts received from others. When giver and receiver had close connections, however, the receiver perceived higher economic value in the gift.[114]

The Amount of Time Spent Searching The amount of time spent searching for a gift symbolizes the nature and intensity of the giver's relationship with the recipient. Men and women differ in how much time and effort they invest in the search for a gift. Women are reportedly more involved in holiday gift shopping than are men.[115] Women also appear to spend more time searching for the perfect gift, whereas men are more likely to settle for something that "will do."[116]

The Presentation Stage

The presentation stage describes the actual exchange of the gift. Here, the ritual or ceremonial aspects of the giving process become very important.[117]

Ceremony During the presentation stage, the giver decides whether to wrap the gift and, if so, how. Wrapping the present nicely in appropriate paper helps to decommodify, or make more personal, a mass-produced product.[118] However, the importance of the gift packaging depends on the formality and spontaneity of the occasion. For example, unanticipated gifts, such as a boss's surprise gift to an assistant or a wife's surprise gift to her husband, may be less formally wrapped and may even be appropriate if left unwrapped.

Timing and Surprise Both the timing and the possibility of surprise may be important in gift giving. For example, although we know that gift giving is part of the Christmas ritual and that the wrapped gifts are even prominently displayed under the tree—sometimes for days before the actual exchange—being surprised by what they contain is often a key element. The excitement of unwrapping an item is heightened by having the recipient guess what the package contains. Although surprise is a valued part of the ritual, it is not always achieved. One study found that right before Christmas, some husbands purchase items that have been chosen in advance by their wives. Here, the gift giving is an orchestrated event with the husband playing the role of "purchasing agent."[119]

Attention to the Recipient Paying attention to the recipient can be a critical dimension in the presentation stage. For example, attendees at wedding showers are expected to watch closely as the bride-to-be opens her gifts.

Recipient's Reaction Another aspect is the reaction that the giver hopes to elicit from the recipient, the recipient's actual reaction, and the giver's response to the recipient's reaction. If you spent a lot of time and effort looking for the perfect gift and then the recipient opens the package quickly and goes on to the next gift without a word, you will probably feel hurt. As noted earlier, you may also feel anxious at the presentation stage if you are not sure about whether the recipient will like your gift.[120]

The Reformulation Stage

The reformulation stage marks the third and final stage of the gift-giving process. At this stage, the giver and the recipient reevaluate their relationship based on the gift-giving process.

Relationship Bonding A gift may affect the relationship between giver and recipient in different ways, as shown in Exhibit 17.13. A gift can either maintain, strengthen, or weaken the relationship between the giver and receiver. One study found that gifts could strengthen a relationship by communicating feelings of connection, bonding, and commitment. Gifts can also affirm the relationship, validating existing feelings of commitment. Research suggests that a romantic relationship is likely to last longer when one member gives the other a gift to publicly announce their relationship. On the negative side, inappropriate gifts or those showing limited search effort or interest in the recipient's desires can weaken a relationship, creating the perception that the relationship lacks bonding and connection.[121]

Reciprocation The reformulation stage also has implications for how and whether the recipient will reciprocate on the next gift-giving occasion. If you gave someone a nice gift on one occasion, you would generally expect the recipient to reciprocate on the next occasion. If, on the other hand, you gave a gift that weakened the tie between you and the recipient, the latter may not give you a very nice gift or may give no gift at all on the next gift-giving occasion.

Some kinds of gift-giving situations or recipients are exempt from reciprocation.[122] For example, if you give someone a gift because she is ill or has experienced some tragedy (say, her house burned down), you will not expect her to reciprocate. However, if someone unexpectedly gives you a Christmas gift, you will usually feel guilty and want to rush out and buy him a gift, too. People of limited financial means (children, students) or of lower status (a secretary as opposed to a boss) may be regarded as exempt from giving to higher status people. Thus, it is appropriate for parents to give their children gifts and expect nothing in return. Women have also been reported to feel less obligated to reciprocate in date-related gift giving, perhaps because of culturally prescribed notions regarding men's generally higher economic power.[123] Note that expectations of reciprocation depend on the culture and the relationship between the giver and the recipient. In China and Hong Kong, for instance, where gifts are commonly exchanged during certain festivals and other important occasions, reciprocity is discouraged among family members and close friends because there is no need to build ties through gift giving.[124]

Exhibit 17.13

Possible Effect of Gift Giving on the Relationship

Gifts can have many different effects on a relationship—effects that range from strengthening to severing the relationship.

Relational Effect	Description	Experiential Themes
Strengthening	Gift receipt improves the quality of the relationship between giver and recipient. Feelings of connection, bonding, commitment, and/or shared meaning are intensified.	Epiphany
Affirmation	Gift receipt validates the positive quality of the relationship between giver and recipient. Existing feelings of connection and/or shared meaning are validated.	Empathy Adherence Affirming farewell Recognition
Negligible effect	The gift-receipt experience has a minimal effect on perceptions of relationship quality.	Superfluity "Error" Charity Overkill
Negative confirmation	Gift receipt validates an existing negative quality of the relationship between giver and recipient. A lack of feelings of connection, bonding, and/or shared meaning is validated.	Absentee Control
Weakening	Gift receipt harms the quality of the relationship between giver and recipient. There is a newly evident or intensified perception that the relationship lacks connection, bonding, and/or shared meaning, but the relationship remains.	Burden Insult
Severing	Gift receipt so harms the quality of the relationship between giver and recipient that the relationship is dissolved.	Threat Nonaffirming farewell

Source: Julie A. Ruth, Cele C. Otnes, and Frédéric F. Brunel, "Gift Receipt and the Reformulation of Interpersonal Relationships," *Journal of Consumer Research* 25, March 1999, p. 389. Reprinted by permission of The University of Chicago Press.

MARKETING IMPLICATIONS

Firms can build on several aspects of gift giving to market more effectively to consumers.

Promoting products and services as gifts

Many marketers promote their products for gift-giving occasions, and often gift-giving occasions are the primary focus of their business. Consider the greeting card industry, which gets its biggest U.S. sales boost from the Christmas/Hanukkah/ Kwanzaa season, when more than 2.2 billion cards are bought and sent.[125] In some cases uncommon gifts are promoted as appropriate for various gift-giving occasions. For example, products from blenders and lingerie to stock certificates and power tools are touted as appropriate Mother's Day gifts. Mortgage companies now offer bridal registries to which gift givers can contribute money to the couple's down payment or mortgage. Some retail outlets are known exclusively as "gift stores". Here the services that the store provides to enhance the presentation of the gift and the salespeople's abilities to point out gifts with special meanings may be important.

Technology and gift shopping

Technology has created major changes in the gift-giving process. Online shopping is faster and more convenient than ever, and many retail sites invite consumers to post "wish lists" showing the gifts that they would like to receive for holidays, weddings, and other occasions. Another major change affecting consumers and retailers is the growing use of gift cards, which have become a $26 billion business.[126] Knowing that consumers who receive gift cards for Christmas often go shopping right after the holiday, retailers are stocking new, full-priced products as well as discounting seasonal merchandise for post-holiday shoppers. This strategy improves businesses' profit margins because recipients tend to spend more freely when they have a gift card.[127]

Alternatives to traditional gifts

Knowing that consumers are tiring of the commercialism, hassle, and materialism surrounding gift-giving occasions like Christmas, some charities are asking consumers to instead give gifts to people in need. For example, the nonprofit Heifer International's holiday catalog invites consumers to purchase "gift" animals such as geese or bees to help families around the world become self-sufficient. For similar reasons, travel is being touted as a holiday gift. More two-income families have less time, more money, and more distance separating them from loved ones, creating a trend toward traveling and holding family reunions at posh resorts around the world.[128]

Summary

Some offerings have symbolic meaning. Consumers use some products as conscious or unconscious badges that designate the various social categories to which they belong. Products and rituals hold symbolic significance when people undergo role transitions; serve as symbols of connection to meaningful people, places, and times; and are symbols of individuality and uniqueness. The symbolic uses of products and rituals affect the consumer's self-concept.

Consumers regard some possessions and brands as very special, nonsubstitutable, and irreplaceable. These items may be purchased with little regard for price and are rarely discarded, even if their functional value is gone; they may not even be used for their original purpose. We personify these possessions, may feel powerful emotions in their presence, and feel fear or sadness over their potential or actual loss. In part, possessions are special because they serve as emblems, facilitate role transitions, connect us to others, or express our unique styles. They are special because they indicate personal mastery and achievements or are mood enhancing. Background characteristics such as social class, gender, and age all influence the type of object someone regards as special.

Some entities (possessions, people, places, objects, times, and events) are so special that they are regarded as sacred. Sacred objects transcend time and space and have strong approach/avoidance powers and great fascination. Consumers care for and nurture these possessions and often devise special rituals to handle them. However, sacred objects can be profaned or made ordinary by commercialization, inappropriate usage, or divestment patterns.

Gift giving is a process of transferring meaning in products from one person to another in three phases: gestation, presentation, and reformulation. Such occasions are often culturally prescribed but may vary in the timing. The manner in which the first two phases of gift giving are enacted can affect the long-term viability of the relationship between giver and recipient.

Questions for Review and Discussion

1. Contrast the emblematic function of a product with the role acquisition function; also contrast the connectedness function of a product with the expressive function.

2. What is reflexive evaluation, and how does it affect role acquisition?

3. How does the ideal identity schema relate to a person's actual identity schemas?

4. What are the three main reasons why possessions take on special meaning?

5. Why do consumers engage in possession, grooming, and divestment rituals?

6. What are sacred entities, and how are they profaned?

7. Identify the three stages of gift giving, and explain how gift giving can affect relations between the giver and the recipient.

CL Visit http://cengage.com/marketing/hoyer/ ConsumerBehavior5e to find resources that are available to help you study for the course.

CONSUMER BEHAVIOR CASE

Buying that Special Something Online

Auctioning pieces of the original Hollywood sign from 1923, McDonald's Happy Meals toys from 1979, Hawaiian postcards from 1897, and gum chewed by Britney Spears in 2004, eBay is the world's largest marketplace for collectibles. The site facilitates the purchase of $60 billion worth of goods and services every year, from everyday objects to special somethings that draw hundreds of people eager to make the winning bid; rare Happy Meal toys sell for about $200; the 1897 postcard (one of 160,000 postcards listed on any given day) went for $1,085; and Britney's gum was purchased for more than $15,000.

What makes these items so special? Happy Meals collectibles may tap into adults' nostalgia for childhood visits to McDonald's. Postcards offer an opportunity to own a tiny piece of the past or a memento of a place that has personal meaning, such as the consumer's hometown or honeymoon destination. And possessing gum chewed by Britney gives the purchaser a small but direct connection to a well-known celebrity.

According to eBay's research, consumers who unintentionally build a collection do so, in part, because they get pleasure from using these special items in daily life. Consumers who consider themselves collectors tend to buy more frequently and spend more money to expand their collections than others do. Some seek out specific items that have meaning because of family traditions, whereas others acquire items that represent their interests or aspirations. Even occasional collectors mob the eBay site when particular items are up for bid, as when 60,000 people visited during a weeklong auction of Walt Disney memorabilia to benefit a children's charity. For

$37,500, one consumer won the right to have his name and a funny saying etched on a mock tombstone featured in Disneyland's Haunted Mansion attraction. A Disney spokesperson observed that the company has been part of the childhood experience for many people and "here was a chance to be part of that on a very big scale."

Other online auction events are also satisfying consumers' cravings for acquiring that special something. When the St. Louis Cardinals tore down the old Busch Stadium, the team auctioned off the seats, pieces of the walls, dugout equipment, telephones, bathroom fixtures, pennants, players' lockers, and even the manager's clubhouse desk. After right fielder Larry Walker autographed his locker plus a trash can, a telephone, and several other items, the lot sold for $11,553. In all, more than 17,000 fans bid on more than 50,000 pieces of the old stadium. "People want this stuff. It's not about stuff being fancy or good-looking. It means something to people," says a team official.

Price is not always the primary concern. Consumers who yearn for a piece of history or a seat from a favorite stadium may be willing to pay whatever they must to acquire that special something. Bidders sometimes get so caught up in the excitement that they pay more than they expected to spend. Of course, auction websites like eBay frequently offer consumers the option of paying a fixed price to buy something immediately, a means of avoiding the delay and uncertainty of participating in an auction. For auction enthusiasts, however, the process of buying from an online auction adds to the fun and the suspense—and gives the successful bidder a special story to tell about acquiring that special something. [129]

Case Questions

1. Would a consumer who buys a Busch stadium seat tend to find cultural meaning or emblematic meaning in it? Why?

2. Is it likely to be the symbolic value, mood-altering properties, or utilitarian value that would cause a consumer to bid high to have his name in Disneyland's Haunted Mansion?

3. Under what circumstances might someone giving a gift of a used item bought on eBay be happy to tell the recipient about the price paid?

Ethics, Social Responsibility, and the Dark Side of Consumer Behavior and Marketing

LEARNING OBJECTIVES

After studying this chapter, you will be able to

1. Contrast addictive, compulsive, and impulsive buying, and discuss their implications for marketers.

2. Explain why marketers need to understand the deviant behaviors of consumer theft, black markets, and underage drinking and smoking.

3. Discuss some important ethical questions facing marketers and what companies are doing in response to these issues.

4. Describe what consumer behaviors related to environmental consciousness and conservation mean for marketers today.

INTRODUCTION

Kids' Food Advertising Goes on a Diet

In the United States, Canada, and Europe, more marketers are putting children's food advertising on a diet. Burger King, Cadbury Adams, Campbell, Chuck E. Cheese, Coca-Cola, General Mills, Hershey, Kellogg, Kraft, Mars, McDonald's, Nestlé, Pepsi, and Unilever are among the growing number of companies that have agreed to restrict what and how they advertise to children. Concerned about rising levels of childhood obesity, groups like the Center for Science in the Public Interest, the Campaign for a Commercial-Free Childhood, and the Children's Food Campaign have been pressuring food marketers to change the ways that they target and communicate with children under 12 years old.

In response, food marketers have introduced lower fat, less sugary children's foods and have changed their message and media strategies. For instance, General Mills is only using spokescharacters that appeal to children on healthy snacks and is launching a SpongeBob SquarePants line of frozen vegetables for children. Kellogg has stopped targeting children with print, broadcast, and online advertising for brands that do not meet nutritional criteria for low fat and limited sugar content. Many food marketers are putting half or more of their children's advertising budgets toward promoting healthier eating choices and active life-styles for the under-12 audience. To ensure that kids' food advertising stays on a diet, the

5. Show how consumers can resist marketing practices, both individually and in groups.

Better Business Bureau's Children's Food and Beverage Advertising Initiative will monitor marketers' progress.[1]

As this example indicates, consumers and consumer groups sometimes question the use of certain marketing practices and try to force change. Ethical issues such as whether advertising contributes to obesity represent part of the "dark side" of *marketing*. Other issues discussed in this chapter represent the dark side of *consumer behavior*: deviant consumer behaviors that stem from uncontrollable sources (compulsive buying, compulsive gambling, and smoking and alcohol addictions) as well as behaviors that are deviant because they are illegal (consumer theft, underage drinking and smoking, and black market transactions). The chapter also explores environmentally conscious behavior and conservation behavior, key issues in social responsibility. Finally, the chapter describes ways that consumers can, individually and in groups, resist marketing efforts or pressure marketers to take certain steps. Exhibit 18.1 summarizes these issues.

Deviant Consumer Behavior

Much of this book has focused on the behavior of the average consumer in an everyday consumption context. However, sometimes consumer behavior is regarded as deviant if it is either unexpected or not sanctioned by members of the society. Such behavior may be problematic to the consumer and/or to society. As Exhibit 18.2 indicates, some forms of deviant consumer behavior occur during the *acquisition* of the product, and some forms occur during product *consumption*. Deviant consumer behavior includes addictive, compulsive, and impulsive behavior; consumer theft; use of black markets; and underage drinking and smoking.

Addictive, Compulsive, and Impulsive Behavior

It is important make a distinction between addictive behavior (taking action as a result of a physiological dependency), compulsive behavior (an inability to stop doing something), and impulsive behavior (nonthoughtful action—acting on impulse). Consumers can exhibit any of these behaviors with respect to acquisition or consumption, with problematic outcomes if consumers do not make an effort to exert self-control.[2] The next sections examine each of these types of behavior.

Addictive Behavior

Addiction Excessive behavior typically brought on by a chemical dependency.

Addiction reflects excessive behaviors typically brought on by a chemical dependency. Addicted consumers feel a great attachment to and dependence on a product or activity and believe that they must use it to function.[3] Individuals can become addicted to many goods and services, including cigarettes, drugs, alcohol, Internet use, and video games. In many cases, an addiction involves repeated use of a product, even if consumption is dangerous. Although addicted individuals may want to stop, they believe doing so is beyond their control ("I can't help myself"). Often individuals feel shame and guilt about their addiction and try to hide it. Some addicted consumers find strength in programs like Alcoholics Anonymous and Smoke Enders.

Addictive behaviors can be harmful to addicts and to those around them. For example, cigarette smoking is the number one preventable cause of death in the

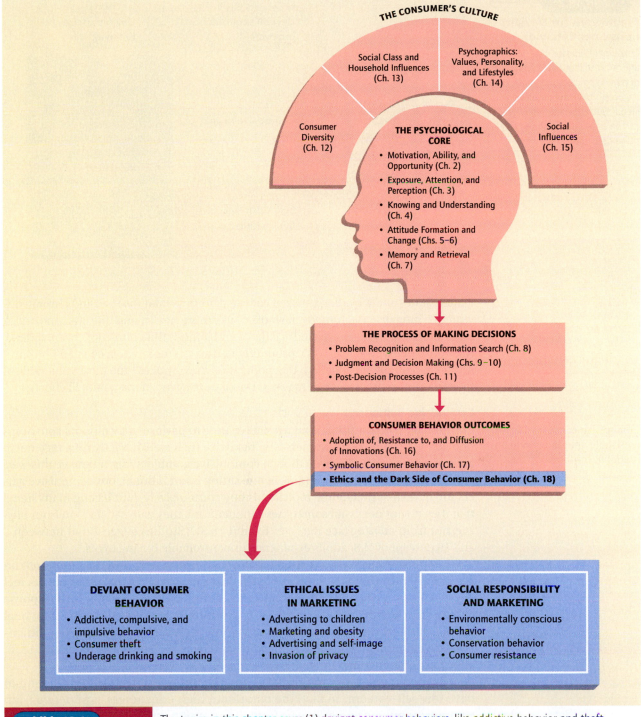

THE CONSUMER'S CULTURE

Social Class and Household Influences (Ch. 13)

Psychographics: Values, Personality, and Lifestyles (Ch. 14)

Consumer Diversity (Ch. 12)

Social Influences (Ch. 15)

THE PSYCHOLOGICAL CORE
- Motivation, Ability, and Opportunity (Ch. 2)
- Exposure, Attention, and Perception (Ch. 3)
- Knowing and Understanding (Ch. 4)
- Attitude Formation and Change (Chs. 5–6)
- Memory and Retrieval (Ch. 7)

THE PROCESS OF MAKING DECISIONS
- Problem Recognition and Information Search (Ch. 8)
- Judgment and Decision Making (Chs. 9–10)
- Post-Decision Processes (Ch. 11)

CONSUMER BEHAVIOR OUTCOMES
- Adoption of, Resistance to, and Diffusion of Innovations (Ch. 16)
- Symbolic Consumer Behavior (Ch. 17)
- **Ethics and the Dark Side of Consumer Behavior (Ch. 18)**

DEVIANT CONSUMER BEHAVIOR
- Addictive, compulsive, and impulsive behavior
- Consumer theft
- Underage drinking and smoking

ETHICAL ISSUES IN MARKETING
- Advertising to children
- Marketing and obesity
- Advertising and self-image
- Invasion of privacy

SOCIAL RESPONSIBILITY AND MARKETING
- Environmentally conscious behavior
- Conservation behavior
- Consumer resistance

Exhibit 18.1

Chapter Overview: Ethics, Social Responsibility, and the Dark Side of Consumer Behavior and Marketing

The topics in this chapter cover (1) deviant consumer behaviors, like addictive behavior and theft, (2) ethical issues like advertising to children, and (3) marketing and social responsibility, such as environmentally conscious behavior.

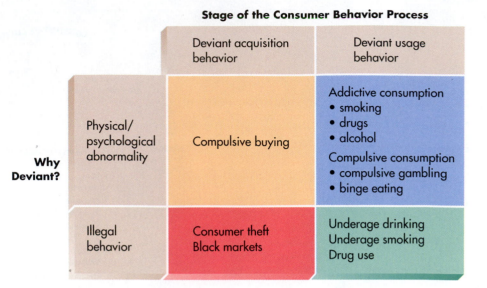

Exhibit 18.2

Framework for Deviant Consumer Behavior

Consumer behavior may be deviant because it involves a physical or psychological abnormality or involves a behavior regarded as illegal. Such deviant behaviors can be associated with the acquisition or usage of offerings.

United States and a leading cause of cancer, cardiovascular disease, and chronic obstructive lung disease. Moreover, smokers use more health benefits, take more sick leave, and have more job-related accidents and injuries than nonsmokers do. Indeed, the annual cost of lower work productivity due to smoking exceeds $90 billion.[4] Although only 20 percent of the U.S. population now smokes,[5] the most vulnerable of those who currently smoke or may soon smoke are aware of the habit's ill effects.

Compulsive Behavior

Compulsive consumption An irresistible urge to perform an irrational consumption act.

Compulsive consumption is an irresistible urge to perform an irrational consumption act. For example, consumers who bet twice their weekly salary on a race horse are not acting rationally, even though compulsive gamblers might behave this way. Similarly, eating two dozen donuts in one sitting is not rational, but compulsive eaters might do just that. Some individuals buy compulsively, purchasing many items that they do not need and sometimes cannot afford; they gain satisfaction from *buying,* not from *owning* (see part a of Exhibit 18.3).[6] Studies suggest that between 2 and 16 percent of U.S. adults experience uncontrollable buying urges.[7]

Compulsive buying has a strong emotional component, and the emotions run the gamut from the most negative to the most positive.[8] Compulsive buyers feel anxious on days when they do not buy; thus, compulsive buying may be a response to tension or anxiety. While in the store, compulsive buyers may feel great emotional arousal at the stimulation evoked by the store's atmosphere. Buying brings an immediate emotional high and a feeling of loss of control (see part b of Exhibit 18.3). This reaction is followed by feelings of remorse, guilt, shame, and depression.

Why do people buy compulsively? For one thing, compulsive buyers tend to have low self-esteem. In fact, the emotional high consumers experience from compulsive buying comes in part from the attention and social approval they get when they buy. The salesperson can provide considerable satisfaction—being a doting helper, telling consumers how attractive they look in a particular outfit. Consumers can also feel that they are pleasing the salesperson and the company by making purchases. This attention and the feeling of pleasing others may temporarily raise compulsive buyers' self-esteem and reinforce buying behavior (see part c of Exhibit 18.3).

Quotes from Compulsive Buyers

Compulsive buying can be an emotionally involving experience. Consumers may engage in compulsive buying to feel a thrill, gain attention, or feel that they are pleasing someone else. But this emotional high may be followed by serious financial and negative emotional consequences.

Emotional Aspects of Compulsive Buying

a. "I couldn't tell you what I bought or where I bought it. It was like I was on automatic."

"I really think it's the spending. It's not that I want it, because sometimes I'll just buy it and I'll think, Ugh, another sweatshirt."

b. "But it was like, it was almost like my heart was palpitating. I couldn't wait to get in to see what was there. It was such a sensation. In the store, the lights, the people; they were playing Christmas music. I was hyperventilating and my hands were starting to sweat, and all of a sudden I was touching sweaters and the whole feel of it was just beckoning to me. And if they had a SALE sign up, forget it; I was gone. You never know when you're going to need it. I bought ten shirts one time for $10.00 each."

"It's almost like you're drunk. You're so intoxicated; . . . I got this great high. It was like you couldn't have given me more of a rush."

Factors Influencing Compulsive Buying

c. "The attention I got there was incredible. She waited on me very nicely, making sure it would fit and if it didn't, they would do this and that. And I guess I enjoyed being on the other end of that. I had no idea how I was going to pay for it. I never do."

"I never bought one of anything. I always buy at least two. I still do. I can never even go into the Jewel and buy one quart of milk. I've always got to buy two . . . It's an act of pleasing. I had been brought up to please everybody and everyone around me because that was the way you got anything was to please. So I thought I was pleasing the store."

Financial and Emotional Consequences of Compulsive Buying

d. "I would always have to borrow between paychecks. I could not make it between paychecks. Payday comes and I'd pay all my bills, but then I'd piss the rest away, and I'd need to borrow money to eat, and I would cry and cry and cry, and everyone would say, 'Well just make a budget.' Get serious. That's like telling an alcoholic not to go to the liquor store. It's not that simple."

e. "My husband said he couldn't deal with this, and he said, 'I'm leaving you. We'll get a divorce. That's it. It's your problem. You did it. You fix it up.'"

"I didn't have one person in the world I could talk to. I don't drink. I don't smoke. I don't do dope. But I can't stop. I can't control it. I said I can't go on like this . . . My husband hates me. My kids hate me. I've destroyed everything. I was ashamed and just wanted to die."

Source: Thomas O'Guinn and Ronald Faber, "Compulsive Buying: A Phenomenological Perspective," *Journal of Consumer Research,* September 1989, pp. 147–157. © 1989 University of Chicago. All rights reserved.

A personality trait called *fantasy orientation* has been linked with compulsive buying. Buying makes compulsive buyers feel more important than they actually are. In addition, compulsive buyers tend to be somewhat alienated from society. Because consumers may feel as though they are friends with a salesperson who has sold them items on repeated occasions, they may feel less alienated than they otherwise would. Family factors can play a role as well: Compulsive buyers are more likely to come from families whose members show compulsive or addictive behaviors, including eating disorders like binge eating.

The financial, emotional, and interpersonal consequences of compulsive buying can be devastating. These consumers rely extensively on credit cards, have high credit card debt, and tend to pay only the minimum monthly balance. They are also more likely to write checks for purchases, even though they know they cannot afford them. And compulsive buyers are more likely to borrow money from others to make it from paycheck to paycheck (see part d of Exhibit 18.3).[9] Finally, as part e of Exhibit 18.3 indicates, children, spouses, and friends can all be hurt by the spending habits of compulsive buyers.

1. Please indicate how much you agree or disagree with the statement below. Place an X on the line that best indicates how you feel.

	Strongly agree (1)	Somewhat agree (2)	Neither agree nor disagree (3)	Somewhat disagree (4)	Strongly disagree (5)
a. If I have any money left at the end of the pay period, I just have to spend it.	_____	_____	_____	_____	_____

2. Please indicate how often you have done each of the following things by placing an X on the appropriate line.

	Very often (1)	Often (2)	Sometimes (3)	Rarely (4)	Never (5)
a. Felt like others would be horrified if they knew of my spending habits	_____	_____	_____	_____	_____
b. Bought things even though I couldn't afford them	_____	_____	_____	_____	_____
c. Wrote a check when I knew I didn't have enough money in the bank to cover it	_____	_____	_____	_____	_____
d. Bought myself something in order to make myself feel better	_____	_____	_____	_____	_____
e. Felt anxious or nervous on days I didn't go shopping	_____	_____	_____	_____	_____
f. Made only the minimum payments on my credit cards	_____	_____	_____	_____	_____

Scoring equation = $-9.69 + (Q1a \times .33) + (Q2a \times .34) + (Q2b \times .50) + (Q2c \times .47) + (Q2d \times .33) + (Q2e \times .38) + (Q2f \times .31)$.
If scoring is ≤ -1.34, subject is classified as a compulsive buyer.

Exhibit 18.4

A Clinical Screening Test for Compulsive Buying

Do you have compulsive buying tendencies? Take this screening test to find out.

A clinical screening test that incorporates many of these elements is shown in Exhibit 18.4.[10]

Another issue relevant to compulsive consumption is compulsive gambling, an affliction affecting an estimated 6 to 9 million Americans. In one study, 85 percent of respondents aged 18 to 24 said that they had gambled, and 5 percent admitted having gambling problems.[11] Nearly one-third of high school students say that they gamble regularly.[12] These consumers are more likely to come from families in which other members have exhibited addictive behavior and they are more likely to be generally impulsive, and to view materialism as a measure of success.[13] Scientists have established a strong link between compulsive gambling and consumption of alcohol, tobacco, and illicit drugs.[14]

Typically, compulsive gambling behavior evolves over a series of stages. Sometimes, but not always, the consumer first experiences the pleasure of a "big win."[15] Next, gambling becomes more reckless, losses pile up, and gambling becomes a central force in the individual's life. The compulsive gambler promises to stop gambling, but cannot. Faced with rising debt and compulsive gambling urges, many gamblers engage in crimes like embezzlement. The final stage occurs when the gambler realizes that he or she has hit rock bottom.

Impulsive Behavior

Two specific types of impulsive behavior related to acquisition and consumption are impulsive buying and impulsive eating. An **impulse** is a sudden urge to act, as would

Impulse A sudden urge to act.

happen when you find yourself doing something based on an emotional whim rather than on a reasoned, nonemotional analysis.[16] Some consumers seem to have impulsive personalities, buying impulsively on a consistent basis.[17] However, other consumers may behave quite rationally in most situations but behave impulsively in situations that make the action (e.g., buying/eating) easy to do or extremely attractive. You might buy a magazine impulsively or order a cupcake from a café just because it is in front of you and looks good[18] or because you see someone else doing so.[19] Interestingly, buying one thing on impulse may make you more likely to buy a second item impulsively, perhaps because the initial purchase creates an impulse-buying mind set.[20]

Impulsive behavior is also affected by the consumer's prevention or promotion focus. Impulsive eaters who are exposed to foods with hedonic appeal, such as chocolate cookies, may develop a promotion focus on the spot. Doing this can cause impulsive eaters to put more emphasis on the positives of consumption (such as enjoying the taste) than on the potential risks (such as gaining weight) when they make their decision to have the treat.[21]

MARKETING IMPLICATIONS

Do marketing activities encourage addictive, compulsive, and impulsive behaviors?

Some might argue that marketing activities encourage such behaviors. For example, cigarettes are heavily promoted in the United States, and the nicotine in cigarettes is addictive. Public policy makers clearly view marketers as perpetuating this form of addictive consumption. Some countries have banned cigarette advertising and require warning labels on cigarette packages, actions that affect marketing practices.

Industry and marketing practices may also perpetuate behaviors like compulsive gambling.[22] Gambling is a fast-growing $900 billion industry, legal in many states and prevalent on many Indian reservations.[23] Seeing the potential for higher revenue, some states spend millions of dollars advertising their lottery programs (see Exhibit 18.5). Singapore recently lifted a ban on casinos to boost tourism and job growth.[24] Online gambling has grown into a $12 billion industry—even though U.S. citizens cannot legally bet in online casinos.[25] And, although research on this issue is scarce, it seems quite likely that enticing sales, attractive displays, doting salespeople, and easily available credit foster compulsive buying.

Marketing activities that deal with addictive and compulsive consumption

Some marketing activities aim to reduce addictive and compulsive consumption. For example, some states and casinos have established hotlines to help compulsive gamblers. Many casinos post signs and distribute flyers mentioning sources of help for gambling problems. Still, some people are

Exhibit 18.5

Forms of Gambling

Casinos and lotteries represent common forms of gambling.

concerned that growth in the gambling industry will be followed by increases in the number of consumers who become compulsive gamblers and/or an increase in gambling opportunities for those already hooked.

Marketing activities that stimulate impulsive behavior

Marketers may also be accused of encouraging consumers to buy or consume impulsively. Indeed, in grocery stores, some goods like candy and magazines are called "impulse items" and are placed right at the cash register so that consumers do not even have to search for them. Other marketing activities may make the product or the environment that it is in so enticing that consumers focus too strongly on how much they want the product rather than on whether they need it. ●▬▬

Consumer Theft

Whereas compulsive buying reflects an uncontrollable desire to *purchase* things, consumer theft reflects a desire to *steal* things.

Prevalence of Consumer Theft

For U.S. retailers, shoplifting is pervasive and significant, with yearly merchandise losses topping $41.6 billion.[26] The average U.S. shoplifting theft involves $855 worth of merchandise (in the United Kingdom, the figure is $312).[27] Consumer theft is a problem for nonretailers as well as for retailers.[28] Automobile insurance fraud; hotel theft; credit card fraud; theft of cable TV services; piracy of music, movies, and software; coupon fraud; fraudulent returns; and switching or altering price tags are just some of the forms of consumer theft with which companies must contend.[29] Of particular concern for many consumers today is theft of their identity (see Exhibit 18.6).[30] Complaints about online auction fraud, in which consumers steal from other consumers, outnumber all other reports of online crimes.[31]

Factors Affecting Consumer Theft

Although you may think that consumer theft is driven by economic need, few demographic variables are associated with theft. Some *forms* of consumer theft are associated with certain demographic groups: shoplifting is most common among teens, and credit card fraud is usually associated with better educated consumers. However, consumers from all walks of life have engaged in theft at one time. For example, roughly two-thirds of the public admit to having shoplifted, and 15 percent admit to concealing income to avoid taxation.[32]

As shown in Exhibit 18.7, two psychological factors seem to explain theft: (1) the temptation to steal and (2) the ability to rationalize theft behavior. As the exhibit indicates, these factors are, in turn, affected by aspects of the product, the purchase environment, and the consumer.

Exhibit 18.6

Identity Theft

Some new product offerings are designed to prevent identity theft.

NOT YOUR PURCHASE? NOT YOUR PROBLEM.

CHASE FRAUD PROTECTION

With **Zero Liability Protection**, you're not held accountable for any fraudulent purchases on your Chase credit card. Learn more at chase.com/matters.

PROTECTION MATTERS CHASE WHAT MATTERS

CHASE ◆

4417 1234 5678 9112

D. BARRETT

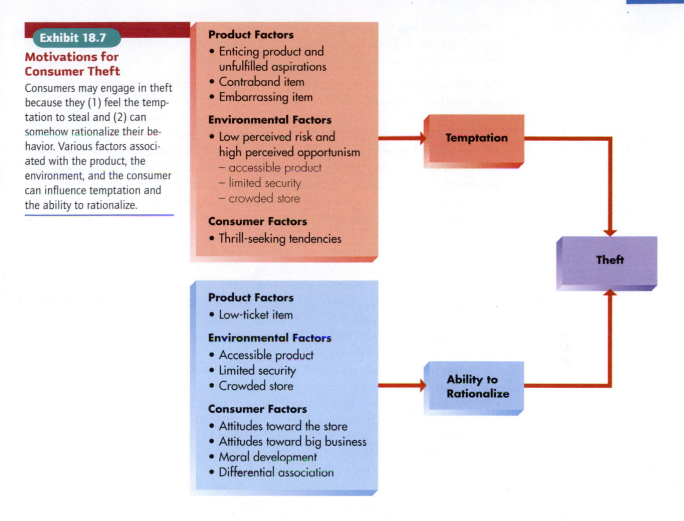

Motivations for Consumer Theft

Consumers may engage in theft because they (1) feel the temptation to steal and (2) can somehow rationalize their behavior. Various factors associated with the product, the environment, and the consumer can influence temptation and the ability to rationalize.

Temptation to Steal The *temptation* to steal arises when consumers want products that they cannot legitimately buy. Some of these desires are driven by real needs, such as the mother who steals baby formula to feed her child. Others reflect greed, as in the case of upper-class consumers who steal money or high-ticket items like jewelry. Some researchers suggest that marketers are involved by perpetuating materialistic tendencies and creating insatiable desires for new goods and services.[33] Consumers may also be tempted to steal items that they are too embarrassed to buy through conventional channels (e.g., condoms) or that they cannot legally buy (e.g., an underage consumer stealing alcohol).[34]

Exhibit 18.7 shows that environmental factors also affect the temptation to steal. Temptation is greater when consumers think that they can get away with stealing and that it is worth doing. Thus, consumers may assess the perceived risks associated with stealing and getting caught and may consider the benefits of having a product or using a service that they did not pay for.[35] Many factors in the environment affect the perceived risks of shoplifting.[36] Stores may be noisy or crowded, have little or no security, have lax return policies, have few salespeople, contain hidden nooks and crannies, or use price tags that are easily switched—leading consumers to believe their theft will be unnoticed. Also, a tendency toward thrill-seeking has been associated with many forms of consumer theft, including price tag switching and shoplifting.[37] The perception that stolen goods can be easily sold through online auction sites may also be a factor.[38]

Rationalizations for Stealing As Exhibit 18.7 shows, consumers also steal because they can somehow *rationalize* their behavior as being either justified or driven by forces outside themselves. For example, consumers may justify stealing a low-ticket item such as a grape from a bunch at the grocery store because the item's cost seems so negligible that the word *stealing* hardly seems to apply. Some consumers may reason that a marketer "asked for it" by keeping merchandise displays open, having no security guards, or using price tags that can be readily switched. Consumers in crowded stores may become so frustrated after waiting for service that they give up and just walk out with their items, justifying their theft as compensation for the inconvenience of the long wait.[39]

Consumers are also likely to rationalize when social influences encourage theft, as in the case of someone who shoplifts on a dare.[40] Interestingly, researchers have found little evidence that dares actually play a large role in the shoplifting behavior of teenagers.[41] "Everybody does it" is another rationalization. In one study, 11 percent of the respondents agreed that it was wrong to download online music without paying and to copy software without paying—but if they believe that "everybody else does it," they may still follow suit.[42]

Consumers are also most likely to rationalize theft when stores have a negative public image. If the store is seen as unfriendly, intimidating, or somehow unfair, consumers may regard theft as a way of getting revenge against the retailer. Similarly, consumers may steal from big businesses because they think that such businesses can absorb the losses. Some consumers may steal because they feel psychologically distanced from the retailer—i.e., they believe that they are dealing with a huge, faceless business, not an individual shop owner.[43]

Consumers who have weak moral development may not regard stealing as wrong. One study found that shoplifters tend to be rule breakers in general. Some speculate that our society's overall level of moral development is changing, so fewer people view theft as wrong. Some evidence suggests that adolescents' moral restraint is weakened simply by observing their peers shoplifting. Thus, socialization can affect moral development, which in turn can affect consumer theft.[44]

MARKETING IMPLICATIONS

Theft is clearly a pervasive and expensive problem for marketers.

Increased usage of theft-reducing devices

Businesses spend billions of dollars every year trying to prevent or reduce theft through the use of antitheft devices and improved security systems (Exhibit 18.8). Some companies combine closed-circuit TVs with sophisticated computer software to track suspicious behavior. The retailer Brookstone, for instance, uses special software to determine the most theft-prone products so that it can rearrange displays and checkout procedures to minimize losses.[45]

Covering the costs of theft

Theft hurts consumers because retailers must raise prices to pay for lost merchandise and equipment, cover the cost of theft insurance, and cover the costs of high-priced security systems.[46] In addition, theft adds to research and development costs as firms

Exhibit 18.8

Theft-Reducing Devices
Devices like in-store mirrors, cameras, and anti-theft tags and clips reduce motivations to steal by letting potential thieves know that they will be caught.

Black market An illegal market in which consumers pay often exorbitant amounts for items not readily available.

experiment with newer and better security systems, a factor that also results in higher prices.

Reducing ability to serve customers

Security systems and procedures may interfere with retailers' abilities to service customers. For example, retailers may have to keep merchandise in glass display cases, locked cabinets, and so on. This added security increases consumers' search costs, making it more difficult and more time-consuming for consumers to examine products and for salespeople to service customers. ▬▬▬

Black Markets

Whereas theft represents situations in which consumers refuse to pay for available items, **black markets** represent situations in which consumers *pay* (often exorbitant amounts) for items *not* readily available. These are called "black" markets because the sellers are unauthorized, which means that the buying-selling process is usually illegal. Black markets for goods like sugar, salt, blankets, matches, and batteries fulfill functional needs; black markets for drugs, entertainment, and sexual services fulfill experiential needs; and black markets for watches and jewelry may fulfill symbolic needs.

Some items sold on the black market are legal but in short supply. For example, some consumers buy blocks of tickets to popular sporting events and concerts and sell them at much higher prices. Princeton University and other universities are cracking down on black-market sales of graduation tickets.[47] Black markets for car air bags and Cuban cigars have also been prevalent in the United States in recent years.[48] Some black markets deal with the trade of basic consumer goods, as evidenced when prisoners trade money and cigarettes for food, books, and clothing.[49]

Some goods and services that *cannot legally be sold* to consumers, such as weapons used to build bombs, are sold on black markets.[50] Black markets for drugs are also common. For example, a large global black market exists for the male potency drug Viagra—as well as a thriving trade in fake Viagra.[51] Counterfeit products such as fake Gucci shoes are also sold through black markets.[52] Consumers in states with high cigarette taxes sometimes use black-market channels to buy cigarettes smuggled in from low-tax states.[53]

(MARKETING IMPLICATIONS)

Marketers are taking a variety of actions to thwart black markets, especially buying and selling online. A lawyer at World Wrestling Entertainment, for example, scours the Internet for auctions that offer fake WWE DVDs and clothing and then takes legal action against the sellers.[54] Online pharmacies cannot stop fake or diluted versions of

Exhibit 18.9

Publicizing the Health Consequences of Smoking

Cigarette smoking at an early age can lead to serious health consequences, including impotence, lung cancer, and heart disease. Public interest groups and government organizations sometimes call attention to these negative health consequences.

Viagra and other drugs from being sold by unscrupulous sites. However, by displaying the seal of certification from the National Association of Boards of Pharmacy, CVS and other pharmacies can reassure consumers that they carry only genuine brand-name drugs.[55]

Underage Drinking and Smoking

As mentioned earlier, addictions to alcohol and tobacco represent one form of deviant consumer behavior. *Illegal use* of these products by minors is another deviant consumer behavior.[56] Half of all junior and senior high school students have consumed alcohol, with the average age of first use below 16.[57] Nearly one-third of high school students and nearly 45 percent of college students have engaged in "binge drinking" (drinking more than five drinks in one sitting). Four million children are alcoholics or problem drinkers, and excessive consumption contributes to the deaths of 4,500 underage drinkers every year.[58] One million young consumers begin smoking every year, and 90 percent of new smokers are teenagers. Nearly 12 percent of middle school students and 28 percent of high school students say they are already smoking.[59] These figures are even higher in countries where there are few bans on cigarette advertising.

Underage drinking and smoking have consequences for the individual and for society.[60] Overuse of alcohol has been implicated in campus violence, campus property damage, academic failures, teen highway fatalities, youth suicides, and campus hazing deaths. Now that colleges are liable for campus drinking incidents, alcohol is a factor in rising tuition costs because schools must cover their insurance costs. Accidents due to drinking also contribute to the high cost of automobile insurance for young consumers.

Cigarette smoking is also harmful, contributing to serious health problems such as lung cancer and heart disease. Moreover, nonsmokers can be harmed through exposure to secondhand smoke. Use of tobacco products also makes young consumers more vulnerable to the problems of addictive consumption, as previously noted. Furthermore, adolescent smokers often find it just as difficult as adults do to quit smoking.[61] As with underage drinking, public interest groups and government organizations are actively publicizing the negative health consequences associated with smoking (see Exhibit 18.9).

MARKETING IMPLICATIONS

A number of marketing issues are related to underage drinking and smoking.

Product availability

Critics say it is too easy for underage consumers to buy alcohol and tobacco since they are not always asked for proof of age when they buy these products.

Exposure to advertising

Others say that kids see too many ads for these products, ads that make the products or the people who use them look attractive.[62] Kids *are* exposed to a large amount of alcohol advertising as well as to non-TV-based tobacco advertising,[63] a situation that has led some to suggest that companies should limit kids' exposure to advertising for these products.[64] Despite the tobacco industry's agreement to avoid marketing to children, some brands continue to be advertised in adult consumer publications that teens also read. Most ads depict drinking alcohol as a positive and appropriate behavior of socially active and beautiful people. Evidence suggests that the more young consumers view alcohol ads, the more they know about these products, and the more likely they are to use them.[65]

Similarly, most youthful smokers choose the most heavily advertised brands—further implicating advertising as a cause of smoking behavior. Adolescents who have the greatest exposure to cigarette advertising in general tend to be the heaviest smokers, and the brands that do the most advertising tend to attract a greater proportion of teenagers than of adults. In particular, tobacco and alcohol ads featuring human actors or models have been found to directly produce more positive attitudes toward the ad, the brand, and the product category.[66] Exposure may be even greater as firms look for ways to get around advertising bans.[67] For example, in countries where tobacco advertising is banned, some advertisers use sponsorships and licensed goods to stay in the public eye.[68]

However, others argue that advertising for these products has little effect on children; more critical determinants are said to include peer influence, parental smoking, and self-esteem. Still, in light of tobacco's addictive qualities and the laws that forbid minors from buying cigarettes, the United States has banned cigarette commercials. Canada bans almost all cigarette advertising, not just TV advertising.

Targeting youth

A third concern is the question of whether cigarette and alcohol manufacturers target young consumers by portraying advertising images that youths find relevant.[69] Many cigarette ads evoke images such as freedom from authority—themes that appeal to young consumers. Advertising content that shows individuals engaged in risky behavior while consuming alcohol has also been criticized.

Some regulators and critics contend that tobacco advertisers target young consumers by using fictional and cartoon characters, although the companies dispute this charge.[70] Suggesting that such character advertising has limited impact on kids, one advertiser noted that children are not demanding Metropolitan Life insurance policies because they are endorsed by Snoopy.[71] The alcohol industry stresses that it does not target young consumers and says that it has invested heavily to promote responsible drinking. Anheuser-Busch alone has spent more than $100 million over the past decade promoting responsible drinking (Exhibit 18.10).[72]

Exhibit 18.10

Health Warning for Alcohol Products

Both companies and public-interest groups promote the negative consequences of drug and alcohol consumption.

Prom '07

"A Night to Remember"

IS IT REALLY FUN IF YOU DON'T REMEMBER?

Live above drugs and alcohol, live abovetheinfluence.com

Inappropriate messages in mainstream media and ads

Fourth, there is concern that mainstream advertisers and entertainment offerings may send inappropriate messages about cigarettes and alcohol. The liquor industry's self-regulatory council enforces its code of responsible practices by acting on complaints about liquor ads, especially the use of overly explicit sexual themes to sell a brand.[73] Meanwhile, tobacco marketers such as Philip Morris are asking movie studios not to feature cigarette brands or brand imagery.[74] Still, research indicates that up to one-third of the children who see smoking in movies rated G, PG, and PG-13 will start to smoke.[75]

Warning labels and ads

Cigarette and alcohol marketers are legally required to display warnings on product packaging and in ads.[76] Some states require additional warnings. Arizona requires businesses that sell alcohol to put up posters warning of the risks of drinking while pregnant. However, these warning labels and posters have not been very effective in changing young consumers' behaviors over long periods.[77] Perhaps one reason is that consumers' perceptual defenses make them tune out these messages. Even when alcohol marketers present messages such as "Don't drink and drive," consumers may react negatively because the source is a corporate sponsor.[78]

The Surgeon General has called for more explicit health warnings on labels. Manufacturers now list alcohol levels on their products so that consumers will clearly understand how strong the beverage is. Some researchers are also experimenting with attention-getting warnings. One study found that when high school students viewed an antismoking ad before a movie in which teen characters smoked, the ad helped reposition the smoking as a tainted activity.[79] Another found that underage consumers who reacted positively to antismoking ads were more likely to curtail their intentions to smoke.[80]

Ethical Issues in Marketing

Does marketing contribute to other negative social outcomes, outcomes not necessarily related to deviant acquisition or consumption? Here we examine four important ethical issues: advertising to children, questions about marketing and obesity, advertising and self-image, and privacy concerns.

Should Marketers Advertise to Children?

Advertising to children has been the subject of considerable controversy focusing on the effects these ads may have on young, impressionable consumers. A recent study found that by the age of two, 90 percent of kids are watching videos or TV on a regular basis[81]; as they get older, kids are more likely to have a TV in their bedroom, making it easy for them to watch TV ads.[82] Networks cluster children's programming in certain time periods, making it easy for marketers to target children and to spend heavily to promote toys and other products for this segment.[83]

One problem with advertising to children is that youngsters, particularly those under seven years old, are not able to distinguish between the ad and the program.[84] Even at an age at which children can recognize this difference, they may not understand that the purpose of the ad is to sell them something.[85] Thus, young children do not possess the same skepticism as adults do and are more likely to believe what

Exhibit 18.11

Should Marketers Advertise to Children?
Advertising to children has come under fire for (among other things) creating materialistic tendencies and causing kids to expect instant gratification.

they see in ads. Note, however, that children are better at understanding the informational intent ("ads tell you about things") than the persuasive intent.[86]

Also, ad messages may prey on children's strong needs for sensual satisfaction, play, and affiliation, influencing them to choose material objects over socially oriented options (Exhibit 18.11).[87] Critics argue that ads teach children to become materialistic, act impulsively, and expect immediate gratification.

Unfortunately, many parents do not watch television with their children and do not educate them about advertising. As a result, children may be particularly impressionable and subject to having their attitudes and behaviors influenced by ads. Exposure to ads often prompts children to step up requests to parents about buying products, particularly toys, leading to family conflict and disappointed children. Children are also exposed to ads for products that shape, often negatively, their impressions of what it means to be an adult.[88] Another controversy centers on the types of products advertised. Until recently, many ads directed at children promoted sugary foods such as candy and sweet cereals; critics say that these ads encourage bad eating habits. Companies are responding to such concerns in a variety of ways, as this chapter's opening example demonstrates.

Concerns have also been raised about the fact that many websites targeting children feature some form of advertising.[89] Although parents can use software to block access to some sites, children may not understand the need to avoid giving out personal data and e-mail addresses. Internet access therefore raises concerns about family privacy as well as about children's ability to differentiate between advertising and nonadvertising material on the Web.

MARKETING IMPLICATIONS

In light of issues related to ads targeting children, both the Federal Trade Commission (FTC) and the Federal Communications Commission (FCC) have recommended that television stations use a separator between the program and the ad whenever the program is directed toward younger children. They recommend including a message prior to and directly after the ads—such as "We will return after these messages" before the commercial break, followed by "We now return to [name of the program]" at the end of the break—to help children to distinguish between ads and programming.[90] The FCC also requires TV stations and cable operators to limit children's advertising to a total of 12 minutes per hour on weekdays and 10.5 minutes per hour on weekends.[91]

The FTC has also encouraged the use of public service announcements (PSAs) to teach children proper nutritional habits. This program has had limited success because the PSAs tend to be shown infrequently and because simply providing children with basic nutritional information is not sufficient to instill good eating habits. Other programs have attempted to educate children about nutrition in schools, hoping that the children will influence their parents to be more conscious of nutrition. Companies such as Red Lobster are providing schools with informational packages about nutrition (in this case, the nutrition of seafood).

The advertising industry has developed guidelines for children's advertising that are enforced by the Children's Advertising Review Unit (CARU), a wing of the Council of Better Business Bureaus; however, not all advertisers seem to adhere to these guidelines.[92] The guidelines encourage truthful and accurate advertising that recognizes children's cognitive limitations and avoids promoting unrealistic expectations about what products can do.

Do Marketing Efforts Promote Obesity?

Some critics argue that marketing is contributing to what scientists are calling a worldwide obesity epidemic.[93] The World Health Organization believes that evidence connecting junk food advertising and childhood obesity is convincing enough that governments should discourage marketing activities that promote unhealthy eating among youngsters.[94] The Center for Science in the Public Interest, an advocacy group, wants a ban on junk-food ads during TV programs that draw 25 percent or more of their audience from consumers under age18.[95] As you saw in the opening example, marketers are responding to these concerns by changing their products and their advertising.

Researchers are investigating a variety of issues that may contribute to overeating and, over time, to obesity. For example, do consumers feel less guilty about eating "low fat" snack foods and therefore overeat? Marketers can help combat this tendency by making serving size information more salient.[96] Do consumers accurately assess the calorie content of the meals that they consume? In fact, they tend to underestimate calorie content, a situation that explains why some legislators and health advocates want restaurants to post nutrition information about the foods that they serve.[97] Another issue is that consumers tend to perceive unhealthy foods as being tastier and more enjoyable than healthy foods. To address this perception, food marketers can reformulate foods to make foods healthier as well as better tasting, as was illustrated in the opening example.[98]

(MARKETING IMPLICATIONS)

More companies and media are using marketing to encourage healthier behaviors. *Sesame Street*'s Cookie Monster now tells kids that cookies are a "sometimes food."[99] Food manufacturers are also emphasizing the good taste of healthy foods and providing nutrition information. Advertising for Unilever's Promise brand margarine spread stresses that it is "endorsed by cardiologists and taste buds" and mentions the amount of fat per serving.[100] Some food marketers are also revamping brand websites to make them less appealing to young children. Kellogg, for instance, removed games from its cereal websites.[101]

Does Advertising Affect Self-Image?

Advertising has long been accused of depicting idealized images of people and their lives. For example, few people have homes like those depicted in ads for household products, and few enjoy holidays in the idealized manner depicted by Hallmark and Royal Caribbean. Advertising may create an idealized image of what one's life *should* be like. If we do not measure up to this idealized image, we may feel dissatisfied. This section considers two questions about advertising and self-image: (1) Does advertising make consumers dissatisfied with their appearance? (2) Does advertising make consumers materialistic?

Idealized Body Images

Most male models shown in advertisements are trim with well-developed muscles and handsome features. The female models in advertisements are mostly young, very thin, and exceedingly beautiful. Because these ads represent society's conception of the ideal man or woman, they exemplify traits that many men and women will never actually achieve. A particularly salient issue for both men and women is how their bodies compare with those of thin models. Indeed, one study found that 11 percent of men said that they would trade more than five years of their lives to achieve personal weight goals—statistics that closely track women's responses.[102]

In many, particularly Westernized, countries thinness is viewed as a characteristic of attractive men and women. Unfortunately, this value can be carried to extremes and can lead to eating disorders such as anorexia and bulimia, disorders that affect approximately 10 million U.S. women and 1 million U.S. men. These disorders are also increasing dramatically among young women in Japan.[103] On the other hand, binge eating is a problem for an estimated 25 million Americans.[104] But do ads with thin models serve as an impetus to consumers with predispositions to eating disorders? Does identification with very thin models create dissatisfaction with one's own body and appearance?[105] Some evidence suggests the answer to these questions is yes.

Social comparison theory A theory that proposes that individuals have a drive to compare themselves with other people.

Social comparison theory proposes that individuals have a drive to compare themselves with other people.[106] Consistent with this theory, research shows that young women do compare themselves with models in ads and that such self-comparisons can affect self-esteem.[107] As a result, consumers feel inadequate if they do not measure up to the comparison person. Consumers who feel threatened by such comparisons will lie about their behavior to protect their self-esteem.[108] Exhibit 18.12 illustrates the statements that female consumers in one study made when they looked at magazine ads that featured beautiful models. Interestingly, some research has also found that consumers who view ads with beautiful models reduce their attractiveness ratings of average-looking women. A potentially strong conclusion, based on the research, is that advertising can have an unintended but negative impact on how satisfied men and women are with their appearance.[109] Note that consumers do not feel bad about the comparison if the models in ads are extremely thin.[110]

MARKETING IMPLICATIONS

Fortunately, some companies are becoming more sensitive to the effects of such messages. In the fashion industry, demand for plus-size models is up—perhaps in response

General Comparison	"God! I wish I looked like that." (written comment about a cosmetic ad before discussion began)
	"There [are] certain [ads] that I look at and say, 'Wow! I'd sure like to look like that.'"
	"In high school, you want to think that you could look like that if you try. Then in college, you realize, 'Oh, forget it.'"
Ads Generating Specific Body Comparisons	"When I see ads, I always look at the chest. I like it when she has no chest. Because, you know, I don't either."
	"I have wide hips. I always look at the hips. I guess I'm just jealous."
	"When I look at a model, I look at the arms because my arms are awful."
Negative Self-Feelings from Viewing Ads	"You look at these ads and you feel inadequate, like you can't measure up."
	"It's frustrating when you start to realize you should look that way—I mean—I can't."
	"I used to go through these magazines every day and look at [models in the ads] and wish I looked like them. I used to go running every day, and really thought maybe I could look like them. I remember, I even picked one model in particular and cut out ads with her in them. I was pretty obsessed. And I finally realized this wasn't realistic. But I sometimes still look and think, 'Well, maybe.'"
	"Sometimes [ads with models] can make you feel a little depressed."
	"They make me feel self-critical." (participant viewing models in swimsuit ads)

Source: Marsha L. Richins, "Social Comparison and the Idealized Images of Advertising," *Journal of Consumer Research*, June 1991, pp. 71–83. © 1991 University of Chicago. All rights reserved.

Exhibit 18.12

Women's Reactions to Idealized Body Images in Ads

One study found that women exposed to ads with beautiful and thin models compared the models with themselves or with specific parts of their bodies. In some cases, the ads made consumers feel bad about themselves.

to consumers' demands for different types of women in fashion products and ads.[111] Also, online retailers give consumers the option of buying and trying on clothing at home.[112] Although some women may be unhappy about how they compare with models in ads, others are comfortable with themselves and are hostile toward advertisers that perpetuate unrealistic images of women.[113] As part of Dove's Campaign for Real Beauty, ads for its Dove Firming body lotion feature curvy rather than super-thin women; the campaign has gained positive attention from consumers and marketing experts alike.[114] However, because some women will still be willing to use products that entail some risk to achieve an idealized body image, marketers must disclose risks (of a pharmaceutical product, for example) so that consumers can evaluate any potential negative outcomes.

Materialism

Advertising has long been criticized for perpetuating materialistic values and making consumers less satisfied with their lives.[115] For example, as advertising content has increasingly depicted materialistic themes, Americans have become more materialistic. Consumers in other countries have also become more materialistic, a trend that coincides with their purchasing of U.S. products and exposure to U.S. ads. Research shows that consumers who watch a lot of TV and who find commercials realistic tend to be more materialistic than consumers who watch less TV.[116] TV shows may provide a biased or distorted view of reality by showing characters who seem to have everything at their disposal.

Family influences can be quite strong: the children of materialistic parents tend to be more materialistic than other children.[117] Materialistic adolescents shop more, save less, and are more responsive to marketing efforts.[118] And with more marketing and media emphasis on brands, it is not surprising that children are aware of more than 200 brands by the time they reach first grade.[119] The materialistic focus of our society may also encourage materialistic values in children.[120]

Social comparison theory would predict that if advertising and the media show individuals with many material possessions, consumers might use advertising as a means of judging their own personal accomplishments. Consumers who perceive that they are less well off than the comparison population may be less satisfied with their lives. Some evidence supports this idea. Consumers exposed to a lot of advertising tend to overestimate how well off the average consumer is.[121] This misperception sets up a potentially false frame of reference regarding how much the average consumer owns. Furthermore, materialistic consumers may pay undue attention to the possessions of others and make inferences about these people based on the possessions that they own.[122]

Because the material "good life" often depicted in advertising is out of reach for many, consumers are set up for potential dissatisfaction. Some governments have been reluctant to show U.S. ads out of fear that the ads will set off a wave of demand for products that the country cannot produce and/or the people cannot afford.[123] Although advertising has not been proven to cause materialism and dissatisfaction, the connection deserves more research attention.

Do Marketing Practices Invade Consumers' Privacy?

Many organizations, including retailers, banks, credit reporting agencies, Internet businesses, telephone companies, and insurance firms, collect and exchange information about consumers through product registration cards, credit applications, product activity monitoring, sales transaction data, and other techniques. Privacy has received more attention lately because the Internet offers the opportunity to collect a great deal of detailed information about consumers.[124]

Consumers have concerns about the amount and type of information that marketers have about them.[125] According to research, consumers believe that businesses collect too much personal information; these consumers are concerned about threats to their personal privacy.[126] In another study, 61 percent of the respondents decided not to use a financial website because of concerns about how their personal data would be handled.[127] They also worry about identity theft, especially in the wake of incidents involving theft of social security numbers and credit card numbers.[128] For instance, after the leak of personal information about 121,000 annual passholders of the Tokyo Disney resorts, hundreds received phony offers by phone or mail.[129]

Consumers also complain that whereas credit card companies, publishers, and catalog companies (among others) earn money by selling their names to other companies, consumers themselves receive nothing. Furthermore, consumers must spend time sifting through mail and e-mail messages from companies that have bought their names and contact information.

The extent of consumer concern and the willingness to give personal information varies according to the type of information that marketers want to collect.[130] However, although consumers often complain about privacy concerns, many still willingly provide information that could compromise their privacy.[131] Research suggests that a company can enhance privacy by providing consumers with more control and information about the benefits they may gain (such as customized offers of products or services) when they allow personal information to be collected.[132] Most websites post privacy policies to explain what consumer data they gather, what they do with it, how consumers can review it, and how it is protected—although often these statements do not offer complete explanations.[133]

SEE HOW EASY IT IS TO SNOOP
ON SOMEONE'S LAPTOP?

Keep wandering eyes off your computer. Get a removable 3M™ Privacy Filter for laptop and desktop monitors. Call 1-888-PRIVACY or go to **3MPrivacyFilter.com**

Vikuiti™

3M
Privacy Filters

Exhibit 18.13

Privacy Protection
Some new products aim to
reduce consumers' concerns
about protecting their privacy.

MARKETING IMPLICATIONS

Why are consumers so concerned about marketers' use of their personal information?

Horror stories hurt all marketers

A few unscrupulous marketers use marketing techniques to defraud consumers, as some companies have done by using telemarketing to defraud elderly consumers of their life savings. These stories get considerable media attention and tarnish the image of all marketers. Consumers also worry about the lack of privacy in general, such as losing a job because their health history has been leaked to an employer.

Communicating how information helps consumers

Consumers need to know more about how the information collected is used and how it will benefit them. For example, catalog companies collect details about consumers' household characteristics, style preferences, and sizes so that they can customize their catalogs. This practice (1) eliminates waste because marketers can more accurately target consumers, (2) better matches products to consumer needs, and (3) keeps costs down so that savings may be passed on to consumers.

Laws and self-imposed regulation

Consumers are gaining more power against unwanted marketing efforts. More than 145 million U.S. consumers have added their phone numbers to the FTC's do-not-call list.[134] U.S. consumers can also write to the Direct Marketing Association or log onto its website (*www.the-dma.org*) and ask that their names not be sold to other companies.

Markets for Privacy Protection

Concerns about privacy also open up the potential for marketers to develop new offerings designed to protect consumer privacy (see Exhibit 18.13). As privacy continues to erode, consumers may be more interested in these services.[135]

Social Responsibility Issues in Marketing

Consumers and companies are increasingly concerned about the environmental consequences of products and marketing. Two social responsibility issues receiving particular attention in this area are how to encourage environmentally conscious behavior and how to encourage conservation behavior. Another key issue is how consumers can resist unwanted or objectionable marketing efforts.

Environmentally Conscious Behavior

Marketers are directly and indirectly involved in efforts to foster environmentally conscious behavior and to address concerns about global warming. Car companies, their suppliers, and gasoline companies all must comply with government requirements such as the use of unleaded gasoline and adherence to stricter emission controls to reduce environmental damage. These efforts sometimes increase marketing costs but may also open new profit opportunities.

Another concern is the increasing amount of trash or garbage in our environment. Now many products (such as Lenor fabric softener in Germany, Jergen's lotion, and Windex cleaners) are sold in refillable containers.[136] Consumers in Romania and other countries reduce waste by using refillable bottles for wine, beer, seltzer, oil, and milk. Many companies are also being pushed by both consumers and retailers to use less product packaging or more environmentally friendly product packaging.[137] Websites like *www.catalogchoice.org* offer consumers the opportunity to opt out of unwanted catalogs, thus saving paper. The trend toward the use of environmentally friendly products is growing, paving the way for companies like Seventh Generation, which markets eco-friendly household cleaning products.[138] Nokia's "Remade" cell phone uses 100 percent recycled pieces, the latest effort in the company's push toward greener products.[139]

Research about recycling demonstrates that specific beliefs about its importance and attitudes toward recycling in general can directly affect whether consumers engage in recycling behaviors and whether they perceive that recycling is inconvenient.[140] On the other hand, environmentally conscious behaviors are most likely to occur when consumers perceive that their actions will make a difference—called *perceived consumer effectiveness*.[141]

Conservation Behavior

Conservation behavior
Limiting the use of scarce natural resources for the purposes of environmental preservation.

A second important aspect of environmental protection is **conservation behavior.** The need to conserve is especially vital in light of the rapidly escalating problems of garbage disposal and depletion of natural resources. Companies are now realizing that garbage has been a misused resource and are finding creative ways to make products more durable and to reuse materials. In particular, consumer researchers have been interested in two aspects of conservation behavior: When are consumers likely to conserve and how can consumers be motivated to act in more environmentally friendly ways?

When Are Consumers Likely to Conserve?

Consumers are most likely to conserve when they accept personal responsibility for the pollution problem.[142] For example, consumers who perceive that there is an energy shortage because of consumption by all consumers (including themselves) are more likely to accept personal responsibility and do something about it. However, consumers often do not feel accountable for many environmental problems and are not motivated to act. Thus, for conservation programs to succeed, messages must make the problem personally relevant. For example, to get consumers to conserve energy by turning down the thermostat, messages could focus on how much energy and money consumers will save each year and over a longer period. Consumers are also most likely to conserve when there are no barriers to doing so.[143]

A study in the Netherlands points out the importance of using social norms to influence consumers' environmental behaviors. This study found that consumers generally perceive that they are more motivated to engage in pro-environmental behavior than other households are but that they have less ability to do so.[144] Furthermore, they believe that ability is the greatest determinant and that their own behavior is influenced by others.

Can Consumers Be Motivated to Be Environmentally Friendly?

Many organizations and agencies are trying to motivate consumers to be environmentally friendly. Ads sometimes encourage consumers to use products or packages that conserve resources or to engage in conservation behaviors. Another approach is to use communications, home audits, and appliance labels to provide consumers with detailed information about how to be environmentally friendly.[145] A more promising approach is to provide consumers with incentives to conserve. Providing consumers with a free shower-water flow device, for instance, significantly increased participation in an energy conservation program. Consumers prefer incentives such as tax credits to coercive tactics such as higher taxes. In addition, setting goals and providing feedback can help consumers curtail their energy use.

MARKETING IMPLICATIONS

Consumers are increasingly aware of conservation efforts and opportunities, thanks to government and business marketing efforts. The Environmental Protection Agency's Energy Star program, promoted through on-package labeling and participating manufacturers' advertising, helps consumers choose energy-efficient appliances and computers. The gradual phase-out of energy-hungry products like incandescent light bulbs in the United States, Australia, Europe, and other nations allows time for educating consumers about conservation alternatives such as compact fluorescent bulbs.[146] In the meantime, marketers are appealing to conservation-minded consumers by having their products certified by independent groups such as Green Seal, which reassures consumers that certain standards for conservation and efficiency are being met.[147] Some companies like Coca-Cola are developing marketing campaigns that publicize the actions that they are undertaking to be more environmentally friendly.[148]

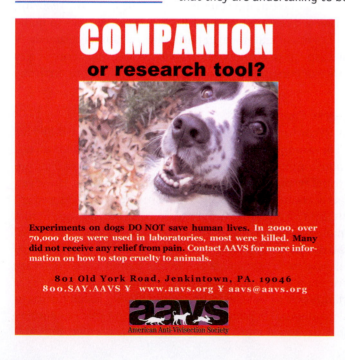

How Can Consumers Resist Marketing Practices?

If consumers are upset about certain marketing practices, they can resist them and try to bring about change individually, through advocacy groups, and through boycotts.[149] Consumers who are dissatisfied or unhappy with marketing practices can choose not to patronize the offending marketer in the future, complain to the marketer, and spread negative word of mouth. These individual consumer resistance strategies can be very effective.

Group strategies are potentially even more powerful than unorganized consumer efforts. Some formally organized advocacy groups engage in resistance by informing the public about business practices that they regard as socially inappropriate (see Exhibit 18.14).[150] The Center for the Study of Commercialism, for example, distributes information and uses lobbying to stop marketing practices such as advertising in schools. *Adbusters,* a magazine published by Canada's Media Foundation, informs consumers about commercial excess.[151] Teens in Minnesota have formed Target Market, an advocacy group to discourage underage smoking.[152]

Boycott An organized activity in which consumers avoid purchasing products or services from a company whose policies or practices are seen as unfair or unjust.

A **boycott** is an organized activity in which consumers avoid purchasing products or services from a company whose policies or practices are seen as unfair or unjust. Boycotting is a way for consumers to hold companies accountable for perceived objectionable actions. Thus, many consumers are motivated by the opportunity and likelihood of making a difference. Also, consumers who are particularly susceptible to the normative influences of the reference group conducting the boycott will be more likely to participate than those who are less susceptible. Finally, consumers may seek to feel less guilty and hope to boost or sustain their self-esteem by joining a particular boycott.[153]

Organized boycotts are able to gain publicity and are likely to have more impact than the same number of consumers acting on their own.[154] Nike, for instance, was boycotted because of poor working conditions at some overseas factories where its sneakers and clothing are made. In response, Nike reviewed the factory conditions, brought in the nonprofit Fair Labor Association to check the factories, and dropped suppliers that did not maintain proper conditions.[155]

Sometimes boycotts are directed against a company's activities rather than against a product. The American Family Association boycotted Ford because some of the company's charitable donations went to groups that support same-sex marriage and some of the company's ads appeared in gay-oriented media. The boycott ended after two years when Ford, struggling with a huge loss unrelated to the boycott, cut its advertising budget and stopped donating to many groups, including those opposed by the American Family Association.[156] The primary indicators that a boycott has been successful are not that it has caused financial effects but rather that it (1) has changed the offending policies, (2) has made businesses more responsible in their plans for future activities, and (3) has forced changes in the behavior of nontargeted businesses that engage in similar practices.

Summary

Deviant consumer behavior covers both illegal and psychologically/physically abnormal behavior. Deviant acquisition behaviors include compulsive buying, consumer theft, and black markets; deviant consumption behaviors include addictive and compulsive consumption and underage drinking and smoking. These behaviors are fairly pervasive, and although some (such as black markets) can provide certain consumer benefits, most have fairly negative effects on consumers and the social groups in which they operate.

Critics have questioned whether and/or how much marketing practices influence these behaviors.

Advertising has been accused of promoting obesity, perpetuating idealized body images, creating materialistic values, and invading consumer privacy. In response, many companies are adopting strategies to reduce public criticism and to put marketing practices in a more favorable light. Marketers are also interested in the social responsibility issues of conservation and environmentally friendly behavior. Consumers are demonstrating their disapproval of practices regarded as unwanted, disreputable, objectionable, and/or unethical through individual resistance, support of advocacy groups, and participation in boycotts.

Questions for Review and Discussion

1. What is compulsive buying, and why is it a problem?

2. How do temptation and rationalization affect consumer theft?

3. How does addictive behavior differ from compulsive behavior and impulsive behavior?

4. What is social comparison theory, and how does it apply to advertising?

5. What influences environmentally conscious consumer behavior?

6. What can consumers do to resist marketing practices that they perceive as unwanted or unethical?

CL Visit http://cengage.com/marketing/hoyer/ConsumerBehavior5e to find resources that are available to help you study for the course.

CONSUMER BEHAVIOR CASE

Is Your Personal Data Private? Is It Safe?

Whenever you use a credit or debit card to buy something—online, in a store, by mail, or over the phone—your purchase is recorded and stored in the retailer's database (as well as in the bank's database). Analyzing your purchasing patterns helps the companies develop more appropriate offers and more targeted communications. A growing number of consumers worry, however, that the names and numbers in these databases might be stolen electronically or through the theft of laptops or computer tapes. That is exactly what happened when hackers broke into the computer network of the parent company of retailer TJ Maxx and stole more than 45 million credit and debit card numbers. Because of that theft, millions of consumers had their banks cancel those cards and issue new cards.

Each year, millions of U.S. consumers fall victim to identity theft, having credit card numbers or other details stolen and used to make fraudulent purchases. The government estimates that $50 billion worth of goods, services, and funds is stolen annually through identity theft. With so much data being gathered and stored by so many companies and government agencies, security is an important concern. Sometimes consumers are hoodwinked into revealing information in response to e-mails, letters, or phone calls that appear to be legitimate but are not.

Even when you are just clicking around the Internet, some sites are collecting personal information about you, and you may not even know it. Many websites place *cookies*—small data files—on your computer's hard drive to track your movement around each site and

to determine which pages and items you looked at, how long you lingered, and which links you clicked on. The benefit gained from this tracking is that sites can customize your online experience by knowing what items you have searched for or looked at. At the same time, your online behavior may be tracked by software that can determine which ads you will see based on the sites you have visited. This situation worries privacy advocates, who want firms to clearly disclose exactly what they are tracking and why and to get the consumer's permission before tracking. The Center for Digital Democracy and other groups have been pushing for a federal "do not track" list—similar to the "do not call" list—so that consumers can opt out of online tracking.

Although many sites post privacy policies to explain their data collection practices, consumers may not always notice these policies or understand what the data is being used for. Google, for example, has addressed such concerns by changing its policy to hold information about searches conducted by consumers for 18 months and then to delete those searches. Consumers can also view their stored Google search data, edit out personal details, and have all search data erased, if they choose.

However, sometimes companies take actions that seem inconsistent with their privacy policies. For instance, the pharmaceutical firm Eli Lilly violated its privacy policy by inadvertently revealing the names of people who had signed up to receive information from its Prozac.com website. In response, the Federal Trade Commission ordered Eli Lilly to set up a system to protect customer data for the next 20 years and to report every year on its security processes.

The social networking site Facebook, where users post all kinds of personal thoughts, photos, videos, and more, has also had problems with privacy. Not long ago, it launched an advertising feature in which a user's actions (such as scoring high on an online game or buying a movie ticket) popped up on the user's page and on the merchant's site. After an outcry from users and privacy advocates, Facebook changed the feature so that such actions would only be visible when users specifically allowed them to be posted.[157]

Case Questions

1. What would you recommend that TJ Maxx do to re-assure shoppers that their credit and debit card data will be safe in the future?

2. From a marketer's perspective, what are the pros and cons of complying with a "do not track" list that would prevent you from collecting online behavioral data about the consumers who are listed?

3. If you were on the marketing staff of Facebook, how would you address the concerns expressed by privacy advocates?

Endnotes

Chapter 1

1. Kenji Hall, "Japan: Google's Real-Life Lab," *Business-Week,* February 25, 2008, pp. 55–58; Ian Rowley, "Testing What's Hot in the Cradle of Cool," *BusinessWeek,* May 7, 2007, p. 46.

2. Jacob Jacoby, "Consumer Psychology: An Octennium," in ed. Paul Mussen and Mark Rosenzweig, *Annual Review of Psychology* (Palo Alto, Calif.: Annual Reviews, 1976), pp. 331–358. With permission from the *Annual Review of Psychology,* vol. 27, © 1976, by Annual Reviews.

3. Pauline Maclaran and Stephen Brown, "The Center Cannot Hold: Consuming the Utopian Marketplace," *Journal of Consumer Research* 32, no. 2, 2005, pp. 311–323; Dawn R. Deeter-Schmelz and Jane L. Sojka, "Wrestling with American Values: An Exploratory Investigation of World Wrestling Entertainment as a Product-Based Subculture," *Journal of Consumer Behaviour* 4, no. 2, 2004, pp. 132–143; Stuart Elliott, "Crossing the Street Is Anything But Pedestrian," *New York Times,* May 25, 2004, *www.nytimes.com.*

4. See, for example, C. A. Russell, A. T. Norman, and S. E. Heckler, "The Consumption of Television Programming: Development and Validation of the Connectedness Scale," *Journal of Consumer Research,* June 2004, pp. 150–161; S. P. Mantel and J. J. Kellaris, "Cognitive Determinants of Consumers' Time Perceptions: The Impact of Resources Required and Available," *Journal of Consumer Research,* March 2003, pp. 531–538; and J. Cotte, S. Ratneshwar, and D. G. Mick, "The Times of Their Lives: Phenomenological and Metaphorical Characteristics of Consumer Lifestyles," *Journal of Consumer Research,* September 2004, pp. 333–345.

5. Joachim Vosgerau, Klaus Wertenbroch, and Ziv Carmon, "Indeterminacy and Live Television," *Journal of Consumer Research* 32, no. 4, 2006, pp. 487–495.

6. Erica Mina Okada and Stephen J. Hoch, "Spending Time Versus Spending Money," *Journal of Consumer Research* 31, no. 2, 2004, pp. 313–323.

7. Morris B. Holbrook, "What Is Consumer Research?" *Journal of Consumer Research,* June 1987, pp. 128–132; Russell W. Belk, "Manifesto for a Consumer Behavior of Consumer Behavior," *Scientific Method in Marketing,* 1984, AMA Winter Educators' Conference, St. Petersburg, FL.

8. Robyn A. LeBoeuf, "Discount Rates for Time Versus Dates: The Sensitivity of Discounting to Time-Interval Description," *Journal of Marketing Research,* February 2006, pp. 59–72.

9. Baba Shiv, Ziv Carmon, and Dan Ariely, "Placebo Effects of Marketing Actions: Consumers May Get What They Pay For," *Journal of Marketing Research,* November 2005, pp. 383–393.

10. Jonathan Arndt, "Role of Product-Related Conversations in the Diffusion of a New Product," *Journal of Marketing Research,* August 1967, pp. 291–295; Vijay Mahajan, Eitan Muller, and Frank M. Bass, "New Product Diffusion Models in Marketing: A Review and Directions," *Journal of Marketing,* January 1990, pp. 1–27.

11. Jacob Jacoby, Carol K. Berning, and Thomas F. Dietworst, "What About Disposition?" *Journal of Marketing,* April 1977, pp. 22–28.

12. Easwar S. Iyer and Rajiv K. Kashyap, "Consumer Recycling: Role of Incentives, Information, and Social Class," *Journal of Consumer Behaviour* 6, no. 1, 2007, pp. 32–47.

13. Nigel F. Maynard, "Waste Not," *Building Products,* July–August 2004, pp. 45+.

14. See Peter Francese, "A New Era of Cold Hard Cash," *American Demographics,* June 2004, pp. 40–41.

15. Joydeep Srivastava and Priya Raghubir, "Debiasing Using Decomposition: The Case of Memory-Based Credit Card Expense Estimates," *Journal of Consumer Psychology* 12, no. 3 (2002), pp. 253–264.

16. "Average Annual Expenditures of All Consumer Units and Percent Changes," U.S. Department of Labor, U.S. Bureau of Labor Statistics, *Consumer Expenditure Survey 2003–2005,* February 2007, Table A.

17. Mathis Chazanov, "Body Language," *Los Angeles Times: Westside News,* April 30, 1995, pp. 10–15.

18. Kristine R. Ehrich and Julie R. Irwin, "Willful Ignorance in the Request for Product Attribute Information," *Journal of Marketing Research,* August 2005, pp. 266–277; Markus Giesler, "Consumer Gift Systems," *Journal of Consumer Research* 33, no. 2, 2006, pp. 283–290.

19. Michael Basnjak, Dirk Obermeier, and Tracy L. Tuten, "Predicting and Explaining the Propensity to Bid in Online Auctions: A Comparison of Two Action-Theoretical Methods," *Journal of Consumer Behaviour* 5, no. 2, 2006, pp. 102–116; Barbara B. Stern and Maria Royne Stafford, "Individual and Social Determinants of Winning Bids in Online Auctions," *Journal of Consumer Behaviour* 5, no. 1, 2006, pp. 43–55; Charles M. Brooks, Patrick J. Kaufmann, and Donald R. Lichtenstein, "Travel Configuration on Consumer Trip-Chained Store Choice," *Journal of Consumer Research* 31, no. 2, 2004, pp. 241–248.

20. Matthew J. Bernthal, David Crockett, and Randall L. Rose, "Credit Cards as Lifestyle Facilitators," *Journal of Consumer Research* 32, no. 1, 2005, pp. 130–145; "President of eBay's PayPal Reportedly Sees No E-commerce Slowdown," *MarketWatch,* March 17, 2008, *www.marketwatch.com.*

21. See, for example, Valerie S. Folkes, Ingrid M. Martin, and Kamal Gupta, "When to Say When: Effects of Supply on Usage," *Journal of Consumer Research,* December 1993, pp. 467–477.

22. Pui-Wing Tam, "Entreaty to Camera-Phone Photographers: Please Print," *Wall Street Journal,* December 28, 2004, pp. B1, B3.

23. Mark A. Le Turck and Gerald M. Goldhaben, "Effectiveness of Product Warning Labels: Effects of Consumer Information Processing Objectives," *Journal of Public Affairs,* Summer 1989, pp. 111–125.

24. Russell W. Belk, "Collecting as Luxury Consumption: Effects on Individuals and Households," *Journal of Economic Psychology,* September 1995, pp. 477–490.

25. Jacoby, Berning, and Dietworst, "What About Disposition?"

26. June Cotte, S. Ratneshwar, and David Glen Mick, "The Times of Their Lives: Phenomenological and Metaphorical Characteristics of Consumer Timestyles," *Journal of Consumer Research* 31, no. 2, 2004, pp. 333–345.

27. Michael Arndt, "McDonald's 24/7," *BusinessWeek,* February 5, 2007, pp. 64+.

28. Rongrong Zhou and Dilip Soman, "Looking Back: Exploring the Psychology of Queuing and the Effect of the Number of People Behind," *Journal of Consumer Research,* March 2003, pp. 517–530.

29. Stephen M. Nowlis, Naomi Mandel, and Deborah Brown McCabe, "The Effect of a Delay Between Choice and Consumption on Consumption Enjoyment," *Journal of Consumer Research,* December 2004, pp. 502–210.

30. Erica Mina Okada, "Trade-ins, Mental Accounting, and Product Replacement Decisions," *Journal of Consumer Research* 27, March 2001, pp. 433–446.

31. John Fetto, "Supershoppers," *American Demographics,* May 2003, p. 17.

32. Ylan Q. Mui, "Paging Through the Holidays," *Washington Post,* December 1, 2007, p. D1.

33. Kuan-Pin Chiang and Ruby Roy Dholakia, "Factors Driving Consumer Intention to Shop Online: An Empirical Investigation," *Journal of Consumer Psychology* 13, no. 1, 2003, pp. 177–183; David Whelan, "A Tale of Two Consumers," *American Demographics,* September 1, 2001, pp. 54–57.

34. Jonathan Birchall, "How to Cut in the Middleman," *Financial Times,* March 12, 2008, p. 12.

35. Rebecca Buckman and David Pringle, "Cellphones Help with Disaster Relief," *Wall Street Journal,* January 3, 2005, p. B5; Hassan Fattah, "America Untethered," *American Demographics,* March 2003, pp. 34–41; Hassan Fattah and Pamela Paul, "Gaming Gets Serious," *American Demographics,* May 2002, pp. 39–43.

36. Linda L. Price, Eric J. Arnould, and Carolyn Folkman Curasi, "Older Consumers' Disposition of Special Possessions," *Journal of Consumer Research,* September 2000, pp. 179–201.

37. Harriet Blake, "Don't Toss It, Freecycle It," *Boston Globe,* March 5, 2008, *www.boston.com.*

38. Morris B. Holbrook and Meryl P. Gardner, "How Motivation Moderates the Effects of Emotion on the Duration of Consumption," *Journal of Business Research,* July 1998, pp. 241–252.

39. Rasul Bailay, "A Hindu Festival Attracts the Faithful and U.S. Marketers," *Wall Street Journal,* February 12, 2001, p. A18.

40. Pierre Chandon and Brian Wansink, "When Are Stockpiled Products Consumed Faster?" *Journal of Marketing Research,* August 2002, pp. 321–335.

41. Joseph C. Nunes, "A Cognitive Model of People's Usage Estimations," *Journal of Marketing Research* 38, November 2000, pp. 397–409.

42. Kathleen D. Vohs and Ronald J. Faber, "Spent Resources: Self-Regulatory Resource Availability Affects Impulse Buying," *Journal of Consumer Research* 33, no. 4, 2007, pp. 537–548; Suresh Ramanathan and Geeta Menon, "Time-Varying Effects of Chronic Hedonic Goals on Impulsive Behavior," *Journal of Marketing Research,* November 2006, pp. 628–641; Fritz Strack, Lioba Werth, and Roland Deutsch, "Reflective and Impulsive Determinants of Consumer Behavior," *Journal of Consumer Psychology* 16, no. 3, 2006, pp. 205–216; Xueming Luo, "How Does Shopping with Others Influence Impulsive Purchasing?" *Journal of Consumer Psychology* 15, no. 4, 2005, pp. 288–294; Rosellina Ferraro, Baba Shiv, and James R. Bettman, "Let Us Eat and Drink, for Tomorrow We Shall Die: Effects of Mortality Salience and Self-Esteem on Self-Regulation in Consumer Choice," *Journal of Consumer Research* 32, no. 1, 2005, pp. 65–75; Anirban Mukhopadhyay and Gita Venkataramani Johar, "Where There Is a Will, Is There a Way? Effects of Lay Theories of Self-Control on Setting and Keeping Resolutions," *Journal of Consumer Research* 31, no. 4, 2005, pp. 779–786.

43. Allison R. Johnson and David W. Stewart, "A Re-Appraisal of the Role of Emotion in Consumer Behavior: Traditional and Contemporary Approaches," in ed. Naresh Malhotra, *Review of Marketing Research,* vol. 1, 2004, pp. 1–33; R. P. Bagozzi, M. Gopinath, and P. U. Nyer, "The Role of Emotions in Marketing," *Journal of the Academy of Marketing Science* 27, no. 2, 1999, pp. 184–206.

44. Deborah J. MacInnis and Gustavo deMello, "The Concept of Hope and its Relevance to Product Evaluation and Choice," *Journal of Marketing,* January 2005, pp. 1–14; Gustavo DeMello, Deborah J. MacInnis, and David W. Stewart, "Threats to Hope: Effects on Reasoning About Product Information," *Journal of Consumer Research* 34, no. 2, 2007, pp. 153–161.

45. Kirsten Passyn and Mita Sujan, "Self-Accountability Emotions and Fear Appeals: Motivating Behavior," *Journal of Consumer Research* 32, March 2006, pp. 583–589; O. Shehryar and D. Hunt, "A Terror Management Perspective on the Persuasiveness of Fear Appeals," *Journal of Consumer Psychology,* 15, no. 4, 2005, pp. 275–287.

46. Eric A. Greenleaf, "Reserves, Regret, and Rejoicing in Open English Auctions," *Journal of Consumer Research* 31, no. 2, 2004, pp. 264–273; Marcel Zeelenberg and Rik Pieters, "A Theory of Regret Regulation 1.0," *Journal of Consumer Psychology* 17, no. 1, 2007, pp. 3–18; Ran

Kivetz and Anat Keinan, "Repenting Hyperopia: An Analysis of Self-Control Regrets," *Journal of Consumer Research* 33, no. 2, 2006, pp. 273–282; Lisa J. Abendroth and Kristin Diehl, "Now or Never: Effects of Limited Purchase Opportunities on Patterns of Regret over Time, "*Journal of Consumer Research* 33, no. 3, 2006, pp. 342–351.

47. Darren W. Dahl, Heather Honea, and Rajesh V. Manchanda, "The Three Rs of Interpersonal Consumer Guilt: Relationship, Reciprocity, Reparation," *Journal of Consumer Psychology* 15, no. 4, 2005, pp. 307–315; Brian Wansink and Pierre Chandon, "Can 'Low-Fat' Nutrition Labels Lead to Obesity?" *Journal of Marketing Research,* November 2006, pp, 605–617.

48. Darren Dahl, Rajesh V. Manchanda, and Jennifer J. Argo, "Embarrassment in Consumer Purchase: The Roles of Social Presence and Purchase Familiarity," *Journal of Consumer Research,* December 2001, pp. 473–483.

49. Georgios A. Bakamitsos, "A Cue Alone or a Probe to Think: The Dual Role of Affect in Product Evaluations," *Journal of Consumer Research,* December 2006, pp. 403–412; Eduardo Andrade, "Behavioral Consequences of Affect: Combining Evaluative and Regulatory Mechanisms," *Journal of Consumer Research,* December 2005, pp. 355–362; Harper A. Roehm and Michelle L. Roehm, "Revisiting the Effect of Positive Mood on Variety Seeking," *Journal of Consumer Research,* September 2005, pp. 330–336.

50. Aaron C. Ahuvia, "Beyond the Extended Self: Loved Objects and Consumers' Identity Narratives," *Journal of Consumer Research* 32, June 2005, pp. 171–184.

51. Joel B. Cohen and Eduardo B. Andrade, "Affective Intuition and Task-Contingent Affect Regulation," *Journal of Consumer Research* 31, no. 2, 2004, pp. 358–367; Nitika G. Barg, Brian Wansink, and J. Jeffrey Inman, "The Influence of Incidental Affect on Consumers' Food Intake," *Journal of Marketing,* January 2007, pp. 194–206.

52. Thorsten Hennig-Thurau, Markus Groth, and Michael Paul, "Are All Smiles Created Equal? How Emotional Contagion and Emotional Labor Affect Service Relationships," *Journal of Marketing,* July 2006, pp. 58–73.

53. Adam Duhachek and Dawn Iacobucci, "Consumer Personality and Coping: Testing Rival Theories of Process," *Journal of Consumer Psychology* 15, no. 1, 2005, pp. 52–63; Adam Duhachek, "Coping: A Multidimensional, Hierarchical Framework of Responses to Stressful Consumption Episodes," *Journal of Consumer Research* 32, no. 1, 2005, pp. 41–53.

54. Sheena Leek and Suchart Chanasawatkit, "Consumer Confusion in the Thai Mobile Phone Market," *Journal of Consumer Behavior* 5, no. 6, 2006, pp. 518–532.

55. Teresa M. Pavia and Marlys J. Mason, "The Reflexive Relationship Between Consumer Behavior and Adaptive Coping," *Journal of Consumer Research* 31, no. 2, 2004, pp. 441–454.

56. Linda L. Price, Eric Arnould, and Carolyn Folkman Curasi, "Older Consumers' Dispositions of Special Possessions," *Journal of Consumer Research,* September 2000, pp. 179–201.

57. Natalie Ross Adkins and Julie L. Ozanne, "The Low Literate Consumer," *Journal of Consumer Research* 32, no. 1, 2005, pp. 93–105.

58. John G. Lynch and G. Zauberman, "Construing Consumer Decision Making," *Journal of Consumer Psychology* 17, no. 2, 2007, pp. 107–112.

59. John A. Bargh, "Losing Consciousness: Automatic Influences on Consumer Judgment, Behavior, and Motivation," *Journal of Consumer Research,* September 2002, pp. 280–285; Stewart Shapiro, "When an Ad's Influence Is Beyond Our Conscious Control: Perceptual and Conceptual Fluency Effects Caused by Incidental Ad Exposure," *Journal of Consumer Research,* June 1999, pp. 16–36; Ap Dijksterhuis, Pamela K. Smith, Rick B. Van Baaren, and Daniel H. J. Wigboldus, "The Unconscious Consumer: Effects of Environment on Consumer Behavior," *Journal of Consumer Psychology* 15, no. 3, 2005, pp. 193–202.

60. Deborah J. MacInnis, Vanessa M. Patrick, and C. Whan Park, "Not as Happy as I Thought I'd Be? Affective Misforecasting and Product Evaluations," *Journal of Consumer Research,* March 2007, pp. 479–490; Deborah J. MacInnis, Vanessa M. Patrick, and C. Whan Park, "Looking Through the Crystal Ball: Affective Forecasting and Misforecasting in Consumer Behavior," *Review of Marketing Research* 2, 2006, pp. 43–80.

61. Vohs and Faber, "Spent Resources: Self-Regulatory Resource Availability Affects Impulse Buying."

62. Lisa Guernsey, "A Site to Bring Parents Up to Speed on Video Games," *New York Times,* January 31, 2008, p. C8; Colin Moynihan, "Council Finds Unfit Games Sold to Youths," *New York Times,* December 19, 2004, p. 53; "Groups Assail 'Most Violent' Video Games, Industry Rating System," *Los Angeles Times,* November 24, 2004, p. A34.

63. "News Analysis: Tobacco's Last Stand?" *Marketing,* October 27, 2004, p. 15.

64. Douglas Bowman, Carrie M. Heilman, and P. B. Seetharaman, "Determinants of Product-Use Compliance Behavior," *Journal of Marketing Research,* August 2004, pp. 324–338.

65. Dipankar Chakravarti, "Voices Unheard: The Psychology of Consumption in Poverty and Development," *Journal of Consumer Psychology* 16, no. 4, 2006, pp. 363–376.

66. James R. Bettman, *An Information Processing Theory of Consumer Choice* (Reading, Mass.: Addison-Wesley, 1979).

67. Michael Marriott, "Gadget Designers Take Aim at Women, and Not Just by Adding Pink," *New York Times,* June 7, 2007, p. C7.

68. Lisa Sanders, "Major Marketers Get Wise to the Power of Assigning Personas," *Advertising Age,* April 9, 2007, p. 36; Lorri Freifeld, "Focus on Retail: Best Buy Connects with Customers," *Training,* August 1, 2007, n.p.; Matthew Boyle, "Best Buy's Giant Gamble," *Fortune,* March 29, 2006, *www.cnnmoney.com*; Brad Anderson, "Minding the Store: Analyzing Customers,

Best Buy Decides Not All Are Welcome," *Wall Street Journal,* November 8, 2004, p. A13; Laura Heller, "The Sound a Big Kid Makes," *DSN Retailing Today,* January 2006, p. 12.

69. Dale Buss, "Can Harley Ride the New Wave?" *Brandweek,* October 25, 2004, p. 203.

70. Robert D. Jewell and H. Rao Unnava, "Exploring Differences in Attitudes Between Light and Heavy Brand Users," *Journal of Consumer Psychology* 14, vol. 1–2, 2004, pp. 75–80.

71. Mike Beirne, "Virgin Mobile Goes After 'Phone Poets,'" *Brandweek,* March 24, 2008, *www.brandweek.com*; Todd Wasserman, "Virgin Mobile's New Call Placed to Teens' Parents," *Brandweek,* December 13, 2004, p. 14.

72. See Claudiu V. Dimofte and Richard F. Yalch, "Consumer Response to Polysemous Brand Slogans," *Journal of Consumer Research* 33, no. 4, 2007, pp. 515–522.

73. See Alexander Chernev, "Jack of All Trades or Master of One? Product Differentiation and Compensatory Reasoning in Consumer Choice," *Journal of Consumer Research* 33, no. 4, 2007, pp. 430–444.

74. Mark Rechtin, "Online Assembly Line Allows Built-to-Order Scions, Delivered Fast," *Automotive News,* February 4, 2008, *www.autonews.com*; Phil Patton, "Mad Scionists: Young, Hip, and a Bit Less Square," *New York Times,* June 17, 2007, p. AU-2.

75. Ellen Byron, "Ad Campaign and Sharper Styles Help Gold Shed Its Frumpy Image," *Wall Street Journal,* December 24, 2004, pp. A7, A9.

76. Stuart Elliott, "And the Winning Flavor Is . . ." *New York Times,* September 20, 2007, p. C3.

77. Rob Walker, "Risky Business," *New York Times Magazine,* November 28, 2004, p. 68.

78. Joe Keohane, "Fat Profits," *Conde Nast Portfolio,* February 2008, pp. 90+.

79. Robert McNatt, "Hey, It's Green—It Must Be Healthy," *BusinessWeek,* July 13, 1998, p. 6.

80. Michael Fielding, "A Clean Slate," *Marketing News,* May 1, 2007, p. 9.

81. Charlotte Clarke, "Language Classes," *Marketing Week,* July 24, 1997, pp. 35–39.

82. Asim Ansari and Carl Mela, "E-Customization," *Journal of Marketing Research,* May 2003, pp. 131–145.

83. Carolyn J. Simmons and Karen L. Becker-Olsen, "Achieving Marketing Objectives Through Social Sponsorships," *Journal of Marketing,* October 2006, pp. 154–169.

84. Brendan I. Koerner, "Frozen Stroganoff in Just 10 Hours," *New York Times,* August 1, 2004, sec. 3, p. 2.

85. Jeff Borden, "Good Cheer," *Marketing News,* March 15, 2008, pp. 24+.

86. Laurence Ashworth, Peter R. Darke, and Mark Schaller, "No One Wants to Look Cheap: Trade-offs Between Social Disincentives and the Economic and Psychological Incentives to Redeem Coupons," *Journal of Consumer Psychology* 15, no. 4, 2005, pp. 295–306.

87. "Del Monte Squeezes Out More Sales," *Incentive Today,* November–December 2004, p. 8.

88. Sucharita Chandran and Vicki G. Morwitz, "The Price of 'Free'-dom: Consumer Sensitivity to Promotions with Negative Contextual Influences," *Journal of Consumer Research* 33, no. 3, 2006, pp. 384–392; Priya Raghubir, "Free Gift with Purchase: Promoting or Discounting the Brand?" *Journal of Consumer Psychology* 14, no. 1/2, pp. 181–186; Luc Wathieu, A. V. Muthukrishnan, and Bart J. Bronnenberg, "The Asymmetric Effect of Discount Retraction on Subsequent Choice," *Journal of Consumer Research* 31, no. 3, 2004, pp. 652–657.

89. Stephanie Dellande, Mary C. Gilly, and John L. Graham, "Gaining Compliance and Losing Weight: The Role of the Service Provider in Health Care Services," *Journal of Marketing* 68, July 2004, pp. 78–91; Sean Dwyer, Orlando Richard, and C. David Shepherd, "An Exploratory Study of Gender and Age Matching in the Salesperson–Prospective Customer Dyad: Testing Similarity-Performance Predictions," *Journal of Personal Selling and Sales Management,* Fall 1998, pp. 55–69.

90. Thomas E. DeCarlo, "The Effects of Sales Message and Suspicion of Ulterior Motives on Salesperson Evaluation," *Journal of Consumer Psychology* 15, no. 3, 2005, pp. 238–249.

91. Thomas Manoj and Vicki Morwitz, "Penny Wise and Pound Foolish: The Left-Digit Effect in Price Cognition," *Journal of Consumer Research* 32, no. 1, 2005, pp. 54–64; Robert M. Schindler and Patrick N. Kirby, "Patterns of Rightmost Digits Used in Advertising Prices: Implications for Nine-Ending Effects," *Journal of Consumer Research,* September 1997, pp. 192–201.

92. Jacob Jacoby, Jerry Olson, and Rafael Haddock, "Price, Brand Name, and Product Composition Characteristics as Determinants of Perceived Quality," *Journal of Applied Psychology,* December 1971, pp. 470–479; Kent B. Monroe, "The Influence of Price Differences and Brand Familiarity on Brand Preferences," *Journal of Consumer Research,* June 1976, pp. 42–49.

93. Devon DelVecchio, H. Shanker Krishnan, and Daniel C. Smith, "Cents or Percent? The Effects of Promotion Framing on Price Expectations and Choice," *Journal of Marketing,* July 2007, pp. 158–170. For more on pricing effects associated with regular and discount prices, see Keith S. Coulter and Robin A. Coulter, "Distortion of Price Discount Perceptions: The Right Digit Effect," *Journal of Consumer Research,* August 2007, pp. 162–173.

94. Laura Bird, "Catalogs Cut Shipping, Handling Fees to Inspire Early Christmas Shopping," *Wall Street Journal,* October 24, 1995, pp. B1, B11.

95. Daniel J. Howard and Roger A. Kerin, "Broadening the Scope of Reference Price Advertising Research: A Field Study of Consumer Shopping Involvement," *Journal of Marketing,* October 2006, pp. 185–204; Tridib Mazumdar, S. P. Raj, and Indrajit Sinha, "Reference Price Research: Review and Propositions," *Journal of Marketing,* October 2005, pp. 84–102; Ziv Carmon and Dan Ariely, "Focusing on the Forgone: How Value Can Appear So Different to Buyers and Sellers," *Journal of Consumer*

Research 27, December 2000, pp. 360–370; Tridib Mazumdar and Purushottam Papatla, "An Investigation of Reference Price Segments," *Journal of Marketing Research* 37, May 2000, pp. 246–258.

96. Dilip Soman and John T. Gourville, "Transaction Decoupling: How Price Bundling Affects the Decision to Consume," *Journal of Marketing Research* 38, February 2001, pp. 30–44.

97. Joseph C. Nunes and Peter Boatwright, "Incidental Prices and Their Effect on Willingness to Pay," *Journal of Consumer Research,* November 2004, pp. 457–466.

98. Dhananjay Nayakankuppam and Himanshu Mishra, "The Endowment Effect: Rose-Tinted and Dark-Tinted Glasses," *Journal of Consumer Research* 32, no. 3, 2005, pp. 390–395.

99. Martha Brannigan, "Sailing on Sale: Travelers Ride a Wave of Discounts on Cruise Ships," *Wall Street Journal,* July 17, 2000, pp. B1, B4.

100. Steven Gray and Amy Merrick, "Latte Letdown: Starbucks Set to Raise Prices," *Wall Street Journal,* September 2, 2004, pp. B1, B5.

101. Ronald E. Milliman, "The Influence of Background Music on the Behavior of Restaurant Patrons," *Journal of Consumer Research,* September 1986, pp. 286–289; Richard Yalch and Eric Spannenberg, "Effects of Store Music on Shopping Behavior," *Journal of Services Marketing,* Winter 1990, pp. 31–39; Joseph A. Bellizi, Ayn E. Crowley, and Ronald W. Hasty, "The Effects of Color in Store Design," *Journal of Retailing,* Spring 1983, pp. 21–45.

102. Velitchka D. Kaltcheva and Barton A. Weitz, "When Should a Retailer Create an Exciting Store Environment?" *Journal of Marketing,* January 2006, pp. 107–118.

103. Risto Moisio and Eric J. Arnould, "Framework in Marketing: Drama Structure, Drama Interaction, and Drama Content in Shopping Experiences," *Journal of Consumer Behavior* 4, no. 4, 2005, pp. 246–256; Robert V. Kozinets, John F. Sherry, Diana Storm, Adam Duhachek, Krittinee Nuttavuthisit, and Benét DeBerry-Spence, "Ludic Agency and Retail Spectacle," *Journal of Consumer Research* 31, no. 3, 2004, pp. 658–672.

104. Timothy C. Barmann, "Apple Polishes Its Store Layout, Design," *Providence Journal,* April 23, 2004, *www. projo.com.*

105. "Swatch Group Sales Up 18 Percent," *National Jeweler,* January 18, 2008, n.p.; Jennifer Fishbein, "An Uptick for Swatch on Tiffany Deal," *BusinessWeek Online,* December 7, 2007, www.businessweek.com; Ed Taylor, "Luxe Lines Drive Swatch Gains," *Wall Street Journal,* August 25, 2004, p. B3; Lorna Strickland, "Time Trials," *Duty-Free International,* October 15, 2004, pp. 190+; Barbara Green, "Watch Retailers Gear Up for Graduation," *National Jeweler,* March 16, 2004, p. 10.

Enrichment

1. Steve Hamm and Kenji Hall, "Perfect: The Quest to Design the Ultimate Portable PC," *BusinessWeek,* February 25, 2008, pp. 42–48; "Lenovo Ranks First in China's PC Market," *China Business News,* January 24, 2008, n.p.; "Lenovo's 'Idea' Brand to Reach China in February," *China Business News,* January 4, 2008, n.p.; Steve Hamm, "Lenovo Thinks Beyond the ThinkPad," *BusinessWeek Online,* January 4, 2008, *www.businessweek.com;* "ZIBA Designs Search for the Soul of the Chinese Consumer," *BusinessWeek Innovation,* September 2006, pp. 6–10.

2. Louise Witt, "Inside Intent," *American Demographics,* March 2004, pp. 35–39.

3. Christopher T. Heun, "Procter & Gamble Readies Market-Research Push," *Information Week,* October 15, 2001, p. 26.

4. Witt, "Inside Intent."

5. Randy Garner, "Post-It Note Persuasion: A Sticky Influence," *Journal of Consumer Psychology* 15, no. 2, 2005, pp. 230–237.

6. Stuart Elliott, "For Marketing, the Most Valuable Player Might Be YouTube," *New York Times,* February 5, 2008, p. C3.

7. "Getting Close to the Customer," *Knowledge@ Wharton,* May 5, 2004, *http://knowledge.wharton.upenn.edu.*

8. Melanie Scarborough, "Customers as Advisers: One Florida Bank Established Community Boards to Give Guidance to Its Staff," *Community Banker,* January 2008, p. 20.

9. Jean Halliday, "Volvo Ads Inspired By . . . Valets," *Advertising Age,* September 17, 2007, *www.adage.com.*

10. Chad Rubel, "Two Research Techniques Probe Shoppers' Minds," *Marketing News,* July 29, 1996, p. 16.

11. Ronald B. Lieber and Joyce E. Davis, "Storytelling: A New Way to Get Close to Your Customer," *Fortune,* February 3, 1997, pp. 102–108.

12. Sandra Yin, "Marketing Tools: The Power of Images," *American Demographics,* November 2001, pp. 32–33.

13. Deborah D. Heisley and Sidney J. Levy, "Autodriving: A Photoelicitation Technique," *Journal of Consumer Research,* December 1991, pp. 257–272.

14. Robin A. Coulter, Gerald Zaltman, and Keith S. Coulter, "Interpreting Consumer Perceptions of Advertising: An Application of the Zaltman Metaphor Elicitation Technique," *Journal of Advertising* 30, Winter 2001, pp. 1–21; Morris B. Holbrook, "Collective Stereographic Photo Essays: An Integrated Approach to Probing Consumption Experiences in Depth," *International Journal of Research in Marketing,* July 1998, pp. 201–221.

15. "How Sweet It Is," *American Demographics,* March 2000, p. S18.

16. Christine Bittar, "Up in Arms," *Brandweek,* June 18, 2001, pp. 17–18.

17. Faith Keenan, "Dear Diary, I Had Jell-O Today," *BusinessWeek,* April 10, 2001, *www.businessweek.com/ technology/icontent/apr2001/tc20010410_958.htm.*

18. Julie Schlosser, "Scanning for Dollars," *Fortune,* January 10, 2005, p. 60.

19. Kortney Stringer, "Dallas Is Hurdle, Testing Ground for Players in Restaurant Game," *Wall Street Journal,* January 3, 2005, p. B4.

20. Roy C. Anderson and Eric N. Hansen, "The Impact of Environmental Certification on Preferences for Wood Furniture: A Conjoint Analysis Approach," *Forest Products Journal,* March 2004, pp. 42–50.

21. Ellen Byron, "A Virtual View of the Store Aisle," *Wall Street Journal,* October 3, 2007, p. B1.

22. Robyn Weisman, "Web Trackers: The Spies in Your Computer," *NewsFactor Network,* November 8, 2001, *www.newsfactor.com/perl/story/14662.html.*

23. Patrick Thibodeau, "Senate Panel Spars over Internet Privacy," *ComputerWorld,* July 13, 2001, *www.cnn.com/2001/TECH/industry/07/13/privacy.legislation.idg.*

24. Alison Stein Wellner, "Watch Me Now," *American Demographics,* October 2002, pp. S1–S4.

25. Jack Neff, "IRI Snares Campbell Soup Market-Research Account," *Advertising Age,* April 26, 2004, p. 8.

26. Emily Steel, "The New Focus Groups: Online Networks," *Wall Street Journal,* January 14, 2008, p. B6.

27. Jennifer Lach, "Data Mining Digs In," *American Demographics,* July 1999, pp. 38–45.

28. Steve Lohr, "Reaping Results: Data-Mining Goes Mainstream," *New York Times,* May 20, 2007, p. BU-3; Constance L. Hays, "What They Know About You," *New York Times,* November 14, 2004, sec. 3, pp. 1, 9.

29. Janet Logan, "Most E-mail Marketing Never Gets Read," *East Bay Business Times,* October 22, 2001, *eastbay.bcentral.com/eastbay/stories/2001/10/22/ smallb4.html.*

30. "Frederick's Retention E-Mail Program," *Internet Week,* June 30, 2004, n.p.

31. Caterina Sismeiro and Randolph E. Bucklin, "Modeling Purchase Behavior at an E-Commerce Web Site: A Task-Completion Approach," *Journal of Marketing Research,* August 2004, pp. 306–323.

32. Carolyn Yoon, Angela H. Gutchess, Fred Feinberg, and Thad A. Polk, "A Functional Magnetic Resonance Imaging Study of Neural Dissociations Between Brand and Person Judgments," *Journal of Consumer Research* 33, no. 1, 2006, pp. 31–40; Colin F. Camerer, George F. Loewenstein, and Drazen Prelec, "Neuroeconomics: How Neuroscience Can Inform Economics," *Journal of Economic Literature,* March 2005, pp. 9–64.

33. Amber Haq, "This Is Your Brain on Advertising," *BusinessWeek Online,* October 8, 2007, *www.businessweek.com.*

34. Laurel Wentz, "Best Buy's First Hispanic Ads Target Family Elders," *AdAge.com,* August 2, 2004, *www.adage.com.*

35. Brooks Barnes, "TV Drama: For Nielsen, Fixing Old Ratings System Causes New Static," *Wall Street Journal,* September 16, 2004, p. A1.

36. Rebecca Dana, "Fox Scores Super Bowl Record: 97 Million Viewers," *Wall Street Journal,* February 5, 2008, p. B3.

37. Nick Wingfield, "Nielsen Tracker May Benefit Videogames as an Ad Medium," *Wall Street Journal,* July 26, 2007, p. B2.

38. Christopher Lawton, "We Are All Marketers Now," *Wall Street Journal,* August 1, 2007, p. D9.

39. *www.arfsite.org,* January 1, 2003.

40. Jacob Jacoby and George J. Szybillo, "Consumer Research in FTC Versus Kraft (1991): "A Case of Heads We Win, Tails You Lose," *Journal of Public Policy and Marketing,* Spring 1995, pp. 1–14; David W. Stewart, "Deception, Materiality, and Survey Research: Some Lessons from Kraft," *Journal of Public Policy and Marketing,* Spring 1995, pp. 15–28.

41. Chris Pullig, Carolyn J. Simmons, and Richard G. Netemeyer, "Brand Dilution: When Do New Brands Hurt Existing Brands?" *Journal of Marketing,* April 2006, pp. 52–66.

42. Joe Mandese, "Observers Rock Research," *Television Week,* March 1, 2004, p. 35.

43. Marlise Simons, "In the Netherlands, Eat, Drink, and Be Monitored," *New York Times,* November 26, 2007, p. A4.

44. John F. Gaski and Michael J. Etzel, "National Aggregate Consumer Sentiment Toward Marketing: A Thirty-Year Retrospective and Analysis," *Journal of Consumer Research* 31, no. 4, 2005, pp. 859–867.

45. Kenneth C. Schneider and Cynthia K. Holm, "Deceptive Practices in Marketing Research: The Consumer's Viewpoint," *California Management Review,* Spring 1982, pp. 89–97.

46. "Office Max Brings Back Elf Viral Campaign," *Promo,* December 11, 2007, *www.promomagazine.com*; "Bob Thacker, Senior VP–Marketing and Advertising, Office-Max," *Advertising Age,* September 17, 2007, p. S-4; Reena Jana, "The Revenge of the Generic," *BusinessWeek Online,* December 27, 2006, *www.businessweek.com*; Kenneth Chang, "Enlisting Science's Lessons to Entice More Shoppers to Spend More," *New York Times,* September 19, 2006, p. F3.

Chapter 2

1. Mark Rechtin, "Which Brand Is Stronger—Scion or Prius?" *Automotive News,* January 21, 2008, p. 24B; Bernard Simon, "Prius Overtakes Explorer in the US," *Financial Times,* January 11, 2008, p. 13; Keith Naughton, "A Case of Prius Envy," *Newsweek,* September 3, 2007, p. 40; Steve Miller, "Supply of Priuses Rebounds, So Toyota Creates Demand," *Brandweek,* April 30, 2007, p. 18; Mark Rechtin, "Spiffs Help Lift Mainstream Sales of Prius," *Automotive News,* April 9, 2007, p. 49.

2. C. Whan Park and Banwari Mittal, "A Theory of Involvement in Consumer Behavior: Problems and Issues," in ed. J. N. Sheth, *Research in Consumer Behavior* (Greenwich, Conn.: JAI Press, 1979), pp. 201–231; Deborah J. MacInnis, Christine Moorman, and Bernard J. Jaworski, "Enhancing and Measuring Consumers' Motivation, Opportunity, and Ability to Process Brand Information from Ads," *Journal of Marketing,* October 1991, pp. 32–53.

3. Deborah J. MacInnis and Bernard J. Jaworski, "Information Processing from Advertisements: Toward an Integrative Framework," *Journal of Marketing,* 53, October 1989, pp. 1–23; Scott B. MacKenzie and Richard A. Spreng, "How Does Motivation Moderate the Impact of

Central and Peripheral Processing on Brand Attitudes and Intentions?" *Journal of Consumer Research*, March 1992, pp. 519–529; Richard E. Petty and John T. Cacioppo, *Communication and Persuasion* (New York: Springer-Verlag, 1986); Anthony Greenwald and Clark Leavitt, "Audience Involvement in Advertising: Four Levels," *Journal of Consumer Research* 11, June 1984, pp. 581–592; Ronald C. Goodstein, "Category-Based Applications and Extensions in Advertising: Motivating More Extensive Ad Processing," *Journal of Consumer Research*, June 1993, pp. 87–99; Ellen Garbarino and Julie A. Edell, "Cognitive Effort, Affect, and Choice," *Journal of Consumer Research*, September 1997, pp. 147–158.

4. Wayne D. Hoyer, "An Examination of Consumer Decision Making for a Common Repeat Purchase Product," *Journal of Consumer Research*, December 1984, pp. 822–829.

5. Kurt A. Carlson, Margaret G. Meloy, and J. Edward Russo, "Leader-Driven Primacy: Using Attribute Order to Affect Consumer Choice," *Journal of Consumer Research* 32, no. 4, 2006, pp. 513–518; Nidhi Agrawal and Durairaj Maheswaran, "Motivated Reasoning in Outcome-Bias Effects," *Journal of Consumer Research* 31, no. 4, 2005, pp. 798–805; Getta Menon, Lauren G. Block, and Suresh Ramanathan, "We're at as Much Risk as We're Led to Believe: The Effect of Message Cues on Judgments of Health Risk," *Journal of Consumer Research*, March 2002, pp. 533–549; Shailendra Jain and Durairai Maheswaran, "Motivated Reasoning: A Depth-of-Processing Perspective," *Journal of Consumer Research*, 2000, 26, no. 4, pp. 358–371; Ziva Kunda, "The Case for Motivated Reasoning," *Psychological Bulletin*, 1990, pp. 480–498.

6. Lisa E. Bolton, Joel B. Cohen, and Paul N. Bloom, "Does Marketing Products as Remedies Create 'Get Out of Jail Free Cards'?" *Journal of Consumer Research* 33, no. 1, 2006, pp. 71–81.

7. Ying-Ching Lin, Chien-Huang Lin, and Priya Raghubir, "Avoiding Anxiety, Being in Denial, or Simply Stroking Self-Esteem: Why Self-Positivity?" *Journal of Consumer Psychology*, 13, no. 4, 2003, pp. 464–477.

8. Gustavo de Mello, Deborah J. MacInnis, and David W. Stewart, "Threats to Hope: Effects on Reasoning About Product Information," *Journal of Consumer Research*, August 2007, pp. 153–161; Deborah J. MacInnis and Gustavo de Mello, "The Concept of Hope and Its Relevance to Product Evaluation and Choice," *Journal of Marketing*, January 2005, pp. 1–14.

9. Richard L. Celsi and Jerry C. Olson, "The Role of Involvement in Attention and Comprehension Processes," *Journal of Consumer Research*, September 1988, pp. 210–224.

10. Marsha L. Richins, Peter H. Bloch, and Edward F. McQuarrie, "How Enduring and Situational Involvement Combine to Create Involvement Responses," *Journal of Consumer Psychology*, September 1992, pp. 143–154; Peter H. Bloch and Marsha L. Richins, "A Theoretical Model for the Study of Product Importance Perceptions," *Journal of Marketing*, Summer 1983, pp. 69–81; Celsi and Olson, "The Role of Involvement in Attention and Comprehension Processes"; Andrew A. Mitchell, "The Dimensions of Advertising Involvement," in ed. Kent Monroe, *Advances in Consumer Research* 8 (Ann Arbor, Mich.: Association for Consumer Research, 1981), pp. 25–30; Marsha L. Richins and Peter H. Bloch, "After the New Wears Off: The Temporal Context of Product Involvement," *Journal of Consumer Research*, September 1986, pp. 280–285.

11. Michael J. Houston and Michael L. Rothschild, "Conceptual and Methodological Perspectives on Involvement," in ed. S. Jain, *Research Frontiers in Marketing: Dialogues and Directions* (Chicago: American Marketing Association, 1978), pp. 184–187; Richins and Bloch, "After the New Wears Off"; Gilles Laurent and Jean-Noel Kapferer, "Measuring Consumer Involvement Profiles," *Journal of Marketing Research*, February 1985, pp. 41–53.

12. C. Whan Park and S. Mark Young, "Consumer Response to Television Commercials: The Impact of Involvement and Background Music on Brand Attitude Formation," *Journal of Marketing Research*, February 1986, pp. 11–24.

13. Judith Lynne Zaichkowsky, "Measuring the Involvement Construct," *Journal of Consumer Research*, December 1985, pp. 341–352; Laurent and Kapferer, "Measuring Consumer Involvement Profiles."

14. Nina Michaelidou and Sally Dibb, "Product Involvement: An Application in Clothing," *Journal of Consumer Behaviour* 5, no. 5, 2006, pp. 442–453.

15. Jennifer Aaker, Susan Fournier, and S. Adam Brasel, "When Good Brands Do Bad," *Journal of Consumer Research*, June 2004, pp. 1–16; Matthew Thomson, Deborah J. MacInnis, and C. W. Park, "The Ties that Bind: Measuring the Strength of Consumers' Emotional Attachments to Brands," *Journal of Consumer Psychology* 15, no. 1, 2005, pp. 77–91.

16. J. Craig Andrews, Syed H. Akhter, Srinivas Durvasula, and Darrel D. Muehling, "The Effect of Advertising Distinctiveness and Message Content Involvement on Cognitive and Affective Responses to Advertising," *Journal of Current Issues and Research in Advertising*, Spring 1992, pp. 45–58; Laura M. Bucholz and Robert E. Smith, "The Role of Consumer Involvement in Determining Cognitive Response to Broadcast Advertising," *Journal of Advertising*, March 1991, pp. 4–17; Darrel D. Muehling, Russell N. Laczniak, and Jeffrey J. Stoltman, "The Moderating Effects of Ad Message Involvement: A Reassessment," *Journal of Advertising*, June 1991, pp. 29–38; Scott B. MacKenzie and Richard J. Lutz, "An Empirical Examination of the Structural Antecedents of Attitude Toward the Ad in an Advertising Pretesting Context," *Journal of Marketing*, April 1989, pp. 48–65.

17. Barbara Mueller, "Standardization vs. Specialization: An Examination of Westernization in Japanese Advertising," *Journal of Advertising Research*, January–February 1992, pp. 15–24.

18. "Arizona Teenager Wins 'American Idol,'" *New York Times,* May 24, 2007, p. A23.

19. Ann E. Schlosser, "Computers as Situational Cues: Implications for Consumers Product Cognitions and Attitudes," *Journal of Consumer Psychology* 13, no. 1&2, 2003, pp. 103–112. Charla Mathwick and Edward Rigdon, "Play, Flow, and the Online Search Experinece," *Journal of Consumer Research* 31, no. 2, 2004, pp. 324–332.

20. Houston and Rothschild, "Conceptual and Methodological Perspectives in Involvement"; Peter H. Bloch, Daniel Sherrell, and Nancy Ridgway, "Consumer Search: An Extended Framework," *Journal of Consumer Research*, June 1986, pp. 119–126; Peter H. Bloch, Nancy M. Ridgway, and Scott A. Dawson, "The Shopping Mall as Consumer Habitat," *Journal of Retailing*, Spring 1994, pp. 23–42; Richard L. Celsi, Randall L. Rose, and Thomas W. Leigh, "An Exploration of High-Risk Leisure Consumption Through Skydiving," *Journal of Consumer Research*, June 1993, pp. 1–23; Eric J. Arnould and Linda L. Price, "River Magic: Extraordinary Experience and the Extended Service Encounter," *Journal of Consumer Research*, June 1993, pp. 24–45; Morris B. Holbrook and Elizabeth C. Hirschman, "The Experiential Aspects of Consumption: Consumer Fantasies, Feelings, and Fun," *Journal of Consumer Research*, September 1982, pp. 132–140; Elizabeth C. Hirschman and Morris B. Holbrook, "Experience Seeking: Emerging Concepts, Methods, and Propositions," *Journal of Marketing*, Summer 1982, pp. 92–101; Morris B. Holbrook, Robert W. Chestnut, Terence A. Oliva, and Eric A. Greenleaf, "Play as a Consumption Experience: The Roles of Emotions, Performance, and Personality in the Enjoyment of Games," *Journal of Consumer Research*, September 1984, pp. 728–739.

21. Yinlong Zhang and Vikas Mittal, "Decision Difficulty: Effects of Procedural and Outcome Accountability," *Journal of Consumer Research* 32, no. 3, 2005, pp. 465–472.

22. Celsi and Olson, "The Role of Involvement in Attention and Comprehension Processes"; Greenwald and Leavitt, "Audience Involvement in Advertising"; Laurent and Kapferer, "Measuring Consumer Involvement Profiles"; Zaichkowsky, "Measuring the Involvement Construct"; Michael L. Rothschild, "Perspectives on Involvement: Current Problems and Future Directions," in ed. Tom Kinnear, *Advances in Consumer Research* 11 (Ann Arbor, Mich.: Association for Consumer Research, 1984), pp. 216–217; Andrew A. Mitchell, "Involvement: A Potentially Important Mediator of Consumer Behavior," in ed. William L. Wilkie, *Advances in Consumer Research*, vol. 6 (Ann Arbor, Mich.: Association for Consumer Research, 1979), pp. 191–196; Petty and Cacioppo, *Communication and Persuasion.*

23. Tiffany Barnett White, "Consumer Disclosure and Disclosure Avoidance: A Motivational Framework," *Journal of Consumer Psychology* 14, no. 1&2, 2004, pp. 41–51.

24. Banwari Mittal, "I, Me, and Mine: How Products Become Consumers' Extended Selves," *Journal of Consumer Behaviour* 5, no. 6, 2006, pp. 550–562.

25. Americus Reed II, "Activating the Self-Importance of Consumer Selves: Exploring Identity Salience Effects on Judgments," *Journal of Consumer Research* 31, no. 2, 2004, pp. 286–295.

26. Lorna Stevens, Pauline Maclaran, and Stephen Brown, "Red Time Is Me Time," *Journal of Advertising*, Spring 2003, pp. 35–45.

27. Randall L. Rose and Stacy L. Wood, "Paradox and the Consumption of Authenticity Through Reality Television," *Journal of Consumer Research* 32, no. 2, 2005, pp. 284–296.

28. C. Miguel Brendl, Arthur B. Markman, and Claude Messner, "The Devaluation Effect: Activating a Need Devalues Unrelated Objects," *Journal of Consumer Research*, March 2003, pp. 463–473.

29. Abraham H. Maslow, *Motivation and Personality*, 2nd ed. (New York: Harper & Row, 1970).

30. C. Whan Park, Bernard J. Jaworski, and Deborah J. MacInnis, "Strategic Brand Concept–Image Management," *Journal of Marketing*, October 1986, pp. 135–145.

31. Martha Visser, "Entrée New," *American Demographics*, December 2003–January 2004, pp. 20–23.

32. Judy Harris and Michael Lynn, "The Manifestations and Measurement of the Desire to Be a Unique Consumer," Proceedings of the 1994 AMA Winter Educators' Conference, Chicago; Kelly Tepper, "Need for Uniqueness: An Individual Difference Factor Affecting Nonconformity in Consumer Responses," Proceedings of the 1994 AMA Winter Educators' Conference, Chicago. Kelly Tepper Tian, William O. Bearden, and Gary L. Hunter, "Consumers' Need For Uniqueness: Scale Development and Validation," *Journal of Consumer Research* 28, June 2001, pp. 50–66.

33. Russell W. Belk, Güliz Ger, and Soren Askegaard, "The Fire of Desire: A Multisited Inquiry into Consumer Passion," *Journal of Consumer Research*, December 2003, pp. 632–351.

34. Benjamin Spillman, "Shiny New Shoppes at Palazzo," *Las Vegas Review-Journal*, January 18, 2008, *http://www.lvrj.com/business/13890922.html.*

35. John T. Cacioppo and Richard E. Petty, "The Need for Cognition," *Journal of Personality and Social Psychology*, February 1982, pp. 116–131; Douglas M. Stayman and Frank R. Kardes, "Spontaneous Inference Processes in Advertising: Effects of Need for Cognition and Self-Monitoring on Inference Generation and Utilization," *Journal of Consumer Psychology* 1, no. 2, 1992, pp. 125–142; John T. Cacioppo, Richard Petty, and Katherine Morris, "Effects of Need for Cognition on Message Evaluation, Recall, and Persuasion," *Journal of Personality and Social Psychology*, October 1993, pp. 805–818.

36. P. S. Raju, "Optimum Stimulation Level: Its Relationship to Personality, Demographics, and Exploratory Behavior," *Journal of Consumer Research*, December 1980, pp. 272–282; Jan-Benedict E. M. Steenkamp and Hans Baumgartner, "The Role of Optimum Stimulation Level in Exploratory Consumer Behavior," *Journal of Consumer Research*, December 1992, pp. 434–448.

37. Stuart Elliott, "Study Tries To Help Retailers Understand What Drives the Shopping Habits of Women," *New York Times*, January 17, 2001, p. C6.

38. Robert Roth, *International Marketing Communications* (Chicago: Crain Books, 1982), p. 5.

39. H. Murray, *Thematic Apperception Test Manual* (Cambridge, Mass.: Harvard University Press, 1943); Harold Kassarjian, "Projective Methods," in ed. Robert Ferber, *Handbook of Marketing Research* (New York: McGraw-Hill, 1974), pp. 85–100; Ernest Dichter, *Packaging the Sixth Sense: A Guide to Identifying Consumer Motivation* (Boston: Cahners Books, 1975); Dennis Rook, "Researching Consumer Fantasy," in ed. Elizabeth C. Hirschman, *Research in Consumer Behavior*, vol. 3 (Greenwich, Conn.: JAI Press, 1990), pp. 247–270; David Mick, M. De Moss, and Ronald Faber, "A Projective Study of Motivations and Meanings of Self-Gifts: Implications for Retail Management," *Journal of Retailing*, Summer 1992, pp. 122–144; Mary Ann McGrath, John F. Sherry, and Sidney J. Levy, "Giving Voice to the Gift: The Use of Projective Techniques to Recover Lost Meanings," *Journal of Consumer Psychology* 2, no. 2, 1993, pp. 171–191.

40. Harold H. Kassarjian and Joel B. Cohen, "Cognitive Dissonance and Consumer Behavior: Reaction to the Surgeon General's Report on Smoking and Health," *California Management Review*, Fall 1965, pp. 55–65; see also Kenneth E. Runyon and David W. Stewart, *Consumer Behavior*, 3rd ed. (Columbus, Ohio: Merrill, 1987).

41. Sharon Shavitt, Suzanne Swan, Tina M. Lowrey, and Michaela Wanke, "The Interaction of Endorser Attractiveness and Involvement in Persuasion Depends on the Goal That Guides Message Processing," *Journal of Consumer Psychology* 3, no. 2, 1994, pp. 137–162; Robert Lawson, "Consumer Decision Making Within a Goal-Driven Framework," *Psychology and Marketing*, August 1997, pp. 427–449; Ingrid W. Martin and David W. Stewart, "The Differential Impact of Goal Congruency on Attitudes, Intentions, and the Transfer of Brand Equity," *Journal of Marketing Research*, November 2001, pp. 471–484.

42. Richard P. Bagozzi and Utpal Dholakia, "Goal Setting and Goal Striving in Consumer Behavior," *Journal of Marketing* 63, 1999, pp. 19–32.

43. Dilip Soman and Amar Cheema, "When Goals Are Counterproductive: The Effects of Violation of a Behavioral Goal on Subsequent Performance," *Journal of Consumer Research*, June 2004, pp. 52–62.

44. Ayelet Fishbach and Ravi Dhar, "Goals as Excuses or Guides: The Liberating Effect of Perceived Goal Progress on Choice," *Journal of Consumer Research* 32, no. 3, 2005, pp. 370–377;

45. Joseph C. Nunes and Xavier Drèze, "The Endowed Progress Effect: How Artificial Advancement Increases Effort," *Journal of Consumer Research* 32, no. 4, 2006, pp. 504–512.

46. Richard P. Bagozzi and Utpal Dholakia, "Goal Setting and Goal Striving in Consumer Behavior," *Journal of Marketing* 63, 1999, pp. 19–32.

47. Rui (Juliet) Zhu and Joan Meyers-Levy, "Exploring the Cognitive Mechanism that Underlies Regulatory Focus Effects," *Journal of Consumer Research* 34, no. 1, 2007, pp. 89–98; Jing Wang and Angela Y. Lee, "The Role of Regulatory Focus in Preference Construction," *Journal of Marketing Research*, February 2006, pp. 28–38; Utpal M. Dholakia, Mahesh Gopinath, Richard P. Bagozzi, and Rajan Nataraajan, "The Role of Regulatory Focus in the Experience and Self-Control of Desire for Temptations," *Journal of Consumer Psychology* 16, no. 2, 2006, pp. 163–175; Jens Förster, E. Tory Higgins, and Lorraine Chen Idson, "Approach and Avoidance Strength During Goal Attainment: Regulatory Focus and the 'Goal Looms Larger' Effect," *Journal of Personality and Social Psychology*, November 1998, pp. 1115–1131.

48. Eduardo B. Andrade, "Behavioral Consequences of Affect: Combining Evaluative and Regulatory Mechanisms," *Journal of Consumer Research* 32, no. 2, 2005, pp. 355–362.

49. Nathan Novemsky and Ravi Dhar, "Goal Fulfillment and Goal Targets in Sequential Choice," *Journal of Consumer Research* 32, no. 3, 2005, pp. 396–404.

50. Anirban Mukhopadhyay and Gita Venkataramani Johar, "Where There Is a Will, Is There a Way? Effects of Lay Theories of Self-Control on Setting and Keeping Resolutions," *Journal of Consumer Research* 31, no. 4, 2005, pp. 779–786.

51. Allison R. Johnson and David W. Stewart, "A Reappraisal of the Role of Emotion in Consumer Behavior: Traditional and Contemporary Approaches," in ed. Naresh K. Malhotra, *Review of Marketing Research*, (London: M.E. Sharpe, 2005), pp. 3–34.

52. Seunghee Han, Jennifer S. Lerner, and Dacher Keltner, "Feelings and Consumer Decision Making: The Appraisal-Tendency Framework," *Journal of Consumer Psychology* 17, no. 3, 2007, pp. 158–168.

53. Tiffany Barnett White, "Consumer Disclosure and Disclosure Avoidance: A Motivational Framework," *Journal of Consumer Psychology* 14, no. 1&2, 2004, pp. 41–51.

54. Jane L. Levere, "Public Service Ads Are Seeking Young Blood," *New York Times*, July 20, 2004, *www.nytimes.com*.

55. Jennifer Edson Escalas, "Narrative Processing: Building Consumer Connections to Brands," *Journal of Consumer Psychology* 14, no. 1/2, 2004, pp. 168–180.

56. Nidhi Agrawal and Durairaj Maheswaran, "The Effects of Self-Construal and Commitment on Persuasion," *Journal of Consumer Research* 31, no. 4, 2005, pp. 841–849; S. Christian Wheeler, Richard E. Petty, and George Y. Bizer, "Self-Schema Matching and Attitude Change: Situational and Dispositional Determinants of Message Elaboration," *Journal of Consumer Research* 31, no. 4, 2005, pp. 787–797.

57. Sara Schaefer Munoz, "'Whole Grain': Food Labels' New Darling?" *Wall Street Journal*, January 12, 2005, pp. B1, B4.

58. Jonathan Welsh, "Checkered-Flag Past Helps Ferrari Unload a Fleet of Used Cars," *Wall Street Journal*, January 11, 2005, pp. A1, A10.

59. Eric Wilson, "Goes Well with Eggnog," *New York Times,* December 21, 2006, p. G12; Rob Walker, "Quack Addicts," *New York Times Magazine,* October 10, 2004, p. 30.

60. Kim Painter, "Grasping at Strands," *USA Today,* March 19, 2007, p. 4D.

61. Ravi Dhar and Itamar Simonson, "Making Complementary Choices in Consumption Episodes: Highlighting Versus Balancing," *Journal of Marketing Research* 36, February 1999, pp. 29–44.

62. "Subway Launches Program to Help Consumers Keep Diet Resolutions," *Nation's Restaurant News,* January 2, 2006, p. 18.

63. Park, Jaworski, and MacInnis, "Strategic Brand Concept–Image Management." *Journal of Marketing,* 50, October, pp. 135–145

64. Alexander Chernev, "Goal Orientation and Consumer Preference for the Status Quo," *Journal of Consumer Research* 31, no. 3, 2004, pp. 557–565.

65. Raymond A. Bauer, "Consumer Behavior as Risk Taking," in ed. Robert S. Hancock, *Dynamic Marketing for a Changing World* (Chicago: American Marketing Association, 1960), pp. 389–398; Grahame R. Dowling, "Perceived Risk: The Concept and Its Measurement," *Psychology and Marketing,* Fall 1986, pp. 193–210; Lawrence X. Tarpey and J. Paul Peter, "A Comparative Analysis of Three Consumer Decision Strategies," *Journal of Consumer Research,* June 1975, pp. 29–37.

66. James R. Bettman, "Perceived Risk and Its Components: A Model and Empirical Test," *Journal of Marketing Research,* May 1973, pp. 184–190.

67. Dana L. Alden, Douglas M. Stayman, and Wayne D. Hoyer, "The Evaluation Strategies of American and Thai Consumers: A Cross Cultural Comparison," *Psychology and Marketing,* March–April 1994, pp. 145–161; Ugur Yavas, Bronislaw J. Verhage, and Robert T. Green, "Global Consumer Segmentation Versus Local Market Orientation: Empirical Findings," *Management International Review,* July 1992, pp. 265–272.

68. Vincent W. Mitchell and Michael Greatorex, "Consumer Purchasing in Foreign Countries: A Perceived Risk Analysis," *International Journal of Advertising* 9, no. 4, 1990, pp. 295–307.

69. Anonymous, "Marketing Briefs," *Marketing News,* March 1995, p. 11.

70. Jacob Jacoby and Leon Kaplan, "The Components of Perceived Risk," in ed. M. Venkatesan, *Advances in Consumer Research,* vol. 3 (Chicago: Association for Consumer Research, 1972), pp. 382–383; Tarpey and Peter, "A Comparative Analysis of Three Consumer Decision Strategies."

71. Jean Halliday, "GM Ads Assure Used Car Buyer," *Advertising Age,* June 11, 2001, p. 10.

72. Vanitha Swaminathan, "The Impact of Recommendation Agents on Consumer Evaluation and Choice," *Journal of Consumer Psychology* 13, no. 1&2, 2003, pp. 93–102.

73. Michael Tsiros and Carrie M. Heilman, "The Effect of Expiration Dates and Perceived Risk on Purchasing Behavior in Grocery Store Perishable Categories," *Journal of Marketing,* April 2005, pp. 114–129.

74. Cornelia Pechmann, Guangzhi Zhao, Marvin E. Goldberg, and Ellen Thomas Reibling, "What to Convey in Antismoking Advertisements for Adolescents," *Journal of Marketing,* April 2003, pp. 1–18.

75. Craig J. Thompson, "Consumer Risk Perceptions in a Community of Reflexive Doubt," *Journal of Consumer Research* 32, no. 2, 2005, pp. 235–248.

76. "Campaign Summary: Flu 2006/07 Post-campaign Evaluation," Scottish Government Publications, July 2007, *http://www.scotland.gov.uk/Publications/2007/07/31095955/1.*

77. Priya Raghubir and Geeta Menon, "AIDS and Me, Never the Twain Shall Meet: The Effects of Information Accessibility on Judgments of Risk and Advertising Effectiveness," *Journal of Consumer Research,* June 1998, pp. 52–63.

78. Shailendra Pratap Jain and Durairaj Maheswaran, "Motivated Reasoning: A Depth-of-Processing Perspective," *Journal of Consumer Research* 26, March 2000, pp. 358–371; Joan Meyers-Levy and Alice Tybout, "Schema-Congruity as a Basis for Product Evaluation," *Journal of Consumer Research,* June 1989, pp. 39–54.

79. MacInnis and Jaworski, "Information Processing from Advertisements." *Journal of Marketing,* 53, October 1989, pp. 1–23.

80. Joseph W. Alba and J. Wesley Hutchinson, "Dimensions of Consumer Expertise," *Journal of Consumer Research,* March 1987, pp. 411–454. For an excellent overview of measures of consumer knowledge or expertise, see Andrew A. Mitchell and Peter A. Dacin, "The Assessment of Alternative Measures of Consumer Expertise," *Journal of Consumer Research,* December 1996, pp. 219–239.

81. Eric J. Johnson and J. Edward Russo, "Product Familiarity and Learning New Information," *Journal of Consumer Research,* June 1984, pp. 542–550; Merrie Brucks, "The Effects of Product Class Knowledge on Information Search Behavior," *Journal of Consumer Research,* June 1985, pp. 1–16; Alba and Hutchinson, "Dimensions of Consumer Expertise." *Journal of Consumer Research,* March 1987, pp. 411–454.

82. Oscar Suris, "New Data Help Car Lessees Shop Smarter," *Wall Street Journal,* July 11, 1995, pp. 1, B12.

83. Durairaj Maheswaran and Brian Sternthal, "The Effects of Knowledge, Motivation, and Type of Message on Ad Processing and Product Judgments," *Journal of Consumer Research,* June 1990, pp. 66–73.

84. Jennifer Gregan-Paxton and Deborah Roedder John, "Consumer Learning by Analogy: A Model of Internal Knowledge Transfer," *Journal of Consumer Research,* December 1997, pp. 266–284.

85. Michelle L. Roehm and Brian Sternthal, "The Moderating Effect of Knowledge and Resources on the Persuasive Impact of Analogies," *Journal of Consumer Research,* September 2001, pp. 257.

86. Michael K. Hui, Xiande Zhao, Xiucheng Fan, and Kevin Au, "When Does the Service Process Matter? A Test of Two Competing Theories," *Journal of Consumer Research* 31, no. 2, 2004, pp. 465–475.

87. Richard Yalch and Rebecca Elmore-Yalch, "The Effect of Numbers on the Route to Persuasion," *Journal of Consumer Research*, June 1984, pp. 522–527.

88. Noel Capon and Roger Davis, "Basic Cognitive Ability Measures as Predictors of Consumer Information Processing Strategies, *Journal of Consumer Research*, June 1984, pp. 551–564.

89. Nicole H. Lurie and Charlotte H. Mason, "Visual Representation: Implications for Decision Making," *Journal of Marketing*, January 2007, pp. 160–177.

90. Joe Goldeen, "Spanish-Language Web Site Aims to Educate California Latinos on Health Care," *The Record (Stockton, CA)*, April 6, 2004, *www.recordnet.com*.

91. Jennifer Gregan-Paxton and Deborah Roedder John, "Are Young Children Adaptive Decision Makers? A Study of Age Differences in Information Search Behavior," *Journal of Consumer Research*, March 1995, pp. 567–580.

92. Catherine A. Cole and Gary J. Gaeth, "Cognitive and Age-Related Differences in the Ability to Use Nutrition Information in a Complex Environment," *Journal of Marketing Research*, May 1990, pp. 175–184.

93. Elizabeth Olson, "Catching the Bouquet, in a Dress You Bought Online," *New York Times,* September 2, 2007, p. B-7.

94. Cynthia Crossen, "'Merry Christmas to Moi' Shoppers Say," *Wall Street Journal,* December 11, 1997, pp. B1, B14.

95. June Fletcher and Sarah Collins, "The Lazy Gardener," *Wall Street Journal,* June 6, 2001, pp. W1, W16.

96. Peter Wright, "The Time Harassed Consumer: Time Pressures, Distraction, and the Use of Evidence," *Journal of Applied Psychology*, October 1974, pp. 555–561.

97. Rajneesh Suri and Kent B. Monroe, "The Effects of Time Constraints on Consumers' Judgments of Prices and Products," *Journal of Consumer Research,* June 2003, pp. 92–104.

98. C. Page Moreau and Darren W. Dahl, "Designing the Solution: The Impact of Constraints on Consumers' Creativity," *Journal of Consumer Research* 32, no. 1, 2005, pp. 13–22.

99. Danny L. Moore, Douglas Hausknecht, and Kanchana Thamodaran, "Time Compression, Response Opportunity, and Persuasion," *Journal of Consumer Research*, June 1986, pp. 85–99; Priscilla LaBarbera and James Mac-Laughlin, "Time Compressed Speech in Radio Advertising," *Journal of Marketing*, January 1979, pp. 30–36; Shelly Chaiken and Alice Eagly, "Communication Modality as a Determinant of Message Persuasiveness and Message Comprehensibility," *Journal of Personality and Social Psychology*, March 1976, pp. 605–614; Herbert Krugman, "The Impact of Television Advertising: Learning Without Involvement," *Public Opinion Quarterly*, Fall 1965, pp. 349–356; Patricia A. Stout and Benedicta Burda, "Zipped Commercials: Are They Effective?" *Journal of Advertising*, Fall 1989, pp. 23–32.

100. Park and Young, "Consumer Response to Television Commercials"; Deborah J. MacInnis and C. Whan Park, "The Differential Role of Characteristics of Music on High- and Low-Involvement Consumers' Processing of Ads," *Journal of Consumer Research*, September 1991, pp. 161–173; Shelly Chaiken and Alice Eagly, "Communication Modality as a Determinant of Persuasion: The Role of Communicator Salience," *Journal of Personality and Social Psychology*, August 1983, pp. 605–614.

101. Kenneth Lord and Robert Burnkrant, "Attention Versus Distraction: The Interactive Effect of Program Involvement and Attentional Devices on Commercial Processing," *Journal of Advertising*, March 1993, pp. 47–61; Kenneth R. Lord and Robert E. Burnkrant, "Television Program Effects on Commercial Processing," in ed. Michael J. Houston, *Advances in Consumer Research* 15 (Provo, Utah: Association for Consumer Research, 1988), pp. 213–218; Gary Soldow and Victor Principe, "Response to Commercials as a Function of Program Context," *Journal of Advertising Research*, February–March 1981, pp. 59–65.

102. Baba Shiv and Stephen M. Nowlis, "The Effect of Distractions While Tasting a Food Sample: The Interplay of Informational and Affective Components in Subsequent Choice," *Journal of Consumer Research*, December 2004, pp. 599–608.

103. Rajeev Batra and Michael L. Ray, "Situational Effects of Advertising Repetitions: The Moderating Influence of Motivation, Ability, and Opportunity to Respond," *Journal of Consumer Research*, March 1986, pp. 432–435; Carl Obermiller, "Varieties of Mere Exposure: The Effects of Processing Style and Repetition on Affective Response," *Journal of Consumer Research*, June 1985, pp. 17–30; Arno Rethans, John L. Swazy, and Lawrence J. Marks, "The Effects of Television Commercial Repetition, Receiver Knowledge, and Commercial Length: A Test of the Two-Factor Model," *Journal of Marketing Research*, February 1986, pp. 50–61; Sharmistha Law and Scott A. Hawkins, "Advertising Repetition and Consumer Beliefs: The Role of Source Memory," in ed. William Wells, *Measuring Advertising Effectiveness* (Mahwah, N.J.: Lawrence Erlbaum Associates, 1997), pp. 67–75; Giles D'Sousa and Ram C. Rao, "Can Repeating an Advertisement More Frequently Than the Competition Affect Brand Preference in a Mature Market?" *Journal of Marketing* 59, no. 2, 1995, pp. 32–43.

104. Margaret C. Campbell and Kevin Lane Keller, "Brand Familiarity and Advertising Repetition Effects," *Journal of Consumer Research*, September 2003, pp. 292–304.

105. Dan Ariely, "Controlling the Information Flow: Effects on Consumers' Decision Making and Preferences," *Journal of Consumer Research* 27, September 2000, pp. 233–248.

106. Ibid.

107. Fred Vogelstein, "Can Schwab Get Its Mojo Back?" *Fortune*, September 17, 2001, pp. 93–97.

108. Linda Daily, "Umpqua Bank Debuts Innovation Lab," *Community Banker*, January 2008, p. 11; Renee Kimmel, "Bank Aids Early Entrepreneurs," *Brandweek*, July 23, 2007, p. 38; Karen Krebsbach, "Is Umpqua Cool? Maybe. Quirky? Yup. Successful? No Question About It," *U.S. Banker*, June 2007, p. 24; Bill Breen, "The Mind Reader," *Fast Company*, October 2006, pp. 71–72; Rob Walker, "Branching Out: Umpqua Bank," *New York Times Magazine*, September 24, 2006, p. 21.

Chapter 3

1. Dianna Dilworth, "Is In-Game Advertising Ready to Take the Next Step?" *DM News*, January 21, 2008, *www.dmnews.com*; Allison Enright, "Inside In-game Advertising," *Marketing News*, September 15, 2007, pp. 26+; Abbey Klaassen, "Buying In-Game Ads? Be Sure They're at Eye Level," *Advertising Age*, July 23, 2007, *www.adage.com*.

2. Mike Molesworth, "Real Brands in Imaginary Worlds: Investigating Players' Experiences of Brand Placement in Digital Games," *Journal of Consumer Behaviour* 5, no. 4, 2006, pp. 355–366.

3. "Visa Rolls with New Multimedia Advertising Campaign," *Wireless News*, September 20, 2007; "'Game of Life' Takes Visa," *San Francisco Chronicle*, March 27, 2007, p. B6; Maria Aspan, "Small and Plastic, with an Upscale Tilt," *New York Times*, February 13, 2007, p. C7; "Visa Will Relaunch Advertising Campaign Aimed at Hispanics," *Cardline*, August 20, 2004, p. D2.

4. Adam Finn, "Print Ad Recognition Readership Scores: An Information Processing Perspective," *Journal of Marketing Research*, May 1988, pp. 168–177.

5. John Battle, "Cashing in at the Register," *Aftermarket Business*, September 1, 1994, pp. 12–13.

6. Laura Petrecca, "Wal-Mart TV Sells Marketers Flexibility," *USA Today*, March 29, 2007, p. 3B; Ann Zimmerman, "Wal-Mart Adds In-Store TV Sets, Lifts Advertising," *Wall Street Journal*, September 22, 2004, p. A20.

7. Douglas A. Blackmon, "New Ad Vehicles: Police Cars, School Buses, Garbage Trucks," *Wall Street Journal*, February 20, 1996, pp. B1, B6; Suzanne Vranica, "Think Graffiti Is All That's Hanging in Subway Tunnels? Look Again," *Wall Street Journal*, April 4, 2001, pp. B1, B6; Leslie Chang, "Online Ads in China Go Offline," *Wall Street Journal*, July 30, 2000, pp. B1, B6.

8. "Panasonic Signs Deal with Road Ads," *Marketing*, January 8, 2004, p. 6.

9. For more about consumer control of e-mail advertising, see Ray Kent and Hege Brandal, "Improving Email Response in a Permission Marketing Context," *International Journal of Market Research*, Winter 2003, pp. 489–504.

10. Steven M. Edwards, Hairong Li, and Joo-Hyun Lee, "Forced Exposure and Psychological Reactance," *Journal of Advertising*, Fall 2002, pp. 83–95.

11. Paul Surgi Speck and Michael T. Elliott, "Predictors of Advertising Avoidance in Print and Broadcast Media," *Journal of Advertising*, Fall 1997, pp. 61–76.

12. Amy L. Webb, "More Consumers Are Ignoring Ads, Survey Shows," *Wall Street Journal Europe*, June 18, 2001, p. 29.

13. Kevin Downey, "Commercial Zapping Doesn't Matter," *Broadcasting & Cable*, September 3, 2007, p. 8.

14. Steve McClellan, "It's Inescapable: DVRs Here to Stay," *Television Week*, November 29, 2004, p. 17.

15. Brian Steinberg, "How to Stop Them from Skipping: TiVo Tells All," *Advertising Age*, July 16, 2007, p. 1; Gina Piccalo, "TiVo Will No Longer Skip Past Advertisers," *Los Angeles Times*, November 17, 2004, p. A1.

16. Dean M. Krugman, Glen T. Cameron, and Candace McKearney White, "Visual Attention to Programming and Commercials: The Use of In-Home Observations," *Journal of Advertising*, Spring 1995, pp. 1–12; S. Siddarth and Amitava Chattopadhyay, "To Zap or Not to Zap: A Study of the Determinants of Channel Switching During Commercials," *Marketing Science* 17, no. 2, 1998, pp. 124–138.

17. Bill Carter, "NBC Is Hoping Short Movies Keep Viewers from Zapping," *New York Times*, August 4, 2003, p. C1.

18. "Kids See, Kids Do? TV Ads and Obesity," *Marketing News*, December 15, 2007, p. 4.

19. Sarah Ellison, "Kraft Limits on Kids' Ads May Cheese Off Rivals," *Wall Street Journal*, January 13, 2005, p. B3; Todd Wasserman, "Curbing Their Appetite," *Brandweek*, December 6, 2004, pp. 24–26; 28; Annie Seeley and Martin Glenn, "Kids and Junk Food: Are Ads to Blame?" *Grocer*, May 15, 2004, p. 30.

20. Burt Helm, "Cutting the Stack of Catalogs, *Business-Week*, December 20, 2007, *www.businessweek.com*.

21. Christopher Conkey, "FTC Wins Order to Shut Down Spam from Adult Web Sites," *Wall Street Journal*, January 12, 2005, p. D2; "FCC Adopts Rules Under the CAN-SPAM Act to Protect Wireless Subscribers," *Computer & Internet Lawyer*, October 2004, p. 39.

22. Allison Enright, "(Third) Screen Tests," *Marketing News*, March 15, 2007, pp. 17–18.

23. Bob Tedeschi, "Reaching More Customers with a Simple Text Message," *New York Times*, July 16, 2007, p. C6.

24. Cynthia H. Cho, "Outdoor Ads, Here's Looking at You," *Wall Street Journal*, July 12, 2004, p. B3; Bradley Johnson, "Cracks in the Foundation," *Advertising Age*, December 8, 2003, pp. 1, 10.

25. "New TiVo Service Monitors Skipping Habits," *MediaWeek*, November 12, 2007, p. 3; Brian Steinberg, "How to Stop Them from Skipping: TiVo Tells All," *Advertising Age*, July 16, 2007, p. 1.

26. Sarah Lacy, "Web Numbers: What's Real?" *BusinessWeek*, October 23, 2007, p. 98; Jessi Hempel, "The Online Numbers Game," *Fortune*, September 3, 2007, p. 18.

27. Rik Pieters, Edward Rosbergen, and Michel Wedel, "Visual Attention to Repeated Print Advertising: A Test of Scanpath Theory," *Journal of Marketing Research* 36, November 1999, pp. 424–438.

28. Rik Pieters and Michel Wedel, "Goal Control of Attention to Advertising: The Yarbus Implication," *Journal of Consumer Research*, August 2007, pp. 224–233.

29. Trebor Banstetter, "American Sues Google over 'Sponsored Links,'" *Fort Worth Star-Telegram*, August 18, 2007, *www.dfw.com.*

30. Scott B. MacKenzie, "The Role of Attention in Mediating the Effect of Advertising on Attribute Importance," *Journal of Consumer Research*, September 1986, pp. 174–195; Richard E. Petty and Timothy C. Brock, "Thought Disruption and Persuasion: Assessing the Validity of Attitude Change Experiments," in eds. Richard E. Petty, Thomas Ostrom, and Timothy C. Brock, *Cognitive Responses in Persuasion* (Hillsdale, N.J.: Lawrence Erlbaum, 1981), pp. 55–79.

31. Joe Flint, "Disappearing Act: The Amount of TV Screen Devoted to Show Shrinks," *Wall Street Journal*, March 29, 2001, pp. B1, B6.

32. L. Hasher and R. T. Zacks, "Automatic and Effortful Processes in Memory," *Journal of Experimental Psychology: General*, September 1979, pp. 356–388; W. Schneider and R. M. Shiffrin, "Controlled and Automatic Human Information Processing: I. Detection, Search, and Attention," *Psychological Review*, January 1977, pp. 1–66; R. M. Shiffrin and W. Schneider, "Controlled and Automatic Human Information Processing: II. Perceptual Learning, Automatic Attending, and a General Theory," *Psychological Review*, March 1977, pp. 127–190.

33. Chris Janiszewski, "Preconscious Processing Effects: The Independence of Attitude Formation and Conscious Thought," *Journal of Consumer Research*, September 1988, pp. 199–209; Joan Meyers-Levy, "Priming Effects on Product Judgments: A Hemispheric Interpretation," *Journal of Consumer Research*, June 1989, pp. 76–87.

34. Janiszewski, "Preconscious Processing Effects"; Chris Janiszewski, "The Influence of Print Advertisement Organization on Affect Toward a Brand Name," *Journal of Consumer Research*, June 1990, pp. 53–65.

35. Chris Janiszewski, "Preattentive Mere Exposure Effects," *Journal of Consumer Research*, December 1993, pp. 376–392; Janiszewski, "Preconscious Processing Effects"; Janiszewski, "The Influence of Print Advertisement Organization on Affect Toward a Brand Name."

36. Janiszewski, "Preattentive Mere Exposure Effects"; Stewart Shapiro and Deborah J. MacInnis, "Mapping the Relationship Between Preattentive Processing and Attitudes," in eds. John Sherry and Brian Sternthal, *Advances in Consumer Research*, vol. 19 (Provo, Utah: Association for Consumer Research, 1992), pp. 505–513.

37. Stewart Shapiro, "When an Ad's Influence Is Beyond Our Conscious Control: Perceptual and Conceptual Fluency Effects Caused by Incidental Ad Exposure," *Journal of Consumer Research* 26, June 1999, pp. 16–36; Stewart Shapiro, Deborah J. MacInnis, and Susan E. Heckler, "The Effects of Incidental Ad Exposure on the Formation of Consideration Sets," *Journal of Consumer Research*, June 1997, pp. 94–104.

38. Richard L. Celsi and Jerry C. Olson, "The Role of Involvement in Attention and Comprehension Processes," *Journal of Consumer Research*, September 1988, pp. 210–224.

39. Paula Lehman, "Social Networks That Break a Sweat," *BusinessWeek*, February 4, 2008, p. 68.

40. Arch Woodside and J. William Davenport Jr., "The Effect of Salesman Similarity and Expertise on Consumer Purchasing Behavior," *Journal of Marketing Research*, May 1974, pp. 198–202.

41. Robert E. Burnkrant and Daniel J. Howard, "Effects of the Use of Introductory Rhetorical Questions Versus Statements on Information Processing," *Journal of Personality and Social Psychology*, December 1984, pp. 1218–1230.

42. Grant McCracken, "Who Is the Celebrity Endorser? Cultural Foundations of the Endorsement Process," *Journal of Consumer Research*, December 1989, pp. 310–321; Jeffrey Burroughs and Richard A. Feinberg, "Using Response Latency to Assess Spokesperson Effectiveness," *Journal of Consumer Research*, September 1987, pp. 295–299.

43. Martin Lindstrom, "Martin Lindstrom's Weekly Video Reports: Spotlighting Branding Practices from Around the World," *Advertising Age*, June 4, 2007, *www.adage.com.*

44. Deborah J. MacInnis and C. Whan Park, "The Differential Role of Characteristics of Music on High- and Low-Involvement Consumers' Processing of Ads," *Journal of Consumer Research*, September 1991, pp. 161–173; David W. Stewart and David H. Furse, *Effective Television Advertising: A Study of 1000 Commercials* (Lexington, Mass.: Lexington Books, 1986); James J. Kellaris and Robert J. Kent, "An Exploratory Investigation of Responses Elicited by Music Varying in Tempo, Tonality, and Texture," *Journal of Consumer Psychology*, March 1993, pp. 381–402; James J. Kellaris, Anthony Cox, and Dena Cox, "The Effects of Background Music on Ad Processing Contingency Explanation," *Journal of Consumer Research*, October 1993, pp. 114–126.

45. Chris Gaerig, "With Feist and The Books, Ads Take Aim at New Audience, *The Michigan Daily,* January 15, 2008, *www.michigandaily.com;* Jamie LaReau, "Music Is Key to Carmakers' Marketing," *Automotive News*, December 20, 2004, p. 22.

46. Brian Sternthal and Samuel Craig, "Humor in Advertising," *Journal of Marketing*, October 1973, pp. 12–18; Thomas Madden and Marc G. Weinberger, "The Effect of Humor on Attention in Magazine Advertising," *Journal of Advertising*, September 1982, pp. 8–14.

47. Martin Lindstrom, "Martin Lindstrom's Weekly Video Reports: Spotlighting Branding Practices from Around the World," *Advertising Age*, June 4, 2007, *www.adage.com.*

48. Josephine L. C. M. Woltman Elpers, Ashesh Mukherjee, and Wayne D. Hoyer, "Humor in Television Advertising: A Moment-to-Moment Analysis," *Journal of Consumer Research*, December 2004, pp. 592–598.

49. Sherman So, "Unsolicited Messages Still a Novelty in the Mainland," *Asia Africa Intelligence Wire*, November 9, 2004, n.p.

50. Kate Fitzgerald, "In-Stadium Tech Reinvents Ad Game," *Advertising Age*, October 27, 2003, p. S-6.

51. Satya Menon and Dilip Soman, "Managing the Power of Curiosity for Effective Web Strategies," *Journal of Advertising*, Fall 2002, pp. 1–14; Yih Hwai Lee, "Manipulating Ad Message Involvement Through Information Expectancy: Effects on Attitude Evaluation and Confidence," *Journal of Advertising* 29, no. 2, Summer 2000, pp. 29–42; Joan Meyers-Levy and Alice Tybout, "Schema Congruity as a Basis for Product Evaluation," *Journal of Consumer Research*, June 1989, pp. 39–54. Characteristics of Music can also Cause Surprise; see James Kellaris and Ronald Rice (1993), "The Influence of Tempo, Loudness and Gender of Listener on Responses to Music," *Psychology and Marketing* 10, no. 1, pp. 15–29.

52. Dana L. Alden, Ashesh Mukherjee, and Wayne D. Hoyer, "The Effects of Incongruity, Surprise and Positive Moderators on Perceived Humor in Television Advertising," *Journal of Advertising* 29, no. 2, Summer 2000, pp. 1–15; Elpers, Mukherjee, and Hoyer, "Humor in Television Advertising: A Moment-to-Moment Analysis."

53. Anthony Malakian, "Ad Beat: Provident Introduces the Iconoclastic 'Mrs. P,'" *Banking Wire,* November 19, 2007, p. 34.

54. Nigel K. Li Pope, Kevin E. Voges, and Mark R. Brown, "The Effect of Provocation in the Form of Mild Erotica on Attitude to the Ad and Corporate Image," *Journal of Advertising*, Spring 2004, pp. 69–82.

55. Edward F. McQuarrie and David Glen Mick, "Visual Rhetoric in Advertising: Text-Interpretive, Experimental, and Reader-Response Analyses," *Journal of Consumer Research* 26, June 1999, pp. 37–54.

56. Finn, "Print Ad Recognition Readership Scores."

57. Avery M. Abernethy and David N. Laband, "The Impact of Trademarks and Advertisement Size on Yellow Page Call Rates," *Journal of Advertising Research*, March 2004, pp. 119–125.

58. Rik Pieters and Michel Wedel, "Attention Capture and Transfer in Advertising: Brand, Pictorial, and Text-size Effects," *Journal of Marketing*, April 2004, pp. 36–50.

59. Roseanne Harper, "Secondary Produce Displays Boost Sales," *Supermarket News,* November 15, 2004, p. 54.

60. S. Shyam Sundar and Sriram Kalyanaraman, "Arousal, Memory, and Impression-Formation Effects of Animation Speed in Web Advertising," *Journal of Advertising,* Spring 2004, pp. 7–17; Werner Krober-Riel, "Activation Research: Psychobiological Approaches in Consumer Research," *Journal of Consumer Research*, March 1979, pp. 240–250; Morris B. Holbrook and Donald R. Lehmann, "Form vs. Content in Predicting Starch Scores," *Journal of Advertising Research*, August 1980, pp. 53–62.

61. Mackenzie, "The Role of Attention in Mediating the Effect of Advertising on Attribute Importance."

62. Walter Nicholls, "The U.S. Is Turned On to Wine," *Washington Post*, January 2, 2008, *www.washingtonpost.com.*

63. Karen V. Fernandez and Dennis L. Rosen, "The Effectiveness of Information and Color in Yellow Pages Advertising," *Journal of Advertising* 29, no. 2, Summer 2000, pp. 61–73.

64. Chris Janiszewski, "The Influence of Display Characteristics on Visual Exploratory Search Behavior," *Journal of Consumer Research*, December 1998, pp. 290–301.

65. Edward Rosbergen, Rik Pieters, and Michel Wedel, "Visual Attention to Advertising: A Segment-Level Analysis," *Journal of Consumer Research*, December 1997, pp. 305–314.

66. Jean Halliday, "Auto Shopping Website Vehix to Now Fill Three Screens," *Advertising Age*, July 26, 2007, *www.adage.com;* Louise Story, "Toyota's Latest Commercial Is Not on TV. Try the Xbox Console," *New York Times,* October 8, 2007, p. C6.

67. Priya Raghubir and Eric A. Greenleaf, "Ratios in Proportion: What Should the Shape of the Package Be?" *Journal of Marketing*, April 2006, pp. 95–107; Priya Raghubir and Aradhna Krishna, "Vital Dimensions in Volume Perception: Can the Eye Fool the Stomach?" *Journal of Marketing Research* 36, August 1999, pp. 313–326; Aradhna Krishna, "Interaction of Senses: The Effect of Vision Versus Touch on the Elongation Bias," *Journal of Consumer Research* 32, no. 4, 2006, pp. 557–566.

68. Valerie Folkes and Shashi Matta, "The Effect of Package Shape on Consumers' Judgments of Product Volume," *Journal of Consumer Research,* September 2004, pp. 390–401.

69. John R. Doyle, Paul A. Bottomley, "Dressed for the Occasion: Font-Product Congruity in the Perception of Logotype," *Journal of Consumer Psychology* 16, no. 2, 2006, pp. 112–123.

70. Peter H. Lindsay and Donald A. Norman, *Human Information Processing: An Introduction to Psychology* (New York: Academic Press, 1973).

71. Ibid.

72. Ibid.

73. Gerald J. Gorn, Amitava Chattopadhyay, and Tracey Yi, "Effects of Color as an Executional Cue: They're in the Shade," *Management Science*, October 1997, pp. 1387–1401.

74. Greg Morago, "Shapely Stuff Makes Waves," *Hartford Courant*, March 23, 2007, p. H1.

75. Cathy Horyn, "A New Year, A New Color. But Are We Blue?" *New York Times*, December 20, 2007, p. G1.

76. Marnell Jameson, "The Palette Patrol," *Los Angeles Times*, June 13, 1997, pp. E1, E8.

77. Lindsay and Norman, *Human Information Processing.*

78. Amitava Chattopadhyay, Darren W. Dahl, Robin J. B. Ritchie, and Kimary N. Shahin, "Hearing Voices: The Impact of Announcer Speech Characteristics on Consumer Response to Broadcast Advertising," *Journal of Consumer Psychology* 13, no. 3, 2003, pp. 198–204.

79. Hannah Booth, "Sound Minds: Brands These Days Need to Sound Good as Well as Look Good," *Design Week,* April 15, 2004, p. 163.

80. Eric Yorkston and Geeta Menon, "A Sound Idea: Phonetic Effects of Brand Names on Consumer Judgments," *Journal of Consumer Research,* June 2004, pp. 43–51.

81. Ronald E. Milliman, "Using Background Music to Affect the Behavior of Supermarket Shoppers," *Journal of Marketing*, Summer 1982, pp. 86–91.

82. Colleen Bazdarich, "In a Buying Mood? Maybe It's the Muzak," *Business 2.0*, March 2002, p. 100.

83. Ronald E. Millman, "The Influence of Background Music on the Behavior of Restaurant Patrons," *Journal of Consumer Research*, September 1986, pp. 286–289; Richard Yalch and Eric Spannenberg, "Effects of Store Music on Shopping Behavior," *Journal of Services Marketing*, Winter 1990, pp. 31–39.

84. Mark I. Alpert and Judy Alpert, "The Effects of Music in Advertising on Mood and Purchase Intentions," Working paper No. 85/86–5–4, Department of Marketing Administration, University of Texas, 1986.

85. Gerald J. Gorn, "The Effects of Music in Advertising on Choice Behavior," *Journal of Marketing*, Winter 1982, pp. 94–101; C. Whan Park and S. Mark Young, "Consumer Response to Television Commercials: The Impact of Involvement and Background Music on Brand Attitude Formation," *Journal of Marketing Research*, February 1986, pp. 11–24; MacInnis and Park, "The Differential Role of Characteristics of Music on High- and Low-Involvement Consumers' Processing of Ads."

86. Kate Fitzgerald, "In-Store Media Ring Cash Register," *Advertising Age*, February 9, 2004, p. 43.

87. "Kellogg's Launches On-Pack Promotion for Nutri-Grain," *Talking Retail*, January 8, 2008, *www.talkingretail.com*.

88. JoAndrea Hoegg and Joseph W. Alba, "Taste Perception: More (and Less) than Meets the Tongue," *Journal of Consumer Research*, March 2007, pp. 490–498.

89. Jeanne Whalen, "Foul Taste Is Part of the Cure," *Wall Street Journal*, November 5, 2007, p. B4.

90. Trygg Engen, *The Perception of Odors* (New York: Academic Press, 1982); Trygg Engen, "Remembering Odors and Their Names," *American Scientist*, September–October 1987, pp. 497–503.

91. T. Schemper, S. Voss, and W. S. Cain, "Odor Identification in Young and Elderly Persons," *Journal of Gerontology*, December 1981, pp. 446–452; J. C. Stevens and W. S. Cain, "Smelling via the Mouth: Effect of Aging," *Perception and Psychophysics*, September 1986, pp. 142–146.

92. W. S. Cain, "Odor Identification by Males and Females: Prediction vs. Performance," *Chemical Senses*, February 1982, pp. 129–142.

93. Beryl Leiff Benderly, "Aroma," *Health*, December 1988, pp. 62–77.

94. M. S. Kirk-Smith, C. Van Toller, and G. H. Dodd, "Unconscious Odor Conditioning in Human Subjects," *Biological Psychology* 17, 1983, pp. 221–231.

95. Pamela Weentraug, "Sentimental Journeys: Smells Have the Power to Arouse Our Deepest Memories, Our Most Primitive Drives," *Omni*, August 1986, p. 815; Howard Erlichman and Jack N. Halpern, "Affect and Memory: Effects of Pleasant and Unpleasant Odors on Retrieval of Happy and Unhappy Memories," *Journal of Personality and Social Psychology*, May 1988, pp. 769–779; Frank R. Schab, "Odors and the Remembrance of Things Past," *Journal of Experimental Psychology: Learning, Memory and Cognition*, July 1990, pp. 648–655.

96. Theresa Howard, "Who Needs Ads When You've Got Hot Doughnuts Now?" *USA Today*, May 31, 2001, p. B3.

97. Anick Bosmans, "Scents and Sensibility: When Do (In)Congruent Ambient Scents Influence Product Evaluations?" *Journal of Marketing*, July 2006, pp. 32–43.

98. Marty Hair, "Artificial Tree Owners Hunt for Smell of Christmas," *Detroit Free Press*, November 26, 2004, *www.freep.com*.

99. Maureen Morrin and S. Ratneshwar, "Does It Make Sense to Use Scents to Enhance Brand Memory?" *Journal of Marketing Research*, February 2003, pp. 10–25.

100. Susan Reda, "Dollars and Scents," *Stores*, August 1994, p. 38.

101. Thomas K. Grose, "That Odd Smell May Be Your E-mail," *U.S. News & World Report*, August 6, 2001, p. 33.

102. Karen A. Newman, "Parry and Advance: P&G's Martin Hettich Builds on the Febreze Promise One Move at a Time," *Global Cosmetic Industry*, December 2007, pp. 46+.

103. Maxine Wilkie, "Scent of a Market," *American Demographics*, August 1995, pp. 40–49.

104. Joann Peck and Terry L. Childers, "Individual Differences in Haptic Information Processing," *Journal of Consumer Research*, December 2003, pp. 430–442.

105. Jacob Hornik, "Tactile Stimulation and Consumer Response," *Journal of Consumer Research*, December 1992, pp. 449–458.

106. Sak Onkvisit and John J. Shaw, *International Marketing: Analysis and Strategy* (Columbus, Ohio: Merrill, 1989).

107. Joann Peck and Jennifer Wiggins, "It Just Feels Good: Customers' Affective Response to Touch and Its Influence on Persuasion," *Journal of Marketing*, October 2006, pp. 57–69.

108. Deborah Brown McCabe and Stephen M. Nowlis, "The Effect of Examining Actual Products or Product Descriptions on Consumer Preference," *Journal of Consumer Psychology* 13, no. 4, 2003, pp. 431–439.

109. M. Eastlake Stevens, "REI's X-Treme Sports Retailing," *Colorado Biz*, August 2000, pp. 56–57.

110. Alison Fahey, "Party Hardly," *Brandweek*, October 26, 1992, pp. 24–25.

111. "Selling It: Nips Are Nipped," *Consumer Reports*, December 2007, p. 67.

112. Richard Gibson, "Bigger Burger by McDonald's: A Two Ouncer," *Wall Street Journal*, April 18, 1996, p. B1.

113. Stuart Rogers, "How a Publicity Blitz Created the Myth of Subliminal Advertising," *Public Relations Quarterly*, Winter 1992, pp. 12–18.

114. Martha Rogers and Christine A. Seiler, "The Answer Is No," *Journal of Advertising Research*, March–April 1994, pp. 36–46; W. B. Key, *Subliminal Seduction* (Englewood Cliffs, N.J.: Prentice-Hall, 1973); Matthew Fitzgerald, *Media Sex-ploitation* (Englewood Cliffs, N.J.: Prentice-Hall, 1976); W. B. Key, *The Clamplate Orgy* (Englewood Cliffs, N.J.: Prentice-Hall, 1980); Martha Rogers and Kirk

H. Smith, "Public Perceptions of Subliminal Advertising: Why Practitioners Shouldn't Ignore This Issue," *Journal of Advertising Research*, March–April 1993, pp. 10–19; Michael Lev, "No Hidden Meaning Here: Survey Sees Subliminal Ads," *New York Times*, June 16, 1991, pp. 22, S12.

115. Sharon Beatty and Del I. Hawkins, "Subliminal Stimulation: Some New Data and Interpretation," *Journal of Advertising*, June 1989, pp. 4–9; Myron Gable, Henry T. Wilkens, Lynn Harris, and Richard Feinberg, "An Evaluation of Subliminally Embedded Sexual Stimuli and Graphics," *Journal of Advertising*, March 1987, pp. 26–32; Dennis L. Rosen and Surendra N. Singh, "An Investigation of Subliminal Embed Effect on Multiple Measures of Advertising Effectiveness," *Psychology and Marketing*, March–April 1992, pp. 157–173; J. Steven Kelly, "Subliminal Embeds in Print Advertising: A Challenge to Advertising Ethics," *Journal of Advertising*, September 1979, pp. 20–24; Anthony R. Pratkanis and Anthony G. Greenwald, "Recent Perspectives on Unconscious Processing: Still No Marketing Applications," *Psychology and Marketing*, Winter 1988, pp. 337–353; Joel Saegert, "Why Marketing Should Quit Giving Subliminal Advertising the Benefit of the Doubt," *Psychology and Marketing*, March–April 1987, pp. 157–173.

116. A. J. Marcel, "Conscious and Unconscious Perception: Experiments on Visual Masking and Word Recognition," *Cognitive Psychology*, June 1983, pp. 197–237; A. J. Marcel, "Conscious and Unconscious Perception: An Approach to the Relations Between Phenomenal Experience and Perceptual Processes," *Cognitive Psychology*, September 1983, pp. 238–300.

117. Ronald C. Goodstein and Ajay Kalra, "Incidental Exposure and Affective Reactions to Advertising," Working paper No. 239, School of Management, University of California at Los Angeles, January 1994.

118. Timothy E. Moore, "Subliminal Advertising: What You See Is What You Get," *Journal of Marketing*, Spring 1982, pp. 38–47.

119. David Penn, "Looking for the Emotional Unconscious in Advertising," *International Journal of Market Research* 48, no. 5, 2006, pp. 515–524.

120. Laura A. Peracchio and Joan Meyers-Levy, "How Ambiguous Cropped Objects in Ad Photos Can Affect Product Evaluations," *Journal of Consumer Research*, June 1994, pp. 190–204.

121. Himanshu Mishra, Arul Mishra, and Dhananjay Nayakankuppam, "Money: A Bias for the Whole," *Journal of Consumer Research* 32, no. 4, 2006, pp. 541–549.

122. "Cathay Pacific's Change for Good Programme Collects Millions for UNICEF," *Asia Travel Tips*, January 18, 2008, *www.aisatraveltips.com*.

123. Daniel Lovering, "Heinz Expands Global Tastes," *Associated Press*, February 4, 2008, *www.ohio.com*; Carrie Coolidge, "Anticipation: H. J. Heinz," *Forbes*, December 10, 2007, p. 188; Donna Kardos and Matt Andrejczak, "Food: Heinz Net Rises as Sales Offset Costs," *Wall Street Journal*, November 30, 2007, p. C11; Christopher Megerian, "The Prize in the Parking Lot," *BusinessWeek*, September 3, 2007, p. 11; The Sauces and Condiments Aisle Was Shaken Up in March This Year by Heinz," *Grocer*, September 22, 2007, p. 44; "Ketchup Passed as Art," *UPI News Track*, April 6, 2007, www.*upi.com/newstrack;* Louise Story, "Putting Amateurs in Charge," *New York Times*, May 26, 2007, pp. C1, C9; "Heinz Launches Its Organic Tomato Ketchup," *Marketing*, February 7, 2007, p. 45.

Chapter 4

1. Steven Scheer, "De Beers Sees 'Challenging' 2008 for Diamond Sector," *Reuters*, February 11, 2008, *www.reuters.com*; Christina Passariello, "European Jewelers Engage in Global Battle for Brides," *Wall Street Journal*, August 3, 2007, p. B1; "De Beers Uses Consumer Site to Push Diamond Quality Standard," *New Media Age*, May 17, 2007, p. 2; "Changing Facets: Diamonds," *The Economist*, February 24, 2007, p. 76.

2. Kevin Lane Keller, "Brand Synthesis: The Multidimensionality of Brand Knowledge," *Journal of Consumer Research*, March 2003, pp. 595–600.

3. Brian T. Ratchford, "The Economics of Consumer Knowledge," *Journal of Consumer Research*, March 2001, pp. 397–411.

4. Lawrence W. Barsalou, *Cognitive Psychology: An Overview for Cognitive Scientists* (Hillsdale, N.J.: Lawrence Erlbaum, 1992); James R. Bettman, "Memory Factors in Consumer Choice: A Review," *Journal of Marketing*, Spring 1979, pp. 37–53; Merrie Brucks and Andrew A. Mitchell, "Knowledge Structures, Production Systems and Decision Strategies," in ed. Kent B. Monroe, *Advances in Consumer Research*, vol. 8 (Ann Arbor, Mich.: Association for Consumer Research, 1982), pp. 750–757.

5. Kevin L. Keller, "Conceptualizing, Measuring, and Managing Customer-Based Brand Equity," *Journal of Marketing*, January 1993, pp. 1–22; Deborah J. MacInnis, Kent Nakamoto, and Gayathri Mani, "Cognitive Associations and Product Category Comparisons: The Role of Knowledge Structure and Context," in eds. John F. Sherry and Brian Sternthal, *Advances in Consumer Research*, vol. 19 (Provo, Utah: Association for Consumer Research, 1992), pp. 260–267.

6. Janet Adamy, "For McDonald's, It's a Wrap," *Wall Street Journal*, January 30, 2007, p. B1.

7. Stephanie Kang, "Regaining Footing: After a Slump, Payless Tries On Fashion for Size," *Wall Street Journal*, February 10, 2007, p. A1.

8. Stijn M. J. Van Osselaer, and Chris Janiszewski, "Two Ways of Learning Brand Associations," *Journal of Consumer Research*, September 2001, pp. 202–223.

9. Vanitha Swaminathan, Karen L. Page, and Zeynep Gurhan-Canli, "'My' Brand or 'Our' Brand: The Effects of Brand Relationship Dimensions and Self-Construal on Brand Evaluations," *Journal of Consumer Research*, August 2007, pp. 248–259.

10. Burleigh B. Gardner and Sidney Levy, "The Product and the Brand," *Harvard Business Review*, March–April 1955,

pp. 33–39; see also David Ogilvy, *Confessions of an Advertising Man* (New York: Atheneum, 1964).

11. Zeynep Gurhan-Canli and Rajeev Batra, "When Corporate Image Affects Product Evaluations: The Moderating Role of Perceived Risk," *Journal of Marketing Research,* May 2004, pp. 197–205.

12. Joseph T. Plummer, "How Personality Makes a Difference," *Journal of Advertising Research,* December 1984–January 1985, pp. 27–31; William D. Wells, Frank J. Andriuli, Fedele J. Goi, and Stuart Seader, "An Adjective Check List for the Study of 'Product Personality,'" *Journal of Applied Psychology,* October 1957, pp. 317–319; Jennifer L. Aaker, "Dimensions of Brand Personality," *Journal of Marketing Research,* August 1997, pp. 347–356.

13. Tim Triplett, "Brand Personality Must Be Managed or It Will Assume a Life of Its Own," *Marketing News,* May 9, 1994, p. 9.

14. Katheryn Kranhold, "Whirlpool Conjures Up Appliance Divas," *Wall Street Journal,* April 27, 2000, p. B14.

15. Rajeev Batra and Pamela Miles Homer, "The Situational Impact of Brand Image Beliefs," *Journal of Consumer Psychology* 14, no. 3, 2004, pp. 318–330.

16. Yongjun Sung and Spencer F. Tinkham, "Brand Personality Structures in the United States and Korea: Common and Culture-Specific Factors," *Journal of Consumer Psychology* 15, no. 4, 2005, pp. 334–350.

17. Gita V. Johar, Jaideep Sengupta, and Jennifer L. Aaker, "Two Roads to Updating Brand Personality Impressions: Trait Versus Evaluative Inferencing," *Journal of Marketing Research,* November 2005, pp. 458–469.

18. See Girish N. Punj and Clayton L. Hillyer, "A Cognitive Model of Customer-Based Brand Equity for Frequently Purchased Products: Conceptual Framework and Empirical Results," *Journal of Consumer Psychology* 14, no. 1&2, 2004, pp. 124–131; Kevin Lane Keller, *Building, Measuring, and Managing Brand Equity,* 2d ed. (Upper Saddle River, N.J.: Prentice-Hall, 2003), p. 60; Roland T. Rust, Valarie Z. Zeithaml, and Katherine N. Lemon, *Driving Customer Equity* (New York: Free Press, 2000), pp. 80–87.

19. Deborah Roedder John, Barbara Loken, Kyeongheui Kim, and Alokparna Basu Monga, "Brand Concept Maps: A Methodology for Identifying Brand Association Networks," *Journal of Marketing Research,* November 2006, pp. 549–563.

20. Lan Nguyen Chaplin and Deborah Roedder John, "The Development of Self-Brand Connections in Children and Adolescents," *Journal of Consumer Research* 32, no. 1, 2005, pp. 119–129.

21. David Gianatasio, "Benefit Plan: Colonial Life Chases Aflac," *Adweek,* February 6, 2008, *www.adweek.com*; Bethany McLean, "Duck and Coverage," *Fortune,* August 13, 2001, pp. 142–143.

22. Peter Valdes-Dapena, "Can That Stroller Run the Rubicon Trail?" *CNN Money,* August 25, 2005, *money.cnn.com*; Gregory L. White, "New Jeep Is Sure to Turn Heads, on the Playground," *Wall Street Journal,* January 9, 2001, pp. B1, B4.

23. Tom Meyvis and Chris Janiszewski, "When Are Broader Brands Stronger Brands? An Accessibility Perspective on the Success of Brand Extensions," *Journal of Consumer Research* 31, no. 2, 2004, pp. 346–357; Sheri Bridges, Kevin Lane Keller, and Sanjay Sood, "Communication Strategies for Brand Extensions: Enhancing Perceived Fit by Establishing Explanatory Links," *Journal of Advertising* 29, no. 4, Winter 2000, pp. 1–11; Elyette Roux and Frederic Lorange, "Brand Extension Research: A Review," in eds. Fred von Raiij and Gary Bamoussy, *European Advances in Consumer Research,* vol. 1 (Provo, Utah: Association for Consumer Research, 1993), pp. 492–500; C. Whan Park, Bernard J. Jaworski, and Deborah J. MacInnis, "Strategic Brand Concept–Image Management," *Journal of Marketing,* October 1986, pp. 135–145; David A. Aaker and Kevin L. Keller, "Consumer Evaluations of Brand Extensions," *Journal of Marketing,* January 1990, pp. 27–41; Bernard Simonin and Julie A. Ruth, "Is a Company Known by the Company It Keeps?: Assessing the Spillover Effects of Brand Alliances on Consumer Brand Attitudes," *Journal of Marketing Research,* February 1998, pp. 30–42; C. Whan Park, Sung Youl Jun, and Allan D. Shocker, "Composite Branding Alliances: An Investigation of Extension and Feedback Effects," *Journal of Marketing Research,* November 1996, pp. 453–466; MacInnis, Nakamoto, and Mani, "Cognitive Associations and Product Category Comparisons," pp. 260–267; David M. Bousch et al., "Affect Generalization to Similar and Dissimilar Brand Extensions," *Psychology and Marketing,* 1987, pp. 225–237; Susan M. Baroniarczyk and Joseph W. Alba, "The Importance of the Brand in Brand Extension," *Journal of Marketing Research,* May 1994, pp. 214–228.

24. Catherine W. M. Yeung and Robert S. Wyer Jr., "Does Loving a Brand Mean Loving Its Products? The Role of Brand-Elicited Affect in Brand Extension Evaluations," *Journal of Marketing Research,* November 2005, pp. 495–506.

25. Stijn M. J. Van Osselaer and Joseph W. Alba, "Locus of Equity and Brand Extension," *Journal of Consumer Research,* March 2003, pp. 539–550.

26. Huifang Mao and H. Shanker Krishnan, "Effects of Prototype and Exemplar Fit on Brand Extension Evaluations: A Two-Process Contingency Model," *Journal of Consumer Research* 33, no. 1, 2006, pp. 41–49; Franziska Volkner and Henrik Sattler, "Drivers of Brand Extension Success," *Journal of Marketing,* April 2006, pp. 18–34; David Bousch, Shannon Shipp, Barbara Loken, Esra Genturk, Susan Crocket, Ellen Kennedy, Bettie Minshall, Dennis Misurell, Linda Rochford, and John Strobel, "Affect Generalization to Similar and Dissimilar Brand Extensions," *Psychology and Marketing* 4, no. 3, 1987, pp. 225–237; Rainer Greifender, Herbert Bless, and Thorston Kurschmann, "Extending the Brand Image on New Products: The Facilitative Effect of Happy Mood States," *Journal of Consumer Behavior* 6, no. 1, 2007, pp. 19–31.

27. Ingrid Martin and David Stewart, "The Differential Impact of Goal Congruence on Attitudes, Intentions, and the Transfer of Brand Equity," *Journal of Marketing Research*, November 2001, pp. 471–484; Sandra Milberg, C. W. Park, and Robert Lawson, "Evaluation of Brand Extensions: The Differential Impact of Goal Congruence on Attitudes, Intentions, and the Transfer of Brand Equity," *Journal of Consumer Research* 18, no. 2, 1991, pp. 185–193.

28. Alokparna Basu Monga and Deborah Roedder John, "Cultural Differences in Brand Extension Evaluation: The Influence of Analytic Versus Holistic Thinking," *Journal of Consumer Research* 33, no. 4, 2007, pp. 529–536. See also Shailendra Pratap Jain, Kalpesh Kaushik Desai, and Huifang Mao, "The Influence of Chronic and Situational Self-Construal on Categorization," *Journal of Consumer Research* 34, no. 1, 2007, pp. 66–76.

29. Mao and Krishnan, "Effects of Prototype and Exemplar Fit on Brand Extension Evaluations."

30. Michael J. Barone, "The Interactive Effects of Mood and Involvement on Brand Extension Evaluations," *Journal of Consumer Psychology* 15, no. 3, 2005, pp. 263–270.

31. Deborah Roedder John, Barbara Loken, and Christopher Joiner, "The Negative Impact of Extensions: Can Flagship Products Be Diluted?" *Journal of Marketing* 62, January 1998, pp. 19–32.

32. Tom Meyvis and Chris Janiszewski, "When Are Broader Brands Stronger Brands? An Accessibility Perspective on the Success of Brand Extensions," *Journal of Consumer Research*, September 2004, pp. 346–357.

33. Subramanian Balachander and Sanjoy Ghose, "Reciprocal Spillover Effects: A Strategic Benefit of Brand Extensions," *Journal of Marketing*, January 2003, pp. 4–13.

34. Rohini Ahluwalia and Zeynep Gürhan-Canli, "The Effects of Extensions on the Family Brand Name: An Accessibility–Diagnosticity Perspective," *Journal of Consumer Research*, December 2000, pp. 371–381; Zeynep Gürhan-Canli and Durairaj Maheswaran, "The Effects of Extensions on Brand Name Dilution and Enhancement," *Journal of Marketing Research*, November 1998, pp. 464–473; Sandra Milberg, C. Whan Park, and Michael S. McCarthy, "Managing Negative Feedback Effects Associated with Brand Extensions: The Impact of Alternative Branding Strategies," *Journal of Consumer Psychology* 6, no. 2, 1997, pp. 119–140; Barbara Loken and Deborah Roedder-John, "Diluting Brand Beliefs: When Do Brand Extensions Have a Negative Impact?" *Journal of Marketing*, July 1993, pp. 71–84; David A. Aaker, *Managing Brand Equity* (New York: The Free Press, 1991).

35. C. Whan Park, Bernard J. Jaworski, and Deborah J. MacInnis, "Strategic Brand Concept-Image Management."

36. Kathryn A. LaTour and Michael S. LaTour, "Assessing the Long-term Impact of a Consistent Advertising Campaign on Consumer Memory," *Journal of Advertising*, Summer 2004, pp. 49–61.

37. Kevin P. Gwinner and John Eaton, "Building Brand Image Through Event Sponsorship: The Role of Image Transfer," *Journal of Advertising* 28, no. 4, Winter 1999, pp. 47–57.

38. Claudia H. Deutsch, "Two Growing Markets That Start at Your Tap," *New York Times*, November 10, 2007, p. C6.

39. Jay Greene, "Return of the Easy Rider," *BusinessWeek*, September 17, 2007, pp. 78–81.

40. Abbey Klaassen, "St. Joseph: From Babies to Boomers," *Advertising Age*, July 9, 2001, pp. 1, 38.

41. Niraj Dawar and Madan M. Pillutla, "Impact of Product-Harm Crises on Brand Equity: The Moderating Role of Consumer Expectations," *Journal of Marketing Research*, May 2000, pp. 215–226.

42. Jennifer Aaker, Susan Fournier, and S. Adam Brasel, "When Good Brands Do Bad," *Journal of Consumer Research*, June 2004, pp. 1–16.

43. Narayan Janakiraman, Robert J. Meyer, and Andrea C. Morales, "Spillover Effects: How Consumers Respond to Unexpected Changes in Price and Quality," *Journal of Consumer Research* 33, no. 3, 2006, pp. 361–369.

44. Thomas W. Leigh and Arno J. Rethans, "Experiences in Script Elicitation Within Consumer Decision-Making Contexts," in eds. Richard P. Bagozzi and Alice M. Tybout, *Advances in Consumer Research*, vol. 10 (Ann Arbor, Mich.: Association for Consumer Research, 1983), pp. 667–672; Roger C. Shank and Robert P. Abelson, *Scripts, Plans, Goals, and Understanding: An Inquiry into Human Knowledge Structures* (Hillsdale, N.J.: Lawrence Erlbaum, 1977); Ruth Ann Smith and Michael J. Houston, "A Psychometric Assessment of Measures of Scripts in Consumer Memory," *Journal of Consumer Research*, September 1985, pp. 214–224; R. A. Lakshmi-Ratan and Easwar Iyer, "Similarity Analysis of Cognitive Scripts," *Journal of the Academy of Marketing Science*, Summer 1988, pp. 36–43; C. Whan Park, Easwar Iyer, and Daniel C. Smith, "The Effects of Situational Factors on In-Store Grocery Shopping Behavior: The Role of Store Environment and Time Available for Shopping," *Journal of Consumer Research*, March 1989, pp. 422–432.

45. Eleanor Rosch, "Principles of Categorization," in eds. E. Rosch and B. Lloyd, *Cognition and Categorization* (Hillsdale, N.J.: Lawrence Erlbaum, 1978), pp. 119–160; Barsalou, *Cognitive Psychology*.

46. Rosch, "Principles of Categorization"; Barsalou, *Cognitive Psychology*; Madhubalan Viswanathan and Terry L. Childers, "Understanding How Product Attributes Influence Product Categorization: Development and Validation of Fuzzy Set-Based Measures of Gradedness in Product Categories," *Journal of Marketing Research*, February 1999, pp. 75–94.

47. Lawrence Barsalou, "Ideals, Central Tendency, and Frequency of Instantiation as Determinants of Graded Structure in Categories," *Journal of Experimental Psychology: Learning, Memory and Cognition*, October 1985, pp. 629–649; Barbara Loken and James Ward,

"Alternative Approaches to Understanding the Determinants of Typicality," *Journal of Consumer Research*, September 1990, pp. 111–126; James Ward and Barbara Loken, "The Quintessential Snack Food: Measurement of Product Prototypes," in ed. Richard J. Lutz, *Advances in Consumer Research*, vol. 13 (Provo, Utah: Association for Consumer Research, 1986), pp. 126–131; Gregory S. Carpenter and Kent Nakamoto, "Consumer Preference Formation and Pioneering Advantage," *Journal of Marketing Research*, August 1989, pp. 285–298.

48. Hyeong Min Kim, "Evaluations of Moderately Typical Products: The Role of Within- Versus Cross-Manufacturer Comparisons," *Journal of Consumer Psychology* 16, no. 1, 2006, pp. 70–78.

49. Luk Warlop and Joseph W. Alba, "Sincere Flattery: Trade-Dress Imitation and Consumer Choice," *Journal of Consumer Psychology* 14, no. 1/2, 2004, pp. 21–27.

50. Gerald J. Gorn and Charles B. Weinberg, "The Impact of Comparative Advertising on Perception and Attitude: Some Positive Findings," *Journal of Consumer Research*, September 1984, pp. 719–727; Cornelia Pechmann and S. Ratneshwar, "The Use of Comparative Advertising for Brand Positioning: Association Versus Differentiation," *Journal of Consumer Research*, September 1991, pp. 145–160; Rita Snyder, "Comparative Advertising and Brand Evaluation: Toward Developing a Categorization Approach," *Journal of Consumer Psychology* 1, no. 1, 1992, pp. 15–30.

51. Sholnn Remand and Norihiko Shirouzu, "Toyota's Gen Y Gamble," *Wall Street Journal*, July 30, 2003, p. B1.

52. Ronald W. Niedrich, Subhash Sharma, and Douglas H. Wedell, "Reference Price and Price Perceptions: A Comparison of Alternative Models," *Journal of Consumer Research*, December 2001, pp. 339–354.

53. See Amos Tversky and Daniel Kahneman, "Extensional Versus Intuitive Reasoning: The Conjunction Fallacy," *Psychological Review*, October 1983, pp. 293–315.

54. Bob Garfield, "Softly Lit or Blunt, 'Less Toxic' Cigarette Ads Hint at Health," *Advertising Age*, November 12, 2001, p. 58; Gordon Fairclough, "Tobacco Titans Bid for 'Organic' Cigarette Maker," *Wall Street Journal*, December 10, 2001, pp. B1, B4; Suein Hwang, "Smokers May Mistake 'Clean' Cigarette for Safe," *Wall Street Journal*, September 30, 1995, pp. B1, B2.

55. Hans Baumgartner, "On the Utility of Consumers' Theories in Judgments of Covariation," *Journal of Consumer Research*, March 1995, pp. 634–643; James R. Bettman, Deborah Roedder John, and Carol A. Scott, "Covariation Assessment by Consumers," *Journal of Consumer Research*, December 1986, pp. 316–326; Susan M. Broniarczyk and Joseph W. Alba, "Theory Versus Data in Prediction and Correlation Tasks," *Organizational Behavior and Human Decision Processes*, January 1994, pp. 117–139.

56. Barbara Loken, Christopher Joiner, and Joann Peck, "Category Attitude Measures: Exemplars as Inputs," *Journal of Consumer Psychology*, no. 2, 2002, pp. 149–161.

57. Lea Goldman, "A Cry in the Wilderness," *Forbes*, May 15, 2000, p. 322.

58. Barsalou, "*Cognitive Psychology.*"

59. Yaacov Trope, Nira Liberman, and Cheryl Wakslak, "Construal Levels and Psychological Distance: Effects on Representation, Prediction, Evaluation, and Behavior," *Journal of Consumer Psychology* 17, no. 2, 2007, pp. 83–95.

60. John G. Lynch and G. Zauberman, "Construing Consumer Decision Making, *Journal of Consumer Psychology* 17, no. 2, 2007, pp. 107–112.

61. Klaus Fiedler, "Construal Level Theory as an Integrative Framework for Behavioral Decision-Making Research and Consumer Psychology," *Journal of Consumer Psychology* 17, no. 2, 2007, pp. 101–106.

62. Frank R. Kardes, Maria L. Cronley, and John Kim, "Construal-Level Effects on Preference Stability, Preference–Behavior Correspondence, and the Suppression of Competing Brands," *Journal of Consumer Psychology* 16, no. 2, 2006, pp. 135–144.

63. Michael Fitzpatrick, "Japan: Kit Kat Sales Boosted by Lucky Translation," *Just-Food.com*, February 3, 2005, *www.just-food.com*.

64. Eleanor Rosch, "Human Categorization," in ed. N. Warren, *Studies in Cross-Cultural Psychology* (New York: Academic Press, 1977), pp. 1–49; A. D. Pick, "Cognition: Psychological Perspectives," in eds. H. C. Triandis and W. Lonner, *Handbook of Cross-Cultural Psychology* (Boston: Allyn & Bacon, 1980), pp. 117–153; Bernd Schmitt and Shi Zhang, "Language Structure and Categorization: A Study of Classifiers in Consumer Cognition, Judgment and Choice," *Journal of Consumer Research*, September 1998, pp. 108–122.

65. Beth Snyder Bulik, "Philips: We're Not Just Light Bulbs," *Advertising Age*, June 25, 2007, *www.adage.com*.

66. Joseph W. Alba and J. Wesley Hutchinson, "Dimensions of Consumer Expertise," *Journal of Consumer Research*, March 1987, pp. 411–454; Deborah Roedder John and John Whitney Jr., "The Development of Consumer Knowledge in Children: A Cognitive Structure Approach," *Journal of Consumer Research*, March 1986, pp. 406–417; Merrie Brucks, "The Effects of Product Class Knowledge on Information Search Behavior," *Journal of Consumer Research*, June 1985, pp. 1–16; Deborah Roedder John and Mita Sujan, "Age Differences in Product Categorization," *Journal of Consumer Research*, March 1990, pp. 452–460. See also Andrew A. Mitchell and Peter A. Dacin, "The Assessment of Alternative Measures of Consumer Expertise," *Journal of Consumer Research*, December 1996, pp. 219–239; C. Whan Park, David L. Mothersbaugh, and Lawrence Feick, "Consumer Knowledge Assessment," *Journal of Consumer Research*, June 1994, pp. 71–82.

67. Elizabeth Cowley and Andrew A. Mitchell, "The Moderating Effect of Product Knowledge on the Learning and Organization of Product Information," *Journal of Consumer Research*, December 2003, pp. 443–454; Stacy L.

Wood and John G. Lynch Jr., "Prior Knowledge and Complacency in New Product Learning," *Journal of Consumer Research*, December 2002, pp. 416–426.

68. Joseph W. Alba and J. Wesley Hutchinson, "Knowledge Calibration: What Consumers Know and What They Think They Know," *Journal of Consumer Research*, September 2000, pp. 123–156.

69. Chingching Chang, "The Interplay of Product Class Knowledge and Trial Experience in Attitude Formation," *Journal of Advertising*, Spring 2004, pp. 83–92.

70. Maureen Morrin, "The Impact of Brand Extensions on Parent Brand Memory Structures and Retrieval Processes," *Journal of Marketing Research*, November 1999, pp. 517–525.

71. Yumiko Ono, "Will *Good Housekeeping* Translate into Japanese?" *Wall Street Journal*, December 30, 1997, pp. B1, B6.

72. Stuart Elliott, "Timberland's Cause-Related Marketing," *New York Times*, November 16, 2004, *www.nytimes.com*.

73. Shashi Matta and Valerie S. Folkes, "Inferences About the Brand from Counterstereotypical Service Providers," *Journal of Consumer Research* 32, no. 2, 2005, pp. 196–206.

74. "The Fruit Formerly Known as . . . Prunes to Be Sold as 'Dried Plums' in Bid to Sweeten Image," *Washington Post*, April 15, 2001, p. A4; Lee Gomes, "Korean Knock-offs, Prunes vs. Dried Plums, and Intel's New Hire," *Wall Street Journal*, September 20, 2004, p. B1.

75. C. Page Moreau, Arthur B. Markman, and Donald R. Lehmann, "'What Is It?' Categorization Flexibility and Consumers' Responses to Really New Products," *Journal of Consumer Research*, March 2001, pp. 489–498.

76. Ronald C. Goodstein, "Category-Based Applications and Extensions in Advertising: Motivating More Extensive Ad Processing," *Journal of Consumer Research*, June 1993, pp. 87–99; Mita Sujan, "Consumer Knowledge: Effects on Evaluation Strategies Mediating Consumer Judgments," *Journal of Consumer Research*, June 1985, pp. 31–46.

77. Susan T. Fiske, "Schema Triggered Affect: Applications to Social Perception," in eds. Margaret S. Clark and Susan T Fiske, *Affect and Cognition: The 17th Annual Carnegie Symposium on Cognition* (Hillsdale, N.J.: Lawrence Erlbaum, 1984), pp. 55–78; Susan T. Fiske and Mark A. Pavelchak, "Category-Based vs. Piecemeal-Based Affective Responses: Developments in Schema-Triggered Affect," in eds. Richard M. Sorrentino and E. Tory Higgins, *Handbook of Motivation and Cognition* (New York: Guilford, 1986), pp. 167–203; Joel B. Cohen, "The Role of Affect in Categorization: Toward a Reconsideration of the Concept of Attitude," in ed. Andrew A. Mitchell, *Advances in Consumer Research*, vol. 9 (Ann Arbor, Mich.: Association for Consumer Research, 1982), pp. 94–100.

78. Douglas M. Stayman, Dana L. Alden, and Karen H. Smith, "Some Effects of Schematic Processing on Consumer Expectations and Disconfirmation Judgments," *Journal of Consumer Research*, September 1992, pp. 245–255.

79. David G. Mick, "Levels of Subjective Comprehension in Advertising Processing and Their Relations to Ad Perceptions, Attitudes, and Memory," *Journal of Consumer Research*, March 1992, pp. 411–424.

80. Jacob Jacoby, Wayne D. Hoyer, and David A. Sheluga, *Miscomprehension of Televised Communication* (New York: American Association of Advertising Agencies, 1980); Jacob Jacoby and Wayne D. Hoyer, *The Comprehension and Miscomprehension of Print Communications: An Investigation of Mass Media Magazines* (New York: Advertising Education Foundation, 1987); see also Jacob Jacoby and Wayne D. Hoyer, "The Miscomprehension of Mass-Media Advertising Claims: A Re-Analysis of Benchmark Data," *Journal of Advertising Research*, June–July 1990, pp. 9–17; Jacob Jacoby and Wayne D. Hoyer, "The Comprehension–Miscomprehension of Print Communication: Selected Findings," *Journal of Consumer Research*, March 1989, pp. 434–444; Fliece R. Gates, "Further Comments on the Miscomprehension of Televised Advertisements," *Journal of Advertising*, Winter 1986, pp. 4–10.

81. Suzanne Vranica, "Aflac Partly Muzzles Iconic Duck," *Wall Street Journal*, December 2, 2004, p. B8.

82. Gary J. Gaeth and Timothy B. Heath, "The Cognitive Processing of Misleading Advertising in Young and Old Adults," *Journal of Consumer Research*, June 1987, pp. 43–54; Deborah Roedder and John and Catherine A. Cole, "Age Differences in Information Processing: Understanding Deficits in Young and Elderly Consumers," *Journal of Consumer Research*, December 1986, pp. 297–315; Catherine A. Cole and Michael J. Houston, "Encoding and Media Effects on Consumer Learning Deficiencies in the Elderly," *Journal of Marketing Research*, February 1987, pp. 55–63.

83. Richard L. Celsi and Jerry C. Olson, "The Role of Involvement in Attention and Comprehension Processes," *Journal of Consumer Research*, September 1988, pp. 210–224.

84. Jacob Jacoby, Robert W. Chestnut, and William Silberman, "Consumer Use and Comprehension of Nutrition Information," *Journal of Consumer Research*, September 1977, pp. 119–127.

85. C. Page Moreau, Donald R. Lehmann, and Arthur B. Markman, "Entrenched Knowledge Structures and Consumer Response to New Products," *Journal of Marketing Research*, February 2001, pp. 14–29.

86. Edward T. Hall, *Beyond Culture* (Garden City, N.Y.: Anchor Press/Doubleday, 1976); Sak Onkvisit and John J. Shaw, *International Marketing: Analysis and Strategy* (Columbus, Ohio: Merrill, 1989), pp. 223–224.

87. Robert Frank, "Big Boy's Adventures in Thailand," *Wall Street Journal*, April 12, 2000, pp. B1, B4.

88. Scott Baldauf, "A Hindi-English Jumble, Spoken by 350 Million," *Christian Science Monitor*, November 23, 2004, p. 1.

89. Onkvisit and Shaw, *International Marketing*.

90. Wayne D. Hoyer, Rajendra K. Srivastava, and Jacob Jacoby, "Examining Sources of Advertising Miscomprehension," *Journal of Advertising,* June 1984, pp. 17–26; Julie A. Edell and Richard Staelin, "The Information Processing of Pictures in Print Advertisements," *Journal of Consumer Research,* June 1983, pp. 45–61; Ann Beattie and Andrew A. Mitchell, "The Relationship Between Advertising Recall and Persuasion: An Experimental Investigation," in eds. Linda F. Alwitt and Andrew A. Mitchell, *Psychological Processes and Advertising Effects* (Hillsdale, N.J.: Lawrence Erlbaum, 1985), pp. 129–156.

91. David Luna, "Integrating Ad Information: A Text-Processing Perspective," *Journal of Consumer Psychology* 15, no. 1, pp. 38–51.

92. Angela Y. Lee and Aparna A. Labroo, "The Effect of Conceptual and Perceptual Fluency on Brand Evaluation," *Journal of Marketing Research,* May 2004, pp. 151–165.

93. Mick, "Levels of Subjective Comprehension in Advertising Processing and Their Relations to Perceptions, Attitudes, and Memory"; Deborah J. MacInnis and Bernard J. Jaworski, "Information Processing from Advertisements: Toward an Integrative Framework," *Journal of Marketing,* October 1989, pp. 1–23.

94. Caroline E. Mayer, "KFC Misled Consumers on Health Benefits, FTC Says," *Washington Post,* June 4, 2004, p. E1.

95. Mick, "Levels of Subjective Comprehension in Advertising Processing and Their Relations to Ad Perceptions, Attitudes, and Memory"; David G. Mick and Claus Buhl, "A Meaning-Based Model of Advertising Experiences," *Journal of Consumer Research,* December 1992, pp. 317–338.

96. Jennifer Gregan-Paxton and Deborah Roedder John, "Consumer Learning by Analogy: A Model of Internal Knowledge Transfer," *Journal of Consumer Research,* December 1997, pp. 266–284.

97. Richard D. Johnson and Irwin P. Levin, "More Than Meets the Eye: The Effect of Missing Information on Purchase Evaluations," *Journal of Consumer Research,* September 1985, pp. 169–177; Frank Kardes, "Spontaneous Inference Processes in Advertising: The Effects of Conclusion Omission and Involvement in Persuasion," *Journal of Consumer Research,* September 1988, pp. 225–233; Alba and Hutchinson, "Dimensions of Consumer Expertise."

98. Pamela W. Henderson, Joan L. Giese, and Joseph A. Cote, "Impression Management Using Typeface Design," *Journal of Marketing,* October 2004, pp. 60–72.

99. Michaela Wänke, Herbert Bless, and Norbert Schwarz, "Context Effects in Product Line Extensions: Context Is Not Destiny," *Journal of Consumer Psychology* 7, no. 4, 1998, pp. 299–322.

100. Shi Zhang and Bernd H. Schmitt, "Creating Local Brands in Multilingual International Markets," *Journal of Marketing Research,* August 2001, pp. 313–325.

101. Teresa Pavia and Janeen Arnold Costa, "The Winning Number: Consumer Perceptions of Alpha-Numeric Brand Names," *Journal of Marketing,* July 1993, pp. 85–99; France Leclerc, Bernd H. Schmitt, and Laurette Dube, "Foreign Branding and Its Effects on Product Perceptions and Attitudes," *Journal of Marketing Research,* May 1994, pp. 263–270; Mary Sullivan, "How Brand Names Affect the Demand for Twin Automobiles," *Journal of Marketing Research,* May 1998, pp. 154–165.

102. Akshay R. Rao, Lu Qu, and Robert W. Ruekert, "Signaling Unobservable Product Quality Through a Brand Ally," *Journal of Marketing Research,* May 1999, pp. 258–268.

103. Bonnie B. Reece and Robert H. Ducoffe, "Deception in Brand Names," *Journal of Public Policy and Marketing* 6, 1987, pp. 93–103.

104. Marilyn Chase, "Pretty Soon the Word 'Organic' on Foods Will Mean One Thing," *Wall Street Journal,* August 18, 1997, p. B1.

105. Benjamin A. Holden, "Utilities Pick New, Nonutilitarian Names," *Wall Street Journal,* April 7, 1997, pp. B1, B5.

106. Wendy M. Grossman, "Generic Names Lose Their Luster," *Smart Business,* April 2001, p. 58.

107. "The Culinary Institute of America (CIA) and American Culinary Institute, Inc. (ACI) Have Settled the Lawsuit the CIA Filed in February," *Food Management,* September 2004, p. 22.

108. Susan M. Broniarczyk and Joseph W. Alba, "The Role of Consumers' Intuitions in Inference Making," *Journal of Consumer Research,* December 1994, pp. 393–407.

109. Gary T. Ford and Ruth Ann Smith, "Inferential Beliefs in Consumer Evaluations: An Assessment of Alternative Processing Strategies," *Journal of Consumer Research,* December 1987, pp. 363–371.

110. Rajagopal Raghunathan, Rebecca Walker Naylor, and Wayne D. Hoyer, "The Unhealthy = Tasty Intuition and Its Effects on Taste Inferences, Enjoyment, and Choice of Food Products," *Journal of Marketing,* October 2006, pp. 170–184.

111. Elizabeth G. Miller and Barbara E. Kahn, "Shades of Meaning: The Effect of Color and Flavor Names on Consumer Choice," *Journal of Consumer Research* 32, no. 1, 2005, pp. 86–92.

112. Irwin P. Levin and Aron M. Levin, "Modeling the Role of Brand Alliances in the Assimilation of Product Evaluations," *Journal of Consumer Psychology* 9, no. 1, 2000, pp. 43–52.

113. Tom Meyvis and Chris Janiszewski, "Consumers' Beliefs About Product Benefits: The Effect of Obviously Irrelevant Information," *Journal of Consumer Research,* March 2002, pp. 618–635.

114. Alexander Chernev and Gregory S. Carpenter, "The Role of Market Efficiency Intuitions in Consumer Choice: A Case of Compensatory Inferences," *Journal of Marketing Research,* August 2001, pp. 349–361.

115. Peeter W. J. Verlegh, Jan-Benedict E. M. Steenkamp, and Matthew T. G. Meulenberg, "Country-of-origin Effects in Consumer Processing of Advertising Claims,"

International Journal of Research in Marketing, June 2005, pp. 127–139; Sung-Tai Hong and Robert S. Wyer Jr., "Determinants of Product Evaluation: Effects of Time Interval Between Knowledge of a Product's Country of Origin and Information about Its Specific Attributes," *Journal of Consumer Research,* December 1990, pp. 277–288; Durairaj Maheswaran, "Country of Origin as a Stereotype: Effects of Consumer Expertise and Attribute Strength on Product Evaluations," *Journal of Consumer Research,* September 1994, pp. 354–365; Sung-Tai Hong and Robert S. Wyer Jr., "Effects of Country of Origin and Product-Attribute Information on Product Evaluation: An Information Processing Perspective," *Journal of Consumer Research,* September 1989, pp. 175–187; Johny K. Johansson, Susan P. Douglas, and Ikujiro Nonaka, "Assessing the Impact of Country of Origin on Product Evaluations," *Journal of Marketing Research,* November 1985, pp. 388–396; Maheswaran, "Country of Origin as a Stereotype"; Wai-Kwan Li and Robert S. Wyer Jr., "The Role of Country of Origin in Product Evaluations: Informational and Standard-of-Comparison Effects," *Journal of Consumer Psychology* 2, 1994, pp. 187–212.

116. Rajeev Batra, Venkatram Ramaswamy, Dana L. Alden, Jan-Benedict E. M. Steenkamp, and S. Ramachander, "Effects of Brand Local and Non-local Origin on Consumer Attitudes in Developing Countries," *Journal of Consumer Psychology* 9, no. 2, 2000, pp. 83–95.

117. Sung-Tai Hong and Dong Kyoon Kang, "Country-of-Origin Influences on Product Evaluations: The Impact of Animosity and Perceptions of Industriousness Brutality on Judgments of Typical and Atypical Products," *Journal of Consumer Psychology* 16, no. 3, 2006, pp. 232–239.

118. Zeynep Gürhan-Canli and Durairaj Maheswaran, "Cultural Variations in Country of Origin Effects," *Journal of Marketing Research,* August 2000, pp. 309–317.

119. Zeynep Gürhan-Canli and Durairaj Maheswaran, "Determinants of Country-of-Origin Evaluations," *Journal of Consumer Research,* June 2000, pp. 96–108.

120. Luk Warlop and Joseph W. Alba, "Sincere Flattery: Trade-Dress Imitation and Consumer Choice," *Journal of Consumer Psychology,* 2004, pp. 21–27.

121. Paul Glader and Christopher Lawton, "Beer and Wine Makers Use Fancy Cans to Court New Fans," *Wall Street Journal,* August 24, 2004, pp. B1–B2.

122. Simon Mowbray, "Spot the Difference: Tesco Once Told Suppliers That Its Days of Copying Their Brands Were Over," *Grocer,* September 2004, pp. 363.

123. Maxine S. Lans, "Supreme Court to Rule on Colors as Trademarks," *Marketing News,* January 2, 1995, p. 28.

124. Ayn Crowley, "The Two-Dimensional Impact of Color on Shopping," *Marketing Letters,* 1993, pp. 59–69.

125. Donald Lichtenstein and Scott Burton, "The Relationship Between Perceived and Objective Price-Quality," *Journal of Marketing Research,* November 1989, pp. 429–443; Etian Gerstner, "Do Higher Prices Signal Higher Quality?" *Journal of Marketing Research,* May 1985, pp. 209–215; Kent Monroe and R. Krishnan, "The Effects of Price on Subjective Product Evaluations," in eds. Jacob Jacoby and Jerry C. Olson, *Perceived Quality: How Consumers View Stores and Merchandise* (Lexington, Mass.: D. C. Heath, 1985), pp. 209–232; Susan M. Petroshius and Kent B. Monroe, "Effect of Product-Line Pricing Characteristics on Product Evaluations," *Journal of Consumer Research,* March 1987, pp. 511–519; Akshay R. Rao and Kent B. Monroe, "The Moderating Effect of Prior Knowledge on Cue Utilization in Product Evaluations," *Journal of Consumer Research,* September 1988, pp. 253–264; Cornelia Pechmann and S. Ratneshwar, "Consumer Covariation Judgments: Theory or Data Driven?" *Journal of Consumer Research,* December 1992, pp. 373–386.

126. Thomas T. Nagle and Reed K. Holden, *The Strategy and Tactics of Pricing,* 2nd ed. (Englewood Cliffs, N.J.: Prentice-Hall, 1995), pp. 84–85.

127. Maria L. Cronley, Steven S. Posavac, Tracy Meyer, Frank R. Kardes, and James J. Kellaris, "Selective Hypothesis Testing Perspective on Price–Quality Inference and Inference-Based Choice," *Journal of Consumer Psychology* 15, no. 2, 2005, pp. 159–169.

128. Frank R. Kardes, Maria L. Cronley, James J. Kellaris, and Steven S. Posavac, "The Role of Selective Information Processing in Price–Quality Inference," *Journal of Consumer Research,* September 2004, pp. 368–374.

129. Priya Raghubir, "Free Gift with Purchase: Promoting or Discounting the Brand?" *Journal of Consumer Psychology,* 2004, pp. 181–186.

130. Ann E. Schlosser, "Applying the Functional Theory of Attitudes to Understanding the Influence of Store Atmosphere on Store Inferences," *Journal of Consumer Psychology* 7, no. 4, 1998, pp. 345–369.

131. Lauranne Buchanan, Carolyn J. Simmons, and Barbara A. Bickart, "Brand Equity Dilution: Retailer Display and Context Brand Effects," *Journal of Marketing Research,* August 1999, pp. 345–355.

132. Becky Sunshine, "Temporary Shops Make Lasting Impressions," *Financial Times,* February 18, 2008, *www.lat.com/business;* Amanda Fortini, "Anti-Concept Concept Store," *New York Times Magazine,* December 12, 2004, p. 54.

133. Tsune Shirai, "What Is an 'International' Mind?" *PHP,* June 1980, p. 25.

134. Barbara Mueller, "Standardization vs. Specialization: An Examination of Westernization in Japanese Advertising," *Journal of Advertising Research,* January–February 1992, pp. 15–22.

135. Margaret C. Campbell and Amna Kirmani, "Consumers' Use of Persuasion Knowledge: The Effects of Accessibility and Cognitive Capacity on Perceptions of an Influence Agent," *Journal of Consumer Research,* June 2000, pp. 69–83.

136. Onkvisit and Shaw, *International Marketing.*

137. Laura A. Peracchio and Joan Meyers-Levy, "Using Stylistic Properties of Ad Pictures to Communicate with Consumers," *Journal of Consumer Research* 32, no. 1, 2005, pp. 29–40.

138. John W. Pracejus, G. Douglas Olsen, and Thomas C. O'Guinn, "How Nothing Became Something: White Space, Rhetoric, History, and Meaning," *Journal of Consumer Research* 33, no. 1, 2006, pp. 82–90.

139. Richard J. Harris, Julia C. Pounds, Melissa J. Maiorelle, and Maria Mermis, "The Effect of Type of Claim, Gender, and Buying History on the Drawing of Pragmatic Inferences from Advertising Claims," *Journal of Consumer Psychology* 2, no. 1, 1993, pp. 83–95; Richard J. Harris, R. E. Sturm, M. L. Kalssen, and J. I. Bechtold, "Language in Advertising: A Psycholinguistic Approach," *Current Issues and Research in Advertising* (Ann Arbor: University of Michigan Press, 1986), pp. 1–26; Raymond R. Burke, Wayne S. DeSarbo, Richard L. Oliver, and Thomas S. Robertson, "Deception by Implication: An Experimental Investigation," *Journal of Consumer Research*, March 1988, pp. 483–494.

140. J. Craig Andrews, Scot Burton, and Richard G. Netemeyer, "Are Some Comparative Nutrition Claims Misleading? The Role of Nutrition Knowledge, Ad Claim Type, and Disclosure Conditions," *Journal of Advertising* 29, no. 3 (Fall 2000), pp. 29–42; Terence Shimp, "Do Incomplete Comparisons Mislead?" *Journal of Advertising Research*, December 1978, pp. 21–27; Harris et al., "The Effect of Type of Claim, Gender, and Buying History on the Drawing of Pragmatic Inferences from Advertising Claims"; Gita Johar, "Consumer Involvement and Deception from Implied Advertising Claims," *Journal of Marketing Research*, August 1995, pp. 267–279.

141. Ken Bensinger and Alana Semuels, "A Pivotal Play for Hyundai," *Los Angeles Times,* February 2, 2008, *www.latimes.com;* Jean Halliday and Brian Steinberg, "Why Hyundai Didn't Forfeit Spots," *Advertising Age,* January 21, 2008, p. 4; Moon Ihlwan, "Hyundai Targets the Lexus Set," *BusinessWeek Online,* December 10, 2007, *www.businessweek.com;* Stuart Elliott, "A Brand Tries to Invite Thought," *New York Times,* September 7, 2007, p. C7; "Hyundai in £10m 'Quality' Drive to Shed Budget Tag," *Marketing,* January 5, 2005, p. 3.

Chapter 5

1. Matt Higgins, "It's a Kids' World on the Halfpipe," *New York Times,* July 15, 2007, sec. 8, pp. 1, 6; "Cycling Team's Anti-Doping Stance Prompts Chipotle to Increase Sponsorship," *Nation's Restaurant News,* October 1, 2007, p. 20; "By Georgie! Mapei to Back Olympic Hopeful," *Contract Flooring Journal,* September 2007, p. 50.

2. Richard E. Petty, H. Rao Unnava, and Alan J. Strathman, "Theories of Attitude Change," in eds. Thomas S. Robertson and Harold H. Kassarjian, *Handbook of Consumer Behavior* (Englewood Cliffs, N.J.: Prentice-Hall, 1991), pp. 241–280.

3. Ida E. Berger and Andrew A. Mitchell, "The Effect of Advertising on Attitude Accessibility, Attitude Confidence, and the Attitude–Behavior Relationship," *Journal of Consumer Research*, December 1989, pp. 269–279; Joel B. Cohen and Americus Reed II, "A Multiple Pathway Anchoring and Adjustment (MPAA) Model of Attitude Generation and Recruitment," *Journal of Consumer Research* 33, no. 1, 2006, pp. 1–15.

4. Rohini Ahluwalia, "Examination of Psychological Processes Underlying Resistance to Persuasion," *Journal of Consumer Research*, September 2000, pp. 217–232.

5. Joseph R. Priester and Richard E. Petty, "The Gradual Threshold Model of Ambivalence," *Journal of Personality and Social Psychology* 71, 1996, pp. 431–449; Joseph R. Priester, Richard E. Petty, and Kiwan Park, "Whence Univalent Ambivalence? From the Anticipation of Conflicting Reactions," *Journal of Consumer Research* 34, no. 1, 2007, pp. 11–21; Martin R. Zemborain and Gita Venkataramani Johar, "Attitudinal Ambivalence and Openness to Persuasion: A Framework for Interpersonal Influence," *Journal of Consumer Research* 33, no. 4, 2007, pp. 506–514.

6. Martin Fishbein and Icek Ajzen, *Belief, Attitude, Intention, and Behavior: An Introduction to Theory and Research* (Reading, Mass.: Addison-Wesley, 1975).

7. Lizbieta Lepkowska-White, Thomas G. Brashear, and Marc G. Weinberger, "A Test of Ad Appeal Effectiveness in Poland and the United States," *Journal of Advertising*, Fall 2003, pp. 57–67.

8. Kevin E. Voss, Eric R. Spangenburg, and Bianca Grohmann, "Measuring the Hedonic and Utilitarian Dimensions of Consumer Attitude," *Journal of Marketing Research*, August 2003, pp. 310–320.

9. Petty, Unnava, and Strathman, "Theories of Attitude Change"; Richard Petty and John T. Cacioppo, *Communication and Persuasion* (New York: Springer, 1986).

10. Cohen and Reed, "A Multiple Pathway Anchoring and Adjustment (MPAA) Model of Attitude Generation and Recruitment;" F. P. Bone and S. P. Ellen, "The Generation and Consequences of Communication-evoked Imagery," *Journal of Consumer Research*, June 1992, pp. 93–104; Punam Anand Keller and Ann L. McGill (1994), "Differences in the Relative Influence of Product Attributes under Alternative Processing Conditions: Attribute Importance Versus Attribute Ease of Imagability," *Journal of Consumer Psychology* 3, no. 1, pp. 29–49; Pham, Michel Tuan, Joel B. Cohen, John W. Pracejus, and G. David Hughes, "Affect Monitoring and the Primacy of Feelings in Judgment," *Journal of Consumer Research* 28, September 2001, pp. 167–188.

11. Jennifer Gregan-Paxton and Deborah Roedder John, "Consumer Learning by Analogy: A Model of Internal Knowledge Transfer," *Journal of Consumer Research* 24, December 1997, pp. 266–284.

12. Cohen and Reed, "A Multiple Pathway Anchoring and Adjustment (MPAA) Model of Attitude Generation and Recruitment."

13. Americus Reed II, "Activating the Self-Importance of Consumer Selves: Exploring Identity Salience Effects on Judgments," *Journal of Consumer Research* 31,

September 2004, pp. 286–295; Sharon Shavitt and Michelle R. Nelson, "The Social-Identity Function in Person Perception: Communicated Meanings of Product Preferences," in eds. Gregory Maio and James M. Olson, *Why We Evaluate: Functions of Attitudes,* (Mahwah, N.J.: Lawrence Erlbaum, 2000), pp. 37–57.

14. Peter L. Wright, "Message-Evoked Thoughts: Persuasion Research Using Thought Verbalizations," *Journal of Consumer Research,* September 1980, pp. 151–175.

15. Jerry C. Olson, Daniel R. Toy, and Philip A. Dover, "Do Cognitive Responses Mediate the Effects of Advertising Content on Cognitive Structure?" *Journal of Consumer Research,* December 1982, pp. 245–262.

16. Marian Friestad and Peter Wright, "The Persuasion Knowledge Model: How People Cope with Persuasion Attempts," *Journal of Consumer Research,* June 1994, pp. 1–31.

17. Peter Wright, "Marketplace Metacognition and Social Intelligence," *Journal of Consumer Research,* March 2002, pp. 677–682.

18. Zakary L. Tormala and Richard E. Petty, "Source Credibility and Attitude Certainty: A Metacognitive Analysis of Resistance to Persuasion," *Journal of Consumer Psychology* 14, no. 4 (2004), pp. 427–442.

19. Daniel R. Toy, "Monitoring Communication Effects: Cognitive Structure/Cognitive Response Approach," *Journal of Consumer Research,* June 1982, pp. 66–76.

20. Petty, Unnava, and Strathman, "Theories of Attitude Change."

21. Punam Anand and Brian Sternthal, "The Effects of Program Involvement and Ease of Message Counterarguing on Advertising Persuasiveness," *Journal of Consumer Psychology* 1, no. 3, 1992, pp. 225–238; Kenneth R. Lord and Robert E. Burnkrant, "Attention Versus Distraction: The Interactive Effect of Program Involvement and Attentional Devices on Commercial Processing," *Journal of Advertising,* March 1993, pp. 47–60.

22. Bob M. Fennis, Enny H. H. J. Das, and Ad Th. H. Pruyn, "'If You Can't Dazzle Them with Brilliance, Baffle Them with Nonsense': Extending the Impact of the Disrupt-Then-Reframe Technique of Social Influence," *Journal of Consumer Psychology* 14, no. 3 (2004), pp. 280–290; B. P. Davis and E. S. Knowles, "A Disrupt-Then-Reframe Technique of Social Influence," *Journal of Personality and Social Psychology* 76 (1999), pp. 192–199.

23. Deborah J. MacInnis and C. Whan Park, "The Differential Role of Characteristics of Music on High- and Low-Involvement Consumers' Processing of Ads," *Journal of Consumer Research,* September 1991, pp. 161–173; Rajeev Batra and Douglas M. Stayman, "The Role of Mood in Advertising Effectiveness," *Journal of Consumer Research,* September 1990, pp. 203–214.

24. William L. Wilkie and Edgar A. Pessemier, "Issues in Marketing's Use of Multi-Attribute Models," *Journal of Marketing Research,* November 1973, pp. 428–441.

25. Richard P. Bagozzi, Nancy Wong, Shuzo Abe, and Massimo Bergami, "Cultural and Situational Contingencies and the Theory of Reasoned Action: Application to Fast-Food Restaurant Consumption," *Journal of Consumer Psychology* 9, no. 2, 2000, pp. 97–106.

26. Icek Ajzen and Martin Fishbein, "Prediction of Goal-Directed Behavior: Attitudes, Intentions, and Perceived Behavioral Control," *Journal of Experimental Social Psychology,* September 1980, pp. 453–474; Blair H. Sheppard, Jon Hartwick, and Paul R. Warshaw, "The Theory of Reasoned Action: A Meta-Analysis of Past Research with Recommendations for Modifications and Future Research," *Journal of Consumer Research,* December 1988, pp. 325–342.

27. Cohen and Reed, "A Multiple Pathway Anchoring and Adjustment (MPAA) Model of Attitude Generation and Recruitment."

28. Arti Sahni Notani, "Moderators of Perceived Behavioral Control's Predictiveness in the Theory of Planned Behavior: A Meta-Analysis," *Journal of Consumer Psychology* 7, no. 3, 1998, pp. 247–271.

29. Nick Bunkley, "Another Spin for 'Made American,'" *New York Times,* June 14, 2007, p. C5; David Welch, "Will These Rockets Rescue Saturn?" *BusinessWeek,* January 17, 2005, pp. 78–79.

30. Neil Eisberg, "US Companies Are Misunderstood, Says ACC (American Chemistry Council)," *Chemistry and Industry,* October 8, 2007, p. 12; Thaddeus Herrick, "Ads' Aim Is to Fix Bad Chemistry," *Wall Street Journal,* October 8, 2003, p. B6.

31. Amitav Chakravarti and Chris Janiszewski, "The Influence of Generic Advertising on Brand Preferences," *Journal of Consumer Research,* March 2004, pp. 487–502.

32. Stephen M. Nowlis and Itamar Simonson, "The Effect of New Product Features on Brand Choice," *Journal of Marketing Research,* February 1996, pp. 36–46.

33. Ashesh Mukherjee and Wayne D. Hoyer, "The Effect of Novel Attributes on Product Evaluation," *Journal of Consumer Research,* December 2001, pp. 462–472.

34. Petia K. Petrova and Robert B. Cialdini, "Fluency of Consumption Imagery and the Backfire Effects of Imagery Appeals," *Journal of Consumer Research* 32, no. 3 (2005), pp. 442–452; Punam Anand Keller and Ann L. McGill "Differences in the Relative Influence of Product Attributes Under Alternative Processing Conditions: Attribute Importance Versus Attribute Ease of Imagability," *Journal of Consumer Psychology* 3, no. 1 (1994), pp. 29–49; Michel Tuan Pham, "Representativeness, Relevance, and the Use of Feelings in Decision Making," *Journal of Consumer Research* 25, September 1998, pp. 144–159.

35. "YouTube Videos Stir Up New Sales for 'Will It Blend' Maker," *InformationWeek,* September 27, 2007, *www.informationweek.com.*

36. Mark Frauenfelder, "Social-Norms Marketing," *New York Times Magazine,* December 9, 2001, p. 100.

37. Laura Bird, "Condom Campaign Fails to Increase Sales," *Wall Street Journal,* June 23, 1994, p. B7

38. Barbara Mueller, "Reflections of Culture: An Analysis of Japanese and American Advertising Appeals," *Journal of Advertising Research*, June–July 1987, pp. 51–59.

39. Yong-Soon Kang and Paul M. Herr, "Beauty and the Beholder: Toward an Integrative Model of Communication Source Effects," *Journal of Consumer Research* 33, no. 1, 2006, pp. 123–130; Ronald E. Goldsmith, Barbara A. Lafferty, and Stephen J. Newell, "The Impact of Corporate Credibility and Celebrity Credibility on Consumer Reaction to Advertisements and Brands," *Journal of Advertising* 29, no. 3, Fall 2000, pp. 43–54; also see Brian Sternthal, Ruby R. Dholakia, and Clark Leavitt, "The Persuasive Effect of Source Credibility: A Situational Analysis," *Public Opinion Quarterly*, Fall 1978, pp. 285–314.

40. Joseph R. Priester, "The Influence of Spokesperson Trustworthiness on Message Elaboration, Attitude Strength, and Advertising Effectiveness," *Journal of Consumer Psychology* 13, no. 4, 2003, pp. 408–421.

41. Bob Tedeschi, "For BizRate, a New Identity and a New Site, Shopzilla.com," *New York Times*, November 15, 2004, p. C4; Rob Pegoraro, "Logging On: Comparison Shop Till You Just Must Stop," *Washington Post*, November 14, 2000, p. G16.

42. Ignacio Galceran and Jon Berry, "A New World of Consumers," *American Demographics*, March 1995, p. 263. "Pepsi Signs Multi-Year Pact with Colombian Pop Star," *Brandweek*, June 11, 2001, p. 10.

43. Amna Kirmani and Baba Shiv, "Effects of Source Congruity on Brand Attitudes and Beliefs: The Moderating Role of Issue-Relevant Elaboration," *Journal of Consumer Psychology* 7, no. 1, 1998, pp. 25–48; Matt Higgins, "It's a Kids' World on the Halfpipe," *New York Times*, July 15, 2007, sec. 8, pp. 1, 6.

44. Pablo Briñol, Richard E. Petty, and Zakary L. Tormala, "Self-Validation of Cognitive Responses to Advertisements," *Journal of Consumer Research*, March 2004, pp. 559–573.

45. Chenghuan Wu and David R. Schaffer, "Susceptibility to Persuasive Appeals as a Function of Source Credibility and Prior Experience with the Attitude Object," *Journal of Personality and Social Psychology*, April 1987, pp. 677–688.

46. Carolyn Tripp, Thomas D. Jensen, and Les Carlson, "The Effects of Multiple Endorsements by Celebrities on Consumers' Attitudes and Intentions," *Journal of Consumer Research*, March 1994, pp. 535–547.

47. Judith A. Garretson and Ronald W. Niedrich, "Spokes-Characters: Creating Character Trust and Positive Brand Attitudes," *Journal of Advertising* 33, no. 2, Summer 2004, pp. 25–36.

48. Bob Garfield, "Amex Spots Make Emotional Connections . . . But to What?" *Advertising Age*, January 17, 2005, p. 29; Arlene Weintraub, "Marketing Champ of the World," *BusinessWeek*, December 20, 2004, p. 64.

49. Joan Voight, "Selling Confidence," *Adweek Southwest*, August 20, 2001, p. 9.

50. Ignacio Galceran and Jon Berry, "A New World of Consumers," *American Demographics*, March 1995, pp. 26–33.

51. Joe Nocera, "Buy It and Be Great," *New York Times Magazine Play*, September 2007, p. 34; Greg Johnson, "He Won't Be Sold Short," *Los Angeles Times*, January 30, 2007, p. D1.

52. Kevin Goldman, "Women Endorsers More Credible Than Men, a Survey Suggests," *Wall Street Journal*, October 22, 1995, p. B1.

53. Cathy Yingling, "Beware the Lure of Celebrity Endorsers: Not Worth It," *Advertising Age*, September 24, 2007, p. 19.

54. Sternthal, Dholakia, and Leavitt, "The Persuasive Effect of Source Credibility."

55. Darlene B. Hannah and Brian Sternthal, "Detecting and Explaining the Sleeper Effect," *Journal of Consumer Research*, September 1984, pp. 632–642.

56. Marvin E. Goldberg and Jon Hartwick, "The Effects of Advertiser Reputation and Extremity of Advertising Claim on Advertising Effectiveness," *Journal of Consumer Research*, September 1990, pp. 172–179.

57. Karen L. Becker-Olsen, "And Now, a Word from Our Sponsor," *Journal of Advertising*, Summer 2003, pp. 17–32.

58. Tülin Erdem and Joffre Swait, "Brand Credibility, Brand Consideration, and Choice," *Journal of Consumer Research*, June 2004, pp. 191–198.

59. "BP's Chief to Retire Early After a Series of Problems," *Los Angeles Times*, January 13, 2007, p. C3.

60. Petty, Unnava, and Strathman, "Theories of Attitude Change"; Charles S. Areni and Richard J. Lutz, "The Role of Argument Quality in the Elaboration Likelihood Model," in ed. Michael J. Houston, *Advances in Consumer Research*, vol. 15 (Provo, Utah: Association for Consumer Research, 1987), pp. 197–203.

61. Parthasarathy Krishnamurthy and Anuradha Sivararman, "Counterfactual Thinking and Advertising Responses," *Journal of Consumer Research*, March 2002, pp. 650–658.

62. Jennifer Edson Escalas and Mary Frances Luce, "Process Versus Outcome Thought Focus and Advertising," *Journal of Consumer Psychology*, 2003, pp. 246–254; Jennifer Edson Escalas and Mary Frances Luce, "Understanding the Effects of Process-Focused Versus Outcome-Focused Thought in Response to Advertising," *Journal of Consumer Research*, September 2004, pp. 274–285.

63. Brett A. S. Martin, Bodo Lang, and Stephanie Wong, "Conclusion Explicitness in Advertising," *Journal of Advertising*, Winter 2003–2004, pp. 57–65.

64. Keith S. Coulter and Girish N. Punj, "The Effects of Cognitive Resource Requirements, Availability, and Argument Quality on Brand Attitudes," *Journal of Advertising* 33, no. 4, Winter 2004, pp. 53–64.

65. Sally Beatty, "Companies Push for Much Bigger, More Complicated On-Line Ads," *Wall Street Journal*, August 20, 1998, p. B1.

66. Timothy B. Heath, Michael S. McCarthy, and David L. Mothersbaugh, "Spokesperson Fame and Vividness Effects in the Context of Issue-Relevant Thinking: The Moderating Role of Competitive Setting," *Journal of Consumer Research*, March 1994, pp. 520–534.

67. Laura A. Peracchio, "Evaluating Persuasion-Enhancing Techniques from a Resource Matching Perspective," *Journal of Consumer Research*, September 1997, pp. 178–191.

68. Jeanne Whalen, "Foul Taste Is Part of the Cure," *Wall Street Journal*, November 5, 2007, p. B4.

69. See Gerd Bohner, Sabine Einwiller, Hans-Peter Erb, and Frank Siebler, "When Small Means Comfortable: Relations Between Product Attributes in Two-Sided Advertising," *Journal of Consumer Psychology*, 13(4), 2003, pp. 454–463.

70. Martin Eisend, "Two-Sided Advertising: A Meta-Analysis," *International Journal of Research in Marketing* 23, no. 2, June 2006, pp. 187–198.

71. Michael A. Kamins and Henry Assael, "Two-Sided Versus One-Sided Appeals: A Cognitive Perspective on Argumentation, Source Derogation, and the Effect of Disconfirming Trial on Belief Change," *Journal of Marketing Research*, February 1984, pp. 29–39.

72. Stephanie Kang, "Hardee's Fesses Up to Shortcomings," *Wall Street Journal*, June 24, 2003, p. B4.

73. Cornelia Pechmann and David W. Stewart, "The Effects of Comparative Advertising on Attention, Memory, and Purchase Intentions," *Journal of Consumer Research*, September 1990, pp. 180–191.

74. Pechmann and Stewart, "The Effects of Comparative Advertising on Attention, Memory, and Purchase Intentions"; Rita Snyder, "Comparative Advertising and Brand Evaluation: Toward Developing a Categorization Approach," *Journal of Consumer Psychology* 1, no. 1, 1992, pp. 15–30.

75. Yung Kyun Choi and Gordon E. Miracle, "The Effectiveness of Comparative Advertising in Korea and the United States," *Journal of Advertising* 33, no. 4, Winter 2004, pp. 75–87.

76. Matthew Creamer, "Microsoft Plans Blitz to Fend Off Apple," *Advertising Age*, December 3, 2007, *www.adage.com*.

77. Patrick Meirick, "Cognitive Responses to Negative and Comparative Political Advertising," *Journal of Advertising*, Spring 2002, pp. 49–62.

78. Bruce E. Pinkleton, Nam-Hyun Um, and Erica Weintraub Austin, "An Exploration of the Effects of Negative Political Advertising on Political Decision Making," *Journal of Advertising*, Spring 2002, pp. 13–25.

79. Dhruv Grewal, Sukumar Kavanoor, Edward F. Fern, Carolyn Costley, and James Barnes, "Comparative Versus Noncomparative Advertising: A Meta-Analysis," *Journal of Marketing*, October 1997, pp. 1–15.

80. Pechmann and Stewart, "The Effects of Comparative Advertising on Attention, Memory, and Purchase Intentions."

81. Kenneth C. Manning, Paul W. Miniard, Michael J. Barone, and Randall L. Rose, "Understanding the Mental Representations Created by Comparative Advertising," *Journal of Advertising* 3, no. 2, Summer 2001, pp. 27–39.

82. Joseph R. Priester, John Godek, D. J. Nayankuppum, and Kiwan Park, "Brand Congruity and Comparative Advertising: When and Why Comparative Advertisements Lead to Greater Elaboration," *Journal of Consumer Psychology* 14, no. 1–2, 2004, pp. 115–123.

83. Jerry B. Gotlieb and Dan Sarel, "Comparative Advertising Effectiveness: The Role of Involvement and Source Credibility," *Journal of Advertising* 20, no. 1, 1991, pp. 38–45; Koprowski, "Theories of Negativity."

84. Cornelia Pechmann and S. Ratneshwar, "The Use of Comparative Advertising for Brand Positioning: Association Versus Differentiation," *Journal of Consumer Research*, September 1991, pp. 145–160.

85. Paul W. Miniard, Michael J. Barone, Randall L. Rose, and Kenneth C. Manning, "A Further Assessment of Indirect Comparative Advertising Claims of Superiority Over All Competitors," *Journal of Advertising* 35, no. 4, Winter 2006, pp. 53–64.

86. A. V. Muthukrishnan and S. Ramaswami, "Contextual Effects on the Revision of Evaluative Judgments: An Extension of the Omission-Detection Framework," *Journal of Consumer Research*, June 1999, pp. 70–84.

87. Shailendra Pratap Jain and Steven S. Posavac, "Valenced Comparisons," *Journal of Marketing Research* 41, no. 1, February 2004, pp. 46–58.

88. Shailendra Pratap Jain, Nidhi Agrawal, and Durairaj Maheswaran, "When More May Be Less: The Effects of Regulatory Focus on Responses to Different Comparative Frames," *Journal of Consumer Research* 33, no. 1, 2006, pp. 91–98.

89. Shailendra Pratap Jain, Charles Lindsey, Nidhi Agrawal, and Durairaj Maheswaran, "For Better or For Worse? Valenced Comparative Frames and Regulatory Focus," *Journal of Consumer Research* 34, no. 1, 2007, pp. 57–65.

90. Anne L. Roggeveen, Dhruv Grewal, and Jerry Gotlieb, "Does the Frame of a Comparative Ad Moderate the Effectiveness of Extrinsic Information Cues?" *Journal of Consumer Research* 33, no. 1, 2006, pp. 115–122.

91. Pechmann and Stewart, "The Effects of Comparative Advertising on Attention, Memory, and Purchase Intentions."

92. Debora Viana Thompson and Rebecca W. Hamilton, "The Effects of Information Processing Mode on Consumers' Responses to Comparative Advertising," *Journal of Consumer Research* 32, no. 4, 2006, pp. 530–540.

93. Kate Macarthur, "Why Big Brands Are Getting into the Ring," *Advertising Age*, May 21, 2007, p. 6.

94. A. V. Muthukrishnan and Amitava Chattopadhyay, "Just Give Me Another Chance: The Strategies for Brand Recovery from a Bad First Impression," *Journal of Marketing Research*, May 2007, pp. 334–345.

95. John Tylee, "New 'Honesty' Laws Could Render Many Campaigns Illegal," *Campaign*, March 17, 2000, p. 16.

96. Barbara Mueller, "Reflections of Culture: An Analysis of Japanese and American Advertising Appeals," *Journal of Advertising Research*, June–July 1987, pp. 51–59.

97. Paschalina (Lilia) Ziamou and S. Ratneshwar, "Innovations in Product Functionality: When and Why Are Explicit Comparisons Effective?" *Journal of Marketing*, April 2003, pp. 49–61.

98. H. Onur Bodur, David Brinberg, and Eloïse Coupey, "Belief, Affect, and Attitude: Alternative Models of the Determinants of Attitude," *Journal of Consumer Psychology* 9, no. 1, 2000, pp. 17–28.

99. Stephen D. Rappaport, "Lessons from Online Practice: New Advertising Models," *Journal of Advertising Research*, June 2007, pp. 135–141.

100. Michel Tuan Pham, "Representativeness, Relevance, and the Use of Feelings in Decision Making," *Journal of Consumer Research*, September 1998, pp. 144–159.

101. MacInnis and Park, "The Differential Role of Characteristics of Music on High- and Low-Involvement Consumers' Processing of Ads."

102. Deborah J. MacInnis and Douglas M. Stayman, "Focal and Emotional Integration: Constructs, Measures and Preliminary Evidence," *Journal of Advertising*, December 1993, pp. 51–66; Chris T. Allen, Karen A. Machleit, and Susan Schultz Kleine, "A Comparison of Attitudes and Emotions as Predictors of Behavior at Diverse Levels of Behavioral Experience," *Journal of Consumer Research*, March 1992, pp. 493–504.

103. Deborah J. MacInnis and Bernard J. Jaworski, "Two Routes to Persuasion in Advertising: Review, Critique, and Research Directions," *Review of Marketing* 10, 1990, pp. 1–25.

104. See Nancy Spears and Richard Germain, "1900–2000 in Review: The Shifting Role and Face of Animals in Print Advertisements in the Twentieth Century," *Journal of Advertising*, Fall 2007, pp. 19ff.

105. Tamar Avnet and E. Tory Higgins, "How Regulatory Fit Affects Value in Consumer Choices and Opinions," *Journal of Marketing Research*, February 2006, pp. 1–10; Tamar Avnet and E. Tory Higgins, "Response to Comments on 'How Regulatory Fit Affects Value in Consumer Choices and Opinions,'" *Journal of Marketing Research*, February 2006, pp. 24–27; Jennifer L. Aaker and Angela Y. Lee, "Understanding Regulatory Fit," *Journal of Marketing Research*, February 2006, pp. 15–19; Aparna A. Labroo and Angela Y. Lee, "Between Two Brands: A Goal Fluency Account of Brand Evaluation," *Journal of Marketing Research*, August 2006, pp. 374–385; Junsang Yeo and Jongwon Park, "Effects of Parent-Extension Similarity and Self-Regulatory Focus on Evaluations of Brand Extensions," *Journal of Consumer Psychology* 16, no. 3, 2006, pp. 272–282.

106. C. Whan Park and S. Mark Young, "Consumer Response to Television Commercials: The Impact of Involvement and Background Music on Brand Attitude Formation," *Journal of Marketing Research*, February 1986, pp. 11–24.

107. Rajeev Batra and Michael L. Ray, "Affective Responses Mediating Acceptance of Advertising," *Journal of Consumer Research*, September 1986, pp. 234–249.

108. Jooyoung Kim and Jon D. Morris, "The Power of Affective Response and Cognitive Structure in Product-Trial Attitude Formation," *Journal of Advertising* 36, no. 1, Spring 2007, pp. 95–106.

109. Hans Baumgartner, Mita Sujan, and Dan Padgett, "Patterns of Affective Reactions to Advertisements: The Integration of Moment-to-Moment Responses into Overall Judgments," *Journal of Marketing Research*, May 1997, pp. 219–232.

110. Deborah J. MacInnis and Bernard J. Jaworski, "Information Processing from Advertisements: Toward an Integrative Framework," *Journal of Marketing*, October 1989, pp. 1–23.

111. Michel Tuan Pham and Tamar Avnet, "Ideals and Oughts and the Reliance on Affect Versus Substance in Persuasion," *Journal of Consumer Research*, March 2004, pp. 503–518.

112. Jennifer L. Aaker and Patti Williams, "Empathy Versus Pride: The Influence of Emotional Appeals Across Cultures," *Journal of Consumer Research*, December 1998, pp. 241–261.

113. Richard P. Bagozzi and David J. Moore, "Public Service Announcements: Emotions and Empathy Guide Prosocial Behavior," *Journal of Marketing*, January 1994, pp. 56–57.

114. May Frances Luce, "Choosing to Avoid: Coping with Negatively Emotion-Laden Consumer Decisions," *Journal of Consumer Research*, March 1998, pp. 409–433.

115. Joel B. Cohen and Charles S. Areni, "Affect and Consumer Behavior," in eds. Thomas S. Robertson and Harold H. Kassarjian, *Handbook of Consumer Behavior* (Englewood Cliffs, N.J.: Prentice-Hall, 1991), pp. 188–240.

116. Robert D. Jewell and H. Rao Unnava, "Exploring Differences in Attitudes Between Light and Heavy Brand Users," *Journal of Consumer Psychology* 14, no. 1/2, 2004, pp. 75–80.

117. James Lardner, "Building a Customer-Centric Company," *Business 2.0*, July 10, 2001, pp. 55–59.

118. Petty, Unnava, and Strathman, "Theories of Attitude Change."

119. Harry C. Triandis, *Attitudes and Attitude Change* (New York: Wiley, 1971).

120. Stuart Elliott, "American Express Gets Specific and Asks, 'Are You a Cardmember?'" *New York Times*, April 6, 2007, p. C3.

121. Brian D. Till and Michael Busler, "The Match-Up Hypothesis: Physical Attractiveness, Expertise, and the Role of Fit on Brand Attitude, Purchase Intent, and Brand Beliefs," *Journal of Advertising* 29, no. 3, Fall 2000, pp. 1–13.

122. Peter H. Reingen and Jerome B. Kernan, "Social Perception and Interpersonal Influence: Some Consequences of the Physical Attractiveness Stereotype in a Personal Selling Situation," *Journal of Consumer Psychology* 2, no. 1, 1993, pp. 25–38.

123. Scott Ward and Frederick E. Webster Jr., "Organizational Buying Behavior," in eds. Thomas S. Robertson and Harold H. Kassarjian, *Handbook of Consumer Behavior* (Englewood Cliffs, N.J.: Prentice-Hall, 1991), pp. 419–458.

124. Herbert Simon, Nancy Berkowitz, and John Moyer, "Similarity, Credibility, and Attitude Change," *Psychological Bulletin*, January 1970, pp. 1–16.

125. Mei Fong, "Yao Gives Reebok an Assist in China," *Wall Street Journal*, September 28, 2007, p. B1; Eric Pfanner, "For 2008 Olympics Campaigns, the Starter's Gun Went Off This Month," *New York Times*, August 23, 2007, p. C3; "China Unicom Sells Motorola Z1 Handsets Endorsed by Yao Ming," *China Business News*, April 27, 2006.

126. Terence A. Shimp and Elnora W. Stuart, "The Role of Disgust as an Emotional Mediator of Advertising Effects," *Journal of Advertising*, Spring 2004, pp. 43–53.

127. Sally Goll Beatty, "Just What Goes In a Viagra Ad? Dancing Couples," *Wall Street Journal*, June 17, 1998, pp. B1, B8.

128. Betsy Spethmann, "Value Ads," *Promo*, March 1, 2001, p. 743.

129. Jennifer Edson Escalas, Marian Chapman Moore, and Julie Edell Britton, "Fishing for Feelings? Hooking Viewers Helps!" *Journal of Consumer Psychology* 14, no. 1 and 2, 2004, pp. 105–114.

130. Patti Williams and Jennifer L. Aaker, "Can Mixed Emotions Peacefully Coexist?" *Journal of Consumer Research*, March 2002, pp. 636–649.

131. Batra and Stayman, "The Role of Mood in Advertising Effectiveness."

132. "'Enjoy Life'? Hey, We're Trying!" *Automotive News*, September 10, 2001, p. 4; Kevin Goldman, "Volvo Seeks to Soft-Pedal Safety Image," *Wall Street Journal*, March 16, 1993, p. B7.

133. Rajesh K. Chandy, Gerard J. Tellis, Deborah J. MacInnis, and Pattana Thaivanich, "'What to Say When' Advertising Appeals in Evolving Markets," *Journal of Marketing Research*, November 2001, pp. 399–414.

134. Moinak Mitra, "Emotion 'Ads' More Value than Celebrities," *Economic Times*, October 3, 2007.

135. "Vicks Push Drops Jargon to Refocus on 'Emotion,'" *Marketing*, October 3, 2007, p. 6.

136. Valerie S. Folkes and Tina Kiesler, "Social Cognition: Consumers' Inferences about the Self and Others," in eds. Thomas S. Robertson and Harold H. Kassarjian, *Handbook of Consumer Behavior* (Englewood Cliffs, N.J.: Prentice-Hall, 1991), pp. 281–315.

137. John F. Tanner, James B. Hunt, and David R. Eppright, "The Protection Motivation Model: A Normative Model of Fear Appeals," *Journal of Marketing*, July 1991, pp. 36–45.

138. Michael L. Ray and William L. Wilkie, "Fear: The Potential of an Appeal Neglected by Marketing," *Journal of Marketing*, January 1970, pp. 54–62.

139. Ibid.

140. Kirsten Passyn and Mita Sujan, "Self-Accountability Emotions and Fear Appeals: Motivating Behavior," *Journal of Consumer Research* 32, no. 4 (2006), pp. 583–589.

141. Omar Shehryar and David M. Hunt, "A Terror Management Perspective on the Persuasiveness of Fear Appeals," *Journal of Consumer Psychology* 15, no. 4, 2005, pp. 275–287.

142. Herbert J. Rotfeld, "Fear Appeals and Persuasion: Assumptions and Errors in Advertising Research," in eds. James H. Leigh and Claude R. Martin, *Current Issues and Research in Advertising* (Ann Arbor, Mich.: Graduate School of Business Administration, University of Michigan, 1990), pp. 155–175.

143. John J. Wheatley, "Marketing and the Use of Fear- or Anxiety-Arousing Appeals," *Journal of Marketing*, April 1971, pp. 62–64; Peter L. Wright, "Concrete Action Plans in TV Messages to Increase Reading of Drug Warnings," *Journal of Consumer Research*, December 1979, pp. 256–269.

144. John J. Burette and Richard L. Oliver, "Fear Appeal Effects in the Field: A Segmentation Approach," *Journal of Marketing Research*, May 1979, pp. 181–190.

145. MacInnis and Jaworski, "Two Routes to Persuasion in Advertising."

146. Thomas J. Olney, Morris B. Holbrook, and Rajeev Batra, "Consumer Responses to Advertising: The Effects of Ad Content, Emotions, and Attitude Toward the Ad on Viewing Time," *Journal of Consumer Research*, March 1991, pp. 440–453.

147. Paul W. Miniard, Sunil Bhatla, and Randall L. Rose, "On the Formation and Relationship of Ad and Brand Attitudes: An Experimental and Causal Analysis," *Journal of Marketing Research*, August 1990, pp. 290–303.

148. Sally Goll Beatty, "Executive Fears Effects of Political Ads," *Wall Street Journal*, April 29, 1996, p. B6.

149. Julie A. Edell and Richard E. Staelin, "The Information Processing of Pictures in Print Advertisements," *Journal of Consumer Research*, June 1983, pp. 45–60.

150. Scott B. MacKenzie, Richard J. Lutz, and George E. Belch, "The Role of Attitude Toward the Ad as a Mediator of Advertising Effectiveness: A Test of Competing Explanations," *Journal of Marketing Research*, May 1986, pp. 130–143; Pamela M. Homer, "The Mediating Role of Attitude Toward the Ad: Some Additional Evidence," *Journal of Marketing Research*, February 1990, pp. 78–86.

151. Stuart Elliott, "Mercury, a Division of Ford Motor, Tries an Online Campaign in an Effort to Create a Cooler Image," *New York Times*, December 30, 2004, p. C3.

152. Matthew Haeberle, "More Than Holiday," *Chain Store Age*, November 2004, p. 74.

153. Richard E. Petty, John T. Cacioppo, and David W. Schumann, "Central and Peripheral Routes to Advertising Persuasion," *Journal of Consumer Research*, September 1983, pp. 134–148.

154. Jaideep Sengupta and Gita Venkataramani Johar, "Effects of Inconsistent Attribute Information on the Predictive Value of Product Attitudes: Toward a Resolution of Opposing Perspectives," *Journal of Consumer Research,* June 2002, pp. 39–56.

155. Robert E. Smith and William R. Swinyard, "Attitude-Behavior Consistency: The Impact of Product Trial Versus Advertising," *Journal of Marketing Research* 20, no. 3 (August 1983), pp. 257–267; Russell H. Fazio and Mark P. Zanna, "Direct Experience and Attitude–Behavior Consistency," in ed. Leonard Berkowitz, *Advances in Experimental Social Psychology* (New York: Academic Press, 1981), pp. 162–202.

156. Jaideep Sengupta and Gavan J. Fitzsimons, "The Effects of Analyzing Reasons for Brand Preferences: Disruption or Reinforcement?" *Journal of Marketing Research* 37, August 2000, pp. 318–330.

157. Russell H. Fazio, Martha C. Powell, and Carol J. Williams, "The Role of Attitude Accessibility in the Attitude-to-Behavior Process," *Journal of Consumer Research,* December 1989, pp. 280–288; Berger and Mitchell, "The Effect of Advertising on Attitude Accessibility, Attitude Confidence, and the Attitude–Behavior Relationship."

158. Smith and Swinyard, "Attitude–Behavior Consistency"; Alice A. Wright and John G. Lynch, "Communication Effects of Advertising vs. Direct Experience When Both Search and Experience Attributes Are Present," *Journal of Consumer Research,* March 1995, pp. 708–718.

159. Vicki G. Morwitz and Gavan J. Fitzsimons, "The Mere-Measurement Effect: Why Does Measuring Intention Change Actual Behavior?" *Journal of Consumer Psychology* 14, no. 1/2, 2004, pp. 64–74; Pierre Chandon, Vicki G. Morwitz, and Werner J. Reinartz, "Do Intentions Really Predict Behavior? Self-Generated Validity Effects in Survey Research," *Journal of Marketing* 69, no. 2 (April 2005), pp. 1–14.

160. Berger, "The Nature of Attitude Accessibility and Attitude Confidence."

161. Joseph R. Priester, Dhananjay Nayakankuppam, Monique A. Fleming, and John Godek, "The A^2SC^2 Model: The Influence of Attitudes and Attitude Strength on Consideration and Choice," *Journal of Consumer Research,* March 2004, pp. 574–587.

162. Fishbein and Ajzen, *Belief, Attitude, Intention, and Behavior.*

163. H. Shanker Krishnan and Robert E. Smith, "The Relative Endurance of Attitudes, Confidence, and Attitude–Behavior Consistency: The Role of Information Source and Delay," *Journal of Consumer Psychology* 7, no. 3, 1998, pp. 273–298.

164. Matt Thomson, Deborah J. MacInnis, and C. W. Park, "The Ties that Bind: Measuring the Strength of Consumers' Emotional Attachments to Brands," *Journal of Consumer Psychology* 15, no. 1 (2005), pp. 77–91; C. W. Park and Deborah J. MacInnis, "What's In and What's Out: Questions on the Boundaries of the Attitude Construct," *Journal of Consumer Research* 33, no. 1 (2006), pp. 16–18; C. W. Park, Deborah J. MacInnis, and Joseph Priester, "Brand Attachment as a Strategic Brand Exemplar," forthcoming in ed. Bernd H. Schmitt, *Handbook of Brand and Experience Management;* Rohini Ahluwalia, Robert Burnkrant, and H. Rao Unnava, "Consumer Response to Negative Publicity: The Moderating Role of Commitment," *Journal of Marketing Research* 37, no. 2 (May 2000), pp. 203–214; Michael D. Johnson, Andreas Herrmann, and Frank Huber, "The Evolution of Loyalty Intentions," *Journal of Marketing* 70, April 2006, 122–132; Matthew Thomson, "Human Brands: Investigating Antecedents to Consumers' Strong Attachments to Celebrities," *Journal of Marketing* 70, no. 3 (July 2006), pp. 104–119.

165. Sekar Raju and H. Rao Unnava, "The Role of Arousal in Commitment: An Explanation for the Number of Counterarguments," *Journal of Consumer Research* 33, no. 2 (2006), pp. 173–178.

166. Krishnan and Smith, "The Relative Endurance of Attitudes, Confidence, and Attitude–Behavior Consistency."

167. John T. Cacioppo, Richard E. Petty, Chuan Fang Kao, and Regina Rodriguez, "Central and Peripheral Routes to Persuasion: An Individual Difference Perspective," *Journal of Personality and Social Psychology* 51, 1986, pp. 1032–1043.

168. Mark Snyder and William B. Swan Jr., "When Actions Reflect Attitudes: The Politics of Impression Management," *Journal of Personality and Social Psychology* 34, 1976, pp. 1034–1042.

169. Mya Frazier, "GEICO: Runner-Up," *Advertising Age,* October 15, 2007, p. 50; Mya Frazier, "Geico's $500M Outlay Pays Off," *Advertising Age,* July 9, 2007, p. 8; Frank Ahrens, "Geico Goes Cruising for Motorcyclists in Cyberspace," *Washington Post,* July 2, 2007, p. D1; *www.geico.com.*

Chapter 6

1. Jeremiah McWilliams, "A-B Sees Web as Fertile Ground for Advertising Efforts," *St. Louis Post-Dispatch,* December 19, 2007, *www.stltoday.com;* Suzanne Vranica, "Anheuser-Busch Kicks Edgy Super Bowl Ad to Curb," *Wall Street Journal,* January 26, 2005, p. B3; Eleftheria Parpis, "Truly Tasteless Jokes," *Adweek,* April 26, 2004, p. 28; Christopher Lawton, "Beck's Hopes Sexy, Brainy Ads Get Attention But Not Catcalls," *Wall Street Journal,* March 14, 2003, p. B2.

2. Norbert Schwarz, "Attitude Research: Between Ockham's Razor and the Fundamental Attribution Error," *Journal of Consumer Research* 33, no. 1, 2006, pp. 19–21.

3. Richard E. Petty and John T. Cacioppo, *Attitudes and Persuasion: Classic and Contemporary Approaches* (Dubuque, Iowa: William C. Brown, 1981); Richard E. Petty, John T. Cacioppo, and David Schumann, "Central and Peripheral Routes to Advertising Effectiveness: The Moderating Role of Involvement," *Journal of Consumer Research,* September 1983, pp. 135–146.

4. Jaideep Sengupta, Ronald C. Goodstein, and David S. Boninger, "All Cues Are Not Created Equal: Obtaining Attitude Persistence Under Low Involvement Conditions," *Journal of Consumer Research*, March 1997, pp. 315–361.

5. Ap Dijksterhuis, Pamela K. Smith, Rick B. Van Baaren, and Daniel H. J. Wigboldus, "The Unconscious Consumer: Effects of Environment on Consumer Behavior," *Journal of Consumer Psychology* 15, no. 3, 2005, pp. 193–202.

6. Nalini Ambady, Mary Ann Krabbenhoft, and Daniel Hogan, "The 30-Sec Sale: Using Thin-Slice Judgments to Evaluate Sales Effectiveness," *Journal of Consumer Psychology* 16, no. 1, 2006, pp. 4–13.

7. Frank R. Kardes, "When Should Consumers and Managers Trust Their Intuition?" *Journal of Consumer Psychology* 16, no. 1, 2006, pp. 20–24.

8. Jens Förster, "How Body Feedback Influences Consumers' Evaluation of Products," *Journal of Consumer Psychology* 14, no. 4, 2004, pp. 416–426. See also Ronald S. Friedman and Jens Förster, "The Effects of Approach and Avoidance Motor Actions on the Elements of Creative Insight," *Journal of Personality and Social Psychology* 79, no. 4, 2000, pp. 477–492.

9. Itamar Simonson, "In Defense of Consciousness: The Role of Conscious and Unconscious Inputs in Consumer Choice," *Journal of Consumer Psychology* 15, no. 3, 2005, pp. 211–217.

10. Gita V. Johar and Anne L. Roggeveen, "Changing False Beliefs from Repeated Advertising: The Role of Claim-Refutation Alignment," *Journal of Consumer Psychology* 17, no. 2, 2007, pp. 118–127.

11. Jennifer Edson Escalas and Mary Frances Luce, "Understanding the Effects of Process-Focused Versus Outcome-Focused Thought in Response to Advertising," *Journal of Consumer Research* 13, no. 2, 2004, pp. 274–285.

12. Ronald C. Goodstein, "Category-Based Applications and Extensions in Advertising: Motivating More Extensive Ad Processing," *Journal of Consumer Research*, June 1993, pp. 87–99.

13. Valerie S. Folkes, "Recent Attribution Research in Consumer Behavior: A Review and New Directions," *Journal of Consumer Research*, March 1988, pp. 548–656.

14. Scott Boeck, "Marbury Shoe Line Gaining Steam," *USA Today*, February 7, 2007, p. 7C.

15. Shelly Chaiken, "Heuristic Versus Systematic Information Processing and the Use of Source Versus Message Cues in Persuasion," *Journal of Personality and Social Psychology* 39, 1980, pp. 752–766; see also "The Heuristic Model of Persuasion," in eds. Mark P. Zanna, J. M. Olson, and C. P. Herman, *Social Influence: The Ontario Symposium*, vol. 5 (Hillsdale, N.J.: Lawrence Erlbaum, 1987), pp. 3–49.

16. Amna Kirmani, "Advertising Repetition as a Signal of Quality: If It's Advertised So Much, Something Must Be Wrong," *Journal of Advertising*, Fall 1997, pp. 77–86.

17. Joseph W. Alba and Howard Marmorstein, "The Effects of Frequency Knowledge on Consumer Decision Making," *Journal of Consumer Research*, June 1987, pp. 14–25.

18. Scott A. Hawkins and Stephen J. Hoch, "Low-Involvement Learning: Memory Without Evaluation," *Journal of Consumer Research*, September 1992, pp. 212–225; Lynn Hasher, David Goldstein, and Thomas Toppino, "Frequency and the Conference of Referential Validity," *Journal of Verbal Learning and Verbal Behavior*, February 1977, pp. 107–112.

19. S. Ratneshwar and Shelly Chaiken, "Comprehension's Role in Persuasion: The Case of Its Moderating Effect on the Persuasive Impact of Source Cues," *Journal of Consumer Research*, June 1991, pp. 52–62.

20. Alice M. Tybout, Brian Sternthal, Prashant Malaviya, Georgios A. Bakamitsos, and Se-Bum Park, "Information Accessibility as a Moderator of Judgments: The Role of Content Versus Retrieval Ease," *Journal of Consumer Research* 32, no. 1, 2005, pp. 76–85.

21. Nancy Spears, "On the Use of Time Expressions in Promoting Product Benefits," *Journal of Advertising*, Summer 2003, pp. 33–44.

22. Jennifer Edson Escalas, "Self-Referencing and Persuasion: Narrative Transportation Versus Analytical Elaboration," *Journal of Consumer Research* 33, no. 4, 2007, pp. 421–429.

23. Patricia M. West, Joel Huber, and Kyeong Sam Min, "Altering Experienced Utility: The Impact of Story Writing and Self-Referencing on Preferences," *Journal of Consumer Research* 31, no. 3, 2004, pp. 623–630; Robert E. Burnkrant and H. Rao Unnava, "Effects of Self-Referencing on Persuasion," *Journal of Consumer Research*, June 1995, pp. 17–26; Sharon Shavitt and Timothy C. Brock, "Self-Relevant Responses in Commercial Persuasion," in eds. Jerry C. Olson and Keith Sentis, *Advertising and Consumer Psychology* (New York: Praeger, 1986), pp. 149–171; Kathleen Debevec and Jean B. Romeo, "Self-Referent Processing in Perceptions of Verbal and Visual Commercial Information," *Journal of Consumer Psychology* 1, no. 1, 1992, pp. 83–102; Joan Myers-Levy and Laura A. Peracchio, "Moderators of the Impact of Self-Reference on Persuasion," *Journal of Consumer Research*, March 1996, pp. 408–423.

24. Daniel J. Howard, Charles Gengler, and Ambuj Jain, "What's in a Name? A Complimentary Means of Persuasion," *Journal of Consumer Research*, September 1995, pp. 200–211.

25. Jennifer L. Aaker, "The Malleable Self: The Role of Self-Expression in Persuasion," *Journal of Marketing Research* 36, February 1999, pp. 45–57.

26. Jenn Abelson, "Sneaker Company Taps Chief," *Boston Globe*, April 18, 2007, p. F1.

27. Anne M. Brumbaugh, "Source and Nonsource Cues in Advertising and Their Effects on the Activation of Cultural and Subcultural Knowledge on the Route to Persuasion," *Journal of Consumer Research*, September 2002, pp. 258+.

28. Robert E. Burnkrant and Daniel J. Howard, "Effects of the Use of Introductory Rhetorical Questions Versus

Statements on Information Processing," *Journal of Personality and Social Psychology,* December 1984, pp. 1218–1230; James M. Munch, Gregory W. Boller, and John L. Swazy, "The Effects of Argument Structure and Affective Tagging on Product Attitude Formation," *Journal of Consumer Research,* September 1993, pp. 294–302.

29. Rohini Ahluwalia and Robert E. Burnkrant, "Answering Questions About Questions: A Persuasion Knowledge Perspective for Understanding the Effects of Rhetorical Questions," *Journal of Consumer Research*, June 2004, pp. 26–42.

30. Russell H. Fazio, Paul M. Herr, and Martha C. Powell, "On the Development and Strength of Category-Brand Associations in Memory: The Case of Mystery Ads," *Journal of Consumer Psychology* 1, no. 1, 1992, pp. 1–14.

31. Liz C. Wang, Julie Baker, Judy A. Wagner, and Kirk Wakefield, "Can a Retail Website Be Social?" *Journal of Marketing,* July 2007, pp. 143–157.

32. David A. Griffin and Qimei Chen, "The Influence of Virtual Direct Experience (VDE) on On-Line Ad Message Effectiveness," *Journal of Advertising,* Spring 2004, pp. 55–68.

33. Hiawatha Bray, "'Advergames' Spark Concerns of Kids Being Targeted," *Boston Globe*, July 30, 2004, *www.boston.com/globe.*

34. Gregory Solman, "2nd Splash for 'Got Milk?' Steroid Parodies," *Adweek*, December 28, 2007, *www.adweek.com.*

35. Joseph W. Alba, J. Wesley Hutchinson, and John G. Lynch, "Memory and Decision Making," in eds. Thomas S. Robertson and Harold H. Kassarjian, *Handbook of Consumer Behavior* (Englewood Cliffs, N.J.: Prentice-Hall, 1991).

36. Chris Janiszewski and Tom Meyvis, "Effects of Brand Logo Complexity, Repetition, and Spacing on Processing Fluency and Judgment," *Journal of Consumer Research,* June 2001, pp. 18–32; H. Rao Unnava and Robert E. Burnkrant, "Effects of Repeating Varied Ad Executions on Brand Name Memory," *Journal of Marketing Research,* November 1991, pp. 406–416.

37. Ida E. Berger and Andrew A. Mitchell, "The Effect of Attitude Accessibility, Attitude Confidence, and the Attitude–Behavior Relationship," *Journal of Consumer Research*, December 1989, pp. 269–279.

38. Prashant Malaviya and Brian Sternthal, "The Persuasive Impact of Message Spacing," *Journal of Consumer Psychology* 6, no. 3, 1997, pp. 233–256.

39. Patrick De Pelsmacker, Maggie Geuens, and Pascal Anckaert, "Media Context and Advertising Effectiveness: The Role of Context Appreciation and Context/Ad Similarity," *Journal of Advertising,* September 2002, pp. 49–61.

40. Marjolein Moorman, Peter C. Neijens, and Edith G. Smit, "The Effects of Magazine-Induced Psychological Responses and Thematic Congruence on Memory and Attitude Toward the Life in a Real-Life Setting," *Journal of Advertising,* Winter 2002, pp. 27–40.

41. See, for instance, Xiang Fang, Surendra Singh, and Rohini Ahluwalia, "An Examination of Different Explanations for the Mere Exposure Effect," *Journal of Consumer Research* 34, no. 1, 2007, pp. 99–103.

42. Carl Obermiller, "Varieties of Mere Exposure: The Effects of Processing Style and Repetition in Affective Response," *Journal of Consumer Research,* June 1985, pp. 17–30.

43. Arno Rethans, John L. Swazy, and Lawrence J. Marks, "The Effects of Television Commercial Repetition, Receiver Knowledge, and Commercial Length: A Test of a Two Factor Model," *Journal of Marketing Research,* February 1986, pp. 50–61.

44. William E. Baker, "When Can Affective Conditioning and Mere Exposure Directly Influence Brand Choice?" *Journal of Advertising* 28, no. 4, Winter 1999, pp. 31–46.

45. Chris Janiszewski and Tom Meyvis, "Effects of Brand Logo Complexity, Repetition, and Spacing on Processing Fluency and Judgment," *Journal of Consumer Research* 28, June 2001, pp. 18–32.

46. Bruce Mohl, "Humor Not Part of Their Policies; New to Ads, Mass. Insurers Emphasize Safety," *Boston Globe,* October 2, 2007, p. C1.

47. Herbert Krugman, "Why Three Exposures May Be Enough," *Journal of Advertising Research,* December 1972, pp. 11–14.

48. George E. Belch, "The Effects of Television Commercial Repetition on Cognitive Response and Message Acceptance," *Journal of Consumer Research,* June 1982, pp. 56–65.

49. Margaret Henderson Blair, "An Empirical Investigation of Advertising Wearin and Wearout," *Journal of Advertising Research* 40, November 2000, p. 95.

50. Margaret C. Campbell and Kevin Lane Keller, "Brand Familiarity and Advertising Repetition Effects," *Journal of Consumer Research,* September 2003, pp. 292–304.

51. Deborah J. MacInnis, Ambar G. Rao, and Allen M. Weiss, "Assessing When Increased Media Weight of Real-World Advertisements Helps Sales," *Journal of Marketing Research,* November 2002, pp. 391–407.

52. Christie L. Nordhielm, "The Influence of Level of Processing on Advertising Repetition Effects," *Journal of Consumer Research,* December 2002, pp. 371–373.

53. Marian Burke and Julie A. Edell, "Ad Reactions over Time: Capturing Changes in the Real World," *Journal of Consumer Research,* June 1986, pp. 114–118; Curtis P. Haugtvedt, David W. Schumann, Wendy L. Schneier, and Wendy L. Warren, "Advertising Repetition and Variation Strategies: Implications for Understanding Attitude Strength," *Journal of Consumer Research,* June 1994, pp. 176–189.

54. Stuart Elliott, "The Pursuit of Happiness in a Grilled Cheese Sandwich," *New York Times,* October 1, 2007, p. C6.

55. Prashant Malaviya, "The Moderating Influence of Advertising Context on Ad Repetition Effects: The Role of Amount and Type of Elaboration," *Journal of Consumer Research* 34, no. 1, 2007, pp. 32–40.

56. Gerald J. Gorn, "The Effects of Music in Advertising on Choice Behavior: A Classical Conditioning Approach," *Journal of Marketing,* Winter 1982, pp. 94–101.

57. Calvin Bierley, Frances K. McSweeny, and Renee Vannieuwkerk, "Classical Conditioning of Preferences for Stimuli," *Journal of Consumer Research,* December 1985, pp. 316–323; James J. Kellaris and Anthony D. Cox, "The Effects of Background Music in Advertising: A Reassessment," *Journal of Consumer Research,* June 1989, pp. 113–118: Chris T. Allen and Thomas J. Madden, "A Closer Look at Classical Conditioning," *Journal of Consumer Research,* December 1985, pp. 301–315.

58. Bierley, McSweeny, and Vannieuwkerk, "Classical Conditioning of Preferences for Stimuli"; Elnora W. Stuart, Terence A. Shimp, and Randall W. Engle, "Classical Conditioning of Consumer Attitudes: Four Experiments in an Advertising Context," *Journal of Consumer Research,* December 1987, pp. 334–349; Terence A. Shimp, Elnora W. Stuart, and Randall W. Engle, "A Program of Classical Conditioning Experiments Testing Variations in the Conditioned Stimulus and Context," *Journal of Consumer Research,* June 1991, pp. 1–12; Chris T. Allen and Chris A. Janiszewski, "Assessing the Role of Contingency Awareness in Attitudinal Conditioning with Implications for Advertising Research," *Journal of Marketing Research,* February 1989, pp. 30–43.

59. Randi Priluck Grossman and Brian D. Till, "The Persistence of Classically Conditioned Brand Attitudes," *Journal of Advertising,* Spring 1998.

60. Terence A. Shimp, "Neo-Pavlovian Conditioning and Its Implications for Consumer Theory and Research," in eds. Thomas S. Robertson and Harold H. Kassarjian, *Handbook of Consumer Behavior* (Englewood Cliffs, N.J.: Prentice-Hall, 1991), pp. 162–187; Steve DiMeglio, "Tiger Pulls Nike's Latest Drivers from Bag of Tricks," *USA Today,* December 6, 2007, *www.usatoday.com.*

61. Mike Hughlett, "Tiger Puts New Face on Tie-ins," *Chicago Tribune,* October 17, 2007, *www.chicagotribune.com.*

62. Aparna A. Labroo and Suresh Ramanathan, "The Influence of Experience and Sequence of Conflicting Emotions on Ad Attitudes," *Journal of Consumer Research* 33, no. 4, 2007, pp. 523–528; Steven P. Brown and Douglas M. Stayman, "Antecedents and Consequences of Attitude Toward the Ad: A Meta-analysis," *Journal of Consumer Research,* June 1993, pp. 34–51; Andrew A. Mitchell and Jerry C. Olson, "Are Product Attributes Beliefs the Only Mediator of Advertising Effects on Brand Attitudes?" *Journal of Marketing Research,* August 1981, pp. 318–322; Terence A. Shimp, "Attitude Toward the Ad as a Mediator of Consumer Brand Choice," *Journal of Advertising* 10, no. 2, 1981, pp. 9–15; Christian M. Derbaix, "The Impact of Affective Reactions on Attitudes Toward the Advertisement and the Brand: A Step Toward Ecological Validity," *Journal of Marketing Research,* November 1995, pp. 470–479.

63. Mitchell and Olson, "Are Product Attributes Beliefs the Only Mediator of Advertising Effects on Brand Attitudes?"

64. Srinivas Durvasula, J. Craig Andrews, Steven Lysonski, and Richard G. Netemeyer, "Assessing the Cross-National Applicability of Consumer Behavior Models: A Model of Attitude Toward Advertising in General," *Journal of Consumer Research,* March 1993, pp. 626–636.

65. Russell I. Haley and Allan L. Baldinger, "The ARF Copy Research Validity Project," *Journal of Advertising Research,* April–May 1991, pp. 11–32.

66. Elizabeth S. Moore and Richard J. Lutz, "Children, Advertising, and Product Experiences: A Multimethod Inquiry," *Journal of Consumer Research* 27, June 2000, pp. 31–48; Scott B. MacKenzie, Richard J. Lutz, and George E. Belch, "The Role of Attitude Toward the Ad as a Mediator of Advertising Effectiveness: A Test of Competing Explanations," *Journal of Marketing Research,* May 1986, pp. 130–143; Pamela M. Homer, "The Mediating Role of Attitude Toward the Ad: Some Additional Evidence," *Journal of Marketing Research,* February 1990, pp. 78–86; Brown and Stayman, "Antecedents and Consequences of Attitude Toward the Ad."

67. Ellen Byron, "How P&G Led Also-Ran To Sweet Smell of Success," *Wall Street Journal,* September 4, 2007, p. B2.

68. Brown and Stayman, "Antecedents and Consequences of Attitude Toward the Ad."

69. Marian Chapman Burke and Julie A. Edell, "Ad Reactions over Time: Capturing Changes in the Real World," *Journal of Consumer Research,* June 1986, pp. 114–118; Amitava Chattopadhyay and Prakash Nedungadi, "Does Attitude Toward the Ad Endure? The Moderating Effects of Attention and Delay," *Journal of Consumer Research,* June 1992, pp. 26–33.

70. Margaret G. Meloy, "Mood Driven Distortion of Product Information," *Journal of Consumer Research* 27, December 2000, pp. 345–359.

71. Michael J. Barone, Paul W. Miniard, and Jean B. Romeo, "The Influence of Positive Mood on Brand Extension Evaluations," *Journal of Consumer Research* 26, March 2000, pp. 386–400.

72. Anick Bosmans and Hans Baumgartner, "Goal-Relevant Emotional Information: When Extraneous Affect Leads to Persuasion and When It Does Not," *Journal of Consumer Research* 32, no. 3 (2005), pp. 424–434.

73. Rashmi Adaval, "Sometimes It Just Feels Right: The Differential Weighting of Affect-Consistent and Affect-Inconsistent Product Information," *Journal of Consumer Research* 28, June 2001, pp. 1–17.

74. Charles S. Areni and David Kim, "The Influence of In-Store Lighting on Consumers' Examination of Merchandise in a Wine Store," *International Journal of Research in Marketing,* March 1994, pp. 117–125.

75. Ayn E. Crowley, "The Two-Dimension Impact of Color on Shopping," *Marketing Letters* 4, no. 1, 1993, pp. 59–69.

76. Nancy M. Puccinelli, "Putting Your Best Face Forward: The Impact of Customer Mood on Salesperson Evaluation," *Journal of Consumer Psychology* 16, no. 2, 2006, pp. 156–162.

77. Julie A. Edell and Marian Chapman Burke, "The Power of Feelings in Understanding Advertising Effects," *Journal of Consumer Research*, December 1987, pp. 421–433; Douglas M. Stayman and David A. Aaker, "Are All Effects of Ad-Induced Feelings Mediated by Aad?" *Journal of Consumer Research*, December 1988, pp. 368–373; Morris B. Holbrook and Rajeev Batra, "Assessing the Role of Emotions as Mediators of Consumer Responses to Advertising," *Journal of Consumer Research*, December 1987, pp. 404–420.

78. Rajeev Batra and Michael L. Ray, "Affective Responses Mediating Acceptance of Advertising," *Journal of Consumer Research*, September 1986, pp. 234–249.

79. David A. Aaker, Douglas M. Stayman, and Michael R. Hagerty, "Warmth in Advertising: Measurement, Impact, and Sequence Effects," *Journal of Consumer Research*, March 1986, pp. 365–381.

80. Joseph A. Bellizzi, Ayn E. Crowley, and Ronald W. Hasty, "The Effects of Color in Store Design," *Journal of Retailing*, Spring 1983, pp. 21–45.

81. Arik Hesseldahl, "Apple Forecasts: Not Just Hype," *BusinessWeek Online*, December 10, 2007, *www.businessweek.com.*

82. Curt Haugtvedt, Richard E. Petty, John T. Cacioppo, and T. Steidley, "Personality and Ad Effectiveness: Exploring the Utility of Need for Cognition," in ed. Michael J. Houston, *Advances in Consumer Research*, vol. 15 (Provo, Utah: Association for Consumer Research, 1988), pp. 209–212.

83. Susan M. Petroshius and Kenneth E. Crocker, "An Empirical Analysis of Spokesperson Characteristics on Advertisement and Product Evaluations," *Journal of the Academy of Marketing Science*, Summer 1989, pp. 217–225; Lynn R. Kahle and Pamela M. Homer, "Physical Attractiveness of the Celebrity Endorser: A Social Adaptation Perspective," *Journal of Consumer Research*, March 1985, pp. 954–961.

84. Michael A. Kamins, "An Investigation into the 'Match-Up' Hypothesis in Celebrity Advertising: When Beauty May Be Only Skin Deep," *Journal of Advertising* 19, no. 1, 1990, pp. 4–13: Marjorie J. Caballero and Paul J. Solomon, "Effects of Model Attractiveness on Sales Response," *Journal of Advertising* 13, no. 1, 1984, pp. 17–23.

85. Kahle and Homer, "Physical Attractiveness of the Celebrity Endorser"; Kathleen Debevec and Jerome B. Kernan, "More Evidence on the Effects of a Presenter's Physical Attractiveness: Some Cognitive, Affective, and Behavioral Consequences," in ed. Thomas C. Kinnear, *Advances in Consumer Research*, vol. 11 (Provo, Utah: Association for Consumer Research, 1984), pp. 127–132; Caballero and Solomon, "Effects of Model Attractiveness on Sales Response"; Marjorie J. Caballero and William M. Pride, "Selected Effects of Salesperson Sex and Attractiveness in Direct Mail Advertising," *Journal of Marketing*, January 1984, pp. 94–100; Shelly Chaiken, "Communicator Physical Attractiveness and Persuasion," *Journal of Personality and Social Psychology*, August 1979, pp. 1387–1397; Peter H. Reingen and Jerome B. Kernan, "Social Perception and Interpersonal Influence: Some Consequences of the Physical Attractiveness Stereotype in a Personal Selling Situation," *Journal of Consumer Psychology* 2, no. 1, 1993, pp. 25–38.

86. Tommy E. Whittler and Joan Scattone Spira, "Model's Race: A Peripheral Cue in Advertising Messages?" *Journal of Consumer Psychology* 12, no. 4, 2002, pp. 291–301.

87. M. Reinhard, M. Messner, and S. Ludwig Sporer, "Explicit Persuasive Intent and Its Impact on Success at Persuasion—the Determining Roles of Attractiveness and Likeableness," *Journal of Consumer Psychology* 16, no. 3, 2006, pp. 249–259.

88. Yong-Soon Kang and Paul M. Herr, "Beauty and the Beholder: Toward an Integrative Model of Communication Source Effects," *Journal of Consumer Research* 33, no. 1, 2006, pp. 123–130; Richard E. Petty, H. Rao Unnava, and Alan J. Strathman, "Theories of Attitude Change," in eds. Thomas S. Robertson and Harold H. Kassarjian, *Handbook of Consumer Behavior* (Englewood Cliffs, N.J.: Prentice-Hall, 1991), pp. 241–280; Kahle and Homer, "Physical Attractiveness of the Celebrity Endorser."

89. Anthony Faiola, "U.S. Stars Shine Again in Japan Ads," *Washington Post*, January 14, 2007, p. A1.

90. Mark R. Forehand and Andrew Perkins, "Implicit Assimilation and Explicit Contrast: A Set/Reset Model of Response to Celebrity Voice-Overs," *Journal of Consumer Research* 32, no. 3, 2005, pp. 435–441.

91. Joshua Harris Prager, "Disability Can Enable a Modeling Career," *Wall Street Journal*, October 17, 1997, pp. B1, B6.

92. Sengupta, Goodstein, and Boninger, "All Cues Are Not Created Equal."

93. Greg Sandoval, "James's Value Shows in Numbers," *Washington Post*, April 16, 2004, p. D8.

94. Alan J. Bush, Craig A. Martin, and Victoria D. Bush, "Sports Celebrity Influence on the Behavioral Intentions of Generation Y," *Journal of Advertising Research*, March 2004, pp. 108–118.

95. Claire Atkinson, "Brawny Man Now a Metrosexual," *Advertising Age*, February 16, 2004, p. 8.

96. Judith A. Garretson and Ronald W. Niedrich, "Spokes-Characters," *Journal of Advertising*, Summer 2004, pp. 25–36.

97. Marla Royne Stafford, Thomas F. Stafford, and Ellen Day, "A Contingency Approach: The Effects of Spokesperson Type and Service Type on Service Advertising Perceptions," *Journal of Advertising*, Summer 2002, pp. 17–34.

98. Peter Ford and Gloria Goodale, "Why Stars and Charities Need Each Other," *Christian Science Monitor*, January 13, 2005, p. 1.

99. Therese A. Louie and Carl Obermiller, "Consumer Response to a Firm's Endorser (Dis)Association Decisions," *Journal of Advertising*, Winter 2002, pp. 41–52.

100. Mitchell and Olson, "Are Product Attributes Beliefs the Only Mediator of Advertising Effects on Brand Attitudes?"

Andrew A. Mitchell, "The Effect of Verbal and Visual Components of Advertisements on Brand Attitudes and Attitude Toward the Advertisement," *Journal of Consumer Research,* March 1986, pp. 12–24; Paul W. Miniard, Sunil Bhatla, Kenneth R. Lord, Peter R. Dickson, and H. Rao Unnava, "Picture-Based Persuasion Processes and the Moderating Role of Involvement," *Journal of Consumer Research,* June 1991, pp. 92–107.

101. Paul W. Miniard, Deepak Sirdeshmukh, and Daniel E. Innis, "Peripheral Persuasion and Brand Choice," *Journal of Consumer Research,* September 1992, pp. 226–239.

102. Andrea Petersen, "The Quest to Make URL's Look Cool in Ads," *Wall Street Journal,* February 26, 1997, pp. B1, B3.

103. Brian Steinberg, "The Times Are A-Changin' for Musicians and Marketers," *Advertising Age,* October 29, 2007, p. 1.

104. "Mark Sandman, An Instant Classic; a Familiar Sound; a Dead Man's Legacy," *Wall Street Journal,* December 28, 2004, p. D8.

105. Gordon C. Bruner, "Music, Mood, and Marketing," *Journal of Marketing,* October 1990, pp. 94–104; Gorn, "The Effects of Music in Advertising on Choice Behavior"; Judy I. Alpert and Mark I. Alpert, "Background Music as an Influence in Consumer Mood and Advertising Responses," in ed. Thomas K. Srull, *Advances in Consumer Research,* vol. 16 (Provo, Utah: Association for Consumer Research, 1989), pp. 485–491; Meryl Paula Gardner, "Mood States and Consumer Behavior: A Critical Review," *Journal of Consumer Research,* December 1985, pp. 281–300; C. Whan Park and S. Mark Young, "Consumer Response to Television Commercials: The Impact of Involvement and Background Music on Brand Attitude Formation," *Journal of Marketing Research,* February 1986, pp. 11–24.

106. Juliet Rui and Joan Meyers-Levy, "Distinguishing Between the Meanings of Music: When Background Music Affects Product Perceptions," *Journal of Marketing Research,* August 2005, pp. 333–345.

107. Mark Alpert and Judy Alpert, "Background Music as an Influence in Consumer Mood and Advertising Responses,"*Advances in Consumer Research* 16, Fall 1989, pp. 485–491; Stout and Leckenby, "Let the Music Play."

108. Noel M. Murray and Sandra B. Murray, "Music and Lyrics in Commercials: A Cross-Cultural Comparison Between Commercials Run in the Dominican Republic and the United States," *Journal of Advertising,* Summer 1996, pp. 51–64.

109. Marc G. Weinberger and Harlan E. Spotts, "Humor in U.S. vs. U.K. TV Advertising," *Journal of Advertising* 18, no. 2, 1989, pp. 39–44; Paul Surgi Speck, "The Humorous Message Taxonomy: A Framework for the Study of Humorous Ads," in eds. James H. Leigh and Claude R. Martin, *Current Research and Issues in Advertising* (Ann Arbor, Mich.: University of Michigan, 1991), pp. 1–44.

110. Thomas J. Madden and Marc G. Weinberger, "Humor in Advertising: A Practitioner View," *Journal of Advertising Research,* August–September 1984, pp. 23–29; Stewart and Furse, *Effective Television Advertising;* Thomas J. Madden and Marc C. Weinberger, "The Effects of Humor on Attention in Magazine Advertising," *Journal of Advertising* 1, no. 3, 1982, pp. 8–14; Marc C. Weinberger and Leland Campbell, "The Use and Impact of Humor in Radio Advertising," *Journal of Advertising Research,* December–January 1991, pp. 44–52.

111. George E. Belch and Michael A. Belch, "An Investigation of the Effects of Repetition on Cognitive and Affective Reactions to Humorous and Serious Television Commercials," in ed. Thomas C. Kinnear, *Advances in Consumer Research,* vol. 11 (Provo, Utah: Association for Consumer Research, 1984), pp. 4–10; Calvin P. Duncan and James E. Nelson, "Effects of Humor in a Radio Advertising Experiment," *Journal of Advertising* 14, no. 2, 1985, pp. 33–40, 64; Betsy D. Gelb and Charles M. Pickett, "Attitude-toward-the-Ad: Links to Humor and to Advertising Effectiveness," *Journal of Advertising* 12, no. 2, 1983, pp. 34–42; Betsy D. Gelb and George M. Zinkhan, "The Effect of Repetition on Humor in a Radio Advertising Study," *Journal of Advertising* 15, no. 2, 1986, pp. 15–20, 34.

112. Harlan E. Spotts, Marc. G. Weinberger, and Amy L. Parsons, "Assessing the Use and Impact of Humor on Advertising Effectiveness: A Contingency Approach," *Journal of Advertising,* Fall 1997, pp. 17–32.

113. Brian Sternthal and Samuel Craig, "Humor in Advertising," *Journal of Marketing* 37, no. 4, 1973, pp. 12–18; Calvin P. Duncan, "Humor in Advertising: A Behavioral Perspective," *Journal of the Academy of Marketing Science* 7, no. 4, 1979, pp. 285–306; Weinberger and Campbell, "The Use and Impact of Humor in Radio Advertising."

114. Thomas W. Cline and James J. Kellaris, "The Influence of Humor Strength and Humor–Message Relatedness on Ad Memorability," *Journal of Advertising,* Spring 2007, pp. 55–67.

115. Thomas W. Cline, Moses B. Altsech, and James J. Kellaris, "When Does Humor Enhance or Inhibit Ad Responses?" *Journal of Advertising,* Fall 2003, pp. 31–45.

116. Josephine L. C. M. Woltman Elpers, Ashesh Mukherjee, and Wayne D. Hoyer, "Humor in Television Advertising: A Moment-to-Moment Analysis," *Journal of Consumer Research,* December 2004, pp. 592–598.

117. Madden and Weinberger, "Humor in Advertising"; Weinberger and Campbell, "The Use and Impact of Humor in Radio Advertising"; Weinberger and Spotts, "Humor in U.S. vs. U.K. TV Advertising."

118. Stuart Elliott, "Old Spice Tries a Dash of Humor to Draw Young Men," *New York Times,* January 8, 2007, p. C6.

119. Madden and Weinberger, "Humor in Advertising"; Thomas W. Whipple and Alice E. Courtney, "How Men and Women Judge Humor: Advertising Guidelines for Action and Research," in eds. James H. Leigh and Claude R. Martin, *Current Research and Issues in Advertising* (Ann Arbor, Mich.: University of Michigan, 1981), pp. 43–56.

120. Yong Zhang, "Responses to Humorous Advertising: The Moderating Effect of Need for Cognition," *Journal of Advertising,* Spring 1996: Amitava Chattopadhyay and Kunal Basu, "Prior Brand Evaluation as a Moderator of the Effects of Humor in Advertising," *Journal of Marketing Research,* November 1989, pp. 466–476.

121. Dana L. Alden, Wayne D. Hoyer, and Chol Lee, "Identifying Global and Culture-Specific Dimensions of Humor in Advertising: A Multi-national Analysis," *Journal of Marketing,* April 1993, pp. 64–75; Dana L. Alden, Wayne D. Hoyer, Chol Lee, and Guntalee We-chasara, "The Use of Humor in Asian and Western Advertising: A Four-Country Comparison," *Journal of Asian-Pacific Business* 1, no. 2, 1995, pp. 3–23.

122. Weinberger and Spotts, "Humor in U.S. vs. U.K. TV Advertising."

123. "Durex Kicks Off Integrated Ad Push for Pleasure Max," *New Media Age,* November 25, 2004, p. 2; Alessandra Galloni, "In New Global Campaign, Durex Maker Uses Humor to Sell Condoms," *Wall Street Journal,* July 27, 2001, p. B1.

124. Yumiko Ono, "Can Racy Ads Help Revitalize Old Fragrances?" *Wall Street Journal,* November 26, 1996, pp. B1, B10.

125. Nigel K., L1. Pope, Kevin E. Voges, and Mark R. Brown, "The Effect of Provocation in the Form of Mild Erotica on Attitude to the Ad and Corporate Image," *Journal of Advertising,* Spring 2004, pp. 69–82.

126. Lawrence Soley and Gary Kurzbard, "Sex in Advertising: A Comparison of 1964 and 1984 Magazine Advertisements," *Journal of Advertising* 15, no. 3, 1986, pp. 46–54.

127. Cyndee Miller, "We've Been 'Cosbyized,'" *Marketing News,* April 16, 1990, pp. 1–2; Joshua Levine, "Marketing: Fantasy, Not Flesh," *Forbes,* January 22, 1990, pp. 118–120.

128. Vranica, "Anheuser-Busch Kicks Edgy Super Bowl Ad to Curb."

129. Robert S. Baron, "Sexual Content and Advertising Effectiveness: Comments on Belch et al. (1981) and Caccavale et al. (1981)," in ed. Andrew A. Mitchell, *Advances in Consumer Research,* vol. 9 (Ann Arbor, Mich.: Association for Consumer Research, 1982), pp. 428–430.

130. Michael S. LaTour, Robert E. Pitts, and David C. Snook-Luther, "Female Nudity, Arousal, and Ad Response: An Experimental Investigation," *Journal of Advertising* 19, no. 4, 1990, pp. 51–62.

131. Laura Petrecca, "Axe Ads Turn Up the Promise of Sex Appeal," *USA Today,* April 17, 2007, p. 3B.

132. Marilyn Y. Jones, Andrea J. S. Stanaland, and Betsy D. Gelb, "Beefcake and Cheesecake: Insights for Advertisers," *Journal of Advertising,* Summer 1998, pp. 33–52.

133. Rebecca Piirto, "The Romantic Sell," *American Demographics,* August 1989, pp. 38–41.

134. John Fetto, "Where's the Lovin'?" *American Demographics,* February 28, 2001.

135. Miller, "We've Been 'Cosbyized.'"

136. "Poll on Ads: Too Sexy," *Wall Street Journal,* March 8, 1993, p. B5.

137. Robert A. Peterson and Roger A. Kerin, "The Female Role in Advertisements: Some Experimental Evidence," *Journal of Marketing,* October 1977, pp. 59–63.

138. Sak Onkvisit and John J. Shaw, "A View of Marketing and Advertising Practices in Asia and Its Meaning for Marketing Managers," *Journal of Consumer Marketing,* Spring 1985, pp. 5–17.

139. Sarah Ellison, "Sex-Themed Ads Often Don't Travel Well," *Wall Street Journal,* March 31, 2000, p. B7.

140. M. Friestad and Esther Thorson, "Emotion-Eliciting Advertising: Effect on Long-Term Memory and Judgment," in ed. R. J. Lutz, *Advances in Consumer Research,* vol. 13 (Provo, Utah: Association for Consumer Research, 1986), pp. 111–116.

141. Theresa Howard, "Coke Adds Spark to Ad Campaign," *USA Today,* April 3, 2006, p. 3B; Christina Cheddar Berk, "Coke to Debut 'Real' Ad on 'Idol,'" *Wall Street Journal,* January 17, 2005, p. B3; Betsy McKay, "Coke Aims to Revive 'Feel Good' Factor," *Wall Street Journal,* April 20, 2001, p. B8.

142. Barbara B. Stern, "Classical and Vignette Television Advertising Dramas: Structural Models, Formal Analysis, and Consumer Effects," *Journal of Consumer Research,* March 1994, pp. 601–615; William D. Wells, "Lectures and Dramas," in eds. Pat Cafferata and Alice M. Tybout, *Cognitive and Affective Responses to Advertising* (Lexington, Mass.: D. C. Heath, 1988); John Deighton, Daniel Romer, and Josh McQueen, "Using Dramas to Persuade," *Journal of Consumer Research,* December 1989, pp. 335–343.

143. Jennifer Edson Escalas and Barbara B. Stern, "Sympathy and Empathy: Emotional Responses to Advertising Dramas," *Journal of Consumer Research,* March 2003, pp. 566–578.

144. Eleftheria Parpis, "A Bite-Size Series," *Adweek,* November 12, 2007, p. 19; Becky Ebenkamp and Todd Wasserman, "Sunsilk's 'Micro Series' Offers Latest Twist for Soap Operas," *Brandweek,* September 11, 2006, p. 10.

145. Marvin E. Goldberg and Gerald J. Gorn, "Happy and Sad TV Programs: How They Affect Reactions to Commercials," *Journal of Consumer Research,* December 1987, pp. 387–403; John P. Murray Jr. and Peter A. Dacin, "Cognitive Moderators of Negative-Emotion Effects: Implications for Understanding Media Context," *Journal of Consumer Research,* March 1996, pp. 439–447.

146. John P. Murray, John L. Lastovicka, and Surendra Singh, "Feeling and Liking Responses to Television Programs: An Examination of Two Explanations for Media-Context Effects," *Journal of Consumer Research,* March 1992, pp. 441–451.

147. S. N. Singh and Gilbert A. Churchill, "Arousal and Advertising Effectiveness," *Journal of Advertising* 16, no. 1, 1987, pp. 4–10.

148. Mark A. Pavelchak, John H. Antil, and James M. Munch, "The Super Bowl: An Investigation into the Relationship Among Program Context, Emotional Experience, and

Ad Recall," *Journal of Consumer Research,* December 1988, pp. 360–367.

149. Sally Beatty, "Madison Avenue Should Rethink Television Violence, Study Finds," *Wall Street Journal,* December 1, 1998, p. B8.

150. Suzanne Vranica, "Ad Houses Will Need to Be More Nimble," *Wall Street Journal,* January 2, 2008, p. B3; Gary McWilliams and Suzanne Vranica, "Wal-Mart Raises Its Emotional Pitch," *Wall Street Journal,* July 20, 2007, p. B3; Michael Barbaro, "Old Notions Put Aside, Penney Takes Aim at the Heartstrings," *New York Times,* July 11, 2007, p. C4; Bob Garfield, "Is It Love? Saatchi's Penney Ads Make Bob Go All Gooey Inside," *Advertising Age,* March 19, 2007, p. 29; Stuart Elliott and Michael Barbaro, "Wal-Mart Wants to Carry Its Christmas Ads Beyond Price," *New York Times,* November 1, 2007, p. C3.

Chapter 7

1. Natasha Singer, "The U.S.S.R. Is Coming Back (At Least on Clothing Racks)," *New York Times,* November 27, 2007, p. A1; Carla Bova, "Latina Clothing Line for Girls in Stores Next Month," *Marin Independent Journal,* June 30, 2007, *www.marinij.com;* Rachel Brown, "Eyeing Hispanic Market, Palomita Line Seeks to Build on Nostalgia (Licen-Zing)," *WWD,* January 31, 2007, p. 13.; Jamie LaReau, "Mustang Ads Blend Nostalgia, Newness," *Automotive News,* December 6, 2004, p. 24 "Ostalgie: East German Products," *The Economist,* September 13, 2003, p. 57.

2. Darrel D. Muehling and David E. Sprott, "The Power of Reflection: An Empirical Examination of Nostalgia Advertising Effects," *Journal of Advertising,* Fall 2004, pp. 25–36.

3. Loraine Lau-Gesk, "Understanding Consumer Evaluations of Mixed Affective Experiences," *Journal of Consumer Research* 32, no. 1, 2005, pp. 23–28.

4. G. Sperling, "The Information Available in Brief Visual Presentations," *Psychological Monographs,* vol. 74, 1960, pp. 1–25; U. Neisser, *Cognitive Psychology* (New York: Appleton-Century-Crofts, 1967).

5. R. N. Haber, "The Impending Demise of the Icon: A Critique of the Concept of Iconic Storage in Visual Information Processing," *The Behavioral and Brain Sciences,* March 1983, pp. 1–54.

6. William James (1890) as described in Henry C. Ellis and R. Reed Hunt, *Fundamentals of Human Memory and Cognition* (Dubuque, Iowa: William C. Brown, 1989), pp. 65–66.

7. Nader T. Tavassoli and Jin Ki. Han, "Scripted Thought: Processing Korean Hancha and Hangul in a Multimedia Context," *Journal of Consumer Research,* December 2001, pp. 482–493.

8. Deborah J. MacInnis and Linda L. Price, "The Role of Imagery in Information Processing: Review and Extensions," *Journal of Consumer Research,* March 1987, pp. 473–491.

9. Allan Paivio, "Perceptual Comparisons Through the Mind's Eye," *Memory and Cognition,* November 1975, pp. 635–647; Stephen M. Kosslyn, "The Medium and the Message in Mental Imagery: A Theory," *Psychological Review,* January 1981, pp. 46–66; MacInnis and Price, "The Role of Imagery in Information Processing."

10. Morris B. Holbrook and Elizabeth C. Hirschman, "The Experiential Aspects of Consumption: Consumer Fantasies, Feelings, and Fun," *Journal of Consumer Research,* September 1982, pp. 132–140; MacInnis and Price, "The Role of Imagery in Information Processing"; Alan Richardson, "Imagery: Definitions and Types," in ed. Aness Sheikh, *Imagery: Current Theory, Research, and Application* (New York: Wiley, 1983), pp. 3–42.

11. Martin S. Lindauer, "Imagery and the Arts," in ed. Aness Sheikh, *Imagery: Current Theory, Research, and Application* (New York: Wiley, 1983), pp. 468–506.

12. Jennifer Edson Escalas, "Imagine Yourself in the Product," *Journal of Advertising,* Summer 2004, pp. 37–48.

13. Victor Godinez, "Game Review: 'Pac-Man Championship Edition,'" *Dallas Morning News,* June 26, 2007, *www.dallasnews.com.*

14. Amy Martinez, "Online Seattle Jeweler Sparkles, Traditional Jewelers Bristle," *Seattle Times,* December 22, 2007, *www.seattletimes.com.*

15. E. Tulving, "Episodic and Semantic Memory," in eds. E. Tulving and W. Donaldson, *Organization and Memory* (New York: Academic Press, 1972), pp. 381–403.

16. Hans Baumgartner, Mita Sujan, and James R. Bettman, "Autobiographical Memories, Affect, and Consumer Information Processing," *Journal of Consumer Psychology* 1, no. 1, 1992, pp. 53–82.

17. See Kathryn A. Braun-LaTour, Michael S. LaTour, and George M. Zinkham, "Using Childhood Memories to Gain Insight into Brand Meaning," *Journal of Marketing,* April 2007, pp. 45–60.

18. Keith S. Coulter and Robin A. Coulter, "Size Does Matter: The Effects of Magnitude Representation Congruency on Price Perceptions and Purchase Likelihood," *Journal of Consumer Psychology* 15, no. 1, 2005, pp. 64–76.

19. Marc Vanhuele, Gilles Laurent, and Xavier Drèze, "Consumers' Immediate Memory for Prices," *Journal of Consumer Research* 33, no. 2, 2006, pp. 163–172.

20. Morris B. Holbrook, "Nostalgia and Consumer Preferences: Some Emerging Patterns of Consumer Tastes," *Journal of Consumer Research,* September 1993, pp. 245–256; Morris B. Holbrook and Robert M. Schindler, "Echoes of the Dear Departed Past: Some Work in Progress on Nostalgia," in eds. Rebecca H. Holman and Michael R. Solomon, *Advances in Consumer Research,* vol. 18 (Provo, Utah: Association for Consumer Research, 1991), pp. 330–333.

21. Kelly Crow, "Wanted: A Few Good Men (with Scissors)," *Wall Street Journal,* April 6, 2007, p. W1.

22. Annamma Joy and Ruby Roy Dholakia, "Remembrances of Things Past: The Meaning of Home and Possessions of Indian Professionals in Canada," in ed. Floyd W. Rudmin, *To Have Possessions: A Handbook on Ownership and Property, Journal of Social Behavior and Personality* [Special Issue], November 1991, pp. 385–402;

Melanie Wallendorf and Eric J. Arnould, "My Favorite Things: A Cross-Cultural Inquiry into Object Attachment, Possessiveness, and Social Linkage," *Journal of Consumer Research*, March 1988, pp. 531–547.

23. Kathryn A. Braun-LaTour, Michael S. LaTour, Jacqueline E. Pickrell, and Elizabeth F. Loftus, "How and When Advertising Can Influence Memory for Consumer Experience," *Journal of Advertising*, Winter 2004, pp. 7–25.

24. Kathryn A. Braun, "Postexperience Advertising Effects on Consumer Memory," *Journal of Consumer Research*, March 1999, pp. 319–334.

25. R. C. Atkinson and R. M. Shiffrin, "Human Memory: A Proposed System and Its Control Processes," in eds. K. W. Spence and J. T. Spence, *The Psychology of Learning and Motivation: Advances in Theory and Research*, vol. 2 (New York: Academic Press, 1968), pp. 89–195.

26. George A. Miller, "The Magical Number Seven, Plus or Minus Two: Some Limits on Our Capacity for Processing Information," *Psychological Review*, March 1956, pp. 81–97; James N. McGregor, "Short-Term Memory Capacity: Limitations or Optimization?" *Psychological Review*, January 1987, pp. 107–108.

27. Noel Hayden, "The Spacing Effect: Enhancing Memory for Repeated Marketing Stimuli," *Journal of Consumer Psychology* 16, no. 3, 2006, pp. 306–320.

28. F. I. M. Craik and R. S. Lockhart, "Levels of Processing: A Framework for Memory Research," *Verbal Learning and Verbal Behavior*, December 1972, pp. 671–684.

29. Ylan Q Mui, "Equipping a New Wave of Female Athletes: Under Armour's Ads Target Nascent Sector," *Washington Post*, August 6, 2007, p. D1.

30. Dilip Soman, "Effects of Payment Mechanism on Spending Behavior: The Role of Rehearsal and Immediacy of Payments," *Journal of Consumer Research* 27, March 2001, pp. 460–474.

31. Alan G. Sawyer, "The Effects of Repetition: Conclusions and Suggestions About Experimental Laboratory Research," in eds. G. David Hughes and Michael L. Ray, *Buyer/Consumer Information Processing* (Chapel Hill, N.C.: University of North Carolina Press, 1974), pp. 190–219; George E. Belch, "The Effects of Television Commercial Repetition on Cognitive Response and Message Acceptance," *Journal of Consumer Research*, June 1982, pp. 56–66; H. Rao Unnava and Robert E. Burnkrant, "Effects of Repeating Varied Ad Executions on Brand Name Memory," *Journal of Marketing Research*, November 1991, pp. 406–416; Murphy S. Sewall and Dan Sarel, "Characteristics of Radio Commercials and Their Recall Effectiveness," *Journal of Marketing*, January 1986, pp. 52–60.

32. Eileen Gunn, "Product Placement Prize: Repetition Factor Makes Videogames Valuable Medium," *Advertising Age*, February 12, 2001, p. S10.

33. Chris Janiszewski, Hayden Noel, and Alan G. Sawyer, "Re-Inquiries: A Meta-Analysis of the Spacing Effect in Verbal Learning: Implications for Research on Advertising Repetition and Consumer Memory," *Journal of Consumer Research*, June 2003, pp. 138–149 ; see also Sara L. Appleton, Robert A. Bjork, and Thomas D. Wickens, "Examining the Spacing Effect in Advertising: Encoding Variability, Retrieval Processes and Their Interaction," *Journal of Consumer Research* 32, no. 2, 2005, pp. 266–276.

34. Sharmistha Law, "Can Repeating a Brand Claim Lead to Memory Confusion? The Effects of Claim Similarity and Concurrent Repetition," *Journal of Marketing Research*, August 2002, pp. 366–378.

35. Susan E. Heckler and Terry L. Childers, "The Role of Expectancy and Relevancy in Memory for Verbal and Visual Information: What Is Incongruency?" *Journal of Consumer Research*, March 1992, pp. 475–492.

36. Sally Beatty, "Ogilvy's TV-Ad Study Stresses 'Holding Power' Instead of Ratings," *Wall Street Journal*, June 4, 1999, p. B2.

37. Catherine A. Cole and Michael J. Houston, "Encoding and Media Effects on Consumer Learning Deficiencies in the Elderly," *Journal of Marketing Research*, February 1987, pp. 55–64; Deborah Roedder John and John C. Whitney Jr., "The Development of Consumer Knowledge in Children: A Cognitive Structure Approach," *Journal of Consumer Research*, March 1986, pp. 406–418.

38. H. Shanker Krishnan, "A Process Analysis of the Effects of Humorous Advertising Executions on Brand Claims Memory," *Journal of Consumer Psychology*, 2003, pp. 230–245.

39. Gabriel Biehal and Dipankar Chakravarti, "Consumers' Use of Memory and External Information in Choice: Macro and Micro Perspectives," *Journal of Consumer Research*, March 1986, pp. 382–405; John G. Lynch, Howard Marmorstein, and Michael F. Weigold, "Choices from Sets Including Remembered Brands: Use of Recalled Attributes and Prior Overall Evaluations," *Journal of Consumer Research*, September 1988, pp. 225–233; Valerie S. Folkes, "The Availability Heuristic and Perceived Risk," *Journal of Consumer Research*, June 1988, pp. 13–23.

40. A. M. Collins and E. F. Loftus, "A Spreading Activation Theory of Semantic Processing," *Psychological Review*, November 1975, pp. 407–428; Lawrence W. Barsalou, *Cognitive Psychology: An Overview for Cognitive Scientists* (Hillsdale, N.J.: Lawrence Erlbaum, 1991); John R. Anderson, *Cognitive Psychology and Its Implications* (New York: W. H. Freeman, 1990); Michael Pham and Gita Venkataramani Johar, "Contingent Processes of Source Identification," *Journal of Consumer Research*, December 1997, pp. 249–265.

41. Jack Neff, "S. C. Johnson Ads to Stress 'Family Owned,'" *Advertising Age*, November 13, 2001, *www.adage.com*.

42. Joseph W. Alba and J. Wesley Hutchinson, "Dimensions of Consumer Expertise," *Journal of Consumer Research*, March 1987, pp. 411–454.

43. David C. Riccio, Vita C. Rabinowitz, and Shari Axelrod, "Memory: When Less Is More," *American Psychologist*, November 1994, pp. 917–926.

44. Anthony Pratkanis, Anthony G. Greenwald, M. R. Leipe, and M. Hans Baumgartner, "In Search of Reliable Persuasion Effects: III. The Sleeper Effect Is Dead: Long Live the Sleeper Effect," *Journal of Personality and Social Psychology*, February 1988, pp. 203–218.

45. Raymond Burke and Thomas K. Srull, "Competitive Interference and Consumer Memory for Advertisements," *Journal of Consumer Research*, June 1988, pp. 55–68; Kevin Keller, "Memory and Evaluation Effects in Competitive Advertising Environments," *Journal of Consumer Research*, March 1991, pp. 463–476; Rik G. M. Pieters and Tammo H. A. Bijmolt, "Consumer Memory for Television Advertising: A Field Study of Duration, Serial Position and Competition Effects," *Journal of Consumer Research*, March 1997, pp. 362–372; Tom J. Brown and Michael L. Rothschild, "Reassessing the Impact of Television Advertising Clutter," *Journal of Consumer Research*, June 1993, pp. 138–147; Robert J. Kent and Chris T. Allen, "Competitive Interference Effects in Consumer Memory for Advertising: The Role of Brand Familiarity," *Journal of Marketing*, July 1994, pp. 97–105; H. Rao Unnava and Deepak Sirdeshmukh, "Reducing Competitive Ad Interference," *Journal of Marketing Research*, August 1994, pp. 403–411.

46. Anand Kumar and Shanker Krishnan, "Memory Interference in Advertising: A Replication and Extension," *Journal of Consumer Research*, March 2004, pp. 602–61; Anand Kumar, "Interference Effects of Contextual Cues in Advertisements on Memory for Ad Content," *Journal of Consumer Psychology* 9, no. 3, 2000, pp. 155–166.

47. Robert D. Jewell and H. Rao Unnava, "When Competitive Interference Can Be Beneficial," *Journal of Consumer Research*, September 2003, pp. 283–291.

48. David Luna and Laura A. Peracchio, "Moderators of Language Effects in Advertising to Bilinguals: A Psycholinguistic Approach," *Journal of Consumer Research*, September 2001, pp. 28–43.

49. Joseph W. Alba and Amitava Chattopadhyay, "Effects of Context and Part-Category Cues on Recall of Competing Brands," *Journal of Marketing Research*, August 1985, pp. 340–349; Joseph W. Alba and Amitava Chattopadhyay, "Salience Effects in Brand Recall," *Journal of Marketing Research*, November 1986, pp. 363–369; Manoj Hastak and Anusre Mitra, "Facilitating and Inhibiting Effects of Brand Cues on Recall, Consideration Set, and Choice," *Journal of Business Research*, October 1996, pp. 121–126.

50. Burke and Srull, "Competitive Interference and Consumer Memory for Advertising"; Rik Pieters and Tammo H. A. Bijmolt, "Consumer Memory for Television Advertising: A Field Study of Duration, Serial Position, and Competition Effects," *Journal of Consumer Research*, March 1997, pp. 362–372.

51. Elizabeth F. Loftus, "When a Lie Becomes Memory's Truth: Memory and Distortion after Exposure to Misinformation," *Current Directions in Psychological Science*, August 1992, pp. 121–123.

52. Ann E. Schlosser, "Learning Through Virtual Product Experiences: The Role of Imagery on True Versus False Memories," *Journal of Consumer Research* 33, no. 3, 2006, pp. 377–383.

53. Larry Percy and John R. Rossiter, "A Model of Brand Awareness and Brand Attitude in Advertising Strategies," *Psychology and Marketing*, July–August 1992, pp. 263–274.

54. Mui, "Equipping a New Wave of Female Athletes: Under Armour's Ads Target Nascent Sector."

55. John Furniss, "Rating American Banks in Japan: Survey Shows Importance of Image," *International Advertiser*, April 1986, pp. 22–23.

56. Bonnie Tsui, "Bowl Poll: Ads Don't Mean Sales," *Advertising Age*, February 5, 2001, p. 33.

57. Marc Vanhuele and Xavier Drèze, "Measuring the Price Knowledge Shoppers Bring to the Store," *Journal of Marketing*, October 2002, pp. 72–85.

58. H. Shanker Krishnan and Dipankar Chakravarti, "Memory Measures for Pretesting Advertisements: An Integrative Conceptual Framework and a Diagnostic Template," *Journal of Consumer Psychology* 8, no. 1, 1999, pp. 1–37.

59. Angela Y. Lee, "Effects of Implicit Memory on Memory-Based Versus Stimulus-Based Brand Choice," *Journal of Marketing Research*, November 2002, pp. 440–454.

60. Susan T. Fiske and Shelley E. Taylor, *Social Cognition* (New York: McGraw-Hill, 1991).

61. Stewart Shapiro and Mark T. Spence, "Factors Affecting Encoding, Retrieval, and Alignment of Sensory Attributes in a Memory-Based Brand Choice Task," *Journal of Consumer Research*, March 2002, pp. 603–617.

62. Joseph W. Alba, J. Wesley Hutchinson, and John G. Lynch Jr., "Memory and Decision Making," in eds. Thomas S. Robertson and Harold Kassarjian, *Handbook of Consumer Behavior* (Englewood Cliffs, N.J.: Prentice-Hall, 1991), pp. 1–49.

63. Rik G. M. Pieters and Tammo H. A. Bijmolt, "Consumer Memory for Television Advertising: A Field Study of Duration, Serial Position, and Competition Effects," *Journal of Consumer Research*, March 1997, pp. 362–372; David W. Stewart and David H. Furse, *Effective Television Advertising: A Study of 1000 Commercials* (Cambridge, Mass.: Marketing Science Institute, 1986); Pamela Homer, "Ad Size as an Indicator of Perceived Advertising Costs and Effort: The Effects on Memory and Perceptions," *Journal of Advertising*, Winter 1995, pp. 1–12.

64. Frank R. Kardes and Gurumurthy Kalyanaram, "Order of Entry Effects on Consumer Memory and Judgment: An Information Integration Perspective," *Journal of Marketing Research*, August 1992, pp. 343–357; Frank Kardes, Murali Chandrashekaran, and Ronald Dornoff, "Brand Retrieval, Consideration Set Composition, Consumer Choice, and the Pioneering Advantage," *Journal of Consumer Research*, June 1993, pp. 62–75; Frank H. Alpert and Michael A. Kamins, "An Empirical Investigation of Consumer Memory, Attitude, and Perceptions Toward Pioneer and Follower Brands," *Journal of Marketing*, October 1995, pp. 34–44.

65. Claudia Penteado, "Coca-Cola Expects to Grow by 7% in Brazil," *Advertising Age*, May 16, 2001, *www.adage.com*; Hillary Chura and Richard Linnett, "Coca-Cola Readies

Massive Global Campaign," *Advertising Age*, April 2, 2001, *www.adage.com.*

66. Sridar Samu, H. Shankar Krishnan, and Robert E. Smith, "Using Advertising Alliances for New Product Introduction: Interactions Between Product Complementarity and Promotional Strategies," *Journal of Marketing*, January 1999, pp. 57–74.

67. T. Bettina Cornwell, Michael S. Humphreys, Angela M. Maguire, Clinton S. Weeks, and Cassandra L. Tellegen, "Sponsorship-Linked Marketing: The Role of Articulation in Memory," *Journal of Consumer Research* 33, no. 3, 2006, pp. 312–321.

68. Gita Venkatatarmani Johar and Michel Tuan Pham, "Relatedness, Prominence, and Constructive Sponsor Identification," *Journal of Marketing Research* 36, August 1999, pp. 299–312.

69. Rex Briggs and Nigel Hollis, "Advertising on the Web: Is There Response Before Click-Through?" *Journal of Advertising Research*, March–April 1997, pp. 33–45.

70. Michael Pham and Gita Venkataramani Johar, "Contingent Processes of Source Identification," *Journal of Consumer Research*, December 1997, pp. 249–265.

71. Deborah D. Heisley and Sidney J. Levy, "Autodriving: A Photoelicitation Technique," *Journal of Consumer Research*, December 1991, pp. 257–272.

72. Nader T. Tavassoli and Yih Hwai Lee, "The Differential Interaction of Auditory and Visual Advertising Elements with Chinese and English," *Journal of Marketing Research*, November 2003, pp. 468–480.

73. Charles D. Lindsey and H. Shanker Krishnan, "Retrieval Disruption in Collaborative Groups due to Brand Cues," *Journal of Consumer Research* 33, no. 4, 2007, pp. 470–478.

74. William E. Baker, Heather Honea, and Cristel Antonia Russell, "Do Not Wait to Reveal the Brand Name," *Journal of Advertising*, Fall 2004, pp. 77–85.

75. Joan Meyers-Levy, "The Influence of a Brand Name's Association Set Size and Word Frequency on Brand Memory," *Journal of Consumer Research*, September 1989, pp. 197–207; Alba and Hutchinson, "Dimensions of Consumer Expertise."

76. Tina M. Lowrey, L. J. Shrum, and Tony M. Dubitsky, "The Relation Between Brand-Name Linguistic Characteristics and Brand-Name Memory," *Journal of Advertising*, Fall 2003, pp. 7–17.

77. Jaideep Sengupta and Gerald J. Gorn, "Absence Makes the Mind Grow Sharper: Effects of Element Omission on Subsequent Recall," *Journal of Marketing Research*, May 2002, pp. 186–201.

78. Terry L. Childers and Jeffrey Jass, "All Dressed Up with Something to Say: Effects of Typeface Semantic Associations on Brand Perceptions and Consumer Memory," *Journal of Consumer Psychology*, 2002, pp. 93–106.

79. Cathy J. Cobb and Wayne D. Hoyer, "The Influence of Advertising at the Moment of Brand Choice," *Journal of Advertising*, December 1986, pp. 5–27.

80. Keller, "Memory Factors in Advertising," *Journal of Consumer Research*, December 1987, pp. 316–333; J. Wesley Hutchinson and Daniel L. Moore, "Issues Surrounding the Examination of Delay Effects of Advertising," in ed. Thomas C. Kinnear, *Advances in Consumer Research*, vol. 11 (Provo, Utah: Association for Consumer Research, 1984), pp. 650–655.

81. Carolyn Costley, Samar Das, and Merrie Brucks, "Presentation Medium and Spontaneous Imaging Effects on Consumer Memory," *Journal of Consumer Psychology* 6, no. 3, 1997, pp. 211–231; David W. Sewart and Girish N. Punj, "Effects of Using a Nonverbal (Musical) Cue on Recall and Playback of Television Advertising: Implications for Advertising Tracking," *Journal of Business Research*, May 1998, pp. 39–51.

82. Cole and Houston, "Encoding and Media Effects on Consumer Learning Deficiencies in the Elderly"; Sharmistha Law, Scott A. Hawkins, and Fergus I. M. Craik, "Repetition-Induced Belief in the Elderly: Rehabilitating Age-Related Memory Deficits," *Journal of Consumer Research*, September 1998, pp. 91–107.

83. H. Rao Unnava and Robert E. Burnkrant, "An Imagery-Processing View of the Role of Pictures in Print Advertisements," *Journal of Marketing Research*, May 1991, pp. 226–231.

84. Sara L. Appleton-Knapp, Robert A. Bjork, and Thomas D. Wickens, "Examining the Spacing Effect in Advertising: Encoding Variability, Retrieval Processes, and Their Interaction," *Journal of Consumer Research* 32, no. 2, 2005, pp. 266–276.

85. Alice M. Isen, "Some Ways in Which Affect Influences Cognitive Processes: Implications for Advertising and Consumer Behavior," in eds. Alice M. Tybout and P. Cafferata, *Advertising and Consumer Psychology* (Lexington, Mass.: Lexington Books, 1989), pp. 91–117; see also Patricia A. Knowles, Stephen J. Grove, and W. Jeffrey Burroughs, "An Experimental Examination of Mood Effects on Retrieval and Evaluation of Advertisement and Brand Information," *Journal of the Academy of Marketing Science*, Spring 1993, pp. 135–143; Gordon H. Bower, "Mood and Memory," *American Psychologist*, February 1981, pp. 129–148; Gordon H. Bower, Stephen Gilligan, and Kenneth Montiero, "Selectivity of Learning Caused by Affective States," *Journal of Experimental Psychology: General*, December 1981, pp. 451–473; Alice M. Isen, Thomas Shalker, Margaret Clark, and Lynn Karp, "Affect, Accessibility of Material in Memory, and Behavior: A Cognitive Loop?" *Journal of Personality and Social Psychology*, 1978, pp. 1–12.

86. Alice M. Isen, "Toward Understanding the Role of Affect in Cognition," in eds. Robert S. Wyer and Thomas K. Srull, *Handbook of Social Cognition* (Hillsdale, N J.: Lawrence Erlbaum, 1984), pp. 179–236.

87. Alice M. Isen, "Some Ways in Which Affect Influences Cognitive Processes: Implications for Advertising and Consumer Behavior," in eds. Patricia Cafferata and Alice M. Tybout, *Cognitive and Affective Responses to Advertising* (Lexington, Mass.: Lexington Books, 1989), pp. 91–118.

88. Angela Y. Lee and Brian Sternthal, "The Effects of Positive Mood on Memory," *Journal of Consumer Research* 26, September 1999, pp. 115–127.

89. Alba and Hutchinson, "Dimensions of Consumer Expertise."

90. Dan Moren, "Apple's Ad Game," *MacWorld*, February 2008, pp. 32+; Mike Elgan, "Elgan: A New iPhone This Summer?" *ComputerWorld*, January 25, 2008, *www.computerworld.com*; Saul Hensell, "Can the Touch Revive Apple's iPod Sales?" *New York Times*, January 22, 2008, *www.nytimes.com*; Troy Wolverton, "Meet Apple's New Star, the Mac Computer," *San Jose Mercury News*, October 26, 2007, *www.mercurynews.com*; Anastasia Goodstein, "Teen Marketing: Apple's the Master," *BusinessWeek Online*, August 17, 2007, *www.businessweek.com*.

Chapter 8

1. Cliff Edwards, "A One-Stop Guide to Gadgets," *BusinessWeek*, December 10, 2007, p. 76; Joe Sharkey, "An Inspector Calls, and Hotels Listen," *New York Times*, September 9, 2007, p. BU2; Jessica Mintz, "Stores Lean More on Shopper Reviews," *International Business Times*, December 6, 2006, *www.ibtimes.com*.

2. Micheline Maynard, "Wrapping a Familiar Name Around a New Product," *New York Times*, May 22, 2004, p. C1.

3. Betsy Lowther, "Vietnam's Changing Retail Landscape," *WWD*, April 25, 2007, p. 10.

4. Michael Barbaro, "Never Mind What's in Them, Bags Are the Fashion," *New York Times*, December 16, 2007, *www.nytimes.com*.

5. "Pret a Manger: Bread Winners," *Marketing Week*, August 2, 2007, p. 24.

6. Joseph W. Alba, J. Wesley Hutchinson, and John G. Lynch, "Memory and Decision Making," in eds. Thomas C. Roberton and Harold H. Kassarjian, *Handbook of Consumer Behavior* (Englewood Cliffs, N.J.: Prentice-Hall, 1991).

7. John R. Hauser and Birger Wernerfelt, "An Evaluation Cost Model of Consideration Sets," *Journal of Consumer Research*, March 1990, pp. 393–408.

8. Emily Bryson York, "Nestle, Pepsi and Coke Face Their Waterloo," *Advertising Age*, October 8, 2007, p. 1.

9. Heather Timmons, "For India's Airlines, Passengers Are Plentiful but Profits Are Scarce," *New York Times*, May 8, 2007, p. C8; Susan Carey, "Even When It's Quicker to Travel by Train, Many Fly," *Wall Street Journal*, August 29, 1997, pp. B1, B5.

10. Emma Reynolds, "Nestlé Moves Away from Indulgence Angle for Aero Ad," *Marketing*, June 21, 2001, p. 22.

11. Kalpesh Kaushik Desai and Wayne D. Hoyer, "Descriptive Characteristics of Memory-Based Consideration Sets: Influence of Usage Occasion Frequency and Usage Location Familiarity," *Journal of Consumer Research* 27, December 2000, pp. 309–323.

12. Prakash Nedungadi and J. Wesley Hutchinson, "The Prototypicality of Brands: Relationships with Brand Awareness, Preference, and Usage," in eds. Elizabeth C. Hirschman and Morris B. Holbrook, *Advances in Consumer Research*, vol. 12 (Provo, Utah: Association for Consumer Research, 1985), pp. 498–503; Prakash Nedungadi, "Recall and Consumer Consideration Sets: Influencing Choice Without Altering Brand Evaluations," *Journal of Consumer Research*, December 1990, pp. 263–276.

13. Alba, Hutchinson, and Lynch, "Memory and Decision Making."

14. Nedungadi and Hutchinson, "The Prototypicality of Brands"; James Ward and Barbara Loken, "The Quintessential Snack Food: Measurement of Product Prototypes," in ed. Richard J. Lutz, *Advances in Consumer Research*, vol. 13 (Provo, Utah: Association for Consumer Research, 1986), pp. 126–131.

15. "Armor All Wants to Clean Some Son of a Gun's Clock," *Brandweek*, October 18, 1993, pp. 32–33.

16. Siew Meng Leong, Swee Hoon Ang, and Lai Leng Tham, "Increasing Brand Name Recall in Print Advertising Among Asian Consumers," *Journal of Advertising*, Summer 1996, pp. 65–82.

17. Stewart Shapiro, Deborah J. MacInnis, and Susan E. Heckler, "The Effects of Incidental Ad Exposure on the Formation of Consideration Sets," *Journal of Consumer Research*, June 1997, pp. 94–104.

18. Alba, Hutchinson, and Lynch, "Memory and Decision Making."

19. S. Ratneshwar and Allan D. Shocker, "Substitution in Use and the Role of Usage Context in Product Category Structures," *Journal of Marketing Research*, August 1991, pp. 281–295.

20. Jason DeParle, "A Western Union Empire Moves Migrant Cash Home," *New York Times*, November 22, 2007, pp. A1, A20.

21. Nedungadi and Hutchinson, "The Prototypicality of Brands"; Ward and Loken, "The Quintessential Snack Food."

22. Bernd Schmitt, "To Build Truly Global Brands, You've Got to Break the Rules," *Advertising Age*, February 11, 2008, *www.adage.com*.

23. Louise Story, "Product Packages Now Shout to Grab Your Fickle Attention," *New York Times*, August 10, 2007, pp. A1, A16; Arlene Weintraub, "J&J's New Baby," *BusinessWeek*, June 18, 2007, pp. 48+.

24. Gabriel Biehal and Dipankar Chakravarti, "Consumers' Use of Memory and External Information in Choice: Macro and Micro Perspectives," *Journal of Consumer Research*, March 1986, pp. 382–405.

25. Gabriel Biehal and Dipankar Chakravarti, "Information Accessibility as a Moderator of Consumer Choice," *Journal of Consumer Research*, June 1983, pp. 1–14.

26. Michaela Waenke, Gerd Bohner, and Andreas Jurkowitsch, "There Are Many Reasons to Drive a BMW: Does Imagined Ease of Argument Generation Influence Attitudes?" *Journal of Consumer Research*, September 1997, pp. 170–177.

27. Shai Danziger, Simone Moran, and Vered Rafaely, "The Influence of Ease of Retreival on Judgment as a Function of Attention to Subjective Experience," *Journal of Consumer Psychology* 16, no. 2, 2006, pp. 191–195.

28. Meryl Paula Gardner, "Advertising Effects on Attributes Recalled and Criteria Used for Brand Evaluations," *Journal of Consumer Research*, December 1983, pp. 310–318; Scott B. MacKenzie, "The Role of Attention in Mediating the Effect of Advertising on Attribute Importance," *Journal of Consumer Research*, September 1986, pp. 174–195; Priya Raghubir and Geeta Menon, "AIDS and Me, Never the Twain Shall Meet: The Effects of Information Accessibility on Judgments of Risk and Advertising Effectiveness," *Journal of Consumer Research*, June 1998, pp. 52–63.

29. Fellman and Lynch, "Self-Generated Validity and Other Effects of Measurement"; John G. Lynch, Howard Marmorstein, and Michael F. Weigold, "Choices from Sets Including Remembered Brands: Use of Recalled Attributes and Prior Overall Evaluations," *Journal of Consumer Research*, September 1988, pp. 169–184.

30. Carolyn L. Costley and Merrie Brucks, "Selective Recall and Information Use in Consumer Preferences," *Journal of Consumer Research*, March 1992, pp. 464–474; Geeta Menon, Priya Raghubit, and Norbert Schwarz, "Behavioral Frequency Judgments: An Accessibility–Diagnosticity Framework," *Journal of Consumer Research*, September 1995, pp. 212–228.

31. Paul M. Herr, Frank R. Kardes, and John Kim, "Effects of Word-of-Mouth and Product-Attribute Information on Persuasion: An Accessibility–Diagnosticity Perspective," *Journal of Consumer Research*, March 1991, pp. 454–462.

32. Bernard Simon, "Prius Overtakes Explorer in the US," *Financial Times*, January 11, 2008, p. 13.

33. Walter Kintsch and Tuen A. Van Dyk, "Toward a Model of Text Comprehension and Production," *Psychological Review*, September 1978, pp. 363–394; S. Ratneshwar, David G. Mick, and Gail Reitinger, "Selective Attention in Consumer Information Processing: The Role of Chronically Accessible Attributes," in eds. Marvin E. Goldberg, Gerald Gorn, and Richard W. Pollay, *Advances in Consumer Research*, vol. 17 (Provo, Utah: Association for Consumer Research, 1990), pp. 547–553.

34. Jacob Jacoby, Tracy Troutman, Alfred Kuss, and David Mazursky, "Experience and Expertise in Complex Decision Making," in ed. Richard J. Lutz, *Advances in Consumer Research*, vol. 13 (Provo, Utah: Association for Consumer Research, 1986), pp. 469–475.

35. Stewart Shapiro and Mark T. Spence, "Factors Affecting Encoding, Retrieval, and Alignment of Sensory Attributes in a Memory-Based Brand Choice Task," *Journal of Consumer Research*, March 2002, pp. 603–617.

36. Gardner, "Advertising Effects on Attributes Recalled"; Mackenzie, "The Role of Attention in Mediating the Effect of Advertising."

37. Vanessa O'Connell, "Labels Suggesting the Benefits of Drinking Wine Look Likely," *Wall Street Journal*, October 26, 1998, pp. B1, B3.

38. Mark I. Alpert, "Identification of Determinant Attributes: A Comparison of Methods," *Journal of Marketing Research*, May 1971, pp. 184–191.

39. Brendan I. Koerner, "The Mercedes of Trash Bags," *New York Times*, January 23, 2005, *www.nytimes.com.*

40. Jolita Kiselius and Brian Sternthal, "Examining the Vividness Controversy: An Availability–Valence Interpretation," *Journal of Consumer Research*, March 1986, pp. 418–431; Herr, Kardes, and Kim, "Effects of Word-of-Mouth and Product-Attribute Information."

41. Punam Anand Keller and Lauren G. Block, "Vividness Effects: A Resource-Matching Perspective," *Journal of Consumer Research*, December 1997, pp. 295–304.

42. Christian Caryl, "Visitors Wanted Now," *Newsweek*, October 15, 2007, p. 14.

43. Reid Hastie and Bernadette Park, "The Relationship Between Memory and Judgment Depends on Whether the Judgment Task Is Memory-Based or On-Line," *Psychological Review*, June 1986, pp. 258–268; Barbara Loken and Ronald Hoverstad, "Relationships Between Information Recall and Subsequent Attitudes: Some Exploratory Findings," *Journal of Consumer Research*, September 1985, pp. 155–168.

44. Biehal and Chakravarti, "Consumers' Use of Memory and External Information in Choice"; Jong-Won Park and Manoj Hastak, "Memory-Based Product Judgments: Effects of Involvement at Encoding and Retrieval," *Journal of Consumer Research*, December 1994, pp. 534–547.

45. Zeynep Gürhan-Canli, "The Effect of Expected Variability of Product Quality and Attribute Uniqueness on Family Brand Evaluations," *Journal of Consumer Research*, June 2003, pp. 105–114.

46. Hans Baumgartner, Mita Sujan, and James R. Bettman, "Autobiographical Memories, Affect, and Consumer Information Processing," *Journal of Consumer Psychology* 1, no. 1, 1992, pp. 53–82.

47. Rodney Ho, "Bowling for Dollars, Alleys Try Updating," *Wall Street Journal*, January 24, 1997, pp. B1, B2.

48. Elizabeth Cowley and Eunika Janus, "Not Necessarily Better, But Certainly Different: A Limit to the Advertising Misinformation Effect on Memory," *Journal of Consumer Research*, June 2004, pp. 229–235.

49. Fara Warner, "The Place to Be This Year," *Brandweek*, November 30, 1992, p. 24.

50. Michael J. Houston, Terry L. Childers, and Susan E. Heckler, "Picture–Word Consistency and the Elaborative Processing of Advertisements," *Journal of Marketing Research*, November 1987, pp. 359–369.

51. Joseph W. Alba and Amitava Chattopadhyay, "Salience Effects in Brand Recall," *Journal of Marketing Research*, November 1986, pp. 363–369; Kiselius and Sternthal, "Examining the Vividness Controversy."

52. Alba and Chattopadhyay, "Salience Effects in Brand Recall"; Kiselius and Sternthal, "Examining the Vividness Controversy."

53. Gordon H. Bower, "Mood and Memory," *American Psychologist,* February 1981, pp. 129–148; Gordon H. Bower, Stephen Gilligan, and Kenneth Montiero, "Selectivity of Learning Caused by Affective States," *Journal of Experimental Psychology: General,* December 1981, pp. 451–473; Alice M. Isen, Thomas Shalker, Margaret Clark, and Lynn Karp, "Affect, Accessibility of Material in Memory, and Behavior: A Cognitive Loop?" *Journal of Personality and Social Psychology,* January 1978, pp. 1–12.

54. Matthew Creamer, "Microsoft Plans Blitz to Fend Off Apple," *Advertising Age,* December 3, 2007, *www.adage.com.*

55. "Game Farmers Brand Deer Meat So It's Less Gamey," *Brandweek,* January 11, 1993, p. 7.

56. Robert L. Simison and Joseph B. White, "Reputation for Poor Quality Still Plagues Detroit," *Wall Street Journal,* May 4, 2000, pp. B1, B4.

57. Peter H. Bloch, Daniel L. Sherrell, and Nancy M. Ridgway, "Consumer Search: An Extended Framework," *Journal of Consumer Research,* June 1986, pp. 119–126.

58. Sharon E. Beatty and Scott M. Smith, "External Search Effort: An Investigation Across Several Product Categories," *Journal of Consumer Research,* June 1987, pp. 83–95.

59. Charles M. Brooks, Patrick J. Kaufmann, and Donald P. Lichtenstein, "Travel Configuration on Consumer Trip-Chained Store Choice," *Journal of Consumer Research* 31, no. 2, 2004, pp. 241–248.

60. Beatty and Smith, "External Search Effort."

61. See Judi Strebel, Tulim Erdem, and Joffre Swait, "Consumer Search in High Technology Markets: Exploring the Use of Traditional Information Channels," *Journal of Consumer Psychology* 14, no. 1–2, 2004, pp. 96–104.

62. Lorraine Mirabella, "As Shoppers Change Ways, Retailers Lag," *Baltimore Sun,* January 21, 2001, p. 1D.

63. David F. Midgley, "Patterns of Interpersonal Information Seeking for the Purchase of a Symbolic Product," *Journal of Marketing Research,* February 1983, pp. 74–83.

64. Michael Arndt, "Burrito Buzz—And So Few Ads," *BusinessWeek,* March 12, 2007, pp. 84–85.

65. Denver D'Rozario and Susan P. Douglas, "Effect of Assimilation on Prepurchase External Information-Search Tendencies," *Journal of Consumer Psychology* 8, no. 2, 1999, pp. 187–209.

66. Niranjan J. Raman, "A Qualitative Investigation of Web-Browsing Behavior," in eds. Merrie Brucks and Deborah J. MacInnis, *Advances in Consumer Research,* vol. 24 (Provo, Utah: Association for Consumer Research, 1997), pp. 511–516.

67. Peter J. Danaher, Guy W. Mullarkey, and Skander Essegaier, "Factors Affecting Web Site Visit Duration: A Cross-Domain Analysis," *Journal of Marketing Research,* May 2006, pp. 182–194.

68. Sally J. McMillan and Jang-Sun Hwang, "Measures of Perceived Interactivity: An Exploration of the Role of Direction of Communication, User Control, and Time in Shaping Perceptions of Interactivity," *Journal of Advertising,* Fall 2002, pp. 29–42; Yuping Liu and L. J. Shrum, "What Is Interactivity and Is It Always Such a Good Thing? Implications of Definition, Person, and Situation for the Influence of Interactivity on Advertising Effectiveness," *Journal of Advertising,* Winter 2002, pp. 53–64.

69. Gerald J. Gorn, Amitava Chattopadhyay, Jaideep Sengupta, and Shashank Tripathi, "Waiting for the Web: How Screen Color Affects Time Perception," *Journal of Marketing Research,* May 2004, pp. 215–225.

70. Charla Mathwick and Edward Rigdon, "Play, Flow, and the Online Search Experience," *Journal of Consumer Research,* September 2004, pp. 324–332.

71. Martin Holzwarth, Chris Janiszewski, and Marcus M. Neumann, "The Influence of Avatars on Online Consumer Shopping Behavior," *Journal of Marketing,* June 2006, pp. 19–36.

72. Puneet Manchanda, Jean-Pierre Dubé, Khim Yong Goh, and Pradeep K. Chintagunta, "The Effect of Banner Advertising on Internet Purchasing," *Journal of Marketing Research,* February 2006, pp. 98–108.

73. Andrew D. Gershoff, Susan M. Broniarczyk, and Patricia M. West, "Recommendation or Evaluation? Task Sensitivity in Information Source Selection," *Journal of Consumer Research,* December 2001, pp. 418–438.

74. Alan D. J. Cooke, Harish Sujan, Mita Sujan, and Barton A. Weitz, "Marketing the Unfamiliar: The Role of Context and Item-Specific Information in Electronic Agent Recommendations," *Journal of Marketing Research,* November 2002, pp. 499+.

75. Dan Ariely, John G. Lynch Jr., and Manuel Aparicio IV, "Learning by Collaborative and Individual-Based Recommendation Agents," *Journal of Consumer Psychology* 14, no. 1–2, 2004, pp. 81–95.

76. Caterina Sismeiro and Randolph E. Bucklin, "Modeling Purchase Behavior at an E-Commerce Web Site: A Task-Completion Approach," *Journal of Marketing Research,* August 2004, pp. 306–323.

77. Nicholas H. Lurie, "Decision Making in Information-Rich Environments: The Role of Information Structure," *Journal of Consumer Research,* March 2004, pp. 473–486.

78. Ross Kerber, "Direct Hit Uses Popularity to Narrow Internet Searches," *Wall Street Journal,* July 2, 1998, p. B4.

79. Kristen Diel, "When Two Rights Make a Wrong: Searching Too Much in Ordered Environments," *Journal of Marketing Research,* August 2005, pp. 313–322; Kristen Diel and Gal Zauberman, "Searching Ordered Sets: Evaluations from Sequences Under Search," *Journal of Consumer Research* 31, no. 4, 2005, pp. 824–832.

80. Michelle Slatalla, "Price-Comparison Sites Do the Legwork," *New York Times,* February 3, 2005, p. G3.

81. Robyn Weisman, "Technologies That Changed 2001," *Newsfactor.com*, January 3, 2002, *www.newsfactor.com/perl/story/?id=15569;* Sally Beatty, "IBM HotMedia Aims to Speed Online Ads," *Wall Street Journal*, October 27, 1998, p. B8.

82. Hairong Li, Terry Daugherty, and Frank Biocca, "Impact of 3-D Advertising on Product Knowledge, Brand Attitude, and Purchase Intention: The Mediating Role of Presence," *Journal of Advertising*, Fall 2002, pp. 43–57.

83. Rebecca Fairley Raney, "Forget Gimmicks: Buyers Want Numbers," *New York Times*, February 11, 2007, sec. 11, p. 1; June Fletcher, "The Home Front: Blind Date with a Bungalow," *Wall Street Journal*, May 7, 2004, p. W14.

84. Eileen Fischer, Julia Bristor, and Brenda Gainer, "Creating or Escaping Community? An Exploratory Study of Internet Consumers' Behaviors," in eds. Kim P. Corfman and John G. Lynch, *Advances in Consumer Research*, vol. 23 (Provo, Utah: Association for Consumer Research, 1996), pp. 178–182; John Buskin, "Tales from the Front," *Wall Street Journal*, December 7, 1998, p. R6.

85. Neil A. Granitz and James C. Ward, "Virtual Community: A Sociocognitive Analysis," in eds. Kim P. Corfman and John G. Lynch, *Advances in Consumer Research*, vol. 23 (Provo, Utah: Association for Consumer Research, 1996), pp. 161–166.

86. Brady, "Cult Brands."

87. Holly Vanscoy, "Life after Living.com," *Smart Business*, February 2001, pp. 68–10; Clare Saliba, "With Webvan Gone, Where Will Online Shoppers Turn?" *E-Commerce Times*, July 10, 2001, *www.ecommercetimes.com/perl/story/11884.html.*

88. John C. Ryan, "Dipping into Books Online," *Christian Science Monitor*, November 13, 2003, p. 12.

89. Fletcher, "The Home Front: Blind Date with a Bungalow."

90. Stacy L. Wood, "Remote Purchase Environments: The Influence of Return Policy Leniency on Two-Stage Decision Process," *Journal of Marketing Research* 38, May 2001, pp. 157–169.

91. Marcelo Prince, "Online Retailers Try to Streamline Checkout Process," *Wall Street Journal*, November 11, 2004, p. D2.

92. Jayne O'Donnell, "Online Shopping: A Blessing and a Curse?" *USA Today*, December 2, 2007, *www.usatoday.com.*

93. Michael Totty, "So Much Information . . .," *Wall Street Journal*, December 9, 2002, p. R4; Subodh Bhat, Michael Bevans, and Sanjit Sengupta, "Measuring Users' Web Activity to Evaluate and Enhance Advertising Effectiveness," *Journal of Advertising*, Fall 2002, pp. 97–106.

94. Bruce Einhorn and Chi-Chu Tschang, "China's E-Tail Awakening," *BusinessWeek*, November 19, 2007, p. 44.

95. Jacob Jacoby, Robert W. Chestnut, Karl Weigl, and William A. Fisher, "Prepurchase Information Acquisition: Description of a Process Methodology, Research Paradigm, and Pilot Investigation," in ed. Beverlee B. Anderson, *Advances in Consumer Research*, vol. 3 (Cincinnati: Association for Consumer Research, 1976), pp. 306–314; Jacob Jacoby, Robert W. Chestnut, and William Silberman, "Consumer Use and Comprehension of Nutrition Information," *Journal of Consumer Research*, September 1977, pp. 119–128.

96. John O. Claxton, Joseph N. Fry, and Bernard Portis, "A Taxonomy of Prepurchase Information Gathering Patterns," *Journal of Consumer Research*, December 1974, pp. 35–42.

97. Bloch, Sherrell, and Ridgway, "Consumer Search."

98. R. A. Bauer, "Consumer Behavior as Risk Taking," in ed. Robert S. Hancock, *Dynamic Marketing for a Changing World* (Chicago: American Marketing Association, 1960), pp. 389–398; Rohit Deshpande and Wayne D. Hoyer, "Consumer Decision Making: Strategies, Cognitive Effort, and Perceived Risk," in *1983 Educators' Conference Proceedings* (Chicago: American Marketing Association, 1983), pp. 88–91.

99. Keith B. Murray, "A Test of Services Marketing Theory: Consumer Information Acquisition Activities," *Journal of Marketing*, January 1991, pp. 10–25; Joel E. Urbany, Peter R. Dickson, and William L. Wilkie, "Buyer Uncertainty and Information Search," *Journal of Consumer Research*, September 1989, pp. 208–215.

100. David J. Furse, Girish N. Punj, and David W. Stewart, "A Typology of Individual Search Strategies Among Purchasers of New Automobiles," *Journal of Consumer Research*, March 1984, pp. 417–431; Narasimhan Srinivasan and Brian T. Ratchford, "An Empirical Test of a Model of External Search for Automobiles," *Journal of Consumer Research*, September 1991, pp. 233–242; Jacob Jacoby, James J. Jaccard, Imran Currim, Alfred Kuss, Asim Ansari, and Tracy Troutman, "Tracing the Impact of Item-by-Item Information Accessing on Uncertainty Reduction," *Journal of Consumer Research*, September 1994, pp. 291–303.

101. Calmetta Y. Coleman, "Selling Jewelry, Dolls, and TVs Next to Corn Flakes," *Wall Street Journal*, November 19, 1997, pp. B1, B8.

102. Diehl and Zauberman, "Searching Ordered Sets."

103. Gal Zauberman, "The Intertemporal Dynamics of Consumer Lock-In," *Journal of Consumer Research*, December 2003, pp. 405–419.

104. Sridhar Moorthy, Brian T. Ratchford, and Debabrata Talukdar, "Consumer Information Search Revisited: Theory and Empirical Analysis," *Journal of Consumer Research*, March 1997, pp. 263–277.

105. Calvin P. Duncan and Richard W. Olshavsky, "External Search: The Role of Consumer Beliefs," *Journal of Marketing Research*, February 1982, pp. 32–43; Girish N. Punj and Richard Staelin, "A Model of Information Search Behavior for New Automobiles," *Journal of Consumer Research*, September 1983, pp. 181–196.

106. Duncan and Olshavsky, "External Search."

107. Kathy Hammond, Gil McWilliam, and Andrea Narholz Diaz, "Fun and Work on the Web: Differences in Attitudes Between Novices and Experienced Users," in eds. Joseph W. Alba and J. Wesley Hutchinson, *Advances in Consumer Research*, vol. 25 (Provo, Utah: Association for Consumer Research, 1998), pp. 372–378.

108. Joan E. Rigdon, "Advertisers Give Surfers Games to Play," *Wall Street Journal*, October 28, 1996, pp. B1, B6.

109. Laura A. Peracchio and Alice M. Tybout, "The Moderating Role of Prior Knowledge in Schema-Based Product Evaluation," *Journal of Consumer Research*, December 1996, pp. 177–192.

110. Joan Meyers-Levy and Alice Tybout, "Schema-Congruity as Basis for Product Evaluation," *Journal of Consumer Research*, June 1989, pp. 39–54.

111. Jonathan Welsh, "Vacuums Make Sweeping Health Claims," *Wall Street Journal*, September 9, 1996, pp. B1, B2.

112. Julie L. Ozanne, Merrie Brucks, and Dhruv Grewal, "A Study of Information Search Behavior During Categorization of New Products," *Journal of Consumer Research*, March 1992, pp. 452–463.

113. Punj and Staelin, "A Model of Consumer Information Search Behavior for New Automobiles"; Kiel and Layton, "Dimensions of Consumer Information Seeking."

114. Christine Moorman, Kristin Diehl, David Brinberg, and Blair Kidwell, "Subjective Knowledge, Search Locations, and Consumer Choice," *Journal of Consumer Research*, December 2004, pp. 673–680.

115. Merrie Brucks, "The Effects of Product Class Knowledge on Information Search Behavior," *Journal of Consumer Research*, June 1985, pp. 1–16; James R. Bettman and C. Whan Park, "Effects of Prior Knowledge and Experience and Phase of the Choice Process on Consumer Decision Processes: A Protocol Analysis," *Journal of Consumer Research*, December 1980, pp. 234–248; Eric J. Johnson and J. Edward Russo, "Product Familiarity and Learning New Information," *Journal of Consumer Research*, June 1984, pp. 542–550; P. S. Raju, Subhas C. Lonial, and W. Glyn Mangold, "Differential Effects of Subjective Knowledge, Objective Knowledge, and Usage Experience on Decision Making; An Exploratory Investigation," *Journal of Consumer Psychology* 4, no. 2, 1995, pp. 153–180; Joseph W. Alba and J. Wesley Hutchinson, "Dimensions of Consumer Expertise," *Journal of Consumer Research*, March 1987, pp. 411–454.

116. Noel Capon and Roger Davis, "Basic Cognitive Ability Measures as Predictors of Consumer Information Processing Strategies," *Journal of Consumer Research*, June 1984, pp. 551–563.

117. For a summary of a number of studies, see Joseph W. Newman, "Consumer External Search: Amount and Determinants," in eds. Arch Woodside, Jagdish Sheth, and Peter Bennett, *Consumer and Industrial Buying Behavior* (New York: North-Holland, 1977), pp. 79–94; Charles M. Schaninger and Donald Sciglimpaglia, "The Influences of Cognitive Personality Traits and Demographics on Consumer Information Acquisition," *Journal of Consumer Research*, September 1981, pp. 208–216.

118. Scott Painton and James W. Gentry, "Another Look at the Impact of Information Presentation Format," *Journal of Consumer Research*, September 1985, pp. 240–244.

119. J. Edward Russo, Richard Staelin, Catherine A. Nolan, Gary J. Russell, and Barbara L. Metcalf, "Nutrition Information in the Supermarket," *Journal of Consumer Research*, June 1986, pp. 48–70.

120. Christine Moorman, "The Effects of Stimulus and Consumer Utilization of Nutrition Information," *Journal of Consumer Research*, December 1990, pp. 362–374.

121. Chris Janiszewski, "The Influence of Display Characteristics on Visual Exploratory Search Behavior," *Journal of Consumer Research*, December 1998, pp. 290–301.

122. William L. Moore and Donald L. Lehman, "Validity of Information Display Boards: An Assessment Using Longitudinal Data," *Journal of Marketing Research*, November 1980, pp. 296–307; C. Whan Park, Easwar S. Iyer, and Daniel C. Smith, "The Effects of Situational Factors on In-Store Grocery Shopping Behavior: The Role of Store Environment and Time Available for Shopping," *Journal of Consumer Research*, March 1989, pp. 422–433.

123. John R. Hauser, Glen L. Urban, and Bruce D. Weinberg, "How Consumers Allocate Their Time When Searching for Information," *Journal of Marketing Research*, November 1993, pp. 452–466.

124. Randolph E. Bucklin and Catarina Sismeiro, "A Model of Web Site Browsing Behavior Estimated on Click-stream Data," *Journal of Marketing Research*, August 2003, pp. 249–267.

125. Alhassan G. Abdul-Muhmin, "Contingent Decision Behavior: Effect of Number of Alternatives to Be Selected on Consumers' Decision Processes," *Journal of Consumer Psychology* 8, no. 1, 1999, pp. 91–111.

126. Laura Lorber, "Raising Your Profile: Beyond the Basics," *Wall Street Journal*, August 27, 2007, p. B4.

127. Naomi Mandel and Eric J. Johnson, "When Web Pages Influence Choice: Effects of Visual Primes on Experts and Novices," *Journal of Consumer Research*, September 2002, pp. 235–245.

128. Furse, Punj, and Stewart, "A Typology of Individual Search Strategies Among Purchasers of New Automobiles."

129. Brian T. Ratchford, Myung-Soo Lee, and Debabrata Talukdar, "The Impact of the Internet on Information Search for Automobiles," *Journal of Marketing Research*, May 2003, pp. 193–209.

130. Judi Strebel, Tülin Erdem, and Joffre Swait, "Consumer Search in High Technology Markets: Exploring the Use of Traditional Information Channels," *Journal of Consumer Psychology*, 2004, pp. 96–104.

131. Nanette Byrnes, "More Clicks at the Bricks," *BusinessWeek*, December 17, 2007, pp. 50–52.

132. "Office Depot," *Chain Store Age*, November 2007, p. 72.

133. Troy Wolverton and Greg Sandoval, "Net Shoppers Wooed by In-Store Deals," *CNET News.com*, December 12, 2001, *http://news.cnet.com/news/0–1007–200–8156745.html*.

134. Jacob Jacoby, Robert W. Chestnut, and William A. Fisher, "A Behavioral Process Approach to Information Acquisition in Nondurable Purchasing," *Journal of Marketing Research*, November 1978, pp. 532–544.

135. Kent B. Monroe, "The Influence of Price Differences and Brand Familiarity on Brand Preferences," *Journal of Consumer Research*, June 1976, pp. 42–49.

136. Kristin Diehl, Laura J. Kornish, and John G. Lynch Jr., "Smart Agents: When Lower Search Costs for Quality Information Increase Price Sensitivity," *Journal of Consumer Research*, June 2003, pp. 56–71.

137. Dhruv Grewal and Howard Marmorstein, "Market Price Variation, Perceived Price Variation, and Consumers' Price Search Decision for Durable Goods," *Journal of Consumer Research*, December 1994, pp. 453–460.

138. "Japan's Fast Retailing Rebuilds Units by Tapping Uniqlo Strength," *AsiaPulse News*, December 27, 2007, n.p.

139. Cynthia Huffman, "Goal Change, Information Acquisition, and Transfer," *Journal of Consumer Psychology* 5, no. 1, 1996, pp. 1–26.

140. Deborah Roedder John, Carol A. Scott, and James R. Bettman, "Sampling Data for Covariation Assessment," *Journal of Consumer Research*, March 1986, pp. 406–417.

141. J. Edward Russo and France Leclerc, "An Eye-Fixation Analysis of Choice for Consumer Nondurables," *Journal of Consumer Research*, September 1994, pp. 274–290.

142. Jacoby et al., "Prepurchase Information Acquisition."

143. J. Edward Russo, Margaret G. Meloy, and Husted Medvec, "Predecisional Distortion of Product Information," *Journal of Marketing Research*, November 1998, pp. 438–452.

144. Carol A. Berning and Jacob Jacoby, "Patterns of Information Acquisition in New Product Purchases," *Journal of Consumer Research*, September 1974, pp. 18–22.

145. Itamar Simonson, Joel Huber, and John Payne, "The Relationship Between Prior Brand Knowledge and Information Acquisition Order," *Journal of Consumer Research*, March 1988, pp. 566–578.

146. Wendy W. Moe, "An Empirical Two-Stage Choice Model with Varying Decision Rules Applied to Internet Clickstream Data," *Journal of Marketing Research*, November 2006, pp. 680–692; Amitav Chakravarti, Chris Janiszewski, and Gulden Ulkumen, "The Neglect of Prescreening Information," *Journal of Marketing Research*, November 2006, pp. 642–653.

147. Carrie M. Heilman, Douglas Bowman, and Gordon P. Wright, "The Evolution of Brand Preference and Choice Behaviors of Consumers New to a Market," *Journal of Marketing Research* 37, May 2000, pp. 139–155.

148. Jacoby et al., "Prepurchase Information Acquisition"; James R. Bettman, *An Information Processing Theory of Consumer Choice* (Reading, Mass.: Addison-Wesley, 1979).

149. Eric J. Johnson and J. Edward Russo, "Product Familiarity and Learning New Information," *Journal of Consumer Research*, June 1984, pp. 542–550; James R. Bettman and P. Kakkar, "Effects of Information Presentation Format on Consumer Information Acquisition Strategies," *Journal of Consumer Research*, March 1977, pp. 233–240.

150. Raj Sethuraman, Catherine Cole, and Dipak Jain, "Analyzing the Effect of Information Format and Task on Cutoff Search Strategies," *Journal of Consumer Psychology* 3, 1994, pp. 103–136.

151. Jacoby et al., "Tracing the Impact of Item-by-Item Information Accessing on Uncertainty Reduction."

152. Joydeep Srivastava and Nicholas Lurie, "A Consumer Perspective on Price-Matching Refund Policies: Effect on Price Perceptions and Search Behavior," *Journal of Consumer Research*, September 2001, pp. 296–307.

153. Elizabeth Woyke, "Wireless: The Next Killer Mobile App," *Forbes.com*, April 3, 2008, www.forbes.com; Jayne O'Donnell, "Shop by Phone Gets New Meaning," *USA Today*, December 18, 2007, www.usatoday.com; Louise Story, "Brokering a Deal, Carefully, Between Malls and the Web," *New York Times*, October 18, 2007, www.nytimes.com; www.frucall.com; www.nearbynow.com; www.cellfire.com.

Chapter 9

1. "Suzuki Motor/Nissan Motor: Thailand Allows Tax Break for Eco-Car Projects," *Wall Street Journal*, December 10, 2007, *www.wsj.com*; James Hookway, "Thailand Shows Signs of Economic Revival; Ford–Mazda Plan Reflects Optimism Ahead of Elections," *Wall Street Journal*, October 10, 2007, p. A13; "Thailand's Eco-Drive," *Global Agenda*, June 21, 2007, n.p.; "Mercedes-Benz (Thailand) Sees Slower Growth," *Asia Africa Intelligence Wire*, February 4, 2005, n.p.; Evelyn Iritani, "Road Warriors," *Los Angeles Times*, July 9, 1995, pp. D1, D6.

2. Michael D. Johnson and Christopher P. Puto, "A Review of Consumer Judgment and Choice," in ed. Michael J. Houston, *Review of Marketing* (Chicago: American Marketing Association, 1987), pp. 236–292.

3. Eloise Coupey, Julie R. Irwin, and John W. Payne, "Product Category Familiarity and Preference Construction," *Journal of Consumer Research*, March 1998, pp. 459–468.

4. Itamar Simonson, Joel Huber, and John Payne, "The Relationship Between Prior Brand Knowledge and Information Acquisition Order," *Journal of Consumer Research*, March 1988, pp. 566–578.

5. Eric J. Johnson and J. Edward Russo, "Product Familiarity and Learning New Information," *Journal of Consumer Research*, June 1984, pp. 528–541.

6. Michel Tuan Pham, Joel B. Cohen, John W. Pracejus, and G. David Hughes, "Affect Monitoring and the Primacy of Feelings in Judgment," *Journal of Consumer Research*, September 2001, pp. 167–188.

7. Gita Venkataramani Johar, Kamel Jedidi, and Jacob Jacoby, "A Varying-Parameter Averaging Model of Online Brand Evaluations," *Journal of Consumer Research*, September 1997, pp. 232–247; Daniel Kahneman and Amos

Tversky, "On the Psychology of Prediction," *Psychology Review,* July 1973, pp. 251–275.

8. Joan Meyers-Levy and Alice M. Tybout, "Context Effects at Encoding and Judgment in Consumption Settings: The Role of Cognitive Resources," *Journal of Consumer Research,* June 1997, pp. 1–14.

9. "Starbucks Coffee Company," *Food Engineering and Ingredients,* June 2004, p. 7.

10. John Carroll, "The Effect of Imagining an Event on Expectations for the Event," *Journal of Experimental Social Psychology,* January 1978, pp. 88–96.

11. Deborah J. MacInnis and Linda L. Price, "The Role of Imagery in Information Processing: Review and Extensions," *Journal of Consumer Research,* March 1987, pp. 473–491.

12. Baba Shiv and Joel Huber, "The Impact of Anticipating Satisfaction on Consumer Choice," *Journal of Consumer Research* 27, September 2000, pp. 202–216.

13. Arul Mishra and Dhananjay Nayakankuppam, "Consistency and Validity Issues in Consumer Judgments," *Journal of Consumer Research* 33, no. 3, 2006, pp. 291–303.

14. Calvin P. Duncan and Richard W. Olshavsky, "External Search: The Role of Consumer Beliefs," *Journal of Marketing Research,* February 1982, pp. 32–43.

15. Geeta Menon, Lauren G. Block, and Suresh Ramanathan, "We're at as Much Risk as We Are Led to Believe: Effects of Message Cues on Judgments of Health Risk," *Journal of Consumer Research,* March 2002, pp. 533–549.

16. Rohini Ahluwalia, "Re-Inquiries: How Prevalent Is the Negativity Effect in Consumer Environments?" *Journal of Consumer Research,* September 2002, pp. 270–279; Rohini Ahluwalia, H. Rao Unnava, and Robert E. Burnkrant, "The Moderating Effect of Commitment on the Spillover Effect of Marketing Communications," *Journal of Marketing Research,* November 2001, pp. 458–470.

17. Meryl Paula Gardner, "Mood States and Consumer Behavior: A Critical Review," *Journal of Consumer Research,* December 1985, pp. 281–300.

18. Margaret G. Meloy, J. Edward Russo, and Elizabeth Gelfand, "Monetary Incentives and Mood," *Journal of Marketing Research,* May 2006, pp. 267–275.

19. Stijn M. J. Van Osselaer and Joseph W. Alba, "Consumer Learning and Brand Equity," *Journal of Consumer Research* 27, June 2000, pp. 1–16.

20. Paul M. Herr, "Priming Price: Prior Knowledge and Context Effects," *Journal of Consumer Research,* June 1989, pp. 67–75.

21. Jim Henry, "Bentley Is King of Ultraluxury Sales in America," *Automotive News,* February 4, 2007, p. 78; "Conspicuous Non-consumption," *The Economist,* January 8, 2005, pp. 56–57.

22. Sung-Tai Hong and Robert S. Wyer Jr., "Effects of Country-of-Origin and Product-Attribute Information: An Information Processing Perspective," *Journal of Consumer Research,* September 1989, pp. 175–187.

23. Normandy Madden, "Study: Chinese Youth Aren't Patriotic Purchasers," *Advertising Age,* January 5, 2004, p. 6; Craig S. Smith, "Chinese Government Struggles to Rejuvenate National Brands," *Wall Street Journal,* June 24, 1996, pp. B1, B6.

24. James R. Bettman and Mita Sujan, "Effects of Framing on Evaluation of Comparable and Noncomparable Alternatives by Expert and Novice Consumers," *Journal of Consumer Research,* September 1987, pp. 141–151.

25. Naomi Mandel, "Shifting Selves and Decision Making: The Effects of Self-Construal Priming on Consumer Risk-Taking," *Journal of Consumer Research,* June 2003, pp. 30–40.

26. Raghubir and Menon, "AIDS and Me, Never the Twain Shall Meet."

27. Menon, Block, and Ramanathan, 2002.

28. Ravi Dhar and Itamar Simonson, "The Effect of Forced Choice on Choice," *Journal of Marketing Research,* May 2004, pp. 146–160; Ravi Dhar, "Consumer Preference for a No-Choice Option," *Journal of Consumer Research,* September 1997, pp. 215–231.

29. Ravi Dhar and Stephen M. Nowlis, "To Buy or Not to Buy," *Journal of Marketing Research,* November 2004, pp. 423–432.

30. "The Rise of the Superbrands," *The Economist,* February 5, 2005, pp. 63–65.

31. F. May and R. Homans, "Evoked Set Size and the Level of Information Processing in Product Comprehension and Choice Criteria," in ed. William D. Perrault, *Advances in Consumer Research,* vol. 4 (Chicago: Association for Consumer Research, 1977), pp. 172–175.

32. Amitav Chakravarti and Chris Janiszewski, "The Influence of Macro-Level Motives on Consideration Set Composition in Novel Purchase Situations," *Journal of Consumer Research,* September 2003, pp. 244–258.

33. Frank R. Kardes, David M. Sanbonmatsu, Maria L. Cronley, and David C. Houghton, "Consideration Set Overvaluation: When Impossibly Favorable Ratings of a Set of Brands Are Observed," *Journal of Consumer Psychology,* 2002, pp. 353–361.

34. Steven S. Posavac, David M. Sanbonmatsu, and Edward A. Ho, "The Effects of Selective Consideration of Alternatives on Consumer Choice and Attitude–Decision Consistency," *Journal of Consumer Psychology,* 2002, pp. 203–213.

35. Steven S. Posavac, David M. Sanbonmatsu, Frank R. Kardes, and Gavan J. Fitzsimons, "The Brand Positivity Effect: When Evaluation Confers Preference," *Journal of Consumer Research,* December 2004, pp. 643–651.

36. Ryan Hamilton, Jiewen Hong, and Alexander Chernev, "Perceptual Focus Effects in Choice," *Journal of Consumer Research,* August 2007, pp. 187–199; Itamar Simonson and Amos Tversky, "Choice in Context: Tradeoff Contrast and Extremeness Aversion," *Journal of Marketing Research,* August 1992, pp. 281–295.

37. Jongwon Park and JungKeun Kim, "The Effects of Decoys on Preference Shifts: The Role of Attractiveness and Providing Justification," *Journal of Consumer Psychology* 15,

no. 2, 2005, pp. 94–107; Joel Huber, John W. Payne, and Christopher Puto, "Adding Asymmetrically Dominated Alternatives: Violations of Regularity and the Similarity Hypothesis," *Journal of Consumer Research,* June 1982, pp. 90–98; Srinivasan Ratneshwar, Allan D. Shocker, and David W. Stewart, "Toward Understanding the Attraction Effect: The Implications of Product Stimulus Meaningfulness and Familiarity," *Journal of Consumer Research,* March 1987, pp. 520–533; Sanjay Mishra, U. N. Umesh, and Donald E. Stem, "Antecedents of the Attraction Effect: An Information Processing Approach," *Journal of Marketing Research,* August 1993, pp. 331–349; Yigang Pan, Sue O'Curry, and Robert Pitts, "The Attraction Effect and Political Choice in Two Elections," *Journal of Consumer Psychology* 4, no. 1, 1995, pp. 85–101; Sankar Sen, "Knowledge, Information Mode, and the Attraction Effect," *Journal of Consumer Research,* June 1998, pp. 64–77; Timothy B. Heath and Subimal Chatterjee, "Asymmetric Decoy Effects on Lower-Quality Versus Higher-Quality Brands: Meta-analytic and Experimental Evidence," *Journal of Consumer Research,* December 1995, pp. 268–284; Elizabeth Cowley and John R. Rossiter, "Range Model of Judgments," *Journal of Consumer Psychology* 15, no. 3, 2005, pp. 250–262.

38. Simonson, "Get Closer to Your Consumers by Understanding How They Make Choices."

39. Jim Wang and Robert S. Wyer Jr., "Comparative Judgment Processes: The Effects of Task Objectives and Time Delay on Product Evaluations," *Journal of Consumer Psychology,* 2002, pp. 327–340.

40. Alexander Chernev, "Decision Focus and Consumer Choice Among Assortments," *Journal of Consumer Research* 33, no. 1, 2006, pp. 50–59.

41. Rebecca W. Hamilton, "Why Do People Suggest What They Do Not Want? Using Context Effects to Influence Others' Choices," *Journal of Consumer Research,* March 2003, pp. 492–506.

42. Leonard Lee and Dan Ariely, "Shopping Goals, Goal Concreteness, and Conditional Promotions," *Journal of Consumer Research* 33, no. 1, 2006, pp. 60–70.

43. Punam A. Keller, "Regulatory Focus and Efficacy of Health Messages," *Journal of Consumer Research* 33, no. 1, 2006, pp. 109–114.

44. John G. Lynch and G. Zauberman, "Construing Consumer Decision Making," *Journal of Consumer Psychology* 17, no. 2, 2007, pp. 107–112.

45. Ran Kivetz and Itamar Simonson, "Self-Control for the Righteous: Toward a Theory of Precommitment to Indulgence," *Journal of Consumer Research,* September 2002, pp. 199–217.

46. Daniel Kahneman and Amos Tversky, "Prospect Theory: An Analysis of Decisions Under Risk," *Econometrica,* March 1979, pp. 263–291.

47. Punan Anand Keller, Isaac M. Lipkus, and Barbara K. Rimer, "Affect, Framing, and Persuasion," *Journal of Marketing Research,* February 2003, pp. 54–64.

48. Ashwani Monga and Rui Zhu, "Buyers Versus Sellers: How They Differ in Their Responses to Framed Outcomes," *Journal of Consumer Psychology* 15, no. 4, 2005, pp. 325–333.

49. Levin, "Associative Effects of Information Framing."

50. Sucharita Chandran and Geeta Menon, "When a Day Means More Than a Year: Effects of Temporal Framing on Judgments of Health Risk," *Journal of Consumer Research,* September 2004, pp. 375–389.

51. Christopher P. Puto, W. E. Patton, and Ronald H. King, "Risk Handling Strategies in Industrial Vendor Selection Decisions," *Journal of Marketing,* January 1987, pp. 89–98.

52. John T. Gourville, "Pennies-a-Day: The Effect of Temporal Reframing on Transaction Evaluation," *Journal of Consumer Research,* March 1998, pp. 395–408.

53. Rashmi Adaval and Kent B. Monroe, "Automatic Construct and Use of Contextual Information for Product and Price Evaluations," *Journal of Consumer Research,* March 2002, pp. 572–588.

54. Yaacov Schul and Yoav Ganzach, "The Effects of Accessibility of Standards and Decision Framing on Product Evaluations," *Journal of Consumer Psychology* 4, no. 1, 1995, pp. 61–83.

55. Baba Shiv, Julie A. Edell, and John W. Payne, "Factors Affecting the Impact of Negatively and Positively Framed Ad Messages," *Journal of Consumer Research,* December 1997, pp. 285–294.

56. Bettman and Sujan, "Effects of Framing on Evaluation of Comparable and Noncomparable Alternatives by Expert and Novice Consumers."

57. Donald P. Green and Irene V. Blair, "Framing and Price Elasticity of Private and Public Goods," *Journal of Consumer Psychology* 4, no. 1, 1995, pp. 1–32.

58. Paul M. Herr and Christine M. Page, "Asymmetric Association of Liking and Disliking Judgments: So What's Not to Like?" *Journal of Consumer Research,* March 2004, pp. 588–601.

59. Robert Berner, "Welcome to Procter & Gamble," *BusinessWeek,* February 7, 2005, pp. 76–77.

60. Brian Steinberg, "Western Union to Court Immigrants," *Wall Street Journal,* May 2, 2003, p. B2.

61. Itamar Simonson, "Get Closer to Your Consumers by Understanding How They Make Choices," *California Management Review,* Summer 1993, pp. 68–84; John W. Payne, James R. Bettman, and Eric J. Johnson, "The Adaptive Decision-Maker," in ed. Robin M. Hogarth, *Insights in Decision Making: A Tribute to Hillel Einhorn* (Chicago: University of Chicago Press, 1990).

62. Aimee Drolet, "Inherent Rule Variability in Consumer Choice: Changing Rules for Change's Sake," *Journal of Consumer Research,* December 2002, pp. 293–305. James R. Bettman, Mary Frances Luce, and John W. Payne, "Constructive Consumer Choice Processes," *Journal of Consumer Research,* December 1998, pp. 187–217; James R. Bettman, Mary Frances Luce, and John W.

Payne, "Constructive Consumer Choice Processes," *Journal of Consumer Research,* December 1998, pp. 187–217; Denis A. Lussier and Richard W. Olshavsky, "Task Complexity and Contingent Processing in Brand Choice," *Journal of Consumer Research,* September 1979, pp. 154–165; Eric J. Johnson and Robert J. Meyer, "Compensatory Choice Models of Noncompensatory Processes: The Effect of Varying Context," *Journal of Consumer Research,* June 1984, pp. 542–551.

63. Sanjay Sood, Yuval Rottenstreich, and Lyle Brenner, "On Decisions That Lead to Decisions: Direct and Derived Evaluations of Preference," *Journal of Consumer Research,* June 2004, pp. 17–18.

64. Seymour Epstein, "Integration of the Cognitive and the Psychodynamic Unconscious," *American Psychologist,* August 1994, pp. 709–724.

65. Mariele K. De Mooij and Warren Keegan, *Worldwide Advertising* (London: Prentice-Hall International, 1991).

66. Peter Wright, "Consumer Choice Strategies: Simplifying vs. Optimizing," *Journal of Marketing Research,* February 1975, pp. 60–67; Noreen Klein and Stewart W. Bither, "An Investigation of Utility-Directed Cutoff Selection," *Journal of Consumer Research,* September 1987, pp. 240–256.

67. Simonson, "Get Closer to Your Consumers by Understanding How They Make Choices."

68. Becky Aikman, "Steve & Barry's Gets Boost with Star Power," *Newsday,* March 3, 2008, *www.newsday.com.*

69. For a review of multiattribute models, see William L. Wilkie and Edgar A. Pessemier, "Issues in Marketing's Use of Multiattribute Models," *Journal of Marketing Research,* November 1983, pp. 428–441; Blair H. Sheppard, Jon Hartwick, and Paul R. Warshaw, "The Theory of Reasoned Action: A Meta-analysis of Past Research with Recommendations for Modifications and Future Research," *Journal of Consumer Research,* December 1988, pp. 325–342.

70. Alexander Chernev, "Goal-Attribute Compatibility in Consumer Choice," *Journal of Consumer Psychology,* 2004, pp. 141–150.

71. Mary Frances Luce, "Choosing to Avoid: Coping with Negatively Emotion-Laden Consumer Decisions," *Journal of Consumer Research,* March 1998, pp. 409–433; Ellen C. Garbarino and Julie A. Edell, "Cognitive Effort, Affect, and Choice," *Journal of Consumer Research,* September 1997, pp. 147–158.

72. Mary Frances Luce, John W. Payne, and James R. Bettman, "Emotional Trade-off Difficulty and Choice," *Journal of Marketing Research* 36, May 1999, pp. 143–159.

73. Aimee Drolet and Mary Frances Luce, "The Rationalizing Effects of Cognitive Load on Emotion-Based Tradeoff Avoidance," *Journal of Consumer Research,* June 2004, pp. 63–77; see also Tiffany Barnett White, "Consumer Trust and Advice Acceptance: The Moderating Roles of Benevolence, Expertise, and Negative Emotions," *Journal of Consumer Psychology* 15, no. 2, 2005, pp. 141–148.

74. David Grether and Louis Wilde, "An Analysis of Conjunctive Choice: Theory and Experiments," *Journal of Consumer Research,* March 1984, pp. 373–385.

75. Evan Perez, "Cruising on Credit: Carnival Introduces Vacation Financing to Get More Aboard," *Wall Street Journal,* April 12, 2001, p. B12.

76. Lussier and Olshavsky, "Task Complexity and Contingent Processing in Brand Choice"; Johnson and Meyer, "Compensatory Choice Models of Noncompensatory Processes."

77. John Hagel and John Seely Brown, "Learning from Tata's Nano," *BusinessWeek,* February 27, 2008, *www.businessweek.com.*

78. Timothy B. Heath, Gangseog Ryu, Subimal Chatterjee, Michael S. McCarthy, David L. Mothersbaugh, Sandra Milberg, and Gary J. Gaeth, "Asymmetric Competition in Choice and the Leveraging of Competitive Disadvantages," *Journal of Consumer Research* 27, December 2000, pp. 291–308.

79. Rohini Ahluwalia, Robert E. Burnkrant, and H. Rao Unnava, "Consumer Response to Negative Publicity: The Moderating Role of Commitment," *Journal of Marketing Research* 37, May 2000, pp. 203–214.

80. "Home Depot's Quarterly Net Off 27% with 'Challenging' Outlook," *Reuters,* February 26, 2008, *www.cnnmoney.com;* Chad Terhune, "Home Depot's Home Improvement," *Wall Street Journal,* March 8, 2001, pp. B1, B4.

81. Gerald Häubl and Kyle B. Murray, "Preference Construction and Persistence in Digital Marketplaces: The Role of Electronic Recommendation Agents," *Journal of Consumer Psychology,* 2003, pp. 75–91.

82. Amos Tversky, "Intransitivity of Preferences," *Psychological Review,* January 1969, pp. 31–48.

83. Amos Tversky, "Elimination by Aspects: A Theory of Choice," *Psychological Review,* July 1972, pp. 281–299.

84. Donna Bryson, "Traditional Fare Goes Fast-Food in S. Africa," *Austin American Statesman,* June 4, 1994, p. A16.

85. John Reed, "ZXAuto to Lead Chinese Assault on US Market," *Financial Times,* January 16, 2008, *www.ft.com;* Joseph B. White, "China's SUV Surge," *Wall Street Journal,* June 10, 2004, pp. B1, B3.

86. Irwin Levin, "Associative Effects of Information Framing," *Bulletin of the Psychonomic Society,* March 1987, pp. 85–86.

87. Nathan Novemsky and Daniel Kahneman, "The Boundaries of Loss Aversion," *Journal of Marketing Research,* May 2005, pp. 119–128; Colin Camerer, "Three Cheers—Psychological, Theoretical, Empirical—for Loss Aversion," *Journal of Marketing Research,* May 2005, pp. 129–133; Dan Ariely, Joel Huber, and Klaus Wertenbroch, "When Do Losses Loom Larger Than Gains?" *Journal of Marketing Research,* May 2005, pp. 134–138.

88. Alexander Chernev, "Goal Orientation and Consumer Preference for the Status Quo," *Journal of Consumer Research* 31, no. 3, 2004, pp. 557–565.

89. Douglas E. Allen, "Toward a Theory of Consumer Choice as Sociohistorically Shaped Practical Experience: The Fits-Like-a-Glove (FLAG) Framework," *Journal of Consumer Research*, March 2002, pp. 515–532.

90. Peter R. Darke, Amitava Chattopadhyay, and Laurence Ashworth, "The Importance and Functional Significance of Affective Cues in Consumer Choice," *Journal of Consumer Research* 33, no. 3, 2006, pp. 322–328; Stephen J. Hoch and George F. Lowenstein, "Time-Inconsistent Preferences and Consumer Self-Control," *Journal of Consumer Research*, March 1991, pp. 492–507.

91. Michel Tuan Pham, "The Logic of Feeling," *Journal of Consumer Psychology* 14, no. 4, 2004, pp. 360–369.

92. Michel Tuan Pham, "Representativeness, Relevance, and the Use of Feelings in Decision Making," *Journal of Consumer Research*, September 1998, pp. 144–159.

93. Epstein, "Integration of the Cognitive and the Psychodynamic Unconscious."

94. Yuval Rottenstreich, Sanjay Sood, and Lyle Brenner, "Feeling and Thinking in Memory-Based Versus Stimulus-Based Choices," *Journal of Consumer Research* 33, no. 4, 2007, pp. 461–469.

95. Pham, "Representativeness, Relevance, and the Use of Feelings in Decision Making"; Morris B. Holbrook and Elizabeth C. Hirschman, "The Experiential Aspects of Consumption: Consumer Fantasies, Feelings, and Fun," *Journal of Consumer Research*, September 1982, pp. 132–140; Erica Mina Okada, "Justification Effects on Consumer Choice of Hedonic and Utilitarian Goods," *Journal of Marketing Research*, February 2005, pp. 43–53,

96. Stacy L. Wood and James R. Bettman, "Predicting Happiness: How Normative Feeling Rules Influence (and Even Reverse) Durability Bias," *Journal of Consumer Psychology* 17, no. 3, 2007, pp. 188–201; Morris B. Holbrook and Meryl P. Gardner, "An Approach to Investigating the Emotional Determinants of Consumption Durations: Why Do People Consume What They Consume for as Long as They Consume It?" *Journal of Consumer Psychology* 2, no. 2, 1993, pp. 123–142.

97. See Jennifer S. Lerner, Seunghee Han, and Dacher Keltner, "Feelings and Consumer Decision Making: Extending the Appraisal-Tendency Framework," *Journal of Consumer Psychology* 17, no. 3, 2007, pp. 184–187; J. Frank Yates, "Emotional Appraisal Tendencies and Carryover: How, Why, and . . . Therefore?" *Journal of Consumer Psychology* 17, no. 3, 2007, pp. 179–183; Baba Shiv, "Emotions, Decisions, and the Brain," *Journal of Consumer Psychology* 17, no. 3, pp. 174–178.

98. Seunghee Han, Jennifer S. Lerner, and Dacher Keltner, "Feelings and Consumer Decision Making: The Appraisal-Tendency Framework," *Journal of Consumer Psychology* 17, no. 3, 2007, pp. 158–168.

99. Lisa A. Cavanaugh, James R. Bettman, Mary Frances Luce, and John W. Payne, "Appraising the Appraisal-Tendency Framework," *Journal of Consumer Psychology* 17, no. 3, 2007, pp. 169–173.

100. Deborah J. MacInnis, Vanessa M. Patrick, and C. Whan Park, "Not as Happy as I Thought I'd Be? Affective Misforecasting and Product Evaluations," *Journal of Consumer Research*, March 2007, pp. 479–490; Deborah J. MacInnis, Vanessa M. Patrick, and C. Whan Park, "Looking Through the Crystal Ball: Affective Forecasting and Misforecasting in Consumer Behavior," *Review of Marketing Research* 2, 2006, pp. 43–80.

101. Eric A. Greenleaf, "Reserves, Regret, and Rejoicing in Open English Auctions," *Journal of Consumer Research* 31, no. 2, 2004, pp. 264–273.

102. I. Simonson, "The Influence of Anticipating Regret and Responsibility on Purchase Decisions," *Journal of Consumer Research* 19, 1992, pp. 105–118.

103. Ann L. McGill and Punam Anand Keller, "Differences in the Relative Influence of Product Attributes under Alternative Processing Conditions: Attribute Importance Versus Ease of Imaginability," *Journal of Consumer Psychology* 3, no. 1, 1994, pp. 29–50; MacInnis and Price, "The Role of Imagery in Information Processing."

104. Russell W. Belk, Güliz Ger, and Søren Askegaard, "The Fire of Desire: A Multisited Inquiry into Consumer Passion," *Journal of Consumer Research*, December 2003, pp. 326+.

105. Ann E. Schlosser, "Experiencing Products in the Virtual World: The Role of Goal and Imagery in Influencing Attitudes Versus Purchase Intentions," *Journal of Consumer Research*, September 2003, pp. 184–198.

106. Jennifer Edson Escalas, "Imagine Yourself in the Product," *Journal of Advertising*, Summer 2004, pp. 37–48.

107. Darren W. Dahl, Amitava Chattopadhyay, and Gerald J. Gorn, "The Use of Visual Mental Imagery in New Product Design," *Journal of Marketing Research* 36, February 1999, pp. 18–28.

108. Carmine Gallo, "Employee Motivation the Ritz-Carlton Way," *BusinessWeek Online*, February 29, 2008, *www.businessweek.com*.

109. Lewis Lazare, "Nike Remains at Top of Advertising Game," *Chicago Sun-Times*, February 7, 2008, *www.suntimes.com*.

110. Eric A. Greenleaf and Donald R. Lehmann, "Reasons for Substantial Delay in Consumer Decision Making," *Journal of Consumer Research*, September 1995, pp. 186–199.

111. Greenleaf and Lehmann, "Reasons for Substantial Delay in Consumer Decision Making."

112. Thomas A. Brunner and Michaela Wänke, "The Reduced and Enhanced Impact of Shared Features on Individual Brand Evaluations," *Journal of Consumer Psychology* 16, no. 2, 2006, pp. 101–111.

113. Olga Kharif, "Making the iPhone Mean Business," *BusinessWeek*, July 23, 2007, p. 30.

114. Michael D. Johnson, "Consumer Choice Strategies for Comparing Noncomparable Alternatives," *Journal of Consumer Research*, December 1984, pp. 741–753; Michael D. Johnson, "Comparability and Hierarchical Processing in Multialternative Choice," *Journal of Consumer Research*, December 1988, pp. 303–314.

115. Kim P. Corfman, "Comparability and Comparison Levels Used in Choices Among Consumer Products," *Journal of Marketing Research*, August 1991, pp. 368–374.

116. C. Whan Park and Daniel Smith, "Product-Level Choice: A Top-Down or Bottom-Up Process?" *Journal of Consumer Research*, December 1989, pp. 289–299.

117. "Visit Scotland Targets Golfers with Latest Tourism Campaign," *New Media Age,* January 31, 2008, n.p.

118. Girish N. Punj and David W. Stewart, "An Interaction Framework of Consumer Decision Making," *Journal of Consumer Research*, September 1983, pp. 181–196.

119. Patricia M. West, Christina L. Brown, and Stephen J. Hoch, "Consumption Vocabulary and Preference Formation," *Journal of Consumer Research,* September 1996, pp. 120–135.

120. Johnson and Russo, "Product Familiarity and Learning New Information"; James R. Bettman and C. Whan Park, "Effects of Prior Knowledge and Experience and Phase of the Choice Process on Consumer Decision Processes, A Protocol Analysis," *Journal of Consumer Research,* December 1980, pp. 234–248.

121. Joffre Swait and Wiktor Adamowicz, "The Influence of Task Complexity on Consumer Choice: A Latent Choice Model of Decision Strategy Switching," *Journal of Consumer Research,* June 2001, pp. 135–148.

122. Elaine Sherman and Ruth Belk Smith, "Mood States of Shoppers and Store Image: Promising Interactions and Possible Behavioral Effects," in eds. Paul Anderson and Melanie Wallendorf, *Advances in Consumer Research,* vol. 14 (Provo, Utah: Association for Consumer Research, 1987), pp. 251–254.

123. Rashmi Adaval, "How Good Gets Better and Bad Gets Worse: Understanding the Impact of Affect on Evaluations of Known Brands," *Journal of Consumer Research,* December 2003, pp. 352–367.

124. Stewart Shapiro, Deborah J. MacInnis, and C. Whan Park, "Understanding Program-Induced Mood Effects: Decoupling Arousal from Valence," *Journal of Advertising,* Winter 2002, pp. 15–26.

125. Catherine W. M. Yeung and Robert S. Wyer Jr., "Affect, Appraisal, and Consumer Judgment," *Journal of Consumer Research,* September 2004, pp. 412+.

126. Gerald J. Gorn, Marvin E. Goldberg, and Kunal Basu, "Mood, Awareness, and Product Evaluation," *Journal of Consumer Psychology* 2, no. 3, 1993, pp. 237–256.

127. Joel B. Cohen and Eduardo B. Andrade, "Affective Intuition and Task-Contingent Affect Regulation," *Journal of Consumer Research,* September 2004, pp. 358–367.

128. Alexander Fedorikhin and Catherine A. Cole, "Mood Effects on Attitudes, Perceived Risk, and Choice: Moderators and Mediators," *Journal of Consumer Psychology* 14, no. 1/2, 2004, pp. 2–12.

129. Payne, Bettman, and Johnson, "The Adaptive Decision-Maker."

130. C. Whan Park, Easwar S. Iyer, and Daniel C. Smith, "The Effects of Situational Factors on In-Store Grocery Shopping Behavior: The Role of Store Environment and Time Available for Shopping," *Journal of Consumer Research,* March 1989, pp. 422–433.

131. Ravi Dhar and Stephen M. Nowlis, "The Effect of Time Pressure on Consumer Choice Deferral," *Journal of Consumer Research* 25, March 1999, pp. 369–384.

132. Michelle M. Bergadaa, "The Role of Time in the Action of the Consumer," *Journal of Consumer Research,* December 1990, pp. 289–302.

133. Simonson, "Get Closer to Your Consumers by Understanding How They Make Choices."

134. Alexander Chernev, "Extremeness Aversion and Attribute-Balance Effects in Choice," *Journal of Consumer Research,* September 2004, pp. 249–263.

135. Ran Kivetz, Oded Netzer, and V. Srinivasan, "Alternative Models for Capturing the Compromise Effect," *Journal of Marketing Research,* August 2004, pp. 237–257; Ravi Dhar, Anil Menon, and Bryan Maach, "Toward Extending the Compromise Effect to Complex Buying Contexts," *Journal of Marketing Research,* August 2004, pp. 258–261.

136. Alexander Chernev, "Context Effects Without a Context: Attribute Balance as a Reason for Choice," *Journal of Consumer Research* 32, no. 2, 2005, pp. 213–223.

137. Norbert Schwarz, "Metacognitive Experiences in Consumer Judgment and Decision Making," *Journal of Consumer Psychology* 14, no. 4, 2004, pp. 332–348.

138. Rolf Reber and Norbert Schwarz, "Effects on Perceptual Fluency on Judgments of Truth," *Consciousness and Cognition,* 8, 1999, 338–342; Matthew S. McGlone and Jessica Tofighbakhsh, "Birds of a Feather Flock Conjointly?: Rhyme as Reason in Aphorisms," *Psychological Science* 11, no.1, 2000, 424–428.

139. See Joel Huber, "A Comment on Metacognitive Experiences and Consumer Choices," *Journal of Consumer Psychology* 14, no. 4, 2004, pp. 356–359; Norbert Schwarz, "Metacognitive Experiences: Response to Commentaries," *Journal of Consumer Psychology* 14, no. 4, 2004, pp. 370–373.

140. Jacob Jacoby, "Perspectives on Information Overload," *Journal of Consumer Research,* March 1984, pp. 569–573; Kevin Lane Keller and Richard Staelin, "Effects of Quality and Quantity of Information on Decision Effectiveness," *Journal of Consumer Research,* September 1987, pp. 200–213.

141. Keller and Staelin, "Effects of Quality and Quantity of Information on Decision Effectiveness."

142. Ran Kivetz and Itamar Simonson, "The Effects of Incomplete Information on Consumer Choice," *Journal of Marketing Research* 37, November 2000, pp. 427–448.

143. A. V. Muthukrishnan, "Decision Ambiguity and Incumbent Brand Advantage," *Journal of Consumer Research,* June 1995, pp. 98–109.

144. Madhubalan Viswanathan and Sunder Narayanan, "Comparative Judgments of Numerical and Verbal Attribute Labels," *Journal of Consumer Psychology* 3, no. 1, 1994, pp. 79–100.

145. Joseph R. Priester, Utpal M. Dholakia, and Monique A. Fleming, "When and Why the Background Contrast

Effect Emerges: Thought Engenders Meaning by Influencing the Perception of Applicability," *Journal of Consumer Research* 31, no. 3, 2004, pp. 491–501; Joel Huber, John W. Payne, and Christopher Puto, "Adding Asymmetrically Dominated Alternatives: Violations of Regularity and the Similarity Hypothesis," *Journal of Consumer Research*, June 1982, pp. 90–98; Ravi Dhar and Itamar Simonson (1999), "Making Complementary Choices in Consumption Episodes: Highlighting Versus Balancing," *Journal of Marketing Research*, February 1999, pp. 29–44.

146. Itamar Simonson and Russell S. Winer, "The Influence of Purchase Quantity and Display Format on Consumer Preference for Variety," *Journal of Consumer Research*, June 1992, pp. 133–138.

147. Itamar Simonson, Stephen Nowlis, and Katherine Lemon, "The Effect of Local Consideration Sets on Global Choice Between Lower Price and Higher Quality," *Marketing Science*, Fall 1993.

148. Rashmi Adaval and Robert S. Wyer Jr., "The Role of Narratives in Consumer Information Processing," *Journal of Consumer Psychology* 7, no. 3, 1998, pp. 207–245.

149. Christina L. Brown and Gregory S. Carpenter, "Why Is the Trivial Important? A Reasons-Based Account for the Effects of Trivial Attributes on Choice," *Journal of Consumer Research*, March 2000, pp. 372–385.

150. Dan Ariely and Jonathan Levav, "Sequential Choice in Group Settings: Taking the Road Less Traveled and Less Enjoyed," *Journal of Consumer Research* 27, December 2000, pp. 279–290.

151. Stijn M. J. van Osselaer, Joseph W. Alba, and Puneet Manchanda, "Irrelevant Information and Mediated Intertemporal Choice," *Journal of Consumer Psychology* 14, no. 3, 2004, pp. 257–270.

152. Guliz Ger, "Problems of Marketization in Romania and Turkey," in eds. Clifford Schultz, Russell Belk, and Guliz Ger, *Consumption in Marketizing Economies* (Greenwich, Conn.: JAI Press, 1995).

153. Sabrina Tavernise, "In Russia, Capitalism of a Certain Size," *New York Times*, July 29, 2001, sec. 3, p. 6; Guliz Ger, Russell Belk, and Dana-Nicoleta Lascu, "The Development of Consumer Desire in Marketing and Developing Economies: The Cases of Romania and Turkey," in eds. Leigh McAlister and Michael L. Rothschild, *Advances in Consumer Research*, vol. 20 (Provo, Utah: Association for Consumer Research, 1993), pp. 102–107.

154. Bernadine Williams, "RV Deliveries Decline 3.4% in December," *Automotive News*, March 3, 2008, p. 30; Bob Ashley, "ARC's Derrick Crandall Identifies Top 10 Challenges Facing Outdoor Recreation—and the RV Industry," *RV Business*, March 2008, p. 18; Juston Jones, "Rolling Homes Aren't Just for the Rich," *New York Times*, April 28, 2007, p. C3; Mark Yost, "Luxury RVs with All the Comforts of Home," *Wall Street Journal*, February 20, 2007, p. D7; Martin Zimmerman, "RVs Retaining Their Luster," *Los Angeles Times*, August 4, 2007, p. C3;

Henry Sanderson, "Winnebago Rides a 'Knife Edge' In Its Attempt to Regain Business," *Wall Street Journal*, November 1, 2006, p. B3E; *www.winnebagoind.com.*

Chapter 10

1. Minet Schindehutte, "Understanding Market-Driving Behavior: The Role of Entrepreneurship," *Journal of Small Business Management*, January 23, 2008, pp. 46+; Ben Steverman, "Jones Soda: On Ice," *BusinessWeek Online*, December 6, 2007, *www.businessweek.com*; Christopher C. Williams, "Sales Pressures Could Take the Fizz Out of Jones Soda," *Wall Street Journal*, June 3, 2007, p. A3; Kate Macarthur, "Quirky Jones Soda Steps into Mainstream," *Advertising Age*, March 27, 2006, p. 12.

2. Rohit Deshpande, Wayne D. Hoyer, and Scott Jeffries, "Low Involvement Decision Processes: The Importance of Choice Tactics," in eds. R. F. Bush and S. D. Hunt, *Marketing Theory: Philosophy of Science Perspectives* (Chicago: American Marketing Association, 1982), pp. 155–158; Alan Newell and Herbert A. Simon, *Human Problem Solving* (Englewood Cliffs, N.J.: Prentice-Hall, 1972); Daniel Kahneman and Amos Tversky, "On the Psychology of Prediction," *Psychological Review*, July 1973, pp. 237–251.

3. Daniel Kahneman and Amos Tversky, "Subjective Probability: A Judgment of Representativeness," *Cognitive Psychology*, July 1972, pp. 430–454.

4. Janet Amady, "For McDonald's, It's a Wrap," *Wall Street Journal*, January 30, 2007, p. B.1.

5. Valerie S. Folkes, "The Availability Heuristic and Perceived Risk," *Journal of Consumer Research*, June 1988, pp. 13–23; Johnson and Puto, "A Review of Consumer Judgment and Choice," in ed. Michael J. Houston, *Review of Marketing* (Chicago: American Marketing Association, 1987), pp. 236–292.

6. Geeta Menon and Priya Raghubir, "Ease-of-Retrieval as an Automatic Input in Judgments: A Mere-Accessibility Framework?" *Journal of Consumer Research*, September 2003, pp. 230–243.

7. Peter R. Dickson, "The Impact of Enriching Case and Statistical Information on Consumer Judgments," *Journal of Consumer Research*, March 1982, pp. 398–408.

8. Chezy Ofir and John G. Lynch Jr., "Context Effects on Judgment Under Uncertainty," *Journal of Consumer Research*, September 1984, pp. 668–679.

9. Amos Tversky and Daniel Kahneman, "Belief in the Law of Small Numbers," *Psychological Bulletin*, August 1971, pp. 105–110; Amos Tversky and Daniel Kahneman, "Judgment Under Uncertainty: Heuristics and Biases," *Science*, September 1974, pp.1124–1131.

10. David Welch, David Kiley, and Moon Ihlwan, "My Way or the Highway at Hyundai," *BusinessWeek*, March 17, 2008, pp. 48–51; "The Hyundai Syndrome," *Adweek's Marketing Week*, April 20, 1992, pp. 20–21.

11. "Samsung: As Good As It Gets?" *The Economist*, March 10, 2005; Claudia Deutsch, "To Change Its Image and Attract New Customers, Samsung Electronics Is

Putting on a Show," *New York Times,* September 20, 2004, p. C11.

12. Sam Diaz, "A New Way to Create Buzz," *Washington Post,* August 25, 2007, p. D1

13. Wayne D. Hoyer, "An Examination of Consumer Decision Making for a Common Repeat Purchase Product," *Journal of Consumer Research,* December 1984, pp. 822–829.

14. Ap Dijksterhuis, Pamela K. Smith, Rick B. van Baaren, and Daniel H. J. Wigboldus, "The Unconscious Consumer: Effects of Environment on Consumer Behavior," *Journal of Consumer Psychology* 15, no. 3, 2005, pp. 193–202.

15. James Vlahos, "Scent and Sensibility," *Key (New York Times Real Estate Magazine),* Fall 2007, pp. 68–73.

16. Tanya L. Chartrand, "The Role of Conscious Awareness in Consumer Behavior," *Journal of Consumer Psychology* 15, no. 3, pp. 203–210.

17. Chris Janiszewski and Stijn M. J. van Osselaer, "Behavior Activation Is Not Enough," *Journal of Consumer Psychology* 15, no. 3, 2005, pp. 218–224.

18. Ap Dijksterhuis and Pamela K. Smith, "What Do We Do Unconsciously? And How?" *Journal of Consumer Psychology* 15, no. 3, 2005, pp. 225–229.

19. Herbert E. Krugman, "The Impact of Television Advertising: Learning Without Involvement," *Public Opinion Quarterly,* Fall 1965, pp. 349–356.

20. Michael L. Ray, *Marketing Communications and the Hierarchy of Effects* (Cambridge, Mass.: Marketing Science Institute, 1973).

21. Robert B. Zajonc, "Feeling and Thinking: Preferences Need No Inferences," *American Psychologist,* February 1980, pp. 151–175; Robert B. Zajonc and Hazel B. Markus, "Affective and Cognitive Factors in Preferences," *Journal of Consumer Research,* September 1982, pp. 122–131.

22. Hoyer, "An Examination of Consumer Decision Making for a Common Repeat Purchase Product."

23. Cathy J. Cobb and Wayne D. Hoyer, "Direct Observation of Search Behavior in the Purchase of Two Nondurable Products," *Psychology and Marketing,* Fall 1983, pp. 161–179.

24. Richard W. Olshavsky and Donald H. Granbois, "Consumer Decision Making: Fact or Fiction?" *Journal of Consumer Research,* September 1979, pp. 93–100.

25. Andrew D. Gershoff and Gita Venkataramani Johar, "Do You Know Me? Consumer Calibration of Friends' Knowledge," *Journal of Consumer Research* 32, no. 4, 2006, pp. 496–503.

26. Baba Shiv, Julie A. Edell Britton, and John W. Payne, "Re-Inquiries: Does Elaboration Increase or Decrease the Effectiveness of Negatively Versus Positively Framed Messages?" *Journal of Consumer Research,* June 2004, pp. 199–208.

27. Yong Zhang and Richard Buda, "Moderating Effects of Need for Cognition on Responses to Positively Versus Negatively Framed Advertising Messages," *Journal of Advertising,* Summer 1999, pp. 1–15.

28. C. Whan Park, Sung Youl Jun, and Deborah J. MacInnis, "Choosing What I Want Versus Rejecting What I Do Not Want: An Application of Decision Framing to Product Option Choice Decisions," *Journal of Marketing Research,* May 2000, pp. 187–202.

29. William E. Baker and Richard J. Lutz, "An Empirical Test of an Updated Relevance–Accessibility Model of Advertising Effectiveness," *Journal of Advertising* 29, no. 1, Spring 2000, pp. 1–13.

30. Deshpande, Hoyer, and Jeffries, "Low Involvement Decision Processes."

31. Hoyer, "An Examination of Consumer Decision Making for a Common Repeat Purchase Product."

32. Siew Meng Leong, "Consumer Decision Making for Common, Repeat-Purchase Products: A Dual Replication," *Journal of Consumer Psychology* 2, no. 2, 1993, pp. 193–208; Dana L. Alden, Wayne D. Hoyer, and Guntalee Wechasara, "Choice Strategies and Involvement, A Cross-Cultural Analysis," in ed. Thomas K. Srull, *Advances in Consumer Research,* vol. 16 (Provo, Utah: Association for Consumer Research, 1989), pp. 119–126.

33. James Vlahos, "Scent and Sensibility," *Key (New York Times Real Estate Magazine),* Fall 2007, pp. 68–73.

34. Walter A. Nord and J. Paul Peter, "A Behavior Modification Perspective on Marketing," *Journal of Marketing,* Spring 1980, pp. 36–47; Michael Rothschild and William C. Gaidis, "Behavioral Learning Theory: Its Relevance to Marketing and Promotions," *Journal of Marketing,* Spring 1981, pp. 70–78.

35. Holly Heline, "Brand Loyalty Isn't Dead—But You're Not Off the Hook," *Brandweek,* June 7, 1994, p. 14.

36. Robert E. Smith and William R. Swinyard, "Information Response Models: An Integrated Approach," *Journal of Marketing,* Winter 1982, pp. 81–93; Robert E. Smith and William R. Swinyard, "Attitude–Behavior Consistency: The Impact of Product Trial vs. Advertising," *Journal of Marketing Research,* August 1983, pp. 257–267.

37. Deanna S. Kempf and Robert E. Smith, "Consumer Processing of Product Trial and the Influence of Prior Advertising: A Structural Modeling Approach," *Journal of Marketing Research,* August 1998, pp. 325–338.

38. Ran Kivetz, Oleg Urminsky, and Yuhuang Zheng, "The Goal-Gradient Hypothesis Resurrected: Purchase Acceleration, Illusionary Goal Progress, and Customer Retention," *Journal of Marketing Research,* February 2006, pp. 39–58.

39. Michael L. Rothschild and Michael J. Houston, "The Consumer Involvement Matrix: Some Preliminary Findings," in eds. Barnett A. Greenberg and Danny N. Bellenger, *Proceedings of the American Marketing Association Educators' Conference,* Series no. 41, 1977, pp. 95–98.

40. Wayne D. Hoyer, "Variations in Choice Strategies Across Decision Contexts: An Examination of Contingent Factors," in ed. Richard J. Lutz, *Advances in Consumer Research,* vol. 13 (Provo, Utah: Association for Consumer Research, 1986), pp. 32–36.

41. Wayne D. Hoyer and Cathy J. Cobb-Walgren, "Consumer Decision Making Across Product Categories: The Influence of Task Environment," *Psychology and Marketing,* Spring 1988, pp. 45–69.

42. Leong, "Consumer Decision Making for Common, Repeat-Purchase Products."

43. Janet Adamy, "Starbucks Closes Stores To Retrain Baristas," *Wall Street Journal,* February 26, 2008, *www.wsj.com.*

44. Robert E. Smith, "Integrating Information from Advertising and Trial: Processes and Effects on Consumer Response to Product Information," *Journal of Marketing Research,* May 1993, pp. 204–219.

45. Jenn Abelson, "Were 5 Blades Worth the Wait for Women?" *Boston Globe,* February 22, 2008, p. C1.

46. Norihiko Shirouzu, "Snapple in Japan: How a Splash Dried Up," *Wall Street Journal,* April 15, 1996, pp. B1, B3.

47. Priya Raghubir and Kim Corfman, "When Do Price Promotions Affect Pretrial Brand Evaluations?" *Journal of Marketing Research* 36, May 1999, pp. 211–222.

48. Adwait Khare and J. Jeffrey Inman, "Habitual Behavior in American Eating Patterns: The Role of Meal Occasions," *Journal of Consumer Research* 32, no. 4, 2006, pp. 567–575; Jacob Jacoby and David B. Kyner, "Brand Loyalty vs. Repeat Purchasing Behavior," *Journal of Marketing Research,* February 1973, pp. 1–9.

49. Ted Roselius, "Consumer Rankings of Risk Reduction Methods," *Journal of Marketing,* January 1971, pp. 56–61.

50. P. B. Seetharaman, Andrew Ainslie, and Pradeep K. Chintagunta, "Investigating Household State Dependence Effects Across Categories," *Journal of Marketing Research* 36, November 1999, pp. 488–500.

51. Rothschild and Gaidis, "Behavioral Learning Theory."

52. "No Bar to Expansion," *Grocer,* January 22, 2005, p. 54.

53. Jack Neff, "Coupons Get Clipped," *Advertising Age,* November 5, 2001, pp. 1, 47.

54. Joe Keohane, "Fat Profits," *Condé Naste Portfolio,* February 2008, pp. 90.

55. Gary F. McKinnon, J. Patrick Kelly, and E. Doyle Robinson, "Sales Effects of Point-of-Purchase In-Store Signing," *Journal of Retailing,* Summer 1981, pp. 49–63.

56. Kathleen Deveny, "Displays Pay Off for Grocery Marketers," *Wall Street Journal,* October 15, 1992, pp. B1, B5.

57. "Study Claims Effectiveness of Point-of-Purchase," *Advertising Age,* July 24, 2001, *www.adage.com.*

58. "Brand Loyalty in the Food Industry," *The Food Institute Report,* November 5, 2001, p. 3.

59. George S. Day, "A Two-Dimensional Concept of Brand Loyalty," *Journal of Advertising Research,* August–September 1969, pp. 29–36; Jacoby and Kyner, "Brand Loyalty vs. Repeat Purchasing Behavior"; Jacob Jacoby and Robert W. Chestnut, *Brand Loyalty: Measurement and Management* (New York: Wiley, 1978).

60. Kyle B. Murray and Gerald Häubl, "Explaining Cognitive Lock-In: The Role of Skill-Based Habits of Use in Consumer Choice," *Journal of Consumer Research* 34, no. 1, 2007, pp. 77–88.

61. Jacob Jacoby, "A Model of Multi-Brand Loyalty," *Journal of Advertising Research,* June–July 1971, p. 26.

62. Ronald E. Frank, William F. Massy, and Thomas L. Lodahl, "Purchasing Behavior and Personal Attributes," *Journal of Advertising Research,* December 1969–January 1970, pp. 15–24.

63. R. M. Cunningham, "Brand Loyalty—What, Where, How Much," *Harvard Business Review,* January–February 1956, pp. 116–128; "Customer Loyalty to Store and Brand," *Harvard Business Review,* November–December 1961, pp. 127–137.

64. Day, "A Two-Dimensional Concept of Brand Loyalty."

65. Marnik G. Dekimpe, Martin Mellens, Jan-Benedict E. M. Steenkamp, and Piet Vanden Abeele, "Erosion and Variability in Brand Loyalty," *Marketing Science Institute Report No. 96–114,* August 1996, pp. 1–25.

66. Heline, "Brand Loyalty Isn't Dead."

67. Michelle L. Roehm, Ellen Bolman Pullins, and Harper A. Roehm Jr., "Designing Loyalty-Building Programs for Packaged Goods Brands," *Journal of Marketing Research,* May 2002, pp. 202–213.

68. Ran Kivetz and Itamar Simonson, "The Idiosyncratic Fit Heuristic: Effort Advantage as a Determinant of Consumer Response to Loyalty Programs," *Journal of Marketing Research,* November 2003, pp. 454–467.

69. Ran Kivetz and Itamar Simonson, "Earning the Right to Indulge: Effort as a Determinant of Customer Preferences Toward Frequency Program Rewards," *Journal of Marketing Research,* May 2002, pp. 155–170.

70. Kenneth Hein, "McD's, Sam Adams in Line with Shifting Loyalty Drivers," *Brandweek,* February 18, 2008, p. 8.

71. Laurie Petersen, "The Strategic Shopper," *Adweek's Marketing Week,* March 30, 1992, pp. 18–20.

72. Peter D. Dickson and Alan G. Sawyer, "Methods to Research Shoppers' Knowledge of Supermarket Prices," in ed. Richard J. Lutz, *Advances in Consumer Research,* vol. 12 (Provo, Utah: Association for Consumer Research, 1986), pp. 584–587.

73. Tulin Erdem, Glenn Mayhew, and Baohung Sun, "Understanding Reference-Price Shoppers: A Within- and Cross-Category Analysis," *Journal of Marketing Research,* November 2001, pp. 445–457.

74. Chris Janiszewski and Donald R. Lichtenstein, "A Range Theory Account of Price Perception," *Journal of Consumer Research* 25, March 1999, pp. 353–368; Kent B. Monroe and Susan M. Petroshius, "Buyers' Perception of Price: An Update of the Evidence," in eds. Harold H. Kassarjian and Thomas S. Robertson, *Perspectives in Consumer Behavior,* 3rd ed. (Dallas: Scott-Foresman, 1981), pp. 43–55.

75. Adrian Atterby, "Household Wipes Market Struggles to Win Over New Customers," *Nonwovens Industry,* February 2008, pp. 26–28.

76. Baba Shiv, Julie A. Edell Britton, and John W. Payne, "Re-Inquiries: Does Elaboration Increase or Decrease the Effectiveness of Negatively Versus Positively Framed Messages?" *Journal of Consumer Research,* June 2004, pp. 199–208.

77. Julie Baker, A. Parasuraman, Dhruv Grewal, and Glenn B. Voss, "The Influence of Multiple Store Environment Cues on Perceived Merchandise Value and Patronage Intentions," *Journal of Marketing*, April 2002, pp. 120–141.

78. Jiwoong Shin, "The Role of Selling Costs in Signaling Price Image," *Journal of Marketing Research*, August 2005, pp. 302–312.

79. Lisa E. Bolton, Luk Warlop, and Joseph W. Alba, "Consumer Perceptions of Price (Un)Fairness," *Journal of Consumer Research*, March 2003, pp. 474+; Joseph C. Nunes and Peter Boatwright, "Incidental Prices and Their Effect on Willingness to Pay," *Journal of Marketing Research*, November 2004, pp. 457–466.

80. Tuo Wang, R. Venkatesh, and Rabikar Chatterjee, "Reservation Price as a Range: An Incentive-Compatible Measurement Approach," *Journal of Marketing Research*, May 2007, pp. 200–213.

81. Mark Stiving and Russell S. Winer, "An Empirical Analysis of Price Endings with Scanner Data," *Journal of Consumer Research*, June 1997, pp. 57–76; Zarrel V. Lambert, "Perceived Prices as Related to Odd and Even Price Endings," *Journal of Retailing*, Fall 1975, pp. 13–22.

82. Aradhna Krishna, Mary Wagner, Carolyn Yoon, and Rashmi Adaval, "Effects of Extreme-Priced Products on Consumer Reservation Prices," *Journal of Consumer Psychology* 16, no. 2, 2006, pp. 176–190.

83. Kent B. Monroe, "The Influence of Price Differences and Brand Familiarity on Brand Preferences," *Journal of Consumer Research*, June 1976, pp. 42–49.

84. Joseph W. Alba, Carl F. Mela, Terence A. Shimp, and Joel E. Urbany, "The Effect of Discount Frequency and Depth on Consumer Price Judgments," *Journal of Consumer Research*, September 1999, pp. 99–114.

85. J. Jeffrey Inman, Anil C. Peter, and Priya Raghubir, "Framing the Deal: The Role of Restrictions in Accentuating Deal Value," *Journal of Consumer Research*, June 1997, pp. 68–79.

86. Dhruv Grewal, Howard Marmorstein, and Arun Sharma, "Communicating Price Information Through Semantic Cues: The Moderating Effects of Situation and Discount Size," *Journal of Consumer Research*, September 1996, pp. 148–155.

87. Priya Raghubir and Joydeep Srivastava, "Effect of Face Value on Product Valuation in Foreign Currencies," *Journal of Consumer Research*, December 2002, pp. 335–347.

88. Margaret C. Campbell, "'Says Who?!' How the Source of Price Information and Affect Influence Perceived Price (Un)fairness," *Journal of Marketing Research*, May 2007, pp. 261–271.

89. *Supermarket Shoppers in a Period of Economic Uncertainty* (New York: Yankelovich, Skelly, & White, 1982), p. 53; Robert Blattberg, Thomas Buesing, Peter Peacock, and Subrata K. Sen, "Who Is the Deal-Prone Consumer?" in ed. H. Keith Hunt, *Advances in Consumer Research*, vol. 5 (Ann Arbor, Mich.: Association for Consumer Research, 1978), pp. 57–62.

90. Donald R. Lichtenstein, Richard G. Netemeyer, and Scot Burton, "Assessing the Domain Specificity of Deal Proneness: A Field Study," *Journal of Consumer Research*, December 1995, pp. 314–326.

91. "Vox Pop: What Does the Future Hold for Price Comparison on the Web?" *Revolution*, May 18, 2004, p. 22.

92. Betsy Spethmann, "Re-Engineering the Price–Value Equation," *Brandweek*, September 20, 1993, pp. 44–47.

93. Christine Bittar, "Tablets, Scents, and Sensibility," *Brandweek*, June 4, 2001, p. S59.

94. Nelson Schwartz, "Colgate Cleans Up," *Fortune*, April 2000, *www.adage.com;* Tara Parker-Pope, "Colgate Places a Huge Bet on a Germ-Fighter," *Wall Street Journal*, December 29, 1997, pp. B1, B2.

95. Kathleen Deveny, "How Country's Biggest Brands Are Faring at the Supermarket," *Wall Street Journal*, March 24, 1994, p. B1.

96. "Manufacturers Offered More Than $250 Billion in Coupons in 2003 at a Cost of $7 Billion, According to the Promotion Marketing Association," *Incentive*, January 2005, p. 14.

97. Dan Levin, "Shifting Coupons, from Clip and Save to Point and Click," *New York Times*, December 27, 2007, p. C3.

98. "International Coupon Trends," *Direct Marketing*, August 1993, pp. 47–49, 83.

99. William J. Holstein, "Why Wal-Mart Can't Find Happiness in Japan," *Fortune*, August 6, 2007, p. 73.

100. "Wal-Mart Opening More Retail Outlets (China Expansion)," *World Trade*, February 2008, p. 12.

101. Daniel J. Howard and Charles Gengler, "Emotional Contagion Effects on Product Attitudes," *Journal of Consumer Research*, September 2001, pp. 189–201.

102. Susan T. Fiske, "Schema Triggered Affect: Applications to Social Perception," in eds. Margaret S. Clark and Susan T. Fiske, *Affect and Cognition: The 17th Annual Carnegie Symposium on Cognition* (Hillsdale, N.J.: Lawrence Erlbaum, 1982), pp. 55–77; Mita Sujan, James R. Bettman, and Harish Sujan, "Effects of Consumer Expectations on Information Processing and Selling Encounters," *Journal of Marketing Research*, November 1986, pp. 346–353.

103. Peter L. Wright, "An Adaptive Consumer's View of Attitudes and Choice Mechanisms as Viewed by an Equally Adaptive Advertiser," in ed. William D. Wells, *Attitude Research at Bay* (Chicago: American Marketing Association, 1976), pp. 113–131.

104. Baba Shiv and Alexander Fedorikhin, "Heart and Mind in Conflict: The Interplay of Affect and Cognition in Consumer Decision Making," *Journal of Consumer Research* 26, December 1999, pp. 278–292.

105. Rebecca Walker Naylor, Rajagopal Raghunathan, and Suresh Ramanathan, "Promotions Spontaneously Induce a Positive Evaluative Response," *Journal of Consumer Psychology* 16, no. 3, 2006, pp. 295–305.

106. Susan T. Fiske and Mark A. Pavelchak, "Category-Based Versus Piecemeal-Based Affective Responses:

Developments in Schema-Triggered Affect," in eds. R. M. Sorrentino and E. T. Higgins, *The Handbook of Motivation and Cognition: Foundations of Social Behavior* (New York: Guilford, 1986), pp. 167–203; David M. Boush and Barbara Loken, "A Process-Tracing Study of Brand Extension Evaluation," *Journal of Marketing Research,* February 1991, pp. 16–28.

107. Fiske, "Schema Triggered Affect"; Mita Sujan, "Consumer Knowledge: Effects on Evaluation Strategies Mediating Consumer Judgments," *Journal of Consumer Research,* June 1985, pp. 31–46.

108. Claire Atkinson, "Whiten Your Teeth Even While Walking the Dog," *New York Times,* July 27, 2007, p. C5.

109. Ralph I. Allison and Kenneth P. Uhl, "Influence of Beer Brand Identification on Taste Perception," *Journal of Marketing Research,* August 1964, pp. 36–39.

110. Wayne D. Hoyer and Stephen P. Brown, "Effects of Brand Awareness on Choice for a Common, Repeat-Purchase Product," *Journal of Consumer Research,* September 1990, pp. 141–148.

111. Leong, "Consumer Decision Making for Common, Repeat-Purchase Products."

112. M. Carole Macklin, "Preschoolers' Learning of Brand Names from Visual Cues," *Journal of Consumer Research,* December 1996, pp. 251–261.

113. Jim Stafford, "Fame of Brand Names Has Changed with Time," *Daily Oklahoman,* February 2, 2005, *www.newsok.com;* Richard W. Stevenson, "The Brands with Billion Dollar Names," *New York Times,* October 28, 1988, p. A1.

114. Eric Yang, "Co-brand or Be Damned," *Brandweek,* November 21, 1994, pp. 21–24.

115. "Frozen Breakfast: Kid Power," *Frozen Food Age,* January 2005, p. S6.

116. "T.G.I. Friday's, Based Here, Has Added Two Dishes to Its Jack Daniel's Grill Line," *Nation's Restaurant News Daily NewsFax,* October 18, 2006, n.p.; Laurie Snyder and Elizabeth Jensen, "Liquor Logos Pop Up in Some Surprising Places," *Wall Street Journal,* August 26, 1997, pp. B1, B15.

117. Karen V. Fernandez and Dennis L. Rosen, "The Effectiveness of Information and Color in Yellow Pages Advertising," *Journal of Advertising* 29, no. 2, Summer 2000, pp. 61–73.

118. Robert W. Veryzer and J. Wesley Hutchinson, "The Influence of Unity and Prototypicality on Aesthetic Responses to New Product Designs," *Journal of Consumer Research,* March 1998, pp. 374–394.

119. "McDonald's China Strategy," *Los Angeles Times,* September 17, 2007, p. C4.

120. "Big Portions: Barilla," *The Economist,* June 23, 2007, p. 75.

121. M. Venkatesan, "Cognitive Consistency and Novelty Seeking," in eds. Scott Ward and Thomas S. Robertson, *Consumer Behavior: Theoretical Sources* (Englewood Cliffs, N.J.: Prentice-Hall, 1973), pp. 354–384; Leigh McAlister, "A Dynamic Attribute Satiation Model of

Variety Seeking Behavior," *Journal of Consumer Research,* September 1982, pp. 141–150.

122. Rebecca K. Ratner, Barbara E. Kahn, and Daniel Kahneman, "Choosing Less-Preferred Experiences for the Sake of Variety," *Journal of Consumer Research* 26, June 1999, pp. 1–15.

123. Rebecca K. Ratner and Barbara E. Kahn, "The Impact of Private Versus Public Consumption on Variety-Seeking Behavior," *Journal of Consumer Research,* September 2002, pp. 246+.

124. Rosario Vázquez-Carrasco and Gordon R. Foxall, "Positive Versus Negative Switching Barriers: The Influence of Service Consumers' Need for Variety," *Journal of Consumer Behavior* 5, no. 4, 2006, pp. 367–379.

125. Hans C. M. Van Trijp, Wayne D. Hoyer, and J. Jeffrey Inman, "Why Switch? Product Category-Level Explanations for True Variety Seeking," *Journal of Marketing Research,* August 1996, pp. 281–292; Wayne D. Hoyer and Nancy M. Ridgway, "Variety Seeking as an Explanation for Exploratory Purchase Behavior: A Theoretical Model," in ed. Thomas C. Kinnear, *Advances in Consumer Research,* vol. 11 (Ann Arbor, Mich.: Association for Consumer Research, 1984), pp. 114–119.

126. J. Jeffrey Inman, "The Role of Sensory-Specific Satiety in Attribute-Level Variety Seeking," *Journal of Consumer Research* 28, June 2001, pp. 105–120.

127. Saatya Menon and Barbara E. Kahn, "The Impact of Context on Variety Seeking in Product Choices," *Journal of Consumer Research,* December 1995, pp. 285–295.

128. Erich A. Joachimsthaler and John L. Lastovicka, "Optimal Stimulation Level–Exploratory Behavior Models," *Journal of Consumer Research,* December 1984, pp. 830–835.

129. Albert Mehrabian and James Russell, *An Approach to Environmental Psychology* (Cambridge, Mass.: MIT Press, 1974).

130. Linda L. Price and Nancy M. Ridgway, "Use Innovativeness, Vicarious Exploration and Purchase Exploration: Three Facets of Consumer Varied Behavior," in ed. Bruce Walker, *American Marketing Association Educators' Conference Proceedings* (Chicago: American Marketing Association, 1982), pp. 56–60.

131. "Brewing Variety," *Beverage Industry,* November 2004, p. 39.

132. Barbara E. Kahn and Brian Wansink, "The Influence of Assortment Structure on Perceived Variety and Consumption Quantities," *Journal of Consumer Research,* March 2004, pp. 519–533.

133. Fritz Strack, Lioba Werth, and Roland Deutsch, "Reflective and Impulsive Determinants of Consumer Behavior," *Journal of Consumer Psychology* 16, no. 2, 2006, pp. 205–216; Dennis W. Rook, "The Buying Impulse," *Journal of Consumer Research,* September 1987, pp. 189–199; Craig J. Thompson, William B. Locander, and Howard R. Pollio, "The Lived Meaning of Free Choice: Existential–Phenomenological Description of

Everyday Consumer Experiences of Contemporary Married Women," *Journal of Consumer Research,* December 1990, pp. 346–361.

134. Jacqueline J. Kacen and Julie Anne Lee, "The Influence of Culture on Consumer Impulsive Buying Behavior," *Journal of Consumer Psychology* 12, no. 2, 2002, pp. 163–176.

135. See Suresh Ramanathan and Geeta Menon, "Time-Varying Effects of Chronic Hedonic Goals on Impulsive Behavior," *Journal of Marketing Research,* November 2006, pp. 628–641.

136. Roy F. Baumeister, "Yielding to Temptation: Self-Control Failure, Impulsive Behavior, and Consumer Behavior," *Journal of Consumer Research,* March 2002, pp. 670–676.

137. Kathleen D. Vons and Ronald J. Faber, "Spent Resources: Self-Regulatory Resource Availability Affects Impulse Buying," *Journal of Consumer Research* 33, no. 4, 2007, pp. 537–548.

138. Kathleen D. Vohs, "Self-Regulatory Resources Power the Reflective System: Evidence from Five Domains," *Journal of Consumer Psychology* 16, no. 3, 2006, pp. 217–223.

139. Deborah J. MacInnis and Vanessa M. Patrick, "Spotlight on Affect: Affect and Affective Forecasting in Impulse Control," *Journal of Consumer Psychology* 16, no. 3, 2006, pp. 224–231.

140. J. Jeffrey Inman and Russell S. Winer, "Where the Rubber Meets the Road: A Model of In-store Consumer Decision Making," *Marketing Science Institute Report Summary,* December 1998, pp. 98–122; "How We Shop . . . From Mass to Market," *Brandweek,* January 9, 1995, p. 17; Danny Bellenger, D. H. Robertson, and Elizabeth C. Hirschman, "Impulse Buying Varies by Product," *Journal of Advertising Research,* December 1978–January 1979, pp. 15–18.

141. Cathy J. Cobb and Wayne D. Hoyer, "Planned vs. Impulse Purchase Behavior," *Journal of Retailing,* Winter 1986, pp. 384–409.

142. Rook, "The Buying Impulse."

143. Russell W. Belk, "Materialism: Trait Aspects of Living in a Material World," *Journal of Consumer Research,* December 1985, pp. 265–280; P. S. Raju, "Optimum Stimulation Level: Its Relationship to Personality, Demographics, and Exploratory Behavior," *Journal of Consumer Research,* December 1980, pp. 272–282; Danny Bellenger and P. K. Korgaonkar, "Profiling the Recreational Shopper," *Journal of Retailing,* Fall 1980, pp. 77–92.

144. Dennis W. Rook and Robert J. Fisher, "Normative Influences on Impulsive Buying Behavior," *Journal of Consumer Research,* December 1995, pp. 305–313; Radhika Puri, "Measuring and Modifying Consumer Impulsiveness: A Cost–Benefit Accessibility Framework," *Journal of Consumer Psychology* 5, no. 2, 1996, pp. 87–114.

145. Xueming Luo, "How Does Shopping with Others Influence Impulsive Purchasing?" *Journal of Consumer Psychology* 15, no. 4, 2005, pp. 288–294.

146. Inman and Winer, "Where the Rubber Meets the Road."

147. Andrew Adam Newman, "A Package That Lights Up on the Shelf," *New York Times,* March 4, 2008, p. C2.

148. Bussey, "Japan's Wary Shoppers Worry Two Capitals."

149. Patricia O'Connell, "The Middle Class's Urge to Splurge," *BusinessWeek Online,* December 3, 2003, *www.businessweek.com.*

150. Melissa Allison, "Starbucks to Offer Free Cups of New Brew Today," *Seattle Times,* April 8, 2008, *www.seattletimes.com;* Korky Vann, "Buying into Free Samples," *Hartford Courant,* March 6, 2008, p. G1; Kate Macarthur, "Banking on a Free Lunch," *Crain's Chicago Business,* June 25, 2007, p. 14; "Sampling Lets Fast-Food Chains Engage New, Existing Customers," *PR Week (US),* June 18, 2007, p. 11; Jack Neff, "Viva Viva! K-C Boosts Brand's Marketing," *Advertising Age,* June 11, 2007, p. 4; Libby Copeland, "An Ocean of Promotion: For Spring Breakers, the Selling Never Stops," *Washington Post,* March 28, 2007, p. A1.

Chapter 11

1. Amy Bickers, "Put Costco on Your 'To Buy' List?" *WashingtonPost.com,* March 28, 2008, *www.washingtonpost.com;* Kris Hudson, "Turning Shopping Trips into Treasure Hunts," *Wall Street Journal,* August 27, 2007, p. B1; Kris Hudson, "Costco Seeks to Lift Margins by Tightening Return Policy," *Wall Street Journal,* February 27, 2007, p. B4; *costco.com.*

2. For a review, see William H. Cummings and M. Venkatesan, "Cognitive Dissonance and Consumer Behavior: A Review of the Evidence," *Journal of Marketing Research,* August 1976, pp. 303–308; also see Dieter Frey and Marita Rosch, "Information Seeking After Decisions: The Roles of Novelty of Information and Decision Reversibility," *Personality and Social Psychology Bulletin,* March 1984, pp. 91–98.

3. Michael Tsiros and Vikas Mittal, "Regret: A Model of Its Antecedents and Consequences in Consumer Decision Making," *Journal of Consumer Research* 26, March 2000, pp. 401–417.

4. Lisa J. Abendroth and Kristin Diehl, "Now or Never: Effects of Limited Purchase Opportunities on Patterns of Regret over Time, " *Journal of Consumer Research* 33, no. 3, 2006, pp. 342–351.

5. Ran Kivetz and Anat Keinan, "Repenting Hyperopia: An Analysis of Self-Control Regrets," *Journal of Consumer Research* 33, no. 2, 2006, pp. 273–282.

6. J. Jeffrey Inman and Marcel Zeelenberg, "Regret in Repeat Purchase Versus Switching Decisions: The Attenuating Role of Decision Justifiability," *Journal of Consumer Research,* June 2002, pp. 116–128.

7. Rik Pieters and Marcel Zeelenberg, "A Theory of Regret Regulation 1.0," *Journal of Consumer Psychology* 17, no. 1, 2007, pp. 3–18; J. Jeffrey Inman, "Regret Regulation: Disentangling Self-Reproach from Learning," *Journal of Consumer Psychology* 17, no. 1, 2007, pp. 19–24; Rik Pieters and Marcel Zeelenberg, "A Theory of Regret Regulation 1.1," *Journal of Consumer Psychology* 17, no. 1, 2007, pp. 29–35.

8. Neal J. Roese, Amy Summerville, and Florian Fessel, "Regret and Behavior: Comment on Zeelenberg and

Pieters," *Journal of Consumer Psychology* 17, no. 1, 2007, pp. 25–28.

9. Stephen J. Hoch and John Deighton, "Managing What Consumers Learn from Experience," *Journal of Marketing,* April 1989, pp. 1–20.

10. Ziv Carmon, Klaus Wertenbroch, and Marcel Zeelenberg, "Option Attachment: When Deliberating Makes Choosing Feel Like Losing," *Journal of Consumer Research,* June 2003, pp. 15–29.

11. Allan Pavio, *Imagery and Verbal Processes* (New York: Holt, Rinehart, & Winston, 1981).

12. Eric M. Eisenstein and J. Wesley Hutchinson, "Action-Based Learning: Goals and Attention in the Acquisition of Market Knowledge," *Journal of Marketing Research,* May 2006, pp. 244–258.

13. Robert E. Smith and William R. Swinyard, "Information Response Models: An Integrated Approach," *Journal of Marketing,* Winter 1982, pp. 81–93; Deanna S. Kempf and Robert E. Smith, "Consumer Processing of Product Trial and the Influence of Prior Advertising: A Structural Modeling Approach," *Journal of Marketing Research,* August 1998, pp. 325–338.

14. Ida E. Berger and Andrew A. Mitchell, "The Effect of Advertising on Attitude Accessibility, Attitude Confidence, and the Attitude-Behavior Relationship," *Journal of Consumer Research,* December 1989, pp. 269–279; Alice A. Wright and John G. Lynch Jr., "Communication Effects of Advertising vs. Direct Experience When Both Search and Experience Attributes Are Present," *Journal of Consumer Research,* March 1995, pp. 708–718.

15. Patricia M. West, "Predicting Preferences: An Examination of Agent Learning," *Journal of Consumer Research,* June 1996, pp. 68–80.

16. Jennifer Aaker, Susan Fournier, and S. Adam Brasel, "When Good Brands Do Bad," *Journal of Consumer Research,* June 2004, pp. 1–16.

17. Bob Tedeschi, "To Raise Shopper Satisfaction, Web Merchants Turn to Videos," *New York Times,* July 2, 2007, p. C4.

18. Merrie Brucks, "The Effects of Product Class Knowledge on Information Search Behavior," *Journal of Consumer Research,* June 1985, pp. 1–16.

19. Joseph W. Alba and J. Wesley Hutchinson, "Dimensions of Consumer Expertise," *Journal of Consumer Research,* March 1987, pp. 411–454.

20. Eric J. Johnson and J. Edward Russo, "Product Familiarity and Learning New Information," *Journal of Consumer Research,* June 1984, pp. 542–551.

21. Stephen J. Hoch and Young-Won Ha, "Consumer Learning: Advertising and the Ambiguity of Product Experience," *Journal of Consumer Research,* October 1986, pp. 221–233.

22. A. V. Muthukrishnan and Frank R. Kardes, "Persistent Preferences for Product Attributes: The Effects of the Initial Choice Context and Uninformative Experience," *Journal of Consumer Research,* June 2001, pp. 89–104.

23. Paul Herr, Steven J. Sherman, and Russell H. Fazio, "On the Consequences of Priming: Assimilation and Contrast Effects," *Journal of Experimental Social Psychology,* July 1983, pp. 323–340; Hoch and Ha, "Consumer Learning."

24. Reid Hastie, "Causes and Effects of Causal Attributions," *Journal of Personality and Social Psychology,* July 1984, pp. 44–56; Thomas K. Srull, Meryl Lichtenstein, and Myron Rothbart, "Associative Storage and Retrieval Processes in Person Memory," *Journal of Experimental Psychology: General* 11, no. 6, 1985, pp. 316–435.

25. Durairaj Maheswaran, "Country of Origin as a Stereotype: Effects of Consumer Expertise and Attribute Strength on Product Evaluations," *Journal of Consumer Research,* September 1994, pp. 354–365.

26. John Deighton, "The Interaction of Advertising and Evidence," *Journal of Consumer Research,* December 1984, pp. 763–770; Hoch and Ha, "Consumer Learning."

27. Bernard Weiner, "Spontaneous Causal Thinking," *Psychological Bulletin,* January 1985, pp. 74–84.

28. Hoch and Deighton, "Managing What Consumers Learn from Experience."

29. Kenneth Hein, "This Fine Wine Is Worth a Cool Million," *Brandweek,* February 5, 2001, p. 40.

30. Youjae Yi, "A Critical Review of Consumer Satisfaction," *Review of Marketing* (Chicago: American Marketing Association, 1992), pp. 68–123.

31. Richard L. Oliver, "Processing of the Satisfaction Response in Consumption: A Suggested Framework and Research Propositions," *Journal of Consumer Satisfaction, Dissatisfaction, and Complaining Behavior* 2, 1989, pp. 1–16; Haim Mano and Richard L. Oliver, "Assessing the Dimensionality and Structure of the Consumption Experience: Evaluation, Feeling, and Satisfaction, *Journal of Consumer Research,* December 1993, pp. 451–466.

32. Haim Mano and Richard L. Oliver, "Assessing the Dimensionality and Structure of the Consumption Experience: Evaluation, Feeling, and Satisfaction," *Journal of Consumer Research,* December 1993, pp. 451–466.

33. Michael D. Johnson, Eugene W. Anderson, and Claes Fornell, "Rational and Adaptive Performance Expectations in a Customer Satisfaction Framework," *Journal of Consumer Research,* March 1995, pp. 695–707.

34. Marsha L. Richins and Peter H. Bloch, "Post-purchase Satisfaction: Incorporating the Effects of Involvement and Time," *Journal of Business Research,* September 1991, pp. 145–158; Vikas Mittal and Wagner A. Kamakura, "Satisfaction, Repurchase Intent, and Repurchase Behavior: Investigating the Moderating Effect of Customer Characteristics," *Journal of Marketing Research,* February 2001, pp. 131–142.

35. Christian Homburg, Nicole Koschate, and Wayne D. Hoyer, "Do Satisfied Customers Really Pay More? A Study of the Relationship Between Customer Satisfaction and Willingness to Pay," *Journal of Marketing,* April 2005, pp. 84–96.

36. David M. Szymanski and David H. Henard, "Customer Satisfaction: A Meta-Analysis of the Empirical Evidence," *Journal of the Academy of Marketing Science* 29,

no. 1, 2001, pp. 16–35; Anders Gustafsson, Michael D. Johnson, and Inger Roos, "The Effects of Customer Satisfaction, Relationship Commitment Dimensions, and Triggers on Customer Retention," *Journal of Marketing*, October 2005, pp. 210–218.

37. Todd A. Mooradian and James M. Oliver, "'I Can't Get No Satisfaction': The Impact of Personality and Emotion on Postpurchase Processes," *Psychology and Marketing* 14, no. 4, 1997, pp. 379–393; Xueming Luo and Christian Homburg, "Neglected Outcomes of Customer Satisfaction," *Journal of Marketing*, April 2007, pp. 133–149.

38. Gustafsson et al., "The Effects of Customer Satisfaction, Relationship Commitment Dimensions, and Triggers on Customer Retention."

39. Kathleen Seiders, Glenn B. Voss, and Dhruv Grewal, "Do Satisfied Customers Buy More? Examining Moderating Influences in a Retailing Context," *Journal of Marketing*, October 2005, pp. 26–43.

40. Bruce Cooil, Timothy L. Keiningham, and Lerzan Aksoy, "A Longitudinal Analysis of Customer Satisfaction and Share of Wallet: Investigating the Moderating Effect of Customer Characteristics," *Journal of Marketing*, January 2007, pp. 67–83.

41. Tom Edmonds, "Speakers Examine Caring, Loyalty Issues," *Furniture Today*, February 25, 2005, *www.furnituretoday.com*.

42. Gail Kachadourian, "NADA Promotes 24-hour Surveys," *Automotive News*, January 31, 2005, p. 32.

43. Douglas Bowman and Das Narayandas, "Managing Customer-Initiated Contacts with Manufacturers: The Impact of Share of Category Requirements and Word-of-Mouth Behavior," *Journal of Marketing Research*, August 2001, pp. 281–297.

44. Vavra, "Learning from Your Losses."

45. Klopp and Sterlickhi, "Customer Satisfaction Just Catching On in Europe."

46. Richard L. Oliver, "A Cognitive Model of the Antecedents and Consequences of Satisfaction Decisions," *Journal of Marketing Research*, November 1980, pp. 460–469; Yi, "A Critical Review of Consumer Satisfaction," p. 92; see also Douglas M. Stayman, Dana L. Alden, and Karen H. Smith, "Some Effects of Schematic Processing on Consumer Expectations and Disconfirmation Judgments," *Journal of Consumer Research*, September 1992, pp. 240–255.

47. Yi, "A Critical Review of Consumer Satisfaction," p. 92; see also Stayman, Alden, and Smith, "Some Effects of Schematic Processing on Consumer Expectations and Disconfirmation Judgments," pp. 240–255.

48. Praveen K. Kopalle and Donald R. Lehman, "The Effects of Advertised and Observed Quality on Expectations About New Product Quality," *Journal of Marketing Research*, August 1995, pp. 280–291; Stephen A. LaTour and Nancy C. Peat, "The Role of Situationally-Produced Expectations, Others' Experiences, and Prior Experiences in Determining Satisfaction," in ed. Jerry C. Olson, *Advances in Consumer Research* (Ann Arbor, Mich.: Association for Consumer Research, 1980), pp. 588–592; Ernest R. Cadotte, Robert B. Woodruff, and Roger L. Jenkins, "Expectations and Norms in Models of Consumer Satisfaction," *Journal of Marketing Research*, August 1987, pp. 305–314.

49. Ruth N. Bolton and James H. Drew, "A Multistage Model of Customers' Assessments of Service Quality and Value," *Journal of Consumer Research*, March 1991, pp. 375–384; Michael D. Johnson, Eugene W. Anderson, and Claes Fornell, "Rational and Adaptive Performance Expectations in a Customer Satisfaction Framework," *Journal of Consumer Research*, March 1995, pp. 695–707.

50. Glenn B. Voss, A. Parasuraman, and Dhruv Grewal, "The Roles of Price, Performance, and Expectations in Determining Satisfaction in Service Exchanges," *Journal of Marketing*, October 1998, pp. 46–61; A. Parasuraman, Valerie A. Zeithaml, and Leonard L. Berry, "SERVQUAL: A Multiple-Item Scale for Measuring Consumer Perceptions of Service Quality," *Journal of Retailing*, Spring 1988, pp. 12–36.

51. Bob Tedeschi, "Online Retailers Say They Are Ready to Deliver Goods to Christmas Shoppers Who Waited Until the Last Minute," *New York Times*, December 20, 2004, p. C4.

52. Stephanie Dellande, Mary C. Gilly, and John L. Graham, "Gaining Compliance and Losing Weight: The Role of the Service Provider in Health Care Services," *Journal of Marketing*, July 2004, pp. 78–91.

53. Susan Fournier and David Glen Mick, "Rediscovering Satisfaction," *Journal of Marketing* 63, October 1999, pp. 5–23.

54. Simona Botti and Ann L. McGill, "When Choosing Is Not Deciding: The Effect of Perceived Responsibility on Satisfaction," *Journal of Consumer Research* 33, no. 2, 2006, pp. 211–219.

55. Ashwani Monga and Michael J. Houston, "Fading Optimism in Products: Temporal Changes in Expectations About Performance," *Journal of Marketing Research*, November 2006, pp. 654–663.

56. Chezy Ofir and Itamar Simonson, "In Search of Negative Customer Feedback: The Effect of Expecting to Evaluate on Satisfaction Evaluations," *Journal of Marketing Research* 38, May 2001, pp. 170–182.

57. Baba Shiv, Ziv Carmon, and Dan Ariely, "Placebo Effects of Marketing Actions: Consumers May Get What They Pay For," *Journal of Marketing Research*, November 2005, pp. 383–393.

58. Caglar Irmak, Lauren G. Block, and Gavan J. Fitzsimons, "The Placebo Effect in Marketing: Sometimes You Just Have to Want It to Work," *Journal of Marketing Research*, November 2005, pp. 406–409.

59. David K. Tse and Peter C. Wilson, "Models of Consumer Satisfaction Formation: An Extension," *Journal of Marketing Research*, May 1988, pp. 204–212; Richard L. Oliver, "Cognitive, Affective, and Attribute Bases of the Satisfaction Response," *Journal of Consumer Research*, December 1993, pp. 418–430; Richard L. Oliver and

Wayne S. DeSarbo, "Response Determinants in Satisfaction Judgments," *Journal of Consumer Research*, March 1988, pp. 495–507.

60. Gilbert A. Churchill and Carol Supranant, "An Investigation into the Determinants of Customer Satisfaction," *Journal of Marketing Research*, November 1982, pp. 491–504; Richard L. Oliver and William O. Bearden, "The Role of Involvement in Satisfaction Processes," in eds. Richard P. Bagozzi and Alice M. Tybout, *Advances in Consumer Research*, vol. 10 (Ann Arbor, Mich.: Association for Consumer Research, 1983), pp. 250–255; Paul G. Patterson, "Expectations and Product Performance as Determinants of Satisfaction for a High Involvement Purchase," *Psychology and Marketing*, September–October 1993, pp. 449–465.

61. Robert A. Westbrook and Michael D. Reilly, "Value-Percept Disparity: An Alternative to the Disconfirmation of Expectations Theory of Consumer Satisfaction," in eds. Richard P. Bagozzi and Alice M. Tybout, *Advances in Consumer Research*, vol. 10 (Ann Arbor, Mich.: Association for Consumer Research, 1983), pp. 256–261.

62. Richard W. Olshavsky and John A. Miller, "Consumer Expectations, Product Performance, and Perceived Product Quality," *Journal of Marketing Research*, February 1972, pp. 469–499.

63. Goll, "Pizza Hut Tosses Its Pies into the Ring."

64. Diane Halstead, Cornelia Droge, and M. Bixby Cooper, "Product Warranties and Post-purchase Service," *Journal of Services Marketing* 7, no. 1, 1993, pp. 33–40; Joshua Lyle Wiener, "Are Warranties Accurate Signals of Product Reliability?" *Journal of Consumer Research*, September 1985, pp. 245–250.

65. Gavin Off, "Renovated Englewood, Fla., Golf Course Back in Business," *The Sun (Port Charlotte, Florida)*, November 20, 2004, *www.sun-herald.com*.

66. Bernard Weiner, "Reflections and Reviews: Attributional Thoughts About Consumer Behavior," *Journal of Consumer Research* 27, December 2000, pp. 382–287; Valerie S. Folkes, "Consumer Reactions to Product Failure: An Attributional Approach," *Journal of Consumer Research*, March 1984, pp. 398–409; Valerie S. Folkes, "Recent Attribution Research in Consumer Behavior: A Review and New Directions," *Journal of Consumer Research*, March 1988, pp. 548–565; Richard W. Mizerski, Linda L. Golden, and Jerome B. Kernan, "The Attribution Process in Consumer Decision Making," *Journal of Consumer Research*, September 1979, pp. 123–140.

67. Mary Jo Bitner, "Evaluating Service Encounters: The Effects of Physical Surroundings and Employee Responses," *Journal of Marketing*, April 1990, pp. 69–82.

68. Valerie S. Folkes, Susan Koletsky, and John L. Graham, "A Field Study of Causal Inferences and Consumer Reaction: The View from the Airport," *Journal of Consumer Research*, March 1987, pp. 534–539.

69. Neeli Bendapudi and Robert P. Leone, "Psychological Implications of Customer Participation in Co-Production," *Journal of Marketing*, January 2003, pp. 14–28.

70. Michael Tsiros, Vikas Mittal, and William T. Ross Jr., "The Role of Attributions in Customer Satisfaction: A Reexamination," *Journal of Consumer Research*, September 2004, pp. 476–483.

71. Andrea C. Morales, "Giving Firms an E for Effort: Consumer Responses to High-Effort Firms," *Journal of Consumer Research* 31, no. 4, 2005, pp. 806–812.

72. David L. Margulius, "Going to the A.T.M. for More Than a Fistful of Twenties," *New York Times*, January 17, 2002, p. D7; Eleena de Lisser, "Banks Court Disenchanted Customers," *Wall Street Journal*, August 30, 1993, p. B1.

73. Richard L. Oliver and John E. Swan, "Equity and Disconfirmation Paradigms as Influences on Merchant and Product Satisfaction," *Journal of Consumer Research*, December 1989, pp. 372–383; Elaine G. Walster, G. William Walster, and Ellen Berscheid, *Equity: Theory and Research* (Boston: Allyn & Bacon, 1978).

74. Peter R. Darke and Darren W. Dahl, "Fairness and Discounts: The Subjective Value of a Bargain," *Journal of Consumer Psychology* 13, no. 3, 2003, pp. 328–338.

75. Richard L. Oliver and John L. Swan, "Consumer Perceptions of Interpersonal Equity and Satisfaction in Transactions, A Field Survey Approach," *Journal of Marketing*, April 1989, pp. 21–35.

76. Ruth N. Bolton and Katherine N. Lemon, "A Dynamic Model of Customers' Usage of Services: Usage as an Antecedent and Consequence of Satisfaction," *Journal of Marketing Research* 36, May 1999, pp. 171–186.

77. Rebecca J. Slotegraaf and J. Jeffrey Inman, "Longitudinal Shifts in the Drivers of Satisfaction with Product Quality: The Role of Attribute Resolvability," *Journal of Marketing Research*, August 2004, pp. 269–280.

78. James G. Maxhamm III and Richard G. Netemeyer, "Firms Reap What They Sow: The Effects of Shared Values and Perceived Organizational Justice on Customers' Evaluations of Complaint Handling," *Journal of Marketing*, January 2003, pp. 46–62.

79. Diane M. Phillips and Hans Baumgartner, "The Role of Consumption Emotions in the Satisfaction Response," *Journal of Consumer Psychology* 12, no. 3, 2002, pp. 243–252; Westbrook, "Product/Consumption-Based Affective Responses and Postpurchase Processes"; Robert A. Westbrook and Richard L. Oliver, "The Dimensionality of Consumption Emotion Patterns and Consumer Satisfaction," *Journal of Consumer Research*, June 1991, pp. 84–91; Mano and Oliver, "Assessing the Dimensionality and Structure of the Consumption Experience."

80. Westbrook, "Product/Consumption-Based Affective Responses and Postpurchase Processes."

81. Westbrook and Oliver, "The Dimensionality of Consumption Emotion Patterns."

82. Thorsten Hennig-Thurau, Markus Groth, and Michael Paul, "Are All Smiles Created Equal? How Emotional Contagion and Emotional Labor Affect Service Relationships," *Journal of Marketing*, July 2006, pp. 58–73.

83. Adam Duhachek and Dawn Iacobucci, "Consumer Personality and Coping: Testing Rival Theories of Process,"

Journal of Consumer Psychology 15, no. 1, 2005, pp. 52–63; Adam Duhachek, "Coping: A Multidimensional, Hierarchical Framework of Responses to Stressful Consumption Episodes," *Journal of Consumer Research* 32, June 2005, pp. 41–53.

84. Richard L. Oliver, "Measurement and Evaluation of Satisfaction Processes in Retail Settings," *Journal of Retailing*, Fall 1981, pp. 25–48.

85. Christian Homburg, Nicole Koschate, and Wayne D. Hoyer, "The Role of Cognition and Affect in the Formation of Customer Satisfaction: A Dynamic Perspective," *Journal of Marketing*, July 2006, pp. 21–31; Stacy L. Wood and C. Page Moreau, "Loathing? How Emotion Influences the Evaluation and Early Use of Innovations," *Journal of Marketing*, July 2006, pp. 44–57.

86. Sarah Fisher Gardial, D. Scott Clemons, Robert B. Woodruff, David W. Schumann, and Mary Jane Burns, "Comparing Consumers' Recall of Prepurchase and Postpurchase Evaluation Experiences," *Journal of Consumer Research*, March 1994, pp. 548–560.

87. Vanessa M. Patrick, Deborah J. MacInnis, and C. Whan Park, "Not As Happy As I Thought I'd Be? Affective Misforecasting and Product Evaluations," *Journal of Consumer Research* 33, no. 4, 2007, pp. 479–489; Daniel T. Gilbert, Elizabeth C. Pinel, Timothy D. Wilson, Stephen J. Blumberg, and Thalia P. Wheatley, "Immune Neglect: A Source of Durability Bias in Affective Forecasting," *Journal of Personality and Social Psychology* 75, no. 3, 1998, pp. 617–638; George Loewenstein and David A. Schkade, "Wouldn't It Be Nice? Predicting Future Feelings," in *Well-Being: The Foundations of Hedonic Psychology* eds. N. Schwartz, D. Kahneman, and E. Diener, (New York: Russell Sage Foundation, 1999), pp. 85–105.

88. Susan Greco, "Saints Alive!" *Inc.*, August 2001, pp. 44–45.

89. C. B. Bhattacharya and Sankar Sen, "Consumer-Company Identification: A Framework for Understanding Consumers' Relationships with Companies," *Journal of Marketing*, April 2003, pp. 76–88; Dennis B. Arnett, Steve D. German, and Shelby D. Hunt, "The Identify Salience Model of Relationship Marketing Success: The Case of Nonprofit Marketing," *Journal of Marketing*, April 2003, pp. 89–105.

90. Day, "Modeling Choices Among Alternative Responses to Dissatisfaction"; Marsha L. Richins, "Word-of-Mouth Communication as Negative Information," *Journal of Marketing*, Winter 1983, pp. 68–78.

91. Day, "Modeling Choices Among Alternative Responses to Dissatisfaction"; Arthur Best and Alan R. Andreasen, "Consumer Response to Unsatisfactory Purchases," *Law and Society*, Spring 1977, pp. 701–742.

92. William O. Bearden and Jesse E. Teel, "Selected Determinants of Consumer Satisfaction and Complaint Reports," *Journal of Marketing Research*, February 1983, pp. 21–28.

93. Cathy Goodwin and Ivan Ross, "Consumer Evaluations of Responses to Complaints: What's Fair and Why," *Journal of Services Marketing*, Summer 1990, pp. 53–61.

94. Day, "Modeling Choices Among Alternative Responses to Dissatisfaction"; Jagdip Singh and Roy D. Howell, "Consumer Complaining Behavior: A Review," in eds. H. Keith Hunt and Ralph L. Day, *Consumer Satisfaction, Dissatisfaction, and Complaining Behavior* (Bloomington, Ind.: Indiana University Press, 1985).

95. S. Krishnan and S. A. Valle, "Dissatisfaction Attributions and Consumer Complaint Behavior," in ed. William L. Wilkie, *Advances in Consumer Research* (Miami: Association for Consumer Research, 1979), pp. 445–449.

96. Folkes, "Consumer Reactions to Product Failure."

97. Nada Nasr Bechwati and Maureen Morrin, "Outraged Customers: Getting Even at the Expense of Getting a Good Deal," *Journal of Consumer Psychology* 13, no. 4, 2003, pp. 440–453.

98. Kjell Gronhaug and Gerald R. Zaltman, "Complainers and Noncomplainers Revisited: Another Look at the Data," in ed. Kent B. Monroe, *Advances in Consumer Research* (Ann Arbor, Mich.: Association for Consumer Research, 1981), pp. 159–165.

99. Jagdip Singh, "A Typology of Consumer Dissatisfaction Response Styles," *Journal of Retailing*, Spring 1990, pp. 57–99.

100. Dan Fost, "On the Internet, Everyone Can Hear Your Complaint," *New York Times*, February 25, 2008, p. C6.

101. Tiffany Kary, "Online Retailers Fumble on Customer Care," *CNET News.com*, January 3, 2002, *http://news.com.com/2100–1017–801668.html.*

102. Marlon A. Walker, "Online Service Lags at Big Firms," *Wall Street Journal*, July 1, 2004, p. B4.

103. Lou Hirsh, "Consumer Gripe Sites—Hidden Treasure?" *CRM Daily.com*, January 2, 2002, *www.crmdaily.com/perl/story/?id=15555.*

104. James G. Maxham III and Richard G. Netemeyer, "A Longitudinal Study of Complaining Customers' Evaluations of Multiple Service Failures and Recovery Efforts," *Journal of Marketing*, October 2002, pp. 57–71.

105. Halstead, Droge, and Cooper, "Product Warranties and Post-purchase Service."

106. Claes Fornell and Nicholas M. Didow, "Economic Constraints on Consumer Complaining Behavior," in ed. Jerry C. Olson, *Advances in Consumer Research*, vol. 7 (Ann Arbor, Mich.: Association for Consumer Research, 1980), pp. 318–323; Claes Fornell and Birger Wernerfelt, "Defensive Marketing Strategy by Customer Complaint Management," *Journal of Marketing Research*, November 1987, pp. 337–346.

107. Claes Fornell and Robert A. Westbrook, "The Vicious Cycle of Consumer Complaints," *Journal of Marketing*, Summer 1984, pp. 68–78.

108. Torsten Ringberg, Gaby Odekerken-Schröder, and Glenn L. Christensen, "A Cultural Models Approach to Service Recovery," *Journal of Marketing*, July 2007, pp. 194–214.

109. Amy K. Smith, Ruth N. Bolton, and Janet Wagner, "A Model of Customer Satisfaction with Service Encounters Involving Failure and Recovery," *Journal of Marketing Research* 36, August 1999, pp. 356–372.

110. Bitner, "Evaluating Service Encounters."

111. Richins, "Word-of-Mouth Communication as Negative Information."

112. Yi, "A Critical Review of Consumer Satisfaction"; Johan Arndt, "Word-of-Mouth Advertising and Perceived Risk," in eds. Harold H. Kassarjian and Thomas R. Robertson, *Perspectives in Consumer Behavior* (Glenview, Ill.: Scott-Foresman, 1968).

113. Fost, "On the Internet, Everyone Can Hear Your Complaint."

114. James McNair, "Company Backlash Strikes Gripe Sites," *Cincinnati Enquirer*, February 7, 2005, *www.usatoday.com*.

115. Keith L. Alexander, "Consumers Exercise Their Growing Clout," *Washington Post*, February 22, 2005, p. E1; Keith L. Alexander, "Hertz Kills Fee for Bookings; Car-Rental Firm Cites Complaints," *Washington Post*, February 16, 2005, p. E3.

116. Frederick F. Reichheld, *The Loyalty Effect: The Hidden Force Behind Growth* (Boston: Harvard Business School Press, 1996).

117. Murali Chandrashekaran, Kristin Rotte, Stephen S. Tax, and Rajdeep Grewal, "Satisfaction Strength and Customer Loyalty," *Journal of Marketing Research*, February 2007, pp. 153–163.

118. Priscilla La Barbera and David W. Mazursky, "A Longitudinal Assessment of Consumer Satisfaction/Dissatisfaction: The Dynamic Aspect of Cognitive Processes," *Journal of Marketing Research*, November 1983, pp. 393–404; Ruth Bolton, "A Dynamic Model of the Duration of the Customer's Relationship with a Continuous Service Provider," *Marketing Science* 17, no. 1, 1998, pp. 45–65.

119. Thomas O. Jones and W. Earl Sasser, "Why Customers Defect," *Harvard Business Review*, November–December 1995, pp. 88–99.

120. Richard L. Oliver, "Whence Consumer Loyalty?" *Journal of Marketing* 63, 1999, pp. 33–44.

121. Michael Lewis, "The Influence of Loyalty Programs and Short-Term Promotions on Customer Retention," *Journal of Marketing Research*, August 2004, pp. 281–292.

122. Frederick F. Reichheld and W. Earl Sasser, "Zero Defections: Quality Comes to Services," *Harvard Business Review*, September 1990, pp. 105–111; Eugene Anderson, Claes Fornell, and Donald H. Lehman, "Customer Satisfaction, Market Share, and Profitability: Findings from Sweden," *Journal of Marketing*, July 1994, pp. 53–66; Rajendra K. Srivastava, Tassadduq A. Shervani, and Liam Fahey, "Market-Based Assets and Shareholder Value: A Framework for Analysis," *Journal of Marketing* 62, no. 1, 1998, pp. 2–18.

123. Werner Reinartz, Manfred Krafft, and Wayne D. Hoyer, "The Customer Relationship Management Process: Its Measurement and Impact on Performance," *Journal of Marketing Research*, August 2004, pp. 293–305; Suni Mithas, M. S. Krishnan, and Claes Fornell, "Why Do Customer Relationship Management Applications Affect Customer Satisfaction?" *Journal of Marketing*, October 2005, pp. 201–209.

124. Becky Ebenkamp, "The Complaint Department," *Brandweek*, June 18, 2001, p. 21; Reichheld, *The Loyalty Effect*.

125. Abigail Sullivan Moore, "Cream and Sugar, and the Milk of Human Kindness," *New York Times*, March 28, 2004, sec. 14, p. 5.

126. Vikki Bland, "Keeping the Customer (Satisfied)," *NZ Business*, September 2004, pp. 16–20.

127. Todd R. Weiss, "Craig Newmark," *ComputerWorld*, February 4, 2008, p. 17; Tom Spring, "The Craig Behind Craigslist," *PC World*, November 2004, p. 32; Elizabeth Millard, "Making the List," *Computer User*, November 2004, p. 24; Matt Richtel, "Craig's To-Do List," *New York Times*, September 6, 2004, pp. C1, C3.

128. Corilyn Shropshire, "More Mom and Pop Stores Use New Technology to Boost Customer Satisfaction," *Pittsburgh Post-Gazette*, February 10, 2005, *www.post-gazette.com*.

129. Dan Zehr, "Dell Opening High-Tech Service Center in China," *Austin American-Statesman*, September 8, 2004, pp. B1, C3.

130. Melissa Martin Young and Melanie Wallendorf, "Ashes to Ashes, Dust to Dust: Conceptualizing Consumer Disposition of Possessions," in *Proceedings, Marketing Educators' Conference* (Chicago: American Marketing Association, 1989), pp. 33–39.

131. Young and Wallendorf, "Ashes to Ashes, Dust to Dust: Conceptualizing Consumer Disposition of Possessions;" see also Erica Mina Okada, "Trade-Ins, Mental Accounting, and Product Replacement Decisions," *Journal of Consumer Research*, March 2001, pp. 433–446; Jacob Jacoby, Carol K. Berning, and Thomas F. Dietvorst, "What About Disposition?" *Journal of Marketing*, April 1977, pp. 22–28; Gilbert D. Harrell and Diane M. McConocha, "Personal Factors Related to Consumer Product Disposal," *Journal of Consumer Affairs*, Winter 1992, pp. 397–417.

132. Jacoby, Berning, and Dietvorst, "What About Disposition?"; Young and Wallendorf, "Ashes to Ashes, Dust to Dust."

133. Harrell and McConocha, "Personal Factors Related to Consumer Product Disposal Tendencies."

134. Jacoby, Berning, and Dietvorst, "What About Disposition?"

135. John B. Sherry, Mary Ann McGrath, and Sidney J. Levy, "The Disposition of the Gift and Many Unhappy Returns," *Journal of Retailing*, Spring 1992, pp. 40–65.

136. Young and Wallendorf, "Ashes to Ashes, Dust to Dust."

137. Russell W. Belk, "Possessions and the Extended Self," *Journal of Consumer Research*, September 1988, pp. 139–168.

138. Young and Wallendorf, "Ashes to Ashes, Dust to Dust."

139. Okada, "Trade-Ins, Mental Accounting, and Product Replacement Decisions."

140. Melissa Martin Young, "Disposition of Possessions During Role Transitions," in eds. Rebecca H. Holman and Michael R. Solomon, *Advances in Consumer Research*,

vol. 18 (Provo, Utah: Association for Consumer Research, 1991), pp. 33–39.

141. James H. Alexander, "Divorce, the Disposition of the Relationship, and Everything," in eds. Rebecca H. Holman and Michael R. Solomon, *Advances in Consumer Research*, vol. 18 (Provo, Utah: Association for Consumer Research, 1991), pp. 43–48.

142. Ibid; Russell W. Belk, John F. Sherry, and Melanie Wallendorf, "A Naturalistic Inquiry into Buyer and Seller Behavior at a Swap Meet," *Journal of Consumer Research*, March 1988, pp. 449–470.

143. Michael D. Reilly and Melanie Wallendorf, "A Comparison of Group Differences in Food Consumption Using Household Refuse," *Journal of Consumer Research*, September 1987, pp. 289–294.

144. For a review, see L. J. Shrum, Tina M. Lowrey, and John A. McCarty, "Recycling as a Marketing Problem: A Framework for Strategy Development," *Psychology and Marketing*, July–August 1994, pp. 393–416.

145. Abhijit Biswas, Jane W. Licata, Daryl McKee, Chris Pullig, and Christopher Daughtridge, "The Recycling Cycle: Waste Recycling and Recycling Shopping Behaviors," *Journal of Public Policy and Marketing* 19, Spring 2000, pp. 93–105.

146. Rik G. M. Pieters, "Changing Garbage Disposal Patterns of Consumers: Motivation, Ability, and Performance," *Journal of Public Policy and Marketing*, Fall 1991, pp. 59–76.

147. Richard P. Bagozzi and Pratibha Dabholkar, "Consumer Recycling Goals and Their Effect on Decisions to Recycle," *Psychology and Marketing*, July–August 1994, pp. 313–340.

148. E. Howenstein, "Marketing Segmentation for Recycling," *Environment and Behavior*, March 1993, pp. 86–102.

149. Shrum, Lowrey, and McCarty, "Recycling as a Marketing Problem."

150. Susan E. Heckler, "The Role of Memory in Understanding and Encouraging Recycling Behavior," *Psychology and Marketing*, July–August 1994, pp. 375–392.

151. Pieters, "Changing Garbage Disposal Patterns of Consumers."

152. Susan Warren, "Recycler's Nightmare: Beer in Plastic," *Wall Street Journal*, November 16, 1999, pp. B1, B4.

153. Kenneth R. Lord, "Motivating Recycling Behavior: A Quasi-Experimental Investigation of Message and Source Strategies," *Psychology and Marketing*, July–August 1994, pp. 341–358.

154. Heckler, "The Role of Memory in Understanding and Encouraging Recycling Behavior."

155. Peter Pae, "JetBlue's Expansion Has Rivals Scrambling," *Los Angeles Times*, April 16, 2008, p. A1; "The Customer Service Elite," *BusinessWeek*, February 21, 2008, *www.businessweek.com;* Jena McGregor, "An Extraordinary Stumble at JetBlue," *BusinessWeek*, March 5, 2007, pp. 58–59; Dan Reed, "JetBlue Tries to Make Up with Fliers," *USA Today*, February 21, 2007, p. 1B; Jeff Bailey, "Chief 'Mortified' by JetBlue Crisis," *New York Times*, February 19, 2007, p. A1.

Chapter 12

1. Chandra Johnson-Greene, "Hispanic Magazine Advertising Up 22 Percent," *Folio*, March 28, 2008, *www.foliomag.com;* "In Hispanic Ritual, A Place for Faith and Celebration," *New York Times*, January 5, 2008, p. B5; Walter Nicholls, "A Rite of Passage, a Slice of Tradition," *Washington Post*, August 23, 2006, p. F1; Becky Tiernan, "Understanding Quinceañera Can Mean Business," *Daily Oklahoman*, February 20, 2005, *www.newsok.com;* Deborah Hirsch, "Quinceañera Parties Evolve as Hispanics Assimilate into American Culture," *Orlando Sentinel*, August 25, 2003; Amy Chozick, "Fairy-Tale Fifteenths," *Wall Street Journal*, October 15, 2004, pp. B1, B6.

2. Charles D. Schewe and Geoffrey Meredith, "Segmenting Global Markets by Generational Cohorts: Determining Motivations by Age," *Journal of Consumer Behavior* 4, no. 1, 2004, pp. 51–63.

3. Peter Francese, "Trend Spotting," *American Demographics*, July–August 2002, pp. 50+; Vickery, Greene, Branch, and Nelson, "Marketers Tweak Strategies as Age Groups Realign."

4. Laura Zinn, "Teens: Here Comes the Biggest Wave Yet," *BusinessWeek*, April 11, 1994, pp. 76–86; Lisa Marie Petersen, "I Bought What Was on Sale," *Brandweek*, February 22, 1993, pp. 12–13.

5. Dennis H. Tootelian and Ralph M. Gaedecke, "The Teen Market: An Exploratory Analysis of Income, Spending, and Shopping Patterns," *Journal of Consumer Marketing*, Fall 1994, pp. 35–44; George P. Moschis and Roy L. Moore, "Decision Making Among the Young: A Socialization Perspective," *Journal of Consumer Research*, September 1979, pp. 101–112.

6. Rick Garlick and Kyle Langley, "Reaching Gen Y on Both Sides of the Cash Register," *Retailing Issues Letter*, Center for Retailing Studies at Texas A&M University, vol. 18, no. 2, 2007, pp. 1–2.

7. Dannie Kjeldgaard and Søren Askegaard, "The Globalization of Youth Culture: The Global Youth Segment as Structures of Common Difference," *Journal of Consumer Research* 33, no. 2, 2006, pp. 231–247.

8. "The Six Value Segments of Global Youth," *Brandweek*, May 22, 2000, pp. 38–44.

9. David Murphy, "Connecting with Online Teenagers," *Marketing*, September 27, 2001, pp. 31–32.

10. Noah Rubin Brier, "Coming of Age," *American Demographics*, November 2004, pp. 16–19.

11. Peter Francese, "Ahead of the Next Wave," *American Demographics*, September 2003, pp. 42–43; Robert Guy Matthews, "Spirits Makers Aim to Shake Up Stodgy Brands with Youth Push," *Wall Street Journal*, November 11, 2004, p. B5.

12. "Resident Population Projections by Sex and Age: 2010 to 2050," *U.S. Interim Projections by Age, Sex, Race, and Hispanic Origin,* U.S. Census Bureau, March 2004, *www.census.gov.*

13. "Teen Clout Grows; Chains React," *MMR,* August 20, 2001, pp. 29.

14. Kerry Capell, "MTV's World," *BusinessWeek,* February 18, 2001, pp. 81–84; Sally Beatty and Carol Hymowitz, "How MTV Stays Tuned In to Teens," *Wall Street Journal,* March 21, 2000, pp. B1, B4.

15. Paula Dwyer, "The Euroteens (and How to Sell to Them)," *BusinessWeek,* April 11, 1994, p. 84.

16. Stephanie Clifford, "An Online Game So Mysterious Its Famous Sponsor Is Hidden," *New York Times,* April 1, 2008, p. C5.

17. Murphy, "Connecting with Online Teenagers"; Fara Warner, "Booming Asia Lures Credit-Card Firms," *Wall Street Journal,* November 24, 1995, p. B10.

18. Beatty and Hymowitz, "How MTV Stays Tuned In to Teens."

19. Maureen Tkacik, "Fast Times for Retail Chain Behind the 'Euro' Shoe Trend," *Wall Street Journal,* November 21, 2002, p. B1.

20. Matthew Grimm, "Irvington, 10533," *Brandweek,* August 17, 1993, pp. 11–13.

21. Helene Cooper, "Once Again, Ads Woo Teens with Slang," *Wall Street Journal,* March 29, 1993, pp. B1, B6; Adrienne Ward Fawcett, "When Using Slang in Advertising: BVC," *Advertising Age,* August 23, 1993, p. S-6.

22. Barbara Martinez, "Antismoking Ads Aim to Gross Out Teens," *Wall Street Journal,* March 21, 1997, pp. B1, B8.

23. Jennie L. Phipps, "Networks Drill Deeper into Teen Market," *Electronic Media,* March 12, 2001, p. 20; Erin White, "Teen Mags for Guys, Not Dolls," *Wall Street Journal,* August 10, 2000, pp. B1, B4; Wendy Bounds, "Teen-Magazine Boom: Beauty, Fashion, Stars, and Sex," *Wall Street Journal,* December 7, 1998, pp. B1, B10.

24. Cristina Merrill, "Keeping Up with Teens," *American Demographics,* October 1999, pp. 27–31.

25. Bob Tedeschi, "Online Retailers Say They Are Ready to Deliver Goods to Christmas Shoppers Who Waited Until the Last Minute," *New York Times,* December 20, 2004, p. C4.

26. Jennifer Gill, "Contagious Commercials," *Inc.,* November 2006, *www.inc.com;* Leigh Muzslay, "Shoes That Morph from Sneakers to Skates Are Flying out of Stores," *Wall Street Journal,* July 26, 2001, p. B1.

27. Jeffrey A. Trachtenberg, "Targeting Young Adults," *Wall Street Journal,* October 4, 2004, pp. B1, B5.

28. Christina Duff, "It's Sad but True: Good Times Are Bad for Real Slackers," *Wall Street Journal,* August 6, 1998, pp. A1, A5; Carol Angrisani, "X Marks the Spot," *Brandmarketing,* April 2001, pp. 18+.

29. "Farther Along the Axis," *American Demographics,* May 2004, pp. 21+.

30. Pamela Paul, "Echo Boomerang," *American Demographics,* June 2001, pp. 45–49.

31. Debra O'Connor, "Home Stretch: Families Remodel Houses to Accommodate Parents or 'Boomerang' Children," *Pioneer Press,* March 18, 2003, *www.twincities.com/mld/pioneerpress.*

32. Angrisani, "X Marks the Spot."

33. Cyndee Miller, "X Marks the Lucrative Spot, But Some Advertisers Can't Hit Target," *Marketing News,* August 2, 1993, pp. 1, 14; Pat Sloan, "Xers Brush Off Cosmetics Marketers," *Advertising Age,* September 27, 1993, p. 4.

34. Alfred Schreiber, "Generation X the Next Big Event Target," *Advertising Age,* June 21, 1993, p. S-3; Robert Gustafson, "Marketing to Generation X? Better Practice Safe Sex," *Advertising Age,* March 7, 1994, p. 26.

35. Joseph B. White, "Toyota, Seeking Younger Drivers, Uses Hip Hop, Web, Low Prices," *Wall Street Journal,* September 22, 1999, p. B10.

36. Horst Stipp, "Xers Are Not Created Equal," *Mediaweek,* March 21, 1994, p. 20; Lisa Marie Petersen, "Previews of Coming Attractions," *Brandweek,* March 1993, pp. 22–23.

37. Angrisani, "X Marks the Spot."

38. Laura Koss-Feder, "Want to Catch Gen X? Try Looking on the Web," *Marketing News,* June 8, 1998, p. 20.

39. "Insurance Gets Hip," *American Demographics,* January 1, 2002, p. 48.

40. Cheryl Russell, "The Power of One," *Brandweek,* October 4, 1993, pp. 27–28, 30, 32.

41. Pamela Paul, "Targeting Boomers," *American Demographics,* March 2003, pp. 24+.

42. Alison Stein Wellner, "Generational Divide," *American Demographics,* October 2000, pp. 52–58.

43. Pamela Paul, "Global Generation Gap," *American Demographics,* March 2002, pp. 18–19.

44. "More at Home on the Road," *American Demographics,* June 2003, pp. 26–27.

45. Ken Brown, "After Roaring Through the '90s, Harley's Engine Could Sputter," *Wall Street Journal,* February 12, 2002, *www.wsj.com;* Joseph Weber, "Harley Investors May Get a Wobbly Ride," *BusinessWeek,* February 11, 2002, p. 65.

46. Peter Francese, "Trend Ticker: Big Spenders," *American Demographics,* September 2001, pp. 30–31; Susan Mitchell, "How Boomers Save," *American Demographics,* September 1994, pp. 22–29; "Baby Boomers Are Top Dinner Consumers," *Frozen Food Age,* February 1994, p. 33.

47. Shirley Leung, "Fast-Food Chains Upgrade Menus, and Profits, with Pricey Sandwiches," *Wall Street Journal,* February 5, 2002, pp. B1–B3.

48. Cyndee Miller, "Jeans Marketers Loosen Up, Adjust to Expanding Market," *Marketing News,* August 31, 1992, pp. 6–7.

49. John Finotti, "Back in Fashion: After a Strong Start and Then a Stumble, Specialty Retailer Chico's FAS Is Riding

the Baby Boomer Wave," *Florida Trend*, January 2002, pp. 16.

50. Michael J. Weiss, "Chasing Youth," *American Demographics*, October 2002, pp. 35+; John Fetto, "Queen for a Day," *American Demographics*, March 2000, pp. 31–32.

51. Michelle Edgar, "Olay Ramping Up Skin Care Offering," *WWD*, May 4, 2007, p. 7; Cris Prystay and Sarah Ellison, "Time for Marketers to Grow Up?" *Wall Street Journal*, February 27, 2003, pp. B1, B4.

52. Carol M. Morgan, "The Psychographic Landscape of 50-Plus," *Brandweek*, July 19, 1993, pp. 28–32; Phil Goodman, "Marketing to Age Groups Is All in the Mind Set," *Marketing News*, December 6, 1993, p. 4.

53. Catherine A. Cole and Gary J. Gaeth, "Cognitive and Age-Related Differences in the Ability to Use Nutritional Information in a Complex Environment," *Journal of Marketing Research*, May 1990, pp. 175–184; Catherine A. Cole and Siva K. Balasubramanian, "Age Differences in Consumers' Search for Information: Public Policy Implications," *Journal of Consumer Research*, June 1993, pp. 157–169; Deborah Roedder John and Catherine A. Cole, "Age Differences in Information Processing: Understanding Deficits in Young and Elderly Consumers," *Journal of Consumer Research*, December 1986, pp. 297–315.

54. Carolyn Yoon, "Age Differences in Consumers' Processing Strategies: An Investigation of Moderating Differences," *Journal of Consumer Research*, December 1997, pp. 329–342.

55. Sharmistha Law, Scott A. Hawkins, and Fergus I. M. Craik, "Repetition-Induced Belief in the Elderly: Rehabilitating Age-Related Memory Deficits," *Journal of Consumer Research*, September 1998, pp. 91–107.

56. Catherine A. Cole and Gary J. Gaeth, "Cognitive and Age-Related Differences in the Ability to Use Nutritional Information in a Complex Environment," *Journal of Marketing Research*, May 1990, pp. 175–184; Cole and Balasubramanian, "Age Differences in Consumers' Search for Information: Public Policy Implications,"; John and Cole, "Age Differences in Information Processing: Understanding Deficits in Young and Elderly Consumers."

57. Michael Moss, "Leon Black Bets Big on the Elderly," *Wall Street Journal*, July 24, 1998, pp. B1, B8.

58. Raphaelle Lambert-Pandraud, Gilles Laurent, and Eric Lapersonne, "Repeat Purchasing of New Automobiles by Older Consumers: Empirical Evidence and Interpretations," *Journal of Marketing*, April 2005, pp. 97–113.

59. Patrick M. Reilly, "What a Long Strange Trip It's Been," *Wall Street Journal*, April 7, 1999, pp. B1, B4.

60. Ronald E. Milliman and Robert C. Erffmeyer, "Improving Advertising Aimed at Seniors," *Journal of Advertising Research*, December 1989–January 1990, pp. 31–36.

61. Robin T. Peterson, "The Depiction of Senior Citizens in Magazine Advertisements: A Content Analysis," *Journal of Business Ethics*, September 1992, pp. 701–706;

Anthony C. Ursic, Michael L. Ursic, and Virginia L. Ursic, "A Longitudinal Study of the Use of the Elderly in Magazine Advertising," *Journal of Consumer Research*, June 1986, pp. 131–133; John J. Burnett, "Examining the Media Habits of the Affluent Elderly," *Journal of Advertising Research*, October–November 1991, pp. 33–41.

62. Patti Williams and Aimee Drolet, "Age-Related Differences in Responses to Emotional Advertisements," *Journal of Consumer Research* 32, no. 3, 2005, pp. 343–354.

63. "America's Aging Consumers," *Discount Merchandiser*, September 1993, pp. 16–28; John and Cole, "Age Differences in Information Processing."

64. Amy Merrick, "Gap's Greatest Generation?" *Wall Street Journal*, September 15, 2004, pp. B1, B3.

65. Lisa D. Spiller and Richard A. Hamilton, "Senior Citizen Discount Programs: Which Seniors to Target and Why," *Journal of Consumer Marketing*, Summer 1993, pp. 42–51; Kelly Tepper, "The Role of Labeling Processes in Elderly Consumers' Responses to Age Segmentation Cues," *Journal of Consumer Research*, March 1994, pp. 503–519.

66. Jinkook Lee and Loren V. Geistfeld, "Elderly Consumers' Receptiveness to Telemarketing Fraud," *Journal of Public Policy & Marketing* 18, no. 2, Fall 1999, pp. 208–217; John R. Emshwiller, "Having Lost Thousands to Con Artists, Elderly Widow Tells Cautionary Tale," *Wall Street Journal*, August 9, 1996, pp. B1, B5.

67. Joan Meyers-Levy, "The Influence of Sex Roles on Judgment," *Journal of Consumer Research*, March 1988, pp. 522–530.

68. Charles S. Areni and Pamela Kiecker, "Gender Differences in Motivation: Some Implications for Manipulating Task-Related Involvement," in ed. Janeen Arnold Costa, *Gender and Consumer Behavior* (Salt Lake City, Utah: University of Utah Printing Service, 1993), pp. 30–43; Brenda Giner and Eileen Fischer, "Women and Arts, Men and Sports: Two Phenomena or One?" in ed. Janeen Arnold Costa, *Gender and Consumer Behavior* (Salt Lake City, Utah: University of Utah Printing Service, 1993), p. 149.

69. Douglas B. Holt and Craig J. Thompson, "Man-of-Action Heroes: The Pursuit of Heroic Masculinity in Everyday Consumption," *Journal of Consumer Research*, September 2004, pp. 425–440.

70. Elia Kacapyr, "The Well-Being of American Women," *American Demographics*, August 1998, pp. 30, 32; "Women in the United States: March 2000 (PPL-121)," *U.S. Department of Commerce*, March 2000, *www.census.gov/population/www/socdemo/ppl-121.html*.

71. Chen May Yee, "High-Tech Lift for India's Women," *Wall Street Journal*, November 1, 2000, pp. B1, B4; Al-ladi Venkatesh, "Gender Identity in the Indian Context, a Socio-Cultural Construction of the Female Consumer," in ed. Costa, *Gender and Consumer Behavior*, pp. 119–129.

72. Timothy M. Smith, Srinath Gopalakrishna, and Paul M. Smith, "Men's and Women's Responses to Sex Role

Portrayals in Advertisements," *Journal of Marketing Research*, March 2004, pp. 61–77.

73. Lynn J. Jaffe and Paul D. Berger, "Impact on Purchase Intent of Sex-Role Identity and Product Positioning," *Psychology and Marketing*, Fall 1988, pp. 259–271.

74. David Whelan, "Do Ask, Do Tell," *American Demographics*, November 2001, p. 41.

75. John Fetto, "In Broad Daylight," *American Demographics*, February 2001, pp. 16–20; Ronald Alsop, "Cracking the Gay Market Code," *Wall Street Journal*, June 29, 1999, p. B1.

76. Steven M. Kates, "The Dynamics of Brand Legitimacy: An Interpretive Study in the Gay Men's Community," *Journal of Consumer Research*, September 2004, pp. 455–464.

77. Stuart Elliott, "A Whole New Meaning for the Phrase 'City of Brotherly Love,'" *New York Times*, June 22, 2004, *www.nytimes.com*.

78. Joan Meyers-Levy and Durairaj Maheswaran, "Exploring Differences in Males' and Females' Processing Strategies," *Journal of Consumer Research*, June 1991, pp. 63–70; William K. Darley and Robert E. Smith, "Gender Differences in Information Processing Strategies: An Empirical Test of the Selectivity Model in Advertising Response," *Journal of Advertising*, Spring 1995, pp. 41–56; Barbara B. Stern, "Feminist Literary Criticism and the Deconstruction of Ads: A Postmodern View of Advertising and Consumer Responses," *Journal of Consumer Research*, March 1993, pp. 556–566.

79. Meyers-Levy, "The Influence of Sex Roles on Judgment"; Joan Meyers-Levy, "Priming Effects on Product Judgments: A Hemispheric Interpretation," *Journal of Consumer Research*, June 1989, pp. 76–86.

80. Laurette Dube and Michael S. Morgan, "Trend Effects and Gender Differences in Retrospective Judgments of Consumption Emotions," *Journal of Consumer Research*, September 1996, pp. 156–162.

81. Richard Elliot, "Gender and the Psychological Meaning of Fashion Brands," in ed. Janeen Arnold Costa, *Gender and Consumer Behavior* (Salt Lake City, Utah: University of Utah Printing Service, 1993), pp. 99–105.

82. Suzanne C. Grunert, "On Gender Differences in Eating Behavior as Compensatory Consumption," in ed. Costa, *Gender and Consumer Behavior*, pp. 74–86.

83. Clifford Krauss, "Women, Hear Them Roar," *New York Times*, July 25, 2007, pp. C1, C9.

84. Linda Bock, "Bye-Bye Barber," *Telegram & Gazette* (Worcester, MA), April 1, 2008, *www.telegram.com*.

85. Michael Schwirtz, "Russian Vodka with a Feminine Kick," *New York Times*, March 30, 2008, p. ST-2.

86. Amy Tsao, "Retooling Home Improvement," *BusinessWeek*, February 14, 2005, *www.businessweek.com*.

87. Robert J. Fisher and Laurette Dubé, "Gender Differences in Responses to Emotional Advertising: A Social Desirability Perspective," *Journal of Consumer Research* 31, no. 4, 2005, pp. 850–858.

88. John B. Ford, Patricia Kramer, Earl D. Honeycutt Jr., and Susan L. Casey, "Gender Role Portrayals in Japanese Advertising: A Magazine Content Analysis," *Journal of Advertising*, Spring 1998, pp. 113–124.

89. Geoffrey A. Fowler, "Marketers Take Heed: The Macho Chinese Man Is Back," *Wall Street Journal*, December 18, 2002, p. B1.

90. Thomas W. Whipple and Mary K. McManamon, "Implications of Using Male and Female Voices in Commercials: An Exploratory Study," *Journal of Advertising*, Summer 2002, pp. 79–91.

91. "An All-women Fitness Event," *Malaysia Star*, March 20, 2008, *http://thestar.com.my*.

92. Patrick M. Reilly, "Hard-Nosed Allure Wins Readers and Ads," *Wall Street Journal*, August 27, 1992, p. B8; Seema Nayyar, "Net TV Soap Ads: Lever Alone Hit Men," *Brandweek*, July 13, 1992, p. 10.

93. Sandra Yin, "Home and Away," *American Demographics*, March 2004, p. 15.

94. Ignacio Vazquez, "Mexicans Are Buying 'Made in USA' Food," *Marketing News*, August 31, 1998, p. 14.

95. Susan Mitchell, "Birds of a Feather," *American Demographics*, February 1995, pp. 40–48.

96. Michael Weiss, "Parallel Universe," *American Demographics*, October 1999, pp. 58–63.

97. Adapted from Claritas, "PRIZM NE Target Finder Report Ranked by Segment."

98. Greg Johnson, "Beyond Burgers: New McDonald's Menu Makes Run for the Border," *Los Angeles Times*, August 13, 2000, pp. C1.

99. Chad Terhune, "Snack Giant's Boats Sting Regional Rivals," *Wall Street Journal*, July 29, 2004, pp. B1–B2.

100. Mitchell, "Birds of a Feather."

101. Ray Schultz, "ZIP + 4 + 2 = ZIP + 6," *Direct* Magazine, February 1, 2007, n.p.

102. Mike Freeman, "Clusters of Customers," *San Diego Union-Tribune*, December 19, 2004, *www.signosandiego.com*.

103. Weiss, "Parallel Universe."

104. Haipeng (Allan) Chen, Sharon Ng, and Akshay R. Rao, "Cultural Differences in Consumer Impatience," *Journal of Marketing Research*, August 2005, pp. 291–301.

105. See Daphna Oyserman, "High Power, Low Power, and Equality: Culture Beyond Individualism and Collectivism," *Journal of Consumer Psychology* 16, no. 4, 2006, pp. 352–356.

106. Sharon Shavitt, Ashok K. Lalwani, Jing Zhang, and Carlos J. Torelli, "The Horizontal/Vertical Dimension in Cross-Cultural Consumer Research," *Journal of Consumer Psychology* 16, no. 4, 2006, pp. 325–342; Joan Meyers-Levy, "Using the Horizontal/Vertical Distinction to Advance Insights into Consumer Psychology," *Journal of Consumer Psychology* 16, no. 4, 2006, pp. 347–351; Jennifer L. Aaker, "Delineating Culture," *Journal of Consumer Psychology* 16, no. 4, 2006, pp. 343–347; Sharon Shavitt, Ashok K. Lalwani, Jing Zhang, and Carlos J. Torelli, "Reflections on the Meaning and Structure of the Horizontal/Vertical Dimension," *Journal of Consumer Psychology* 16, no. 4, 2006, pp. 357–362.

107. Michelle R. Nelson, Frédéric F. Brunel, Magne Supphel-len, and Rajesh V. Manchanda, "Effects of Culture, Gender, and Moral Obligations on Responses to Charity Advertising Across Masculine and Feminine Cultures," *Journal of Consumer Psychology* 16, no. 1, 2006, pp. 45–56.

108. Donnel A. Briley and Jennifer L. Aaker, "When Does Culture Matter? Effects of Personal Knowledge on the Correction of Culture-Based Judgments," *Journal of Marketing Research*, August 2006, pp. 395–408.

109. Steven M. Kates and Charlene Goh, "Brand Morphing," *Journal of Advertising*, Spring 2003, pp. 59–68.

110. Yumiko Ono, "U.S. Superstores Find Japanese Are a Hard Sell," *Wall Street Journal*, February 14, 2000, pp. B1, B4.

111. Normandy Madden, "Inside the Asian Colossus," *Advertising Age*, August 16, 2004, *www.adage.com.*

112. George P. Moschis, *Consumer Socialization* (Lexington, Mass.: D. C. Heath, 1987); Lisa Penaloza, "Atravesando Fronteras/Border Crossings: A Critical Ethnographic Exploration of the Consumer Acculturation of Mexican Immigrants," *Journal of Consumer Research*, June 1994, pp. 32–54.

113. Sonya A. Grier, Anne M. Brumbaugh, and Corliss G. Thornton, "Crossover Dreams: Consumer Responses to Ethnic-Oriented Products," *Journal of Marketing*, April 2006, pp. 35–51.

114. Jean-Francois Ouellet, "Consumer Racism and Its Effects on Domestic Cross-Ethnic Product Purchase: An Empirical Test in the United States, Canada, and France," *Journal of Marketing*, January 2007, pp. 113–128.

115. U.S. Census Bureau, "Projected Population of the United States, by Race and Hispanic Origin: 2000–2050," March 18, 2004, *www.census.gov/ipc/www/usinterimproj.*

116. Rebecca Gardyn, "Habla English?" *American Demographics*, April 2001, pp. 54–57.

117. Rebecca Gardyn and John Fetto, "Race, Ethnicity, and the Way We Shop," *American Demographics,* February 2003, pp. 30–33; Joan Raymond, "The Multicultural Report," *American Demographics*, November 2001, pp. S3–S6; Rebecca Gardyn, "True Colors," *American Demographics*, April 2001, pp. 14–17.

118. Kimberly Palmer, "Ads for Ethnic Hair Care Show a New Face," *Wall Street Journal,* July 21, 2003, pp. B1, B3.

119. Marlene Rossman, "Inclusive Marketing Shows Sensitivity," *Marketing News*, October 10, 1994, p. 4.

120. "Nation's Population One-Third Minority," *U.S. Census Bureau News*, May 10, 2006, *www.census.gov.*

121. Pamela Paul, "Hispanic Heterogenity," *Forecast*, June 4, 2001, pp. 1; Geoffrey Paulin, "A Growing Market: Expenditures by Hispanics," *Monthly Labor Review*, March 1998, pp. 3–21.

122. Carrie Goerne, "Go the Extra Mile to Catch Up with Hispanics," *Marketing News*, December 24, 1990, p. 13; Marlene Rossman, *Multicultural Marketing* (New York: American Management Association, 1994).

123. Penaloza, "Atravesando Fronteras/Border Crossings."

124. Humberto Valencia, "Developing an Index to Measure Hispanicness," in eds. Elizabeth C. Hirschman and Morris B. Holbrook, *Advances in Consumer Research*, vol. 12 (Provo, Utah: Association for Consumer Research, 1981), pp. 18–21; Rohit Deshpande, Wayne D. Hoyer, and Naveen Donthu, "The Intensity of Ethnic Affiliation: A Study of the Sociology of Hispanic Consumption," *Journal of Consumer Research*, September 1986, pp. 214–220.

125. Cynthia Webster, "Effects of Hispanic Ethnic Identification on Marital Roles in the Purchase Decision Process," *Journal of Consumer Research*, September 1994, pp. 319–331.

126. Cynthia Webster, "The Effects of Hispanic Subcultural Identification on Information Search Behavior," *Journal of Advertising Research*, September–October 1992, pp. 54–62; Naveen Donthu and Joseph Cherian, "Hispanic Coupon Usage: The Impact of Strong and Weak Ethnic Identification," *Psychology and Marketing*, November–December 1992, pp. 501–510.

127. Dianne Solis, "Latino Buying Power Still Surging: It Will Exceed That of Blacks in 2007, Report Says," *Dallas Morning News,* September 1, 2006, *www.dallasnews.com.*

128. Hillary Chura, "Sweet Spot," *Advertising Age*, November 12, 2001, pp. 1, 16; Roberta Bernstein, "Food For Thought," *American Demographics*, May 2000, pp. 39–42.

129. Claire Hoffman, "Small Business; Taking a Shine to Hair Care Business," *Los Angeles Times*, September 13, 2006, p. C1.

130. Suzanne Vranica, "Miller Turns Eye Toward Hispanics," *Wall Street Journal*, October 8, 2004, p. B3.

131. "The Best Way to Court Hispanics May Be to Get Granular and Local," *MediaWeek*, March 3, 2008, *www.mediaweek.com.*

132. "10 Largest Advertisers to the Hispanic Market, 1999 vs. 2000," *Marketing News*, July 2, 2001, p. 17.

133. Jones, "Translating for the Hispanic Market."

134. Rossman, *Multicultural Marketing.*

135. Rohit Deshpande and Douglas M. Stayman, "A Tale of Two Cities: Distinctiveness Theory and Advertising Effectiveness," *Journal of Marketing Research*, February 1994, pp. 57–64.

136. See Claudia V. Dimofte, Mark R. Forehand, and Rohit Deshpandé, "Ad Schema Incongruity as Elicitor of Ethnic Self-Awareness and Differential Advertising Response," *Journal of Advertising*, Winter 2003–2004, pp. 7–17; Mark R. Forehand and Rohit Deshpandé, "What We See Makes Us Who We Are: Priming Ethnic Self-Awareness and Advertising Response," *Journal of Marketing Research*, August 2001, pp. 336–348.

137. Anne M. Brumbaugh, 'Source and Nonsource Cues in Advertising and Their Effects on the Activation of Cultural and Subcultural Knowledge on the Route to Persuasion," *Journal of Consumer Research*, September 2002, pp. 258–269.

138. Robert E. Wilkes and Humberto Valencia, "Hispanics and Blacks in Television Commercials," *Journal of Advertising*, March 1989, pp. 19–25.

139. Scott Koslow, Prem N. Shamdasani, and Ellen E. Touchstone, "Exploring Language Effects in Ethnic Advertising: A Sociolinguistic Perspective," *Journal of Consumer Research*, March 1994, pp. 575–585.

140. Laurel Wentz, "Cultural Cross Over," *Advertising Age*, July 7, 2003, pp. S-4+.

141. David Luna and Laura A. Peracchio, "Advertising to Bilingual Consumers: The Impact of Code-switching on Persuasion," *Journal of Consumer Research* 31, no. 4, 2005, pp. 760–765; David Luna, Dawn Lerman, and Laura A. Peracchio, "Structural Constraints in Code-Switched Advertising," *Journal of Consumer Research* 32, no. 3, 2005, pp. 416–423.

142. Kris Hudson and Ana Campoy, "Hispanics' Hard Times Hit Wal-Mart," *Wall Street Journal*, August 29, 2007, p. A8.

143. "The DNR List: Latino Logistics," *Daily News Record*, August 23, 2004, p. 136.

144. "Nation's Population One-Third Minority."

145. William H. Frey, "Revival," *American Demographics*, October 2003, pp. 27+; "Black Population Surged During '90s: U.S. Census," *Jet*, August 27, 2001, p. 18.

146. "Where Blacks, Whites Diverge," *Brandweek*, May 3, 1993, p. 22.

147. Howard Schlossberg, "Many Marketers Still Consider Blacks 'Dark-Skinned Whites,'" *Marketing News*, January 18, 1993, pp. 1, 13.

148. Alan J. Bush, Rachel Smith, and Craig Martin, "The Influence of Consumer Socialization Variables on Attitude Toward Advertising: A Comparison of African-Americans and Caucasians," *Journal of Advertising* 28, no. 3, Fall 1999, pp. 13–24.

149. Solis, "Latino Buying Power Still Surging: It Will Exceed That of Blacks in 2007, Report Says."

150. Corliss L. Green, "Ethnic Evaluations of Advertising: Interaction Effects of Strength of Ethnic Identification, Media Placement, and Degree of Racial Composition," *Journal of Advertising* 28, no. 1, Spring 1999, pp. 49–64; Pepper Miller and Ronald Miller, "Trends Are Opportunities for Targeting African-Americans," *Marketing News*, January 20, 1992, p. 9.

151. "African-Americans Go Natural," *MMR*, December 17, 2001, p. 43.

152. Alan J. Bush, Rachel Smith, and Craig Martin, "The Influence of Consumer Socialization Variables on Attitude Toward Advertising: A Comparison of African-Americans and Caucasians," *Journal of Advertising* 28, no. 3, Fall 1999, pp. 13–24.

153. Green, "Ethnic Evaluations of Advertising."

154. Jake Holden, "The Ring of Truth," *American Demographics*, October 1998, p. 14.

155. Mary Connelly, "Lincoln Ads Target Blacks; Campaign Features Stories of Success," *Automotive News*, October 30, 2006, p. 6.

156. Mike Shields, "BET Digital Launches New African-American Ad Net," *Mediaweek*, January 14, 2008, p. 8.

157. "10 Largest Advertisers to the African American Market, 2000," *Marketing News*, July 2, 2001, p. 17.

158. Jennifer L. Aaker, Anne M. Brumbaugh, and Sonya A. Grier, "Nontarget Markets and Viewer Distinctiveness: The Impact of Target Marketing on Advertising Attitudes," *Journal of Consumer Psychology* 9, no. 3, 2000, pp. 127–140.

159. Donnel A. Briley, L. J. Shrum, and Robert S. Wyer Jr., "Subjective Impressions of Minority Group Representation in the Media: A Comparison of Majority and Minority Viewers' Judgments and Underlying Processes," *Journal of Consumer Psychology* 17, no. 1, 2007, pp. 36–48; William J. Qualls and David J. Moore, "Stereotyping Effects on Consumers' Evaluation of Advertising: Impact of Racial Difference Between Actors and Viewers," *Psychology and Marketing*, Summer 1990, pp. 135–151.

160. Sonia Alleyne, "The Magic Touch," *Black Enterprise*, June 1, 2004, n.p.

161. Tommy E. Whittler and Joan DiMeo, "Viewers' Reactions to Racial Cues in Advertising Stimuli," *Journal of Advertising Research*, December 1991, pp. 37–46.

162. Tommy E. Whittler, "Viewers' Processing of Source and Message Cues in Advertising Stimuli," *Psychology & Marketing*, July–August 1989, pp. 287–309.

163. "Nation's Population One-Third Minority."

164. "Diversity in America: Asians," *American Demographics*, November 2002, p. S14; William H. Frey, "Micro 165. Melting Pots," *American Demographics* 25, no. 6, 2001, pp. 20–23.

165. "Diversity in America: Asians."

166. Jonathan Burton, "Advertising Targeting Asians," *Far Eastern Economic Review*, January 21, 1993, pp. 40–41.

167. Saul Gitlin, "An Optional Data Base," *Brandweek*, January 5, 1998, p. 16.

168. Bill Kossen, "Japanese-Language Ads Demonstrate Novel Marketing Approach," *Seattle Times*, July 3, 2001, *www.seattletimes.com*.

169. Rebecca Gardyn and John Fetto, "The Way We Shop," *American Demographics*, February 2003, pp. 31+.

170. "Asian Americans Lead the Way Online," *Min's New Media Report*, December 31, 2001.

171. Rebecca Gardyn and John Fetto, "The Way We Shop," *American Demographics*, February 2003, pp. 31+.

172. U.S. Census Bureau, "Income 2002," *Current Population Survey, 2002, www.census.gov*; "Diversity in America: Asians."

173. Chui Li, "The Asian Market for Personal Products," *Drug & Cosmetic Industry*, November 1992, pp. 32–36; William Dunn, "The Move Toward Ethnic Marketing," *Nation's Business*, July 1992, pp. 39–41; Rossman, *Multicultural Marketing*.

174. Mark Peters, "An Asian Niche at Mohegan Sun," *Hartford Courant*, August 11, 2007, p. E1.

175. Marty Bernstein, "Auto Advertisers Shift Some Attention to Asian-Americans," *Automotive News,* October 13, 2003, p. 4M; Julie Cantwell, "Zero Gives New Life to Big 3 in the West; New Plans Include More Dealer Ad Money and Multicultural Marketing," *Automotive News,* November 12, 2001, p. 35.

176. "HSBC Banks on World Cup Soccer Web Site, in Chinese," *Brandweek,* April 1, 2002, p. 30.

177. Wayne Karrfalt, "Case Study: Cruising to New Customers," *Cable TV: The Multicultural Connection,* n.d., p. S10.

178. "NBA Drops Chinese Insert to Salute Yao, Wang, and Bateer," *People's Daily Online,* October 30, 2003, *www .english.people.com.cn.*

179. Jonathan Burton, "Advertising Targeting Asians," *Far Eastern Economic Review,* January 21, 1993, pp. 40–41; Brett A. S. Martin, Christina Kwai-Choi Lee, and Yang Feng, "The Influence of Ad Model Ethnicity and Self-Referencing on Attitudes," *Journal of Advertising,* Winter 2004, pp. 27–37.

180. Linda Laban, "Crossing Cultures," *Boston Globe,* April 5, 2007, p. 6.

181. Onkvisit and Shaw, *International Marketing;* Charles M. Schaninger, Jacques C. Bourgeois, and W. Christian Buss, "French-English Canadian Subcultural Consumption Differences," *Journal of Marketing,* Spring 1985, pp. 82–92.

182. Brian Dunn, "Nationalism in Advertising: Dead or Alive?" *Adweek,* November 22, 1993.

183. Hans Hoefer, *Thailand* (Boston: Houghton Mifflin, 1993).

184. Saritha Rai, "India's Boom Spreads to Smaller Cities," *New York Times,* January 4, 2005, p. C5.

185. Pamela Paul, "Religious Identity and Mobility," *American Demographics,* March 2003, pp. 20–21; Pamela Paul, "One Nation, Under God?" *American Demographics,* January 2002, pp. 16–17.

186. Priscilla L. Barbera, "Consumer Behavior and Born-Again Christianity," in eds. Jagdish N. Sheth and Elizabeth C. Hirschman, *Research in Consumer Behavior* (Greenwich, Conn.: JAI Press, 1988), pp. 193–222.

187. "Salem Communications Income Down in 4Q," *Los Angeles Business,* March 4, 2008, *www.bizjournals.com;* Rodney Ho, "Rappin' and Rockin' for the Lord," *Wall Street Journal,* February 28, 2001, pp. B1, B4.

188. Jennifer Youssef, "New Wal-Mart Draws Crowd," *Detroit News,* March 6, 2008, *www.detnews.com.*

189. Lisa Miller, "Registers Ring in Sanctuary Stores," *Wall Street Journal,* December 17, 1999, pp. B1, B4; Elizabeth Bernstein, "Holy Frappuccino!" *Wall Street Journal,* August 3, 2001, pp. W1, W8.

190. Stephanie Kang, "Pop Culture Gets Religion," *Wall Street Journal,* May 5, 2004, pp. B1, B2.

191. Julie Jargon, "Can M'm, M'm Good Translate?" *Wall Street Journal,* July 9, 2007, p. A16; "Campbell Soup Aims at China, Russia," *Los Angeles Times,* July 10, 2007, p. C2; "Campbell Soup Entering Russia and China with Customized Products and Promotions," *The Food Institute Report,* July 16, 2007, p. 1.

Chapter 13

1 John Hagel and John Seely Brown, "Learning from Tata's Nano," *BusinessWeek Online,* February 28, 2008, *www .businessweek.com;* Greg Keenan, "Car Sales 'Epicentre' Shifts to New Ground," *The Globe and Mail,* March 28, 2008, w*ww.theglobeandmail.com;* "The In-Betweeners: Economics Focus," *The Economist,* February 2, 2008, p. 88; Diana Farrell and Eric Beinhocker, "The World's Next Big Spenders," *Newsweek International,* May 28, 2007, n.p.; Joe Sharkey, "Indian Airline Makes Its Case as a Premier-Class Contender," *New York Times,* July 31, 2007, p. C8.

2. Pierre Bourdieu, *Language and Symbolic Power* (Cambridge, Mass.: Harvard University Press, 1991).

3. Richard P. Coleman, "The Continuing Significance of Social Class to Marketing," *Journal of Consumer Research,* December 1983, pp. 265–280; Wendell Blanchard, *Thailand, Its People, Its Society, Its Culture* (New Haven, Conn.: HRAF Press, 1990), as cited in Sak Onkvisit and John J. Shaw, *International Marketing: Analysis and Strategy* (Columbus, Ohio: Merrill, 1989), p. 293.

4. Edward W. Cundiff and Marye T. Hilger, *Marketing in the International Environment* (Englewood Cliffs, N.J.: Prentice-Hall, 1988), as cited in Mariele K. DeMooij and Warren Keegan, *Advertising Worldwide* (Englewood Cliffs, N.J.: Prentice-Hall, 1991), p. 96.

5. Onkvisit and Shaw, *International Marketing.*

6. Ernst Dichter, "The World Consumer," *Harvard Business Review,* July–August 1962, pp. 113–123, as cited in Cundiff and Hilger, *Marketing in the International Environment,* p. 135.

7. Richard P. Coleman, "The Significance of Social Stratification in Selling," in ed. Martin L. Bell, *Marketing: A Maturing Discipline* (Chicago: American Marketing Association, 1960), pp. 171–184.

8. Douglas E. Allen and Paul F. Anderson, "Consumption and Social Stratification: Bourdieu's Distinction," in eds. Chris T. Allan and Deborah Roedder John, *Advances in Consumer Research,* vol. 21 (Provo, Utah: Association for Consumer Research, 1994), pp. 70–73.

9. Pierre Bourdieu, *Distinction: A Social Critique of the Judgment of Taste* (Cambridge, Mass.: Harvard University Press, 1984).

10. Michael R. Solomon, "Deep Seated Materialism: The Case of Levi's 501 Jeans," in ed. Richard J. Lutz, *Advances in Consumer Research,* vol. 13 (Provo, Utah: Association for Consumer Research, 1986), pp. 619–622.

11. Coleman, "The Continuing Significance of Social Class to Marketing."

12. See Joan M. Ostrove and Elizabeth R. Cole, "Privileging Class: Toward a Critical Psychology of Social Class in the Context of Education," *Journal of Social Issues,* Winter 2003, pp. 677+; and Charles M. Schaninger, "Social Class

Versus Income Revisited: An Empirical Investigation," *Journal of Marketing Research,* May 1981, pp. 192–208.

13. Gillian Stevens and Joo Hyun Cho, "Socioeconomic Indexes and the New 1980 Census Occupational Classification Scheme," *Social Science Research,* March 1985, pp. 142–168; Charles B. Nam and Mary G. Powers, *The Socioeconomic Approach to Status Measurement* (Houston: Cap and Gown Press, 1983).

14. Diane Crispell, "The Real Middle Americans," *American Demographics,* October 1994, pp. 28–35; Michael Hout, "More Universalism, Less Structural Mobility: The American Occupational Structure in the 1980s," *American Journal of Sociology,* May 1988, pp. 1358–1400.

15. Peter Francese, "The College–Cash Connection," *American Demographics,* March 2002, pp. 42+; Patricia Cohen, "Forget Lonely. Life Is Healthy at the Top," *New York Times,* May 15, 2004, p. B9.

16. William L. Wilkie, *Consumer Behavior,* 2nd ed. (New York: Wiley, 1990).

17. Güliz Ger, Russell W. Belk, and Dana-Nicoleta Lascu, "The Development of Consumer Desire in Marketizing and Developing Economies: The Cases of Romania and Turkey," in eds. Leigh McAlister and Michael L. Rothschild, *Advances in Consumer Research,* vol. 20 (Provo, Utah: Association for Consumer Research, 1992), pp. 102–107.

18. M. R. Haque, "Marketing Opportunities in the Middle East," in ed. V. H. Manek Kirpalani, *International Business Handbook* (New York: Haworth Press, 1990), pp. 375–416.

19. W. Lloyd Warner, Marchia Meeker, and Kenneth Eells, *Social Class in America* (Chicago: Science Research Associates, 1949); August B. Hollingshead and Fredrick C. Redlich, *Social Class and Mental Illness, A Community Study* (New York: Wiley, 1958).

20. Gerhard Lenski, "Status Crystallization: A Non-Vertical Dimension of Social Status," *American Sociological Review,* August 1956, pp. 458–464.

21. Alison Stein Wellner, "The Money in the Middle," *American Demographics,* April 2000, pp. 56–64.

22. Benita Eisler, *Class Act: America's Last Dirty Secret* (New York: Franklin Watts, 1983); David L. Featherman and Robert M. Hauser, *Opportunity and Change* (New York: Academic Press, 1978).

23. See Mary Ellen Slayter, "Succeeding with an Upbringing That's Not Upper Crust," *Washington Post,* May 2, 2004, p. K1; and Aaron Bernstein, "Waking Up from the American Dream," *BusinessWeek,* December 1, 2003, p. 54.

24. Allen and Anderson, "Consumption and Social Stratification."

25. Jake Ryan and Charles Sackrey, *Strangers in Paradise: Academics from the Working Class* (Boston: South End Press, 1984).

26. Mary Janigan, Ruth Atherley, Michelle Harries, Brenda Branswell, and John Demont, "The Wealth Gap: New Studies Show Canada's Rich Really Are Getting Richer—and the Poor Poorer—as the Middle Class Erodes," *Maclean's,* August 28, 2000, pp. 42; Bernstein, "Waking Up from the American Dream."

27. Roger Burbach and Steve Painter, "Restoration in Czechoslovakia," *Monthly Review,* November 1990, pp. 36–49; Rahul Jacob, "The Big Rise," *Fortune,* May 30, 1994, pp. 74–80.

28. Haque, "Marketing Opportunities in the Middle East."

29. Jacob, "The Big Rise."

30. David Wessel, "Barbell Effect: The Future of Jobs," *Wall Street Journal,* April 2, 2004, p. A1; Matt Murray, "Settling for Less," *Wall Street Journal,* August 13, 2003, p. A1; Greg J. Duncan, Martha Hill, and Willard Rogers, "The Changing Fortunes of Young and Old," *American Demographics,* August 1986, pp. 26–33; Katherine S. Newman, *Falling from Grace: The Experience of Downward Mobility in the American Middle Class* (New York: Free Press, 1988); Kenneth Labich, "Class in America," *Fortune,* February 7, 1994, pp. 114–126.

31. Newman, *Falling from Grace;* Eisler, *Class Act.*

32. Michael J. Weiss, "Great Expectations," *American Demographics,* May 2003, pp. 26–35.

33. Scott D. Roberts, "Consumer Responses to Involuntary Job Loss," in eds. Rebecca H. Holman and Michael R. Solomon, *Advances in Consumer Research,* vol. 18 (Provo, Utah: Association for Consumer Research, 1988), pp. 40–42.

34. Deborah Ball, "Despite Downturn, Japanese Are Still Having Fits for Luxury Goods," *Wall Street Journal,* April 24, 2001, pp. B1, B4.

35. Labich, "Class in America."

36. Labich, "Class in America."

37. John Brooks, *Showing Off in America: From Conspicuous Consumption to Parody Display* (Boston: Little, Brown, 1981); for those interested in reading more about the theory of conspicuous consumption, see Thorstein Veblen, *The Theory of the Leisure Class* (New York: Macmillan, 1899).

38. Aron O'Cass and Hmily McEwen, "Exploring Consumer Status and Conspicuous Consumption," *Journal of Consumer Behavior* 4, no. 1, 2004, pp. 25–39.

39. Wilfred Amaldoss and Sanjay Jain, "Pricing of Conspicuous Goods: A Competitive Analysis of Social Effects," *Journal of Marketing Research,* February 2005, pp. 30–42.

40. Jamie Arndt, Sheldon Solomon, Tim Kasser, and Kennon M. Sheldon, "The Urge to Splurge: A Terror Management Account of Materialism and Consumer Behavior," *Journal of Consumer Psychology* 14, no. 3, 2004, pp. 198–212.

41. Christine Page, "A History of Conspicuous Consumption," in eds. Floyd Rudmin and Marsha Richins, *Meaning, Measure, and Morality of Materialism* (Provo, Utah: Association for Consumer Research, 1993), pp. 82–87.

42. Ger, Belk, and Lascu, "The Development of Consumer Desire in Marketizing and Developing Economies."

43. Janeen Arnold Costa and Russell W. Belk, "Nouveaux Riches as Quintessential Americans: Case Studies of Consumption in the Extended Family," in ed. Russell W. Belk, *Advances in Nonprofit Marketing,* vol. 3 (Greenwich, Conn.: JAI Press, 1990), pp. 83–140.

44. Christina Duff, "Indulging in Inconspicuous Consumption," *Wall Street Journal,* April 14, 1997, pp. B1, B4.

45. Peter Francese, "The Exotic Travel Boom," *American Demographics,* June 2002, pp. 48–49.

46. Rebecca H. Holman, "Product Use as Communication: A Fresh Appraisal of a Venerable Topic," in eds. Ben M. Enis and Kenneth J. Roering, *Review of Marketing* (Chicago: American Marketing Association, 1981), pp. 106–119.

47. John Tagliabue, "For the Yachting Class, the Latest Amenity Can Take Flight," *New York Times,* October 2, 2007, pp. C1, C4.

48. J. R. Whitaker Penteado, "Fast Food Franchises Fight for Brazilian Aficionados," *Brandweek,* June 7, 1993, pp. 20–24.

49. Naomi Mandel, Petia K. Petrova, and Robert B. Cialdini, "Images of Success and the Preference for Luxury Brands," *Journal of Consumer Psychology* 16, no. 1, 2006, pp. 57–69.

50. Rebecca Gardyn, "Oh, the Good Life," *American Demographics,* November 2002, pp. 30–35.

51. Brooks, *Showing Off in America.*

52. Stephen Buckley, "Brazil Rediscovers Its Culture; Poor Man's Cocktail, Martial Art Hip Among Middle Class," *Washington Post,* April 15, 2001, p. A16.

53. Teri Agins, "Now, Subliminal Logos," *Wall Street Journal,* July 20, 2001, p. B1.

54. Sigmund Gronmo, "Compensatory Consumer Behavior: Theoretical Perspectives, Empirical Examples and Methodological Challenges," in eds. Paul F. Anderson and Michael J. Ryan, *1984 American Marketing Association Winter Educators' Conference* (Chicago: American Marketing Association, 1984), pp. 184–188.

55. Russell W. Belk, "Yuppies as Arbiters of the Emerging Consumption Style," in ed. Richard J. Lutz, *Advances in Consumer Research,* vol. 13 (Provo, Utah: Association for Consumer Research, 1986), pp. 514–519.

56. Scott Cendrowski, "Extreme Retailing: Midlevel Luxury Brands Flee for the High End or the Low," *Fortune,* March 31, 2008, p. 14; "Tiffany's Boutique Risk; By Breaking Mall Fast, High-End Exclusivity May Gain Touch of Common," *Wall Street Journal,* October 20, 2007, p. B14.

57. Russell W. Belk and Melanie Wallendorf, "The Sacred Meanings of Money," *Journal of Economic Psychology,* March 1990, pp. 35–67.

58. Abraham McLaughlin, "Africans' New Motto: 'Charge It,'" *Christian Science Monitor,* February 14, 2005, p. 6.

59. "Rabobank Deploys Siebel CRM On Demand," *Canadian Corporate News,* November 17, 2004, *www.comtextnews.com.*

60. C. Rubenstein, "Your Money or Your Life," *Psychology Today* 12, 1980, pp. 47–58.

61. Adrian Furnham and Alan Lewis, *The Economic Mind: The Social Psychology of Economic Behavior* (Brighton, Sussex: Harvester Press, 1986); Belk and Wallendorf, "The Sacred Meanings of Money."

62. H. Goldberg and R. Lewis, *Money Madness: The Psychology of Saving, Spending, Loving, and Hating Money* (London: Springwood, 1979).

63. Rebecca Gardyn, "Generosity and Income," *American Demographics,* December 2002–January 2003, pp. 46–47.

64. Mark Scott, "For Nokia, Excess Is a Vertu," *BusinessWeek Online,* December 24, 2007, *www.businessweek.com.*

65. "Spectacular Results," *The Economist,* August 18, 2007, p. 55.

66. Bert Archer, "Still Upwardly Mobile," *Toronto Life,* November 2007, p. 95.

67. Ronald J. Mann, "The Plastic Revolution," *Foreign Policy,* March–April 2008, pp. 34–35.

68. C. W. Young, "Bijan Designs a Very Exclusive Image," *Advertising Age,* March 13, 1986, pp. 18, 19, 21, as cited in LaBarbera, "The Nouveaux Riches"; V. Kanti Prasad, "Socioeconomic Product Risk and Patronage Preferences of Retail Shoppers," *Journal of Marketing,* July 1975, pp. 42–47.

69. Mercedes M. Cardona, "Affluent Shoppers Like Their Luxe Goods Cheap," *Advertising Age,* December 1, 2003, p. 6.

70. John Fetto, "Sensible Santas," *American Demographics,* December 2000, pp. 10–11.

71. See "Old Money," *American Demographics,* June 2003, pp. 34–37.

72. Jean Halliday, "Ultra-luxury Car Marketers Roll Out Red Carpet for Buyers," *Advertising Age,* February 2, 2004, p. 6.

73. Daniel McGinn, "Friendly Skies," *Newsweek,* October 1, 2007, p. E8.

74. Kathryn Kranhold, "Marketing to the New Millionaire," *Wall Street Journal,* October 11, 2000, pp. B1, B6.

75. Carole Ann King, "The New Wealthy: Younger, Richer, More Proactive," *National Underwriter Life & Health–Financial Services Edition,* February 12, 2001, p. 4.

76. "U.S. Millionaires Grow at Slowest Rate Since 2003," *Trusts & Estates,* March 13, 2008, n.p.

77. Paul C. Henry, "Social Class, Market Situation, and Consumers' Metaphors of (Dis)Empowerment," *Journal of Consumer Research* 31, no. 4, 2005, pp. 766–778.

78. John Fetto, "I Want My MTV," *American Demographics,* March 2003, p. 8.

79. Elisabeth Malkin, "Mexico's Working Poor Become Homeowners," *New York Times,* December 17, 2004, p. W1.

80. Dave Montgomery, "Ten Years After Russia's Failed Coup, Middle Class Is Small but Growing," *Knight Ridder,* August 11, 2001.

81. Jacob, "The Big Rise."

82. Rebecca Piirto Heath, "The New Working Class," *American Demographics* 20, no. 1, January 1998, pp. 51–55.

83. Coleman, "The Continuing Significance of Social Class to Marketing."

84. Paul C. Henry, "Social Class, Market Situation, and Consumers' Metaphors of (Dis)Empowerment," *Journal of Consumer Research* 31, no. 4, 2005, pp. 766–778.

85. Prasad, "Socioeconomic Product Risk and Patronage Preferences of Retail Shoppers"; Stuart Rich and Subhish Jain, "Social Class and Life Cycle as Predictors of Shopping Behavior," *Journal of Marketing Research,* June–July 1987, pp. 51–59.

86. John Fetto, "Watering Holes," *American Demographics,* June 2003, p. 8.

87. Ronald Paul Hill and Mark Stamey, "The Homeless in America: An Examination of Possessions and Consumption Behaviors," *Journal of Consumer Research,* December 1990, pp. 303–321; Frank Caro, *Estimating the Numbers of Homeless Families* (New York: Community Service Society of New York, 1981).

88. "Federal Report Takes Snapshot of Country's Homeless Population," *The Nation's Health,* May 2007, p. 10; National Coalition for the Homeless, "How Many People Experience Homelessness?" February 1999, *http://nch. ari.net/numbers.html.*

89. Lakshmi Bhargave, "Homeless Help Themselves with 'Advocate,'" *Daily Texan (Austin),* February 16, 2000, pp. 1, 8.

90. Richard B. Freeman and Brian Hall, "Permanent Homelessness in America?" *Population Research and Policy Review* 6, 1987, pp. 3–27.

91. Ronald Paul Hill, "Homeless Women, Special Possessions, and the Meaning of 'Home': An Ethnographic Case Study," *Journal of Consumer Research,* December 1991, pp. 298–310.

92. David A. Snow and Leon Anderson, "Identity Work among the Homeless: The Verbal Construction and Avowal of Personal Identities," *American Journal of Sociology,* May 1987, pp. 1336–1371.

93. Marla Dickerson, "Mexican Retailer, Partner to Build Cars," *Los Angeles Times,* November 23, 2007, p. C1; Peter Katel, "Petro Padillo Longoria: A Retailer Focused on Working-Class Needs," *Time International,* October 15, 2001, p. 49.

94. Jack Neff, "Value Positioning Becomes a Priority," *Advertising Age,* February 23, 2004, pp. 24, 30.

95. Teri Agins, "New Kors Line Stars Luxury Look-Alikes: 'Carpool Couture,'" *Wall Street Journal,* August 20, 2004, pp. B1, B3.

96. Sonya A. Grier and Rohit Deshpandé, "Social Dimensions of Consumer Distinctiveness: The Influence of Social Status on Group Identity and Advertising Persuasion," *Journal of Marketing Research* 38, May 2001, pp. 216–224.

97. David Carr, "For the Rich, Magazines Fat on Ads," *New York Times,* October 1, 2007, p. C1.

98. Kelly Shermach, "Study Identifies Types of Interactive Shoppers," *Marketing News,* September 25, 1995, p. 22; *eMarketer,* February 3, 2000 (online reference).

99. Rich and Jain, "Social Class and Life Cycle as Predictors of Shopping Behavior."

100. Jessica Brinton, "People Like Them," *The Sunday Times,* March 16, 2008, *www.timesonline.co.uk;* Teri Agins and Deborah Ball, "Designer Stores, in Extra Large," *Wall Street Journal,* June 6, 2001, pp. B1, B12.

101. Page, "A History of Conspicuous Consumption."

102. Matthew Grimm, "Target Hits Its Mark," *American Demographics,* November 2002, pp. 42–43.

103. "Multigenerational Households Number 4 Million According to Census 2000," *U.S. Department of Commerce News,* September 7, 2001, *www.census.gov/pressrelease/www/2001/cb01cn182.html.*

104. Sak Onkvisit and John J. Shaw, *International Marketing: Analysis and Strategy* (Columbus, Ohio: Merrill, 1989).

105. Patrick Barta, "Looming Need for Housing a Big Surprise," *Wall Street Journal,* May 15, 2001, pp. B1, B4.

106. "The Future of Households," *American Demographics,* December 1993, pp. 27–40.

107. Steven Bodzin, "Home Alone: Households of Singles Go to First in U.S.," *Los Angeles Times,* August 18, 2005, p. A12.

108. "Nation's Median Age Highest Ever, But 65-and-Over Population's Growth Lags, Census 2000 Shows," *United States Department of Commerce News* (soundbite), May 15, 2001.

109. Pamela Paul, "Childless by Choice," *American Demographics,* November 2001, pp. 45–50.

110. Rex Y. Du and Wagner A. Kamakura, "Household Life Cycles and Lifestyles in the United States," *Journal of Marketing Research,* February 2006, pp. 121–132; Mary C. Gilly and Ben M. Enis, "Recycling the Family Life Cycle," in ed. Andrew A. Mitchell, *Advances in Consumer Research,* vol. 9 (Ann Arbor, Mich.: Association for Consumer Research, 1982), pp. 271–276; William D. Danko and Charles M. Schaninger, "An Empirical Evaluation of the Gilly-Enis Updated Household Life Cycle Model," *Journal of Business Research,* August 1990, pp. 39–57.

111. Robert E. Wilkes, "Household Life-Cycle Stages, Transitions, and Product Expenditures," *Journal of Consumer Research,* June 1995, pp. 27–42.

112. John Fetto, "The Baby Business," *American Demographics,* May 2003, p. 40.

113. Alan R. Andreasen, "Life Status Changes and Changes in Consumer Preferences and Satisfaction," *Journal of Consumer Research,* December 1984, pp. 784–794.

114. Rebecca Gardyn, "A Market Kept in the Closet," *American Demographics,* November 2001, pp. 37–43.

115. "The Mommies, in Numbers," *Brandweek,* November 13, 1993, p. 17; Lee Smith, "The New Wave of Illegitimacy," *Fortune,* April 18, 1994, pp. 81–94.

116. Diane Brady and Christopher Palmeri, "The Pet Economy," *BusinessWeek,* August 6, 2007, pp. 44–54.

117. Peter Francese, "Marriage Drain's Big Cost," *American Demographics,* April 2004, pp. 40–41; Matthew Grimm, "Hitch Switch," *American Demographics,* November 2003, pp. 34–36.

118. James Morrow, "A Place for One," *American Demographics,* November 2003, pp. 25+; "Multigenerational Households Number 4 Million According to Census 2000," *U.S. Department of Commerce news release,* September 7, 2001.

119. Patricia Braus, "Sex and the Single Spender," *American Demographics*, November 1993, pp. 28–34.

120. Morrow, "A Place for One."

121. Peter Francese, "Well Enough Alone," *American Demographics*, November 2003, pp. 32–33.

122. Barbara Carton, "It's a Niche! Twins, Triplets and Beyond," *Wall Street Journal*, February 2, 1999, pp. B1, B4.

123. Rebecca Gardyn, "Unmarried Bliss," *American Demographics*, December 2000, pp. 56–61.

124. David Whelan, "Do Ask, Do Tell," *American Demographics*, November 2001, p. 41.

125. Clark D. Olson, "Materialism in the Home: The Impact of Artifacts on Dyadic Communication," in eds. Elizabeth C. Hirschman and Morris B. Holbrook, *Advances in Consumer Research*, vol. 12 (Provo, Utah: Association for Consumer Research, 1985), pp. 388–393.

126. Jeanne L. Hafstrom and Marilyn M. Dunsing, "Socio-economic and Social–Psychological Influences on Reasons Wives Work," *Journal of Consumer Research*, December 1978, pp. 169–175; Rena Bartos, *The Moving Target: What Every Marketer Should Know About Women* (New York: Free Press, 1982).

127. Rose M. Rubin, Bobye J. Riney, and David J. Molina, "Expenditure Pattern Differentials Between One-Earner and Dual-Earner Households: 1972–1973 and 1984," *Journal of Consumer Research*, June 1990, pp. 43–52; Horacio Soberon-Ferrer and Rachel Dardis, "Determinants of Household Expenditures for Services," *Journal of Consumer Research*, March 1991, pp. 385–397; Don Bellante and Ann C. Foster, "Working Wives and Expenditure on Services," *Journal of Consumer Research*, September 1984, pp. 700–707.

128. Suraj Commuri and James W. Gentry, "Resource Allocation in Households with Women as Chief Wage Earner," *Journal of Consumer Research* 32, no. 2, 2005, pp. 185–195.

129. See John Fetto, "Does Father Really Know Best?" *American Demographics*, June 2002, pp. 10–11; Pamela Paul, "Meet the Parents," *American Demographics*, January 2002, pp. 42–43; Linda Thompson and Alexis Walker, "Gender in Families: Women and Men in Marriage, Work, and Parenthood," *Journal of Marriage and the Family*, November 1989, pp. 845–871.

130. Joan Raymond, "The Ex-Files," *American Demographics*, February 2001, pp. 60–64.

131. "Do Us Part," *American Demographics*, September 2002, p. 9.

132. James H. Alexander, John W. Shouten, and Scott D. Roberts, "Consumer Behavior and Divorce," in eds. Janeen Costa and Russell W. Belk, *Research in Consumer Behavior*, vol. 6 (Greenwich, Conn.: JAI Press, 1993), pp. 153–184.

133. Kalpana Srinivasan, "More Single Fathers Raising Kids, Though Moms Far More Common," *Austin (Tex.) American Statesman*, December 11, 1998, p. A23.

134. Raymond, "The Ex-Files."

135. Barbara Rosewicz, "Here Comes the Bride . . . and for the Umpteenth Time," *Wall Street Journal*, September 10, 1996, pp. B1, B10.

136. Jan Larson, "Understanding Stepfamilies," *American Demographics*, July 1992, pp. 36–40.

137. "Profiles of General Demographic Characteristics: 2000 Census of Population and Housing," *United States Department of Commerce News*.

138. Paul, "Childless by Choice."

139. Lyle V. Harris, "Shopping by Male," *Austin (Tex.) American Statesman*, April 27, 1999, pp. E1, E2.

140. Gardyn, "Unmarried Bliss."

141. Jen Christensen, "Grocery Store Provides Dinner (and Maybe a Date)," *Atlanta Journal Constitution*, March 13, 2008, *www.ajc.com*.

142. Sandra Yin, "Coming Out in Print," *American Demographics*, February 2003, pp. 18+; Ronald Alsop, "Corporate Sponsorships at Gay Pride Parades Alienate Some Activists," *Wall Street Journal*, June 22, 2001, p. B1.

143. Jean Halliday, "Cadillac Takes Tentative Step Toward Targeting Gay Market," *Advertising Age*, February 2, 2004, p. 8.

144. Ronald Alsop, "As Same-Sex Households Grow More Mainstream, Businesses Take Note," *Wall Street Journal*, August 8, 2001, pp. B1, B4.

145. Robert E. Wilkes and Debra A. Laverie, "Purchasing Decisions in Non-Traditional Households: The Case of Lesbian Couples," *Journal of Consumer Behavior* 6, no. 1, 2007, pp. 60–73.

146. Harry L. Davis, "Dimensions of Marital Roles in Consumer Decision Making," *Journal of Marketing Research*, May 1970, pp. 168–177; Conway Lackman and John M. Lanasa, "Family Decision Making Theory: An Overview and Assessment," *Psychology and Marketing*, March–April 1993, pp. 81–93.

147. P. Doyle and P. Hutchinson, "Individual Differences in Family Decision Making," *Journal of the Market Research Society*, October 1973, pp. 193–206; Jagdish N. Sheth, "A Theory of Family Buying Decisions," in ed. J. N. Sheth, *Models of Buyer Behavior* (New York: Harper & Row, 1974), pp. 17–33; Daniel Seymour and Greg Lessne, "Spousal Conflict Arousal: Scale Development," *Journal of Consumer Research*, December 1984, pp. 810–821.

148. Neal Templin, "The PC Wars: Who Gets to Use the Family Computer?" *Wall Street Journal*, October 5, 1996, pp. B1, B2.

149. Alice Gronhoj, "Communication About Consumption: A Family Process Perspective on 'Green' Consumer Practices," *Journal of Consumer Behavior* 5, no. 6, 2006, pp. 491–503.

150. Sheth, "A Theory of Family Buying Decisions"; Michael A. Belch, George E. Belch, and Donald Sciglimpaglia, "Conflict in Family Decision Making: An Exploratory Investigation," in ed. Jerry C. Olson, *Advances in Consumer Research*, vol. 7 (Chicago: Association for Consumer Research, 1980), pp. 475–479.

151. W. Christian Buss and Charles M. Schaninger, "The Influence of Family Decision Processes and Outcomes," in eds. Richard P. Bagozzi and Alice M. Tybout, *Advances in Consumer Research*, vol. 10 (Ann Arbor, Mich.: Association for Consumer Research, 1983), pp. 439–444.

152. Terry L. Childers and Akshay R. Rao, "The Influence of Familial and Peer-Based Reference Groups on Consumer Decisions," *Journal of Consumer Research*, September 1992, pp. 198–211.

153. Harry L. Davis and Benny P. Rigaux, "Perception of Marital Roles in Decision Processes," *Journal of Consumer Research*, June 1974, pp. 5–14; Mandy Putnam and William R. Davidson, *Family Purchasing Behavior: 11 Family Roles by Product Category* (Columbus, Ohio: Management Horizons, Inc., a Division of Price Waterhouse, 1987).

154. Rosann Spiro, "Persuasion in Family Decision Making," *Journal of Consumer Research*, March 1983, pp. 393–402; Alvin Burns and Donald Granbois, "Factors Moderating the Resolution of Preference Conflict," *Journal of Marketing Research*, February 1977, pp. 68–77.

155. Pierre Filiarault and J. R. Brent Ritchie, "Joint Purchasing Decisions: A Comparison of Influence Structure in Family and Couple Decision Making Units," *Journal of Consumer Research*, September 1980, pp. 131–140; Dennis Rosen and Donald Granbois, "Determinants of Role Structure in Financial Management," *Journal of Consumer Research*, September 1983, pp. 253–258; Spiro, "Persuasion in Family Decision Making"; Kim P. Corfman and Donald R. Lehmann, "Models of Cooperative Group Decision-Making and Relative Influence: An Experimental Investigation of Family Purchase Decisions," *Journal of Consumer Research*, June 1987, pp. 1–13.

156. William J. Qualls, "Household Decision Behavior: The Impact of Husbands' and Wives' Sex Role Orientation," *Journal of Consumer Research*, September 1987, pp. 264–279; Giovanna Imperia, Thomas O'Guinn, and Elizabeth MacAdams, "Family Decision Making Role Perceptions Among Mexican-American and Anglo Wives: A Cross-Cultural Comparison," in eds. Elizabeth C. Hirschman and Morris B. Holbrook, *Advances in Consumer Research*, vol. 12 (Provo, Utah: Association for Consumer Research, 1985), pp. 71–74.

157. Michael Flagg, "Asian Marketing," Asian *Wall Street Journal*, March 19, 2001, p. A12.

158. Robert T. Green, Jean-Paul Leonardi, Jean-Louis Chandon, Isabella C. M. Cunningham, Bronis Verhage, and Alain Strazzieri, "Societal Development and Family Purchasing Roles: A Cross-National Study," *Journal of Consumer Research*, March 1983, pp. 436–442; Leonidas C. Leonidou, "Understanding the Russian Consumer," *Marketing and Research Today*, March 1992, pp. 75–83; Sak Onkvisit and John J. Shaw, *International Marketing: Analysis and Strategy* (Columbus, Ohio: Merrill, 1989).

159. Michael B. Menasco and David J. Curry, "Utility and Choice: An Empirical Study of Wife/Husband Decision Making," *Journal of Consumer Research*, June 1989, pp. 87–97; Qualls, "Household Decision Behavior."

160. C. Whan Park, "Joint Decisions in Home Purchasing: A Muddling-Through Process," *Journal of Consumer Research*, September 1982, pp. 151–162; Harry L. Davis, Stephen J. Hoch, and E. K. Easton Ragsdale, "An Anchoring and Adjustment Model of Spousal Predictions," *Journal of Consumer Research*, June 1986, pp. 25–37; Gary M. Munsinger, Jean E. Weber, and Richard W. Hansen, "Joint Home Purchasing by Husbands and Wives," *Journal of Consumer Research*, March 1975, pp. 60–66; Lakshman Krisnamurthi, "The Salience of Relevant Others and Its Effect on Individual and Joint Preferences: An Experimental Investigation," *Journal of Consumer Research*, June 1983, pp. 62–72; Robert F. Krampf, David J. Burns, and Dale M. Rayman, "Consumer Decision Making and the Nature of the Product: A Comparison of Husband and Wife Adoption Process Location," *Psychology and Marketing*, March–April 1993, pp. 95–109.

161. Davy Lerouge and Luk Warlop, "Why It Is So Hard to Predict Our Partner's Product Preferences: The Effect of Target Familiarity on Prediction Accuracy," *Journal of Consumer Research* 33, no. 3, 2006, pp. 393–402; Chenting Su, Edward F. Fern, and Keying Ye, "A Temporal Dynamic Model of Spousal Family Purchase-Decision Behavior," *Journal of Marketing Research*, August 2003, pp. 268–281.

162. Tamara F. Mangleburg, "Children's Influence in Purchase Decisions: A Review and Critique," in eds. Marvin E. Goldberg, Gerald Gorn, and Richard W. Pollay, *Advances in Consumer Research*, vol. 17 (Provo, Utah: Association for Consumer Research, 1990), pp. 813–825; Ellen R. Foxman, Patriya S. Tansuhaj, and Karin M. Ekstrom, "Family Members' Perceptions of Adolescents' Influence in Family Decision Making," *Journal of Consumer Research*, March 1989, pp. 481–490; George Belch, Michael A. Belch, and Gayle Ceresino, "Parental and Teenage Influences in Family Decision Making," *Journal of Business Research*, April 1985, pp. 163–176; Lackman and Lanasa, "Family Decision Making Theory."

163. Selina S. Guber and Jon Berry, "War Stories from the Sandbox: What Kids Say," *Brandweek*, July 5, 1993, pp. 26–30; Andre Caron and Scott Ward, "Gift Decisions by Kids and Parents," *Journal of Advertising Research*, August–September 1975, pp. 15–20.

164. Mary Lou Roberts, Lawrence H. Wortzel, and Robert L. Berkeley, "Mothers' Attitudes and Perceptions of Children's Influence and Their Effect on Family Consumption," in ed. Jerry C. Olson, *Advances in Consumer Research*, vol. 8 (Ann Arbor, Mich.: Association for Consumer Research, 1981), pp. 730–735; Ellen Foxman and Patriya Tansuhaj, "Adolescents' and Mothers' Perceptions of Relative Influence in Family Purchase

Decisions: Patterns of Agreement and Disagreement," in ed. Michael J. Houston, *Advances in Consumer Research*, vol. 15 (Provo, Utah: Association for Consumer Research, 1988), pp. 449–453.

165. Sharon E. Beatty and Salil Talpade, "Adolescent Influence in Family Decision Making: A Replication with Extension," *Journal of Consumer Research*, September 1994, pp. 332–341; Christopher Power, "Getting 'Em While They're Young," *BusinessWeek*, September 9, 1991, pp. 94–95; Scott Ward and Daniel B. Wackman, "Children's Purchase Influence Attempts and Parental Yielding," *Journal of Marketing Research*, November 1972, pp. 316–319.

166. William K. Darley and Jeen-Su Lim, "Family Decision Making in Leisure Time Activities: An Exploratory Analysis of the Impact of Locus of Control, Child Age Influence Factor and Parental Type on Perceived Child Influence," in ed. Richard J. Lutz, *Advances in Consumer Research*, vol. 13 (Ann Arbor, Mich.: Association for Consumer Research, 1986), pp. 370–374; George P. Moschis and Linda G. Mitchell, "Television Advertising and Interpersonal Influences on Teenagers' Participation in Family Consumer Decisions," in ed. Lutz, *Advances in Consumer Research*, vol. 13, pp. 181–186; Beatty and Talpade, "Adolescent Influence in Family Decision Making."

167. Jeff Brazil, "Play Dough," *American Demographics*, December 1999, pp. 57–61.

168. June Cotte and Stacy L. Wood, "Families and Innovative Consumer Behavior: A Triadic Analysis of Sibling and Parental Influence," *Journal of Consumer Research*, June 2004, pp. 78–86.

169. Kay M. Palan and Robert E. Wilkes, "Adolescent–Parent Interaction in Family Decision Making," *Journal of Consumer Research*, September 1997, pp. 159–169.

170. Les Carlson and Sanford Grossbart, "Parental Style and Consumer Socialization of Children," *Journal of Consumer Research*, June 1988, pp. 77–94.

171. Belch, Belch, and Ceresino, "Parental and Teenage Influences in Family Decision Making."

172. Miho Inada, "Playing at Professions," *Wall Street Journal*, February 9, 2007, p. B1.

173. Amanda C. Kooser, "Virtual Playground," *U.S. News & World Report*, April 1, 2008, *www.usnews.com.*

174. Brooks Barnes, "Web Playgrounds of the Very Young," *New York Times*, December 31, 2007, pp. C1, C3.

175. Claire Cain Miller, "The New Back Fence," *Forbes*, April 7, 2008, p. 66; Gregg Cebrzynski, "McD Turns to Moms for Family Marketing Advice," *Nation's Restaurant News*, May 22, 2006, p. 6; Emily Steel, "The New Focus Groups," *Wall Street Journal*, January 14, 2008, p. B6; *www.kfc.com;* Gregg Cebrzynski, "KFC Sets Up Moms' Panel to Offer Advice on Family Issues," *Nation's Restaurant News*, September 4, 2006, p. 14; Robert Berner, "I Sold It Through the Grapevine," *BusinessWeek*, May 29, 2006, *www.businessweek.com.*

Chapter 14

1. Rachel Dodes and Christina Passariello, "Luxury Labels Hit in the Pocketbook," *Wall Street Journal*, January 24, 2008, p. B1; Christina Binkley, "The Psychology of the $14,000 Handbag," *Wall Street Journal*, August 9, 2007, p. D8; "Back Down to the Basics—the Affordable Basics," *Retailing Today*, March 17, 2008, p. 32; Mike Vogel, "Four Segments Star Performers," *Chain Drug Review*, November 5, 2007, p. 25; Joseph Rago, "Taste—de Gustibus: Conspicuous Virtue and the Sustainable Sofa," *Wall Street Journal*, March 23, 2007, p. W13.

2. Milton Rokeach, *The Nature of Human Values* (New York: Free Press, 1973), p. 5.

3. Wagner A. Kamakura and Jose Alfonso Mazzon, "Value Segmentation: A Model for the Measurement of Values and Value Systems," *Journal of Consumer Research*, September 1991, pp. 208–218; see also Milton Rokeach and Sandra J. Ball-Rokeach, "Stability and Change in American Value Priorities, 1968–1981," *American Psychologist*, May 1989, pp. 775–784; Milton Rokeach, *Understanding Human Values* (New York: Free Press, 1979); Shalom H. Schwartz and Wolfgang Bilsky, "Toward a Universal Psychological Structure of Human Values," *Journal of Personality and Social Psychology*, September 1987, pp. 550–562.

4. Kim A. Nelson, "Consumer Decision Making and Image Theory: Understanding Value-Laden Decisions," *Journal of Consumer Psychology* 14, no. 1/2, 2004, pp. 28–40.

5. Francesco M. Nicosia and Robert N. Mayer, "Toward a Sociology of Consumption," *Journal of Consumer Research*, September 1976, pp. 65–75; Hugh E. Kramer, "The Value of Higher Education and Its Impact on Value Formation," in eds. Robert E. Pitts and Arch G. Woodside, *Personal Values and Consumer Psychology* (Lexington, Mass.: Lexington Books, 1984), pp. 239–251.

6. Mary Gilly and Lisa Penaloza, "Barriers and Incentives in Consumer Acculturation," in eds. W. Fred van Raaij and Gary J. Bamossy, *European Advances in Consumer Research*, vol. 1 (Provo, Utah: Association for Consumer Research, 1993), pp. 278–286.

7. Rokeach, *The Nature of Human Values;* Schwartz and Bilsky, "Toward a Universal Psychological Structure of Human Values."

8. Russell W. Belk, "Materialism: Trait Aspects of Living in the Material World," *Journal of Consumer Research*, December 1985, pp. 265–280; Russell W. Belk, "Three Scales to Measure Constructs Related to Materialism: Reliability, Validity, and Relationships to Happiness," in ed. Thomas P. Kinnear, *Advances in Consumer Research*, vol. 11 (Provo, Utah: Association for Consumer Research, 1984), pp. 291–297.

9. Marsha L. Richins, "Special Possessions and the Expression of Material Values," *Journal of Consumer Research*, December 1994, pp. 522–533.

10. James A. Roberts, John F. Tanner Jr., and Chris Manolis, "Materialism and the Family Structure–Stress Relation,"

Journal of Consumer Psychology 15, no. 2, 2005, pp. 183–190.

11. Jamie Arndt, Sheldon Solomon, Tim Kasser, and Kennon M. Sheldon, "The Urge to Splurge: A Terror Management Account of Materialism and Consumer Behavior," *Journal of Consumer Psychology* 14, no. 3, 2004, pp. 198–212; Jamie Arndt, Sheldon Solomon, Tim Kasser, and Kennon M. Sheldon, "The Urge to Splurge Revisited: Further Reflections on Applying Terror Management Account to Materialism and Consumer Behavior," *Journal of Consumer Psychology* 14, no. 3, 2004, pp. 225–229; Durairaj Maheswaran and Nidhi Agrawal, "Motivational and Cultural Variations in Mortality Salience Effects: Contemplations on Terror Management Theory and Consumer Behavior," *Journal of Consumer Psychology* 14, no. 3, 2004, pp. 213–218; Aric Rindfleisch and James E. Burroughs, "Terrifying Thoughts, Terrible Materialism? Contemplations on a Terror Management Account of Materialism and Consumer Behavior," *Journal of Consumer Psychology* 14, no. 3, 2004, pp. 219–224.

12. Marsha L. Richins and Scott Dawson, "A Consumer Values Orientation for Materialism and Its Measurement: Scale Development and Validation," *Journal of Consumer Research*, December 1992, pp. 303–316.

13. James E. Burroughs and Aric Rindfleisch, "Materialism and Well-Being: A Conflicting Values Perspective," *Journal of Consumer Research*, December 2002, pp. 348–370.

14. Mary Yoko Brannen, "Cross Cultural Materialism: Commodifying Culture in Japan," in eds. Floyd Rudmin and Marsha Richins, *Meaning, Measure, and Morality of Materialism* (Provo, Utah: The Association for Consumer Research, 1992), pp. 167–180; Dorothy E. Jones, Dorinda Elliott, Edith Terry, Carla A. Robbins, Charles Gaffney, and Bruce Nussbaum, "Capitalism in China," *BusinessWeek*, January 1985, pp. 53–59; see also Tse, Belk, and Zhou, "Becoming a Consumer Society."

15. Meg Dupont, "Cocooning Morphs into Hiving," *Hartford Courant*, October 29, 2004, p. H2.

16. "One Third of Americans Regularly Bank Online," *Information Week*, February 19, 2008, *www.informationweek.com*.

17. "Ikea Ads Home in on Soul Objective," *Marketing Week*, September 20, 2007, p. 12; Suzanne Vranica, "Ikea to Tug at Heartstrings," *Wall Street Journal*, September 18, 2007, p. B6.

18. John Fetto, "Nowhere to Hide," *American Demographics*, July–August 2002, pp. 12.

19. Allison Enright, "FreshDirect: The Internet-Only Grocer," *Marketing News*, September 1, 2007, p. 11; Lisa Fickenscher, "Online Grocer Clicks," *Crain's New York Business*, February 21, 2005, p. 3.

20. Michelle Higgins, "To Plug In or Unplug for the Pedicure," *New York Times*, September 16, 2007, sec. 5, p. 6.

21. Elizabeth C. Hirschman, "Men, Dogs, Guns, and Cars," *Journal of Advertising*, Spring 2003, pp. 9–22.

22. Mohan J. Dutta-Bergman and William D. Wells, "The Values and Lifestyles of Idiocentrics and Allocentrics in an Individualist Culture: A Descriptive Approach," *Journal of Consumer Psychology*, 12 (3), 2002, pp. 232–242.

23. Sue Shellenbarger, "Technology Is Helping 'Commuter Families' to Stay in Touch," *Wall Street Journal*, February 14, 2001, p. B1.

24. Merissa Marr, "Disney Reaches to the Crib to Extend Princess Magic," *Wall Street Journal*, November 19, 2007, p. B1.

25. Hilary Stout, "Monogram This: Personalized Clothes, Toys Are on the Rise," *Wall Street Journal*, March 17, 2005, p. D6.

26. Chad Terhune, "Gatorade Works on Endurance," *Wall Street Journal*, March 21, 2005, p. B6.

27. Jay Krall, "Big-Brand Logos Pop Up in Organic Aisle," *Wall Street Journal*, July 29, 2003, p. B1.

28. Becky Ebenkamp, "Veggie Tales," *Brandweek*, March 24, 2008, pp. 16–17.

29. James Kanter, "Opponents of Genetically Modified Crops Win Victory in France," *International Herald Tribune*, March 19, 2008, *www.iht.com*.

30. Diane McCartney, "Even Dogs on Diets Can Splurge on These Treats," *The Wichita Eagle*, April 3, 2008, *www.kansas.com*.

31. Milt Freudenheim, "Wal-Mart Will Expand In-Store Medical Clinics," *New York Times*, February 7, 2008, p. C4.

32. Gregory Lopes, "Study Shows U.S. Outweighs Europe," *Washington Times*, October 2, 2007, p. C8.

33. David Sterrett, "Apple Dippers for Small Fries," *Crain's Chicago Business*, March 10, 2008, p. 1; Paul Kurnit, "The Advertising Diet," *Adweek Online*, December 3, 2007, *www.adweek.com*.

34. Keiko Morris, "Finding Both Fashion and Fit," *Newsday*, May 28, 2007, n.p.

35. Derek Gale, "High Rolling (Restaurant Sales at the Highest at Las Vegas)," *Restaurants & Institutions*, April 15, 2007, p. 47.

36. "Haagen Dazs: Coming In from the Cold," *Marketing Week*, April 3, 2008, p. 29; "Low-Fat Chance," *Advertising Age*, February 19, 2007, p. 14.

37. Raj Raghunathan, Rebecca Walker- Naylor, and Wayne D. Hoyer, "The 'Unhealthy = Tasty Intuition' and Its Effects on Taste Inferences, Enjoyment, and Choice of Food Products," *Journal of Marketing* 70, no. 4, 2006, pp. 170–184.

38. Renee Schettler, "America's Artificial Sweetheart," *Washington Post*, February 23, 2005, p. F1.

39. Susan Jakes, "From Mao to Maybelline," *Time*, March 8, 2005, p. 22; Diane Solis, "Cost No Object for Mexico's Makeup Junkies," *Wall Street Journal*, June 6, 1994, p. B1.

40. Heather Landi, "Meet Me in the Yard," *Beverage World*, July 15, 2007, p. 8.

41. Kent Grayson and Radan Martinec, "Consumer Perceptions of Iconicity and Indexicality and Their Influence on Assessments of Authentic Market Offerings," *Journal of Consumer Research* 31, no. 2, 2004, pp. 296–312.

42. Craig J. Thompson, Aric Rindfleisch, and Zrsel Zeynep, "Emotional Branding and the Strategic Value of the Doppelganger Brand Image," *Journal of Marketing,* January 2006, pp. 50–64.

43. David J. Lipke, "Green Homes," *American Demographics,* January 2001, pp. 50–55.

44. Sandra Block, "Gas Prices, Taxes Got You Down? Buying a Hybrid Could Provide a Break," *USA Today,* March 11, 2008, p. 3B.

45. Rebecca Gardyn, "Saving the Earth, One Click at a Time," *American Demographics,* January 2001, pp. 30–34.

46. Jon Mooallem, "The Afterlife of Cellphones," *New York Times Magazine,* January 13, 2008, p. 38.

47. Stephen Baker and Adam Aston, "The Business of Nanotech," *BusinessWeek,* February 14, 2005, pp. 64–71.

48. Paul Schweitzer, "The Third Millennium: Riding the Waves of Turbulence," *News Tribune,* December 1993, pp. 5–27.

49. Sak Onkvisit and John J. Shaw, *International Marketing: Analysis and Strategy* (Columbus, Ohio: Merrill, 1989), p. 243.

50. Robert Wilk, "INFOPLAN: The New Rich: A Psychographic Approach to Marketing to the Wealthy Japanese Consumer," ESOMAR Conference, Venice, Italy, June 1990, reported in de Mooij and Keegan, *Advertising Worldwide,* pp. 122–129.

51. K. S. Yang, "Expressed Values of Chinese College Students," in eds. K. S. Yang and Y. Y. Li, *Symposium on the Character of the Chinese: An Interdisciplinary Approach* (Taipei, Taiwan: Institute of Ethnology Academic Sinica, 1972), pp. 257–312; see also Oliver H. M. Yau, *Consumer Behavior in China: Customer Satisfaction and Cultural Values* (New York: Rutledge, 1994).

52. Alfred S. Boote, cited in Rebecca Piirto, *Beyond Mind Games* (Ithaca, N.Y.: American Demographic Books, 1991).

53. Geert Hofstede, "National Cultures in Four Dimensions," *International Studies of Management and Organization,* Spring–Summer 1983, pp. 46–74.

54. Michael Lynn, George M. Zinkhan, and Judy Harris, "Consumer Tipping: A Cross-Country Study," *Journal of Consumer Research,* December 1993, pp. 478–488.

55. Dana L. Alden, Wayne D. Hoyer, and Chol Lee, "Identifying Global and Culture-Specific Dimensions of Humor in Advertising: A Multinational Analysis," *Journal of Marketing,* April 1993, pp. 64–75.

56. Douglas B. Holt and Craig J. Thompson, "Man-of-Action Heroes: The Pursuit of Heroic Masculinity in Everyday Consumption," *Journal of Consumer Research* 31, no. 2, 2004, pp. 425–440.

57. Van R. Wood and Roy Howell, "A Note on Hispanic Values and Subcultural Research: An Alternative View," *Journal of the Academy of Marketing Science,* Winter 1991, pp. 61–67; see also Humberto Valencia, "Hispanic Values and Subcultural Research," *Journal of the Academy of Marketing Science,* Winter 1989, pp. 23–28; Thomas E. Ness and Melvin T. Smith, "Middle-Class Values in Blacks and Whites," in eds. Pitts and Woodside, *Personal Values and Consumer Psychology,* pp. 231–237.

58. "China's Golden Oldies," *The Economist,* February 26, 2005, p. 65.

59. Richard P. Coleman, "The Continuing Significance of Social Class to Marketing," *Journal of Consumer Research,* December 1983, pp. 265–280.

60. William Strauss and Neil Howe, "The Cycle of Generations, *American Demographics,* April 1991, pp. 25–33, 52; see also William Strauss and Neil Howe, *Generations: The History of America's Future, 1584 to 2069* (New York: William Morrow, 1992); Lawrence A. Crosby, James D. Gill, and Robert E. Lee, "Life Status and Age as Predictors of Value Orientation," in eds. Pitts and Woodside, *Personal Values and Consumer Psychology,* pp. 201–218.

61. Sharon Beatty, Lynn R. Kahle, Pamela Homer, and Shekhar Misra, "Alternative Measurement Approaches to Consumer Values: The List of Values and the Rokeach Value Survey," *Psychology and Marketing,* Fall 1985, pp. 181–200.

62. Lynn R. Kahle, *Social Values and Social Change: Adaptation to Life in America* (New York: Praeger, 1983).

63. Heather Green and Kerry Capell, "Carbon Confusions," *BusinessWeek,* March 17, 2008, pp. 52–55.

64. "Face Value: At the Sharp End," *The Economist,* March 3, 2007, p. 73.

65. Brendan I. Koerner, "Mr. Clean and the Future of Mopping," *New York Times,* March 20, 2005, sec. 3, p. 2.

66. Patricia F. Kennedy, Roger J. Best, and Lynn R. Kahle, "An Alternative Method for Measuring Value-Based Segmentation and Advertisement Positioning," in eds. James H. Leigh and Claude R. Martin Jr., *Current Issues and Research in Advertising,* vol. 11 (Ann Arbor, Mich.: Division of Research, School of Business Administration, University of Michigan, 1988), pp. 139–156; Daniel L. Sherrell, Joseph F. Hair Jr., and Robert P. Bush, "The Influence of Personal Values on Measures of Advertising Effectiveness: Interactions with Audience Involvement," in eds. Pitts and Woodside, *Personal Values and Consumer Psychology,* pp. 169–185.

67. Bob Garfield, "Dove's New 'Onslaught' Ad a Triumph," *Advertising Age,* October 8, 2007, *www.adage.com.*

68. Pichayaporn Utumporn, "Ad with Hitler Brings Outcry in Thailand," *Wall Street Journal,* June 5, 1995, p. C1.

69. Robert E. Pitts, John K. Wong, and D. Joel Whalen, "Consumers' Evaluative Structures in Two Ethical Situations: A Means–End Approach," *Journal of Business Research,* March 1991, pp. 119–130.

70. Russell W. Belk and Richard W. Pollay, "Materialism and Status Appeals in Japanese and U.S. Print Advertising," *International Marketing Review,* Winter 1985, pp. 38–47; see also Russell W. Belk, Wendy J. Bryce, and Richard W. Pollay, "Advertising Themes and Cultural Values: A Comparison of U.S. and Japanese Advertising," in eds. K. C. Mun and T. S. Chan, *Proceedings of the Inaugural Meeting of the Southeast Asia Region*

Academy of International Business (Hong Kong: The Chinese University of Hong Kong, 1985), pp. 11–20.

71. David K. Tse, Russell W. Belk, and Nan Zhou, "Becoming a Consumer Society: A Longitudinal and Cross-Cultural Content Analysis of Print Ads from Hong Kong, the People's Republic of China, and Taiwan," *Journal of Consumer Research*, March 1989, pp. 457–472.

72. For more on means–end chain analysis, see Beth A. Walker and Jerry C. Olson, "Means–End Chains: Connecting Products with Self," *Journal of Business Research*, March 1991, pp. 111–118; Thomas J. Reynolds and John P. Richon, "Means–End Based Advertising Research: Copy Testing Is Not Strategy Assessment," *Journal of Business Research*, March 1991, pp. 131–142; Jonathan Gutman, "Exploring the Nature of Linkages Between Consequences and Values," *Journal of Business Research*, March 1991, pp. 143–148; Thomas J. Reynolds and Jonathan Gutman, "Laddering Theory, Method, Analysis and Interpretation," *Journal of Advertising Research*, February/March 1988, pp. 11–31; Thomas J. Reynolds and Jonathan Gutman, "Laddering: Extending the Repertory Grid Methodology to Construct Attribute–Consequence–Value Hierarchies," in eds. Pitts and Woodside, *Personal Values and Consumer Psychology*, pp. 155–167.

73. Dawn R. Deeter-Schmelz and Jane L. Sojka, "Wrestling with American Values," *Journal of Consumer Behavior* 4, no. 2, 2004, pp. 132–143.

74. Thomas J. Reynolds and J. P. Jolly, "Measuring Personal Values: An Evaluation of Alternative Methods," *Journal of Marketing Research*, November 1980, pp. 531–536; Reynolds and Gutman, "Laddering"; Jonathan Gutman, "A Means–End Model Based on Consumer Categorization Processes," *Journal of Marketing*, Spring 1982, pp. 60–72.

75. T. L. Stanley, "Death of the Sports Car?" *Brandweek*, January 2, 1995, p. 38.

76. Frenkel Ter Hofstede, Jan-Benedict E. M. Steenkamp, and Michel Wedel, "International Market Segmentation Based on Consumer–Product Relations," *Journal of Marketing Research* 36, February 1999, pp. 1–17.

77. Marsha L. Richins, "The Material Values Scale: Measurement Properties and Development of a Short Form," *Journal of Consumer Research,* June 2004, pp. 209–219.

78. J. Michael Munson and Edward F. McQuarrie, "Shortening the Rokeach Value Survey for Use in Consumer Research," in ed. Michael J. Houston, *Advances in Consumer Research*, vol. 15 (Provo, Utah: Association for Consumer Research, 1988), pp. 381–386.

79. Lynn R. Kahle, Sharon Beatty, and Pamela Homer, "Alternative Measurement Approaches to Consumer Values: The List of Values (LOV) and Values and Life Style (VALS)," *Journal of Consumer Research*, December 1986, pp. 405–409; Kahle, *Social Values and Social Change*.

80. Wagner Kamakura and Thomas P. Novak, "Value-System Segmentation: Exploring the Meaning of LOV," *Journal of Consumer Research*, June 1992, pp. 119–132.

81. Sigmund Freud, *Collected Papers*, vols. I–V (New York: Basic Books, 1959); Erik Erickson, *Childhood and Society* (New York: Norton, 1963); Erik Erickson, *Identity: Youth and Crisis* (New York: Norton, 1968).

82. Yumiko Ono, "Marketers Seek the 'Naked' Truth," *Wall Street Journal*, May 30, 1997, pp. B1, B13.

83. Gordon Allport, *Personality: A Psychological Interpretation* (New York: Holt, Rinehart, & Winston, 1937); Raymond B. Cattell, *The Scientific Analysis of Personality* (Baltimore: Penguin, 1965).

84. Carl G. Jung, *Man and His Symbols* (Garden City, N.Y.: Doubleday, 1964); see also Hans J. Eysenck, "Personality, Stress and Disease: An Interactionistic Perspective," *Psychological Inquiry*, vol. 2, 1991, pp. 221–232.

85. For example, see Lara K. Kammrath, Daniel R. Ames, and Abigail R. Scholer, "Keeping Up with Impressions: Inferential Rules for Impression Change Across the Big Five," *Journal of Experimental Social Psychology* 43, 2007, pp. 450–457; William Fleeson, "Situation-Based Contingencies Underlying Trait-Content Manifestation in Behavior," *Journal of Personality* 75, no. 4, 2007, pp. 825–862.

86. Carl R. Rogers, "Some Observations on the Organization of Personality," *American Psychologist*, September 1947, pp. 358–368; George A. Kelly, *The Psychology of Personal Constructs*, vols. 1 and 2 (New York: Norton, 1955).

87. Bernard Weiner, "Attribution in Personality Psychology," in ed. Lawrence A. Pervin, *Handbook of Personality: Theory and Research* (New York: Guilford, 1990), pp. 465–484; Harold H. Kelly, "The Processes of Causal Attribution," *American Psychologist*, February 1973, pp. 107–128.

88. David Glen Mick and Claus Buhl, "A Meaning-Based Model of Advertising Experiences," *Journal of Consumer Research*, December 1992, pp. 317–338.

89. Karen B. Horney, *Our Inner Conflicts* (New York: Norton, 1945).

90. Joel B. Cohen, "An Interpersonal Orientation to the Study of Consumer Behavior," *Journal of Marketing Research*, August 1967, pp. 270–277; Jon P. Noerager, "An Assessment of CAD—A Personality Instrument Developed Specifically for Marketing Research," *Journal of Marketing Research*, February 1979, pp. 53–59.

91. Marsha L. Richins, "An Analysis of Consumer Interaction Styles in the Marketplace," *Journal of Consumer Research*, June 1983, pp. 73–82.

92. Richard P. Bagozzi, Hans Baumgartner, and Youjae Yi, "State Versus Action Orientation and the Theory of Reasoned Action, An Application to Coupon Usage," *Journal of Consumer Research*, March 1992, pp. 505–518; William O. Bearden and Randall L. Rose, "Attention to Social Comparison Information: An Individual Difference Factor Affecting Consumer Conformity," *Journal of Consumer Research*, March 1990, pp. 461–471; Bobby J. Calder and Robert E. Burnkrant, "Interpersonal Influence on Consumer Behavior: An Attribution Theory Approach," *Journal of Consumer Research*, December 1979, pp. 29–38.

93. B. F. Skinner, *About Behaviorism* (New York: Knopf, 1974); B. F. Skinner, *Beyond Freedom and Dignity* (New York: Knopf, 1971).

94. Jacob Jacoby, "Multiple Indicant Approaches for Studying New Product Adopters," *Journal of Applied Psychology*, August 1971, pp. 384–388; Harold H. Kassarjian, "Personality and Consumer Behavior: A Review," *Journal of Marketing Research*, November 1971, pp. 409–418; see also Harold H. Kassarjian, "Personality: The Longest Fad," in ed. William L. Wilkie, *Advances in Consumer Research*, vol. 6 (Ann Arbor, Mich.: Association for Consumer Research, 1979), pp. 122–124.

95. John L. Lastovicka and Erich A. Joachimsthaler, "Improving the Detection of Personality–Behavior Relationships in Consumer Research," *Journal of Consumer Research*, March 1988, pp. 583–587; Kathryn E. A. Villani and Yoram Wind, "On the Usage of 'Modified' Personality Trait Measures in Consumer Research," *Journal of Consumer Research*, December 1975, pp. 223–228.

96. William O. Bearden, David M. Hardesty, and Randall L. Rose, "Consumer Self-Confidence: Refinements in Conceptualization and Measurement," *Journal of Consumer Research* 28, June 2001, pp. 121–134.

97. D. E. Berlyne, *Conflict, Arousal and Curiosity* (New York: McGraw-Hill, 1960); D. E. Berlyne, "Novelty, Complexity, and Hedonic Value," *Perception and Psychophysics*, November 1970, pp. 279–286.

98. Marvin Zuckerman, *Sensation Seeking: Beyond the Optimal Level of Arousal* (Hillsdale, N.J.: Lawrence Erlbaum, 1979); Elizabeth C. Hirschman, "Innovativeness, Novelty Seeking, and Consumer Creativity," *Journal of Consumer Research*, December 1980, pp. 283–295.

99. R. A. Mittelstadt, S. L. Grossbart, W. W. Curtis, and S. P. DeVere, "Optimal Stimulation Level and the Adoption Decision Process," *Journal of Consumer Research*, September 1976, pp. 84–94; P. S. Raju, "Optimum Stimulation Level: Its Relationship to Personality, Demographics, and Exploratory Behavior," *Journal of Consumer Research*, December 1980, pp. 272–282; Jan-Benedict E. M. Steenkamp and Hans Baumgartner, "The Role of Optimum Stimulation Level in Exploratory Consumer Behavior," *Journal of Consumer Research*, December 1992, pp. 434–448; Erich A. Joachimsthaler and John Lastovicka, "Optimal Stimulation Level—Exploratory Behavior Models," *Journal of Consumer Research*, December 1984, pp. 830–835.

100. Leon G. Schiffman, William R. Dillon, and Festus E. Ngumah, "The Influence of Subcultural and Personality Factors on Consumer Acculturation," *Journal of International Business Studies*, Fall 1981, pp. 137–143.

101. Kelly Tepper Tian, William O. Bearden, and Gary L. Hunter, "Consumers' Need for Uniqueness: Scale Development and Validation," *Journal of Consumer Research* 28, June 2001, pp. 50–66.

102. Itamar Simonson and Stephen M. Nowlis, "The Role of Explanations and Need for Uniqueness in Consumer Decision Making: Unconventional Choices Based on Reasons," *Journal of Consumer Research* 27, June 2000, pp. 49–68.

103. Craig J. Thompson and Zeynep Arsel, "The Starbucks Brandscape and Consumers' (Anticorporate) Experiences of Globalization," *Journal of Consumer Research* 31, no. 3, 2004, pp. 631–642.

104. James E. Burroughs and David Glen Mick, "Exploring Antecedents and Consequences of Consumer Creativity in a Problem-Solving Context," *Journal of Consumer Research*, September 2004, pp. 402–411.

105. Ibid., and Alice M. Isen, "Positive Effect," in eds. Tim Dageleisch and Mick Power, *Handbook of Cognition and Emotion*, (New York: Wiley, 1999), pp. 521–539.

106. John T. Cacioppo, Richard E. Petty, and Chuan F. Kao, "The Efficient Assessment of Need for Cognition," *Journal of Personality Assessment*, June 1984, pp. 306–307; Curtis R. Haugtvedt, Richard E. Petty, and John T. Cacioppo, "Need for Cognition and Advertising: Understanding the Role of Personality Variables in Consumer Behavior," *Journal of Consumer Psychology* 1, no. 3, 1992, pp. 239–260; Rajeev Batra and Douglas M. Stayman, "The Role of Mood in Advertising Effectiveness," *Journal of Consumer Research*, September 1990, pp. 203–214; John T. Cacioppo, Richard E. Petty, and K. Morris, "Effects of Need for Cognition on Message Evaluation, Recall and Persuasion," *Journal of Personality and Social Psychology*, October 1983, pp. 805–818.

107. Susan Powell Mantel and Frank R. Kardes, "The Role of Direction of Comparison, Attribute-Based Processing, and Attitude-Based Processing in Consumer Preference," *Journal of Consumer Research* 25, March 1999, pp. 335–352.

108. William O. Bearden, Richard G. Netemeyer, and Jesse H. Teel, "Measurement of Consumer Susceptibility to Interpersonal Influence," *Journal of Consumer Research*, March 1989, pp. 472–480; Peter Wright, "Factors Affecting Cognitive Resistance to Ads," *Journal of Marketing Research*, June 1975, pp. 1–9.

109. John L. Lastovicka, Lance A. Bettencourt, Renée Shaw Hughner, and Ronald J. Kuntze, "Lifestyle of the Tight and Frugal: Theory and Measurement," *Journal of Consumer Research* 26, June 1999, pp. 85–98.

110. Terrence H. Witkowski, "World War II Poster Campaigns," *Journal of Advertising*, Spring 2003, pp. 69–82.

111. "Free Magazines Popping Up All Over Japan," *Japan Close-Up*, March 2005, p. 7.

112. Richard C. Becherer and Lawrence C. Richard, "Self-Monitoring as a Moderating Variable in Consumer Behavior," *Journal of Consumer Research*, December 1978, pp. 159–162; Mark Snyder and Kenneth G. DeBono, "Appeals to Image and Claims about Quality: Understanding the Psychology of Advertising," *Journal of Personality and Social Psychology*, September 1985, pp. 586–597.

113. Dean Peabody, *National Characteristics* (Cambridge, England: Cambridge University Press, 1985); Allan B. Yates, "Americans, Canadians Similar but Vive La Difference," *Direct Marketing*, October 1985, p. 152.

114. Terry Clark, "International Marketing and National Character: A Review and Proposal for an Integrative Theory," *Journal of Marketing*, October 1990, pp. 66–79.

115. Greg Sandoval, "China Bans LeBron James Nike Ad," *Washington Post*, December 7, 2004, p. E2.

116. John C. Mowen, "Exploring the Trait of Competitiveness and its Consumer Behavior Consequences," *Journal of Consumer Psychology* 14, no. 1/2, 2004, pp. 52–63.

117. Rob Walker, "For Kicks," *New York Times Magazine*, March 20, 2005, p. 38.

118. Tom Lowry, "The Game's the Thing at MTV Networks," *BusinessWeek*, February 18, 2008, pp. 51–52.

119. David Crockett, "The Role of Normative Political Ideology in Consumer Behavior," *Journal of Consumer Research* 31, no. 3, 2004, pp. 511–528.

120. Morris B. Holbrook, "Nostalgia and Consumption Preferences: Some Emerging Patterns of Consumer Tastes," *Journal of Consumer Research*, September 1993, pp. 245–256.

121. Sandra Yin, "Going to Extremes," *American Demographics*, June 1, 2001, p. 26.

122. Michelle Moran, "Category Analysis: Small Electrics & Consumer Lifestyles Dictate Trends," *Gourmet Retailer*, June 2001, p. 34. .

123. Onkvisit and Shaw, *International Marketing*, p. 283.

124. Leonidas C. Leonidou, "Understanding the Russian Consumer," *Marketing and Research Today*, March 1992, pp. 75–83.

125. "Sip and Sup: Ideas for Quick Noshing," *Arizona Republic*, April 9, 2008, *www.azcentral.com*.

126. See Leonard L. Berry, Kathleen Seiders, and Dhruv Grewal, "Understanding Service Convenience," *Journal of Marketing Research*, July 2002, pp. 1–17.

127. Cynthia Crossen, "Marketing Panache, Plant Lore Invigorate Independent Garden Center's Sales," *Wall Street Journal*, May 25, 2004, pp. B1, B4.

128. ACE Brochure 1989, published by RISC, Paris, France; see also de Mooij and Keegan, *Advertising Worldwide*.

129. Jerri Stroud, "'Bankers' Hours' Now Include Evenings and Sundays," *St. Louis Post-Dispatch*, September 4, 2007, n.p.

130. Basil G. Englis and Michael R. Solomon, "To Be and Not to Be: Life Style Imagery, Reference Groups, and the Clustering of America," *Journal of Advertising*, Spring 1995, pp. 13–28.

131. Jacob Hornik and Mary Jane Schlinger, "Allocation of Time to the Mass Media," *Journal of Consumer Research*, March 1981, pp. 343–355.

132. Eben Shapiro, "Web Lovers Love TV, Often Watch Both," *Wall Street Journal*, June 12, 1998, p. B9.

133. Michael J. Weiss, Morris B. Holbrook, and John Habich, "Death of the Arts Snob," *American Demographics*, June 2001, pp. 40–42.

134. Jeff Borden, "High-Quality Ingredients," *Marketing News*, October 1, 2007, pp. 13.

135. SRI Consulting Business Intelligence, *VALS Framework and Segment Descriptions*, *www.sricbi.com/VALS/types .shtml*.

136. Pamela Paul, "Sell It to the Psyche," *Time*, September 15, 2003, p. A23.

137. Louise Witt, "Inside Intent," *American Demographics*, March 1, 2004.

138. David J. Lipke, "Head Trips," *American Demographics*, October 2000, pp. 38–39; Yankelovich Web site, *http:// www.yankelovich.com*.

139. Douglas B. Holt, "Poststructuralist Lifestyle Analysis: Conceptualizing the Social Patterning of Consumption in Postmodernity," *Journal of Consumer Research*, March 1997, pp. 326–350.

140. Marvin Shoenwald, "Psychographic Segmentation: Used or Abused?" *Brandweek*, January 22, 2001, p. 34.

141. Pamela Paul, "Sell It to the Psyche."

142. Antoinette Alexander, "Tech-Savvy Young Shoppers May Be Untapped Market," *Drug Store News*, June 21, 2004, pp. 973.

143. Joanna Weiss, "'Psychographics' Enters Brave New World of TV Marketing," *Boston Globe*, June 10, 2005, *www.boston.com*.

144. Vicki Mabrey and Deborah Apton, "From McMuffins to McLattes," *ABC News*, March 31, 2008, *www.abcnews .go.com*; Dave Carpenter, "Breakfast, Europe a Winning Combo," *Houston Chronicle*, March 11, 2008, p. 3; "Profile: Pierre Woreczek, Man of Many Tastes,'" *Brand Strategy*, March 7, 2008, p. 17; Dagmar Mussey and Laurel Wentz, "Want a Quiet Cup of Coffee in Germany? Head to McDonald's," *Advertising Age*, September 10, 2007, p. 32; Julia Werdigier, "McDonald's, But with Flair," *New York Times*, August 25, 2007, p. C1, C4; Michael Arndt, "Knock Knock, It's Your Big Mac," *BusinessWeek Online*, July 13, 2007, *www.businessweek.com*.

Chapter 15

1. Douglas Quenqua, "Word of Mouth," *DM News*, February 4, 2008, *www.dmnews.com*; Leo Benedictus, "Psst! Have You Heard?" *The Guardian*, January 30, 2007, *www.guardian.co.uk*.

2. Greg Metz Thomas, "Building the Buzz with the Hive in Mind," *Journal of Consumer Behavior* 4, no. 1, 2004, pp. 64–72.

3. Seth Schiesel, "Gamers, on Your Marks: Halo 3 Arrives," *New York Times*, September 24, 2007, p. E1.

4. Amna Kirmani and Margaret C. Campbell, "Goal Seeker and Persuasion Sentry: How Consumer Targets Respond to Interpersonal Marketing Persuasion," *Journal of Consumer Research*, December 2004, pp. 573–582.

5. Robert L. Simison and Joseph B. White, "Reputation for Poor Quality Still Plagues Detroit," *Wall Street Journal*, May 4, 2000, pp. B1, B4.

6. Utpal M. Dholakia, Richard P. Bagozzi, and Lisa Klein Pearo, "A Social Influence Model of Consumer Participation in Network- and Small-Group-Based Virtual Communities," *International Journal of Research in Marketing* 21, 2004, pp. 241–263.

7. See Mehdi Mourali, Michel Larouche, and Frank Pons, "Antecedents of Consumer Relative Preference for

Interpersonal Information Sources in Pre-Purchase Search," *Journal of Consumer Behaviour* 4, no. 5, 2005, pp. 307–318.

8. Rebecca Gardyn, "How Does This Work?" *American Demographics*, December 2002/January 2003, pp. 18–19.

9. Frederick Koenig, *Rumor in the Marketplace: The Social Psychology of Commercial Hearsay* (Dover, Mass.: Auburn House, 1985); Paul M. Herr, Frank R. Kardes, and John Kim, "Effects of Word-of-Mouth and Product-Attribute Information on Persuasion: An Accessibility-Diagnosticity Perspective," *Journal of Consumer Research*, March 1991, pp. 454–462.

10. Paul F. Lazarsfeld, Bernard Berelson, and Hazel Gaudet, *The People's Choice; How the Voter Makes Up His Mind in a Presidential Campaign* (New York: Columbia University Press, 1948); see also Herr, Kardes, and Kim, "Effects of Word-of-Mouth and Product-Attribute Information on Persuasion."

11. David Pogue, "Reconsidering Pixel Envy," *New York Times*, March 24, 2005, *tech.nytimes.com/2005/03/24/technology/circuits/24read.html.*

12. Dale Duhan, Scott Johnson, James Wilcox, and Gilbert Harrell, "Influences on Consumer Use of Word-of-Mouth Recommendation Sources," *Journal of the Academy of Marketing Science* 25, Fall 1997, pp. 283–295.

13. Vicki Clift, "Systematically Solicit Testimonial Letters," *Marketing News*, June 6, 1994, p. 7.

14. Wendy Bounds, "Keeping Teens from Smoking, with Style," *Wall Street Journal*, May 6, 1999, p. B6.

15. Bob Tedeschi, "Readers Are Key Ingredient as Virtual Kitchen Heats Up," *New York Times,* June 25, 2007, p. C6.

16. See Robert V. Kozinets, "E-Tribalized Marketing? The Strategic Implications of Virtual Communities of Consumption," *European Management Journal*, 1999, pp. 252–264.

17. Susan B. Garland, "So Glad You Could Come. Can I Sell You Anything?" *New York Times*, December 19, 2004, sec. 3, p. 7.

18. Michael Barbaro, "Unbound, Wal-Mart Tastemakers Write a Blunt and Unfiltered Blog," *New York Times,* March 3, 2008, pp. C1, C8; David Kirkpatrick and Daniel Roth, "Why There's No Escaping the Blog," *Fortune,* January 10, 2005, p. 44.

19. John W. Milligan, "Choosing Mediums for the Message," *US Banker*, February 1995, pp. 42–45.

20. Gangseog Ryu and Lawrence Feick, "A Penny for Your Thoughts: Referral Reward Programs and Referral Likelihood," *Journal of Marketing*, January 2007, pp. 84–94.

21. Cris Prystay, "Companies Market to India's Have-Littles," *Wall Street Journal*, June 5, 2003, pp. B1, B12.

22. Robert McMillan, "Bill Gates Says Internet Censorship Won't Work," *Computerworld*, February 20, 2008, *www.computerworld.com;* "Wave of Internet Surfers Has Chinese Censors Nervous," *Los Angeles Times*, June 26, 1995, p. D6; Jeffrey A. Trachtenberg, "Time Warner Unit Sets Joint Venture to Market TV Programming in China," *Wall Street Journal*, March 8, 1995, p. B2.

23. Jacob Jacoby and Wayne D. Hoyer, "What If Opinion Leaders Didn't Really Know More: A Question of Nomological Validity," in ed. Kent B. Monroe, *Advances in Consumer Research*, vol. 8 (Chicago: Association for Consumer Research, 1980), pp. 299–302; Robin M. Higie, Lawrence F. Feick, and Linda L. Price, "Types and Amount of Word-of-Mouth Communications about Retailers," *Journal of Retailing*, Fall 1987, pp. 260–277; regarding innovativeness, Terry L. Childers ("Assessment of the Psychometric Properties of an Opinion Leadership Scale," *Journal of Marketing Research*, May 1986, pp. 184–187).

24. Marsha L. Richins and Teri Root-Shafer, "The Role of Involvement and Opinion Leadership in Consumer Word of Mouth: An Implicit Model Made Explicit," in ed. Michael J. Houston, *Advances in Consumer Research*, vol. 15 (Provo, Utah: Association for Consumer Research, 1988), pp. 32–36.

25. Audrey Guskey-Federouch and Robert L. Heckman, "The Good Samaritan in the Marketplace: Motives for Helpful Behavior," Paper presented at the Society for Consumer Psychology Conference, St. Petersburg, Fla., February 1994.

26. Lawrence F. Feick, Linda L. Price, and Robin Higie, "People Who Use People: The Opposite Side of Opinion Leadership," in ed. Richard J. Lutz, *Advances in Consumer Research*, vol. 13 (Provo, Utah: Association for Consumer Research, 1986), pp. 301–305; see also Jagdish N. Sheth, "Word-of-Mouth in Low-Risk Innovations," *Journal of Advertising Research*, June–July 1971, pp. 15–18.

27. Ronald E. Goldsmith, Ronald A. Clark, and Elizabeth Goldsmith, "Extending the Psychological Profile of Market Mavenism," *Journal of Consumer Behavior* 5, no. 5, 2006, pp. 411–419; Lawrence F. Feick and Linda L. Price, "The Market Maven: A Diffuser of Marketplace Information," *Journal of Marketing*, January 1987, pp. 83–97.

28. See, for example, Dorothy Leonard-Barton, "Experts as Negative Opinion Leaders in the Diffusion of a Technological Innovation," *Journal of Consumer Research*, March 1985, pp. 914–926.

29. Joanne Kaufman, "Publishers Seek to Mine Book Circles," *New York Times,* November 19, 2007, p. C5.

30. Laura Bird, "Consumers Smile on Unilever's Mentadent," *Wall Street Journal,* May 31, 1994, p. B9; Joseph R. Mancuso, "Why Not Create Opinion Leaders for New Product Introduction?" *Journal of Marketing*, July 1969, pp. 20–25.

31. "Smoking Cessation: GSK Strikes a Chord with Reality Ads," *Chemist and Druggist*, March 5, 2005, p. 40.

32. Christopher Reynolds, "Up on the Envy Meter," *American Demographics,* June 2004, pp. 6–7.

33. Jennifer Edson Escalas and James R. Bettman, "Self-Construal, Reference Groups, and Brand Meaning," *Journal of Consumer Research* 32, no. 3, 2005, pp. 378–389.

34. Albert M. Muniz Jr. and Thomas C. O'Guinn, "Brand Community," *Journal of Consumer Research* 27, March 2001, pp. 412–432; James H. McAlexander, John W.

Schouten, and Harold F. Koenig, "Building Brand Community," *Journal of Marketing,* January 2002, pp. 38–54.

35. Richard P. Bagozzi and Utpal M. Dholakia, **"Antecedents and Purchase Consequences of Customer Participation in Small Group Brand Communities,"** *International Journal of Research in Marketing* 23, 2006, pp. 45–61.

36. Albert M. Muniz Jr. And Hope Jensen Schau, "Religiosity in the Abandoned Apple Newton Brand Community," *Journal of Consumer Research* 31, no. 4, 2005, pp. 737–747.

37. Jim Patterson, "Branding Campaign Meant to Take Stigma off Country Music," *Associated Press Newswires,* May 1, 2001.

38. Katherine White and Darren W. Dahl, "To Be or Not Be? The Influence of Dissociative Reference Groups on Consumer Preferences," *Journal of Consumer Psychology* 16, no. 4, 2006, pp. 404–414.

39. T. L. Stanley, "Heavies of Hip-Hop Lend Phat to Nokia," *Advertising Age,* December 15, 2003, p. 6.

40. Basil G. Englis and Michael R. Solomon, "To Be and Not to Be: Lifestyle Imagery, Reference Groups, and the Clustering of America," *Journal of Advertising,* March 1995, pp. 13–28.

41. Stefan Fatsis, "'Rad' Sports Give Sponsors Cheap Thrills," *Wall Street Journal,* May 12, 1995, p. B8.

42. Jonathan Fahey, "Love Into Money," *Forbes,* January 7, 2002, pp. 60–65.

43. Paul White, "Red Sox Nation New King of the Road," *USA Today,* August 22, 2007, *www.usatoday.com.*

44. Todd Nissen, "McDonald's Sees Good Results in Middle East," *ClariNet Electronic News Service,* February 20, 1994.

45. A. Benton Cocanougher and Grady D. Bruce, "Socially Distant Referent Groups and Consumer Aspiration," *Journal of Marketing Research,* August 1971, pp. 379–383.

46. Linda L. Price, Lawrence Feick, and Robin Higie, "Preference Heterogeneity and Coorientation as Determinants of Perceived Informational Influence," *Journal of Business Research,* November 1989, pp. 227–242; Jacqueline J. Brown and Peter Reingen, "Social Ties and Word-of-Mouth Referral Behavior," *Journal of Consumer Research,* December 1987, pp. 350–362; Mary C. Gilly, John L. Graham, Mary Wolfinbarger, and Laura Yale, "A Dyadic Study of Interpersonal Information Search," *Journal of the Academy of Marketing Science* 26, no. 2, pp. 83–100; George Moschis, "Social Comparison and Informal Group Influence," *Journal of Marketing Research,* August 1976, pp. 237–244.

47. Randall L. Rose, William O. Bearden, and Kenneth C. Manning, "Attributions and Conformity in Illicit Consumption: The Mediating Role of Group Attractiveness," *Journal of Public Policy & Marketing* 20, no. 1, Spring 2001, pp. 84–92.

48. Rohit Deshpande, Wayne D. Hoyer, and Naveen Donthu, "The Intensity of Ethnic Affiliation: A Study of the Sociology of Hispanic Consumption," *Journal of Consumer Research,* September 1986, pp. 214–220; Douglas M.

Stayman and Rohit Deshpande, "Situational Ethnicity and Consumer Behavior," *Journal of Consumer Research,* December 1989, pp. 361–371.

49. Robert Madrigal, "The Influence of Social Alliances with Sports Teams on Intentions to Purchase Corporate Sponsors' Products," *Journal of Advertising* 29, no. 4, Winter 2000, pp. 13–24.

50. Americus Reed II, "Activating the Self-Importance of Consumer Selves: Exploring Identity Salience Effects on Judgments," *Journal of Consumer Research,* September 2004, pp. 286–295.

51. Jonathan K. Frenzen and Harry L. Davis, "Purchasing Behavior in Embedded Markets," *Journal of Consumer Research,* June 1990, pp. 1–12; see also Mark S. Granovetter, "The Strength of Weak Ties," *American Journal of Sociology,* May 1973, pp. 1360–1380; Brown and Reingen, "Social Ties and Word-of-Mouth Referral Behavior"; Jonathan K. Frenzen and Kent Nakamoto, "Structure, Cooperation, and the Flow of Market Information," *Journal of Consumer Research,* December 1993, pp. 360–375.

52. "Theme Parks: Finally, the Year of the Mouse," *BusinessWeek,* April 4, 2005, p. 16.

53. Reingen and Kernan, "Analysis of Referral Networks in Marketing"; Brown and Reingen, "Social Ties and Word-of-Mouth Referral Behavior"; see also Frenzen and Nakamoto, "Structure, Cooperation, and the Flow of Market Information."

54. Walker, "The Hidden (in Plain Sight) Persuaders."

55. Nicole Woolsey Biggart, *Charismatic Capitalism* (Chicago: University of Chicago Press, 1989); see also Jonathan K. Frenzen and Harry L. Davis, "Purchasing Behavior in Embedded Markets," *Journal of Consumer Research,* June 1990, pp. 1–12.

56. Frenzen and Davis, "Purchasing Behavior in Embedded Markets."

57. Scott Ward, "Consumer Socialization," *Journal of Consumer Research,* September 1974, pp. 1–16; George P. Moschis, "The Role of Family Communication in Consumer Socialization of Children and Adolescents," *Journal of Consumer Research,* March 1985, pp. 898–913; George P. Moschis, *Consumer Socialization: A Life Cycle Perspective* (Lexington, Mass.: Lexington Books, 1987); Scott Ward, "Consumer Socialization," in eds. Harold H. Kassarjian and Thomas S. Robertson, *Perspectives in Consumer Behavior* (Glenview, Ill.: Scott-Foresman, 1980), pp. 380–396; Les Carlson and Sanford Grossbart, "Parental Style and Consumer Socialization of Children," *Journal of Consumer Research,* June 1988, pp. 77–92.

58. Deborah Roedder John, "Consumer Socialization of Children: A Retrospective Look at Twenty-Five Years of Research," *Journal of Consumer Research* 26, December 1999, pp. 183–213.

59. Elizabeth S. Moore, William L. Wilkie, and Richard J. Lutz, "Passing the Torch: Intergenerational Influences as a Source of Brand Equity," *Journal of Marketing,* April 2002, pp. 17–37.

60. Gwen Bachmann Achenreiner and Deborah Roedder John, "The Meaning of Brand Names to Children: A Developmental Investigation," *Journal of Consumer Psychology*, 13 (3), 2003, pp. 205–219.

61. Gregory M. Rose, Vassilis Dalakas, and Fredric Kropp, "Consumer Socialization and Parental Style Across Cultures: Findings from Australia, Greece, and India," *Journal of Consumer Psychology* 13 (4), 2003, pp. 366–376.

62. John, "Consumer Socialization of Children: A Retrospective Look at Twenty-Five Years of Research."

63. Ann Walsh, Russell Laczniak, and Les Carlson, "Mothers' Preferences for Regulating Children's Television," *Journal of Advertising*, Fall 1998, pp. 23–36.

64. Dave Howland, "Ads Recruit Grandparents to Help Keep Kids from Drugs," *Marketing News*, January 18, 1999, p. 6.

65. Moschis, "The Role of Family Communication in Consumer Socialization of Children and Adolescents"; Conway Lackman and John M. Lanasa, "Family Decision Making Theory: An Overview and Assessment," *Psychology and Marketing*, March–April 1993, pp. 81–93; George P. Moschis, *Acquisition of the Consumer Role by Adolescents* (Atlanta: Georgia State University, 1978).

66. Beverly A. Browne, "Gender Stereotypes in Advertising on Children's Television in the 1990s: A Cross-National Analysis," *Journal of Advertising*, Spring 1998, pp. 83–96.

67. See, for example, Greta Fein, David Johnson, Nancy Kosson, Linda Stork, and Lisa Wasserman, "Sex Stereotypes and Preferences in the Toy Choices of 20-Month-Old Boys and Girls," *Developmental Psychology*, July 1975, pp. 527–528; Lenore A. DeLucia, "The Toy Preference Test: A Measure of Sex-Role Identification," *Child Development*, March 1963, pp. 107–117; Judith E. O. Blackmore and Asenath A. LaRue, "Sex-Appropriate Toy Preference and the Ability to Conceptualize Toys as Sex-Role Related," *Developmental Psychology*, May 1979, pp. 339–340; Nancy Eisenberg-Berg, Rita Boothby, and Tom Matson, "Correlates of Preschool Girls' Feminine and Masculine Toy Preferences," *Developmental Psychology*, May 1979, pp. 354–355.

68. Donna Rouner, "Rock Music Use as a Socializing Function," *Popular Music and Society*, Spring 1990, pp. 97–108; Thomas L. Eugene, "Clothing and Counterculture: An Empirical Study," *Adolescence*, Spring 1973, pp. 93–112.

69. Fein et al., "Sex Stereotypes and Preferences in the Toy Choices of 20-Month-Old Boys and Girls"; Eisenberg-Berg, Boothby, and Matson, "Correlates of Preschool Girls' Feminine and Masculine Toy Preferences"; Sheila Fling and Main Manosevitz, "Sex Typing in Nursery School Children's Play," *Developmental Psychology* 7, September 1972, pp. 146–152.

70. Tamara Mangleburg and Terry Bristol, "Socialization and Adolescents' Skepticism Toward Advertising," *Journal of Advertising*, Fall 1998, pp. 11–21.

71. Robert E. Burnkrant and Alain Cousineau, "Informational and Normative Social Influence in Buyer Behavior," *Journal of Consumer Research*, December 1975, pp. 206–215; Morton Deutsch and Harold B. Gerard, "A Study of Normative and Informational Influence upon Individual Judgment," *Journal of Abnormal and Social Psychology*, November 1955, pp. 629–636.

72. Dennis Rook and Robert Fisher, "Normative Influences on Impulsive Buying Behavior," *Journal of Consumer Research*," December 1995, pp. 305–313.

73. Paul Rozin and Leher Singh, "The Moralization of Cigarette Smoking in the United States," *Journal of Consumer Psychology* 8, no. 3, 1999, pp. 321–337.

74. David B. Wooten, "From Labeling Possessions to Possessing Labels: Ridicule and Socialization Among Adolescents," *Journal of Consumer Research* 33, no. 2, 2006, pp. 188–198.

75. Margaret Talbot, "Girls Just Want to Be Mean," *New York Times Magazine*, February 24, 2002, p. 24.

76. Peter Reingen, Brian Foster, Jacqueline Brown, and Stephen B. Seidman, "Brand Congruence in Interpersonal Relations: A Social Network Analysis," *Journal of Consumer Research*, December 1984, pp. 771–783.

77. Rajagopal Raghunathan and Kim Corfman, "Is Happiness Shared Doubled and Sadness Shared Halved? Social Influence on Enjoyment of Hedonic Experiences," *Journal of Marketing Research*, August 2006, pp. 386–394.

78. Tina M. Lowrey, Cele C. Otnes, and Julie A. Ruth, "Social Influences on Dyadic Giving over Time: A Taxonomy from the Giver's Perspective," *Journal of Consumer Research*, March 2004, pp 547–558.

79. Ann E. Schlosser and Sharon Shavitt, "Anticipating Discussion About a Product: Rehearsing What to Say Can Affect Your Judgments," *Journal of Consumer Research*, June 2002, pp. 101–115.

80. James E. Stafford, "Effects of Group Influence on Consumer Brand Preferences," *Journal of Marketing Research*, February 1966, pp. 68–75.

81. Pankaj Aggarwal, "The Effects of Brand Relationship Norms on Consumer Attitudes and Behavior," *Journal of Consumer Research*, June 2004, pp. 87–101.

82. Randall L. Rose, William O. Bearden, and Jesse E. Teel, "An Attributional Analysis of Resistance to Group Pressure Regarding Illicit Drug and Alcohol Consumption," *Journal of Consumer Research*, June 1992, pp. 1–13; see also Bobby J. Calder and Robert E. Burnkrant, "Interpersonal Influences on Consumer Behavior: An Attribution Theory Approach," *Journal of Consumer Research*, June 1977, pp. 29–38, 71; Solomon E. Asch, "Effects of Group Pressure upon the Modification and Distortion of Judgment," in ed. H. Guetzkow, *Groups, Leadership and Men* (Pittsburgh, Pa.: Carnegie Press, 1951); Sak Onkvisit and John J. Shaw, *International Marketing: Analysis and Strategy* (Columbus, Ohio: Merrill, 1989); see also Chin Tiong Tan and John U. Farley, "The Impact of Cultural Patterns on Cognition and Intention in Singapore," *Journal of Consumer Research*, March 1987, pp. 540–544.

83. Lisa E. Bolton and Americus Reed II, "Sticky Priors: The Perseverance of Identity Effects on Judgment," *Journal of Marketing Research,* November 2004, pp. 397–410.

84. Utpal M. Dholakia, Richard P. Bagozzi, and Lisa Klein Pearo, "A Social Influence Model of Consumer Participation in Network- and Small-Group-Based Virtual Communities," *International Journal of Research in Marketing* 21, 2004, pp. 241–263.

85. For a general discussion of reactance behavior, see Mona A. Clee and Robert A. Wicklund, "Consumer Behavior and Psychological Reactance," *Journal of Consumer Research,* March 1980, pp. 389–405.

86. Rene Algesheimer, Utpal M. Dholakia, and Andreas Hermann, "The Social Influence of Brand Community: Evidence from European Car Clubs," *Journal of Marketing,* July 2005, pp. 19–34.

87. A. Peter McGraw and Philip E. Tetlock, "Taboo Trade-Offs, Relational Framing, and the Acceptability of Exchanges," *Journal of Consumer Psychology* 15, no. 1, 2005, pp. 2–15. See also Gita Venkataramani Johar, "The Price of Friendship: When, Why, and How Relational Norms Guide Social Exchange Behavior," *Journal of Consumer Psychology* 15, no. 1, 2005, pp. 22–27; and Barbara E. Kahn, "The Power and Limitations of Social Relational Framing for Understanding Consumer Decision Processes," *Journal of Consumer Psychology* 15, no. 1, 2005, pp. 28–34; and Philip E. Tetlock and A. Peter McGraw, "Theoretically Framing Relational Framing," *Journal of Consumer Psychology* 15, no. 1, 2005, pp. 35–37.

88. Russell W. Belk, "Exchange Taboos from an Interpretive Perspective," *Journal of Consumer Psychology* 15, no. 1, 2005, pp. 16–21.

89. White and Dahl, "To Be or Not Be? The Influence of Dissociative Reference Groups on Consumer Preferences."

90. William O. Bearden and Michael J. Etzel, "Reference Group Influence on Product and Brand Purchase Decisions," *Journal of Consumer Research* 9, no. 2, 1982, pp. 183–194.

91. Robert E. Witt and Grady D. Bruce, "Group Influence and Brand Choice Congruence," *Journal of Marketing Research,* November 1972, pp. 440–443.

92. Jennifer J. Argo, Darren W. Dahl, and Rajesh V. Manchanda, "The Influence of a Mere Social Pressure in a Retail Context," *Journal of Consumer Research* 32, no. 2, 2005, pp. 207–212; Darren W. Dahl, Rajesh V. Manchanda, and Jennifer J. Argo, "Embarrassment in Consumer Purchase: The Roles of Social Presence and Purchase Familiarity," *Journal of Consumer Research,* December 2001, pp. 473–481.

93. Bobby J. Calder and Robert E. Burnkrant, "Interpersonal Influences on Consumer Behavior: An Attribution Theory Approach," *Journal of Consumer Research,* June 1977, pp. 29–38; William O. Bearden, Richard G. Netemeyer, and Jesse E. Teel, "Measurement of Consumer Susceptibility to Interpersonal Influence," *Journal of Consumer Research,* March 1989, pp. 473–481; William O. Bearden and Randall L. Rose, "Attention to Social Comparison Information: An Individual Difference Factor Affecting Conformity," *Journal of Consumer Research,* March 1990, pp. 461–471.

94. John C. Mowen, "Exploring the Trait of Competitiveness and Its Consumer Behavior Consequences," *Journal of Consumer Psychology,* 2004, pp. 52–63.

95. Brendan I. Koerner, "Neighbors, Start Your Lawn Mowers," *New York Times,* October 17, 2004, sec. 3, p. 2.

96. Charles S. Gulas and Kim McKeage, "Extending Social Comparison: An Examination of the Unintended Consequences of Idealized Advertising Imagery," *Journal of Advertising* 29, no. 2, Summer 2000, pp. 17–28.

97. David B. Wooten and Americus Reed II, "Playing It Safe: Susceptibility to Normative Influence and Protective Self-Presentation," *Journal of Consumer Research,* December 2004, pp. 551–556.

98. C. Whan Park and Parker Lessig, "Students and Housewives: Differences in Susceptibility to Reference Group Influence," *Journal of Consumer Research,* September 1977, pp. 102–110.

99. Robert Fisher and Kirk Wakefield, "Factors Leading to Group Identification: A Field Study of Winners and Losers," *Psychology and Marketing,* January 1998, pp. 23–40.

100. John R. French and Bertram Raven, "The Bases of Social Power," in ed. D. Cartwright, *Studies in Social Power* (Ann Arbor, Mich.: Institute for Social Research, 1969), pp. 150–167.

101. Reingen et al., "Brand Congruence in Interpersonal Relations"; Park and Lessig, "Students and Housewives."

102. Donnel A. Briley and Robert S. Wyer Jr., "The Effect of Group Membership Salience on the Avoidance of Negative Outcomes: Implications for Social and Consumer Decisions," *Journal of Consumer Research,* December 2002, pp. 400–415.

103. Dana-Nicoleta Lascu, William O. Bearden, and Randall L. Rose, "Norm Extremity and Interpersonal Influences on Consumer Conformity," *Journal of Business Research,* March 1995, pp. 200–212.

104. Social influence, attitudes toward the ads, and prior trial behavior all affect antismoking beliefs, as discussed in J. Craig Andrews, Richard G. Netemeyer, Scot Burton, D. Paul Moberg, and Ann Christiansen, "Understanding Adolescent Intentions to Smoke: An Examination of Relationships Among Social Influence, Prior Trial Behavior, and Antitobacco Campaign Advertising," *Journal of Marketing,* July 2004, pp. 110–123.

105. J. L. Freeman and S. Fraser, "Compliance Without Pressure: The Foot-in-the-Door Technique," *Journal of Personality and Social Psychology,* August 1966, pp. 195–202.

106. Robert B. Cialdini, J. E. Vincent, S. K. Lewis, J. Caalan, D. Wheeler, and B. L. Darby, "Reciprocal Concessions Procedure for Inducing Compliance: The Door-in-the-Face Effect," *Journal of Personality and Social Psychology,* February 1975, pp. 200–215; John C. Mowen and Robert Cialdini, "On Implementing the Door-in-the-Face

Compliance Strategy in a Marketing Context," *Journal of Marketing Research,* May 1980, pp. 253–258; see also Edward Fern, Kent Monroe, and Ramon Avila, "Effectiveness of Multiple Request Strategies: A Synthesis of Research Results," *Journal of Marketing Research,* May 1986, pp. 144–152.

107. Alice Tybout, Brian Sternthal, and Bobby J. Calder, "Information Availability as a Determinant of Multiple Request Effectiveness," *Journal of Marketing Research,* August 1983, pp. 279–290; John T. Gourville, "Pennies-a-Day: The Effect of Temporal Reframing on Transaction Evaluation," *Journal of Consumer Research,* March 1998, pp. 395–408.

108. Eric R. Spangenberg and David E. Sprott, "Self-Monitoring and Susceptibility to the Influence of Self-Prophecy," *Journal of Consumer Research* 32, no. 4, 2006, pp. 550–556; Eric R. Spangenberg and Anthony G. Greenwald, "Social Influence by Requesting Self-Prophecy," *Journal of Consumer Psychology* 8, no. 1, 1999, pp. 61–89.

109. For more about self-prophecy, see Eric R. Spangenberg, David E. Sprott, Bianca Grohmann, and Ronn J. Smith, "Mass-Communicated Prediction Requests: Practical Application and a Cognitive Dissonance Explanation for Self-Prophecy," *Journal of Marketing,* July 2003, pp. 47–62.

110. Stephanie Dellande, Mary C. Gilly, and John L. Graham, "Gaining Compliance and Losing Weight: The Role of the Service Provider in Health Care Services," *Journal of Marketing,* July 2004, pp. 78–91.

111. Deutsch and Gerard, "A Study of Normative and Informational Influence upon Individual Judgment"; C. Whan Park and Parker Lessig, "Students and Housewives: Differences in Susceptibility to Reference Group Influences" *Journal of Consumer Research* 4, September 1977, 102–110. Dennis L. Rosen and Richard W. Olshavsky, "The Dual Role of Informational Social Influence: Implications for Marketing Management," *Journal of Business Research,* April 1987, pp. 123–144.

112. Jeffrey D. Ford and Elwood A. Ellis, "A Re-examination of Group Influence on Member Brand Preference," *Journal of Marketing Research* 17, no. 1, 1980, pp. 125–133; Linda L. Price and Lawrence F. Feick, "The Role of Interpersonal Sources in External Search: An Informational Perspective," in ed. Thomas Kinnear, *Advances in Consumer Research,* vol. 11 (Ann Arbor, Mich.: Association for Consumer Research, 1984), pp. 250–255.

113. Arch G. Woodside and M. Wayne DeLosier, "Effects of Word-of-Mouth Advertising on Consumer Risk Taking," *Journal of Advertising,* September 1976, pp. 17–26.

114. Henry Assael, *Consumer Behavior and Marketing Action,* 4th ed. (Boston: PWS-Kent, 1992).

115. John R. French and Bertram Raven, "The Bases of Social Power," in ed. D. Cartwright, *Studies in Social Power* (Ann Arbor, Mich.: Institute for Social Research, 1959), pp. 150–167; Dana-Nicoleta Lascu, William Bearden, and Randall Rose, "Norm Extremity and Interpersonal Influences on Consumer Conformity," *Journal of Business Research,* March 1995, pp. 200–212; David B. Wooten and Americus Reed II, "Informational Influence and the Ambiguity of Product Experience: Order Effects on the Weighting of Evidence," *Journal of Consumer Psychology* 7, no. 1, 1998, pp. 79–99.

116. Bearden, Netemeyer, and Teel, "Measurement of Consumer Susceptibility to Interpersonal Influence"; Bearden and Rose, "Attention to Social Comparison Information."

117. Gerald Zaltman and Melanie Wallendorf, *Consumer Behavior: Basic Findings and Management Implications,* 2d ed. (New York: Wiley, 1983); Reingen et al., "Brand Congruence in Interpersonal Relations."

118. Charles R. Taylor, Gordon E. Miracle, and R. Dale Wilson, "The Impact of Information Level on the Effectiveness of U.S. and Korean Television Commercials," *Journal of Advertising,* Spring 1997, pp. 1–18.

119. Jane L. Levere, "Wisdom of the Web," January 29, 2008, p. C8. For more about Web-based chatting, see George M. Zinkhan, Hyokjin Kwak, Michelle Morrison, and Cara Okleshen Peters, "Web-Based Chatting: Consumer Communications in Cyberspace," *Journal of Consumer Psychology* 13 (1&2), 2003, pp. 17–27.

120. Stephen A. LaTour and Ajay Manrai, "Interactive Impact of Informational and Normative Influence on Donations," *Journal of Marketing Research,* August 1989, pp. 327–335.

121. Asim Ansari, Skander Essegaier, and Rajeev Kohli, "Internet Recommendation Systems," *Journal of Marketing Research* 37, August 2000, pp. 363–375.

122. Johan Arndt, "Role of Product-Related Conversations in the Diffusion of a New Product," *Journal of Marketing Research,* August 1967, pp. 291–295.

123. Marsha L. Richins, "Negative Word of Mouth by Dissatisfied Consumers: A Pilot Study," *Journal of Marketing,* January 1983, pp. 68–78.

124. Ann E. Schlosser, "Posting Versus Lurking: Communication in a Multiple Audience Context," *Journal of Consumer Research* 32, no. 2, 2005, pp. 260–265.

125. Herr, Kardes, and Kim, "Effects of Word-of-Mouth and Product-Attribute Information on Persuasion"; Richard W. Mizerski, "An Attribution Explanation of the Disproportionate Influence of Unfavorable Information," *Journal of Consumer Research,* December 1982, pp. 301–310.

126. See Suman Basuroy, Subimal Chatterjee, and S. Abraham Ravid, "How Critical Are Critical Reviews? The Box Office Effects of Film Critics, Star Power, and Budgets," *Journal of Marketing,* October 2003, pp. 103–117.

127. Daniel Laufer, Kate Gillespie, Brad McBride, and Silvia Gonzalez, "The Role of Severity in Consumer Attributions of Blame: Defensive Attributions in Product-Harm Crises in Mexico," *Journal of International Consumer Marketing* 17, no. 2/3, 2005, pp. 33–50.

128. Brown and Reingen, "Social Ties and Word-of-Mouth Referral Behavior"; Arndt, "Role of Product-Related Conversations in the Diffusion of a New Product"; Laura Yale and Mary C. Gilly, "Dyadic Perceptions in Personal

Source Information Search," *Journal of Business Research*, March 1995, pp. 225–238.

129. Yong Liu, "Word of Mouth for Movies: Its Dynamics and Impact on Box Office Revenue," *Journal of Marketing*, July 2006, pp. 74–89.

130. Chip Walker, "Word of Mouth," *American Demographics*, July 1995, pp. 39–46.

131. Robert East, Kathy Hammond, and Malcolm Wright, "The Relative Incidence of Positive and Negative Word of Mouth: A Multi-Category Study," *International Journal of Research in Marketing*, June 2007, pp. 175–184.

132. Herr, Kardes, and Kim, "Effects of Word-of-Mouth and Product-Attribute Information on Persuasion."

133. Elihu Katz and Paul F. Lazarsfeld, *Personal Influence* (Glencoe, Ill.: Free Press, 1955).

134. Beth Snyder Bulik, "Who Blogs? Odds Are Marketers Have No Idea," *Advertising Age*, June 4, 2007, *www.adage.com*.

135. Tom A. Peter, "Automakers Put Bloggers in the Driver's Seat," *Christian Science Monitor*, January 17, 2008, p. 15.

136. Joann Klimkiewicz, "Carving Out New Space: Girl Scouts Pitch Cookies on MySpace and Other Social Networks, But Will It Work?" *Hartford Courant*, March 5, 2007, p. D1.

137. A. Coskun and Cheryl J. Frohlich, "Service: The Competitive Edge in Banking," *Journal of Services Marketing*, Winter 1992, pp. 15–23; Jeffrey G. Blodgett, Donald H. Granbois, and Rockney Waters, "The Effects of Perceived Justice on Complainants' Negative Word-of-Mouth Behavior and Repatronage Intentions," *Journal of Retailing*, Winter 1993, pp. 399–429; Karen Maru File, Ben B. Judd, and Russ A. Prince, "Interactive Marketing: The Influence of Participation on Positive Word-of-Mouth Referrals," *Journal of Services Marketing*, Fall 1992, pp. 5–15; Gary L. Clark, Peter F. Kaminski, and David R. Rink, "Consumer Complaints: Advice on How Companies Should Respond Based on an Empirical Study," *Journal of Services Marketing*, Winter 1992, pp. 41–51.

138. Justin Scheck and Ben Worthen, "When Animals Go AWOL, Zoos Try To Tame Bad PR," *Wall Street Journal*, January 5, 2008, p. A1.

139. Kathryn Kranhold and Erin White, "The Perils and Potential Rewards of Crisis Managing for Firestone," *Wall Street Journal*, September 8, 2000, pp. B1, B4.

140. Mara Adelman, "Social Support in the Service Sector: The Antecedents, Processes, and Outcomes of Social Support in an Introductory Service," *Journal of Business Research*, March 1995, pp. 273–283; Jerry D. Rogers, Kenneth E. Clow, and Toby J. Kash, "Increasing Job Satisfaction of Service Personnel," *Journal of Services Marketing*, Winter 1994, pp. 14–27.

141. Abbey Klaassen, "What Happens in Vegas Matters for Marketers," *Advertising Age*, January 7, 2008, p. 6.

142. Michael Kamins, Valerie Folkes, and Lars Perner, "Consumer Responses to Rumors: Good News, Bad News," *Journal of Consumer Psychology* 6, no. 2, 1997, 165–187.

143. Michelle L. Roehm and Alice M. Tybout, "When Will a Brand Scandal Spill Over, and How Should Competitors Respond?" *Journal of Marketing Research*, August 2006, pp. 366–373.

144. Richard Morochove, "Monitor Your Web Reputation," *PC World*, March 3, 2008, *www.pcworld.com*.

145. Koenig, *Rumor in the Marketplace*; see also Alice M. Tybout, Bobby J. Calder, and Brian Sternthal, "Using Information Processing Theory to Design Marketing Strategies," *Journal of Marketing Research*, February 1981, pp. 73–79.

146. Stephanie Kang, "Nike Warns of Soccer-Ball Shortage; Sporting-Goods Firm Cuts Ties with a Big Supplier, Citing Labor Violations," *Wall Street Journal*, November 21, 2006, p. B5.

147. Beth Bragg, "Alaska Staple Is Safe: Rumors of Pilot Bread's Demise Are False," *Anchorage Daily News*, November 6, 2007, *www.adn.com*.

148. Reingen and Kernan, "Analysis of Referral Networks in Marketing."

149. Steve Pounds, "Verizon Tries Unlimited Without Voice," *Austin American-Statesman*, April 16, 2008, *www.statesman.com*; Kim Leonard, "More People Let Fingers Do Talking," *Pittsburgh Tribune-Review*, April 4, 2008, n.p.; Spencer E. Ante and Bruce Meyerson, "Verizon Wireless' Grand Opening," *BusinessWeek*, December 10, 2007, p. 36; Angel Jennings, "What's Good for a Business Can Be Hard on Friends," *New York Times*, August 4, 2007, p. C1.

Chapter 16

1. Carolyn Walkup, "Panera Readies Price Hike, Menu Revamp to Combat Soft Sales," *Nation's Restaurant News*, November 12, 2007, p. 8; Micheline Maynard, "Wasabi to the People: Big Chains Evolve or Die," *New York Times*, July 11, 2007, pp. F1, F8; Janet Adamy, "For McDonald's, It's a Wrap," *Wall Street Journal*, January 30, 2007, p. B1; Michael Arndt, "Giving Fast Food a Run for Its Money," *BusinessWeek*, April 17, 2006, p. 62.

2. Tom Yager, "Apple iPhone SDK Upends Mobile Market," *Infoworld*, March 12, 2008, *www.infoworld.com*; Roger O. Crockett and Cliff Edwards, "Making the iPhone Mean Business," *BusinessWeek*, July 23, 2007, p. 30.

3. Deborah Ball, "After Buying Binge, Nestlé Goes on a Diet," *Wall Street Journal*, July 23, 2007, p. 1.

4. Hubert Gatignon and Thomas S. Robertson, "Innovative Decision Processes," in eds. Thomas S. Robertson and Harold H. Kassarjian, *Handbook of Consumer Behavior* (New York: Prentice-Hall, 1991), pp. 316–317; see also Everett M. Rogers, *The Diffusion of Innovations* (New York: Free Press, 1983).

5. Dave McCaughan, "To Win Hearts of Japanese Men, Focus on Their Hair," *Advertising Age*, October 15, 2007, p. 38; Robert Langreth, "From a Prostate Drug Comes a Pill for Baldness," *Wall Street Journal*, March 20, 1997, pp. B1, B4.

6. Characteristics of employees involved in new product development can also affect innovativeness; see, for example, Rajesh Sethi, Daniel C. Smith, and C. Whan Park,

"Cross-Functional Product Development Teams, Creativity, and the Innovativeness of New Consumer Products," *Journal of Marketing Research*, February 2001, pp. 73–85.

7. Yumiko Ono, "Overcoming the Stigma of Dishwashers in Japan," *Wall Street Journal*, May 19, 2000, pp. B1, B4.

8. Sonoo Singh, "Interactive/Ecommerce: Net Lifts High Street Blues," *Marketing Week*, February 28, 2008, n.p.

9. Thomas S. Robertson, "The Process of Innovation and the Diffusion of Innovation," *Journal of Marketing*, January 1967, pp. 14–19; Thomas S. Robertson, *Innovative Behavior and Communication* (New York: Holt, Reinhart, & Winston, 1971).

10. Katie Hafner, "Film Drop-Off Sites Fading Fast as Digital Cameras Dominate," *New York Times*, October 9, 2007, pp. C1, C11.

11. C. Page Moreau, Arthur B. Markman, and Donald R. Lehmann, "'What Is It?' Categorization Flexibility and Consumers' Responses to Really New Products," *Journal of Consumer Research* 27, March 2001, pp. 489–498.

12. Alfred R. Petrosky, "Extending Innovation Characteristic Perception to Diffusion Channel Intermediaries and Aesthetic Products," in eds. Rebecca Holman and Michael Solomon, *Advances in Consumer Research*, vol. 17 (Provo, Utah: Association for Consumer Research, 1991), pp. 627–634.

13. Noah Rothbaum, "Catalog Critic: Oven-Mitt Technology Heats Up," *Wall Street Journal*, August 25, 2006, p. W9C; Wilton Woods, "Dressed to Spill," *Fortune*, October 17, 1995, p. 209.

14. S. Ram, "A Model of Innovation Resistance," in eds. Melanie Wallendorf and Paul Anderson, *Advances in Consumer Research*, vol. 14 (Provo, Utah: Association for Consumer Research, 1987), pp. 208–212; Jagdish N. Sheth, "Psychology of Innovation Resistance: The Less Developed Concept (LDC) in Diffusion Research," in *Research in Marketing* (Greenwich, Conn.: JAI Press, 1981), pp. 273–282.

15. Amitav Chakravarti and Jinhong Xie, "The Impact of Standards Competition on Consumers: Effectiveness of Product Information and Advertising Formats," *Journal of Marketing Research*, May 2006, pp. 224–236.

16. David Glen Mick and Susan Fournier, "Paradoxes of Technology: Consumer Cognizance, Emotions, and Coping Strategies," *Journal of Consumer Research*, September 1998, pp. 123–143.

17. Stacy L. Wood and Joffre Swait, "Psychological Indicators of Innovation Adoption: Cross-Classification Based on Need for Cognition and Need for Change," *Journal of Consumer Psychology*, Vol. 12 (1), 2002, pp. 1–13.

18. Alexander Chernev, "Goal Orientation and Consumer Preference for the Status Quo," *Journal of Consumer Research* 31, no. 3, 2004, pp. 557–565.

19. Michal Herzenstein, Steven S. Posavac, and J. Joško Brakus, "Adoption of New and Really New Products: The Effects of Self-Regulation Systems and Risk Salience," *Journal of Marketing Research*, May 2007, pp. 251–260.

20. C. Page Moreau, Donald R. Lehmann, and Arthur B. Markman, "Entrenched Knowledge Structures and Consumer Response to New Products," *Journal of Marketing Research*, February 2001, pp. 14–29.

21. Glen Urban and Gilbert A. Churchill, "Five Dimensions of the Industrial Adoption Process," *Journal of Marketing Research*, August 1971, pp. 322–327; Charles R. O'Neal, Hans B. Thorelli, and James M. Utterback, "Adoption of Innovation by Industrial Organizations," *Industrial Marketing Management*, March 1973, pp. 235–250; Gerald Zaltman, Robert Duncan, and Jonny Holbek, *Innovations and Organizations* (New York: Wiley, 1973).

22. Eric Newman, "Meow Mix Educates Cat-loving Consumers," *Brandweek*, November 19, 2007, p. 48; Tim Parry, "Teaching Tools," *Promo*, April 1, 2005, n.p.

23. "The Segway, Billed As the Next Big Thing, Is Still Finding Its Place After Hype," *Canadian Press*, February 27, 2008, n.p.; Rachel Metz, "Oft-Scorned Segway Finds Friends Among the Disabled," *New York Times*, October 14, 2004, p. G5.

24. Rogers, *The Diffusion of Innovations*.

25. Geoffrey A. Moore, *Crossing the Chasm* (New York: HarperBusiness, 1991).

26. Adam Lashinsky, "Early Adopters' Paradise," *Fortune*, January 10, 2005, p. 52.

27. Cristina Lourosa, "Understanding the User: Who Are the First Ones Out There Buying the Latest Gadgets?" *Wall Street Journal*, June 15, 1998, p. R17a.

28. Bill Machrone, "The Most Memorable Tech Flops," *PC Magazine*, January 2008, pp. 88–89.

29. Robert A. Peterson, "A Note on Optimal Adopter Category Determination," *Journal of Marketing Research*, August 1973, pp. 325–329; see also William R. Darden and Fred D. Reynolds, "Backward Profiling of Male Innovators," *Journal of Marketing Research*, February 1974, pp. 79–85; Steven A. Baumgarten, "The Innovative Communicator in the Diffusion Process," *Journal of Marketing Research*, February 1975, pp. 12–17a. Schemes based on consumers' involvement in the new-product development process, for example, might be utilized by managers (see Jerry Wind and Vijay Mahajan, "Issues and Opportunities in New Product Development: An Introduction to the Special Issue," *Journal of Marketing Research*, February 1997, pp. 1–12).

30. David F. Midgley and Grahame R. Dowling, "Innovativeness: The Concept and Its Measurement," *Journal of Consumer Research*, March 1978, pp. 229–242; Mary Dee Dickerson and James W. Gentry, "Characteristics of Adopters and Non Adopters of Home Computers," *Journal of Consumer Research*, September 1983, pp. 225–235; see also Vijay Mahajan, Eitan Muller, and Rajendra Srivastava, "Determination of Adopter Categories by Using Innovation Diffusion Models," *Journal of Marketing Research*, February 1990, pp. 37–50; Kenneth C. Manning, William O. Bearden, and Thomas J. Madden, "Consumer Innovativeness and the Adoption

Process," *Journal of Consumer Psychology* 4, no. 4, 1995, pp. 329–345.

31. Chuan-Fong Shih and Alladi Venkatesh, "Beyond Adoption: Development and Application of a Use-Diffusion Model," *Journal of Marketing,* January 2004, pp. 59–72.

32. See review in Thomas S. Robertson, Joan Zielinski, and Scott Ward, *Consumer Behavior* (Glenview, Ill.: Scott, Foresman, 1984); see also Dickerson and Gentry, "Characteristics of Adopters and Non Adopters of Home Computers"; Duncan G. Labay and Thomas C. Kinnear, "Exploring the Consumer Decision Process in the Adoption of Solar Energy Systems," *Journal of Consumer Research*, December 1981, pp. 271–277; Kenneth Uhl, Roman Andrus, and Lance Poulsen, "How Are Laggards Different? An Empirical Inquiry," *Journal of Marketing Research*, February 1970, pp. 51–54; Rogers, *The Diffusion of Innovations*, pp. 383–384.

33. Moon Ihlwan, "The Mobile Internet's Future Is East," *BusinessWeek Online,* January 29, 2007, *www.businessweek.com;* Robert A. Guth, "Can Your Cell Phone Shop, Play or Fish?" *Wall Street Journal*, August 3, 2000, p. B1.

34. Rogers, *The Diffusion of Innovations;* see also Mark S. Granovetter, "The Strength of Weak Ties," *American Journal of Sociology*, May 1973, pp. 1360–1380; John A. Czepiel, "Word-of-Mouth Processes in the Diffusion of a Major Technological Innovation," *Journal of Marketing Research*, May 1974, pp. 172–181.

35. Manning, Bearden, and Madden, "Consumer Innovativeness and the Adoption Process"; Jan-Benedict E. M. Steenkamp and Hans Baumgartner, "The Role of Optimum Stimulation Level in Exploratory Consumer Behavior," *Journal of Consumer Research*, December 1992, pp. 434–448; P. S. Raju, "Optimum Stimulation Level: Its Relationship to Personality, Demographics, and Exploratory Behavior," *Journal of Consumer Research*, December 1980, pp. 272–282.

36. Thomas S. Robertson and James H. Myers, "Personality Correlates of Opinion Leadership and Innovative Buying Behavior," *Journal of Marketing Research*, May 1969, pp. 164–167.

37. Gordon R. Foxall and Christopher G. Haskins, "Cognitive Style and Consumer Innovativeness," *Marketing Intelligence and Planning*, January 1986, pp. 26–46; Gordon R. Foxall, "Consumer Innovativeness: Novelty Seeking, Creativity and Cognitive Style," in eds. Elizabeth C. Hirschman and Jagdish N. Sheth, *Research in Consumer Behavior*, vol. 3 (Greenwich, Conn.: JAI Press, 1988), pp. 79–114.

38. Ronald E. Goldsmith and Charles F. Hofacker, "Measuring Consumer Innovativeness," *Journal of the Academy of Marketing Science*, Summer 1991, pp. 209–221.

39. Jan-Benedict E. M. Steenkamp, Frenkel ter Hofstede, and Michael Wedel, "A Cross-National Investigation into the Individual and National Cultural Antecedents of Consumer Innovativeness," *Journal of Marketing*, April 1999, pp. 55–69.

40. Hubert Gatignon and Thomas S. Robertson, "A Propositional Inventory for New Diffusion Research," *Journal of Consumer Research*, March 1985, pp. 849–867; see also John O. Summers, "Media Exposure Patterns of Consumer Innovators," *Journal of Marketing*, January 1972, pp. 43–49.

41. James J. Engel, Robert J. Kegerreis, and Roger D. Blackwell, "Word-of-Mouth Communication by the Innovator," *Journal of Marketing*, July 1969, pp. 15–19.

42. Dickerson and Gentry, "Characteristics of Adopters and Non Adopters of Home Computers"; Robertson, *Innovative Behavior and Communication;* James W. Taylor, "A Striking Characteristic of Innovators," *Journal of Marketing Research*, February 1977, pp. 104–107; see also Gatignon and Robertson, "A Propositional Inventory for New Diffusion Research"; Elizabeth C. Hirschman, "Innovativeness, Novelty Seeking and Consumer Creativity," *Journal of Consumer Research*, December 1980, pp. 283–295; Engel, Kegerreis, and Blackwell, "Word-of-Mouth Communication by the Innovator."

43. Zweli Mokgata, "Vodacom Ready to Ring the Changes," *The Times (South Africa)*, February 26, 2008, n.p.; Reinhardt Krause, "America Movil Accelerating Push Into 3G," *Investor's Business Daily*, February 26, 2008, *www.investors.com.*

44. Frank M. Bass, "New Product Growth Models for Consumer Durables," *Management Science*, September 1969, pp. 215–227; Wellesley Dodds, "An Application of the Bass Model in Long-Term New Product Forecasting," *Journal of Marketing Research*, August 1973, pp. 308–311; Roger M. Heeler and Thomas P. Hustad, "Problems in Predicting New Product Growth for Consumer Durables," *Management Science*, October 1980, pp. 1007–1020; Douglas Tigart and Behrooz Farivar, "The Bass New Product Growth Model: A Sensitivity Analysis for a High Technology Product," *Journal of Marketing*, Fall 1981, pp. 81–90.

45. William E. Cox Jr., "Product Life Cycles as Marketing Models," *Journal of Business*, October 1967, pp. 375–384; Rolando Polli and Victor Cook, "Validity of the Product Life Cycle," *Journal of Business*, October 1969, pp. 385–400; D. R. Rink and J. E. Swan, "Product Life Cycle Research: A Literature Review," *Journal of Business Research*, September 1979, pp. 219–242; Robertson, *Innovative Behavior and Communication.*

46. Mike Hughlett, "Mapmaker Rand McNally Sets Out on Digital Road," *Chicago Tribune*, June 27, 2007, *www.chicagotribune.com.*

47. Hillary Chura, "Grabbing Bull by Tail: Pepsi, Snapple Redouble Efforts to Take on Red Bull Energy Drink," *Advertising Age*, June 11, 2001, p. 4.

48. Rayna McInturf, "Crash Course: Fitness Goals Lagging a Bit?" *Los Angeles Times*, February 17, 2005, p. E23.

49. Patricia Leigh Brown, "For Fans of Trader Vic's, an Adventure in Tikiland," *New York Times*, March 5, 2008, *www.nytimes.com;* Rick Ramseyer, "Tiki Reigns Again," *Restaurant Business*, February 1, 2005, p. 34.

50. David H. Henard and David M. Szymanski, "Why Some New Products Are More Successful Than Others," *Journal of Marketing Research,* August 2001, pp. 362–375.

51. "An Elusive Goal: Identifying New Products that Consumers Actually Want," *Marketing at Wharton,* December 15, 2004, *knowledge.wharton.upenn.edu.*

52. James E. Burroughs and David Glen Mick, "Exploring Antecedents and Consequences of Consumer Creativity in a Problem-Solving Context," *Journal of Consumer Research* 31, no. 2, 2004, pp. 402–411.

53. Elliot Spagat, "At $70 a Pop, Consumers Put Discount DVD Players on Holiday List," *Wall Street Journal,* December 13, 2001, pp. B1, B4.

54. Randall Stross, "Freed from the Page, but a Book Nonetheless," *New York Times,* January 27, 2008, p. BU3.

55. Rich Thomaselli, "Scare Revives FluMist Health," *Advertising Age,* December 15, 2004, pp. 1, 31.

56. Se Young Lee and Jay Alabaster, "Sony's PS3 Gets Boost From Its Blu-ray Drive," *Wall Street Journal,* March 12, 2008, p. D7.

57. Jan-Benedict E. M. Steenkamp and Katrijn Gielens, "Consumer and Market Drivers of the Trial Probability of New Consumer Packaged Goods," *Journal of Consumer Research,* December 2003, pp. 368–384.

58. Steve Hoeffler, "Measuring Preferences for Really New Products," *Journal of Marketing Research,* November 2003, pp. 406–420.

59. Paschalina Ziamou and S. Ratneshwar, "Promoting Consumer Adoption of High-Technology Products: Is More Information Always Better?" *Journal of Consumer Psychology,* Vol. 12 (4), 2002, pp. 341–351.

60. Gatignon and Robertson, "A Propositional Inventory for New Diffusion Research"; Vijay Mahajan, Eitan Muller, and Frank M. Bass, "New Product Diffusion Models in Marketing: A Review and Directions for Research," *Journal of Marketing,* April 1990, pp. 1–27.

61. Greg Jacobson, "Proven Brands Rule," *MMR,* January 14, 2002, p. 29.

62. "10 Problem Products from 2003," *Advertising Age,* December 22, 2003, p. 27.

63. Rogers, *The Diffusion of Innovations.*

64. Rogers, *The Diffusion of Innovations.*

65. Debora Viana Thompson, Rebecca W. Hamilton, and Roland T. Rust, "Feature Fatigue: When Product Capabilities Become Too Much of a Good Thing," *Journal of Marketing Research,* November 2005, pp. 431–442.

66. Ashesh Mukherjee and Wayne D. Hoyer, "The Effect of Novel Attributes on Product Evaluation," *Journal of Consumer Research,* December 2001, pp. 462–472.

67. Katherine A. Burson, "Consumer–Product Skill Matching: The Effects of Difficulty on Relative Self-Assessment and Choice," *Journal of Consumer Research* 34, no. 1, 2007, pp. 104–110.

68. Al Doyle, "Getting the Perfect Picture," *Technology & Learning,* January 2002, pp. 9–11.

69. Jagdish N. Sheth and S. Ram, *Bringing Innovation to Market,* 1987 (New York: Wiley).

70. John Naughton, "How Flickr Developed into a Classic Web 2.0 Success," *The Observer (U.K.),* March 9, 2008, *www.guardian.co.uk;* "Flickr Adds Location Info to Photos," *PC Magazine Online,* November 19, 2007, *www.pcmag.com.*

71. Sheth and Ram, *Bringing Innovation to Market.*

72. Sheth and Ram, *Bringing Innovation to Market.*

73. "Car Wash Tech," *DSN Retailing Today,* July 19, 2004, p. 15.

74. Kranhold, "Toyota Makes a Bet on New Hybrid Prius."

75. Raymund Flandez, "Lights! Camera! Sales! How to Use Video to Expand Your Business in a YouTube World," *Wall Street Journal,* November 29, 2007, *ww.wsj.com.*

76. Robert J. Fisher and Linda L. Price, "An Investigation into the Social Context of Early Adoption Behavior," *Journal of Consumer Research,* December 1992, pp. 477–486.

77. Sandra D. Atchison, "Lifting the Golf Bag Burden," *BusinessWeek,* July 25, 1994, p. 84.

78. June Fletcher, "New Machines Measure That Holiday Flab at Home," *Wall Street Journal,* December 26, 1997, p. B8.

79. Rogers, *The Diffusion of Innovations,* p. 99.

80. C. Whan Park, Bernard J. Jaworski, and Deborah J. MacInnis, "Strategic Brand Concept–Image Management," *Journal of Marketing,* October 1986, pp. 135–145.

81. Fisher and Price, "An Investigation into the Social Context of Early Adoption Behavior."

82. Petrosky, "Extending Innovation Characteristic Perception to Diffusion Channel Intermediaries and Aesthetic Products."

83. Alfred Petrosky labels this factor *genrefication* and discusses it in the context of aesthetic innovations in "Extending Innovation Characteristic Perception to Diffusion Channel Intermediaries and Aesthetic Products."

84. Diane Brady, "A Thousand and One Noshes," *BusinessWeek,* June 14, 2004, pp. 54–56.

85. Sheth and Ram, *Bringing Innovation to Market.*

86. Everett M. Rogers and F. Floyd. Shoemaker, *Communication of Innovations* (New York: Free Press, 1971); Elizabeth C. Hirschman, "Consumer Modernity, Cognitive Complexity, Creativity and Innovativeness," in ed. Richard P. Bagozzi, *Marketing in the 80s: Changes and Challenges* (Chicago: American Marketing Association, 1980), pp. 152–161.

87. Jaishankar Ganesh, V. Kumar, and Velavan Subramaniam, "Learning Effect in Multinational Diffusion of Consumer Durables: An Exploratory Investigation," *Journal of the Academy of Marketing Science* 25, Summer 1997, pp. 214–228; Gatignon and Robertson, "A Propositional Inventory for New Diffusion Research."

88. Seth Stevenson, "I'd Like to Buy the World a Shelf-Stable Children's Lactic Drink," *New York Times Magazine,*

March 10, 2002, p. 38; John C. Jay, "The Valley of the New," *American Demographics*, March 2000, pp. 58–59; Norihiko Shirouzu, "Japan's High-School Girls Excel in Art of Setting Trends, *Wall Street Journal*, April 24, 1998, pp. B1, B7.

89. Gatignon and Robertson, "A Propositional Inventory for New Diffusion Research"; Lawrence A. Brown, Edward J. Malecki, and Aron N. Spector, "Adopter Categories in a Spatial Context: Alternative Explanations for an Empirical Regularity," *Rural Sociology*, Spring 1976, pp. 99–117a.

90. Dorothy Leonard-Barton, "Experts as Negative Opinion Leaders in the Diffusion of a Technological Innovation," *Journal of Consumer Research*, March 1985, pp. 914–926.

91. Everett Rogers and D. Lawrence Kincaid, *Communication Networks: Toward a New Paradigm for Research* (New York: Free Press, 1981).

92. Rogers and Kincaid, *Communication Networks*.

93. Frank M. Bass, "The Relationship Between Diffusion Curves, Experience Curves, and Demand Elasticities for Consumer Durable Technological Innovations," *Journal of Business*, July 1980, pp. s51–s57; Dan Horskey and Leonard S. Simon, "Advertising and the Diffusion of New Products," *Marketing Science*, Winter 1983, pp. 1–17; Vijay Mahajan and Eitan Muller, "Innovation Diffusion and New Product Growth Models in Marketing," *Journal of Marketing*, Fall 1979, pp. 55–68; Mahajan, Muller, and Bass, "New Product Diffusion Models in Marketing."

94. Lauriston Sharp, "Steel Axes for Stone Age Australians," in ed. Edward H. Spicer, *Human Problems in Technological Change* (New York: Russell Sage Foundation, 1952).

95. H. David Banta, "The Diffusion of the Computer Tomography (CT) Scanner in the United States," *International Journal of Health Services* 10, 1980, pp. 251–269, as reported in Rogers, *The Diffusion of Innovations*, pp. 231–237.

96. Steven Mufson, "Power Switch: The New Energy Law Will Change Light Bulbs, Appliances, and How We Save Electricity in the Home," *Washington Post*, January 20, 2008, p. F1; "Utilities: PG&E Giving Away Energy-Saver Bulbs," *Los Angeles Times*, October 4, 2007, p. C6; Jenn Abelson, "For This Fall, Green Is In: Stores Hope New Products Will Lure Crowds of Eco-Conscious Teens Headed Back to School," *Boston Globe*, August 17, 2007, p. C1; Marc Lifsher and Adrian G. Uribarri, "How Much Savings Does It Take to Change One?" *Los Angeles Times*, February 24, 2007, p. A1; John J. Fialka and Kathryn Kranhold, "Households Would Need New Bulbs to Meet Lighting-Efficiency Rule," *Wall Street Journal*, May 5, 2007, p. A1; J. Fialka and Kathryn Kranhold, "Lights Out for Old Bulbs?" *Wall Street Journal*, September 13, 2007, p. A8.

Chapter 17

1. Phyllis Korkki, "Cost Is No Object When It Comes to Your Pet," *New York Times*, January 13, 2008, p. BU2; Diane Brady and Christopher Palmeri, "The Pet Economy," *BusinessWeek*, August 6, 2007, pp. 44–54; Frederick Kaufman, "They Eat What We Are," *New York Times Magazine*, September 2, 2007, pp. 20+; John Fetto, "In the Doghouse," *American Demographics*, January 2002, p. 7; John Fetto, "Pets Can Drive," *American Demographics*, March 2000, pp. 10–12.

2. Grant McCracken, "Culture and Consumption: A Theoretical Account of the Structure and Movement of the Cultural Meaning of Consumer Goods," *Journal of Consumer Research*, June 1986, pp. 71–84; Grant McCracken, *Culture and Consumption* (Indianapolis, Ind.: Indiana University Press, 1990).

3. Lisa Peñaloza, "Consuming the American West: Animating Cultural Meaning and Memory at a Stock Show and Rodeo," *Journal of Consumer Research*, December 2001, pp. 369–398.

4. See Craig J. Thompson, "Marketplace Mythology and Discourses of Power," *Journal of Consumer Research*, June 2004, pp. 162–175; Elizabeth C. Hirschman, Linda Scott, and William B. Wells, "A Model of Product Discourse: Linking Consumer Practice to Cultural Texts," *Journal of Advertising*, Spring 1998, pp. 33–50; Barbara A. Phillips, "Thinking into It: Consumer Interpretation of Complex Advertising Images," *Journal of Advertising*, Summer 1997, pp. 77–86; Cele Otnes and Linda Scott, "Something Old, Something New: Exploring the Interaction between Ritual and Advertising," *Journal of Advertising*, Spring 1996, pp. 33–50; Jonna Holland and James W. Gentry, "The Impact of Cultural Symbols on Advertising Effectiveness: A Theory of Intercultural Accommodation," in eds. Merrie Brucks and Debbie MacInnis, *Advances in Consumer Research*, vol. 24 (Provo, Utah: Association for Consumer Research, 1997), pp. 483–489.

5. "Sarah Jessica Parker Coming to Town," *Cincinnati Enquirer*, March 5, 2008, *www.news.enquirer.com*.

6. Ruth La Ferla, "Young Shoppers Chase Up-from-the-Asphalt Niche Designers," *New York Times*, December 21, 2007, pp. G1, G10.

7. Elizabeth Weinstein, "Style & Substance: Graffiti Cleans Up at Retail," *Wall Street Journal*, November 12, 2004, p. B1; Lauren Goldstein, "Urban Wear Goes Suburban," *Fortune*, December 21, 1998, pp. 169–172.

8. Jennifer Edson Escalas and James R. Bettman, "You Are What They Eat: The Influence of Reference Groups on Consumers' Connections to Brands," *Journal of Consumer Psychology* 13, no. 3, 2003, pp. 339–348.

9. For a discussion of how consumers use fashion to both characterize their identity and infer aspects of others' identities, see Craig J. Thompson and Diana L. Haytko, "Speaking of Fashion: Consumers' Use of Fashion Discourses and the Appropriation of Countervailing Cultural Meanings," *Journal of Consumer Research*, June 1997, pp. 15–42.

10. Keith Naughton, "Roots Gets Rad: Trading in Earth Shoes for Hot Berets, the Canadian Firm Plans a U.S. Invasion

After Its Olympic Triumph," *Newsweek*, February 25, 2002, p. 36; Larry M. Greenberg, "Marketing the Great White North, Eh?" *Wall Street Journal*, April 21, 2000, p. B1.

11. Laura R. Oswald, "Culture Swapping: Consumption and the Ethnogenesis of Middle-Class Haitian Immigrants," *Journal of Consumer Research*, March 1999, pp. 303–318.

12. Elisabeth Furst, "The Cultural Significance of Food," in ed. Per Otnes, *The Sociology of Consumption: An Anthology* (Oslo, Norway: Solum Forlag, 1988), pp. 89–100.

13. "Breaching the Grape Wall of China," *BusinessWeek Online*, February 10, 2005, *www.businessweek.com*; Kathleen Brewer Doran, "Symbolic Consumption in China: The Color Television as a Life Statement," in eds. Merrie Brucks and Debbie MacInnis, *Advances in Consumer Research*, vol. 24 (Provo, Utah: Association for Consumer Research, 1997), pp. 128–131.

14. Amy Cortese, "My Jet Is Bigger Than Your Jet," *BusinessWeek*, August 25, 1997, p. 126.

15. Tina A. Brown, "Kids Uniformly Love the Clothes, Parents Love the Prices," *Hartford Courant*, August 9, 2007, p. B2.

16. Pierre Bourdieu, *Distinction: A Social Critique of the Judgment of Taste* (Cambridge, Mass.: Harvard University Press, 1984); for other research on gender associations with food, see Deborah Heisley, "Gender Symbolism in Food," doctoral dissertation, Northwestern University, 1991.

17. Sidney Levy, "Interpreting Consumer Mythology: A Structural Approach to Consumer Behavior," *Journal of Marketing* 45, no. 3, 1982, pp. 49–62.

18. David Welch, "Why Toyota Is Afraid of Being Number One," *BusinessWeek*, March 5, 2007, pp. 42+.

19. Americus Reed II, "Activating the Self-Importance of Consumer Selves: Exploring Identity Salience Effects on Judgments," *Journal of Consumer Research* 31, no. 2, 2004, pp. 286–295.

20. Jeffrey Ball, "Detroit Worries Some Consumers Are Souring on Big SUVs," *Wall Street Journal*, January 8, 2003, pp. B1, B4.

21. Jennifer Edison Escalas, "The Consumption of Insignificant Rituals: A Look at Debutante Balls," in eds. Leigh McAlister and Michael L. Rothschild, *Advances in Consumer Research*, vol. 20 (Provo, Utah: Association for Consumer Research, 1993), pp. 709–716.

22. Jon Gertner, "From 0 to 60 to World Domination," *New York Times Magazine*, February 18, 2007, pp. 34+.

23. James B. Arndorfer, "Miller Lite: Bob Mikulay," *Advertising Age*, November 1, 2004, p. S12; "Miller Lite," *Beverage Dynamics*, January–February 2002, p. 40.

24. Michael R. Solomon, "Building Up and Breaking Down: The Impact of Cultural Sorting on Symbolic Consumption," in eds. Elizabeth C. Hirschman and Jagdish N. Sheth, *Research in Consumer Behavior* (Greenwich, Conn.: JAI Press, 1988), pp. 325–351; McCracken, "Culture and Consumption"; McCracken, *Culture and Consumption*.

25. Alex Taylor III, "America's Best Car Company," *Fortune*, March 19, 2007, pp. 98+.

26. Solomon, "Building Up and Breaking Down"; James H. Leigh and Terrace G. Gabel, "Symbolic Interactionism: Its Effects on Consumer Behavior and Implications for Marketing Strategy," *Journal of Consumer Marketing*, Winter 1992, pp. 27–39.

27. Myrna L. Armstrong and Donata C. Gabriel, "Motivation for Tattoo Removal," *Archives of Dermatology*, April 1996, pp. 412–416.

28. John W. Schouten, "Personal Rites of Passage and the Reconstruction of Self," in eds. Rebecca H. Holman and Michael R. Solomon, *Advances in Consumer Research*, vol. 18 (Provo, Utah: Association for Consumer Research, 1991), pp. 49–51.

29. Melissa Martin Young, "Dispositions of Possessions During Role Transitions," in eds. Rebecca H. Holman and Michael R. Solomon, *Advances in Consumer Research*, vol. 18 (Provo, Utah: Association for Consumer Research, 1991), pp. 33–39.

30. Robert A. Wicklund and Peter M. Gollwitzer, *Symbolic Self-Completion* (Hillsdale, N.J.: Lawrence Erlbaum, 1982).

31. Diane Ackerman, *A Natural History of Love* (New York: Random House, 1994).

32. See, for example, Samuel K. Bonsu and Russell W. Belk, "Do Not Go Cheaply into That Good Night: Death-Ritual Consumption in Asante, Ghana," *Journal of Consumer Research*, June 2003, pp. 41–55.

33. James H. McAlexander, John W. Schouten, and Scott D. Roberts, "Consumer Behavior and Divorce," in eds. Janeen Arnold Costa and Russell W. Belk, *Research in Consumer Behavior*, vol. 6 (Greenwich, Conn.: JAI Press, 1993), pp. 162; see also Rita Fullerman and Kathleen Debevec, "Till Death Do We Part: Family Dissolution, Transition, and Consumer Behavior," in eds. John F. Sherry and Brian Sternthal, *Advances in Consumer Research*, vol. 19 (Provo, Utah: Association for Consumer Research, 1992), pp. 514–521.

34. Melanie Wallendorf and Michael D. Reilly, "Ethnic Migration, Assimilation, and Consumption," *Journal of Consumer Research*, December 1983, pp. 292–302; Rohit Deshpande, Wayne Hoyer, and Naveen Donthu, "The Intensity of Ethnic Affiliation: A Study of the Sociology of Hispanic Consumption," *Journal of Consumer Research*, September 1986, pp. 214–220; for a discussion of acculturation of Chinese Americans, see Wei-Na Lee, "Acculturation and Advertising Communication Strategies: A Cross-Cultural Study of Chinese Americans," *Psychology and Marketing*, September–October 1993, pp. 381–397; for an interesting study on the immigration of Haitian consumers, see Laura R. Oswald, "Culture Swapping: Consumption and the Ethnogenesis of Middle-Class Haitian Immigrants."

35. Annamma Joy and Ruby Roy Dholakia, "Remembrances of Things Past: The Meaning of Home and Possessions

of Indian Professionals in Canada," in ed. Floyd W. Rudmin, *To Have Possessions: A Handbook of Ownership and Property*, Special Issue, *Journal of Social Behavior and Personality* 6, no. 6, 1991, pp. 385–402; see also Raj Mehta and Russell W. Belk, "Artifacts, Identity, and Transition: Favorite Possessions of Indians and Indian Immigrants to the United States," *Journal of Consumer Research*, March 1991, pp. 398–411.

36. Craig J. Thompson and Siok Kuan Tambyah, "Trying to Be Cosmopolitan," *Journal of Consumer Research* 26, December 1999, pp. 214–241.

37. Priscilla A. LaBarbera, "The Nouveaux Riches: Conspicuous Consumption and the Issue of Self-Fulfillment," in eds. Elizabeth C. Hirschman and Jagdish N. Sheth, *Research in Consumer Behavior* (Greenwich, Conn.: JAI Press, 1988), pp. 181–182.

38. Sarah Ellison and Carlos Tejada, "Mr., Mrs., Meet Mr. Clean," *Wall Street Journal,* January 30, 2003, pp. B1, B3.

39. Blythe Yee, "Ads Remind Women They Have Two Hands," *Wall Street Journal*, August 14, 2003, pp. B1, B5; for an extensive discussion of consumer life transitions and related products, see Paula Mergenhagen, *Targeting Transitions* (Ithaca, N.Y.: American Demographics Books, 1995).

40. Ian Mount, "Alternative Gift Registries," *Wall Street Journal,* March 2, 2004, p. D1; Julie Flaherty, "Freedom to Marry, and to Spend on It," *New York Times*, May 16, 2004, sec. 9, p. 2; Miller, "'Til Death Do They Part."

41. Pamela Paul, "What to Expect When Expecting? A Whole Lot of Loot," *New York Times*, June 24, 2007, p. BU5.

42. Otnes and Scott, "Something Old, Something New."

43. In line with our notion that the meaning of the symbol may derive from the culture instead of from the individual and that symbols may have public or private meaning, see Marsha L. Richins, "Valuing Things: The Public and Private Meaning of Possessions," *Journal of Consumer Research*, December 1994, pp. 504–521.

44. N. Laura Kamptner, "Personal Possessions and Their Meanings: A Life Span Perspective," *Journal of Social Behavior and Personality* 6, no. 6, 1991, pp. 209–228; see also Richins, "Valuing Things."

45. Adam Kuper, "The English Christmas and the Family: Time Out and Alternative Realities," in ed. Daniel Miller, *Unwrapping Christmas* (Oxford, England: Oxford University Press, 1993), pp. 157–175; Barbara Bodenhorn, "Christmas Present: Christmas Public," in ed. Miller, *Unwrapping Christmas*, pp. 193–216.

46. Carolyn Folkman Curasi, Linda L. Price, and Eric J. Arnould, "How Individuals' Cherished Possessions Become Families' Inalienable Wealth," *Journal of Consumer Research,* December 2004, pp. 609–622.

47. Kelly Tepper Tian, William O. Bearden, and Gary L. Hunter, "Consumers' Need for Uniqueness: Scale Development and Validation," *Journal of Consumer Research* 28, June 2001, pp. 50–66; Howard L. Fromkin and C. R. Snyder, "The Search for Uniqueness and Valuation of Scarcity," in eds. Kenneth Gergen, Martin S. Green-

berg, and Richard H. Willis, *Social Exchanges: Advances in Theory and Research* (New York: Plenum, 1980), pp. 57–75; Csikszentmihalyi and Rochberg-Halton, *The Meaning of Things*; see also Richins, "Valuing Things."

48. Gabriel Bar-Haim, "The Meaning of Western Commercial Artifacts for Eastern European Youth," *Journal of Contemporary Ethnography*, July 1987, pp. 205–226.

49. Jonah Berger and Chip Heath, "Where Consumers Diverge from Others: Identity Signaling and Product Domains," *Journal of Consumer Research,* August 2007, pp. 121–134.

50. Robert P. Libbon, "Datadog," *American Demographics*, September 2000, p. 26.

51. Stacy Baker and Patricia Kennedy, "Death by Nostalgia," in *Advances in Consumer Research*, vol. 21 (Provo, Utah: Association for Consumer Research, 1994), pp.169–174; Morris B. Holbrook and Robert Schindler, "Echoes of the Dear Departed Past," in *Advances in Consumer Research*, vol. 18 (Provo, Utah: Association for Consumer Research, 1991), pp. 330–333.

52. Stuart Elliott, "A Two-Wheeled Ride Down Memory Lane," *New York Times,* May 4, 2004, *www.nytimes.com.*

53. Vanitha Swaminathan, Karen L. Page, and Zeynep Gürhan-Canli, "'My' Brand or 'Our' Brand: The Effects of Brand Relationship Dimensions and Self-Construal on Brand Evaluations," *Journal of Consumer Research*, August 2007, pp. 2348–259; Matthew Thomson, Deborah J. MacInnis, and C. Whan Park, "The Ties That Bind: Measuring the Strength of Consumers' Emotional Attachments to Brands," *Journal of Consumer Psychology* 15, no. 1, 2005, pp. 77–91; Jennifer Edson Escalas, "Narrative Processing: Building Consumer Connections to Brands," *Journal of Consumer Psychology* 14, no. 1/2, 2004, pp. 168–180; Jennifer Edson Escalas and James R. Bettman, "Self-Construal, Reference Groups, and Brand Meaning," *Journal of Consumer Research* 32, no. 3, 2005, pp. 378–389; Russell W. Belk, "Possessions and the Extended Self," *Journal of Consumer Research*, September 1988, pp. 139–168; A. Dwayne Ball and Lori H. Tasaki, "The Role and Measurement of Attachment in Consumer Behavior," *Journal of Consumer Psychology* 1, no. 2, 1992, pp. 155–172; Robert E. Kleine, Susan Schultz Kleine, and Jerome B. Kernan, "Mundane Consumption and the Self: A Social Identity Perspective," *Journal of Consumer Psychology* 2, no. 3, 1993, pp. 209–235.

54. Kleine, Kleine, and Kernan, "Mundane Consumption and the Self"; see also Sirgy, "Self-Concept and Consumer Behavior"; George M. Zinkhan and J. W. Hong, "Self-Concept and Advertising Effectiveness: A Conceptual Model of Congruence, Conspicuousness, and Response Mode," in eds. Rebecca Holman and Michael Solomon, *Advances in Consumer Research*, vol. 18 (Provo, Utah: Association for Consumer Research, 1991), pp. 348–354.

55. For example, see Robert V. Kozinets, "Utopian Enterprise: Articulating the Meanings of *Star Trek*'s Culture of Consumption," *Journal of Consumer Research*, June

2001, pp. 67–88; Douglas B. Holt, "Why Do Brands Cause Trouble? A Dialectical Theory of Consumer Culture and Branding," *Journal of Consumer Research,* June 2002, pp. 70–90.

56. Kelly Tian and Russell W. Belk, "Extended Self and Possessions in the Workplace," *Journal of Consumer Research* 32, no. 2, 2005, pp. 297–310.

57. Kleine, Kleine, and Kernan, "Mundane Consumption and the Self."

58. C. R. Snyder and Howard L. Fromkin, *Uniqueness: Human Pursuit of Difference* (New York: Plenum, 1981).

59. Hope Jensen Schau and Mary C. Gilly, "We Are What We Post? Self-Presentation in Personal Web Space," *Journal of Consumer Research,* December 2003, pp. 385–404.

60. Stuart Elliott, "Carpet Spots Feature a Confident and Reflective Andie MacDowell," February 24, 2004, *www.nytimes.com.*

61. Sirgy, "Self-Concept and Consumer Behavior"; Sirgy, *Social Cognition and Consumer Behavior.*

62. Ian Rowley, "Here, Kid, Take the Wheel," *BusinessWeek,* July 23, 2007, p. 37.

63. Cheng Lu Wang, Terry Bristol, John C. Mowen, and Goutam Chakraborty, "Alternative Modes of Self-Construal: Dimensions of Connectedness–Separateness and Advertising Appeals to the Cultural and Gender-Specific Self," *Journal of Consumer Psychology* 9, no. 2, 2000, pp. 107–115.

64. Matthew Thomson, Deborah J. MacInnis, and C. Whan Park, "The Ties That Bind: Measuring the Strength of Consumers' Emotional Attachments to Brands," *Journal of Consumer Psychology* 15, no. 1, 2005, p. 77–91; Jennifer Edson Escalas, "Narrative Processing: Building Consumer Connections to Brands," *Journal of Consumer Psychology* 14, no. 1/2, 2004, pp. 168–180; Jennifer Edson Escalas and James R. Bettman, "Self-Construal, Reference Groups, and Brand Meaning," *Journal of Consumer Research* 32, no. 3, 2005, pp. 378–389.

65. Richins, "Valuing Things"; Marsha L. Richins, "Special Possessions and the Expression of Material Values," *Journal of Consumer Research*, December 1994, pp. 522–533.

66. Richins, "Valuing Things."

67. Thomson, MacInnis, and Park, "The Ties that Bind: Measuring the Strength of Consumers' Emotional Attachments to Brands; C. W. Park and Deborah J. MacInnis, "What's In and What's Out: Questions on the Boundaries of the Attitude Construct," *Journal of Consumer Research* 33, no. 1, 2006, pp. 16–18; Rohini Ahluwalia, Robert Burnkrant, and H. Rao Unnava, "Consumer Response to Negative Publicity: The Moderating Role of Commitment," *Journal of Marketing Research* 37, no. 2, May 2000, pp. 203–214; Michael D. Johnson, Andreas Herrmann, and Frank Huber, "The Evolution of Loyalty Intentions," *Journal of Marketing* 70, April 2006, 122–132; Matthew Thomson, "Human Brands: Investigating Antecedents to Consumers'

Strong Attachments to Celebrities," *Journal of Marketing* 70, no. 3 ,July 2006, pp. 104–119.

68. Richins, "Valuing Things."

69. Diane Brady and Christopher Palmeri, "The Pet Economy," *BusinessWeek,* August 6, 2007, pp. 44–54; Richard C. Morais, "Dog Days," *Forbes Global,* June 21, 2004, p. 30; Rebecca Gardyn, "VIPs (Very Important Pets)," *American Demographics*, March 2001, pp. 16–18.

70. Morais, "Dog Days"; Fetto, "In the Doghouse."

71. Belk, "Possessions and the Sense of Past"; Susan Schultz Kleine, Robert E. Kleine III, and Chris T. Allen, "How Is a Possession 'Me' or 'Not Me'? Characterizing Types and an Antecedent of Material Possession Attachment," *Journal of Consumer Research*, December 1995, pp. 327–343; McAlexander, Schouten, and Roberts, "Consumer Behavior and Divorce"; Lisa L. Love and Peter S. Sheldon, "Souvenirs: Messengers of Meaning," in eds. Joseph W. Alba and Wesley Hutchinson, *Advances in Consumer Research*, vol. 25 (Provo, Utah: Association for Consumer Research, 1998), pp. 170–175.

72. Belk, "Possessions and the Sense of Past."

73. Russell W. Belk, "Moving Possessions: An Analysis Based on Personal Documents from the 1847–1869 Mormon Migration," *Journal of Consumer Research*, December 1992, pp. 339–361.

74. Russell W. Belk, Melanie Wallendorf, John F. Sherry Jr., and Morris B. Holbrook, "Collecting in a Consumer Culture," in ed. Belk, *Highways and Buyways* (Provo, Utah: Association for Consumer Research), pp.178–215.

75. John Waggoner, "Which Way Does the Wind Blow for Hot Collectibles?" *USA Today*, August 18, 2006, p. 3B.

76. Russell W. Belk, Melanie Wallendorf, John F. Sherry Jr., Morris Holbrook, and Scott Roberts, "Collectors and Collecting," in ed. Michael J. Houston, *Advances in Consumer Research*, vol. 15 (Provo, Utah: Association for Consumer Research, 1988), pp. 548–553.

77. Belk, Wallendorf, Sherry, Holbrook, and Roberts, "Collectors and Collecting."

78. Russell W. Belk, "The Ineluctable Mysteries of Possessions," in ed. Floyd W. Rudmin, *To Have Possessions: A Handbook on Ownership and Property,* Special Issue, *Journal of Social Behavior and Personality* 6, no. 6, 1991, pp. 17–55.

79. Kent Grayson and David Shulman, "Indexicality and the Verification Function of Irreplaceable Possessions: A Semiotic Analysis," *Journal of Consumer Research* 27, June 2000, pp. 17–30.

80. Daniel Terdiman, "Curiously High-Tech Hacks for a Classic Tin," *New York Times*, February 3, 2005, *www.nytimes.com.*

81. Belk et al., "Collecting in a Consumer Culture."

82. Fournier, "The Development of Intense Consumer–Product Relationships."

83. Csikszentmihalyi and Rochberg-Halton, *The Meaning of Things*; M. Wallendorf, and E. J. Arnould, "My Favorite Things: A Cross-Cultural Inquiry into Object

Attachment, Possessiveness, and Social Linkage," *Journal of Consumer Research*, March 1988, pp. 531–547; Belk, "Moving Possessions."

84. A. Peter McGraw, Philip E. Tetlock, and Orie V. Kristel, "The Limits of Fungibility: Relational Schemata and the Value of Things," *Journal of Consumer Research*, September 2003, pp. 219–228.

85. Csikszentmihalyi and Rochberg-Halton, *The Meaning of Things*.

86. Csikszentmihalyi and Rochberg-Halton, *The Meaning of Things*.

87. Helga Dittmar, "Meaning of Material Possessions as Reflections of Identity: Gender and Social-Material Position in Society," in ed. Rudmin, *To Have Possessions*, pp. 165–186; see also Helga Dittmar, *The Social Psychology of Material Possessions* (New York: St. Martin's, 1992).

88. Jaideep Sengupta, Darren W. Dahl, and Gerald J. Gorn, "Misrepresentation in the Consumer Context," *Journal of Consumer Psychology* 12 (2), 2002, pp. 69–79.

89. Dittmar, "Meaning of Material Possessions as Reflections of Identity"; Kamptner, "Personal Possessions and Their Meanings."

90. Wallendorf and Arnould, "My Favorite Things."

91. Russell W. Belk and Melanie Wallendorf, "Of Mice and Men: Gender Identity in Collecting," in eds. K. Ames and K. Martinez, *The Gender of Material Culture* (Ann Arbor, Mich.: University of Michigan Press), reprinted in ed. Susan M. Pearce, *Objects and Collections* (London: Routledge, 1994), pp. 240–253; Belk et al., "Collectors and Collecting."

92. McCracken, "Culture and Consumption"; McCracken, *Culture and Consumption*.

93. McCracken, "Culture and Consumption"; McCracken, *Culture and Consumption*.

94. McCracken, "Culture and Consumption"; McCracken, *Culture and Consumption*.

95. John L. Lastovicka and Karen V. Fernandez, "Three Paths to Disposition: The Movement of Meaningful Possessions to Strangers," *Journal of Consumer Research* 31, no. 4, 2005, pp. 813–823.

96. Linda L. Price, Eric J. Arnold, and Carolyn Folkman Curasi, "Older Consumers' Disposition of Special Possessions," *Journal of Consumer Research* 27, September 2000, pp. 179–201.

97. Russell W. Belk, Melanie Wallendorf, and John F. Sherry Jr., "The Sacred and the Profane in Consumer Behavior: Theodicy on the Odyssey," *Journal of Consumer Research*, June 1989, pp. 1–38.

98. Maya Kaneko, "Seattle Tries to Extend Appeal to Japanese Visitors Beyond Baseball Superstar," *Kyodo News International*, January 9, 2005, *www.kyodonews.com*.

99. Belk, "Possessions and the Sense of Past."

100. Belk, Wallendorf, and Sherry, "The Sacred and the Profane in Consumer Behavior."

101. Amitai Etzioni, "The Socio-Economics of Property," in ed. Rudmin, *To Have Possessions, : A Handbook on Ownership and Property,* Special Issue, *Journal of Social Behavior and Personality* 6, no. 6, 1991, pp. 465–468.

102. Robert V. Kozinets, "Utopian Enterprise: Articulating the Meanings of *Star Trek*'s Culture of Consumption," *Journal of Consumer Research* 28, June 2001, pp. 67–88.

103. Jackie Clarke, "Different to 'Dust Collectors'? The Giving and Receiving of Experience Gifts," *Journal of Consumer Behavior* 5, no. 6, 2006, pp. 533–549.

104. See, for example, Leigh Schmidt, "The Commercialization of the Calendar," *Journal of American History*, December 1991, pp. 887–916.

105. For fascinating historical and sociological accounts of Christmas, see Daniel Miller, "A Theory of Christmas," in ed. Miller, *Unwrapping Christmas*, pp. 3–37; Claude Levi-Strauss, "Father Christmas Executed," in ed. Miller, *Unwrapping Christmas*, pp. 38–54; Belk, "Materialism and the Making of the Modern American Christmas"; Barbara Bodenhorn, "Christmas Present: Christmas Public," in ed. Miller, *Unwrapping Christmas*, pp. 193–216; William B. Waits, *The Modern Christmas in America* (New York: New York University Press, 1993); and Stephen Nissenbaum, *The Battle for Christmas* (New York: Vantage Books, 1997).

106. John F. Sherry Jr., "Gift Giving in Anthropological Perspective," *Journal of Consumer Research*, September 1983, pp. 157–168.

107. For a discussion of several of these motives, see Sherry, "Gift Giving in Anthropological Perspective"; for research on gender differences in motives, see Mary Ann McGrath, "Gender Differences in Gift Exchanges: New Directions from Projections," *Psychology and Marketing*, August 1995, pp. 229–234; Cele Otnes, Kyle Zolner, and Tina M. Lowry, "In-Laws and Outlaws: The Impact of Divorce and Remarriage upon Christmas Gift Exchange," in eds. Chris Allen and Debbie Roedder-John, *Advances in Consumer Research*, vol. 21 (Provo, Utah: Association for Consumer Research, 1994), pp. 25–29; Russell W. Belk, "The Perfect Gift," in eds. Cele Otnes and Richard Beltrami, *Gift Giving Behavior: An Interdisciplinary Anthology* (Bowling Green, Ohio: Bowling Green University Popular Press, 1996); for a discussion of the roles played by gift givers (the pleaser, the provider, the compensator, the socializer, and the acknowledger), see Cele Otnes, Tina M. Lowrey, and Young Chan Kim, "Gift Selection for Easy and Difficult Recipients," *Journal of Consumer Research*, September 1993, pp. 229–244; Kleine, Kleine, and Allen, "How Is a Possession 'Me' or 'Not Me'?"

108. McAlexander, Schouten, and Roberts, "Consumer Behavior and Divorce."

109. David B. Wooten, "Qualitative Steps Toward an Expanded Model of Anxiety in Gift-Giving," *Journal of Consumer Research* 27, June 2000, pp. 84–95.

110. Russell W. Belk and Gregory S. Coon, "Gift Giving as Agapic Love: An Alternative to the Exchange Paradigm Based on Dating Experiences," *Journal of Consumer Research*, December 1993, pp. 393–417.

111. Sherry, "Gift Giving in Anthropological Perspective"; Mary Searle-Chatterjee, "Christmas Cards and the Construction of Social Relations in Britain Today," in ed. Miller, *Unwrapping Christmas*, pp. 176–192.

112. Belk and Coon, "Gift Giving as Agapic Love"; see also Sherry, "Gift Giving in Anthropological Perspective."

113. Sak Onkvisit and John J. Shaw, *International Marketing: Analysis and Strategy* (Columbus, Ohio: Merrill, 1989), pp. 241–242.

114. "The Efficiency of Gift Giving: Is It Really Better to Give than to Receive?" *Marketing: Knowledge at Wharton,* December 15, 2004, *knowledge.wharton.upenn.edu.*

115. Sandra Yin, "Give and Take," *American Demographics,* November 2003, pp. 12–13; Eileen Fischer and Stephen J. Arnold, "More Than a Labor of Love: Gender Roles and Christmas Shopping," *Journal of Consumer Research,* December 1990, pp. 333–345.

116. John F. Sherry Jr. and Mary Ann McGrath, "Unpacking the Holiday Presence: A Comparative Ethnography of Two Gift Stores," in ed. Elizabeth C. Hirschman, *Interpretive Consumer Research* (Provo, Utah: Association for Consumer Research, 1989), pp. 148–167.

117. See, for example, Theodore Caplow, "Rule Enforcement Without Visible Means: Christmas Gift Giving in Middletown," *American Journal of Sociology,* March 1984, pp. 1306–1323.

118. James G. Carrier, "The Rituals of Christmas Giving," in ed. Miller, *Unwrapping Christmas*, pp. 55–74.

119. Mary Ann McGrath, "An Ethnography of a Gift Store: Trappings, Wrappings, and Rapture," *Journal of Retailing,* Winter 1989, p. 434.

120. Wooten, "Qualitative Steps Toward an Expanded Model of Anxiety in Gift-Giving."

121. Julie A. Ruth, Cele C. Otnes, and Frederic F. Brunel, "Gift Receipt and the Reformulation of Interpersonal Relationships," *Journal of Consumer Research,* March 1999, pp. 385–402; Ming-Hui Huang and Shihti Yu, "Gifts in a Romantic Relationship: A Survival Analysis," *Journal of Consumer Psychology* 9, no. 3, 2000, pp. 179–188.

122. Belk, "Gift Giving Behavior"; see also Sherry, "Gift Giving in Anthropological Perspective."

123. Belk and Coon, "Gift Giving as Agapic Love."

124. Annamma Joy, "Gift Giving in Hong Kong and the Continuum of Social Ties," *Journal of Consumer Research,* September 2001, pp. 239–256.

125. "Holiday Cards More than 2.2 . . . " *Washington Post,* November 29, 2007, p. H5.

126. Anne D'Innocenzio, "What's in Your Wallet? Empty Gift Cards?" *Chicago Tribune,* March 4, 2008, *www.chicagotribune.com.*

127. Louise Lee, "What's Roiling the Selling Season," *BusinessWeek,* January 10, 2005, p. 38.

128. Susan Carey, "Over the River, Through the Woods, to a Posh Resort We Go," *Wall Street Journal,* November 21, 1997, pp. B1, B4.

129. Amanda Fehd, "Executive Who Steered eBay's Rise to Retire," *Washington Post,* January 24, 2008, p. D2; Matthew Summers-Sparks, "When Old Stadiums Go, Everything Must Go!" *New York Times,* February 16, 2006, p. F4; "Britney's Gum Is Hot eBay Item," *UPI NewsTrack,* September 2, 2004, n.p.; Michele Himmelberg, "Disney Fan Pays $37,400 to Have Name Placed on Haunted Mansion Tombstone," *Orange County Register,* October 23, 2004, *www.ocregister.com;* Daniel P. Finney, "Happy 25 for the Happy Meal!" *St. Louis Post-Dispatch,* June 14, 2004, *www.stltoday.com;* Meredith Schwartz, "The Accidental Collector: eBay Offers Insights into Two Types of Collectors," *Gifts & Decorative Accessories,* June 2004, p. 1003; *ebay.com.*

Chapter 18

1. Eric Pfanner, "In Britain, A Campaign Against Obesity Is Snarled in Controversy," *New York Times,* February 11, 2008, p. C7; "Leading Food and Beverage Companies Release Commitments on Children's Advertising," *CNW Group,* February 6, 2008, n.p.; "Brands Move to Reduce Advertising to Children," *New Media Age,* January 10, 2008, p. 10; Emily Bryson York, "You Want Apple Fries with That?" *Advertising Age,* September 11, 2007, *www.adage.com;* Paul Kurnit, "Art & Commerce: The Advertising Diet," *Adweek Online,* December 3, 2007, *www.adweek.com;* Karen Robinson-Jacobs, "Chuck E. Cheese's Chain Joins Fight Against Childhood Obesity," *Dallas Morning News,* October 16, 2007, *www.dallasnews.com;* Ira Teinowitz, "More Major Food Marketers Establish Kids-Advertising Limits," *Advertising Age,* July 18, 2007, *www.adage.com.*

2. Kathleen D. Vohs, "Self-Regulatory Resources Power the Reflective System: Evidence from Five Domains," *Journal of Consumer Psychology* 16, no. 3, 2006, pp. 217–223.

3. Elizabeth C. Hirschman, "The Consciousness of Addiction: Toward a General Theory of Compulsive Consumption," *Journal of Consumer Research,* September 1992, pp. 155–179.

4. Ron Panko, "By the Numbers: Smoking's Cost in the United States," *Best's Review,* December 2007, p. 20.

5. "Cigarette Smoking Among Adults—United States, 2006," *Morbidity and Mortality Weekly Report,* Centers for Disease Control and Prevention, November 2, 2007, *www.cdc.gov/mmwr.*

6. Thomas C. O'Guinn and Ronald J. Faber, "Compulsive Buying: A Phenomenological Exploration," *Journal of Consumer Research,* September 1989, pp. 147–157.

7. Lorrin M. Koran, Ronald J. Faber, Elias Aboujaoude, Michael D. Large, and Richard T. Serpe, "Estimated Prevalence of Compulsive Buying Behavior in the United States," *The American Journal of Psychiatry,* October 2006, pp. 1806–1812.

8. Ronald Faber, Gary Christenson, Martina DeZwaan, and James Mitchell, "Two Forms of Compulsive Consumption: Comorbidity of Compulsive Buying and Binge Eating," *Journal of Consumer Research,* December 1995, pp. 296–304; O'Guinn and Faber, "Compulsive Buying"; Ronald J. Faber and Thomas C. O'Guinn, "Compulsive

Consumption and Credit Abuse," *Journal of Consumer Policy*, March 1988, pp. 97–109; Gilles Valence, Alain D'Astous, and Louis Fortier, "Compulsive Buying: Concept and Measurement," *Journal of Consumer Policy*, December 1988, pp. 419–433; Rajan Nataraajan and Brent G. Goff, "Compulsive Buying: Toward a Reconceptualization," in ed. Floyd W. Rudman, *To Have Possessions: A Handbook on Ownership and Property* (Corte Madera, Calif.: Select Press, 1991), pp. 307–328; "Compulsive Shopping Could Be Hereditary," *Marketing News*, September 14, 1998, p. 31; Wayne S. DeSarbo and Elizabeth A. Edwards, "Typologies of Compulsive Buying Behavior: A Constrained Cluster-wise Regression Approach," *Journal of Consumer Psychology* 5, no. 3, 1996, pp. 231–262.

9. Faber and O'Guinn, "Compulsive Consumption and Credit Abuse"; Ronald J. Faber and Thomas C. O'Guinn, "A Clinical Screener for Compulsive Buying," *Journal of Consumer Research*, December 1992, pp. 459–469; O'Guinn and Faber, "Compulsive Buying"; James A. Roberts, "Compulsive Buying Among College Students: An Investigation of Its Antecedents, Consequences, and Implications for Public Policy," *Journal of Consumer Affairs*, Winter 1998, pp. 295–319.

10. Hyokjin Kwak, George M. Zinkhan, and Melvin R. Crask, "Diagnostic Screener for Compulsive Buying: Applications to the USA and South Korea," *Journal of Consumer Affairs*, Summer 2003, pp. 161+.

11. Hannah Karp, "The Senior Trip to the Strip," *Wall Street Journal*, April 8, 2005, p. W4.

12. "Risky Gamble," *Prevention*, May 2006, p. 42.

13. Richard G. Netemeyer, Scot Burton, Leslie K. Cole, Donald A. Williamson, Nancy Zucker, Lisa Bertman, and Gretchen Diefenbach, "Characteristics and Beliefs Associated with Probably Pathological Gambling: A Pilot Study with Implications for the National Gambling Impact and Policy Commission," *Journal of Public Policy and Marketing* 17, no. 2, Fall 1998, pp. 147–160.

14. Laurence Arnold, "Link to Other Addictions Raises New Questions About Gambling," *Associate Press*, June 12, 2001.

15. Jeffrey N. Weatherly, John M. Sauter, and Brent M. King, "The 'Big Win' and Resistance to Extinction When Gambling," *Journal of Psychology*, November 2004, pp. 495+.

16. Dennis Rook, "The Buying Impulse," *Journal of Consumer Research* 14, September 1987, pp. 189–199; S. J. Hoch and G. F. Loewenstein, "Time-inconsistent Preferences and Consumer Self-control," *Journal of Consumer Research* 17 no. 4, 1991, pp. 492–507; Kathleen D. Vohs and Ronald J. Faber, "Spent Resources: Self-Regulatory Resource Availability Affects Impulse Buying," *Journal of Consumer Research* 33, 2007, pp. 537–548; Suresh Ramanathan and Geeta Menon, "Time-Varying Effects of Chronic Hedonic Goals on Impulsive Behavior," *Journal of Marketing Research*, November 2006, pp. 628–641.

17. Dennis W. Rook and Robert J. Fisher, "Normative Influences on Impulsive Buying Behavior," *Journal of Consumer Research* 22, December 1995, pp. 305–315; Sharon E. Beatty and M. Elizabeth Ferrell, "Impulse Buying: Modeling Its Precursors," *Journal of Retailing* 74, no. 2, 1998, pp. 169–191.

18. W. Walter Mischel and O. Ayduk, "Willpower in a Cognitive-Affective Processing System: The Dynamics of Delay of Gratification," in eds. R. F. Baumeister and K. D. Vohs, *Handbook of Self-Regulation: Research, Theory, and Applications* (New York, N.Y.: Guilford Press, 2004), pp. 99–129; Fritz Strack, Lioba Werth, and Roland Deutsch, "Reflective and Impulsive Determinants of Consumer Behavior," *Journal of Consumer Psychology* 16, no. 3, 2006, pp. 205–216; Vohs and Faber, "Spent Resources."

19. Xueming Luo, "How Does Shopping with Others Influence Impulsive Purchasing?" *Journal of Consumer Psychology* 15, no. 4, 2005, pp. 288–294; Ramanathan and Menon, "Time-Varying Effects of Chronic Hedonic Goals on Impulsive Behavior."

20. Ravi Dhar, Joel Huber, and Uzma Khan, "The Shopping Momentum Effect," *Journal of Marketing Research* 44 no. 3, 2007, pp. 370–378.

21. Jaideep Sengupta and Rongrong Zhou, "Understanding Impulsive Eaters' Choice Behaviors: The Motivational Influences of Regulatory Focus," *Journal of Marketing Research*, May 2007, pp. 297–308.

22. Kevin Heubusch, "Taking Chances on Casinos," *American Demographics*, May 1997, pp. 35–40; Tom Gorman, "Indian Casinos in Middle of Battle over Slots," *Los Angeles Times*, May 9, 1995, pp. A3, A24; Max Vanzi, "Gambling Industry Studies the Odds," *Los Angeles Times*, May 9, 1995, pp. A3, A24; James Popkin, "America's Gambling Craze," *US News and World Report*, March 14, 1994, pp. 42–45; Iris Cohen Selinger, "The Big Lottery Gamble," *Advertising Age*, May 10, 1993, pp. 22–26; Tony Horwitz, "In a Bible Belt State, Video Poker Mutates into an Unholy Mess," *Wall Street Journal*, December 2, 1997, pp. A1, A13; Rebecca Quick, "For Sports Fans, The Internet Is a Whole New Ball Game," *Wall Street Journal*, September 3, 1998, p. B9; Stephen Braun, "Lives Lost in a River of Debt," *Los Angeles Times*, June 22, 1997, pp. A1, A14–A15.

23. Dan Seligman, "In Defense of Gambling," *Forbes*, June 23, 2003, p. 86.

24. "World Watch," *Wall Street Journal*, April 19, 2005, p. A18.

25. Matt Viser, "Internet Gambling Is a Target of Patrick Bill; Casino Initiative Makes It Illegal," *Boston Globe*, November 10, 2007, p. A1.

26. Anne D'Innocenzio and Marcus Kabel, "Retail: Crime Eating More Profits," *Houston Chronicle*, June 14, 2007, p. 3.

27. Elizabeth Woyke, "Attention, Shoplifters," *BusinessWeek*, September 11, 2006, p. 46.

28. Julia Angwin, "Credit-Card Scams Bedevil E-Stores," *Wall Street Journal*, September 19, 2000, pp. B1, B4;

Ronald A. Fullerton and Girish Punj, "Choosing to Misbehave: A Structural Model of Aberrant Consumer Behavior," in eds. Leigh McAlister and Michael Rothschild, *Advances in Consumer Research*, vol. 20 (Provo, Utah: Association for Consumer Research, 1993), pp. 570–574; Ronald A. Fullerton and Girish Punj, "The Unintended Consequences of the Culture of Consumption: An Historical-Theoretical Analysis of Consumer Misbehavior," *Consumption, Markets and Culture* 1, no. 4, 1998, pp. 393–423.

29. Joseph C. Nunes, Christopher K. Hsee, and Elke U. Weber, "Why Are People So Prone to Steal Software? The Effect of Cost Structure on Consumer Purchase and Payment Intentions," *Journal of Public Policy and Marketing* 23, Spring 2004, pp. 43–53.

30. Keith B. Anderson, "Who Are the Victims of Identity Theft: The Effect of Demographics," *Journal of Public Policy and Marketing* 25, Fall 2006, pp. 160–171.

31. Cynthia Ramsaran, "ID Theft Hits Paper Harder," *Bank Systems and Technology,* March 2005, p. 14; Robert P. Libbon, "Datadog," *American Demographics*, July 2001, p. 26.

32. David Myron, "What Uncle Sam Doesn't Know," *American Demographics,* November 2004, pp. 10–11; Dena Cox, Anthony P. Cox, and George P. Moschis, "When Consumer Behavior Goes Bad: An Investigation of Adolescent Shoplifting," *Journal of Consumer Research*, September 1990, pp. 149–159; Fullerton and Punj, "The Unintended Consequences of the Culture of Consumption"; George P. Moschis, Dena S. Cox, and James J. Kellaris, "An Exploratory Study of Adolescent Shoplifting Behavior," in eds. Melanie Wallendorf and Paul Anderson, *Advances in Consumer Research*, vol. 14 (Provo, Utah: Association for Consumer Research, 1987), pp. 526–530.

33. Fullerton and Punj, "The Unintended Consequences of the Culture of Consumption."

34. Cox, Cox, and Moschis, "When Consumer Behavior Goes Bad."

35. Paul Bernstein, "Cheating—The New National Pastime?" *Business*, October–December 1985, pp. 24–33; Fullerton and Punj, "Some Unintended Consequences of the Culture of Consumption."

36. Fullerton and Punj, "Choosing to Misbehave"; Donald R. Katz, *The Big Store* (New York: Penguin, 1988).

37. Cox, Cox, and Moschis, "When Consumer Behavior Goes Bad"; Moschis, Cox, and Kellaris, "An Exploratory Study of Adolescent Shoplifting Behavior"; Fullerton and Punj, "Some Unintended Consequences of the Culture of Consumption."

38. Jessica Silver-Greenberg, "Shoplifters Get Smarter," *BusinessWeek*, November 19, 2007, p. 42.

39. Katz, *The Big Store.*

40. Cox, Cox, and Moschis, "When Consumer Behavior Goes Bad"; Moschis, Cox, and Kellaris, "An Exploratory Study of Adolescent Shoplifting Behavior."

41. Anthony D. Cox, Dena Cox, Ronald D. Anderson, and George P. Moschis, "Social Influences on Adolescent Shoplifting—Theory, Evidence, and Implications for the Retail Industry," *Journal of Retailing*, Summer 1993, p. 234.

42. John Fetto, "Penny for Your Thoughts," *American Demographics*, September 2000, pp. 8–9.

43. Chok C. Hiew, "Prevention of Shoplifting: A Community Action Approach," *Canadian Journal of Criminology*, January 1981, pp. 57–68.

44. Cox, Cox, and Moschis, "When Consumer Behavior Goes Bad"; Fullerton and Punj, "The Unintended Consequences of the Culture of Consumption"; Fullerton and Punj, "Choosing to Misbehave"; Cox, Cox, Anderson, and Moschis, "Social Influences on Adolescent Shoplifting."

45. Daniel McGinn, "Shoplifting: The Five-Finger Fix?" *Newsweek,* December 20, 2004, p. 13.

46. "Retailers to Tighten Up Security," *Retail World*, February 22–26, 1999; Charles Goldsmith, "Less Honor, More Case at Europe Minibars," *Wall Street Journal*, March 22, 1996, p. B6; Steve Weinstein, "The Enemy Within," *Progressive Grocer*, May 1994, pp. 175–179.

47. Diana Ransom, "The Black Market in College-Graduation Tickets," *Wall Street Journal,* May 8, 2007, p. D1.

48. Joel Engardio, "L.A. Air Bag Thieves May Be Popping Up in East County," *Los Angeles Times*, July 1, 1998, p. 1; Ann Marie O'Connon, "Where There's Smoke," *Los Angeles Times*, September 7, 1997, p. A3R.

49. Lisa R. Szykman and Ronald P. Hill, "A Consumer-Behavior Investigation of a Prison Economy," in eds. Janeen Costa Arnold and Russell W. Belk, *Research in Consumer Behavior*, vol. 6 (Greenwich, Conn.: JAI Press, 1993), pp. 231–260; David Bevan, Paul Collier, and Jan Willem Gunning, "Black Markets: Illegality, Information, and Rents," *World Development*, December 1989, pp. 1955–1963.

50. "Hey, Anybody Want a Gun?" *The Economist*, May 16, 1998, pp. 47–48; Mark Hosenball and Daniel Klaidman, "A Deadly Mix of Drugs and Firepower," *Newsweek*, April 19, 1999, p. 27.

51. Arik Hesseldahl, "Profiting from Fake Pharma," *BusinessWeek Online*, August 21, 2007, *www.businessweek.com;* Jonathan Karp, "Awaiting Knockoffs, Indians Buy Black-Market Viagra," *Wall Street Journal*, July 10, 1998, pp. B1, B2; M. B. Sheridan, "Men Around the Globe Lust After Viagra," *Los Angeles Times*, May 26, 1998, p. 1.

52. Ken Bensinger, "Can You Spot the Fake?" *Wall Street Journal*, February 16, 2001, pp. W1, W14.

53. Gordon Fairclough, "Pssst! Wanna Cheap Smoke?" *Wall Street Journal*, December 27, 2002, pp. B1, B4.

54. Maija Palmer, "Cyberspace Fakes Make Brands Truly Worried," *Financial Times,* April 11, 2007, p. 10.

55. Hesseldahl, "Profiting from Fake Pharma."

56. George A. Hacker, "Liquor Advertisements on Television: Just Say No," *Journal of Public Policy and Marketing*, Spring 1998, pp. 139–142; William K. Eaton, "College Binge Drinking Soars, Study Finds," *Los Angeles Times*, June 8, 1994, p. A21; Mike Fuer and Rita Walters, "Mixed Message Hurts Kids: Ban Tobacco, Alcohol Billboards: The Targeting of Children Is Indisputable and Intolerable,"

Los Angeles Times, June 8, 1997, p. M5; Joseph Coleman, "Big Tobacco Still Calls the Shots in Japan," *Marketing News*, August 4, 1997, p. 12.

57. Richard J. Bonnie, "Reducing Underage Drinking: The Role of Law," *Journal of Law, Medicine, and Ethics*, Winter 2004, pp. S38+.

58. "Underage Drinking in the United States: A Status Report, 2004," *Georgetown University Center on Alcohol Marketing and Youth*, February 2005, p. 2; Mindy Sink, "Drinking Deaths Draw Attention to Old Campus Problem," *New York Times*, November 9, 2004, p. A16.

59. "Tobacco Use, Access, and Exposure to Tobacco in Media Among Middle and High School Students, United States, 2004," *Morbidity and Mortality Weekly Report, Centers for Disease Control and Prevention*, April 1, 2005, *www.cdc.gov/mmwr.*

60. Charles S. Clark, "Underage Drinking," *The CQ Researcher* 2, no. 10, 1992, pp. 219–244; Courtney Leatherman, "College Officials Are Split on Alcohol Policies: Some Seek to End Underage Drinking; Others Try to Encourage 'Responsible Use,'" *Chronicle of Higher Education*, January 31, 1990, pp. A33–A35.

61. Antonia C. Novello, "Alcohol and Tobacco Advertising," *Vital Speeches of the Day*, May 15, 1993, pp. 454–459.

62. Alyssa Bindman, "Children Exposed to Alcohol Ads More Likely to Drink," *The Nation's Health* 37, no. 6, 2007, p. 24; Cornelia Pechmann and Susan J. Knight, "An Experimental Investigation of the Joint Effects of Advertising and Peers on Adolescents' Beliefs and Intentions About Cigarette Consumption," *Journal of Consumer Research*, June 2002, pp. 5–19.

63. Joan Ryan, "Steroids? Alcohol Is the Real Problem," *San Francisco Chronicle*, March 17, 2005, *www.sfgate.com*; Vanessa O'Connell and Christopher Lawton, "Alcohol TV Ads Ignite Bid to Curb," *Wall Street Journal*, December 18, 2002, p. B2; Associated Press, "Study: Kids Remember Beer Ads," *ClariNet Electronic News Service*, February 11, 1994; Fara Warner, "Cheers! It's Happy Hour in Cyberspace," *Wall Street Journal*, March 15, 1995, pp. B1, B4; Kirk Davidson, "Looking for Abundance of Opposition to TV Liquor Ads," *Marketing News*, January 6, 1997, pp. 4, 30.

64. Nicholas Bakalar, "Ad Limits Seen as Way to Curb Youth Smoking and Drinking," *New York Times*, May 22, 2007, p. F5.

65. Bindman, "Children Exposed to Alcohol Ads More Likely to Drink"; Elizabeth M. Botvin, Gilbert J. Botvin, John L. Michela, Eli Baker, and Anne D. Filazolla, "Adolescent Smoking Behavior and the Recognition of Cigarette Advertisements," *Journal of Applied Social Psychology*, November 1991, pp. 919–932; Botvin et al., "Smoking Behavior of Adolescents Exposed to Cigarette Advertising"; Richard W. Pollay, S. Siddarth, Michael Siegel, Anne Hadix, Robert K. Merritt, Gary A. Giovino, and Michael P. Eriksen, "The Last Straw? Cigarette Advertising and Realized Market Shares Among Youths and Adults, 1979–1993," *Journal of Marketing*, April 1996, pp. 1–16; Joseph DiFranza, John W. Richards, Paul M. Paulman, Nancy Wolf-Gillespie, Christopher Fletcher, Robert D. Jaffe, and David Murray, "RJR Nabisco's Cartoon Camel Promotes Camel Cigarettes to Children," *Journal of the American Medical Association*, December 11, 1991, p. 314.; K. M. Cummings, E. Sciandra, T. F. Pechacek, J. P. Pierce, L. Wallack, S. L. Mills, W. R. Lynn, and S. E. Marcus, "Comparison of the Cigarette Brand Preferences of Adult and Teenaged Smokers—United States, 1989, and 10 U.S. Communities, 1988 and 1990," *Journal of the American Medical Association*, April 8, 1992, p. 189.

66. Kathleen J. Kelly, Michael D. Slater, and David Karan, "Image Advertisements' Influence on Adolescents' Perceptions of the Desirability of Beer and Cigarettes," *Journal of Public Policy and Marketing*, Fall 2002, pp. 295–304.

67. "Alcohol Ads Face Close Scrutiny by Government," *Marketing Week*, November 15, 2007, p. 5.

68. Betsy Spethmann, "Five States Sue RJR," *Promo*, May 2001, p. 22.

69. Richard W. Pollay and Ann M. Lavack, "The Targeting of Youths by Cigarette Marketers: Archival Evidence on Trial," in eds. Leigh McAlister and Michael Rothschild, *Advances in Consumer Research*, vol. 20 (Provo, Utah: Association for Consumer Research, 1993), pp. 266–271.

70. See Kathleen J. Kelly, Michael D. Slater, David Karan, and Liza Hunn, "The Use of Human Models and Cartoon Characters in Magazine Advertisements for Cigarettes, Beer, and Nonalcoholic Beverages," *Journal of Public Policy and Marketing* 19, no. 2, Fall 2000, pp. 189–200.

71. Richard Morgan, "Is Old Joe Taking Too Much Heat?" *Adweek*, March 16, 1992, p. 44.

72. Clark, "Underage Drinking."

73. Stuart Elliott, "Hoping to Show It Can Police Itself, the Liquor Industry Takes the Wraps Off Its Review Board," *New York Times*, March 8, 2005, p. C3.

74. Vanessa O'Connell, "Tobacco Makers Want Cigarettes Cut from Films," *Wall Street Journal*, June 13, 2004, pp. B1, B4.

75. "Smoking in Movies Linked to Kids Lighting Up," *Health Day*, January 8, 2008, *www.nlm.nih.gov/medlineplus*.

76. Debra L. Scammon, Robert N. Mayer, and Ken R. Smith, "Alcohol Warnings: How Do You Know When You've Had One Too Many?" *Journal of Public Policy and Marketing*, Spring 1991, pp. 214–228; Michael B. Mazis, Louis A. Morris, and John L. Swasy, "An Evaluation of the Alcohol Warning Label: Initial Survey Results," *Journal of Public Policy and Marketing*, Spring 1991, pp. 229–241; Novello, "Alcohol and Tobacco Advertising"; Richard Gibson and Marj Charlier, "Anheuser Leads the Way in Listing Alcohol Levels," *Wall Street Journal*, March 11, 1993, pp. B1, B2; Richard J. Fox, Dean M. Krugman, James E. Fletcher, and Paul M. Fischer, "Adolescents' Attention to Beer and Cigarette Print Ads and Associated Product Warnings," *Journal of Advertising*, Fall 1998, pp. 57–68.

77. David P. MacKinnon, Rhonda M. Williams-Avery, Kathryn L. Wilcox, and Andrea M. Fenaughty, "Effects of the Arizona Alcohol Warning Poster," *Journal of Public Policy and Marketing* 18, no. 1, Spring 1999, pp. 77–88.

78. Lisa R. Szykman, Paul N. Bloom, and Jennifer Blazing, "Does Corporate Sponsorship of a Socially Oriented Message Make a Difference? An Investigation of the Effects of Sponsorship Identity on Responses to an Anti-Drinking and Driving Message," *Journal of Consumer Psychology* 14, no. 1/2, 2004, pp. 13–20.

79. Cornelia Pechmann and Chuan-Fong Shih, "Smoking Scenes in Movies and Antismoking Advertisements Before Movies: Effects on Youth," *Journal of Marketing* 63, July 1999, pp. 1–13.

80. J. Craig Andrews, Richard G. Netemeyer, and Scot Burton, "Understanding Adolescent Intentions to Smoke: An Examination of Relationships Among Social Influence, Prior Trial Behavior, and Antitobacco Campaign Advertising," *Journal of Marketing,* July 2004, pp. 110–123.

81. F. J. Zimmerman et al., *Archives of Pediatric and Adolescent Medicine* 161, no. 5, 2007, pp. 473–479.

82. E. A. Vandewater et al., *Pediatrics,* 119, May 2007, pp. 1006–1015.

83. W. Melody, *Children's Television: The Economics of Exploitation* (New Haven, Conn.: Yale University Press, 1973); Ellen Notar, "Children and TV Commercials: Wave After Wave of Exploitation," *Childhood Education,* Winter 1989, pp. 66–67.

84. Scott Ward, "Consumer Socialization," *Journal of Consumer Research,* September 1974, pp. 1–13; Laurene Krasney Meringoff and Gerald S. Lesser, "Children's Ability to Distinguish Television Commercials from Program Material," in ed. R. P. Adler, *The Effect of Television Advertising on Children* (Lexington, Mass.: Lexington Books, 1980), pp. 29–42; S. Levin, T. Petros, and F. Petrella, "Preschoolers' Awareness of Television Advertising," *Child Development,* August 1982, pp. 933–937.

85. M. Carole Macklin, "Preschoolers' Understanding of the Informational Function of Advertising," *Journal of Consumer Research,* September 1987, pp. 229–239; Merrie Brucks, Gary M. Armstrong, and Marvin E. Goldberg, "Children's Use of Cognitive Defenses Against Television Advertising: A Cognitive Response Approach," *Journal of Consumer Research,* March 1988, pp. 471–482.

86. Mary C. Martin, "Children's Understanding of the Intent of Advertising: A Meta-Analysis," *Journal of Public Policy and Marketing,* Fall 1997, pp. 205–216.

87. Jon Berry, "The New Generation of Kids and Ads," *Adweek's Marketing Week,* April 15, 1991, pp. 25–28; Marvin E. Goldberg and Gerald J. Gorn, "Some Unintended Consequences of TV Advertising to Children," *Journal of Consumer Research,* June 1978, pp. 22–29; Gary M. Armstrong and Merrie Brucks, "Dealing with Children's Advertising: Public Policy Issues and Alternatives," *Journal of Public Policy and Marketing* 7, 1988, pp. 98–113.

88. Gerald J. Gorn and Renee Florsheim, "The Effects of Commercials for Adult Products on Children," *Journal of Consumer Research,* March 1985, pp. 962–967.

89. "For Kids on the Web, It's an Ad, Ad, Ad, Ad World," *BusinessWeek,* August 13, 2001, p. 108.

90. Meringoff and Lesser, "Children's Ability to Distinguish Television Commercials from Program Material."

91. Doug Halonen, "FCC Urged to Monitor Total Hours of Kids TV," *Electronic Media,* September 24, 2002, p. 2; Jon Berry, "Kids' Advocates to TV: 'We've Only Begun to Fight,'" *Adweek's Marketing Week,* April 15, 1991, p. 25.

92. Dale Kunkel and Walter Granz, "Assessing Compliance with Industry Self-Regulation of Television Advertising to Children," *Journal of Applied Communication Research,* May 1993, pp. 148–162.

93. Ron Winslow and Peter Landers, "Obesity: A WorldWide Woe," *Wall Street Journal,* July 1, 2002, pp. B1, B4.

94. Betsy McKay, "The Children's Menu: Do Ads Make Kids Fat?" *Wall Street Journal,* January 27, 2005, pp. B1, B7.

95. Caroline E. Mayer, "Group Takes Aim at Junk-Food Marketing," *Washington Post,* January 7, 2005, p. E3.

96. Brian Wansink and Pierre Chandon, "Can 'Low-Fat' Nutrition Labels Lead to Obesity?" *Journal of Marketing Research,* November 2006, pp. 605–617.

97. Pierre Chandon and Brian Wansink, "Is Obesity Caused by Calorie Underestimation? A Psychophysical Model of Meal Size Estimation," *Journal of Marketing Research,* February 2007, pp. 84–99.

98. Rajagopal Raghunathan, Rebecca Walker Naylor, and Wayne D. Hoyer, "The Unhealthy = Tasty Intuition and Its Effects on Taste Inferences, Enjoyment, and Choice of Food Products," *Journal of Marketing,* October 2006, pp. 170–184.

99. Claudia Kalb and Karen Springen, "Pump Up the Family," *Newsweek,* April 25, 2005, pp. 62+.

100. Promise Advertisement, *Cooking Light,* March 2008, p. 145.

101. "Brands Move to Reduce Advertising to Children."

102. Catherine Fitzpatrick, "How Buff Is Enough? Reality Check Is in the Male," *Milwaukee Journal Sentinel,* June 24, 2001, p. 1-L.

103. Isabel Reynolds, "Japan: Feature—Eating Disorders Plague Young Japanese," *Reuters,* June 20, 2001, *www .reuters.com.*

104. Laura Landro, "The Informed Patient: Amid Focus on Obesity and Diet, Anorexia, Bulimia Are on the Rise," *Wall Street Journal,* March 30, 2004, p. D1.

105. See also Debra Lynn Stephens, Ronald P. Hill, and Cynthia Hanson, "The Beauty Myth and Female Consumers: The Controversial Role of Advertising," *Journal of Consumer Affairs,* Summer 1994, pp. 137–154.

106. Leon Festinger, "A Theory of Social Comparison Processes," *Human Relations,* May 1954, pp. 117–140.

107. Michael Häfner, "How Dissimilar Others May Still Resemble the Self: Assimilation and Contrast After Social Comparison," *Journal of Consumer Psychology* 14, no. 2, 2004,

pp. 187–196; Mary C. Martin and James W. Gentry, "Stuck in the Model Trap: The Effects of Beautiful Models in Ads on Female Pre-Adolescents and Adolescents," *Journal of Advertising*, Summer 1997, pp. 19–33; Marsha L. Richins, "Social Comparison and the Idealized Images of Advertising," *Journal of Consumer Research*, June 1991, pp. 71–83; Richard W. Pollay, "The Distorted Mirror: Reflections on the Unintended Consequences of Advertising," *Journal of Marketing*, April 1986, pp. 18–36.

108. Jennifer J. Argo, Katherine White, and Darren W. Dahl, "Social Comparison Theory and Deception in the Interpersonal Exchange of Consumption Information," *Journal of Consumer Research* 33, no. 1, 2006, pp. 99–108.

109. Charles S. Gulas and Kim McKeage, "Extending Social Comparison: An Examination of the Unintended Consequences of Idealized Advertising Imagery," *Journal of Advertising* 29, no. 2, Summer 2000, pp. 17–28.

110. Dirk Smeesters and Naomi Mandel, "Positive and Negative Media Image Effects on the Self," *Journal of Consumer Research* 32, no. 4, 2006, pp. 576–582.

111. Calmetta Y. Coleman, "Can't Be Too Thin, but Plus-Size Models Get More Work Now," *Wall Street Journal*, May 3, 1999, pp. A1, A10.

112. José Antonio Rosa, Ellen C. Garbarino, and Alan J. Malter, "Keeping the Body in Mind: The Influence of Body Esteem and Body Boundary Aberration on Consumer Beliefs and Purchase Intentions," *Journal of Consumer Psychology* 16, no. 1, 2006, pp. 79–91.

113. Sally Goll Beatty, "Women's Views of Their Lives Aren't Reflected by Advertisers," *Wall Street Journal*, December 19, 1995, p. B2.

114. Joseph Jaffe, "Marketing's Big Bang Theory: Why So Many Campaigns That Begin with A Sizzle End with A Fizzle," *Adweek Online*, March 3, 2008, *www.adweek.com*.

115. M. Joseph Sirgy, Dong-Jin Lee, Rustan Kosenko, H. Lee Meadow, Don Rahtz, et al., "Does Television Viewership Play a Role in the Perception of Quality of Life?" *Journal of Advertising*, Spring 1998, pp. 125–143; Pollay, "The Distorted Mirror: Reflections on the Unintended Consequences of Advertising"; Russell W. Belk and Richard W. Pollay, "Images of Ourselves: The Good Life in Twentieth Century Advertising," *Journal of Consumer Research*, March 1985, pp. 887–897; Russell W. Belk, "Materialism: Trait Aspects of Living in a Material World," *Journal of Consumer Research*, December 1985, pp. 265–280; Mary Yoko Brannen, "Cross-Cultural Materialism: Commodifying Culture in Japan," in eds. Floyd Rudmin and Marsha L. Richins, *Meaning, Measure, and Morality of Materialism* (Provo, Utah: Association for Consumer Research, 1992), pp. 167–180; Güliz Ger and Russell W. Belk, "Cross-Cultural Differences in Materialism," *Journal of Economic Psychology*, February 1996, pp. 55–77; Marsha L. Richins, "Media, Materialism, and Human Happiness," in eds. Melanie Wallendorf and Paul Anderson, *Advances in Consumer Research*, vol. 14 (Provo, Utah: Association for

Consumer Research, 1986), pp. 352–356; Thomas C. O'Guinn and Ronald J. Faber, "Mass Mediated Consumer Socialization: Non-Utilitarian and Dysfunctional Outcomes," in eds. Melanie Wallendorf and Paul Anderson, *Advances in Consumer Research*, vol. 14 (Provo, Utah: Association for Consumer Research, 1987), pp. 473–477; Ronald J. Faber and Thomas C. O'Guinn, "Expanding the View of Consumer Socialization: A Non-Utilitarian Mass Mediated Perspective," in eds. Elizabeth C. Hirschman and Jagdish N. Sheth, *Research in Consumer Behavior*, vol. 3 (Greenwich, Conn.: JAI Press, 1988), pp. 49–78.

116. Richins, "Media, Materialism, and Human Happiness," in eds. Melanie Wallendorf and Paul Anderson, *Advances in Consumer Research*, vol. 14 (Provo, Utah: Association for Consumer Research, 1987), pp. 352–356.

117. Aaron C. Ahuvia and Nancy Y. Wong, "Personality and Values Based Materialism: Their Relationship and Origins," *Journal of Consumer Psychology* 12, no. 4, 2002, pp. 389–402; Marvin E. Goldberg, Gerald J. Gorn, Laura A. Peracchio, and Gary Bamossy, "Understanding Materialism Among Youth," *Journal of Consumer Psychology* 13, no. 3, 2003, pp. 278–288.

118. Goldberg, Gorn, Peracchio, and Bamossy, "Understanding Materialism Among Youth."

119. Noel C. Paul, "Branded for Life?" *Christian Science Monitor*, April 1, 2002, *www.csmonitor.com/2002/0401/p15s02-wmcn.html*.

120. Julie B. Schor, *Born to Buy* (New York: Scribner, 2005).

121. Richins, "Media, Materialism, and Human Happiness."

122. See, for example, James M. Hunt, Jerome B. Kernan, and Deborah J. Mitchell, "Materialism as Social Cognition: People, Possessions, and Perception," *Journal of Consumer Psychology* 5, no. 1, 1996, pp. 65–83.

123. Russell W. Belk, "The Third World Consumer Culture," in ed. Jagdish N. Sheth, *Research in Marketing* (Greenwich, Conn.: JAI Press, 1988), pp. 103–127.

124. Eve M. Caudill and Patrick E. Murphy, "Consumer Online Privacy: Legal and Ethical Issues," *Journal of Public Policy and Marketing* 19, no. 1, Spring 2000, pp. 7–19.

125. Ellen Foxman and Paula Kilcoyne, "Information Technology, Marketing Practice, and Consumer Privacy: Ethical Issues," *Journal of Public Policy and Marketing*, Spring 1993, p. 106; Kim Bartel Sheehan and Mariea Grubbs Hoy, "Dimensions of Privacy Concern Among Online Consumers," *Journal of Public Policy and Marketing* 19, no. 1, Spring 2000, pp. 62–73.

126. Carol Krol, "Consumers Reach the Boiling Point Over Privacy Issues," *Advertising Age,* March 29, 1999, p. 22; "Survey Results Show Consumers Want Privacy," *Direct Marketing*, March 1999, p. 10.

127. Michael Moss, "A Web CEO's Elusive Goal: Privacy," *Wall Street Journal*, February 7, 2000, pp. B1, B6.

128. Bob Tedeschi, "Poll Says Identity Theft Concerns Rose After High-Profile Breaches," *New York Times*, March 10, 2005, p. G5.

129. "Personal Data on Over 120,000 Tokyo Disney Resort Customers Leaked," *Japan Today*, March 17, 2005, *www.japantoday.com.*

130. Pamela Paul, "Mixed Signals," *American Demographics*, July 2001, pp. 45–49; Joseph Phelps, Glen Nowak, and Elizabeth Ferrell, "Privacy Concerns and Consumer Willingness to Provide Personal Information," *Journal of Public Policy and Marketing* 19, no. 1, Spring 2000, pp. 27–41.

131. Patricia A. Norberg and Daniel R. Horne, "Privacy Attitudes and Privacy-Related Behavior, *Psychology and Marketing* 24, no. 10, 2007, pp. 829–847.

132. George R. Milne, "Privacy and Ethical Issues in Database/Interactive Marketing and Public Policy: A Research Framework and Overview of the Special Issue," *Journal of Public Policy and Marketing* 19, no. 1, Spring 2000, pp. 1–6.

133. Mary J. Culnan, "Protecting Privacy Online: Is Self-Regulation Working?" *Journal of Public Policy and Marketing* 19, no. 1, Spring 2000, pp. 20–26; Anthony D. Miyazaki and Ana Fernandez, "Internet Privacy and Security: An Examination of Online Retailer Disclosures," *Journal of Public Policy and Marketing* 19, no. 1, Spring 2000, pp. 54–61.

134. "Current Do Not Call Registrations by Consumer State/Territory," U.S. Federal Trade Commission, September 30, 2007, *www.ftc.gov.*

135. Roland T. Rust, P. K. Kannan, and Peng Na, "The Customer Economics of Internet Privacy," *Journal of the Academy of Marketing Science* 30, Fall 2002, pp. 455–464.

136. Seema Nayyar, "Refillable Pouch a Lotions First," *Brandweek*, October 26, 1992, p. 3; Seema Nayyar, "L&F Cleaner Refills Greener," *Brandweek*, September 14, 1992, p. 5; Belk, "Daily Life in Romania."

137. Jack Neff, "Eco-Wal-Mart Costs Marketers Green," *Advertising Age*, October 1, 2007, pp. 3, 42.

138. Jack Neff, "Seventh Generation," *Advertising Age*, November 12, 2007, p. S13.

139. "Nokia Unveils Recycled Handset," *Wall Street Journal*, February 13, 2008, *www.wsj.com.*

140. John A. McCarty and L. J. Shrum, "The Influence of Individualism, Collectivism, and Locus of Control on Environmental Beliefs and Behavior," *Journal of Public Policy and Marketing* 20, no. 1, Spring 2001, pp. 93–104.

141. Pam Scholder Ellen, Joshua Lyle Wiener, and Cathy Cobb-Walgren, "The Role of Perceived Consumer Effectiveness in Motivating Environmentally Conscious Behaviors," *Journal of Public Policy and Marketing*, Fall 1991, pp. 102–117; Thomas C. Kinnear, James R. Taylor, and Sadrudin A. Ahmed, "Ecologically Concerned Consumers: Who Are They?" *Journal of Marketing*, April 1972, pp. 46–57.

142. Russell Belk, John Painter, and Richard Semenik, "Preferred Solutions to the Energy Crisis as a Function of Causal Attributions," *Journal of Consumer Research*, December 1981, pp. 306–312.

143. C. Dennis Anderson and John D. Claxton, "Barriers to Consumer Choice of Energy-Efficient Products," *Journal of Consumer Research*, September 1982, pp. 163–170.

144. Rik Peters, Tammo Bijmo, H. Fred van Raaij, and Mark de Kruijk, "Consumers' Attributions of Proenvironmental Behavior, Motivation, and Ability to Self and Others," *Journal of Public Policy and Marketing*, Fall 1998, pp. 215–225.

145. Ibid; Dennis L. McNeill and William L. Wilkie, "Public Policy and Consumer Information: Impact of the New Energy Labels," *Journal of Consumer Research*, June 1979, pp. 1–11.

146. Daniel Gross, "Edison's Dimming Bulbs," *Newsweek*, October 15, 2007, p. E22.

147. "How Green Is Your Stuff?" *Newsweek*, March 3, 2008, p. 50.

148. Michael Bush, "Sustainability and a Smile," *Advertising Age*, February 25, 2008, pp. 1, 25.

149. N. Craig Smith and Elizabeth Cooper-Martin, "Ethics and Target Marketing: The Role of Product Harm and Consumer Vulnerability," *Journal of Marketing*, July 1997, pp. 1–20; Robert O. Hermann, "The Tactics of Consumer Resistance: Group Action and Marketplace Exit," in eds. Leigh McAlister and Michael Rothschild, *Advances in Consumer Research*, vol. 20 (Provo, Utah: Association for Consumer Research, 1993), pp. 130–134; Lisa Penaloza and Linda L. Price, "Consumer Resistance: A Conceptual Overview," in eds. Leigh McAlister and Michael L. Rothschild, *Advances in Consumer Research*, vol. 20 (Provo, Utah: Association for Consumer Research, 1993), pp. 123–128.

150. Robert V. Kozinets and Jay M. Handelman, "Adversaries of Consumption: Consumer Movements, Activism, and Ideology," *Journal of Consumer Research* 31, no. 3, 2004, pp. 691–704.

151. Richard W. Pollay, "Media Resistance to Consumer Resistance: On the Stonewalling of 'Adbusters' and Advocates," in eds. Leigh McAlister and Michael Rothschild, *Advances in Consumer Research*, vol. 20 (Provo, Utah: Association for Consumer Research, 1993), p. 129.

152. H. J. Cummins, "Judging a Book Cover," *Star-Tribune of the Twin Cities*, January 17, 2001, p. 1E.

153. Jill Gabrielle Klein, N. Craig Smith, and Andrew John, "Why We Boycott: Consumer Motivations for Boycott Participation," *Journal of Marketing Research*, July 2004, pp. 92–109; Sakar Sen, Zeynep Gürhan-Canli, and Vicki Morwitz, "Withholding Consumption: A Social Dilemma Perspective on Consumer Boycotts," *Journal of Consumer Research*, December 2001, pp. 399+.

154. Jonathan Baron, "Consumer Attitudes About Personal and Political Action," *Journal of Consumer Psychology* 8, no. 3, 1999, pp. 261–275.

155. Stephanie Kang, "Just Do It: Nike Gets Revelatory," *Wall Street Journal*, April 13, 2005, p. 11.

156. Ruthie Ackerman, "Anti-Gay Group Ends Ford Boycott," *Forbes*, March 11, 2008, *www.forbes.com.*

157. Grant Gross, "Privacy Advocates: Consumer Education Isn't Enough," *PC World,* April 17, 2008, *www.pcworld.com;* "Consumer Groups Push 'Do Not Track' Registry," *PC Magazine Online,* April 15, 2008, *www.pcmag.com;* Bob Wice, "Who's Mining the Store?" *Best's Review,* August 2007, pp. 93+; Dan Tynan, "Watch Out for Online Ads That Watch You," *PC World,* March 2007, p. 26; Peter O'Connor, "Online Consumer Privacy: An Analysis of Hotel Company Behavior," *Cornell Hotel and Restaurant Administration Quarterly,* May 2007, pp. 183+; Frank Davies, "Report: Internet Privacy Protection Improving," *San Jose Mercury News,* August 8, 2007, *www.mercurynews.com;* David Myron, "Stolen Names, Big Numbers," *American Demographics,* September 2004, p. 363; Cliff Saran, "Eli Lilly Case Raises Privacy Fears," *Computer Weekly,* January 31, 2002, p. 6.

Ad/Photo Credits

Chapter 17

Chapter Opener, **p.440:** © Phil McCarten/Reuters/Landov

Exhibit 17.4, **p.445:** © Peter Turnley/Corbis

Exhibit 17.6, **p.450:** Fisher-Price ad and logo used with permission of Fisher-Price, Inc.

Exhibit 17.7, **p.451:** © Larry Williams/Larry Williams and Associates/Corbis

Exhibit 17.8, **p.454:** Courtesy GovMint.com

Exhibit 17.11, **p.460:** © Lucas Jackson/Reuters/Corbis

Chapter 18

Chapter Opener, **p.469:** © Somos Images/Corbis

Exhibit 18.5, **p.475:** © Bill Aron/PhotoEdit

Exhibit 18.6, **p.476:** Courtesy of Chase Card Services

Exhibit 18.8, **p.479:** © Helen King/Corbis

Exhibit 18.9, **p.480:** © David Young-Wolff/PhotoEdit

Exhibit 18.10, **p.481:** Office of National Drug Control Policy/ The Partnership for a Drug-Free America

Exhibit 18.11, **p.483:** © Ace Stock Limited/Alamy

Exhibit 18.13, **p.488:** Reproduced with permission from 3M Company

Exhibit 18.14, **p, 490:** Courtesy of the American Anti-Vivisection Society

Text Credits

Chapter 1

Excerpt, **p.16:** Reprinted with permission of the American Marketing Association.

Chapter 2

Exhibit 2.6, **p.55:** From Richard P. Bagozzi and Utpal Dholakia, "Goal Setting and Goal Striving in Consumer Behavior," *Journal of Marketing*, Vol. 63, 1999, p. 20. Reprinted with permission of American Marketing Association.

Exhibit 2.7, **p.57:** Adapted from Allison Johnson and David Stewart (2005), "A Re-Appraisal of the Role of Emotion in Consumer Behavior: Traditional and Contemporary Approaches," in Review of Marketing Research, Vol. 1, M.E. Sharpe, 3–34.

Chapter 3

Exhibit 3.5, **p.79:** From Paivio, et al., *Journal of Experimental Psychology, Monograph Supplement*, January 1968, pp. 1–25. Reprinted with permission.

Exhibit 3.7, **p.82:** From Kate Fitzgerald, "In-Store Media Ring Cash Register," *Advertising Age*, February 9, 2004, p.43. Reprinted with permission from Advertising Age. Copyright, Crain Communications, Inc.

Chapter 4

Exhibit 4.3, **p.96:** Reprinted from August 15, 2008 issue of *BusinessWeek* by special permission, copyright © 2008 by The McGraw-Hill Companies, Inc.

Exhibit 4.4, **p.96:** Reprinted with permission from *Journal of Marketing research*, published by the American Marketing Association, Jennifer L. Aaker, August 1997, Vol. 34, pp. 347–356.

Exhibit 4.12, **p.115:** From Hitoshi Taira, "More Japanese People Want 'Made in Japan,'" Japan Close-Up, December 2004, p. 31. Reprinted with permission of PHP Institute, Inc.

Exhibit 4.14, **p.117:** From "Measuring Shopper Response," *Chain Store Age*, January 2004, pp. 3B+. Reprinted with permission of Lebhar-Friedman, Inc.

Chapter 5

Exhibit 5.5, **p.133:** Reprinted with permission from *American Demographics*, October 2003, p. 13. Copyright, Crain Communications, Inc.

Chapter 6

Exhibit 6.9, **p.164:** From Gordon C. Bruner, "Music, Mood, and Marketing," *Journal of Marketing*, October 1990. Reprinted with permission of American Marketing Association.

Chapter 7

Exhibit 7.7, **p.185:** Copyright © 2004–2008 IAG Research, http://www.iagra.net/data_total_market.jsp. Reprinted with permission.

Chapter 8

Exhibit 8.7, **p.206:** From Peter H. Bloch, Daniel L. Sherrell and Nancy M. Ridgeway, "Consumer Search: An Extended Framework," *Journal of Consumer Research*, June 1986, p. 120. Reprinted with permission of University of Chicago Press.

Chapter 9

Exhibit 9.13, **p.243:** From Dan Ariely and Jonathan Levav, "Sequential Choice in Group Settings: Taking the Road Less Traveled and Less Enjoyed," *Journal of Consumer Research*, December 2000, p. 281. Reprinted with permission of The University of Chicago Press.

Chapter 11

Exhibit 11.3, **p.276:** Stephen J. Hoch and John Deighton, "Managing What Consumers Learn from Experience," *Journal of Marketing*, April 1989, pp. 1–20. Reprinted by permission.

Exhibit 11.11, **p.292:** From: Melissa Martin Young and Melanie Wallendorf, "Ashes to Ashes, Dust to Dust: Conceptualizing Consumer Disposition of Possessions," In PROCEDDINGS, MARKETING EDUCATORS' CONFERENCE, (Chicago: American Maketing Association, 1989): 33–9.

Chapter 13

Exhibit 13.2, **p.328:** From Richard P. Coleman, "The Continuing Significance of Social Class to Marketing," *Journal of Consumer Research*, December 1983, p. 277. Reprinted with permission of The University of Chicago Press.

Exhibit 13.4, **p.331:** Reproduced with permission from Julie McMillan and F.L. Jones, "The ANU3_2 Scale: A Revised Occupational Status Scale for Australia," *Journal of Sociology*, March 2000, Appendix on pp. 69–80, by permission of Sage Publications Ltd.

Exhibit 13.6, **p.334:** Mariele De Mooij and Warren Kegan, *Advertising Worldwide* (Englewood Cliffs, NJ: Prentice Hall, 1991), p. 116. Reprinted by permission of Pearson Education Limited.

Exhibit 13.12, **p.345:** Adapted from Joe Schwartz, "Family Traditions: Although Radically Changed, the American-Family Is as Strong as Ever," *American Demographics*, March 1987, p. 9. American Demographics, 1987. Reprinted with permission.

Exhibit 13.13, **p.346:** From Rex Y. Du and Wagner A. Kamakura, "Household Life Cycles and Lifestyles in the United States," *Journal of Marketing Research*, February 2006. Reprinted with permission of American Marketing Association.

Exhibit 13.15, **p.350:** Robert Boutilier, "Pulling the Family's Strings," *American Demographics*, August 1993, pp. 44–48. American Demographics © 1993. Reprinted with permission.

Chapter 14

Exhibit 14.5, **p.363:** Reprinted with permission from *American Demographics*, March 2004, p. 29. Copyright, Crain Communications, Inc.

Exhibit 14.10, **p.372:** Adapted from Hans Eysenck and S. Rachman, The Causes and Cures of Neurosis: An Introduction to Modern Behavior Therapy Based on Learning Theory and Principles of Conditioning (San Diego: Calif.: Knapp. 1965, p. 16.) Reprinted by permission from EdITS.

Exhibit 14.13, **p.379:** Joseph T. Plumer, "The Concept and Application of Life Style Segmentation," *Journal of Marketing*, January 1974. Reprinted with permission of American Marketing Association.

Exhibit 14.14, **p.381:** Reprinted with permission from VALS™ Program. SRI Consulting Business Intelligence (SRIC-BI); www.sric-bi.com/VALS.

Chapter 15

Exhibit 15.3, **p.390:** Copyright © 2008 by Consumers Union of U.S., Inc. Yonkers, NY 10703-1057, a nonprofit organization. Reprinted with permission from ConsumerReports.org® for educational purposes only. No commercial use or reproduction permitted, www.ConsumerReports.org.

Exhibit 15.5, **p.393:** Reprinted from Addictive Behaviors, Volume 32, Issue #8, by Steve Sussman, Pallav Pokhrel, Richard D. Ashmore, and B. Bradford Brown, "Adolescent Peer Group Identification and Characteristcs: A Review of the Literature," Addictive Behaviors, August 2007, pp. 1620–1627. Copyright © 2007 with permission of Elsevier.

Exhibit 15.6, **p.394:** From R. James H. McAlexander, John W. Schouten, and Harold F. Koenig, "Building Brand Community" *Journal of Marketing*, January 2002, p. 39. Reprinted with permission of American Marketing Association.

Exhibit 15.11, **p.403:** Susceptibility to Interpersonal Influence Scale from William O. Bearden, Richard G. Netemeyer and Jesse E. Teel, "Measurement of Consumer Susceptibility to Interpersonal Influence," *Journal of Consumer Research*, March 1989, pp. 472–481.Reprinted with permission of The University of Chicago Press.

Exhibit 15.13, **p.409:** From Kathryn Kranbold and Erin White, "The Perils and Potential Rewards of Crisis Management for Firestone," *Wall Street Journal*, September 8, 2000, p. B1. Copyright © 2000 by Dow Jones & Company, Inc. Reproduced with permission of Dow Jones & Company, Inc. via Copyright Clearance Center.

Chapter 16

Exhibit 16.4, **p.420:** From David Glen Mick and Susan Fornier, "Paradoxes of Technology: Consumer Cognizance, Emotions, and Coping Strategies," *Journal of Consumer Research*, Vol. 25, September 1998, p. 126. Reprinted with permission of The University of Chicago Press.

Exhibit 16.6, **p.422:** Adapted with the permission of The Free Press, a Division of Simon & Schuster Adult Publishing Group, from Diffusion of Innovations, 3rd Edition by Everett M. Rogers. Copyright © 1962, 1971, 1983 by The Free Press. All rights reserved.

Exhibit 16.7, **p.424:** From R. James H. McAlexander, John W. Schouten, and Harold F. Koenig, "Building Brand Community" *Journal of Marketing*, January 2004. Reprinted with permission of American Marketing Association.

Chapter 17

Exhibit 17.3, **p.444:** Adapted from Grant McCracken, "Culture and Consumption: A Theoretical Account of the Structure and Movement of the Cultural Meaning of Consumer Goods," *Journal of Consumer Research*, 1986, pp. 71–84. Reprinted with permission of The University of Chicago Press.

Exhibit 17.5, **p.448:** Adapted from Michael Solomon, "The Role of Products as Social Stimuli: A Symbolic Interactionism Perspective," *Journal of Consumer Research*, December 1983, pp. 319–329. Reprinted with permission of The University of Chicago Press.

Exhibit 17.10, **p.458:** Adapted with permission from N. Laura Kamptner, "Personal Possessions and Their Meanings: A Life-Span Perspective," in ed. Floyd W. Rudmin, To Have Possessions: A Handbook on Ownership and Property, Special Issue, *Journal of Social Behavior and Personality 6*, no. 6, 1991, p. 215.

Exhibit 17.13, **p.465:** From Julie A. Ruth, Cele C. Otnes, and Frederic F. Brunel, "Gift Receipt and the Reformulation of Interpersonal Relationships," *Journal of Consumer Research*, Vol. 25, March 1999, p. 389. Reprinted with permission of The University of Chicago Press.

Chapter 18

Exhibit 18.3, **p.473:** From Thomas O'Guinn and Ronald Faber, "Compulsive Buying: A Phenomenological Perspective," *Journal of Consumer Research*, September 1989, pp. 147–157. Reprinted with permission of The University of Chicago Press.

Exhibit 18.12, **p.486:** From Marsha L. Richins, "Social Comparison and the Idealized Images of Advertising," *Journal of Consumer Research*, June 1991, pp. 71–93. Reprinted with permission of The University of Chicago Press.

Glossary

A

Ability The extent to which consumers have the resources needed to make an outcome happen. (2)

Absolute threshold The minimal level of stimulus intensity needed to detect a stimulus. (3)

Accessible The extent to which an association or link is retrievable from memory. (7)

Accommodation theory The more effort one puts forth in trying to communicate with an ethnic group, the more positive the reaction. (12)

Acculturation Learning how to adapt to a new culture. (12)

Acquisition The process by which a consumer comes to own an offering. (1)

Activities, interests, and opinions (AIOs) The three components of lifestyles. (14)

Actual identity schemas The set of multiple, salient identities that reflect our self-concept. (17)

Actual state The way things actually are. (8)

Adaptability The extent to which the innovation can foster new styles. (16)

Addiction Excessive behavior typically brought on by a chemical dependency. (18)

Additive difference model Compensatory model in which brands are compared by attribute, two brands at a time. (9)

Adoption A purchase of an innovation by an individual consumer or household. (16)

Aesthetic or hedonic innovation An innovation that appeals to our aesthetic, pleasure-seeking, and/or sensory needs. (16)

Affect referral A simple type of affective tactic whereby we simply remember our feelings for the product or service. (10)

Affect Low-level feelings. (10)

Affective decision-making models The process by which consumers base their decision on feelings and emotions. (9)

Affective decision making Decisions based on feelings and emotions. (9)

Affective forecasting A prediction of how you will feel in the future. (9)

Affective forecasting When we try to predict how a product will make us feel. (11)

Affective function How attitudes influence our feelings. (5)

Affective involvement Expending emotional energy and heightened feelings regarding an offering or activity. (5)

Affective involvement Interest in expending emotional energy and evoking deep feelings about an offering, activity, or decision. (2)

Affective responses When consumers generate feelings and images in response to a message. (5)

Affect-related tactics Tactics based on feelings. (10)

Agentic goals Goals that stress mastery, self-assertiveness, self-efficacy, strength, and no emotion. (12)

Alternative-based strategy Making a noncomparable choice based on an overall evaluation. (9)

Ambiguity of information When there is not enough information to confirm or disprove hypotheses. (11)

Ambivalence When our evaluations regarding a brand are mixed (both positive and negative). (5)

Anchoring and adjustment process Starting with an initial evaluation and adjusting it with additional information. (9)

Appraisal theory A theory of emotion that proposes that emotions are based on an individual's assessment of a situation or an outcome and its relevance to his or her goals. (2)

Approach-approach conflict A feeling of conflictedness about which offering to acquire when each can satisfy an important but different need. (2)

Approach-avoidance conflict A feeling of conflictedness about acquiring or consuming an offering that fulfills one need but fails to fulfill another. (2)

Aspirational reference group A group that we admire and desire to be like. (15)

Associative reference group A group to which we currently belong. (15)

Attention The process by which an individual allocates part of his or her mental activity to a stimulus. (3)

Attitude accessibility How easily an attitude can be remembered. (5)

Attitude confidence How strongly we hold an attitude. (5)

Attitude persistence How long our attitude lasts. (5)

Attitude resistance How difficult it is to change an attitude. (5)

Attitude toward the act (A_{act}) How we feel about doing something. (5)

Attitude toward the ad (A_{ad}) Whether the consumer likes or dislikes an ad. (5)

Attitude A relatively global and enduring evaluation of an object, issue, person, or action. (5)

Attraction effect When adding of an inferior brand to a consideration set increases the attractiveness of the dominant brand. (9)

Attractiveness A source characteristic that evokes favorable attitudes if source is physically attractive, likable, familiar, or similar to ourselves. (5)

Attribute balancing Picking a brand because it scores equally well on certain attributes rather than faring unequally on these attributes. (9)

Attribute determinance Attributes that are both salient and diagnostic. (8)

Attribute processing Comparing brands, one attribute at a time. (9)

Attribute-based strategy Making noncomparable choices by making abstract representations of comparable attributes. (9)

Attribution theory A theory of how individuals find explanations for events. (11)

Autobiographical or episodic memory Knowledge we have about ourselves and our personal experiences. (7)

Autonomic decision Decision equally likely to be made by the husband or wife, but not by both. (13)

Availability heuristic Basing judgments on events that are easier to recall. (10)

Avoidance-avoidance conflict A feeling of conflictedness about which offering to acquire when neither can satisfy an important but different need. (2)

B

Baby boomers Individuals born between 1946 and 1964. (12)

Bargaining A fair exchange of preferences. (13)

Base-rate information How often an event really occurs on average. (10)

Basic level A level of categorization below the superordinate category that contains objects in more refined categories. (4)

Behavior (B) What we do. (5)

Behavioral intention (BI) What we intend to do. (5)

Belief discrepancy When a message is different from what consumers believe. (5)

Bias for the whole The tendency to perceive more value in a whole than in the combined parts that make up a whole. (3)

Black market An illegal market in which consumers pay often exorbitant amounts for items not readily available. (18)

Boycott An organized activity in which consumers avoid purchasing products or services from a company whose policies or practices are seen as unfair or unjust. (18)

Brand community A specialized group of consumers with a structured set of relationships involving a particular brand, fellow customers of that brand, and the product in use. (15)

Brand familiarity Easy recognition of a well-known brand. (10)

Brand image A subset of salient and feeling-related associations stored in a brand schema. (4)

Brand loyalty Buying the same brand repeatedly because of a strong preference for it. (10)

Brand personality The set of associations that reflect the personification of the brand. (4)

Brand processing Evaluating one brand at a time. (9)

Brand-choice congruence Purchase of the same brand as members of a group. (15)

C

Categorization The process of labeling or identifying an object. Involves relating what we perceive in our external environment to what we already know. (4)

Central-route processing The attitude formation and change process when effort is high. (5)

Choice tactics Simple rules of thumb used to make low-effort decisions. (10)

Chunk A group of items that can be processed as a unit. (7)

Class average Families with an average income in a particular class. (13)

Classic A successful innovation that has a lengthy product life cycle. (16)

Classical conditioning Producing a response to a stimulus by repeatedly pairing it with another stimulus that automatically produces this response. (6)

Closure According to this principle, individuals have a need to organize perceptions so that they form a meaningful whole. (3)

Clustering The grouping of consumers according to common characteristics using statistical techniques. (12)

Co-branding An arrangement by which the two brands form a partnership to benefit from the power of both. (10)

Coercive power The extent to which the group has the capacity to deliver rewards and sanctions. (15)

Cognitive decision-making models The process by which consumers combine items of information about attributes to reach a decision. (9)

Cognitive function How attitudes influence our thoughts. (5)

Cognitive involvement Interest in thinking about and learning information pertinent to an offering, activity, or decisions. (2)

Cognitive responses Thoughts we have in response to a communication. (5)

Communal goals Goals that stress affiliation and fostering harmonious relations with others, submissiveness, emotionality, and home orientation. (12)

Comparative messages Messages that make direct comparisons with competitors. (5)

Compatibility The extent to which an innovation is consistent with one's needs, values, norms, or behaviors. (16)

Compensatory consumption The consumer behavior of buying products or services to offset frustrations or difficulties in life. (13)

Compensatory eating Making up for depression or lack of social contact by eating. (12)

Compensatory model A mental cost-benefit analysis model in which negative features can be compensated for by positive ones. (9)

Complexity The extent to which an innovation is complicated and difficult to understand or use. (16)

Compliance Doing what the group or social influencer asks. (15)

Comprehension The process of deepening understanding. Involves using prior knowledge to understand more about what we have categorized. (4)

Compromise effect When a brand gains share because it is an intermediate rather than an extreme option. (9)

Compulsive consumption An irresistible urge to perform an irrational consumption act. (18)

Computerized Status Index (CSI) A modern index used to determine social class through education, occupation, residence, and income. (13)

Concession Giving in on some points to get what one wants in other areas. (13)

Concreteness The extent to which a stimulus is capable of being imagined. (3)

Confirmation bias Tendency to recall information that reinforces or confirms our over-all beliefs rather than contradicting them, thereby making our judgment or decision more positive than it should be. (8)

Conformity The tendency to behave in an expected way. (15)

Conjoint analysis A research technique to determine the relative importance and appeal of different levels of an offering's attributes. (EN)

Conjunctive model A noncompensatory model that sets minimum cutoffs to reject "bad" options. (9)

Connative function How attitudes influence our behavior. (5)

Connectedness function The use of products as symbols of our personal connections to significant people, events, or experiences. (17)

Conservation behavior Limiting the use of scarce natural resources for the purposes of environmental preservation. (18)

Consideration or evoked set The subset of top-of-mind brands evaluated when making a choice. (8)

Consideration set The subset of top-of-mind brands evaluated when making a choice. (9)

Conspicuous consumption The acquisition and display of goods and services to show off one's status. (13)

Conspicuous waste Visibly buying products and services that one never uses. (13)

Consumer behavior The totality of consumers' decisions with respect to the acquisition, consumption, and disposition of goods, services, time, and ideas by human decision-making units (over time). (1)

Consumer memory A personal storehouse of knowledge about products and services, shopping, and consumption experiences. (7)

Consumer socialization The process by which we learn to become consumers. (15)

Continuous innovation An innovation that has a limited effect on existing consumption patterns. (16)

Correlated associations The extent to which two or more associations linked to a schema go together. (4)

Counterarguments (CAs) Thoughts that disagree with the message. (5)

Credibility Extent to which the source is trustworthy, expert, or has status. (5)

Cultural categories The natural grouping of objects that reflect our culture. (17)

Cultural principles Ideas or values that specify how aspects of our culture are organized and/or how they should be perceived or evaluated. (17)

Culture The typical or expected behaviors, norms, and ideas that characterize a group of people. (1)

Customer retention The practice of keeping customers by building long-term relationships. (11)

Cutoff levels For each attribute, the point at which a brand is rejected with a noncompensatory model. (9)

D

Data mining Searching for patterns in a company database that offer clues to customer needs, preferences, and behaviors. (EN)

Deal-prone consumers Consumers who are more likely to be influenced by price. (10)

Decay The weakening of memory nodes or links over time. (7)

Decision framing The initial reference point or anchor in the decision process. (9)

Decision making Making a selection among options or courses of action. (9)

Diagnostic information That which helps us discriminate among objects. (8)

Differential threshold/just noticeable difference (j.n.d.) The intensity difference needed between two stimuli before they are perceived to be different. (3)

Diffusion The percentage of the population that has adopted an innovation at a specific point in time. (16)

Disconfirmation The existence of a discrepancy between expectations and performance. (11)

Discontinuous innovation An offering that is so new that we have never known anything like it before. (16)

Discursive processing The processing of information as words. (7)

Disjunctive model A noncompensatory model that sets acceptable cutoffs to find options that are "good." (9)

Disposition The process by which a consumer discards an offering. (1)

Dissatisfaction The feeling that results when consumers make a negative evaluation or are unhappy with a decision. (11)

Dissociative reference group A group we do not want to emulate. (15)

Divestment rituals Rituals enacted at the disposition stage that are designed to wipe away all traces of our personal meaning in a product. (17)

Dogmatism A tendency to be resistant to change or new ideas. (14)

Domain-specific values Values that may only apply to a particular area of activities. (14)

Door-in-the-face technique A technique designed to induce compliance by first asking an individual to comply with a very large and possibly outrageous request, followed by a smaller and more reasonable request. (15)

Downward mobility Losing one's social standing. (13)

Dramas Ads with characters, a plot, and a story. (6)

Dual coding The representation of a stimulus in two modalities, e.g., pictures and words in memory. (7)

Dual-mediation hypothesis Explains how attitudes toward the ad influence brand attitudes. (6)

Dynamically continuous innovation An innovation that has a pronounced effect on consumption practices and often involves a new technology. (16)

E

Earned status Status acquired later in life through achievements. (13)

Echoic memory Very brief memory for things we hear. (7)

Elaboration Transferring information into long-term memory by processing it at deeper levels. (7)

Elimination-by-aspects model Similar to the lexicographic model but adds the notion of acceptable cutoffs. (9)

Embedded markets Markets in which the social relationships among buyers and sellers change the way the market operates. (15)

Emblematic function The use of products to symbolize membership in social groups. (17)

Emotional appeals Messages designed to elicit an emotional response. (5)

Emotional detachment Emotionally disposing of a possession. (11)

Encoding of evidence Processing the information one experiences. (11)

Endowment effect When ownership increases the value of an item. (9)

Enduring involvement Long-term interest in an offering, activity, or decision. (2)

Equity theory A theory that focuses on the fairness of exchanges between individuals, which helps in understanding consumer satisfaction and dissatisfaction. (11)

Estimations of likelihood Judging how likely it is that something will occur. (9)

Ethnic groups Subcultures with a similar heritage and values. (12)

Ethnographic research In-depth qualitative research using observations and interviews (often over repeated occasions) of consumers in real world surroundings. Often used to study the meaning that consumers ascribe to a product or consumption phenomenon. (EN)

Even-a-penny-will-help technique A technique designed to induce compliance by asking individuals to do a very small favor—one that is so small that it almost does not qualify as a favor. (15)

Expectancy-value model A widely used model that explains how attitudes form and change. (5)

Expectations Beliefs about how a product/service will perform. (11)

Explicit memory Memory for some prior episode achieved by active attempts to remember. (7)

Exponential diffusion curve A diffusion curve characterized by rapid initial growth. (16)

Exposure to evidence Actually experiencing the product or service. (11)

Exposure The process by which the consumer comes in physical contact with a stimulus. (3)

Expressive roles Roles that involve an indication of family norms. (13)

Expressiveness function The use of products as symbols to demonstrate our uniqueness—how we stand out as different from others. (17)

Extended family The nuclear family plus relatives such as grandparents, aunts, uncles, and cousins. (13)

External search The process of collecting information from outside sources, e.g., magazines, dealers, ads. (8)

Extremeness aversion Options that are extreme on some attributes are less attractive than those with a moderate level of those attributes. (9)

F

Fad A successful innovation that has a very short product life cycle. (16)

Fairness in the exchange The perception that people's inputs are equal to their outputs in an exchange. (11)

Family life cycle Different stages of family life, depending on the age of the parents and how many children are living at home. (13)

Fashion A successful innovation that has a moderately long and potentially cyclical product life cycle. (16)

Favorability The degree to which we like or dislike something. (5)

Fear appeals Messages that stress negative consequences. (5)

Felt involvement Self--reported arousal or interest in an offering, activity, or decision. (2)

Figure and ground According to this principle, people interpret stimuli in the context of a background. (3)

Financial risk The extent to which buying, using, or disposing of an offering is perceived to have the potential to create financial harm. (2)

Focus group A form of interview involving 8 to 12 people; a moderator leads the group and asks participants to discuss a product, concept, or other marketing stimulus. (EN)

Foot-in-the-door technique A technique designed to induce compliance by getting an individual to agree first to a small favor, then to a larger one, and then to an even larger one. (15)

Fraudulent symbols Symbols that become so widely adopted that they lose their status. (13)

Frequency heuristic Belief based simply on the number of supporting arguments or amount of repetition. (6)

Functional innovation A new product, service, attribute, or idea that offers better or different utilitarian benefits than existing alternatives. (16)

Functional needs Needs that motivate the search for offerings that solve consumption-related problems. (2)

G

Gatekeepers Sources that control the flow of information. (15)

Gender Biological state of being male or female. (12)

Generation X Individuals born between 1965 and 1976. (12)

Generation Y Mini population explosion from the children of baby boomers. (12)

Gestation stage The first stage of gift giving, when we consider what to give someone. (17)

Global values A person's most enduring, strongly held, and abstract values that hold in many situations. (14)

Goal-derived category Things that are viewed as belonging in the same category because they serve the same goals. (4)

Goals Outcomes that we would like to achieve. (2)

Graded structure The fact that category members vary in how well they represent a category. (4)

Gray market Individuals over 65. (12)

Grooming rituals Rituals we engage in to bring out or maintain the best in special products. (17)

Grouping The tendency to group stimuli to form a unified picture or impression. (3)

H

Habit Doing the same thing time after time. (10)

Habituation The process by which a stimulus loses its attention-getting abilities by virtue of its familiarity. (3)

Hedonic dimension When an ad creates positive or negative feelings. (5)

Hedonic needs Needs that relate to sensory pleasure. (2)

Hedonism The principle of pleasure seeking. (14)

Heuristics Simple rules of thumb that are used to make judgments. (6)

High-effort hierarchy of effects A purchase of an innovation based on considerable decision-making effort. (16)

Homeless People at the low end of the status hierarchy. (13)

Homophily The overall similarity among members in the social system. (15)

Household decision roles Roles that different members play in a household decision. (13)

Household A single person living alone or a group of individuals who live together in a common dwelling, regardless of whether they are related. (13)

Husband-dominant decision Decision made primarily by the male-head-of-household. (13)

Hypothesis generation Forming expectations about the product or service. (11)

Hypothesis testing Testing out expectations through experience. (11)

I

Iconic memory Very brief memory for things we see. (7)

Ideal identity schema A set of ideas about how the identity would be indicated in its ideal form. (17)

Ideal state The way we want things to be. (8)

Imagery processing The processing of information in sensory form. (7)

Imagery Imagining an event in order to make a judgment. (9)

Implicit memory Memory for things without any conscious attempt at remembering them. (7)

Impulse purchase An unexpected purchase based on a strong feeling. (10)

Impulse A sudden urge to act. (18)

Incidental learning Learning that occurs from repetition rather than from conscious processing. (6)

Independent variable The "treatment" or the entity that researchers vary in a research project. (EN)

Inept set Options that are unacceptable when making a decision. (9)

Inert set Options toward which consumers are indifferent. (9)

Informational influence The extent to which sources influence consumers simply by providing information. (15)

Inherited status Status that derives from parents at birth. (13)

Inhibition The recall of one attribute inhibiting the recall of another. (8)

Innovation An offering that is perceived as new by consumers within a market segment and that has an effect on existing consumption patterns. (16)

Instrumental roles Roles that relate to tasks affecting the buying decision. (13)

Instrumental values The values needed to achieve the desired end states such as ambition and cheerfulness. (14)

Integration of evidence Combining new information with stored knowledge. (11)

Intensity of ethnic identification How strongly people identify with their ethnic group. (12)

Interference That which causes us to confuse which features go with which brand or concept due to semantic networks being too closely aligned. (7)

Internal search The process of recalling stored information from memory. (8)

J

Judgments of goodness/badness Evaluating the desirability of something. (9)

Judgments of likelihood Evaluations of an object or estimates of likelihood of an outcome or event. (9)

K

Knowledge content Information we already have in memory. (4)

Knowledge structure The way in which knowledge is organized. (4)

L

Law of small numbers The expectation that information obtained from a small number of people represents the larger population. (10)

Legitimacy The extent to which the innovation follows established guidelines for what seems appropriate in the category. (16)

Lexicographic model A noncompensatory model that compares brands by attributes, one at a time in order of importance. (9)

Lifestyles People's patterns of behavior. (14)

List of Values (LOV) A survey that measures nine principal values in consumer behavior. (14)

Locus of control How people interpret why things happen (internal versus external). (14)

Long-term memory (LTM) The part of memory where information is placed for later use; permanently stored knowledge. (7)

Low-effort hierarchy of effects A purchase of an innovation based on limited decision-making effort. (16)

Low-effort hierarchy of effects Sequence of thinking-behaving-feeling. (10)

M

Market maven A consumer on whom others rely for information about the marketplace in general. (15)

Market test A study in which the effectiveness of one or more elements of the marketing mix is examined by evaluating sales of the product in an actual market, e.g., a specific city. (EN)

Marketing A social and managerial process through which individuals and groups obtain what they need and want by creating and exchanging products and value with others. (1)

Marketing source Influence delivered from a marketing agent, e.g., advertising, personal selling. (15)

Marketing stimuli Information about offerings communicated either by the marketer via ads, salespeople, brand symbols, packages, signs, prices, and so on or by nonmarketing sources, e.g., the media or word of mouth. (3)

Match-up hypothesis The idea that the source must be appropriate for the product/service. (5)

Materialism Placing importance on money and material goods. (14)

Means-end chain analysis A technique that helps us understand how values link to attributes in products and services. (14)

Mere exposure effect When familiarity leads to a consumer's liking an object. (6)

Metacognitive experiences How the information is processed beyond the content of the decision. (9)

Middle class Primarily white-collar workers. (13)

Miscomprehension Inaccurate understanding of a message. (4)

Modernity The extent to which consumers in the social system have positive attitudes toward change. (16)

Motivated reasoning Processing information in a way that allows consumers to reach the conclusion that they want to reach. (2)

Motivation An inner state of arousal that provides energy needed to achieve a goal. (2)

Multiattribute expectancy-value model A type of brand-based compensatory model. (9)

Multibrand loyalty Buying two or more brands repeatedly because of a strong preference for them. (10)

Multicultural marketing Strategies used to appeal to a variety of cultures at the same time. (12)

Mystery ad An ad in which the brand is not identified until the end of the message. (6)

N

National character The personality of a country. (14)

Need for cognition (NFC) A trait that describes how much people like to think. (14)

Need for uniqueness (NFU) The desire for novelty through the purchase, use, and disposition of products and services. (14)

Needs An internal state of tension caused by disequilibrium from an ideal/desired physical or psychological state. (2)

Negative word-of-mouth communication The act of consumers saying negative things about a product or service to other consumers. (11)

Noncomparable decisions The process of making decisions about products or services from different categories. (9)

Noncompensatory model Simple decision model in which negative information leads to rejection of the option. (9)

Nonmarketing source Influence delivered from an entity outside a marketing organization, e.g., friends, family, the media. (15)

Normative choice tactics Low-elaboration decision making that is based on others' opinions. (10)

Normative influences How other people influence our behavior through social pressure. (5)

Norms Collective decisions about what constitutes appropriate behavior. (15)

Nuclear family Father, mother, and children. (13)

O

Objective comprehension The extent to which the receiver accurately understands the message a sender intended to communicate. (4)

Offering A product, service, activity, or idea offered by a marketing organization to consumers. (1)

One-sided message A marketing message that presents only positive information. (5)

Ongoing search A search that occurs regularly, regardless of whether the consumer is making a choice. (8)

Online processing When consumer are actively evaluating a brand as they view an ad for it. (8)

Operant conditioning The view that behavior is a function of reinforcements and punishments received in the past. (10)

Opinion leader An individual who acts as an information broker between the mass media and the opinions and behaviors of an individual or group. (15)

Optimal stimulation level (OSL) The level of arousal that is most comfortable for an individual. (10)

Optimum stimulation level (OSL) People's preferred level of stimulation, which is usually moderate. (14)

Overprivileged Families with an income higher than the average in their social class. (13)

P

Parody display Status symbols that start in the lower social classes and move upward. (13)

Perceived risk The extent to which the consumer is uncertain about the consequences of an action, e.g., buying, using, or disposing of an offering. (2)

Perception The process by which incoming stimuli activate our sensory receptors: eyes, ears, taste buds, skin, and so on. (3)

Perceptual fluency The ease with which information is processed. (4)

Perceptual organization The process by which stimuli are organized into meaningful units. (3)

Performance risk Uncertainty about whether the offering will perform as expected. (2)

Performance The measurement of whether the product/service actually fulfills consumers' needs. (11)

Performance-related tactics Tactics based on benefits, features, or evaluations of the brand. (10)

Peripheral cues Easily processed aspects of a message, such as music, an attractive source or picture, or humor. (6)

Peripheral route to persuasion Aspects other than key message arguments that are used to influence attitudes. (6)

Peripheral-route processing The attitude formation and change process when effort is low. (5)

Personal relevance Something that has a direct bearing on the self and has potentially significant consequences or implications for our lives. (2)

Personality An internal characteristic that determines how individuals behave in various situations. (14)

Physical detachment Physically disposing of an item. (11)

Physical or safety risk The extent to which buying, using, or disposing of an offering is perceived to have the potential to create physical harm or harm one's safety. (2)

Possession rituals Rituals we engage in when we first acquire a product that help to make it "ours." (17)

Post-decision dissonance A feeling of anxiety over whether the correct decision was made. (11)

Post-decision feelings Positive or negative emotions experienced while using the products or services. (11)

Post-decision regret A feeling that one should have purchased another option. (11)

Preattentive processing The nonconscious processing of stimuli in peripheral vision. (3)

Prepurchase search A search for information that aids a specific acquisition decision. (8)

Presentation stage The second stage of gift giving, when we actually give the gift. (17)

Price-related tactics Simplifying decision heuristics that are based on price. (10)

Primacy and Recency effect The tendency to show greater memory for information that comes first or last in a sequence. (7)

Primary data Data originating from a researcher and collected to provide information relevant to a specific research project. (EN)

Primary reference group Group with whom we have physical face-to-face interaction. (15)

Prime Activation of a node in memory, often without conscious awareness. (7)

Problem recognition The perceived difference between an actual and an ideal state. (8)

Product life cycle A concept that suggests that products go through an initial introductory period followed by periods of sales growth, maturity, and decline. (16)

Profane things Things that are ordinary and hence have no special power. (17)

Prominence The intensity of stimuli that causes them to stand out relative to the environment. (3)

Prototype The best example of a cognitive (mental) category. (4)

Prototypicality When an object is representative of its category. (10)

Psychographics A description of consumers based on their psychological and behavioral characteristics. (14)

Psychological risk The extent to which buying, using, or disposing of an offering is perceived to have the potential to create negative emotions or harm one's sense of self. (2)

R

Reactance Doing the opposite of what the individual or group wants us to do. (15)

Recall The ability to retrieve information from memory. (7)

Recirculation The process by which information is remembered via simple repetition without active rehearsal. (7)

Recognition The process of determining whether a stimulus has or has not been encountered before. (7)

Reference group A group of people we compare ourselves with for information regarding behavior, attitudes, or values. (1)

Reflexive evaluation Feedback from others that tells us whether we are fulfilling the role correctly. (17)

Reformulation stage The final stage of gift giving, when we reevaluate the relationship based on the gift-giving experience. (17)

Rehearsal The process of actively reviewing material in an attempt to remember it. (7)

Relative advantage Benefits in an innovation superior to those found in existing products. (16)

Representativeness heuristic Making a judgment by simply comparing a stimulus with the category prototype or exemplar. (10)

Research foundation A nonprofit organization that sponsors research on topics relevant to the foundation's goals. (EN)

Resistance A desire not to buy the innovation, even in the face of pressure to do so. (16)

Response involvement Interest in certain decisions and behaviors. (2)

Retrieval cue A stimulus that facilitates a node's activation in memory. (7)

Retrieval The process of remembering or accessing what we have stored in memory. (7)

Rokeach Value Survey (RVS) A survey that measures instrumental and terminal values. (14)

Role acquisition function The use of products as symbols to help us feel more comfortable in a new role. (17)

S

Sacred entities People, things, and places that are set apart, revered, worshiped, and treated with great respect. (17)

Salient attributes Attributes that are "top of mind" or more important. (8)

Satisfaction The feeling that results when consumers make a positive evaluation or feel happy with their decision. (11)

Satisfice Finding a brand that satisfies a need even though the brand may not be the best brand. (10)

Schema The set of associations linked to a concept. (4)

Script A special type of schema that represents knowledge of a sequence of actions involved in performing an activity. (4)

Searching by attribute Comparing brands on attributes, one at a time. (8)

Searching by brand Collecting information on one brand before moving to another. (8)

Secondary data Data collected for some other purpose that is subsequently used in a research project. (EN)

Secondary reference group Group with whom we do not have direct contact. (15)

Self-concept Our mental view of who we are. (2)

Self-referencing Relating a message to one's own experience or self-image. (6)

Semantic memory General knowledge about an entity, detached from specific episodes. (7)

Semantic or associative network A set of associations in memory that are linked to a concept. (7)

Sensation seekers Those who actively look for variety. (10)

Sensory memory Sensory experiences stored temporarily in memory. (7)

Sexual orientation A person's preference toward certain behaviors. (12)

Shaping Leading consumers through a series of steps to create a desired response. (10)

Short-term memory (STM) The portion of memory where incoming information is encoded or interpreted in light of existing knowledge. (7)

Simple inferences Beliefs based on peripheral cues. (6)

Situational involvement Temporary interest in an offering, activity, or decision, often caused by situational circumstances. (2)

Sleeper effect Consumers forget the source of a message more quickly than they forget the message. (5)

Social class fragmentation The disappearance of class distinctions. (13)

Social class hierarchy The grouping of members of society according to status high to low. (13)

Social comparison theory A theory that proposes that individuals have a drive to compare themselves with other people. (18)

Social influences Information by and implicit or explicit pressures from individuals, groups, and the mass media that affect how a person behaves. (15)

Social relevance The extent to which an innovation can be observed or the extent to which having others observe it has social cachet. (16)

Social risk The extent to which buying, using, or disposing of an offering is perceived to have the potential to do harm to one's social standing. (2)

Source derogations (SDs) Thoughts that discount or attack the source of the message. (5)

Spreading of activation The process by which retrieving one concept or association spreads to the retrieval of a related concept or association. (7)

S-shaped diffusion curve A diffusion curve characterized by slow initial growth followed by a rapid increase in diffusion. (16)

Status crystallization When consumers are consistent across indicators of social class income, education, occupation, etc. (13)

Status float Trends that start in the lower and middle classes and move upward. (13)

Status panic The inability of children to reach their parents' level of social status. (13)

Status symbols Products or services that tell others about someone's social class standing. (13)

Storytelling A research method by which consumers are asked to tell stories about product acquisition, usage, or disposition experiences. These stories help marketers gain insights into consumer needs and identify the product attributes that meet these needs. (EN)

Strong argument A presentation that features the best or central merits of an offering in a convincing manner. (5)

Subjective comprehension Reflects what we understand, regardless of whether this understanding is accurate. (4)

Subjective norms (SN) How others feel about our doing something. (5)

Subliminal perception The activation of sensory receptors by stimuli presented below the perceptual threshold. (3)

Subordinate level A level of categorization below the basic level that contains objects in very finely differentiated categories. (4)

Superordinate level The broadest level of category organization containing different objects that share few associations but are still members of the category. (4)

Support arguments (SAs) Thoughts that agree with the message. (5)

Survey A written instrument that asks consumers to respond to a predetermined set of research questions. (EN)

Symbolic innovation A product, service, attribute, or idea that has new social meaning. (16)

Symbolic needs Needs that relate to how we perceive ourselves, how we are perceived by others, how we relate to others, and the esteem in which we are held by others. (2)

Symbols External signs that we use to express our identity. (1)

Syncratic decision Decision made jointly by the husband and wife. (13)

T

Taxonomic category A group of objects that are classified in an orderly and often hierarchically based scheme based on their similarity to one another. (4)

Terminal values Highly desired end states such as social recognition and pleasure. (14)

Terror management theory (TMT) A theory which deals with how we cope with the threat of death by defending our world view of values and beliefs. (5)

Terror management theory Theory that explains how individuals try to deal with anxiety over the inevitability of death. (14)

Theory of planned behavior An extension of the TORA model that predicts behaviors over which consumers perceive they have control. (5)

Theory of reasoned action (TORA) A model that provides an explanation of how, when, and why attitudes predict behavior. (5)

Thin-slice judgments Evaluations made after very brief observations. (6)

Tie-strength The extent to which a close, intimate relationship connects people. (15)

Time risk Uncertainties over the length of time consumers must invest in buying, using, or disposing of the offering. (2)

Top dog A market leader or brand that has a large market share. (11)

Trace strength The extent to which an association or link is strongly or weakly linked to a concept in memory. (7)

Trade group A professional organization made up of marketers in the same industry. (EN)

Traditional hierarchy of effects Sequential steps used in decision making involving thinking, then feeling, then behavior. (10)

Transformational advertising Ads that try to increase emotional involvement with the product or service. (6)

Trialability The extent to which an innovation can be tried on a limited basis before it is adopted. (16)

Trickle-down effect Trends that start in the upper classes and then are copied by lower classes. (13)

Truth effect When consumers believe a statement simply because it has been repeated a number of times. (6)

Two-sided message A marketing message that presents both positive and negative information. (5)

U

Underdogs Lower-Share brands. (11)

Underprivileged Families below the average income in their class. (13)

Unity When all the visual parts of a design fit together. (10)

Upper class The aristocracy, new social elite, and upper middle class. (13)

Upward mobility Raising one's status level. (13)

Usage The process by which a consumer uses an offering. (1)

Use innovativeness Finding use for a product that differs from the product's original intended usage. (16)

Utilitarian (functional) dimension When an ad provides information. (5)

V

Valence Whether information about something is good (positive valence) or bad (negative valence). (15)

Value segmentation The grouping of consumers by common values. (14)

Value system Our total set of values and their relative importance. (14)

Values and Life Style Survey (VALS) A psychographic tool that measures demographic, value, attitude, and lifestyle variables. (14)

Values Beliefs about what is right, important, or good. (2)

Values Enduring beliefs regarding what is right or wrong. (14)

Variety seeking Trying something different. (10)

Vicarious exploration Seeking information simply for stimulation. (10)

Viral marketing Rapid spread of brand/product information among a population of people. (15)

W

Wearout Becoming bored with a stimulus. (6)

Weber's law The stronger the initial stimulus, the greater the additional intensity needed for the second stimulus to be perceived as different. (3)

Wife-dominant decision Decision made primarily by the female head-of-household. (13)

Word of mouth Influence delivered verbally from one person to another person or group of people. (15)

Working class Primarily blue-collar workers. (13)

Z

Zapping Use of a remote control to switch channels during commercial breaks. (3)

Zipping Fast-forwarding through the commercials recorded on a VCR or DVR. (3)

Zone of acceptance The acceptable range of prices for any purchase decision. (10)

Name/Author Index

Company/Product Index

Subject Index

Chapter Closing Cases

▶ At the end of each chapter, there is a short case about real-world situations that show consumer behavior at work.

▶ *Student Companion Site*

The Student Companion Site includes materials to help students study and test their learning. Highlights of the site include Interactive Flash-cards that allow students to easily review key terms and concepts; and Interactive Quizzes that give students an opportunity to prepare for exams through a number of chapter self-assessments.